FAMILY LAW

ASPEN CASEBOOK SERIES

FAMILY LAW

SEVENTH EDITION

LESLIE JOAN HARRIS
Dorothy Kliks Fones Professor of Law Emerita
University of Oregon School of Law

JUNE CARBONE
Robina Chair in Law, Science, and Technology
University of Minnesota Law School

RACHEL REBOUCHÉ
Dean and James E. Beasley Professor of Law
Temple University Beasley School of Law

To contact Customer Service, e-mail customer.service@aspenpublishing.com, call 1-800-950-5259, or mail correspondence to:

    Aspen Publishing
    Attn: Order Department
    PO Box 990
    Frederick, MD 21705

Printed in the United States of America.

2 3 4 5 6 7 8 9 0

ISBN 978-1-5438-3888-6

Library of Congress Cataloging-in-Publication Data

Names: Harris, Leslie J., 1952- author. | Carbone, June, author. |
  Rebouché, Rachel, author.
Title: Family law / Leslie Joan Harris, Dorothy Kliks Fones Professor of
  Law EmeritaUniversity of Oregon School of Law; June Carbone, Robina
  Chair in Law, Science, and Technology University of Minnesota Law
  School; Rachel Rebouché, Dean and James E. Beasley Professor of Law,
  Temple University Beasley School of Law.
Description: Seventh Edition. | Frederick, MD: Aspen Publishing, 2023. |
  Series: Aspen casebook series | Includes bibliographical references and
  index. | Summary: "Family law casebook for law school students enrolled
  in family law courses"—Provided by publisher.
Identifiers: LCCN 2023001253 (print) | LCCN 2023001254 (ebook) | ISBN
  9781543838886 (hardback) | ISBN 9781543838893 (ebook)
Subjects: LCSH: Domestic relations—United States. | LCGFT: Casebooks (Law)
Classification: LCC KF505 .H37 2023 (print) | LCC KF505 (ebook) | DDC
  346.7301/5—dc23/eng/20230403
LC record available at https://lccn.loc.gov/2023001253
LC ebook record available at https://lccn.loc.gov/2023001254

About Aspen Publishing

Aspen Publishing is a leading provider of educational content and digital learning solutions to law schools in the U.S. and around the world. Aspen provides best-in-class solutions for legal education through authoritative textbooks, written by renowned authors, and breakthrough products such as Connected eBooks, Connected Quizzing, and PracticePerfect.

The Aspen Casebook Series (famously known among law faculty and students as the "red and black" casebooks) encompasses hundreds of highly regarded textbooks in more than eighty disciplines, from large enrollment courses, such as Torts and Contracts to emerging electives such as Sustainability and the Law of Policing. Study aids such as the *Examples & Explanations* and the *Emanuel Law Outlines* series, both highly popular collections, help law students master complex subject matter.

Major products, programs, and initiatives include:

- **Connected eBooks** are enhanced digital textbooks and study aids that come with a suite of online content and learning tools designed to maximize student success. Designed in collaboration with hundreds of faculty and students, the Connected eBook is a significant leap forward in the legal education learning tools available to students.
- **Connected Quizzing** is an easy-to-use formative assessment tool that tests law students' understanding and provides timely feedback to improve learning outcomes. Delivered through CasebookConnect.com, the learning platform already used by students to access their Aspen casebooks, Connected Quizzing is simple to implement and integrates seamlessly with law school course curricula.
- **PracticePerfect** is a visually engaging, interactive study aid to explain commonly encountered legal doctrines through easy-to-understand animated videos, illustrative examples, and numerous practice questions. Developed by a team of experts, PracticePerfect is the ideal study companion for today's law students.
- The **Aspen Learning Library** enables law schools to provide their students with access to the most popular study aids on the market across all of their courses. Available through an annual subscription, the online library consists of study aids in e-book, audio, and video formats with full text search, note-taking, and highlighting capabilities.
- Aspen's **Digital Bookshelf** is an institutional-level online education bookshelf, consolidating everything students and professors need to ensure success. This program ensures that every student has access to affordable course materials from day one.
- **Leading Edge** is a community centered on thinking differently about legal education and putting those thoughts into actionable strategies. At the core of the program is the Leading Edge Conference, an annual gathering of legal education thought leaders looking to pool ideas and identify promising directions of exploration.

SUMMARY OF CONTENTS

Contents   xi
Preface   xxv
Acknowledgments   xxvii

PART I
MARRIAGE AND ITS ALTERNATIVES   1

CHAPTER 1
Defining Family   3

CHAPTER 2
The Importance of Being a Family   27

CHAPTER 3
Entering Ceremonial Marriage   97

CHAPTER 4
Legal Recognition of Informal Family Partnerships   165

PART II
FAMILY DISSOLUTION   201

CHAPTER 5
Divorce Grounds and Procedures   203

CHAPTER 6
Property Division and Spousal Support   231

CHAPTER 7
Parent-Child Support Duties   325

CHAPTER 8
**Modification, Termination, Enforcement, and Tax
and Bankruptcy Treatment of Orders**   363

CHAPTER 9
Child Custody   411

CHAPTER 10
Family Contracts   483

CHAPTER 11
Lawyers and Family Dispute Resolution   545

CHAPTER 12
Jurisdiction   593

PART III
CHILDREN, PARENTS, AND THE STATE   659

CHAPTER 13
Determining Legal Parenthood: Marriage, Biology, and Function   661

CHAPTER 14
Adoption and Alternative Reproductive Technologies   733

Table of Cases   785
Index   797

CONTENTS

Preface xxv
Acknowledgments xxvii

PART I
MARRIAGE AND ITS ALTERNATIVES 1

CHAPTER 1
Defining Family 3

June Carbone & Naomi Cahn, Uncoupling 4
Martha Albertson Fineman, Why Marriage? 5
Carol Sanger, A Case for Civil Marriage 5
Cynthia Grant Bowman, Social Science and Legal Policy:
 The Case of Heterosexual Cohabitation 7
Braschi v. Stahl Associates Company 8
Notes and Questions 11
Obergefell v. Hodges 12
Notes and Questions 14
City of Ladue v. Horn 16
Notes and Questions 19
Armstrong v. Mayor 21
Notes and Questions 25

CHAPTER 2
The Importance of Being a Family 27

A. Marital Property 28
 1. Ownership and Control of Wealth 29
  a. The Common Law Tradition 30
   Problem 31
   Adams v. Jankouskas 31
   Notes and Questions 34
   Problems 35
  b. Community Property 35
   Elizabeth R. Carter, The Illusion of Equality: The Failure of the
    Community Property Reform to Achieve Management Equality 37
   Notes and Questions 38
   Problems 39
  2. Employment-Related and Public Benefits 40
   Boggs v. Boggs 41

Notes and Questions   45
3. Family Support Duties   46
   McGuire v. McGuire   46
   Mary Anne Case, Enforcing Bargains in an Ongoing Marriage   49
   Lee E. Teitelbaum, Family History and Family Law   51
   Bruce C. Hafen, The Family as an Entity   52
   Notes and Questions   53
   Sharpe Furniture, Inc. v. Buckstaff   54
   John Kenneth Galbraith, Economics and the Public Purpose   56
   Elizabeth R. Carter, The Illusion of Equality: The Failure of the
      Community Property Reform to Achieve Management Equality   57
   Notes and Questions   59
   Problem   60
   "Necessaries" and Public and Private Benefits   61
   Notes and Questions   62
4. Constitutional Limits on Gender-Based Classifications   62
   Problem   62
      a. Relevant Statutes   63
      b. Empirical Data   63
         Naomi Cahn, June Carbone & Nancy Levit, Gender and the
            Tournament: Reinventing Antidiscrimination Law in an
            Age of Inequality   63
         Kevin Miller, The Simple Truth About the Gender Pay Gap   64
      c. Constitutional Decisions on Gender Equality   64
B. Domestic Violence   68
   Elizabeth Pleck, Domestic Tyranny: The Making of Social Policy
      Against Family Violence from Colonial Times to the Present   69
1. Responses by the Criminal Justice System   69
   Williams v. State   70
   Notes and Questions   72
   Problem   73
   Note: The Impact of Mandatory Arrest and No-Drop Policies   74
2. Protective Orders   75
   J.D. v. M.D.F.   75
   Notes and Questions   81
   Note: Federal Domestic Violence Legislation   84
C. Reproductive Choice   85
1. Overturning Constitutional Protection for Abortion   85
   Dobbs v. Jackson Women's Health Organization   86
   Notes and Questions   92
2. Substantive Due Process Rights after *Dobbs*   93
   Notes and Questions   93
   Problem   95

CHAPTER 3
Entering Ceremonial Marriage   97

A. The Agreement to Marry   97
   Lutwak v. United States   97
   Notes and Questions   100
   Note: "Void" and "Voidable" Marriages   101

Problems	102
Note: Marriage-Related Immigration Rules	102
In re Marriage of Ramirez	103
Notes and Questions	106
Problems	108
B. Constitutional Protection for the Right to Marry	109
Loving v. Virginia	109
Notes and Questions	111
Obergefell v. Hodges	113
Notes and Questions	124
Note: Free Exercise Claims Colliding with Same-Sex Couples' Rights	126
Note: International Legal Recognition of Same-Sex Couples	128
C. Restrictions on Marrying	128
1. Formalities	128
Duncan v. Duncan	128
Notes and Questions	132
Problem	133
2. Mental Capacity	133
In re Marriage of Oakley	133
Notes and Questions	136
3. Relationship	138
Nguyen v. Holder	138
Notes and Questions	140
Problems	143
4. Age	143
Porter v. Dep't of Health & Human Services	143
Notes and Questions	146
5. One at a Time	147
State v. Holm	148
Notes and Questions	154
Problem	158
D. Interstate Recognition of Marriage	158
Matter of Geraghty	158
Notes and Questions	161
Problems	163

CHAPTER 4
Legal Recognition of Informal Family Partnerships   **165**

Mary Ann Glendon, Marriage and the State: The Withering Away of Marriage	165
A. Common Law Marriage, Presumptions About Marriage, and the Putative Spouse Doctrine	166
1. Common Law Marriage	166
Stone v. Thompson	166
Notes and Questions	171
Problems	173
2. Presumptions About Marriage and Putative Spouses	174
Spearman v. Spearman	174
Notes and Questions	176
Problem	178

B. Unmarried Cohabitants   178
          Cynthia Grant Bowman, Social Science and Legal Policy:
                The Case of Heterosexual Cohabitation   178
          Eleanor Brown, Naomi Cahn & June Carbone, The Price of Exit   179
    1. Contractual and Equitable Remedies   181
          Marvin v. Marvin   181
          Notes and Questions   182
        a. Applying Contract Theories   183
          Boulds v. Nielsen   184
          Notes and Questions   186
        b. Applying Equitable Theories   187
          Cates v. Swain   187
          Notes and Questions   190
          Uniform Cohabitants Economic Remedies Act   191
          Problems   191
    2. Other Legal Statuses for Intimate Partners?   193
          Connell v. Francisco   193
          Katharine K. Baker, What Is Nonmarriage?   195
          Notes and Questions   196
          Problems   197
          Erez Aloni, Registering Relationships   197
          Notes and Questions   198

PART II
FAMILY DISSOLUTION   201

CHAPTER 5
Divorce Grounds and Procedures   203

A. The Traditional Divorce System   204
          Kucera v. Kucera   205
          Notes and Questions   207
          Problems   211
B. The Adoption of No-Fault Divorce   212
          Lawrence Friedman, Rights of Passage: Divorce Law in Historical
                Perspective   212
    1. No-Fault Grounds for Divorce: Irretrievable Breakdown   213
          Uniform Marriage and Divorce Act §§302, 305   214
          Desrochers v. Desrochers   215
          Notes and Questions   216
    2. The Coexistence of Fault and No-Fault Grounds   217
          Flanagan v. Flanagan   217
          Notes and Questions   221
    3. No-Fault Divorce Procedure and Collusion   221
          Vandervort v. Vandervort   221
          Notes and Questions   223
          California Family Code Summary Dissolution   224
          Notes and Questions   225
          Problems   226

C. Divorce Commentary   226
        Stéphane Mechoulan, Divorce Laws and the Structure
            of the American Family   227
        Eleanor Brown, Naomi Cahn & June Carbone, The Price of Exit   228
        Notes and Questions   229

CHAPTER 6
Property Division and Spousal Support   **231**

A. Overview   231
    1. Historical Justifications of and Criteria for Economic Awards   231
    2. Economic Orders in the No-Fault Era   232
    3. Criticism of No-Fault Economics   233
        Susan W. Prager, Sharing Principles and the Future
            of Marital Property Laws   235
        J. Thomas Oldham, Putting Asunder in the 1990s   236
        June Carbone & Naomi Cahn, Nonmarriage   236
B. Property Division at Divorce   237
        Uniform Marriage and Divorce Act §307   238
        Notes and Questions   239
        Problem   240
    1. The Meaning of "Equitable Distribution"   240
        Arneault v. Arneault   241
        Notes and Questions   246
        Problems   251
    2. Characterization of Property as Separate or Marital   252
        Siefert v. Siefert   252
        Notes and Questions   254
        Problem   255
        O'Brien v. O'Brien   255
        Notes and Questions   260
        Note: Challenges to the Classification Regime—Marital
            Partnership Theory Revisited   262
        Problems   263
    3. Property Division and a Cohabitation Remedy?   264
        Thieme v. Aucoin-Thieme   265
        Notes and Questions   267
    4. Choice-of-Law Issues   268
    5. Dividing Debts   268
        Geldmeier v. Geldmeier   269
        Notes and Questions   270
        Problem   271
    6. The Marital Home   272
C. Spousal Support at Divorce   272
        Uniform Marriage and Divorce Act §308   273
        Paula England & George Farkas, Households, Employment and Gender   274
        Herma Hill Kay, Equality and Difference: A Perspective
            on No-Fault Divorce and Its Aftermath   275
        Ira Mark Ellman, The Theory of Alimony   275
        J. Thomas Oldham, Putting Asunder in the 1990s   276
        Joan Williams, Is Coverture Dead? Beyond a New Theory of Alimony   276

	Twila Perry, Alimony: Race, Privilege, and Dependency in the Search	
	for Theory	277
	In Re Marriage of Pazhoor	278
	Notes and Questions	285
	Problems	285
3.	The Emergence of Alimony Guidelines	286
	Zaleski v. Zaleski	286
	Notes and Questions	290
4.	Fault Revisited	292
5.	Spousal Support for the Caregiving Parent?	292
	Problem	292
	Empirical Data on Working Parents	293
	Overview of Governing Legal Principles and Practical Realities	293
	The Politics and Social Value of Caregiving	293
D.	Divorce and New Property	295
1.	Basic Principles	295
	Note: Valuing Streams of Payments	296
2.	Pensions and Other Employment-Related Benefits	297
	Mickey v. Mickey	297
	Notes and Questions	303
	Note: Dividing Benefits Into Marital and Nonmarital Shares	306
	A Comparison: Survivorship Rights and Death Benefits	307
	Note: Social Security, Military, and Other Pensions	308
	Problems	311
3.	Professional Practices and Other Closely Held Businesses	311
	McReath v. McReath	312
	Notes and Questions	316
	Problems	318
4.	Degrees, Licenses, Jobs, and Earning Capacity	319
	Marriage of Harris and Harris	319
	Notes and Questions	323

CHAPTER 7
Parent-Child Support Duties — **325**

	Leslie Harris, Dennis Waldrop & Lori R. Waldrop, Making and	
	Breaking Connections Between Parents' Duty to Support and	
	Right to Control Their Children	325
A.	The Current Child Support Model	327
	Robert G. Williams, Guidelines for Setting Levels	
	of Child Support Orders	328
	Jane C. Venohr, Child Support Guidelines and Guidelines Reviews:	
	State Differences and Common Issues	330
	Notes and Questions	332
B.	Challenges to the Continuity of Expenditures Model	333
	Leslie Joan Harris, The Proposed ALI Child Support Principles	334
	Jo Michell Beld & Len Biernat, Federal Intent for State	
	Child Support Guidelines: Income Shares, Cost Shares,	
	and the Realities of Shared Parenting	336

Notes and Questions 337
C. Applying Child Support Formulas 339
Tuckman v. Tuckman 339
Notes and Questions 342
Problems 344
In re Marriage of Turk 345
Notes and Questions 348
Note: Child Support Obligations of Low-Income Parents 348
D. Post-Majority Child Support 349
Leslie Harris, Dennis Waldrop & Lori R. Waldrop, Making and
Breaking Connections Between Parents' Duty to Support and
Right to Control Their Children 349
McLeod v. Starnes 350
Ruth N. Lopez Turley & Matthew Desmond, Contributions to
College Costs by Married, Divorced, and Remarried Parents 353
Notes and Questions 354
Problems 356
E. Adult Children's Legal Obligation to Support Parents 357
American Healthcare Center v. Randall 357
Swoap v. Superior Court 359
Notes and Questions 360

CHAPTER 8

Modification, Termination, Enforcement, and Tax
and Bankruptcy Treatment of Orders 363

A. Modification and Termination of Support 363
1. "Foreseeable" Changes in Circumstances 364
2. "Voluntary" versus "Involuntary" Decreases in the Payor's Income 365
Sharpe v. Sharpe 365
Notes and Questions 369
Problems 371
3. New Families—Spousal Support, Remarriage, and Cohabitation 372
Peterson v. Peterson 372
Notes and Questions 374
Problems 376
In the Matter of Raybeck 376
Notes and Questions 379
Problem 380
4. New Families—Child Support 381
Harte v. Hand 381
Notes and Questions 383
Problems 385
B. Enforcement 385
Timothy Grall, Custodial Mothers and Fathers and Their Child
Support: 2017 385
1. Private Enforcement Mechanisms—Liens, Trusts, and Insurance 387
2. Jailing "Deadbeat" Parents 388
Turner v. Rogers 388
Notes and Questions 392

Note: Civil or Criminal Contempt?	395
Problem	396
3. The State-Federal Child Support Enforcement Program	397
4. The Continuing Challenge of Childhood Poverty	398
Timothy Grall, Custodial Mothers and Fathers and Their Child Support: 2017	398
Leslie Joan Harris, Questioning Child Support Enforcement Policy for Poor Families	399
C. Taxes	400
1. Taxation of the Ongoing Family	401
2. Taxation of the Family After Divorce	402
a. Property Division—IRC §1041	403
b. Spousal Support—Former IRC §§71 and 215	403
c. Child Support, Child Tax Credits, Child Care Credits, Earned Income Credits, and Children's Medical Expenses	404
D. Bankruptcy	405
In re Chamberlain	406
Notes and Questions	408

CHAPTER 9
Child Custody — 411

A. Introduction	411
Michael Grossberg, Governing the Hearth: Law and the Family in Nineteenth Century America	411
B. Standards for Custody Determination	412
1. An Introduction to the "Best Interests" Standard	412
Painter v. Bannister	413
Anna Freud, Painter v. Bannister: Postscript by a Psychoanalyst	416
Notes and Questions	419
2. Shared Custody	421
J.R. v. M.S.	422
Notes and Questions	427
Note: Shared Custody Presumptions	429
Note: Children's Preferences	430
Note: Parental Alienation and Joint Custody	430
Note: Parenting Plans and Parenting Coordinators	432
American Law Institute, Principles of the Law of Family Dissolution	433
Notes and Questions	433
Problems	434
3. Primary Caretaker	435
Deyle v. Deyle	435
Notes and Questions	439
Problems	442
4. Managing Shared Parenting	443
a. Relocation and Changed Circumstances	443
Arnott v. Arnott	443
Notes and Questions	446
Problems	448

    b. Unfriendly Co-Parenting: Domestic Violence, Abuse, and Alienation   448
       Niemann v. Niemann   448
       Notes and Questions   451
       Problems   454
       In the Matter of Miller   456
       Notes and Questions   460
       June Carbone, From Partners to Parents: The Second Revolution in
          Family Law   462
       Note: Visitation and Parenting Plans   462
       Problems   463
    c. Choosing Between Parents: Religion, Race, and Caretaking   464
       Weisberger v. Weisberger   464
       Notes and Questions   469
       Note: Free Exercise of Religion and Custody Decisionmaking   470
       Problems   471
       Note: New Partners   472
       Note: Race   473
       Problems   475
C. Visitation and Its Enforcement   476
       Morgan v. Foretich   476
       Notes and Questions   478
       Problem   479
       Note: Attorney-Client Confidentiality and Duties to Disclose   480

CHAPTER 10
Family Contracts   **483**

A. Premarital Agreements   484
       Simeone v. Simeone   484
       Notes and Questions   488
       Lane v. Lane   490
       Notes and Questions   494
       Brian Bix, Bargaining in the Shadow of Love: The Enforcement of
          Premarital Agreements and How We Think About Marriage   499
       Uniform Premarital and Marital Agreements Act (UPMAA)   500
       Uniform Premarital Agreement Act (UPAA)   502
       Notes and Questions   503
       American Law Institute Principles of the Law of Family Dissolution   505
       Notes and Questions   506
       Problems   507
B. Spousal Contracts During Marriage   508
       Borelli v. Brusseau   508
       Notes and Questions   513
       Bedrick v. Bedrick   515
       Notes and Questions   518
C. Agreements at the End of Relationships   520
    1. The Permissible Scope of Settlement Agreements   520
       Uniform Marriage and Divorce Act §306   520
       American Law Institute Principles of the Law of Family
          Dissolution §7.09   521

Robert H. Mnookin & Lewis Kornhauser, Bargaining in the Shadow of the Law: The Case of Divorce	521
Huss v. Weaver	521
Notes and Questions	528
2. Post-Decree Attacks on Separation Agreements	531
Hresko v. Hresko	531
Notes and Questions	533
Problems	534
3. Modification of Settlement Agreements	535
Toni v. Toni	535
Notes and Questions	541
Problem	543

CHAPTER 11
Lawyers and Family Dispute Resolution — 545

A. Lawyers' Duties to Clients and the Court	545
In re the Discipline of Ortner	545
Notes and Questions	549
B. Conflicts of Interest	549
ABA Model Rule of Professional Conduct 1.7, Conflict of Interest: Current Clients	549
Notes and Questions	550
ABA Model Rule of Professional Conduct Rule 1.9, Duties to Former Clients	554
Notes and Questions	554
Problems	556
Note: Fee Arrangements	557
Problems	559
C. Counseling, Negotiation, and Client Relations	559
American Academy of Matrimonial Lawyers (AAML), Bounds of Advocacy: Goals for Family Lawyers, Preliminary Statement	560
Notes and Questions	562
Problem	563
Timothy Hedeen & Peter Salem, What Should Family Lawyers Know? Results of a Survey of Practitioners and Students	563
Notes and Questions	564
Problems	567
D. Alternative Dispute Resolution	568
Jana B. Singer, Dispute Resolution and the Post-divorce Family: Implications of a Paradigm Shift	568
1. Arbitration	570
Fawzy v. Fawzy	570
Notes and Questions	574
Problem	577
2. Mediation	577
In re Lee	579
Notes and Questions	583
Problems	587

3. Collaborative Practice	587
Notes and Questions	590
Problems	591

CHAPTER 12

Jurisdiction 593

A. Divorce Jurisdiction	594
Sherrer v. Sherrer	597
Notes and Questions	598
Problems	600
B. Divisible Divorce	601
Vanderbilt v. Vanderbilt	601
Notes and Questions	602
Note: Property Division — Jurisdiction and Full Faith and Credit	603
Problems	603
Note: Jurisdiction to Enter Domestic Violence Protective Orders	604
C. Jurisdiction and Full Faith and Credit for Support Duties	605
1. Long-Arm Jurisdiction in Support Cases	605
Kulko v. Superior Court	605
Notes and Questions	608
Problems	609
2. Interstate Modification and Enforcement of Support	609
OCS/Pappas v. O'Brien	610
Notes and Questions	616
Problems	619
Note: International Support Enforcement	619
D. Child Custody Jurisdiction	620
1. Initial Jurisdiction	621
Ex parte Siderius	621
Notes and Questions	625
Problem	626
2. Interstate Enforcement and Modification Jurisdiction	627
Brandt v. Brandt	628
Notes and Questions	633
Note: Domestic Violence Cases and the UCCJEA	636
Problems	637
3. Adoption Jurisdiction	637
4. International Enforcement of Custodial Rights	639
Monasky v. Taglieri	639
Notes and Questions	644
Golan v. Saada	646
Notes and Questions	649
E. Federal Court Jurisdiction over Domestic Relations	650
Ankenbrandt v. Richards	650
Judith Resnik, "Naturally" Without Gender: Women, Jurisdiction,	
and the Federal Courts	653
Notes and Questions	654

PART III
CHILDREN, PARENTS, AND THE STATE   659

CHAPTER 13
Determining Legal Parenthood: Marriage, Biology, and Function   661

A. The Constitutional Rights of Parents   663
    Troxel v. Granville   663
    Notes and Questions   668
    Problems   669
B. Determining Parentage in the Context of Custodial Rights and Support Duties   670
    Leslie Joan Harris, Reforming Paternity Law to Eliminate Gender,
        Status and Class Inequality   670
   1. Establishing Legal Parenthood   672
      Uniform Parentage Act   673
      Greer ex rel. Farbo v. Greer   674
      Notes and Questions   680
      Pavan v. Smith   682
      Notes and Questions   683
      Problems   684
   2. Unmarried Parents' Rights—Adoption and Custody   685
      Lehr v. Robertson   685
      Notes and Questions   690
      In re Adoption of S.D.W.   691
      Notes and Questions   695
      Problems   696
   3. Biological Parenthood and Child Support   697
      McGee v. Gonyo   699
      Notes and Questions   705
      Problem   707
C. Legal Recognition of Functional Parents   708
    David Chambers, Stepparents, Biologic Parents, and the Law's
        Perceptions of "Family" After Divorce   708
    Courtney G. Joslin & Douglas NeJaime, How Parenthood Functions   710
    Elisa B. v. Superior Court   711
    Notes and Questions   714
    In re Custody of B.M.H.   715
    Notes and Questions   721
    Note: Second Parent Adoption   724
    Problems   725
D. More Than Two Parents?   726
    T.D. v. M.M.M.   726
    Notes and Questions   729
    Cal. Fam. Code §7612(c)   729
    Problems   732

CHAPTER 14
Adoption and Alternative Reproductive Technologies   733

A. Adoption   733
        Burton Z. Sokoloff, Antecedents of American Adoption   733
  1. Terminating the First Parent-Child Relationship   736
     a. Consent to Adopt   736
        Monty S. v. Jason W.   737
        Notes and Questions   738
        Note: Open Adoption and Open Records   740
     b. Adoption Without Consent   741
        Rodgers v. Rodgers   742
        Notes and Questions   744
        Problems   745
  2. Establishing the New Parent-Child Relationship — Independent versus Agency
     Adoption and Adoption of Special-Needs Children   746
  3. Child Placement, Native American Heritage, Race, and Religion   747
     Mississippi Band of Choctaw Indians v. Holyfield   748
     Notes and Questions   749
     Note: *Adoptive Couple v. Baby Girl*   751
     Note: Transracial Placement   752
     Twila L. Perry, Transracial and International Adoption: Mothers,
        Hierarchy, Race and Feminist Legal Theory   753
     Elizabeth Bartholet, International Adoption: The Child's Story 754
     Notes and Questions   755
     Religious Matching   758
     Problem   759
B. Alternative Reproductive Technologies   760
  1. Artificial Insemination and In Vitro Fertilization   760
     Uniform Parentage Act   760
     Gatsby v. Gatsby   761
     Notes and Questions   768
     Problems   771
  2. Surrogate Motherhood and Gestational Carriers   772
     P.M. v. T.B.   773
     Notes and Questions   780
     Problems   783

Table of Cases   785
Index   797

PREFACE

This casebook is intended for a basic course in family law. In the preface to every edition since the first we have commented on how rapidly the law concerning families, parents and children, spouses, and domestic partners is changing. This seems truer today than ever. The last edition incorporated the wide-ranging effects of the Supreme Court's decision that the Constitution protects the right of same-sex couples to marry. Long-standing principles and practices regarding marriage, divorce, marital property, spousal support, and custody have been abandoned or substantially modified and continue to change. This edition touches on another transformation in an area covered by almost every family law casebook: the reversal of Roe v. Wade and the elimination of constitutional protection for abortion rights.

This book compares innovative developments across states with the reaffirmation of traditional principles in others and does so in the context of a wider focus on family and the state, the role of mediating institutions, and the efficacy of law and particular methods of enforcing the law. In assessing these developments, we present many different voices and arguments without, we hope, privileging any particular account as representing that of the book as a whole. Perspectives in this book shift regularly, through the notes and questions. In this volume, in particular, we see two issues on the horizon: the growing class divide in family formation, and the tensions between relatively conservative versus relatively liberal states about the foundations of family law, including how varying forms of families are recognized and defined.

Understanding family law requires appreciation of the difficult social and theoretical issues underlying changes in legal doctrine, as well as the settings in which family law practice occurs. Many students will practice domestic relations shortly after graduation, and a family law course must introduce them to the doctrine, procedures, and techniques they will encounter in law offices and courts.

Although family law has its own distinct body of doctrine, it also draws on doctrines from a number of other areas, including property, contracts, torts, criminal law, conflict of laws, public benefits, bankruptcy, tax, civil procedure, and constitutional law. The book introduces or reviews principles from those areas to enable students to understand how they play out when they encounter problems in family law.

The practice of family law is—even more than most other areas—cross-disciplinary. The foundation of family wealth has changed from land, cars, and bank accounts to employment and benefits—and therefore retirement accounts, businesses, and degrees. Some notion of financial principles (such as the time value of money) is essential to the valuation of property at divorce. As parentage has become more contested and complicated, knowledge of genetics and assisted reproductive technologies, for example, has become more important, and some understanding of child development is regularly necessary in custody disputes. Social history is important to understanding the context in which the law has developed and to the interpretation of current bodies of doctrine. And discussions of legal and policy responses to domestic violence, for instance, must draw on social scientific evidence regarding the incidence, distribution, and causes of such violence.

Moreover, family law cannot be effectively taught without some attention to process. The text incorporates materials that address jurisdiction, alternative dispute resolution, and ethics. The role of contract and of privately ordered processes are increasingly important in resolving disputes between partners and parents.

The casebook deals with the complexity of family law both in the organization of the chapters and in the diversity of materials within each chapter. Each unit combines primary cases with comprehensive notes, supplemented with academic and policy analyses that provide a foundation for evaluation. Detailed problems extend the coverage or apply the commentary to real world examples.

We hope the casebook conveys our continued excitement about the study of family law, and our conviction that family practice requires appreciation of the complex interaction between human relations and legal process.

Leslie J. Harris
June Carbone
Rachel Rebouché

September 2022

Editors' note: Throughout the book, footnotes to the text, to opinions, and to other quoted materials are numbered consecutively from the beginning of each chapter. Some footnotes in opinions and secondary authorities are omitted. Editors' footnotes added to quoted materials are indicated by the abbreviation: — Eds.

ACKNOWLEDGMENTS

We thank members of The Froebe Group for editorial assistance.

June Carbone thanks her research assistants David Edholm and Emma Kruger. Rachel Rebouché thanks Isabelle Aubrun, Carleigh Belardo, Paul Gugliuzza, Alyssa Holt, and Emily Lawson for comments.

The late Lee Teitelbaum, former professor and dean of the University of Utah, was a principal author of the first two editions of this book, and his contributions to the book continue to be important. Professor Carol A. Weisbrod was a coauthor of the first edition of this book, and we gratefully acknowledge her contributions.

AAML. Sections from Bounds of Advocacy: Goals for Family Lawyers, Preliminary Statement. Copyright © 2000 American Academy of Matrimonial Lawyers (AAML). Reprinted with permission.

American Law Institute. Principles of the Law of Family Dissolution: Analysis and Recommendations. Copyright © 2002 by The American Law Institute. Reproduced with permission. All rights reserved.

Bartholet, Elizabeth. "The Child's Story." *Georgia State University Law Review*, Vol. 24, Issue 2 (Winter 2007). Reprinted with permission of the author.

Beld, Jo Michelle & Len Biernat. "Federal Intent for State Child Support Guidelines: Income Shares, Cost Shares, and the Realities of Shared Parenting." *Family Law Quarterly*, Vol. 37, No. 2 (Summer 2003). Reprinted with permission of the authors.

Bix, Brian. "Bargaining in the Shadow of Love: The Enforcement of Premarital Agreements and How We Think About Marriage." *William & Mary Law Review*, Vol. 40, Issue 1 (1998). Reprinted with permission of the author.

Bowman, Cynthia Grant. Social Science and Legal Policy: The Case of Heterosexual Cohabitation, *Journal of Law and Family Studies*, Vol. 9 (2007). Reprinted with permission of the author.

Brown, Eleanor, Naomi Cahn, and June Carbone. The Price of Exit. *Washington University Law Review*, Vol. 99 (2022).

Carbone, June. *From Partners to Parents: The Second Revolution in Family Law* (2000). Columbia University Press.

Carbone, June & Naomi Cahn. Nonmarriage. *Maryland Law Review*, Vol. 76, Issue 1 (2016).
_____. Uncoupling, *Arizona State Law Journal*, Vol. 53, Issue 1 (Spring 2021).

Carter, Elizabeth R. "The Illusion of Equality: The Failure of the Community Property Reform to Achieve Management Equality." *Indiana Law Review*, Vol. 48 No. 3 (2015). Reprinted with permission of the author.

Chambers, David. "Stepparents, Biologic Parents, and the Law's Perceptions of 'Family' After Divorce," in *Divorce Reform at the Crossroads* (Stephen D. Sugarman & Herma Hill Kay eds., 1990). Copyright © 1990 Yale University Press.

Davis, Peggy Cooper. "Challenge and Tradition." *New York University Journal of Legislation and Public Policy*, Vol. 19. Reprinted with permission of the author.

England, Paula & George Farkas. *Households, Employment and Gender*. Copyright © 1986 Taylor & Francis.

Fineman, Martha Albertson. "Why Marriage?" *Virginia Journal of Social Policy and the Law*, Vol. 9, No. 1 (2001). Reprinted with permission of the author.

Friedman, Lawrence. "Rights of Passage: Divorce in Historical Perspective." *Oregon Law Review*, Vol. 63 (1984). Reprinted with permission of the author.

Glendon, Mary Ann. "Marriage and the State: The Withering Away of Marriage." *Virginia Law Review*, Vol. 62, No. 4 (1976). Reprinted with permission of the author.

Grossberg, Michael. *Governing the Hearth: Law and the Family in Nineteenth Century America*. Copyright © 1985 University of North Carolina Press.

Harris, Leslie Joan. "The Proposed ALI Child Support Principles." *Willamette Law Review*, Vol. 35 (1999).

_____ . "Reforming Paternity Law to Eliminate Gender, Status, and Class Inequality." *Michigan State Law Review*, Vol. 2013, Issue 4 (2013).

_____ . "Questioning Child Support Enforcement Policy for Poor Families." *Family Law Quarterly*, Vol. 45, No. 2 (Summer 2011).

Harris, Leslie, Dennis Waldrop, & Lori R. Waldrop. "Making and Breaking Connections Between Parents' Duty to Support and Right to Control Their Children." *Oregon Law Review*, Vol. 69 (1990). Reprinted with permission.

Hedeen, Timothy & Peter Salem. "What Should Family Lawyers Know? Results of a Survey of Practitioners and Students." *Family Court Review*, Vol. 44, Issue 4 (October 2006). Copyright © 2006 John Wiley & Sons.

Joslin, Courtney G. & Douglas NeJaime. "How Parenthood Functions." *Columbia Law Review* (forthcoming 2023). Reprinted with permission of the authors.

Kay, Herma Hill. "Equality and Difference: A Perspective on No-Fault Divorce and Its Aftermath." *University of Cincinnati Law Review*, Vol. 56 (1987). Reprinted with permission.

López Turley, Ruth N. & Matthew Desmond. "Contributions to College Costs by Married, Divorced, and Remarried Parents." *Journal of Family Issues*, Vol. 32, Issue 6 (2011). Copyright © 2011 SAGE Publications.

Mechoulan, Stéphane. "Divorce Laws and the Structure of the American Family." *The Journal of Legal Studies*, Vol. 35, No. 1, (2006). Reprinted with permission of the author.

Oldham, J. Thomas. "Putting Asunder in the 1990s." *California Law Review*, Vol. 80, No. 4 (1992). California Law Review, Inc. Reprinted with permission of the author.

Paul, Diane B. & Hamish G. Spencer. "'It's OK, We're Not Cousins by Blood': The Cousin Marriage Controversy in Historical Perspective," 6(12) *PLoS Biol e320*. doi:10.1371/journal.pbio.0060320 (2008). Copyright © 2008. Paul and Spencer. This is an open-access article distributed under the terms of the Creative Commons Attribution License, which permits unrestricted use, distribution, and reproduction in any medium, provided the original author and source are credited.

Perry, Twila L. "Alimony: Race, Privilege, and Dependency in the Search for Theory." *Georgetown Law Journal*, Vol. 82 (1994). Reprinted with permission of the author.

_____ . "Transracial and International Adoption: Mothers, Hierarchy, Race, and Feminist Legal Theory." *Yale Journal of Law and Feminism*, Vol. 10 (1998). Reprinted with permission of the author.

Prager, Susan W. "Sharing Principles and the Future of Marital Property Law." *UCLA Law Review*, Vol. 25 (1981). Reprinted with permission.

Rebouché, Rachel. "A Case Against Collaboration." *Maryland Law Review*, Vol. 76, Issue 3 (2017).

Resnik, Judith. "'Naturally' Without Gender: Women, Jurisdiction, and the Federal Courts." *New York University Law Review*, Vol. 66 (December 1991). Reprinted with permission of the author.

Sanger, Carol. "A Case for Civil Marriage." *Cardozo Law Review*, Vol. 27 (2006). Reprinted with permission of the author.

Scott, Elizabeth S. & Robert E. Emery. "Gender Politics and Child Custody: The Puzzling Persistence of the Best-Interests Standard." *Law and Contemporary Problems*, Vol. 77, Issue 1 (2014). Reprinted with permission.

Singer, Jana B. "Dispute Resolution and the Postdivorce Family: Implications of a Paradigm Shift." *Family Court Review*, Vol. 47, Issue 3 (July 2009). Reprinted with permission of the author.

Sokoloff, Burton Z. "Antecedents of American Adoption." *The Future of Children*, Vol. 3, No. 1 (1993). Copyright © 1993 The Trustees of Princeton University. Licensed under CC BY-ND 3.0, https://creativecommons.org/licenses/by-nd/3.0/.

Starnes, Cynthia Lee. "Lovers, Parents, and Partners: Disentangling Spousal and Co-Parenting Commitments." *Arizona Law Review*, Vol. 54 (2012). Reprinted with permission.

Teitelbaum, Lee E. "Family History and Family Law." *Wisconsin Law Review* (1981). Copyright © 1985 by The Board of Regents of the University of Wisconsin System. Reprinted by permission of the Wisconsin Law Review.

Uniform State Laws: The following have been reproduced in whole or in part: Uniform Marriage and Divorce Act, Uniform Parentage Act (2017), Uniform Premarital and Marital Agreements Act (2012). Copyright © The National Conference of Commissioners on Uniform State Laws. Reprinted by permission of the National Conference of Commissioners on Uniform State Laws.

Venohr, Jane C. "Child Support Guidelines and Guidelines Reviews: State Differences and Common Issues." *Family Law Quarterly*, Vol. 47, No. 3 (Fall 2013). Reprinted with permission from the author.

Williams, Joan C. "Is Coverture Dead? Beyond a New Theory of Alimony." *Georgetown Law Journal*, Vol. 82 (1994). Reprinted with permission of the author.

Williams, Robert G. "Guidelines for Setting Levels of Child Support Orders." *Family Law Quarterly*, Vol. 21, No. 3 (Fall 1987). Reprinted with permission from the author.

FAMILY LAW

PART I

MARRIAGE AND ITS ALTERNATIVES

CHAPTER 1

DEFINING FAMILY

A generation or two ago, *family* had a fairly clear connotation, although many people even then did not live in families that fit the standard image. Today, however, the meaning of *family* is contested across various realms of life. In 2017, for instance, only 19 percent of all households consisted of married couples with children, down from 44 percent in 1960, and 30 percent consisted of married couples without children, closer to the 31 percent in 1960. Mark Mather et al., America's Changing Population: What to Expect in the 2020 Census, 74 Population Bulletin 13 (2019). What do these statistics suggest? Significant shifts in family formation have occurred in the last twenty years: a move away from marriage, with income level correlating with the decision to marry; individuals, at least those with financial means, living far longer; and lower overall fertility, with low income families experiencing the largest drops after 2009. *See* Naomi Cahn, Clare Huntington, & Elizabeth Scott, Family Law for the One-Hundred Year Life, 132 Yale L.J. __ (2023). Taken together, current trends suggest that the period of adulthood devoted to raising children has shrunk with even those who marry spending less of their lives in households organized around childrearing. In addition, a larger portion of adults, including adults with children, will never marry, with income level as a major factor in marriage decisions. Commenting on this trend six years earlier, a demographer stated, "We seem to be reverting to a much older pattern, when elites marry and a great many others live together and have kids." Blaine Harden, Numbers Drop for the Married with Children: Institution Becoming the Choice of the Educated, Affluent, Wash. Post, Mar. 4, 2007.

Said another way, many people cohabitate without marrying. Between the years of 2017 and 2019, nearly 60 percent of women between the ages of 15 and 49 reported having cohabited with a partner of the opposite sex at some point in time. Cohabitation With the Opposite Sex: 2015-2019, Key Statistics from the National Survey of Family Growth (Nov. 2021). And between 2006 and 2010, almost half of all women lived with a partner rather than marrying as their first family-like union, compared to about a third of women in 1995. Cohabitation was especially common among women without higher educations; 70 percent of them cohabited as a first union, compared to 47 percent of women with a bachelor's degree. Casey E. Copen et al., First Premarital Cohabitation in the United States: 2006-2010 National Survey of Family Growth (National Health Statistics Reports No. 64, Apr. 4, 2013).

This chapter introduces legal questions that arise in defining what a family is and the legal rights that should be accorded to families defined by marriage, cohabitation, or function.

- Should the law make distinctions among people based on their family status at all?
- When family membership matters, how should it be determined? On the basis of markers such as blood relationship or legal ceremony, or on the roles and responsibilities people assume?
- If family is defined by function, what kinds of behavior indicate that people belong to a family?

These questions will continue to arise throughout the following three chapters in this part. Chapter 2 explores in some detail the ways in which the law treats adults differently if they are "married" or in an equivalent relationship and how laws have changed that regulate violence between intimates and reproductive decision making. Chapter 3 examines the law of formal marriage, and Chapter 4 deals with nonmarriage domestic arrangements among adults. Chapter 13 returns to some of these issues in the context of the parent-child relationship. Consider the following excerpts as you think about these themes.

June Carbone & Naomi Cahn

Uncoupling
53 Ariz. St. L.J. 1 (2021)

Just as the industrial age destabilized the sources of stability in the agrarian age, so too has the information age dismantled the family wage of the industrial era. A growing academic literature describes the different components—women's greater economic independence and changing family dynamics, the disappearance of high-paid manufacturing jobs for blue collar men and the corresponding increase in economic insecurity and inequality, and the increasing inability of social insurance to provide an effective social safety net, as fewer people have secure jobs or stable personal relationships. What no one has discussed, however, is the way that these elements contribute not just to increased family insecurity, but to a change in the dynamics of the entire system. The new system rewards those who manage the human capital investments necessary to achieve labor market nimbleness and family relationships based on flexibility, reciprocity and trust—qualities beyond the reach of much of the population. Seeing the changes in these terms underscores the conclusion not just that the family wage system of the industrial era is gone, but that it cannot be resurrected. Neither long term employment nor marriage can work as a foundation for family security and stability in the information age; they have become markers of success rather than pathways to security. . . . The upwardly mobile middle class responded to these changes, just as the upwardly mobile middle class of the industrial era did: with a new family strategy. . . .

The legal regulation of marriage reinforces this strategy. The changed marital terms are egalitarian in form as they assume a partnership with equal contributions. At divorce, the couple's assets are equally divided, and shared parenting has become the norm. For couples in unequal, unhappy, unfair, or unstable relationships, however, legal commitments may undermine security. . . .

While better off couples may have the resources to respond to a job loss by going back to school or taking a lower paying job that supplies new skills, working class men have more difficulty recovering financially and layoffs often exacerbate substance abuse, violence and other behavioral issues. Even without such issues, many individuals are reluctant to commit to a partner who is not financially stable for fear that the relationship will deplete their own resources.

Practically this means that while marriage is a source of strength for couples who can trade off childcare and workforce participation in ways that allow the family to marshal the resources necessary for investment in children and in adult "employability," it can be a threat to working class families. It also means that the working class have little ability to form families on middle-class terms and that marriage without those terms does not and cannot serve as the foundation for family security and stability.

Martha Albertson Fineman

Why Marriage?
9 Va. J. Soc. Pol'y & L. 239, 245-246 (2001)

. . . I argue that for all relevant and appropriate societal purposes we do not need marriage, per se, at all. To state that we do not need marriage to accomplish many societal objectives is not the same thing as saying that we do not need a family to do so for some. However, family as a social category should not be dependent on having marriage as its core relationship. Nor is family synonymous with marriage. Although both of these things might historically have been true, things have changed substantially in the past several decades. Marriage does not have the same relevance as a societal institution as it did even fifty years ago, when it was the primary means of protecting and providing for the legal and structurally devised dependency of wives.

The pressing problems today do not revolve around the marriage connection, but the caretaker-dependent relationship. In a world in which wives are equal partners and participants in the market sphere, and in which the consensus is that bad marriages should end, women do not need the special protection of legal marriage. Rather than marriage, we should view the parent-child relationship as the quintessential or core family connection, and focus on how policy can strengthen this tie. Thus, in a responsive society, one could have a marriage [or other long-term sexual affiliation] without necessarily constituting a "family" entitled to special protection and benefits under law. Correspondingly, one might have dependents, thereby creating a family and gaining protection and benefits, without having a marriage.

If this suggestion seems extreme and radical, it only serves to demonstrate the extent to which marriage continues to be uncritically central to our thinking about the family. What is bizarre is that it remains central in spite of the fact that the traditional marital family has become a statistical minority of family units in our society. The tenacity of marriage as a concept explains the relatively unsophisticated and uninformed policy debates. Marriage, as the preferred societal solution, has become the problem. The very existence of this institution eclipses discussion and debate about the problems of dependency and allows us to avoid confronting the difficulty of making the transformations necessary to address these problems.

Carol Sanger

A Case for Civil Marriage
27 Cardozo L. Rev. 1311, 1311-1322 (2006)

. . . Should civil marriage simply be abolished? In this mini-symposium, Professors Edward Zelinsky and Daniel Crane have provided two answers to his question: yes and yes. . . . Both are content to use contract to create enforceable marriage-like obligations. . . .

As a Contracts professor, I am honored that my subject has been chosen for this important assignment. At the same time, I am wary about just how well it is going to perform. . . .

. . . I agree with Professor Zelinsky that many couples, even those who are represented by lawyers, will contract incompletely and then turn to gap fillers provided by the state. It is interesting to think for a moment about why parties to a marriage contract may be especially unlikely to provide for the range of likely disputes. As Lynn Baker and Robert Emery discovered in their study of newlyweds, there is an enormous optimism about marriage by those standing on its cusp. Although the study's subjects were well aware of the general dismal statistics on divorce, not one of them thought that their own marriage would bust up. In addition to the optimism bias, all the standard reasons that contracting parties leave things out apply: fear of introducing the deal breaker and a reluctance of parties in on-going relationships to spell out every expectation, demand, or obligation. For all these reasons, there is likely to be substantial recourse to gap fillers.

I wonder, however, whether the default rules will begin to operate as a shadow regime, establishing baselines for marital obligation and support so that the law of marriage contract will over time not differ much from the law of civil marriage. If, as Professor Zelinsky acknowledges, marriage contracts are a unique kind of contract and therefore "require . . . unique rules," I would prefer to have the rules straight up rather than through indirect resort to contract.

My greater concern, however, is not about the terms parties leave out but about the enforcement of terms they explicitly include. What is a court to do with provisions that limit the number of children to the marriage or that forbid the use of contraception by either spouse? What about a contract that provides only fault-based grounds for dissolution or no grounds for divorce at all? The immediate answer is that the complaining parties consented to the agreement and are stuck with their bargain. But how will courts handle breach in cases where the wife has used a diaphragm or the husband has had an affair in violation of contract terms? Should judges enforce liquidated damage clauses that deny the breaching spouse property? Can a plaintiff sue for specific performance so that the defendant spouse might be enjoined from marrying again, just as defecting sports players cannot sign with other teams?

There is also a deeper question about the contract-based marital regime. Professor Zelinsky envisions an array of standard form contracts from which couples may choose. I am sure this will be so should his proposal prevail; we are energetic capitalists and just as umbrellas appear for sale on every Manhattan corner within two minutes of a thundershower, marriage entrepreneurs will be out there faster than you can say "Party of the First Part." There will be contract options to cater to every relationship taste and preference. But how customized can a marriage contract be before it falls outside the marital regime altogether? Is there a list of topics or terms that must be included before the arrangement is not marriage but something else, something perhaps closer to an employment contract or a property transfer or a friendship pact? Must the contracting parties reside together or be economically interdependent? Must there be provision for mutual support? . . .

It may be that this question — what have we got here? — is no longer the state's business. If states get out of the marriage business, they would seem to have little room to object to whatever arrangements substitute in. . . .

. . . Each religious tradition can offer and can "realize its own vision with respect to . . . marital obligation, divorce, and remarriage," limited only by respect for "the minimal norms of a liberal democratic society." When disputes arise, the parties turn, for arbitrated resolution, to "tribunals specialized in the religious traditions of the relevant family." . . . But the matter is not quite so simple.

. . . In few religions do women and men participate equally with one another, whether as celebrants, members, and certainly as founders. As political theorist Susan Okin has stressed,

Christianity, Judaism, and Islam, certainly in their more orthodox forms, are organized around the authority of husbands and the subservience of women. . . .

Participatory norms are also challenged by religious marriage. Not all religions permit marriage outside the faith so that marriage to one's chosen partner may not be permitted at all. . . . Civil marriage performs [the opposite] function: it provides a "basis on which individuals . . . can reconstitute their relations and take new initiatives in social life without having to count on the affective support of the communities to which they have hitherto belonged."

Just as some religious traditions restrict entrance to marriage, not all faiths permit exit from the institution. Restrictions on divorce implicate issues of autonomy and of equal participation, particularly for women. As Okin has explained, women's vulnerability within a marriage is intensified by their inability to leave it. The distribution of power at home impacts significantly on participation and influence in the public realm: "the more a culture requires or expects of women in the domestic sphere, the less opportunity they have of achieving equality with men in either sphere." . . .

For all these reasons, it is therefore not enough simply to invoke minimum norms to satisfy concerns about unjust practices in religious marriage. Religions are markedly undemocratic, concerned not with rights or equality or principles of non-discrimination but with the demands of faith. Moreover, I suspect few religions would accept the importation of democratic norms, minimal or not, as a condition of governance. It means nothing to cede authority to religious tradition if the religion must first sign on to an incompatible set of civic values and practices. . . .

. . . However, I think it is worth letting all committed couples ask this of one another: to commit to the full extent that is possible at law. And it is marriage law — not contract law — that ought to do the heavy lifting here, not as a functional matter — we can probably kick contract law into sufficient shape to do the job if necessary — but as a matter of the legitimacy of state authority over marriage. Just as the state has interests in marriage, citizens have an interest in the state articulating and defending its interests, as it was eventually unable to do with miscegenation, prohibitions on contraception, or as an absolute requirement for parenting. The nature of the state's interest in marriage is often contested, as it should be. As historian Nancy Cott has pointed out, "the public benefit of governmental involvement in marriage no longer goes without saying." But the explication of the state's interest is less likely to be produced by adjusting the definition of consideration or narrowing the application of injunctive relief.

Cynthia Grant Bowman

Social Science and Legal Policy: The Case of Heterosexual Cohabitation
9 J.L. & Fam. Stud. 1, 36-42 (2007)

If, as recent studies indicate, cohabitants are more likely to merge their finances than to keep them separate, and the presence of a cohabitant in the household adds substantially to the ability of an otherwise single mother to support her child, then we need to worry about vulnerability of the parties if the relationship ends. Legal remedies for the custodial parent (usually the mother) — remedies beyond the child support she can presumably command from the child's biological father — may be very important for the welfare of the children involved. . . .

The argument that to give legal status to cohabitants will harm the ideal embodied in marriage assumes that refusal to recognize cohabitation will lead people to marry instead, and that marriage by many of the people currently cohabiting would not be characterized by the bad effects that accompany their cohabitation. Arguments to this effect are seriously flawed in a number of respects.

First, legal incentives do not seem to affect people's private behavior in this way. Indeed, most people are unlikely even to know what their legal rights and obligations are, at least until they get divorced. . . . Many people in the United States mistakenly believe that the law in fact does protect them after a certain period of cohabitation, although common law marriage is recognized only in a handful of states. . . .

We now have a number of studies, primarily in the context of welfare reform, about the impact of legal incentives upon the rate of marriage. Without exception they show that welfare programs designed to encourage marriage have had no statistically significant effect on the marriage rate. Indeed, one study suggests that entry into marriage is *negatively* associated with the incentives offered by the new federal welfare initiatives which drastically limit payment of benefits to unmarried mothers. These results are consistent with evidence that variations in welfare benefits do not affect the non-marital birth rate either. Human beings apparently do not regulate behavior as private as union formation and childbirth in response to incentives from the state.

If people did think and act in this way, however, the incentive structure provided by the current legal treatment of cohabitation in this country is perverse. By not imposing any legal obligations on cohabitants, the stronger partner economically is given an incentive *not* to marry, because to do so would mean being required to share his or her property upon dissolution of the relationship and possibly to support the former partner in the short or long run. . . .

In sum, offering legal recognition and support to cohabitants and making their lives easier does not appear to discourage marriage, and in fact the opposite may be true. . . .

While people's familial choices have been changing, the law of marriage, cohabitation, and parentage has changed too. Perhaps the most dramatic change was opening marriage to couples of the same sex, a process that culminated with the Supreme Court decision in Obergefell v. Hodges in 2015, excerpted below. Consider first a case that tests how family is defined without marriage in an era when couples of the same sex were prohibited from marrying.

Braschi v. Stahl Associates Company
543 N.E.2d 49 (N.Y. 1989)

Titone, J. Appellant, Miguel Braschi, was living with Leslie Blanchard in a rent-controlled apartment located at 405 East 54th Street from the summer of 1975 until Blanchard's death in September of 1986. In November of 1986, respondent, Stahl Associates Company, the owner of the apartment building, served a notice to cure on appellant contending that he was a mere licensee with no right to occupy the apartment since only Blanchard was the tenant of record. In December of 1986 respondent served appellant with a notice to terminate informing appellant that he had one month to vacate the apartment and that, if the apartment was not vacated, respondent would commence summary proceedings to evict him.

Appellant then initiated an action seeking a permanent injunction and a declaration of entitlement to occupy the apartment. By order to show cause appellant then moved for a preliminary injunction, pendente lite, enjoining respondent from evicting him until a court could determine whether he was a member of Blanchard's family within the meaning of

9 NYCRR 2204.6(d). After examining the nature of the relationship between the two men, Supreme Court concluded that appellant was a "family member" within the meaning of the regulation and, accordingly, that a preliminary injunction should be issued. . . .

The Appellate Division reversed, concluding that section 2204.6(d) provides noneviction protection only to "family members within traditional, legally recognized familial relationships." . . . We now reverse.

The present dispute arises because the term "family" is not defined in the rent-control code and the legislative history is devoid of any specific reference to the noneviction provision. All that is known is the legislative purpose underlying the enactment of the rent-control laws as a whole. Rent control was enacted to address a "serious public emergency" created by "an acute shortage in dwellings," which resulted in "speculative, unwarranted and abnormal increases in rents." These measures were designed to regulate and control the housing market so as to "prevent exactions of unjust, unreasonable and oppressive rents and rental agreements and to forestall profiteering, speculation and other disruptive practices tending to produce threats to the public health . . . [and] to prevent uncertainty, hardship and dislocation." . . .

To accomplish its goals, the Legislature recognized that not only would rents have to be controlled, but that evictions would have to be regulated and controlled as well. Hence, section 2204.6 of the New York City Rent and Eviction Regulations (9 NYCRR 2204.6), which authorizes the issuance of a certificate for the eviction of persons occupying a rent-controlled apartment after the death of the named tenant, provides, in subdivision (d), noneviction protection to those occupants who are either the "surviving spouse of the deceased tenant or some other member of the deceased tenant's family who has been living with the tenant [of record]." The manifest intent of this section is to restrict the landowners' ability to evict a narrow class of occupants other than the tenant of record. The question presented here concerns the scope of the protections provided. Juxtaposed against this intent favoring the protection of tenants is the over-all objective of a gradual "transition from regulation to a normal market of free bargaining between landlord and tenant." One way in which this goal is to be achieved is "vacancy decontrol," which automatically makes rent-control units subject to the less rigorous provisions of rent stabilization upon the termination of the rent-control tenancy.

Emphasizing the latter objective, respondent argues that the term "family member" as used in 9 NYCRR 2204.6(d) should be construed, consistent with this State's intestacy laws, to mean relationships of blood, consanguinity and adoption in order to effectuate the over-all goal of orderly succession to real property. Under this interpretation, only those entitled to inherit under the laws of intestacy would be afforded noneviction protection. . . .

Contrary to all of these arguments, we conclude that the term "family," as used in 9 NYCRR 2204.6(d), should not be rigidly restricted to those people who have formalized their relationship by obtaining, for instance, a marriage certificate or an adoption order. The intended protection against sudden eviction should not rest on fictitious legal distinctions or genetic history, but instead should find its foundation in the reality of family life. In the context of eviction, a more realistic, and certainly equally valid, view of a family includes two adult lifetime partners whose relationship is long term and characterized by an emotional and financial commitment and interdependence. This view comports both with our society's traditional concept of "family" and with the expectations of individuals who live in such nuclear units. In fact, Webster's Dictionary defines "family" first as "a group of people united by certain convictions or common affiliation." Hence, it is reasonable to conclude that, in using the term "family," the Legislature intended to extend protection to those who reside in households having all of the normal familial characteristics. Appellant Braschi should therefore be afforded the opportunity to prove that he and Blanchard had such a household.

This definition of "family" is consistent with both of the competing purposes of the rent-control laws: the protection of individuals from sudden dislocation and the gradual transition to a free market system. Family members, whether or not related by blood or law, who have always treated the apartment as their family home will be protected against the hardship of eviction following the death of the named tenant, thereby furthering the Legislature's goals of preventing dislocation and preserving family units which might otherwise be broken apart upon eviction. This approach will foster the transition from rent control to rent stabilization by drawing a distinction between those individuals who are, in fact, genuine family members, and those who are mere roommates or newly discovered relatives hoping to inherit the rent-controlled apartment after the existing tenant's death.

The determination as to whether an individual is entitled to noneviction protection should be based upon an objective examination of the relationship of the parties. In making this assessment, the lower courts of this State have looked to a number of factors, including the exclusivity and longevity of the relationship, the level of emotional and financial commitment, the manner in which the parties have conducted their everyday lives and held themselves out to society, and the reliance placed upon one another for daily family services. These factors are most helpful, although it should be emphasized that the presence or absence of one or more of them is not dispositive since it is the totality of the relationship as evidenced by the dedication, caring and self-sacrifice of the parties which should, in the final analysis, control. Appellant's situation provides an example of how the rule should be applied.

Appellant and Blanchard lived together as permanent life partners for more than 10 years. They regarded one another, and were regarded by friends and family, as spouses. The two men's families were aware of the nature of the relationship, and they regularly visited each other's families and attended family functions together, as a couple. Even today, appellant continues to maintain a relationship with Blanchard's niece, who considers him an uncle. In addition to their interwoven social lives, appellant clearly considered the apartment his home. He lists the apartment as his address on his driver's license and passport, and receives all his mail at the apartment address. Moreover, appellant's tenancy was known to the building's superintendent and doormen, who viewed the two men as a couple. Financially, the two men shared all obligations including a household budget. The two were authorized signatories of three safe-deposit boxes, they maintained joint checking and savings accounts, and joint credit cards. In fact, rent was often paid with a check from their joint checking account. Additionally, Blanchard executed a power of attorney in appellant's favor so that appellant could make necessary decisions — financial, medical and personal — for him during his illness. Finally, appellant was the named beneficiary of Blanchard's life insurance policy, as well as the primary legatee and coexecutor of Blanchard's estate. Hence, a court examining these facts could reasonably conclude that these men were much more than mere roommates.

. . . Accordingly, the order of the Appellate Division should be reversed and the case remitted to that court for a consideration of undetermined questions. The certified question should be answered in the negative.

SIMONS, J. (dissenting). I would affirm. The plurality has adopted a definition of family which extends the language of the regulation well beyond the implication of the words used in it. In doing so, it has expanded the class indefinitely to include anyone who can satisfy an administrator that he or she had an emotional and financial "commitment" to the statutory tenant. Its interpretation is inconsistent with the legislative scheme underlying rent regulation, goes well beyond the intended purposes of 9 NYCRR 2204.6(d), and produces an unworkable test that is subject to abuse. . . .

. . . [T]here are serious practical problems in adopting the plurality's interpretation of the statute. Any determination of rights under it would require first a determination of whether protection should be accorded the relationship (i.e., unmarrieds, nonadopted occupants, etc.)

and then a subjective determination in each case of whether the relationship was genuine, and entitled to the protection of the law, or expedient, and an attempt to take advantage of the law. Plaintiff maintains that the machinery for such decisions is in place and that appropriate guidelines can be constructed. He refers particularly to a formulation outlined by the court in 2-4 Realty Assocs. v. Pittman, 137 Misc. 2d 898, 902, 523 N.Y.S.2d 7, which sets forth six different factors to be weighed. The plurality has essentially adopted his formulation. The enumeration of such factors, and the determination that they are controlling, is a matter best left to Legislatures because it involves the type of policy making the courts should avoid, but even if these considerations are appropriate and exclusive, the application of them cannot be made objectively and creates serious difficulties in determining who is entitled to the statutory benefit. Anyone is potentially eligible to succeed to the tenant's premises and thus, in each case, the agency will be required to make a determination of eligibility based solely on subjective factors such as the "level of emotional and financial commitment" and "the manner in which the parties have conducted their everyday lives and held themselves out to society."

[The concurring opinion of Bellacosa, J., is omitted.]

NOTES AND QUESTIONS

1. The governing statute in this case provides protections to members of a decedent's "family." Upon what theory does the majority find that Miguel Braschi and Leslie Blanchard were a family?

2. How does the majority determine whether a relationship constitutes a family? How would the dissent determine this question? What role do stereotypes and cultural norms play in these definitions? If Miguel and Leslie had been a heterosexual couple who lived apart for half the year, maintained separate finances, and kept their relationship secret from family and friends, would Miguel have been a surviving family member for purposes of the statute as interpreted by the majority?

3. What values are promoted by the majority's test for serving the functions of "family"? The dissent says that the state legislature should define who is a family member, not the court. Do you agree? Why or why not?

4. Today, Miguel Braschi and Leslie Blanchard could marry in New York. If they had exactly the same relationship described in the case, but *chose* not to marry, would that change the outcome of the case? *See* Matter of 530 Second Ave Co., LLC v. Zenker, 160 A.D.3d 160 (N.Y. App. Div. 2018) (reaffirming the *Braschi* holding and holding that an unmarried couple who had been together for years, broken up, but still lived together were considered family).

5. The New York City Rent Stabilization Code definition of "family" was amended to incorporate the holding of *Braschi* after the decision. Most of the cases decided under the code involve claims by long-term romantic partners. *See, e.g.*, WSC Riverside Drive Owners LLC v. Williams, 3 N.Y.S.3d 342 (App. Div. 2015) (tenant's opposite-sex partner of eight years); *see also* RHM Estates v. Hampshire, 795 N.Y.S.2d 214 (App. Div. 2005) (male roommate of female tenant who did not commingle finances but who celebrated holidays and birthdays, traveled with her, and who cared for the tenant through her cancer battle). The statute has not been limited to just long-term romantic partners. For example, In re Davidson, 903 N.Y.S.2d 685 (Sup. Ct. 2010), held that the niece of the tenant who was unable to live alone and who had lived with the tenant for 38 years and "did everything" with the tenant was a "non-traditional family member" entitled to remain in the apartment after the death of the tenant concerned.

6. Although New York courts have not broadly applied *Braschi* outside of the rent-control context, they have considered the majority's test in the child custody context. In 1991, the Court of Appeals refused to apply *Braschi*'s analytical approach to a custody dispute between a biological mother and her former partner, even though the two women had agreed to have the child and parented together for the first two years of the child's life. Alison D. v. Virginia M., 572 N.E.2d 27 (N.Y. 1991). Subsequent cases affirmed the decision: "*Alison D.*, in conjunction with second-parent adoption, creates a bright-line rule that promotes certainty in the wake of domestic breakups otherwise fraught with the risk of 'disruptive . . . battle[s].'" Matter of Jacob, 660 N.E.2d 397 (N.Y. 1995); *see also* Debra H. v. Janice R., 930 N.E.2d 184 (N.Y. 2010) (applying *Alison D.* to a couple in a civil union). In 2016, however, the Court of Appeals overruled *Alison D.* Brooke S.B. v. Elizabeth A.C.C., 61 N.E.3d 488 (N.Y. 2016). The court held that when clear and convincing evidence showed that the biological mother of a child and her partner agreed to conceive and raise a child together, the partner had standing as a parent to seek custody and visitation. Cases following *Brooke S.B.* are considered further in Chapter 13.

7. Whether cohabitants are entitled to public benefits has arisen in a number of other situations with mixed results. *See, e.g.*, MacGregor v. Unemployment Insurance Appeals Board, 689 P.2d 453 (Cal. 1984) (allowing unemployment compensation benefits to a woman who quit work to follow fiancé); Norman v. Unemployment Insurance Appeals Board, 663 P.2d 904 (Cal. 1983) (denying unemployment benefits to a woman who quit work to follow cohabitant because this was not "good cause"). Some jurisdictions have statutes that provide relief in specific instances. *See, e.g.*, Or. Rev. Stat. §656.226 (effective 2023) (treating cohabitants living together for over a year the same as married couples for workers' compensation).

Marriage continues to play a central role in defining family for legal purposes. But should a relationship recognized by a marriage license be the only thing that counts as a legally recognized status of intimate rights and responsibilities? In the not-too-distant past, sexual relationships outside marriage were criminal, punished under laws that prohibited fornication and adultery, for example. While this is no longer true today in many states, in all states unmarried cohabitation is allowed but does not give rise to all the legal advantages (and disadvantages) of marriage. Does this amount to treating nonmarriage as lesser than marriage? Consider how the Supreme Court describes the history and importance of the institution of marriage below.

Obergefell v. Hodges
576 U.S. 644 (2015)
[Another excerpt of this opinion appears on page 113.]

Justice KENNEDY delivered the opinion of the Court. . . . From their beginning to their most recent page, the annals of human history reveal the transcendent importance of marriage. The lifelong union of a man and a woman always has promised nobility and dignity to all persons, without regard to their station in life. Marriage is sacred to those who live by their religions and offers unique fulfillment to those who find meaning in the secular realm. Its dynamic allows two people to find a life that could not be found alone, for a marriage becomes greater than just the two persons. Rising from the most basic human needs, marriage is essential to our most profound hopes and aspirations.

The centrality of marriage to the human condition makes it unsurprising that the institution has existed for millennia and across civilizations. Since the dawn of history, marriage has transformed strangers into relatives, binding families and societies together. Confucius taught that marriage lies at the foundation of government. This wisdom was echoed centuries later and half a world away by Cicero, who wrote, "The first bond of society is marriage; next, children; and then the family." There are untold references to the beauty of marriage in religious and philosophical texts spanning time, cultures, and faiths, as well as in art and literature in all their forms. It is fair and necessary to say these references were based on the understanding that marriage is a union between two persons of the opposite sex.

That history is the beginning of these cases. The respondents say it should be the end as well. To them, it would demean a timeless institution if the concept and lawful status of marriage were extended to two persons of the same sex. Marriage, in their view, is by its nature a gender-differentiated union of man and woman. This view long has been held—and continues to be held—in good faith by reasonable and sincere people here and throughout the world. . . .

Choices about marriage shape an individual's destiny. As the Supreme Judicial Court of Massachusetts has explained, because "it fulfills yearnings for security, safe haven, and connection that express our common humanity, civil marriage is an esteemed institution, and the decision whether and whom to marry is among life's momentous acts of self-definition." *Goodridge*, 440 Mass., at 322, 798 N.E.2d, at 955.

The nature of marriage is that, through its enduring bond, two persons together can find other freedoms, such as expression, intimacy, and spirituality. This is true for all persons, whatever their sexual orientation. There is dignity in the bond between two men or two women who seek to marry and in their autonomy to make such profound choices. Cf. *Loving, supra*, at 12 ("[T]he freedom to marry, or not marry, a person of another race resides with the individual and cannot be infringed by the State").

A second principle in this Court's jurisprudence is that the right to marry is fundamental because it supports a two-person union unlike any other in its importance to the committed individuals. This point was central to Griswold v. Connecticut, which held the Constitution protects the right of married couples to use contraception. 381 U.S., at 485. Suggesting that marriage is a right "older than the Bill of Rights," *Griswold* described marriage this way:

> "Marriage is a coming together for better or for worse, hopefully enduring, and intimate to the degree of being sacred. It is an association that promotes a way of life, not causes; a harmony in living, not political faiths; a bilateral loyalty, not commercial or social projects. Yet it is an association for as noble a purpose as any involved in our prior decisions." *Id.*, at 486.

And in *Turner*, the Court again acknowledged the intimate association protected by this right, holding prisoners could not be denied the right to marry because their committed relationships satisfied the basic reasons why marriage is a fundamental right. The right to marry thus dignifies couples who "wish to define themselves by their commitment to each other." Marriage responds to the universal fear that a lonely person might call out only to find no one there. It offers the hope of companionship and understanding and assurance that while both still live there will be someone to care for the other. . . .

A first premise of the Court's relevant precedents is that the right to personal choice regarding marriage is inherent in the concept of individual autonomy. . . . Like choices concerning contraception, family relationships, procreation, and childrearing, all of which are protected by the Constitution, decisions concerning marriage are among the most intimate that an individual can make. . . .

A third basis for protecting the right to marry is that it safeguards children and families and thus draws meaning from related rights of childrearing, procreation, and education. See

Pierce v. Society of Sisters, 268 U.S. 510 (1925); *Meyer*, 262 U.S., at 399. The Court has recognized these connections by describing the varied rights as a unified whole: "[T]he right to 'marry, establish a home and bring up children' is a central part of the liberty protected by the Due Process Clause." *Zablocki*, 434 U.S., at 384 (quoting *Meyer, supra*, at 399). Under the laws of the several States, some of marriage's protections for children and families are material. But marriage also confers more profound benefits. By giving recognition and legal structure to their parents' relationship, marriage allows children "to understand the integrity and closeness of their own family and its concord with other families in their community and in their daily lives." Marriage also affords the permanency and stability important to children's best interests. . . .

Fourth and finally, this Court's cases and the Nation's traditions make clear that marriage is a keystone of our social order. Alexis de Tocqueville recognized this truth on his travels through the United States almost two centuries ago:

> "There is certainly no country in the world where the tie of marriage is so much respected as in America. . . . [W]hen the American retires from the turmoil of public life to the bosom of his family, he finds in it the image of order and of peace. . . . [H]e afterwards carries [that image] with him into public affairs." 1 Democracy in America 309 (H. Reeve transl., rev. ed. 1990).

In Maynard v. Hill, 125 U.S. 190, 211 (1888), the Court echoed de Tocqueville, explaining that marriage is "the foundation of the family and of society, without which there would be neither civilization nor progress." Marriage, the *Maynard* Court said, has long been "'a great public institution, giving character to our whole civil polity.'" *Id.*, at 213, 8 S. Ct. 723. This idea has been reiterated even as the institution has evolved in substantial ways over time, superseding rules related to parental consent, gender, and race once thought by many to be essential. . . .

No union is more profound than marriage, for it embodies the highest ideals of love, fidelity, devotion, sacrifice, and family. In forming a marital union, two people become something greater than once they were. As some of the petitioners in these cases demonstrate, marriage embodies a love that may endure even past death. It would misunderstand these men and women to say they disrespect the idea of marriage. Their plea is that they do respect it, respect it so deeply that they seek to find its fulfillment for themselves. Their hope is not to be condemned to live in loneliness, excluded from one of civilization's oldest institutions. . . .

NOTES AND QUESTIONS

1. How does Justice Kennedy view the modern purpose of marriage? In explaining the importance of marriage, he describes principles tied to self-determination—the choice of selecting a mate for a "two-person union unlike any other" and the right to "shape an individual's destiny." The traditional approach to marriage, which Chief Justice Roberts' dissent emphasized, involved marriage as command: those who engage in sexual intercourse that may result in pregnancy have an obligation to marry because marriage is the institution designed to deal with the consequences of pregnancy. And, historically, marriage as "a command" involved not just the obligation to marry, but the assumption of gendered obligations within it. Does this concept of self-definition mean that marriage has become a choice not a command?

2. Scholars like Marsha Garrison have defended the signaling function of marriage and the clarity it brings to a couple's legal rights and obligations: "Formal marriage signals intention. It signals each partner who enters into a new marital union, their friends, and their families. It also signals strangers; those who meet or do business with the married couple understand that each spouse has entered into a binding commitment that entails expectations of fidelity, sharing, and lifetime partnership. Formal marriage also signals intention to the state; government officials can and do assume that the married couple has undertaken obligations to each other that both justify treating them as an economic unit and assuming that a deceased spouse would want his or her marital partner to obtain the lion's share of the decedent spouse's assets." The Decline of Formal Marriage: Inevitable or Reversible?, 49 Fam. L.Q. 491, 493-499, 501-503, 516-519 (2007). State courts have also held that intimate cohabitation, even if long and marriage-like, should not receive the same status as marriage under law. The Supreme Court of Illinois, in dismissing common law claims between never-married, long-term cohabitants of the same sex, wrote:

> [T]his court finds that the current legislative and judicial trend is to uphold the institution of marriage. Most notably, within the past year, the United States Supreme Court in Obergefell v. Hodges, 135 S. Ct. 2584, 2604-05 (2015), held that same-sex couples cannot be denied the right to marry. In doing so, the Court found that "new insights [from the developments in the institution of marriage over the past centuries] have strengthened, not weakened, the institution of marriage." For the institution of marriage has been a keystone of our social order and "remains a building block of our national community." Accordingly, the Court invalidated any state legislation prohibiting same-sex marriage because excluding same-sex couples from marriage would be excluding them "from one of civilization's oldest institutions." . . .
>
> It is well settled that the policy of the [Illinois] Marriage and Dissolution Act gives the state a strong continuing interest in the institution of marriage and the ability to prevent marriage from becoming in effect a private contract terminable at will, by disfavoring the grant of mutually enforceable property rights to knowingly unmarried cohabitants. . . .

Blumenthal v. Brewer, 69 N.E.3d 834 (Ill. 2016).

Can marriage be a "keystone of the social order" if it is not mandatory or if it is principally a matter of self-definition, per Justice Kennedy's opinion? Does choice alter the role of the "signaling function" of marriage or does it mean that a couple can signal commitment, fidelity, and permanence without assuming defined roles within marriage?

3. Some legal scholars have reacted negatively to Justice Kennedy's praise of marriage, interpreting it as denigrating people who choose not to. They argue that the law must recognize and protect at least some familial rights for those who do not marry. Others believe it makes sense to keep some legal distinctions between married and unmarried couples, though they differ about what such distinctions should be. *See, e.g.*, June Carbone & Naomi Cahn, Nonmarriage, 76 Md. L. Rev. 55 (2016); Clare Huntington, Obergefell's Conservatism: Reifying Familial Fronts, 84 Fordham L. Rev. 23 (2015); Courtney G. Joslin, The Gay Rights Canon and the Right to Nonmarriage, 97 B.U. L. Rev. 425 (2017); Melissa Murray, Obergefell v. Hodges and Nonmarriage Inequality, 104 Calif. L. Rev. 1207 (2016). What might it mean to protect the right to nonmarriage? Many of the harms Justice Kennedy cites stem as much from law's failure to recognize the parentage of a second, nonmarried parent as they do from the inability to marry. Is marriage necessary for law to recognize families with children?

4. As Justice Kennedy makes clear in *Obergefell,* the right to marry is bound up with other rights that the Supreme Court has interpreted as fundamental and protected by the Constitution, such as rights to make decisions related to childbearing and childrearing and to engage in intimate or sexual conduct. Can rights to marry be disentangled from other rights to make familial and intimate decisions? Consider that question as you read Dobbs v.

Jackson Women's Health Org., 142 S. Ct. 2228 (2022), overturning constitutional protection for abortion, in Chapter 2.

5. One of the important legal effects of marriage is that both spouses are recognized as parents of children born during the marriage, and the parents generally have equal legal rights to custody and responsibility for children. Is marriage important to the definition of family and children's well-being because there is something important about marriage itself or is it because, at the time of the decision, many states required marriage to recognize parental status on the basis of something other than biology? As we will see, resolving legal questions becomes more complicated when children are born to unmarried parents. These issues are considered at length in Chapters 13 and 14.

The previous cases have considered definitions of family based on whether or not the parties are married or appeared to be "like" married couples. A host of laws govern how family is defined for purposes of private and public benefits. The following cases consider zoning laws—regulations that prohibit or permit groups of people to live together in a household. Consider the opposite conclusions drawn by the following two decisions.

City of Ladue v. Horn
720 S.W.2d 745 (Mo. App. E.D. 1986)

CRANDALL, Judge. Defendants, Joan Horn and E. Terrence Jones, appeal from the judgment of the trial court in favor of plaintiff, City of Ladue (Ladue), which enjoined defendants from occupying their home in violation of Ladue's zoning ordinance and which dismissed defendants' counterclaim. We affirm.

The case was submitted to the trial court on stipulated facts. Ladue's Zoning Ordinance No. 1175 was in effect at all times pertinent to the present action. Certain zones were designated as one-family residential. The zoning ordinance defined family as: "One or more persons related by blood, marriage or adoption, occupying a dwelling unit as an individual housekeeping organization." The only authorized accessory use in residential districts was for "[a]ccommodations for domestic persons employed and living on the premises and home occupations." The purpose of Ladue's zoning ordinance was broadly stated as to promote "the health, safety, morals and general welfare" of Ladue.

In July, 1981, defendants purchased a seven-bedroom, four-bathroom house which was located in a single-family residential zone in Ladue. Residing in defendants' home were Horn's two children (aged 16 and 19) and Jones's one child (age 18). The two older children attended out-of-state universities and lived in the house only on a part-time basis. Although defendants were not married, they shared a common bedroom, maintained a joint checking account for the household expenses, ate their meals together, entertained together, and disciplined each other's children. Ladue made demands upon defendants to vacate their home because their household did not comprise a family, as defined by Ladue's zoning ordinance, and therefore they could not live in an area zoned for single-family dwellings. When defendants refused to vacate, Ladue sought to enjoin defendants' continued violation of the zoning ordinance. Defendants counterclaimed, seeking a declaration that the zoning ordinance was constitutionally void. They also sought attorneys' fees and costs. The trial court entered a permanent injunction in favor of Ladue and dismissed defendants' counterclaim. Enforcement of the injunction was stayed pending this appeal. . . .

. . . Defendants allege that the United States and Missouri Constitutions grant each of them the right to share his or her residence with whomever he or she chooses. They assert that Ladue has not demonstrated a compelling, much less rational, justification for the overly proscriptive blood or legal relationship requirement in its zoning ordinance.

Defendants posit that the term "family" is susceptible to several meanings. They contend that, since their household is the "functional and factual equivalent of a natural family," the ordinance may not preclude them from living in a single-family residential Ladue neighborhood. Defendants argue in their brief as follows:

> The record amply demonstrates that the private, intimate interests of Horn and Jones are substantial. Horn, Jones, and their respective children have historically lived together as a single family unit. They use and occupy their home for the identical purposes and in the identical manners as families which are biologically or maritally related.

To bolster this contention, defendants elaborate on their shared duties, as set forth earlier in this opinion. Defendants acknowledge the importance of viewing themselves as a family unit, albeit a "conceptual family" as opposed to a "true non-family," in order to prevent the application of the ordinance.

The fallacy in defendants' syllogism is that the stipulated facts do not compel the conclusion that defendants are living as a family. A man and woman living together, sharing pleasures and certain responsibilities, does not *per se* constitute a family in even the conceptual sense. To approximate a family relationship, there must exist a commitment to a permanent relationship and a perceived reciprocal obligation to support and to care for each other. Only when these characteristics are present can the conceptual family, perhaps, equate with the traditional family. In a traditional family, certain of its inherent attributes arise from the legal relationship of the family members. In a non-traditional family, those same qualities arise in fact, either by explicit agreement or by tacit understanding among the parties.

While the stipulated facts could arguably support an inference by the trial court that defendants and their children comprised a non-traditional family, they do not compel that inference. Absent findings of fact and conclusions of law, we cannot assume that the trial court's perception of defendants' familial status comported with defendants' characterization of themselves as a conceptual family. In fact, if a finding by the trial court that defendants' living arrangement constituted a conceptual family is critical to a determination in defendants' favor, we can assume that the court's finding was adverse to defendants' position. Ordinarily, given our deference to the decision of the trial court, that would dispose of this appeal. We decline, however, to restrict our ruling to such a narrow basis. We therefore consider the broader issues presented by the parties. We assume, *arguendo*, that the sole basis for the judgment entered by the trial court was that defendants were not related by blood, marriage or adoption, as required by Ladue's ordinance.

We first consider whether the ordinance violates any federally protected rights of the defendants. Generally, federal court decisions hold that a zoning classification based upon a biological or a legal relationship among household members is justifiable under constitutional police powers to protect the public health, safety, morals or welfare of the community.

More specifically, the United States Supreme Court has developed a two-tiered approach by which to examine legislation challenged as violative of the equal protection clause. If the personal interest affected by the ordinance is fundamental, "strict scrutiny" is applied and the ordinance is sustained only upon a showing that the burden imposed is necessary to protect a compelling governmental interest. If the ordinance does not contain a suspect class or impinge upon a fundamental interest, the more relaxed "rational basis" test is applied and the classification imposed by the ordinance is upheld if any facts can reasonably justify it. Defendants urge this court to recognize that their interest in choosing their own living arrangement inexorably involves their fundamental rights of freedom of association and of privacy. . . .

In the Village of Belle Terre v. Boraas, 416 U.S. 1 (1974), the court addressed a zoning regulation of the type at issue in this case. The court held that the Village of Belle Terre ordinance involved no fundamental right, but was typical of economic and social legislation which is upheld if it is reasonably related to a permissible governmental objective. The challenged zoning ordinance of the Village of Belle Terre defined family as:

> One or more persons related by blood, adoption or marriage, living and cooking together as a single housekeeping unit [or] a number of persons but not exceeding two (2) living and cooking together as a single housekeeping unit though not related by blood, adoption, or marriage. . . .

The court upheld the ordinance, reasoning that the ordinance constituted valid land use legislation reasonably designed to maintain traditional family values and patterns.

The importance of the family was reaffirmed in Moore v. City of East Cleveland, 431 U.S. 494 (1977), wherein the United States Supreme Court was confronted with a housing ordinance which defined a "family" as only certain closely related individuals. Consequently, a grandmother who lived with her son and two grandsons was convicted of violating the ordinance because her two grandsons were first cousins rather than brothers. The United States Supreme Court struck down the East Cleveland ordinance for violating the freedom of personal choice in matters of marriage and family life. The court distinguished Belle Terre by stating that the ordinance in that case allowed all individuals related by blood, marriage or adoption to live together; whereas East Cleveland, by restricting the number of related persons who could live together, sought "to regulate the occupancy of its housing by slicing deeply into the family itself." The court pointed out that the institution of the family is protected by the Constitution precisely because it is so deeply rooted in the American tradition and that "[o]urs is by no means a tradition limited to respect for the bonds uniting the members of the nuclear family."

Here, because we are dealing with economic and social legislation and not with a fundamental interest or a suspect classification, the test of constitutionality is whether the ordinance is reasonable and not arbitrary and bears a rational relationship to a permissible state objective.

Ladue has a legitimate concern with laying out guidelines for land use addressed to family needs. "It is ample to lay out zones where family values, youth values, and the blessings of quiet seclusion and clean air make the area a sanctuary for people." The question of whether Ladue could have chosen more precise means to effectuate its legislative goals is immaterial. Ladue's zoning ordinance is rationally related to its expressed purposes and violates no provisions of the Constitution of the United States. Further, defendants' assertion that they have a constitutional right to share their residence with whomever they please amounts to the same argument that was made and found unpersuasive by the court in *Belle Terre*. . . .

For purposes of its zoning code, Ladue has in precise language defined the term "family." It chose the definition which comports with the historical and traditional notions of family; namely, those people related by blood, marriage or adoption. That definition of family has been upheld in numerous Missouri decisions. *See, e.g.*, London v. Handicapped Facilities Board of St. Charles County, 637 S.W.2d 212 (Mo. App. 1982) (group home not a "family" as used in restrictive covenant); Feely v. Birenbaum, 554 S.W.2d 432 (Mo. App. 1977) (two unrelated males not a "family" as used in restrictive covenant); Cash v. Catholic Diocese, 414 S.W.2d 346 (Mo. App. 1967) (nuns not a "family" as used in a restrictive covenant).

Decisions from other state jurisdictions have addressed identical constitutional challenges to zoning ordinances similar to the ordinance in the instant case. The reviewing courts have upheld their respective ordinances on the ground that maintenance of a traditional family environment constitutes a reasonable basis for excluding uses that may impair the stability of that environment and erode the values associated with traditional family life.[1]

The essence of zoning is selection; and, if it is not invidious or discriminatory against those not selected, it is proper. There is no doubt that there is a governmental interest in marriage and in preserving the integrity of the biological or legal family. There is no concomitant governmental interest in keeping together a group of unrelated persons, no matter how closely they simulate a family. Further, there is no state policy which commands that groups of people may live under the same roof in any section of a municipality they choose.

The stated purpose of Ladue's zoning ordinance is the promotion of the health, safety, morals, and general welfare in the city. Whether Ladue could have adopted less restrictive means to achieve these same goals is not a controlling factor in considering the constitutionality of the zoning ordinance. Rather, our focus is on whether there exists some reasonable basis for the means actually employed. In making such a determination, if any state of facts either known or which could reasonably be assumed is presented in support of the ordinance, we must defer to the legislative judgment. We find that Ladue has not acted arbitrarily in enacting its zoning ordinance which defines family as those related by blood, marriage or adoption. Given the fact that Ladue has so defined family, we defer to its legislative judgment.

The judgment of the trial court is affirmed.

NOTES AND QUESTIONS

1. Why did the City of Ladue limit buildings in this part of town to "single family dwellings"? How does the Ladue zoning ordinance define "single family"? What assumptions about the meaning of "family" does this definition make? Is this definition of "family" consistent with the goal of the ordinance? If Horn and Jones had lived together without their children, would they be able to meet the requirements of the single-family ordinance? If they had married, but not adopted each other's children, would this have changed the result? Which arrangement—two unmarried adults or a married couple with adult children from prior relationships—better fits the idea of family in the Ladue ordinance and in the readings above?

2. The court in *City of Ladue* relies on the Supreme Court decision in Belle Terre v. Boraas to reject the Horns' claim that their right to live together was protected under Moore v. City of East Cleveland. What is the extent of the right recognized in *Moore*? Some lower courts and many advocates have relied on *Moore* as a basis for legal protection for functional families, as we will see later in this book. For a summary of the racial and other assumptions about the nature and composition of family made in the *Moore* decision, *see* R.A. Lenhardt & Clare Huntington, Symposium: Moore Kinship, 85 Fordham L. Rev. 2251, 2254-2256 (2017).

---

1. *See, e.g.,* City of White Plains v. Ferraioli, 34 N.Y.2d 300, 357 N.Y.S.2d 449, 313 N.E.2d 756 (1974) (married couple, their two children and 10 foster children not a family under city's ordinance); Rademan v. City and County of Denver, 186 Colo. 250, 526 P.2d 1325 (1974) (two married couples living as a "communal family" not a family); Town of Durham v. White Enterprises, Inc., 115 N.H. 645, 348 A.2d 706 (1975) (student renters not a family); Prospect Gardens Convalescent Home, Inc. v. City of Norwalk, 32 Conn. Supp. 214, 347 A.2d 637 (1975) (nursing home employees living together not a family). *See generally* Annot., 12 A.L.R.4th 238 (1985). A number of jurisdictions have found restrictive zoning ordinances invalid. *See, e.g.,* City of Des Plaines v. Trottner, 34 Ill. 2d 432, 216 N.E.2d 116 (1970) (ordinance with restrictive definition of family violates authority delegated by state legislature in the enabling statute); City of Santa Barbara v. Adamson, 27 Cal. 3d 123, 164 Cal. Rptr. 539, 610 P.2d 436 (1982) (zoning ordinance limiting the number of unrelated persons who could live together, but not related persons, did not further legislative goals); Charter Township of Delta v. Dinolfo, 419 Mich. 253, 351 N.W.2d 831 (1984) (restrictive definition of family not rationally related to achieving township's goals).

3. A few state courts have held that zoning ordinances based on traditional definitions of "family" required a heightened level of scrutiny under the state constitution. City of Santa Barbara v. Adamson, 610 P.2d 436 (Cal. 1980); Charter Township of Delta v. Dinolfo, 351 N.W.2d 831 (Mich. 1984); State v. Baker, 405 A.2d 368 (N.J. 1979); Baer v. Town of Brookhaven, 537 N.E.2d 819 (N.Y. 1989). However, most state courts have followed *Belle Terre* and upheld single-family dwelling unit ordinances with restrictive definitions of "family" against constitutional challenges, relying on rational basis scrutiny. *See, e.g.*, Schwartz v. Philadelphia Zoning Bd. of Adjustment, 126 A.3d 1032 (Pa. Commw. Ct. 2015); City of Baton Rouge v. Myers, 145 So. 3d 320 (La. 2014); McMaster v. Columbia Bd. of Zoning Appeals, 719 S.E.2d 660 (S.C. 2011). Consider this comment on such ordinances:

> Zoning urban, suburban, and rural areas has proven a useful tool for local and state governments to control population, traffic, pollution, and other social problems. Unfortunately, zoning has also been used to control the identity of the population, and with some success. The ordinance at issue in *Belle Terre* was a common instance of this kind of control; it limited the number of unrelated people that could live in a home, but put no such limit on the number of related people that may live together. Using this type of zoning ordinance, many municipalities have successfully kept out or forced out unrelated people living communally and other non-traditional families. This sort of discrimination, although purportedly for the lawful purpose of protecting traditional family values, effectively imposes the municipality's social preferences on the individuals in the community. Not only does this seem contrary to the most basic and often quoted American themes of plurality and individuality, it summarily dismisses the value of the voluntary family. . . .
>
> No doubt the law-abiding citizens of Belle Terre believed that the Supreme Court had saved their neighborhood. After all, if those students were allowed to live there, others could follow, until the streets were lined with traffic and empty beer bottles. Once the "weirdos" got in, they might never be able to get rid of them, and the quiet of their waterfront enclave would be forever lost.
>
> Those students were not the weirdos the villagers thought, however. In fact, they were probably making better use of the six-bedroom house than anyone else had ever made of it. They shared responsibilities and intellectual conversations, and lived as efficiently as they could on their limited means. During the summer, they, like everyone else in town, looked forward to relaxing on the beach with their family. This family was simply a little bit different in character than the others: there were no noisy children and no wedding rings. Instead there was friendship, camaraderie, and a well-run household.

Rebecca Ginzburg, Note, Altering "Family": Another Look at the Supreme Court's Narrow Protection of Families in *Belle Terre*, 83 B.U. L. Rev. 875, 877, 896 (2003). Single-family zoning also tends to increase segregation, since people of color are more likely to live in duplexes and multifamily dwellings. Solangel Maldonado, Sharing a House but Not a Household: Extended Families and Exclusionary Zoning Forty Years After *Moore*, 85 Fordham L. Rev. 2641 (2017). *See also* Rigel C. Oliveri, Single-Family Zoning, Intimate Association, and the Right to Choose Household Companions, 67 Fla. L. Rev. 1402 (2015).

4. Twenty-one states have statutes prohibiting discrimination on the basis of marital status in housing, employment, or both. A few of the statutes explicitly provide that they do not protect unmarried cohabiting couples; in most of the remaining states, courts have interpreted the statutes to achieve the same result. Courtney G. Joslin, Marital Status Discrimination 2.0, 95 B.U. L. Rev. 805, 808 (2015). In some states, however, the statutes have been construed to provide protection. *E.g.*, Richardson v. Northwest Christian University, 242 F. Supp. 3d 1132, (D. Or. 2017) (policy prohibiting extramarital sex or cohabitation is marital status discrimination).

The federal Fair Housing Act prohibits discrimination on the basis of "familial status." 42 U.S.C. §3602(k) (2022). However, the statute is generally interpreted as prohibiting only discrimination against families with minor children, and the House Report states that "family status" does not include marital status. Joslin, *supra*, at 810-811.

Armstrong v. Mayor
979 A.2d 98 (Md. 2009)

HARRELL, Judge. The land use dispute engendering the present case (and its predecessors, contemporaries, and what may come yet) represents Baltimore City's version of the Hundred Years' War.[2] The present skirmish involves the interpretation and application of the term "family" as defined by the Baltimore City Zoning Code ("the Code" or "BCZC").

The Code provides that a "dwelling unit" may be occupied by no more than one "family." Four unrelated individuals (and no more) who live together comprise a "family," if they form a "single housekeeping unit." . . .

Cresmont Properties Ltd. ("Cresmont") owns a 28,132 square-foot parcel of land (the "Property") located at 2807-35 Cresmont Avenue in Baltimore City. Petitioners, a group of neighborhood residents opposed to Cresmont's development of and particular use established on the Property, challenge here the last of three construction permits, as well as an occupancy permit, issued to Cresmont by the Baltimore City Department of Housing and Community Development ("DHCD") for a multi-unit residential building known as Cresmont Loft. . . .

. . . Petitioners argued that the Property was not going to house the twenty-six dwelling units for which the construction permit was issued. Although there were twenty-six four-bedroom suites, Petitioners urged that the suites were not dwelling units. They claimed that the developer intended to lease separately each of the four bedrooms in each of the suites. Thus, as this argument proceeded, the Property actually housed 104 individual "rooming units."

Cresmont countered that each of the twenty-six suites satisfied the Code definition of a "dwelling unit." A "dwelling unit," Cresmont observed, is a rental unit that contains a bathroom, kitchen facilities, and is occupied by a "family." Cresmont proffered that the tenants of each suite would constitute a "family," despite having separate leases, because they would be "living together as a single housekeeping unit," as required by the Code definition of "family." Thus, according to Cresmont, the project complied with the construction permit's allowance of twenty-six dwelling units. . . .

At the hearing, Petitioners introduced several of Cresmont Loft's promotional materials which made clear that Cresmont intended to rent the twenty-six suites to a total of 104 individual tenants. One advertisement listed a total of 104 "units" available for rent. A website provided that "[e]ach unrelated resident will sign a separate lease." Petitioners also introduced the affidavit of a "potential tenant" who inquired about renting at Cresmont Loft. She stated that "[t]he woman who answered the phone said, 'You have to understand that [you] would only be renting the bedroom.'" . . .

On 2 November 2006, the Board issued its third (and final) written decision affirming the issuance of the April 2004 construction permit. In pertinent part, the Board concluded: . . . that the use of each of the dwelling units by four unrelated people who live

---

2. The Hundred Years' War (1337-1453) was a prolonged series of conflicts between the royal Houses of Valois and Plantagenet, each vying to rule France after the extinction of the Capetian line of French kings. The House of Valois (the ultimate victors) were native French. The Plantagenets were French-English and ruled England at the time. The Hundred Years' War gave history Joan of Arc. The instant case also has a central figure named Joan (one of the Petitioners), who, like her saintly antecedent, faithfully presses her cause, having battled the Mayor and City Council of Baltimore numerous times. Although Joan of Arc suffered an unfortunate fate, her principals, the House of Valois, ultimately succeeded. As this case probably will not be the last combat between these litigants, time will tell whether the modern Joan ultimately will hoist the banner of victory in the war over the Cresmont Loft apartment building.

together as a single housekeeping unit in a dwelling unit complies with the definition of "Family" in Section 1-142 of the Zoning Code. . . .

On 9 May 2007, the Circuit Court affirmed the decisions of the Board. Petitioners timely noted an appeal to the Court of Special Appeals, which, in an unreported decision, affirmed in part and reversed in part. . . .

We granted Petitioners' petition for a writ of certiorari. . . .

The Code defines a "dwelling unit" as "1 or more rooms in a dwelling that: (1) are used as living quarters for occupancy by 1 family; and (2) contain permanently installed bathroom and kitchen facilities reserved for the occupants of the room or rooms." BCZC §1-137. Thus, for the City to prevail in its assertion that the suites are "dwelling units," the tenants of each suite must meet the Code's land use definition of a "family." The definition of "family," therefore, is the focal point of this case. It provides:

(a) *In general.*
"Family" means one of the following, together with usual household helpers:
(1) an individual;
(2) or more people related by blood, marriage, or adoption, living together as a single housekeeping unit in a dwelling unit; or
(3) *a group of not more than 4 people, who need not be related by blood, marriage, or adoption, living together as a single housekeeping unit in a dwelling unit.* . . .

The Code does not define the phrase "single housekeeping unit"; however, it is the pivotal term in our assessment of whether the Board concluded properly that the tenants of a suite at Cresmont Loft constitute a "family," and, in turn, that each suite is a "dwelling unit" for purposes of the Code's Bulk Regulations. . . . [T]he phrase "single housekeeping unit" is found with some frequency in the zoning codes of other municipalities and local governments across the country, and the attendant judicial opinions interpreting those codes help us to triangulate on a common and ordinary sense of the phrase as used in comparable land use settings. . . .

. . . In those cases interpreting zoning ordinances wherein the "family" limitation had been defined as a "single housekeeping unit," many extended family groups were deemed to fall within that category. The use of this test was viewed as extending beyond the occupancy by a one-family unit to a determination as to whether it was a one-housekeeping unit. The focus was on whether the unit functioned as a family unit, rather than on the respective relationships that existed between the members of the unit. *See, e.g.*, City of Syracuse v. Snow, 123 Misc. 568, 205 N.Y.S. 785 (Sup. Ct. 1924) ("single housekeeping unit" held not to exclude a college sorority); Robertson v. Western Baptist Hospital, 267 S.W.2d 395 (Ct. of Appeals of Ky. 1954) (use of a residence as a home for about 20 nurses constituted a permitted use under a "single housekeeping unit" test); Boston-Edison Protective Ass'n v. Paulist Fathers, 306 Mich. 253, 10 N.W.2d 847 (1943), 306 Mich. 253, 10 N.W.2d 847, 148 A.L.R. 364 (approved the use of a dwelling house in a highly restricted district as a residence for Roman Catholic priests).

As noted in Rathkopf's treatise on zoning, "[i]n the past, courts have interpreted [the phrase 'single housekeeping unit'] in a rather elastic way, generally ruling that any living arrangement which makes use of unified house-keeping facilities satisfies such an ordinance." 3 Edward H. Ziegler, Jr. et al., Rathkopf's The Law of Zoning and Planning 23-33 (Thompson Reuters 2009). A survey of relevant case law from other jurisdictions confirms this.

In *Miller*, the Pennsylvania Supreme Court held that a homeowner, who allowed unrelated elderly and handicapped persons to live with her, did not violate a local ordinance limiting the occupation of a home in her zoning district to one "family," where "family" was defined by the ordinance as "any number of persons living and cooking together as a single house-keeping unit." That court opined, based on the extensive history of the term, that "the 'single housekeeping unit' evolved as a term limiting the use [of a property] to a unit that functions in the manner of a family residence." The court reasoned that the unrelated individuals living with the homeowner constituted a single housekeeping unit because the evidence established that they lived and cooked together, shared meals together, and had shared access to all areas of the premises. . . . In another case, Linn County v. City of Hiawatha, 311 N.W.2d 95 (Iowa 1981), the Supreme Court of Iowa held that a foster home in which a married couple cared for six unrelated, developmentally-disabled children constituted a "single housekeeping unit." There, the court rejected the argument that, because the children's Social Security benefits covered the cost of maintaining them in the home, the setting was akin to a boarding house. The court reasoned that, in effect, "'the duties and responsibilities of the occupants [of the foster home] in . . . maintaining a household . . . cannot be distinguished from those performed by other home dwellers in the community.'"

In Borough of Glassboro v. Vallorosi, 117 N.J. 421, 568 A.2d 888 (1990), the Supreme Court of New Jersey affirmed a trial court's finding that ten unrelated college students were a "single housekeeping unit." There, the parents of a college student purchased a house near campus in which they allowed their son and nine of his friends to live while attending school. The student roommates shared the common areas of the house, as well as a telephone line; they "often ate meals together in small groups, cooked for each other, and generally shared the household chores, grocery shopping, and yard work." Like the tenants of Cresmont Loft, the roommates in *Vallorosi* had separate lease agreements with the landlord. Each lease was for a term of four months (the length of a semester) and was renewable at the term's end.

The *Vallorosi* court framed the "narrow issue before [it]" as "whether there [wa]s sufficient credible evidence in th[e] record to sustain the trial court's factual finding that the occupancy of the defendants' dwelling by these ten college students constituted a single house-keeping unit as defined by the Glassboro ordinance." Answering in the affirmative, the court highlighted that

> The students ate together, shared household chores, and paid expenses from a common fund. Although the students signed four-month leases, the leases were renewable if the house was "in order" at the end of the term. Moreover, the students testified to their own intention to remain in the house throughout college, and there was no significant evidence of defections up to the time of trial.

The "narrow issue" before this Court is whether the Board's decisions affirming the issuance of the April 2004 construction permit and the August 2004 occupancy permit were supported by substantial evidence. Viewing the evidence of record in a light most favorable to the Board, we hold that they were. The Cresmont Loft form lease agreement provides that a tenant has the sole use of her or his bedroom and the "shared use and occupancy of the bathroom(s), kitchen and living/dining areas" of the apartment in which she or he resides. It further establishes that the tenant is "liable for a pro-rata share of any damages to the common areas of the apartment unit . . . unless the party solely responsible for any such damage can be reasonably ascertained." Moreover, according to the undisputed testimony of the property manager, Brian Swift, Cresmont Loft leases are for a term of one year. Mr. Swift also echoed that a tenant has "the exclusive right to th[e] entire four bedroom unit" and that she or he is equally "responsible for the care and maintenance of the apartment unit." As observed in the cases discussed herein, shared access to the premises and joint responsibility for the care thereof are significant considerations. . . .

Petitioners' flagship argument in opposition to the Board's conclusion lies in the Cresmont Loft lease agreement. Petitioners maintain that the tenants of a suite may not be a "single housekeeping unit" because each has a separate lease agreement "tied to" an individual bedroom, and, under those agreements, Cresmont reserves the right to move any of them to another suite at any time. We are not persuaded that these considerations compel a different conclusion than that reached by the Board. In *Vallorosi*, the ten college students residing together had separate lease agreements with their landlord.

In addition, the fact that the Cresmont Loft leases are "tied to" individual bedrooms, with Cresmont reserving the right to move a tenant to another suite, is not inconsistent with the rights and obligations of the tenants *with respect to one another* (namely the right to shared use of the common areas of the apartment and the joint obligation to maintain the apartment). Petitioners do not offer any reason for concluding that four unrelated individuals whose leases are "tied to" individual bedrooms are in a living arrangement that, for purposes of the "single housekeeping unit" analysis, differs materially from an arrangement in which four unrelated individuals, in similar circumstances, collectively sign a lease for a four-bedroom apartment. Furthermore, by signing a Cresmont Loft lease agreement, a tenant ordinarily may expect to share an apartment with the same three suitemates for the one-year duration of the lease. The mere possibility that one (or more) of the suitemates may be removed from the housekeeping unit in less than one year's time does not undermine the unit's stability or permanence to such a degree as to warrant reversal of the Board's decision. . . .

. . . [T]he "single housekeeping unit" standard ordinarily does not embrace circumstances in which one or more of the members of the purported unit are transient. *See* Open Door Alcoholism Program, Inc. v. Bd. of Adjustment, 200 N.J. Super. 191, 491 A.2d 17, 19, 22 (App. Div. 1985) (holding that eleven people staying in a group home for alcoholics did not qualify as a "family" under the "single housekeeping unit" standard because they "could leave at any time" and the average length of stay was only six months). The Board's decisions do not deviate from that general proposition, as the testimony of the property manager established that each of Cresmont Loft's tenants signs a one-year lease. . . .

Petitioners also direct our attention to Prospect Gardens Convalescent Home, Inc. v. City of Norwalk, 32 Conn. Supp. 214, 347 A.2d 637 (1975), as support for the proposition that the tenants of a Cresmont Loft apartment are not a "single housekeeping unit." In that case, the owner of a convalescent home leased three houses near the convalescent home to as many as thirty of its employees. After the local health department notified the owner that the employee housing facilities constituted rooming houses, the owner filed suit against the city seeking declaratory and injunctive relief. The owner alleged that the employee-occupants of the houses were "families" under an ordinance defining the term as "any number of individuals living and cooking together as a single housekeeping unit." The Superior Court rejected the owner's argument, reasoning that the employee-occupants were not families because they each paid rent individually to their employer, there was no showing that they cooked and/or ate together, and they rarely were together as a group due to the fact that they worked different shifts at the convalescent home.

We reject Petitioners' favored comparison of *Prospect Gardens* to the present case. In *Prospect Gardens*, the three houses at issue housed, respectively, seven, ten, and eleven employees. Because controlling population density is one of the objectives of limiting what constitutes a "family," the court observed that the high number of people comprising each purported housekeeping unit mitigated against finding that they constitute a family. In the instant case, however, there are only four tenants comprising the "single housekeeping unit." It is not apparent whether the *Prospect Gardens* court would have resolved that case in the same way if the houses at issue housed only four employees each. . . .

For the reasons discussed, we affirm the judgment of the Court of Special Appeals. . . .

NOTES AND QUESTIONS

1. How does the Baltimore "single family" zoning ordinance differ from the City of Ladue ordinance? What explains the difference?

2. Consider the definition of family in the Baltimore ordinance. What is a "single housekeeping unit"? Do the cases discussed in *Armstrong* make the meaning clear? Under these definitions, what is the role of the court in defining "family"? Zoning law has evolved, in some ways, from defining households in terms of dyads and their offspring to recognizing "functional families" — households not defined by blood or legal status. Sara Bronin, Zoning for Families, 95 Ind. L.J. 6, 6 (2020) (tracking "judicial decisions that have rejected restrictive definitions of family and analyzes sociological and anthropological literature demonstrating that definitions excluding functional families are unreasonable as a matter of law").

3. Does the "single housekeeping unit" test of *Armstrong* adequately protect a community's interests in restricting some areas to single-family dwellings? Under the Baltimore ordinance, the inhabitants of an apartment could easily change every school term or even more often. What does this suggest about the utility of this definition? On the other hand, would there be any question that a married couple who divorced after a few months was still, while they were married, a "single housekeeping unit"?

4. Professors Courtney Joslin and Douglas NeJaime have questioned why laws do not recognize multi-parent families when "multi-parent families exist across society . . . [and] the reality is that there have always been children who have had more than two parental figures in their lives," such as stepparents, extended family, or families formed through assisted reproductive technologies. As put by Joslin ad NeJaime, "What would it mean to take a fuller range of families and legal developments into account in assessing the reality and consequences of multi-parent families?" Courtney Joslin & Douglas NeJaime, Multi-Parent Families, Real and Imagined, 90 Fordham L. Rev. 2561, 2572-2574 (2022). Chapters 13 and 14 consider answers to their question.

CHAPTER 2

THE IMPORTANCE OF BEING A FAMILY

More than a thousand federal statutes factor marital status into determining individual rights and responsibilities, such as immigration preferences and Social Security benefits. GAO, Defense of Marriage Act: Update to Prior Report (Jan. 23, 2004). As we saw in Chapter 1, state statutes also use marital status or its equivalent or sometimes familial status as a basis for granting benefits to and imposing responsibilities on people in dozens of ways. One of the consequences of Obergefell v. Hodges, 576 U.S. 644 (2015), is that same-sex couples who had been married in one state but whose marriages were not recognized by the federal government or by the state in which they lived suddenly found themselves married and subject to state and federal statutes that treat married people differently. Some couples in domestic partnerships whose relationships were automatically converted to marriage under state law had the same experience.

Invoking the doctrine of family privacy or the marital or family unit, courts also routinely treat adults differently because they are in a marital relationship or its equivalent. The metaphor of the "marital unit" has ancient roots. Bracton, writing in the thirteenth century, said that husband and wife "are *quasi* one person, for they are one flesh and one blood." 4 Bracton on the Laws and Customs of England 335 (Samuel E. Thorne trans., 1977). Blackstone wrote, "By marriage, the husband and wife are one person in law: that is, the very being or legal existence of the woman is suspended during the marriage, or at least incorporated and consolidated into that of the husband." William Blackstone, Commentaries on the Laws of England *442 (W. Lewis ed., 1897). The first American treatise on Husband and Wife explained the common law identity of spouses as a fiction designed to protect wives from coercion. Tapping Reeve, The Law of Baron and Femme: of Parent and Child, of Guardian and Ward, of Master and Servant, and of the Powers of Courts of Chancery 98 (1816).

However, courts never employed the myth of marital unity to the maximum extent that its logic would imply, and it does not provide a satisfactory analytical basis for family law doctrine. Pollock and Maitland, for example, observed:

> If we look for any one thought which governs the whole of this province, we shall hardly find it. In particular we must be on our guard against the common belief that the ruling principle is that which sees an "unity of person" between husband and wife. This is a principle which suggests itself from time to time; it has the warrant of holy writ; it will serve to round a paragraph; and may now and again lead us out of or into a difficulty; but a consistently operative principle it can not be. We do not treat the wife as a thing or as somewhat that is neither thing nor person; we treat her as a person. Thus Bracton tells us that if either the husband without the wife, or the wife without the husband, brings an action for the wife's land, the defendant can take exception to this "for they are *quasi* one person, for they are one flesh and one blood." But this impracticable proposition is followed by a real working principle: — "for the thing is the wife's own and the husband is guardian as being the head of the wife." The husband is the wife's

guardian:—that we believe to be the fundamental principle; and it explains a great deal, when we remember that guardianship is a profitable right.

2 Frederick Pollock & Frederic W. Maitland, The History of English Law 405-406 (2d ed. 1968).

Still, the myth of marital unity has substantially influenced the development of family law. Courts often invoke the idea of the "family unit" to explain doctrines once justified by reference to the doctrine of marital unity. In many settings "the family" seems to be conceived as an entity having claims separate from those of the state and the individual members of the family. This usage suggests that the family stands independent of the state and even that it is a vehicle for governance with claims to "sovereignty." At the least, regard for the family unit suggests that governmental agencies—whether courts, legislatures, or others—should carefully consider the extent to which and the ways in which their rules affect relations within the family.

The idea of the family as a "unit" or "entity" is itself subject to question, since these terms tend to make legal treatment of the family seem inevitable or "natural" and to obscure the effects of that treatment on family members. *See* Lee E. Teitelbaum, Family History and Family Law, 1985 Wis. L. Rev. 1135. Moreover, the treatment of the traditional married family as a unit has also served to justify much greater state intervention into less conventional families. Martha Albertson Fineman, The Neutered Mother, the Sexual Family and Other Twentieth Century Tragedies (1995). The materials in this chapter provide an opportunity to consider the meaning of a couple being legally regarded as a family and the tension between a traditional view of the family as a unit and a more recent tendency to view the family as an association of independent actors. Most of the cases involve couples who are formally married, but the same issues may arise for other couples who are regarded as being a family.

Section A, dealing with family property, introduces the common law and community property systems. The section explores the doctrines that allocate ownership and management of wealth between married couples. Notions of family privacy and family protection will compete with the interests of individual family members in making decisions about how wealth is used. The section concludes with an overview of constitutional decisions regarding gender equality.

Section B, which addresses the legal treatment of violence between adult family members, presents the same tension as courts and legislatures consider whether notions of family privacy or other concerns should prevent criminal or civil prosecution of one intimate partner for assault of another.

Section C reviews key cases establishing and then dismantling the constitutional right to abortion and considers the claim that society as a whole has an interest in affecting or controlling these decisions.

A. MARITAL PROPERTY

This section provides an overview of the significance of marriage or its equivalent for ownership, management, control, and distribution of property or, more generally, wealth. More particularly, the first part deals with doctrines relating to the ownership of real and personal property, including public and private entitlements related to employment. The next part concerns the power of spouses to manage and control family wealth with respect to each other and with respect to creditors.

The concepts and doctrines discussed here are, of course, relevant when the parties' relationship is dissolved, and, accordingly, this section provides a background for the extensive treatments of property distribution upon dissolution of a marriage or cohabiting relationship later in this book. However, the subject of family property is important not only at dissolution. Management and control of wealth during the relationship may be highly significant for the partners themselves. The doctrines that determine management and control during a marriage may affect the ability of creditors to reach the assets of each party. While we expect and hope that family members arrange their financial affairs by mutual agreement, whether articulated or not, questions of right and power may nonetheless arise in ways that couples do not necessarily anticipate.

Moreover, for each case when questions arise overtly, there are many more relationships where the fact or appearance of lawful control defines how each person understands the allocation of decisional authority within the family. If, for example, husbands possess the legal authority to manage available family wealth (as was once true in common law and community property jurisdictions alike), wives may accept — perhaps without even conscious thought about it — their husbands' ultimate responsibility for determining where and how they will live, who will work at what and how much, and the myriad other matters that involve decisions about the acquisition and expenditure of wealth.

The location and character of property ownership may also substantially affect the position of third parties who deal with a married person. Creditors, for example, may find themselves situated differently with respect to property owned by a single person or the "nonmarital" wealth of a spouse than they are with respect to property characterized as "marital."

Finally, consideration of family property, broadly understood, includes kinds of wealth that may or may not be distributable at dissolution and may or may not be available to a surviving spouse upon the other's death. This aspect of marital property includes public, and some private, benefit schemes that are as important to the economic condition of beneficiary families as are farms and bonds for other families.

1. Ownership and Control of Wealth

The marital property systems of Western nations today are divided into two types: "those in which [spouses] own all property separately except those items that they have expressly agreed to hold jointly (in a nontechnical sense) and those in which [spouses] own a substantial portion or even all of their property jointly unless they have expressly agreed to hold it separately." Charles Donahue, Jr., What Causes Fundamental Legal Ideas? Marital Property in England and France in the Thirteenth Century, 78 Mich. L. Rev. 59 (1979). The scheme of separate property ownership is the common law system, which operates or has operated in some fashion in most Anglo-American jurisdictions. The system of joint property is found, in some fashion, in many countries of Western Europe and in nine American states.[1]

These labels — "common law property" and "community property" — capture certain substantial differences in the ways the two systems treat wealth acquired during the marriage. However, there are important aspects in which both regimes in their traditional forms treat the property of married persons alike, particularly with respect to the management of wealth generated during the marriage.

---

1. The nine states are Arizona, California, Idaho, Louisiana, Nevada, New Mexico, Texas, Washington, and (by legislation enacted in the 1980s) Wisconsin. Puerto Rico has also adopted community property. Almost a third of the U.S. population lives in these jurisdictions. J. Thomas Oldham, Everything Is Bigger in Texas, Except the Community Property Estate: Must Texas Remain a Divorce Haven for the Rich?, 44 Fam. L.Q. 293 (2010). In addition, Alaska, Tennessee, and Kentucky allow married couples to opt into community property. Alaska Stat. Ann. §34.77.030 (enacted in 1998); Tenn. Stat. Ann. §§35-17-101 et seq. (enacted in 2010); Ky. Rev. Stat. §§386.620, 622, 624 (enacted in 2020).

a. *The Common Law Tradition*[2]

In a common law property state, the law that applies during the marriage and the law that applies at divorce differ substantially. During the marriage, a separate property regime applies; each spouse owns the property that he or she buys or is given. Spouses can own property jointly as tenants in common, joint tenants, or, in some states, tenants by the entirety. These forms of joint ownership must be expressly created, either at the time the property is originally conveyed to the spouses or later, when one spouse "adds the other to the title" of property that had been separately owned.

Under the common law principles that prevailed before the middle of the nineteenth century, a single woman could manage the property that she owned, and she could enter into contracts and sue and be sued. However, a woman lost these rights when she married. For the duration of the marriage, her husband was entitled to manage her real property and to use any revenue it produced as he saw fit.

The situation changed, however, when one of the spouses died. A wife who survived her husband recaptured her rights with respect to the real property she brought into the marriage. Equally important, her husband could not, during his life, alienate that property without her active participation. Moreover, a married woman had an inchoate life interest in the land that her husband had owned and possessed (of which he was "seised") during the time of their marriage. If the couple had children, the wife had this dower right in one-third of the husband's property and in one-half if they had no children. A wife's dower interest was a life estate (or in some places a life estate unless she remarried) in the dower lands, including the right to rents and profits generated by those lands. A wife's dower was jealously protected against alienation by her husband, who could not sell his land free of that interest unless his wife consented. Moreover, her consent was valid only if given in a judicial proceeding, during which she would be examined privately to ensure that her consent was voluntary. If a husband sold land during the marriage without the wife's valid consent, the wife would still acquire a life estate at his death, perhaps to the surprise of the buyer. If a husband survived his wife and the couple had no children, her real property passed to her heirs. If they had children, however, the husband had the right to possession and enjoyment of her real property for the rest of his life. Only at death did it pass to her heirs.

The husband's rights in the wife's personal property were even more extensive. Except for certain personal items (such as clothing, jewelry, and the like), he owned and could do as he wished with her personal wealth. Concomitantly, a married man assumed responsibility for his wife's debts and civil wrongs.

By about 1840, state legislatures began to enact statutes that had the effect of reducing or eliminating the more obvious disabilities associated with marriage. Generally, these laws, called Married Women's Property Acts, gave married women the same legal capacity to deal with their property that single women had. The 1861 Illinois Married Women's Act, for example, provided as follows:

> Section 1. *Be it enacted* . . . That all property, both real and personal, belonging to any married woman, as her sole and separate property, or which any woman hereafter married owns at the time of her marriage, or which any married woman, during coverture, acquires, in good faith,

---

2. To talk of the "common law tradition," however conventional, risks two kinds of errors. One is to suggest that the common law treatment of marital property was static, that is, that marital property was treated alike over a lengthy period and that this treatment was the province of courts rather than legislation. The other is to suggest that the common law at a single point in time treated all forms of property alike. Both of these are untrue. English law developed significantly in this as in other respects over time, and by statute as well as by judicial decision. *See, e.g.,* Charles Donahue, Jr., What Causes Fundamental Legal Ideas? Marital Property in England and France in the Thirteenth Century, 78 Mich. L. Rev. 59 (1979), on early developments of marital property doctrine.

from any person, other than her husband, by descent, devise or otherwise, together with all the rents, issues, increase and profits thereof, shall, notwithstanding her marriage, be and remain, during coverture, her sole and separate property, under her sole control, and be held, owned, possessed and enjoyed by her the same as though she was sole and unmarried; and shall be exempt from execution or attachment for the debts of her husband.

1861 Ill. Laws 1433. These acts, which are still in effect generally, address only a married woman's *separate* property — that is, property she acquired before marriage or by her efforts or gift during marriage. They do not create any interest for the wife in her husband's separate property. Accordingly, this legislation did not affect the wife's position in the common situation where she did not bring wealth into the marriage, inherit wealth, or work in the paid economy during marriage.

PROBLEM

George and Martha were married in 1990. At that time, Martha owned a small portfolio of stocks (worth approximately $25,000) given to her by her parents; George owned nothing. During their marriage, Martha was a homemaker, and George was first an employee and then a partner in a real estate group. Fifteen years after their marriage, George and Martha decided to evaluate their financial arrangements because George is concerned about a potential liability as a result of some recent unsuccessful investments on his part. Assuming that the stocks remain titled in Martha's name, that the current value of the real estate partnership is approximately $100,000, and that George has over the years purchased a house and made investments in his own name that amount to approximately $250,000, advise them on the following questions. Under a Married Women's Property Act like the Illinois statute quoted above, who owns what property? Under the statute, which of their assets can George's creditors reach to collect what he owes them?

Married Women's Property Acts address only property given to or earned by women; they generally have no effect on property titled in one spouse's name to which both spouses have in some way contributed. In this situation, spouses sometimes seek relief through generally applicable equitable remedies,[3] particularly resulting and constructive trusts.

Adams v. Jankouskas
452 A.2d 148 (Del. 1982)

MOORE, J. . . . On December 23, 1944 John married Stella in Elkton, Maryland. Both had been married before, and each had children by their prior marriages. . . .

---

3. The terms *equity* and *equitable* appear in a number of property contexts. Their meanings within each are specific, and the meaning within one context cannot safely be employed in another. Sometimes these terms refer to remedies created by courts of equity, such as the wife's separate estate in equity (based on an express trust), or the resulting and constructive trust remedies described immediately below, which are extensions, with some modification, of generally applicable doctrines recognizing ownership interests that are not reflected in the legal title. Such equitable interests in specific items of wealth may be recognized at any time.

These uses should be distinguished from "equitable distribution," which is *not* intended to reflect ownership interests in particular items of property but deals only with the distribution of all family property at divorce. Equitable distribution is discussed in detail in Chapter 6.

At the time of the marriage, Stella was the owner and operator of a small beauty shop which she had purchased a few months earlier. She apparently saved parsimoniously to buy the shop (even putting her 2 young sons by her previous marriage in an orphanage), but when she married John it was not a particularly profitable enterprise. Before the marriage John had held a string of jobs with various companies and, at the time of the marriage, he was earning approximately $150 a week. In 1948, he secured employment with the duPont Company where he worked until his retirement in 1978.

With the assistance of counsel Stella set up a corporation in July 1947 named "Jan's Apartments," and all 100 shares of the common stock of the corporation were issued in her name. In addition to accumulating other assets, the initial investment of "Jan's Apartments" was in an apartment building at 829 Washington Street which John renovated. About five years later Stella moved her beauty parlor to this building. The corporation also acquired a house at 2409 Franklin Street, which became John and Stella's family residence. John paid monthly rent to the Corporation for their joint use of the house.

Stella was clearly the dominant partner in the marriage and she mainly controlled the family finances. From the beginning of the marriage John surrendered his paycheck to Stella, who then deposited it either in their joint account or the corporate account of Jan's Apartments. John in turn received a nominal sum from Stella for spending money. Early in the marriage the funds in the joint account were used primarily for basic living expenses, but later some of these funds were invested by Stella in stocks, bonds, certificates of deposit and other assets.

The trial testimony indicates that John and Stella voluntarily pooled John's earnings from duPont, and the earnings of the beauty parlor and the corporation. Several witnesses testified that John and Stella were saving "so that they could enjoy their retirement together." In effect they were "planning for the future" and setting aside a "nest egg" for their old age. John testified that the pooling was based upon their agreement that, "what's mine is yours and what's yours is mine." According to John, the understanding was "if [he] died she had everything and if she died [he] had everything."

Stella died in October 1977 leaving an estate valued at over $350,000, approximately $40,000 of which consisted of personal property held in their joint names. Except for this property, a diamond ring, an automobile and $10,000 in cash, all bequeathed to John, Stella's will purported to make her niece, Dolores Adams, the daughter of Stella's sister and executrix, her sole ultimate beneficiary. Virtually all the assets acquired by either party during the marriage were considered by the executrix to be assets of Stella's estate.

. . . John brought this action on September 27, 1979, almost two years after Stella's death. Following trial, the former Chancellor awarded John 50% of the estate left by Stella on the theory that the transactions between Stella and John created a constructive or resulting trust on Stella's part for the benefit of John. . . .

The Chancellor imposed a constructive or resulting trust over the assets of the estate held by Stella's executrix. These two trust theories are similar in that they are both "implied" trusts, that is, their existence is not based upon a valid written trust agreement. Although a constructive trust and a resulting trust are similar in effect, they are based upon entirely different theories.

A resulting trust arises from the presumed intentions of the parties and upon the circumstances surrounding the particular transaction. In imposing a resulting trust, the court presumes, absent contrary evidence, that the person supplying the purchase money for property intends that its purchase will inure to his benefit, and the fact that title is in the name of another is for some incidental reason. Conversely, a constructive trust does not arise from the presumed intent of the parties, but is imposed when a defendant's fraudulent, unfair or unconscionable conduct causes him to be unjustly enriched at the expense of another to whom he owed some duty.[4]

Although most resulting trust cases involve the purchase of real property, the theory upon which they are based equally applies to acquisitions of personality. It has also been applied to situations in which the purchase price for property has been paid out of partnership or community assets. In a case involving purchases made with partnership or community funds, the trust "results" in favor of the partnership or the community. This rule is applicable when, as here, the property was bought with joint funds.

In reviewing the evidence, the Chancellor found:

> Here, it is established by the evidence adduced at trial that at the inception of their marriage both parties contributed their earnings to a species of joint account, petitioner's contributions initially constituting a large percentage of such funding. The evidence also establishes that title to such acquisitions was placed in the name of the decedent. I am satisfied after trial that the source of funds used by the decedent to acquire her initial holdings was from the parties' pooled funds since there is no other credible source of money for such acquisitions.

[In addition,] Stella's ultimate beneficiary, Dolores Adams, an apparently hostile witness, conceded the occurrence of three transactions during the later years of the marriage in which Stella withdrew funds from the joint account and deposited them in a savings account in her name only. Presumably, other such transactions could have been proven, but many of the records pertaining to Stella's affairs were destroyed by the executrix, or someone purportedly acting on advice of her counsel.[5]

---

4. A good discussion of the differences between these two trusts is as follows:

> *Resulting trusts* arise where the legal estate is disposed of or acquired, not fraudulently or in the violation of any fiduciary duty, but the intent in theory of equity appears or is inferred or assumed from the terms of the disposition, or from the accompanying facts and circumstances, that the beneficial interest is not to go with the legal title. In such a case a trust "results" in favor of the person from whom the equitable interest is thus assumed to have been intended, and whom equity deems to be the real owner (see §§1031 et seq.).
>
> *Constructive trusts* are by equity for the purpose of working out right and justice, where there was no intention of the party to create such a relation, and often directly contrary to the intention of the one holding the legal title. All instances of constructive trust may be referred to what equity denominates fraud, either actual or constructive, including acts or omissions in violation of fiduciary obligations. If one party obtains the legal title to property, not only by fraud or by violation of confidence or of fiduciary relations, but in any other unconscientious manner, so that he cannot equitably retain the property which really belongs to another, equity carries out its theory of a double ownership, equitable and legal, by impressing a constructive trust upon the property in favor of the one who is in good conscience entitled to it, and who is considered in equity as the beneficial owner (see §§1044 et seq.). Courts of equity, by thus extending the fundamental principle of trusts—that is, the principle of a division between the legal estate in one and the equitable estate in another—to cases of actual or constructive fraud and breaches of good faith, are enabled to wield a remedial power of tremendous efficacy in protecting the rights of property.

1 Pomeroy's Equity Jurisprudence §166, at 210-211 (5th ed. 1941) (emphasis in original).

5. There also was sufficient competent evidence that Stella never intended to keep her word to John about the ultimate use of the assets accumulated from their joint funds, thus supporting the Chancellor's conclusion that grounds existed for the imposition of a constructive trust. One of Stella's former employees testified:

> A. . . . The only thing she talked about all the time was her will, and she changed her mind about that so many times.
> Q. What did she say about her will?
> A. Well she told me on several occasions that when she died Mr. Jann was going to be in for a real surprise; that he wasn't going to get half of what he thought he was going to get (T-38).

Stella's son also testified:

> Basically one of the things that I always felt irritable about is the fact that I knew that she was trying to cut Mr. Jann out from the will.

Thus, the Court of Chancery properly imposed either a resulting or constructive trust on the assets accumulated from joint contributions. It is important to note that this is not a case where a party was disappointed with what he received under a will. Rather, it is one in which joint funds were committed in obvious trust to one partner and then pooled to purchase property and make investments for the mutual benefit of both. Under these circumstances Chancery may impose this trust upon the accumulated assets in whatever form they now take. . . .

Affirmed. . . .

NOTES AND QUESTIONS

1. The court indicates that the evidence showed that Stella lied to John about her intentions regarding the investment assets and that she never planned to leave them to him. If, instead, Stella originally intended to leave the assets to John but just changed her mind, would that justify imposing a constructive trust in his favor?

2. The chancellor found that the money used to purchase the assets that were in Stella's name came from the parties' pooled funds and that, therefore, Stella held part of the assets on resulting trust for the benefit of John. Why didn't the court simply find that John had made a gift to Stella of the money that he put into the account in her name?

Any time one person hands over property to another, the question can arise as to whether the transaction was intended as a gift or whether the original owner intended for the person who received the property to hold the beneficial interest in the property on resulting trust for the original owner. In theory, the answer depends on the intent of the original owner, but often the evidence regarding intent is unclear. Therefore, the outcome will often be decided on the basis of whether or not the transaction was presumed to be a gift.

If a person purchases property and titles it in the name of another, unrelated person, the presumption will be that the person whose name is not on the title did not intend to make a gift; in other words, the presumption will be in favor of a resulting trust.

At common law, a distinct body of law developed in connection with gifts between spouses. Transfers from husband to wife, such as when the husband purchased property from wealth he controlled and placed title in the wife's name alone or in joint ownership, were generally presumed to be gifts to her or to the marital estate. *See* Maxwell v. Maxwell, 109 Ill. 588 (1884) (gift presumed although both parties treated property as husband's); Brown v. Brown, 507 A.2d 1223 (Pa. Super. 1986) (titling property jointly is strong evidence of intent of donor to make gift to marital estate). Where, however, the wife transferred wealth to her husband, courts often treated the transfer as a loan or as a bailment for safekeeping and would impose a constructive trust for her benefit on that property. *See* Comment, Transfers from Wife to Husband: A Reexamination of Presumptions in Illinois, 53 Nw. U. L. Rev. 781 (1959). Today inconsistent treatment of transfers by spouses based on gender is considered to violate equal protection. *See* Butler v. Butler, 347 A.2d 477 (Pa. 1975).

In what direction should the presumption concerning transfers between spouses run, assuming that the presumption will apply to all transfers between spouses?

3. Assume that John had not contributed money to the bank account from which the assets were purchased, but he had done a great deal of work on the real property that Stella purchased and titled in her name. While John's work added significant value, he did not contribute cash or its equivalent to the property and so would not be entitled to claim a share of the beneficial interest on a resulting trust theory.

4. As we will see in Chapter 6, in most states divorce courts have authority to distribute property acquired during the marriage through labor of either spouse "equitably," which would allow a court to award some of the property to John. However, states do not allow equitable distribution when a marriage ends because of the death of one of the parties. The estate of the decedent consists of property the decedent owned during life, and the only way that the surviving spouse can lay claim to any of the decedent's property (which is not subject to a will) is by establishing the basis for a resulting or constructive trust or by claiming the surviving spouse's elective share. For more information, *see* Naomi Cahn, What's Wrong About the Elective Share "Right"?, 53 U.C. Davis L. Rev. 2087 (2020).

PROBLEMS

1. For the course of their marriage, Paul and Tim worked and pooled their earnings. After some time, however, Paul started a "crash" savings program for, as he told his spouse, "our latter days." From then on, Tim's earnings were used for family expenses and Paul's earnings were invested, entirely in his name. The family house was also in Paul's name, having been purchased with a down payment of $6500 supplied by his mother. Does Tim have any interest in these properties? What arguments would be made for Tim's position?

2. William and Mary were married in 1957. Shortly afterward, William, together with a partner, established a business. William's initial investment came from savings the couple had accumulated over the first few years of their marriage. During the early years of the business, the wife helped out as a business advisor and bookkeeper. After the birth of their children, she still assisted with the bookkeeping. She has been paid a salary by the company for these services. In conversations with his wife, William often referred to the business as "our company" and its profits as "our security blanket." However, Mary never owned any of the stock in this closely held corporation, nor did she hold any management office in it. The business is now worth approximately one-half million dollars. Assuming that all of the stock in the company is held in the husband's name, does the wife have any legal or equitable interest in the company?

3. Stephanie inherited $170,000 from her aunt before her marriage, which she used to purchase a home for herself and her partner, Danny. The home was titled solely in the name of Danny, who later became Stephanie's spouse. Stephanie said that she put sole title in Danny's name because she feared that if her name were on the title, her former spouse's creditors would try to attach the home. Danny has recently died, and the estate's executor claims the house. Stephanie seeks an order imposing a constructive trust on the house for her benefit. Danny's best friend would testify that Danny had said shortly before dying that Stephanie claimed she never meant to give the house to Danny, but that earlier, when they were first married, she had said something different, that the house was a gift to the marriage. What arguments should the parties make?

b. Community Property

The law of community property, which is often traced to Visigothic Spain, generally recognizes that both spouses own wealth acquired by the labor of either of them during the marriage. As with common law property, the notion of community property has been understood and applied differently at different times and in different places. Community property jurisdictions differ in their treatment of debts and of property owned prior to or inherited during marriage. In one scheme (the Roman-Dutch), all property becomes community property upon marriage; in the Spanish form commonly followed in U.S. community property states and in South America, premarital wealth is regarded as separate property, and its ownership is not affected by marriage. And there are also, as one would expect, intermediate schemes as well as differences with respect to the treatment of the income produced by premarital (separate) assets.

Despite these variations, community property interests seem very different from those in a separate property system. During the marriage, in common law states, each spouse *owns* separately what each spouse has been given or earns during the marriage,[6] while in community property states the spouses jointly own property that is the product of either spouse's labor from the beginning of the marriage. Moreover, community and common law property schemes differ substantially in their treatment of wealth *not* earned during the marriage but brought into the marriage as separate property. Whereas a married woman lost her right to manage her real and personal property during marriage at common law, that was never the case under community property principles. Except for her dowry, a wife has always enjoyed the exclusive rights to control, manage, and dispose of her separate property and can, without her husband's consent, convey her separate property.[7]

Similarly, wives have always had the right to deal with the rents and profits of their separate property in jurisdictions where such rents and profits are separate rather than community property.

Lest one believe, however, that wives under community property principles stood entirely equal to husbands, it should be added that wives occupied much the same position as married women in common law jurisdictions before Married Women's Property Acts with respect to management of wealth generated *during* the marriage. While a wife held an ownership interest in that wealth that wives in common law states did not possess, her interest was passive as long as her husband was alive; the husband possessed full power to manage all of the community property, absent an agreement to the contrary. This state of the law resulted, according to the leading commentators on community property principles, "from the consideration of the husband as head of the family, as the one who due to economic and biological factors has been the member of the marital partnership more practiced and experienced in the acquisition and management of property." W. de Funiak & M. Vaughan at 276 (noting, without reference to a doctrine of marital unity, that Spanish law—quite as clearly as English law—declared that "the husband was head of the family, with the duty to provide for its wants and the right to choose its place of residence").

Sole management power in the husband disappeared during the 1970s as legislatures, either on principle or in anticipation of equal protection challenges, revised their statutes to provide that each spouse or both spouses could manage community wealth. In Kirchberg v. Feenstra, 450 U.S. 455 (1981), the U.S. Supreme Court upheld a Fifth Circuit decision holding the Louisiana "head-and-master" rule unconstitutional:

---

6. *See* Dana V. Kaplan, Note: Women of the West: The Evolution of Marital Property Laws in the Southwestern United States and Their Effect on Mexican-American Women, 26 Women's Rts. L. Rep. 139 (2005) (describing the development of community property systems in the Southwest and analyzing how rights of married women in those jurisdictions compared to rights in the common law states during the nineteenth century).

7. The Spanish law recognized three kinds of property at the time of marriage: dowry, paraphernalia, and other separate property. The dowry was, of course, the consideration, or part of the consideration, paid the husband for marrying his wife. Accordingly, the right of management and control was placed in his hands. However, as with the wife's realty at common law, neither the husband nor his heirs (assuming they were not also hers) had any interest in dower property after dissolution of the marriage.

Paraphernalia included personal property brought by the wife into the marriage, but for her separate use. She retained all rights of control in this property unless she placed the management in her husband's hands by an express writing. *Other separate property* included wealth owned by the wife but not brought by her into the marriage for common use. Here again, the husband had no right of management.

If the wife received property by gift or inheritance, this was treated as other separate property, and the donee wife retained the power of management and distribution. *See* William Q. de Funiak & Michael J. Vaughan, Principles of Community Property 270-273 (2d ed. 1971).

By granting the husband exclusive control over the disposition of property, Art. 2404 clearly embodies the type of express gender-based discrimination that we have found unconstitutional absent a showing that the classification is tailored to further an important governmental interest. . . . [Appellant's claim that wives may choose to avoid the impact of Art. 2404] overlooks the critical question: Whether Art. 2404 substantially furthers an important government interest. As we have previously noted, the "absence of an insurmountable barrier" will not redeem an otherwise unconstitutionally discriminatory law. Instead the burden remains on the party seeking to uphold the statute that expressly discriminates on the basis of sex to advance an "exceedingly persuasive justification" for the challenged classification. Because appellant has failed to offer such a justification . . . we affirm the judgment of the Court of Appeals invalidating Art. 2404.

450 U.S. at 459-461.

However, equalization of authority over community wealth has not been easy to accomplish in practice. Professor Elizabeth Carter reviews the current systems in use in the United States in the following excerpt. As she notes, the exception from the systems that she describes in the excerpt below is the Texas dual management system, which grants exclusive management authority to the spouse who acquired an item of property. The Texas system results in management authority much like that in a common law property state.

Elizabeth R. Carter

The Illusion of Equality: The Failure of the Community Property Reform to Achieve Management Equality
48 Ind. L. Rev. 853, 875, 878-884 (2015)

a. *Equal management.* — Equal management is the default rule of management in every [community property] state except Texas. Those acts and transactions that do not require joinder and are not subject to the exclusive management by one spouse are subject to the residual rule of equal management. . . . As a practical matter, however, relatively few transactions actually fall within the scope of this residual rule.

b. *Joinder required.* — . . . All equal management states require the joinder of both spouses in various transactions affecting community real property. . . . A handful of states continue to require joinder or concurrence in the transfer or encumbrance of household furnishings. . . . The equal management states also carried forward various restrictions on a spouse's ability to make gratuitous transfers of community property to third parties. . . .

c. *Exclusive management by one spouse.* — . . . California, Louisiana, Nevada, and Washington specifically recognize a "business exception" to management. In these states, the spouse who is the "manager" of a sole proprietorship has the exclusive right to engage in various acts of management affecting that business. . . . [T]he business exception states adopted procedural safeguards to "protect the nonacting spouse (and thus the community) from imprudent and arbitrary decisions involving 'blue chip' community assets." California requires the managing spouse "give prior written notice to the other spouse of the sale, lease, exchange, encumbrance, or other disposition of all or substantially all of the personal property used in the operation of the business." Louisiana requires the joinder of both spouses for the alienation, encumbrance, or lease of "all or substantially all of the assets of a community enterprise." Nevada and Washington require the consent of the nonparticipating spouse for transactions that are not in the ordinary course of business. . . .

Today, many business owners elect to incorporate their sole proprietorships into limited liability companies — an option that was not available at the time of the revision. Management of community interests in corporations, partnerships, limited liability companies and other business entities typically falls under the exclusive management of one spouse because of concepts of privity and title. Once a spouse incorporates his sole proprietorship as a business entity, the procedural safeguards of the business exception no longer apply. Statutes in Louisiana and Washington make it clear that community personal property registered or titled in the name of one spouse is subject to that spouse's exclusive control. This includes interests in business entities. Basic title concepts and notions of privity mean that, as a practical matter, this is the case in all community property jurisdictions. . . .

This "practical matter" exception to equal management is more far reaching than registered stocks and business interests. It is an exception that swallows the default rule of equal management. . . .

Approximately two-thirds of a couple's net worth is attributed to non-financial assets. The most commonly owned non-financial assets are vehicles, primary residence property, other residential property, and business equity. . . . Vehicles and business equity are typically subject to the rule of privity and fall under the exclusive management of the spouse whose name is on the title to the asset. Both types of residential property require the joinder of both spouses in most major acts of management.

On average, financial assets account for more than one-third of an American family's net worth. . . . Today, financial assets are almost always subject to the exclusive management of one spouse unless the spouses affirmatively elect to take a different approach.

The most commonly owned financial assets are transaction accounts (checking accounts, savings accounts, and money market accounts) and retirement accounts (such as 401(k) accounts and IRAs). . . .

. . . No law requires a spouse to deposit community funds into a joint bank account with his or her spouse. Spouses are free to deposit their earnings and other community funds into any combination of joint accounts and individual accounts that they see fit and research shows that they most often do so in a manner that is detrimental to the wife. . . .

NOTES AND QUESTIONS

1. A good starting point for understanding community property is that any property acquired by the productive efforts of either spouse during the marriage is community property, while property owned before marriage or given to only one spouse during marriage is separate property. Because life is more complicated than this simple formula, classification of property as community or separate is also more complicated. We will look at the major points of difficulty in Chapter 6.

On the level of principle, community property seems more consistent with the idea of "marital unity." However, efforts to convince common law property states to change to a community property system have been spectacularly unsuccessful. The Uniform Marital Property Act, promulgated in 1984, would create a community property system during marriage. Only one state, Wisconsin, has enacted the Uniform Act. What might explain the persistence of the common law system in most states?

For more on these issues, *see* Alicia Brokars Kelly, Money Matters in Marriage: Unmasking Interdependence in Ongoing Spousal Economic Relations, 47 Louisville L. Rev. 113 (2008).

2. Assume that you were a married woman living in the era before Kirchberg v. Feenstra was decided. Would you be better off living in Louisiana or Alabama, a state with common law property, from the perspective of being able to manage your financial affairs independently of your husband? How much control would you have in a modern community property state using a joint management system? An equal management system?

3. In some community property states the law explicitly provides that a spouse who manages community property has a fiduciary duty to the other spouse. This principle is well-developed in California. Family Code §721(b) (2022) provides:

[I]n transactions between themselves, spouses are subject to the general rules governing fiduciary relationships that control the actions of persons occupying confidential relations with each other. This confidential relationship imposes a duty of the highest good faith and fair dealing on each spouse, and neither shall take any unfair advantage of the other. This confidential relationship is a fiduciary relationship subject to the same rights and duties of nonmarital business partners, as provided in . . . the Corporations code, including, but not limited to, the following:

> (1) Providing each spouse access at all times to any books kept regarding a transaction for the purposes of inspection and copying.
> (2) Rendering upon request, true and full information of all things affecting any transaction that concerns the community property. Nothing in this section is intended to impose a duty for either spouse to keep detailed books and records of community property transactions.
> (3) Accounting to the spouse, and holding as a trustee, any benefit or profit derived from any transaction by one spouse without the consent of the other spouse that concerns the community property.

Family Code §1100 (2022) further provides:

Each spouse shall act with respect to the other spouse in the management and control of the community assets and liabilities in accordance with the general rules governing fiduciary relationships which control the actions of persons having relationships of personal confidence as specified in Section 721, until such time as the assets and liabilities have been divided by the parties or by a court. This duty includes the obligation to make full disclosure to the other spouse of all material facts and information regarding the existence, characterization, and valuation of all assets in which the community has or may have an interest and debts for which the community is or may be liable, and to provide equal access to all information, records, and books that pertain to the value and character of those assets and debts, upon request.

In *In re Marriage of DeSouza*, 266 Cal.Rptr.3d 890 (Cal. App. 2020), the court held that a husband breached his fiduciary duty to his wife because he did not tell her that he was investing substantial amounts of community funds in bitcoin during the marriage. He filed for divorce, and by the time the property division was finalized, thousands of dollars' worth of the cryptocurrency was tied up in the bankruptcy of the issuing company, and the husband had not taken adequate steps to protect the bitcoins, failing to disclose all the relevant facts to his soon-to-be ex-wife during the divorce process. *DeSouza* has been called the first major bitcoin case, resulting in a court ordering a spouse to transfer cryptocurrency still in the husband's possession. David Yaffe-Bellamy, One More Divorce Argument: How to Split Up the Bitcoin, N.Y. Times (Feb. 14, 2022).

For more information on divorce courts' authority to provide remedies when a spouse commits economic fraud during the marriage, *see* note 8 following Arneault v. Arneault beginning on page 250.

PROBLEMS

1. If George and Martha, the couple in the problem on page 31 above, lived at all times in a community property state, which assets would be community property, and which would be the separate property of George or Martha? Who would have the ability to sell the assets under a joint management system? An equal management system?

2. How would problems 1, 2, and 3 on page 35 above be analyzed in a community property state?

2. Employment-Related and Public Benefits

To this point, we have largely been concerned with traditional forms of property: houses, ranches, bank accounts, and the like. A great deal of wealth, however, takes a different form; many of these assets provide streams of income for people who are working, retired, or unable to work, and others provide access to insurance at relatively low cost. As Professor Reich observed, "[T]oday more and more of our wealth takes the form of rights or status rather than of tangible goods. An individual's profession or occupation is a prime example. To many others, a job with a particular employer is the principal form of wealth." Charles Reich, The New Property, 73 Yale L.J. 733, 738 (1964). Peter Drucker described the importance of this form of wealth when he characterized the modern American economy as "pension socialism":

> If "socialism" is defined as "ownership of the means of production by the workers"—and this is the most orthodox definition—then the United States is the most "socialist" country in the world. . . .
>
> [T]he largest employee pension funds . . . own a controlling interest in practically every single one of the "command positions" in the economy. . . . Indeed, a larger sector of the American economy (outside of farming) today is owned by the American worker—through his investment agent, the pension fund—than Allende in Chile proposed to bring under government ownership to make Chile a "socialist country. . . ."

Peter Drucker, Pension Fund "Socialism," *in* The Public Interest 3-6 (Winter 1976).

The importance of this form of property for its holders as well as for the economy has grown enormously. Professor Glendon explained:

> [F]or the majority in modern welfare states, old property (in the sense of traditional assets of real and personal property) is less important than individual earning power and public and private benefits based on such labor. To the extent that there are savings apart from home equity in a middle-aged middle-income family, they tend less to be represented by bank accounts or tangible assets than by employment-related pension plans, profit-sharing plans, insurance or other benefits. . . .

Mary Ann Glendon, The New Family and the New Property 93-94 (1981).

In 2020, 71 percent of all workers had access to an employer-sponsored pension plan, up from 59 percent in 2009, but only 55 percent actually participated in a plan. Management and professional workers were the most likely to have coverage, and service workers the least likely. Full-time employees were more likely to be covered than part-time workers, and 94 percent of unionized workers were covered, compared to 67 percent of nonunion workers. Rates of access and participation are higher in firms with larger numbers of employees. U.S. Bureau of Labor Statistics, U.S. Dept. of Labor, Employee Benefits in the United States, March 2020 Tbl. 2 (Sept. 2020), available at https://www.bls.gov/ncs/ebs/benefits/2020/employee-benefits-in-the-united-states-march-2020.pdf. Access and participation rates increased as workers' wages increased. Young and less educated workers are less likely to participate, and "Hispanic, African-American, and Asian workers are less likely to have access to a plan than white workers." Pew Charitable Trusts, Who's In, Who's Out: A Look at Access to Employer-Based Retirement Plans and Participation in the States (Jan. 2016).

Federal and state government programs also provide social insurance benefits, as well as other means of income maintenance and protections for health and welfare. Together, all these employment-related benefits constitute significant forms of wealth. Family law statutes and judicial decisions have increasingly come to recognize the importance of these assets.

For example, the Employee Retirement Income Security Act of 1974 (ERISA), 29 U.S.C. §§1001 et seq., sets forth a comprehensive scheme for the regulation of private pension plans to protect their participants and beneficiaries. Government pension plans are not covered, although they often include provisions similar to those found in the federal statute.

The relationship between ERISA, as modified by the Retirement Equity Act of 1984, and state laws generally governing the ownership of wealth by family members is of great importance. In general, state laws define the treatment of wealth earned or held by one or more members of a family and the extent to which family members may dispose of that wealth. ERISA, however, incorporates a critical principle that affects the power of pension plan participants to deal with their pension funds and, concomitantly, the power of others—particularly spouses and creditors—to reach or use those funds. ERISA §206(d)(1) requires that "[e]ach pension plan shall provide that benefits provided under the plan may not be assigned or alienated." The relationship between that principle and other aspects of ERISA to state laws governing marital property (and especially community property) is explored in the following case.

Boggs v. Boggs
520 U.S. 833 (1997)

Kennedy, J., delivered the opinion of the Court, in which Stevens, Scalia, Souter and Thomas, JJ., joined, and in which Rehnquist, C.J., and Ginsburg, J., joined as to Part III. Breyer, J., filed a dissenting opinion, in which O'Connor, J., joined, and in which Rehnquist, C.J., and Ginsburg, J., joined except as to Part II-B-3. . . .

Isaac Boggs worked for South Central Bell from 1949 until his retirement in 1985. Isaac and Dorothy, his first wife, were married when he began working for the company, and they remained husband and wife until Dorothy's death in 1979. They had three sons. Within a year of Dorothy's death, Isaac married Sandra, and they remained married until his death in 1989.

Upon retirement, Isaac received various benefits from his employer's retirement plans. One was a lump-sum distribution from the Bell System Savings Plan for Salaried Employees (Savings Plan) of $151,628.94, which he rolled over into an Individual Retirement Account (IRA). He made no withdrawals and the account was worth $180,778.05 when he died. He also received 96 shares of AT&T stock from the Bell South Employee Stock Ownership Plan (ESOP). In addition, Isaac enjoyed a monthly annuity payment during his retirement of $1,777.67 from the Bell South Service Retirement Program.

The instant dispute over ownership of the benefits is between Sandra (the surviving wife) and the sons of the first marriage. The sons' claim to a portion of the benefits is based on Dorothy's will. Dorothy bequeathed to Isaac one-third of her estate, and a lifetime usufruct in the remaining two-thirds. A lifetime usufruct is the rough equivalent of a common-law life estate. She bequeathed to her sons the naked ownership in the remaining two-thirds, subject to Isaac's usufruct. All agree that, absent pre-emption, Louisiana law controls and that under it Dorothy's will would dispose of her community property interest in Isaac's undistributed pension plan benefits. A Louisiana state court, in a 1980 order entitled "Judgment of Possession," ascribed to Dorothy's estate a community property interest in Isaac's Savings Plan account valued at the time at $21,194.29.

Sandra contests the validity of Dorothy's 1980 testamentary transfer, basing her claim to those benefits on her interest under Isaac's will and 29 U.S.C. §1055. Isaac bequeathed to Sandra outright certain real property including the family home. His will also gave Sandra a lifetime usufruct in the remainder of his estate, with the naked ownership interest being held by the sons. Sandra argues that the sons' competing claim, since it is based on Dorothy's 1980 purported testamentary transfer of her community property interest in undistributed pension plan benefits, is pre-empted by ERISA. The Bell South Service Retirement Program monthly annuity is now paid to Sandra as the surviving spouse.

After Isaac's death, two of the sons filed an action in state court requesting the appointment of an expert to compute the percentage of the retirement benefits they would be entitled to as a result of Dorothy's attempted testamentary transfer. They further sought a judgment awarding them a portion of: the IRA; the ESOP shares of AT&T stock; the monthly annuity payments received by Isaac during his retirement; and Sandra's survivor annuity payments, both received and payable.

In response, Sandra Boggs filed a complaint in the United States District Court for the Eastern District of Louisiana, seeking a declaratory judgment that ERISA pre-empts the application of Louisiana's community property and succession laws to the extent they recognize the sons' claim to an interest in the disputed retirement benefits. The District Court granted summary judgment against Sandra Boggs. It found that, under Louisiana community property law, Dorothy had an ownership interest in her husband's pension plan benefits built up during their marriage. The creation of this interest, the court explained, does not violate 29 U.S.C. §1056(d)(1), which prohibits pension plan benefits from being "assigned" or "alienated," since Congress did not intend to alter traditional familial and support obligations. In the court's view, there was no assignment or alienation because Dorothy's rights in the benefits were acquired by operation of community property law and not by transfer from Isaac. . . .

A divided panel of the Fifth Circuit affirmed. . . .

. . . In large part the number of ERISA pre-emption cases reflects the comprehensive nature of the statute, the centrality of pension and welfare plans in the national economy, and their importance to the financial security of the Nation's workforce. ERISA is designed to ensure the proper administration of pension and welfare plans, both during the years of the employee's active service and in his or her retirement years.

This case lies at the intersection of ERISA pension law and state community property law. None can dispute the central role community property laws play in the nine community property States. It is more than a property regime. It is a commitment to the equality of husband and wife and reflects the real partnership inherent in the marital relationship. State community property laws, many of ancient lineage, "must have continued to exist through such lengths of time because of their manifold excellences and are not lightly to be abrogated or tossed aside." 1 W. de Funiak, Principles of Community Property 11 (1943). . . .

. . . This case involves a community property claim, but our ruling will affect as well the right to make claims or assert interests based on the law of any State, whether or not it recognizes community property. . . .

ERISA is an intricate, comprehensive statute. Its federal regulatory scheme governs employee benefit plans, which include both pension and welfare plans. All employee benefit plans must conform to various reporting, disclosure and fiduciary requirements, while pension plans must also comply with participation, vesting, and funding requirements. The surviving spouse annuity and QDRO provisions, central to the dispute here, are part of the statute's mandatory participation and vesting requirements. These provisions provide detailed protections to spouses of plan participants which, in some cases, exceed what their rights would be were community property law the sole measure.

ERISA's express pre-emption clause states that the Act "shall supersede any and all State laws insofar as they may now or hereafter relate to any employee benefit plan. . . ." §1144(a). We can begin, and in this case end, the analysis by simply asking if state law conflicts with the provisions of ERISA or operates to frustrate its objects. . . .

Sandra Boggs, as we have observed, asserts that federal law pre-empts and supersedes state law and requires the surviving spouse annuity to be paid to her as the sole beneficiary. We agree.

The annuity at issue is a qualified joint and survivor annuity mandated by ERISA. . . . ERISA requires that every qualified joint and survivor annuity include an annuity payable to a nonparticipant surviving spouse. The survivor's annuity may not be less than 50% of the amount of the annuity which is payable during the joint lives of the participant and spouse. Provision of the survivor's annuity may not be waived by the participant, absent certain limited circumstances, unless the spouse consents in writing to the designation of another beneficiary, which designation also cannot be changed without further spousal consent, witnessed by a plan representative or notary public. Sandra Boggs, as the surviving spouse, is entitled to a survivor's annuity under these provisions. She has not waived her right to the survivor's annuity, let alone consented to having the sons designated as the beneficiaries.

Respondents say their state-law claims are consistent with these provisions. Their claims, they argue, affect only the disposition of plan proceeds after they have been disbursed by the Bell South Service Retirement Program, and thus nothing is required of the plan. . . .

We disagree. The statutory object of the qualified joint and survivor annuity provisions . . . is to ensure a stream of income to surviving spouses. . . .

ERISA's solicitude for the economic security of surviving spouses would be undermined by allowing a predeceasing spouse's heirs and legatees to have a community property interest in the survivor's annuity. Even a plan participant cannot defeat a nonparticipant surviving spouse's statutory entitlement to an annuity. It would be odd, to say the least, if Congress permitted a predeceasing nonparticipant spouse to do so. Nothing in the language of ERISA supports concluding that Congress made such an inexplicable decision. . . .

Beyond seeking a portion of the survivor's annuity, respondents claim a percentage of: the monthly annuity payments made to Isaac Boggs during his retirement; the IRA; and the ESOP shares of AT&T stock. As before, the claim is based on Dorothy Boggs' attempted testamentary transfer to the sons of her community interest in Isaac's undistributed pension plan benefits. Respondents argue further — and somewhat inconsistently — that their claim again concerns only what a plan participant or beneficiary may do once plan funds are distributed, without imposing any obligations on the plan itself. Both parties agree that the ERISA benefits at issue here were paid after Dorothy's death, and thus this case does not present the question whether ERISA would permit a nonparticipant spouse to obtain a devisable community property interest in benefits paid out during the existence of the community between the participant and that spouse. . . .

ERISA confers beneficiary status on a nonparticipant spouse or dependent in only narrow circumstances delineated by its provisions. For example, as we have discussed, §1055(a) requires provision of a surviving spouse annuity in covered pension plans, and, as a consequence the spouse is a beneficiary to this extent. Section 1056's QDRO provisions likewise recognize certain pension plan community property interests of nonparticipant spouses and dependents. A QDRO is a type of domestic relations order which creates or recognizes an alternate payee's right to, or assigns to an alternate payee the right to, a portion of the benefits payable with respect to a participant under a plan. . . . A domestic relations order must meet certain requirements to qualify as a QDRO. QDRO's, unlike domestic relations orders in general, are exempt from both the pension plan anti-alienation provision, and ERISA's general pre-emption clause. . . . These provisions are essential to one of REA's central purposes, which is to give enhanced protection to the spouse and dependent children in the event of divorce or separation, and in the event of death the surviving spouse. Apart from these detailed provisions, ERISA does not confer beneficiary status on nonparticipants by reason of their marital or dependent status. . . .

The surviving spouse annuity and QDRO provisions, which acknowledge and protect specific pension plan community property interests, give rise to the strong implication that other community property claims are not consistent with the statutory scheme. ERISA's silence with respect to the right of a nonparticipant spouse to control pension plan benefits by testamentary transfer provides powerful support for the conclusion that the right does not exist. . . .

We conclude the sons have no claim under ERISA to a share of the retirement benefits. To begin with, the sons are neither participants nor beneficiaries. A "participant" is defined as an "employee or former employee of an employer, or any member or former member of an employee organization, who is or may become eligible to receive a benefit." A "beneficiary" is a "person designated by a participant, or by the terms of an employee benefit plan, who is or may become entitled to a benefit thereunder." §1002(8). Respondents' claims are based on Dorothy Boggs' attempted testamentary transfer, not on a designation by Isaac Boggs or under the terms of the retirement plans. . . .

The conclusion that Congress intended to pre-empt respondents' nonbeneficiary, nonparticipant interests in the retirement plans is given specific and powerful reinforcement by the pension plan anti-alienation provision. Section 1056(d)(1) provides that "[e]ach pension plan shall provide that benefits provided under the plan may not be assigned or alienated." Statutory anti-alienation provisions are potent mechanisms to prevent the dissipation of funds. . . . The anti-alienation provision can "be seen to bespeak a pension law protective policy of special intensity: Retirement funds shall remain inviolate until retirement."

Dorothy's 1980 testamentary transfer, which is the source of respondents' claimed ownership interest, is a prohibited "assignment or alienation." An "assignment or alienation" has been defined by regulation, with certain exceptions not at issue here, as "[a]ny direct or indirect arrangement whereby a party acquires from a participant or beneficiary" an interest enforceable against a plan to "all or any part of a plan benefit payment which is, or may become, payable to the participant or beneficiary." Those requirements are met. Under Louisiana law community property interests are enforceable against a plan. If respondents' claims were allowed to succeed they would have acquired, as of 1980, an interest in Isaac's pension plan at the expense of plan participants and beneficiaries.

As was true with survivors' annuities, it would be inimical to ERISA's purposes to permit testamentary recipients to acquire a competing interest in undistributed pension benefits, which are intended to provide a stream of income to participants and their beneficiaries. Pension benefits support participants and beneficiaries in their retirement years, and ERISA's pension plan safeguards are designed to further this end. . . . Under respondents' approach, retirees could find their retirement benefits reduced by substantial sums because they have been diverted to testamentary recipients. Retirement benefits and the income stream provided for by ERISA-regulated plans would be disrupted in the name of protecting a nonparticipant spouse's successors over plan participants and beneficiaries. Respondents' logic would even permit a spouse to transfer an interest in a pension plan to creditors, a result incompatible with a spendthrift provision such as §1056(d)(1). . . .

Reversed.

Justice BREYER, with whom Justice O'CONNOR joins, and with whom THE CHIEF JUSTICE and Justice GINSBURG join except as to Part II-B-3, dissenting. The question in this case is whether the Employee Retirement Income Security Act of 1974 (ERISA), 29 U.S.C. §1001, et seq., "pre-empts," and thereby nullifies, state community property law. . . .

The state law in question concerns the ownership of benefits. I concede that a primary concern of ERISA is the proper financial management of pension and welfare benefit funds themselves, and that payment of benefits (which amounts to the writing of checks from those funds) is closely "connected with" that management. . . . But, even so, I cannot say that the state law at issue here concerns a subject that Congress wished to place outside the State's legal reach.

My reason in part lies in the fact that the state law in question involves family, property, and probate—all areas of traditional, and important, state concern. When this Court considers pre-emption, it works "on the 'assumption that the historic police powers of the States were not to be superseded by the Federal Act unless that was the clear and manifest purpose of Congress.'"

I can find no reasonably defined relevant category of state law that Congress would have intended to displace. Obviously, Congress did not intend to pre-empt all state laws that govern property ownership. After all, someone must own an interest in ERISA plan benefits. Nor, for similar reasons, can one believe that Congress intended to pre-empt state laws concerning testamentary bequests . . . . The question, "who owns the property?" needs an answer. Ordinarily, where federal law does not provide a specific answer, state law will have to do so.

Nor can I find some appropriately defined forbidden category by looking to the congressional purpose of establishing uniform laws to regulate the administration of pension funds. This case does not involve a lawsuit against a fund. I agree with the majority that ERISA would likely pre-empt state law that permitted such a suit. But this is not such a case; nor is there reason to believe Louisiana law would produce such a case. . . .

NOTES AND QUESTIONS

1. The Supreme Court in *Boggs* concludes that recognizing Dorothy's community property interests in the pensions at Isaac's death would undermine Congress's purposes in requiring that pensions be inalienable. What are these purposes, according to the Court? Do you agree with the Court's conclusion as to each of the three kinds of rights—the lump sum distribution that Isaac took at retirement and rolled into an IRA, the shares of stock purchased through the employee stock ownership plan, and the surviving spouse's annuity?

If Dorothy and Isaac had divorced, the divorce court would have been able to award Dorothy her community property interests in the pensions that Isaac earned during marriage, as we will see in Chapter 6. For this reason, Professor Andrea Carroll criticizes ERISA as interpreted by *Boggs* as giving spouses in Dorothy's position an incentive to divorce. Andrea B. Carroll, Incentivizing Divorce, 30 Cardozo L. Rev. 1925 (2009).

2. The supremacy clause of the United States Constitution states that the "laws of the United States . . . shall be the supreme law of the Land." Accordingly, state laws inconsistent with federal law are void. Federal legislation may preempt state law in two ways. It may undertake to provide the sole body of law in a field, either by express statutory provision or by implication. Even if Congress has not expressly or implicitly undertaken to occupy the entire field, state law is preempted to the extent of any conflict with a federal statute. Such a "conflict preemption" arises when a private party cannot comply with both federal and state law or when compliance with the challenged state law will frustrate accomplishment of important federal purposes embodied in congressional legislation.

For an analysis of subsequent Supreme Court decisions in cases related to *Boggs*, *see* Albert Feuer, How the Supreme Court and the Department of Labor May Dispel Myths About ERISA's Family Law Provisions and Protect the Benefit Entitlements That Arise Thereunder, 45 J. Marshall L. Rev. 635 (2012).

3. Other federal laws sometimes conflict with a state's treatment of property as community or marital property, again raising a preemption issue. For example, cases have considered whether federal law precludes copyrighted or patented work from being treated as community property. In Rodrigue v. Rodrigue, 218 F.3d 432 (5th Cir. 2000), *cert. denied*, 532 U.S. 905 (2001), the question was whether the wife of a highly successful Louisiana artist was entitled to rights in the husband's copyrighted works created during the marriage. The husband argued that the Copyright Act of 1976 provided that ownership of a copyright "vests initially in the author" at the time of the creation of the work. From this, the husband contended, it follows that the community property principle that property acquired during marriage is owned equally by the spouses had been preempted by federal law assigning full ownership solely in the author, and thus his copyrighted works were separate property not subject to division at divorce.

While Section 301 of the Copyright Act provides that the Act governs "all legal or equitable rights that are equivalent to any of the exclusive rights with the general scope of copyright," the Fifth Circuit concluded that this language did not amount to a preemption of the entire field of marital property. Rather, it held that the Copyright Act protects five exclusive rights: reproduction, adaptation, publication, performance, and display of protected works.

Accordingly, the question was whether the operation of Louisiana community property law conflicted with the purposes of the Act. The strongest argument for finding a conflict was that Louisiana state law would give the nonauthor spouse equal management rights to copyrighted works, which was functionally inconsistent with Copyright Act's grant to authors of exclusive rights related to management. The Fifth Circuit agreed that dividing these management rights, as opposed to the right to enjoy income or other economic benefits from copyrighted works, would conflict with the federal scheme. However, the court held that Louisiana community property law was not preempted to the extent that it allowed a nonauthor spouse to share in the economic benefits created by copyrighted works during the existence of the marriage. For more information, *see* Llewellyn Joseph Gibbons, Love's Labor's Lost: Marry for Love, Copyright Work Made-for-Hire, and Alienate at Your Leisure, 101 Ky. L.J. 113 (2012-2013); Sarah Coates, Comment, I Do, I Did, I'm Done: Copyright and Termination of Transfer in Divorce, 23 Or. Rev. Int'l L. 183 (2022). *See also* Daniel H. Shulman & Angela Upchurch, Spousal Rights to Inventions: A Latent Threat to Corporate Patent Portfolios, 50 Seton Hall L. Rev. 1 (2019).

4. ERISA covers only benefit plans established by (1) employers who are engaged in or affect interstate commerce or (2) employee organizations representing employees engaged in or affecting commerce, or both. While many of its provisions apply to all benefit plans, including welfare benefit plans such as health insurance or vacation plans, the anti-alienation provision applies only to pension benefit plans. Mackey v. Lanier Collection Agency & Service, Inc., 486 U.S. 825 (1988). As the Court notes in *Boggs*, however, benefits other than annuity payments, such as employee stock option benefits and profit sharing plans, may qualify as "pension benefits" and therefore come under the anti-alienation provisions of ERISA.

3. Family Support Duties

McGuire v. McGuire
59 N.W.2d 336 (Neb. 1953)

Messmore, J. The plaintiff, Lydia McGuire, brought this action in equity in the district court for Wayne County against Charles W. McGuire, her husband, as defendant, to recover suitable maintenance and support money, and for costs and attorney's fees. Trial was had to the court and a decree was rendered in favor of the plaintiff.

The district court decreed that the plaintiff was legally entitled to use the credit of the defendant and obligate him to pay for certain items in the nature of improvements and repairs, furniture, and appliances for the household in the amount of several thousand dollars; required the defendant to purchase a new automobile with an effective heater within 30 days; ordered him to pay travel expenses of the plaintiff for a visit to each of her daughters at least once a year; that the plaintiff be entitled in the future to pledge the credit of the defendant for what may constitute necessaries of life; awarded a personal allowance to the plaintiff in the sum of $50 a month; awarded $800 for services for the plaintiff's attorney; and as an alternative to part of the award so made, defendant was permitted, in agreement with plaintiff, to purchase a modern home elsewhere. . . .

The record shows that the plaintiff and defendant were married in Wayne, Nebraska, on August 11, 1919. At the time of the marriage the defendant was a bachelor 46 or 47 years of age and had a reputation for more than ordinary frugality, of which the plaintiff was aware. She had visited in his home and had known him for about 3 years prior to the marriage. After the marriage the couple went to live on a farm of 160 acres located in Leslie precinct, Wayne County, owned by the defendant and upon which he had lived and farmed since 1905. The parties have lived on this place ever since. The plaintiff had been previously married. Her first husband died in October 1914, leaving surviving him the plaintiff and two daughters. . . .

At the time of trial plaintiff was 66 years of age and the defendant nearly 80 years of age. No children were born to these parties. The defendant had no dependents except the plaintiff.

The plaintiff testified that she was a dutiful and obedient wife, worked and saved, and cohabited with the defendant until the last 2 or 3 years. She worked in the fields, did outside chores, cooked, and attended to her household duties such as cleaning the house and doing the washing. For a number of years she raised as high as 300 chickens, sold poultry and eggs, and used the money to buy clothing, things she wanted, and for groceries. She further testified that the defendant was the boss of the house and his word was law; that he would not tolerate any charge accounts and would not inform her as to his finances or business; and that he was a poor companion. The defendant did not complain of her work, but left the impression to her that she had not done enough. On several occasions the plaintiff asked the defendant for money. He would give her very small amounts, and for the last 3 or 4 years he had not given her any money nor provided her with clothing, except a coat about 4 years previous. The defendant had purchased the groceries the last 3 or 4 years, and permitted her to buy groceries, but he paid for them by check. There is apparently no complaint about the groceries the defendant furnished. The defendant had not taken her to a motion picture show during the past 12 years. They did not belong to any organizations or charitable institutions, nor did he give her money to make contributions to any charitable institutions. The defendant belongs to the Pleasant Valley Church, which occupies about 2 acres of his farm land. At the time of trial there was no minister for this church, so there were no services. For the past 4 years or more, the defendant had not given the plaintiff money to purchase furniture or other household necessities. Three years ago he did purchase an electric, wood-and-cob combination stove which was installed in the kitchen, also linoleum floor covering for the kitchen. The plaintiff further testified that the house is not equipped with a bathroom, bathing facilities, or inside toilet. The kitchen is not modern. She does not have a kitchen sink. Hard and soft water is obtained from a well and cistern. She has a mechanical Servel refrigerator, and the house is equipped with electricity. There is a pipeless furnace, which she testified had not been in good working order for 5 or 6 years, and she testified she was tired of scooping coal and ashes. She had requested a new furnace, but the defendant believed the one they had to be satisfactory. She related that the furniture was old and she would like to replenish it, at least to be comparable with some of her neighbors; that her silverware and dishes were old and were primarily gifts, outside of what she purchased; that one of her daughters was good about furnishing her clothing, at least a dress a year, or sometimes two; that the defendant owns a 1929 Ford coupe equipped with a heater which is not efficient, and on the average of every 2 weeks he drives the plaintiff to Wayne to visit her mother; and that he also owns a 1927 Chevrolet pickup which is used for different purposes on the farm. The plaintiff was privileged to use all of the rent money she wanted to from the 80-acre farm, and when she goes to see her daughters, which is not frequent, she uses part of the rent money for that purpose, the defendant providing no funds for such use. . . . At the present time the plaintiff is not able to raise chickens and sell eggs. She has about 25 chickens. The plaintiff has had three abdominal operations for which the defendant has paid. She selected her own doctor, and there were no restrictions placed in that respect. When she has requested various things for the home or personal effects, defendant has informed her on many occasions that he did not have the money to pay for the same. She would like to have a new car. She visited one daughter in Spokane, Washington, in March 1951 for 3 or 4 weeks, and visited the other daughter living in Fort Worth, Texas, on three occasions for 2 to 4 weeks at a time. She had visited one of her daughters when she was living in Sioux City some weekends. The plaintiff further testified that she had very little funds, possibly $1,500 in the bank, which was chicken money and money which her father furnished her, he having departed this life a few years ago; and that use of the telephone was restricted, indicating that defendant did not desire that she make long distance calls; otherwise she had free access to the telephone.

It appears that the defendant owns 398 acres of land with 2 acres deeded to a church, the land being of the value of $83,960; that he has bank deposits in the sum of $12,786.81 and government bonds in the amount of $104,500; and that his income, including interest on the bonds and rental for his real estate, is $8,000 or $9,000 a year. There are apparently some Series E United States Savings Bonds listed and registered in the names of Charles W. McGuire or Lydia M. McGuire purchased in 1943, 1944, and 1945, in the amount of $2,500. Other bonds seem to be in the name of Charles W. McGuire, without a beneficiary or co-owner designated. The plaintiff has a bank account of $5,960.22. This account includes deposits of some $200 and $100, which the court required the defendant to pay his wife as temporary allowance during the pendency of these proceedings. One hundred dollars was withdrawn on the date of each deposit. . . .

The defendant assigns as error that the decree is not supported by sufficient evidence; that the decree is contrary to law; [and] that the decree is an unwarranted usurpation and invasion of defendant's fundamental and constitutional rights. . . .

The plaintiff relies upon the following cases from this jurisdiction, which are clearly distinguishable from the facts in the instant case, as will become apparent.

In the case of Earle v. Earle, the plaintiff's petition alleged . . . that the defendant sent his wife away from him, did not permit her to return, contributed to her support and maintenance separate and apart from him, and later refused and ceased to provide for her support and the support of his child. The wife instituted a suit in equity against her husband for maintenance and support without a prayer for divorce or from bed and board. The question presented was whether or not the wife should be compelled to resort to a proceeding for a divorce, which she did not desire to do, or from bed and board. On this question, in this state the statutes are substantially silent and at the present time there is no statute governing this matter. The court stated that it was a well-established rule of law that it is the duty of the husband to provide his family with support and means of living — the style of support, requisite lodging, food, clothing, etc., to be such as fit his means, position, and station in life — and for this purpose the wife has generally the right to use his credit for the purchase of necessaries. The court held that if a wife is abandoned by her husband, without means of support, a bill in equity will lie to compel the husband to support the wife without asking for a decree of divorce. . . .

In the instant case the marital relation has continued for more than 33 years, and the wife has been supported in the same manner during this time without complaint on her part. The parties have not been separated or living apart from each other at any time. In the light of the cited cases it is clear, especially so in this jurisdiction, that to maintain an action such as the one at bar, the parties must be separated or living apart from each other.

The living standards of a family are a matter of concern to the household, and not for the courts to determine, even though the husband's attitude toward his wife, according to his wealth and circumstances, leaves little to be said in his behalf. As long as the home is maintained and the parties are living as husband and wife it may be said that the husband is legally supporting his wife and the purpose of the marriage relation is being carried out. Public policy requires such a holding. It appears that the plaintiff is not devoid of money in her own right. She has a fair-sized bank account and is entitled to use the rent from the 80 acres of land left by her first husband, if she so chooses. . . .

For the reasons given in this opinion, the judgment rendered by the district court is reversed and the cause remanded with directions to dismiss the cause.

Reversed and remanded with directions to dismiss.

YEAGER, J. (dissenting). I respectfully dissent. . . . From the beginning of the married life of the parties the defendant supplied only the barest necessities and there was no change thereafter. He did not even buy groceries until the last 3 or 4 years before the trial, and neither did he buy clothes for the plaintiff. . . .

There is and can be no doubt that, independent of statutes relating to divorce, alimony, and separate maintenance, if this plaintiff were living apart from the defendant she could in equity and on the facts as outlined in the record be awarded appropriate relief.

The principle supporting the right of a wife to maintain an action in equity, independent of statute, for maintenance was first announced in this jurisdiction in Earle v. Earle, 27 Neb. 277, 43 N.W. 118, 119, 20 Am. St. Rep. 667. In the opinion it was said: "While the statute books of this and other states amply provide for the granting of divorces in meritorious cases, yet we do not apprehend that it is the purpose of the law to compel a wife, when the aggrieved party, to resort to this proceeding, and thus liberate her husband from all obligations to her, in order that the rights which the law gives her, by reason of her marital relations with her husband, may be enforced. Such a conclusion would not generally strike the conscience of a court of equity as being entirely equitable.". . .

If relief is to be denied to plaintiff under this principle it must be denied because of the fact that she is not living separate and apart from the defendant and is not seeking separation.

In the light of what the decisions declare to be the basis of the right to maintain an action for support, is there any less reason for extending the right to a wife who is denied the right to maintenance in a home occupied with her husband than to one who has chosen to occupy a separate abode?

The *McGuire* case raises central questions about the relationship of the state, particularly courts, to family governance. These questions, and the case itself, have been the subjects of wide comment and some disagreement. The following materials explore some aspects of that debate, including the importance, utility, and implications of treating the family as an economic and social unit.

Mary Anne Case

Enforcing Bargains in an Ongoing Marriage
35 Wash. U. J.L. & Pol'y 225, 239-242 (2011)

The inability to obtain enforcement in an ongoing marriage is far from a universal feature of the law of marriage in all legal systems at all times. For example, Montesquieu declared at the beginning of the eighteenth century that, in France, "husbands have only a vestige of authority over wives," because "the law intervenes in every dispute between them." Indeed, historians of late medieval and early modern France and Italy provide evidence of a pattern of judicial enforcement of women's rights within an ongoing marriage that seems to resemble the U.S. corporate law norm:

> For women, property separations emerged as a more viable option than separations of person and property. The relative ease with which property separations were granted provided married women with the leverage to counter, whether by threat or by actual petition, the legal privileges their husbands had over marital property and to check other kinds of behavior than the narrow management of property.
>
> . . . [In litigated cases, h]usbands' competence was questioned rather than assumed; indeed, some women in these cases . . . were able to use separation petitions to reshape the political economies of their households to protect their own interests if their husbands came up short. . . .
>
> . . . For the state as represented by its judges, for the local community, and for kin anxious to protect their lineage property, separations were a means of disciplining and regulating households. But all three parties sought to limit the disruption by trying to reconcile husbands and wives and by favoring property separations as checks on the internal problems of households over the disintegration of households that separations of person and property entailed.

Perhaps one reason why continental judges were more willing than their English contemporaries to follow what became the modern rule for corporations is that continental marriages, particularly among the urban bourgeoisie, resembled closely held corporations more than did those of the English landed gentry. Women in intact marriages in early modern France, for example, had their own capital in the form of lineage property, and the level of detailed judicial decision making required to vest control of such property in a wife was far less than the micromanagement inevitably involved in determining, for example, the appropriate living standards of the McGuire household. "In England, by contrast, where there was no lineage property, there was also no common-law right to separate property and no separate property agreement until the nineteenth century, and separate domicile was easier for women to obtain than separate property."

The historians' evidence suggests that bargaining in the shadow of possible judicial enforcement—as the modern law and economics literature would predict—strengthened the hand of women in continental Europe negotiating with recalcitrant husbands, not only over property issues such as household expenditures and investments, but also when it came to matters such as domestic violence. For example, in her study of separated couples in fourteenth-century Venice, historian Linda Guzzetti describes cases settled before judicial proceedings were brought, in which:

> it was a question of the husband undertaking, for the future, neither to beat his wife, nor to abuse her, but to treat her well. The promises were made with the aim that the wives accept living again with the husbands from whom they had fled. These reconciliation agreements contained formulas similar to those in all other notarial contracts: for non-fulfilment of promise a financial penalty was envisaged, and each party could take the other to court.

Whereas differences in marital property regimes between England and the continent may help account for the comparative willingness of courts in early modern continental Europe to enforce bargains in an ongoing marriage, the fact that their approach to marriage is more thoroughgoingly contractual and juridical may help explain why Jewish and Islamic legal systems have also long been more willing to enforce bargains in an ongoing marriage than the Anglo-American legal system, whose approach to civil marriage evolved from Christian canonical notions of marriage as a sacrament of union.

According to Elimelech Westreich, the McGuire case would have been decided very differently under Jewish law: "The living standards are definitely a matter for the courts to determine. [This] is accepted without reservations by the Misnah, Talmud, Mishneh Torah, Sefer Ha-Turim, Shulchan Aruch, and in other Jewish law sources including the verdicts of the rabbinical courts of Israel."

Lee E. Teitelbaum

Family History and Family Law
1985 Wis. L. Rev. 1135, 1144-1145, 1174-1178

[The social history of the nineteenth- and twentieth-century American family] is developmental, moving from hierarchically-ordered households closely integrated with the community towards an egalitarian, companionate family sharply separated from the public world. The trend is not so much toward a nuclear as an enucleated family. . . .

. . . "[P]rivacy" for the household is often given an objective meaning. . . . The meaning given to privacy . . . is the familiar one of autonomy or freedom from governmental control. A clear statement of this association has been provided by Judith Stiehm:

> In this country, intrafamily relations are a private rather than a governmental concern. The state does establish a legal basis for the family's existence, but this defining function is exercised principally when families are either being founded, as in marriage or adoption, or dissolved, as in divorce or death. Even then, the state's role is minimal unless property is involved. The government is only too happy to avoid having either to forbid or to require particular interpersonal behavior.

Judith Stiehm, Government and the Family: Justice and Acceptance, in Changing Images of the Family 361, 362 (V. Tufte & B. Myerhoff eds., 1979).

Both the notion of family privacy and its meaning of autonomy or freedom from governmental concern are used in legal discussions as well. . . . Generally, the notion of family privacy includes two situations: those in which courts decline to intervene to resolve intra-familial disputes for prudential reasons and those in which they say that law may not properly regulate certain aspects of family relationships. The most familiar illustration of the first situation is the reluctance of courts to order the financial and personal arrangements of spouses. Where the marriage is "intact," meaning that proceedings for separation or divorce have not been instituted, courts traditionally have refused to enter support decrees unless gross and dangerous neglect is proved. . . .

. . . When courts refuse to resolve intra-spousal financial disputes, that decision is founded on the principle of family autonomy. . . . However, the practical consequence of many, if not all, of these decisions is to confer or ratify the power of one family member over others. . . . Certainly Mrs. McGuire was not "free to work out her own role" in the marriage if Mr. McGuire had all the money. She could not get the new cloth coat she wanted, or new linoleum for the kitchen, or a warm heater for their old car. Her only choice lay without the marriage, in seeking a judicial separation or divorce. When the majority in *McGuire* say that "the living standards of the family are a matter of concern to the household," they mean only that they propose to leave the parties where they are. The "household" does not make decisions about living standards, unless that is informally agreed. Otherwise, the husband will make those decisions. . . .

[Analysis that assumes that the state does not intervene in the family unit] depends on a particular conceptualization of law. We mean by intervention public activity through proscriptive and prescriptive rules: "Thou shalt not steal" or "Thou shalt support thy wife." Commands of these kinds are sharply distinguished from facilitative rules and from silence or abstention, which are considered instances of nonregulation. A rule that says "Fathers must leave at least one-third of their wealth to their children at death" is considered different in kind from one that says "Any testamentary provision made in a certain form will be enforced." Similarly, a rule reciting that "Husbands shall adequately support their wives" is different, not only in its content but in its nature, from one that says, "The state will not resolve financial disputes between spouses." The first of these pairs of rules would be considered an instance of intervention because each manifestly limits individual choice; the second of these pairs would ordinarily be regarded as facilitating or conveying autonomy. . . .

The entity approach . . . hides decisions about family relationships that are worth examining. Although only prescriptive and proscriptive rules are taken as cases of intervention, it is surely true that all forms of societal behavior—including facilitative rules and silence—involve policy choices. Moreover, the choice of strategies is not simply between domination (intervention) and freedom (nonintervention), but between two kinds of authority. When government acts by commands, it thereby authorizes an exercise of public authority. . . .

Facilitative rules and silence, by contrast, leave people to their own strengths and thereby authorize personal authority. If bargains will always be enforced, the making of that bargain reflects only the power, skill, and knowledge of the parties. When the parties are in fact unequal in these characteristics, the weaker party is subject to the domination of the stronger. That domination is personal rather than public; law only ratifies the naturally existing or socially created inequalities which have led to the victory of one over the other.

By regarding the family as an entity which is left free by governmental silence, the effects of a policy permitting personal domination are obscured. When . . . Mrs. McGuire is left to her own resources in dealing with her husband, she is subject to his personal authority in seeking a car or a coat. No rules require that he treat her as other husbands treat their wives, or as he treated a former wife, had he married previously. It does not in principle matter that her neighbors have bought cars, coats, or an electric range for their wives. . . . Because we focus on "the family" rather than on Mrs. McGuire, however, her condition becomes invisible.

Bruce C. Hafen

The Family as an Entity
22 U.C. Davis L. Rev. 865, 909, 912 (1989)

We might help to restore a more familistic perspective on family relationships by regarding the family as a structurally significant and legally meaningful entity that affects both individual and social interests. . . .

This notion of entity is nothing more mysterious than what most Americans still assume (even if partly as myth) is "the dominant American ideal"—namely, relationships based upon marriage and kinship in which legal, biological, and social expectations convey long-term, normative, familistic assumptions. Those who accept membership in such an entity implicitly accept in a general—even if, in many ways, unenforceable—sense the familistic model's characteristics. . . .

Emphasizing the family's "internal" institutional autonomy may leave some deserving individuals without legal recourse for unequal treatment or other wrongs (short of actual abuse) that they may suffer within the sphere of family privacy. However, unless we to some degree assume that risk, constant legal intervention (or the threat of it) will destroy the continuity that is critically necessary for meaningful, ongoing relationships and developmental nurturing. Even the "direct, prolonged conflict" that may characterize some family continuity may play a significant role in "forging communal bonds." . . .

Moreover, when we increase state intervention in an ongoing family to protect the autonomy of some family members against others, we may be simply exchanging one threat to autonomy for another. We must then ask which threat is worse—the state or other family members? In cases of serious spousal or child abuse, the threat from within the family is obviously worse. Over the long run, however, liberal thought has usually, and accurately, perceived the state as a more frightening enemy of personal liberty.

NOTES AND QUESTIONS

1. During the 34 years of marriage before Mrs. McGuire brought this suit, she and her children paid for the things that she needed that Mr. McGuire did not provide. Was she not entitled to support during the marriage? A number of cases say that a married woman was entitled to support even when she had earnings or property of her own or when her children provided her with funds. *See* Pezas v. Pezas, 201 A.2d 192 (Conn. 1964); Ewell v. State, 114 A.2d 66 (Md. 1955); Ulrich v. State, 59 A.2d 460 (Del. 1948).

2. Mrs. McGuire relied on the earlier decision in Earle v. Earle to support her claim. How did the court distinguish that case? Why did the difference matter?

3. If you had represented Mrs. McGuire after this decision, what would you have advised her to do if she still wanted to remain in a relationship with Mr. McGuire but for him to pay for more household expenses? In Nebraska in the 1950s, divorce was granted only for fault, and Mr. McGuire's conduct would very likely not have been sufficiently bad to justify granting Mrs. McGuire a divorce.

4. Courts in North Carolina and South Carolina have held that courts should not entertain suits in which a wife who is living with her husband seeks spousal support because separate maintenance statutes assume that the parties are in fact living separately. Baumann-Chacon v. Baumann, 710 S.E.2d 431 (N.C. App. 2011); Theisen v. Theisen, 716 S.E.2d 271 (S.C. 2011). In addition, the *Theisen* court explained that it was concerned about

> the relative ease with which parties might otherwise bring their minor disputes into the spotlight of the family court, thereby working irreparable damage to the family unit. The potential for unnecessary litigation will work more harm to a marriage than the requirement that a spouse's discontent with the marriage ordinarily must be sufficient for him or her to leave the marital home prior to receiving separate maintenance.

716 S.E.2d at 279. The dissent responded:

> In my opinion, public policy does not require parties live in separate residences in order to bring a separate maintenance and support suit. Instead, I would allow such a suit where the parties no longer have a "romantic" relationship. We allow a divorce action to be brought where the parties share a residence, *Watson, supra*, and have allowed a separate maintenance and support suit under the same circumstances. *Murray, supra*. Both *Watson* and *Murray* recognize the hardship placed on a parent in a custody situation if the parent must leave the home in order to commence marital litigation. In a similar vein, public policy should recognize that financial impossibility may prevent a spouse from establishing a separate residence prior to receiving court-ordered support. We should not deny access to the family court to a party who must, of financial necessity, remain in the marital abode.

716 S.E.2d at 278. How would a court determine whether the parties no longer have a "romantic relationship"?

Sharpe Furniture, Inc. v. Buckstaff
299 N.W.2d 219 (Wis. 1980)

BEILFUSS, C.J. This controversy centers around the purchase of a sofa from Sharpe Furniture, Inc. (Sharpe). The purchase was made by Karen Buckstaff on August 15, 1973. On that date, Mrs. Buckstaff signed in her own name a special order for a "Henredon 6800 Sofa." Under the terms of the order she was to pay $621.50 within 60 days after the item was received from the factory. Interest at a rate of 1.5 percent per month was charged on the unpaid balance after that 60-day period. No representations were made to Sharpe at the time of the purchase that Mrs. Buckstaff was acting on behalf of her husband in purchasing the furniture. Indeed, John Buckstaff had previously written to the local credit bureau service to advise that office that he would not be responsible for any credit extended to his wife.

The Henredon sofa was received from the factory and delivered to the residence of the defendants on February 8, 1974. This piece of furniture has been a part of the Buckstaff home ever since its delivery. Despite this fact, neither John Buckstaff nor his wife have tendered payment for the sofa.

On November 20, 1975, Sharpe commenced this action against both Buckstaffs. The parties agreed to allow the trial court to decide the dispute on the basis of the undisputed facts as they appeared in the trial memoranda submitted by counsel. In addition to the facts already stated above, the informal stipulation of the parties reveals that John Buckstaff, Jr., is the president of Buckstaff Company of Oshkosh, Wisconsin. Mrs. Buckstaff is a housewife. Mr. Buckstaff earns a substantial income and the Buckstaff family is one of social and economic prominence in the Oshkosh area. It was further set forth that Mr. Buckstaff has always provided his wife with the necessaries of life and has never failed or refused to provide his wife with items which could be considered necessaries.

On the basis of these facts, the trial court found that Karen Buckstaff was liable on her contract and that John Buckstaff was also liable for the amount due on the sofa under the common law doctrine of necessaries. . . .

There are two issues which we must consider in reviewing the decision of the court of appeals:

1. Whether, under the common law doctrine of necessaries and in the absence of any contractual obligation on his part, a husband may be held liable for sums due as payment for necessary items purchased on credit by his wife.

2. Whether, in an action for recovery of the value of necessaries supplied on credit to a wife, it is essential for the plaintiff-creditor to prove either that the husband has failed, refused or neglected to provide the items which have been supplied by the plaintiff-creditor or that the items supplied were reasonably needed by the wife or the family.

Before proceeding to a discussion of the merits of this case, we examine the substance of the doctrine of necessaries.

The Wisconsin Supreme Court restated the common law rule of necessaries early on in the history of the jurisprudence of this state. In 1871, in the case of Warner and Ryan v. Heiden, 28 Wis. 517, 519 (1871), the court wrote:

> The husband is under legal obligations to support his wife, and nothing but wrongful conduct on her part can free him from such obligation. If he fails to provide her with suitable and proper necessaries, any third person who does provide her therewith, may maintain an action against him for the same. 1 Bishop on Mar. and Div., sec. 553. The same learned author, in the next section (sec. 554), thus defines what are necessaries which the husband is bound to furnish to his wife: "And, in general, we may say, that necessaries are such articles of food, or apparel, or medicine, or such medical attendance and nursing, or such provided means of

locomotion, or provided habitation and furniture, *or such provision for her protection in society*, and the like, as the husband, considering his ability and standing, ought to furnish to his wife for her sustenance, and the preservation of her health and comfort."

This doctrine traditionally required the creditor to show that he supplied to the wife an item that was, in fact, a necessary and that the defendant had previously failed or refused to provide his wife with this item. . . . When such a showing was made, the creditor was entitled to recovery as against the husband despite the fact that the husband had not contractually bound himself by his own act or by the act of an agent. The doctrine of necessaries is not imposed by the law of agency. This duty is placed upon a husband by virtue of the legal relationship of marriage. It arises as an obligation placed on him as a matter of public policy.

The appellant challenges the continued vitality of this common law rule. Mr. Buckstaff charges that the necessaries doctrine conflicts with contemporary trends toward equality of the sexes and a sex neutral society. . . .

It is true that the necessaries rule has been justified in the past on the basis of a social view of the married woman as a person without legal capacity. However, the nature of the woman's obligations under the necessary rule in relation to the obligation of her husband is not at issue here. That question has been treated in our decision in Estate of Stromsted, 299 N.W.2d 226 (1980), wherein we concluded the husband was primarily liable for necessities and the wife secondarily liable. The question presented in this case involves a consideration of the nature of the husband's obligation. We must decide whether such a liability imposed upon the husband furthers a proper purpose in contemporary society.

We are of the opinion that the doctrine of necessaries serves a legitimate and proper purpose in our system of common law. The heart of this common law rule is a concern for the support and the sustenance of the family and the individual members thereof. The sustenance of the family unit is accorded a high order of importance in the scheme of Wisconsin law. . . . The necessaries rule encourages the extension of credit to those who in an individual capacity may not have the ability to make these basic purchases. In this manner it facilitates the support of the family unit and its function is in harmony with the purposes behind the support laws of this state. The rule retains a viable role in modern society. . . .

We conclude that when an item or service is obtained for the benefit of the family which is necessary and no payment for that item or service has been made, the elements of an action for an implied-in-law contract exist and the husband is primarily liable. . . .

Mr. Buckstaff's second argument is that, as a matter of law, he is not liable for the necessaries purchased by his wife because Sharpe did not plead or prove that he as a husband failed, refused or neglected to provide a sofa for his wife. It is also argued that liability cannot be found in the face of the parties' stipulation which states that Mr. Buckstaff has always provided his wife with the necessaries of life and has never failed or refused to provide her with items which would constitute necessaries. . . .

In the case of Eder v. Grifka, 149 Wis. 606, 136 N.W. 154 (1912), it was held that, besides demonstrating that necessaries were furnished by the creditor to the defendant's spouse, a plaintiff-creditor must also plead and prove that the defendant willfully refused to provide the necessaries for his wife. . . .

The merchant's burden of proof was modified by the decision in Simpson Garment Co. v. Schultz, 182 Wis. 506, 196 N.W. 783 (1924). . . .

The *Simpson Garment Company* rule required only that the creditor show that the item was "reasonably needed" by the wife or family, and not that the husband willfully refused to provide his wife with the necessary item as suggested by Eder v. Grifka, supra. . . .

Buckstaff's first argument, that the court's judgment of liability is invalid in the absence of a finding of refusal or neglect by a husband, must be rejected. Under *Simpson Garment Company*, the refusal or neglect of the husband is not an element essential to recovery by the creditor. Mr.

Buckstaff's second contention is that the sofa should not be considered a necessary in view of the stipulation that he as a husband provided his wife with all necessaries. Whether or not, as a general matter, a man provides his wife with necessaries is irrelevant to a determination of whether a particular item is reasonably needed under the *Simpson Garment Company* rule. . . .

We have reviewed the stipulation of the parties in this matter and we are satisfied that ample evidence supported the trial court's conclusion that the Henredon sofa was a legally necessary item. The Buckstaffs are a prominent family and their socio-economic standing justifies a finding that the sofa at issue here was a suitable and proper item for their household. With reference to the element of reasonable need, we note that the sofa has been in use in the Buckstaff home since its delivery. Such continued use gives rise to an inference of reasonable need. This inference is not rebutted by the stipulation stating that Mr. Buckstaff provided his wife with "all necessaries." . . .

The decision of the court of appeals is affirmed.

ABRAHAMSON, J. (concurring). I join the court in retaining the doctrine of necessaries and imposing liability on Mr. Buckstaff for the cost of the sofa. I do not agree, however, with that portion of the opinion in which the court adopts a rule placing primary liability on the husband to the creditor for necessaries supplied to the family. . . .

. . . [I]f the common law doctrine of necessaries is to survive as a rule of law it must be modified in accordance with the developing laws recognizing equal rights and responsibilities of both marital partners and the changes in the economic and social conditions of society. The common law doctrine of necessaries was premised on the legal disability of the married woman and on the husband's duty to support. Today, the married woman is free to contract, and the duty of support rests not on the husband alone but on both the husband and wife. While these changes in the law will require an alteration of the doctrine of necessaries, I would leave that alteration to a case in which the application of the common law doctrine conflicts with the married women statutes and the support statutes. This is not the case.

I believe the court has erred in adopting a flat, general rule which places primary liability on the husband to the creditor who supplies necessaries to the family. In my opinion, the rule suffers from two infirmities: First, the rule is not in harmony with the legislatively established public policy of this state, which is to impose the obligation to support on both the husband and wife on the basis of their respective economic resources and not on one spouse or the other on the basis of gender. Second, the rule discriminates against men and thus contravenes the state and federal constitutional guarantees of equal protection of law. . . .

I am persuaded that the majority rule which effects an unequal distribution of economic benefits and burdens on the basis of gender cannot pass muster under the federal and Wisconsin constitutions. Craig v. Boren, 429 U.S. 190 (1977); Weinberger v. Wiesenfeld, 420 U.S. 636 (1975).

John Kenneth Galbraith

Economics and the Public Purpose
31-37 (1973)

Industrialization eliminated the need for women in such cottage employments as spinning, weaving or the manufacture of apparel. . . . Meanwhile rising standards of popular consumption, combined with the disappearance of the menial personal servant, created an urgent need for labor to administer and otherwise manage consumption. In consequence a new social virtue came to attach to household management—the intelligent shopping for goods, their preparation, use and maintenance and the care and maintenance of the dwelling and other possessions. The virtuous woman became the good housekeeper or, more comprehensively, the good homemaker. . . .

The conversion of women into a crypto-servant class was an economic accomplishment of the first importance. . . . The value of services of housewives has been calculated, somewhat impressionistically, at roughly one fourth of total Gross National Product. . . . If it were not for this service, all forms of household consumption would be limited by the time required to manage such consumption—to select, transport, prepare, repair, maintain, clean, service, store, protect and otherwise perform the tasks that are associated with the consumption of goods. . . .

As just noted, the labor of women to facilitate consumption is not valued in national income or product. This is of some importance for its disguise; what is not counted is often not noticed. The neoclassical model has, however, a much more sophisticated disguise for the role of women. That is the household. . . .

The household having been made identical with the individual, it then distributes its income to various uses so that satisfactions are roughly equal at the margin. This, as observed, is the optimal state of enjoyment, the neoclassical consumer equilibrium. An obvious problem arises as to whose satisfactions are equated at the margin—those of the husband, the wife, the children with some allowance for age or the resident relatives, if any. But on this all accepted theory is silent. Between husband and wife there is evidently a compromise which accords with the more idyllic conception of the sound marriage. . . .

In fact, the modern household does not allow expression of individual personality and preference. It requires extensive subordination of preference by one member or another. The notion that economic society requires something approaching half of its adult members to accept subordinate status is not easily . . . reconciled with a system of social thought which not only esteems the individual but acclaims his or her power. So neoclassical economics resolves the problem by burying the subordination of the individual within the household, the inner relationships of which it ignores. Then it recreates the household as an individual consumer. There the matter remains. The economist does not invade the privacy of the household.

The common reality is that the modern household involves a simple but highly important division of labor. With the receipt of the income, in the usual case, goes the *basic* authority over its use. This usually lies with the male. Some of this authority is taken for granted. The place where the family lives depends overwhelmingly on the convenience or necessity of the member who makes the income. And both the level and nature or style of expenditure are also extensively influenced by its source—by whether the recipient is a business executive, lawyer, artist, accountant, civil servant, artisan, assembly-line worker or professor. More important, in a society which sets store by pecuniary achievement, a natural authority resides with the person who earns the money. This entitles him to be called the *head* of the family.

The administration of the consumption resides with the woman. This involves much choice as to purchases. . . . The conventional wisdom celebrates this power; it is women who hold the purse strings. In fact this is normally the power to implement decisions, not to make them. Action, within the larger strategic framework, is established by the man. . . .

Elizabeth R. Carter

The Illusion of Equality: The Failure of the Community Property Reform to Achieve Management Equality
48 Ind. L. Rev. 853, 855-857, 871-872 (2015)

The manner in which spouses actually manage their assets has always been more nuanced than the law suggests. To better describe what happens to money once it enters the home, sociologists have identified six distinct "allocative systems." These allocative systems classify spousal money control and management along a continuum by reference to two factors. The first basis of classification looks at whether and to what extent the spouses combine their money into a common pot or account. Spouses may entirely combine their money into a common pot, they may keep their money entirely separate, or they may combine only a portion of their money. The second basis of classification considers which spouse has control over the money. One spouse may control all of the money or the spouses may jointly manage the money. At the spousal level, the manner in which spouses manage their money is an "indicator of the level of equality in a relationship." . . .

The six allocative systems identified by sociologists are: (1) separate money/women's control; (2) separate money/men's control; (3) separate money/equal control; (4) pooled money/women's control; (5) pooled money/men's control; and (6) pooled money/equal control. A brief description of each follows.

1. *Separate Money/Women's Control.* — Spouses utilizing the separate money/women's control allocative system typically combine all of the wife's income, if any, with a portion of the husband's income into a single pot or account. The wife has control over that combined fund and uses it for household expenditures. The husband, however, retains a portion of his earnings for his own discretionary spending. "The implication of women's control, in conjunction with segregated money, is that most of the money for household spending is managed by the woman but that she does not have access to all of the man's earnings." At first blush, the separate money/women's control allocative system appears to give the wife substantial control over the couple's finances and, in turn, control in the relationship. Research, however, suggests the exact opposite to be the case. Today, the separate money/women's control allocative system is most common in low-income households, "where there is insufficient money to meet the bills and the task is likely to be a chore or a burden rather than a source of power."

2. *Separate Money/Men's Control.* — Under the separate money/men's control allocative system the husband retains control over his own earnings and is responsible for paying the household expenses. The wife typically has little or no income of her own and has no meaningful access to her husband's income. The husband may provide the wife with a "housekeeping allowance" so that she may buy groceries and perform other household errands. Research indicates that the separate money/men's control allocative system is particularly unequal and unfavorable to women with respect to women's access to personal spending money.

3. *Separate Money/Equal Control.* — The separate money/equal control allocative system is sometimes referred to as a "partial pooling" system. Under this allocative system, money is segregated and each spouse controls his or her funds independently. "[N]either partner has full access to the other's money, and household expenses are taken care of either by having each individual pay certain bills or by both pooling some portion of income for household expenses while each keeps his or her remaining income separate." The separate money/equal control allocative system is more common when both spouses are employed full-time and have higher income levels.

4. *Pooled Money/Women's Control.* — The pooled money/women's control allocative system is one in which the spouses combine all of their money into a common pot that is controlled by the wife. Just like the separate money/women's control allocative system, the pooled money/women's control allocative system is less advantageous to women than its name suggests. The pooled money/women's control allocative system is associated with lower-income households where controlling money is a chore rather than a source of power or independence.

5. *Pooled Money/Men's Control.* — The pooled money/men's control allocative system is the opposite of the pooled money/women's control allocative system. Under this system all money is combined into a single account or pot that is controlled by the husband. Research suggests this system is associated with higher income levels where only the man is employed.

6. *Pooled Money/Equal Control.* — The final allocative system, pooled money/equal control, is one in which the spouses combine all of their funds into a joint account or pool and then share management responsibility equally. . . .

Several studies suggest that truly equal management of pooled income is not common. Qualitative studies have found that "among male breadwinner-female homemaker couples using joint accounts, inequalities remain in access to money because nonearning women feel uncomfortable spending on themselves using money they did not earn or because breadwinning men retain primary decision-making power over money that is nominally pooled." A 1997 study based on data collected by telephone interviews found that, although wives are primarily responsible for shopping and paying the bills, "financial decision making is a domain in which husbands report, on average, that they exercise greater control than is reported by wives." Nearly three-fourths of the husbands surveyed reported that they were responsible for making major financial decisions. Yet, the same survey showed a widespread belief in gender equality and shared decision-making. . . .

NOTES AND QUESTIONS

1. The obligation to supply necessaries is sometimes said to rest on a theory that the wife acts as the husband's agent for the purchase of such items. That theory has the appeal of preserving a notion of family unity. Is *Buckstaff* consistent with such a theory? With changing gender roles and definitions of marriage?

The court describes the sofa as a "suitable and proper item for [the Buckstaff] household." Did the Buckstaff "household" make this purchase? Is the "household" sued for the price in this case? Does the "household" now own the sofa? Is a "household" a legal entity for any purpose?

2. Discussions of *McGuire* frequently observe that Mrs. McGuire could have pledged her husband's credit to purchase necessaries, *e.g.*, Bruce C. Hafen, The Family as an Entity, 22 U.C. Davis L. Rev. 865 (1989). How useful is the power to pledge a husband's credit for the wife who does not possess independent financial means? Consider the situation from the creditor's point of view. If the husband did not pay, what would the creditor have to prove to recover from him? Consider also that it was traditionally a defense to an action for necessaries that the wife had forfeited her right to support by adultery or abandonment of her husband. *See* Homer H. Clark, Jr., The Law of Domestic Relations in the United States 252-257 (2d ed. 1988).

If the Buckstaffs had discussed the purchase of the sofa, had disagreed, and Mr. Buckstaff had then told Sharpe Furniture not to sell the sofa to his wife, would he be liable if the store nonetheless sold the sofa to Mrs. Buckstaff?

3. The Henredon sofa cost $621.50 (in 1973 dollars or over $4,000 in 2022 dollars). On what basis does the court decide that this, rather than a less expensive piece of furniture, is a suitable and proper item for the Buckstaff household? Could a designer coat be a "necessary"? *See* Gimbel Bros., Inc. v. Pinto, 145 A.2d 865 (Pa. Super. 1958). On the other hand, would Mr. McGuire likely be required to pay for a $621.50 sofa if Mrs. McGuire charged it?

After reading *McGuire*, how would one describe the level of support to which a married woman who works only in the home is entitled? What level does *Buckstaff* suppose? How does one explain the difference?

4. A spouse's liability for necessaries is explained in *Buckstaff* and most other cases as a device for enforcing the duty of support. Why are supported spouses allowed to use this method of enforcing the right to support but not to sue their mates, which would allow a court to order a comprehensive remedy? Is either strategy more respectful of "family autonomy"?

Some courts have abolished the necessaries doctrine on the basis that, in modern conditions, it is no longer necessary or even useful as a means of providing for the support of dependents. Do you agree?

5. There are at least four schemes of ordering the liability of spouses for "necessaries" purchased by one of them. At common law the husband was liable for both his own debts and those incurred by his wife: a perhaps inevitable result having regard to his virtually plenary control over the wife's wealth during the marriage. A second approach is that developed in Estate of Stromsted, 299 N.W.2d 226 (Wis. 1980), and employed in *Buckstaff*: The husband is primarily liable for necessaries and the wife only secondarily responsible. Accordingly, a creditor must first seek satisfaction from the husband and can go against the wife only if the husband's assets are inadequate. A third possibility is to impose joint and several liability, allowing the creditor to choose either or both spouses as the target(s) for collection. *See* Cooke v. Adams, 183 So. 2d 925 (Miss. 1966). The fourth is to hold that the creditor should seek to recover first against the spouse incurring the obligation, making the other secondarily liable. This is the result reached in Jersey Shore Medical Center v. Baum, 417 A.2d 1003 (N.J. 1980), discussed by Justice Abrahamson.

6. Two-thirds of the states retain the necessaries doctrine, have enacted a family expense statute, or both. Marie T. Reilly, In Good Times and in Debt: The Evolution of Marital Agency and the Meaning of Marriage, 87 Neb. L. Rev. 373, 400 (2008).

7. In Klotz v. Celentano Stadtmauer & Walentowicz LLP, 991 Fed. 3d 458 (3rd Cir. 2021), a hospital sued a surviving wife under the necessaries doctrine for medical services it had provided to her husband, who had died without an estate. She argued that the federal Equal Credit Opportunity Act, 15 U.S.C. §§1691 et seq., which prohibits creditors from seeking to collect debts that are not authorized by law, conflicted with the state necessaries doctrine and was, therefore, preempted by it. The Third Circuit rejected her argument, finding no express conflict between the federal and state law and that enforcing the state law would not conflict with a purpose of the federal statute.

PROBLEM

Anita and Lawrence were married 30 years ago, when he was 61 and she was 41. He was very wealthy and ready to retire. At his request, Anita quit her work to spend all her time with him. Because both of them had children from a former marriage, they entered a valid premarital agreement providing that each person's assets and the proceeds from those assets would remain his or her separate property. The agreement also provided that Lawrence would give Anita $2 million outright and $15,000 a month thereafter. The monthly stipend was not intended to be her sole means of support, but rather to provide her the means to build up some assets of her own. Lawrence paid all the expenses of their lavish life together for the next 25 years. Five years ago his health and mental faculties had deteriorated, and he gave his son a general power of attorney to manage his affairs. He is now living in a long-term care facility, and everyone agrees that he is legally incompetent. Over the years the son has been increasingly less generous to Anita. Now he only authorizes dispersal of $15,000 a month to her and refuses to pay any expenses beyond that. Anita cannot support the lifestyle to which she has become accustomed on that amount and is using her own assets to support herself. She has filed suit against Lawrence under a state statute providing that a married person must support his or her spouse when in need and that the obligee spouse or the state on behalf of the obligee spouse may bring an action against the obligor spouse to enforce the duty. What arguments can Lawrence's son, as representative of Lawrence, make? How should Anita respond?

"Necessaries" and Public and Private Benefits

The obligation to provide necessaries is not always invoked only in the comfortable middle-class setting of *Buckstaff* or even in the less comfortable setting of *McGuire*. It can also arise in connection with employment and other public and private benefits.

Consider, for example, the situation of a person needing long-term care. Medicare, a federal program available to everyone 65 or older who is eligible for Social Security benefits (and to certain others on Social Security disability), is regarded as an insurance program on which one may draw as a matter of right. Medicare coverage does not, however, cover the costs of custodial care for a disabled person.

A person without enough money to pay for needed long-term care may turn to Medicaid, a joint federal and state program that provides medical assistance to the poor. Because Medicaid is a welfare program for the poor, persons with property or income above certain levels do not qualify. For those who do qualify, most of their income must be used to pay for care, and Medicaid picks up the remaining cost. Determining the income of a married applicant brings into play spousal support issues.

If the institutionalized spouse is the primary income producer, federal law provides that the community spouse is entitled to a portion of that income for his or her living expenses. The amount of the community spouse's living allowance is determined by a standardized formula that is updated annually, and all the rest of the institutionalized spouse's income goes toward his or her care. The amount of the community spouse's allowance is low enough that the spouse's standard of living may decline significantly when his or her mate goes into the long-term care. Generally, however, states exempt from the eligibility calculation portions of the institutionalized spouse's income that must be paid to support dependents pursuant to a court order. This rule clearly applies to court orders that preexist the application for Medicaid. What is not so clear is whether the community spouse can circumvent the income rules discussed above by getting a court order for a higher level of support than the rules allow.

The New York Court of Appeals held in In the Matter of Gomprecht, 652 N.E.2d 936 (N.Y. 1995), that if the community spouse initiates an action in state court for support after the institutionalized spouse has applied for Medicaid, the court must apply the Medicaid rule that support above the formula amount is ordered only if the community spouse proves exceptional circumstances resulting in financial duress. In *Gomprecht*, an institutionalized husband had income of $5721.31 per month. His wife, who had two residences assessed at more than $430,000, was entitled to a standard community spouse allowance of only $306.71 from her husband's income. She sought an increase in order to maintain her standard of living before her husband was institutionalized. The trial and intermediate appellate courts held that Family Court was not limited by the Medicaid rules and awarded her an increased allowance of $3339.26. The Court of Appeals reversed, saying that the purpose of the federal provisions for the community spouse is to "end the pauperization of the community spouse by assuring that the community spouse has a sufficient — but not excessive — amount of income and resources available." On the facts of the case, the court concluded that allowing the wife such a large portion of her husband's income was inconsistent with the purposes of the federal act.

In contrast, the New Jersey intermediate appellate court has held that state courts have more discretion under domestic relations law to enter an order providing for the community spouse. M.E.F. v. A.B.F., 925 A.2d 12 (N.J. Super. 2007).

Now consider the situation in which the community spouse has most of the income. To what extent is that spouse obligated to contribute that income to pay for nursing home care of the institutionalized spouse? Since 1988, federal law has said that the community spouse has no obligation; only the institutionalized spouse's income is considered in determining Medicaid eligibility. However, this is a special rule applicable only to long-term care cases. In other situations, if one spouse applies for Medicaid, the income of the other is deemed to be available to the applicant, and eligibility is determined on the basis of the combined income of the spouses. In Schweiker v. Gray Panthers, 453 U.S. 34 (1981), the Supreme Court upheld these spousal income deeming rules as consistent with the statutory language and with legislative history indicating a congressional intent to hold spouses responsible for each other's support.

NOTES AND QUESTIONS

1. In what ways do the Medicaid rules regarding spousal support obligations differ from those in *McGuire* and *Buckstaff*? What might explain the difference in approaches?

2. What is the theory behind "deeming" the income of one spouse to be available to the other? Is it simply an application of the general rule that a creditor may recover against one spouse for the necessaries supplied to the other? Are the positions of the creditor and the state Medicaid administrator alike?

3. Federal and state statutes also allow for setting aside a portion of an institutionalized person's income to support the person's or the person's spouse's minor child, dependent child, dependent parent, or dependent sibling if more than half of the needs of the child, parent, or sibling have been provided by the institutionalized person or the person's spouse. 42 U.S.C. §1396r-5(d)(1)(C).

4. For further information, *see* Sean R. Bleck et al., Preserving Wealth and Inheritance Through Medicaid Planning for Long-Term Care, 17 Mich. St. U. J. Med. & L. 153, 153-196 (2013).

4. Constitutional Limits on Gender-Based Classifications

PROBLEM

Your office represents Dr. Willa Sanchez, an oral surgeon. She has recently treated Ms. Alicia Duran, whom she has also known socially for some time. Dr. Sanchez has billed Ms. Duran $2300 for this surgery but would prefer to collect from Ms. Duran's husband, Roberto, both because she would like to accommodate Ms. Duran's desire that she do so and because she thinks Mr. Duran ought to pay the bill.

Interviews with Dr. Sanchez and Ms. Duran, who is cooperative, reveal the following facts. Ms. Duran has been married to Roberto for five years. Before and during her marriage, Ms. Duran has been employed as a caseworker in the state Department of Human Services, an occupation she enjoys and thinks worthwhile, and in which she has had considerable success. She is well on her way to achieving a Master's of Social Work degree, which is the standard professional credential for personnel occupying supervisory positions in the department. Reviews of her performance to this point suggest that she will achieve a promotion when or soon after she receives this degree.

Mr. Duran is a contractor and a native of Florida. The construction business has been in decline in your state for the last several years, and no substantial improvement is in sight. Mr. Duran has essentially given up — in his own words, "no more" — and decided to return to Florida, where construction continues to boom. Ms. Duran has repeatedly urged him to remain here and equally often declares that she had no desire to leave her job and go to Florida.

Three months ago, Mr. Duran took the car and most of their liquid assets with him to Fort Lauderdale. His departure followed an argument during which he insisted that Alicia go with him and her refusal to do so. Ms. Duran has, since her husband's departure, been able to manage on her salary except for the expenses associated with oral surgery.

She notified Mr. Duran of this bill, and he has refused to pay it while repeating his insistence that she join him in Florida. He has also consulted a lawyer in Florida — not for purposes of divorce, which is for religious reasons unacceptable to both him and Ms. Duran — but in order to cut off any financial obligations he may have as long as she remains away from him.

Your research has disclosed the statutory provisions set out immediately below. Please prepare a memorandum analyzing the legal possibility of collecting the debt from Mr. Duran, assuming that he will (as seems likely) return to the state at least temporarily. Your analysis should incorporate the materials considered to this point, as well as the following materials.

a. Relevant Statute

Section 1. Both wives and husbands have the duty to support each other during marriage. However, when either party to a marriage incurs a debt for purchase of an item or service that is reasonably necessary to maintenance of the household, the husband shall be primarily liable for that debt and the wife shall be secondarily liable for that debt.

Section 2. Notwithstanding the provisions of Section 1, there shall be no liability for debts incurred by a spouse if the spouse incurring the debt has been given adequate resources to purchase the item or service, nor shall a husband be liable for the debts incurred by his wife if she has abandoned the marital home.

Section 3. If the parties cannot agree upon the location of the marital home, the spouse earning the most money shall determine its location.

b. Empirical Data

In 1980 women working full- or part-time in the United States earned only 64 cents for every dollar men earned. In 2020, the most recent year for which data are available, women were paid 84 percent of what men were paid. The size of the gap has held relatively steady over the last 15 years. Amanda Barroso & Anna Brown, Gender Pay Gap in U.S. Held Steady in 2020, Pew Research Center, (May 25, 2021), available at https://www.pewresearch.org/fact-tank/2021/05/25/gender-pay-gap-facts. However, women are overrepresented in lower-paying jobs, and the pay gap is wider for older women than for younger ones. Earlene K.P. Dowell, Women Consistently Earn Less Than Men (U.S. Census Bureau, Jan. 27, 2022), available at https://www.census.gov/library/stories/2022/01/gender-pay-gap-widens-as-women-age.html.

Naomi Cahn, June Carbone & Nancy Levit

Gender and the Tournament: Reinventing Antidiscrimination Law in an Age of Inequality
96 Tex. L. Rev. 425, 454-458 (2018)

[A]s a measure of women's economic standing, the composite numbers are misleading. While the wage gap has narrowed, it has done so overwhelmingly at the bottom, in part because of the drop in blue collar male wages. Since 1990, the gendered wage gap has grown where it matters most — at the top. In 1990, the gendered gap in wages did not vary much by education; to the extent that there was a difference, college graduate women earned a slightly higher percentage of the male wage than less educated women. Today, that relationship has reversed; the percentage of the male wage that female college graduates earn has declined, while it has increased for all other women.

This is precisely where there has been the most substantial growth in income inequality in the United States. Between 2000 and 2014, weekly wages for the top 10% of the workforce rose by 9.7%, the place where women had "lost substantial ground," while falling 3.7% for workers in the lowest tenth of the earnings distribution, and 3% for those in the lowest quarter.

Kevin Miller

The Simple Truth About the Gender Pay Gap
American Association of University Women, Spring 2017,
http://www.aauw.org/resource/the-simple-truth-about-the-gender-pay-gap/

The gender pay gap has lifelong financial effects. For one, it contributes directly to women's poverty. In 2015, 14 percent of American women ages 18-64 were living below the federal poverty level, compared with 11 percent of men. For ages 65 and older, 10 percent of women and 7 percent of men were living in poverty. Eliminating the gender pay gap by increasing women's levels of pay to those of their male counterparts could cut the poverty rate for working women in half.

Even after women leave the workforce, the pay gap follows them. Because women typically are paid less than men during working years, when women retire they receive less income from Social Security, pensions, and other sources than do retired men. Other benefits such as disability and life insurance are also smaller for women, because these benefits usually are based on earnings.

The impact of the pay gap has also deepened in recent years as a result of changes in family structure. Between 1967 and 2012, the proportion of mothers bringing home at least a quarter of the family's earnings rose from less than a third (28 percent) to nearly two-thirds (63 percent). Today, 40 percent of mothers with children under the age of 18 are their families' primary or sole breadwinners. As families increasingly rely on women's wages to make ends meet, the gender pay gap directly affects men and children as well.

c. Constitutional Decisions on Gender Equality

Craig v. Boren, 429 U.S. 190, 197-200 (1976): Brennan, J. [Oklahoma law prohibited the sale of 3.2 percent beer to males under the age of 21 and to females under the age of 18.] To withstand constitutional challenge, previous cases establish that classifications by gender must serve important governmental objectives and must be substantially related to achievement of those objectives. Thus, in [Reed v. Reed, 404 U.S. 71 (1971),] the objectives of "reducing the workload on probate courts" and "avoiding intrafamily controversy" were deemed of insufficient importance to sustain use of an overt gender criterion in the appointment of administrators of intestate decedents' estates. Decisions following *Reed* similarly have rejected administrative ease and convenience as sufficiently important objectives to justify gender-based classifications. . . . And only two terms ago, Stanton v. Stanton expressly stating that Reed v. Reed was "controlling," held that *Reed* required invalidation of a Utah differential age-of-majority statute, notwithstanding the statute's coincidence with and furtherance of the State's purpose of fostering "old notions" of role typing and preparing boys for their expected performance in the economic and political worlds.

Reed v. Reed has also provided the underpinning for decisions that have invalidated statutes employing gender as an inaccurate proxy for other, more germane bases of classification. Hence, "archaic and overbroad" generalizations concerning the financial position of servicewomen and working women could not justify use of a gender line in determining eligibility for certain governmental entitlements. Similarly, increasingly outdated misconceptions concerning the role of females in the home rather than in the "marketplace and world of ideas" were rejected as loose-fitting characterizations incapable of supporting state statutory schemes that were premised upon their accuracy. . . .

We accept for purposes of discussion the District Court's identification of the objective underlying [the statute] as the enhancement of traffic safety. Clearly, the protection of public health and safety represents an important function of state and local governments. However, appellees' statistics in our view cannot support the conclusion that the gender-based distinction closely serves to achieve that objective and therefore the distinction cannot under *Reed* withstand equal protection challenge. . . .

The most focused and relevant of the statistical surveys, arrests of 18–20-year-olds for alcohol-related driving offenses, exemplifies the ultimate unpersuasiveness of this evidentiary record. Viewed in terms of the correlation between sex and the actual activity that Oklahoma seeks to regulate . . . the statistics establish that .18% of females and 2% of males in that age group were arrested for that offense. While such a disparity is not trivial in a statistical sense, it hardly can form the basis for employment of a gender line as a classifying device. Certainly if maleness is to serve as a proxy for drinking and driving, a correlation of 2% must be considered an unduly tenuous "fit." Indeed, prior cases have consistently rejected the use of sex as a decision making factor even though the statutes in question certainly rested on far more predictive empirical relationships than this.

Orr v. Orr, 440 U.S. 268 (1979): Brennan, J. The question presented is the constitutionality of Alabama alimony statutes which provide that husbands, but not wives, may be required to pay alimony upon divorce. . . .

In authorizing the imposition of alimony obligations on husbands, but not on wives, the Alabama statutory scheme provides that different treatment be accorded . . . on the basis of . . . sex. The fact that the classification expressly discriminates against men rather than women does not protect it from scrutiny. Craig v. Boren, 429 U.S. 190 (1976). To withstand scrutiny under the Equal Protection Clause, "classifications by gender must serve important governmental objectives and must be substantially related to achievement of those objectives." We shall, therefore, examine the three governmental objectives that might arguably be served by Alabama's statutory scheme.

Appellant views the Alabama alimony statutes as effectively announcing the State's preference for an allocation of family responsibilities under which the wife plays a dependent role, and as seeking for their objective the reinforcement of that model among the State's citizens. . . . We agree, as he urges, that prior cases settle that this purpose cannot sustain the statutes. Stanton v. Stanton, 421 U.S. 7, 10 (1975), held that the "old notion" that "generally it is the man's primary responsibility to provide a home and its essentials," can no longer justify a statute that discriminates on the basis of gender. "No longer is the female destined solely for the home and the rearing of the family, and only the male for the marketplace and the world of ideas. . . ."

The opinion of the Alabama Court of Civil Appeals suggests other purposes that the statute may serve. . . . One is a legislative purpose to provide help for needy spouses, using sex as a proxy for need. The other is a goal of compensating women for past discrimination during marriage, which assertedly has left them unprepared to fend for themselves in the working world following divorce. We concede, of course, that assisting needy spouses is a legitimate and important governmental objective. We have also recognized "[r]eduction of the disparity in economic condition between men and women caused by the long history of discrimination against women . . . as . . . an important governmental objective," Califano v. Webster, 430 U.S., at 317. It only remains, therefore, to determine whether the classification at issue here is "substantially related to achievement of those objectives."

Ordinarily, we would begin the analysis of the "needy spouse" objective by considering whether sex is a sufficiently "accurate proxy," Craig v. Boren, 429 U.S. at 204, for dependency to establish that the gender classification rests "upon some ground of difference having a fair and substantial relation to the object of the legislation. . . . Similarly, we would initially approach the 'compensation' rationale by asking whether women had in fact been significantly discriminated against in the sphere to which the statute applied a sex-based classification, leaving the sexes *not* similarly situated with respect to opportunities in that sphere."

But in this case, even if sex were a reliable proxy for need, and even if the institution of marriage did discriminate against women, these factors still would "not adequately justify the salient features of" Alabama's statutory scheme. Under the statute, individualized hearings at which the parties' relative financial circumstances are considered *already* occur. There is no reason, therefore, to use sex as a proxy for need. . . . In such circumstances, not even an administrative convenience rationale exists to justify operating by generalization or by proxy. Similarly, since individualized hearings can determine which were in fact discriminated against vis-à-vis their husbands, as well as which family units defied the stereotype and left the husband dependent on the wife, Alabama's alleged compensatory purpose may be effectuated without placing burdens solely on husbands. . . . "Thus, the gender-based distinction is gratuitous. . . ."

Legislative classifications which distribute benefits and burdens on the basis of gender carry the inherent risk of reinforcing stereotypes about the "proper place" of women and their need for special protection. Thus, even statutes purportedly designed to compensate for and ameliorate the effects of past discrimination must be carefully tailored. Where, as here, the State's compensatory and ameliorative purposes are as well served by a gender-neutral classification as one that gender classifies and therefore carries with it the baggage of sexual stereotypes, the State cannot be permitted to classify on the basis of sex.

Kirchberg v. Feenstra, 450 U.S. 455 (1981): See above, page 36.

United States v. Virginia, 518 U.S. 515 (1996): [The United States sued Virginia Military Institute (VMI) and the state of Virginia, claiming that VMI's exclusively male admissions policy violated the equal protection clause. After the Fourth Circuit reversed a trial court decision in VMI's favor, the state proposed establishment of a parallel program for women. The district court found that this proposal satisfied the equal protection requirement and the Fourth Circuit affirmed, although it recognized that the new school would lack the historical benefit and prestige of VMI.

The United States Supreme Court reversed, holding that any gender-based government action must rest on an "exceedingly persuasive justification." To meet this burden, a state must demonstrate "at least that the classification serves 'important governmental objectives' and that the discriminatory means employed are 'substantially related to the achievement of those objectives.'" The justification must be genuine and not merely pretextual or post hoc, and must not rely on overbroad generalizations about the different talents, abilities, or preferences of men and women. The majority also observed that, under its decisions, sex classifications may be used to compensate women for particular economic disabilities they have suffered, to promote equality of employment opportunity, but not to create or perpetuate the legal, social, and economic inferiority of women.

The categorical exclusion of women from VMI did not meet this test. The state's claim that VMI's "adversative" method of training to instill physical and mental discipline could neither be made available to women nor modified sufficiently without great compromise to VMI's program was not proved and thus rested on overbroad notions concerning the roles and abilities of males and females. The Supreme Court also held that the creation of a separate program for women did not cure the constitutional violation. The violation was the categorical exclusion of women, without regard for their individual capacities, from an educational opportunity provided to men. The proposed alternative institution was different in kind and unequal in tangible and intangible resources, and thus did not provide substantial equality in educational opportunities.]

The above cases deal with explicit sex-based classifications in law. When law has a discriminatory impact but is neutral on its face as to sex or a suspect classification, the Supreme Court has been less willing to strike down laws and policies or offer a remedy, as seen in the case excerpts that follow.

Washington v. Davis, 426 U.S. 229 (1976): White, J. [Respondents, unsuccessful African-American applicants for positions on the District of Columbia police force, claimed that a test measuring verbal ability, reading comprehension, and vocabulary resulted in a higher percentage of African-Americans failing the test and therefore unconstitutionally discriminated against them. There was no claim that use of the test was an intentional or purposeful act of discrimination.]

The central purpose of the Equal Protection Clause of the Fourteenth Amendment is the prevention of official misconduct discriminating on the basis of race. [However,] our cases have not embraced the proposition that a law or other official act, without regard to whether it reflects a racially discriminatory purpose, is unconstitutional *solely* because it has a racially disproportionate impact. . . .

This is not to say that the necessary discriminatory racial purpose must be express or appear on the face of the statute, or that a law's disproportionate impact is irrelevant in cases involving Constitution-based claims of racial discrimination. A statute, otherwise neutral on its face, must not be applied so as invidiously to discriminate on the basis of race. . . .

Necessarily, an invidious discriminatory purpose may often be inferred from the totality of the relevant facts, including the fact, if it is true, that the law bears more heavily on one race than another. Nevertheless, we have not held that a law, neutral on its face and serving ends otherwise within the power of government to pursue, is invalid under the Equal Protection Clause simply because it may affect a greater proportion of one race than of another. Disproportionate impact is not irrelevant, but it is not the sole touchstone of an invidious racial discrimination forbidden by the Constitution. Standing alone, it does not trigger the rule, that racial classifications are to be subjected to the strictest scrutiny and are justifiable only by the weightiest of considerations. . . .

Personnel Administrator v. Feeney, 442 U.S. 256 (1979): Stewart, J. This case presents a challenge to the constitutionality of the Massachusetts veterans' preference statute on the ground that it discriminates against women in violation of the Equal Protection Clause of the Fourteenth Amendment. Under [the statute], all veterans who qualify for state civil service positions must be considered for appointment ahead of any qualifying nonveterans. The preference operates overwhelmingly to the advantage of males. . . .

If the impact of this statute could not be plausibly explained on a neutral ground, impact itself would signal that the real classification made by the law was in fact not neutral. But there can be but one answer to the question whether this veteran preference excludes significant numbers of women from preferred state jobs because they are women or because they are nonveterans. Apart from the facts that the definition of "veterans" in the statute has always been neutral as to gender and that Massachusetts has consistently defined veteran status in a way that has been inclusive of women who have served in the military, this is not a law that can plausibly be explained only as a gender-based classification. Indeed, it is not a law that can rationally be explained on that ground. Veteran status is not uniquely male. Although few women benefit from the preference, the nonveteran statute is not substantially all female. . . .

. . . [It] cannot seriously be argued that the Legislature of Massachusetts could have been unaware that most veterans are men. . . . It would thus be disingenuous to say that the adverse consequences of this legislation for women were unintended, in the sense that they were not volitional or in the sense that they were not foreseeable.

"Discriminatory purpose," however, implies more than intent as volition or intent as awareness of consequences. It implies that the decisionmaker [chose] or reaffirmed a particular course of action at least in part "because of," not merely "in spite of," its adverse effects upon an identifiable group. Yet nothing in the record demonstrates that this preference for veterans was originally devised or subsequently reenacted because it would accomplish the collateral goal of keeping women in a stereotypic and predefined place in the Massachusetts Civil Service.

B. DOMESTIC VIOLENCE

"No doubt, acts of violence and willful neglect within families have been occurring as long as there have been human families." Lloyd Ohlin & Michael Tonry, Family Violence in Perspective, *in* Family Violence 1 (Lloyd Ohlin & Michael Tonry eds., 1989). But what counts as a "legal response" to violence within families has evolved dramatically. The historian Elizabeth Pleck reports that the "first law against wife abuse anywhere in the Western World was written into a new criminal code of the Massachusetts Bay Colony [during the middle of the seventeenth century]." Elizabeth Pleck, Criminal Approaches to Family Violence: 1640-1980, *in* Family Violence, above, at 19, 22. However, ecclesiastical courts had long recognized serious physical abuse as a ground for legal separation, allowing the victim to live apart from the abuser while requiring the abuser to continue providing financial support.

For domestic violence, enforcement of the law involvement often depends on whether the victims identify themselves to law enforcement and whether they wish to become involved in the formal processing of a complaint. Thus, the identification of domestic violence is largely in the control of family members. Police officers, lawyers, social workers, and judges all have some role in the response to complaints of domestic violence. How they respond will be influenced by both institutional and personal views of the gravity of the behavior, the perceived utility of various kinds of response, and interpretations of the outcomes that will likely be associated with judicial processing of the complaint.

In considering the following materials, it may be useful not only to consider the doctrinal issues that arise in connection with family violence, and how those doctrines have changed over time, but also the issues that complicate defining and responding to conduct between spouses and domestic partners.

Elizabeth Pleck

Domestic Tyranny: The Making of Social Policy Against Family Violence from Colonial Times to the Present
7-9 (1987)

The history of reform against family violence . . . , although similar in some respects to many [other social movements in the United States], has had one aspect that necessarily limited it and made it more controversial.

The single most consistent barrier to reform against domestic violence has been the Family Ideal—that is, [related] but nonetheless distinct ideas about family privacy, conjugal and parental rights, and family instability. In this ideal with origins possibly extending into antiquity, the "family" consists of a two-parent household with minor children. Other constellations, such as a mother and her two children, were seen not as a family but as a deviation from it.

One crucial element of the Family Ideal was belief in domestic privacy. . . .

By the 1830s the private sphere came to acquire a deeply emotional texture; it became a refuge from the hard, calculating dealings of the business world. . . . Even more than before, intervention in the family was viewed as problematic, a violation of family intimacy. Although there have been many periods of American history since the 1830s when family privacy has declined in importance, belief in it has persisted to the present day. Modern defenders are likely to argue that the family has a constitutional right to privacy or insist that the home is the only setting where intimacy can flourish, providing meaning, coherence, and stability in personal life.

A second element of the Family Ideal is a belief in conjugal and parental rights. In ancient times, the head of the household had the power to compel obedience from his wife, children, and servants and maintain domestic harmony. . . .

The Romans had the most extensive legal definition of these traditional rights. A Roman wife remained under the guardianship of her husband, who possessed *patria potestas*, including the power to sell his wife and children into slavery or put them to death. Since Roman times, the husband's power has been gradually restricted, and the rights of women and children have correspondingly increased. Yet in many areas of law a stranger is entitled to more legal protection than a family member. . . .

A third element of the Family Ideal is belief in the preservation of the family. Marriage was supposed to be life long, for religious reasons and for the responsibility of raising children. Conservatives of the nineteenth century argued that women were dependent on the family for their happiness. They were tethered to it because of their children and in order to make the home a place of affection. . . .

. . . [R]eform against family violence is an implicit critique of each element of the Family Ideal. It inevitably asserts that family violence is a public matter, not a private issue. Public policy against domestic violence offers state intervention in the family as a major remedy for abuse, challenges the view that marriage and family should be preserved at all costs, and asserts that children and women are individuals whose liberties must be protected.

1. Responses by the Criminal Justice System

Well into the 1970s, police forces commonly treated domestic violence calls differently from other reports of crimes. Officers were taught to try to defuse the situation by getting the alleged aggressor to "cool off" and to use arrest only as a last resort. Laurie S. Kohn, The Justice System and Domestic Violence: Engaging the Case but Divorcing the Victim, 32 N.Y.U. Rev.

L. & Soc. Change 191, 212 (2008) (quoting International Association of Chiefs of Police, Training Key 16: Handling Disturbance Calls (1967), and American Bar Ass'n, Standards Relating to the Urban Police Function 107 (1973)). In addition to the family privacy rationale, many police and prosecutors believed that domestic violence complainants were unreliable, prone to return to their attackers, and likely to refuse to cooperate as witnesses. Even if the aggressor was arrested, if the alleged victim asked to have the case dismissed, the charges would be dropped.

Lawyers and advocates have criticized these practices, arguing that sometimes victims' requests to drop charges were coerced; that leaving the decision about whether to prosecute in their hands placed them at greater risk of harm from their assailants; and that domestic violence victims are often ambivalent for good reasons, including lack of independent financial resources and social support, desire to preserve their families, and post-traumatic stress. The efforts of these advocates, as well as data from an influential empirical study, led to mandatory arrest and no-drop policies. These policies were also supported by the argument that the public has an interest independent of the victim's in seeing a person who has committed a crime brought to justice. *See generally* Deborah Epstein, Effective Intervention in Domestic Violence Cases: Rethinking the Roles of Prosecutors, Judges, and the Court System, 11 Yale J.L. & Feminism 3 (1999); Cheryl Hanna, No Right to Choose: Mandated Victim Participation in Domestic Violence Prosecutions, 109 Harv. L. Rev. 1849 (1996).

Williams v. State
151 P.3d 460 (Alaska App. 2006)

Coats, Chief Judge. . . . Thomas A. Williams was charged almost two and one-half years ago with assaulting his wife of twenty-three years. He is apparently still awaiting trial. As required by AS 12.30.027(b), one of the conditions of his pre-trial release forbids him from returning to the residence he shared with his wife and daughter. . . .

On April 21, 2004, the police responded to a report by a passerby that a man was strangling a woman in a house on Henderson Loop in Anchorage. When the police arrived at the house, they contacted Terese Williams. Williams said her husband, Thomas Williams, had grabbed her around the neck during an argument and pushed her to the ground. She said he kept a firm grip on her throat and squeezed for several minutes and that she was very scared. Then he let go and she got up. She was shaken and went to smoke a cigarette; her husband grabbed his bags and left. . . . The investigating officer noted that Terese Williams was "visibly shaken" and had a scratch on her chin, a finger impression under her right ear, and a small red mark on the left of her neck.

Based on these allegations, Thomas Williams was charged with fourth-degree assault. The conditions of his pre-trial release barred him from contacting his wife or returning to the residence they had shared.

Several weeks after his release, Williams asked the court to modify his release conditions so he could have contact with his wife. His attorney said Williams and his wife had been together for more than twenty years and that both parties wished to renew contact. The State did not oppose the request. The prosecutor told the court that "in looking at Mr. Williams's record and the facts in this case, the State [is] confident or at least hopeful that it was an isolated incident." The court modified the bail conditions to allow contact, but emphasized that, by statute, Williams was still barred from the residence.

Several months later, Williams asked the court for permission to stay in the residence to care for the house and dog while his wife and daughter were in London. Williams's wife supported the request, and the State did not oppose. The court also granted that request.

On December 23, 2004—eight months after the incident—Williams, again with his wife's support, asked the court for permission to return to the residence for Christmas. He also filed a motion challenging the constitutionality of AS 12.30.027(b). Williams argued that the statute infringed his fundamental right to maintain his marital relationship and violated his rights to both due process and equal protection of the laws. . . .

Relying on AS 12.30.027(b), District Court Judge Sigurd E. Murphy denied Williams's request to return to the residence. The court then scheduled a hearing on Williams's motion challenging the constitutionality of the statute.

That hearing was held in January 2005. At the hearing, Terese Williams reiterated that she had been in regular contact with her husband and that she did not feel he was a threat. She said Williams was in counseling and that it was her wish that he return to the residence. She also asserted that the police and witnesses had exaggerated the seriousness of the incident. The State opposed the motion but did not present any evidence. The prosecutor simply observed that the domestic violence in the home had escalated, noting that Williams had threatened his wife with a fire poker in 2002 (he was convicted of disorderly conduct for that offense), and was now charged with assault for strangling his wife.

On February 2, 2005, Judge Murphy denied the motion. . . .

We have previously subjected restrictions on marital association to heightened scrutiny. In Dawson v. State, we observed that "[a] condition of probation restricting marital association plainly implicates the constitutional rights of privacy, liberty, and freedom of association and . . . must be subjected to special scrutiny."

The State nevertheless argues that no fundamental right is at stake in this case because Williams's conditions of release permit him to see his wife—just not in their home. Hence, the State argues, the residence restriction has "at most a modest, incidental, and temporary effect" on the marital relationship. This argument understates the integral relationship between cohabitation and marriage. Moreover, apart from any burden imposed on Williams's relationship with his wife and family, Williams has a liberty interest in choosing his family living arrangements. . . .

This liberty interest does not disappear because a person has been charged with a crime. We hold based on this authority that Williams has an important, if not fundamental, right to live in his home with his wife and family while on pre-trial release, and that any state infringement of that right must be carefully scrutinized. . . .

The State argues that a blanket prohibition on returning to the alleged victim's residence is necessary because of the peculiar dynamics of domestic violence—in particular, the well-documented tendency of victims to remain with their abusers. The State argues that the victims of domestic violence are influenced by psychological and emotional forces that "too often make impossible an accurate assessment of whether the victim's safety can be assured if the defendant is allowed to return to [the] residence." The State concludes that a court's evaluation of whether a defendant poses a risk to the alleged victim is therefore likely to be "little more than an educated guess." We agree that it can be difficult for judges to accurately predict whether a particular defendant will be dangerous in the future. But judges confront this task "countless times each day throughout the American system of criminal justice." . . .

As the State points out, courts are not obliged to credit a victim's assertion that her abuser is no threat—even if that testimony is undisputed. And in this case, in urging us to affirm the district court, the State lists ample circumstantial evidence Judge Murphy could have relied on to discredit Terese Williams's statements: the couple's lengthy marriage; Terese Williams's testimony about the financial strain of maintaining separate residences; Williams's prior conviction for threatening his wife with a fire poker; the fact that Terese Williams had resumed living with Williams after that prior incident; the eyewitness reports that Williams had strangled his wife; and the investigating officer's observations of Terese Williams's injuries. . . .

Of course, the residence restriction in AS 12.30.027(b) generally will only burden the liberty interest of a person who was living with the alleged victim at the time of the offense. But even within this narrower context, it is easy to imagine situations in which the condition would serve no legitimate governmental purpose. . . .

As the above examples illustrate, under Alaska's far-reaching definition of domestic violence, probable cause to believe a person has committed a domestic violence offense cannot necessarily be equated with probable cause to believe that the person poses an ongoing risk to the alleged victim's safety. . . .

Moreover, it appears that other jurisdictions have found less restrictive alternatives adequate to protect the victims of domestic violence. The Model Code on Domestic and Family Violence, which served as a blueprint for Alaska's 1996 Domestic Violence Prevention and Victim Protection Act (the law that authorized the residence restriction at issue in this case), contains no blanket prohibition on a person charged with domestic violence returning to the residence of the alleged victim. Rather, the Model Code gives courts discretion to remove the accused from the home if the court finds that doing so is necessary to protect the alleged victim. Apparently no other state follows Alaska's rule. At least two states restrict a person charged with domestic violence from returning to the alleged victim's residence for one to three days after the incident—but the victim can waive that requirement. . . .

We therefore hold that AS 12.30.027(b), as applied to individuals on pre-trial release, violates article I, section 1 of the Alaska Constitution. (We express no opinion as to whether this statute is constitutional as applied to individuals on post-conviction release.) . . .

NOTES AND QUESTIONS

1. According to *Williams*, what constitutional right did the condition on Thomas's pre-trial release violate?

In Kerry v. Din, 576 U.S. 86 (2015), the State Department denied a visa to the noncitizen husband of a U.S. citizen; without the visa, he could not join her in the United States. She argued that the action violated her constitutionally protected "liberty interest in her marriage," "right of association with one's spouse," "liberty interest in being reunited with certain blood relatives," and "the liberty interest of a U.S. citizen under the Due Process Clause to be free from arbitrary restrictions on his right to live with his spouse." 576 U.S. at 93. Justice Scalia, writing for himself, the Chief Justice and Justice Thomas, rejected the wife's claim; they would have held that she had no constitutionally protected interest. Four dissenting justices said that she had such a right that was unjustifiably infringed upon, and two concurring justices assumed for purposes of discussion that she had a right but that the State Department's process satisfied due process.

2. Does the court in *Williams* use the doctrine of family privacy in the same way that the court in *McGuire* did? Would the *Williams* court have held that Thomas's constitutional rights were violated if Terese had not supported his request that he be allowed to return home?

Professor Suk argues that an unintended consequence of efforts to change police policies in domestic violence cases has been to criminalize conduct that is ordinarily not criminal—being in one's home—and that prosecutions for violations of restraining orders have become a surrogate for punishing domestic violence itself. When orders are issued incidental to arrests and prosecutions, they deny women autonomy and effectively reallocate property in the home, impose de facto divorce (if the couple was married), and criminalize decisions to live as intimate partners. Jeannie Suk, Criminal Law Comes Home, 116 Yale L.J. 2 (2006). *See also* Leigh Goodmark, A Troubled Marriage: Domestic Violence and the Legal System 106-35 (2012); Aya Gruber, The Feminist War on Crime: The Unexpected Role of Women's Liberation in Mass Incarceration 67-93 (2021).

3. *Williams* indicates that a statute would be constitutional if it gave a court discretion to decide whether to exclude a defendant charged with a crime of domestic violence from the home he shared with the victim. What is the constitutional significance of the difference between a blanket rule and a discretionary rule? Could it have been argued in support of the statute that the legislature had determined that a person charged with a crime of domestic violence always posed a risk to the victim?

If the statute in *Williams* had granted the judge discretion about whether to exclude the husband from the home, and the prosecution had asked for an order, should it have been granted? How much weight should the court give to the wife's expressed wish that her husband be allowed to return home? To the fact that Mr. Williams had been violent toward his wife before? That this time, in strangling her, he had injured her severely? How should courts consider evidence about the cyclic nature of violence, in which abuse abates and reoccurs, that some victims experience? Professor Leigh Goodmark offers additional evidence that complicates theories of cyclical abuse and its effects. Decriminalizing Domestic Violence: A Balanced Policy Approach to Intimate Partner Violence 121-56 (2018).

4. Other provisions of the Constitution besides due process limit the state's authority to define conduct as domestic violence that can be sanctioned. The First Amendment and state constitutional protections for free speech prevent the state from entering certain orders that prohibit communication. For example, in In re Marriage of Suggs, 93 P.3d 161 (Wash. 2d 2004), a court restrained a woman from "knowingly and willfully making invalid and unsubstantiated allegations or complaints to third parties which are designed for the purpose of annoying, harassing, vexing, or otherwise harming" her former husband. The appellate court held that the order, which imposed a prior restraint, violated the First Amendment. It said that the trial court could restrain the woman from slandering her former husband, the language in the order was so broad and vague that it could be interpreted as covering protected speech. *See also* In re Marriage of Meredith, 201 P.3d 1056 (Wash. App. 2009).

5. One of the most notorious expressions of the family privacy doctrine with regard to domestic violence was the common law rule that a man could not legally rape his wife. 1 Matthew Hale, History of Pleas of the Crown 629 (1736). All states have abandoned this rule in its absolute form. Lalenya Weintraub Siegel, Note, The Marital Rape Exemption: Evolution to Extinction, 43 Clev. St. L. Rev. 351, 367-369 (1995). However, many states subject marital rape to less serious sanctions than nonmarital rape and/or create special procedural requirements for prosecutions of marital rape. Jill Elaine Hasday, A Legal History of Marital Rape, 88 Cal. L. Rev. 1373, 1375, 1484-1485 (2000).

6. Until the middle of the twentieth century, tort suits between spouses were barred by the doctrine of spousal immunity, which was justified, in part, as protecting family unity and marital privacy. The first case abolishing immunity was decided by the Alabama Supreme Court in 1932. Bennett v. Bennett, 140 So. 378 (Ala. 1932). Almost all states have abolished or severely limited the doctrine. *See generally* Camille Carey, Domestic Violence Torts: Righting a Civil Wrong, 62 U. Kan. L. Rev. 695 (2014); Fernanda G. Nicola, Intimate Liability: Emotional Harm, Family Law, and Stereotyped Narratives in Interspousal Torts, 19 Wm. & Mary J. Women & L. 445 (2013).

The Restatement (Second) of Torts says that some conduct that would be tortious between strangers is not actionable between spouses, giving the example of "family roughhousing." Does this principle express a vestige of the marital privacy doctrine, or is there another reason for it?

PROBLEM

Scott and Janet had a stormy marriage, marked by frequent heated arguments, many of which ended with Scott threatening Janet. Last year she filed for a restraining order against him but dropped it within a few days. In May they fought again, and she became frightened that he was going to hurt her badly. She left their home and went to stay with her parents in Canada, taking their son and some belongings. Two months later, she returned at Scott's request and after he promised that he had changed and would not hit her any more. On the third day after she came home, Janet and Scott began fighting again, and Scott took the baby and left the house. Janet called the police, reporting the fight and her fear for her child's safety. When the police arrived, she opened the door a crack and told the officers that her call had been a misunderstanding, that nothing was wrong. She refused to answer the officer's questions, kept glancing furtively over her shoulder, and finally said, "Go! Just please go!"

The Fourth Amendment limits the ability of police officers to enter a dwelling without a warrant, but one exception to the requirement allows them to enter if they have probable cause to believe that an immediate response is necessary to protect someone's life or safety. On these facts, would the exception apply so that the police can enter, despite what Janet said?

NOTE: THE IMPACT OF MANDATORY ARREST AND NO-DROP POLICIES

The first study of the impact of arrest on domestic violence showed that arrest significantly reduced the violence, compared to more traditional "cooling-off strategies." However, replications of the study produced a more complicated picture. Effectiveness of arrest varied from city to city, and arrest was much more effective in stopping violence committed by men who were employed, married, high school graduates, and white than with other populations. The validity of these replication studies has, in turn, been challenged. *See* sources cited in Kimberly D. Bailey, The Aftermath of Crawford and Davis: Deconstructing the Sound of Silence, 2009 BYU L. Rev. 1, 9-10.

Some victims' rights advocates have challenged mandatory arrest and prosecutorial no-drop policies for "ignoring victims" without necessarily making them safer. Laurie S. Kohn, The Justice System and Domestic Violence: Engaging the Case but Divorcing the Victim, 32 N.Y.U. Rev. L. & Soc. Change 191 (2008); Aya Gruber, A "Neo-Feminist" Assessment of Rape and Domestic Violence Law Reform, 15 J. Gender Race & Just. 583 (2012). Some critics also argue that the common view that the only solution is for the victim to leave the relationship oversimplifies domestic violence and illegitimately disregards the wishes of people who want to end the violence but preserve the relationship. *See, e.g.*, Sally F. Goldfarb, Reconceiving Civil Protection Orders for Domestic Violence: Can Law Help End the Abuse Without Ending the Relationship?, 29 Cardozo L. Rev. 1487 (2008). For a review of the history of the criminal justice system's response to domestic violence and an assessment of arguments for decriminalization, *see* Leigh Goodmark, Should Domestic Violence Be Decriminalized?, 40 Harv. J.L. & Gender 53 (2017).

The majority of domestic violence victims do not report to police. The victim may believe that the matter is personal or private, may wish to protect the offender, may fear reprisal, or may believe that police would do nothing or would be ineffective. Andrea L. Dennis & Carol E. Jordan, Encouraging Victims: Responding to a Recent Study of Battered Women Who Commit Crimes, 15 Nev. L.J. 1, 12 (2014). Regardless of whether a victim decides to seek redress from the criminal justice system, prosecutors may take action to elicit their testimony in the name of protecting the victim or the population at large. This behavior often criminalizes the victim, perhaps even more so than the perpetrator, by subjecting victims to fines or incarceration unless they testify. When victims become defendants, they are systematically overcharged and over-sentenced when their attempts at self-defense harm or kill their abuser. Leigh Goodmark, The Impact of Prosecutorial Misconduct, Overreach, and Misuse of Discretion on Gender Violence Victims, 123 Dick. L. Rev. 627 (2019).

If a victim of domestic violence is unwilling to testify against the defendant, a prosecutor may try to proceed without the victim's testimony, relying on physical evidence and the victim's hearsay statements at or near the time of the violence. However, this option is limited by a line of Supreme Court decisions beginning with Crawford v. Washington, 541 U.S. 36 (2004), where the Supreme Court held that "testimonial" hearsay cannot be admitted against a criminal defendant unless the declarant is presently available for cross-examination, or is presently unavailable but was once available for cross-examination by the defendant. In Davis v. Washington, 547 U.S. 813 (2006), the Supreme Court held that statements made to police officers when "the primary purpose of interrogation is to enable police assistance to meet an ongoing emergency" are not testimonial and are not inadmissible under *Crawford*. More recent decisions have eased the strict application of these rules. *See* Tom Lininger, The Sound of Silence: Holding Batterers Accountable for Silencing Their Victims, 87 Tex. L. Rev. 857 (2009); A. Ann Ratnayake, The Confrontation Clause After Ohio v. Clark: The Path to Reinvigorating Evidence-Based Prosecution in Intimate Partner Violence Cases, 84 Geo. Wash. L. Rev. Arguendo 18 (2016).

2. Protective Orders

The most widely used judicial response to domestic violence is the protective order. Protective orders are civil orders restraining the offender from conduct that endangers the person seeking the order. Such orders are available in every state for threats to the safety of a domestic partner. The statutes typically authorize courts to grant temporary protective orders after a hearing or ex parte; if the latter is authorized, a respondent is entitled to a full due process hearing within a few days. In some states, these hearings are automatic, as in the next case; in other states, the respondent must ask for a hearing. At the full hearing, the petitioner has the burden of proof. The next case considers the type of notice that a petition for a restraining order must provide, as well as what kind of conduct can provide the basis for an order.

J.D. v. M.D.F.
25 A.3d 1045 (N.J. 2011)

Justice HOENS delivered the opinion of the Court. . . . From 1993 until 2006, plaintiff, J.D., and defendant, M.D.F., were engaged in a long-term relationship. Although they never married, they resided together and two children were born to them. After they ended their relationship, they sought the assistance of the courts in a variety of disputed proceedings, including a litigated palimony suit, the details of which are not apparent from the record on appeal in this matter. What is clear from the record is that following their separation, their relationship continued to deteriorate and they were on the verge of becoming embroiled in a custody dispute when the events that gave rise to this appeal occurred.

Throughout the proceedings relating to the domestic violence allegations in the trial court, the parties appeared without attorneys. As a result, the record has presented challenges to courts at every level. Relevant to this dispute, it appears that at all times since the end of the relationship, plaintiff continued to reside in the home that she and defendant had purchased together. The couple's two children resided with her, as did an older child of hers that she had from a relationship prior to the one with defendant. By the time of the events in issue, plaintiff had begun a relationship with a new person, R.T., who she referred to as her boyfriend, and who was present during the events in question.

. . . Plaintiff's domestic violence complaint, which was filed on September 19, 2008, was apparently compiled with the assistance of court personnel based on information plaintiff supplied and was transcribed on a court-approved form. According to the complaint, plaintiff and her boyfriend, R.T., observed defendant outside of plaintiff's residence at 1:42 A.M. taking flash photographs. In the complaint, plaintiff alleged that as soon as her boyfriend pulled aside the curtain to look, defendant drove away. According to the complaint, "[p]lain[tiff] reports def[endant] did this for the sole purpose of harassing plain[tiff] and attempting to cause strain in plain[tiff]'s present relationship." . . .

In the section of the complaint form that requested identification of prior incidents of domestic violence, plaintiff referred to several. These were: (1) a June 2008 incident in which defendant was outside of the residence taking pictures and asked her boyfriend "how the accommodations were"; (2) an undated incident in which defendant climbed in her window and "attempted to have relations w[ith]" her; (3) an assertion that during "their separation def[endant] would come to the residence at various times"; and (4) an allegation that "[d]uring another occasion pla[intiff] had locked her doors and yet def[endant] was able to gain entry & harass" her.

Based on that complaint, a Temporary Restraining Order (TRO) was issued and a return date was set for the following week. For reasons not apparent from the record, the matter was adjourned and a new return date fixed for a few days later. Plaintiff, accompanied by R.T., and defendant appeared on the adjourned return date.

After administering the oath to plaintiff and defendant, the trial court began to hear testimony from plaintiff about the basis of her complaint. Plaintiff briefly described the events that took place on September 19, explaining that her boyfriend, after emerging from the shower, went to hang a towel at the bedroom window. According to plaintiff, as R.T. was looking out of the window, he told her that he saw defendant outside taking pictures. Plaintiff further testified that she then "went to the window and [defendant] was in his white Dodge, outside the house and you could see flash photography. And he—then my boyfriend proceeded to pull the curtains back and [defendant] pulled away."

After that explanation of the basis for her request for a restraining order, the court inquired further of plaintiff, asking whether there was "[a]nything else you think I should know?" Plaintiff responded by referring to "multiple incidents," none of which had been identified in the complaint as being part of the prior history of domestic violence between the two. The prior incidents that were outside of the complaint have been referred to by the parties as the "videotape," the "lacrosse field," and the "Wawa" incidents. The "videotape" refers to an incident in which defendant left an embarrassing home videotape, created with plaintiff's knowledge and consent, in her mailbox with a message indicating that her new boyfriend should see it. The "lacrosse field" incident refers to a series of verbal arguments between the parties about parenting styles and about one child's missed practice sessions and included one dispute between defendant and R.T. about R.T.'s role in the lives of the children. The "Wawa" incident refers to a conversation between defendant and R.T. in a convenience store parking lot during which plaintiff was not present.

In describing those incidents, plaintiff recited the contents of text messages she asserted she had received and she reported the substance of conversations to which defendant and her boyfriend alone had been parties. . . .

As plaintiff's testimony proceeded, the trial court repeated the earlier inquiry, asking "anything else you think I should know?" In response, plaintiff continued to add to her factual testimony, expanding to include her views that the communications were "threats" and were "annoying" and offering her impression that the conversation between defendant and her boyfriend was defendant's effort to harass him as well.

When plaintiff concluded her series of responses to the trial court's repeated inquiries by saying, "that's basically it," the court offered defendant an opportunity to respond. Defendant immediately said that many of the incidents about which plaintiff had just testified had occurred long ago and asserted that he had not known that plaintiff would be referring to them. As part of that answer, defendant told the court that he "really wasn't prepared." Notwithstanding that, defendant attempted to respond and the court inquired in detail about several of those earlier incidents that had not been identified in the complaint.

After hearing defendant's responses to those questions, the trial court inquired about the early morning photography incident. . . .

Defendant did not deny that he had gone to plaintiff's residence and had taken photographs in the early morning hours, but his response concerning that incident was two-fold. In part, he sought to attack plaintiff's credibility by challenging her testimony that his car was parked while he was taking the photographs. He testified that he was driving slowly by, offering that as evidence in support of his testimony that he intended not to be detected.

Second, defendant attempted to suggest that he had an innocent motive for taking the photographs as proof that he did not intend to harass plaintiff. Although he was reluctant to reveal his motive, it was apparent that defendant had been preparing to file, and on the same day when he was served with the TRO he had filed, a motion seeking to challenge plaintiff's custody of their two children. It was readily apparent from his testimony that he was taking late-night photographs of R.T.'s truck parked outside the home because defendant hoped that gathering photographic evidence that plaintiff's boyfriend was residing there would assist him in his quest to have custody of the two minor children transferred to him. . . .

The trial court then permitted defendant to inquire of plaintiff briefly. Defendant used that opportunity to try to undercut plaintiff's credibility by focusing on whether he was parked or not. After a time, the trial court concluded that both that line of attack, as well as defendant's assertion that he was only taking photographs for his custody motion and his suggestion that plaintiff was aware of his motive, were irrelevant. . . .

[New Jersey's Prevention of Domestic Violence Act] defines domestic violence by referring to a list of predicate acts that are otherwise found within the New Jersey Code of Criminal Justice. It provides that the commission of a predicate act, if the plaintiff meets the definition of a "victim of domestic violence," constitutes domestic violence and authorizes the court to impose restraints and related forms of relief. . . .

Although the restraints imposed pursuant to the Act are essentially civil, they are backed by the threat of enforcement through a contempt proceeding, and are accompanied by the possibility of the imposition of criminal sanctions.

Sadly, in spite of decades of careful and consistent enforcement of the Act by our courts, domestic violence remains a significant problem in our society. In 2009, the most recent year for which statistics were available for inclusion in the statutorily mandated annual report, reports of domestic violence offenses had increased. Although a year-by-year comparison for the period from 2005 through 2009 demonstrates that there had been a slight downward trend in domestic violence incidents through 2008, that trend was reversed for the most recent reporting year, with total reported incidents in most categories exceeding most prior years.

Among the predicate offenses that may serve as the basis for domestic violence purposes, one of the most frequently reported is harassment. In 2009, harassment was not only the most frequently reported of all predicate offenses, but it exceeded its incidence as compared to all prior reporting years. At the same time, however, harassment is the predicate offense that presents the greatest challenges to our courts as they strive to apply the underlying criminal statute that defines the offense to the realm of domestic discord. Drawing the line between acts that constitute harassment for purposes of issuing a domestic violence restraining order and those that fall instead into the category of "ordinary domestic contretemps" presents our courts with a weighty responsibility and confounds our ability to fix clear rules of application.

In part, the decision about which acts constitute domestic violence and which do not can be found not in the analysis of the predicate acts themselves, but in the second inquiry required of courts considering complaints seeking protection pursuant to the Act. Our Appellate Division has ably explained the appropriate approach:

The second inquiry, upon a finding of the commission of a predicate act of domestic violence, is whether the court should enter a restraining order that provides protection for the victim. . . .

Because all of the arguments raised on appeal rest only on a claimed act of harassment, we begin with a review of the body of law that has developed concerning this most challenging basis for a domestic violence complaint. The predicate act of harassment is defined by statute to be a criminal offense:

> Harassment. Except as provided in subsection e., a person commits a petty disorderly persons offense if, with purpose to harass another, he:
>
> a. Makes, or cause to be made, a communication or communications anonymously or at extremely inconvenient hours, or in offensively coarse language, or any other manner likely to cause annoyance or alarm;
>
> b. Subjects another to striking, kicking, shoving or other offensive touching, or threatens to do so; or
>
> c. Engages in any other course of alarming conduct or of repeatedly committed acts with purpose to alarm or seriously annoy such other person. . . .

Defendant's argument that permitting plaintiff to testify about numerous incidents she asserted were evidence of a prior history of domestic violence, but that were not identified in her complaint, violated his due process rights is a variation of an argument that we have previously addressed. As we have held, ordinary due process protections apply in the domestic violence context, notwithstanding the shortened time frames for conducting a final hearing that are imposed by the statute. What that means is that "[a]t a minimum, due process requires that a party in a judicial hearing receive 'notice defining the issues and an adequate opportunity to prepare and respond.'" More particularly, we held that due process forbids the trial court "'to convert a hearing on a complaint alleging one act of domestic violence into a hearing on other acts of domestic violence which are not even alleged in the complaint.'"

The fact remains, however, that plaintiffs seeking protection under the Act often file complaints that reveal limited information about the prior history between the parties, only to expand upon that history of prior disputes when appearing in open court. And it is frequently the case that the trial court will attempt to elicit a fuller picture of the circumstances either to comply with the statutory command to consider the previous history, if any, of domestic violence between the parties or to be certain of the relevant facts that may give content to otherwise ambiguous communications or behavior.

That reality is not inconsistent with affording defendants the protections of due process to which they are entitled. Instead, ensuring that defendants are not deprived of their due process rights requires our trial courts to recognize both what those rights are and how they can be protected consistent with the protective goals of the Act. To begin with, trial courts should use the allegations set forth in the complaint to guide their questioning of plaintiffs, avoiding the sort of questions that induced plaintiff in this appeal to abandon the history revealed in the complaint in favor of entirely new accusations. That does not mean that trial courts must limit plaintiffs to the precise prior history revealed in a complaint, because the testimony might reveal that there are additional prior events that are significant to the court's evaluation, particularly if the events are ambiguous. Rather, the court must recognize that if it allows that history to be expanded, it has permitted an amendment to the complaint and must proceed accordingly.

To be sure, some defendants will know full well the history that plaintiff recites and some parties will be well-prepared regardless of whether the testimony technically expands upon the allegations of the complaint. Others, however, will not, and in all cases the trial court must ensure that defendant is afforded an adequate opportunity to be apprised of those allegations and to prepare.

When permitting plaintiff to expand upon the alleged prior incidents and thereby allowing an amendment to the complaint, the court also should have recognized the due process implication of defendant's suggestion that he was unprepared to defend himself. Although defendant's assertion that he needed time to prepare was not cloaked in the lawyer-like language of an adjournment request and was made as part of a longer response to a question, it was sufficient to raise the due process question for the trial court and it should have been granted. . . .

This is especially true because there is no risk to plaintiff based on such a procedure; courts are empowered to continue temporary restraints during the pendency of an adjournment, thus fully protecting the putative victim while ensuring that defendant's due process rights are safeguarded as well. . . .

Defendant's final argument relates to the sufficiency of the evidence on which the trial court relied in concluding that he had committed the predicate act of harassment and that plaintiff therefore was entitled to protection under the Act. Our courts have struggled with the proofs needed to support a domestic violence restraining order based on claims of harassment. In part, the challenge comes from litigants, often representing themselves, who use the word "harassment" as it is used in common parlance rather than in the sense meant by either the New Jersey Code of Criminal Justice or the Prevention of Domestic Violence Act. Often, a party's accusation that another's actions are "harassing" is vague and conclusory, making it particularly difficult for a trial court to discern on which side of the line running between domestic violence and ordinary "contretemps" a particular act properly falls.

In our efforts to be faithful to the strong expressions of our Legislature and to protect the rights of both parties we have vested great discretion in our Family Part judges. We have observed that they are judges who have been specially trained to detect the difference between domestic violence and more ordinary differences that arise between couples, and we have recognized that their findings are entitled to deference.

Many published decisions have addressed questions concerning what conduct constitutes harassment and what does not. Our Appellate Division has concluded that sending explicit photographs of plaintiff to her sister and threatening to send them to plaintiff's son and to her workplace was harassment. Similarly, there was sufficient evidence to support a finding of harassment when defendant found plaintiff's new telephone number and sent her a text message that told her that he could see her watching a particular television show. Even though defendant was not in fact watching plaintiff and therefore was unable to see her, the content of the message was such that it was intended to cause her "annoyance, which means 'to disturb, irritate, or bother.'"

A history of domestic violence may serve to give content to otherwise ambiguous behavior and support entry of a restraining order. For example, in part based on the parties' history, a defendant who was angry because plaintiff rebuffed his efforts to talk to her, and who blocked her from leaving in her car, using coarse and vulgar language to express his frustration, committed an act of harassment.

Not all offensive or bothersome behavior, however, constitutes harassment. In the criminal context, our Appellate Division has cautioned against "overextending a criminal statute to rude behavior which is not directed to anyone specifically but only towards an institution in general." That observation convinced the appellate panel that "venting of frustration or irritation" and using obscenities during a 911 call did not demonstrate a purpose to harass, thus making a restraining order inappropriate. . . .

With these principles and these examples of their application to guide us, we turn to a consideration of whether the facts in the record support the court's finding that defendant committed an act or a series of acts of harassment sufficient to entitle plaintiff to issuance of a domestic violence restraining order. Our analysis must begin by restating the findings that the trial court made. Boiled down to its essence, the court first noted that the critical facts were not contested, because defendant conceded that he had been outside of the residence early in the morning taking photographs. Based on that alone, the trial court concluded that "being there . . . at quarter to two in the morning . . . in and of itself, [is] harassment." Supplementing that finding, however, the court relied on three incidents about which plaintiff had testified, none of which had been identified in the complaint. Finally, the court rejected defendant's repeated assurances that his purpose was only to gather evidence for his planned custody motion, concluding instead that he acted with the requisite purpose to harass.

The trial court did not specify which of the two subsections of the harassment statute it was applying to the factual assertions being raised by plaintiff. Although the appellate panel applied subsection c., because the trial court's recitation of findings and conclusions appears to be an alternative analysis that might have been intended to support issuance of the restraining order pursuant to either subsection, we consider each separately.

It is possible that the court meant to apply subsection a., based on the reference to the fact that defendant's presence outside the residence alone sufficed. For purposes of subsection a., a single act can be enough and the act, given that it took place at what could clearly qualify as an "extremely inconvenient hour," could theoretically constitute a predicate act. Nevertheless, it would only qualify as a predicate act if it were both committed with a purpose to harass and if the act was "likely to cause annoyance or alarm."

The evidence in this record, however, is insufficient to support a finding under subsection a. Merely being outside of the home in the early morning hours is not an act of harassment. More to the point, plaintiff's own clear testimony about the incident demonstrates that she was completely unaware that defendant was outside until R.T. walked over to the window and happened to look out. Only then did he notice defendant taking photographs and tell plaintiff what he saw. Plaintiff also conceded that as R.T. pulled aside the curtain, defendant immediately left. Far from a record suggesting that defendant's camera created a series of bright flashes that drew plaintiff's attention and caused her alarm, the undisputed facts are that plaintiff saw nothing until R.T. called to her and that defendant beat a hasty retreat when the curtain moved and he realized that they had seen him.

In the alternative, as the appellate panel surmised, the trial court might have meant to apply subsection c. That test for harassment would require a course of alarming conduct or a series of repeated acts, along with proof of a purpose to alarm or seriously annoy plaintiff. Utilizing the test set forth in subsection c., there is no evidence of a repeated act, with the result that defendant can only be in violation of subsection c. if he engaged in a "course of alarming conduct" within the meaning of the statute.

The trial court did not articulate precise findings of fact and conclusions of law and therefore did not explain what it was in the series of past incidents that led it to conclude that defendant's purpose when he engaged in late-night photography was to harass plaintiff. Certainly, the series of events that plaintiff testified were part of the history between the parties shows that defendant's behavior was hardly praiseworthy. But those events may or may not suffice to demonstrate defendant's intent and absent the trial court's explanation of its reasoning or its analysis, we cannot be confident that they do.

First, the statute requires that the victim, in this instance, the plaintiff, be the target of the harassing intent. Many of the incidents set forth by plaintiff in this record, including defendant's snide remarks to the new beau about the comfort of the accommodations, are ones in which plaintiff was not even present. Those incidents, therefore, could not serve as evidence of an intent to annoy or alarm plaintiff. Moreover, there is nothing in those acts that objectively rises to the level of "alarming" or "seriously annoying" as the statute demands.

Turning to the other past incidents, the trial court placed particular emphasis on defendant's delivery of the videotape to plaintiff. Although referring to it as "a dirty trick," the trial court did not explain how it demonstrated that defendant acted with the purpose to harass plaintiff when he went to take photographs, which is the incident claimed to be the predicate act. Although a purpose to harass can be inferred from a history between the parties, that finding must be supported by some evidence that the actor's conscious object was to alarm or annoy; mere awareness that someone might be alarmed or annoyed is insufficient. The victim's subjective reaction alone will not suffice; there must be evidence of the improper purpose. Moreover, when evaluating whether an individual acted with the requisite purpose, our courts must be especially vigilant in cases involving, as do many domestic violence disputes, the interactions of a couple in the midst of a breakup of a relationship.

It is significant as well that defendant in fact was preparing a motion for a change in custody that was based on plaintiff's cohabitation and the effect he believed that her new relationship was having on his children. That motion, which defendant testified was the reason for his decision to go to the home and take photographs, was filed within hours of the event, and its implications should have been considered and addressed by the court. We do not imply that, in evaluating claims of domestic violence, an individual can have only one motive or intent. On the contrary, domestic violence often presents circumstances in which a party may mask an intent to harass with what could otherwise be an innocent act. But some domestic violence complainants may perceive an entirely innocent act to be a harassing one as well. Our courts must examine the record with care lest an abuser hiding behind an apparently innocent act be overlooked. But they must be equally careful lest a plaintiff be permitted to seize upon what is truly an innocent act in an effort to gain an advantage in litigation between parties.

Finally, although not directly raised by defendant, the record does not include an analysis of "the second inquiry," and thus lacks the required consideration of whether entry of restraints is "necessary" to protect plaintiff from harm. That inquiry serves to ensure that the protective purposes of the Act are served, while limiting the possibility that the Act, or the courts, will become inappropriate weapons in domestic warfare. Although, as our Appellate Division noted, there will be cases in which the risk of harm is so great that the inquiry can be perfunctory, in others, including this one, it is not. In those cases, overlooking that important step in the analysis poses the risk of unfairness and error.

In entering the [Final Restraining Order], the trial court did not sufficiently articulate findings and conclusions consistent with the statutory standards and our independent review of the record leaves us unsure that there is sufficient evidence to sustain the issuance of the order. Therefore, in an abundance of caution, and mindful of the Family Court's "special expertise" and the Act's protective purposes, we are constrained to remand this matter to the trial court for a re-hearing, both to protect defendant's due process rights and to permit the trial court to evaluate the testimony and the evidence in accordance with the principles we have expressed. . . .

NOTES AND QUESTIONS

1. Why did the trial court and appellate court disagree about whether M.D.F. had committed harassment? On remand, what arguments should the parties make about whether the evidence is sufficient to show harassment?

The statute in *J.D.* defines domestic violence for purposes of obtaining a restraining order by reference to criminal statutes. The appellate court observes that harassment is one of the most common predicate crimes alleged in petitions for restraining orders and says that it "presents the greatest challenges to our courts as they strive to apply the underlying criminal statute that defines the offense to the realm of domestic discord. Drawing the line between acts that constitute harassment for purposes of issuing a domestic violence restraining order and those that fall instead into the category of 'ordinary domestic contretemps' presents our courts with a weighty responsibility and confounds our ability to fix clear rules of application." Why is it necessary to draw this line? Is the harassment statute's emphasis on the actor's motive a good vehicle for making this distinction?

In other states, restraining order statutes do not incorporate criminal definitions but instead base availability of an order on proof that the respondent has caused or attempted to cause harm to the petitioner or put the petitioner in fear of harm. *See, e.g.*, National Council of Juvenile and Family Court Judges, Model Code on Domestic and Family Violence §§102(1), 301; Or. Rev. Stat. §107.705(1) (2022). What are the advantages and disadvantages of this approach? Would the evidence in *J.D.* have been sufficient for an order in such a jurisdiction?

2. The New Jersey Supreme Court had previously held that issuing a restraining order based on incidents that were not specifically pled in the petition violates the respondent's right to notice, but, as the *J.D.* court says, courts must also consider the context of conduct that is pled to determine whether a restraining order is warranted. At what point does evidence of "context" become an allegation of conduct that must be pled? If such evidence comes in during a hearing on the order, what should the court do to protect the respondent's right to notice while also ensuring the safety of the petitioner? The petitioner in this case drafted the petition with the assistance of court personnel, but often petitioners draft petitions alone, and such petitions may be even less complete than this one. Do the New Jersey courts strike the right balance between the respondent's right to due process and the petitioner's need to be able to explain the situation to the judge? How important should specific events be in determining whether a petition for a restraining order should be granted?

3. When restraining order statutes were introduced, the provisions allowing ex parte orders on an emergency or temporary basis were challenged as violating due process, usually without success. For example, in Kampf v. Kampf, 603 N.W.2d 295 (Mich. App. 1999), the court analyzed the issue as follows:

> There is no procedural due process defect in obtaining an emergency order of protection without notice to a respondent when the petition for the emergency protection order is supported by affidavits that demonstrate exigent circumstances justifying entry of an emergency order without prior notice, see, e.g., Mitchell v. W.T. Grant, 416 U.S. 600 (1974), and where there are appropriate provisions for notice and an opportunity to be heard after the order is issued. Here, subsection 12 permits a court to issue an *ex parte* order only if it clearly appears from specific facts shown by verified complaint, written motion, or affidavit that *immediate and irreparable injury, loss, or damage will result from the delay required to effectuate notice or that the notice will itself precipitate adverse action before a personal protection order can be issued* [emphasis added].
>
> Further, [the statute] gives a respondent the right to bring a motion to rescind a PPO within fourteen days of being served with notice or receiving actual notice of the PPO, and requires the court to schedule a hearing on the motion within five or fourteen days, depending on whether the PPO enjoins the respondent from purchasing and possessing a firearm. Clearly, the procedural safeguards employed under the statute are sufficient to meet respondent's due process challenge.

603 N.W.2d at 299. *See also* State v. Fernando A., 981 A.2d 427 (Conn. 2009) (when statute authorizes restraining order incident to criminal prosecution, due process satisfied by evidentiary hearing conducted after order issued to determine continued necessity of order).

4. Most domestic violence protective order statutes reach cohabitant or former cohabitant relationships as well as former spouses. For example, the California Domestic Violence Prevention Act, §§6200 et seq., defines "domestic violence" as abuse against a spouse, former spouse, cohabitant, former cohabitant, a person with whom the respondent is having or has had a dating or engagement relationship, a person with whom the respondent has had a child or presumed child, or any other person related by consanguinity or affinity within the second degree. Cal. Fam. Code §6211 (2022). The South Carolina Supreme Court held that the state statute which applied to unmarried opposite-sex cohabitants but not those of the same sex violated equal protection in Doe v. State, 808 S.E.2d 807 (S.C. 2017). A New Jersey court found that the restraining order statute that applied to people in a "dating relationship" included a couple who never had a traditional, in-person date. Their relationship consisted of intense communication, including almost 1300 highly personal text messages. In footnote 6, the court observed, "We need look no further than the impact of the COVID-19 pandemic on the inability to meet in-person on traditional 'dates.' Instead, many people access internet websites and applications to 'meet,' sustain, and develop relationships virtually." C.C. v. J.A.H., 232 A.3d 505 (N.J. App. Div. 2020), *cert. denied*, 240 A.3d 389 (2020).

5. For information about civil protective order and stalking statutes in all 50 states, *see* American Bar Association Commission on Domestic & Sexual Violence, Statutory Summary Charts, https://www.americanbar.org/groups/domestic_violence/Initiatives/statutory_summary_charts/.

6. In Gonzales v. City of Castle Rock, 545 U.S. 748 (2005), the Supreme Court held that there is no constitutional remedy against police officers who fail to enforce a domestic violence restraining order, notwithstanding a state mandatory arrest statute. Jessica Gonzales had obtained a restraining order limiting her husband Simon's contact with her and their daughters, aged 10, 9, and 7. Shortly after the order was issued, the children disappeared from the front of Jessica's home. She suspected (correctly) that her husband had taken the children and she called the Castle Rock Police Department. Two officers came to the home, where she showed them a copy of the restraining order and asked that it be enforced and her children returned to her immediately. The officers "stated that there was nothing they could do about the TRO and suggested that Plaintiff call the Police Department again if the children did not return home by 10:00 P.M." Subsequently, Jessica heard from her husband that he was at an amusement park with the children. She called the police, who told her to wait until 8 P.M. At 8 P.M. she was told to wait until 10 P.M., a pattern that continued all evening. At approximately 3:20 A.M., Simon arrived at the Castle Rock police station in his truck. He got out and opened fire on the station with a semi-automatic handgun he had purchased soon after abducting his daughters. He was shot dead at the scene. The police found the bodies of the three girls, who had been murdered by their father earlier that evening, in the cab of the truck.

Jessica Gonzales brought a 1983 action on behalf of herself and her deceased daughters against the City of Castle Rock, Colorado, and three Castle Rock police officers. She claimed her due process rights were violated by the officers' failure to enforce the restraining order against her husband. The district court dismissed the case, holding that there was no violation of either substantive or procedural due process. The Supreme Court ultimately upheld the trial court ruling on the basis of the well-established tradition of police discretion to determine whether to make arrests. The Court rejected the argument that domestic violence statutes calling for arrest are intended by the legislature to be different from other criminal statutes in this regard.

Gonzales then successfully petitioned the Inter-American Commission on Human Rights, which found that the United States violated several of her rights under the American Declaration on the Rights and Duties of Man. Lenahan (Gonzales) v. United States, Inter-Am. C.H.R., Report No. 80/11 ¶5 (2011). Commentary on *Castle Rock* includes Julie Goldscheid, Rethinking Civil Rights and Gender Violence, 14 Geo. J. Gender & L. 43 (2013); G. Kristian Miccio, The Death of the Fourteenth Amendment: *Castle Rock* and Its Progeny, 17 Wm. & Mary J. Women & L. 277 (2011); Atinuke O. Awoyomi, The State-Created Danger Doctrine in Domestic Violence Cases: Do We Have a Solution in Okin v. Village of Cornwall-on-Hudson Police Department?, 20 Colum. J. Gender & L. 1 (2011).

7. Cook v. Cole, 795 Fed.Appx. 906 (5th Cir. 2019), held that a victim of domestic violence had not been intentionally discriminated against, in violation of the Fourteenth Amendment's equal protection and due process clauses, when she was killed by her abuser after the police did not respond to her 911 call in a timely manner. Deanna Cook's ex-husband broke into her home, in violation of the protection order against him, and Deanna called 911, screaming for help as she was being attacked. Even though the call was marked as "urgent," officers were not dispatched to her home for nearly an hour. When Deanna did not answer the door, they left and marked the incident as resolved. Her mother, Vickie, who went to check on Deanna after she did not appear in church, found Deanna's body days after the attack.

Vickie, Deanna's two minor daughters, and the Administrator of Deanna's estate sued the employees of the 911 call center on the day of Deanna's call, the police dispatcher, the responding police officers, and the City of Dallas. Plaintiffs claimed defendants violated Deanna's due process and equal protection rights, as well as offended §1983 and state tort law.

The Fifth Circuit held that the city had not created a "special relationship" with Deanna when its officers "promised" they would arrest her abuser because these assurances were too far removed from the incident that led to Deanna's death. Moreover, defendants could not be found to have "exacerbated the danger" she faced in violation of the due process clause and the plaintiffs did not raise sufficient evidence of discrimination on the basis of race, gender, socioeconomic status, or status as a victim of domestic violence. Finally, the city could not be held liable under §1983 because no constitutional deprivations had occurred or under state tort law because the city had governmental immunity for the government functions of emergency and police services.

8. As discussed in Chapter 9, when the domestic violence and abusive behavior of one spouse is an element in a custody dispute, a 2019 study found that mothers' claims of abuse were widely dismissed in family court, often to the psychological and physical detriment of the children. Joan Meier identifies that courts often privilege custody for a father against whom credible allegations of abuse have been made in order to avoid so-called parental alienation. Joan S. Meier, U.S. Child Custody Outcomes in Cases Involving Parental Alienation and Abuse Allegations: What Do the Data Show?, 42 J. Social Welfare & Fam. L. 92-105 (2020).

NOTE: FEDERAL DOMESTIC VIOLENCE LEGISLATION

The Violence Against Women Act of 1994 (VAWA), Pub. L. No. 103-322, codified as amended in various sections of 8, 18, and 42 U.S.C. (2022), provides federal civil and criminal remedies for victims of violence motivated by gender-based animus. VAWA also requires that states give full faith and credit to and enforce domestic violence restraining orders from other states. 18 U.S.C. §2265. An order that is valid according to the law of the state that issued it must be enforced, even if it includes terms or applies to parties that the law of the forum state would not permit. VAWA was reauthorized in March 2022.

State and federal laws also limit the availability of firearms to domestic violence offenders. The federal Gun Control Act prohibits a person who is subject to a domestic violence restraining order from possessing a firearm during the life of the order, and a person convicted of a misdemeanor crime of domestic violence is barred for life from possessing a firearm. 18 U.S.C. §922(g)(8), (9). In United States v. Hayes, 555 U.S. 415 (2009), the Supreme Court held that this prohibition applies to a person who was convicted of a generic misdemeanor of violence where the victim was the offender's spouse or intimate partner, even if the existence of a domestic relationship between the victim and offender was not an element of the misdemeanor. However, the Court said, in a prosecution for violating the gun law, the prosecution must prove beyond a reasonable doubt that the domestic relationship existed. In Voisine v. United States, 579 U.S. 686 (2016), the Supreme Court held that 18 U.S.C. §922(g)(9), which bars a person convicted of a felony or misdemeanor crime of domestic violence from possessing a firearm, is triggered by a conviction for a reckless domestic assault. Previously, in United States v. Castleman, 572 U.S. 157 (2014), the Court had held that any intentional domestic violence crime that includes an offensive touching is a crime of violence for purposes of the statute, rejecting the argument that "violent force" must have been used.

C. REPRODUCTIVE CHOICE

In Dobbs v. Jackson Women's Health Organization, 142 S.Ct. 2228 (2022), the Supreme Court overturned constitutional protection for pre-viability abortion and initiated a sea change in the legal protection for reproductive decisionmaking by pregnant people. *Dobbs* upended almost 50 years of precedent, reversing Roe v. Wade, 410 U.S. 113 (1973), which established that the Fourteenth Amendment due process clause protected the right to seek an abortion.

This section provides the background for *Dobbs*, including *Roe* and Planned Parenthood v. Casey, 505 U.S. 833 (1992), which upheld *Roe* with a refashioned constitutional test for abortion rights. It then considers the future of reproductive rights now that states may ban all abortion from the earliest stages of pregnancy. The concluding material considers the potential effect of *Dobbs* on other rights—to marry, to use contraceptives, or to engage in intimate behavior—that are important to family law. These materials raise once again difficult problems in conceptualizing the family and in defining its internal relations and its relationship with the state.

1. Overturning Constitutional Protection for Abortion

The roots of a constitutional right to abortion are in cases that protect a right for married and unmarried persons to use contraceptives. In Griswold v. Connecticut, 381 U.S. 479 (1965), the Supreme Court recognized a constitutionally protected interest in privacy. Appellant Griswold, the executive director of Planned Parenthood of Connecticut, challenged the constitutionality of a Connecticut statute making it an offense to use, or to assist another in using, "any drug, medicinal article, or instrument for the purpose of preventing conception." A majority of the Court held the law unconstitutional. Justice Douglas, writing for the Court, concluded that certain constitutional guarantees generated "penumbras," which, although not mentioned in specific terms by the Constitution, nonetheless were entitled to constitutional protection. Justice Douglas found that a number of specific guarantees—the First Amendment's protection of speech and belief; the Third Amendment's prohibition against the quartering during peacetime of soldiers in any house; the Fourth Amendment's protection of persons, houses, and property against unreasonable search and seizure; and the Fifth Amendment privilege against self-incrimination—created zones of privacy that are entitled to constitutional protection. This right to privacy, Justice Douglas concluded, reached the law forbidding the *use* of contraceptives:

> We deal with a right of privacy older than the Bill of Rights—older than our political parties, older than our school system. Marriage is a coming together for better or for worse, hopefully enduring, and intimate to the degree of being sacred. It is an association that promotes a way of life, not causes; a harmony in living, not political faiths; a bilateral loyalty, not commercial or social projects. Yet it is an association for as noble a purpose as any involved in our prior decisions.

381 U.S. at 486. Justice Goldberg, joined by Chief Justice Warren and Justice Brennan, concurred. They agreed that the concept of liberty in the Fourteenth Amendment due process

clause was not confined to the specific terms of the Bill of Rights and, moreover, that it "embraced the right of marital privacy."

In Roe v. Wade, 410 U.S. 113 (1973), the Court further defined the scope of, and state power with respect to, the privacy right. The appellant sought a declaratory judgment that the Texas criminal abortion statutes were unconstitutional on their face. Justice Blackmun's majority opinion held that the right to privacy is broad enough to encompass a woman's decision whether or not to terminate her pregnancy, and that right is a "fundamental right" that can be restricted by the state only when it can show a "compelling interest" and that its regulations are "narrowly drawn to express only the legitimate state interests at stake." 410 U.S. at 155.

Justice Blackmun applied this analytical framework to the Texas statute. The state argued that a fetus is a "person" and therefore its protection under the Fourteenth Amendment was a compelling state interest. Justice Blackmun found no consensus in either state laws or other sources for the proposition that the "unborn" are persons in the whole sense and held that Texas could not, by adopting one of the various theories of life, generally override the rights of the pregnant woman. Justice Rehnquist dissented. He did not agree that the right of privacy recognized in earlier cases included a right to terminate a pregnancy, nor that any liberty interest the woman might have was entitled to the high level of protection accorded fundamental rights.

Roe v. Wade was followed by a wide variety of statutes seeking to define (or limit) the conditions under which women could obtain abortions. In Planned Parenthood of Southeastern Pennsylvania v. Casey, 505 U.S. 833 (1992), Justice O'Connor announced the judgment of the Court and concluded, after lengthy consideration of the policy embodied in *stare decisis*, that *Roe* should not be entirely abandoned.

Justice O'Connor's opinion upheld that the basic decision in *Roe*— that is, recognizing a constitutional liberty to decide whether to terminate a pregnancy, at least before a fetus is viable. However, the opinion rejected the test for a law's constitutionality announced in *Roe*. *Casey* held that states could regulate to protect a person's health or respect for potential life throughout pregnancy so long as the regulation did not impose an undue burden on the right to abortion: "A finding of an undue burden is a shorthand for the conclusion that a state regulation has the purpose or effect of placing a substantial obstacle in the path of a woman seeking an abortion of a nonviable fetus." 505 U.S. at 877.

In the case that follows, the Supreme Court abandoned that test.

Dobbs v. Jackson Women's Health Organization
142 S. Ct. 2228 (2022)

ALITO, J., delivered the opinion of the Court, in which THOMAS, GORSUCH, KAVANAUGH, and BARRETT, JJ., joined. THOMAS, J., and KAVANAUGH, J., filed concurring opinions. ROBERTS, C. J., filed an opinion concurring in the judgment. BREYER, SOTOMAYOR, and KAGAN, JJ., filed a dissenting opinion.

In 1973, this Court decided Roe v. Wade, 410 U.S. 113. Even though the Constitution makes no mention of abortion, the Court held that it confers a broad right to obtain one. . . .

We hold that Roe and Casey must be overruled. The Constitution makes no reference to abortion, and no such right is implicitly protected by any constitutional provision, including the one on which the defenders of Roe and Casey now chiefly rely—the Due Process Clause of the Fourteenth Amendment. That provision has been held to guarantee some rights that are not mentioned in the Constitution, but any such right must be "deeply rooted in this Nation's history and tradition" and "implicit in the concept of ordered liberty." Washington v. Glucksberg, 521 U.S. 702, 721 (1997).

The right to abortion does not fall within this category. Until the latter part of the 20th century, such a right was entirely unknown in American law. Indeed, when the Fourteenth Amendment was adopted, three quarters of the States made abortion a crime at all stages of pregnancy. The abortion right is also critically different from any other right that this Court has held to fall within the Fourteenth Amendment's protection of "liberty." Roe's defenders characterize the abortion right as similar to the rights recognized in past decisions involving matters such as intimate sexual relations, contraception, and marriage, but abortion is fundamentally different, as both Roe and Casey acknowledged, because it destroys what those decisions called "fetal life" and what the law now before us describes as an "unborn human being." Stare decisis, the doctrine on which Casey's controlling opinion was based, does not compel unending adherence to Roe's abuse of judicial authority. Roe was egregiously wrong from the start. Its reasoning was exceptionally weak, and the decision has had damaging consequences. And far from bringing about a national settlement of the abortion issue, Roe and Casey have enflamed debate and deepened division.

It is time to heed the Constitution and return the issue of abortion to the people's elected representatives. . . . That is what the Constitution and the rule of law demand. . . .

We begin by considering the critical question whether the Constitution, properly understood, confers a right to obtain an abortion. . . .

First, we explain the standard that our cases have used in determining whether the Fourteenth Amendment's reference to "liberty" protects a particular right. Second, we examine whether the right at issue in this case is rooted in our Nation's history and tradition and whether it is an essential component of what we have described as "ordered liberty." Finally, we consider whether a right to obtain an abortion is part of a broader entrenched right that is supported by other precedents. . . .

[O]ur decisions have held that the Due Process Clause protects two categories of substantive rights.

The first consists of rights guaranteed by the first eight Amendments. Those Amendments originally applied only to the Federal Government, but this Court has held that the Due Process Clause of the Fourteenth Amendment "incorporates" the great majority of those rights and thus makes them equally applicable to the States. The second category—which is the one in question here—comprises a select list of fundamental rights that are not mentioned anywhere in the Constitution.

In deciding whether a right falls into either of these categories, the Court has long asked whether the right is "deeply rooted in [our] history and tradition" and whether it is essential to our Nation's "scheme of ordered liberty." . . . "

Historical inquiries of this nature are essential whenever we are asked to recognize a new component of the "liberty" protected by the Due Process Clause because the term "liberty" alone provides little guidance. "Liberty" is a capacious term. . . .

Until the latter part of the 20th century, there was no support in American law for a constitutional right to obtain an abortion. No state constitutional provision had recognized such a right. Until a few years before Roe was handed down, no federal or state court had recognized such a right. Nor had any scholarly treatise of which we are aware. . . . [A]bortion had long been a crime in every single State. [The majority opinion then provides an extensive assessment of how common law, early U.S. court decisions, and state statutes regulated abortion. — Eds.]

The inescapable conclusion is that a right to abortion is not deeply rooted in the Nation's history and traditions. On the contrary, an unbroken tradition of prohibiting abortion on pain of criminal punishment persisted from the earliest days of the common law until 1973. . . .

Nor does the right to obtain an abortion have a sound basis in precedent. Casey relied on cases involving the right to marry a person of a different race, Loving v. Virginia, 388 U.S.

1 (1967); the right to marry while in prison, Turner v. Safley, 482 U.S. 78 (1987); the right to obtain contraceptives, Griswold v. Connecticut, 381 U.S. 479 (1965), Eisenstadt v. Baird, 405 U.S. 438 (1972), Carey v. Population Services Int'l, 431 U.S. 678 (1977); the right to reside with relatives, Moore v. East Cleveland, 431 U.S. 494 (1977); the right to make decisions about the education of one's children, Pierce v. Society of Sisters, 268 U.S. 510 (1925), Meyer v. Nebraska, 262 U.S. 390 (1923); the right not to be sterilized without consent, Skinner v. Oklahoma ex rel. Williamson, 316 U.S. 535 (1942); and the right in certain circumstances not to undergo involuntary surgery, forced administration of drugs, or other substantially similar procedures, Winston v. Lee, 470 U.S. 753 (1985). Respondents and the Solicitor General also rely on post-Casey decisions like Lawrence v. Texas, 539 U.S. 558 (2003) (right to engage in private, consensual sexual acts), and Obergefell v. Hodges, 576 U.S. 644 (2015) (right to marry a person of the same sex).

These attempts to justify abortion through appeals to a broader right to autonomy and to define one's "concept of existence" prove too much. Casey. Those criteria, at a high level of generality, could license fundamental rights to illicit drug use, prostitution, and the like. None of these rights has any claim to being deeply rooted in history.

What sharply distinguishes the abortion right from the rights recognized in the cases on which Roe and Casey rely is something that both those decisions acknowledged: Abortion destroys what those decisions call "potential life" and what the law at issue in this case regards as the life of an "unborn human being." See Roe (abortion is "inherently different"); Casey (abortion is "a unique act"). None of the other decisions cited by Roe and Casey involved the critical moral question posed by abortion. . . . They do not support the right to obtain an abortion, and by the same token, our conclusion that the Constitution does not confer such a right does not undermine them in any way. . . .

Americans who believe that abortion should be restricted press countervailing arguments about modern developments. They note that attitudes about the pregnancy of unmarried women have changed drastically; that federal and state laws ban discrimination on the basis of pregnancy; that leave for pregnancy and childbirth are now guaranteed by law in many cases; that the costs of medical care associated with pregnancy are covered by insurance or government assistance; that States have increasingly adopted "safe haven" laws, which generally allow women to drop off babies anonymously; and that a woman who puts her newborn up for adoption today has little reason to fear that the baby will not find a suitable home. They also claim that many people now have a new appreciation of fetal life and that when prospective parents who want to have a child view a sonogram, they typically have no doubt that what they see is their daughter or son.

Both sides make important policy arguments, but supporters of Roe and Casey must show that this Court has the authority to weigh those arguments and decide how abortion may be regulated in the States. They have failed to make that showing, and we thus return the power to weigh those arguments to the people and their elected representatives. . . .

We next consider whether the doctrine of stare decisis counsels continued acceptance of Roe and Casey. . . . We have long recognized . . . that stare decisis is "not an inexorable command," and it "is at its weakest when we interpret the Constitution." . . .

Some of our most important constitutional decisions have overruled prior precedents. . . . In Brown v. Board of Education, 347 U.S. 483 (1954), the Court repudiated the "separate but equal" doctrine, which had allowed States to maintain racially segregated schools and other facilities. In so doing, the Court overruled the infamous decision in Plessy v. Ferguson, 163 U.S. 537 (1896), along with six other Supreme Court precedents that had applied the separate-but-equal rule. . . .

In this case, five factors weigh strongly in favor of overruling Roe and Casey: the nature of their error, the quality of their reasoning, the "workability" of the rules they imposed on the country, their disruptive effect on other areas of the law, and the absence of concrete reliance. [Arguments applying the five factors have been omitted. — EDS.]

. . . Having shown that traditional stare decisis factors do not weigh in favor of retaining Roe or Casey, we must address one final argument that featured prominently in the Casey plurality opinion.

The argument . . . was essentially as follows. The American people's belief in the rule of law would be shaken if they lost respect for this Court as an institution that decides important cases based on principle, not "social and political pressures." There is a special danger that the public will perceive a decision as having been made for unprincipled reasons when the Court overrules a controversial "watershed" decision, such as Roe. . . . [T]herefore the preservation of public approval of the Court weighs heavily in favor of retaining Roe. . . .

We do not pretend to know how our political system or society will respond to today's decision overruling Roe and Casey. And even if we could foresee what will happen, we would have no authority to let that knowledge influence our decision. We can only do our job, which is to interpret the law, apply longstanding principles of stare decisis, and decide this case accordingly.

We therefore hold that the Constitution does not confer a right to abortion. Roe and Casey must be overruled, and the authority to regulate abortion must be returned to the people and their elected representatives. . . .

We must now decide what standard will govern if state abortion regulations undergo constitutional challenge and whether the law before us satisfies the appropriate standard.

Under our precedents, rational-basis review is the appropriate standard for such challenges. As we have explained, procuring an abortion is not a fundamental constitutional right because such a right has no basis in the Constitution's text or in our Nation's history.

A law regulating abortion, like other health and welfare laws, is entitled to a "strong presumption of validity." Heller v. Doe, 509 U.S. 312, 319 (1993). It must be sustained if there is a rational basis on which the legislature could have thought that it would serve legitimate state interests. Williamson v. Lee Optical of Okla., Inc., 348 U.S. 483, 491 (1955). . . . These legitimate interests include respect for and preservation of prenatal life at all stages of development, the protection of maternal health and safety; the elimination of particularly gruesome or barbaric medical procedures; the preservation of the integrity of the medical profession; the mitigation of fetal pain; and the prevention of discrimination on the basis of race, sex, or disability. Roe, cf. Glucksberg (identifying similar interests). . . . These legitimate interests provide a rational basis for [Mississippi's] Gestational Age Act, and it follows that respondents' constitutional challenge must fail. . . .

We end this opinion where we began. Abortion presents a profound moral question. The Constitution does not prohibit the citizens of each State from regulating or prohibiting abortion. Roe and Casey arrogated that authority. We now overrule those decisions and return that authority to the people and their elected representatives.

The judgment of the Fifth Circuit is reversed, and the case is remanded for further proceedings consistent with this opinion.

Justice THOMAS, concurring.

I join the opinion of the Court because it correctly holds that there is no constitutional right to abortion. . . .

I write separately to emphasize a second, more fundamental reason why there is no abortion guarantee lurking in the Due Process Clause. [T]he Due Process Clause at most guarantees process. It does not, as the Court's substantive due process cases suppose, "forbi[d] the government to infringe certain 'fundamental' liberty interests at all, no matter what process is provided." Reno v. Flores, 507 U.S. 292, 302 (1993). . . .

[I]n future cases, we should reconsider all of this Court's substantive due process precedents, including Griswold, Lawrence, and Obergefell. Because any substantive due process decision is "demonstrably erroneous," we have a duty to "correct the error" established in those precedents. . . . (citations omitted.)

Because the Court properly applies our substantive due process precedents to reject the fabrication of a constitutional right to abortion, and because this case does not present the opportunity to reject substantive due process entirely, I join the Court's opinion. But, in future cases, we should "follow the text of the Constitution, which sets forth certain substantive rights that cannot be taken away, and adds, beyond that, a right to due process when life, liberty, or property is to be taken away." Carlton, 512 U.S. at 42 (opinion of Scalia, J.). Substantive due process conflicts with that textual command and has harmed our country in many ways. Accordingly, we should eliminate it from our jurisprudence at the earliest opportunity.

(The concurring opinions of Justice Kavanaugh and Chief Justice Roberts are omitted.)

Justice BREYER, Justice SOTOMAYOR, and Justice KAGAN, dissenting.

. . . Roe and Casey well understood the difficulty and divisiveness of the abortion issue. The Court knew that Americans hold profoundly different views about the "moral[ity]" of "terminating a pregnancy, even in its earliest stage." Casey. And the Court recognized that "the State has legitimate interests from the outset of the pregnancy in protecting" the "life of the fetus that may become a child." So the Court struck a balance, as it often does when values and goals compete. It held that the State could prohibit abortions after fetal viability, so long as the ban contained exceptions to safeguard a woman's life or health. It held that even before viability, the State could regulate the abortion procedure in multiple and meaningful ways. But until the viability line was crossed, the Court held, a State could not impose a "substantial obstacle" on a woman's "right to elect the procedure" as she (not the government) thought proper, in light of all the circumstances and complexities of her own life. . . .

Today, the Court discards that balance. It says that from the very moment of fertilization, a woman has no rights to speak of. A State can force her to bring a pregnancy to term, even at the steepest personal and familial costs. An abortion restriction, the majority holds, is permissible whenever rational, the lowest level of scrutiny known to the law. And because, as the Court has often stated, protecting fetal life is rational, States will feel free to enact all manner of restrictions. The Mississippi law at issue here bars abortions after the 15th week of pregnancy. Under the majority's ruling, though, another State's law could do so after ten weeks, or five or three or one — or, again, from the moment of fertilization. States have already passed such laws, in anticipation of today's ruling. More will follow. Some States have enacted laws extending to all forms of abortion procedure, including taking medication in one's own home. They have passed laws without any exceptions for when the woman is the victim of rape or incest. Under those laws, a woman will have to bear her rapist's child or a young girl her father's — no matter if doing so will destroy her life. So too, after today's ruling, some States may compel women to carry to term a fetus with severe physical anomalies — for example, one afflicted with Tay-Sachs disease, sure to die within a few years of birth. States may even argue that a prohibition on abortion need make no provision for protecting a woman from risk of death or physical harm. Across a vast array of circumstances, a State will be able to impose its moral choice on a woman and coerce her to give birth to a child.

Enforcement of all these draconian restrictions will also be left largely to the States' devices. A State can of course impose criminal penalties on abortion providers, including lengthy prison sentences. But some States will not stop there. Perhaps, in the wake of today's decision, a state law will criminalize the woman's conduct too, incarcerating or fining her for daring to seek or obtain an abortion. And as Texas has recently shown, a State can turn neighbor against neighbor, enlisting fellow citizens in the effort to root out anyone who tries to get an abortion, or to assist another in doing so.

The majority tries to hide the geographically expansive effects of its holding. Today's decision, the majority says, permits "each State" to address abortion as it pleases. That is cold comfort, of course, for the poor woman who cannot get the money to fly to a distant State for a procedure. Above all others, women lacking financial resources will suffer from today's decision. In any event, interstate restrictions will also soon be in the offing. After this decision, some States may block women from traveling out of State to obtain abortions, or even from receiving abortion medications from out of State. Some may criminalize efforts, including the provision of information or funding, to help women gain access to other States' abortion services. Most threatening of all, no language in today's decision stops the Federal Government from prohibiting abortions nationwide, once again from the moment of conception and without exceptions for rape or incest. If that happens, "the views of [an individual State's] citizens" will not matter. The challenge for a woman will be to finance a trip not to "New York [or] California" but to Toronto. [citing Kavanaugh, J., concurring]. . . .

And no one should be confident that this majority is done with its work. The right Roe and Casey recognized does not stand alone. To the contrary, the Court has linked it for decades to other settled freedoms involving bodily integrity, familial relationships, and procreation. Most obviously, the right to terminate a pregnancy arose straight out of the right to purchase and use contraception. See Griswold v. Connecticut, 381 U.S. 479 (1965); Eisenstadt v. Baird, 405 U.S. 438 (1972). In turn, those rights led, more recently, to rights of same-sex intimacy and marriage. See Lawrence v. Texas, 539 U.S. 558 (2003); Obergefell v. Hodges, 576 U.S. 644 (2015). They are all part of the same constitutional fabric, protecting autonomous decisionmaking over the most personal of life decisions. The majority (or to be more accurate, most of it) is eager to tell us today that nothing it does "cast[s] doubt on precedents that do not concern abortion." cf. (Thomas, J., concurring). But how could that be? The lone rationale for what the majority does today is that the right to elect an abortion is not "deeply rooted in history": Not until Roe, the majority argues, did people think abortion fell within the Constitution's guarantee of liberty. The same could be said, though, of most of the rights the majority claims it is not tampering with. The majority could write just as long an opinion showing, for example, that until the mid- 20th century, "there was no support in American law for a constitutional right to obtain [contraceptives]." So one of two things must be true. Either the majority does not really believe in its own reasoning. Or if it does, all rights that have no history stretching back to the mid-19th century are insecure. Either the mass of the majority's opinion is hypocrisy, or additional constitutional rights are under threat. It is one or the other.

One piece of evidence on that score seems especially salient: The majority's cavalier approach to overturning this Court's precedents. Stare decisis . . . is a doctrine of judicial modesty and humility. Those qualities are not evident in today's opinion. The majority has no good reason for the upheaval in law and society it sets off. Roe and Casey have been the law of the land for decades, shaping women's expectations of their choices when an unplanned pregnancy occurs. Women have relied on the availability of abortion both in structuring their relationships and in planning their lives. The legal framework Roe and Casey developed to balance the competing interests in this sphere has proved workable in courts across the country. No recent developments, in either law or fact, have eroded or cast doubt on those precedents. Nothing, in short, has changed. . . . Today, the proclivities of individuals rule. The Court departs from its obligation to faithfully and impartially apply the law. We dissent.

NOTES AND QUESTIONS

1. The majority opinion's history of abortion regulation, omitted in large part from the excerpt above, has received substantial criticism. *See* Aziz Huq, Alito's Case for Overturning Roe Is Weak for a Reason, Politico, May 3, 2022. Does a prior history of criminalization of conduct bar later constitutional protection for it?

2. How do the majority and dissenting opinions approach the impact of pregnancy on people's equal standing and opportunity? Justice Alito, writing for the majority, implies that federal legislation (the Pregnancy Discrimination Act and the Family Medical Leave Act, for example) and state policies (allowing "safe haven" drop-offs of newborns at pre-determined sites and adoption laws) have reduced the burdens of pregnancy. Why would the burden that pregnancy imposes matter to the question of whether the constitution protects a right to abortion?

3. At the time this book was written, over a dozen states have enacted laws that restrict abortion in almost all circumstances from the earliest stages of pregnancy. Before *Dobbs*, research demonstrated that the majority of people who seek abortions live just at or below the poverty line. The Turnaway Study tracked people over a five year period who sought an abortion but were denied one. They suffered financially, socially, and developmentally when compared to a similar group that terminated their pregnancies. The cohort "turned away" from terminating a pregnancy was more likely to report debt, missed educational and employment opportunities, problems in raising the children they had, and mental as well as physical health problems. Diana Greene Foster, The Turnaway Study: Ten Years, A Thousand Women, and the Consequences of Having—or Being Denied—an Abortion (2021).

4. The maternal mortality rate in the United States is higher than in other high-income countries. The dissenting justices in *Dobbs* wrote:

> Mississippi's own record illustrates how little facts on the ground have changed since Roe and Casey, notwithstanding the majority's supposed "modern developments." Sixty-two percent of pregnancies in Mississippi are unplanned, yet Mississippi does not require insurance to cover contraceptives and prohibits educators from demonstrating proper contraceptive use. The State neither bans pregnancy discrimination nor requires provision of paid parental leave. It has strict eligibility requirements for Medicaid and nutrition assistance, leaving many women and families without basic medical care or enough food. Although 86 percent of pregnancy-related deaths in the State are due to postpartum complications, Mississippi rejected federal funding to provide a year's worth of Medicaid coverage to women after giving birth. Perhaps unsurprisingly, health outcomes in Mississippi are abysmal for both women and children. Mississippi has the highest infant mortality rate in the country, and some of the highest rates for preterm birth, low birthweight, cesarean section, and maternal death. It is approximately 75 times more dangerous for a woman in the State to carry a pregnancy to term than to have an abortion (citations omitted).

Numerous reports have documented the scarcity of maternal care providers and services in various regions across the country. How might bans on abortion affect the number of births and thus the availability of maternal healthcare? How will decreased access to maternal healthcare affect people's decisions to terminate pregnancies outside the law, using self-managed means? *See* Rachel Rebouché, The Public Health Turn in Reproductive Rights, 78 Wash. & Lee L. Rev. 1355 (2021) (tracing the trajectory of self-managed abortion with or without a constitutional right to abortion).

5. The dissenting opinion in *Dobbs* notes the racial disparity in maternal mortality rates: a ban on abortions increases maternal mortality by 21 percent, with white women facing a 13 percent increase and Black women facing a 33 percent increase. What role does race play in the *Dobbs* opinions?

2. Substantive Due Process Rights after *Dobbs*

The dissenting Justices in *Dobbs* expressed deep skepticism that other rights protected by the due process clause of the Fourteenth Amendment would not be affected by the majority's holding:

> Throughout our history, the sphere of protected liberty has expanded, bringing in individuals formerly excluded. In that way, the constitutional values of liberty and equality go hand in hand; they do not inhabit the hermetically sealed containers the majority portrays. So before Roe and Casey, the Court expanded in successive cases those who could claim the right to marry — though their relationships would have been outside the law's protection in the mid-19th century. See, e.g., Loving (interracial couples); Turner v. Safley, 482 U.S. 78 (1987) (prisoners); see also, e.g., Stanley v. Illinois, 405 U.S. 645, 541-542 (1972) (offering constitutional protection to untraditional "family unit[s]"). And after Roe and Casey, of course, the Court continued in that vein . . .
>
> Faced with all these connections between Roe/Casey and judicial decisions recognizing other constitutional rights, the majority tells everyone not to worry. It can (so it says) neatly extract the right to choose from the constitutional edifice without affecting any associated rights. (Think of someone telling you that the Jenga tower simply will not collapse.) . . . Should the audience for these too-much-repeated protestations be duly satisfied? We think not . . . .
>
> Even placing the concurrence to the side, the assurance in today's opinion still does not work. Or at least that is so if the majority is serious about its sole reason for overturning Roe and Casey: the legal status of abortion in the 19th century. . . . According to the majority, no liberty interest is present — because (and only because) the law offered no protection to the woman's choice in the 19th century. But here is the rub. The law also did not then (and would not for ages) protect a wealth of other things. It did not protect the rights recognized in Lawrence and Obergefell to same-sex intimacy and marriage. It did not protect the right recognized in Loving to marry across racial lines. It did not protect the right recognized in Griswold to contraceptive use. For that matter, it did not protect the right recognized in Skinner v. Oklahoma ex rel. Williamson, 316 U.S. 535 (1942), not to be sterilized without consent. So if the majority is right in its legal analysis, all those decisions were wrong, and all those matters properly belong to the States too — whatever the particular state interests involved. And if that is true, it is impossible to understand (as a matter of logic and principle) how the majority can say that its opinion today does not threaten — does not even "undermine" — any number of other constitutional rights. . . .
>
> By overruling Roe, Casey, and more than 20 cases reaffirming or applying the constitutional right to abortion, the majority abandons stare decisis, a principle central to the rule of law.

142 S. Ct. at 2329 – 2333. Justice Thomas, in his concurring opinion, argued that, "[I]n future cases, we should reconsider all of this Court's substantive due process precedents, including *Griswold, Lawrence,* and *Obergefell.* Because any substantive due process decision is 'demonstrably erroneous,' we have a duty to 'correct the error' established in those precedents. After overruling these demonstrably erroneous decisions, the question would remain whether other constitutional provisions guarantee the myriad rights that our substantive due process cases have generated." 142 S. Ct. at 2301-2302.

NOTES AND QUESTIONS

1. Given Justice Thomas's concurrence and the test employed by the majority opinion regarding the "history and tradition" of constitutional protection, do you agree with the dissent that "no one should be confident that the majority is done with its work"?

2. *Dobbs* sets out a rational basis test for abortion regulation. Under that test, "States may regulate abortion for legitimate reasons, and when such regulations are challenged under the

Constitution, courts cannot 'substitute their social and economic beliefs for the judgment of legislative bodies'" 142 S. Ct. at 2283-2284. Legitimate reasons include "respect for and preservation of prenatal life at all stages of development; the protection of maternal health and safety; the elimination of particularly gruesome or barbaric medical procedures; the preservation of the integrity of the medical profession; the mitigation of fetal pain; and the prevention of discrimination on the basis of race, sex, or disability." *Id.*

These interests allow states not only to ban abortion but potentially to enact requirements that *Roe* and *Casey* prohibited. For example, *Casey* invalidated the legislative provision that required married women to notify spouses of their intent to seek an abortion. *Casey* followed the earlier case, Planned Parenthood of Central Missouri v. Danforth 428 U.S. 52 (1976). In *Danforth*, the Court held:

> It seems manifest that, ideally, the decision to terminate a pregnancy should be one concurred in by both the wife and her husband. No marriage may be viewed as harmonious or successful if the marriage partners are fundamentally divided on so important and vital an issue. But it is difficult to believe that the goal of fostering mutuality and trust in a marriage, and of strengthening the marital relationship and the marriage institution, will be achieved by giving the husband a veto power exercisable for any reason whatsoever or for no reason at all. Even if the State had the ability to delegate to the husband a power it itself could not exercise, it is not at all likely that such action would further, as the District Court majority phrased it, the "interest of the state in protecting the mutuality of decisions vital to the marriage relationship." . . . The obvious fact is that when the wife and the husband disagree on this decision, the view of only one of the two marriage partners can prevail. Inasmuch as it is the woman who physically bears the child and who is the more directly and immediately affected by the pregnancy, as between the two, the balance weighs in her favor.

428 U.S. at 71. Is a spousal notification law constitutional under the rational-basis test of *Dobbs*? Suppose that a husband brought an action to enjoin a wife from having a legal abortion, but the state in which the abortion would occur required spousal notification. Suppose he announced a readiness to take sole custody of the child upon delivery, if the mother so desired. What legal arguments might a pregnant person make against spousal notification or consent?

3. States may now restrict abortion from the earliest stages of pregnancy, ban it altogether, and place any number of restrictions on abortion access, including, presumably, requiring spousal notification. The *Dobbs* dissent highlighted the interstate and interjurisdictional conflicts that will arise as each state legislates abortion rights without federal constitutional protection for pre-viability abortion:

> Anyone concerned about workability should consider the majority's substitute standard. The majority says a law regulating or banning abortion "must be sustained if there is a rational basis on which the legislature could have thought that it would serve legitimate state interests." [T]he majority lists interests like "respect for and preservation of prenatal life," "protection of maternal health," elimination of certain "medical procedures," "mitigation of fetal pain," and others. This Court will surely face critical questions about how that test applies. Must a state law allow abortions when necessary to protect a woman's life and health? And if so, exactly when? How much risk to a woman's life can a State force her to incur, before the Fourteenth Amendment's protection of life kicks in? Suppose a patient with pulmonary hypertension has a 30-to-50 percent risk of dying with ongoing pregnancy; is that enough? And short of death, how much illness or injury can the State require her to accept, consistent with the Amendment's protection of liberty and equality? Further, the Court may face questions about the application of abortion regulations to medical care most people view as quite different from abortion. What about the morning-after pill? IUDs? In vitro fertilization? And how about the use of dilation and evacuation or medication for miscarriage management?

Finally, the majority's ruling today invites a host of questions about interstate conflicts. [S]ee generally D. Cohen, G. Donley & R. Rebouché, The New Abortion Battleground, 123 Colum. L. Rev. (forthcoming 2023). Can a State bar women from traveling to another State to obtain an abortion? Can a State prohibit advertising out-of-state abortions or helping women get to out-of-state providers? Can a State interfere with the mailing of drugs used for medication abortions? The Constitution protects travel and speech and interstate commerce, so today's ruling will give rise to a host of new constitutional questions. Far from removing the Court from the abortion issue, the majority puts the Court at the center of the coming "interjurisdictional abortion wars."

In short, the majority does not save judges from unwieldy tests or extricate them from the sphere of controversy.

142 S. Ct. at 2336-2337. A number of states have passed laws, so-called shield laws, that anticipate attacks on their providers and those that assist providers who offer services to out-of-state patients. At the same time, states like Texas are weighing measures to have their laws reach outside of state borders to penalize abortion travel.

4. Most states have kept their pre-*Dobbs* abortion laws in place, including parental involvement requirements. These laws require a minor, usually under 18 years of age, to notify and seek permission from a parent before an abortion. Thus, the end of *Roe* has not meant the end of abortion regulation even in states that have not banned abortion. Rachel Rebouché & Mary Ziegler, There's No Knowing What Will Happen When *Roe* Falls, The Atlantic, Apr. 25, 2022, https://www.theatlantic.com/ideas/archive/2022/04/abortion-access-states-scotus-roe-casey-reverse/629579/.

5. Overturning constitutional protection for abortion on due process grounds does not mean that other federal and state constitutional provisions might not be violated by a state limit on abortion. At the time of writing, several state laws have been enjoined under state constitutional rights to bodily autonomy or equality, for example. Guttmacher Institute, Abortion Policy in the Absence of Roe, August 1, 2022, https://www.guttmacher.org/state-policy/explore/abortion-policy-absence-roe.

6. Can constitutional protection for contraceptives survive Justice Alito's test as the dissent suggests may not? Contraceptives, like abortion, have a history of criminalization until fairly recently. *See* Lara V. Marks, Sexual Chemistry: A History of the Contraceptive Pill xiii-xvii (2011). What about constitutional protection for newer forms of reproductive health decisionmaking, such as receiving gender-affirming care? Does *Dobbs* close the door to constitutional protection for rights that have not, until this point, been accorded constitutional recognition?

PROBLEM

You are a law clerk to Justice Groat of your state supreme court. The court has taken an appeal in a case of consolidated matters arising under a recently adopted law that bans abortion from the earliest stages of pregnancy. The law also creates a private cause of action, which can be pursued by any state resident, to sue any person "aiding and abetting" an illegal abortion as defined by the state. Groups opposing abortion have sued several parents and spouses who assisted their children or spouses in seeking abortion care out of state. Groups supportive of abortion rights argue that the statute encroaches on constitutional protections for family rights and the right to travel protected under the due process clause of the Fourteenth Amendment. Prepare a memorandum that will assist your judge in understanding the relevant constitutional law and family law issues.

CHAPTER 3

ENTERING CEREMONIAL MARRIAGE

To state the requirements for getting married seems simplicity itself. The parties must agree to marry; they must be generally eligible ("competent") to marry; they must be eligible to marry each other; and they must go through whatever forms are required for marriage in the state where they intend to marry. As we examine the law in this area, what seems simple will become more complex. States differ regarding the nature of the requisite agreement. The weight given to compliance with statutory forms for marriage also differs. Laws regarding eligibility to marry differ from state to state and are potentially qualified by constitutional doctrines concerning the power of the state to limit entrance into marriage. Moreover, people tend not to stay put, creating circumstances in which a court in one jurisdiction must decide what effect will be given to marriages contracted in another state or nation.

Finally, whether any given marriage is valid may vary from time to time and from purpose to purpose. As we will see in this chapter, marriage can be—and perhaps ordinarily is—viewed in terms of the social and economic rights and duties of spouses. However, that relationship also is as important for determining the various rights, incidents, and benefits that depend on marital or family relationships as it is for its own sake. A variety of social institutions employ familial terms to express the relationships and obligations with which these institutions are concerned; for example, immigration law accords to "spouses of American citizens" a special position, and "spouses" of decedents have an established priority for inheritance purposes and for possible entitlements of workers' compensation and Social Security benefits. To some considerable extent, "one can accurately imagine the family as a hub around which [various intermediate social systems] turn . . . in [their] reliance . . . on family relationships." Lee E. Teitelbaum, Placing the Family in Context, 22 U.C. Davis L. Rev. 801, 818 (1989). Because the various institutional interests that draw on family relationships have their own purposes, however, it is not surprising to find that a marriage may be considered valid for one purpose but not for another.

A. THE AGREEMENT TO MARRY

Lutwak v. United States
344 U.S. 604 (1952)

MINTON, J. The petitioners, Marcel Max Lutwak, Munio Knoll, and Regina Treitler, together with Leopold Knoll and Grace Klemtner, were indicted on six counts in the Northern District of Illinois, Eastern Division. The first count charged conspiracy to commit substantive offenses set forth in the remaining five counts and conspiracy "to defraud the United States of and concerning its governmental function and right of administering" the immigration laws and the Immigration and Naturalization Service, by obtaining the illegal entry into this country of three aliens as spouses of honorably discharged veterans. Grace Klemtner was dismissed from the indictment before the trial. . . . The jury acquitted Leopold Knoll and convicted the three petitioners on the conspiracy count. The Court of Appeals affirmed, and we granted certiorari.

We are concerned here only with the conviction of the petitioners of the alleged conspiracy. Petitioner Regina Treitler is the sister of Munio Knoll and Leopold Knoll, and the petitioner Lutwak is their nephew. Munio Knoll had been married in Poland in 1932 to one Maria Knoll. There is some evidence that Munio and Maria were divorced in 1942, but the existence and validity of this divorce are not determinable from the record. At the time of the inception of the conspiracy, in the summer of 1947, Munio, Maria and Leopold were refugees from Poland, living in Paris, France, while Regina Treitler and Lutwak lived in Chicago, Illinois. Petitioner Treitler desired to get her brothers into the United States.

Alien spouses of honorably discharged veterans of World War II were permitted to enter this country under the provisions of the so-called War Brides Act. . . .

The first count of the indictment charged that the petitioners conspired to have three honorably discharged veterans journey to Paris and go through marriage ceremonies with Munio, Leopold and Maria. The brothers and Maria would then accompany their new spouses to the United States and secure entry into this country by representing themselves as alien spouses of World War II veterans. It was further a part of the plan that the marriages were to be in form only, solely for the purpose of enabling Munio, Leopold and Maria to enter the United States. The parties to the marriages were not to live together as husband and wife, and thereafter would take whatever legal steps were necessary to sever the legal ties. It was finally alleged that the petitioners conspired to conceal these acts in order to prevent disclosure of the conspiracy to the immigration authorities.

The conspiracy to commit substantive offenses consisted in that part of the plan by which each of the aliens was to make a false statement to the immigration authorities by representing in his application for admission that he was married to his purported spouse, and to conceal from the immigration authorities that he had gone through a marriage ceremony solely for the purpose of gaining entry into this country with the understanding that he and his purported spouse would not live together as man and wife, but would sever the formal bonds of the ostensible marriage when the marriage had served its fraudulent purpose. . . .

From the evidence favorable to the Government, the jury could reasonably have believed that the following acts and transactions took place, and that the petitioners conspired to bring them about. Lutwak, a World War II veteran, was selected to marry Maria Knoll, his aunt by marriage. He went to Paris where he went through a marriage ceremony with Maria. They traveled to the United States, entering the port of New York on September 9, 1947. They represented to the immigration authorities that Maria was the wife of Lutwak, and upon that representation Maria was admitted. They never lived together as man and wife, and within a few months Munio and Maria commenced living together in this country as man and wife, holding themselves out as such. Lutwak, in the meantime, represented himself to friends as an unmarried man. Lutwak and Maria were divorced on March 31, 1950.

Lutwak and Mrs. Treitler also found two women — Bessie Benjamin Osborne and Grace Klemtner — who were honorably discharged veterans of World War II, and who were willing to marry Munio and Leopold so that the brothers could come to the United States. Bessie Osborne was introduced to Treitler by Lutwak, and went to Paris accompanied by Treitler. There she went through a pretended marriage ceremony with Munio Knoll, and on their arrival at New York City, Munio was admitted on November 13, 1947, on the representation that he was married to Bessie Osborne. The marriage was never consummated and was never intended to be. The parties separated after entering the United States, and they never lived together as husband and wife at any time. Bessie Osborne's suit for divorce from Munio was pending at the time of the trial.

Still later, Grace Klemtner, who was also a World War II veteran and an acquaintance of Regina Treitler, went to Paris and went through a pretended marriage ceremony with Leopold. They then traveled to the United States, where Leopold was admitted on December 5, 1947, upon the representation that he was the husband of Grace Klemtner. They immediately separated after their entry into this country, and they never lived together as husband and wife at any time until about the time Grace Klemtner appeared before the grand jury which returned the indictment. This was approximately April 1, 1950, more than two years after the marriage ceremony in Paris. Bessie Osborne and Grace Klemtner received a substantial fee for participating in these marriage ceremonies. . . .

At the trial, it was undisputed that Maria, Munio and Leopold had gone through formal marriage ceremonies with Lutwak, Bess Osborne and Grace Klemtner, respectively. Petitioners contended that, regardless of the intentions of the parties at the time of the ceremonies, the fact that the ceremonies were performed was sufficient to establish the validity of the marriages, at least until the Government proved their invalidity under French law. They relied on the general American rule of conflict of laws that a marriage valid where celebrated is valid everywhere unless it is incestuous, polygamous or otherwise declared void by statute. Neither side presented any evidence of the French law, and the trial court ruled that in the absence of such evidence, the French law would be presumed to be the same as American law. The court later instructed the jury that "if the subjects agree to a marriage only for the sake of representing it as such to the outside world and with the understanding that they will put an end to it as soon as it has served its purpose to deceive, they have never really agreed to be married at all." The petitioners claim that the trial court erred in presuming that the French law relating to the validity of marriages is the same as American law, and they further contend that even under American law these marriages are valid.

We do not believe that the validity of the marriages is material. No one is being prosecuted for an offense against the marital relation. We consider the marriage ceremonies only as a part of the conspiracy to defraud the United States and to commit offenses against the United States. In the circumstances of this case, the ceremonies were only a step in the fraudulent scheme and actions taken by the parties to the conspiracy. By directing in the War Brides Act that "alien spouses" of citizen war veterans should be admitted into this country, Congress intended to make it possible for veterans who had married aliens to have their families join them in this country without the long delay involved in qualifying under the proper immigration quota. Congress did not intend to provide aliens with an easy means of circumventing the quota system by fake marriages in which neither of the parties ever intended to enter into the marital relationship; that petitioners so believed is evidenced by their care in concealing from the immigration authorities that the ostensible husbands and wives were to separate immediately after their entry into this country and were never to live together as husband and wife. The common understanding of a marriage, which Congress must have had in mind when it made provision for "alien *spouses*" in the War Brides Act, is that the two parties have undertaken to establish a life together and assume certain duties and obligations. Such was not the case here, or so the jury might reasonably have found. Thus, when one of the aliens stated that he was married, and omitted to explain the true nature of his marital relationship, his statement did, and was intended to, carry with it implications of a state of facts which were not in fact true.

Because the validity of the marriages is not material, the cases involving so-called limited purpose marriages,[1] cited by petitioners to support their contention that the marriages in the

---

1. *E.g.*, Schibi v. Schibi, 136 Conn. 196, 69 A.2d 831; Hanson v. Hanson, 287 Mass. 154, 191 N.E. 673. These and other cases cited by petitioners are collected and discussed in a note, 14 A.L.R.2d 624 (1950).

instant case are valid, are inapplicable. All of those cases are suits for annulment in which the court was requested to grant relief to one of the parties to a marriage on the basis of his own admission that the marriage had been a sham. Where the annulment was denied, one or more of the following factors influenced the court: (1) a reluctance to permit the parties to use the annulment procedure as a quick and painless substitute for divorce, particularly because this might encourage people to marry hastily and inconsiderately; (2) a belief that the parties should not be permitted to use the courts as the means of carrying out their own secret schemes; and (3) a desire to prevent injury to innocent third parties, particularly children of the marriage. These factors have no application in the circumstances of the instant case . . . . In the instant case . . . there was no good faith — no intention to marry and consummate the marriages even for a day. With the legal consequences of such ceremonies under other circumstances, either in the United States or France, we are not concerned. . . .

NOTES AND QUESTIONS

1. If Lutwak had sued for an annulment, rather than a divorce, on the basis that he and Maria did not really intend to take on the rights and duties of marriage, should his petition be granted? The defendants in *Lutwak* cited "limited purpose marriage" cases that reject such claims. One of these was Schibi v. Schibi, 69 A.2d 831 (Conn. 1949), in which the parties married solely for the purpose of legitimating an unborn child. They did not intend to, nor did they, assume the relationship of spouses. Subsequently, the husband sought an annulment on the ground that the marriage was void for lack of mutual consent of the parties. The court denied that relief, saying:

> The law is clear that mutual consent is essential to a valid marriage. . . . In his complaint, the plaintiff alleges as the only basis for relief that at the time of the ceremony there was neither consent nor intent to incur the obligations of a marriage contract, and his prayers for relief are that the purported marriage be annulled and declared void. The sole question presented to the court for determination was whether the marriage was void because there was no mutual consent of the parties. That there was such mutual consent is implicit in the court's conclusion that the parties were legally married. Whether this conclusion is supported by the subordinate facts is the question decisive of the appeal.
>
> . . . The result reached is in accord with this general principle relative to the effect of prenuptial agreements: "Once a marriage has been properly solemnized and the obligations of married life undertaken, its validity cannot be affected by an antenuptial agreement not to live together, nor by an agreement previously entered into that the marriage should not be valid and binding, nor because one or even both of the parties did not intend it to be a permanent relation." . . .

69 A.2d at 832-834.

Why does the majority opinion in *Lutwak* treat the validity of the marriages as a matter of domestic relations law as "immaterial" to the immigration prosecution?

Modern cases continue to hold that sham immigration marriages are not void, even though they may violate federal immigration law. The Kansas Court of Appeals has said, however, that such a marriage may be voidable under a statutory provision allowing a court to annul a marriage "for any other reason justifying rescission." An example is a marriage that has an illegal purpose contrary to public policy. In re Marriage of Kidane, 389 P.3d 212 (Kan. App. 2017).

2. Assume that one of the defendants in *Lutwak*, after serving time in prison, married some third person. Would he or she be subject to prosecution for bigamy in New York? If one of the defendants were hospitalized, would the person whom he or she had married in France be responsible for that expense?

3. The validity of a marriage for limited purposes is important in almost any area where marriage confers a benefit or avoids a burden. Consider the following examples:

In United States v. Mathis, the defendant's former wife had cooperated with law enforcement authorities. Mathis told her that, if she would remarry him, friends would give her $25,000; if she did not, she and her baby would be killed. She and the defendant remarried after her (inculpatory) grand jury testimony but before trial. At trial, she invoked the husband-wife testimonial privilege, which the court rejected. "It is well established that an exception to the husband-wife privilege exists if the trial judge determines that the marriage is a fraud. Lutwak v. United States, 344 U.S. 604 (1953). . . ." 559 F.2d 294, 298 (5th Cir. 1977).

Mpirilis v. Hellenic Lines, Ltd., 323 F. Supp. 865 (S.D. Tex. 1970), involved a wrongful death action under the Jones Act to recover damages by reason of the fatal injuries suffered by the decedent while working on a ship in New York harbor. The plaintiff and the decedent were married on the day of the latter's arrival in the United States, allegedly so that he could gain entry into this country on a preferred basis. Assuming that the parties agreed not to assume any of the normal duties, obligations, or incidents of marriage, should the plaintiff be entitled to wrongful death recovery? Is the case distinguishable from *Lutwak*?

NOTE: "VOID" AND "VOIDABLE" MARRIAGES

In a simple world, marriages would be either void or valid. This is not, however, a simple world. Analyzing the effect of both the formal and substantive defects in marriage sometimes requires an understanding of one of the genuinely arcane areas of law: the distinction between a "void" and a "voidable" marriage. What makes the distinction difficult is that, while a divorce supposes a valid marriage that is dissolved after some time, an annulment has been understood to declare the *in*validity of the marriage *ab initio*. In point of law, an annulled marriage is one that never existed. One might ask, therefore, how there can be a difference between a void marriage and a voidable marriage, if the result in either case is the nonexistence of the marriage at any time.

The differences between the two kinds of marriage are in substantial respects procedural. A "voidable" marriage has at least potential validity. It is valid unless its nullity has been declared. Moreover, the nullity of a voidable marriage ordinarily can be sought only by one of the parties to the marriage and only during the lifetime of the marriage. If, for example, the parties marry at age 17 when the local law permits marriages only by persons who are 18 years or older, their marriage could be annulled at the instance of at least the underaged spouse, and if the annulment is granted, the formal result is that they were never married. However, the marriage can become a valid marriage, and if the parties never seek its annulment, the marriage will become valid when they continue to live as husband and wife after reaching the age of consent. *See, e.g.*, Powell v. Powell, 86 A.2d 331 (N.J. 1952); Jones v. Jones, 37 S.E.2d 711 (Ga. 1946). *See also* Medlin v. Medlin, 981 P.2d 1087 (Ariz. App. 1999).

A "void" marriage in theory requires no declaration of invalidity. Moreover, the voidness of the marriage can be declared at any time and, generally, at the instance of any interested party. Nor, in principle, can a void marriage ever become a valid marriage.

The distinction between void and voidable marriages has its roots in English ecclesiastical law. Marital disabilities were of two types: civil (which included insanity and prior marriage) and canonical (which included marriages within forbidden degrees of kinship). Civil disabilities rendered a marriage void; canon law disabilities made it voidable. *See* Note, "Void" and "Voidable" Under Marriage Consanguinity Statutes, 17 Iowa L. Rev. 254 (1932). The continued viability of this distinction is doubtful.

Some of the implications of voidness have been eliminated. For example, the children of a void marriage were illegitimate; those of a voidable marriage were legitimate unless the marriage was annulled. *See* Matter of Moncrief's Will, 139 N.E. 550 (N.Y. 1923); 1 Homer H. Clark, Jr., Domestic Relations in the United States 238 (1987). However, modern statutes now generally treat children of an invalid marriage as legitimate under most circumstances. Similarly, alimony is in principle inconsistent with a void marriage; nonetheless, some states provide for alimony upon annulment—*e.g.*, Conn. Gen. Stat. Ann. §46b-60 (2022); Or. Rev. Stat. §§107.095, 107.105 (2022). Despite such a statute, the Colorado Court of Appeals held that courts still have the ultimate responsibility to issue economic orders that are equitable and that a woman who fraudulently induced a man to marry her was not entitled to a share of the property or to spousal support. In re Marriage of Joel & Roohi, 404 P.3d 1251 (Colo. App. 2012). Other states retain the broader traditional rule that spousal support and property division cannot be ordered if the marriage was invalid. *See, e.g.*, Wright v. Hall (Ga. 2013).

PROBLEMS

1. Virgil and Gretta were an unmarried couple who had sex one time. Several months later, Gretta told Virgil that she was pregnant by him. They decided to marry in order to "give the baby a name." They also agreed, however, that they would not cohabit after the marriage, that there would be no sharing of incomes or support (except for the child), and that they would get a divorce after the child turned one year old.

They married and went their separate ways. Virgil has, however, fallen in love with Beatrice in the meantime. Beatrice is Roman Catholic and has serious problems with marrying someone who is divorced. Virgil decides to seek an annulment of his marriage to Gretta rather than a divorce. Will the annulment be granted?

2. Roy and Dale have been friends for some time. At a party one evening, their friends decide to entertain themselves by making fun of Roy and Dale's friendship and whether it will ever "go anywhere." Because they had had a couple of drinks and because they were tired of being teased, Roy and Dale decide to go through a marriage ceremony; but, after a few days, when the joke has worn off, they plan to secure an annulment. They do not intend to cohabit or live together or in any other way act as spouses. They go through a marriage ceremony before a justice of the peace. A week later, Roy brings an annulment action. Should the annulment be granted?

NOTE: MARRIAGE-RELATED IMMIGRATION RULES

A citizen can obtain a K-1 or fiancée visa, allowing a noncitizen to enter the United States for up to 90 days to marry the petitioner. A citizen who marries a noncitizen (either before or after the noncitizen enters the United States) may then petition the U.S. Citizenship and Immigration Services (USCIS) to classify the noncitizen as an "immediate relative." Normally, "immediate relative" status permits a noncitizen to obtain permanent residency and, eventually, citizenship without having to apply and enter the United States as part of his or her country of origin's immigration quota. 8 U.S.C. §1151(b). In 2021, about 740,000 people were granted legal permanent-resident status; of these, 385,396, or 52.1 percent, were spouses of the petitioning citizen. Irene Gibson, U.S. Legal Permanent Residents: 2021 tbl. 2 (Dep't Homeland Sec. Office of Immigration Statistics Apr. 2021). These figures are lower than usual because of the COVID-19 pandemic.

If the citizen spouse dies within the two-year period, surviving spouses may pursue permanent residency on their own. Abused spouses may also file their own petition. 8 U.S.C.

§1151(b)(2)(A)(i). To support a claim of abuse, the spouse must prove evidence of physical battery or extreme cruelty, joint residence with the abusive spouse, that he or she is of good character, and that the marriage was entered into in good faith. 8 U.S.C. §1154(a)(1). If the couple divorces within the first year after the petition is filed, the noncitizen spouse is still eligible if the divorce was connected to abuse.

This set of rules creates a tempting opportunity for immigration fraud, as was alleged in *Lutwak*. The most recent legislation designed to smoke out marriages whose only purpose is to obtain advantageous immigration status is the Marriage Fraud Amendments of 1986, codified in scattered sections of 8 U.S.C. The amendments provide that a foreign national who is not a permanent resident of the United States and who marries a citizen receives only a conditional immigration status, with the bona fides and continuance of the marriage to be reexamined after two years.

Procedures adopted by USCIS may include a visit to the couple's residence to see whether they actually reside together and interviews with neighbors, employers, and others to determine the existence of a marital relationship. Regulations interpreting the good faith marriage requirement say that evidence may include but is not limited to documents showing joint ownership of property, joint tenancy of a common residence, commingling of finances, birth certificates of children born to the petitioner and spouse, and affidavits sworn to or affirmed by third parties having personal knowledge of the bona fides of the marital relationship. 8 C.F.R. §204.2.

The International Marriage Broker Regulation Act (IMBRA), 8 U.S.C. §§1375a, 1184, and other sections scattered in 8 U.S.C., addresses a different problem with international marriages, abuse of women who enter the country as "mail order brides." Congress enacted the law partly in response to the murder of two "mail order brides" by their husbands early in the twenty-first century. The Act regulates marriage broker services and individuals who petition for fiancée visas.

An entity or person covered by IMBRA must collect background information about a citizen who is using its services (including any restraining orders, arrests or criminal convictions for violent crimes or prostitution-related offenses, controlled substances or alcohol abuse, current or previous marriages, the ages of any children younger than 18, and all countries and states in which the citizen has resided within the last 20 years); provide it to the foreign national; and get her consent before disclosing her contact information.

IMBRA also requires all citizens who petition for a fiancée visa to disclose criminal convictions for the offenses listed above, and a citizen will not be granted a fiancée visa more often than once every two years.

For more information, *see* Kerry Abrams, Immigration Law and the Regulation of Marriage, 91 Minn. L. Rev. 1625 (2007); Kerry Abrams, Marriage Fraud, 100 Cal. L. Rev. 1 (2012); Olga Grosh, Foreign Wives, Domestic Violence: U.S. Law Stigmatizes and Fails to Protect "Mail-Order Brides," 22 Hastings Women's L.J. 81 (2011); Christina L. Pollard, Here Come Many More Mail-Order Brides: Why IMBRA Fails Women Escaping the Russian Federation, 46 Cap. U. L. Rev. 609 (2018); Marcia A. Zug, Buying a Bride: An Engaging History of Mail-Order Matches (2016).

In re Marriage of Ramirez
81 Cal. Rptr. 3d 180 (Cal. App. 2008)

RAMIREZ, P.J. . . . Jorge, an immigrant from the State of Michoacán, Mexico, lived in the United States and sought legal residence here. His mother was a permanent resident and sponsored Jorge in his application for that status. He began his application process in 1994 or 1995 but because his mother was not a citizen herself, the process took many years.

In 1999, Jorge and Lilia were married in a religious ceremony in Moreno Valley, California. The ceremony was performed by a priest or other official from the State of Jalisco, Mexico, and an "Acta de Matrimonio" was issued. No marriage license was issued by the State of California. In 2001, Jorge and Lilia became aware that the 1999 marriage was invalid because Lilia's prior divorce had not been final for 300 days prior to the marriage. Additionally, because it was made to look as though the parties were married in Mexico, the Mexican marriage certificate would prevent Jorge from getting his green card because it would make it appear that he had not been in continuous residence in the United States.

The parties were remarried in 2001 and obtained a confidential marriage license. After the death of Jorge's mother, Lilia assumed the position as Jorge's sponsor to pursue his application for permanent residence and citizenship. In 2004, after she signed a document related to his immigration status, Jorge informed Lilia that it would be the last one. Two weeks later, in May 2004, he took Lilia out to dinner and asked for a divorce because he was in love with someone else and always had been. In June 2004, Jorge moved out.

That same month, Lilia found out who the other woman was when she overheard a conversation between Jorge and Lilia's sister Blanca. Jorge had begun an affair with Blanca prior to the 2001 marriage, and it lasted until 2005. The intercepted conversation occurred in 2005. Lilia asked her teenaged son Victor to call Blanca, who babysat for Jorge and Lilia's daughter, on her cell phone to inquire if she would be joining them for lunch with the child. Blanca, at a restaurant with Jorge, had the cell phone in her purse. Instead of pressing the stop key, she pressed the button to answer the call, so the conversation she was having with Jorge was overheard on Victor's cell phone, which Lilia and Victor listened to by activating the loudspeaker. In this conversation, Jorge professed his love for Blanca, assured her that they would be together once he got his share of money and property from Lilia, and told her that he had only married Lilia to gain permanent resident status. This conversation occurred after Jorge had moved out.

Shortly after the parties separated, an attempt was made to reach an agreement with Jorge as to the disposition of assets. Lilia has a real estate broker's license and she and Jorge had worked together in the realty business during their marriage. Lilia's attorney prepared a proposed settlement agreement listing five parcels of real property as community property, and three as Lilia's separate property. Lilia offered Jorge one of the properties, but he declined. He then filed a petition for dissolution of the marriage on April 21, 2005.

On June 22, 2005, Lilia filed a response to the petition and a request for a judgment of nullity of marriage. At the bifurcated trial relating to the status of the marriage, Jorge demonstrated he had obtained his permanent resident status in 2002. He denied having a relationship with Blanca, although several telephone messages left on Blanca's cell phone and retrieved by a close family friend of Blanca and Lilia—in addition to the conversation overheard by Lilia—belied his protestations.

The trial court concluded the 1999 marriage was void under the laws of Mexico. . . .

The court also found the second marriage was void because Jorge perpetrated a fraud on Lilia by carrying on an extramarital affair with Blanca. The court found that Jorge did not marry Lilia because he was worried about his immigration or work status; instead, the court found Jorge made false statements to Blanca about his reasons for marrying Lilia, including a need for a green card, to string her along and to delay having to make a commitment to her. Thus, the fraud related to Jorge's marrying Lilia while carrying on a sexual relationship with Blanca which he intended to maintain. The court concluded Jorge wanted to "have his cake and eat it too" by carrying on sexual relationships with both women at the same time.

The trial court held that this kind of fraud goes to the heart of the marital relationship and declared the 2001 marriage void on the ground of fraud. . . . Jorge appeals. . . .

A marriage is voidable and may be adjudged a nullity if the consent of either party was obtained by fraud. A marriage may be annulled for fraud only in an extreme case where the particular fraud goes to the very essence of the marriage relation. (In re Marriage of Meagher & Maleki (2005) 131 Cal. App. 4th 1, 3 [31 Cal. Rptr. 3d 663] (*Meagher*).) The fact represented or suppressed to induce consent to marriage will be deemed material if it relates to a matter of substance and directly affects the purpose of the party deceived in entering the marital contract. In other words, the fraud relied upon must be such as directly defeats the marriage relationship and not merely such fraud as would be sufficient to rescind an ordinary civil contract. Fraudulent intent not to perform a duty vital to the marriage state must exist in the offending spouse's mind at the moment the marriage contract is made.

A promise to be a kind, dutiful and affectionate spouse cannot be made the basis of an annulment. (Marshall v. Marshall (1931) 212 Cal. 736, 739-740 [300 P. 816].) Instead, the particular fraudulent intention must relate to the sexual or procreative aspects of marriage. In the absence of this type of fraud, the long-standing rule is that neither party may question the validity of the marriage upon the ground of express or implied representations of the other with respect to such matters as character, habits, chastity, business or social standing, financial worth or prospects, or matters of a similar nature. (*Meagher, supra*, 131 Cal. App. 4th at p. 8.) Concealment of incontinence, temper, idleness, extravagance, coldness or lack of represented fortune will not justify an annulment. (*Marshall, supra*, at p. 740.)

Other decisions demonstrate that to void a marriage, the fraud alleged must show an intention not to perform a duty vital to the marriage, which exists in the mind of the offending spouse at the time of marriage. (Millar v. Millar (1917) 175 Cal. 797 [167 P. 394] [wife concealed from husband at time of marriage that she did not intend to have sexual relations with him]; Hardesty v. Hardesty (1924) 193 Cal. 330 [223 P. 951] [wife concealed from husband at time of marriage that she was pregnant by another man]; Vileta v. Vileta (1942) 53 Cal. App. 2d 794 [128 P.2d 376] [spouse concealed from other spouse known fact of sterility at time of marriage]; In re Marriage of Liu, *supra*, 197 Cal. App. 3d 143 [wife married husband in Taiwan to acquire a green card, and never consummated the marriage].) Thus, historically, annulments based on fraud have only been granted in cases where the fraud relates in some way to the sexual, procreative or child-rearing aspects of marriage.

Here, the trial court specifically found that the fraud was unrelated to the husband's efforts to obtain permanent legal status. Instead, it found the fraud was based on Jorge's intent to continue the ongoing simultaneous sexual relationships with Lilia and Blanca at the time that he and Lilia entered into the 2001 marriage.

In rendering its judgment of nullity, the trial court relied on the decision in Schaub v. Schaub (1945) 71 Cal. App. 2d 467 [162 P.2d 966] (*Schaub*). In that case, a younger woman married an older man to obtain his real property. She had been involved in an intimate relationship with another man for many years, and conspired with her lover to marry the husband, with no intention of fulfilling the obligation of marriage to consummate the marriage. This she did, while continuing her sexual relationship with her lover. The fraud was discovered when an investigator, hired by the husband, found the wife in bed with her lover, both naked.

We read *Schaub* as not standing solely on the intent not to consummate. *Schaub* does not at any point suggest that the intent not to consummate is *the* indicator of fraud. Neither does *Schaub* anywhere indicate that the intent to continue an existing relationship with a third party is enough for a finding of fraud only when accompanied by the intent not to consummate.

Further, the court in *Schaub* points out that "The marriage in itself was a contract under which each of the parties undertook the obligations of mutual respect, *fidelity* and support [citing Civ. Code, former §155]." The *Schaub* court then concludes that the fraud consisted of the wife's intention not to perform her marriage obligations, including the obligation of fidelity, and the concealment of that from the innocent spouse. That is just what happened here. At the time he entered into the 2001 marriage, Jorge manifestly intended not to perform his marriage obligation of fidelity. That is fraud under Family Code sections 720 and 2210, subdivision (d).

Bolstering this interpretation of *Schaub*, the court in *Meagher* in fact refers to *Schaub* as justifying annulment where one party simply has the "intent to continue in an intimate relationship with a third person." That describes exactly Jorge's intent and actions at the time he and Lilia married in 2001.

Finally, as stated above, historically, annulments based on fraud have only been granted in cases where the fraud relates in some way to the sexual, procreative or child-rearing aspects of marriage. Jorge's actions here, in marrying Lilia while continuing to carry on a sexual relationship with her sister Blanca, directly relates to a sexual aspect of marriage — sexual fidelity. For emphasis, we again quote from Family Code section 720: "Husband and wife contract toward each other obligations of mutual respect, fidelity, and support." At the time of the 2001 marriage, Jorge purposely deceived Lilia into thinking that he would perform one of the central obligations of the marriage contract — the obligation of fidelity. Under Family Code sections 720 and 2210, subdivision (d), and under *Schaub* and *Meagher*, Jorge committed fraud and Lilia is entitled to a judgment of annulment.

The judgment is affirmed. Jorge is directed to pay costs on appeal.

GAUT, J., concurring. I concur with the portion of the decision relating to the nullity of the 1999 marriage. However, regarding the nullity of the 2001 marriage, I dissent. I would reverse the judgment annulling the marriage and direct the entry of a judgment of dissolution of marriage.

The majority holds that infidelity alone, disdainful as it may be, may serve as a basis for annulment on the ground of fraud, relying upon the case of Schaub v. Schaub (1945) 71 Cal. App. 2d 467 [162 P.2d 966]. That case involved a plot by a woman and her longtime lover to cheat an unsuspecting older gentleman out of a half-interest in his real property, while the wife maintained illicit extramarital relations with her lover.

In the 63 years since the *Schaub* case was decided, it has never been cited, until today, for the proposition that the infidelity of a spouse, without more, constitutes a fraud which justifies an annulment. Today's decision could have unintended repercussions in family law practice, leading to unnecessary litigation over title to property acquired by spouses during marriage which may not be considered community property if the marriage is deemed a nullity.

I would reverse the judgment of nullity of marriage and order the entry of a judgment of dissolution of marriage. Annulment should be the exception, not the rule.

NOTES AND QUESTIONS

1. The law of annulment for fraud has been heavily influenced by the law applied in English ecclesiastical courts until 1857. Even after civil courts assumed jurisdiction over matrimonial affairs, the rule was that a marriage could be annulled only for "error personae," which meant that the wrong person was married. Errors of condition or quality ("error fortunae") were not sufficient to avoid the marriage. *See* Harry W. Vanneman, Annulment of Marriage for Fraud, 9 Minn. L. Rev. 497 (1925), reprinted in Association of American Law Schools, Selected Essays on Family Law 335, 336 (1950).

Although American cases do not go as far as the traditional English view, most have restricted annulment for fraud to misrepresentations going to the "essentials" of marriage. An influential early American case, Reynolds v. Reynolds, 85 Mass. (3 Allen) 605 (1862), expressed the following rationale for this limitation:

> The great object of marriage in a civilized and Christian community is to secure the existence and permanence of the family relation, and to insure the legitimacy of offspring. It would tend to defeat this object, if error or disappointment in personal qualities or character was allowed to be the basis of proceedings on which to found a dissolution of the marriage tie. The law therefore wisely requires that persons who act on representations or belief in regard to such matters should bear the consequences which flow from contracts into which they have voluntarily entered, after they have been executed, and affords no relief for the results of a "blind credulity, however it may have been produced."

85 Mass. at 607. The plaintiff in *Reynolds*, who had never engaged in sexual relations with the defendant prior to marriage, received an annulment based on his wife's undisclosed pregnancy by another. Where is the misrepresentation? And why does this misrepresentation go to the "essentials" of marriage? Under this test, would Lilia Ramirez be entitled to an annulment?

Under the traditional view of fraud, in what sense is agreement necessary to marriage? A cause of action for fraud in an ordinary contracts case involves a representation of fact, known to be false, that is intended to and does deceive the other party to his or her detriment. How does this approach to fraud compare to the way that fraud was defined for purposes of annulling a marriage?

2. The traditional English view of the fraud that will justify annulment stands at one end of the spectrum of possible positions. New York, which sharply restricted divorce until relatively recently, is usually said to stand at the other end:

> [T]he fraud [required for annulment] need no longer "necessarily concern what is commonly called the essentials of the marriage *relation* — the rights and duties connected with cohabitation and consortium attached by law to the marital status. Any fraud is adequate which is 'material, to that degree that, had it not been practiced, the party deceived would not have consented to the marriage' and is 'of such nature as to deceive an ordinarily prudent person.'" Although it is not enough to show merely that one partner married for money and the other was disappointed [citing Woronzoff-Daschkoff v. Woronzoff-Daschkoff, 104 N.E.2d 877, 880 (N.Y. 1952)], and the decisions upon the subject of annulment have not always been uniform, there have been circumstances where misrepresentations of love and affection, with intention to make a home, were held sufficient, likewise in case of fraudulent representations concerning the legitimacy of children of the wife of a supposedly prior marriage, or concerning prior marital status. Concealment of prior marital status was held to be sufficient in Costello v. Costello; concealment of affliction with tuberculosis in Yelin v. Yelin; failure to reveal treatment of a mental disorder (schizophrenia, catatonic type) was held to be enough in Schaeffer v. Schaeffer; material misrepresentation of age in Tacchi v. Tacchi. . . .

Kober v. Kober, 211 N.E.2d 817, 819 (N.Y. 1965). In *Kober* itself, the New York Court of Appeals held that the husband's fraudulent concealment of his membership in the Nazi party during World War II and fanatical anti-Semitism were sufficient bases for annulment. *Kober* endorses a test similar to that used for ordinary contracts cases. If that is the test applied in New York, why cannot false representations regarding wealth or social position suffice? How does this test differ from the test adopted in *Ramirez*, or does it? Under either test, would falsely claiming to be in love with a would-be spouse warrant an annulment?

3. Duress, like fraud, is usually said to vitiate the consent necessary for marriage. This claim arises only occasionally now. However, the older cases generally held that duress did not exist when a man agreed to marry after being threatened with prosecution for the crimes of seduction or bastardy. Under this approach, to what extent is entrance into marriage a matter of "contract"?

4. The British Forced Marriage (Civil Protection) Act of 2007 addresses duress in a modern context. The law allows family courts to make Forced Marriage Protection Orders to protect someone from being forced into marriage. An order can also be made to protect someone who has already been forced into marriage, to help remove the person from the situation. Those who fail to obey an order may be found in contempt of court and sent to prison for up to two years. One of the first orders was issued against the father of a 22-year-old woman who tried to force her to go to Pakistan to marry one of his relatives. In another early case, a mother forced her two teenage daughters to marry their first cousins in Pakistan in July 2007. After the girls returned to the UK, they told a teacher, who called the police. The mother was convicted of inciting or causing a child to engage in sexual activity, arranging or facilitating the commission of a child sex offense, and intending to pervert the course of justice. Houriya Ahmed, Landmark Case on Forced Marriage: Mother Jailed (Centre for Social Cohesion blog, May 22, 2009).

For a discussion of the problem of forced marriages in the United States, assessment of the utility of domestic violence protective orders in such cases, and the need for legislation like that in the United Kingdom, *see* Lisa V. Martin, Restraining Forced Marriage, 18 Nev. L.J. 919 (2018).

PROBLEMS

1. Plaintiff Elizabeth Princess married the defendant, Kermit, two years ago. Prior to the marriage, Kermit seemed the ideal spouse: handsome, sober, hard-working, and sympathetic. Over the last two years, however, Elizabeth has found that her husband has a serious drinking problem, which he did not reveal; has no genuine interest in seeking a job; and is entirely unconcerned about his physical appearance or his manners. She has filed a complaint seeking an annulment on the ground that he failed to disclose his drinking problem and misrepresented his interest in seeking employment. Kermit has filed a motion to dismiss the bill for failure to state a claim. What arguments would be made by the parties in the hearing on that motion? *See* Johnston v. Johnston, 22 Cal. Rptr. 2d 253 (Cal. App. 1993) (where plaintiff alleged that defendant had "turned from a prince into a frog").

2. In 2012 Napoleon and Josephine were divorced after 30 years of marriage. In 2020 Napoleon told Josephine that he had a terminal illness from which he would die within a few years, and she agreed to remarry him so that he would not die alone. After the wedding, Napoleon did not seem to be ill, and Josephine and their son came to believe that Napoleon had lied to her. She also found a 2021 insurance form that Napoleon had signed, saying he had no medical problems. In 2022 Napoleon filed for a divorce, and Josephine cross-petitioned for a declaration that the marriage was not valid. What result under the traditional fraud test? Under *Ramirez*? Under *Kober*?

3. Jerry and Nancy had sex once while each was married to someone else; Nancy was also carrying on a long-term affair with a third man, Sam. Nine months later she gave birth to a child, but she did not tell Jerry until three years later that he was the father. At that point, Jerry and Nancy began an affair, got divorces from their spouses, and married. Twenty years later, Nancy filed for divorce, and Jerry cross-petitioned for an annulment on the basis that Nancy had fraudulently induced him to marry her by telling him that he was the father of the baby. DNA testing had proved Nancy's lover Sam to be the actual biological father. If Nancy knew that Jerry was not the biological father, does her misrepresentation amount to fraud going to the essentials of the marriage? What if she honestly thought that Jerry was the father?

4. Angela, a citizen of Colombia, met Raul, an American citizen, through an online dating service. After a brief courtship, they married, and Angela came to the United States. Raul began the process to allow Angela to obtain permanent resident status immediately. As soon as she received final approval for her green card, Angela left Raul and filed for divorce. Raul counterclaimed for annulment, claiming fraud. If the court finds that Angela never loved Raul and married him only to obtain legal residency, should the annulment be granted?

B. CONSTITUTIONAL PROTECTION FOR THE RIGHT TO MARRY

Loving v. Virginia
388 U.S. 1 (1967)

Mr. Chief Justice WARREN delivered the opinion of the Court. . . . In June 1958, two residents of Virginia, Mildred Jeter, a Negro woman, and Richard Loving, a white man, were married in the District of Columbia pursuant to its laws. Shortly after their marriage, the Lovings returned to Virginia and established their marital abode in Caroline County. At the October Term, 1958, of the Circuit Court of Caroline County, a grand jury issued an indictment charging the Lovings with violating Virginia's ban on interracial marriages. On January 6, 1959, the Lovings pleaded guilty to the charge and were sentenced to one year in jail; however, the trial judge suspended the sentence for a period of 25 years on the condition that the Lovings leave the State and not return to Virginia together for 25 years. . . .

After their convictions, the Lovings took up residence in the District of Columbia. On November 6, 1963, they filed a motion in the state trial court to vacate the judgment and set aside the sentence on the ground that the statutes which they had violated were repugnant to the Fourteenth Amendment. . . . On January 22, 1965, the state trial judge denied the motion to vacate the sentences, and the Lovings perfected an appeal to the Supreme Court of Appeals of Virginia. . . .

The Supreme Court of Appeals upheld the constitutionality of the antimiscegenation statutes and, after modifying the sentence, affirmed the convictions. The Lovings appealed this decision, and we noted probable jurisdiction. . . .

The two statutes under which appellants were convicted and sentenced are part of a comprehensive statutory scheme aimed at prohibiting and punishing interracial marriages. The Lovings were convicted of violating §20-58 of the Virginia Code:

> "Leaving State to evade law. — If any white person and colored person shall go out of this State, for the purpose of being married, and with the intention of returning, and be married out of it, and afterwards return to and reside in it, cohabiting as man and wife, they shall be punished as provided in §20-59, and the marriage shall be governed by the same law as if it had been solemnized in this State. The fact of their cohabitation here as man and wife shall be evidence of their marriage."

Section 20-59, which defines the penalty for miscegenation, provides:

> "Punishment for marriage. — If any white person intermarry with a colored person, or any colored person intermarry with a white person, he shall be guilty of a felony and shall be punished by confinement in the penitentiary for not less than one nor more than five years."

. . .

In upholding the constitutionality of these provisions in the decision below, the Supreme Court of Appeals of Virginia referred to its 1955 decision in Naim v. Naim, 197 Va. 80, 87 S.E.2d 749, as stating the reasons supporting the validity of these laws. In *Naim*, the state court concluded that the State's legitimate purposes were "to preserve the racial integrity of its citizens," and to prevent "the corruption of blood," "a mongrel breed of citizens," and "the obliteration of racial pride," obviously an endorsement of the doctrine of White Supremacy. The court also reasoned that marriage has traditionally been subject to state regulation without federal intervention, and, consequently, the regulation of marriage should be left to exclusive state control by the Tenth Amendment.

While the state court is no doubt correct in asserting that marriage is a social relation subject to the State's police power, Maynard v. Hill, 125 U.S. 190 (1888), the State does not contend in its argument before this Court that its powers to regulate marriage are unlimited notwithstanding the commands of the Fourteenth Amendment. Nor could it do so in light of Meyer v. State of Nebraska, 262 U.S. 390 (1923), and Skinner v. State of Oklahoma, 316 U.S. 535 (1942). Instead, the State argues that the meaning of the Equal Protection Clause, as illuminated by the statements of the Framers, is only that state penal laws containing an interracial element as part of the definition of the offense must apply equally to whites and Negroes in the sense that members of each race are punished to the same degree. Thus, the State contends that, because its miscegenation statutes punish equally both the white and the Negro participants in an interracial marriage, these statutes, despite their reliance on racial classifications do not constitute an invidious discrimination based upon race. The second argument advanced by the State assumes the validity of its equal application theory. The argument is that, if the Equal Protection Clause does not outlaw miscegenation statutes because of their reliance on racial classifications, the question of constitutionality would thus become whether there was any rational basis for a State to treat interracial marriages differently from other marriages. On this question, the State argues, the scientific evidence is substantially in doubt and, consequently, this Court should defer to the wisdom of the state legislature in adopting its policy of discouraging interracial marriages.

Because we reject the notion that the mere "equal application" of a statute containing racial classifications is enough to remove the classifications from the Fourteenth Amendment's proscription of all invidious racial discriminations, we do not accept the State's contention that these statutes should be upheld if there is any possible basis for concluding that they serve a rational purpose. The mere fact of equal application does not mean that our analysis of these statutes should follow the approach we have taken in cases involving no racial discrimination. . . . In these cases, involving distinctions not drawn according to race, the Court has merely asked whether there is any rational foundation for the discriminations, and has deferred to the wisdom of the state legislatures. In the case at bar, however, we deal with statutes containing racial classifications, and the fact of equal application does not immunize the statute from the very heavy burden of justification which the Fourteenth Amendment has traditionally required of state statutes drawn according to race. . . .

There can be no question but that Virginia's miscegenation statutes rest solely upon distinctions drawn according to race. The statutes proscribe generally accepted conduct if engaged in by members of different races. Over the years, this Court has consistently repudiated "(d)istinctions between citizens solely because of their ancestry" as being "odious to a free people whose institutions are founded upon the doctrine of equality." At the very least, the Equal Protection Clause demands that racial classifications, especially suspect in criminal statutes, be subjected to the "most rigid scrutiny," and, if they are ever to be upheld, they must be shown to be necessary to the accomplishment of some permissible state objective, independent of the racial discrimination which it was the object of the Fourteenth Amendment to eliminate. . . .

There is patently no legitimate overriding purpose independent of invidious racial discrimination which justifies this classification. The fact that Virginia prohibits only interracial marriages involving white persons demonstrates that the racial classifications must stand on their own justification, as measures designed to maintain White Supremacy. We have consistently denied the constitutionality of measures which restrict the rights of citizens on account of race. There can be no doubt that restricting the freedom to marry solely because of racial classifications violates the central meaning of the Equal Protection Clause.

II.

These statutes also deprive the Lovings of liberty without due process of law in violation of the Due Process Clause of the Fourteenth Amendment. The freedom to marry has long been recognized as one of the vital personal rights essential to the orderly pursuit of happiness by free men.

Marriage is one of the "basic civil rights of man," fundamental to our very existence and survival. Skinner v. State of Oklahoma, 316 U.S. 535, 541 (1942). See also Maynard v. Hill, 125 U.S. 190 (1888). To deny this fundamental freedom on so unsupportable a basis as the racial classifications embodied in these statutes, classifications so directly subversive of the principle of equality at the heart of the Fourteenth Amendment, is surely to deprive all the State's citizens of liberty without due process of law. The Fourteenth Amendment requires that the freedom of choice to marry not be restricted by invidious racial discriminations. Under our Constitution, the freedom to marry or not marry, a person of another race resides with the individual and cannot be infringed by the State.

These convictions must be reversed. It is so ordered.

NOTES AND QUESTIONS

1. Is the holding in *Loving* based on equal protection (classification by race) or due process (limitation on access to marriage)? What does it mean to say that it is both? Consider this commentary by Professor Cooper Davis:

> In looking both to the equal protection and the substantive due process grounds for invalidating anti-miscegenation laws, the Court called forth principles that speak to two conspicuous ways that marriage rights of African-Americans have been constrained in the United States: they speak not only to the racial restrictions that were at issue in *Loving* but also to the slave laws under which recognition of the marriages of African-American people were denied entirely. Marriage is not just something that must be granted to different kinds of people equally; it is a right *that must be granted* unless there is a compelling interest in denying it. The difference is significant. In the same-sex marriage context, it is the difference between saying that singling out same-sex couples for exclusion from the institution of marriage would have to be strongly justified and saying that the institution of marriage is so important that *any* significant constraints upon it must be specially justified. In the African-American context, it is the difference between recognizing, as *Loving* did, a right of choice in marriage partners regardless of race and understanding, as *Loving* also did, that participation in the institution of marriage is a civic entitlement. . . .
>
> The centrality of family status denials to practices of enslavement is now well recognized. Orlando Patterson, one of slavery's most thoughtful and learned students, has described enslavement as a *social death* attributable to three overlapping factors: degradation, powerlessness, and "natal alienation." Natal alienation is classification, not as child or parent, but as rootless object, available for sale or exploitation. It was a defining feature of enslavement in the United States. . . .
>
> The understanding that free citizenship entailed family recognition seems to have gone unquestioned in the post-war period. Indeed, between 1865 and 1870, all eleven states of the former Confederacy revised their laws to recognize marriages between former slaves who had become free citizens by virtue of the Reconstruction amendments.
>
> By contrast, the laws prohibiting marriage between black and white people were not immediately understood to have been incompatible with Reconstruction's declaration of multi-racial United States citizenship, but survived until they were invalidated by the *Loving* Court a century after the Civil War. To note this is not to defend anti-miscegenation laws or belittle their subordinating effect. Anti-miscegenation laws were, as the *Loving* court recognized, a supremacist

insult conceived to maintain racial hierarchy. Nonetheless, the laws that made enslaved people officially rootless were more potent and more plainly incompatible with free citizenship than were the laws forbidding interracial marriage. Anti-miscegenation laws signaled degradation. But the social death achieved by natal alienation was something more. It marked a distinction between people and property. It didn't just separate enslaved people and free people; it legitimized disregard of any of an enslaved person's intimate choices and relationships. This disregard was an even greater affront to human dignity than the mandatory segregation that was its sequel.

Peggy Cooper Davis, Challenge and Tradition, 19 N.Y.U. J. Legis. & Pub. Pol'y 563, 565, 566, 567-568 (2016). *See also* Dorothy Roberts, Loving v. Virginia as a Civil Rights Decision, 59 N.Y.L. Sch. L. Rev. 175, 178 (2014/2015). The Supreme Court's interpretation of the Due Process Clause under the Fourteenth Amendment in Dobbs v. Jackson Women's Health Organization, 142 S. Ct. 2228 (2022), stripped abortion rights of constitutional protection. *See* Chapter 2 and below for what the decision may mean for protection of family and intimate rights, such as the right to marry.

2. Does *Loving* support the conclusion that all restrictions on access to marriage are subject to strict scrutiny?

3. After *Loving*, the Supreme Court addressed the constitutionality of bars to marriage twice, in Zablocki v. Redhail, 434 U.S. 374 (1978), and Turner v. Safley, 482 U.S. 78 (1987).

Zablocki concerned the constitutionality of a state law barring child support obligors from marrying if they owed back due child support or if their children were receiving public assistance. Redhail was denied permission to marry his pregnant girlfriend because he owed support for a child from an earlier relationship. Using an equal protection analysis, the Court held that marriage is a "fundamental right" and applied heightened scrutiny to strike down the law. The Court said that the denial of marriage was not sufficiently closely related to the state goals of counseling people against taking on more support duties than they can pay, encouraging obligors to pay up, and preventing people from incurring new support obligations when they are unable to provide for existing dependents.

Turner held that a state regulation that allowed prisoners to marry only if the superintendent found a compelling reason to grant permission violated due process because it was not reasonably related to legitimate penological interests. The Court adhered to a line of cases using the rational-basis test to assess due process challenges to prison regulations out of deference to the particular needs of prison authorities.

4. In the same term that it decided *Zablocki*, the Supreme Court used a rational-basis standard of scrutiny to assess the constitutionality of a section of the Social Security Act challenged as infringing on the right to marry. Califano v. Jobst, 434 U.S. 47 (1977). The Court applied the rational-basis standard and held that the rule was "not rendered invalid simply because some persons who might otherwise have married were deterred by the rule or because some who did marry were burdened thereby." 434 U.S. at 54. In *Zablocki* the Court explained:

> As the opinion for the Court [in *Jobst*] expressly noted, the rule terminating benefits upon marriage was not "an attempt to interfere with the individual's freedom to make a decision as important as marriage." The Social Security provisions placed no direct obstacle in the path of persons desiring to get married, and . . . there was no evidence that the laws significantly discouraged, let alone made "practically impossible," any marriages. Indeed, the provisions had not deterred the individual who challenged the statute from getting married, even though he and his wife were both disabled. 434 U.S. at 374, n. 12.
>
> [Justice Stevens (concurring in the judgment):] When a state allocates benefits or burdens, it may have valid reasons for treating married and unmarried persons differently. Classification based on marital status has been an accepted characteristic of tax legislation, Selective Service rules, and Social Security regulations. As cases like *Jobst* demonstrate, such laws may "significantly interfere with decisions to enter into the marital relationship." That kind of interference, however,

is not a sufficient reason for invalidating every law reflecting a legislative judgment that there are relevant differences between married persons as a class and unmarried persons as a class.

A classification based on marital status is fundamentally different from a classification which determines who may lawfully enter into a marriage relationship. The individual's interest in making the marriage decision independently is sufficiently important to merit special constitutional protection. It is not, however, an interest which is constitutionally immune from evenhanded regulation. Thus, laws prohibiting marriage to a child, a close relative, or a person afflicted with venereal disease, are unchallenged even though they "interfere directly and substantially with the right to marry." The Wisconsin statute has a different character.

434 U.S. at 403-404.

5. For more on the Lovings' story, *see* The Case of Mr. and Mrs. Loving: Reflections on the Fortieth Anniversary of Loving v. Virginia, in Family Law Stories 7 (Carol Sanger ed., 2008); Peter Wallenstein, Tell the Court I Love My Wife (2002). Issue 3 of volume 5 of the Virginia Journal of Social Policy and the Law (2018) is a symposium on the occasion of the fiftieth anniversary of *Loving*.

Obergefell v. Hodges
135 S. Ct. 2584 (2015)
[Portions of the majority opinion are reproduced above on pages 12–14.]

Justice KENNEDY delivered the opinion of the Court. . . . These cases come from Michigan, Kentucky, Ohio, and Tennessee, States that define marriage as a union between one man and one woman. The petitioners are 14 same-sex couples and two men whose same-sex partners are deceased. The respondents are state officials responsible for enforcing the laws in question. The petitioners claim the respondents violate the Fourteenth Amendment by denying them the right to marry or to have their marriages, lawfully performed in another State, given full recognition.

Petitioners filed these suits in United States District Courts in their home States. Each District Court ruled in their favor. The respondents appealed the decisions against them to the United States Court of Appeals for the Sixth Circuit. It consolidated the cases and reversed the judgments of the District Courts. . . .

The ancient origins of marriage confirm its centrality, but it has not stood in isolation from developments in law and society. The history of marriage is one of both continuity and change. That institution—even as confined to opposite-sex relations—has evolved over time.

For example, marriage was once viewed as an arrangement by the couple's parents based on political, religious, and financial concerns; but by the time of the Nation's founding it was understood to be a voluntary contract between a man and a woman. As the role and status of women changed, the institution further evolved. Under the centuries-old doctrine of coverture, a married man and woman were treated by the State as a single, male-dominated legal entity. As women gained legal, political, and property rights, and as society began to understand that women have their own equal dignity, the law of coverture was abandoned. These and other developments in the institution of marriage over the past centuries were not mere superficial changes. Rather, they worked deep transformations in its structure, affecting aspects of marriage long viewed by many as essential.

These new insights have strengthened, not weakened, the institution of marriage. Indeed, changed understandings of marriage are characteristic of a Nation where new dimensions of freedom become apparent to new generations, often through perspectives that begin in pleas or protests and then are considered in the political sphere and the judicial process.

This dynamic can be seen in the Nation's experiences with the rights of gays and lesbians. Until the mid-20th century, same-sex intimacy long had been condemned as immoral by the state itself in most Western nations, a belief often embodied in the criminal law. For this reason, among others, many persons did not deem homosexuals to have dignity in their own distinct identity. A truthful declaration by same-sex couples of what was in their hearts had to remain unspoken. Even when a greater awareness of the humanity and integrity of homosexual persons came in the period after World War II, the argument that gays and lesbians had a just claim to dignity was in conflict with both law and widespread social conventions. Same-sex intimacy remained a crime in many States. Gays and lesbians were prohibited from most government employment, barred from military service, excluded under immigration laws, targeted by police, and burdened in their rights to associate.

For much of the 20th century, moreover, homosexuality was treated as an illness. When the American Psychiatric Association published the first Diagnostic and Statistical Manual of Mental Disorders in 1952, homosexuality was classified as a mental disorder, a position adhered to until 1973. Only in more recent years have psychiatrists and others recognized that sexual orientation is both a normal expression of human sexuality and immutable.

In the late 20th century, following substantial cultural and political developments, same-sex couples began to lead more open and public lives and to establish families. This development was followed by a quite extensive discussion of the issue in both governmental and private sectors and by a shift in public attitudes toward greater tolerance. As a result, questions about the rights of gays and lesbians soon reached the courts, where the issue could be discussed in the formal discourse of the law.

This Court first gave detailed consideration to the legal status of homosexuals in Bowers v. Hardwick, 478 U.S. 186 (1986). There it upheld the constitutionality of a Georgia law deemed to criminalize certain homosexual acts. Ten years later, in Romer v. Evans, 517 U.S. 620 (1996), the Court invalidated an amendment to Colorado's Constitution that sought to foreclose any branch or political subdivision of the State from protecting persons against discrimination based on sexual orientation. Then, in 2003, the Court overruled *Bowers*, holding that laws making same-sex intimacy a crime "demea[n] the lives of homosexual persons." Lawrence v. Texas, 539 U.S. 558, 575.

Against this background, the legal question of same-sex marriage arose. In 1993, the Hawaii Supreme Court held Hawaii's law restricting marriage to opposite-sex couples constituted a classification on the basis of sex and was therefore subject to strict scrutiny under the Hawaii Constitution. Baehr v. Lewin, 852 P.2d 44. Although this decision did not mandate that same-sex marriage be allowed, some States were concerned by its implications and reaffirmed in their laws that marriage is defined as a union between opposite-sex partners. So too in 1996, Congress passed the Defense of Marriage Act (DOMA), defining marriage for all federal-law purposes as "only a legal union between one man and one woman as husband and wife."

The new and widespread discussion of the subject led other States to a different conclusion. In 2003, the Supreme Judicial Court of Massachusetts held the State's Constitution guaranteed same-sex couples the right to marry. See Goodridge v. Department of Public Health, 440 Mass. 309, 798 N.E.2d 941 (2003). After that ruling, some additional States granted marriage rights to same-sex couples, either through judicial or legislative processes. These decisions and statutes are cited in Appendix B, *infra* [omitted]. Two Terms ago, in United States v. Windsor, 570 U.S. ___ (2013), this Court invalidated DOMA to the extent it barred the Federal Government from treating same-sex marriages as valid even when they were lawful in the State where they were licensed. DOMA, the Court held, impermissibly disparaged those same-sex couples "who wanted to affirm their commitment to one another before their children, their family, their friends, and their community."

Numerous cases about same-sex marriage have reached the United States Courts of Appeals in recent years. . . . With the exception of the opinion here under review and one other, see Citizens for Equal Protection v. Bruning, 455 F.3d 859, 864-868 (C.A. 8 2006), the Courts of Appeals have held that excluding same-sex couples from marriage violates the Constitution. There also have been many thoughtful District Court decisions addressing same-sex marriage — and most of them, too, have concluded same-sex couples must be allowed to marry. In addition the highest courts of many States have contributed to this ongoing dialogue in decisions interpreting their own State Constitutions. . . .

After years of litigation, legislation, referenda, and the discussions that attended these public acts, the States are now divided on the issue of same-sex marriage.

Under the Due Process Clause of the Fourteenth Amendment, no State shall "deprive any person of life, liberty, or property, without due process of law." The fundamental liberties protected by this Clause include most of the rights enumerated in the Bill of Rights. In addition these liberties extend to certain personal choices central to individual dignity and autonomy, including intimate choices that define personal identity and beliefs.

The identification and protection of fundamental rights is an enduring part of the judicial duty to interpret the Constitution. That responsibility, however, "has not been reduced to any formula." Rather, it requires courts to exercise reasoned judgment in identifying interests of the person so fundamental that the State must accord them its respect. That process is guided by many of the same considerations relevant to analysis of other constitutional provisions that set forth broad principles rather than specific requirements. History and tradition guide and discipline this inquiry but do not set its outer boundaries. That method respects our history and learns from it without allowing the past alone to rule the present.

The nature of injustice is that we may not always see it in our own times. The generations that wrote and ratified the Bill of Rights and the Fourteenth Amendment did not presume to know the extent of freedom in all of its dimensions, and so they entrusted to future generations a charter protecting the right of all persons to enjoy liberty as we learn its meaning. When new insight reveals discord between the Constitution's central protections and a received legal stricture, a claim to liberty must be addressed.

Applying these established tenets, the Court has long held the right to marry is protected by the Constitution. In Loving v. Virginia, 388 U.S. 1, 12 (1967), which invalidated bans on interracial unions, a unanimous Court held marriage is "one of the vital personal rights essential to the orderly pursuit of happiness by free men." The Court reaffirmed that holding in Zablocki v. Redhail, 434 U.S. 374, 384 (1978), which held the right to marry was burdened by a law prohibiting fathers who were behind on child support from marrying. The Court again applied this principle in Turner v. Safley, 482 U.S. 78, 95 (1987), which held the right to marry was abridged by regulations limiting the privilege of prison inmates to marry. Over time and in other contexts, the Court has reiterated that the right to marry is fundamental under the Due Process Clause.

It cannot be denied that this Court's cases describing the right to marry presumed a relationship involving opposite-sex partners. The Court, like many institutions, has made assumptions defined by the world and time of which it is a part. This was evident in Baker v. Nelson, 409 U.S. 810, a one-line summary decision issued in 1972, holding the exclusion of same-sex couples from marriage did not present a substantial federal question.

Still, there are other, more instructive precedents. This Court's cases have expressed constitutional principles of broader reach. In defining the right to marry these cases have identified essential attributes of that right based in history, tradition, and other constitutional liberties inherent in this intimate bond. And in assessing whether the force and rationale of its cases apply to same-sex couples, the Court must respect the basic reasons why the right to marry has been long protected.

This analysis compels the conclusion that same-sex couples may exercise the right to marry. The four principles and traditions to be discussed demonstrate that the reasons marriage is fundamental under the Constitution apply with equal force to same-sex couples.

A first premise of the Court's relevant precedents is that the right to personal choice regarding marriage is inherent in the concept of individual autonomy. This abiding connection between marriage and liberty is why *Loving* invalidated interracial marriage bans under the Due Process Clause. Like choices concerning contraception, family relationships, procreation, and childrearing, all of which are protected by the Constitution, decisions concerning marriage are among the most intimate that an individual can make. Indeed, the Court has noted it would be contradictory "to recognize a right of privacy with respect to other matters of family life and not with respect to the decision to enter the relationship that is the foundation of the family in our society."

Choices about marriage shape an individual's destiny. As the Supreme Judicial Court of Massachusetts has explained, because "it fulfills yearnings for security, safe haven, and connection that express our common humanity, civil marriage is an esteemed institution, and the decision whether and whom to marry is among life's momentous acts of self-definition."

The nature of marriage is that, through its enduring bond, two persons together can find other freedoms, such as expression, intimacy, and spirituality. This is true for all persons, whatever their sexual orientation. There is dignity in the bond between two men or two women who seek to marry and in their autonomy to make such profound choices.

A second principle in this Court's jurisprudence is that the right to marry is fundamental because it supports a two-person union unlike any other in its importance to the committed individuals. This point was central to Griswold v. Connecticut, which held the Constitution protects the right of married couples to use contraception. Suggesting that marriage is a right "older than the Bill of Rights," *Griswold* described marriage this way:

> "Marriage is a coming together for better or for worse, hopefully enduring, and intimate to the degree of being sacred. It is an association that promotes a way of life, not causes; a harmony in living, not political faiths; a bilateral loyalty, not commercial or social projects. Yet it is an association for as noble a purpose as any involved in our prior decisions." . . .

As this Court held in *Lawrence*, same-sex couples have the same right as opposite-sex couples to enjoy intimate association. *Lawrence* invalidated laws that made same-sex intimacy a criminal act. And it acknowledged that "[w]hen sexuality finds overt expression in intimate conduct with another person, the conduct can be but one element in a personal bond that is more enduring." But while *Lawrence* confirmed a dimension of freedom that allows individuals to engage in intimate association without criminal liability, it does not follow that freedom stops there. Outlaw to outcast may be a step forward, but it does not achieve the full promise of liberty.

A third basis for protecting the right to marry is that it safeguards children and families and thus draws meaning from related rights of childrearing, procreation, and education. The Court has recognized these connections by describing the varied rights as a unified whole: "[T]he right to 'marry, establish a home and bring up children' is a central part of the liberty protected by the Due Process Clause." Under the laws of the several States, some of marriage's protections for children and families are material. But marriage also confers more profound benefits. By giving recognition and legal structure to their parents' relationship, marriage allows children "to understand the integrity and closeness of their own family and its concord with other families in their community and in their daily lives." Marriage also affords the permanency and stability important to children's best interests.

As all parties agree, many same-sex couples provide loving and nurturing homes to their children, whether biological or adopted. And hundreds of thousands of children are presently being raised by such couples. Most States have allowed gays and lesbians to adopt, either as individuals or as couples, and many adopted and foster children have same-sex parents. This provides powerful confirmation from the law itself that gays and lesbians can create loving, supportive families.

Excluding same-sex couples from marriage thus conflicts with a central premise of the right to marry. Without the recognition, stability, and predictability marriage offers, their children suffer the stigma of knowing their families are somehow lesser. They also suffer the significant material costs of being raised by unmarried parents, relegated through no fault of their own to a more difficult and uncertain family life. The marriage laws at issue here thus harm and humiliate the children of same-sex couples.

That is not to say the right to marry is less meaningful for those who do not or cannot have children. An ability, desire, or promise to procreate is not and has not been a prerequisite for a valid marriage in any State. In light of precedent protecting the right of a married couple not to procreate, it cannot be said the Court or the States have conditioned the right to marry on the capacity or commitment to procreate. The constitutional marriage right has many aspects, of which childbearing is only one.

Fourth and finally, this Court's cases and the Nation's traditions make clear that marriage is a keystone of our social order. Alexis de Tocqueville recognized this truth on his travels through the United States almost two centuries ago:

> "There is certainly no country in the world where the tie of marriage is so much respected as in America. . . . [W]hen the American retires from the turmoil of public life to the bosom of his family, he finds in it the image of order and of peace. . . . [H]e afterwards carries [that image] with him into public affairs." 1 Democracy in America 309 (H. Reeve transl., rev. ed. 1990).

In Maynard v. Hill, 125 U.S. 190, 211 (1888), the Court echoed de Tocqueville, explaining that marriage is "the foundation of the family and of society, without which there would be neither civilization nor progress." Marriage, the *Maynard* Court said, has long been "'a great public institution, giving character to our whole civil polity.'" This idea has been reiterated even as the institution has evolved in substantial ways over time, superseding rules related to parental consent, gender, and race once thought by many to be essential.

For that reason, just as a couple vows to support each other, so does society pledge to support the couple, offering symbolic recognition and material benefits to protect and nourish the union. Indeed, while the States are in general free to vary the benefits they confer on all married couples, they have throughout our history made marriage the basis for an expanding list of governmental rights, benefits, and responsibilities. These aspects of marital status include: taxation; inheritance and property rights; rules of intestate succession; spousal privilege in the law of evidence; hospital access; medical decisionmaking authority; adoption rights; the rights and benefits of survivors; birth and death certificates; professional ethics rules; campaign finance restrictions; workers' compensation benefits; health insurance; and child custody, support, and visitation rules. Valid marriage under state law is also a significant status for over a thousand provisions of federal law. The States have contributed to the fundamental character of the marriage right by placing that institution at the center of so many facets of the legal and social order.

There is no difference between same- and opposite-sex couples with respect to this principle. Yet by virtue of their exclusion from that institution, same-sex couples are denied the constellation of benefits that the States have linked to marriage. This harm results in more than just material burdens. Same-sex couples are consigned to an instability many opposite-sex couples would deem intolerable in their own lives. As the State itself makes marriage all the more precious by the significance it attaches to it, exclusion from that status has the effect of teaching that gays and lesbians are unequal in important respects. It demeans gays and lesbians for the State to lock them out of a central institution of the Nation's society. Same-sex couples, too, may aspire to the transcendent purposes of marriage and seek fulfillment in its highest meaning.

The limitation of marriage to opposite-sex couples may long have seemed natural and just, but its inconsistency with the central meaning of the fundamental right to marry is now manifest. With that knowledge must come the recognition that laws excluding same-sex couples from the marriage right impose stigma and injury of the kind prohibited by our basic charter. . . .

The right to marry is fundamental as a matter of history and tradition, but rights come not from ancient sources alone. They rise, too, from a better informed understanding of how constitutional imperatives define a liberty that remains urgent in our own era. Many who deem same-sex marriage to be wrong reach that conclusion based on decent and honorable religious or philosophical premises, and neither they nor their beliefs are disparaged here. But when that sincere, personal opposition becomes enacted law and public policy, the necessary consequence is to put the imprimatur of the State itself on an exclusion that soon demeans or stigmatizes those whose own liberty is then denied. Under the Constitution, same-sex couples seek in marriage the same legal treatment as opposite-sex couples, and it would disparage their choices and diminish their personhood to deny them this right.

The right of same-sex couples to marry that is part of the liberty promised by the Fourteenth Amendment is derived, too, from that Amendment's guarantee of the equal protection of the laws. The Due Process Clause and the Equal Protection Clause are connected in a profound way, though they set forth independent principles. Rights implicit in liberty and rights secured by equal protection may rest on different precepts and are not always co-extensive, yet in some instances each may be instructive as to the meaning and reach of the other. In any particular case one Clause may be thought to capture the essence of the right in a more accurate and comprehensive way, even as the two Clauses may converge in the identification and definition of the right. This interrelation of the two principles furthers our understanding of what freedom is and must become.

The Court's cases touching upon the right to marry reflect this dynamic. In *Loving* the Court invalidated a prohibition on interracial marriage under both the Equal Protection Clause and the Due Process Clause. . . .

In *Lawrence* the Court acknowledged the interlocking nature of these constitutional safeguards in the context of the legal treatment of gays and lesbians. Although *Lawrence* elaborated its holding under the Due Process Clause, it acknowledged, and sought to remedy, the continuing inequality that resulted from laws making intimacy in the lives of gays and lesbians a crime against the State. . . .

This dynamic also applies to same-sex marriage. It is now clear that the challenged laws burden the liberty of same-sex couples, and it must be further acknowledged that they abridge central precepts of equality. Here the marriage laws enforced by the respondents are in essence unequal: same-sex couples are denied all the benefits afforded to opposite-sex couples and are barred from exercising a fundamental right. Especially against a long history of disapproval of their relationships, this denial to same-sex couples of the right to marry works a grave and continuing harm. The imposition of this disability on gays and lesbians serves to disrespect and subordinate them. And the Equal Protection Clause, like the Due Process Clause, prohibits this unjustified infringement of the fundamental right to marry.

These considerations lead to the conclusion that the right to marry is a fundamental right inherent in the liberty of the person, and under the Due Process and Equal Protection Clauses of the Fourteenth Amendment couples of the same-sex may not be deprived of that right and that liberty. The Court now holds that same-sex couples may exercise the fundamental right to marry. No longer may this liberty be denied to them. . . .

There may be an initial inclination in these cases to proceed with caution—to await further legislation, litigation, and debate. The respondents warn there has been insufficient democratic discourse before deciding an issue so basic as the definition of marriage. . . .

Yet there has been far more deliberation than this argument acknowledges. There have been referenda, legislative debates, and grassroots campaigns, as well as countless studies, papers, books, and other popular and scholarly writings. There has been extensive litigation in state and federal courts. Judicial opinions addressing the issue have been informed by the contentions of parties and counsel, which, in turn, reflect the more general, societal discussion of same-sex marriage and its meaning that has occurred over the past decades. As more than 100 *amici* make clear in their filings, many of the central institutions in American life—state and local governments, the military, large and small businesses, labor unions, religious organizations, law enforcement, civic groups, professional organizations, and universities—have devoted substantial attention to the question. This has led to an enhanced understanding of the issue—an understanding reflected in the arguments now presented for resolution as a matter of constitutional law. . . .

This is not the first time the Court has been asked to adopt a cautious approach to recognizing and protecting fundamental rights. In *Bowers*, a bare majority upheld a law criminalizing same-sex intimacy. . . . Although *Bowers* was eventually repudiated in *Lawrence*, men and women were harmed in the interim, and the substantial effects of these injuries no doubt lingered long after *Bowers* was overruled. Dignitary wounds cannot always be healed with the stroke of a pen.

A ruling against same-sex couples would have the same effect—and, like *Bowers*, would be unjustified under the Fourteenth Amendment. . . .

The respondents also argue allowing same-sex couples to wed will harm marriage as an institution by leading to fewer opposite-sex marriages. This may occur, the respondents contend, because licensing same-sex marriage severs the connection between natural procreation and marriage. That argument, however, rests on a counterintuitive view of opposite-sex couple's decisionmaking processes regarding marriage and parenthood. Decisions about whether to marry and raise children are based on many personal, romantic, and practical considerations; and it is unrealistic to conclude that an opposite-sex couple would choose not to marry simply because same-sex couples may do so. The respondents have not shown a foundation for the conclusion that allowing same-sex marriage will cause the harmful outcomes they describe. . . .

Finally, it must be emphasized that religions, and those who adhere to religious doctrines, may continue to advocate with utmost, sincere conviction that, by divine precepts, same-sex marriage should not be condoned. The First Amendment ensures that religious organizations and persons are given proper protection as they seek to teach the principles that are so fulfilling and so central to their lives and faiths, and to their own deep aspirations to continue the family structure they have long revered. The same is true of those who oppose same-sex marriage for other reasons. In turn, those who believe allowing same-sex marriage is proper or indeed essential, whether as a matter of religious conviction or secular belief, may engage those who disagree with their view in an open and searching debate. The Constitution, however, does not permit the State to bar same-sex couples from marriage on the same terms as accorded to couples of the opposite sex.

These cases also present the question whether the Constitution requires States to recognize same-sex marriages validly performed out of State. . . .

. . . The Court, in this decision, holds same-sex couples may exercise the fundamental right to marry in all States. It follows that the Court also must hold—and it now does hold—that there is no lawful basis for a State to refuse to recognize a lawful same-sex marriage performed in another State on the ground of its same-sex character. . . .

The judgment of the Court of Appeals for the Sixth Circuit is reversed.

Chief Justice ROBERTS, with whom Justice SCALIA and Justice THOMAS join, dissenting. . . .
[T]his Court is not a legislature. Whether same-sex marriage is a good idea should be of no
concern to us. Under the Constitution, judges have power to say what the law is, not what
it should be. The people who ratified the Constitution authorized courts to exercise "neither
force nor will but merely judgment." . . .

Petitioners and their *amici* base their arguments on the "right to marry" and the
imperative of "marriage equality." There is no serious dispute that, under our precedents, the
Constitution protects a right to marry and requires States to apply their marriage laws equally.
The real question in these cases is what constitutes "marriage," or—more precisely—*who
decides* what constitutes "marriage"? . . .

As the majority acknowledges, marriage "has existed for millennia and across civilizations."
For all those millennia, across all those civilizations, "marriage" referred to only one
relationship: the union of a man and a woman. . . .

This universal definition of marriage as the union of a man and a woman is no historical
coincidence. Marriage did not come about as a result of a political movement, discovery,
disease, war, religious doctrine, or any other moving force of world history—and certainly
not as a result of a prehistoric decision to exclude gays and lesbians. It arose in the nature
of things to meet a vital need: ensuring that children are conceived by a mother and father
committed to raising them in the stable conditions of a lifelong relationship.

The premises supporting this concept of marriage are so fundamental that they rarely
require articulation. The human race must procreate to survive. Procreation occurs through
sexual relations between a man and a woman. When sexual relations result in the conception
of a child, that child's prospects are generally better if the mother and father stay together
rather than going their separate ways. Therefore, for the good of children and society, sexual
relations that can lead to procreation should occur only between a man and a woman
committed to a lasting bond.

Society has recognized that bond as marriage. And by bestowing a respected status and
material benefits on married couples, society encourages men and women to conduct sexual
relations within marriage rather than without. . . .

As the majority notes, some aspects of marriage have changed over time. . . .

The majority observes that these developments "were not mere superficial changes" in
marriage, but rather "worked deep transformations in its structure." They did not, however,
work any transformation in the core structure of marriage as the union between a man and
a woman. If you had asked a person on the street how marriage was defined, no one would
ever have said, "Marriage is the union of a man and a woman, where the woman is subject to
coverture." The majority may be right that the "history of marriage is one of both continuity
and change," but the core meaning of marriage has endured. . . .

The majority purports to identify four "principles and traditions" in this Court's due
process precedents that support a fundamental right for same-sex couples to marry. In
reality, however, the majority's approach has no basis in principle or tradition, except for the
unprincipled tradition of judicial policymaking that characterized discredited decisions such
as Lochner v. New York, 198 U.S. 45. . . .

The need for restraint in administering the strong medicine of substantive due process is
a lesson this Court has learned the hard way. The Court first applied substantive due process
to strike down a statute in Dred Scott v. Sandford, 19 How. 393 (1857). There the Court
invalidated the Missouri Compromise on the ground that legislation restricting the institution
of slavery violated the implied rights of slaveholders. The Court relied on its own conception
of liberty and property in doing so. It asserted that "an act of Congress which deprives a citizen
of the United States of his liberty or property, merely because he came himself or brought his

property into a particular Territory of the United States . . . could hardly be dignified with the name of due process of law." . . .

Dred Scott's holding was overruled on the battlefields of the Civil War and by constitutional amendment after Appomattox, but its approach to the Due Process Clause reappeared. In a series of early 20th-century cases, most prominently Lochner v. New York, this Court invalidated state statutes that presented "meddlesome interferences with the rights of the individual," and "undue interference with liberty of person and freedom of contract." . . .

In the decades after *Lochner*, the Court struck down nearly 200 laws as violations of individual liberty, often over strong dissents contending that "[t]he criterion of constitutionality is not whether we believe the law to be for the public good." By empowering judges to elevate their own policy judgments to the status of constitutionally protected "liberty," the *Lochner* line of cases left "no alternative to regarding the court as a . . . legislative chamber."

Eventually, the Court recognized its error and vowed not to repeat it. "The doctrine that . . . due process authorizes courts to hold laws unconstitutional when they believe the legislature has acted unwisely," we later explained, "has long since been discarded. We have returned to the original constitutional proposition that courts do not substitute their social and economic beliefs for the judgment of legislative bodies, who are elected to pass laws." Thus, it has become an accepted rule that the Court will not hold laws unconstitutional simply because we find them "unwise, improvident, or out of harmony with a particular school of thought."

Rejecting *Lochner* does not require disavowing the doctrine of implied fundamental rights, and this Court has not done so. But to avoid repeating *Lochner*'s error of converting personal preferences into constitutional mandates, our modern substantive due process cases have stressed the need for "judicial self-restraint." Our precedents have required that implied fundamental rights be "objectively, deeply rooted in this Nation's history and tradition," and "implicit in the concept of ordered liberty, such that neither liberty nor justice would exist if they were sacrificed." . . .

The majority acknowledges none of this doctrinal background, and it is easy to see why: Its aggressive application of substantive due process breaks sharply with decades of precedent and returns the Court to the unprincipled approach of *Lochner*. . . .

When the majority turns to the law, it relies primarily on precedents discussing the fundamental "right to marry." These cases do not hold, of course, that anyone who wants to get married has a constitutional right to do so. They instead require a State to justify barriers to marriage as that institution has always been understood. . . .

None of the laws at issue in those cases purported to change the core definition of marriage as the union of a man and a woman. . . .

The majority suggests that "there are other, more instructive precedents" informing the right to marry. Although not entirely clear, this reference seems to correspond to a line of cases discussing an implied fundamental "right of privacy." . . .

The Court also invoked the right to privacy in Lawrence v. Texas, 539 U.S. 558 (2003), which struck down a Texas statute criminalizing homosexual sodomy. *Lawrence* relied on the position that criminal sodomy laws, like bans on contraceptives, invaded privacy by inviting "unwarranted government intrusions" that "touc[h] upon the most private human conduct, sexual behavior . . . in the most private of places, the home."

Neither *Lawrence* nor any other precedent in the privacy line of cases supports the right that petitioners assert here. Unlike criminal laws banning contraceptives and sodomy, the marriage laws at issue here involve no government intrusion. They create no crime and impose no punishment. Same-sex couples remain free to live together, to engage in intimate conduct, and to raise their families as they see fit. No one is "condemned to live in loneliness" by the laws challenged in these cases — no one. At the same time, the laws in no way interfere with the "right to be let alone." . . .

In sum, the privacy cases provide no support for the majority's position, because petitioners do not seek privacy. Quite the opposite, they seek public recognition of their relationships, along with corresponding government benefits. Our cases have consistently refused to allow litigants to convert the shield provided by constitutional liberties into a sword to demand positive entitlements from the State. Thus, although the right to privacy recognized by our precedents certainly plays a role in protecting the intimate conduct of same-sex couples, it provides no affirmative right to redefine marriage and no basis for striking down the laws at issue here. . . .

One immediate question invited by the majority's position is whether States may retain the definition of marriage as a union of two people. . . .

It is striking how much of the majority's reasoning would apply with equal force to the claim of a fundamental right to plural marriage. If "[t]here is dignity in the bond between two men or two women who seek to marry and in their autonomy to make such profound choices," why would there be any less dignity in the bond between three people who, in exercising their autonomy, seek to make the profound choice to marry? If a same-sex couple has the constitutional right to marry because their children would otherwise "suffer the stigma of knowing their families are somehow lesser," why wouldn't the same reasoning apply to a family of three or more persons raising children? If not having the opportunity to marry "serves to disrespect and subordinate" gay and lesbian couples, why wouldn't the same "imposition of this disability," serve to disrespect and subordinate people who find fulfillment in polyamorous relationships? . . .

The legitimacy of this Court ultimately rests "upon the respect accorded to its judgments." That respect flows from the perception — and reality — that we exercise humility and restraint in deciding cases according to the Constitution and law. The role of the Court envisioned by the majority today, however, is anything but humble or restrained. Over and over, the majority exalts the role of the judiciary in delivering social change. In the majority's telling, it is the courts, not the people, who are responsible for making "new dimensions of freedom . . . apparent to new generations," for providing "formal discourse" on social issues, and for ensuring "neutral discussions, without scornful or disparaging commentary." . . .

Federal courts are blunt instruments when it comes to creating rights. They have constitutional power only to resolve concrete cases or controversies; they do not have the flexibility of legislatures to address concerns of parties not before the court or to anticipate problems that may arise from the exercise of a new right. Today's decision, for example, creates serious questions about religious liberty. Many good and decent people oppose same-sex marriage as a tenet of faith, and their freedom to exercise religion is — unlike the right imagined by the majority — actually spelled out in the Constitution.

Respect for sincere religious conviction has led voters and legislators in every State that has adopted same-sex marriage democratically to include accommodations for religious practice. The majority's decision imposing same-sex marriage cannot, of course, create any such accommodations. . . .

Hard questions arise when people of faith exercise religion in ways that may be seen to conflict with the new right to same-sex marriage — when, for example, a religious college provides married student housing only to opposite-sex married couples, or a religious adoption agency declines to place children with same-sex married couples. Indeed, the Solicitor General candidly acknowledged that the tax exemptions of some religious institutions would be in question if they opposed same-sex marriage. There is little doubt that these and similar questions will soon be before this Court. Unfortunately, people of faith can take no comfort in the treatment they receive from the majority today. . . .

Justice SCALIA, with whom Justice THOMAS joins, dissenting. . . . When the Fourteenth Amendment was ratified in 1868, every State limited marriage to one man and one woman, and no one doubted the constitutionality of doing so. That resolves these cases. . . .

But what really astounds is the hubris reflected in today's judicial Putsch. The five Justices who compose today's majority are entirely comfortable concluding that every State violated the Constitution for all of the 135 years between the Fourteenth Amendment's ratification and Massachusetts' permitting of same-sex marriages in 2003. They have discovered in the Fourteenth Amendment a "fundamental right" overlooked by every person alive at the time of ratification, and almost everyone else in the time since. They see what lesser legal minds—minds like Thomas Cooley, John Marshall Harlan, Oliver Wendell Holmes, Jr., Learned Hand, Louis Brandeis, William Howard Taft, Benjamin Cardozo, Hugo Black, Felix Frankfurter, Robert Jackson, and Henry Friendly—could not. They are certain that the People ratified the Fourteenth Amendment to bestow on them the power to remove questions from the democratic process when that is called for by their "reasoned judgment." These Justices *know* that limiting marriage to one man and one woman is contrary to reason; they *know* that an institution as old as government itself, and accepted by every nation in history until 15 years ago, cannot possibly be supported by anything other than ignorance or bigotry. And they are willing to say that any citizen who does not agree with that, who adheres to what was, until 15 years ago, the unanimous judgment of all generations and all societies, stands against the Constitution. . . .

Hubris is sometimes defined as o'erweening pride; and pride, we know, goeth before a fall. The Judiciary is the "least dangerous" of the federal branches because it has "neither Force nor Will, but merely judgment; and must ultimately depend upon the aid of the executive arm" and the States, "even for the efficacy of its judgments." With each decision of ours that takes from the People a question properly left to them—with each decision that is unabashedly based not on law, but on the "reasoned judgment" of a bare majority of this Court—we move one step closer to being reminded of our impotence.

Justice THOMAS, with whom Justice SCALIA joins, dissenting. . . . I have elsewhere explained the dangerous fiction of treating the Due Process Clause as a font of substantive rights. It distorts the constitutional text, which guarantees only whatever "process" is "due" before a person is deprived of life, liberty, and property. Worse, it invites judges to do exactly what the majority has done here—"'roa[m] at large in the constitutional field' guided only by their personal views" as to the "'fundamental rights'" protected by that document. . . .

Justice ALITO, with whom Justice SCALIA and Justice THOMAS join, dissenting. . . . The Constitution says nothing about a right to same-sex marriage, but the Court holds that the term "liberty" in the Due Process Clause of the Fourteenth Amendment encompasses this right. . . .

To prevent five unelected Justices from imposing their personal vision of liberty upon the American people, the Court has held that "liberty" under the Due Process Clause should be understood to protect only those rights that are "'deeply rooted in this Nation's history and tradition.'" And it is beyond dispute that the right to same-sex marriage is not among those rights. . . .

Attempting to circumvent the problem presented by the newness of the right found in these cases, the majority claims that the issue is the right to equal treatment. Noting that marriage is a fundamental right, the majority argues that a State has no valid reason for denying that right to same-sex couples. This reasoning is dependent upon a particular understanding of the purpose of civil marriage. Although the Court expresses the point in loftier terms, its argument is that the fundamental purpose of marriage is to promote the well-being of those who choose to marry. . . . This understanding of marriage, which focuses almost entirely on the happiness of persons who choose to marry, is shared by many people today, but it is not the traditional one. For millennia, marriage was inextricably linked to the one thing that only an opposite-sex couple can do: procreate.

. . . Here, the States defending their adherence to the traditional understanding of marriage have explained their position using the pragmatic vocabulary that characterizes most American political discourse. Their basic argument is that States formalize and promote marriage, unlike other fulfilling human relationships, in order to encourage potentially procreative conduct to take place within a lasting unit that has long been thought to provide the best atmosphere for raising children. They thus argue that there are reasonable secular grounds for restricting marriage to opposite-sex couples.

If this traditional understanding of the purpose of marriage does not ring true to all ears today, that is probably because the tie between marriage and procreation has frayed. Today, for instance, more than 40% of all children in this country are born to unmarried women. This development undoubtedly is both a cause and a result of changes in our society's understanding of marriage.

While, for many, the attributes of marriage in 21st-century America have changed, those States that do not want to recognize same-sex marriage have not yet given up on the traditional understanding. They worry that by officially abandoning the older understanding, they may contribute to marriage's further decay. It is far beyond the outer reaches of this Court's authority to say that a State may not adhere to the understanding of marriage that has long prevailed, not just in this country and others with similar cultural roots, but also in a great variety of countries and cultures all around the globe. . . .

The system of federalism established by our Constitution provides a way for people with different beliefs to live together in a single nation. If the issue of same-sex marriage had been left to the people of the States, it is likely that some States would recognize same-sex marriage and I others would not. It is also possible that some States would tie recognition to protection for conscience rights. The majority today makes that impossible. By imposing its own views on the entire country, the majority facilitates the marginalization of the many Americans who have traditional ideas. Recalling the harsh treatment of gays and lesbians in the past, some may think that turnabout is fair play. But if that sentiment prevails, the Nation will experience bitter and lasting wounds. . . .

NOTES AND QUESTIONS

1. Does *Obergefell* use the same kind of equal protection analysis that *Loving* does? Is the due process analysis the same? What is the relationship between due process and equal protection in *Obergefell*?

2. *Obergefell* identifies four principles and traditions that support the conclusion that the right to marry is a fundamental right protected by the Constitution. What are the principles and traditions? Does *Obergefell* mean that any restriction on marriage fails if it impinges on all these interests? What if a restriction interferes with some but not all of the interests?

3. Two years before *Obergefell*, the Supreme Court held 5-4 in United States v. Windsor, 570 U.S. 744 (2013), that one clause of the federal Defense of Marriage Act (DOMA) violates equal protection. The clause provided that the federal government would not recognize same-sex marriages valid under state law for purposes of the myriad federal statutes allocating rights and duties based on marital status. The majority opinion, written by Justice Kennedy, held that the provision failed to satisfy equal protection because it lacked a legitimate purpose:

. . . The Constitution's guarantee of equality "must at the very least mean that a bare congressional desire to harm a politically unpopular group cannot" justify disparate treatment of that group. In determining whether a law is motived by an improper animus or purpose, "'[d]iscriminations of an unusual character'" especially require careful consideration. DOMA cannot survive under these principles. The responsibility of the States for the regulation of domestic relations is an important indicator of the substantial societal impact the State's classifications have in the daily lives and customs of its people. DOMA's unusual deviation from the usual tradition of recognizing and accepting state definitions of marriage here operates to deprive same-sex couples of the benefits and responsibilities that come with the federal recognition of their marriages. This is strong evidence of a law having the purpose and effect of disapproval of that class. The avowed purpose and practical effect of the law here in question are to impose a disadvantage, a separate status, and so a stigma upon all who enter into same-sex marriages made lawful by the unquestioned authority of the States.

570 U.S. at 770. Why doesn't *Obergefell* invoke this argument in support of its holding?

4. *Obergefell* holds that states must recognize same-sex marriages from other states, which is unremarkable, since they must allow same-sex marriages within their borders. What it means to recognize a marriage became the subject of litigation. In a brief per curiam opinion, the Supreme Court held that a state that recognizes a married woman's husband as the legal father of a child born by artificial insemination must also recognize the wife of a married woman who gives birth by artificial insemination as the child's legal parent. Pavan v. Smith, 137 S. Ct. 2075 (2017). On the implications of *Obergefell* for legal parentage generally, *see* Leslie Joan Harris, *Obergefell's* Ambiguous Impact on Legal Parentage, 92 Chi.-Kent L. Rev. 55 (2017). This issue is covered in depth in Chapter 13.

5. After *Obergefell*, the only governmental entities in the United States that may prohibit same-sex couples from marrying are Native tribes, since tribes are sovereign. Many tribes do not issue marriage certificates, and some are unlikely to have laws relating to same-sex marriage. Most tribes allow same-sex marriage under their own laws or because they tie their marriage laws to state law. A dozen tribes prohibit same-sex marriage, including the largest tribe, the Navajo Nation. While a federal statute requires tribes to adhere to equal protection and due process principles, the tribes are allowed to interpret those rights according to their own cultures and traditions. For a discussion of the difficulties created when a tribe does not allow same-sex marriage, *see* Suzanne D. Painter-Thorne, Fraying the Knot: Marital Property, Probate, and Practical Problems with Tribal Marriage Bans, 85 Brook. L. Rev. 471 (2020).

6. As discussed in Chapter 2, the majority decision in Dobbs v. Jackson Women's Health Organization, 142 S. Ct. 2228 (2022), says that stripping constitutional protection for abortion rights under the Fourteenth Amendment's due process clause did not call into question rights protected under the same clause, such as the right to marry. However, Justice Thomas, in his concurring opinion, wrote that "in future cases, we should reconsider all of this Court's substantive due process precedents, including Griswold, Lawrence, and Obergefell." If a future majority of the Supreme Court adopted Justice Thomas's view, would *Loving* remain good law? Would *Obergefell*? Are there other constitutional provisions, such as the equal protection clause, that would secure a right to marry for couples of the same sex? In view of the uncertainty about these issues, in 2022 Congress enacted legislation to protect same-sex and interracial marriage. The legislation does not require states to permit such marriages to occur within their borders, but it requires all states to recognize and give full effect to marriages validly entered into in other states. It also provides that such marriages will be recognized for all purposes of federal law.

7. State law also provides some protection for marriage rights. At the time *Obergefell* was decided, high courts in seven states had held that denial of access to the benefits of marriage to same-sex couples violated the state constitutions, and three other states' highest courts have rejected such claims. The difference in outcomes turned on the level of scrutiny the courts applied and the way the courts applied prior cases. Cases holding that the same-sex marriage ban was unconstitutional were Kerrigan v. Comm'r Pub. Health, 957 A.2d 407 (Conn. 2008); Baehr v. Lewin, 852 P.2d 44 (Haw. 1993) and Baehr v. Miike, 1996 WL 694235 (Haw. 1st Cir. 1996), *aff'd* 950 P.2d 1234 (Haw. 1997), (superseded by constitutional amendment); Varnum v. Brien, 763 N.W.2d 862 (Iowa 2009); Goodridge v. Department of Public Health, 798 N.E.2d 941 (Mass. 2003); Lewis v. Harris, 908 A.2d 196 (N.J. 2006) and Garden State Equality v. Dow, 79 A.3d 1036 (N.J. 2013); and Griego v. Oliver, 316 P.3d 865 (N.M. 2013). The cases upholding the ban were Conaway v. Dean, 932 A.2d 571 (Md. App. 2007); Hernandez v. Robles, 855 N.E.2d 1 (N.Y. 2006); and Andersen v. King County, 138 P.3d 963 (Wash. 2006).

Some of these states had enacted legislation allowing same-sex marriage, and other states had enacted legislation without the spur of litigation. *Obergefell*, Appendix B, 135 S. Ct. at 2611. However, three-fifths of the states have constitutional provisions that ban same-sex marriage that could be revived if *Obergefell* were overruled.

Between 1999 and 2014, at least 15 states and the District of Columbia enacted civil union or other statutes creating a status relationship for same-sex couples that provided some or all the rights and duties of marriage under state law but without calling the relationship marriage. The clear impetus for most of this legislation was providing some protection to same-sex couples while denying them access to marriage. Most of these statuses were open only to same-sex couples and provided all or almost all the state law benefits and obligations of marriage without being called marriage. Domestic partnerships were open to opposite-sex couples where at least one partner was 62 or older in only a few states. The Hawaii legislation was unique in being open to any couple not eligible to marry until California changed its domestic partnership statute to open it to almost all couples in 2020. Hawaii Reciprocal Beneficiaries Legislation, H.B. 118 (1997), codified as Haw. Rev. Stat. Ch. 572c. Cal. Fam. Code §297 (2020). After *Obergefell*, some states repealed their civil union and domestic partnership laws. If *Obergefell* were overruled, statutes in a number of states that prohibit same-sex civil unions and other relationships could be revived.

8. The Census Bureau estimated that in 2019, there were 980,000 same-sex couple households in the United States, and about 58 percent were married. Laquitta Walker & Danielle Taylor, Same-Sex Couple Households: 2019 (U.S. Census Bureau Rpt. No. ACSBR-005, Feb. 23, 2021), available at https://www.census.gov/library/publications/2021/acs/acsbr-005.html.

In comparison, civil unions and domestic partnerships have not been so popular. In 2011, two years before *Windsor*, 22 percent of all same-sex couples in the United States had a formalized relationship under state law; 47 percent of couples who lived in states that offered relationship recognition entered into the status at some point. They preferred marriage over civil unions or domestic partnerships even when the latter offered full rights. On average, 30 percent of same-sex couples married in the first year their state allowed marriage, compared to 18 percent who entered civil unions or comprehensive domestic partnerships in the first year possible. Only 8 percent entered limited domestic partnerships or reciprocal beneficiary or other limited relationships. In the states that allow opposite-sex couples to enter partnerships other than marriage, only 1 percent entered civil unions. M.V. Lee Badgett & Jody L. Herman, Patterns of Relationship Recognition by Same-Sex Couples in the United States at 1 (Nov. 2011). On the shift in popular and legal perception of civil unions and domestic partnerships in the United States, *see* Melissa Murray, Paradigms Lost: How Domestic Partnership Went from Innovation to Injury, 37 N.Y.U. Rev. L. & Soc. Change 291 (2013). In contrast, in some other countries, civil unions and domestic partnerships have continued to expand in popularity even after the countries adopted marriage equality. Nausica Palazzo, Marriage Apostates: Why Heterosexuals Seek Same-Sex Registered Partnerships, 42 Colum. J. Gender & L. 186 (2021).

NOTE: FREE EXERCISE CLAIMS COLLIDING WITH SAME-SEX COUPLES' RIGHTS

Dissenting opinions in *Obergefell* ask whether businesses and other entities with religious or other objections to same-sex marriage will be able to refuse to provide goods or services for this reason. Two cases that raise this question directly have reached the Supreme Court, but neither has yielded a decision on the merits. In Masterpiece Cakeshop, Ltd. v. Colorado Civil

Rights Comm'n, 138 S. Ct. 1719 (2018), the Court ruled in favor of a baker who refused to provide services to same-sex couples on religious grounds and who was charged with violating state civil rights laws. The Court held that the state civil rights commission which adjudicated the case showed "clear and impermissible" hostility toward the baker's religious beliefs, avoiding the question of how to resolve a clash between the rights recognized in *Obergefell* and those protected by the Free Exercise Clause. In Arlene's Flowers, Inc. v. Washington, a florist refused to provide flowers to a same-sex couple for their wedding on religious grounds. State v. Arlene's Flowers, Inc., 389 P.3d 543 (Wash. 2017). The Supreme Court of Washington ruled against the florist, and the Supreme Court remanded for reconsideration in light of *Masterpiece Cakeshop*. The Washington court affirmed its prior holding that the florist violated Washington's antidiscrimination law. 441 P.3d 1203 (Wash. 2019) *cert. denied* 41 S. Ct. 2884 (2021).

In a case raising related issues, the Supreme Court unanimously held that when the city of Philadelphia terminated a contract with Catholic Social Services because the agency would not certify same-sex couples as foster parents, it violated the agency's free exercise rights. Fulton v. City of Philadelphia, 141 S. Ct. 1868 (2021). The governing statute in this case permitted the city to make exceptions in its sole discretion to the requirement that agencies provide services to people without regard to their sexual orientation. Prior cases had held that where a rule provides a means for making individualized exceptions to a requirement, the state "may not refuse to extend that system to cases of 'religious hardship' without compelling reason." Employment Division v. Smith, 494 U.S. 872, 884 (1990). The Court further held that the city of Philadelphia's reasons for denying Catholic Services an exception were not compelling. The reasons offered were maximizing the number of foster families, protecting the city from liability, and treating equally prospective foster parents and foster children.

Public officials have also been sued for refusing to participate in same-sex weddings. The Wyoming Supreme Court held in In re Neely, 390 P.3d 728 (Wyo. 2017), that a magistrate who refused to perform weddings violated the rules of judicial conduct and that she should be censured, though not removed from office, provided that she committed to performing weddings in the future. The magistrate claimed that punishing her violated her free exercise and free speech rights, but the court said the state interest in judicial impartiality justified the ruling. In Ermold v. Davis, 936 F.3d 429 (6th Cir. 2019), *cert. denied*, 141 S. Ct. 3 (2020) a same-sex couple sued a county clerk for refusing to issue them a marriage license because of her religious beliefs. The Sixth Circuit held that she was protected from suit by sovereign immunity, since she acted on behalf of the state, but it held that she was not entitled to qualified immunity from suit in her personal capacity. Justice Thomas, joined by Justice Alito, issued a statement regarding the denial of certiorari, saying, "By choosing to privilege a novel constitutional right over the religious liberty interests explicitly protected in the First Amendment, and by doing so undemocratically, the Court has created a problem that only it can fix. Until then, *Obergefell* will continue to have 'ruinous consequences for religious liberty.'" 141 S. Ct. at 4.

Commentary on the tension between same-sex rights and free exercise includes Netta Barak-Corren, A License to Discriminate? The Market Response to Masterpiece Cakeshop, 56 Harv. C.R.-C.L. L. Rev. 315 (2021); Pamela S. Karlan, Just Desserts?: Public Accommodations, Religious Accommodations, Racial Equality, and Gay Rights, 2018 S.Ct. Rev. 145; Douglas Laycock, The Broader Implications of Masterpiece Cakeshop, 2019 BYU L. Rev. 167; Kaiponanea T. Matsumura, The Integrity of Marriage, 61 Wm. & Mary L. Rev. 453 (2019); Mark L. Movsesian, Masterpiece Cakeshop and the Future of Religious Freedom, 42 Harv. J.L. & Pub. Pol'y 711 (2019); Melissa Murray, Inverting Animus: Masterpiece Cakeshop and the New Minorities, 2018 S. Ct. Rev. 257; Arianna Nord, Comment, Queer and Convincing: Reviewing Freedom of Religion and LGBTQ+ Protections Post-Fulton v. City of Philadelphia, 97 Wash. L. Rev. 265, 280-281 (2022); Lawrence G. Sager & Nelson Tebbe, The Reality Principle, 34 Const. Comm. 171 (2019).

NOTE: INTERNATIONAL LEGAL RECOGNITION OF SAME-SEX COUPLES

Canada, Australia, and New Zealand   All three of these countries allow same-sex marriage. Some Canadian provinces recognize civil unions or domestic partnerships for same- and opposite-sex couples. In New Zealand, same-sex couples who had previously entered civil unions can convert them to marriages. Australian federal law recognizes de facto unions for same-sex as well as opposite-sex couples that have legal consequences similar to marriage. Most states and territories have civil unions or domestic partnerships as well.

Europe   Same-sex couples can marry in Austria, Belgium, Denmark, England and Wales, Finland, France, Germany, Greenland, Iceland, Ireland, Luxembourg, Malta, Netherlands, Norway, Portugal, Scotland, Slovenia, Spain, Sweden, and Switzerland. Eleven of the countries that allow same-sex marriage also recognize civil unions or domestic partnerships. Several other countries have legislation creating domestic partnerships or civil unions. Some of these acts give registrants all the rights of marriage, while others are limited; the most common difference is not allowing registered partners to adopt children.

Africa   South Africa enacted legislation in 2006 that allows same-sex and opposite-sex couples to enter a marriage or a civil union. In some portions of Spanish, Portuguese, French, and British territories same-sex marriage is allowed, along with domestic partnerships or de facto unions.

Central and South America   Argentina, Brazil, Chile, Colombia, Costa Rica, Cuba, Ecuador, and Uruguay, and most Mexican states allow same-sex marriage.

Asia   In 2017 the highest court of Taiwan ruled a ban on same-sex marriages is unconstitutional. The effective date of the ban was delayed for two years to allow the legislature to amend marriage laws.

C. RESTRICTIONS ON MARRYING

1. Formalities

The formal requirements for marriage vary somewhat from state to state. Ordinarily, the parties must secure a license. Many states impose a minimum waiting period between the issuance of a license and the marriage celebration, but this can often be waived. A ceremony is also generally required in all states that do not recognize common law marriage. However, the form of ceremony is rarely specified. Statutes typically require that an authorized person conduct the wedding, often with exceptions to recognize the practices of various religious groups or, as in the next case, Native tribes.

Duncan v. Duncan
754 S.E.2d 451 (N.C. App. 2014)

DILLON, Judge. . . . Barbara R. Duncan (Plaintiff) and John H. Duncan (Defendant) exchanged vows in two separate marriage ceremonies in North Carolina occurring twelve years apart. The first ceremony occurred on 15 October 1989 (the 1989 ceremony) and was presided over by Hawk Littlejohn, who held himself out to be a Cherokee medicine man and who was ordained as a minister by the Universal Life Church. In 2001, the parties' estate planning attorney expressed his concern that the 1989 ceremony was not valid; and, accordingly, on 14 October 2001, Plaintiff and Defendant participated in a second ceremony at the First Presbyterian Church in Franklin, North Carolina (the 2001 ceremony).

In 2005, Plaintiff commenced this action seeking, *inter alia*, divorce, equitable distribution, alimony, and child support, alleging that the parties' date of marriage was 15 October 1989, the date of the 1989 ceremony. Defendant filed responsive pleadings alleging, *inter alia*, that Hawk Littlejohn was not authorized under North Carolina law to perform a valid marriage ceremony; and, therefore, the parties' date of marriage was 14 October 2001, the date of the 2001 ceremony. . . .

Following a hearing, the trial court entered an order on 15 October 2007 (the 2007 order), concluding that the 1989 ceremony resulted in a valid marriage, that 15 October 1989 was "the date of marriage for all matters related to this Chapter 50 action" and that Defendant was estopped from contesting the validity of the 1989 ceremony.

. . . Defendant appeals from the 2007 order . . .

. . . A marriage based on a ceremony in North Carolina not properly solemnized pursuant to the requirements of N.C. Gen. Stat. § 51–1 is voidable. . . .

Regarding the validity of the 1989 ceremony, Defendant does *not* argue that the ceremony did not take place. Rather, he contends that Hawk Littlejohn, who officiated the ceremony, was not authorized under the North Carolina law in effect at that time to solemnize a marriage.

Our Supreme Court has held that "[a] common law marriage or marriage by consent is not recognized by this State." *State v. Lynch*, 272 S.E.2d 349, 354 (N.C. 1980). . . . The version of N.C. Gen. Stat. § 51–1 in effect in 1989 required, in pertinent part, that the parties "'express their solemn intent to marry in the presence of (1) an ordained minister of any religious denomination; or (2) a minister authorized by his church; or (3) a magistrate.'" . . .

. . . [T]he parties stipulated that Hawk Littlejohn had performed the 1989 ceremony, that he was a minister ordained by the Universal Life Church, and that the relevant facts regarding the Universal Life Church as it applies in this case were essentially the same as described by the Supreme Court in *Lynch*.

In *Lynch*, our Supreme Court reversed a bigamy conviction of a defendant where one of his two marriages was solemnized before a Universal Life Church minister. . . . In reversing the bigamy conviction, the Court stated as follows:

> A ceremony solemnized by a [layman] who bought for $10.00 a mail order certificate giving him 'credentials of minister' in the Universal Life Church, Inc.—whatever that is—is not a ceremony of marriage to be recognized for purposes of a bigamy prosecution in the State of North Carolina. *The evidence does not establish—rather, it negates the fact—that [the "minister"] was authorized under the laws of this State to perform a marriage ceremony.*

Since the record shows that Plaintiff stipulated that the "relevant facts" concerning the Universal Life Church and Hawk Littlejohn's ordination as a minister therein were essentially the same as described by our Supreme Court in *Lynch*, and since our Supreme Court in *Lynch* stated that evidence that an individual was ordained by the Universal Life Church—as the Church is described in that case—"negates the fact that [the individual] was authorized under the laws of this State to perform a marriage ceremony," we are compelled in the present case to conclude that Defendant met his high burden of demonstrating that Hawk Littlejohn was not authorized under the applicable version of N.C. Gen. Stat. § 51–1 to solemnize the 1989 ceremony.

We do not agree with the trial court's conclusion that N.C. Gen. Stat. § 51–1.1 passed by our Legislature in 1981, the year after *Lynch* was decided, renders the 1989 ceremony valid. Specifically, the trial court correctly found that "the Legislature passed N.C. Gen. Stat. Sec. 51–1.1 in 1981, prior to the parties [sic] marriage, which expressly validated all marriages performed by ministers of the Universal Life Church prior to July 3, 1981[,]" but then erroneously concluded that "the effect of [N.C. Gen. Stat. § 51–1.1] is to give legislative approval to marriages performed by ministers of the Universal Life Church[.]". . . .

Indeed, in *Fulton v. Vickery*, this Court described N.C. Gen. Stat. § 51–1.1 as a "curative statute." In other words, by limiting the scope of the statute only to those marriages performed prior to 3 July 1981, the Legislature intended to provide relief to any "innocent" couple whose marital status was suddenly put in doubt by the *Lynch* decision. However, had the Legislature intended to validate otherwise voidable marriages solemnized by the Universal Life Church *for all time*, it could have easily done so.

. . . Accordingly, the parties' marriage—as based on the 1989 ceremony—was voidable . . .

Defendant argues that the trial court erred by concluding that, even if the 1989 ceremony was voidable, Defendant was judicially estopped from contesting its validity. We agree.

Our Supreme Court has stated that three factors are to be considered in applying the doctrine of judicial estoppel: (1) whether a party's position in a legal proceeding is clearly inconsistent with an earlier position taken in a legal proceeding; (2) whether the party succeeded in persuading a court to accept the party's earlier position; and (3) whether the party seeking to assert the inconsistent position would derive some unfair advantage or impose an unfair detriment on the opposing party.

In this case, the trial court's order does not contain any finding that Defendant took the position in this or any other judicial proceeding that the 1989 ceremony was valid. Rather, the record reflects that Defendant *denied* in his initial pleading in this action Plaintiff's allegation that they were married in 1989. . . .

Defendant argues that the trial court erred by concluding that he is equitably estopped from challenging the validity of the 1989 ceremony. Specifically, he argues that Plaintiff is barred from asserting equitable estoppel because she has "unclean hands" by having participated in the 1989 ceremony. . . .

Whether principles of estoppel apply "turn[s] on the particular facts of each case." . . .

We believe that the facts in the present case—as found by the trial court in the 2007 order— . . . suggest that both Plaintiff and Defendant were equally negligent in relying on Hawk Littlejohn's credentials. Accordingly, we believe that the trial court correctly applied the law in concluding that Defendant was equitably estopped from challenging the validity of the 1989 ceremony.

The scales of equity might have tipped towards Defendant had the evidence shown that Plaintiff had actually known at the time of the 1989 ceremony that Hawk Littlejohn was not authorized to solemnize a North Carolina marriage *or* that she had misrepresented to Defendant prior to the 1989 ceremony that she had engaged in some due diligence to determine the validity of Hawk Littlejohn's credentials where she, in fact, had not done so. Further, had Plaintiff not agreed to participate in the 2001 ceremony, the scales of equity would have swayed against her, at least with respect to any benefit she seeks in this action that relates to the period of the marriage occurring after she had learned in 2001 that her marriage was voidable. . . . We note that Defendant has pled allegations that might enhance Plaintiff's culpability, including allegations about her expertise in Native American culture and her desire and insistence that she and Defendant participate in the traditional Cherokee ceremony officiated by Hawk Littlejohn. However, there is nothing . . . indicating that any testimony or other evidence was presented to the trial court regarding these allegations. . . .

Accordingly, we affirm the trial court's determination that the date of marriage for purposes of this action is 15 October 1989. . . .

McGee, Judge, concurring in result with separate opinion. . . . I agree that the trial court did not err in ruling that Defendant was equitably estopped from denying 15 October 1989 as the date of marriage. I write separately because I believe the remainder of Section II of the majority opinion is dicta, which unnecessarily, and perhaps erroneously, addresses issues better left to future panels of this Court, should these issues again arise.

Though I do not believe we need to, or should, address any issues beyond equitable estoppel in Section II, I am concerned with the statement of the majority that "Defendant met his high burden [of] show[ing] that Hawk Littlejohn was not authorized under the applicable version of N.C. Gen. Stat. § 51–1 to solemnize the 1989 ceremony." I am not at all certain Defendant met his burden in this regard, and would much prefer we not address this issue in dicta.

Initially, pursuant to N.C. Gen. Stat. § 51–1, a marriage ceremony results in a valid marriage if, *inter alia*, it is conducted "[i]n the presence of a minister authorized by a church[.]" . . . [T]he majority fails to consider Hawk Littlejohn's uncontested status as a Cherokee Medicine Man.

The trial court made the following relevant findings of fact in its 15 October 2007 order:
10. That, on . . . October 15th, 1989, . . . Plaintiff and Defendant participated in a marriage ceremony performed by Hawk Littlejohn, a Cherokee Medicine Man; . . .

12. That the ceremony was attended by friends and family, had several sweat lodges, there was an exchange of corn and blankets, bagpipes were played and the exchanging of gold wedding bands took place. Further, . . . Defendant wore a kilt for the ceremony; . . .

27. That the parties in this case expressed their solemn intent to marry at a traditional Cherokee ceremony attended by family and friends[.] . . .

29. That . . . Defendant failed to produce any evidence or offer controlling law that Hawk Littlejohn was not . . . "authorized by his church" to perform weddings in accordance with the traditions of the Cherokee Indian Nation or in accordance with N.C. Gen. Stat. Sec. 51–1. . . .

I would also note that the issue of whether Hawk Littlejohn, or another Native American religious figure, could validly perform marriages pursuant to N.C.G.S. § 51–1, before its amendment on 1 October 2001, has never been answered by our appellate courts. In dissenting from the majority opinion in *Pickard v. Pickard, 625 S.E.2d 869 (N.C. App. 2006)*, that a marriage performed by Hawk Littlejohn in 1991 was valid through the application of judicial estoppel, the dissenting judge made the argument that the marriage was valid as performed, due in part to Hawk Littlejohn's status as a Cherokee Medicine Man. . . .

Finally, though not an issue argued on this appeal, I disagree with the definitive statement of the majority declaring the 1989 ceremony invalid, and thus the resulting marriage "voidable," because I recognize a possibility, as of yet undecided by any appellate court of this state, that the 1989 ceremony resulted in a valid marriage by action of statute.

Our General Assembly, on 10 May 2001, approved legislation to amend N.C.G.S. § 51–1 and other statutes ("the Act"). . . . By Section 1 of H.B. 142, N.C.G.S. § 51–1 was amended in part to read:

> A valid and sufficient marriage is created by the consent of a male and female person who may lawfully marry, presently to take each other as husband and wife, freely, seriously and plainly expressed by each in the presence of the other, either:
>
> (1) a. In the presence of an ordained minister of any religious denomination, a minister authorized by a church, or a magistrate; and
> b. With the consequent declaration by the minister or magistrate that the persons are husband and wife; or
> (2) *In accordance with any mode of solemnization recognized by any religious denomination, or federally or State recognized Indian Nation or Tribe.*

The relevant enacting language of H.B. 142 is as follows: "[Section 1] of this act becomes effective October 1, 2001." Because the Act was enacted in part to *validate* marriages performed in accordance with recognized Native American nations or tribes, and because there is no temporal restriction in the enacting language, I would not declare the 1989 marriage in this matter invalid and voidable, and would not imply that other marriage ceremonies performed in a similar manner before 1 October 2001, are invalid and therefore voidable. . . .

NOTES AND QUESTIONS

1. What is the purpose of requiring that a wedding ceremony be conducted by a minister, a magistrate, or other authorized person? Was this purpose satisfied in this case?

The North Carolina Supreme Court, in State v. Lynch, held that the Universal Life Church is not a church that can ordain ministers authorized to perform weddings. How does a court decide what constitutes a "real" church?

Center for Inquiry, Inc. v. Marion Cir. Ct. Clerk, 758 F.3d 869 (7th Cir. 2014), held that an Indiana statute that allowed officials designated by religious groups to officiate at marriages, but not officials of secular groups such as humanist societies violated the establishment clause of the First Amendment. Three other states (Florida, Maine, and South Carolina) allow people to solemnize marriages by becoming notaries public, but Indiana does not. Four states (Alaska, Massachusetts, Vermont, and Virginia) allow anyone to solemnize a marriage, and six (Colorado, Kansas, Montana, Pennsylvania, New York, and Wisconsin) allow a couple to solemnize their own marriage. 758 F.3d at 871.

2. After *Lynch* was decided, the North Carolina legislature enacted a statute that validates marriages celebrated by Universal Life Church ministers before July 3, 1981. Does this mean that marriages performed after that date are invalid?

According to the dissent in *Duncan*, what was the legal impact of the legislature's enactment of H.B. 142 in 2001, regarding marriage ceremonies conducted according to the law of a Native American nation or tribe? Why do you suppose the majority apparently did not agree?

3. Many jurisdictions recognize the "mock priest" rule, which provides that if either party believed in good faith that the officiant was authorized to perform the wedding, the marriage is valid. If this rule were applied in *Duncan*, what outcome?

4. Ms. Duncan argued that Mr. Duncan was judicially estopped from denying that Hawk Littlejohn was authorized to perform marriages, but there was no evidence that Mr. Duncan had ever represented that he believed he was validly married in any legal proceeding. In an earlier case cited by *Duncan*, the court found that a man was judicially estopped to deny Littlejohn's authority because he had earlier represented in an adoption proceeding that he was married. Pickard v. Pickard, 625 S.E.2d 869 (N.C. App. 2006). A principal purpose of the doctrine of judicial estoppel is to preserve the authority of legal proceedings.

5. The *Duncan* court concluded that Mr. Duncan was equitably estopped to deny Littlejohn's authority because he participated in the wedding ceremony, which constituted an implicit assertion that Littlejohn had that authority. In some states, parties asserting an equitable estoppel claim must show that they detrimentally relied on an assertion to obtain relief. Could Ms. Duncan show detrimental reliance? In North Carolina, a line of cases says that if the parties are equally negligent in failing to discover that some representation is false, either can be equitably estopped to deny the truth of the representation without providing detrimental reliance. However, a party who was more negligent than the other cannot claim the benefit of equitable estoppel.

6. A number of cases concern the validity of weddings conducted without a license, with mixed results. In one of the best known, Carabetta v. Carabetta, 438 A.2d 109 (Conn. 1980), the governing statute provided that "[n]o persons shall be married without a license." However, the Connecticut Supreme Court held that the statutory requirement was "directory" rather than "mandatory" and that the marriage was therefore not "null and void." The court further suggested that it would hold a marriage void only if the legislature expressly required that result. *See also* Levick v. MacDougall, 805 S.E.2d 775 (Va. 2017); In re Estate of Peacock, 788 S.E.2d 191 (N.C. App. 2016); Vlach v. Vlach, 835 N.W.2d 72 (Neb. 2013); Rivera v. Rivera, 243 P.3d 1148 (N.M. App. 2010) (although parties' Texas license did not authorize marriage in New Mexico, license requirement is only directory, collecting cases from other jurisdictions. *Contra* Estate of DePasse, 118 Cal. Rptr. 2d 143 (Cal. App. 2002) (marriage license requirement is mandatory, and its absence cannot be cured by petition to declare the existence of the marriage after the death of one of the parties); Yaghoubinejad v. Haghighi, 894 A.2d 1173 (N.J. Super. App. 2006) (applying statute that makes any marriage performed without a license "absolutely void").

What value does a regulation that is merely "directory" have? What reasons would support making a regulation "directory" rather than "mandatory"?

PROBLEM

Devorah and Steven participated in a hurriedly arranged wedding ceremony before their rabbi without first obtaining a license because the rabbi did not want them to move into an apartment together without being married. He told the couple to be sure to get a license and have another ceremony, but they never did. After the ceremony, Steven tore up the form ketubah (marriage contract) that the two had signed, but when they applied to join a synagogue, he said Devorah and he were married. Devorah received public assistance as a single parent and described herself as single in a lawsuit. She worked in Steven's law firm as a paralegal without being paid. After living together ten years, they separated, and Devorah sued for divorce. Steven replied that they were not married. What arguments should the parties make?

2. Mental Capacity

The classic test for mental capacity to marry is similar to legal capacity tests in other circumstances: whether the person has the ability to understand the rights and duties of marriage. Other concerns, including protecting vulnerable people from exploitation, doubts about the ability of disabled people to raise children, and eugenics are also sometimes in play in the cases.

In re Marriage of Oakley
340 S.W.3d 628 (Mo. App. 2011)

GARY W. LYNCH, Judge. Christopher C. Oakley ("Husband"), through his legal guardian and father, Lester Oakley ("Father"), appeals the Circuit Court of Howell County's denial of his petition for annulment of marriage. Father contends, first, that the trial court plainly erred in denying the petition because Husband had been declared incapacitated in the State of Florida and was therefore legally unable to consent to marry under the Florida judgment and, second, that the trial court's judgment was against the weight of the evidence. Finding no error as alleged, we affirm.

. . . [T]he following evidence was adduced at trial.

In 1986, Husband—a child at the time—was hit by a truck and suffered a traumatic brain injury. Father was first appointed Husband's plenary guardian in Florida in 1988. Father alleged that in 1995, he was appointed Husband's legal guardian in Florida, pursuant to a petition for determination of incapacity. A third party, Donald E. Brown, was named Husband's conservator. Brown is responsible for managing Husband's settlement funds from the truck accident, paying Husband's bills, and giving Husband an allowance. Father and Husband moved to Missouri in 1989, but Father was not issued letters of guardianship in Missouri until October 2009.

Husband resides at Lamplighter Village ("Lamplighter"), an assisted-living facility in Howell County, Missouri. Husband actually lives in a Lamplighter-owned residence that is located across the street from its main facility. Lamplighter is responsible for ensuring that Husband is bathed, has clean clothes, has adequate nutrition, and takes any prescribed medication. Husband receives an allowance and does not pay his own bills.

Sometime before 1997, Husband became involved with another Lamplighter resident, Melissa D. Warren, now Melissa D. Oakley ("Wife"). Husband and Wife live together in the independent residence across from Lamplighter. Wife has a limited guardian and conservator in Charm Eagleman, the Howell County Public Administrator. Thus, Wife also does not pay her own bills or manage her own money.

Husband and Wife approached each guardian seeking permission to marry. Both Father and Eagleman declined to grant permission. After deciding that they "wanted to get married like everybody else[,]" Husband and Wife had a friend drive them to Salem, Arkansas, where they obtained a marriage license on October 5, 2006. They then drove back to Missouri and returned to Salem the following day and got married. Upon returning to Missouri after their marriage, Husband and Wife continued to live together at the Lamplighter residence and held themselves out as a married couple.

Although Father knew about the marriage within two or three months after it occurred, he waited nearly two years before filing the underlying action for annulment. He did so after consulting with Husband's conservator and their discussion that the marriage might be considered valid. In his petition, Father claimed that the Florida guardianship papers expressly removed from Husband the right to marry without court approval, and therefore the marriage was void. A photocopy of the Florida guardianship orders was attached to the petition.

Trial was held February 9, 2010. Father presented the testimony of Dr. Dale Halfaker, a psychologist who examined Husband on two occasions, first on November 26, 2002, and again on August 26, 2008. Dr. Halfaker initially met with Husband to tour Lamplighter and make sure Husband's needs were being addressed there. At that time, Dr. Halfaker determined Husband's IQ to be 71, which is just above the level of mild retardation but below the average range. He stated that Husband's "capacity to think, reason, problem-solve, use language to draw conclusions and that sort of thing was significantly diminished." During his second examination of Husband, undertaken to ensure that Husband's needs were still being met at Lamplighter, Dr. Halfaker determined Husband's IQ to be 70 and "basically unchanged"; he felt Husband's answers to objective test questions were "[a] little bit better[.]" Dr. Halfaker acknowledged, however, that simply having an IQ in the borderline range does not disqualify an individual from entering into a marriage. After opining that he feels he has the capacity to judge whether Husband "could understand the total ramifications of being married[,]" Dr. Halfaker stated,

> I think [Husband] understands marriage in a general sense of that it's a relationship and that you perhaps live with someone, you spend time together, you perhaps have meals together, sleep together and that sort of thing. My concern would be that he does not or would not have the full capacity to take into account all of the legal, financial and just practical ramifications for what a marriage might be. Things like issues of taxes or inheritance or health insurance, those kinds of pieces.

Dr. Halfaker never asked Husband any questions pertaining to his marriage and believes that, although they may not fully comprehend all of the legal and financial consequences of marriage, Husband and Wife appear to have a happy and successful "marriage kind of thing." Dr. Halfaker never had any communication with Wife regarding Husband, and admitted that he would have asked Husband different, more specific questions if he had evaluated him with the specific purpose of determining Husband's capacity to marry. He also admitted that there could be significant emotional consequences for Husband if the marriage was suddenly declared void.

Father, who resides in Eminence, Missouri, testified that he has no objection to Husband and Wife living together, but he does not believe they should be married, primarily because of potential difficulty in moving Husband if Father should relocate from the area. Father also does not believe that Husband understands "the full scenario[,]" asking, "What happens if he decides ten years from now that if somebody else—another girl comes in his life and it's better and bigger and everything than what he had[?]" Father expressly denied his permission as guardian when Husband and Wife sought his approval to get married, stating, "Why would you buy the cow when you get the milk for free[?]"

Eagleman, Wife's limited guardian and conservator, testified that she, too, denied the couple permission to marry. Eagleman has observed Husband and Wife's relationship on many occasions, stating that they live together as husband and wife and behave as a married couple, doing such activities as going grocery shopping and taking walks; they share the household responsibilities, and do a "pretty good job" of taking care of themselves. Although she did not grant her permission for them to marry, Eagleman did sit down with Husband and Wife to discuss the emotional and financial meaning of getting married, and she believes they both understood the conversation. In her opinion, Husband and Wife made a conscious decision to marry in spite of her admonitions regarding the possible negative financial consequences. In her testimony, Eagleman emphasized that neither Husband nor Wife deal with financial issues on a daily basis because both have conservators. She requested that the trial court uphold the marriage as valid, and stated her intent to seek court approval to allow Husband and Wife to marry if the trial court did annul the marriage.

Husband testified that he "want[s] to stay married[,] . . . [b]ecause [he] love[s Wife] and, hopefully, she feels the same about [him]." He further stated that when he married Wife, he wanted to take care of her, and he still wants to take care of her to the best of his ability. Wife testified that she is happier being married to Husband and that she is committed to taking care of Husband. She stated that she and Husband "want to grow old together[,]" and that both would do whatever they could to take care of the other.

The trial court entered its judgment on March 9, 2010, finding that Father had not met his burden of demonstrating that Husband was not legally able to consent to marry. The trial court stated that it "accepted some of the testimony of each witness as credible and rejected other parts of the testimony of each witness as not credible." The trial court applied Arkansas law in reaching its decision.

Father filed a motion for new trial on April 8, 2010. . . . The trial court denied the motion. This appeal timely followed.

Father presents two points for our review. We review them in the order presented.

In his first point, Father contends:

> The trial court erred in denying the Petition for Annulment and declaring the marriage of [Husband] and [Wife] to be valid because the court's denial of the Petition for Annulment and declaration of the validity of the marriage were plain error in that the marriage was void; [Husband] had, prior to the marriage, been declared incapacitated and unable to enter into contracts or to marry under the guardianship entered in the State of Florida; no court approval was obtained prior to the marriage; and the Florida guardianship is granted full faith and credit in Missouri.

Because the Florida order of guardianship was not properly before the trial court, Father's first point is denied. . . .

In his second point Father claims:

> The trial court erred in finding that [Father] had not met his burden of rebutting the presumption of a valid marriage between [Husband] and [Wife] because the weight of the evidence supported a finding that the marriage was invalid in that [Husband] was incapacitated at the time he became married to [Wife]; [Husband] had sustained a severe closed head injury

as a result of an automobile accident and suffered significant neurological damage including reduced I.Q., difficulty with memory, problem solving, money management; [Husband] was and is unable to understand the legal and financial concepts of marriage; and he was previously declared incapacitated and incapable of entering into contracts and marrying.

We disagree.

This Court reviews judgments in annulment cases under the standard articulated in *Murphy [v. Carron*, 536 S.W.2d 30, 32 (Mo. banc 1976)] "[T]he decree or judgment of the trial court will be sustained by the appellate court unless there is no substantial evidence to support it, unless it is against the weight of the evidence, unless it erroneously declares the law, or unless it erroneously applies the law." We defer "to the trial court's credibility determinations, recognizing that the [trial] court is free to believe all, part, or none of the testimony presented. . . . The trial court's determinations are entitled to deference even if some of the evidence supports a different conclusion." . . .

Father's failure to fully identify and develop the evidence favorable to the trial court's judgment necessarily undermines his ability to demonstrate how that evidence was so lacking in probative value that, when considered in the context of the totality of the evidence, it failed to induce belief in the existence of a valid marriage. Granting Father's point would require this Court to compile its own demonstration of how the omitted favorable evidence is lacking in probative value so as to be against the weight of the evidence, which would transform this Court into an advocate for Father, a role we are prohibited from assuming. Father's second point is denied.[2]

The trial court's judgment is affirmed.

NOTES AND QUESTIONS

1. Nominally, Christopher brought the action to annul his own marriage through his guardian. However, of course, Christopher very much did not want an annulment, and the real party seeking an order invalidating the marriage was the guardian.

Persons who lack the capacity to manage their affairs independently may be placed under the care of a conservator, guardian, or both. The use of these terms, and the powers that go with them, differ greatly from jurisdiction to jurisdiction. A guardian has legal authority to make personal decisions for the protected person, such as where the person will live. A plenary guardian has much the same powers that a parent has with regard to a child. *See, e.g.*, UPC §5-315. A conservator is appointed to protect the financial interests of a person and

---

2. An *ex gratia* review of the record reveals that the trial court's judgment was not against the weight of the evidence. Under applicable Arkansas law, a party lacks the requisite mental capacity to marry if the party is "incapable of understanding the nature, effect, and consequences of the marriage." "[C]lear reason, discernment, and sound judgment" are not necessary to enter into a marriage. Furthermore, there is a presumption of validity:

> Annulment of a marriage is the exception and not the rule, and must be granted only upon extraordinary facts. . . . The burden of proving the invalidity of a marriage rests upon him who asserts such invalidity, and a marriage will not be declared invalid except upon clear, cogent and convincing proof. The evidence presented to the trial court demonstrates that Husband and Wife are, and have been for over a decade, in a long-term, committed relationship; Husband desired to get married for some time before actually doing so; Husband repeatedly attempted to marry Wife and wants to remain married; Husband loves Wife and wants to take care of her for the rest of his life; and Husband may not understand the financial ramifications and responsibilities of marriage, but he does not handle his own finances nor those of Wife. Although Father includes the Florida order of guardianship as support for his argument, it cannot be considered for the reasons stated *supra*. The totality of the evidence—including the lack of an authenticated Florida order of guardianship—demonstrates that the trial court's finding that Father failed to meet his burden was not against the weight of the evidence.

has a duty to receive a ward's income, to decide how much of the estate should be used for living expenses, and to prevent loss or waste of the ward's property or business. *See, e.g.*, UPC §5-401 (Official 2010 Text).

Ordinarily, the fact that a guardian or conservator has been appointed for someone does not automatically mean that the person lacks the capacity to marry. However, the 2006 Florida statute under which Christopher's father was originally appointed his guardian provides that if a guardianship order removes a person's legal capacity to contract, the person can marry only with court approval. Fla. Stat. §744.3215(2)(a) (2022). Christopher's father tried to get the Missouri court to recognize and enforce the Florida court order that removed Christopher's capacity to contract but failed because his attorney did not properly validate the order. Even if the order had been admitted into evidence in the Missouri case, it is not clear that Christopher's marriage would have been annulled. In Smith v. Smith, 224 So.3d 740 (Fla. 2017), the Florida Supreme Court held that a marriage entered into without complying with this statute is neither void nor voidable, but it is invalid. However, the court said that the ward and the intended spouse may seek court approval after they marry, and if approval is granted, the marriage is valid.

2. Why did the guardian object to Christopher being married if he didn't mind that Christopher lived with Melissa? Why did Melissa's guardian originally refuse to consent to the marriage? Did they believe that Christopher and Melissa lacked capacity to marry under the test discussed in footnote 2? What does it mean to understand the nature, effect, and consequences of the marriage? Why do you suppose Melissa's guardian changed her mind and asked the court not to annul the marriage?

3. State restrictions on marriage by the developmentally disabled and the mentally ill may reflect a eugenic concern that found strong support during the late nineteenth and early twentieth centuries. Belief in the hereditary sources of mental illness and faith in scientific solutions to social evils, combined with a growing concern about the health of the American family, seemed to suggest the value of standards for conjugal fitness that would reduce the incidence of "feeble-minded" children.

> Advocates of hereditary restrictions touted them as necessary weapons to defend the nation from degeneration. Feminist and pioneering social scientist Elizabeth Cady Stanton declared in 1879 that the "law of heredity should exclude many from entering the marriage relation." Ten years earlier she had insisted that only those "who can give the world children with splendid physique, strong intellect, and high moral sentiment, may conscientiously take on themselves the responsibility of marriage and maternity." Similarly, sociologist George Howard complained in 1904 that "under pleas of 'romantic love' we blandly yield to sexual attraction in choosing our mates, ignoring the welfare of the race." Appealing for a "higher standard of conjugal choice," he contended that experience "shows that in wedlock natural and sexual selection should play a smaller and artificial selection a larger role." Here, he declared, "the state has a function to perform."

Michael Grossberg, Governing the Hearth: Law and the Family in Nineteenth Century America 148 (1985).

4. The other large category of cases in which competence to marry is challenged, in addition to those involving people with mental disabilities, concern elderly people who marry those in a position to take advantage of them, often caretakers or others who provide services. An example is Malousek v. Meyer, 962 N.W.2d 676 (Neb. 2021). Greg Meyer and Molly Stacey began living together in 2009. In 2015 she was diagnosed with cancer, and she died in 2017. Greg and Molly married nine days before her death, and the next day she changed beneficiary designations on accounts and insurance policies to favor Greg, rather than her adult children from a former relationship, who had been the beneficiaries. She also executed quit claim deeds on her homes to Greg. Until the marriage Molly had repeatedly said that she wanted her property to go to her adult children and that she would never marry again. After her death Molly's adult children and the administrator of her estate filed a declaratory judgment action seeking declarations that the marriage and the property transactions were invalid because they were procured by Greg's undue influence and because Molly lacked capacity. The evidence was divided about whether Molly had capacity and acted freely. The Nebraska Supreme Court affirmed the trial court findings in favor of Molly's children because of the abrupt change in her plans near the end of her life which were kept secret by Greg, evidence that she was delirious during part of the time the changes were made, and the trial court's findings that the children's witnesses were more credible.

5. Professor Knaplund argues that most cases, dealing with similar fact patterns, do not provide enough protection for vulnerable elders in the community. On the other hand, she finds that elders who live in care facilities face the problem of too much "protection"—rules and practices that deny residents opportunities for intimacy, not only because facilities fear they will be sued for failing to protect residents with declining competence but also because families don't want to think about grandma or grandpa being sexually active. Kristine S. Knaplund, The Right of Privacy and America's Aging Population, 86 Denv. U. L. Rev. 439 (2009). *See also* Gayle Doll, Dementia and Consent for Sex Reconsidered, 12 NAELA J. 133 (2016); Terry L. Turnipseed, How Do I Love Thee, Let Me Count the Days: Deathbed Marriages in America, 96 Ky. L.J. 275 (2007-2008).

3. Relationship

All states prohibit marriage between persons closely related by blood—that is, through a common ancestor—and most states criminalize sexual relationships between close relatives. Moreover, most states interpret these prohibitions as applying to persons related by the half as well as the whole blood. The relationships that result in domestic relations litigation typically are those between first cousins, uncles and nieces, and aunts and nephews, as well as certain nonconsanguineous relations—that is, between people related by marriage or "affinity" rather than by blood.

Nguyen v. Holder
21 N.E.3d 1023 (N.Y. 2014)

MEMORANDUM. Following certification of a question by the United States Court of Appeals for the Second Circuit and acceptance of the question by this Court pursuant to section 500.27 of the Rules of Practice of the Court of the Court of Appeals and after hearing argument by counsel for the parties and consideration of the briefs and the record submitted, certified question answered in the negative. A marriage where a husband is the half brother of the wife's mother is not void as incestuous under Domestic Relations Law §5(3).

SMITH, J. (concurring). . . . Petitioner is a citizen of Vietnam. In January of 2000, at the age of 19, she was married in Rochester, New York to Vu Truong, who was 24 and a naturalized American citizen. Later that year, petitioner was granted the status of a conditional permanent resident in the United States on the basis of her marriage.

According to the factual findings of the United States Board of Immigration Appeals, which the Second Circuit accepted as supported by substantial evidence, petitioner's mother was born in 1950 to a woman named Nguyen Thi Ba. Twenty-five years later, Nguyen Thi Ba gave birth to Vu Truong. Petitioner's mother and Vu Truong had different fathers. Thus petitioner's mother was Vu Truong's half sister, and petitioner is his half niece.

An immigration judge ordered petitioner removed from the country on the ground that her purported marriage to an American citizen was void, and the Board of Immigration

Appeals affirmed. Petitioner sought review of that ruling in the Second Circuit, and the Second Circuit certified the following question to us:

"Does section 5(3) of New York's Domestic Relations Law void as incestuous a marriage between an uncle and niece 'of the half blood' (that is, where the husband is the half-brother of the wife's mother)?"

Section 5 of the Domestic Relations Law reads in full:

"A marriage is incestuous and void whether the relatives are legitimate or illegitimate between either:
"1. An ancestor and a descendant;
"2. A brother and sister of either the whole or the half blood;
"3. An uncle and niece or an aunt and nephew.
"If a marriage prohibited by the foregoing provisions of this section be solemnized it shall be void, and the parties thereto shall each be fined not less than fifty nor more than one hundred dollars and may, in the discretion of the court in addition to said fine, be imprisoned for a term not exceeding six months. Any person who shall knowingly and wilfully solemnize such marriage, or procure or aid in the solemnization of the same, shall be deemed guilty of a misdemeanor and shall be fined or imprisoned in like manner."

We must decide whether subdivision (3) of this statute should be read to include a half uncle and half niece (or half aunt and half nephew). There is something to be said on both sides of this question.

In common speech, the half brother of one's mother or father would usually be referred to as an uncle, and the daughter of one's half sister or half brother would usually be referred to as a niece; the terms "half uncle" and "half niece" are not in common use. Thus it is perfectly plausible to read subdivision (3) as including half blood relatives. On the other hand, the authors of Domestic Relations Law §5(2), when prohibiting brother-sister marriages, went to the trouble of adding the words "of either the whole or the half blood." No similar words appear in section 5(3), arguably implying that the legislature did not intend the uncle-niece prohibition to reach so far. The statute is ambiguous. Perhaps the likeliest inference is that the authors of section 5(3) gave no particular thought to the half uncle/half niece question, since if they had they could easily have clarified it either way.

Nor does New York case law point to any clear conclusion. . . . I would resolve the issue by considering the nature and the purpose of the statute we interpret.

Domestic Relations Law §5 is in part a criminal statute: it says that the participants in a prohibited marriage may be fined, and may be imprisoned for up to six months. Penal Law §255.25, using language very similar to that of Domestic Relations Law §5 ("ancestor, descendant, brother or sister of either the whole or the half blood, uncle, aunt, nephew or niece"), makes entry into a prohibited marriage a class E felony. Where a criminal statute is ambiguous, courts will normally prefer the more lenient interpretation, and the courts of several other states have followed that rule in interpreting their criminal laws not to prohibit relationships between uncles and nieces, or aunts and nephews, of the half blood. The government says that these cases are distinguishable because they were criminal cases; but we are here interpreting a statute that applies in both civil and criminal cases, and it would be strange at best to hold that the same words in the same statute mean different things in different kinds of litigation.

I also conclude that the apparent purpose of section 5(3) supports a reading that excludes half uncle/half niece marriages from its scope. Section 5 as a whole may be thought of as serving two purposes: it reflects long-held and deeply-rooted values, and it is also concerned with preventing genetic diseases and defects. Section 5(1) and (2), prohibiting primarily parent-child and brother-sister marriages, are grounded in the almost universal horror with which such marriages are viewed — a horror perhaps attributable to the destructive effect on normal family life that would follow if people viewed their parents, children, brothers and sisters as potential sexual partners. . . .

There is no comparably strong objection to uncle-niece marriages. Indeed, until 1893 marriages between uncle and niece or aunt and nephew, of the whole or half blood, were lawful in New York. And 60 years after the prohibition was enacted we affirmed, in *May*, a judgment recognizing as valid a marriage between a half uncle and half niece that was entered into in Rhode Island and permitted by Rhode Island law. It seems from the Appellate Division's reasoning in *May* that the result would have been the same even if a full uncle and full niece had been involved. Thus Domestic Relations Law §5(3) has not been viewed as expressing strong condemnation of uncle-niece and aunt-nephew relationships.

The second purpose of section 5's prohibition of incest is to prevent the increased risk of genetic disorders generally believed to result from "inbreeding." (It may be no coincidence that the broadening of the incest statute in 1893 was roughly contemporaneous with the development of the modern science of genetics in the late nineteenth century.) We are not geneticists, and the record and the briefs in this case do not contain any scientific analysis; but neither party disputes the intuitively correct-seeming conclusion that the genetic risk in a half uncle, half niece relationship is half what it would be if the parties were related by the full blood. Indeed, both parties acknowledged at oral argument that the risk in a half uncle/half niece marriage is comparable to the risk in a marriage of first cousins. First cousins are allowed to marry in New York, and I conclude that it was not the legislature's purpose to avert the similar, relatively small, genetic risk inherent in relationships like this one.

GRAFFEO, J. (concurring). Under our long-standing principles of statutory construction, I conclude that a marriage between a half uncle and half niece, or a half aunt and half nephew, is permissible in New York based on the structure of Domestic Relations Law §5. . . .

Nevertheless, I write separately to emphasize that the legislature may see fit to revisit this provision. The record before us does not address the question of genetic ramifications for the children of these unions. Some of my colleagues assert that marriages between half uncles and half nieces, or half aunts and half nephews, are no different than marriages between first cousins. Perhaps there is no genetic basis for precluding such unions, but this Court was not presented with any scientific evidence upon which to draw an informed conclusion on this point.

From a public policy perspective, there may be other important concerns. Such relationships could implicate one of the purposes underlying incest laws, i.e., "maintaining the stability of the family hierarchy by protecting young family members from exploitation by older family members in positions of authority, and by reducing competition and jealous friction among family members." Similar intrafamilial concerns may arise regardless of whether the uncle or aunt in the marriage is of whole or half blood in relation to the niece or nephew. The issue of unequal stature in a family or cultural structure may not be implicated in this case but certainly could exist in other contexts, and a number of states have retained statutory prohibitions involving such marriages. These considerations are more appropriately evaluated in the legislative process.

NOTES AND QUESTIONS

1. How important to Judge Smith's opinion were the criminal penalties within the marriage statute? If only the penal law imposed a punishment, would the analysis have changed? What if incest were not a crime?

The European Court of Human Rights held that a British law forbidding marriage between a couple who had been father-in-law and daughter-in-law to each other before they both divorced violated Article 12 of the European Convention on Human Rights. The court held that because the law did not criminalize sexual relationships or cohabitation between former in-laws, the marriage prohibition was not rationally related to the asserted goals of preventing sexual rivalry between parents and children and preventing harm to minor children who might be adversely affected by such relationships. B and L v. UK (No. 36536/0s, Judgment Sept. 13, 2005, discussed in Ruth Gaffney-Rhys, The Law Relating to Affinity After B and L v. UK, 2005 Fam. L. 955-957).

2. Judge Graffeo is concerned about the implications of loosening the incest prohibition for child abuse. What is the connection?

3. It is common to dismiss genetic bases for incest restrictions on the ground that taboos against incest are far older than the science of genetics. Certainly genetics as a science is relatively recent; most of what we know about genetics has developed since the twentieth century. Nevertheless, observations about inheritance might informally have been made by earlier societies and transformed into taboos. Further, it is quite clear that the mating of closely related persons presents a genuine basis for genetic concern. This concern is particularly strong with respect to the inheritance of harmful recessive alleles (gene forms). A large number of traits in humans have been identified as the result of the expression of recessive alleles. Among these are phenylketonuria (leading to mental disability), amyotrophic lateral sclerosis (Lou Gehrig's disease), Bloom's syndrome (dwarfism with skin changes and susceptibility to cancer), and cystic fibrosis. These examples are taken from Linda R. Maxson & Charles H. Daugherty, Genetics: A Human Perspective 71-73 (2d ed. 1989).

In 2008 a British politician caused an uproar when he claimed that the rate of birth defects among the UK Pakistani population was caused by the frequency of first-cousin marriage. A biologist and a political scientist reviewed the history of bans on first-cousin marriages and whether they are justified by genetic concerns:

> US prohibitions on cousin marriage date to the Civil War and its immediate aftermath. The first ban was enacted by Kansas in 1858, with Nevada, North Dakota, South Dakota, Washington, New Hampshire, Ohio, and Wyoming following suit in the 1860s. Subsequently, the rate of increase in the number of laws was nearly constant until the mid-1920s; only Kentucky (1946), Maine (1985), and Texas (2005) have since banned cousins from marrying.(. . .
>
> . . . In any case, by the late nineteenth century, in Europe as well as the US, marrying one's cousin had come to be viewed as reckless, and today, despite its continued popularity in many societies and among European elites historically, the practice is highly stigmatized in the West (and parts of Asia—the People's Republic of China, Taiwan, and both North and South Korea also prohibit cousin marriage). . . . But is the practice as risky as many people assume?
>
> Until recently, good data on which to base an answer were lacking. . . . In an effort at clarification, the National Society of Genetic Counselors (NSGC) convened a group of experts to review existing studies on risks to offspring and issue recommendations for clinical practice. Their report concluded that the risks of a first-cousin union were generally much smaller than assumed—about 1.7%-2% above the background risk for congenital defects and 4.4% for pre-reproductive mortality—and did not warrant any special preconception testing. In the authors' view, neither the stigma that attaches to such unions in North America nor the laws that bar them were scientifically well-grounded. . . .
>
> . . . Although the report warned against generalizing from (and hence by implication to) more inbred populations, many writers, roughly averaging the statistics for birth defects and pre-reproductive mortality, noted that first-cousin marriage "only" increases the risk of adverse events by about 3%. But for several reasons, any overall calculation of risk is in fact quite complicated.
>
> First, even assuming that the deleterious phenotype arises solely from homozygosity at a single locus, the increased risk depends on the frequency of the allele involved; it is not an immediate consequence of the degree of relatedness between cousins. . . .
>
> Second, children of cousin marriages are likely to manifest an increased frequency of birth defects showing polygenic inheritance and interacting with environmental variation. But as the NSGC report notes, calculating the increased frequency of such quantitative traits is not

straightforward, and properly controlled studies are lacking. Moreover, socio-economic and other environmental influences will vary among populations, which can easily confound the effects of consanguinity. . . .

Third, . . . whether first-cousin marriage is an occasional or regular occurrence in the study population matters, and it is thus inappropriate to extrapolate findings from largely outbred populations with occasional first-cousin marriages to populations with high coefficients of inbreeding and vice-versa. Standard calculations, such as the commonly cited 3% additional risk, examine a pedigree in which the ancestors (usually grandparents) are assumed to be unrelated. In North America, marriages between consanguineal kin are strongly discouraged. But such an assumption is unwarranted in the case of UK Pakistanis, who have emigrated from a country where such marriage is traditional and for whom it is estimated that roughly 55%-59% of marriages continue to be between first cousins. . . .

Diane B. Paul & Hamish G. Spencer, "It's OK, We're Not Cousins by Blood": The Cousin Marriage Controversy in Historical Perspective, 6 PLoS Biol e320 (2008).

4. Whatever weight we give to genetic concerns, it is plain that social concerns strongly influence restrictions on sexual relations and marriage between close kin. For one thing, cultural restrictions are not always understandable in terms that make genetic sense. Historians and anthropologists have long wondered why a number of societies allow marriage between children born to the same father and different mothers but proscribe marriages in the reverse situation. This was the law among the Athenians, where one might marry a half-sister by the father but not by the mother, the Jews (*see* Genesis 20:12), and the Kwakiutl Indians of British Columbia. Claude Lévi-Strauss, On Marriage Between Close Kin, *in* The View from Afar 88-89 (Joachim Neugroschel & Phoebe Hoss trans., 1985). Concern for heredity certainly does not explain an incest prohibition that is stricter on the maternal than on the paternal side.

Lévi-Strauss concludes that the incest prohibition should be regarded not only negatively but positively — that is, as a division of the rights of marriage between families. It arises

> only so that families (however defined by each society) could intermingle. . . . As Edward Burnett Tyler understood a century ago . . . man knew very early that he had to choose between "either marrying-out or being killed-out": the best, but not the only, way for biological families not to be driven to reciprocal extermination is to link themselves by ties of blood. Biological families that wished to live in isolation, side by side with one another, would each form a closed group, self-perpetuating and inevitably prey to ignorance, fear, and hatred. In opposing the separatist tendency of consanguinity, the incest prohibition succeeded in weaving the web of affinity that sustains societies and without which none could survive.

Lévi-Strauss, *supra*, at 54-55. Does Lévi-Strauss's location of the deep structure of incest prohibitions in a universal need for social links adopt a particular view of human nature?

5. In Muth v. Frank, 412 F.3d 808 (7th Cir. 2005), a biological brother and sister who married and had three children were prosecuted for the crime of incest. The brother and sister were in and out of foster care as children and were separated for some years. When the sister, who was considerably younger than the brother, reached the age of majority, they reunited and married. They came to the attention of authorities when they abandoned one of the children. The court rejected their argument that under Lawrence v. Texas, the criminalization of incest is unconstitutional: "*Lawrence* did not announce a fundamental right of adults to engage in all forms of private consensual sexual conduct." 412 F.3d at 818. *See also* Lowe v. Swanson, 663 F.3d 258 (6th Cir. 2011) (statute that criminalizes consensual sexual relationship between stepparent and adult stepchild is not unconstitutional). Does *Obergefell* change the analysis? *See generally* Cynthia Godsoe, Redrawing the Boundaries of Relational Crime, 69 Ala. L. Rev. 169 (2017); Naomi Cahn, Accidental Incest: Drawing the Line — or the Curtain? — for Reproductive Technology, 32 Harv. J.L. & Gender 59, 97-99 (2009).

PROBLEMS

1. Venus and Adonis are adopted sister and brother. They come from different birth families, but were adopted when they were very young and have lived together with their adoptive parents for the last ten years. Venus is now 20 and Adonis 21. They have fallen in love and wish to marry. Should they be barred from marrying? If they have sex, would they be guilty under *Muth v. Frank*?

2. Murray was married for many years to Aphrodite, who died last year. Aphrodite brought a daughter, Delilah, to the marriage. Delilah lived and grew up in the home with Murray and Aphrodite. After her mother's death, Delilah moved back into the house to take care of Murray. Murray proposed marriage to Delilah, and she accepted. They sought a marriage license but were turned down by the county clerk, who knows them both. State law prohibits marriage between a father and his "daughter." What arguments might be made in connection with their challenge to the denial of their application to marry?

3. Henry and Fiona are high school sweethearts. Their mothers discover that they conceived the two children with sperm from the same sperm bank, and when they inquire further, they learn that they used the same donor. Thus, Henry and Fiona are half-siblings. If Henry and Fiona nevertheless want to marry, is there any reason to distinguish their situation from that in *Nguyen*?

4. Age

At common law, the age of consent to marriage for males was 14 and for females, 12. Early English legislation also required that parents consent to the marriage of a child younger than 21, the age of majority. Vivian E. Hamilton, The Age of Marital Capacity: Reconsidering Civil Recognition of Adolescent Marriage, 92 B.U. L. Rev. 1817, 1825-1828 (2012). The parental consent requirement protected parental and familial interests in controlling family property, which was profoundly affected by marriage. The American colonies adopted statutes that mirrored these provisions, but they frequently did not invalidate marriages by young people over the minimum age of consent who did not have parental permission. *Id.* at 1829.

Today most states establish a minimum age below which no one may marry (most often 16), and a window between that minimum age and the age of full consent, during which marriage is allowed only with parental permission. Some statutes also require a court to approve a marriage in the "window." In addition, some states allow courts to authorize marriages for young people below 18 without parental consent upon a finding that it is in the person's best interests. Tahirih Justice Center, Understanding State Statutes on Minimum Marriage Age and Exceptions (Aug. 26, 2021), https://www.tahirih.org/wp-content/uploads/2021/09/August-2021-State-Statutory-Compilation-1.pdf.

Porter v. Dep't of Health & Human Services
286 S.W.3d 686 (Ark. 2008)

ROBERT L. BROWN, Justice. [The state filed a petition in juvenile court alleging that Mark Porter and his ex-wife Diana Rolen neglected their two daughters, D.P., age 16, and S.P., age 12, by allowing them to be truant. At the initial hearing on the petition, the state Department of Human Services ("DHS") presented evidence that on August 10, 2007, Porter and Rolen had consented to the marriage of 16-year-old D.P. to Ralph Rodriguez, a 34-year-old man from Mississippi.]

Rolen testified at the hearing that she believed Rodriguez to be twenty-five years old. Rolen also testified that when she returned home from a vacation during the previous weekend, D.P. and Rodriguez had departed for Mississippi. Rolen added that she had given her consent to the marriage because of her fear that D.P. would "run off" otherwise.

Porter testified at the same hearing that he was called at work and asked to consent to D.P.'s marriage to Rodriguez. He left work and signed the necessary documents that provided his consent to the marriage. Although he testified that he was concerned about the marriage, he also testified that he was generally unfamiliar with Rodriguez and had not inquired into Rodriguez's past. At that point, the trial judge asked Porter why he had consented to his sixteen-year-old daughter's marriage to someone about whom he knew so little. Porter replied that he "was afraid [D.P.] would run off" and he would "never hear from her again." In response, the trial judge said, "Bad answer." . . .

. . . On November 30, 2007, the attorney ad litem for D.P. filed a motion to void the marriage between D.P. and Rodriguez. The attorney ad litem asserted that the marriage should be voided because the parents' consent was given in disregard for the health and safety of D.P. and without knowledge of Rodriguez's true age.

. . . [T]he trial judge determined D.P. . . . [was] dependent-neglected. D.P. . . . [was] ordered to remain in DHS custody. . . . The judge, in addition, voided the marriage of D.P. and Rodriguez on the basis that the parental consent was obtained through coercion and misrepresentation of Rodriguez's age and that D.P. lacked the mental capacity to enter into a contract of marriage. Porter now appeals both the finding of dependency-neglect and the court's order voiding the marriage. . . .

Porter contends that the trial judge's decision to remove the children from his custody was grounded entirely upon his consent to his daughter's marriage. This reliance was in error, he claims, because his consent was lawful under Act 441. Thus, Porter maintains that the trial judge violated his Fourteenth Amendment due-process right to make child-care decisions. . . .

A "dependent-neglected juvenile" is defined by the Juvenile Code as one "who is at substantial risk of serious harm as a result of" abuse, sexual abuse, neglect, or parental unfitness to the juvenile, or a sibling. The statute goes on to define "abuse" as "injury to a juvenile's intellectual, emotional, or psychological development as evidenced by observable and substantial impairment of the juvenile's ability to function within the juvenile's normal range of performance and behavior."

The statute also describes "neglect" as: . . .

> (vii) Failure to appropriately supervise the juvenile that results in the juvenile's being left alone at an inappropriate age or in inappropriate circumstances, creating a dangerous situation or a situation that puts the juvenile at risk of harm.

We first address whether the trial judge erred in considering Porter's consent to his daughter's marriage as evidence of dependency-neglect. Parents, of course, have a fundamental right to direct the care and upbringing of their children. But the State of Arkansas has an equally compelling interest in the protection of its children. . . .

The evidence before the trial judge was that D.P.'s parents allowed her, as a fifteen-year-old, to date a thirty-four-year-old man, without appropriate supervision. The evidence showed that D.P. and Rodriguez had inappropriate sexual contact before their marriage, including the posting of sexually exploitative pictures on the internet. Moreover, D.P.'s parents consented to her marriage without inquiring into Rodriguez's age or background and allowed her to drop out of school and move to Mississippi. This easily qualifies as evidence of Porter's "failure to appropriately supervise D.P.," which resulted in her being "left alone . . . in inappropriate circumstances, creating a dangerous situation." The trial judge was correct to consider this factor in determining dependency-neglect.

We turn next to the issue of whether there is sufficient evidence overall to support the trial judge's finding of dependency-neglect. In addition to D.P.'s relationship with Rodriguez, the trial judge placed great weight on the testimony of D.P.'s therapist, Linda VanBlaricom, who testified that she believed D.P. had been neglected. Ms. VanBlaricom stated that D.P.'s problems were 95% to 99% the result of her parents' failure to provide a stable and nurturing environment and her exposure to substance abuse. . . .

Even if D.P.'s marriage to Rodriguez is found to be valid, which we hold that it is in this opinion, the result in this case regarding DHS's custody of D.P. will not change. . . .

At the dependency-neglect adjudication hearing, the trial judge declared the marriage between D.P. and Rodriguez void on the following grounds: (1) misrepresentation of Rodriguez's age under §9-11-104; (2) the marriage was not in D.P.'s best interest and was incompatible with the goal of reunification with her parents; and (3) D.P., a necessary party to the marriage contract, lacked the mental capacity to enter into the marriage. Porter contends that the trial judge had no authority under Arkansas law to declare D.P.'s marriage void. . . .

A. Misrepresentation

It is true that a marriage contract may be set aside and annulled upon the application of a parent or guardian, where there has been a misrepresentation of age by a contracting party. . . .

In the present case, there is no clear and convincing evidence that Rodriguez misrepresented his age or that D.P. misrepresented his age to her parents. Both of D.P.'s parents testified at the FINS hearing that they believed Rodriguez to be in his twenties, but neither asserted that a misrepresentation had taken place. Porter testified, "I had the impression he was in his mid-20s, but when I seen him he looks like he's over 30." Additionally, the marriage certificate that both parents signed listed Rodriguez's true age as thirty-four.

Nor does it appear from the record that either parent relied upon Rodriguez's age in giving his or her consent to the marriage. Porter's ex-wife, Rolen, testified at the FINS hearing that she allowed her daughter to date a thirty-four-year-old man and, again, Porter noted that Rodriguez appeared to be over thirty. Furthermore, Porter testified that he had reservations about allowing his daughter to date a thirty-four-year-old man and had voiced these reservations to D.P. The facts simply do not rise to the level of clear and convincing evidence that either Rodriguez or D.P. misrepresented his age, but rather exhibit extreme carelessness on the part of the parents in supervising D.P.

B. Incompatibility with Reunification and the Best Interests of D.P.

The trial judge's stated ground for declaring the marriage void included her finding that the marriage was incompatible with the goal of reunification of D.P. with her father and that the marriage was not in D.P.'s best interests. This is not a ground for voidance set out by statutory law. Hence, there is simply no statutory basis for granting an annulment on these grounds.

C. Mental Capacity

Arkansas Code Annotated §9-12-201 (Repl. 2008) provides:

> When either of the parties to a marriage is incapable from want of age or understanding of consenting to any marriage, . . . or when the consent of either party shall have been obtained by force or fraud, the marriage shall be void from the time its nullity shall be declared by a court of competent jurisdiction.

The trial judge found D.P.'s marriage to be void on grounds that D.P. lacked the mental capacity to enter into marriage based on this statute. In support of this finding, the trial judge pointed to the testimony of D.P.'s therapist regarding D.P.'s emotional state and unfitness to make decisions; the fact that D.P. had met Rodriguez on the internet; D.P.'s immaturity based on her testimony that she was ready to have children and was not using contraception; and

D.P.'s behavior at trial, which included outbursts, making faces at attorneys, refusal to coop-erate, and an inability to control her emotions that was so disruptive that it eventually lead to D.P.'s being handcuffed and placed in a holding cell.

Generally, a party lacks the mental capacity to enter into a contract for marriage if that party is "incapable of understanding the nature, effect, and consequences of the marriage." The relevant inquiry is whether mental incapacity existed at the very time the parties entered into the marriage. As a collateral point, immaturity of the parties is not sufficient to establish a party's inability to consent to marriage. Nor does the mental capacity necessary to enter into marriage require the ability to exercise "clear reason, discernment, and sound judgment."

Here, no inquiry was made by the trial judge into D.P.'s mental capacity at the time the parties entered into the marriage. The trial judge based the majority of her decision upon D.P.'s behavior at trial, which is an insufficient basis for finding mental incapacity. Further-more, D.P.'s therapist, Linda VanBlaricom, testified that D.P. had a "strong sense of herself," was a "bright girl" and "had learned to make decisions . . . and been responsible for herself in a lot of ways for a long time." Ms. VanBlaricom added that D.P. was not necessarily able to use the judgment of an adult, but the immaturity of D.P. or her inability to exercise sound judgment are not factors for mental incapacity. As a final point, in response to the question of whether she believed D.P. mature enough to marry, Ms. VanBlaricom responded that she would have a very hard time answering that question about most people.

Taken together, the evidence from the record does not show that D.P. was incapable of understanding the nature, effect, and consequences of marriage. We hold that the trial judge erred in declaring the marriage void on the basis of misrepresentation, best interest of D.P., or mental incapacity. We reverse the trial judge on this point and remand for entry of a judgment in accordance with this opinion. . . .

Affirmed in part. Reversed and remanded in part.

NOTES AND QUESTIONS

1. What state interests support a law prohibiting people younger than 18 to marry with-out parental consent? Why would the law today allow a young person to marry with parental permission? What functions does parental consent serve?

2. Considerable evidence shows that teenage marriages are high-risk enterprises, in terms of both the likelihood of divorce and the quality of marital satisfaction. Generally speak-ing, youthful marriages correlate with the participants' lower educational attainment, lower income, higher unemployment, increased risk of mental health disorders, and poorer physical health. Vivian E. Hamilton, The Age of Marital Capacity: Reconsidering Civil Recognition of Adolescent Marriage, 92 B.U. L. Rev. 1817, 1843-1848 (2012). Correlation does not prove causation, however, and it is possible that other factors contribute both to the marital instabil-ity and unhappiness and to these other social outcomes. What factors might these be?

The riskiness of early marriage has increased over the last 30 years. In 1980 the divorce risk leveled off after the age of 21 so that couples marrying in their early 20s were no more likely to divorce than those who married in their late 20s. By 2000, however, couples experienced greater marital happiness and less divorce risk the older they were, with the improvements continu-ing into the 30s. Paul R. Amato et al., Alone Together: How Marriage in America Is Changing (2009). Why might age matter more to marital happiness in the twenty-first century than it did in 1980?

3. What does it mean for the young woman in *Porter* to be subject to the authority of the juvenile court as a neglected child if her marriage is valid?

After *Porter* was decided, Arkansas Code §9-11-102 was amended to provide, "The consent of the parent may be voided by the order of a circuit court on a showing by clear and convincing evidence that: (i) The parent is not fit to make decisions concerning the child; and (ii) The marriage is not in the child's best interest." How would a court determine whether a parent is "fit to make decisions concerning the child"?

4. If a minor's parents are divorced or unmarried, typically the statute provides that either parent or the parent with custody has authority to consent to the child's underage marriage. Kirkpatrick v. Dist. Ct., 64 P.3d 1056 (Nev. 2003), considered the constitutionality of a statute permitting a minor under the age of 16 to marry with the consent of one parent and the district court's authorization. Under that statute, the district court permitted petitioner's 15-year-old daughter to marry her 48-year-old guitar teacher. Although the daughter's mother had provided consent, the father—who had joint legal custody and maintained an ongoing personal and custodial relationship with his daughter—had no knowledge that his daughter was planning to marry. Because he received neither notice nor an opportunity to be heard before his daughter was given judicial permission to marry, he argued that the statute as applied violated his rights to substantive and procedural due process. The Nevada Supreme Court originally ruled in his favor but then withdrew that opinion and issued a new decision, rejecting his claims. It found that the statute appropriately balanced the minor's constitutionally protected interest in access to marriage, "the interest of the mother in her daughter's welfare and happiness," and "the father's interest in the legal control of his daughter for the remainder of her minority." 64 P.3d at 1062.

5. Recent highly publicized cases have focused on the problem of forced marriage of young girls and teenagers in the United States. *See, e.g.*, Nicholas Kristof, 11 Years Old, a Mom, and Pushed to Marry Her Rapist in Florida, N.Y. Times, May 26, 2017. *See also* Teri Dobbins Baxter, Child Marriage as Constitutional Violation, 19 Nev. L.J. 39 (2018); Erin K. Jackson, Addressing the Inconsistency Between Statutory Rape Laws and Underage Marriage and Removing the Spousal Exemption to Statutory Rape, 85 UMKC L. Rev. 343 (2017).

A national campaign against child marriage has achieved some success. In 2017 all states permitted some people younger than 18 to marry under some circumstances. Since then, seven states have adopted legislation forbidding anyone younger than 18 to marry with no exceptions. The states are Delaware, Massachusetts, Minnesota, New Jersey, New York, Pennsylvania, and Rhode Island. In another six states—Georgia, Indiana, Kentucky, Ohio, Texas, and Virginia—a person must be 18 or legally emancipated and at least 16 or 17 to marry. Would an age restriction on marriage be unconstitutional under *Obergefell*?

5. One at a Time

Bans on marrying more than one person apply to very different fact patterns, including people who appear monogamous but who have a living spouse whom they do not divorce before marrying again; traditional polygyny, where one man marries and lives with multiple wives; and polyamorous groups, i.e., three or more sexually intimate adults in a committed relationship. Legal bars to plural marriage, like other limits on marriage that we have examined, include both marriage laws that invalidate marriages entered into by people with living spouses and criminal laws that punish marrying, or sometimes living with, a new mate without divorcing a living spouse.

Adultery is still a crime in 19 states and under United States military law. Edward Stein, Adultery, Infidelity, and Consensual Non-Monogamy, 55 Wake Forest L. Rev. 147, 148-149, nn. 4, 52 (2020). Bigamy is a crime in every state, and no state recognizes the validity of more than one simultaneous marriage as matter of family law. Some states provide a defense to a person charged with the crime of bigamy who mistakenly believed that an earlier spouse was dead because the spouse had been missing without explanation for a statutory period, usually five to seven years. These statutes only provide a defense to the crime of bigamy; they do not make the second marriage valid. In some states statutes provide a procedure for judicial declaration of the death of the absent spouse and, accordingly, offer protection to a marriage contracted subsequent to the proceeding. *E.g.*, N.Y. Dom. Rel. Law §§220, 221 (2022); 23 Pa. Con. Stat. Ann. §1701 (2022).

State v. Holm
137 P.3d 726 (Utah 2006)

DURRANT, Justice: In this case, we are asked to determine whether Rodney Hans Holm was appropriately convicted for bigamy. . . .

Holm was legally married to Suzie Stubbs in 1986. Subsequent to this marriage, Holm, a member of the Fundamentalist Church of Jesus Christ of Latter-day Saints (the "FLDS Church"),[3] participated in a religious marriage ceremony with Wendy Holm. Then, when Rodney Holm was thirty-two, he participated in another religious marriage ceremony with then-sixteen-year-old Ruth Stubbs, Suzie Stubbs's sister. After the ceremony, Ruth moved into Holm's house, where her sister Suzie Stubbs, Wendy Holm, and their children also resided. By the time Ruth turned eighteen, she had conceived two children with Holm, the second of which was born approximately three months after her eighteenth birthday. . . .

At trial, Ruth Stubbs testified that although she knew that the marriage was not a legal civil marriage under the law, she believed that she was married. Stubbs's testimony included a description of the ceremony she had participated in with Holm. Stubbs testified that, at the ceremony, she had answered "I do" to the following question:

> Do you, Sister [Stubbs], take Brother [Holm] by the right hand, and give yourself to him to be his lawful and wedded wife for time and all eternity, with a covenant and promise on your part, that you will fulfil all the laws, rites and ordinances pertaining to this holy bond of matrimony in the new and everlasting covenant, doing this in the presence of God, angels, and these witnesses, of your own free will and choice?

Stubbs testified that she had worn a white dress, which she considered a wedding dress; that she and Holm exchanged vows; that Warren Jeffs, a religious leader in the FLDS religion, conducted the ceremony; that other church members and members of Holm's family attended the ceremony; and that photographs were taken of Holm, Stubbs, and their guests who attended the ceremony.

Stubbs also testified about her relationship with Holm after the ceremony. She testified that she had moved in with Holm; that Holm had provided, at least in part, for Stubbs and their children; and that she and Holm had "regularly" engaged in sexual intercourse at the house in Hildale, Utah. Evidence was also introduced at trial that Holm and Stubbs "regarded each other as husband and wife." . . .

Holm appealed his conviction on all charges. . . .

Holm was convicted pursuant to Utah's bigamy statute, which provides that "[a] person is guilty of bigamy when, knowing he has a husband or wife or knowing the other person has a husband or wife, the person purports to marry another person or cohabits with another person." The jury weighing the case against Holm indicated on a special verdict form its

---

3. The FLDS Church is one of a number of small religious communities in Utah that continue to interpret the early doctrine of the Church of Jesus Christ of Latter-day Saints (the "LDS Church" or "Mormon Church") as supporting the practice of "plural marriage," or polygamy. Though often referred to as "fundamentalist Mormons," these groups have no connection to the LDS Church, which renounced the practice of polygamy in 1890.

conclusion that Holm had both "purported to marry another person" and "cohabited with another person" knowing that he already had a wife. . . .

[The court rejected Holm's argument that the bigamy statute applied only if a defendant purported to enter more than one legally recognized marriage. It concluded that the legislature intended the bigamy statute to cover Holm's religiously but not legally sanctioned marriages and then turned to the constitutional issues.]

. . . [T]he Utah Constitution offers no protection to polygamous behavior and, in fact, shows antipathy towards it by expressly prohibiting such behavior. Specifically, article III, section 1, entitled "Religious toleration — Polygamy forbidden," states as follows: "First: — Perfect toleration of religious sentiment is guaranteed. No inhabitant of this State shall ever be molested in person or property on account of his or her mode of religious worship; but polygamous or plural marriages are forever prohibited." Utah Const. art. III, §1. This language, known commonly as the "irrevocable ordinance," unambiguously removes polygamy from the realm of protected free exercise of religion. . . .

1. The Bigamy Statute Does Not Impermissibly Infringe Holm's Federal Free Exercise Right

Although the United States Supreme Court, in Reynolds v. United States, 98 U.S. 145, (1879), upheld the criminal prosecution of a religiously motivated polygamist as nonviolative of the Free Exercise Clause, Holm contends on appeal that his federal free exercise right is unduly infringed upon by his conviction in this case. Holm argues that *Reynolds* is "nothing more than a hollow relic of bygone days of fear, prejudice, and Victorian morality," and that modern free exercise jurisprudence dictates that no criminal penalty can be imposed for engaging in religiously motivated polygamy. This court recently rejected an identical argument in State v. Green, 2004 UT 76, ¶¶18-19, 99 P.3d 820.

As we pointed out in *Green*, *Reynolds*, despite its age, has never been overruled by the United States Supreme Court and, in fact, has been cited by the Court with approval in several modern free exercise cases, signaling its continuing vitality. . . . As we noted in *Green*, the United States Supreme Court held in Employment Division, Department of Human Resources v. Smith, 494 U.S. 872 (1990) . . . that a state may, even without furthering a compelling state interest, burden an individual's right to free exercise so long as the burden is imposed by a neutral law of general applicability. The Court has since clarified that a law is not neutral if the intent of that law "is to infringe upon or restrict practices because of their religious motivation." Church of the Lukumi Babalu Aye, Inc. v. City of Hialeah, 508 U.S. 520, 533 (1993). In *Green*, we concluded that Utah's bigamy statute is a neutral law of general applicability and that any infringement upon the free exercise of religion occasioned by that law's application is constitutionally permissible. . . .

2. Holm's Conviction Does Not Offend the Due Process Clause of the Fourteenth Amendment

Holm argues that the State of Utah is foreclosed from criminalizing polygamous behavior because the freedom to engage in such behavior is a fundamental liberty interest that can be infringed only for compelling reasons and that the State has failed to identify a sufficiently compelling justification for its criminalization of polygamy. We disagree and conclude that there is no fundamental liberty interest to engage in the type of polygamous behavior at issue in this case.

In arguing that his behavior is constitutionally protected as a fundamental liberty interest, Holm relies primarily on the United States Supreme Court's decision in Lawrence v. Texas, 539 U.S. 558 (2003). . . .

Despite its use of seemingly sweeping language, the holding in *Lawrence* is actually quite narrow. Specifically, the Court takes pains to limit the opinion's reach to decriminalizing private and intimate acts engaged in by consenting adult gays and lesbians. In fact, the Court went out of its way to exclude from protection conduct that causes "injury to a person or abuse of an institution the law protects." Further, after announcing its holding, the Court noted the following: "The present case does not involve minors. It does not involve persons who might be injured or coerced or who are situated in relationships where consent might not easily be refused. It does not involve public conduct. . . ."

In marked contrast to the situation presented to the Court in *Lawrence*, this case implicates the public institution of marriage, an institution the law protects, and also involves a minor. In other words, this case presents the exact conduct identified by the Supreme Court in *Lawrence* as outside the scope of its holding.

First, the behavior at issue in this case is not confined to personal decisions made about sexual activity, but rather raises important questions about the State's ability to regulate marital relationships and prevent the formation and propagation of marital forms that the citizens of the State deem harmful. . . .

. . . The people of this State have declared monogamy a beneficial marital form and have also declared polygamous relationships harmful. As the Tenth Circuit stated in *Potter*, Utah "is justified, by a compelling interest, in upholding and enforcing its ban on plural marriage to protect the monogamous marriage relationship."

Further, this case features another critical distinction from *Lawrence*; namely, the involvement of a minor. Stubbs was sixteen years old at the time of her betrothal, and evidence adduced at trial indicated that she and Holm regularly engaged in sexual activity. Further, it is not unreasonable to conclude that this case involves behavior that warrants inquiry into the possible existence of injury and the validity of consent. *See, e.g., Green*, 2004 UT 76, ¶40, 99 P.3d 820 ("The practice of polygamy . . . often coincides with crimes targeting women and children. Crimes not unusually attendant to the practice of polygamy include incest, sexual assault, statutory rape, and failure to pay child support.").

Given the above, we conclude that *Lawrence* does not prevent our Legislature from prohibiting polygamous behavior. The distinction between private, intimate sexual conduct between consenting adults and the public nature of polygamists' attempts to extralegally redefine the acceptable parameters of a fundamental social institution like marriage is plain. The contrast between the present case and *Lawrence* is even more dramatic when the minority status of Stubbs is considered. Given the critical differences between the two cases, and the fact that the United States Supreme Court has not extended its jurisprudence to such a degree as to protect the formation of polygamous marital arrangements, we conclude that the criminalization of the behavior engaged in by Holm does not run afoul of the personal liberty interests protected by the Fourteenth Amendment. . . .

DURHAM, Chief Justice, concurring in part and dissenting in part: I join the majority in upholding Holm's conviction for unlawful sexual conduct with a minor. As to the remainder of its analysis, I respectfully dissent. As interpreted by the majority, Utah Code section 76-7-101 defines "marriage" as acts undertaken for religious purposes that do not meet any other legal standard for marriage—acts that are unlicensed, unsolemnized by any civil authority, acts that are indeed entirely outside the civil law, and unrecognized as marriage for any other purpose by the state—and criminalizes those acts as "bigamy." I believe that in doing so the statute oversteps lines protecting the free exercise of religion and the privacy of intimate, personal relationships between consenting adults. . . .

The majority concludes that Holm may be found guilty of "purport[ing] to marry another person" while already having a wife because he entered a religious union with Ruth Stubbs that the two of them referred to as a "marriage," even though neither believed, represented, or intended that the union would have the legal status of a state-sanctioned marriage. In doing so, the majority deems irrelevant the distinction between the word "marry" when used in a legal context and the same word's idiosyncratic meaning when used as a label for a relationship recognized as significant by a particular individual or group, but not by the state. . . .

The majority's conflation of private relationships with legal unions is also problematic in its analysis of Holm's claim that his bigamy conviction violates the guarantees of individual rights protected by article I of the Utah Constitution. The majority dismisses Holm's claim on the basis that the Utah Constitution "offers no protection to polygamous behavior and, in fact, shows antipathy towards it by expressly prohibiting such behavior" in article III, section 1. . . . Here, as elsewhere in Utah law, I understand the term "marriage" to refer only to a "legal union." Understood in this way, article III, section 1, by its plain language, does not prohibit private individual behavior but instead prevents Utah's state government, to whom the ordinance is addressed, from recognizing a particular form of union as a "marriage." . . .

[The opinion argues that the state constitution provides greater protection for religiously motivated conduct than does the federal constitution and particularly that it guarantees "free exercise of religion to the extent such exercise [is] consistent with public peace and order."]

. . . [T]he burden on the religious conduct at issue must be necessary to serve a strong governmental interest unrelated to the suppression of religious freedom. I do not believe that any of the strong state interests normally served by the Utah bigamy law require that the law apply to the religiously motivated conduct at issue here—entering a religious union with more than one woman.

I note at the outset that the State has not suggested that section 76-7-101 furthers a governmental interest in preserving democratic society. I agree that no such interest is implicated here. . . . [T]he federal government's nineteenth century criminalization of polygamy in the Utah Territory, as construed by the *Reynolds* Court, was intended to address the harm to democratic society that LDS Church polygamy was thought to embody. However, I do not presume that our modern criminal bigamy statute, enacted in 1973, addresses the same fears—which have since been discounted by many as grounded more in bias than in fact—that propelled Congress' legislation a century earlier.

Indeed, this court previously set forth, in *Green*, a list of state interests served by the modern statute that omits any reference to such a concern. There, we first explained that the modern statute serves the state's interest in "regulating marriage" and in maintaining the "network of laws" that surrounds the institution of marriage. . . . Here, the State has emphasized its interest in "protecting" monogamous marriage as a social institution. I agree that the state has an important interest in regulating marriage, but only insofar as marriage is understood as a legal status. . . .

However, I do not believe the state's interest extends to those who enter a religious union with a second person but who do not claim to be legally married. For one thing, the cohabitation of unmarried couples, who live together "as if" they are married in the sense that they share a household and a sexually intimate relationship, is commonplace in contemporary society. Even outside the community of those who practice polygamy for religious reasons, such cohabitation may occur where one person is legally married to someone other than the person with whom he or she is cohabiting. Yet parties to such relationships are not prosecuted under the criminal bigamy statute, the criminal fornication statute, or, as far as I am aware, the criminal adultery statute, even where their conduct violates these laws.

That the state perceives no need to prosecute nonreligiously motivated cohabitation, whether one of the parties to the cohabitation is married to someone else or not, demonstrates that, in the absence of any claim of legal marriage, neither participation in a religious ceremony nor cohabitation can plausibly be said to threaten marriage as a social or legal institution. The state's concern with regulating marriage, as I understand it, has to do with determining who is entitled to enter that legal status, what benefits are accorded, and what obligations and restrictions are imposed thereby. . . . Our state's network of laws may indeed presume a particular domestic structure — whether it be that a man will live with only one woman, that a couple living together will enter a legal union, or that each household will contain a single nuclear family. However, any interest the state has in maintaining this network of laws does not logically justify its imposition of criminal penalties on those who deviate from that domestic structure, particularly when they do so for religious reasons. . . .

Those who choose to live together without getting married enter a personal relationship that resembles a marriage in its intimacy but claims no legal sanction. They thereby intentionally place themselves outside the framework of rights and obligations that surrounds the marriage institution. While some in society may feel that the institution of marriage is diminished when individuals consciously choose to avoid it, it is generally understood that the state is not entitled to criminally punish its citizens for making such a choice, even if they do so with multiple partners or with partners of the same sex. The only distinction in this case is that when Holm consciously chose to enter into a personal relationship that he knew would not be legally recognized as marriage, he used religious terminology to describe this relationship. The terminology that he used — "marriage" and "husband and wife" — happens to coincide with the terminology used by the state to describe the legal status of married persons. That fact, however, is not sufficient for me to conclude that criminalizing this conduct is essential in order to protect the institution of marriage. . . .

The second state interest served by the bigamy law, as recognized in *Green*, is in preventing "marriage fraud," whereby an already-married individual fraudulently purports to enter a legal marriage with someone else, "or attempts to procure government benefits associated with marital status." This interest focuses on preventing the harm caused to the state, to society, and to defrauded individuals when someone purports to have entered the legal status of marriage, but in fact is not eligible to validly enter that status because of a prior legal union. This interest is simply not implicated here, where no claim to the legal status of marriage has been made.

In *Green*, the court cited "protecting vulnerable individuals from exploitation and abuse" as the third state interest served by the bigamy statute. The court concluded that this was a legitimate state interest to which the criminal bigamy statute was rationally related for purposes of our First Amendment Free Exercise Clause analysis. The court rested this conclusion on the idea that perpetrators of other crimes "not unusually attendant to the practice of polygamy" — such as "incest, sexual assault, statutory rape, and failure to pay child support" — could be prosecuted for bigamy in the absence of sufficient evidence to support a conviction on these other charges. . . . However, reviewing this assessment in light of the heightened scrutiny I believe is called for here, I cannot conclude that the restriction that the bigamy law places on the religious freedom of all those who, for religious reasons, live with more than one woman is necessary to further the state's interest in this regard. . . . The State has provided no evidence of a causal relationship or even a strong correlation between the practice of polygamy, whether religiously motivated or not, and the offenses of "incest, sexual assault, statutory rape, and failure to pay child support," cited in *Green*. Moreover, even assuming such a correlation did exist, neither the record nor the recent history of prosecutions of alleged polygamists warrants the conclusion that section 76-7-101 is a necessary tool for the state's attacks on such harms. For one thing, I am unaware of a single instance where the state was forced to bring a charge of bigamy in place of other narrower charges, such as incest or unlawful sexual conduct with a minor, because it was unable to gather sufficient evidence to prosecute these other crimes. The State has suggested that its initial ability to file bigamy charges allows it to gather the evidence required to prosecute those engaged in more specific crimes. Even if there were support for this claim in the record, I would consider it inappropriate to let stand a criminal law simply because it enables the state to conduct a fishing expedition for evidence of other crimes. Further, the State itself has indicated that it does not prosecute those engaged in religiously motivated polygamy under the criminal bigamy statute unless the person has entered a religious union with a girl under eighteen years old. Such a policy of selective prosecution reinforces my conclusion that a blanket criminal prohibition on religious polygamous unions is not necessary to further the state's interests, and suggests that a more narrowly tailored law would be just as effective.

I do not reach this conclusion lightly. I acknowledge the possibility that other criminal conduct may accompany the act of bigamy. Such conduct may even, as was suggested in *Green*, be correlated with the practice of polygamy in a community that has isolated itself from the outside world, at least partially in fear of criminal prosecution for its religious practice. Indeed, the FLDS community in its current form has been likened to a cult, with allegations focusing on the power wielded by a single leader who exerts a high degree of control over followers, ranging from ownership of their property to the determination of persons with whom they may enter religious unions.[4] In the latter regard, reports of forcible unions between underage girls and older men within the FLDS community have recently appeared in the media.[5] Yet, the state does not criminalize cult membership, and for good reason. To do so would be to impose a criminal penalty based on status rather than conduct—long considered antithetical to our notion of criminal justice. Moreover, such a criminal law would require that the state make normative judgments distinguishing between communities that are actually "cults" and those that are voluntary associations based on common religious or other ideological beliefs. . . . The State of Utah has criminal laws punishing incest, rape, unlawful sexual conduct with a minor, and domestic and child abuse. Any restrictions these laws place on the practice of religious polygamy are almost certainly justified. However, the broad criminalization of the religious practice itself as a means of attacking other criminal behavior is not. . . .

Because I conclude that Holm's bigamy conviction violates the Utah Constitution's religious freedom guarantees, my dissenting vote is not based on the majority's analysis of Holm's federal constitutional claims. I do, however, wish to register my disagreement with the majority's treatment of Holm's claim that his conviction violates his Fourteenth Amendment right under the Due Process Clause to individual liberty, as recognized by the United States Supreme Court in Lawrence v. Texas, 539 U.S. 558 (2003). . . .

The majority does not adequately explain how the institution of marriage is abused or state support for monogamy threatened simply by an individual's choice to participate in a religious ritual with more than one person outside the confines of legal marriage. Rather than offering such an explanation, the majority merely proclaims that "the public nature of polygamists' attempts to extralegally redefine the acceptable parameters of a fundamental social institution like marriage is plain." It is far from plain to me.

---

4. Media reports suggest that this situation has worsened since Warren Jeffs, the son of Rulon Jeffs, assumed the leadership position in 2002 following his father's death. Polygamous Church May Pull up Roots, Associated Press, Mar. 5, 2005, available at Rick A. Ross Institute, Polygamist Groups, http://www.rickross.com/groups/polygamy. html [hereinafter Ross Institute site]; Lawsuits and Governmental Scrutiny Increase Pressure on Polygamist Sect, Associated Press, Sept. 17, 2004, available at Ross Institute site, *supra*; Authorities Probe Arizona Polygamist Town, N.Y. Times, Jan. 23, 2004, available at Ross Institute site, *supra*.

5. *E.g.*, FLDS Runaways Speak Out on Dr. Phil Show, S.L. Trib., May 4, 2005, available at ReligionNewsBlog. com, http://www.religionnewsblog.com/11129; Polygamists on Utah-Arizona Border Under Scrutiny, All Things Considered, May 3, 2005, available at http://www.npr.org (search term "polygamy"); Allegations Abound: Colorado City's Polygamous Community Comes Under Increasing Scrutiny, Havasu News-Herald, Sept. 25, 2004, available at Ross Institute site, *supra*.

I am concerned that the majority's reasoning may give the impression that the state is free to criminalize any and all forms of personal relationships that occur outside the legal union of marriage. While under *Lawrence* laws criminalizing isolated acts of sodomy are void, the majority seems to suggest that the relationships within which these acts occur may still receive criminal sanction. Following such logic, nonmarital cohabitation might also be considered to fall outside the scope of federal constitutional protection. Indeed, the act of living alone and unmarried could as easily be viewed as threatening social norms.

In my view, any such conclusions are foreclosed under *Lawrence*. Essentially, the Court's decision in *Lawrence* simply reformulates the longstanding principle that, in order to "secure individual liberty, . . . certain kinds of highly personal relationships" must be given "a substantial measure of sanctuary from unjustified interference by the State." Whether referred to as a right of "intimate" or "intrinsic" association, a right to "privacy," a right to make "choices concerning family living arrangements," or a right to choose the nature of one's personal relationships, this individual liberty guarantee essentially draws a line around an individual's home and family and prevents governmental interference with what happens inside, as long as it does not involve injury or coercion or some other form of harm to individuals or to society. . . . The Court determined that when "adults . . . with full and mutual consent from each other" enter into particular personal relationships with no threat of injury or coercion, a state may not criminalize the relationships themselves or the consensual intimate conduct that occurs within them.

In conclusion, I agree with the majority that because Holm's conduct in this case involved a minor, he is unable to prevail on his individual liberty claim under the Due Process Clause. However, I disagree with the majority's implication that the same result would apply where an individual enters a private relationship with another adult. . . .

NOTES AND QUESTIONS

1. Holm and other members of the FLDS church were acutely aware of the state prohibition on plural marriage and made sure that they were not purporting to enter into more than one civil marriage that would be recognized by the state. How, then, did he fall afoul of the criminal prohibition?

After *Holm* was decided, the Utah statutes were amended so that bigamy is no longer a felony, but rather an infraction for which the penalties can be fines or community service, but not imprisonment. Inducing bigamy by fraudulent or false pretenses or threats or coercion remains a felony. Utah Code Ann. §76-7-101 (2022).

2. The majority and dissent disagree about whether Holm's relationships were protected under *Lawrence*. What is the basis for their disagreement?

3. The state in *Holm* argues that one of its interests is protecting monogamous marriage. Would this state interest be sufficient if the ban on plural marriage were challenged under *Obergefell*? Consider Reynolds v. United States, 98 U.S. 145 (1878), the nineteenth-century case addressing whether the constitutional protection for freedom of religion precludes punishing polygamy. A Mormon defendant challenged the constitutionality of federal law making bigamy a crime in the territory of Utah as violating his right to free exercise of religion. The Court sustained the statute and defendant's conviction, saying:

> Polygamy has always been odious among the Northern and Western nations of Europe and, until the establishment of the Mormon Church, was almost exclusively a feature of the life of Asiatic and African people. At common law, the second marriage was always void. 2 Kent, Com. 79, and from the earliest history of England polygamy has been treated as an offense against society.

. . . [W]e think it may safely be said there has never been a time in any State of the Union when polygamy has not been offence against society, cognizable by the civil courts and punishable with more or less severity. In the face of all this evidence, it is impossible to believe that the constitutional guaranty of religious freedom was intended to prohibit legislation in respect to this most important feature of social life. Marriage, while from its very nature a sacred obligation, is nevertheless, in most civilized nations, a civil contract, and usually regulated by law. Upon it society may be said to be built, and out of its fruits spring social relations and social obligations and duties, with which government is necessarily required to deal. In fact, according as monogamous or polygamous marriages are allowed, do we find the principles on which the government of the people, to a greater or less extent, rests. Professor Lieber says, polygamy leads to the patriarchal principle, and which, when applied to large communities, fetters the people in stationary despotism, while that principle cannot long exist in connection with monogamy. . . .

98 U.S. at 164-166.

What did Professor Lieber mean when he said that polygamy is related to despotism, and monogamy to democratic forms of government? Is this simply nineteenth-century parochialism, or might something in the nature of polygamous family life be expected to affect attitudes toward social and political organization?

Justice Durham argues in her dissent in *Holm* that the modern ban on polygamy is not based on these political concerns and suggests that if this argument were used to support the ban today, it might not succeed because the fears expressed in *Reynolds* "have since been discounted by many as grounded more in bias than in fact." Do you agree?

4. The state also argued that the law in *Holm* was supported by its interest in preventing fraud. In 2005 the attorneys general of Utah and Arizona reported that 66 percent of the residents in one FLDS community and 78 percent of the residents of a neighboring community received public assistance. The Primer: Helping Victims of Domestic Violence and Child Abuse in Polygamous Communities at 18 (2005). Do these figures suggest that community members are committing welfare fraud? Or are single mothers simply taking advantage of public benefits to which they are legally entitled?

5. The state in *Holm* also asserted an interest in protecting vulnerable individuals, which referred to both women and children. How does polygamy threaten women?

Professor Strassberg has observed that the nineteenth-century Mormon style of polygamy, "was also fundamentally inegalitarian; it was a practice designed to create a political and religious aristocracy. In a society with relatively equal numbers of men and women, polygyny gives some men significantly greater opportunities to reproduce than others because many wives for some men means no wives for others." Maura I. Strassberg, The Crime of Polygamy, 12 Temp. Pol. & Civ. Rts. L. Rev. 353, 362 (2003). *See also* Maura I. Strassberg, Distinctions of Form or Substance: Monogamy, Polygamy, and Same-Sex Marriage, 75 N.C. L. Rev. 1501 (1997); Shayna M. Sigman, Everything Lawyers Know About Polygamy Is Wrong, 16 Cornell J.L. & Pub. Pol'y 101 (2006).

The first session of the United Nations Commission on the Status of Women in 1947 identified as a principal aim, in the field of marriage, "freedom of choice, dignity of the wife, monogamy, and equal right to dissolution of marriage." Legal Status of Married Women (Reports Submitted by the Secretary-General). Forty-five years later, the United National Committee on the Elimination of Discrimination Against Women said, "Polygamous marriage contravenes a woman's right to equality with men, and can have such serious emotional and financial consequences for her and her dependants that such marriages ought to be discouraged and prohibited." 13th Session, General Recommendation 21: Equality in Marriage and Family Relations (1992), U.N. Doc. A/49/38/UNCEDAW. Why might monogamy be regarded as important to the recognition of equal rights for women?

On the other hand, women in Utah gained the franchise in 1870, and the National Woman Suffrage Association (founded by Elizabeth Cady Stanton and Susan B. Anthony) resolved, days after the *Reynolds* decision, that the federal government "should forbear to exercise federal power to disenfranchise the women of Utah, who have had a more just and liberal spirit shown them by Mormon men than Gentile women in the States have yet perceived in their rulers." Carol Weisbrod & Pamela Sheingorn, Reynolds v. United States: Nineteenth Century Forms of Marriage and the Status of Women, 10 Conn. L. Rev. 828, 850-856 (1978).

6. A document prepared by the attorneys general of Utah and Arizona reported that since the 1950s "polygamy laws have not been frequently enforced. However, Utah and Arizona have recently stepped up efforts to enforce laws in polygamous communities involving child abuse, domestic violence and fraud." The Primer, *supra*, at 7. *Holm* was one of the cases prosecuted under this policy. Numerous reports from Holm's community and other polygamous communities in the West consistently described girls as young as 13 or 14 being given as plural wives to much older men.

Girls were not the only children at risk in the community. A 2007 article estimated that between 500 and 1000 young men had been expelled, mostly for religious disobedience, from the FLDS settlements in Utah and Colorado. Social workers providing services to some of the expelled boys believe religious disobedience merely served as a pretext for removing excess males from the community. The article noted that the increase in the number of disobedient male youth expelled from the community of about 6000 people dates to the early 1990s, when Rulon Jeffs, who was then leader of the community, married dozens of young wives. Erik Eckholm, Boys Cast Out by Polygamists Find Help, N.Y. Times (Sept. 9, 2007).

Warren Jeffs, the son of Rulon Jeffs and his successor as leader of the group, was convicted in Texas of sexually assaulting two minor girls whom he had taken as wives and was sentenced to life in prison. Lindsay Whitehurst, Warren Jeffs Gets Life in Prison for Sex with Underage Girls, Salt Lake Tribune (Aug. 10, 2011). Other adult men in the group were convicted of the same offense in 2009 and 2010. A four-part documentary on Netflix entitled Keep Sweet: Pray and Obey examines the FLDS church before and after the time Jeffs led the group.

7. A social psychologist who studied modern practitioners of plural marriage described the diversity among the estimated 30,000 to 50,000 people living in polygamous communities in the North America:

> The capstone theme of our research is that contemporary polygamous families and their participants display a great variety of profiles in managing their day-to-day lives and interpersonal relationships. They vary considerably in how successful they are in their relationships, exhibit diversity in their coping mechanisms and lifestyles, and continually struggle to maintain viable relationships between husband and wives and between wives. In this respect, they are similar to monogamous families, who also do not exhibit complete uniformity in lifestyle.
>
> Yet many critics of polygamous family relationships portray or think about them as identical in certain qualities, especially negative ones. This pattern of stereotyping was evident in nineteenth century writings and legal opinions. . . . Some of these and other stereotypes and caricatures are still used today, with polygamous men labeled as selfish, controlling, and exploitive of women. Common perceptions of polygamist communities are that all or many young girls marry old men; that women in plural families are hateful and jealous of one another, with no recourse to leaving bad marriages; and that young boys are being thrown out of communities in large numbers. As with many stereotypes, such qualities are applied to whole populations, are often exaggerations, and are based on a limited number of cases. . . .
>
> Although our research confirms individual cases consistent with negative stereotypes in contemporary plural families, the major theme of our findings is that diversity and variation of differences abound in plural family life, and that traditional stereotypes do not apply across the board. In much the same way that one can readily accept the idea that monogamous

relationships in contemporary society vary widely in their qualities, so it is that our data reveal the same pattern in polygamous families.

Irwin Altman, Husbands and Wives in Contemporary Polygamy, 8 J.L. & Fam. Stud. 389, 392-393 (2006). *See also* Irwin Altman & Joseph Ginat, Polygamous Families in Contemporary Society (1996); Irwin Altman, Polygamous Family Life: The Case of Contemporary Mormon Fundamentalists, 1996 Utah L. Rev. 367. On FLDS communities in Canada, *see* Angela Campbell, Bountiful's Plural Marriages, 6 Int'l J. Law in Context 343 (2010); Martha Bailey & Amy J. Kaufman, Polygamy in the Monogamous World: Multicultural Challenges for Western Law and Policy (2010).

8. To what extent are the concerns about polygamy present when a married person commits bigamy by leaving his or her spouse without getting a divorce and then begins living with a new intimate partner? To what extent are the concerns present in modern polyamorous relationships such as the one described in Newsweek:

> Terisa Greenan and her boyfriend, Matt, are enjoying a rare day of Seattle sun, sharing a beet carpaccio on the patio of a local restaurant. Matt holds Terisa's hand, as his 6-year-old son squeezes in between the couple to give Terisa a kiss. His mother, Vera, looks over and smiles; she's there with her boyfriend, Larry. Suddenly it starts to rain, and the group must move inside. In the process, they rearrange themselves: Matt's hand touches Vera's leg. Terisa gives Larry a kiss. The child, seemingly unconcerned, puts his arms around his mother and digs into his meal.
>
> Terisa and Matt and Vera and Larry — along with Scott, who's also at this dinner — are not swingers, per se; they aren't pursuing casual sex. Nor are they polygamists of the sort portrayed on HBO's Big Love; they aren't religious, and they don't have multiple wives. But they do believe in "ethical nonmonogamy," or engaging in loving, intimate relationships with more than one person — based upon the knowledge and consent of everyone involved. They are polyamorous, to use the term of art applied to multiple-partner families like theirs, and they wouldn't want to live any other way.

Jessica Bennett, Only You. And You. And You: Polyamory — Relationships with Multiple, Mutually Consenting Partners — Has a Coming-out Party, Newsweek (July 28, 2009), quoted in Michael Lwin, Big Love: Perry v. Schwarzenegger and Polygamous Marriage, 9 Geo. J.L. & Pub. Pol'y 393, 422 (2011). A recent study found that one out of every six single adults in the United States wants to engage in polyamory and one in nine has done so at some point. Amy C. Moors, Amanda N. Gesselman & Justin R. Garcia, Desire, Familiarity, and Engagement in Polyamory: Results from a National Sample of Single Adults in the United States, 12 Frontiers in Psychology 619-640 (2021).

In 2020 Somerville, Massachusetts enacted the first multiple-partner domestic partnership ordinance in the country. Two other Massachusetts cities, Cambridge and Arlington, followed in 2021 and 2022. The ordinances allow polyamorous partners to have access to their mates' health insurance and other benefits under local law. Note, Three's Company, Too: The Emergence of Polyamorous Partnership Ordinances, 135 Harv. L. Rev. 1441 (2022). Does *Obergefell* require states to allow polygamous, state-sanctioned marriage?

9. If the concerns about polygamy vary significantly from setting to setting, what are the consequences for a constitutional challenge to a ban on polygamy? *See generally* Kaiponanea T. Matsumura, Beyond Polygamy, 107 Iowa L. Rev. 1903 (2022); Edward Stein, Adultery, Infidelity, and Consensual Non-Monogamy, 55 Wake Forest L. Rev. 147 (2020); Deborah Zalesne & Adam Dexter, From Marriage to Households: Towards Equal Treatment of Intimate Forms of Life, 66 Buff. L. Rev. 909 (2018); Haddan Aviram & Gwendolyn M. Leachman, The Future of Polyamorous Marriage: Lessons from the Marriage Equality Struggle, 38 Harv. J.L. & Gender 269 (2015); Elizabeth F. Emens, Monogamy's Law: Compulsory Monogamy and Polyamorous Existence, 29 N.Y.U. Rev. L. & Soc. Change 277 (2004); Suzannah Weiss, How Polyamorous People Are Marking Commitment to Multiple Partners (Wash. Post, May 16, 2022).

PROBLEM

Alicia and Betty lived together in the United States in a committed relationship. Karl, a visitor from Denmark, developed a romantic relationship with both women. To be able to move to the United States, Karl married Alicia and after gaining legal residency status, he and Alicia had a child. Karl later fathered a child with Betty. The three adults think of themselves as a "truple," with all three adults living together, jointly raising the two children, sharing expenses, and commingling their financial lives. They would like to receive greater legal recognition of their relationship. Advise them, first, as to whether they risk prosecution and, if so, on what grounds. Second, do they have any grounds on which to contest the state refusal to allow them to marry as a threesome? Third, should they have access to alternative statuses such as domestic partnerships?

D. INTERSTATE RECOGNITION OF MARRIAGE

The traditional choice-of-law rule regarding the validity of a marriage is that a marriage valid where entered into is valid everywhere unless recognizing the marriage would conflict with a strong public policy of the state asked to recognize the marriage. The Second Restatement of Conflicts incorporates this rule but provides that ultimately the governing law is that of the state "which, with respect to the particular issue, has the most significant relationship to the spouses and the marriage." Restatement (Second) of Conflict of Laws §283. The following case is an example of the Second Restatement approach.

Matter of Geraghty
150 A.3d 386 (N.H. 2016)

CONBOY, J. . . . The parties met in 1981 and were married in 1986 in New York. Shortly after marrying, the respondent moved into the petitioner's New York apartment, where they resided for approximately four years. . . .

In 1990, the parties moved to Massachusetts, where they resided for approximately four years. In 1994, they moved to New Jersey and purchased a house, which served as their principal residence until 2007. In 2007, the parties sold their New Jersey house and purchased property in New Hampshire, where, by January 2008, they resided full-time.

In September 2013, the petitioner filed a petition for divorce. The petitioner asserted the fault grounds of "conduct to endanger" and adultery as grounds for the divorce. In February 2015, the respondent filed a petition for annulment of the marriage on the ground that the marriage had been induced by fraud. During the litigation, he claimed that the petitioner had concealed that she had engaged in prostitution, used illegal drugs, and had certain medical procedures prior to their marriage and that had he known about this conduct he would not have married her. He also argued that New York law should apply to the petition for annulment because the parties were married under New York law and annulment of marriage concerns whether a marriage is void at its inception. . . .

. . . [T]he court issued a final decree of divorce, ruling that: (1) "New Hampshire law is the appropriate law to be applied in this case"; (2) under New Hampshire law, the petitioner's prostitution and use of illegal drugs prior to the marriage were insufficient to warrant annulment of the marriage. . . . This appeal followed.

II. CHOICE OF LAW

. . . The choice-influencing considerations adopted by this court in Clark v. Clark, 222 A.2d 205 (N.H. 1966), are: (1) predictability of results; (2) maintenance of reasonable orderliness and good relationship among the states in our federal system; (3) simplification of the judicial task; (4) advancement by the court of its own state's governmental interests rather than those of other states; and (5) the court's preference for what it regards as the sounder rule of law.

"Predictability of results, the first of our choice-influencing criteria, is usually implicated only in suits involving contractual or similar consensual transactions." "It emphasizes the importance of applying to the parties' bargain or other dealings the law on which they agreed to rely at the outset." "The predictability that results when courts apply the same law wherever suit is brought can also discourage forum shopping among plaintiffs."

The respondent argues that "[a]t the *outset* of the parties' marriage, they resided in New York and thus application of New York law and not New Hampshire law would protect the justifiable expectations the parties had when entering their marital contract." We agree that the residence of the parties at the outset of their marriage is relevant to the consideration of the predictability of results.

The respondent also contends that because the parties were married in New York and the alleged fraud which he relies upon to support his annulment petition occurred in New York, "it would have been reasonable for the parties to expect that New York law would be applied to any review of the circumstances that induced the parties to enter their New York marriage contract." We agree.

> To the extent that [parties] think about the matter, they would usually expect that the validity of their marriage would be determined by the local law of the state where it was contracted. In situations where the parties did not give advance thought to the question of which should be the state of the applicable law, or where their intentions in this regard cannot be ascertained, it may at least be said that they expected the marriage to be valid.

Restatement (Second) of Conflict of Laws §283 cmt. b at 234 (1971).
***

Accordingly, we conclude that our first consideration—predictability of results—favors application of New York law.

"The second consideration, which counsels maintenance of reasonable orderliness among the States, requires only that a court not apply the law of a State which does not have a substantial connection with the total facts and the particular issue being litigated." Here, the parties were married in New York and resided there for approximately four years immediately thereafter. At the time of the filing of the annulment petition, the parties resided in New Hampshire and had done so for approximately eight years. Accordingly, as the respondent concedes, both states have a substantial connection to the "total facts" of this case and the particular issue of annulment.

The third consideration, simplification of the judicial task, carries little weight in this case. While New Hampshire judges are accustomed to applying New Hampshire annulment law, they could with relative ease apply New York annulment law.

The fourth consideration, the advancement of the forum's governmental interest, "is a significant consideration in a choice-of-law question." . . .

The respondent argues that "[a]lthough the [trial court] recognized that domicile in New Hampshire was not a sufficient basis upon which to apply New Hampshire law over New York's it erroneously applied New Hampshire law because it concluded the parties were domiciled in New Hampshire." We disagree. In addressing this factor, the trial court stated that "New Hampshire [has] a strong interest in maintaining order in its system of regulating marriage and marital dissolutions." Thus, it is not only the parties' domicile within the state, but also the state's interest in the nature of their dispute that the court relied upon when ruling that New Hampshire has a strong interest in the case.

The respondent also asserts that the court erred in justifying "its application of New Hampshire law based upon the State's interest in the 'protection of offspring'" and "'in ensuring that former spouses will not be destitute and thus a potential drain on the state'" because these justifications are not implicated under the particular facts of this case. We disagree with the respondent's characterization of the trial court's order. At most, the court recognized that such justifications, in general, favor recognizing New Hampshire's governmental interest in the dissolution of its residents' marriages, whether by divorce or annulment, with which we agree. However, the court did not base its decision upon these justifications. . . .

The respondent further contends that because New Hampshire and New York both have "statutory framework[s] governing divorce and annulment proceedings . . . there was no reason to select New Hampshire's statutory divorce framework over New York's to protect New Hampshire's forum interest." Even assuming the respondent's contention is correct, we nevertheless find that New Hampshire's substantial interest in regulating the dissolution of its residents' marriages, whether by divorce or annulment, outweighs any interest New York has in this case. The parties' marriage in New York occurred approximately 29 years before the respondent filed the annulment petition and, at the time he filed the petition, the parties had not resided in New York for approximately 25 years. By contrast, the parties were residents of New Hampshire at the time the annulment petition was filed and had been for approximately eight years.

Upon consideration of all the circumstances, we conclude that this choice-influencing consideration — advancement of the forum's governmental interest — favors application of New Hampshire law.

"The fifth and final consideration concerns our preference for applying the sounder rule of law." This consideration "can play an important role in the ultimate choice made between the two competing laws." . . . The determination of which state's rule of law is the sounder rule requires an examination of the policies behind the conflicting rules and a decision as to which represents "the sounder view of the law in light of the socio-economic facts of life at the time when the court speaks."

Under New York law, "annulments are decreed, not for any and every kind of fraud, but for fraud as to matters 'vital' to the marriage relationship only." The fraud, however, need not go "to the essentials of marriage, that is, consortium and cohabitation." Rather, "[a]ny fraud is adequate which is material, to that degree that, had it not been practiced, the party deceived would not have consented to the marriage, and is of such a nature as to deceive an ordinarily prudent person."

In New Hampshire, "annulment of a marriage for fraud is granted only with extreme caution." "Annulment is not granted for any and every kind of fraud." Fraud "by one of the parties as to character, morality, habits, wealth, or social position is generally held insufficient" to annul a marriage. "Consequently the standard for the annulment of a marriage is both strict and stringent." "The fraudulent representations for which a marriage may be annulled must be of something essential to the marriage relation — of something making impossible the performance of the duties and obligations of that relation or rendering its assumption and continuance dangerous to health or life."

We conclude that our stricter approach to the annulment of marriage upon the basis of fraud is the sounder rule of law for several reasons. First, annulment of a marriage, which vitiates the existence of the marriage, should not be an easy substitute for legal separation or divorce. Second, in Heath v. Heath, 159 A. 418 (N.H. 1932), we ruled that so-called "material" fraud, that is fraud "important enough to be a substantial inducement of the marriage," is insufficient to annul a marriage contract. We explained that such a "material" fraud rule is

> so broad and general in its comprehensive scope that it leaves much to the discretion of the trier and practically each case would be largely decided on its own special merits. The uncertainties and discrepancies that would thus arise would produce an unsatisfactory situation both from the public's and the individual's standpoint.

Finally, we have long recognized that annulment of a marriage contract should be different from the voiding of an ordinary civil contract. "To give [marriage] contractual treatment generally because it has some contractual aspects is to overshadow the greater importance of its institutional character." As we recognized in *Heath*, marriage creates "a status containing more than an ordinary contractual relationship and not subject to the ordinary rules of contract law."

The respondent argues that "New Hampshire's law toward annulment actions . . . is outmoded and unduly restrictive whereas New York law is more progressive and developed." He further argues that New York law is the sounder rule of law because it "reflects an emerging national trend that annulment may be granted when the fraud was material to the parties directly affected by the fraud."

We disagree that our law is outmoded and unduly restrictive. Many states employ laws similar to ours. . . .

Accordingly, our analysis of the five choice-influencing considerations leads us to conclude that the trial court correctly applied New Hampshire law to the respondent's petition for annulment of the marriage. . . .

To the extent that the respondent also challenges the court's denial of his petition for annulment under New Hampshire law, we find no reversible error. To obtain an annulment, the respondent had to demonstrate that the petitioner's alleged fraud concerned something essential to the marriage relation; that is, something making impossible the performance of the duties and obligations of that relation or rendering its assumption and continuance dangerous to health or life. As the appealing party, the respondent has the burden of demonstrating reversible error. Based upon our review of the trial court's order, the respondent's challenges to it, the relevant law, and the record submitted on appeal, we conclude that the respondent has not demonstrated reversible error. . . .

NOTES AND QUESTIONS

1. How does *Geraghty* determine that New Hampshire's law should be applied in the first instance, rather than that of New York, the state in which the wedding occurred? Which considerations were the most important and why?

2. Under the traditional approach, New York law would apply in *Geraghty* unless that law was contrary to a strong public policy of New Hampshire. How would a court determine whether New Hampshire had such a strong public policy regarding marital fraud that applying New York law would conflict with it?

Two of the most famous cases applying the traditional approach are In re May's Estate, 114 N.E.2d 4 (N.Y. 1953), and Catalano v. Catalano, 170 A.2d 726 (Conn. 1961). In both, a state that did not allow marriages between uncles and nieces was asked to recognize such a marriage that had been entered into in a jurisdiction where such marriages were permitted. *May's Estate* held that the law of the state of celebration should apply because recognizing the marriage did not offend New York policy, while *Catalano* held that Connecticut law applied, resulting in the marriage's invalidity. The parties in *May* had been married 32 years and had six children; the Catalanos had been married several years but had lived together only a short time, since for most of the time the husband had lived in Connecticut and the wife in Italy. They had no children. The domestic relations law of both states said that marriages between people too closely related were void. Violation of the New York statute carried a penalty of up to six months in jail; the *May* court did not mention whether incest was a crime. In Connecticut incest carried a sentence of up to ten years in prison. Which of these factors might explain the difference in the two cases?

3. The Indiana Supreme Court applied the Second Restatement in McPeek v. McCardle, 888 N.E.2d 171 (Ind. 2008), to recognize a marriage that was not valid in the state where it was celebrated. A man and woman who lived in Indiana obtained an Indiana marriage license, participated in a marriage ceremony in Ohio, and recorded the completed marriage license in Indiana. Ten years later, when the woman died, children from her first marriage claimed that the marriage was invalid because the marriage was performed in Ohio without an Ohio license. The supreme court held that even though the marriage might not be valid according to the law of the Ohio, the state in which the wedding was celebrated (there being no recent decision about whether the license requirement was "mandatory" or "directory"), it was valid under Indiana law and so Indiana would recognize it. *See also* In re Estate of Shippy, 678 P.2d 848 (Wash. App. 1984) (applying law of Washington, the state with the most significant relationship to the issue, to validate a marriage that was void in the state where it was celebrated).

4. In re Dalip Singh Bir's Estate, 188 P.2d 499 (Cal. App. 1948), concerned the marriages of a native of the Punjab province of India who legally married two wives. He later moved to California, where he died intestate. Both women sought to inherit as his wives. The California Court of Appeal held that recognition of both marriages for inheritance purposes did not violate strong public policy, but that the result would be different "if the decedent had attempted to cohabit with his two wives in California." *See also* Ghazel & Ghazel, (2016) 306 FLR 173 (Australia), holding that an Iranian marriage that permitted the husband to take three more wives should be recognized in Australia.

> . . . [M]any states distinguish between the validity of a marriage and the ability to enjoy its "incidents." There was a time when courts treated marriage as a simple yes-or-no, up-or-down proposition: A marriage was either valid, in which case it was valid for all purposes, or it was not, in which case it was invalid for all purposes. Particularly in this century, however, judges have been willing to draw finer lines, applying the place of celebration rule to the question of validity while saving the public policy exception for particular "incidents" of being married. The right to cohabit, for example, is a usual incident of being married, but not a necessary one. A man married to two wives in India might be able to move to Kansas without being prosecuted for bigamy, but Kansas might forbid the three of them from living together. At the same time, the surviving wives might both be permitted to inherit as spouses under the state's law of succession.

Larry Kramer, Same-Sex Marriage, Conflict of Laws, and the Unconstitutional Public Policy Exception, 106 Yale L.J. 1965, 1971 (1997).

5. The same-sex marriage debate produced renewed interest in the choice-of-law issue, addressed in a rich literature. Rebecca Aviel, Faithful Unions, 69 Hastings L.J. 721 (2018); Mary Patricia Byrn & Morgan L. Holcomb, Wedlocked, 67 U. Miami L. Rev. 1 (2012); Brenda Cossman, Betwixt and Between Recognition: Migrating Same-Sex Marriages and the Turn Toward the Private, 71 Law & Contemp. Probs. 153 (Summer 2008); Larry Kramer, Same-Sex Marriage, Conflict of Laws, and the Unconstitutional Public Policy Exception, 106 Yale L.J. 1965 (1997); Linda Silberman, Same-Sex Marriages: Refining the Conflict of Laws Analysis, 153 U. Pa. L. Rev. 2195 (2005); Gary Simon, Beyond Interstate Recognition in the Same-Sex Marriage Debate, 314 U.C. Davis L. Rev. 40 (2006); Joseph William Singer, Same Sex Marriage, Full Faith and Credit, and the Evasion of Obligation, 1 Stan. J. C.R. & C.L. 1 (2005); Lynn D. Wardle, From Slavery to Same-Sex Marriage: Comity versus Public Policy in Inter-Jurisdictional Recognition of Controversial Domestic Relations, 2008 BYU L. Rev. 1855; Tobias Barrington Wolff, Interest Analysis in Interjurisdictional Marriage Disputes, 153 U. Pa. L. Rev. 2215 (2005).

PROBLEMS

1. John and Susan, a married couple who live in State *A*, believe in plural marriage. They decide that John should also marry Marie, Susan's younger sister, who is willing. John and Marie travel to Country *B*, which allows men to have more than one wife, and are married according to that jurisdiction's law. They return to State *A* after one week and continue to reside together. Two years later, Marie sues John for divorce in State *A* and asks for spousal support. If John contests the divorce on the ground that there was no marriage, what will be the result?

2. Same facts as problem 1, except that after two years of postmarital residence in State *A*, John and Susan are killed in an automobile accident. Marie seeks to inherit as his surviving spouse. What result?

3. Suppose that, in both situations above, the parties were originally residents of the country in which John and Marie were married. All three then moved to State *A*, where they lived together until the events described above. What results?

CHAPTER 4

LEGAL RECOGNITION OF INFORMAL FAMILY PARTNERSHIPS

Most of the time we think of marriage as a relationship clearly distinct from others, begun by a formal ceremony and ended by death or divorce. However, many people who have not gone through a valid ceremonial marriage live together and share their lives much as people who have been ceremonially married do. While this phenomenon is not new, the rate of cohabitation has increased dramatically over the last 50 years throughout the Western world. As the Pew Research Center recently reported, "The share of U.S. adults who are currently married has declined modestly in recent decades, from 58% in 1995 to 53% today. Over the same period, the share of adults who are living with an unmarried partner has risen from 3% to 7%. While the share who are currently cohabiting remains far smaller than the share who are married, the share of adults ages 18 to 44 who have ever lived with an unmarried partner (59%) has surpassed the share who has ever been married (50%) . . ." Juliana Menasce Horowitz, Nikki Graf & Gretchen Livingston, Marriage and Cohabitation in the U.S., Pew Research Center (Nov. 6, 2019). This chapter examines legal doctrines that in some circumstances and to varying extents result in the people in these households being treated as members of families.

Mary Ann Glendon

Marriage and the State: The Withering Away of Marriage
62 Va. L. Rev. 663, 684-687, 692-693 (1976)

Cohabitation, or "living together," is only one aspect of diversity in American marriage behavior, using the word *marriage* broadly. Defining exactly what turns a sexual relation into "marriage" is difficult, but it is useful to follow the lead of the family sociologist Rene Konig, by thinking of the shadow institution of legal marriage as a set of heterosexual unions undertaken with some idea of duration and manifested to the relevant social environment. . . .

Motivations to enter informal rather than legal marriage include economic advantages as in the case of many elderly people, inability to enter a legal marriage, unwillingness to be subject to the legal effects of marriage, desire for a "trial marriage," and lack of concern with the legal institution. This lack of concern is nothing new among groups accustomed to forming and dissolving informal unions without coming into contact with legal institutions. Among these groups legal marriage is but an aspect of the irrelevance of traditional American family law, law that is viewed as being property-oriented and organized around the ideals of a dominant social group. Lack of concern with marriage law has been growing, however, among many who definitely are not outside the mainstream of American life. Until recently these converts accepted unquestioningly the traditional structures of the enacted law, but they now find that on balance the enacted law offers no advantages over informal arrangements.

. . . In the past our legal response to cohabitation has been to pretend it is marriage and then attribute to it the traditional incidents of marriage. Thus, what in effect were cohabitation cases were disguised as cases involving presumptively legal marriage, estoppels, and implied agreements to pay for service. Because informal marriage exists in every society, every legal system has had to provide some ways to deal with the problems it generates. Professor Walter Weyrauch has convincingly demonstrated that this is the correct way to view not only the institution of common law marriage, but the myriad devices of the law of proof and presumptions that are the functional equivalent of common law marriage in those states that do not recognize it. In this view, naturally, the gradual decline in the number of jurisdictions that recognize the doctrine of common law marriage loses significance because other devices have simultaneously arisen to bring about functionally analogous legal effects, usually through the provision of economic benefits, such as alimony, inheritance rights, wrongful death, or workmen's compensation benefits to members of a de facto family.

A. COMMON LAW MARRIAGE, PRESUMPTIONS ABOUT MARRIAGE, AND THE PUTATIVE SPOUSE DOCTRINE

As Professor Glendon says, the traditional legal treatment of cohabitants was either to regard their relationship as wholly unlawful or to assimilate it into marriage through a variety of doctrines. This section considers three of the most important and widely used of these doctrines: common law marriage, the putative spouse doctrine, and presumptions of marriage validity. Other devices include limitations on standing to attack the validity of marriage (see Chapter 3) and the validity of divorce (see Chapter 12).

1. Common Law Marriage

American common law marriage derives from English marriage law prior to the Marriage Act of 1753. Ecclesiastical courts did not require that couples marry in church; they also recognized people as married if they exchanged promises to marry in the present tense (*sponsalia per verba de praesenti*) or in the future followed by consummation (*sponsalia per verba de futuro*). However, the 1753 Marriage Act, known as Lord Hardwicke's Act, which provided that only marriages celebrated in church or in a public chapel in the presence of two witnesses would thereafter be valid, officially abolished nonceremonial marriage. Exceptions were made for the royal family, Quakers, and Jews. Nonceremonial marriages were recognized in the English colonies as well.

Stone v. Thompson
833 S.E.2d 266 (S.C. 2019)

Justice HEARN:

. . . The institution of common-law marriage traces its roots to informal marriage in Europe prior to the Reformation. Cynthia Grant Bowman, A Feminist Proposal to Bring Back Common Law Marriage, 75 Or. L. Rev. 709, 718 (1996); *see also* Ashley Hedgecock, Comment, Untying the Knot: The Propriety of South Carolina's Recognition of Common Law Marriage, 58 S.C. L. Rev. 555, 559-62 (2007). England recognized such unions during colonization, and as a result, common-law marriage migrated to the New World. Some states proceeded to adopt the doctrine, while others did not. A primary reason for those that did was logistical—frontier America was sparsely populated and difficult to travel, making access to officials or ministers impractical for many. States also sought to legitimize "subversive" relationships and the children thereof, as well as to direct women to the family for financial support instead of the public fisc.

South Carolina followed New York's approach in adopting common-law marriage, holding it was a matter of civil contract that did not require ceremony; rather, two people were married when they agreed and intended to be. As Justice Littlejohn explained in 1970, the institution sought to "legitimatize innocent children and adjust property rights between the parties who treated each other the same as husband and wife. Common-law marriage in South Carolina rests upon moral paternalism, as our courts have long recognized. ("The law presumes morality, and not immorality; marriage, and not concubinage; legitimacy, and not bastardy.") While our legislature has not expressly codified common-law marriage, it has recognized the institution by exception to the general requirement to obtain a marriage license.

B. The Modern Trend

The prevailing trend, however, has been repudiation of the doctrine. The reasons have been myriad—from economic to social—including some more nefarious than others. . . .

In 2003, the Pennsylvania Commonwealth Court set forth a thorough explanation for its conclusion that common-law marriage should no longer be recognized in PNC Bank Corp. v. W.C.A.B. (Stamos), 831 A.2d 1269 (Pa. Commw. Ct. 2003). Notably, the court determined:

> The circumstances creating a need for the doctrine are not present in today's society. A woman without dependent children is no longer thought to pose a danger of burdening the state with her support and maintenance simply because she is single, and the right of a single parent to obtain child support is no longer dependent upon his or her marital status. Similarly, the marital status of parents no longer determines the inheritance rights of their children. Access to both civil and religious authorities for a ceremonial marriage is readily available in even the most rural areas of the Commonwealth. The cost is minimal, and the process simple and relatively expedient.

The court also pointed to benefits of standardized formal marriage requirements such as predictability, judicial economy, and upholding the statutes' "salutary" purposes.

C. Modern South Carolina

We find the Pennsylvania court's reasoning and other considerations sufficiently persuasive to adopt a bright-line rule requiring those who wish to be married in South Carolina to obtain a lawful license. . . . The paternalistic motivations underlying common-law marriage no longer outweigh the offenses to public policy the doctrine engenders. By and large, society no longer conditions acceptance upon marital status or legitimacy of children. The current case is emblematic of this shift, as the parties' community of friends was wholly unconcerned with their marital status, and indeed several of their witnesses were in similar relationships.

Meanwhile, courts struggle mightily to determine if and when parties expressed the requisite intent to be married, which is entirely understandable given its subjective and circumstantial nature. The solemn institution of marriage is thereby reduced to a guessing game with significant ramifications for the individuals involved, as well as any third party dealing with them.

Critically, non-marital cohabitation is exceedingly common and continues to increase among Americans of all age groups. The right to marry is a fundamental constitutional right, Obergefell v. Hodges, 135 S. Ct. 2584, 2604-05 (2015), which leads us to believe the right to remain unmarried is equally weighty, particularly when combined with our admonitions that a person cannot enter into such a union accidentally or unwittingly. Further, we must agree with the many observers who have noted that common-law marriage requirements are a mystery to most. The present case is again illustrative. None of the multiple witnesses who were asked understood what was required to constitute a common-law marriage, despite the fact that, as mentioned, several were involved in lengthy cohabiting relationships themselves. Moreover, two of such partners testified in complete opposition to one another, with one reporting they were common-law married, and the other stating emphatically they were not. This further persuades us to reject a mechanism which imposes marital bonds upon an ever-growing number of people who do not even understand its triggers.

Our public policy is to promote predictable, just outcomes for all parties involved in these disputes, as well as to emphasize the sanctity of marital union. We can discern no more efficacious way to fulfill these interests than to require those who wish to be married in our State to comply with our statutory requirements. Our quest to see inside the minds of litigants asserting different motivations and levels of knowledge at varying times must yield to the most reliable measurement of marital intent: a valid marriage certificate.

D. Prospective Application

. . . The Pennsylvania Commonwealth Court . . . elected to apply its decision purely prospectively. The court weighed the purpose of its new rule, the level of reliance on the old rule, and the impact on judicial function by retroactive application. The Pennsylvania court noted the benefits of the new rule should not undermine relationships which were validly entered into at the time, and upending formerly-correct decisions of law served the interests of no one. The court also concluded the old rule had been in effect for such a length of time that citizens undoubtedly relied upon it, including the parties before the court.

We likewise decline to exercise our prerogative to apply our ruling today retroactively. . . . Accordingly, our ruling today is to be applied purely prospectively; no individual may enter into a common-law marriage in South Carolina after the date of this opinion.

E. Refining the Test

Consistent with our observations regarding the institution's validity in modern times, we believe we must update the standards courts are to apply in future common-law marriage litigation. A common-law marriage is formed when the parties contract to be married, either expressly or impliedly by circumstance. The key element in discerning whether parties are common-law married is mutual assent: each party must intend to be married to the other and understand the other's intent. Some factors to which courts have looked to discern the parties' intent include tax returns, documents filed under penalty of perjury, introductions in public, contracts, and checking accounts.

Appellate courts have previously recognized two lines of cases regarding common-law marriage. The first holds that a party proves a common-law marriage by a preponderance of the evidence. The second relies on "a strong presumption in favor of marriage by cohabitation, apparently matrimonial, coupled with social acceptance over a long period of time. This presumption—like common-law marriage itself—is based on a conception of morality and favors marriage over concubinage and legitimacy over bastardy. It can only be overcome by "strong, cogent, satisfactory or conclusive evidence" showing the parties are not married. This Court has held that once a common-law marriage becomes complete, "no act or disavowal" can invalidate it.

Thompson argues the rebuttable presumption of common-law marriage is based on outdated assumptions about cohabitation. Given our foregoing assessment of common-law marriage, it will come as no surprise that we agree. The concerns regarding immorality, illegitimacy, and bastardy are no longer stigmatized by society, and as a result, they can no longer serve as the basis for assuming individuals are married.

Additionally, consistent with our preceding discussion regarding the sanctity of a marital relationship and our reticence to impose one on those who did not fully intend it, we believe a heightened burden of proof is warranted. Therefore, we hold the "clear and convincing evidence" standard utilized in probate matters should also apply to living litigants. This is an intermediate standard—more than a preponderance, but less than beyond a reasonable doubt—and requires a party to show a degree of proof sufficient to produce a firm belief in the allegations sought to be established. . . .

To sum up, in the cases litigated hereafter, a party asserting a common-law marriage is required to demonstrate mutual assent to be married by clear and convincing evidence. Courts may continue to weigh the same circumstantial factors traditionally considered, but they may not indulge in presumptions based on cohabitation, no matter how apparently matrimonial. While we have set forth the law to be applied in future litigation, we apply the principles in effect at the time this action was filed to the case at hand.

II.

A. Factual and Procedural Background

Stone and Thompson met in the early 1980's and began a romantic relationship shortly thereafter. Thompson was married to another man at the time and obtained a divorce from him in 1987. Later that year, Stone and Thompson had their first child. After Hurricane Hugo hit Charleston in 1989, the parties had their second child and started living together. They continued to live, raise their children, and manage rental properties together for approximately twenty years. Thompson worked as a veterinarian and owned multiple practices, while Stone performed contracting work and collected rent from tenants. The parties ultimately ended their relationship after Thompson discovered Stone was having an affair with a woman in Costa Rica.

In 2012, Stone filed an amended complaint in family court seeking a declaratory judgment that the parties were common-law married, a divorce, and an equitable distribution of alleged marital property. Thompson answered, asserting the parties were never common-law married and seeking dismissal. She also asked the court to bifurcate the issues to first determine if a common-law marriage existed if it would not dismiss the case. After a hearing, the family court denied Thompson's motion to dismiss but granted her motion to bifurcate, ordering a trial on the sole issue of whether the parties were married at common law.

The trial involved more than a week of proceedings, testimony from over 40 witnesses, and nearly 200 exhibits. Stone's testimony focused on the parties' cohabitation for approximately twenty years, the fact that they raised their two children together during this time, and their partnership in acquiring, renovating, and renting multiple properties in the Charleston area. He submitted evidence that the parties were jointly titled on real estate, boats, bank accounts, and credit cards, as well as that Thompson had listed herself as married to him on several documents from 2005-2008, including some prescribing criminal penalties for false statements. Stone's witnesses generally testified that the parties were assumed to be married in the community and were introduced as husband and wife by themselves and others on multiple occasions without correction.

Conversely, Thompson testified she never intended to marry Stone and went to great lengths to preserve her unmarried status. She pointed to numerous documents listing both her and Stone as single during the relevant time period, including all of their tax returns, his documents related to a Costa Rican financial venture, and a 2008 agreement signed by both parties. Thompson's witnesses reported that they and others in the community knew she and Stone were not married and they never heard them introduced as such. Several testified Thompson had told them she would never marry again.

The family court concluded the parties were common-law married beginning in 1989 when they began to live together full-time and Thompson introduced Stone as her husband during an art opening. The court found Stone's testimony credible while rejecting Thompson's versions of events on credibility grounds, as it determined Stone's witnesses were longtime friends of both parties and were distressed at having to testify, while many of Thompson's witnesses did not become close to her until after the affair. The family court concluded that Stone presented sufficient evidence of the parties' apparently-matrimonial cohabitation to trigger a presumption of marriage that could only be refuted by strong, cogent evidence they never agreed to marry. The court found Thompson failed to submit such evidence, as once she expressed the intention to be married in December 1989, no subsequent act could change it, as there is no common-law divorce. The family court awarded $125,620.32 in attorney's fees and costs to Stone, reasoning that Thompson's actions and denial of a common-law marriage were "flatly contradicted time and again. . . ."

Thompson appealed to the court of appeals, which determined the family court's order was not final and appealable because it did not end the case. Thompson petitioned for a writ of certiorari, which this Court granted. We issued an opinion on April 3, 2019, finding the order was appealable. . . .

Thompson asserts the record reflects she never intended to be married to Stone. Stone contends the family court correctly found the parties were common-law married in 1989 because the record demonstrates the parties held themselves out and signed multiple documents under threat of criminal penalties as such during the course of their relationship.

The family court found the parties were married in 1989 after they moved in together, had their second child, and held themselves out as a married couple, as this established the requisite meeting of the minds. We disagree. Stone testified Thompson introduced him as her husband to a third party at an art opening around Christmas 1989, but Thompson stated this did not occur. Stone did not produce the third party to confirm that it did, and even respecting the court's credibility finding, we do not believe this rises to a preponderance of the evidence that, at that time, the two intended to be married and knew the other did as well.

Further, no evidence from the subsequent decade and a half demonstrated mutual intent to be married. Even assuming Stone intended to be married to Thompson throughout this time — which the evidence presented does not fully support — the critical inquiry is whether Thompson ever did. The parties continued to live and raise children together — consistent with their agreement to participate in a committed relationship — as well as run their business partnership of purchasing, flipping, and/or managing properties. Although some witnesses testified the two introduced each other as husband and wife, others testified they never heard them do so, and still others testified they knew not to because Thompson had told them they were not married. While acknowledging the family court's credibility determination, we nonetheless disagree with the court's view of the evidence. The court's finding that Thompson's witnesses largely became close to her after the affair is contradicted by fourteen witnesses who were acquainted with her and Stone during the relevant time period and testified they knew the parties were not married, while Stone's merely assumed they were. Significantly, there were no documents from 1989-2004 in which Thompson indicated she was married, and many that reflected she was not. Moreover, the children's birth certificates stated their last name was Thompson. While the children were born shortly before 1989, their legal last name remained Thompson until June 2000, when it was changed to Thompson Stone. Even if a rebuttable presumption the parties were married arose, Thompson refuted it by strong, cogent evidence.

The evidence presented as to the factors appellate courts consider in determining intent was decidedly mixed. For example, Thompson insisted on filing her taxes as "single head of household" during the entirety of her relationship with Stone. On the other hand, both she and Stone filed other documents under penalty of perjury claiming they were married. Both sides presented evidence that the parties did/did not introduce themselves to others as married over the years. The parties signed some contracts jointly, but many more were only in one's name or the other's. Finally, the parties shared at least one checking account, but Thompson disputed Stone's assertion that they shared several.

The closest the parties came to the requisite meeting of the minds, in our opinion, was from 2005-2008, when Thompson indicated she was married to Stone, at least for certain purposes. It began with a medical intake form dated May 31, 2005, which only she signed, but continued that year with several documents both parties signed. These included a mortgage loan application stating they were married followed by mortgage documents listing the parties as husband and wife. Mortgage documents from December 2006 and January 2007 likewise listed the parties as married. Thompson signed a transfer of insurance from Stone to herself that indicated she was his wife as of October 2008. She finally listed herself as married on another medical intake form with a different doctor in December 2008, which she sought to change to "single" two weeks after this case was filed.

However, these documents are undercut by others from the same period, including Thompson's continued tax filings as single, Stone's Costa Rican documents wherein he listed himself as single, and a 2008 reconciliation agreement signed by both parties in which they agreed they had preserved their unmarried status. Thompson further explained the parties signed the financial documents as married during this time because banks were more closely scrutinizing mortgage loans. While we in no way condone false statements in pursuit of a financial benefit, we do not believe these documents evidence the necessary intent to prove the parties were common-law married.

It is clear the parties intended to be in a committed relationship and business partnership together, but their conduct in living together, raising children, and running the business does not demonstrate they each intended to be married and knew the other intended the same. Furthermore, because our decision constitutes a reversal on the merits, we likewise reverse the family court's award of attorney's fees. . . .

NOTES AND QUESTIONS

1. The elements of common law marriage are generally said to be that the parties intended to be married, that they cohabited, and that they represented to the world ("held out") that they were married. South Carolina was unusual in providing that a presumption in favor of a common law marriage arose from cohabitation. More commonly, courts imposed the burden of proof on the party claiming the existence of a common law marriage and said that the most important question was whether the parties held out that they were married.

Stone emphasizes the importance of the parties' intent to be married. What does it mean to intend to be married? In this case Stone asserted that he intended to be married, and thus the dispute was over Thompson's intent. What facts show that Thompson intended to be married? What facts show that she did not?

What should happen if the facts show that one party intended to be married while the other harbored reservations? In this situation holding out may become critical. What facts in *Stone* show that the parties held out to the world that they were married? What facts undercut this claim? Why do you suppose Stone wanted a finding that the parties were married while Thompson did not?

2. For the most part, the doctrine of common law marriage does not provide a way to avoid the substantive requirements for marriage; it addresses only the issue of formalities. For example, Stone and Thompson could not have been common law married before 1987, even though they were romantically involved, because she was married to someone else until then.

With surprising frequency, people purport to marry while they are still legally married to someone else, either because they haven't bothered to get a divorce or because the divorce is not yet final. When the parties reside in a state that permits common law marriage, courts have often found that such a marriage commenced if and when the first marriage ended. *See, e.g.*, Hall v. Duster, 727 So. 2d 834 (Ala. Civ. App. 1999); Thomas v. 5 Star Transportation, 770 S.E.2d 183 (S.C. 2015). For such situations the Uniform Marriage and Divorce Act (UMDA) §207(b) proposes the following statutory remedy for states that do not generally allow common law marriage: "Parties to a marriage prohibited under this section who cohabit after removal of the impediment are lawfully married as of the date of the removal of the impediment."

3. In most states that allow common law marriage, courts have held that it is legally possible for same-sex couples to have entered into a common law marriage prior to the Supreme Court's ruling in Obergefell v. Hodges. LaFleur v. Pyfer, 479 P.3d 869 (Colo. 2021); In re J.K.N.A, 454 P.3d 642 (Mont. 2019); Gil v. Van Nostrand, 206 A.3d 869 (D.C. App. 2019); In re Estate of Carter, 159 A.3d 970 (Pa. Super. 2017). *Contra* Swicegood v. Thompson, 865 S.E.2d 775 (S.C. 2022). For further discussion, *see* Michael J. Higdon, (In) Formal Marriage Equality, 89 Fordham L. Rev. 1351 (2021); Charles W. "Rocky" Rhodes, Loving Retroactivity, 45 Fla. St. U. L. Rev. 383 (2018).

4. In the late 1880s, more than half the states allowed common law marriages to be formed within their boundaries, but today only seven states and the District of Columbia do so. The states recognizing common law marriage are Colorado, Iowa, Kansas, Montana, Rhode Island, Texas, and Utah. Since 1991, seven states—Alabama, Georgia, Idaho, Ohio, Oklahoma, Pennsylvania, and South Carolina—have abolished common law marriage by statute or judicial decision. A New Hampshire statute provides, "Persons cohabiting and acknowledging each other as husband and wife, and generally reputed to be such, for the period of 3 years, and until the decease of one of them, shall thereafter be deemed to have been legally married." N.H. Rev. Stat. §457:39 (2017). Why does the statute only provide rights at death?

What reasons does the South Carolina Supreme Court give for abolishing common law marriage prospectively? Does it matter that lay people often do not understand the requirements for a common law marriage? Does the acceptability today of nonmarital cohabitation mean that there is no need for common law marriage or something like it?

5. Contrary to the trend in other states, in 1987 the Utah legislature enacted a statute providing that a couple is married, even if they have not participated in a valid ceremony, if a court or administrative agency finds that they (a) are capable of giving consent; (b) are legally capable of entering a solemnized marriage under the provisions of this chapter; (c) have cohabited; (d) mutually assume marital rights, duties, and obligations; and (e) hold themselves out as and have acquired a uniform and general reputation as husband and wife. Utah Stat. §30-1-4.5 (2022). Under this statute, would Stone and Thompson have been treated as married?

The Utah statute was intended to reduce public assistance to families with children. In Utah stepparents, but not unmarried cohabitants, are obligated to support their stepchildren during their marriage to the children's custodial parent. Accordingly, a family may be eligible for assistance if the custodial parent is living with but not married to a partner, while the family would become ineligible if the cohabitants were married. Does this statute seem likely to accomplish its purpose? Might it be used to increase other public expenditures for family members? The state of Utah relied on this statute to prosecute individuals for bigamy (Chapter 3, page 148).

6. The federal government uses something like common law marriage to limit people's eligibility for certain means-tested benefits. The Supplemental Security Income program rules require that the income of both spouses be considered in determining a person's eligibility unless the person is in long-term care. For purposes of this rule, spouse includes a person with whom the applicant lives if the couple "leads people to believe" that they are spouses. 20 C.F.R. §§416.1806(3), 416.1826.

7. Common law marriage is more important than one might conclude from looking only at the number of states in which such marriages can be contracted. Under choice-of-law rules, a state may recognize a common law marriage entered into in another jurisdiction even when the forum state itself does not allow common law marriages. As we saw in Chapter 3, the traditional choice-of-law rule is that a marriage is valid where entered into is valid everywhere, but a state may refuse to recognize a marriage entered into in another state if to do so would violate a strong public policy of the forum state. If the parties were domiciled in a state that allows common law marriage, other states will generally recognize the parties' common law marriage. The problem arises when the parties were domiciled in a state that does not allow common law marriage but had some level of contact with a state that does.

According to Professor Clark, the states' approaches can be sorted into three groups. Some states do not have a strong policy against common law marriage; they therefore are willing to treat their domiciliaries as having entered into a common law marriage in another state even when the parties' contact with that state was just a short visit. At the other extreme, some states have such a strong policy against common law marriage that they will not recognize an alleged common law marriage between parties not domiciled in the common law marriage state at the time of the alleged marriage. In the third group of states, parties do not have to have been domiciled in the common law marriage state, but they must have established a residence there; visits alone are not sufficient. Homer H. Clark, Jr., The Law of Domestic Relations in the United States §2.4, at 57-59 (2d ed. 1988).

8. In principle, common law marriage differs from ceremonial marriage only in the way in which it is entered. Consequently, a formal divorce action is necessary to dissolve a common law marriage. However, the Utah statute quoted above provides that a proceeding to establish a common law marriage must be brought within a year after the relationship has ended. Does this statute create a form of common law divorce?

PROBLEMS

1. Nine years ago, John Winegard met Sally Jones, who was single, 13 years his junior, and an employee of his company. Romance blossomed, but after a few months Sally broke off the relationship and married Lonny, with whom she had a baby. About a year later, Sally asked John for a loan to get a divorce from Lonny, which she received. John and Sally dated over the next year and a half before Sally left John and married Frank. Three years later, Sally and Frank separated, and John assisted Sally financially in procuring her second divorce. About six months later John and Sally entered into a premarital agreement and went to Hawaii to get married. However, they did not go through with the wedding. Sally returned briefly to Lonny and then left him again for John. In February of last year John gave Sally an engagement ring, and in March they flew to Las Vegas to be married but again did not go through with the wedding. On the flight home, Sally said that John said they didn't need a ceremony because they were just as married as anybody. John denied saying this, though he admitted he gave her a wedding ring to save her from embarrassment and because he didn't have anything else to do with it.

Upon their return home, Sally began living with John and told various people that she and John were married. They received wedding gifts from several people, including members of his family, and they received mail as and traveled together as Mr. and Mrs. Winegard. They sent out Christmas cards from "Sally and John Winegard." Sally was mentioned several times in the local newspaper society section as "Mrs. Winegard." John bought an insurance policy naming Sally Winegard as the beneficiary, and he endorsed checks to her as "Sally Winegard."

However, their relationship soured when Sally learned that John was seeing another woman. She has sued for divorce, seeking property division and alimony. John denies that they were ever married. Assuming John and Sally lived in a state that recognizes common law marriage, what arguments should be made on Sally's behalf? On John's?

2. Ernest and Irene, who were both widowed and retired, participated in a wedding ceremony performed by a minister, but they did not obtain a marriage license. Irene believed that if she remarried, she would lose her pension benefits as the surviving spouse of her first husband. After the wedding, Ernest and Irene lived together in a state that allows common law marriage, referred to themselves as husband and wife, and were generally known among their friends as spouses. They filed their income taxes as single people and did not notify the Social Security Administration or the administrators of their private pensions that they were married. Ernest has died, and Irene claims rights as his surviving widow on the theory that they had a common law marriage. Ernest's brother, who is executor of his estate, has denied her claim. What arguments should the parties make?

2. Presumptions About Marriage and Putative Spouses

Spearman v. Spearman
482 F.2d 1203 (5th Cir. 1973)

Roney, C.J. At the time of his death, on October 1, 1969, Edward Spearman was insured by Metropolitan Life Insurance Company under Group Policy No. 17000-G in the amount of $10,000. The policy provided that, if no beneficiary were designated, the proceeds were to be paid to the "widow" of the insured. The parties stipulated that the policy designated no beneficiary.

After Spearman's death, both defendants claimed to be his "widow" and claimed the proceeds of his life insurance policy. The first wife, Mary Spearman, is a resident of Alabama and was married to insured on October 2, 1946, in Russell County, Alabama. Two children, twin girls, were born of this marriage, and both carry the surname of Spearman. The second wife, Viva Spearman, a resident of California, married insured on June 7, 1962, in Monterey County, California. This marriage produced no offspring.

Metropolitan filed this interpleader action and paid the proceeds of the policy into the registry of the District Court. . . .

The decision in this case turns on the definition of the term "widow" as used in the life insurance policy. The policy itself does not define "widow," nor does the Federal Employees' Group Life Insurance Act provide any guidance. This question is not however, one of first impression. In Tatum v. Tatum, 241 F.2d 401 (9th Cir. 1957), the Ninth Circuit, by looking to judicial interpretations of an analogous federal statute, the National Service Life Insurance Act, 38 U.S.C.A. §701 et seq., determined that the term "widow" meant "lawful widow." . . .

California law is in accord with the general rule which provides that a second marriage cannot be validly contracted if either spouse is then married.

In a contest between conflicting marriages under California law, once the first wife presents evidence that her marriage has not been dissolved, then the burden of persuasion shifts to the second wife to establish that her spouse's marriage to his first wife had been dissolved. Otherwise, the first wife is deemed to have established her status as the lawful wife. According to the California rule, as in most states, the process of establishing which wife enjoys the status of lawful wife involves these shifting presumptions and burdens of persuasion:

1. Initially, when a person has contracted two successive marriages, a presumption arises in favor of the validity of the second marriage. Absent any contrary evidence, the second wife is deemed to be the lawful wife.

2. The presumption of validity accorded the second marriage is, however, merely a rule of evidence. It is a rebuttable presumption, the effect of which is to cast upon the first wife the burden of establishing the continuing validity of her marriage by demonstrating that it had not been dissolved by death, divorce, or annulment at the time of the second marriage.

3. California formerly required the first wife to prove that her husband had not dissolved their marriage by showing that no record of either divorce or annulment existed in any jurisdiction in which the husband may have resided. This strict burden has now been somewhat relaxed. The current rule is that, to rebut the presumption of validity inuring to the second or subsequent marriage, the first spouse need examine the records of only those jurisdictions in which either she or her husband have been in fact domiciled.

4. If the first wife shows that an examination of the pertinent records of such jurisdictions and all of the available evidence demonstrate that her marriage remains undissolved, the burden of demonstrating the invalidity of the first marriage then shifts to the party asserting its invalidity, the second wife in this case. Unless the second wife then can establish that her husband's first marriage has been dissolved, the first wife qualifies as the "lawful widow." . . .

Even if the second wife cannot qualify as the insured's "widow," she may nevertheless be entitled to one-half of the proceeds of the life insurance policy as insured's "putative spouse."

A putative spouse is one whose marriage is legally invalid but who has engaged in (1) a marriage ceremony or a solemnization, on the (2) good faith belief in the validity of the marriage. According to Estate of Foy, 109 Cal. App. 2d 329, 240 P.2d 685 (1952),

> [t]he term "putative marriage" is applied to a matrimonial union which has been solemnized in due form and good faith on the part of one or of both of the parties but which by reason of some legal infirmity is either void or voidable. The essential basis of such marriage is the belief that it is valid.

109 Cal. App. 2d at 331-332, 240 P.2d at 686.

The theory under which the "putative spouse" is entitled to recover a share of the insurance proceeds is that, as the insured's "putative spouse," she is entitled to share in the property accumulated by the family unit during its existence. The general rule, therefore, is that the "putative spouse" is entitled to the same share in this property as would have been accorded a de jure spouse under the community property laws. . . .

Applying these rules to the facts before it, the District Court first looked to the law of Alabama and concluded that Mary, the first wife, was validly married in Alabama in 1946. The subsequent marriage to Viva in 1962 in California was valid under California law, unless there was a preexisting marriage. At this point, the presumption in favor of the most recent marriage to Viva required Mary to show that her marriage had not been dissolved or annulled at the time of the insured's marriage to Viva. This showing she successfully made by establishing that no petition for annulment or divorce had been filed, by either herself or the insured, in any of their known domiciles since 1946. . . . After Mary had rebutted the presumption of validity initially attaching to Viva's marriage, the burden of persuasion shifted to Viva. This burden failed for want of proof: Viva introduced no credible evidence that either Mary or the insured had ever been a party to any legal proceeding that had annulled or dissolved their marriage. The District Court then correctly ruled that Mary had established the continuing validity of her marriage to the insured and that Viva had failed to establish otherwise.

. . . The District Court found that Viva could not qualify as the insured's "putative spouse" because she could not meet the requirement of a good faith belief in the existence of a valid marriage. . . . The evidence before the District Court showed that Viva knew (1) that the insured had fathered two children by Mary Spearman, (2) that Mary and both children carried the Spearman name, (3) that Mary had secured a support decree against the insured, (4) that the insured returned to Alabama each year on his vacation, and (5) that while on these vacations the insured lived in the same house with Mary and his two children. On these facts, the District Court's finding of an absence of good faith was amply supported. As the District Court stated in its thorough opinion, "Viva admits that she was aware of the possibility, if not the likelihood, of [insured's] prior marriage to Mary, and, yet, she took no steps to perfect her marital status."

Viva contends that the District Court's view of the "bona fide belief requirement rests upon an erroneous interpretation of the California decisions. She argues that these decisions require only that the "putative spouse" have neither actual knowledge of invalidity nor a belief that the marriage was invalid. Under Viva's view, then, so long as she did not actually know of her marriage's invalidity and maintained a belief in its validity, no matter how unreasonable that belief may have been, she qualified as the insured's "putative spouse." We decline to adopt such a test of good faith. Rather, we think that the District Court correctly held that a good faith belief in the validity of the marriage must be posited on a view of the facts known to the spouse in question. . . .

Affirmed.

NOTES AND QUESTIONS

1. *Spearman* invokes the presumption that the most recent of a series of marriages is valid. Another commonly invoked presumption that might apply on facts like these is that a marriage validly entered into continues. Both presumptions are applied in many contexts besides that of *Spearman*. Can you think of any? What factual and policy assumptions underlie these presumptions?

In *Spearman*, Viva benefitted from the presumption that the most recent marriage is valid, while the presumption that a valid marriage continues favored Mary. If both presumptions had been invoked, how should the clash between them have been resolved?

> . . . The Supreme Court of Pennsylvania has specifically instructed courts . . . to perform a balancing test by weighing the evidence in the record to determine which of two presumptions, one in favor of continuation of the first marriage and the other in favor of the validity of the second marriage, is more easily sustained by the evidence. . . . In adjusting that balance, we think no mechanical rule will suffice. Instead, we think the court should consider the conduct of both parties and their respective contributions to the stability of the family each chose to support or deny in light of the value our society attributes to traditional families and evolving conditions of family life in this nation.

Huff v. Director, 40 F.3d 35, 37 (3d Cir. 1994).

2. *Spearman* allows a first spouse to satisfy the burden of proving that the marriage never ended by a search of divorce records in the state where the parties to the first marriage were domiciled because only states in which one spouse or the other was domiciled may constitutionally assert jurisdiction to divorce them. See Chapter 12, Section A. However, not all courts agree that this is sufficient. *See, e.g.,* Yarbrough v. Celebrezze, 217 F. Supp. 943 (M.D.N.C. 1963) (first wife's search of divorce records of various states without finding any divorce obtained by husband did not rebut presumption); Spears v. Spears, 12 S.W.2d 875 (Ark. 1928) (similar). What more could the party alleging the validity of the first marriage do?

3. *Spearman* does not discuss what Mary knew about Edward's relationship with Viva. If evidence showed that Mary knew that Edward and Viva had lived together as spouses for the seven years before his death, should her claim be barred because of her delay in asserting that she, not Viva, was Edward's wife? In Rogers v. Office of Personnel Management, 87 F.3d 471 (Fed. Cir. 1996), the court applied this doctrine to prevent the first wife from asserting a claim to a survivor's annuity. The court held that the second wife was prejudiced because, had the first wife come forward while the man was still alive, the second wife could have taken steps to clarify the situation, to make other financial provision for herself, or both.

4. Applying the putative spouse doctrine, *Spearman* concluded that Viva did not in good faith believe she was married. Even taking an objective view of good faith, as the court does, are there other "reasonable" explanations for Viva's belief that she was married, knowing what she did about Edward's relationship with Mary? The California Supreme Court in Ceja v. Rudolph & Sietten, Inc., 302 P.3d 211 (Cal. 2013), held that under California law, the putative spouse doctrine requires only proof of a subjective good faith belief that the marriage was valid, disapproving of *Spearman* and a number of lower California appellate decisions that applied an objective test. Did Viva have a subjectively good faith belief that she was married?

5. The putative spouse doctrine derives from Spanish and French law and was first recognized in states, such as California, whose domestic relations law derived from civil law. Finding that one is a putative spouse does not necessarily give that person all the rights of a true spouse. Instead, as *Spearman* indicates, the putative spouse doctrine was originally used to provide marital property rights. For example, the Supreme Court of Nevada has held that the putative spouse doctrine permits an award of property but not spousal support when the validity of the marriage is successfully challenged. Williams v. Williams, 97 P.3d 1124 (Nev. 2004). *Williams* reports that a majority of states recognize the doctrine in some form.

6. Section 209 of the UMDA creates a remedy for putative spouses, but unlike the form of the doctrine used in community property states, it does not require that the parties have participated in a wedding ceremony. Xiong v. Xiong, 800 N.W.2d 187 (Minn. App. 2011), applied this section to a traditional Hmong wedding ceremony between a man and a woman who was too young to marry under state law. The two lived together and were regarded as married in the Hmong community, although they knew they were not married under state law. After the woman turned 18, she and the man obtained a marriage license but did not participate in another wedding ceremony. When the couple broke up 15 years later, the court found that the woman was a putative spouse because she believed the man when he told her that obtaining the license constituted a marriage under state law.

7. Both presumptions about the validity of marriage and the putative spouse rule, like common law marriage, are sufficiently indeterminate that courts can apply them flexibly to do justice in individual cases. Why might the court in *Spearman* have favored awarding the insurance proceeds to Mary, rather than to Viva?

8. Application of the presumptions about marriage validity produces a conclusion about which one of two or more marriages is valid. In contrast, the putative spouse doctrine admits of the possibility that two or more people would have spousal rights. In 2013 the South Carolina Supreme Court expressly declined to adopt the putative spouse doctrine because it is inconsistent with state policy prohibiting bigamy. Hill v. Bell, 747 S.E.2d 791 (S.C. 2013). Do you agree? In *Hill*, Thomas married Lavona in 1979; they separated in 1983 but never divorced. In 1986 Thomas obtained a marriage license and participated in a marriage ceremony with Barbara, who did not know about Thomas's prior marriage. They lived together until Thomas died 16 years later, but the surviving spouse benefits from his NFL pension went to Lavona, not Barbara, as a result of this decision. Hill v. Bert Bell/Pete Rozelle NFL Player Retirement Plan, 548 Fed. Appx. 55 (3d Cir. 2013).

PROBLEM

Irene and Bill were ceremonially married in Texas in 1997 when Irene was 17, a year younger than the minimum marriage age. They lived together until she was 22. Under Texas law their marriage was ratified and thus validated by their living together after she became 18. They separated in 2001 without having had children. Bill moved to Pennsylvania. In 2002 Irene filed for divorce from Bill, but the action was dismissed for lack of prosecution and thus the divorce was never finalized.

In 2006 Irene began living with Tom Bennett, with whom she had three children. She is named "Irene Bennett" on the children's birth certificates, even though she was never ceremonially married to Tom.

In 2008 Bill ceremonially married Ethel in Pennsylvania. On the application for the marriage license Bill said that he had never been married. He had told Ethel about his marriage to Irene but said that it had been annulled. Following the wedding ceremony, Bill and Ethel held themselves out and lived as a married couple for 15 years. They had two children. Bill, who was an employee of the federal government, recently died in an automobile accident. Both Irene and Ethel claim benefits as his surviving spouse. What arguments should each make?

B. UNMARRIED COHABITANTS

Unmarried cohabitation has changed dramatically in the United States over the last half century, growing from 450,000 couples in 1960 to about 9 million in 2017. Most young adults will live with an unmarried partner at least once, and more than half of all those who marry live together first, according to the Census Bureau. Nonetheless, "compared to 25 years ago, fewer couples today are engaged or have definite marriage plans when they begin to cohabit, and fewer cohabiting couples make the transition to marriage. In the early 1990s, nearly six in 10 cohabiting couples married within three years; today, about four in 10 do so." Population Reference Bureau, Understanding the Dynamics of Family Change in the United States, 71 Population Bulletin 8 (July 2016).

Cynthia Grant Bowman

Social Science and Legal Policy: The Case of Heterosexual Cohabitation
9 J.L. & Fam. Stud. 1, 10-16, 18-20, 23, 31-32 (2007)

As the numbers of cohabitants have skyrocketed, the number of distinct groups from which they come has also increased, as have the types and functions of these unions. . . .

. . . [W]hile there are some patterns about cohabitation behavior, those patterns are made up of multiple designs; and many of them are changing with the passage of time. As a result of this demographic research, we do know that multiple and differing groups are included within the aggregate data on cohabitation in the United States, including but not limited to the following:

1. Young "dating" singles, often sharing quarters for reasons of convenience and economy;
2. Young adults cohabiting prior to marriage, either with no plans to marry or as some sort of trial marriage which may succeed or fail;
3. Working-class couples without the resources for a wedding ceremony or home ownership;

4. Low-income mothers making rational use of cohabitation to support themselves and their children;
5. Puerto Rican couples in consensual unions, often with children of the union;
6. Divorced persons either screening candidates for remarriage or seeking an alternative to marriage; and
7. Older persons cohabiting for convenience and economy or because they have no particular reason to marry. . . .

A very important point that can be missed in the aggregate data is that the stability, like the rate, of cohabitation differs by subgroups of the population. The average duration of a cohabiting union is longer, for example, for persons who have previously been married. This is also so for cohabitants who are older. CDC data show that women who are older at the start of a cohabiting union (25 or over) are less likely to experience disruption of the relationship, indicating that at least some of the divorces that statistically would have resulted from early marriage have shifted into the statistics about cohabitation instead. The probability of disruption (under the CDC definition) is also higher in communities with high unemployment: 76% of African American cohabitants in communities of high unemployment break up within ten years, as compared with 57% of non-Hispanic whites living in areas of low unemployment. In addition, the probability that a first cohabitation will transition to marriage within five years is 75% for non-Hispanic white women, 61% for Hispanic women, and 48% for African Americans. In short, if you are older, a member of the dominant racial or ethnic group, and have more money, you are more likely to make a long-term success of either cohabitation or marriage. . . .

Similarly, the generalized finding, oft repeated, that premarital cohabitation increases the rate of subsequent divorce looks different when deconstructed. The conclusion usually drawn from the correlation of cohabitation and subsequent divorce is that cohabitation, touted as a way to try out candidates for marriage, is not a very good screening mechanism. However, the correlation between cohabitation and divorce is not very significant for persons who cohabit only with the person they subsequently marry, as the vast majority do. Other studies confirm that premarital cohabitation with the subsequent spouse is not associated with a higher risk of divorce. The implication is that it is only persons who engage in multiple cohabiting relationships prior to marriage who are a bad risk. . . .

Eleanor Brown, Naomi Cahn & June Carbone

The Price of Exit
99 Wash. U. L. Rev. 1897, 1919-1923 (2022)

The distinguishing feature between committed bargains and contingent bargains is interdependence. . . . [C]ommitted couples commingle resources and share an intensive emotional and material investment in children. This interdependence, even without legal recognition, increases the cost of exit as untangling joint undertakings can be complex and contentious. Contingent bargains, in contrast, limit the degree of interdependence, which makes exit easier. A partner who lacks confidence in the other partner is less likely to commit to the relationship, which in turn produces greater wariness about joint undertakings. Instead, the bargains tend to be transactional: the partners may agree to live together so long as there are joint contributions to the rent, to share childcare responsibilities so long as a partner is sober, respectful and responsible, to remain together so long as both partners are employed and do not constitute an undue burden on the other's resources. In many cases, couples report that they are unwilling to enter into an open-ended commitment because they are unsure that these conditions can be met. They accordingly position themselves for the possibility of exit.

Empirical research suggests that these expectations are realistic. . . . [W]omen's and men's job prospects and job quality influence the type of relationships they enter; the more precarious the job and the fewer fringe benefits, the more likely is cohabitation than marriage. . . . A Federal Reserve Report, for example, indicated that close to 40% of Americans would have difficulty paying an unexpected bill of $400. According to the same report, 30% of American adults have income that varies from month to month. . . .

For this group, commitment to a partner may be a source of vulnerability rather than strength. . . . Commingling resources means carrying the partner through layoffs and hard times. Race intersects with the class differences. African American and Latinx families, for example, in comparison with whites and Asians, "are more often the target of growing precarious employment, lower wages, more erratic schedules, and greater job unpredictability." And in the poorest groups, women may have more stable income than men. Indeed, in the bottom quintile of American families by income, wives earned more in 70% of the marriages. These factors influence decisions about commitment. A frequent reason that couples give for wariness of open-ended commitment is that they are not financially ready. . . .

Women are more likely than men to say that "it's very important for a person to have a steady job before getting married (67% vs. 58% of men) or moving in with a partner (66% vs. 54%)." They are also more likely to say that "it's very important for a person to be financially stable before getting married" (48% vs. 40%) or "moving in with a partner" (53% vs. 44%) Income volatility as well as low income destabilizes these relationships. . . .

A second reason for wariness about commitment involves the ability to find the right partner — one who shares the same values about a relationship. Couples generally prefer egalitarian relationships. Couples who see themselves as better off than their partners or see their partners as unreliable tend to be warier of open-ended commitments. Better-educated men are more likely to report concerns about relationships limiting their future opportunities, and to fear that a commitment to their current partner may hold them back. Men are more likely than women to say that if a couple cannot manage the tradeoffs necessary for a dual earner arrangement, their career should come first. Women, on the other hand, are more likely than men to emphasize steady employment or responsible behavior as important from a partner. If they cannot find a partner supportive of their workforce involvement, they are more likely to choose to go it alone. Surveys of cohabitants between the ages of eighteen and twenty-nine reflect these concerns. Among those who have completed at least some college, 68% of women but only 46% of the men report that they expect to marry their current partner. Among those who have not finished high school, the gender breakdown flips; it is the women rather than the men who express greater hesitation to commit to their current partners.

Historically, if a couple lived together without being ceremonially married and were not eligible for or did not satisfy the requirements for a common law marriage or the putative spouse doctrine, their relationship was "meretricious," a word derived from the Latin for "prostitute." Legally, they were at best roommates and at worst outlaws. However, with the dramatic rise in open nonmarital cohabitation, the law has changed. The first part of this section considers judicially created remedies, based on contract and equitable principles, that give the parties some rights against each other. The second part examines possibilities for creating new status relationships between unmarried cohabitants that give them rights and duties between one another, in relation to third parties, or both. Couples who bring these cases typically have property worth fighting over. As you read about the evolution of these doctrines, consider whether they incorporate a vision of cohabitation that does justice to the many types of couples who may cohabit in the future.

1. Contractual and Equitable Remedies

Marvin v. Marvin[1]
557 P.2d 106 (Cal. 1976)

TOBRINER, J. Plaintiff avers that in October of 1964 she and defendant "entered into an oral agreement" that while "the parties lived together they would combine their efforts and earnings and would share equally any and all property accumulated as a result of their efforts whether individual or combined." Furthermore, they agreed to "hold themselves out to the general public as husband and wife" and that "plaintiff would further render her services as a companion, homemaker, housekeeper and cook to . . . defendant."

Shortly thereafter plaintiff agreed to "give up her lucrative career as an entertainer (and) singer" in order to "devote her full time to defendant . . . as a companion, homemaker, housekeeper and cook"; in return defendant agreed to "provide for all of plaintiff's financial support and needs for the rest of her life."

Plaintiff alleges that she lived with defendant from October of 1964 through May of 1970 and fulfilled her obligations under the agreement. During this period the parties as a result of their efforts and earnings acquired in defendant's name substantial real and personal property, including motion picture rights worth over $1 million. In May of 1970, however, defendant compelled plaintiff to leave his household. He continued to support plaintiff until November of 1971, but thereafter refused to provide further support.

On the basis of these allegations plaintiff asserts two causes of action. The first, for declaratory relief, asks the court to determine her contract and property rights; the second seeks to impose a constructive trust upon one half of the property acquired during the course of the relationship. . . .

After hearing argument the court granted defendant's motion [for judgment on the pleadings] and entered judgment for defendant. Plaintiff . . . appealed from the judgment.

2. PLAINTIFF'S COMPLAINT STATES A CAUSE OF ACTION FOR BREACH OF AN EXPRESS CONTRACT

. . . Defendant first and principally relies on the contention that the alleged contract is so closely related to the supposed "immoral" character of the relationship between plaintiff and himself that the enforcement of the contract would violate public policy. . . .

Although the past decisions hover over the issue in the somewhat wispy form of the figures of a Chagall painting, we can abstract from those decisions a clear and simple rule. . . . The fact that a man and woman live together without marriage, and engage in a sexual relationship, does not in itself invalidate agreements between them relating to their earnings, property, or expenses. Neither is such an agreement invalid merely because the parties may have contemplated the creation or continuation of a nonmarital relationship when they entered into it. Agreements between nonmarital partners fail only to the extent that they rest upon a consideration of meretricious sexual services. Thus the rule asserted by defendant, that a contract fails if it is "involved in" or made "in contemplation" of a nonmarital relationship, cannot be reconciled with the decisions. . . .

---

1. While actor Lee Marvin and Michelle Triola Marvin lived together, he won an Oscar for *Cat Ballou* in 1965 and starred in other films, including *The Dirty Dozen* in 1967 and *Paint Your Wagon* in 1969.—Ed.

3. Plaintiff's Complaint Can Be Amended to State a Cause of Action Founded upon Theories of Implied Contract or Equitable Relief

. . . We are aware that many young couples live together without the solemnization of marriage, in order to make sure that they can successfully later undertake marriage. This trial period preliminary to marriage, serves as some assurance that the marriage will not subsequently end in dissolution to the harm of both parties. We are aware, as we have stated, of the pervasiveness of nonmarital relationships in other situations.

The mores of the society have indeed changed so radically in regard to cohabitation that we cannot impose a standard based on alleged moral considerations that have apparently been so widely abandoned by so many. Lest we be misunderstood, however, we take this occasion to point out that the structure of society itself largely depends upon the institution of marriage, and nothing we have said in this opinion should be taken to derogate from that institution. The joining of the man and woman in marriage is at once the most socially productive and individually fulfilling relationship that one can enjoy in the course of a lifetime.

We conclude that the judicial barriers that may stand in the way of a policy based upon the fulfillment of the reasonable expectations of the parties to a nonmarital relationship should be removed. As we have explained, the courts now hold that express agreements will be enforced unless they rest on an unlawful meretricious consideration. We add that in the absence of an express agreement, the courts may look to a variety of other remedies in order to protect the parties' lawful expectations.[2]

The courts may inquire into the conduct of the parties to determine whether that conduct demonstrates an implied contract or implied agreement of partnership or joint venture, or some other tacit understanding between the parties. The courts may, when appropriate, employ principles of constructive trust or resulting trust. Finally, a nonmarital partner may recover in *quantum meruit* for the reasonable value of household services rendered less the reasonable value of support received if he can show that he rendered services with the expectation of monetary reward.

Since we have determined that plaintiff's complaint states a cause of action for breach of an express contract, and, as we have explained, can be amended to state a cause of action independent of allegations of express contract, we must conclude that the trial court erred in granting defendant a judgment on the pleadings.

The judgment is reversed and the cause remanded for further proceedings consistent with the views expressed herein.

(The concurring and dissenting opinion of Justice Clark is omitted.)

NOTES AND QUESTIONS

1. Could Michelle Marvin have argued that she had a common law marriage? Could she have argued that she was a putative spouse? Was her understanding of her situation significantly different from that of Stone and Thompson or the Spearmans?

---

2. We do not seek to resurrect the doctrine of common law marriage, which was abolished in California by statute in 1895. (*See* Norman v. Thomson (1898) 121 Cal. 620, 628, 54 P. 143; Estate of Abate (1958) 166 Cal. App. 2d 282, 292, 333 P.2d 200.) Thus, we do not hold that plaintiff and defendant were "married," nor do we extend to plaintiff the rights which the Family Law Act grants valid or putative spouses; we hold only that she has the same rights to enforce contracts and to assert her equitable interest in property acquired through her effort as does any other unmarried person.

If the Marvins had been married, could Michelle have enforced a contract such as that alleged in this case? Why or why not? Does enforcing express agreements between cohabitants give them greater freedom to determine their relationship than married people have?

2. What aspects of relationships are purely economic? In what sense are they severable from the romantic and sexual aspects of the relationship?

3. Courts in at least 26 states and the District of Columbia allow cohabitants to make contract claims against each other when the relationship ends, at least in principle; a plurality of states "fully embrace *Marvin*'s approach permitting claims as between former cohabitants based on express contract, implied contract, and equitable theories," including Alaska, Arizona, Arkansas, California, Colorado, Connecticut, Indiana, Iowa, Kansas, Massachusetts, Missouri, Nevada, New Hampshire, North Carolina, Pennsylvania, and Wisconsin. Courtney G. Joslin, Autonomy in the Family, 66 UCLA L. Rev. 912, 927-928 (2019). In three states, statutes require that cohabitants' contracts be in writing to be enforceable. Minn. Stat. §§513.075, 513.076 (2022); Tex. Fam. Code §1.108 (2022); N.J. Stat. §25:1-5(h) (2022). The New Jersey statute enacted in 2010 overturned several judicial decisions that liberally interpreted relational contract claims. Maeker v. Ross, 62 A.3d 310 (N.J. 2014). Besides a writing, the New Jersey statute requires that both parties have the advice of counsel before an agreement is enforceable. The New Jersey Supreme Court held that the statute did not impair the right to contract but that the advice of counsel requirement violated due process. Moynihan v. Lynch, 269 A.3d 435 (N.J. 2022).

4. Courts in Illinois, Georgia, and Louisiana have refused to grant remedies to cohabitants based on relational contracts. Hewitt v. Hewitt, 394 N.E.2d 1204 (Ill. 1979); Blumenthal v. Brewer, 69 N.E.3d 834 (Ill. 2016); Rehak v. Mathis, 238 S.E.2d 81 (Ga. 1977); Schwegmann v. Schwegmann, 441 So. 2d 316 (La. App. 1983). Even in these states, though, courts will enforce contracts between cohabitants that the court finds are not founded on the sexual aspects of a relationship. *See, e.g.*, Abrams v. Massell, 586 S.E.2d 435 (Ga. App. 2004) (enforcing contract to make a will for $400,000 at death of first cohabitant). Courts vary in the types of contracts they are willing to enforce, generally declining to enforce "exchanges that inhere in the relationship itself, such as services rendered." Albertina Antognini, Nonmarital Contracts, 73 Stan. L. Rev. 67, 77-78 (2021). What was the nature of the contract alleged in Marvin v. Marvin?

5. Where cohabitants have operated a business together outside the home, courts are generally willing to apply partnership principles to determine ownership of the business when the relationship ends. For example, in Bass v. Bass, 814 S.W.2d 38 (Tenn. 1991), a man and woman worked long hours for a number of years in businesses titled in his name. The woman was never paid for her work. When he died, she successfully claimed ownership of half of the business. Similarly, in In re Estate of Thornton, 499 P.2d 864 (Wash. 1972), a man and woman were treated as business partners where they ran a cattle operation together for many years. The administrator of the man's estate unsuccessfully argued that the woman was not entitled to compensation because of the familial context. Can a cohabitant make a claim on this theory if she is paid for her work in the business? If she is not an equal manager? *See* Harman v. Rogers, 510 A.2d 161 (Vt. 1986), rejecting a cohabitant's partnership claim under these circumstances.

a. Applying Contract Theories

Application of the contract theories varies from state to state. For example, California courts generally interpret the requirements strictly, as illustrated by the outcome of *Marvin* itself. On remand the trial court found no express or implied contract to share property between Lee and Michelle. Affirming the trial court decision, the court of appeal explained:

[T]he parties to this lawsuit never agreed during their cohabitation that they would combine their efforts and earnings or would share equally in any property accumulated as a result of their efforts, whether individual or combined. They also never agreed during this period that plaintiff would relinquish her professional career as an entertainer and singer in order to devote her efforts full time to defendant as his companion and homemaker generally. Defendant did not agree during this period of cohabitation that he would provide all of plaintiff's financial needs and support for the rest of her life.

Furthermore, the trial court specifically found that: (1) defendant has never had any obligation to pay plaintiff a reasonable sum as and for her maintenance; (2) plaintiff suffered no damage resulting from her relationship with defendant, including its termination and thus defendant did not become monetarily liable to plaintiff at all; (3) plaintiff actually benefited economically and socially from the cohabitation of the parties, including payment by defendant for goods and services for plaintiff's sole benefit in the approximate amount of $72,900.00, payment by defendant of the living expenses of the two of them of approximately $221,400.00, and other substantial specified gifts; (4) a confidential and fiduciary relationship never existed between the parties with respect to property; (5) defendant was never unjustly enriched as a result of the relationship of the parties or of the services performed by plaintiff for him or for them; (6) defendant never acquired any property or money from plaintiff by any wrongful act.

Marvin v. Marvin, 176 Cal. Rptr. 555, 557 (Cal. App. 1981). Compare the following case's approach to determining whether the parties have a contract.

Boulds v. Nielsen
323 P.3d 58 (Alaska 2014)

Winfree, Justice. . . . Raymond Boulds and Elena Nielsen began cohabiting in 1993 and separated in 2009; they never married. Boulds and Nielsen have three children together. Boulds also raised Nielsen's son from a prior relationship as his own child. During their relationship, Boulds worked on the North Slope and Nielsen was a stay-at-home mother. Although Nielsen worked as a waitress when the parties met, she began receiving disability income in 1996. This money was spent on the household and children. Boulds claimed Nielsen as a dependent on his taxes for at least some of the years they were together.

During the relationship Boulds accumulated three employment benefits through his employer: an insurance death benefit, a 401(k) retirement account, and a union pension governed by the federal Employee Retirement Income Security Act (ERISA). . . .

The [trial] court determined that the employment death benefit and 401(k) account were Boulds's separate property and that the union pension was partnership property. . . .

Boulds argues that the superior court erred in determining that Nielsen was entitled to part of his union pension for two reasons: (1) ERISA prohibits division of a federal retirement account with a non-spouse; and (2) the court erred by determining that the parties intended the union pension to be a partnership asset.[3] We conclude neither argument has merit.

A. ERISA

ERISA prohibits assignments of pensions except pursuant to a qualified domestic relations order (QDRO). ERISA defines a QDRO as a domestic relations order that "creates or

---

3. "When two people reside together in an intimate relationship, the property they acquire while cohabiting should be distributed according to the parties' express or implied intent." Jaymot v. Skillings-Donat, 216 P.3d 534, 544 (Alaska 2009) (citing Bishop v. Clark, 54 P.3d 804, 811 (Alaska 2002)). . . .

recognizes the existence of an alternate payee's right to, or assigns to an alternate payee the right to, receive all or a portion of the benefits payable with respect to a participant under a plan". . . . A domestic relations order "[r]elates to the provision of . . . marital property rights to a spouse, former spouse, child, or other dependent of a participant." "Alternate payee" as used in the definition of a QDRO is identical to the categories of recipients listed in the domestic relations order definition. . . .

The Court of Appeals for the Ninth Circuit examined a similar situation in Owens v. Auto. Machinists Pension Trust, which concerned an unmarried couple who had cohabited for 30 years. A Washington state court determined that the woman should receive half of the man's monthly payments from an ERISA-covered pension acquired during the relationship. . . .

The Ninth Circuit started its analysis by noting that ERISA only recognizes orders that relate to "marital property rights" and concern an "alternate payee," which is defined to include an "other dependent." The case therefore turned on the meaning of "marital property rights" and whether the woman was an "other dependent." The court reasoned that because federal law does not define "marital property rights," the court must apply Washington law to define the term. . . . The Ninth Circuit concluded that because Washington allows property to be distributed after a cohabitative relationship ends, the state provides "marital property rights" to cohabitants. Under Washington law, the pension was a "marital property right."

Next, the court looked to the Internal Revenue Service's definition of an "other dependent" to determine whether the woman was an "other dependent" under ERISA. The Internal Revenue Code defines "other dependent" to include "[a]n individual (other than . . . the spouse . . . of the taxpayer) who, for the taxable year of the taxpayer, has the same principal place of abode as the taxpayer and is a member of the taxpayer's household." The Ninth Circuit held that the woman was an "other dependent" as defined by the IRS, and therefore an "alternate payee" under ERISA.

We adopt the Ninth Circuit's reasoning. First, we ask whether Alaska provides a "marital property right" to cohabitants. Alaska, like Washington, provides for marital-like property distribution following a cohabitative relationship. Whether Nielsen and Boulds's relationship satisfies the requirements necessary for their property to be "marital" for ERISA's purposes under Alaska law is addressed below. We then ask whether Nielsen falls into one of the qualifying classes of payees under ERISA. Boulds claimed Nielsen as a dependent on his taxes and they shared a residence; Nielsen therefore qualifies as an "other dependent" under I.R.C. §152(d)(2)(H), one of the classes of alternate payees permitted under ERISA. Boulds's argument that an order dividing the union pension cannot meet the requirements of 29 U.S.C. §1056(d)(3)(B) therefore fails. Federal law does not preclude distribution of part of the union pension to Nielsen, provided Nielsen is entitled to it under Alaska law. We now address this question.

B. THE PARTIES' INTENT

We made clear in Bishop v. Clark that the first step in dividing an unmarried couple's property is to examine the couple's intent. We quoted our adoption of the Oregon Supreme Court's standard that "'a division of property accumulated during a period of cohabitation must be begun by inquiring into the intent of the parties, and if an intent can be found, it should control that property distribution.'" We summarized the types of evidence courts have reviewed when determining explicit and implicit intent:

> In determining the intent of cohabiting parties, courts consider, among other factors, whether the parties have (1) made joint financial arrangements such as joint savings or checking accounts, or jointly titled property; (2) filed joint tax returns; (3) held themselves out as husband and wife; (4) contributed to the payment of household expenses; (5) contributed to

the improvement and maintenance of the disputed property; and (6) participated in a joint business venture. Whether they have raised children together or incurred joint debts is also important.

In the present case, the superior court expressly applied *Bishop* to determine the parties' intent with respect to various assets and debts. The court held that the union pension was intended to be a partnership asset and thus subject to division between Boulds and Nielsen. . . .

Our holding in Reed v. Parrish is instructive. There we explained that "the [*Bishop*] factors are not exclusive; they reflect the factual circumstances of the case." Today we further clarify that the intent of the cohabiting parties as articulated in *Bishop* does not mean that each party's intent necessarily must be analyzed separately for every individual piece of property. In some cases, the parties' intent with respect to all or broad classes of property will be easy to infer based on evidence that "the parties formed a domestic partnership and intended to share in the fruits of their relationship as though married justifying an equal division of their property." We emphasize that simply living together is not sufficient to demonstrate intent to share property as though married, and, moreover, that parties who intend to share some property do not presumptively intend to share all property—even when the *Bishop* factors tilt heavily toward finding partnership property, other evidence may show that the parties had no such intent for particular pieces of property. But when the parties have demonstrated through their actions that they intend to share their property in a marriage-like relationship, a court does not need to find specific intent by each cohabitant as to each piece of property.

The superior court's determination that the parties intended to share the union pension as if they were married, like they shared their other property, was not in error. There was testimony that the parties wore wedding and engagement rings at various times. The court heard undisputed testimony that Boulds supported Nielsen financially. Boulds claimed Nielsen as a dependent on his taxes for at least some of the years they were together. Boulds worked outside the home, while Nielsen worked inside the home raising their children. Boulds apparently took on much of the financial responsibility for the couple, while Nielsen saw to other matters. Boulds listed Nielsen as his intended pre-retirement death beneficiary until he was told she could not be listed. The superior court concluded that the couple had a common goal of using the pension fund to finance raising the children. Ample evidence "support[s] a finding that the parties were in a domestic partnership and intended to share property as though married." . . .

NOTES AND QUESTIONS

1. The court did not find that the parties had entered into an express contract; appellate cases involving express contracts are exceedingly rare. Instead, the ruling in favor of Elena Nielsen is based on a finding of an implied in fact contract. What are the terms of this contract? What evidence supports the finding? If you represented Raymond Boulds, how would you argue that these facts do not prove an implied contract?

2. Is it likely that a court following the approach used in *Marvin* would find a contract between Boulds and Nielsen? On the other hand, would the Alaska court have found that Lee and Michelle Marvin had an implied contract to share property? Which approach to determining whether the parties had an implied contract is preferable and why?

3. The *Boulds* court found that Boulds and Nielsen were in a "domestic partnership." What role does that finding play in the determination of the parties' intent? In a subsequent case, the Alaska Supreme Court observed that "[I]n domestic partnership cases, . . . '[w]e have rejected . . . the rule that the party who has title or possession is necessarily entitled to ownership of property, because that rule 'tends to operate purely by accident or perhaps by reason of the cunning, anticipatory designs of just one of the parties.'" Wright v. Dropik, 512 P.3d 655, 660-661 (Alaska 2022). Alternatively, the court observed that if no domestic partnership exists, "[t]here is a presumption that the person with title [to real property] owns the property." *Id.* at 663. Is this consistent with the approach the court took in *Boulds*?

4. In Gunderson v. Golden, 360 P.3d 353 (Idaho App. 2015), a woman sued for a share of property that her domestic partner had accumulated during their 25-year cohabitation. The couple stipulated that the division principles applicable at divorce should be used to resolve the suit, but the trial court refused to accept the stipulation. The court of appeals affirmed, saying that although the stipulation amounted to a contract to share property as if the parties had been married, it was contrary to public policy and therefore unenforceable. Idaho allowed common law marriage until 1996, when the legislature abolished it. The court held that enforcing the contract would be the equivalent of reinstating common law marriage, in contravention of the statute. Do you agree?

b. Applying Equitable Theories

On remand, a trial court found that Michelle Marvin was not entitled to relief in the form of an equitable trust or quantum meruit because she "suffered no damage resulting from her relationship with defendant, including its termination and thus [Lee] did not become monetarily liable to plaintiff at all," that she "actually benefited economically and socially from the cohabitation of the parties," that "a confidential and fiduciary relationship never existed between the parties with respect to property," that Lee Marvin "was never unjustly enriched as a result of the relationship of the parties or of the services performed by plaintiff for him or for them," and that Lee "never acquired any property or money from plaintiff by any wrongful act." Nevertheless, the trial court ordered Lee to pay Michelle $104,000 as rehabilitative support to enable her to get back on her feet. The court relied on footnotes in the supreme court opinion in *Marvin v. Marvin* (above) implying that remedies other than those that the court had specifically endorsed might be available on the right facts. The court of appeal reversed, saying, "The difficulty in applying either of these footnotes in the manner in which the trial court has done in this case is that . . . there is nothing in the trial court's findings to suggest that such an award is warranted to protect the expectations of both parties." Marvin v. Marvin, 176 Cal. Rptr. 555 (Cal. App. 1981).

Cates v. Swain
215 So. 3d 492 (Miss. 2013) (en banc)

CHANDLER, Justice, for the Court. . . . In 2000, [Elizabeth] Swain and [Mona] Cates met though an online dating service and began a relationship while living in different states. Swain was in the Navy and worked as an oceanographer, and Cates was a commercial airline pilot based in New York, New York, where she maintained a separate residence. During the entirety of her relationship with Cates, Swain was married and estranged from her husband. Swain testified that she remained married so that her husband could remain covered under her medical insurance policy, and so that Swain could claim a larger housing allowance from the Navy than she would have been entitled to as a single individual. Swain divorced after her relationship with Cates had ended.

In late 2000, Swain transferred to Pensacola, Florida, and bought a house there. Cates provided $2,000 in earnest money toward the purchase of the house, residing there and in New York. Swain made the monthly mortgage payments and significantly paid down the principal. The two made improvements to the house.

In 2003, Swain and Cates moved to Seattle, Washington. Cates bought a home in Seattle, where the two cohabitated. Swain sold the Florida home and received $32,000 in equity. Swain testified that she gave Cates a check for $34,000, representing the equity in the Florida home, plus an extra $2,000 from Swain's personal checking account as an investment. Swain testified that Cates used this money for the down payment on the Washington home, which Cates purchased for $191,000. In contrast, Cates testified that the check was repayment for undocumented loans. Swain and Cates made various improvements to the Washington home, and in 2005 the residence sold for $300,000.

In 2005, Cates and Swain moved to Tate County, Mississippi, where Cates bought a home for $350,000, using the equity from the sale of the Washington home. Swain provided Cates a check for $5,000 with "closing costs" written in the memo line. She also paid $4,495 to carpet the home. Again, Cates characterized these expenditures as repayments for undocumented loans to Swain.

Subsequently, the parties' relationship deteriorated, and Swain moved out in March 2006. On June 13, 2006, Swain filed a complaint against Cates, alleging that they had been cohabitants, that they had been involved in several joint ventures together, and that they had entered into an agreement for Swain to invest the proceeds from the sale of her Florida home into future purchases of real property in Washington and Mississippi. Swain requested that the chancery court declare a constructive trust or a resulting trust in the Mississippi home, and that Cates had been unjustly enriched.

The chancellor rejected Swain's claims of a constructive trust or a resulting trust. The chancellor found that Cates had been unjustly enriched by Swain's investment contributions. The chancellor rejected Cates's unsupported assertions that these contributions were merely loan repayments. The chancellor found Swain was entitled to recover the equity from her Florida home. . . . The chancellor also found that Swain was entitled to recover the $5,000 she had tendered to Cates for closing costs on the Mississippi home and the $4,495 she had spent to carpet Cates's Mississippi home. . . .

. . . The Court of Appeals reviewed our prior cases pertaining to unmarried cohabitants, and concluded that "Mississippi does not enforce contracts implied from the relationship of unmarried cohabitants." Therefore, the Court of Appeals held that the chancellor had lacked the authority to grant the remedy of unjust enrichment. This Court granted Swain's petition for certiorari to review the legal question of whether the remedy of unjust enrichment was available to Swain. We find that, in the particular circumstances, the chancellor did not err by granting relief on the basis of unjust enrichment. . . .

Unjust enrichment "applies to situations where there is no legal contract and 'the person sought to be charged is in possession of money or property which in good conscience and justice he should not retain but should deliver to another.' " In these circumstances, equity imposes "a duty to refund the money or the use value of the property to the person to whom in good conscience it ought to belong." The amount of recovery for unjust enrichment is "that to which the claimant is equitably entitled."

The chancellor found that Cates had been unjustly enriched by Swain's contributions to the Mississippi home, which consisted of Swain's proceeds gained from the sale of her Florida home, the $5,000 Swain contributed at closing, and the $4,495 Swain had paid to carpet the Mississippi home. The Court of Appeals concluded that the remedy of unjust enrichment was not available to Swain as an unmarried cohabitant. The Court of Appeals primarily relied upon Davis v. Davis, 643 So. 2d 931 (Miss. 1994), and Estate of Alexander v. Alexander, 445 So. 2d 836 (Miss. 1984), to reach this conclusion.

We find *Davis* and *Alexander* to be distinguishable from this case. In *Davis*, the unmarried parties separated, and the woman, Elvis Davis, sought an equitable distribution of assets. Travis Davis had amassed considerable wealth, and Elvis argued that, by virtue of *her* efforts in her live-in, long-term *relationship* with Travis, she was entitled to an equitable division of assets. The Court disagreed, noting that the Legislature has not extended the rights enjoyed by married people to those who cohabit.

In Estate of Alexander v. Alexander, 445 So. 2d 836 (Miss. 1984), Margie and Sam Alexander had cohabitated for thirty years in a house owned by Sam. When Sam died, Margie petitioned the court for a life estate in the residence. The Court found that the Legislature had made no provision for a person in Margie's situation, and that "a mere *'live-in'* *relationship* . . . cannot be allowed to negate the law of descent and distribution." The Court also found that Margie could not recover under an implied-contract theory because no evidence established the existence of an implied contract between Margie and Sam.

In both *Davis* and *Alexander*, the aggrieved party's claim for recovery was based upon a relationship. Both claims were for equitable division of property. In *Davis*, the Court rightly noted that cohabitation is prohibited as against public policy and that the Legislature has not extended the rights of married persons to cohabitants, nor do we today. In this case, Swain's claim was not one for equitable division. Swain made a claim, *inter alia*, for unjust enrichment based upon her monetary contributions to Cates's purchase of the Washington home and the purchase and improvement of the Mississippi home, which Cates retained after Swain moved from the residence. Ultimately, the chancellor adjudicated the case on that theory of relief, and we find no error in the chancellor's legal conclusion.

True, as Presiding Justice Dickinson indicates in his separate opinion, Swain's unjust-enrichment claim was predicated on her assertion that Swain and Cates had entered into an agreement that Swain would invest the proceeds from the sale of her Florida home toward future home purchases. Thus, as Swain contended at trial, she should be entitled to share in the profits Cates earned from the use of Swain's money.

Swain claimed there was a mutual agreement between her and Cates that her Florida equity proceeds were to be used as an investment in both the Washington and Mississippi homes but offered no written evidence to support her testimony. Cates, who disputed Swain's version, claimed that she considered the funds provided by Swain to be reimbursement money for all the "loans" she had provided Swain, but she offered no written evidence to support her testimony. The only proof offered by either party for her claims was her respective testimony. The chancellor, essentially, accepted neither version. We find no abuse of discretion.

Instead, the chancellor focused on readily identifiable assets (or tangible benefits) each party conferred on the other, which, if retained by that party, would, under the circumstances, inequitably benefit (or unjustly enrich) that party. In essence, these particular benefits spoke for themselves, irrespective of how the parties attempted to characterize them after the fact at trial. The chancellor declined to treat these benefits as either investments or gratuitous gifts, as the Court of Appeals mistakenly construed our caselaw to require. Rather, the chancellor sought, as much as the evidence would allow, to restore the status quo and return the parties to the positions they had occupied before the transaction(s). This Court has held that an unjust-enrichment award may consist of a refund, if that is equitable. . . .

. . . We are mindful that the doctrine of unjust enrichment is not "a roving mandate [for a court] to sort through terminated personal relationships in an attempt to nicely judge and balance the respective contributions of the parties." The chancellor astutely recognized that Swain's unjust enrichment claim did not request that the court undertake such a momentous task. We find that the chancellor did not err in granting Swain recovery under the theory of unjust enrichment.

We affirm the judgment of the Court of Appeals to the extent that it affirmed the chancellor's rejection of the constructive trust or resulting trust claim [and] reverse the judgment of the Court of Appeals regarding the unjust-enrichment award. . . .

[The opinion of Justice Dickinson concurring and dissenting is omitted.]

NOTES AND QUESTIONS

1. Elizabeth Swain claimed a share of the Mississippi property based on constructive trust and resulting trust theories, but, as the Mississippi Court of Appeals explained, she did not prove fraud or the equivalent, which is necessary for a constructive trust in Mississippi, nor that she had purchased the property in Cates's name with the intent to retain beneficial ownership, the basis for a resulting trust. Cates v. Swain, 116 So. 3d 1073 (Miss. App. 2012).

If the house purchased in Washington had been titled in the names of both Swain and Cates, would Cates have had a right to the beneficial interest on a resulting trust theory? Or should it be presumed that she intended that each would own half the house? *Compare* Hofstad v. Christie, 240 P.3d 816 (Wyo. 2010) (man who titled house he purchased jointly with cohabitant was in a family relationship and made a gift of half the value), with Jones v. Graphia, 95 So. 3d 751 (Miss. App. 2012) (on similar facts, rejecting presumption of gift and upholding order giving entire value to man because woman did not contribute to acquisition of property).

2. What made it "unjust" for Cates to retain all of the Mississippi property? Why wasn't it "unjust" for her to retain the increase in value of the properties in Washington and Mississippi rather than sharing it with Swain?

3. Mississippi refuses to grant relief based on the relationship itself, noting that "cohabitation is prohibited as against public policy" in the state. For case law throughout the country, *see* George L. Blum, Property Rights Arising from Relationship of Couple Cohabiting Without Marriage, 69 A.L.R.5th 219 (1999 with weekly updates).

How does the court in *Cates* then justify the use of unjust enrichment principles? Would the court in *Cates* have granted relief to Michelle Marvin? How about to the plaintiff in Boulds v. Nielsen?

4. *Cates* is consistent with Section 28(1) of the Restatement (Third) of Restitution and Unjust Enrichment (2011), which provides:

> If two persons have formerly lived together in a relationship resembling marriage, and if one of them owns a specific asset to which the other has made substantial, uncompensated contributions in the form of property or services, the person making contributions has a claim in restitution against the owner as necessary to prevent unjust enrichment upon the dissolution of the relationship.

Critics of this provision argue that it undermines the goal of rationalizing and taming the field of restitution. *See, e.g.*, Emily Sherwin, Love, Money, and Justice: Restitution Between Cohabitants, 77 U. Colo. L. Rev. 711 (2006). They favor the traditional rules, which say that restitution is not available if (1) the claimant intended to make a gift or transferred property under a valid contract, or (2) the claimant could reasonably have negotiated a payment for the benefit conferred but failed to do so. *Id.* at 724. Those who favor the Restatement respond that people in intimate relationships should not be expected to protect themselves by engaging in arm's-length negotiation. Candace Saari Kovacic-Fleischer, Cohabitation and the Restatement (Third) of Restitution and Unjust Enrichment, 68 Wash. & Lee L. Rev. 1407 (2011). For an example of a case applying the Restatement and concluding that a cohabitant's financial contributions to a home titled in his partner's name were not intended as a gift, *see* McLaren v. Gabel, 211 Vt. 591, 609, 229 A.3d 422, 435 (2020). How is the Uniform Cohabitants Economic Remedies Act above similar to or different from the Restatement?

5. If a claimant kept the house, cared for the children, and did other kinds of domestic work, should a court presume that the work was gratuitous? What if one cohabitant works in the other's start-up business, with the understanding that neither will be able to take out money unless and until the business becomes successful? For a case denying recovery on such facts on the theory that a claimant did not prove that she expected to be paid for her work, *see* Featherston v. Steinhoff, 575 N.W.2d 6 (Mich. App. 1997).

6. Would the result in Cates v. Swain been different under the Uniform Cohabitants Economic Remedies Act, below? How would *Marvin* and *Boulds* be analyzed under the Act?

UNIFORM COHABITANTS ECONOMIC REMEDIES ACT (2021)
Section 2. Definitions

In this [act]:

(1) "Cohabitant" means each of two individuals not married to each other who live together as a couple after each has reached the age of majority or been emancipated. The term does not include individuals who are too closely related to marry each other legally . . .

(3) "Contributions to the relationship" means contributions of a cohabitant that benefit the other cohabitant, both cohabitants, or the cohabitants' relationship, in the form of efforts, activities, services, or property. The term:

    (A) includes:

        (i) cooking, cleaning, shopping, household maintenance, conducting errands, and other domestic services for the benefit of the other cohabitant or the cohabitants' relationship; and

        (ii) otherwise caring for the other cohabitant, a child in common, or another family member of the other cohabitant; and

    (B) does not include sexual relations.

(4) "Property" means anything that may be the subject of ownership, whether real or personal, tangible or intangible, legal or equitable, or any interest therein. The term includes responsibility for a debt.

Section 7. Equitable Relief

(a) Unless maintaining the action is inconsistent with a valid cohabitants' agreement, a cohabitant may commence an equitable action against the other cohabitant concerning entitlement to property based on contributions to the relationship. . . .

(c) . . . [T]he court adjudicating a claim under this section shall consider:

    (1) the nature and value of contributions to the relationship by each cohabitant, including the value to each cohabitant and the market value of the contributions;

    (2) the duration and continuity of the cohabitation;

    (3) the extent to which a cohabitant reasonably relied on representations or conduct of the other cohabitant;

    (4) the extent to which a cohabitant demonstrated an intent to share, or not to share, property with the other cohabitant . . .

7. The variety in the states' approaches to the rights and duties of cohabitants presents complex choice-of-law problems. For example, if a couple enters into a cohabiting relationship in California and moves to another state that does not recognize equitable remedies before the relationship ends, which state's law applies? Professor William A. Reppy, Jr., who has written extensively on choice-of-law issues when a marriage ends by death or divorce, addresses the choice-of-law problems attendant to cohabitation in Choice of Law Problems Arising When Unmarried Cohabitants Change Domicile, 55 SMU L. Rev. 273 (2002).

PROBLEMS

1. Harry and Margaret engaged in an intimate relationship for seven years but never actually lived together. He was an executive, she an actress. At the end of the relationship she sued, claiming that he expressly promised to support her in return for her acting as his hostess and companion. He defended on the basis that they had never lived together. Is cohabitation necessary under *Marvin*?

What if Harry and Margaret had lived together for four days a week over a long period but Harry maintained a separate dwelling?

2. Brett and Kerry lived together for 20 years. Both worked throughout the relationship, although Brett always earned much more than Kerry and paid more of the couple's expenses. Two years into the relationship, Brett bought a duplex titled in his name only; the couple lived in one side and rented the other. The rent covered the mortgage. Both parties worked on renovating and maintaining the building, and both contributed to household expenses. Three years later Brett sold the duplex and bought another house, again titled only in his name. The down payment came from the proceeds of the duplex sale and from the savings of both partners. They paid the mortgage from their joint bank account. A few years later they took out a home equity line of credit, with each individually liable for the full amount borrowed. However, as a practical matter only Brett drew on the line of credit. Brett and Kerry have now broken up, and Kerry wishes to sue Brett for a share of the value of the equity in the house. The governing statute provides that "any person owning a present undivided legal or equitable interest in real property shall be entitled to have partition" of the property. The statute continues:

> In entering its decree the court may, in its discretion, award or assign the property or its proceeds on sale as a whole or in such portions as may be fair and equitable. In exercising its discretion in determining what is fair and equitable in a case before it, the court *may* consider: the direct or indirect actions and contributions of the parties to the acquisition, maintenance, repair, preservation, improvement, and appreciation of the property; the duration of the occupancy and nature of the use made of the property by the parties; disparities in the contributions of the parties to the property; any contractual agreements entered into between the parties in relation to sale or other disposition of the property; waste or other detriment caused to the property by the actions or inactions of the parties; tax consequences to the parties; the status of the legal title to the property; and any other factors the court deems relevant.

What arguments should each party make, based on the statute and the cases in this chapter?

3. Fifteen years ago, Wendy, who was single, and Max, who was separated but not divorced from his wife, began living together. At the time both worked for Large Construction Co., he as a machine operator and she as a bookkeeper. Within a few months they decided to start an equipment rental business, W & M Rentals. Max provided the start-up money from his savings and maintained the equipment, and Wendy kept the books and managed the rental end. The business license was issued in Wendy's name alone, in the hopes that this would keep Max's wife from having a claim to the business. Max continued to work for Large Construction Co. and worked at W & M nights and on weekends.

After three years W & M Rentals had become quite successful, and Max had grown tired of working for Large. He and Wendy agreed that he would quit to work only for W & M and that W & M would expand into the construction business. As the business grew larger and more successful, it demanded more sophisticated accounting than Wendy could provide. She was becoming increasingly busy with volunteer work and entertaining business clients, so eight years ago she quit working for W & M and since then has devoted herself to these other endeavors. Since that time all of the assets of the business have been titled in Max's name. He told Wendy that it was too inconvenient to have her name on anything because she was never in the office.

Five years ago Max's wife died. Wendy and Max discussed getting formally married but never went through with the plans, in part because a number of their business and social acquaintances assumed that they were already married. Wendy has, however, always used her birth surname, and she and Max have never filed a joint income tax return. They have joint bank accounts and charge accounts and own their residence as joint tenants with right of survivorship. They have no children.

Wendy and Max's state recognizes common law marriage and the putative spouse doctrine, and it gives cohabitants remedies based on express and implied contract as well as for equitable reasons. The state uses usual business partnership law.

If Wendy becomes ill and is provided emergency medical services, on what theory or theories can the hospital recover the costs of her care from Max? If Max and Wendy are domiciled in a common law property state, on what theory or theories may Wendy claim some or all of the assets of W & M Rentals?

2. Other Legal Statuses for Intimate Partners?

The ALI Principles of the Law of Family Dissolution recommend the adoption of a new status relationship, the domestic partnership. If the parties have a child together, they will qualify as domestic partners once they have maintained a common household for a particular period of time (to be established by the state; the example given in the commentary is two years). If they do not have a child, they are rebuttably presumed to be domestic partners after they have lived together for a (longer) period of time (*e.g.*, three years). If the relationship is established, the Principles provide that the law applicable at the dissolution of a marriage should apply, unless the couple explicitly agree to the contrary. ALI Principles §§6.01, 6.04, 6.05, 6.06.

The drafters of the ALI Principles drew on the law of Canada, Australia, and New Zealand and case law from Washington and Oregon. Following is a leading Washington case.

Connell v. Francisco
898 P.2d 831 (Wash. 1995) (en banc)

GUY, Justice. Petitioner Richard Francisco and Respondent Shannon Connell met in Toronto, Canada, in June 1983. Connell was a dancer in a stage show produced by Francisco. She resided in New York, New York. She owned clothing and a leasehold interest in a New York apartment. Francisco resided in Las Vegas, Nevada. He owned personal property, real property, and several companies, including Prince Productions, Inc. and Las Vegas Talent, Ltd., which produced stage shows for hotels. Francisco's net worth was approximately $1,300,000 in February 1984.

Connell, at Francisco's invitation, moved to Las Vegas in November 1983. They cohabited in Francisco's Las Vegas home from November 1983 to June 1986. While living in Las Vegas, Connell worked as a paid dancer in several stage shows. She also assisted Francisco as needed with his various business enterprises. Francisco managed his companies and produced several profitable stage shows.

In November 1985, Prince Productions, Inc. purchased a bed and breakfast, the Whidbey Inn, on Whidbey Island, Washington. Connell moved to Whidbey Island in June 1986 to manage the Inn. Shortly thereafter Francisco moved to Whidbey Island to join her. Connell and Francisco resided and cohabited on Whidbey Island until the relationship ended in March 1990.

While living on Whidbey Island, Connell and Francisco were viewed by many in the community as being married. Francisco acquiesced in Connell's use of his surname for business purposes. A last will and testament, dated December 11, 1987, left the corpus of Francisco's estate to Connell. Both Connell and Francisco had surgery to enhance their fertility. In the summer of 1986, Francisco gave Connell an engagement ring.

From June 1986 to September 1990 Connell continuously managed and worked at the Inn. She prepared breakfast, cleaned rooms, took reservations, laundered linens, paid bills, and maintained and repaired the Inn. Connell received no compensation for her services at the Inn from 1986 to 1988. From January 1989 to September 1990 she received $400 per week in salary.

Francisco produced another profitable stage show and acquired several pieces of real property during the period from June 1986 to September 1990. . . . Connell did not contribute financially toward the purchase of any of the properties, and title to the properties was held in Francisco's name individually or in the name of Prince Productions, Inc.

Connell and Francisco separated in March 1990. When the relationship ended Connell had $10,000 in savings, $10,000 in jewelry, her clothes, an automobile, and her leasehold interest in the New York apartment. She continued to receive her $400 per week salary from the Inn until September 1990. In contrast, Francisco's net worth was over $2,700,000, a net increase since February 1984 of almost $1,400,000. In March 1990, he was receiving $5,000 per week in salary from Prince Productions, Inc.

Connell filed a lawsuit against Francisco in December 1990 seeking a just and equitable distribution of the property acquired during the relationship. The Island County Superior Court determined Connell and Francisco's relationship was sufficiently long term and stable to require a just and equitable distribution. The Superior Court limited the property subject to distribution to the property that would have been community in character had they been married. The trial court held property owned by each party prior to the relationship could not be distributed. In addition, the Superior Court required Connell to prove by a preponderance of the evidence that the property acquired during their relationship would have been community property had they been married.

. . . [The Court of Appeals reversed both holdings, and Francisco successfully petitioned the Supreme Court for review.]

A meretricious relationship is a stable, marital-like relationship where both parties cohabit with knowledge that a lawful marriage between them does not exist.[4]

Relevant factors establishing a meretricious relationship include, but are not limited to: continuous cohabitation, duration of the relationship, purpose of the relationship, pooling of resources and services for joint projects, and the intent of the parties.

. . . The Superior Court found Connell and Francisco were parties to a meretricious relationship. This finding is not contested.

Historically, property acquired during a meretricious relationship was presumed to belong to the person in whose name title to the property was placed. "[I]n the absence of any evidence to the contrary, it should be presumed as a matter of law that the parties intended to dispose of the property exactly as they did dispose of it." This presumption is commonly referred to as "the *Creasman* presumption."

. . . In 1984, this court overruled *Creasman*. *Lindsey*, 101 Wash. 2d at 304, 678 P.2d 328. In its place, the court adopted a general rule requiring a just and equitable distribution of property following a meretricious relationship. . . .

In *Lindsey*, the parties cohabited for less than 2 years prior to marriage. When they subsequently divorced, the wife argued the increase in value of property acquired during the meretricious portion of their relationship was also subject to an equitable distribution as if the property were community in character. We agreed, citing former RCW 26.09.080 [which governs property division at divorce].

---

4. In Olver v. Fowler, 126 P.3d 69 (Wash. App. 2006), the Washington Court of Appeals announced that it would henceforth use the term "committed intimate relationship." The Washington courts also use the term "equity relationship." Walsh v. Reynolds, 335 P.3d 984 (Wash. App. 2014). — Ed.

. . . Francisco contends the Court of Appeals misinterpreted *Lindsey* when it applied all the principles contained in RCW 26.09.080 to meretricious relationships. We agree. A meretricious relationship is not the same as a marriage. . . . As such, the laws involving the distribution of marital property do not directly apply to the division of property following a meretricious relationship. Washington courts may look toward those laws for guidance.

Once a trial court determines the existence of a meretricious relationship, the trial court then: (1) evaluates the interest each party has in the property acquired during the relationship, and (2) makes a just and equitable distribution of the property. The critical focus is on property that would have been characterized as community property had the parties been married. This property is properly before a trial court and is subject to a just and equitable distribution.

While portions of RCW 26.09.080 may apply by analogy to meretricious relationships, not all provisions of the statute should be applied. The parties to such a relationship have chosen not to get married and therefore the property owned by each party prior to the relationship should not be before the court for distribution at the end of the relationship. However, the property acquired during the relationship should be before the trial court so that one party is not unjustly enriched at the end of such a relationship. We conclude a trial court may not distribute property acquired by each party prior to the relationship at the termination of a meretricious relationship. Until the Legislature, as a matter of public policy, concludes meretricious relationships are the legal equivalent to marriages, we limit the distribution of property following a meretricious relationship to property that would have been characterized as community property had the parties been married. This will allow the trial court to justly divide property the couple has earned during the relationship through their efforts without creating a common law marriage or making a decision for a couple which they have declined to make for themselves. Any other interpretation equates cohabitation with marriage; ignores the conscious decision by many couples not to marry; confers benefits when few, if any, economic risks or legal obligations are assumed; and disregards the explicit intent of the Legislature that RCW 26.09.080 apply to property distributions following a marriage.

Francisco argues the Court of Appeals erred in requiring the application of a community-property-like presumption to property acquired during a meretricious relationship. We disagree.

In a marital context, property acquired during marriage is presumptively community property. When no marriage exists there is, by definition, no community property. However, only by treating the property acquired in a meretricious relationship similarly can this court's reversal of "the *Creasman* presumption" be given effect. Failure to apply a community-property-like presumption to the property acquired during a meretricious relationship places the burden of proof on the non-acquiring partner. . . . The Court of Appeals properly rejected the resurrection of "the *Creasman* presumption." . . .

[The dissenting opinion of Justice Utter is omitted.]

Katharine K. Baker

What Is Nonmarriage?
73 SMU L. Rev. 201, 203-204 (2020)

[W]hat is a nonmarital family, nonmarriage, or a kinship structure? Those calling for the law to recognize alternative families must realize that before the law can recognize those entities it has to decide what they are. What makes two or more people a family? That they have sex with each other? (How often? Need it be monogamous? And why does that matter?) That they share a home? (What if there are "nonfamily" members in the home also? What if there are two homes, and the movement between them is fluid? And what does household have to do with family?) That they share their money and labor? (How much sharing is enough? What counts as labor?) That they are committed to each other? (Measured how? By whom? Must it be mutual?) The law ceased asking these questions of married people long ago. The answer to the question, "Are you a family?" is answered by reference to your marital status.

Numerous critics assail the law's binary treatment of family status — married or not married — but the binary treatment of marital status has benefits not only for people who marry but also for everyone who wants to minimize the state's role in prescribing and judging intimate behavior. Because so much turns on marital status, not the actual behavior of the parties, marriage affords married people protection from invasive state inquiries into their sex lives, their living arrangements, their interpersonal conduct, and much of their financial decision-making. It is not clear that it will be possible to incorporate non-normative families into family law without bringing back that which contemporary family law has effectively banished: moralistic inquiries about what kind of love and care are worthy of recognition, subjective understandings of the value of intimate care work, and necessarily normative inquiries about sexual conduct.

Moreover, there are sound reasons why many people may wish to live without the law's protection of their alternative family. Contemporary family law imposes a set of rights and obligations on those with marital status. Those rights and obligations can create unacceptable constraints and complicated problems for people with little wealth and social stability. The costs of being recognized as family for purposes of family law may well outweigh the benefits. If that is the case, then the numerous calls for greater recognition of nonmarital families, especially for low-income couples, are somewhat misplaced. It is not family law that low-income people need; it is money, education, health care, and the means to acquire the economic security that makes family law relevant.

NOTES AND QUESTIONS

1. What is the basis for finding a "committed intimate relationship" under Washington law in *Connell*? For an argument that the Washington Supreme Court has essentially revived common law marriage through this doctrine, *see* Charlotte K. Goldberg, The Schemes of Adventuresses: The Abolition and Revival of Common-Law Marriage, 13 Wm. & Mary J. Women & L. 483 (2007). Professor Baker suggests that the Washington courts are "more willing to find that a couple that divided their labor along traditional gender lines pooled their income than did a couple in which the woman continued to work but just earned much less than the man."[5] 73 SMU L. Rev. at 222. She also finds that "the emotional interdependence inquiry, under the guise of assessing 'commitment' and 'intent,' is usually tied to sex," including consideration of whether the relationship is monogamous. *Id.* Compare the criteria for finding a domestic partnership under the ALI Principles, which are set out before *Connell*. Would Connell and Francisco's relationship have qualified under the Principles? Would the ALI standards be more or less intrusive than the Washington standard?

2. How is the legal theory used in *Connell* different from that in Boulds v. Nielsen, above? How does the available relief differ? Does *Connell* authorize a court to award support to an economically weaker partner at the end of a committed intimate relationship?

---

5. *Compare* Fenn v. Lockwood, 136 Wash. App. 1017 (Wash. Ct. App., 2006), *with* In re Marriage of Pennington, 14 P.3d 764 (Wash. 2000).

3. As *Connell* indicates, even though Washington is a community property state, all property acquired by either spouse is subject to equitable division when the parties divorce. Why doesn't the court apply this rule to cohabitants? How would you argue for a contrary rule?

4. What are the advantages of allowing a court to find that parties are in a familial relationship based on their conduct, rather than requiring them to register as domestic partners? What are the concerns with this approach?

5. Does the committed intimate spouse doctrine give rights to third parties who deal with one or both of the parties?

6. The Washington Supreme Court limited some of the expansive language in *Connell* in In re Marriage of Pennington, 14 P.3d 764 (Wash. 2000) (en banc), holding that lower courts had erred in finding meretricious (or "committed intimate") relationships in two cases in which one of the parties had a spouse for at least part of the time they lived together. In each relationship, one of the parties was married to someone else at the outset, though by the time the parties broke up divorces had occurred, and in both cases the parties' relationships were unstable to some extent. Based on these facts, the court said that the parties' cohabitation was not "continuous" and that they did not have a mutual intent to live in a committed relationship. Concluding that the committed intimate relationship doctrine is still tied to its equitable underpinnings, the court held that its purpose was to prevent the unjust enrichment of one party at the other's expense and found no basis for granting a remedy in either case. Do these cases validate or assuage the concerns Professor Baker raised above?

7. Professors Carbone and Cahn describe the substantial social science literature on unmarried cohabitants and argue that nonmarriage is becoming a distinct status, often consciously chosen by people who do not want to take on the legal commitments of marriage. They conclude, therefore, that the law should not attach the legal consequences of marriage to such relationships. Instead, default rules should be based on the assumption that parties intend to be financially independent while receiving credit for financial contributions to major assets such as real estate. June Carbone & Naomi Cahn, Nonmarriage, 76 Md. L. Rev. 55 (2016). Professor Antognini, on the other hand, argues that the law of nonmarriage systematically disadvantages women economically and calls for the development of a new system, independent of the marriage model, for assigning property rights to cohabitants. Albertina Antognini, The Law of Nonmarriage, 58 B.C. L. Rev. 2 (2017).

PROBLEMS

1. Would Brett and Kerry in problem 2, page 192 above, be committed intimate partners? If they were, would the equity in the house be subject to equitable division under *Connell*?

2. Would Wendy and Max in problem 3, page 192 above, be committed intimate partners? If they were, would W & M Rentals be subject to equitable division under *Connell*? Would Max be liable for Wendy's medical expenses if the hospital sued him?

Erez Aloni

Registering Relationships
87 Tul. L. Rev. 573, 576-577 (2013)

. . . [T]he legal issues arising from the prevalence of cohabitation and other nonmarital living arrangements would be best addressed if more options for legal recognition of various unions were offered. [This article] argues that if policy makers genuinely care about strengthening the American family, the best way to do that is by offering an additional registration scheme—one that is different from marriage. This scheme needs to respond to and be suitable for the diverse family structures that already exist in the United States and their legal needs. . . .

Accordingly, this Article presents the primary principles of a registration-based marriage alternative. It offers an innovative and sophisticated opt-in model based on contract. I call this model "registered contractual relationships" (RCRs). This legal institution would offer couples the option to sign—and deposit with the state—a contract defining the partners' obligations and rights vis-à-vis each other and changing their status to that of "registered partners." Registered partners would receive most of the rights and benefits that the state provides for married couples, such as the ability to sponsor your registered partner (even if it is a nonintimate partner) for admission to the United States. However, these couples would be able to choose which personal rights and obligations between themselves (such as visitation rights and end-of-life decisions) they want to designate. Registration would not require a solemnization process nor any ceremonial or religious component and would provide an easy way to dissolve the relationship in cases where the couple does not have minor children.

This model enjoys the advantages of both worlds: the flexibility of contracts and the certainty of official registration. It promotes greater autonomy in family formation in two ways: it allows more choice between two state-sanctioned mechanisms (the RCR and marriage), and at the same time, it allows individuals to design the terms of their relationships, rather than imposing the one-size-fits-all structure of marriage. The plasticity of RCRs and the fact that couples set their degree of commitment mean that RCRs could be used by people in different stages of their relationships and in diverse types of families (including registration of nonromantic partners). For example, RCRs could be used by couples in their premarital stage and would include very few obligations between the partners; at the same time, it could serve as a "marriage without the name" for couples who want the commitment to each other but who reject marriage's historical, patriarchal, or religious connotations.

The introduction of a competitive alternative to marriage based on a contract recognized by the state would have far-reaching legal and societal consequences. It would provide a functional model for registration and termination of partnerships, and it would offer an alternative that is not associated with marriage's symbolism and acts to reduce the harm that symbolism creates. At the same time, it would efficiently address the state's need to regulate some aspects of people's relationships in the interest of avoiding and mediating potential conflict and of encouraging couples to think about and negotiate their rights early on in their relationships.

NOTES AND QUESTIONS

1. From the point of view of the individuals involved, what are the advantages of the registered partnership model that Professor Aloni proposes? What are the disadvantages?

2. What social goals would the model advance? Would the model undermine other social policies?

3. Between 1997, when Hawaii enacted a Reciprocal Beneficiaries Statute after the state supreme court held that restricting marriage for same-sex couples violated the state constitution, and 2015, when Obergefell v. Hodges was decided, 15 states and the District of Columbia enacted statutes creating civil unions, domestic partnerships, or other alternative statuses for couples. Most of these statuses were open only to same-sex couples and provided all or almost all of the state law benefits and obligations of marriage without being called marriage. Domestic partnerships were open to opposite-sex couples where at least one partner was 62 or older in only a few states. The Hawaii legislation was unique in being open to any couple not eligible to marry until California changed its domestic partnership statute to open it to almost all couples in 2020. Hawaii Reciprocal Beneficiaries Legislation, H.B. 118 (1997), codified as Haw. Rev. Stat. Ch. 572c. Cal. Fam. Code §297 (2022).

In Connecticut, Delaware, New Hampshire, Rhode Island, and Vermont, the legislation creating domestic partnerships and civil unions was repealed when marriage was opened to same-sex couples. Couples were permitted or required to convert domestic partnerships or civil unions into marriages. Civil unions, domestic partnerships, or reciprocal beneficiaries remain an alternative in California, Colorado, District of Columbia, Hawaii, Illinois, Maine, Maryland, Nevada, New Jersey, Oregon, Washington, and Wisconsin. On the status of civil unions and domestic partnerships after *Obergefell, see* Mark P. Strasser, The Right to Marry and State Marriage Amendments: Implications for Future Families, 45 Stetson L. Rev. 309 (2016); Kaiponanea T. Matsumura, A Right Not to Marry, 84 Fordham L. Rev. 1509 (2016).

4. A number of European countries have enacted legislation creating registered partnerships that give some or, in some cases, all of the rights of marriage. The Scandinavian legislation substantially predates the American statutes, but, as in the United States, the main political impetus for much of this legislation was to create a legally recognized family relationship for same-sex couples. In a number of jurisdictions only same-sex couples may register as partners. However, registered partnerships are also open to opposite-sex couples in the Netherlands, Belgium, and France. In these countries couples have the choice between marriage and registered partnerships, and in both France and the Netherlands the great majority of registered partners are opposite-sex couples. Opposite-sex couples in France often choose a pacte civil de solidarité rather than marriage because it offers tax and inheritance advantages while being associated socially and politically with non-marital unions. Edward Cody, Straight Couples in France Are Choosing Civil Unions Meant for Gays, Wash. Post, Feb. 14, 2009. The legal treatment of cohabitants who do not register as partners varies greatly across Europe. Anna Stepie-Sporek & Margaret Ryznar, The Consequences of Cohabitation, 50 U.S.F. L. Rev. 75 (2016).

5. Commentary exploring options for legal recognition of relationships other than marriage includes David L. Chambers, For the Best of Friends and for Lovers of All Sorts, a Status Other Than Marriage, 76 Notre Dame L. Rev. 1347 (2001); Laura A. Rosenbury, Friends with Benefits?, 106 Mich. L. Rev. 189 (2007); Nancy Polikoff, Beyond (Straight and Gay) Marriage: Valuing All Families Under the Law (2008); Elizabeth F. Emens, Regulatory Fictions: On Marriage and Countermarriage, 99 Cal. L. Rev. 235 (2011); William N. Eskridge Jr., Family Law Pluralism: The Guided-Choice Regime of Menus, Default Rules, and Override Rules, 100 Geo. L.J. 1881 (2012); Melissa Murray, Obergefell v. Hodges and Nonmarriage Inequality, 104 Cal. L. Rev. 1207, 1223 (2016); Courtney G. Joslin, Autonomy in the Family, 66 UCLA L. Rev. 912 (2019).

PART II

FAMILY DISSOLUTION

CHAPTER 5

DIVORCE GROUNDS AND PROCEDURES

The idea of divorce involves centuries-old tensions between two conceptions of marriage: marriage as covenant, involving permanent commitments ordained by God, state, or community; and marriage as contract, resting on the consent of the spouses, and sometimes their families, to a set of reciprocal obligations. The division between these two concepts is older than the United States, and the tension between these ideas has shaped much of the history of American family law. Anglo-American law, to the extent it followed canon law and the English ecclesiastical tradition, primarily reflected the former view. Within this tradition, marriage involves permanent obligations beyond the power of the parties to alter or dissolve. At the time the country began, the states that adopted the English tradition, which included all of the southern states, did not recognize the power of the judiciary to grant divorces at all. Yet American law, starting with the New England colonists who came to the Americas to escape the dominance of the Church of England, has also provided some recognition of the contractual aspects of marriage. A number of these early northeastern colonies adopted liberal divorce laws well before England or many American states. This chapter will examine family dissolution in the context of ongoing differences concerning the permissibility and purposes of divorce.

At the time of the settlement of the colonies, English law recognized annulment and separation, which was known as divorce *a mensa et thoro*, or divorce from bed and board. True divorce, which caused the termination of the marital relationship (and thus the ability to remarry), required an Act of Parliament and was effectively available only to those few persons with enough wealth and influence to secure a private bill of divorce from Parliament.

In the United States, the availability of divorce has always varied by region. "From the earliest periods of American history, the colonies took different approaches to questions of marriage and divorce." Ann Laquer Estin, Family Law Federalism: Divorce and the Constitution, 16 Wm. & Mary Bill Rts. J. 381, 383-384 (2007). The New England colonies, especially those influenced by various Protestant teachings rather than the traditions of the Church of England, treated divorce as a civil matter and started granting divorces during the seventeenth century. Professor Areen links these views to Martin Luther's teachings about the nature of marriage as a civil contract rather than a sacrament, and to the propriety of divorce as a remedy for adultery or desertion. Judith Areen, Uncovering the Reformation Roots of American Marriage and Divorce Law, 26 Yale J.L. & Feminism 29, 37 (2014). After the American Revolution, the northern states began to adopt laws providing for judicial divorce, and by 1800 every New England state and many mid-Atlantic states had done so. The southern colonies, like the English, regarded divorce as an ecclesiastical matter and generally refused to permit complete divorce without an act of the legislature until after the Civil War.

Divorce remained a divisive issue throughout much of the nineteenth century and the first half of the twentieth. One legacy of the English tradition was that the authority to regulate divorce resided with the legislature; the judiciary had no equitable jurisdiction regarding divorce. Legislative debates concerned not just whether judicial divorce should be allowed, but on what terms, since statutory law determined judicial authority to grant divorce even in those states that had allowed courts to grant divorces since the colonial era. State differences remained intense, with states also varying in their willingness to recognize out-of-state decrees. The more conservative states were particularly loath to acknowledge divorces from "divorce mill" states, which granted divorces easily and without much regard for marital domicile. The grounds on which divorce should be allowed caused so much turmoil that legislation to enact a constitutional amendment making family law (or at least divorce) a federal issue was introduced in almost every session of Congress from 1884 until the late 1940s. Nelson M. Blake, The Road to Reno 145-150 (1977).

After World War II, reform movements focused on eliminating fault as a requirement for divorce. These movements were fueled partly by growing support for the principle that if the spouses wanted a divorce, the state should not stand in the way, and partly by concern for the integrity of the judicial system as couples colluded to secure divorces the formal law did not allow. In the 20-year period between 1965 and 1985, every state passed legislation recognizing some form of no-fault ground for divorce. The legislation was far from uniform. Some states followed California and the Uniform Marriage and Divorce Act in substituting "irretrievable breakdown" for fault as the exclusive basis for divorce and, as a practical matter, granted a divorce whenever either party wanted one. Other states simply added no-fault grounds, such as irreconcilable differences or a period of separation, without changing the fault provisions. A few states conditioned availability of the no-fault ground on the mutual agreement of the parties or mandated longer periods of separation in cases where the parties disagreed. Other states required that the courts determine whether the alleged differences between the spouses were truly irreconcilable rather than rely on the pleadings alone. In these debates, the tensions between the secular and the religious interpretations of marriage, and between private freedom to contract and state responsibility to oversee family well-being, reappear and recombine in different ways.

Divorce law continues to evolve. In recent years, some jurisdictions, internationally and domestically, have considered adopting "administrative divorce," extending the contract model of marriage. France, for example, has adopted a non-judicial dissolution process, allowing couples to divorce by "mutual consent." Margaret Ryznar & Angélique Devaux, Voilà! Taking the Judge Out of Divorce, 42 Seattle U. L. Rev. 161, 183 (2018).

This chapter approaches the issue of divorce by, first, exploring fault-based jurisprudence, elements of which remain good law in the majority of U.S. jurisdictions. Second, it considers the implementation of no-fault provisions. Third, it examines the continuing discussion of divorce reforms and proposals for further change.

A. THE TRADITIONAL FAULT DIVORCE SYSTEM

This section examines the grounds for and defenses or bars to divorce under the traditional fault system. Until the last half-century, an action for divorce could be successful only when these conditions were met; a divorce could not be granted without them even if both parties wanted the divorce. In 2010, New York became the last state to adopt no-fault grounds for divorce, permitting the dissolution of a marriage on the basis of irretrievable breakdown. The grounds and defenses themselves retain importance in many jurisdictions, where both fault and no-fault grounds may be asserted in a dissolution proceeding. As of 2016, 35 states retained traditional fault grounds for divorce, including the states with a covenant marriage option. Jana Douglas, Kirk Eby & (Zhiying) Mikaela Feng, Marriage and Divorce, 17 Geo.

J. Gender & L. 325, 344 (2016). The assumptions behind a fault-based system are no less important than the grounds, both in themselves and in assessing the desirability of a return, wholly or in part, to the traditional standards for divorce.

Kucera v. Kucera
117 N.W.2d 810 (N.D. 1962)

STRUTZ, J. (on reassignment). . . . The record discloses that the parties were married on September 17, 1955. At the time of the marriage, the plaintiff was pregnant by another man, a certain Mr. K—, and the child who was born to her, less than seven months after the marriage, admittedly is not the child of the defendant. The plaintiff herself, testifying in this case, stated that she had had no sexual relations with the defendant prior to their marriage. She contends, however, that this child, having been born into the family of the defendant after their marriage and the defendant having married the plaintiff with full knowledge of her pregnant condition, should be held to have been adopted at its birth by the defendant and that the defendant is liable for its support as one standing *in loco parentis.*

The record further discloses that the parties themselves were extremely doubtful whether the marriage would be a successful one, even before it was consummated. The plaintiff testified that they had agreed, before marriage, that "if the marriage didn't work out we could get a divorce in a year, but it would give the child a name."

After the birth of this child, a second child was born and, for a period of more than two years before the commencement of this action, the parties ceased to have any marital relations. The defendant testified positively that:

> We have had no sexual relations since Robin was born.

The plaintiff does not deny this. There is evidence in the record that the defendant did call the plaintiff names and that, on at least one occasion, he struck her. He also called the first child, who admittedly is not his child, some obscene names.

The differences of the parties finally were brought to a head when the defendant, returning home unexpectedly one evening from the college where he was working on a thesis, discovered Mr. K—, the man who had fathered the plaintiff's first child, in the home with the plaintiff. The plaintiff thereupon admitted that Mr. K—had been calling on her for a period of more than six months, as often as once a week. This was in the month of March 1959. The parties continued to live under the same roof until the end of the school year in June, when this action was commenced by the plaintiff.

On this record the trial court granted to the plaintiff a decree of divorce, and ordered the defendant to make monthly payments for the support of the plaintiff and for the support of the two children born during the marriage. From this judgment the defendant has appealed. . . .

The plaintiff's cause of action is based on an allegation of extreme cruelty. "Extreme cruelty" is the infliction by one party to a marriage of grievous bodily injury or grievous mental suffering upon the other.

A divorce may be granted in North Dakota on the grounds of grievous mental suffering, even though such suffering produces no bodily injury.

Does the record disclose conduct on the part of the defendant which would tend to so wound the feelings of the plaintiff that her health was impaired, and were the actions of the defendant such as to destroy the ends of the marriage? We have examined the entire record carefully. The plaintiff did testify to some instances in which the defendant's language and custom was such that she alleges it caused her extreme mental anguish. While the evidence supporting the plaintiff's cause of action is not very strong, the trial court did find that such evidence was sufficient to entitle her to a divorce.

The defendant, however, has counterclaimed for a divorce on grounds of extreme cruelty and on grounds of adultery. On reading the entire record, we believe that the plaintiff also was guilty of conduct which, standing alone, would entitle the defendant to a decree of divorce. For a period of more than six months, the plaintiff was allowing Mr. K—, the man who was the father of her first child, to call on her at the home of the parties. True, the plaintiff contends that he called against her wishes, but the plaintiff does admit that these calls were continued, more or less regularly, for a period of more than six months. The plaintiff must have given some cooperation to Mr. K—, at least to the extent of informing him as to what hours the defendant would be absent from the home.

The plaintiff has denied positively any acts of adultery during the six months of such visits. It is difficult to believe that the man who was the father of her child continued to call on her for more than six months without resuming such relationship as they had had prior to the marriage of the plaintiff and the defendant. While the court, ordinarily, will not require direct evidence on a charge of adultery, the trial court did believe the statements of the plaintiff when she testified that she had had no relations with Mr. K—during these visits. While the evidence is such that it is difficult to believe the plaintiff's testimony on this point, we cannot say that the evidence is so strong that the trial court clearly erred in this finding. . . .

Although the defendant failed to prove his charge of adultery to the satisfaction of the trial court, we do believe that he did prove a cause of action on the ground of extreme cruelty. Here, the defendant had married the plaintiff knowing that she had had previous relations with Mr. K—and that she was pregnant and with child by Mr. K—at the time of the marriage of the parties. Thereafter, he discovered that, for more than six months, the plaintiff was visited by the same Mr. K—in the home of the parties. Certainly that is sufficient evidence to substantiate a charge of extreme cruelty.

But that is not all. The defendant introduced evidence which would have justified a decree of divorce in his favor on grounds of desertion. He testified that "we have had no sexual relations since Robin was born," which was well over two years before the commencement of this action. The plaintiff did not deny this, nor did she try to justify her refusal to have reasonable sexual relations with the defendant, for physical or health reasons. She merely testified, "I couldn't stand to have sexual relations with him," and then admitted that her refusal was not due to physical or health reasons. . . .

Our statute defines "willful desertion" to include "persistent refusal to have reasonable matrimonial intercourse as husband and wife when health or physical condition does not make such refusal reasonably necessary. . . ."

It is true that the defendant alleged only extreme cruelty and adultery as grounds for divorce in his counterclaim. But, under the Rules of Civil Procedure now in force in North Dakota, when issues not raised by the pleadings are tried by express or implied consent of the parties, they shall be tried in all respects as if they had been raised by the pleadings. . . .

Therefore, since the defendant did prove a cause of action for divorce on grounds of desertion as well as on grounds of extreme cruelty, we have a situation where both parties have established a cause of action for divorce.

Section 14-05-10 of the North Dakota Century Code provides:

> "Divorces must be denied upon showing: . . .
> "4. Recrimination; . . ."

Section 14-05-15 reads:

"Recrimination is a showing by the defendant of any cause of divorce against the plaintiff in bar of the plaintiff's cause of divorce. . . ."

This court repeatedly has held that the above statutes are an absolute bar to divorce in a case where both the plaintiff and the defendant plead and prove facts constituting statutory grounds for divorce against each other. . . .

Thus, where recrimination is proved, as it was in this case, a divorce must be denied to both of the parties. This is true even though we believe the legitimate ends of the marriage have been destroyed and a divorce perhaps would be the better solution for the difficulties facing the parties. The provisions of our statute on recrimination are mandatory, and a divorce "must be denied" upon a showing of recrimination. The court has no discretion in the matter and must follow the mandatory wording of the law. . . .

NOTES AND QUESTIONS

1. *Kucera* is an example of the most commonly invoked grounds for divorce under the fault system. In states that had only fault grounds, a court could grant a divorce only when one and *only one* of the spouses could be said to have flouted the bonds of marriage. If both parties wished to dissolve their union without fault by either party, or if both parties had violated their marital obligations, grounds did not exist for divorce. In contrast, if a state has both fault and no-fault grounds, the parties can agree to a divorce or a court can conclude that although fault grounds have not been established, the court can grant a divorce on the basis of no-fault grounds.

What justified the older system's requirement that one and only one party be at fault in order to grant a divorce? Why would a court conclude that, in circumstances where both spouses want the divorce, no divorce can be granted?

2. The states that retain fault generally interpret these grounds in terms of the earlier precedents. As you review these grounds, consider whether the earlier doctrines continue to make sense and whether they serve the same purposes as they did in the fault era.

a. *Adultery.* "Adultery" ordinarily is defined as voluntary sexual intercourse by a married person with a person who is not the spouse. The element of voluntariness excludes rape from the definition of "adultery." In the traditional view, same-sex relations were not defined as adulterous. In 2021, New Hampshire overruled a 2003 precedent, which held that sexual relations with a person of the same sex were not adultery and therefore did not constitute grounds for divorce. Matter of Blaisdell, No. 2020-0211, 2021 WL 1222134 (N.H. 2021) holding that "adultery," as a statutory ground for divorce, is defined as voluntary sexual intercourse between a married person and someone other than that person's spouse, regardless of the sex or gender of either person. For a review of the history of legal definitions of adultery, *see* Peter Nicolas, The Lavender Letter: Applying the Law of Adultery to Same-Sex Couples and Same-Sex Conduct, 63 Fla. L. Rev. 97, 122 (2011). Alison Lefkovitz, in "The Peculiar Anomaly": Same-Sex Infidelity in Postwar Divorce Courts, 33 Law & Hist. Rev. 665, 683 (2015), found that in the era following World War II, judges were more likely to grant divorces if the allegations involved same-sex relations between women rather than between men.

In the fault era, one of the oddities of adultery was that it usually could be proved by direct evidence only when it did not in fact occur—that is, when one supposedly guilty spouse, typically the husband, agreed to provide the other with manufactured evidence that he had committed adultery so that she could establish a ground for divorce. This practice, which became a cottage industry in New York when adultery was the only available basis for absolute divorce, is discussed later in this section. Whether circumstantial proof offered in a divorce case is sufficient is largely a matter for the trial court to decide, as *Kucera*, above, indicates. For additional examples, *compare* Lister v. Lister, 981 So. 2d 340 (Miss. App. 2008), affirming a grant of divorce on the ground of adultery where the husband had an infatuation with his secretary "sufficient to be an adulterous inclination" and there was testimony that the couple "had opportunities to consummate that inclination," *with* Fore v. Fore, 109 So. 3d 137 (Miss. App. 2013), affirming a decision not to grant a divorce on the basis of adultery because there was insufficient proof of the opportunity to act on the inclination. States vary as to whether adultery can be grounds for divorce where the adultery occurred after the parties filed for divorce. *Compare* Tidwell v. Tidwell, 152 So. 3d 1045 (La. 2014), *with* Turner v. Turner, 210 So. 3d 603, 606 (Ala. Civ. App. 2016).

Even today, however, some courts still hold that a party's admission is insufficient to establish adultery and that it requires corroboration. Mayland v. Mayland, 586 S.W.3d 179 (Ark. App. 2019) (holding that wife must offer independent corroboration even when husband admits to the alleged misconduct). South Carolina courts, however, have held that "this rule may be relaxed when it is evident that collusion does not exist." Mick-Skaggs v. Skaggs, 766 S.E.2d 870, 874 (S.C. App. 2014). Texas concluded that a husband's repeated failure to deny "affairs" and "adultery" when confronted by his wife could be considered an "adopted admission." Escalante v. Escalante, 632 S.W.3d 573, 579 (Tex. App. 2020). For a discussion of the modern treatment of adultery, which remains technically illegal in a number of states, *see* Deborah L. Rhode, Adultery: Infidelity and the Law 23 (2016).

b. *Cruelty.* The definition of "cruelty" was originally developed in connection with divorce *a mensa et thoro*, before absolute divorce was judicially available. The older cases on cruelty required violence or at least intentionally and seriously injurious conduct that reasonably led to fear for life or health. After absolute divorce became possible, many, though not all, states expanded the definition of cruelty to include emotional abuse that did not necessarily involve physical conduct. Depending on the jurisdiction, cruelty can encompass a variety of forms of misconduct, including ridicule, harassment, false accusations of unfaithfulness, child abuse, and relative abuse. *See, e.g.*, Stevenson v. Stevenson, 369 P.2d 923 (Utah 1962) (concluding husband falsely accused wife of infidelity, emotional and mental illness, giving him a venereal disease, and — you may think ironically — paranoia). In some states, "extreme cruelty" effectively became an escape hatch allowing unhappy couples to divorce on the basis of allegations of nagging or insults. In 2020, the Supreme Court of South Dakota defined the grounds of extreme cruelty as "the infliction of grievous bodily injury or grievous mental suffering upon the other, by one party of the marriage." The court further held that "in a marital setting, the definition of extreme cruelty differs according to the personalities of the parties involved. [Courts] must view the evidence in light of the full context of the marriage and not in the narrow light of isolated incidents." Evens v. Evens, 951 N.W.2d 268 (S.D. 2020).

New Hampshire's divorce statute, which was adopted in 1840 to provide an easier standard to meet than "extreme cruelty," requires spousal conduct that seriously "injures health" or "endangers reason." The state supreme court, however, affirmed that while the statute "does not require proof of conduct that would have affected an average or reasonable person, it does require proof that the health or reason of the complaining spouse was *actually* affected." Accordingly, the wife's discovery of her husband's sexually suggestive e-mails professing his love to a former girlfriend was not a ground for divorce, even though the wife alleged that the discovery made her feel "angry, upset, and distraught." In re Guy, 969 A.2d 373 (N.H. 2009). In contrast, the same court upheld a finding of extreme cruelty where the wife discovered that her husband had abused their son 30 years earlier, with the discovery causing her to "suffer from depression, insomnia and weight loss." In re Henry, 37 A.3d 320, 321 (N.H. 2012).

c. *Desertion.* This ground, sometimes called "abandonment" and often described in terms of "willful" desertion, requires departure from the home without the consent of the other and without justification.

Justification for departure from the home can be a complicated business. The strictest view is that departure is justified only when the abandoned spouse has engaged in conduct that would itself provide grounds for divorce. Other jurisdictions view justification more broadly to include conduct that in some way makes cohabitation impossible. *See* Brown v. Brown, 142 So. 3d 425 (Miss. App. 2013), *cert. denied,* 141 So. 3d 947 (Miss. 2014) (dismissing divorce action on grounds of desertion because wife's behavior caused husband "stress" precipitating his departure).

Many statutes specify a minimum period, ordinarily between one and five years. And the period must usually be continuous.

Historically, desertion often involved the husband's failure to support the family. In Gardner v. Gardner, 130 So. 3d 1162 (Miss. App. 2013), the dissent objected to grant of a divorce on grounds of desertion because the husband continued to provide some financial support, primarily contributions to the mortgage payments, even though he did not live with the family. Some cases, including *Kucera,* recognize a "constructive" abandonment—meaning, as the term *constructive* always does, that no such thing occurred. In Kreyling v. Kreyling, 23 A.2d 800 (N.J. 1942), for example, the husband refused to engage in sexual intercourse without the use of a contraceptive. This refusal was held an unjustified course of conduct by the defendant and an instance of constructive desertion. For modern treatment of desertion and constructive desertion, *see* discussion of *Flanagan,* in Section B.2. below.

3. The fault scheme recognized several defenses to divorce. Ordinarily, these are treated as affirmative defenses that must be specifically pleaded and proved.

a. *Insanity.* In some jurisdictions, incurable insanity is a ground for divorce; it is also generally recognized as a defense to divorce actions founded on adultery or desertion. Is there any reason for doubt to be expressed with respect to the applicability of that defense to divorce based on cruelty? In Simpson v. Simpson, 716 S.W.2d 27 (Tenn. 1986), the wife sought a divorce on the basis of cruelty following a ten-year pattern of abuse in which the husband harassed and belittled her, stockpiled weapons, and physically threatened her and her family. When she attempted to separate from him, he kidnapped her and told her that he was going to kill her. The husband defended the divorce action on the ground of insanity; that is, he argued that he was not responsible for the acts of cruelty because of mental illness. A psychiatrist testified that he was suffering from paranoid schizophrenia, and the trial court dismissed the divorce action on that basis. The Tennessee Supreme Court, noting that the states varied in their treatment of insanity as a bar to divorce, adopted the same standard that would be applicable in a criminal case: the defendant must establish that, as a result of mental illness, he lacked the capacity to appreciate the wrongfulness of his acts or the volition to prevent them. *See* David Chapus, Insanity as Defense to Divorce or Separate Suit—Post 1950 Cases, 67 A.L.R.4th 277, ¶8b (2017).

b. *Connivance.* The theory of divorce is that the misconduct of one spouse (and only one spouse) has destroyed the marital relationship. One set of circumstances where misconduct otherwise justifying divorce may not suffice arises when the "offending" conduct was in fact agreed to (connived at) by the spouse now seeking the divorce. As a practical matter, this defense is almost entirely limited to adultery, although a similar principle is evident in the requirement that desertion, to support a divorce, must be nonconsensual. For a classic instance, *see* Hollis v. Hollis, 427 S.E.2d 233 (Va. App. 1993). The wife, who wished to divorce her husband, encouraged him to have an affair with someone he met at a holiday party. In particular, she urged him and the correspondent to rent an apartment for a year and live there as a couple and, when they did so, the wife sent flowers and a congratulatory note. She then sought a divorce on the grounds of adultery, which a court denied based on connivance.

c. *Condonation.* Condonation is a defense to most of the grounds of divorce, although its application to cruelty is somewhat unclear. Condonation occurs when the injured spouse, knowing of a marital wrong, continues or resumes marital cohabitation. Although the essence of the defense is said to be forgiveness, that state of mind may be inferred from resumption of marital relations itself.

    However, the circumstances in which marital relations are resumed may be important. The New York Supreme Court, Appellate Division, held that an estranged couple's attempt at reconciliation, even where it involves an isolated resumption of cohabitation, or sexual relations, or both, does not, as a matter of law, preclude granting a divorce to a spouse who otherwise had a valid claim for abandonment. "Rather, the trial court should examine the totality of the circumstances surrounding the purported reconciliation, before determining its effect, if any, upon the pending marital proceeding. Among the many factors for the trial court to consider are whether the reconciliation and any cohabitation were entered into in good faith, whether it was at all successful, who initiated it and with what motivation." Haymes v. Haymes, 646 N.Y.S.2d 315, 319 (App. Div. 1996). *See also* Sullivan v. Sullivan, 950 N.E.2d 906 (Mass. App. 2011) (stating that condonation is a "state of mind" that requires an "intent to forgive"). The Massachusetts court relied in part on prior decisions holding that cohabitation, especially if not in good faith, does not condone a course of cruel conduct in the same way it would condone adultery. *See also* Aronson v. Aronson, 691 A.2d 785 (Md. Spec. App. 1997), *cert. denied and appeal dismissed*, 346 Md. 371, 697 A.2d 111 (1997) (ruling that resumption of sexual relations is evidence of condonation); Ware v. Ware, 7 So. 3d 271 (Miss. App. 2008) (asserting that no condonation from resumption of sexual relations where the husband did not forgive the wife for her adultery); Srivastava v. Srivastava, 769 S.E.2d 442, 450-451 (S.C. App. 2015) (holding that even though the spouses slept in separate bedrooms, condonation occurred where spouses resumed sexual relations after husband learned of wife's adultery, and therefore the adultery did not bar alimony).

    In principle, condonation is conditional; it is forgiveness conditioned on the absence of future wrongdoing. An offense, once condoned, may be "revived" if the offending spouse does not treat the condoning spouse properly. Indeed, the initial wrong may be revived even if the offending spouse's subsequent misconduct is not sufficiently grave to constitute an independent basis for divorce.

d. *Recrimination.* The defense of recrimination was raised in *Kucera.* Professor Clark describes recrimination as "a rare combination of silliness, futility and brutality." Homer H. Clark, Jr., Domestic Relations 704 (2d ed. 1979). What is his point?

Some jurisdictions do not recognize recrimination as a bar to divorce but instead look to "comparative rectitude" when both spouses have committed marital fault. *E.g.*, Jenkins v. Jenkins, 55 So. 3d 1094 (Miss. App. 2010) (recrimination is no longer an absolute bar to divorce; instead the court should determine which party's conduct was the proximate cause of the divorce); Alejandro v. Alejandro, 651 S.E.2d 62 (Ga. 2007) (upholding trial court finding that the wife's adultery did not cause the dissolution of the parties' marriage as there was evidence of adultery by both parties, of physical and injurious violence by the husband toward the wife, and of relocation for the husband's work). In New Hampshire, on the other hand, the state supreme court held that when the husband committed adultery 11 months after the divorce action was filed, his adultery constituted recrimination barring a divorce against the wife on fault grounds. In Matter of Ross, 146 A.3d 1232, 1234 (N.H. 2016).

4. The doctrine of collusion is often listed as a defense to divorce, but in some sense, it is a special doctrine. Unlike the other defenses, collusion need not be pleaded or proved. Rather, for reasons obvious by its nature, this bar is ordinarily raised by the court *sua sponte*. The doctrine of collusion is also the clearest evidence of a public interest in the control of marital dissolution.

Collusion exists when the parties agree to frustrate the divorce procedure in some way. It may take the form of an agreement to create the appearance of marital wrongdoing when none has in fact occurred. The industry of supplying fictitious evidence of adultery is a familiar example. The defendant and plaintiff would arrange for one of them, usually the husband, to be in bed in a hotel room with an anonymous woman, partially clothed. A photographer would gain entry and "surprise" the couple in that position, and the photograph would provide evidence of adultery. In England, the practice was even simpler; the hotel bill was sent home by the husband, and witnesses testified that he stayed at the hotel and occupied a bedroom with a woman not his wife. Lawrence M. Friedman, A Dead Language: Divorce Law and Practice Before No-Fault, 86 Va. L. Rev. 1497, 1512-1515 (2000).

Collusion may also arise, or be inferred, from agreements not to defend a case. On the other hand, consent expressed through an agreement to settle the rights of the parties or to grant suit money to the plaintiff is not necessarily improper. The line between illegal and legal agreement has often been unclear, and this uncertainty has presented problems in the drafting of separation agreements. (*See* Chapter 10, Section C.) Even ordinary provisions that one party will sue and the other will not defend may be dangerous to include. For a discussion of collusion in the context of no-fault grounds for divorce, *see* the discussion in Section B.3, No-Default Divorce Procedure and Collusion, below.

Can the assertion of fault grounds or defenses to divorce justify substantive (and perhaps intrusive) discovery? In 2020, an appellate court in New York reinforced the long-standing rule that absent questions of "egregious fault," discovery is not permitted on divorce grounds. Agulnick v. Agulnick, 136 N.Y.S.3d 462 (N.Y. App. Div. 2020).

PROBLEMS

1. Colin and Marie married at age 21, when Marie became pregnant. They had a second child three years later. Colin works as a manager in a sporting goods store, Marie as an administrative assistant. After seven years of marriage, Marie feels the spark is gone. They do relatively little together, are too exhausted to go out much, and share few interests. One day Marie comes home and tells Colin she would like a divorce. Two weeks later, she serves him with papers alleging extreme cruelty. Colin is shocked and very angry. At the trial, Marie testifies that Colin drinks alcohol daily, often consuming six beers a night. On one occasion, he became so intoxicated that he urinated in the parties' closet and then became angry and verbally abusive when she attempted to clean up after him. Since she first expressed her interest in a divorce, he has criticized and belittled her, provoking arguments. During one of these arguments, he threatened to punch her, and during another, he slapped her. Marie asserts that she finally left the marital home because she had become afraid of Colin's increasingly uncontrolled anger.

Colin responds that his drinking increased only after Marie told him she wanted a divorce; that he slapped her on only one occasion, after she precipitated an argument with him; that she has relentlessly criticized him and blamed him for their marital difficulties; and that after counseling, he has gained better control over his drinking and anger. He does not want a divorce, but maintains that if the court is to grant one, it should be on the basis of her desertion.

Do grounds exist to grant Marie a divorce? If not, what would be the effect of a counterclaim by Colin on the ground of desertion?

2. A divorce action is brought alleging cruel and inhuman treatment. Plaintiff husband testifies that his husband had for several years repeatedly nagged and scolded him for fancied wrongs on his part and had frequently, wrongly accused him of adultery. This, plaintiff says, has resulted in a general decline in his health, loss of sleep, and increased nervousness on his part. Assuming these facts are proved, will a divorce be granted?

3. Plaintiff sues for divorce on the ground of adultery. During the trial, the plaintiff admits having an affair before the parties separated. Defendant denies committing adultery and asserts the affirmative defenses of recrimination and condonation. At trial, plaintiff testifies that the alleged paramour had stayed as a guest at their home and when plaintiff became suspicious, the paramour admitted the affair with defendant spouse. Plaintiff also testifies that the defendant spouse had an earlier affair, but that the plaintiff had forgiven that affair. Plaintiff further states that after the second affair, the two spouses had sexual relations, but there had been no forgiveness for the second affair.

Will a divorce be granted on these facts?

B. THE ADOPTION OF NO-FAULT DIVORCE

Lawrence Friedman

Rights of Passage: Divorce Law in Historical Perspective
63 Or. L. Rev. 649, 662, 666-667 (1984)

. . . In almost every state, perjury or something close to it was a way of life in divorce court. . . . In theory, a collusive divorce was illegal. Certainly, perjury was a crime, and so was the manufacture of evidence. Judges had to be aware of what was going on in front of their noses. Yet the system flourished, and the divorce rate grew steadily. There were 7,380 divorces in 1860, or 1.2 per 1,000 marriages. There were 167,105 divorces in 1920, or 7.7 per 1,000 marriages. The overwhelming majority were collusive and consensual, in fact if not in theory. The legal system winked and blinked and ignored. . . .

. . . The real divorce revolution, arguably, was not the passage of the no-fault statutes. These statutes were a delayed ratification of a system largely in place; a system that was expensive, dirty, and distasteful, perhaps, but a system that more or less worked. If one asks who created that system, the answer is ordinary people and their lawyers. Their demand for easy divorce, their pressure on the system, led to concrete patterns of legal behavior that flourished for a century. Lower court judges, all over the country, accepted the system, but it was not their idea. The structure of divorce law, as it existed between 1870 and 1970, evolved quietly in obscure places, without disturbing the surface of law or altering official norms.

In its middle period, divorce law was a compromise between the instrumental demand for divorce and the opposing moral postulate. The situation was, by common agreement, a mess: costly, ineffective, destructive. Yet it lasted for generations. . . .

In the middle of the twentieth century, it was clear to everybody that the system of divorce was a fake: "a solemn if silly comic melodrama," "beneath the dignity of the American court"; a system that "cheapens not only the tribunal but the members of the legal profession who are . . . involved." The question was: What to do about it? One suggestion was to increase the role of the court and to reduce the element of sham. It was felt that a judge should have authority to deal with the entire human drama that lay behind a bill of divorce, and that skilled professionals should be attached to the court to help him. The goal was to set up a true "divorce court," a court of family justice.

This was indeed the philosophy of the Report of the Governor's Commission on the Family, issued in California in 1966. The report called for the destruction of the old system, and paved the way for the California no-fault law of 1970. The Commission demanded an end to "dissimulation, hypocrisy, and . . . perjury." A new law was needed to "allow the therapeutic processes of the Family Court to function with full effectiveness." The "standard" the Commission suggested would "permit—indeed . . . require—the Court to inquire into the whole picture of the marriage."

California did change its law in 1970, and in the next decade, so did almost every state. Yet the "therapeutic" path was most decidedly not the one taken. Instead, the whole house of cards collapsed. For divorces at least—child custody of course is a different animal—the judge did not gain more power and discretion. Instead, in practice he lost what little power he had. No-fault reduced divorce to even greater routine. The social-work or family-court ideal faded away. . . .

The no-fault divorce revolution was not solely an American phenomenon, as Mary Ann Glendon observes in Abortion and Divorce in Western Law 66-67 (1987):

> Between 1969 and 1985 divorce law in nearly every Western country was profoundly altered. Among the most dramatic changes was the introduction of civil divorce in the predominantly Catholic countries of Italy and Spain, and its extension to Catholic marriages in Portugal. Other countries replaced or amended old strict divorce laws. . . . The chief common characteristics of all these changes were the recognition or expansion of nonfault grounds for divorce, and the acceptance or simplification of divorce by mutual consent. When California in 1969 became the first Western jurisdiction completely to eliminate fault grounds for divorce, the move was thought by some to pre-figure the direction of reforms in other places. But it soon became clear that the purist approach was not to find wide acceptance. That same year England, too, passed a new divorce law which purported to make divorce available only when marriage had irretrievably broken down. But since the English statute permitted marriage breakdown to be proved by evidence of traditional marital offenses as well as by mutual consent or long separation, it did not really repudiate the old fault system. As it turned out, compromise statutes of the English type (resembling those already in place in Australia, Canada, and New Zealand) became the prevailing new approach to the grounds of divorce.

1. No-Fault Grounds for Divorce: Irretrievable Breakdown

"No-fault" divorce means only that the state recognizes some ground for divorce that does not require finding one (and only one) party at fault. These no-fault grounds can take several forms. First, as the Uniform Marriage and Divorce Act (below) indicates, the legislation can require a finding that that the marriage is "irretrievably broken." Alternatively, some states refer to "irreconcilable differences" or "incompatibility." Second, the state can require a period of separation, after which the parties become eligible for no-fault divorce. Third, the state can require mutual consent to the divorce, or it can provide for separation for a longer period if the parties do not agree. This section considers irreconcilable differences, and the following section addresses laws that include both no-fault and fault grounds.

UNIFORM MARRIAGE AND DIVORCE ACT
§302 [Dissolution of Marriage; Legal Separation]

(a) The [_____] court shall enter a decree of dissolution of marriage if:

(1) the court finds that one of the parties, at the time the action was commenced, was domiciled in this State, or was stationed in this State while a member of the armed services, and that the domicil or military presence has been maintained for 90 days next preceding the making of the findings;

(2) the court finds that the marriage is irretrievably broken, if the finding is supported by evidence that (i) the parties have lived separate and apart for a period of more than 180 days next preceding the commencement of the proceeding, or . . .

(ii) there is serious marital discord adversely affecting the attitude of one or both of the parties toward the marriage;

(3) the court finds that the conciliation provisions of Section 305 either do not apply or have been met;

(4) to the extent it has jurisdiction to do so, the court has considered, approved, or provided for child custody, the support of any child entitled to support, the maintenance of either spouse, and the disposition of property; or has provided for a separate, later hearing to complete these matters.

(b) If a party requests a decree of legal separation rather than a decree of dissolution of marriage, the court shall grant the decree in that form unless the other party objects.

§305 [Irretrievable Breakdown]

(a) If both of the parties by petition or otherwise have stated under oath or affirmation that the marriage is irretrievably broken, or one of the parties has so stated and the other has not denied it, the court, after hearing, shall make a finding whether the marriage is irretrievably broken.

(b) If one of the parties has denied under oath or affirmation that the marriage is irretrievably broken, the court shall consider all relevant factors, including the circumstances that gave rise to filing the petition and the prospect of reconciliation, and shall:

(1) make a finding whether the marriage is irretrievably broken; or

(2) continue the matter for further hearing not fewer than 30 nor more than 60 days later, or as soon thereafter as the matter may be reached on the court's calendar, and may suggest to the parties that they seek counseling. The court, at the request of either party shall, or on its own motion may, order a conciliation conference. At the adjourned hearing the court shall make a finding whether the marriage is irretrievably broken.

(c) A finding of irretrievable breakdown is a determination that there is no reasonable prospect of reconciliation.

The following case raises questions about the meaning of "irreconcilable" differences in no-fault provisions. The governing statute provides that no divorce shall be granted when "there is a likelihood for rehabilitation of the marriage" or when "there is a reasonable possibility of reconciliation."

Desrochers v. Desrochers
347 A.2d 150 (N.H. 1975)

KENISON, C.J. The parties married in September 1970. Their only child, a daughter, was born in January 1973. The parties separated in May of that year and the wife brought this libel for divorce the following September. A month later the parties agreed to and the court approved arrangements for custody, visitation and support. The defendant did not support his wife and child from the time of separation until the temporary decree. He made the payments called for by the decree from its entry until June 1975. In July 1974, the Hillsborough County Superior Court, Loughlin, J., held a hearing and made certain findings of fact. The critical portion of these findings is: "[T]he action was originally brought because the defendant did not work steadily and stated that he, when he learned that the plaintiff was pregnant, wanted a boy instead of a girl; if the plaintiff bore a girl he would like to put the child up for adoption. After the birth of the child [a daughter] the defendant became very attached to the child, has visited the child weekly except on two occasions, and has been faithfully making support payments under the temporary order of $25.00 a week. The defendant claims that he loves his wife, does not want a divorce. The wife claims that she no longer loves her husband, but since the filing of the divorce he has been an industrious worker and is very attached to the child." . . . At the [appellate] argument, counsel informed the court that the defendant had stopped making support payments and had gone to Nevada in June 1975. At that time he had written to his attorney expressing his desire to remain married. . . .

RSA 458:7-a (Supp. 1973) is the product of a national discussion regarding the proper grounds for divorce. It follows in important respects the California Family Law Act of 1969. . . . A consensus has emerged that a period of separation due to marital difficulties is strong evidence of the irremediable breakdown of a marriage. . . . When asked to interpret a statute similar to RSA 458:7-a, the Florida court of Appeal stated: "The Legislature has not seen fit to promulgate guidelines as to what constitutes an 'irretrievably broken' marriage. It is suggested that this lack of definitive direction was deliberate and is desirable in an area as volatile as a proceeding for termination of the marital status. Consideration should be given to each case individually and predetermined policy should not be circumscribed by the appellate courts of this State.

"Thus, we are hesitant to set forth specific circumstances which trial courts could utilize as permissible indices of an irretrievable breakdown of the marital status. Were we to attempt to do so, we feel that the basic purpose of the new dissolution of marriage law would be frustrated. Such proceedings would either again become primarily adversary in nature or persons would again fit themselves into tailor-made categories or circumstances to fit judicially defined breakdown situations. It is our opinion that these two problems are the very ones which the Legislature intended to eliminate." Riley v. Riley, 271 So. 2d 181, 183 (Fla. App. 1972).

The existence of irreconcilable differences which have caused the irremediable breakdown of the marriage is determined by reference to the subjective state of mind of the parties. While the desire of one spouse to continue the marriage is evidence of "a reasonable possibility of reconciliation," it is not a bar to divorce. If one spouse resolutely refuses to continue and it is clear from the passage of time or other circumstances that there is no reasonable possibility of a change of heart, there is an irremediable breakdown of the marriage. The defendant may attempt to impeach the plaintiff's evidence of his or her state of mind regarding the relationship. If the trial court doubts plaintiff's evidence that the marriage has irremediably broken down, the court may continue the action to determine if reconciliation is possible. However, if the parties do not reconcile, dissolution should be granted. . . .

The question whether a breakdown of a marriage is irremediable is a question to be determined by the trial court. RSA 458:7-a contemplates the introduction of factual testimony sufficient to permit a finding of irreconcilable differences which have caused the irremediable breakdown of the marriage. Nevertheless there are limits to the inquiry. "In the first place, there is the natural tendency to withhold information of a personal nature from anyone but a trusted and discreet adviser; secondly, any probing into personal matters against the wishes of the party examined would be objectionable . . . ; and thirdly, the parties have come to court for a purpose. Their answers, which may be perfectly honest ones, will inevitably be slanted in the direction of their ultimate goal, which is divorce." Within these limits the trial court must be adequately informed before acting in matters of such importance. But the statute does not contemplate a complete biopsy of the marriage relationship from the beginning to the end in every case. This is a difficult task, but judges face similar problems in other cases.

The separation of the parties for two and one-half years and the plaintiff's persistence in seeking a divorce during that period is evidence from which the trial court could find that this marriage has irremediably broken down.

Remanded.

NOTES AND QUESTIONS

1. In 2010 New York amended its divorce statute to add the following ground for divorce:

Dom. Rel. Law §170. Action for divorce

(7) The relationship between husband and wife has broken down irretrievably for a period of at least six months, provided that one party has so stated under oath. No judgment of divorce shall be granted under this subdivision unless and until the economic issues of equitable distribution of marital property, the payment or waiver of spousal support, the payment of child support, the payment of counsel and experts' fees and expenses as well as the custody and visitation with the infant children of the marriage have been resolved by the parties, or determined by the court and incorporated into the judgment of divorce.

How does the New York statute differ from the New Hampshire statute in *Desrochers*? From the UMDA? If one party files an affidavit that the "relationship between husband and wife has broken down irretrievably for a period of at least six months," can the other party contest it? If so, on what ground? *Compare* Strack v. Strack, 916 N.Y.S.2d 759 (Sup. Ct., Essex County 2011) (irretrievable breakdown is a question of fact that may be subject to a jury trial), *with* Vahey v. Vahey, 940 N.Y.S.2d 824 (Sup. Ct. 2012) (ruling a court can grant divorce on the basis of plaintiff's unilateral declaration of irretrievable breakdown without a trial).

The New York statute also provides that the court may not issue a divorce decree without addressing the economic and custody issues in the case. What impact do you think that will have on the parties' negotiating positions in a divorce? *See* A.C. v. D.R., 927 N.Y.S.2d 496 (Sup. Ct. 2011).

2. In what sense is the marriage broken when one spouse wishes to continue that marriage? Why do the opposing spouses in *Desrochers* wish to prevent divorce? Should it matter?

3. Should parties alleging irretrievable breakdown be required to allege and prove facts that establish the breakdown? How do such allegations differ from "fault"? Mo. Stat. §452.320 authorizes a divorce on the ground that a marriage is irretrievably broken only when both parties agree that it is. In Koon v. Koon, 969 S.W.2d 828 (Mo. App. 1998), the wife alleged that she and her husband had "separated on March 19, 1996," and that the marriage was irretrievably broken "because [Husband] has behaved during the marriage in such a way that [Wife] cannot reasonably be expected to live with him." Under the Missouri statute, a finding that the marriage is irretrievably broken, when contested, must be supported by evidence of various kinds of misconduct by the defendant, such that the wife could not be expected to continue to live with the husband. At trial, the wife testified that her husband tried to control everything she did and that they often argued over how and where money should be spent. She also testified that when the husband was working temporarily in Virginia, she was much happier than when he was at home. In her opinion, there was no hope for reconciliation. The husband testified that he did not believe the marriage was irretrievably broken and that he did not want the court to dissolve the marriage.

In rendering judgment, the trial court found that the parties' marriage was irretrievably broken, but also specifically stated it did "not find that [Husband] has behaved in such a way that [Wife] could not reasonably be expected to live with him." On these findings, the appellate court reversed the trial court, holding that no divorce could be granted on these facts.

How is the Missouri statute different from the statute in *Desrochers*? From the one in New York? In Williams v. Williams, 197 So. 3d 480, 483 (Ala. Civ. App. 2015), the wife's verified complaint "alleged incompatibility, an irretrievable breakdown of the marriage, and verbal abuse as grounds for a divorce." The husband's answer denied the wife's allegations, but he later submitted an affidavit testifying to the parties' incompatibility. The court concluded, "In light of the parties' affidavits, a hearing to elicit testimony establishing incompatibly as the ground for a divorce was not necessary." The dissent argued that "Alabama law provides that a divorce based on incompatibility may not be obtained merely on the agreement of the parties," and therefore that the court needed to receive "testimony" establishing "such a complete incompatibility of temperament that the parties can no longer live together." *Id.* at 484. Given that both parties want the divorce, what testimony would you advise the parties to provide?

4. Do no-fault statutes that permit "unilateral divorce" violate the rights of the party who would prefer to stay married? The Supreme Court of Nebraska declined to find the state's no-fault divorce statute unconstitutional on such grounds. Dycus v. Dycus, 949 N.W.2d 357 (Neb. 2020). The husband had argued that granting divorce based on one party's unilateral assertion that the marriage was "irretrievably broken" deprived him of due process, but the court disagreed, holding that granting the divorce on such grounds required a factual determination based on both parties' presentations.

5. Do these differences in the approach to no-fault divorce reflect the differences between marriage as covenant (and thus an indissoluble bond) versus marriage as contract (and dependent on the consent of the couple) introduced at the beginning of the chapter?

2. The Coexistence of Fault and No-Fault Grounds

Flanagan v. Flanagan
956 A.2d 829 (Md. App. 2008)

HOLLANDER, J. . . . The parties were married on November 23, 1984. It was a second marriage for each, and they have no children together. . . .

At the time of trial on September 19, 2006, appellant was 68 years old and appellee was 64 years of age.

. . . Appellee recounted that she moved out of the marital home on February 2, 2005, leaving appellant a letter explaining her decision. She and appellant had lived separate and apart since that date, with no hope of reconciliation.

The letter was admitted into evidence. . . . [In the letter] appellee commented:

> On the average, we spend 51 waking hours together a week. When you are sober I admire your intelligence, your wit and enjoy being with you. However, I have to deal with your varying degree of intoxication every night for a conservative average of 37 hours per week. This isn't the quality of life I expected to be leading at this stage of my life.

Ms. Flanagan added: "I have resolved not to live my life under these conditions any longer. I want peace."

In her testimony, appellee identified two reasons for her departure from the home, which were consistent with her letter. First, she pointed to appellant's alleged excessive drinking, which often led him to be "accusatory, argumentative, you know, all my faults, real and imagined for twenty years would be paraded out in front of me." Second, she complained about appellant's persistent "internet sexual contacts," which she discovered beginning in 2002. They consisted of visits to pornographic websites, which she characterized as "just nasty," as well as participation in "interactive chat rooms" and activity on dating websites. In December 2002, appellee discovered that appellant had made a date with another couple "to set up a sexual encounter with them at a future date. . . ." She contacted the other couple and arranged, without appellant's knowledge, for the two couples to meet in order to confront appellant. According to appellee, appellant denied his online activity "[u]p until that point no matter what I said. . . ." However, appellee noted that when the other woman, Marianne, "was standing in front of [appellant] with her boyfriend . . . then he could no longer deny it because [the other woman] was there in person." Appellee indicated that she believed appellant's behavior had stopped for a time, but resumed in 2004.

In addition, appellee suggested that appellant was "threatening in his manner." But, she described only one incident of physical force, which occurred in January 2003, when appellant "threw a wallet" at appellee after a session of joint counseling. . . .

Appellant admitted to "prowling" for women on the internet in order to "add a little spice to [his] sex life." He explained that in 2002 he had a "severe prostatitis attack," which rendered him "dysfunctional." This condition prevented the parties from engaging in a physical relationship, and "stupidly" prompted him to visit online chat rooms, through which he conversed with a woman named Marianne. He arranged to meet her at an area restaurant, and she brought her boyfriend, Ron. Appellant testified: "Marianne's demeanor did not appeal to me. She had tattoos. She was rough. . . . [A]nd I really wasn't planning on having sex with another male." So, appellant "bought them a bucket of clams and a couple of beers and left." Appellant claimed that, a week later, appellee told him she was taking him out to dinner. When they arrived at the restaurant, the other couple was there, and appellee "threw her arms around Marianne as if they were ancient friends. . . ." Appellant testified: "I spun on my heel and walked out of [the restaurant] and spent the next two hours sitting in the parking lot by myself." Appellee remained in the restaurant with appellant's car keys.

Mr. Flanagan insisted that he had no other internet encounter after that incident. He maintained that sometime thereafter appellee "helped [him] solve the [sexual dysfunction] problem." . . .

In addition, appellant categorically denied ever striking appellee at any time during their marriage. . . .

With regard to his alcohol consumption, appellant insisted that his drinking at home was limited to "a couple of cocktails" before or with dinner every other day or so, but that "after dinner I didn't drink anything at all." . . .

On February 27, 2007, the court issued a "Memorandum Opinion," in which it found voluntary separation as the grounds for divorce. However, neither party had advanced the ground of voluntary separation. . . .

In Maryland, the permissible grounds for divorce are governed by statute. . . . F.L. §7-103(a) provides the permissible bases for an absolute divorce, which include the following:

> (2) desertion, if:
>> (i) the desertion has continued for 12 months without interruption before the filing of the application for divorce;
>> (ii) the desertion is deliberate and final; and
>> (iii) there is no reasonable expectation of reconciliation;
> (3) voluntary separation, if:
>> (i) the parties voluntarily have lived separate and apart without cohabitation for 12 months without interruption before the filing of the application for divorce; and
>> (ii) there is no reasonable expectation of reconciliation; . . .
> (5) 2-year separation, when the parties have lived separate and apart without cohabitation for 2 years without interruption before the filing of the application for divorce[.]

As noted, appellee's complaint alleged constructive desertion, while appellant alleged actual desertion in his counterclaim. In its Memorandum Opinion, the court awarded a divorce on the basis of "mutual and voluntary separation of more than 12 months." It reasoned that, following appellee's departure from the marital home on February 2, 2005, "[n]either party has attempted reconciliation. Insofar as the separation became mutual and voluntary and both parties indicate there is no reasonable expectation of reconciliation." . . .

We addressed the elements of voluntary separation in Aronson v. Aronson, 115 Md. App. 78, 691 A.2d 785, *cert. denied*, 346 Md. 371, 697 A.2d 111 (1997). We began our analysis by reviewing the Court of Appeals's decision in *Wallace*. . . . We said:

> What the [*Wallace*] Court said is pertinent here:
>
>> In order to establish the existence of the twelve month voluntary separation ground for divorce *a vinculo* . . . three elements must be shown: (i) an express or implied agreement to separate, *accompanied by a mutual intent not to resume the marriage relationship*; (ii) voluntarily living separate and apart without cohabitation for twelve months prior to the filing of the bill of complaint; and (iii) that the separation is beyond any reasonable hope of reconciliation.
>
> Indeed, the Court of Appeals has consistently held that voluntariness requires an agreement to live separate and apart, coupled with a common intent to terminate the marriage. . . .
>
> In contrast, "[a]cquiescence in or assent to what one cannot prevent does not amount to a voluntary agreement to separate." . . . Nevertheless, the elements of mutuality and separation need not coincide at the inception of the separation. Indeed, an involuntary separation may later be transformed into a voluntary separation. Thus, a separation that begins as a desertion may later achieve "voluntary" status.

We noted in *Aronson* that proof of a *mutually* voluntary separation was lacking. We explained:

> [A]ppellee never affirmatively represented that both parties wanted to end the marriage. . . . [A]ppellee's assertion that the parties agreed that she would move out of the marital home does not distinguish between an agreement to separate, which appellant concedes, and an agreement to separate for the particular purpose of terminating the relationship, which appellant contests. . . .

Appellee's position is at odds with *Wallace* and *Aronson*; there was no evidence below of an agreement to separate that existed for the requisite duration. . . . When appellee left the marital home in February 2005, there was no evidence that the parties had a mutual agreement to separate with the intent to end the marriage. To the contrary, the evidence clearly showed that it was a unilateral decision of appellee. . . . Nor was there evidence of such an agreement by April 11, 2005, i.e., one year before appellee filed her Complaint for Absolute Divorce. . . .

Appellee's reliance on the filing by appellant of a Counter-Complaint for Absolute Divorce is also unavailing. That filing, on May 17, 2006, did not demonstrate that appellant agreed to terminate the nuptial bond at the time that is relevant, i.e., at least one year prior to April 11, 2006—or assuming that appellant's Counter-Complaint established a new date by which the separation could be measured, one year prior to May 17, 2006.

Moreover, appellant's Counter-Complaint based on desertion did not establish his agreement to a no-fault divorce. Voluntary separation is a no-fault ground, while appellant counterclaimed based on desertion, which is a fault-based ground. . . . As we recognized in *Aronson*, the fact that a party seeks to end the marriage on the basis of fault does not establish the party's acquiescence to a no-fault termination. . . .

Accordingly, we agree with appellant that the court erred in granting a divorce on the ground of voluntary separation. Nevertheless, we are equally convinced that any error was harmless. We explain. . . .

The court did not specify a ground in the Divorce Order. Although the Memorandum Opinion found a voluntary separation, we discern no substantial injury that accrued to appellant as a result of that finding, rather than a finding of desertion or constructive desertion. As appellee underscores, appellant clearly wanted a divorce, as evidenced by his counter-complaint, and he obtained the relief he sought, i.e., an absolute divorce.

Moreover, there was an adequate factual basis in the record for an absolute divorce on the grounds of either actual or constructive desertion. In Ricketts v. Ricketts, 393 Md. 479, 487-88, 903 A.2d 857 (2006), the Court explained:

> Desertion may be constructive or actual. We have defined actual desertion as
>
>> "the voluntary separation of one of the married parties from the other, or the refusal to renew suspended cohabitation, without justification either in the consent or the wrongful conduct of the other party. . . . [Furthermore,] the separation and intention to abandon must concur, and desertion does not exist without the presence of both. The two need not begin at the same time, but desertion begins whenever to either one the other is added."

Here, the record supported a finding of constructive desertion, the ground alleged by appellee. Moreover, the court made factual findings that were consistent with constructive desertion.

We explained the showing required for a divorce based on the basis of constructive desertion in *Lemley, supra*, 102 Md. App. at 281 (emphasis in original; internal citations omitted):

> The question, as framed by the Court of Appeals, is whether [one spouse] has engaged in "such conduct as would make a continuance of the marital relationship inconsistent with the health, self-respect and reasonable comfort of the other." There must be "a pattern of persistent conduct which is detrimental to the safety or health of the complaining spouse, *or so demeaning to his or her self-respect as to be intolerable*." As the italicized language suggests, it is not necessary in every case to show that the safety or physical health of a spouse is threatened; a grave threat to a spouse's self-respect alone may be sufficient.

The findings of the court below were tantamount to a finding of constructive desertion, and were supported by the record. Notably, the court below found that appellee "decided to leave the marital home . . . after years of her husband's soliciting extramarital sexual relationships on the internet, his heavy drinking and verbal abuse." . . .

NOTES AND QUESTIONS

1. Maryland does not recognize irreconcilable differences or irretrievable breakdown as a ground for divorce. Instead, a voluntary separation of 12 months or a 2-year separation are the only no-fault grounds for divorce. The 12-month separation requires the agreement of the spouses; the 2-year separation does not. What are the advantages and disadvantages of permitting an innocent spouse who does not want a divorce to delay the final decree?

2. The *Flanagan* court recognizes that at some point a unilateral separation may become mutual if the party who initially opposed the separation no longer wants a reconciliation. What standard does the court use for determining when that point occurs?

3. The *Flanagan* court finds that the trial court's erroneous conclusion that the divorce can be granted on the basis of the parties' voluntary separation is "harmless" because the parties met the requirements for a fault divorce: the husband's constructive desertion. How do the elements of desertion, constructive desertion, and a two-year separation differ from each other?

4. By the time the divorce decree was issued, both parties wanted a divorce, but they did not agree on the grounds. The trial court dealt with the issue by choosing a no-fault basis for the divorce; the appellate court insisted on finding that the husband was at fault in part because the parties had not been separated for the two years required in the absence of mutual consent. How would this case have been handled under the UMDA? How does the presence of fault grounds as an alternative basis for divorce change the dynamic of this case?

5. In some states, the grounds for divorce may affect the availability of spousal support, though relatively few states treat fault as an absolute bar. *See, e.g.*, Gardner v. Gardner, 452 P.3d 1134 (Utah 2019) (holding that, when determining alimony, the trial courts should determine the degree to which the alleged fault caused the end of the marriage); Conzelman v. Conzelman, 453 P.3d 773 (Wyo. 2019) (holding that a trial court may, but does not need to, consider the fault of the parties when dividing marital property). In South Carolina, however, proof of adultery is a ground to deny a spouse alimony, even when the divorce is granted on no-fault grounds and both parties were found to have engaged in adultery. Mick-Skaggs v. Skaggs, 766 S.E.2d 870, 874 (S.C. Ct. App. 2014).

6. State statutes give courts various powers to prompt or encourage reconciliation between divorcing spouses. For example, a number of states, like Maryland, mandate periods of separation or cooling-off periods before a divorce. What impact do you think the period of separation had on the parties in the *Flanagan* case? Did it have any impact on their inclination to divorce? Did it make dissolution of their marriage any more amicable? Did it affect their likelihood of remarriage? Cohabitation?

3. No-Fault Divorce Procedure and Collusion

Vandervort v. Vandervort
134 P.3d 892 (Okla. Civ. App. 2005)

Reif, J. This appeal arises from post-decree proceedings in which Wife, Patricia Vandervort, sought to vacate the parties' divorce decree. . . . Husband and Wife had agreed to divorce and to divest Wife of nearly all her marital property in anticipation of her eventual need for care in a nursing home for multiple sclerosis. Both believed Wife's single status and complete lack of assets would enable her to receive social security disability income and Medicaid to pay for her nursing home care.

In the time period between the divorce and Wife's need for nursing home care, Husband and Wife were to continue living together at their Texas County residence in Guymon. Husband was to care for Wife until she required nursing home care. Not long after the divorce, however, acrimony developed and Wife ended up living with her parents. Wife claims she went to visit her parents and Husband refused to allow her to return; Husband claims Wife "abandoned" her right to live with him. After considering these facts, along with other evidence and contentions of the parties, the trial court vacated the divorce decree.

In announcing the ruling from the bench, the trial court vacated the decree on the ground of fraud, but did not elaborate. . . .

The petition signed by Husband affirmatively represented that incompatibility was the ground upon which divorce should be granted, while the "consent decree" signed by both parties reflected their mutual agreement that incompatibility existed between them. However, at the time the divorce was sought and granted, Husband and Wife intended to return to their Texas County residence where they were to continue living together with Husband providing and caring for Wife. In fact, they did so for a short time after the divorce. These facts belie their claim of incompatibility.

"The statutory ground of incompatibility does not permit the court to dissolve a marriage merely because its termination is desired by one or both parties." "Incompatibility [cannot be] dependent in application upon an agreement or stipulation between the parties, and thus furnish a vehicle for a consensual divorce which the law did not intend."

"Actionable incompatibility is determined to exist when there is such a conflict of personalities as to destroy the legitimate ends of matrimony and the possibility of reconciliation." Incompatibility must be established "by proof, objective in its character, of causes to which marital disharmony is attributed [and cannot be] bottomed on a mere subterfuge or afterthought [without] a substantial foundation."

The State of Oklahoma has constitutional authority "to declare and maintain a policy in regard to marriage and divorce as to persons domiciled within its borders." "The statutory grounds of divorce are exclusive, and the courts have authority in this field to do only that which is prescribed by the legislature."

"The State is a silent third party in every divorce proceeding." The State is an interested party because "the rights of the plaintiff and defendant are not isolated from the general interest of society in preserving the marriage relation as the foundation of the home and the state." To protect the State's interest, a divorce decree is properly vacated where there is conduct that "amounts to a fraud . . . upon the state as represented by the court in the administration of justice."

In cases where parties to a divorce collude to procure a judgment and one party later seeks to vacate that judgment, the law generally "will leave them where it finds them." However, the Oklahoma Supreme Court has also observed that "where the jurisdiction of the court is invoked and obtained by a fraudulent 'concoction' and the fraud is consummated through the instrumentality of a court of justice, it would impeach the moral sense and that of justice that courts be not protected against such fraud." We conclude the case at hand falls under the latter rule rather than the former. The parties here colluded to misrepresent incompatibility as a ground for divorce (when they actually intended to continue cohabitating) and, in turn, used the sham divorce to deceive public agencies concerning Wife's eligibility for public benefits. It not only offends public policy for parties to obtain a divorce on a concocted ground, but it also offends public policy to use such a divorce for financial gain. Rather than leave the parties where we find them, we believe equity and justice require they be returned to the state of matrimony. The trial court's judgment accomplishes that purpose. . . .

GABBARD, J., dissenting. This case is a good example of how bad facts sometimes make bad law.

. . . The parties were dealing with a problem common to many middle-class Americans: How do couples preserve their marital assets in the face of a catastrophic illness? Their solution was to obtain a divorce in which Husband received virtually all the marital property, thereby qualifying Wife for government assistance when her progressive illness caused her health to deteriorate to the point that she needed nursing home care. Husband promised to care for her in the home until that time. Only after Husband allegedly breached his promise of care did Wife move to set aside the decree. That relief should not be granted.

As the majority and the trial court have concluded, this case involves mutual fraud. It is not a case in which one spouse practices fraud upon the other in order to obtain an advantageous divorce settlement. Where both parties have participated in fraud upon the court, 24 Am. Jur. 2d Divorce and Separation §438 (1998) sets forth the general rule:

> [A] spouse who *participates* in the fraudulent procurement of a divorce decree, and who freely enjoys the fruits of the decree, will be unable to have it set aside under a rule allowing actions for relief from judgments procured by fraud. . . .
>
> A court of equity will ordinarily refuse to vacate a decree of divorce where its aid is made necessary by the fault or neglect of the applicant. (Emphasis added.)

This rule is based on sound public policy and has been followed by Oklahoma courts since 1910. . . .

Because the majority's decision is contrary to established precedent and public policy, and provides an unnecessary and inappropriate remedy, I dissent.

NOTES AND QUESTIONS

1. If the husband and wife agreed to the divorce, against whom was the fraud committed? The most obvious answer is the public authorities who would provide the wife with greater benefits. These authorities are not a party to this case, however, and it is not clear that the couple violated any law or regulation that pertains to those benefits. The second possible answer is that the husband deceived the wife, but the majority and the dissent agree that the wife knew what she was doing when she agreed to the divorce, and that the real problem is that the husband reneged on his promise to provide for her afterward. The third answer is that the couple deceived the court when they maintained that they were "incompatible." Why should that matter? If both parties have their reasons for wanting a divorce and agree that one should be granted, why should it matter to the state what the reasons are (particularly if they do not violate any other law or regulation)? How does the majority respond to this issue? How does the majority justify continuing the marriage at a point where the parties have demonstrated incompatibility?

2. The dissent, in arguing that the divorce should stand, objects that if no divorce is granted, the wife may recover far more than originally agreed. In the original divorce, the husband received all the marital property, but agreed to care for the wife. If the divorce is vacated, the wife has the opportunity to obtain her share of the marital property. Why might this trouble the dissenting judge?

In Matter of Harmon, 129 A.3d 311, 313 (N.H. 2015), the New Hampshire Supreme Court observed that "a final judgment of divorce may be set aside or vacated when procured by fraud, accident, mistake, or misfortune." Could the wife in *Vandervort* claim the benefit of this doctrine? The court in *Harmon* concluded that the agreement of both parties by itself was insufficient to set aside a final divorce decree. Why? Does this reflect a comment on judicial process, estopping the parties from setting aside a decree they requested, or a comment on the nature of marriage as a product of state action rather than the consent of the parties?

3. Courts in other states have disagreed about the continuing importance of collusion. In McKim v. McKim, 6 Cal. 3d 673, 493 P.2d 868, 872 (1972), the California Supreme Court held that collusion barred the granting of a no-fault divorce. On the other hand, the Iowa Supreme Court concluded that "collusion is no longer relevant [in divorce proceedings]. In truth, if it were demonstrated the parties were in collusion to bring about a termination of the marriage relationship, it would further evidence the fact of marital breakdown." In re Marriage of Collins, 200 N.W.2d 886, 890 (Iowa 1972). Will the role of collusion in New York depend on that state's determination of whether "irretrievable breakdown" is a factual determination or a matter of pleading in which the court must accept the parties' statement of subjective intent? Would the determination affect the outcome in *Vandervort*?

4. Does a divorce obtained through collusion necessarily bind federal authorities? In Boyter v. Commissioner, 74 T.C. 989 (1981), the U.S. Tax Court refused to recognize a Maryland couple's year-end divorce. The couple used the divorce to file as two single individuals rather than as a married couple and thereby incurred lower income taxes. The couple promptly remarried in January, and at trial the wife testified that they divorced only to obtain the tax advantage.

Many cases address the issue of whether third parties with a claim against one spouse can reach the assets the other spouse received in a divorce settlement. In Commodity Futures Trading Comm'n v. Walsh, 951 N.E.2d 369 (N.Y. 2011), the court distinguished between assets that an innocent spouse acquires in a divorce proceeding "where that spouse in good faith and without knowledge of the fraud gave fair consideration for the transferred property" and "fraudulently-obtained assets in a divorce settlement, where it is demonstrated that the transferee-spouse was aware of or participated in the fraud or otherwise failed to act in good faith." Do these principles create any ground for recovery by third parties in *Vandervort*?

For a discussion of these issues and more, *see* Kerry Abrams, Marriage Fraud, 100 Cal. L. Rev. 1 (2012).

Several states have adopted summary dissolution procedures *e.g.*, Cal. Fam. Code §§2400 et seq. (2020); Or. Rev. Stat. §§107.485, 107.490, 107.500 (2022). These procedures, which are often restricted to short-term marriages with no minor children, typically dispense with any requirement of a hearing as long as the parties have agreed to the distribution of marital property and abandoned spousal maintenance claims. The California version follows:

CALIFORNIA FAMILY CODE — SUMMARY DISSOLUTION

§2400. [Conditions]

(a) A marriage may be dissolved by the summary dissolution procedure provided in this chapter if all of the following conditions exist at the time the proceeding is commenced:

(1) Either party has met the jurisdictional requirements of Chapter 3 . . . with regard to dissolution of marriage.

(2) Irreconcilable differences have caused the irremediable breakdown of the marriage and the marriage should be dissolved.

(3) There are no children of the relationship of the parties born before or during the marriage or adopted by the parties during the marriage, and the wife, to her knowledge, is not pregnant.

(4) The marriage is not more than five years in duration at the time the petition is filed.

(5) Neither party has any interest in real property wherever situated [with the exception of a short-term residential lease].

(6) There are no unpaid obligations in excess of four thousand dollars ($4,000) incurred by either or both of the parties after the date of their marriage, excluding the amount of any unpaid obligation with respect to an automobile.

(7) The total fair market value of community property assets, excluding all encumbrances and automobiles . . . is less than twenty-five thousand dollars ($25,000) and neither party has separate property assets, excluding all encumbrances and automobiles, in excess of twenty-five thousand dollars ($25,000).

(8) The parties have executed an agreement setting forth the division of assets and the assumption of liabilities of the community, and have duly executed any documents, title certificates, bills of sale, or other evidence of transfer necessary to effectuate the agreement.

(9) The parties waive any rights to spousal support.

(10) The parties, upon entry of the judgment of dissolution of marriage . . . irrevocably waive their respective rights to appeal and their rights to move for a new trial.

(11) The parties have read and understand the summary dissolution brochure provided for in Section 2406.

(12) The parties desire that the court dissolve the marriage. . . .

§2403. When six months have expired from the date of the filing of the joint petition for summary dissolution, the court may, upon application of either party, enter the judgment dissolving the marriage. The judgment restores to the parties the status of single persons. . . . The clerk shall send a notice of entry of judgment to each of the parties at the party's last known address.

§2406. [Brochure supplied by court.] [This section requires courts to supply a brochure, in "nontechnical" English and Spanish language versions, describing summary dissolution proceedings. The brochure summarizes the procedure. It advises that the parties should consult a lawyer, explains the availability of legal aid lawyers, that spousal support will not be available, and that a permanent adjudication of rights will occur.]

NOTES AND QUESTIONS

1. Do courts need to be involved in the divorce process at all when the parties agree? A statute introduced into the Minnesota legislature would provide for "Cooperative Private Divorce." This statute would allow couples, who create their own divorce agreement, to file for a "certificate of marital termination" to be issued by the commissioner of mediation services. Parties could thus obtain a divorce without judicial involvement, though the statute would also allow married couples to retain the option of seeking a traditional divorce or of obtaining the judicial involvement necessary to enforce the agreement or to secure interstate recognition. What problems do you see with such a proposal? *See* Minnesota State Legislature, HF 1348, posted Mar. 17, 2015, available at https://www.revisor.mn.gov/bills/text.php?number=HF1348&version=0&session_year=2015&session_number=0 (last visited Aug. 11, 2022).

2. How would you expect a contested proceeding to differ from the California summary dissolution procedure above? In the Netherlands, empirical studies indicate that the adoption of simplified procedures increased divorce rates by approximately 11 percent. Jan Kabátek, Divorced in a Flash: The Effect of the Administrative Divorce Option on Marital Stability in the Netherlands, IZA Discussion Papers, No. 12150, Institute of Labor Economics (2019). On the other hand, some U.S. scholars have argued that the difficulty, expense, and substantive provisions of divorce law persuade some Americans not to marry. *See* Eleanor Brown, Naomi Cahn & June Carbone, The Price of Exit, 99 Wash. U. L. Rev. 1 (2022). For further discussion of these procedures, *see* Lynda B. Munro, Johanna S. Katz & Meghan M. Sweeney, Administrative Divorce Trends and Implications, 50 Fam. L. Q. 427 (2016).

PROBLEMS

1. Arthur is a pilot with Centennial Airlines. He has been flying for Centennial for more than two decades and he has accumulated substantial pension benefits, but he is worried about the financial viability of the company. He files for a divorce from Betsy, his wife of 19 years, a full-time homemaker who is two years older than he is. They agree that there are irreconcilable differences between them. They also agree to a settlement that awards Betsy Arthur's pension, and awards Arthur the couple's house and most of their savings. In accordance with federal law, Betsy is to receive the pension benefits immediately in a lump sum payment of $600,000 even though Arthur has no intention of retiring anytime soon.

Centennial suspects that the divorce is a sham that Arthur and Betsy have arranged to secure immediate payment of the pension benefits. If Centennial were to have financial difficulties, the pension would be paid to the Pension Benefit Guarantee Corporation, which would distribute the benefits in lesser sums on an annual basis after Arthur retired. The total value of the pension in that event would likely be less than the lump sum payment.

Centennial would like to intervene in the divorce proceeding to allege that the couple does not in fact have "irreconcilable differences." Does it have standing to do so? If the couple remarry after Betsy receives the pension funds, and Centennial brings that fact to the attention of the court, is there any action the court could take?

2. Walter and Caren have been married for 30 years. Shortly after Caren learned that Walter faced indictment for securities and accounting fraud, she filed for divorce. Walter and Caren have stipulated that their differences are irreconcilable. They have also agreed to a settlement that gives Caren the family home, which Walter arranged to place solely in Caren's name several years ago and which is worth $6 million, as well as bank accounts worth an additional $2 million. Walter is to receive his pension benefits, which he is likely to forfeit; stock options with a face value of $10 million; and an additional $4 million in stocks and bonds. The precise value of Walter's assets, however, is uncertain because the accounting fraud for which he has been indicted has likely distorted the true value of the holdings. In addition, he faces several billion dollars in potential liability as a result of his fraudulent activities and a potential prison sentence of 10 to 15 years. There is no evidence that Caren knew of or engaged in any of Walter's schemes, but the effect of the divorce will be to insulate Caren and the assets she receives in the settlement from Walter's obligations to provide restitution to his victims.

What actions, if any, should the court take to determine whether the differences between Caren and Walter are irreconcilable? To what extent should the court question the settlement to which they have agreed? On what basis could the court either refuse to grant the divorce or alter the property division?

C. DIVORCE COMMENTARY

The adoption of no-fault divorce was controversial partly because it marked the change from marriage as covenant to marriage as contract, contradicting religious teachings about marriage and raising concerns about family stability. Divorce rates rose dramatically in the era immediately following the adoption of no-fault divorce and have plateaued at slightly less than 50 percent of all marriages. These patterns are distinctly different from those in other developed countries. Sociologist Andrew Cherlin observes that:

> Both entry into and exit from marriage are indicators of what Robert Schoen has called a country's "marriage metabolism": the number of marriage- and divorce-related transitions that adults and their children undergo. . . . [T]he United States has by far the highest marriage metabolism of any of the developed countries in question. . . . In other words, what makes the United States most distinctive is the combination of high marriage and high divorce rates—which implies that Americans typically experience more transitions into and out of marriages than do people in other countries.

Andrew J. Cherlin, American Marriage in the Early Twenty-First Century, 15 The Future of Children: Marriage and Child Well-Being 33, 43-46 (Fall 2005). Cherlin notes further that "affluent and well-educated whites—society's most privileged group—still marry at very high rates and bear children predominantly within marriage." *Id.* Indeed, by the mid-nineties, divorce had dropped dramatically for college graduates, returning to the levels that existed before the adoption of no-fault divorce, and for college-educated whites, those rates have remained low. For other groups, however, divorce rates continued to rise, and non-marital birth rates increased dramatically. See discussion of the changing demographics of the family in Chapter 1.

The question is whether the legal changes have anything to do with these developments and how the law respond to them. Some scholars have argued that the change in divorce ushered in a change in marriage.

Stéphane Mechoulan

Divorce Laws and the Structure of the American Family
35 J. Legal Stud. 143, 144-147, 165-166 (2006)

Divorce laws have received much attention lately. . . . A commonly expressed claim in support of a return to a fault rule is that the move to no fault caused the divorce rate to rise. . . .

Since the mid-1970s, a vast body of literature has sought to understand the effects of these divorce laws. . . .

The starting point of this analysis rests on the following observations: not only have aggregate divorce rates decreased since most of the legal changes were passed, but the average difference in divorce rates across different divorce regimes has been narrowing. One should then also investigate why, since the early 1980s, divorce rates have decreased faster, on average, in states where fault is not considered for property [distributions]. . . .

The paper explores the hypothesis that spouses take the law into account and sort themselves differently accordingly to which rule governs their future divorce. . . .

Using cross-sectional micro data . . . (1971-98), the findings first confirm that for couples who married before the changes in the law, there was a significant impact of no fault for property or divorce odds: this is referred to as the "pipeline effect" (that is, the increased divorce rate resulting from the divorces of couples whose marriages were falling apart but who did not divorce until the new law took effect). Most important, among individuals who have not experienced a change in property law since their marriage, the odds of divorce are found not to differ significantly between the two regimes [*i.e.*, fault and no fault]: my interpretation is that the direct effect and the indirect effect (that is, better selection at marriage) cancel out. The law defining divorce grounds, in contrast, has a more limited impact on divorce probabilities.

Further, there is evidence of a delay in marriage for women when fault is irrelevant for property decisions, ceterus paribus, a longer search also points toward better matching.

. . . To summarize, this theory says that the divorce law changes introduced in the early 1970's affected the odds of divorce for those couples who married before these laws were passed. Such couples were more likely to divorce after a change in law from fault to no-fault divorce, and the key variable seems to be the law governing property division and spousal support. Once the first legal changes passed, many poorly matched couples who married before the changes in the law broke up, thus boosting the rate of divorce. The legal changes that appeared later still had some impact for those who had married under a fault regime. Most important, the effect of no-fault divorce was mitigated by those couples who reduced their probability of divorce through better sorting upon marriage. The main conclusion of the paper is that this better sorting decreased the probability of divorce by about as much as the institution of no-fault increased it.

This selection effect is apparent since under no fault for property laws on average women marry when they are significantly older than are women in fault states. This work thus provides an explanation for the observed apparent convergence in divorce rates between fault and no-fault states over the last 20 years. It presents a consistent interpretation for the argument that the effects of unilateral divorce laws on divorce rates died out a decade after their introduction. The results also expand on . . . [those scholars] who found that couples married under unilateral divorce regimes are less likely to divorce than those married under mutual consent regimes, all else being equal, despite living in a state with a more liberal regime, which reinforces the theory of selection into marriage. . . .

Eleanor Brown, Naomi Cahn & June Carbone

The Price of Exit
99 Wash. U. L. Rev. 1, 4-6 (2022)

Today, in the aftermath of liberalized divorce and greater ability to enter into intimate relationships of choice, the terms of exit from intimate relationships remain critical to values associated with autonomy and gender equality. The legal cost of exit from an intimate relationship — the expense and inconvenience of the proceedings, the possibility of being subject to continuing financial obligations, and the risk of loss of control over children or assets — influences the way that differing communities approach family formation; . . . [that is,] the consequences of exit from an intimate relationship affect the willingness to enter various types of relationships in the first place.

The connections between entry and exit reinforce each other. . . .

The modal (that is, the most common) committed intimate bargain is one in which the parties intermingle their lives, based on principles of interdependence, reciprocity, and equal respect. These committed relationships can take one of two forms. The first type pairs a higher earning (typically, but today not inevitably, a man) with a lower-earning spouse who assumes responsibility for the family's nonmarket activities. The second involves two-earner households in which the parties trade off responsibilities for work and family as circumstances change. At the core of these arrangements, whether inside or outside of marriage, is an implicit bargain that makes sense: the combination of the parties' joint efforts in both market and nonmarket investments that create interdependence and a payoff in terms of the accumulation of wealth and investment in the well-being of the next generation. A higher price of exit, whether in terms of shared ownership of family assets, barriers to divorce, or simply a higher implicit price in the form of shared custody rights, accordingly reflects not only the couple's commitment to each other, but the vulnerability that arises from interdependence.

The modal contingent relationship, in contrast, is one in which the parties cohabit, raise children together, or share an intimate relationship without either a long-term commitment to each other or economic interdependence. In many communities, couples organize their relationships to ensure subsistence; they may move in together to save on rent or to make it easier to care for a joint child. And in a world where employment has become less secure and income more volatile, the idea of a reliable single "breadwinner" has disappeared. Instead, many families depend on both parties' incomes, or one party may both earn the more reliable income and assume the primary responsibility for the family's care work, with the other playing a lesser role in each sphere. The implicit bargain reflecting these realities is contingent rather than committed, that is, the partners have not emotionally or practically made an unqualified commitment to each other to stay together. They are less likely to commingle their limited resources, assume equal childcare responsibility, or forego opportunities for individual advancement in reliance on the other partner's earnings.

In the context of these relationships, easier access to exit is critical for the party taking greater responsibility for dependents. Shared ownership and shared custody imposed from without not only increase the cost of exit; they remake the underlying bargain in ways that undercut support for caretaking.

NOTES AND QUESTIONS

1. Both passages above address the relationship between divorce terms and marriage patterns. Are the explanations consistent or inconsistent?

Both articles view no-fault divorce as changing the terms of marriage. Professor Mechoulan suggests that homemakers were most disadvantaged by the changes, and that, in pure no-fault states, couples tended to marry later and to marry partners more like themselves (sociologists call this "assortative mating.") *See* Christine R. Schwartz, Trends and Variation in Assortative Mating: Causes and Consequences, 39 Ann. Rev. Soc. 451, 460 (2013). Why might these changes produce lower divorce rates than younger marriages between couples who are less alike in terms of education or earning capacity?

Professors Brown, Cahn and Carbone argue that "higher costs of exit" involve not just the expense and inconvenience of divorce but also governing legal doctrines that define and dictate marital property and shared custody. In a world where employment is less secure and family roles less rigidly assigned by gender, committed relationships depend on "interdependence, reciprocity, and equal respect." This may make couples less willing to marry, particularly if marrying means losing control of their assets in a relationship when they do not trust their partner to make equal contributions. The big difference is between couples willing to make an unqualified commitment to each other and those who are unwilling to do so. How might this affect marriage and divorce rates?

2. One of the factors that affects divorce rates is the changing role of women. Professors Brinig and Allen found in 2000 that women initiated two-thirds of all divorces, and a factor that affected women's willingness to file was custody: women who feared losing their children were less likely to initiate a divorce. Margaret F. Brinig & Douglas W. Allen, "These Boots Are Made for Walking": Why Most Divorce Filers Are Women, 2 Am. L. & Econ. Rev. 126, 128 tbl. 1, 136-137 (2000). Might these considerations also affect willingness to marry?

3. A cohort of scholars and practitioners argues for divorce education, often coupled with a waiting period, that provides information and sometimes counseling to couples who file for divorce. Some studies report that couples going through divorce find the programs helpful, particularly in resolving custody disputes more amicably, but there is little evidence that they reduce divorce rates. *See, e.g.*, Stephanie R. deLusé & Sanford L. Braver, A Rigorous Quasi-Experimental Design to Evaluate the Causal Effect of a Mandatory Divorce Education Program, 53 Fam. Ct. Rev. 66 (2015) (reporting that 46 states have divorce education programs and that they tend to increase the visitation time of noncustodial parents). For alternative systems promoting reconciliation, *see* Solangel Maldonado, Facilitating Forgiveness and Reconciliation in "Good Enough" Marriages, 13 Pepp. Disp. Resol. L.J. 105 (2013).

Professor William Doherty and Leah Ward Sears, a former justice of the Georgia Supreme Court, have proposed combining a waiting period of a year with required participation in a marriage dissolution program for couples with children. William J. Doherty & Leah Ward Sears, Inst. for Am. Values, Second Chances: A Proposal to Reduce Unnecessary Divorce (2011), available at chrome-extension://efaidnbmnnnibpcajpcglclefindmkaj/https://media1.razorplanet.com/share/511538-7984/siteDocs/second%20chances.pdf (last visited Nov. 5, 2022).

Professor Doherty's earlier research indicates that among samples of divorcing couples, one in four individual parents indicated some belief that their marriage could still be saved, and, in about one in nine matched couples, both partners did. Men tended to be more interested in reconciliation services than women, and the partner who had not initiated the divorce tended to be much more interested than the one who did. William J. Doherty et al., Interest in Marital Reconciliation Among Divorcing Parents, 49 Fam. Ct. Rev. 313 (2011). Doherty and Sears propose designing programs that target the minority of couples who express interest in reconciliation at the outset of the divorce process.

What population is likely to benefit most from such proposals?

4. Family court judges have pioneered other proposals for reform. They observe that over the past several decades marital dissolutions proceedings, post-judgment hearings, and domestic violence proceedings have all increased, producing overcrowded dockets and a backlog of cases. In addition, they report "a drastic increase in the number of self-represented litigants (SRLs)" that now approaches 80 percent of divorce litigants. Hon. Lynda B. Munro (Ret.) et al., Administrative Divorce Trends and Implications, 50 Fam. L.Q. 427 (2016). To remedy the situation, some judges have streamlined divorced procedures. These proposals would allow divorcing couples who meet certain requirements, such as the ability to design parenting plans on their own, to employ streamlined procedures that would be faster, less expensive, and rely to a much greater degree on voluntary settlements with less public involvement of any kind. *Id.* at 428.

5. Some scholars believe that the expense and inconvenience of divorce influences decisions to marry. Miller and colleagues report that about half of their sample expressed concerns about the consequences of leaving a marriage. They found, in particular, that:

> Working-class cohabitors — particularly the women — were more than twice as likely to express concerns regarding how hard marriage was to exit than were middle-class respondents, emphasizing the legal and financial challenges of unraveling a marriage, rather than the social and emotional ramifications or difficulties for children. At least some divorce concerns might be more salient, then, for the working class, as marriage may really be more difficult to exit given their lower incomes. This reality may encourage lower-income individuals with divorce fears to delay or avoid marriage, not only because of the difficulty of paying for the wedding but also because of the financial realities of disentangling the union in the future should things go wrong.

Amanda J. Miller et al., The Specter of Divorce: Views from Working- and Middle-Class Cohabitors, 60 Fam. Rel. 602, 613 (2011). Why might working-class women be more concerned about divorce than working-class men? How might adoption of simplified divorce procedures affect these perceptions?

CHAPTER 6

PROPERTY DIVISION AND SPOUSAL SUPPORT

A. OVERVIEW

This chapter and Chapters 7 and 8 concern orders that courts use to allocate the economic rights and obligations of parents and former spouses. This chapter covers property division and spousal support (also called alimony or maintenance) at the time of divorce. Chapter 7 concerns initial child support orders. Chapter 8 deals with modification, termination, and enforcement of support orders and the federal income tax and bankruptcy treatment of obligations.

As we will see, there is debate about the extent to which the justifications and criteria for making these awards differ. Regardless, courts and lawyers always consider the relationship among these orders to arrive at a complete picture of the post-divorce economic circumstances of former spouses and their children. On the other hand, practicality also dictates distinguishing and labeling these orders because very important "collateral" consequences—an order's modifiability and terminability or its tax and bankruptcy consequences—turn on these distinctions. Property division orders are not modifiable, but support orders are. Property division and child support have no income tax consequences, while spousal support is deductible to the payor and income to the payee if it was ordered before 2019. Support is not dischargeable in bankruptcy, while property division obligations sometimes are.

These issues are the stuff of which a large portion of domestic relations practice is made. This reason alone justifies extended treatment of them. But determination of the economic consequences of divorce is not merely the point at which theoretical and principled understandings about the nature of the family and family law are practically implemented. When courts and legislatures decide what constitutes property and how it should be divided, when and why spousal support is required, and how to divide financial obligations to children between parents who no longer live in the same household, they reexamine fundamental questions about what constitutes a "family," and why and how family membership changes a person's rights and duties.

1. Historical Justifications of and Criteria for Economic Awards

A commonly told story of changes in the law of property division and support over the last century assumes that before the no-fault revolution the law sharply distinguished property from support orders. Property was supposed to have been awarded to the spouse who owned it during marriage, and support orders carried the entire burden of providing for dependent women and children. Moreover, the fault theory of divorce shaped the availability of support, for a wife[1] found at fault was not entitled to alimony and was likely to lose custody of the children and so not be entitled to support for them either. As fault-based divorce covertly turned into consensual divorce, according to this story, the presence or absence of formal grounds became bargaining tools used to shape the economic consequences.

Neither the law nor the reality was ever this simple. In some jurisdictions at some times the criteria for property division were not sharply distinct from those for spousal and child support, and scholarly articles written in the early twentieth century debated whether "alimony" was in the nature of support or property division. F. Granville Munson, Some Aspects of the Nature of Permanent Alimony, 16 Colum. L. Rev. 217 (1916). *See also* Chester G. Vernier & John B. Hurlbut, The Historical Background of Alimony Law and Its Present Structure, 6 Law & Contemp. Probs. 197 (1939). Nor were property awards based solely on simple assessments of who owned what during marriage:

> In the nineteenth century, a property settlement apparently was awarded to the wife under the same theory that ongoing support or alimony would be awarded today (i.e., for future needs), rather than as a division of the accumulated assets of the marriage. The legal profession termed this property settlement "alimony," but because the word often was used rather indiscriminately, authority existed for the proposition that "alimony" was meant to include maintenance not only for the wife but also for those children committed to her custody.

Donna Schuele, Origins and Development of the Law of Parental Child Support, 27 J. Fam. L. 807, 827 (1988-1989).

It is commonly believed that equitable distribution arose in common law property states only in the latter half of the twentieth century, and that community property states do not permit equitable distribution. In fact, a few common law property states have provided for equitable distribution since the nineteenth century. *See, e.g.*, Gen. Stat. Kan. §4756 (1889); 43 Okla. Stat. Ann. §121(B) (2017) (enacted in 1893). These statutes are discussed in Comment, The Development of Sharing Principles in Common Law Property States, 28 UCLA L. Rev. 1269, 1294-1299 (1981). By the early twentieth century, statutes in all the community property states except Louisiana empowered divorce courts to divide community property "equitably." Harriet S. Daggett, Division of Property upon Dissolution of Marriage, 6 Law & Contemp. Probs. 225, 231 (1930), citing McKay, Community Property 39 et seq. (1910). However, today more community property states require title-based distribution, as described in Section B of this chapter.

Thus, the criteria for and purposes of the various types of economic orders in fault-based divorce law overlapped, at least in some jurisdictions, just as they often do today. However, the demise of the fault-based system did generate a conceptual crisis for spousal support and property division orders by eliminating or limiting the effect of a finding of fault on the division of economic resources.

2. Economic Orders in the No-Fault Era

No-fault divorce policy seeks to free spouses of their relationship so that they may seek a new and more satisfying life, which may include new relationships. Given this policy, several propositions seem obvious. One is that judicial decrees should end, as far as possible, all personal and economic ties between the spouses. Second, the abandonment of fault grounds, coupled with the acceptance of gender equality, implies that both spouses should become equal and independent social and economic actors after divorce and that neither spouse should be especially burdened by the divorce decree.

---

1. Traditionally, men were not entitled to alimony. Orr v. Orr, 440 U.S. 268 (1979), excerpted in Chapter 2, held that this limitation violates equal protection.

These principles have a number of theoretical and practical implications for economic orders at divorce. Support as a "pension" for a wronged spouse is obviously inconsistent with disinterest in fault and with the goal of terminating the previous relationship.[2] Fortunately, an approach to marital property emerged along with the change to no-fault divorce that provides a vehicle for distributing wealth without long-term support. Drawing on social perceptions about the importance of work in the (unpaid) domestic economy and the legal theory of community property, during the 1970s and 1980s most legislatures and courts came to regard assets acquired during marriage as the result of the contributions of both spouses as divisible at divorce. While those contributions differ in kind and in origin, they nonetheless are important and, in some approaches, of equal value.

Understood in this way, the theory that property should be distributed according to spousal contribution, rather than according to title or beneficial ownership of specific items of wealth, does not seem controversial in principle. However, application of the theory raises a number of questions.

The first part of this chapter introduces some problems of principle and practice in connection with property distribution. Most obvious are questions about the definition and valuation of the parties' contributions to the acquisition of property. In addition, many property division statutes permit transfers of property from one spouse to the other who is dependent and needy as a qualification of the contribution theory, and spousal support is available for the same reason. A related approach provides support, but only on a limited basis, to allow a spouse who lacks education and training an opportunity to acquire skills. While the need of the would-be recipient is usually apparent, the reason for requiring the former spouse to provide for that need is not clear in a no-fault world. One answer that has developed is to regard support orders at least partially as compensation for contributions to the family. This, in turn, raises questions about how to define and quantify need, as well as raising again the value of nonmonetary contributions.

Finally, the changing nature of wealth adds more complications. Until relatively recently, the principal forms of wealth were tangible or intangible property (such as houses or stocks). However, the most important forms of wealth for many modern families produce streams of income that replace or supplement earned income, such as pension plans and insurance. Should they be regarded as property that is divisible in the same way that more traditional assets are? If so, does dividing them conflict with the goal of ending the ties between former spouses, allowing them to start anew? The third part of this section takes up these questions.

3. Criticism of No-Fault Economics

Less than ten years after states began to adopt no-fault divorce systems, critics argued that the change had caused economic disaster for the women and children of divorce. The earliest well-known critic, Dr. Lenore Weitzman, and her colleagues, studied divorce awards and the post-divorce economic status of men, women, and children in California in the early 1970s.[3]

---

2. However, advocates of no-fault divorce did not intend or even contemplate that this change would undermine the traditional bases for economic awards. Herma Hill Kay, Equality and Difference: A Perspective on No-Fault Divorce and Its Aftermath, 56 U. Cin. L. Rev. 1, 62-63 (1987).

3. Weitzman's book, The Divorce Revolution (1985), collects and analyzes these data. Much of the work was published earlier in a series of articles, including Lenore J. Weitzman & Ruth B. Dixon, Child Custody Awards: Legal Standards and Empirical Patterns for Child Custody, Support and Visitation After Divorce, 12 U.C. Davis L. Rev. 471 (1979); Ruth B. Dixon & Lenore J. Weitzman, Evaluating the Impact of No-Fault Divorce in California, 29 Fam. Rel. 297 (1980); Lenore J. Weitzman & Ruth B. Dixon, The Alimony Myth: Does No-Fault Divorce Make a Difference?, 14 Fam. L.Q. 141 (1980); Lenore J. Weitzman, The Economics of Divorce: Social and Economic Consequences of Property, Alimony and Child Support Awards, 28 UCLA L. Rev. 1181 (1981).

Virtually no one disagrees with Weitzman's fundamental claim that, on average, women and children suffer economically after divorce.

> The short-run economic consequences of divorce are significant, particularly for women. Most studies place the magnitude of the household income drop for women in the range of 23%-40% during the year following divorce. . . . The economic consequences of divorce are comparatively modest for men. Earlier studies revealed economic gains for men, whereas a more recent analysis uncovered a slight decline. . . . Just a handful of studies follow a longer period to examine whether the economic decline is short term or long term. [Studies in 1989 and 2009] found no improvement in standard of living 5 years after divorce, whereas [a 1985 study] showed a modest improvement, overall suggesting that the negative consequences of divorce for financial well-being are long term.

I-Fen Lin & Susan L. Brown, The Economic Consequences of Gray Divorce for Women and Men, 76 J. Gerontol. B. Psychol. Sci. Soc. Sci. 2073 (2021). In 2016, 11 percent of men who had divorced within the last year lived below the poverty level, compared with 20 percent of women who had divorced within the last year, and 19 percent of the men received public assistance, compared to 28 percent of the women. U.S. Census Bureau, Number, Timing, and Duration of Marriages and Divorces: 2016 (Oct. 8, 2021), at 17.

However, the reasons for the gender disparity are disputed. Weitzman largely blamed the change from fault to no-fault divorce grounds for the poor position of women and children. This change in the law, she said, had two adverse effects. She argued that the change in grounds, from consensual to unilateral divorce (see Chapter 5), deprived women of bargaining power—that is, they could no longer extract favorable economic settlements by refusing to go along with a divorce, and no-fault divorce gave judges more discretion over economic awards, which they exercised to the disadvantage of women. Weitzman, The Divorce Revolution at 26-28, 63-66.

The bargaining hypothesis has been criticized on the basis that it incorrectly assumes that most of the people who want out of marriage are husbands and that most wives want, or are at least willing, to stay married. Marygold S. Melli, Constructing a Social Problem: The Post-Divorce Plight of Women and Children, 1986 Am. B. Found. Res. J. 759, 770-771. In fact, over time studies consistently show that wives want most of the divorces. A study based on data collected in 2015 found that women initiated the breakup of opposite-sex marriages almost 70 percent of the time. Michael J. Rosenfeld, Who Wants the Breakup? Gender and Breakup in Heterosexual Couples in Social Networks and the Life Course (Duane F. Alwain, Diane Felmlee & Derek Kreager eds. 2018).

Whether the change in divorce grounds caused or aggravated the post-divorce economic position of women and children is of more than theoretical interest. As Professor Melli observed, "[B]y assuming that the disastrous economic consequences of divorce were caused by a change in the law, The Divorce Revolution makes the problem appear to be a simple one: a few more changes in the law and the problems will be rectified. It is undoubtedly true . . . that changes in some laws may incrementally affect the economic status of divorced women and children. . . . But the consequences of divorce for those women who devote their major energies to homemaking and the children for whom they care is a problem that has long preceded the current controversies. It defies easy solution and has survived any number of divorce reforms." Melli, above, at 772.

Further, Professor Garrison points out, "[N]o divorce law can provide a standard of living for families that experience divorce that is commensurate with that enjoyed by the marital household. With increasing numbers of two-earner families, the economic disadvantage of divorce as compared to marriage will not abate and will likely grow. We can be confident that divorce will almost always occasion a decline in standard of living as compared to marriage. All that divorce law can accomplish is fair apportionment of that disadvantage." Marsha Garrison, The Economic Consequences of Divorce, 32 Fam. & Conciliation Cts. Rev. 10, 18 (1994).

Views about the extent to which care for dependent people is a private, family obligation or a public one also substantially affect judgments about how much we should try to use property division and support orders to restructure families' post-divorce lives.

As you study what the law says or should say about dividing property at the end of a marriage or marriage-like relationship and when, if ever, people should be required to help support their ex-partners, consider the following perspectives.

Susan W. Prager

Sharing Principles and the Future of Marital Property Laws
25 UCLA L. Rev. 1, 5-6, 12 (1981)

Although the views of those favoring separate property and those advocating sharing principles ultimately diverge, both stem from a concern for equality. This preoccupation with equal rights concerns may dangerously skew our vision of marital property policy questions and create a deceptive mode of analysis. The recent literature is dominated by the notion that equality is the critical, perhaps exclusive, factor in *shaping* the property rights of married people. It suggests that to the extent that there is economic inequality a sharing oriented system is required. When inequality is not present, a system based on individual rights is appropriate.

While it is certainly true that in recent years sharing principles have been advanced because of the economic inequalities created by the traditional marriage, it is questionable whether once those inequalities disappear the need for sharing principles will vanish as well. As long as marriage and other similar close personal relationships continue to reflect sharing behavior, there is a place for sharing principles in marital property law. Marital sharing principles are not dependent upon a social structure in which one or the other spouse relinquishes the earner role. Rather the need for the sharing philosophy stems from the dynamics of marriage and similar relationships.

. . . In marriage most of us seek an alliance with another individual who will believe in us, be loyal to us, help us function in a demanding, often hostile world, and who will help make life satisfying. In exchange we will try to do the same. In many senses these needs and the expectations they create shape the frame of mind with which decisions are made during marriage. The expectation of stability and continuity and the desire for a shared life suggest that married people are unlikely to make decisions on an individually oriented basis; rather the needs of each person tend to be taken into account. Thus married people will often make decisions differently than they would if there were no marriage or marriage-like relationship functioning. . . .

. . . The choice of a separate property system may reflect the judgment that, regardless of how the spouses actually make choices, from a societal viewpoint their decisions *ought* to be made on an individual basis. Thus, the marital property law becomes a tool of social engineering, designed to encourage independence. A separate property system encourages each person to function as an earner by refusing to compensate a spouse who remains in the home for some significant period.

The absence of sharing principles can thus be used to discourage the establishment of dependency relationships. But if many couples in fact make decisions with the special exigencies of the marital relationship in mind, a system of property law which assumes decisions ought to be made on an individual basis may produce two quite different ill effects. First, one spouse may ultimately be treated unfairly if the couple does not alter its behavior to conform to the individualistic orientation of the separate property model. Second, if behavior is indeed responsive to a legal structure which dictates putting oneself first, other social values will suffer. By dictating that a married person behave as if unmarried with respect to certain choices or suffer the consequences of subsequent property disadvantage for not doing so, the individually oriented model works to reward self-interested choices which can be detrimental to the continuation of the marriage. At the same time it punishes conduct of accommodation and compromise so important to furthering and preserving the relationship. From a social engineering standpoint, an individualistic property system will begin to produce behavior that is at cross-purposes with other values, such as stability and cooperation in marital relationships.

J. Thomas Oldham

Putting Asunder in the 1990s
80 Cal. L. Rev. 1091, 1125-1126 (1992)

Divorce reform is still struggling to respond to the increasing practice of serial marriage in American society. Most divorcing spouses eventually remarry. Indeed, one argument advanced in support of no-fault divorce was that people should be able to establish a happy domestic life; if a first marriage appeared to be a mistake, the spouses should be free to dissolve the first union and initiate another.

Obviously, such a policy is not unrelated to the post-divorce economic problems of women and children. Many divorcing families already are in a difficult economic situation. Once the divorced father remarries, particularly if he establishes a new family, his connections with the first family will probably diminish. . . .

What posture should divorce law take toward the divorced father? Should he be encouraged to remarry, should substantial barriers to remarriage be created, or should the law be neutral? If the father remarries, this may affect his inclination and ability to provide resources to his former spouse and his children. Many, myself included, would find it unfair to burden unduly the noncustodial parent's ability to remarry. Thus, the challenge for the no-fault divorce system is whether it can adequately provide for the custodial parent and the children without placing unreasonable burdens upon the ex-husband's remarriage options. Satisfying both of these goals may require the talents of the magicians Penn and Teller. Many divorcing families already are pressed financially before they divorce. Maintaining two households frequently is quite difficult, even before a divorcing spouse contemplates establishing a new relationship.

It must be recognized that divorce normally will be a financial hardship for both spouses as well as for the children. Marital roles will change and probably become more onerous for most custodial parents, at least until they remarry; this is unfortunate, but given current American family policy it seems inevitable. About 60% of married women living with their spouse work outside the home. In contrast, about 75% of divorced women are in the work force. It is unrealistic to suggest that a divorcing housewife should not be "forced . . . to play multiple roles against her will after the marriage ends." One must strike a fair balance between a desire to use private law to compensate women for roles assumed during marriage and the concern about unduly burdening men's remarriage prospects.

June Carbone & Naomi Cahn

Nonmarriage
76 Md. L. Rev. 55, 80 (2016)

. . . The laws that apply to marriage adopt a single coherent view of what the institution should be. Today, these laws reinforce marriage as a relationship between equals premised on unqualified commitment, interdependence, and shared parenting.

Spouses no longer vow to love, honor, and obey. Instead, they agree to trust, honor, and cooperate. This change in the nature of marriage accordingly frames both judicial divisions at divorce and couples' decisions to marry or to not marry. In addition, while the law permits individual marital contracting, it does not hesitate to address the normative core of marriage as an institution. This normative vision enshrines the equal status of the spouses. . . .

. . . Until the mid-twentieth century, state and federal law imposed clearly-delineated gender roles within marriage. The husband alone had a duty of support and, during the marriage, he unilaterally controlled not only his own income, upon which the family typically depended, but also the couples' jointly-held property. These legally enforced roles made wives dependent on their husbands and, correspondingly, made it practically as well as legally difficult to leave a marriage. Over the last half-century, Supreme Court and state law reforms have remade marriage in accordance with principles of equality, giving both spouses joint decisionmaking authority over assets and children and dividing both more equally at divorce. The result has changed marriage from a structure that fostered dependency based on rigidly-defined gender roles to an interdependent union that requires greater cooperation and coordination between the couple. . . .

The movements towards marriage as a system of formal equality between two spouses, who to a much greater degree today can choose to enter and leave marriage on terms of their choosing, have fundamentally shifted the legal regulation of marriage. Marriage has come to mean the agreement of the spouses to assume joint and equal responsibility for their financial affairs and any resulting children—a meaning reinforced by property, parentage, and custody laws. . . .

These changes have reshaped marriage. Today, it has become a union for the financially stable and mature. The husband no longer solely generates the family income with the legal authority to determine how it will be spent; instead, both spouses have the obligation to support each other and the need to cooperate in managing the family's assets. . . .

. . . This remaking of marriage along principles of equality does not allow spouses complete freedom to tailor the terms of marriage to their preferences. . . . Marriage remains an institution whose content comes from strong social and legal norms, not just from the agreement of the spouses.

B. PROPERTY DIVISION AT DIVORCE

In all states, the steps in dividing property at divorce are the same. The first is to determine which property is subject to the court's dispositional authority under state law. Then the property is valued, and the court allocates the divisible property between the spouses according to the governing legal principles. The final order implements the decisions and may provide who gets exactly what assets. The most important issues in principle are those that determine which property is divisible and in what shares. States can be divided into three groups based on how they resolve these issues. A key variable that distinguishes these three systems is the amount of discretion available to the judge.

Title-Based Distribution. Under this type of system, courts have little or no express discretion over property division, since the governing principle is that property is awarded to the spouses as they owned it during the marriage. Thus, distribution at divorce depends on the principles of property ownership discussed in Chapter 2. In a common law property jurisdiction using a pure title system, the spouse in whose name property was titled would receive it at divorce, subject to any equitable claims of the other spouse discussed in Chapter 2. A court in a community property jurisdiction using a pure title system would award separate property to the owner and divide the community property equally.

Today, no common law property state relies on title-based distribution. It is used in a limited form in California, Louisiana, and New Mexico, the three community property states that mandate equal division of community property with very few exceptions and require that separate property be awarded to the spouse who owned it during marriage. Cal. Fam. Code §2550 (2022); La. Civ. Code Ann. art. 1290, 1308, 2336, 2341, 2341.1 (2022); Michelson v. Michelson, 520 P.2d 263, 266 (N.M. 1974). Where community property must be divided equally, division in kind is generally not required. *See, e.g.*, In re Marriage of Fink, 603 P.2d 881 (Cal. 1980).

Pure Equitable Distribution. This type of system is at the opposite end of the discretion spectrum, for the judge has discretion to divide all the property of both spouses as is "just and proper" or through some equivalent formula. Despite the similarity in terminology, "equitable distribution" is very different from the "equitable ownership" principles we examined in Chapter 2. Determining who is the equitable owner of property during marriage is critical to implementing a title-based system of divorce property division, since the equitable owner will prevail over a titleholder who is not the equitable owner. In a state that mandates equitable distribution of all property, which spouse owned property legally or equitably during marriage may be relevant but is not determinative of who will get it at divorce. In 2020 Alaska, Arkansas, Connecticut, Hawaii, Indiana, Iowa, Kansas, Massachusetts, Michigan, Minnesota, New Hampshire, North Dakota, Ohio, Oregon, South Dakota, Utah, Vermont, Wisconsin, and Wyoming allowed courts to divide all the parties' property equitably. Family Law Quarterly Editorial Staff, Charts 2020: Family Law in the Fifty States, D.C., and Puerto Rico, Part 2, 55 Fam. L. Q. 211, 214 Chart 5 (2022). In some of these states, however, property is still characterized as marital or separate, and ordinarily only marital property is divided.

Equitable Distribution of Marital or Community Property. This system gives judges more discretion over property division at divorce than does a title system, but less than an equitable distribution system, and it has become the system most commonly used in this country. In most of the community property states—Arizona, Idaho, Nevada, Texas, Washington, and Wisconsin—equitable rather than equal division of community property is mandated. In addition, most common law property states have gone to a form of a "deferred marital property," which was first fully developed in the Nordic countries. In 2020 the common law states using this system were Alabama, Colorado, Delaware, D.C., Florida, Georgia, Illinois, Kentucky, Maine, Maryland, Minnesota, Mississippi, Missouri, Montana, Nebraska, New Jersey, New York, North Carolina, Oklahoma, Pennsylvania, Rhode Island, South Carolina, Tennessee, West Virginia, and Virginia. Family Law Quarterly Staff, above. Under this system, as long as the marriage lasts, each spouse owns and manages assets that he or she brings into or acquires during the marriage. But when the marriage ends, the assets are shared as if they had been acquired in a community property state.

The Uniform Marriage and Divorce Act set out alternative approaches to what property is subject to division and on what basis.

UNIFORM MARRIAGE AND DIVORCE ACT §307
Alternative A (for Common Law Property States)

(a) In a proceeding for dissolution of a marriage . . . the court, without regard to marital misconduct, shall . . . finally equitably apportion between the parties the property and assets belonging to either or both however and whenever acquired, and whether the title thereto is in the name of the husband or wife or both. In making apportionment the court shall consider the duration of the marriage, any prior marriage of either party, any antenuptial agreement of the parties, the age, health, station, occupation, amounts and sources of income, vocational skills, employability, estate, liabilities, and needs of each of the parties, custodial provisions, whether the apportionment is in lieu of or in addition to maintenance, and the opportunity of each for future acquisition of capital assets and income. The court shall also consider the contribution or dissipation of each party in the acquisition, preservation, depreciation, or appreciation in value of the respective estates, and the contribution of a spouse as a homemaker or to the family unit.

Alternative B (for Community Property States)

In a proceeding for dissolution of the marriage . . . the court shall assign each spouse's separate property to that spouse. It also shall divide community property, without regard to marital misconduct, in just proportions after considering all relevant factors including:

(1) contribution of each spouse to acquisition of the marital property, including contribution of a spouse as homemaker;

(2) value of the property set apart to each spouse;

(3) duration of the marriage; and

(4) economic circumstances of each spouse when the division of property is to become effective, including the desirability of awarding the family home or the right to live therein for a reasonable period to the spouse having custody of any children.

NOTES AND QUESTIONS

1. As originally drafted, Section 307 of the Uniform Marriage and Divorce Act (UMDA) did not provide different rules for common law and community property states. Instead, like Alternative B, it provided that spouses receive their separate property and that the marital property was to be divided "without regard to marital misconduct, in such proportions as the court deems just after considering" all the factors listed in Alternative B except the duration of the marriage. The original version defined "marital property" as "all property acquired by either spouse subsequent to the marriage" except (1) property acquired by gift, bequest, devise, or descent; (2) property acquired in exchange for property acquired prior to the marriage or in exchange for property acquired by gift, bequest, devise, or descent; (3) property acquired by a spouse after a decree of legal separation; (4) property excluded by valid agreement of the parties; and (5) the increase in value of property acquired prior to the marriage.

The Family Law Section of the American Bar Association refused to support the initial version of Section 307, and the version you see above was adopted instead. However, the spirit of the original draft prevailed in the end. As described above, most common law property states now divide property into marital and nonmarital shares and allow only the former to be distributed at divorce or also allow nonmarital shares to be divided in compelling circumstances. The American Law Institute Principles of the Law of Family Dissolution also recommend this system, with the notable exception that in long-term marriages the Principles recommend that separate property gradually be converted into marital (and hence divisible) property. ALI, Principles of the Law of Family Dissolution §§4.03, 4.12 (2002).

2. A common law property state that uses the principles of property ownership described in Chapter 2 during the marriage but then provides that at divorce marital property is identified and subject to equitable distribution is called a deferred marital property system. Is such a system illogical, in that it treats spouses as economic individuals while they are married but as an economic unit when they divorce? If a spouse in a state with a deferred marital property system, seeing divorce coming, begins to give away property, perhaps to children or parents, does the other spouse have any remedy? Should the other spouse be able to avoid these transfers while the parties are still married? Should the divorce court be able to avoid them? Taking economic fault into account when dividing property can sometimes provide a partial solution, as this section discusses below.

3. Courts in common law property states have held that a statute providing for equitable distribution of property at divorce does not violate due process, even though it permits a court to award one spouse property that was owned by the other spouse during marriage. The usual explanation is that states have plenary authority to regulate marriage. *See, e.g.*, Rothman v. Rothman, 320 A.2d 496, 499, 501 (N.J. 1974). In contrast, the Arizona Supreme Court in Hatch v. Hatch, 547 P.2d 1044 (Ariz. 1976) (en banc), suggested that an unequal division of community property would violate due process except in unusual circumstances. The Texas courts have suggested that awarding one spouse's separate property to the other would violate due process. Eggemeyer v. Eggemeyer, 554 S.W.2d 137 (Tex. 1977), *appeal after remand*, 623 S.W.2d 462 (Tex. App. 1981); Cameron v. Cameron, 641 S.W.2d 210 (Tex. 1982). *See also* James R. Ratner, Distribution of Marital Assets in Community Property Jurisdictions: Equitable Doesn't Equal Equal, 72 La. L. Rev. 21, 24 (2011) (criticizing equitable distribution of community property as undermining principles of equal ownership and management of community assets from the time of acquisition and creating risk that fault will be considered).

PROBLEM

Hank and Wilma marry when both are 21. Neither brings significant assets into the marriage, and neither inherits nor is given property during the marriage. Throughout the marriage Wilma was a homemaker, and Hank was a well-paid employee who skillfully invested his excess income in stocks and bonds, always taking title in his name alone. When they divorce, their assets consist of the family home, purchased during the marriage from Hank's earnings and titled in joint tenancy, and the securities that Hank purchased.

In a common law state using a pure title system, what property would be divisible? In a community property system using a pure title system? In a common law property state that has adopted Alternative A of Section 307, what property would be subject to division? In a community property state that has adopted Alternative B? In a common law property state that has adopted the original version of Section 307?

1. The Meaning of "Equitable Distribution"

Most states provide for equitable distribution of some or all of the parties' property. Equitable distribution statutes vary considerably in form but little in substance. Some, like UMDA Section 307 above, contain lists of factors that judges must consider, while others do not. Appellate courts often interpret the latter kind of statute as requiring consideration of factors similar to those contained in the statutory lists. Lists of factors do not provide much structure, for they do not tell judges what weight or priority to give to the factors.

What these statutes do, then, is to grant judges discretion without providing either governing principles or ultimate goals. However, as a practical matter, judges will probably adopt, consciously or unconsciously, some framework within which to make decisions, either from a sense that such a framework is necessary to ensure a measure of consistency or to achieve efficiency. And good lawyers will construct a theory of their cases based on a particular version of what "equitable distribution" means so that they can do more than simply present scattered pieces of evidence. As you study the materials that follow, consider what visions of fairness underlie the parties' and the courts' arguments.

Arneault v. Arneault
639 S.E.2d 720 (W. Va. 2006)

Davis, Chief Justice. . . . A brief synopsis of the relevant facts shows that the parties were married on July 12, 1969, and now have two adult children. The parties had been married for thirty-three years when Mr. Arneault filed for divorce on March 22, 2002. By agreement of the parties, they denominated December 20, 2002, as their date of separation. By order of the family court, the parties were granted a divorce on July 22, 2004. The parties' marital home was located in Grand Rapids, Michigan. During the marriage, Mrs. Arneault stayed home with the children until 1990, when she returned to work on a part-time basis as a teacher. In 1995, Mrs. Arneault started her own business as a counselor providing college placement and career consulting services to high school students. While there is discord as to the effort Mrs. Arneault applied to her business, there is no dispute that Mrs. Arneault's business did not generate great income.

Mr. Arneault currently holds the same job position as he did at the time of the divorce. Mr. Arneault is Chairman, President, and Chief Executive Officer of MTR Gaming Group, Inc. (hereinafter "MTR"), which owns and controls Mountaineer Park, Inc., and operates video lottery terminals. Since 1995, Mr. Arneault has worked in Chester, West Virginia, away from the marital home. Prior to the divorce, he returned to Michigan on most weekends. There is no dispute that Mr. Arneault has been responsible for MTR's great success. In return for his achievements, Mr. Arneault has received a lucrative income from MTR, as well as MTR stock. . . .

In the bifurcated case below, the family court determined that because Mr. Arneault had contributed significantly to the marital estate, a 50/50 split of the estate would be inequitable. Thus, the family court ordered that the parties' marital estate be divided 35/65, with Mr. Arneault receiving the larger share. . . . Mrs. Arneault now appeals to this Court. . . .

. . . Mrs. Arneault argues that a 50/50 split of the marital estate is appropriate, and that Mr. Arneault has not overcome the presumption of an equal division of the marital property. Conversely, Mr. Arneault avers that his contribution to the marital estate has been so substantial that it would be inequitable to require him to divide the marital estate equally. The family court accepted Mr. Arneault's argument and found that it was unjust to divide equally the vast accumulation of wealth of the marital estate. Therefore, the family court split the marital estate 35/65, and the circuit court affirmed.

In a divorce proceeding, subject to some limitations, all property is considered marital property,[4] which preference is reflected in our case law.

---

4. W. Va. Code §48-1-233 (2001) (Repl. Vol. 2004) provides as follows:

"Marital property" means:

(1) All property and earnings acquired by either spouse during a marriage, including every valuable right and interest, corporeal or incorporeal, tangible or intangible, real or personal, regardless of the form of ownership, whether legal or beneficial, whether individually held, held in trust by a third party, or whether held by the parties to the marriage in some form of co-ownership such as joint tenancy or tenancy in common, joint tenancy with the right of survivorship, or any other form of shared ownership recognized in other jurisdictions without this state, except that marital property does not include separate property as defined in section 1-238 [§48-1-238]; and

(2) The amount of any increase in value in the separate property of either of the parties to a marriage, which increase results from: (A) an expenditure of funds which are marital property, including an expenditure of such funds which reduces indebtedness against separate property, extinguishes liens, or otherwise increases the net value of separate property; or (B) work performed by either or both of the parties during the marriage. . . .

. . . The parties do not contest the lower courts' classification of the estate as marital or separate; thus, we now address the appropriate percentage of the property to be afforded to each party.

With a few exceptions, all of the parties' property constituted marital property and should have been divided equally absent some compelling reason otherwise. . . . W. Va. Code §48-7-103 (2001) (Repl. Vol. 2004), . . . provides as follows:

In the absence of a valid agreement, the court shall presume that all marital property is to be divided equally between the parties, but may alter this distribution, without regard to any attribution of fault to either party which may be alleged or proved in the course of the action, after a consideration of the following:

(1) The extent to which each party has contributed to the acquisition, preservation and maintenance, or increase in value of marital property by monetary contributions, including, but not limited to:
   (A) Employment income and other earnings; and
   (B) Funds which are separate property.
(2) The extent to which each party has contributed to the acquisition, preservation and maintenance or increase in value of marital property by monetary contributions, including, but not limited to:
   (A) Homemaker services;
   (B) Child care services;
   (C) Labor performed without compensation, or for less than adequate compensation, in a family business or other business entity in which one or both of the parties has an interest;
   (D) Labor performed in the actual maintenance or improvement of tangible marital property; and
   (E) Labor performed in the management or investment of assets which are marital property.
(3) The extent to which each party expended his or her efforts during the marriage in a manner which limited or decreased such party's income-earning ability or increased the income-earning ability of the other party, including, but not limited to:
   (A) Direct or indirect contributions by either party to the education or training of the other party which has increased the income-earning ability of such other party; and
   (B) Forgoing by either party of employment or other income-earning activity through an understanding of the parties or at the insistence of the other party.
(4) The extent to which each party, during the marriage, may have conducted himself or herself so as to dissipate or depreciate the value of the marital property of the parties: Provided, that except for a consideration of the economic consequences of conduct as provided for in this subdivision, fault or marital misconduct shall not be considered by the court in determining the proper distribution of marital property.

When the issue of the equitable distribution of the marital estate was presented to the family court judge, . . . [t]he judge explained the rationale for the unequal distribution by finding that, under the factors set forth in W. Va. Code §48-7-103, Mr. Arneault's contributions to the marital estate overwhelmed the contributions made by Mrs. Arneault. Specifically, the family court reasoned as follows:

. . . [T]his Court finds that the presumption of equal division has been rebutted. The petitioner's own overwhelming contribution as defined by §103(2)(E) and §103(1)(A) make it completely inequitable to divide the marital estate equally. . . . Were subsections 103(2)(E) and (1)(A) the only factors to be considered, the petitioner would be receiving virtually all of the marital estate. However, as [Mrs. Arneault's expert] testified, the respondent engaged in service contributions which gave the petitioner the freedom to focus on his business pursuits. Those contributions and the other factors in §103 create the respondent's entitlement to a portion of the estate. This Court believes her contributions were substantial, but not as overwhelming as the petitioner's contributions. Thus it is equitable that her share of the estate be less, although still substantial, because of her service contributions, and this Court finds equity to require that she receive thirty-five percent (35%) of the marital estate. It is proper that the petitioner must receive an adequate award for his accomplishments, and, at the same time, the respondent be properly rewarded for her contributions to the environment which permitted him to use his personal talents to amass this fortune.

In that same order, the family court further explained that

[t]he petitioner's intelligence and ability are unique to him and the development of these attributes can not [sic] be attributed equally to the petitioner and respondent, regardless of the environment which the respondent created in order to allow the petitioner to achieve the estate that has been amassed. He must be given some additional weight and credit in equitable distribution for existence of those attributes, intelligence, and abilities, which helped him achieve the marital estate currently in question. This Court looks at these personal attributes as substantial service contributions to the marital estate. . . .

In essence, it appears that the family court judge believed Mr. Arneault's intelligence and ability led to his great financial success, and while Mrs. Arneault's homemaking and child-rearing duties were substantial, they did not compare to Mr. Arneault's contribution to the marital estate. . . .

Significantly, we disagree with the family court's undervaluement of the contributions made to the marital estate by Mrs. Arneault. In essence, the family court found that because Mrs. Arneault's contributions were not monetary in nature, they did not count as substantially as Mr. Arneault's contributions to the marital estate. This idea is contrary to West Virginia jurisprudence. We previously have held:

Under equitable distribution, the contributions of time and effort to the married life of the couple—at home and in the workplace—are valued equally regardless of whether the parties' respective earnings have been equal. Equitable distribution contemplates that parties make their respective contributions to the married life of the parties in that expectation.

We likewise have stated that "general contributions, rather than economic contributions [a]re to be the basis for a distribution" of a marital estate. In *Raley* [v. Raley, 437 S.E.2d 770 (1993) (per curiam)] we recognized that the wife "made a significant monetary contribution to the marriage as well as many other contributions, *i.e.*, homemaker skills, in which she did not receive any sort of financial compensation." Thus, based on the value of her homemaker services, we determined that the wife was entitled to fifty percent of the investment account that was at issue before the Court.

The facts of the present case highlight how important the contributions of both parties were to the marital estate. It was conceded that Mr. Arneault and Mrs. Arneault did not have any unusual fortune at the time of their marriage. Mrs. Arneault had recently received an undergraduate degree, and Mr. Arneault earned his undergraduate degree soon after they married. Mrs. Arneault then earned a master's degree, while Mr. Arneault went on to obtain his CPA license and a master's degree in business administration. The family court found that Mr. Arneault's innate abilities led to the financial wealth of the marital estate. However, the facts illustrate that the opposite is more probable. Mr. Arneault and Mrs. Arneault entered the marriage on fairly equal levels. Mr. Arneault earned a professional license and a graduate degree after the marriage commenced. It is very conceivable that this accumulation of knowledge, after the commencement of the marriage, led to the development of Mr. Arneault's innate abilities.

Even though Mrs. Arneault also had an advanced degree, she abandoned her own career in order to stay home with the couple's children. She also was responsible for the majority of the housework and the maintenance of the marital residence. Her responsibilities were manifestly increased by the fact that Mr. Arneault was completely absent from the marital home during the work week, leaving Mrs. Arneault with even greater responsibilities and household duties than is normally encountered in like circumstances. Rather than the conclusion made by the family court, the facts of this case show it is more likely that Mrs. Arneault's contributions to the marriage are precisely the reason that Mr. Arneault was able to succeed in his work.

While this Court has recognized that there are circumstances in which an unequal distribution of a marital estate is appropriate, this is not one of those cases. . . .

In the present case, there is no allegation that Mrs. Arneault did anything to detract from the value of the marital estate, and no suggestion that she did anything to frivolously dispose of marital money or assets. Thus, we conclude that the family court abused its discretion in fixing a 35/65 split of the marital estate. Mr. Arneault's intelligence and financial prowess is not sufficient justification for straying from the presumption of a 50/50 split. This conclusion is especially true under facts such as these where it is clear that Mr. Arneault's success was due in large part to the contributions made to the marriage by Mrs. Arneault. Accordingly, we find that the marital estate should be split 50/50 and reverse the circuit court's contrary ruling. . . .

STARCHER, J., dissenting. . . . This marriage was *not* a standard fifty/fifty marital partnership, where Mrs. Arneault was the homemaker/support mechanism and Mr. Arneault was the income earner outside the home. Although the couple lived together prior to Mr. Arneault's success (which has resulted in this dispute over the MTR Gaming stock), the Arneaults have lived and worked in separate states for more than a decade.

Since 1995, Mrs. Arneault lived in Michigan and Mr. Arneault spent the bulk of his time in West Virginia. He returned to Michigan a few days a week, being actively involved in various activities with his children, including coaching his son's teams in various sports, such as football, wrestling, basketball, and baseball, and performing household duties, while Mrs. Arneault engaged in her counseling business. Mrs. Arneault only visited West Virginia perhaps three times in ten years. The couple's children are now both emancipated adults and Mrs. Arneault, who received her master's degree in 1971, works in her consulting business, which she has maintained on a full-time basis since 1995. There was no evidence that Mrs. Arneault's choices regarding work were compelled by Mr. Arneault or the couple's circumstances. Rather, since 1995, the couple pursued separate lives in separate states.

There is no evidence to support Mrs. Arneault's assertions that she provided substantial assistance in Mr. Arneault's success with MTR Gaming. For example, there is no evidence of record that Mrs. Arneault was a host for her husband's business functions. When Mr. Arneault accumulated the stock which is the subject of this appeal, Mrs. Arneault lived in Michigan and Mr. Arneault lived and worked in West Virginia. Other than residing in the couple's Michigan home while Mr. Arneault toiled in West Virginia, Mrs. Arneault had nothing to do with MTR Gaming, even long after the children had gone to college.

The record is also undisputed that much of MTR's success was due to Mr. Arneault's considerable efforts. The evidence was undisputed that Mr. Arneault is not merely an employee of MTR. He is president, chief executive officer, and chairman of the board of directors. He is also the spokesman and public persona of the corporation. . . . The family court found that Mr. Arneault nearly single-handedly created the gaming industry in West Virginia. Plainly, Mr. Arneault's role in the success of MTR Gaming has been remarkable.

Essentially, Mrs. Arneault makes a "community property" argument, contending that because she was Mr. Arneault's long-time wife, she is automatically entitled to one-half of the stock of a corporation that Mr. Arneault built irrespective of their relative contributions to the corporation.

West Virginia, however, is *not* a "community property" state. Rather, West Virginia is an "equitable distribution" state in which its legislature has prescribed various factors to be considered in making, not an "equal" distribution of marital property, but an "equitable" distribution, based primarily upon the parties' relative contributions. . . .

As held in the family court judge's order, Mrs. Arneault did almost nothing to refute the substantial evidence presented by Mr. Arneault which supported the thirty-five/sixty-five division of the stock. Consequently, there is a paucity of discussion in the majority opinion regarding her contributions to the marriage or the corporation.

No details are provided about Mrs. Arneault's contributions to MTR Gaming because Mrs. Arneault made no contributions to MTR Gaming. Few details are provided about Mrs. Arneault's contributions to the marital home and child rearing because third parties provided many housekeeping and childcare services, and despite Mr. Arneault's business travel, he shared the parenting duties. There is no evidence that Mrs. Arneault ever sacrificed her career for Mr. Arneault's. Instead, as was noted, Mr. Arneault's career involved great sacrifice on his part in leaving the marital residence to earn a living which allowed Mrs. Arneault to enjoy a comfortable lifestyle and to pursue her far less lucrative business interests. In contrast to the overwhelming evidence of Mr. Arneault's sacrifices, there was *no* evidence of Mrs. Arneault's sacrifices. . . .

Once a litigant, like Mr. Arneault, rebuts the presumption of equal division by demonstrating that the evidence satisfies the statutory criteria for an unequal division, the burden shifts to the other party to adduce evidence that the statutory criteria support an equal division. In this case, rather than presenting any evidence, Mrs. Arneault essentially argued and continues to argue for "judicial nullification" of the equitable distribution statute in favor of fifty/fifty presumption that can never be rebutted. Mrs. Arneault likens a marriage to a law partnership whereby both parties are entitled to share in the good fortune of the other. . . .

The West Virginia Legislature, however, has not created a "marital partnership" in which each partner, whatever their relative contributions, is always entitled to share equally in the good fortune of the other. Rather, as this Court stated in Burnside v. Burnside, 460 S.E.2d 264 (W. Va. 1995), "Thus to be equitable, the division need not be equal, but as a starting point, equality is presumptively equitable." . . .

While married to Mr. Arneault, Mrs. Arneault reaped the benefits of his success and would be a multi-millionaire under the judgment of the Circuit Court of Hancock County. It is simply inequitable for her also to receive fifty percent of the stock in light of her negligible contribution to the success of the company, merely as the result of her status as his wife. MTR is not a "lottery ticket," the cost of which was purchased with marital funds and the equal division of which would be equitable. Rather, the overwhelming evidence was that Mr. Arneault was the heart and soul of MTR and it was his extraordinary personal efforts that built the company into what it is today. . . .

What the legislature has instructed is that when the efforts of one spouse are disproportionate to the efforts of another spouse with respect to the acquisition of marital assets, the efforts of the first spouse are *not to be ignored* in the *equitable* distribution of the marital assets; otherwise, slough and neglect would prevail over industry and diligence. The family law judge recognized, based on overwhelming evidence, that Mr. Arneault's contributions to the acquisition and appreciation of the stock were so profound and unique and Mrs. Arneault's contributions were relatively negligible as to justify a relatively unequal distribution of the subject stock. . . .

There are spouses, both husbands and wives, whose contributions to the success of their spouse's businesses are more or less, particularly considering their other contributions to the marriage, such as homemaker services, equal. For those spouses, they absolutely deserve a fifty percent distribution of the value of those businesses. Where one spouse, however, as in the instant case, is so instrumental in building a business, and the other spouse's contributions are relatively insignificant, an unequal distribution of the value of that business is appropriate. Had Mrs. Arneault, in reality, served the role of "corporate spouse" that she alleges, she might be entitled to half of the value of MTR stock.

In most cases, in the ordinary circumstances of divorce — which is that neither party can afford it — a relatively strict application of the presumption of equal distribution may be more appropriate. "Let both parties suffer equally" is not an unreasonable principle. But when the "super rich" start dividing things up, and even a person with the shorter end of the stick will be "rich" after a divorce, then it is less harmful to let the equities have their way. The majority opinion is therefore additionally deficient in its discussion of equitable distribution because it pretends that the enormous wealth that Mr. Arneault has amassed through his work is just like the "house and pension and savings" that ninety-nine percent of us have. . . .

BENJAMIN, J., concurring. It has been said that "[m]otherhood is not a part time job." Yet that is precisely the sentiment the dissenters have expressed in discounting the contributions Mrs. Arneault made to the parties' marriage of 35 years — contributions which freed Mr. Arneault of his obligations to home and family and allowed him to make his weekly travels to West Virginia to develop MTR into the successful institution it is today. Because the majority properly considers Mrs. Arneault's role in maintaining the marital residence and raising the parties' children during Mr. Arneault's extensive absences and awards her equitable distribution of one-half of the marital estate in recognition of her substantial contributions to the parties' marriage, I respectfully concur with the majority's opinion in this case. . . .

NOTES AND QUESTIONS

1. Much of the reform in property division law in the last half century has focused on how to deal with couples in which one partner, usually the woman in opposite-sex families, stayed out of the labor market to work as a homemaker. In a common law property jurisdiction using the traditional title-based system of property division, a spouse who did not work outside the home throughout all or most of the marriage would ordinarily receive little or no property at divorce because homemaking was not recognized as a financial contribution to the acquisition of property. *See* Chapter 2, Section A.1. Though a homemaker might well be in great financial need after a divorce, only alimony was available to satisfy that need. An important reason that common law property states moved to equitable division of property at divorce was a changed understanding of fairness to homemakers.

Most jurisdictions today require that homemaking be considered a contribution to the acquisition of property, raising the question of how homemaking should be valued. In wrongful death suits homemaking is broken down into component jobs, and the market value of each of these jobs is determined. Under this approach, how should the components of homemaking be characterized? Many of the jobs to which a homemaker's work might be compared are very low paying. For example, should the care of young children be compared to babysitting or to teaching? Should running the household be compared to housecleaning or to managing a small business? Should the characterization vary from family to family so that a homemaker who takes care of the home is compared to a cleaning person while one who has hired help is compared to a manager? Should this method of analysis be used for purposes of property distribution at divorce?

In Marvin v. Marvin, 557 P.2d 106 (Cal. 1976), set out in Chapter 4, the California trial court on remand found that Lee Marvin's support of Michelle Marvin adequately compensated her for her services. Has the homemaker spouse similarly been adequately compensated, so that she should have no claim to property that her husband earned during the marriage? Is the spouse different from the cohabitant? If we take the view that marital support can compensate for homemaking, should living a lavish lifestyle be treated as more complete compensation than living simply?

The percentage of families in which one spouse is a full-time homemaker has declined steadily. In 1980, 49.8 percent of all wives were in the labor force. By 2021, only 5.5 percent of married couples had an unemployed member, and in 62.3 percent of families with children, both parents were employed. Bureau of Labor Statistics, Employment Characteristics of Families—2021 (2022). This change does not mean, however, that spouses devote themselves equally to career development. Especially when they have children, one spouse may work part time or take a less demanding job that allows flexibility for dealing with issues at home. Should such a spouse be regarded as making homemaker contributions?

2. How does the majority in *Arneault* determine the value of the wife's homemaking contributions? Is the legal presumption in favor of an equal division of marital property based on the assumption that the contributions of spouses are ordinarily of equal market value?

3. The *Arneault* court, like many others, analogizes marriage to a partnership. What does it mean to call marriage a partnership?

When a business partnership is dissolved and the business is ended, all the assets of the partnership are divided equally after returning the "capital investment" of each partner. Only rarely is an unequal division of the remaining assets justified. The rules in the few community property states that require return of separate property to the owner and equal division of community property produce results similar to the business partnership rules. However, when one partner carries on a business, as frequently happens, the withdrawing partner usually may choose between forcing the remaining partner(s) to buy out the partner's interest and leaving the partner's capital in the business with a right to share future profits. If property division were based on these principles, what would the typical order look like? *See* Cynthia Starnes, Divorce and the Displaced Homemaker: A Discourse on Playing with Dolls, Partnership Buyouts and Dissociation Under No-Fault, 60 U. Chi. L. Rev. 67 (1993). For criticism of analogizing marriage to a business partnership, *see* Ira Mark Ellman, The Theory of Alimony, 77 Cal. L. Rev. 1 (1989).

4. Sometimes spouses are partners in the conventional business sense, and courts may apply business law rather than family law principles to determine ownership of the business assets when the marriage and business partnership both break up. For example, the Nebraska Supreme Court held that when a husband led the wife to believe that they were partners in a business during their marriage, the lower court properly imposed a constructive trust that gave her a share of business assets titled in his name alone. If the court had applied only domestic relations principles, it would probably have been unable to give the wife much or any of the property because of a restrictive premarital agreement the parties had signed. Simons v. Simons, 978 N.W.2d 121 (Neb. 2022). The opinion also discusses cases from other jurisdictions.

5. The dissenting judge in *Arneault* suggests that in a "big money" case in which one spouse was extraordinarily successful at work, the principle of equal sharing no longer applies. Why not? Is the argument of the concurring judge satisfactory? The American cases on this issue are divided; for a discussion, *see* David N. Hofstein et al., Equitable Distribution Involving Large Marital Estates, 26 J. Am. Acad. Matrimonial Law. 311 (2014).

In England the House of Lords interpreted the English property division statute to require considerations of contribution, including homemaker contribution. It further held that an equal division of marital assets was the starting point for property division and that any departure had to be justified. In seminal cases, the court held that departure should not be common and that valid reasons include evidence that the spouses deliberately kept their assets separate when both worked or that one spouse made "special contributions" to the marriage. White v. White [2001] AC 596, Miller v. Miller, McFarlane v. McFarlane [2006] UKHL 24. English courts invoke the special contributions exception infrequently. Margaret Ryznar, All's Fair in Love and War: But What About in Divorce? The Fairness of Property Division in American and English Big Money Divorce Cases, 86 N.D. L. Rev. 115, 143-144 (2010).

The English courts borrowed the "special contributions" principle from Australian law, which emphasizes contribution as the main determinant of property division at divorce. The courts are careful to say that special contributions could be in the realm of homemaking and parenting, but the doctrine is usually applied in favor of entrepreneurial spouses who have built up substantial wealth. Patrick Parkinson, The Yardstick of Equality: Assessing Contributions in Australia and England, 19 Int'l J.L. Pol'y & Fam. 163 (2005).

6. The law in many states provides that equitable distribution should be based on each spouse's contributions to the acquisition of assets during the marriage, but that the court should also take into account the economic needs of the parties after the divorce. For example, in Pierson v. Pierson, 653 P.2d 1258 (Or. 1982), the court awarded the husband more than half of the marital assets, applying a statute that required the court to divide the couple's property

> as may be just and proper in all the circumstances. The court shall consider the contribution of a spouse as a homemaker as a contribution to the acquisition of marital assets. There is a rebuttable presumption that both spouses have contributed equally to the acquisition of property during the marriage, whether such property is jointly or separately held. . . .

The court explained its order this way:

> The equation of property division and the entitlement of a party to individually acquired property may be disturbed in order to accomplish broader purposes of a dissolution. There are social objectives as well as financial ones to be achieved and that may result in an uneven financial division. . . .
> "Dissolution of a marriage is analogous in many ways to dissolution of a partnership or other joint financial venture. . . . The analogy is not complete, however. Unlike a business dissolution, a marital dissolution often requires the achievement of certain social as well as financial objectives which may be unique to the parties. . . . For example, the parties to a long-term marriage should be awarded the resources for self-sufficient, post-dissolution life apart insofar as possible within the limitations of the capabilities and property of the parties. . . ."
> . . . The need in this case is to enable both spouses to emerge from the marriage and recommence life on a sufficient economic footing. Fortunately, there is sufficient property and income to serve that need. Where the income and property of one spouse is greater, the achievement of economic self-sufficiency of both parties is not necessarily best served by an equal division of the marital assets. In dividing the non-inherited marital assets, we therefore take into account that the wife has greater income and, because of the inheritance, greater financial resources.

653 P.2d at 1262.

Some state courts have adopted a preference for using unequal property division to satisfy need where possible. For example, in Hockema v. Hockema, 403 P.3d 1080 (Alaska 2017), the wife strongly preferred spousal support rather than real property located in another state because of the difficulties of managing property from a long distance. The trial court agreed, and the state supreme court reversed, holding that the court must make specific findings to justify awarding support rather than a larger share of the property, and the recipient spouse's wishes are not a sufficient reason.

On the other hand, some jurisdictions do not allow courts to alter property divisions resulting from a contribution analysis to account for need. For example, in Fisher v. Fisher, 278 S.W.3d 732 (Mo. App. 2009), the court reversed a trial court order awarding a wife the marital home in lieu of permanent spousal support because support orders are always modifiable if circumstances change, making an unmodifiable award of property inappropriate.

The ALI Family Dissolution Principles recommend a presumption in favor of dividing marital property equally that can be rebutted by a showing that the former spouse is entitled to compensation for reasons that would justify an award of spousal support. ALI, Principles of the Law of Family Dissolution §4.09 (2002). If need is the controlling factor in property division, a number of questions arise. As this recommendation indicates, questions about the meaning of "need" are more often raised in determining eligibility for and the amount of spousal support, and they are, accordingly, considered in the next section of this chapter.

7. In 15 states a court can consider a party's "non-economic misconduct" in determining an equitable division of property. In some of these states, only domestic violence is included in the list of factors. Family Law Quarterly Editorial Staff, Charts 2020: Family Law in the Fifty States, D.C., and Puerto Rico, Part 2, 55 Fam. L.Q. 211, 215 Chart 5 (2022). Many others, like UMDA Section 307, explicitly exclude "marital misconduct" as a factor. The others either call simply for equitable distribution or for equitable distribution with lists of factors that do not include language clearly connoting fault. Most courts today exclude marital fault as a factor in property division, and even where fault can be considered, courts often relegate it to a minor role. This approach to marital fault is consistent with public opinion, as an empirical study shows. Researchers surveyed 600 people awaiting jury service in Pima County, Arizona, and found that the great majority of them believe that marital fault should not be considered in dividing property at divorce. In even the most egregious case, where a spouse admits adultery and gives no explanation, 65 percent of the respondents said that fault should not be considered. Sanford L. Braver & Ira Mark Ellman, Citizens' Views About Fault in Property Division, 47 Fam. L.Q. 419, 423, 431 (2013). The survey also included questions designed to reveal the reasons for the respondents' judgments. Discussing the results, the authors wrote:

> . . . [T]hose with experience with divorce, or who would have more at stake in a divorce because they had more property or more income, were all more skeptical of allowing courts to consider fault, as were older and more educated respondents. Perhaps these more seasoned respondents worry that, while it might seem fair in the abstract to consider adultery, allowing its consideration in real cases would actually produce *unfair* outcomes because of problems in the judicial process. . . . This interpretation is supported by our respondents' endorsement of [statements] suggesting just such problems. The . . . statement that received the strongest endorsement — the only one with a mean rating over 5 — was that judges should not consider fault because "deciding which spouse is at fault is so subjective that the decision would just depend on which judge heard the case." That concern could apply even to cases in which the misconduct is clear (as where the adultery is admitted) because one must still decide how large a penalty to impose on the offending spouse. Penalties that fluctuated arbitrarily among cases decided by different judges would not be fair.
>
> . . . [I]t was only the simplest case — where a spouse admits adultery and offers no excuse or justification — in which unequal division received any support at all. In all the other cases, the overwhelming majority of respondents chose equal division. . . . Even most of those sympathetic to considering fault apparently concluded that in these cases they weren't prepared to put all the blame for the marital failure on either spouse. One might guess many would also worry about how well judges would do if they were given that task. Our respondents did, on average, agree with other [statements] offering such prudential reasons for not considering fault: "marital relationships are too complicated for judges to figure out" (mean of 4.85); "courts would end up spending too much time and money" (mean of 4.79); and "divorcing spouses would often end up spending too much money for lawyers and other costs required to make such claims, or to defend [against them]" (mean of 4.87). In other words, though fairness is good in concept, it may be too difficult or expensive to achieve in this context.

47 Fam. L.Q. at 433-435. The researchers found that citizens strongly favor equal division of marital assets at divorce or at the end of a long-term cohabiting relationship, regardless of whether the partners had equal or unequal earnings. Opinions did not vary with the respondents' gender, income, education, marital status, parental status, or political affiliation. Ira Mark Ellman & Sanford L. Braver, Should Marriage Matter?, in Marriage at the Crossroads 170 (Elizabeth Scott & Marsha Garrison eds., 2013).

8. Most states allow courts to consider economic misconduct when dividing property at divorce. Under statutes that do not address fault but include lists of factors, courts sometimes justify the consideration of economic fault on the basis that it pertains to the parties' contributions to the acquisition or dissipation of assets. Most courts have defined economic misconduct as one spouse's use of marital property for his or her own benefit for a purpose unrelated to the marriage after the parties have separated, or at a time where the marriage is in serious jeopardy or undergoing an irreconcilable breakdown, although some courts have held that their divorce statutes do not include this temporal limitation. Finan v. Finan, 949 A.2d 468 (Conn. 2008) (collecting and discussing cases).

Some courts require proof that the at-fault spouse intended to deprive the other of a fair share of the assets. *See, e.g.*, Gershman v. Gershman, 943 A.2d 1091 (Conn. 2008) (discussing cases from other jurisdictions). Other courts focus more on economic considerations. Taking the latter approach to determine the effect of a husband's bad investment decisions that resulted in a loss of more than $1 million, the New Hampshire Supreme Court wrote:

> The Court of Appeals of Washington has instructed its trial courts that they may consider "whose negatively productive conduct depleted the couple's assets and . . . apportion a higher debt load or fewer assets to the wasteful marital partner." In re Marriage of Williams, 927 P.2d 679, 683 (Wash. App. 1996) *review denied*, 937 P.2d 1102 (Wash. 1997). In *Williams*, the court approved the trial court's consideration of various factors to determine that the wife's gambling losses throughout the marriage did not amount to a dissipation of marital assets. The factors the trial court considered included: the amount of income the wife brought into the marriage; the nature of the conduct (the court equated legalized gambling to an "entertainment cost[ ]"); and the husband's knowledge of the wife's gambling.
>
> The Supreme Judicial Court of Massachusetts adopted a similar view in *Kittredge*: "[D]etermination whether a spouse's expenditures constitute dissipation considers them in the light of that spouse's over-all contribution, including whether the expenditures have rendered the spouse unable to support the other spouse from the much-diminished estate at the time of divorce." *Kittredge*, 803 N.E.2d at 315.
>
> We find these cases persuasive and hold that . . . to support an unequal distribution of assets due to a spouse's conduct which resulted in a diminution in value of property, a trial court must consider factors such as: conduct which contributed to the growth in value of property; the nature of the conduct; the other spouse's knowledge of the conduct; whether the conduct diminished the total marital assets to such an extent that the other spouse is unable to maintain a similar lifestyle following divorce; and any other factor the court deems relevant.
>
> There is evidence in the record before us, and the trial court found, that the respondent contributed the initial start-up funds deposited into the account from the purchase and sale of properties and businesses. The petitioner also testified that she was aware that the respondent had invested money in the stock market and that he managed the account daily. In addition, there is evidence in the record that the parties had other significant marital assets besides the stock account, and that the stock loss allowed the parties to claim a loss on their taxes, contributing to a tax credit of nearly $131,000. The record fails to show that the trial court considered these factors when it found that "the actions of [the respondent] . . . caused the diminution in value of property owned by the parties."

In re Martel, 944 A.2d 575 (N.H. 2008). For further discussion, including a comparison of the approaches to these issues in community property and common law states, *see* J. Thomas

Oldham, "Romance Without Finance Ain't Got No Chance": Development of the Doctrine of Dissipation in Equitable Distribution States, 21 J. Am. Acad. Matrimonial Law. 501 (2008).

9. Tort suits between spouses or recently divorced former spouses have become increasingly common. Most are for the intentional torts of assault or battery, but successful suits have also been brought for intentional infliction of emotional distress, tortious infliction of a venereal disease, negligence, fraud, and on miscellaneous other theories. For a review of the issues and case law, *see* Michelle L. Evans, Note: Wrongs Committed During a Marriage: The Child That No Area of the Law Wants to Adopt, 66 Wash. & Lee L. Rev. 465 (2009); Ayelet Hoffman Libson, Not My Fault: Morality and Divorce Law in the Liberal State, 93 Tul. L. Rev. 599, 615-623 (2019).

PROBLEMS

1. Theresa and Nandor lived throughout their married life in a state whose statutory and case law create a rebuttable presumption of equal division of the property and mandate that the court consider "the contributions of each spouse to the acquisition of the property, including the contribution of a spouse as homemaker." Both Theresa and Nandor worked, and they contributed roughly equal amounts of money to running the household, but Theresa has done most of the homemaker work. Is Theresa therefore entitled to more than half the property?

Nandor spent his excess earnings on "toys," and Theresa invested hers in stocks. Has Theresa contributed more to the acquisition of the stocks than has Nandor? Has Nandor committed economic waste?

2. Tanya and Jeremy were married three years ago when she was 26 and he was 38. She had just graduated from university, and he had been a sheriff's deputy for 15 years. Shortly after their wedding they moved to another state so that Tanya could attend law school. Jeremy got a job with the local police department at lower pay than he had been earning. He also had to start over at the bottom of the seniority list. She took out loans to pay for school, and after the first year she worked to help support the family. Shortly after Tanya graduated from law school, she filed for divorce. She asked the court to award each spouse the property he or she had brought into the marriage. However, the trial judge awarded almost all the assets to Jeremy; he received net assets worth $90,000, compared to her $1,000. The judge justified the award on the basis that her earning prospects far exceeded his because of her law degree and her age and that he had given up his established career in their home state to move with her for law school. Tanya appealed on the basis that the award is not equitable because it is not based on the parties' contributions to the marriage. How should Jeremy respond?

3. During a time when Betty and Walt were experiencing marital difficulties, Walt gave his son from a prior marriage a very large gift when the son graduated from high school. Betty and Walt divorced six months later. Did Walt's gift amount to "economic misconduct"?

4. Mary and Victor were married four years ago. Before the marriage Victor was a successful psychiatrist earning $50,000 a year; after they were married he quit. Mary is heir to the Johnson & Johnson fortune; she receives more than $1 million annually from a family trust. During the marriage they lived on Mary's income, and they purchased real property worth almost $4 million. At trial Mary presented convincing evidence that Victor was negotiating for her murder. The courts have previously held that the statutes embody a partnership concept of marriage for purposes of property division and that fault is not a factor to be considered in dividing the property. Can Victor's actions be considered in dividing the property?

2. Characterization of Property as Separate or Marital

In states in which only community or marital property is divisible, characterizing assets as "community/marital" or "separate/nonmarital" is crucial. Even in states that permit division of all property, the principles that underlie characterization may affect how a judge exercises discretion because these principles express commonly held beliefs about fairness and the spouses' expectations. Statutes and case law generally provide that separate property includes (1) property owned by either spouse before marriage, (2) property acquired by a spouse after the marriage by gift or inheritance, and (3) property acquired after the marriage in exchange for separate property. However, many assets cannot readily be characterized on the basis of these rules alone. For example, they do not tell us whether income produced by or the increase in value of separate property is separate or marital, whether separate property that has been mixed ("commingled") with marital property is separate or marital, or whether an asset's character has been changed or "transmuted" by a voluntary act of the owner, such as a change in title, issues with which the next case deals.

Courts in community property states, where characterization has been required for a long time, have more experience with issues of characterization than do those in common law property states. However, the resolutions that these courts have reached should not necessarily be imported into common law property states because community property rules are sometimes shaped by considerations of rights and duties of the spouses during marriage or at death. William A. Reppy, Jr., Major Events in the Evolution of American Community Property Law and Their Import to Equitable Distribution States, 23 Fam. L.Q. 163, 164-165 (1989). Texas and California almost always have different rules for resolving a characterization issue, with California's tending to increase the size of the community estate and Texas's rules tending to decrease it. The other community property states vary in which solution they choose. J. Thomas Oldham, Everything Is Bigger in Texas, Except the Community Property Estate: Must Texas Remain a Divorce Haven for the Rich?, 44 Fam. L.Q. 293, 293-294 (2010). This article considers some of the most significant issues and the community property states' solutions.

Siefert v. Siefert
973 N.E.2d 834 (Ohio App. 2012)

TIMOTHY P. CANNON, P.J. Appellant, Susan M. Siefert, appeals the September 23, 2011 judgment of the Trumbull County Court of Common Pleas, Domestic Relations Division. This court must determine whether the trial court abused its discretion in finding that appellant relinquished her separate interest in a 1992 Ford Mustang when she transferred title of the vehicle into the joint names of the parties after their marriage. . . .

The record reveals that appellant purchased the Mustang in 2001, prior to the parties' marriage. The parties testified that, after their marriage on July 13, 2002, they began restoring the vehicle. It is undisputed that the parties spent considerable time, effort, and money during the Mustang's restoration, thereby increasing its value from $7,500 to $27,200, the stipulated appraisal.

At the time of purchase, the Mustang was titled solely in appellant's name. In 2005, however, appellant transferred title of the Mustang from her name to both the parties' names, jointly, with rights of survivorship. . . .

Property is divided into two categories: marital and separate. In this case, it is undisputed that appellant purchased the Mustang prior to the parties' marriage for the sum of $7,500. Although there is evidence that appellant borrowed $500 from appellee, the record demonstrates this amount was paid back to appellee. At the time of purchase, the Mustang was titled solely in appellant's name. As the Mustang was acquired by appellant prior to the marriage, it is deemed separate property.

A spouse, however, may convert separate property to marital property through actions during the marriage. In this case, appellant transferred the title of the vehicle from her name to the parties' joint names in 2005. The trial court found that by transferring the title of the vehicle into the joint names of the parties, appellant converted any separate property claims she may have into a marital asset. As there is a lack of competent, credible evidence to support such a finding, we reverse the trial court's decision.

The most commonly-recognized method for converting separate property into marital property is through an inter vivos gift of the property from the donor spouse to the donee spouse. In Ohio, the elements of an inter vivos gift include: "(1) the intent of the donor to make an immediate gift; (2) the delivery of the property to the donee; and (3) the acceptance of the gift by the donee after the donor has relinquished control of the property." "The donee bears the burden of proving by clear and convincing evidence that the donor made an inter vivos gift."

Based on the findings of fact issued by the trial court, it appears the trial court relied solely on appellant's transfer of the title from her name to the parties' joint names in determining that appellant intended to relinquish by gift to appellee any separate interest she had in the Mustang. The trial court did not cite to any evidence other than the transfer of title; standing alone, this is insufficient to establish an inter vivos gift.

In Frederick v. Frederick, this court found:

> Under prior case law, the presence of both parties' names on a joint title may have given rise to the presumption that appellant had foregone whatever separate interest [she] had in the property by gifting fifty percent of it to appellee as marital property. Since the enactment of R.C. 3105.171 however, the presumption of a gift has been negated. . . . Rather, a trial court may make such a finding only upon an appropriate factual context.

As the donee, appellee had the burden of showing by clear and convincing evidence that appellant, the donor, made an inter vivos gift. Appellee did not provide any evidence or testimony that appellant intended to make an inter vivos gift when she transferred title of the Mustang. Appellee did submit an exhibit of the certificate of transfer of title illustrating the transfer of title. Appellee also testified this transfer was done in conjunction with the execution of the parties' wills; in the event of both of their deaths, the Mustang was to be bestowed to the Ford Motor Company. Appellant, however, gave no testimony regarding the transfer of the vehicle or the circumstances surrounding the transfer.

Appellee did not meet his evidentiary burden. The title of the Mustang in both parties' names is insufficient to establish an inter vivos gift. This is particularly true where the transfer of the asset has a potential alternate purpose, such as estate planning. Here, the evidence does not indicate that appellant intended to present an immediate possessory interest to appellee; rather, in transferring the title, appellant may simply have been planning for the disposition of the vehicle in the event of her death.

. . . This matter is remanded to the trial court for further proceedings consistent with this opinion.

DIANE V. GRENDELL, J., dissents with a Dissenting Opinion. . . . "[T]he holding of title to property by one spouse individually or by both spouses in a form of co-ownership does not determine whether the property is marital property or separate property." Although "[t]he fact that both parties['] names are on the deed is not determinative of whether the property is marital or separate, . . . such evidence may be considered on the issue."

The issue in the present case is whether there is any evidence in the record, beyond the titling of the vehicle, which supports the lower court's determination that Ms. Siefert's separate interest in the Mustang became a marital interest during the course of the marriage. Because such evidence exists, that determination should be affirmed.

In addition to being titled in the name of both parties, the Mustang's Certificate of Title contains the notation WROS, i.e., with right of survivorship. The right of survivorship, while not determinative of ownership, is evidence of a present ownership interest in each party (both Mr. and Ms. Siefert), which would pass to the other in the event of that party's death.

In connection with this right of survivorship, there was testimony that, at the time the Mustang was re-titled, the parties executed wills to ensure that if anything happened to either one or both of them, the vehicle would pass to the Ford Motor Company rather than Ms. Siefert's daughters. As Mr. Siefert testified: "we had the wills done stating that if anything happened to us, the car would go to Ford Motor Company to a museum because she said that her daughters wouldn't know what to do with it." Again, this is evidence of Ms. Siefert's donative intent, rather than merely an estate planning device. Otherwise, Ms. Siefert could have left the vehicle in her name only and devised it directly to the Ford Motor Company, i.e., there would be no need to provide for the contingency "if anything happened to us."

Lastly, the marital nature of the Mustang is evidenced by the joint effort expended by both parties to restore the vehicle and enter it at car show competitions. The lower court's uncontroverted finding was that "the majority of the restoration work performed on this vehicle was done after the parties' marriage and was done with marital money." Ms. Siefert testified that, during the marriage, they took the Mustang to car shows "together." Mr. Siefert testified that he invested his own time, money, and parts from a separately owned vehicle in the Mustang. The parties agree that Ms. Siefert purchased the Mustang prior to the marriage, in part, with money loaned by Mr. Siefert.

While none of these facts are necessarily determinative of the status of the Mustang as separate or marital property, collectively they corroborate the evidence of the vehicle's Title, and are competent and credible evidence supporting the lower court's determination, which, therefore, must be affirmed. Accordingly, I dissent.

NOTES AND QUESTIONS

1. The owner of property may change or transmute its character by a voluntary act manifesting this intent. Marital or community property can be transmuted into the separate property of one or both spouses, and separate property of one spouse can be transmuted into marital or community property or into separate property of the other spouse. In some community property states transmutation of community property into separate property requires a written agreement.

2. Perhaps the most common situation in which the transmutation issue arises is when the owner of an asset changes how it is titled. The owner of separate property may change the title to both spouses' names, as in *Siefert*, or one spouse may agree that a community asset will be titled only in the name of the other. Often the change in title is not accompanied by a clear expression of intent about whether the asset's character is changing, and the issue only arises later, when the marriage is ending. This problem is essentially the same as a problem discussed in Chapter 2: under what circumstances a change in title establishes that one spouse made a gift of property to the other. Because convincing evidence is often unavailable, many cases are decided based on who has the burden of proof on the intent issue. In *Siefert*, who had the burden? Why?

Absent a statute on point, courts tend to hold that when the owner of separate property jointly titles it, intent to transmute the asset's character is presumed. *E.g.*, Smith v. Smith, 93 S.W.3d 871 (Tenn. App. 2002). What arguments support this rule? What arguments would support a presumption that a change in title does not change the character of the asset?

3. In *Siefert* the wife argued that she added her husband's name to the title for estate planning purposes so that he would get the car if she predeceased him. This argument is commonly made by a spouse trying to prove that a jointly titled asset remained separate property. The majority and dissent disagree about the sufficiency of this evidence. Why? In a state that presumed a change in title to both names proved the intent to transmute the asset into marital property, would such evidence be enough to rebut the presumption?

4. If one spouse uses separate funds or community/marital funds to buy a gift for the other, should it be presumed that the gift is the recipient's separate property, since gifts during marriage to only one spouse are usually separate property? Or should this rule apply only to gifts from third parties? In California spousal gifts usually remain marital property, except that gifts of clothes and jewelry are separate unless they are "substantial." Other community property states do not necessarily agree. If separate property is used to make a gift, some courts say that the property is transmuted into marital property, and others say that it becomes the separate property of the other spouse. Common law property states are also divided on the effect of interspousal gifts. In some, case law or statutes say that such a gift is marital property, while in others the gift becomes the separate property of the recipient.

5. If a third party makes a gift that increases the value of community or marital property, should the gift be presumed to be community or marital as well? In a number of cases, the parents of one spouse help make the down payment or pay down the mortgage on the couple's home, and at divorce the spouse whose parents made the gift argues that the gift should be his or her separate property. In re Marriage of Krejci, 297 P.3d 1035 (Colo. App. 2013), holds that the gift is presumed to be marital property and discusses cases from New York, Florida, Illinois, Missouri, and Washington.

6. Jurisdiction-specific discussions of this topic include Sara Craig, Transmutations and the Presumption of Undue Influence: A Quagmire in Divorce Court, 25 Hastings Women's L.J. 81 (2014) (California); Matthew L. Roberts, Transmuting Mississippi's Current Transmutation Doctrines: Establishing Clear and Consistent Precedents to Property Division, 80 Miss. L.J. 709 (2010); Leslie Joan Harris, Tracing, Spousal Gifts and Rebuttable Presumptions: Puzzles of Oregon Property Division Law, 83 Or. L. Rev. 1291 (2004).

PROBLEM

Sam and Ash are divorcing, and they disagree about the character of a piece of real property that Ash inherited during the marriage. The title to the building remained in Ash's name until five years ago, when Sam and Ash applied for a loan to purchase another parcel of property. The lender required that Ash sign a quit claim deed conveying the inherited property to Sam and Ash as joint tenants. The deed was drafted by the lender, and no one explained to Ash what the legal significance of signing the deed was. The title to the inherited property has not been changed again. Sam says that the property is marital property subject to equitable distribution, while Ash says that it is separate property. What arguments should each party make?

O'Brien v. O'Brien
508 S.E.2d 300 (N.C. App. 1998)

HORTON, Judge. Plaintiff-husband and defendant-wife were married on 24 May 1975, separated on 7 August 1995, and divorced on 24 September 1996. No children were born of the marriage. Following their separation, plaintiff instituted this equitable distribution action on 28 December 1995.

The evidence before the trial court tends to show that in 1986, after receiving an inheritance from her father of approximately $163,000.00, defendant opened an investment account with Wheat First Securities. She deposited about $158,000.00 of her inheritance, as well as a $10,000.00 gift from her Aunt Mabel Dozier Stone (Aunt Mabel), into this investment account. On the advice of her broker, defendant had the investment account listed in the joint names of the parties, with a right of survivorship. From November 1986 until July 1989, the parties deposited a total of $4,550.00 of marital funds into this investment account, and withdrew $38,658.00 from the investment account for marital purposes. This investment account remained with Wheat First Securities until July 1989, at which time it was transferred to Interstate Johnson Lane when the parties' investment broker changed firms. At the time of the transfer, the investment account was valued at $138,161.00 or nearly $30,000.00 less than the initial deposit.

The investment account remained at Interstate Johnson Lane until January 1991, when it again followed the investment broker to his new position at Shearson Lehman. At the time of the transfer to Shearson Lehman, the investment account had depreciated as a result of market forces, and was valued at $119,714.00. Also, during this time Aunt Mabel was in poor health and was attempting to deplete her estate by distributing portions to her intended beneficiaries in order to avoid estate tax consequences. Therefore, Aunt Mabel made gifts to plaintiff and defendant in December 1992 and January 1993 for $10,000.00 each, for a total of $40,000.00. Along with each gift Aunt Mabel included a note describing the purpose of her gifts. The 28 December 1992 note to plaintiff read, in pertinent part, as follows:

> Dear Dick:
>   I have enclosed a check for $10,000 which is part of the inheritance I am leaving Mabel. Since the law allows only $10,000 per family member, I am sending this gift for her in your name to remove assets from my estate that would otherwise be taxed at a very high rate if left in the estate. Please deposit upon receipt.
>   Mabel D. Stone

Aunt Mabel's 15 January 1993 note contained similar language, stating that she had "enclosed a check for $10,000 which is part of the inheritance that I am leaving to Mabel." Of this $40,000.00 in gifts from Aunt Mabel, $24,990.00 was deposited into the investment account at Shearson Lehman, and $9,970.00 was used to purchase a 1993 Volvo 850 automobile for defendant.

In addition to the $24,990.00 in gift money invested in the investment account, the investment account increased in value by approximately $44,000.00 due to dividends, share reinvestment gains and market value gains. Further, approximately $6,500.00 in management fees were charged against the investment account, and $1,035.00 was withdrawn from the investment account. In May 1994, the Shearson Lehman investment account was valued at $181,452.00. The investment account remained at Shearson Lehman until May 1994, when it was transferred to Scott & Stringfellow. While the investment account was at Scott & Stringfellow, defendant received an inheritance from Aunt Mabel's estate totaling $62,841.00, of which she deposited $56,851.00 into the investment account. The investment account remained there until the parties' separation in August 1995. After hearing all of the evidence, the trial court found that the $40,000.00 in gifts from Aunt Mabel were intended to be gifts to defendant in the total amount of $40,000.00, and not gifts to plaintiff. Further, the trial court determined that other than $4,550.00 of marital funds deposited in the investment account when it was with Wheat First Security, all of which was withdrawn and spent for marital purposes, no other marital property or earnings of the parties was ever deposited to or invested in the investment account. Consequently, the trial court determined the investment account to be the separate property of defendant and not subject to distribution. In sum, the trial court found $308,465.12 of the total estate to be the separate property of defendant and $277,578.57 to be marital property. After determining that an equal division of the marital property would be equitable, the trial court awarded plaintiff $158,677.28 of the marital estate, and awarded defendant $118,901.29 of the marital estate. In addition, the trial court ordered plaintiff to pay defendant a distributive award of $19,888.00 in order to equalize the distribution. On appeal, plaintiff contends the trial court erred by (1) classifying the investment account and the gifts from Aunt Mabel as defendant's separate property rather than the marital property of the couple; . . . and (4) failing to award plaintiff an unequal distribution of the marital property and debt.

* * *

The main contention raised by plaintiff's appeal is that the trial court improperly classified the investment account as defendant's separate property. According to plaintiff, although the money used to begin the investment account was part of defendant's inheritance, the investment account should nevertheless be classified as marital property for the following reasons: (1) marital funds were commingled with the inherited funds, thus "transmuting" the investment account from separate property to marital property; (2) defendant has failed to "trace out" the $4,550.00 in marital funds which were deposited into the investment account; and (3) plaintiff actively participated with defendant in managing the investment account by making certain decisions which ultimately led to the increased value of the investment account. For purposes of clarity, we will address each of these points separately.

Before addressing plaintiff's contentions, we note that in order to determine the nature of certain property, it is helpful to consult the definitions of marital property and separate property provided in N.C. Gen. Stat. §50-20(b), which defines the terms as follows:

(1) "Marital property" means all real and personal property acquired by either spouse or both spouses during the course of the marriage and before the date of the separation of the parties, and presently owned, except property determined to be separate property . . . in accordance with subdivision (2) . . . of this subsection. . . . It is presumed that all property acquired after the date of marriage and before the date of separation is marital property except property which is separate property under subdivision (2) of this subsection. This presumption may be rebutted by the greater weight of the evidence.

(2) "Separate property" means all real and personal property acquired by a spouse before marriage or acquired by a spouse by bequest, devise, descent, or gift during the course of the marriage. . . . Property acquired in exchange for separate property shall remain separate property regardless of whether the title is in the name of the husband or wife or both and shall not be considered to be marital property unless a contrary intention is expressly stated in the conveyance. The increase in value of separate property and the income derived from separate property shall be considered separate property.

Furthermore, in cases such as this there are dual burdens of proof. First, the party seeking to classify the investment as marital property must show by the preponderance of the evidence that the property is presently owned, and was acquired by either of the spouses during the course of the marriage and before the date of separation. Thereafter, the party seeking to classify the investment account as separate property must show by the preponderance of the evidence that the property falls within the statutory definition of separate property. If both parties meet their burdens, " 'then under the statutory scheme of N.C.G.S. §50-20(b)(1) and (b)(2), the property is excepted from the definition of marital property and is, therefore, separate property.' "

A. "TRANSMUTATION" OF SEPARATE PROPERTY INTO MARITAL PROPERTY

According to plaintiff, although the initial deposit into the investment account was without question the separate property of defendant, the subsequent actions by the parties of commingling marital funds with separate funds "transmuted" the nature of the investment account from separate property to marital property. The doctrine of transmutation is well developed in Illinois, where it was first adopted by judicial decision and later by legislative enactment. Under this theory, "the affirmative act of augmenting nonmarital property by commingling it with marital property" creates a rebuttable presumption that all the property has been transmuted into marital property. In re Marriage of Smith, 86 Ill. 2d 518, 56 Ill. Dec. 693, 427 N.E.2d 1239, 1245-46 (Ill. 1981).

However, as plaintiff concedes, this Court has expressly rejected the theory of transmutation. We find, therefore, that the mere commingling of marital funds with separate funds alone does not automatically transmute the separate property into marital property.

B. "Tracing Out" of Separate Funds

Next, plaintiff contends that regardless of whether the investment account was transmuted into marital property, defendant failed to meet her burden of "tracing out" her separate property. Here, it is clear that the investment account was begun during the marriage and prior to the date of separation. However, it is equally clear that the initial deposit into the investment account was from defendant's separate property, consisting of her inheritance from her father's estate. Therefore, defendant has met her burden of establishing the separate nature of the property.

Despite the fact that defendant has met her burden of proving the separate nature of the investment account, plaintiff contends defendant must also "trace out" her separate property from the $4,550.00 of marital funds which were deposited into the investment account. However, the $4,550.00 of marital funds deposited into the investment account was the only deposit of marital funds into the investment account. Further, soon after this deposit, $38,658.00 was withdrawn from the account.

After considering this evidence, the trial court concluded that the $4,550.00 deposit of marital funds was entirely consumed by the subsequent withdrawal, such that no marital funds remained in the investment account. Since there is competent evidence in the record to support this finding, we are bound by it. Therefore, after these marital funds were removed, the only funds remaining in the investment account were separate funds. This being the case, we find that defendant has met her burden of "tracing out" her separate property.

C. Active vs. Passive Appreciation of the Investment Account

Finally, plaintiff contends that he actively participated in the management of the investment account, such that the account should be treated as marital property. It is well recognized that there is a distinction between active and passive appreciation of separate property. Active appreciation refers to financial or managerial contributions of one of the spouses to the separate property during the marriage; whereas, passive appreciation refers to enhancement of the value of separate property due solely to inflation, changing economic conditions or other such circumstances beyond the control of either spouse. Furthermore, the party seeking to establish that any appreciation of separate property is passive bears the burden of proving such by the preponderance of the evidence.

The issue of the characterization of the appreciation of investment accounts, mutual funds, and other stocks or securities, as active or passive has not been previously addressed in North Carolina. . . . Therefore, we will look to other jurisdictions for guidance.

In *Deffenbaugh*, 877 S.W.2d 186, the Missouri Court of Appeals was presented with the question of whether the appreciated value of 425 shares of a mutual fund was marital or separate property. The evidence tended to show that the shares were originally purchased with the wife's separate property. According to the husband, he regularly looked at the quarterly statements, corresponded with and spoke to the investment broker, and regularly gave advice to his wife. However, the court held that these activities "were within the purview of ordinary and usual spousal duties; and as such, did not transform the increased value of the original shares of the mutual fund into [separate] property." Further, the Missouri Court of Appeals has repeatedly held that several factors must be shown in order for a spouse to be awarded a proportionate share of the increase in value of the other spouse's separate property, including: (1) a contribution of substantial services; (2) a direct correlation between those services and the increase in value; (3) the amount of the increase in value; (4) the performance of the services during the marriage; and (5) the value of the services, lack of compensation, or inadequate compensation.

We believe that the multi-factorial approach of the Missouri Court of Appeals is consistent with the public policy considerations incorporated in our Equitable Distribution Act, and we adopt that approach. We hold, therefore, that if either or both of the spouses perform substantial services during the marriage which result in an increase in the value of an investment account, that increase is to be characterized as an active increase and classified as a marital asset. In making the determination of whether the services of a spouse are substantial, the trial court should consider, among other relevant facts and circumstances of the particular case, the following factors: (1) the nature of the investment; (2) the extent to which the investment decisions are made only by the party or parties, made by the party or parties in consultation with their investment broker, or solely made by the investment broker; (3) the frequency of contact between the investment broker and the parties; (4) whether the parties routinely made investment decisions in accordance with the recommendation of the investment broker, and the frequency with which the spouses made investment decisions contrary to the advice of the investment broker; (5) whether the spouses conducted their own research and regularly monitored the investments in their accounts, or whether they primarily relied on information supplied by the investment broker; and (6) whether the decisions or other activities, if any, made solely by the parties directly contributed to the increased value of the investment account.

Here, the trial court did not find that the actions of the spouses in jointly meeting with the wife's broker and routinely choosing between investment alternatives based on the recommendation of the investment broker rose to the level of substantial activity. The trial court determined that the defendant-wife had established by the preponderance of the evidence that any appreciation of the investment account was purely passive. After careful review, we find that the trial court's findings support its conclusions of law. Therefore, we overrule this assignment of error.

. . . Next, plaintiff contends the trial court erred by finding the two $10,000.00 checks written by Aunt Mabel to plaintiff were the separate property of defendant. In its 2 April 1997 order, the trial court made the following findings with regard to Aunt Mabel's intent:

> 14. In December [1992] and January [1993], defendant's Aunt Mabel Dozier Stone was in ill health. [Aunt Mabel] was attempting to distribute a portion of her estate to intended beneficiaries prior to her death in order to avoid estate tax consequences. In December [1992], [Aunt Mabel] wrote two $10,000 checks—one payable to defendant individually and one payable to plaintiff individually. In January [1993], [Aunt Mabel] wrote two more $10,000 checks—one to plaintiff individually and one to defendant individually. She also wrote a letter to plaintiff describing her intent and design that the checks payable to plaintiff were in fact gifts for the defendant. [Aunt Mabel's] intention in making the $40,000 in payments was to make a gift to defendant in the total amount of $40,000 and not to make any gift to plaintiff of any of said sum. . . . Plaintiff was not an object of [Aunt Mabel's] bounty or gift-giving. He was not the intended recipient of the funds being given. With regard to these checks, plaintiff was merely a conduit for [Aunt Mabel's] gift to defendant.

According to plaintiff, there was no competent evidence in the record to support this finding. Additionally, plaintiff contends that "as a matter of law the aunt's intent is irrelevant given that the aunt had to have been making a gift to [plaintiff] in order to comply with federal gift tax law."

. . . [T]he trial court's findings in this case are adequately supported by the record evidence, and these findings justify its conclusions. It is clear that plaintiff was not the object of Aunt Mabel's bounty, but was a mere conduit for the gift to defendant. As such, we overrule this assignment of error. Further, we find plaintiff's federal estate tax argument to be without merit. . . .

NOTES AND QUESTIONS

1. The statute construed in *O'Brien*, like those in many other states, creates a presumption that all property acquired during the marriage is marital. What is the effect of this presumption? What policies underlie it?

2. How did the court determine the character of the gifts from Aunt Mabel? For purposes of the federal estate and gift tax, half of these transfers were gifts to the husband. Why didn't this characterization control who owned the gifts for purposes of the O'Briens' divorce?

3. The wife in *O'Brien* deposited the money she inherited and was given into a joint account with her husband. Why didn't this change in title change the character of the asset?

4. Separate property may be mixed with marital property intentionally, as in *O'Brien,* or when a separately owned asset is brought into the marriage and is paid off or maintained with marital funds. Commingling of separate and marital property can also occur unintentionally, as when a bank account owned before marriage earns interest in a state that treats the income from separate property as marital. In either situation, the possibility arises that the commingling shows an intent to transmute the separate property into marital property or vice versa. Should commingling create a presumption in favor of transmutation? If so, in which direction?

In *Siefert* the parties restored the wife's vintage Mustang, investing marital funds and effort into the car before its title was changed. Is this commingling evidence that the wife intended to transmute the car into a marital asset?

5. The *O'Brien* court says that it rejects "the doctrine of transmutation." Since the court surely did not mean that the owner of property cannot change its character, just what was it rejecting? In a few states, property cannot be partly separate and partly marital; in these states commingling separate property with marital property automatically converts the separate property into marital property. In most states, it is legally possible to *trace* separate funds in and out of bank accounts and other property. What policy does each approach express? As discussed in *O'Brien*, the Illinois Supreme Court adopted the automatic approach in In re Marriage of Smith, 427 N.E.2d 1239 (Ill. 1981), but *Smith* was overruled by the legislature a few years later. *See* In re Marriage of Malters, 478 N.E.2d 1068 (Ill. App. 1985). *See also* Lambert v. Lambert, 367 S.E.2d 184 (Va. App. 1988).

Tracing can be quite difficult, as, for example, when separate and marital funds are mixed in a bank account and then many deposits and withdrawals are made over the years. Ordinarily, the spouse who claims to own separate property carries the burden of tracing the funds. If the spouse cannot carry this burden, commingled property will be entirely marital.

6. In all states, the increase in value of and income from marital/community property is marital/community. Thus, if the court had found that Mrs. O'Brien's gifts and inheritances had been transmuted into marital property, the increases in value of the assets purchased with them would also have been marital.

However, the court found that the inheritances and gifts remained separate property, requiring it to consider the classification of the increases in value. The governing statute in *O'Brien* said that increases in value of and income from separate property are separate property.

The husband argued, though, that the increases in value were "active" and thus marital. What is the difference between active and passive increases? Active increases are always marital; can you see why? *See also* White v. White, 937 N.W.2d 838 (Neb. 2020).

In some other common law property states, all increases in value of separate property, regardless of the reason, are treated as marital, eliminating the need to distinguish between active and passive increases.[5] However, most community property states treat passive increases in value of separate property as separate and active increases as marital.

7. If the increase in value of an asset is partly separate and partly marital, allocating the increase between the two categories can be very complex. For example, this problem could arise in a state that treats passive increases in the value of separate property as separate and active increases as marital. California case law provides the method most widely used in community property states for dealing with an increase in value of separate property that is partly active and partly passive. Two cases, Pereira v. Pereira, 103 P. 488 (Cal. 1909), and Van Camp v. Van Camp, 199 P. 885 (Cal. App. 1921), applied two different methods. Under *Pereira* a reasonable return on the separate investment is calculated and treated as separate property; the remainder of the increase in value is community property. Under *Van Camp* a fair salary for the labor of the spouse is calculated. If the spouse was paid less than this amount, the community receives enough of the increase to make up the difference, and the rest of the increase in value is separate property. While no hard and fast rules determine when each rule should be used, California case law provides that *Van Camp* should be used when the appreciation in value is primarily attributable to community efforts, and *Pereira* should be used when the primary cause is market factors and the like. In re Lopez, 113 Cal. Rptr. 58 (Cal. App. 1974).

8. The ALI Family Dissolution Principles provide that the increase in value of separate property is marital if attributable to a spouse's labor and separate if due to other causes. In mixed cases the Principles recommend an approach similar to that used in *Pereira*. ALI, Principles of the Law of Family Dissolution §§4.04, 4.05 (2002).

9. If the principal value of an asset is commingled, partly marital/community and partly separate, characterizing increases in value presents still another allocation problem. Most community property states use the "inception of title" rule, which provides that the character of an asset is determined when it is acquired (unless, of course, the owner transmutes it). Thus, property acquired as separate property remains separate property even though community property is invested in it, and vice versa. (Property has a mixed character if it is initially acquired partly with community funds and partly with separate funds.) If the asset's increase is passive, i.e., attributable to market forces, inflation, or the like, the increase in value takes the same character as the original capital investment in the asset. Thus, the separate estate owns all of the increase in value, and the community has no claim to it. If the increase in value of separate property is attributable to the investment of community funds or to the active labor of one of the spouses, the community is entitled to reimbursement for the value of the contribution. The converse is true if separate funds or labor is invested in community property.

Common law property states have not always followed this approach because of its complexity. In states that say that increases due to market forces are separate, many use the "source of funds" rule to allocate market force increases if the principal value of the asset is partly marital and partly nonmarital. Under the source of funds rule, increases in value caused by market or other passive forces are allocated proportionately according to the contributions

---

5. While Section 307 of the UMDA says that increases in value of separate property are separate, one of the reporters for the UMDA has written that the drafters had in mind assets such as bonds, which increase in value without owner effort and for which tracing and identification are easy. Robert J. Levy, An Introduction to Divorce-Property Issues, 23 Fam. L.Q. 147, 154 (1989).

of separate and marital funds to the principal. Other states grant trial courts substantial discretion to resolve the problem on a case-by-case basis.

10. In all states income produced by marital property — rents, dividends, interest, and the like — is also marital property. The states are divided, though, in their treatment of income from separate property. Four community property states — Idaho, Louisiana, Texas, and Wisconsin — treat income from separate property as community property. The other five community property states say that such income is separate property. J. Thomas Oldham, Everything Is Bigger in Texas, Except the Community Property Estate: Must Texas Remain a Divorce Haven for the Rich?, 44 Fam. L.Q. 293, 294 (2010).

Equitable distribution statutes that address this issue usually say that income from nonmarital property is nonmarital. The Comment to UMDA Section 307 says that income from nonmarital property is marital property. The ALI Family Dissolution Principles treat income from separate property as they treat appreciation in value: income is marital if attributable to a spouse's labor and separate if due to other causes. ALI Principles, above. For detailed discussion of these issues, *see* the Reporter's Note to §4.04.

11. A number of legislatures and courts have considered when a marriage ends for purposes of defining "marital property." The possibilities include:

(1) The date of separation (*see, e.g.*, Cal. Fam. Code §771 (2022); N.C. Gen. Stat. §50-20(b)(1)(2022); 23 Pa. Consol. Stat. §3501(a)(4) (2022); Deitz v. Deitz, 436 S.E.2d 463 (Va. App. 1993); In re Estate of Osicka, 461 P.2d 585 (Wash. App. 1969)).

(2) The date the petition for dissolution was filed (*see, e.g.*, Fla. Stat. §61.075(7) (2022); Sanjari v. Sanjari, 755 N.E.2d 1186, 1192 (Ind. App. 2001)).

(3) The date the decree is entered (*see, e.g.*, Askins v. Askins, 704 S.W.2d 632 (Ark. 1986); Centazzo v. Centazzo, 509 A.2d 995 (R.I. 1986)).

What are the advantages and disadvantages of each of these rules?

12. A related but different question is when property is valued for purposes of division. Most jurisdictions appear to value assets as of the date of judgment of divorce, though courts in some states have said that the date of valuation is the date of filing or the date of trial, or is to be decided case by case. Toni Hendricks, Comment: Valuation Date in Divorces: What a Difference a Date Can Make, 21 J. Am. Acad. Matrimonial Law. 747 (2008).

NOTE: CHALLENGES TO THE CLASSIFICATION REGIME — MARITAL PARTNERSHIP THEORY REVISITED

The principles explored in this section for characterizing property as marital/community or nonmarital/separate are based on the economic partnership theory of marriage: parties share the economic fruits of their labors. Under this theory, separate property is any property that does not result from the labor of either spouse during marriage. Some rules, especially the transmutation doctrine, recognize that the parties may choose what to share based on other principles. The ALI Principles of the Law of Family Dissolution modify the transmutation doctrine by adding a new rule: separate property is gradually converted to marital property as it is held over the course of the marriage. ALI Principles §4.12. The rationale for this proposal is that as the parties' lives grow together over the years, they will increasingly expect and intend to share their economic fortunes fully. Carolyn J. Frantz and Hanoch Dagan support this proposal, regarding the passage of time as a good proxy for intent. Properties of Marriage, 104 Colum. L. Rev. 75, 113-114 (2004). They add, "over time, spouses feel less need and less desire to guard against the possibility of divorce and remarriage." *Id.* at 114. However, unlike the ALI Principles, they argue that in one situation separate property should be transmuted into marital property regardless of intent—when it is used during marriage. The foundation of this proposal is their argument that marriage should be understood as an "egalitarian liberal community" and that property division rules should be based on this understanding. They explain:

> The most common example is the family home, but also included are furniture, automobiles, and other items used by the family. . . . A spouse who has lived in a family home (and quite possibly raised children in it) perceives the property as an aspect of personhood—in constitutive rather than merely instrumental terms. Furthermore, it is not only important to individual identity, but also to identity as a member of the marital community. For the spouse who owns this property separately to claim such property as her own and to treat it as such during marriage would undermine marital sharing, trust and commitment.

Id. at 116-117.

Professor Motro has developed a formula for automatically converting separate property into shareable marital or community property as the marriage lengthens. Shari Motro, Labor, Luck, and Love: Reconsidering the Sanctity of Separate Property, 102 Nw. U. L. Rev. 1623 (2008). She proposes that classification of property as separate or marital be based on the idea that marriage is "a commitment by spouses not only to labor for the unit, but also to share more broadly in the opportunities and vulnerabilities that characterize who they are financially for the duration of their union." *Id.* at 1650. She argues:

> Like the partnership theory, the proposed paradigm ensures that homemakers are compensated for their labor. But unlike the partnership theory, this approach does not impose an artificial fiction. Rather than pretending that monetary and nonmonetary contributions have the same value, the proposal matches most people's intuition that husbands' and wives' various contributions to marriage cannot and need not be compared. It also recognizes that spouses often contribute unequally at different points in their relationship as employment and health circumstances change. Indeed, in terms of labor contributed, some marriages are unequal from start to finish. The proposal embodies the notion that matrimony fuses spouses' risks and rewards regardless of their relative contributions of labor.

Id. at 1658-1659. In contrast, Professor Oldham argues that if a spouse does nothing to indicate an intent to transmute separate property into marital or community property, it is not likely that the parties both expected that the property would be shared at divorce. J. Thomas Oldham, Should Separate Property Gradually Become Community Property as a Marriage Continues?, 72 La. L. Rev. 127 (2011). If a state wants to increase the amount of shareable property for policy reasons, he suggests that income from separate property could be classified as community/marital property, that rules for sharing post-divorce income be liberalized, or both. (The latter issue is discussed later in this chapter.)

PROBLEMS

1. A substantial part of the income of Spencer, a server at a high-end restaurant, comes from tips. Are these gifts from a third party and hence separate property or wages and hence marital property?

2. On Sasha and Quincy's wedding day Sasha's father gives them $10,000. Is this Sasha's separate property or marital property? What if Quincy gives Sasha a necklace worth $5000, purchased from premarital funds? If Sasha gives Quincy a valuable painting on their fifth anniversary, purchased from marital funds, does the painting remain marital property or does it become Quincy's separate property?

3. In 2012 Wanda purchased a house, taking title in her own name. She made the down payment and mortgage payments with her own funds. When she married Henry in 2014, the equity in the house was worth $200,000. Two days after the wedding Wanda changed the title of the house to herself and Henry as joint tenants with right of survivorship, and the two began contributing equally to the mortgage payments from their earnings. The equity in the house is now worth $400,000, or $200,000 more than its value when they married. Of this $200,000, $100,000 was attributable to the payoff of principal that they made through their mortgage payments, and $100,000 was attributable to inflation and other market factors. Wanda and Henry are now divorcing. They live in a common law property state where only marital property is divisible at divorce. The statute defines "marital property" as all property acquired by either spouse subsequent to the marriage except (1) property acquired by gift, bequest, devise, or descent and (2) property acquired in exchange for property acquired prior to the marriage or in exchange for property acquired by gift, bequest, devise, or descent. The statute also provides that all property acquired by either spouse subsequent to the marriage is presumed to be marital property regardless of how it is titled and that this presumption may be overcome by showing that the property was acquired in one of the two ways listed above.

Assuming that no cases have interpreted this statute and that Wanda wants as much of the value of the house as possible to be characterized as her separate, nonmarital property, what arguments should she make? How should Henry argue that some or all of the house is marital property?

4. While Max and Riley were married and living together, Riley won the lottery. Riley took the winnings in annual installments over 20 years. If Max and Riley divorce three years later, are the remaining 17 years of payments marital property or Riley's separate property? What if Max and Riley had been living separately for two years when Riley won the lottery?

5. Before his marriage to Kathleen, John inherited a small lakeside resort from his first wife, which was and always has been titled in his name alone. He ran the resort throughout his 20-year marriage to Kathleen, and the parties lived in a house that was part of the resort. Kathleen, who worked as a nurse during the marriage, also helped run the resort. John finished paying the mortgage on the resort with money that it earned during the marriage. The parties had no children, but the wife's ten children from a former marriage lived with the parties and helped run the resort. Over the 20 years, the resort more than doubled in value from $151,000 to $398,000, in part because of market conditions and in part because of improvements that John made over the years. The parties made no attempt to keep their finances separate during the marriage, and each put inherited money, as well as their earnings, into a joint account from which all the bills for the family and for the resort were paid. John's inheritance amounted to $25,000, and Kathleen's to $90,000. The parties dispute the character of the increase in value of the resort property. In this jurisdiction, the passive increase in value of separate property remains separate. What arguments should each party make?

3. Property Division and a Cohabitation Remedy?

As we saw in Chapter 4, the number of people who live together continues to grow, and most people who marry live together for some time before the wedding. In some of these cases, the couple pools their economic resources at least to some extent long before they marry. In addition, many same-sex couples lived together and combined their assets, sometimes for years, before they were legally permitted to marry (or enter a domestic partnership or civil union, where that was possible). In either situation, when the couple divorces, the question arises whether property acquired before the marriage is divisible on some theory. In a state where all property is subject to equitable division at divorce, a court would have discretion to divide assets owned before marriage, though in some of these states the court would have to find that the case was exceptional to do so.

In a state that allows only marital or community property to be divided at divorce, property acquired during premarital cohabitation is generally not treated as divisible. However, some courts have held that property acquired "in anticipation of marriage" is marital property. McCoy v. McCoy, 2013 WL 5925900 (Tenn. App. 2013); Winer v. Winer, 575 A.2d 518 (N.J. App. 1990); In re Marriage of Altman, 530 P.2d 1012 (Colo. App. 1974); Stallings v. Stallings, 393 N.E.2d 1065 (Ill. App. 1979). *See also* Cross v. Cross, 30 S.W.3d 233, 236 (Mo. App. 2000) (debt for wedding acquired in anticipation of marriage is marital debt). In most states, however, this is a limited exception to the general rule.

An Ohio statute provides that ordinarily marital property begins to be acquired on the date of the marriage, but the court has discretion to select another date if necessary to do equity. Ohio Rev. Code Ann. §3105.171(A)(2)(b) (2022); Hornbeck v. Hornbeck, 136 N.E.3d 966 (Ohio App. 2019).

The next case considers another possible solution: when the couple breaks up, divide the marital property and also apply legal principles used for unmarried cohabitants to assets acquired before the marriage.

Thieme v. Aucoin-Thieme
151 A.3d 545 (N.J. 2016)

Justice PATTERSON delivered the opinion of the Court. . . . In this appeal, the Court construes New Jersey's equitable distribution statute, N.J.S.A. 2A:34-23(h) and -23.1, and considers the equitable remedy of a constructive trust, in the setting of a post-judgment dispute over deferred compensation.

Plaintiff Michael J. Thieme (Thieme) and defendant Bernice F. Aucoin-Thieme (Aucoin-Thieme) were briefly married after an eight-year cohabitation. Before and during the marriage, Thieme was a salaried employee of a biotechnology consulting business, International Biometrics Group (IBG). Although Thieme had no ownership interest in IBG, its principals committed in writing to compensate him for his contributions to IBG's success, in the event that they sold their company. Thieme and Aucoin-Thieme made personal and financial decisions with the expectation that if IBG were sold, Thieme would receive substantial compensation. Thieme worked long hours and traveled extensively on IBG's behalf; Aucoin-Thieme devoted her attention to their child and home and did not seek employment. IBG, however, was not sold during the parties' marriage.

When Thieme and Aucoin-Thieme divorced, they agreed upon the terms of a Property Settlement Agreement (PSA), and their assets were divided in accordance with its terms. Three months after the Family Part's entry of a judgment of divorce, IBG was sold. IBG paid Thieme $2.25 million, characterized as a "Closing Bonus" (the Closing Bonus or the Bonus), granted in compensation for his contributions to the business for more than a decade of service.

In post-judgment proceedings before a Family Part judge, Aucoin-Thieme sought a share of the Closing Bonus. After a bench trial, the trial judge ruled that Aucoin-Thieme was entitled to equitable distribution; however, the equitable distribution was limited to the portion of Thieme's Closing Bonus that was attributable to his work during the parties' marriage and excluded any share of the remainder of that compensation. The Appellate Division affirmed the trial court's determination. . . .

We first review the trial court's determination that only the portion of Thieme's Closing Bonus attributed to the work that he performed during the parties' fourteen-month marriage was subject to equitable distribution, and that the remainder of the Bonus, earned prior to the marriage, was exempt from equitable distribution.

The equitable distribution statute authorizes the Family Part to distribute assets "in all actions where a judgment of divorce, dissolution of civil union, divorce from bed and board or legal separation from a partner in a civil union couple is entered." It reflects a public policy that is "at least in part an acknowledgment 'that marriage is a shared enterprise, a joint undertaking, that in many ways [ ] is akin to a partnership.'" The statute clearly addresses the distribution of property only in the context of an action for divorce or the dissolution of a civil union. Thus, the equitable distribution statute does not govern disputes over property between parties who have cohabited but have never entered into a marriage or civil union.

The Legislature has limited the property that is subject to equitable distribution to "property, both real and personal, which was legally and beneficially acquired by them or either of them during the marriage or civil union." Although the language "during the marriage or civil union" is not defined in the statute, it is unambiguous. It is evident that the Legislature did not intend to treat property acquired during a period of cohabitation prior to a marriage or civil union as the equivalent of property acquired during that marriage or civil union, for purposes of equitable distribution. . . .

Our rejection of Aucoin-Thieme's claim for equitable distribution of the portion of the Closing Bonus allocated to the period prior to the parties' marriage does not end the inquiry. Aucoin-Thieme has also asserted claims based on equitable principles. As a remedy for alleged unjust enrichment, Aucoin-Thieme seeks a constructive trust and an allocation of a percentage of the Closing Bonus that was earned by Thieme while they cohabited prior to their marriage. . . .

To prove a claim for unjust enrichment, a party must demonstrate that the opposing party "received a benefit and that retention of that benefit without payment would be unjust." "That quasi-contract doctrine also 'requires that plaintiff show that it expected remuneration from the defendant at the time it performed or conferred a benefit on defendant and that the failure of remuneration enriched defendant beyond its contractual rights.'"

In the event that a court finds unjust enrichment, it may impose a constructive trust. That remedy has been described as "the formula through which the conscience of equity finds expression. When property has been acquired in such circumstances that the holder of the legal title may not in good conscience retain the beneficial interest, equity converts him into a trustee." Equitable remedies such as constructive trusts "are not based on the actual intent of the parties, but 'are arbitrarily imposed by the court to prevent an unjust enrichment.'" As this Court has observed, "[g]enerally all that is required to impose a constructive trust is a finding that there was some wrongful act, usually, though not limited to, fraud, mistake, undue influence, or breach of a confidential relationship, which has resulted in a transfer of property." . . .

. . . As the evidence presented at trial made clear, the prospect that Thieme would be generously compensated was a significant factor in the parties' personal and financial planning from the early stages of their relationship. Thieme and Aucoin-Thieme each relied on the expectation of deferred compensation if IBG were sold as they made important decisions for themselves and their family. . . .

Although the prospects for IBG's sale were for many years uncertain, and the company's owners were not in a position to quantify Thieme's compensation until the September 2012 sale, IBG's commitment to reward him was an important consideration in the decisions made by the parties throughout their cohabitation and marriage. Despite his grueling schedule and its impact on his family, Thieme was determined to retain his job. Although he understood Aucoin-Thieme's desire to work outside of the home, Thieme firmly opposed any suggestion that he pursue less demanding employment and take on a more active role in their daughter's care so that she could seek work outside the home. He reasoned that his work at IBG was crucial to the family's future. In short, as they planned their finances and personal lives, Thieme and Aucoin-Thieme anticipated that they might someday share in the proceeds of the company's sale.

During the parties' eight years of cohabitation, and for most of their brief marriage, Aucoin-Thieme undertook significant efforts to support Thieme's challenging career. As Thieme acknowledged, Aucoin-Thieme ably shouldered almost all of the responsibility for caring for their daughter. She maintained and repaired their homes, managed their rental properties, and paid the bills. With the exception of a brief per diem job substitute teaching at her child's preschool, Aucoin-Thieme did not pursue a career or return to school. She moved with Thieme and their daughter to Virginia to accommodate IBG's need to assign Thieme to an important contract. . . .

Indeed, Thieme himself recognized that Aucoin-Thieme's contributions to their family should be rewarded. He acknowledged Aucoin-Thieme's "great sacrifice" of her "career and educational aspirations" to care for their daughter. He committed to support her "fully." Thieme expressly recognized that his obligation to financially support Aucoin-Thieme implicated, to some extent, any compensation that he would receive in the event that IBG were sold. He assured Aucoin-Thieme that if he received an unexpected bonus, they would split that bonus, after the deduction of taxes. Thieme represented that he viewed Aucoin-Thieme's claim to share in his assets to date back to 2003, when their child was born.

Accordingly, the record supports the conclusion that Aucoin-Thieme's decision not to seek further education and employment was made, at least in part, in reliance on Thieme's financial commitment to her. Aucoin-Thieme clearly made decisions regarding her future in light of IBG's unequivocal expression of its intent to fairly compensate Thieme if it had the opportunity to do so, and Thieme's repeated representations that he would generously support her in return for her efforts on the family's behalf. Even as the parties negotiated the terms of their divorce, Thieme suggested to Aucoin-Thieme that if IBG were sold and he were afforded a portion of the proceeds, that payment would be shared with her. . . .

. . . We conclude that a decision constraining Aucoin-Thieme to the nominal share of the Closing Bonus that is authorized by the equitable distribution statute would result in unjust enrichment, and that Aucoin-Thieme has proven the elements of that equitable claim.

As a remedy, a percentage of the portion of the Closing Bonus that Thieme earned during the period in which the parties cohabited prior to their marriage should be deemed to be held by Thieme in constructive trust for Aucoin-Thieme. We make no determination as to the precise time period for which the Closing Bonus should be shared by the parties, the percentage of the Closing Bonus that should be allocated to Aucoin-Thieme to avoid unjust enrichment, or the impact of taxes imposed on Thieme by virtue of the Closing Bonus.

On remand, the court should make those determinations based on the comprehensive record presented at trial. . . .

NOTES AND QUESTIONS

1. What theory does the court use to justify imposing a constructive trust on the closing bonus?

2. How do Aucoin-Thieme's rights under the constructive trust theory differ from what her rights would be under the Ohio statute discussed before the case?

3. For a discussion of this issue and a proposed solution, *see* Allison Anna Tait, Divorce Equality, 90 Wash. L. Rev. 1245 (2015). Peter Nicolas, Backdating Marriage, 105 Calif. L. Rev. 395 (2017), addresses the legal claims that same-sex couples may make against third parties when they have been together for many years but married only a short time. These claims include rights to receive Social Security dependent benefits, immigration rights, some surviving spouse pension rights, spousal rights in a decedent's estate, and determination of legal parentage. For a proposed new remedy, "equitable marriage," *see* Michael J. Higdon, (In) Formal Marriage Equality, 89 Fordham L. Rev. 1351 (2021).

4. Choice-of-Law Issues

When spouses acquire property in one state but are divorced in another, choice-of-law problems may arise. For example, *H* and *W*, who is a homemaker, marry and live for most of their lives in a common law property state. They own $200,000 in personal property, all of which was saved from *H*'s earnings and all of which remains titled in *H*'s name alone. *H* and *W* retire to a community property state and shortly thereafter divorce. Under traditional choice-of-law principles, the court in the community property state will apply its own law to determine what property is subject to division, but it will apply the law of the state where the property was acquired to determine whether it is community or separate property. Thus, the $200,000 will be characterized as *H*'s separate property. (Remember that even in common law states that characterize property as marital or nonmarital at divorce, the common law title system described in Chapter 2 governs ownership during the marriage.) If the state in which they are living at divorce permits division only of community property, *W* will be entitled to none of the assets even though, had the couple been divorced in their original home state, the court could have awarded her some of these assets.

Legislatures in some community property states have solved this problem by enacting "quasi-community property" statutes, which provide that if property would have been community property had it been acquired in the state, it is treated as community property for purposes of property division at divorce. Cal. Fam. Code §125 (2022); Ariz. Rev. Stat. Ann. §25-318(A) (2022); Tex. Fam. Code §7.002 (2022). In the absence of such legislation, courts in some community property states have solved the problem by applying the substantive property division law of the state in which the property was acquired. Berle v. Berle, 546 P.2d 407 (Idaho 1976); Braddock v. Braddock, 542 P.2d 1060 (Nev. 1975). This approach creates difficult problems of tracing, apportionment, and determining the effect of a post-acquisition change in the law of the state in which the property was acquired.

Similar issues may arise if spouses acquire property in a community property state and are divorced in a common law property/equitable distribution state. In addition, choice-of-law issues may arise in determining whether property should be characterized as marital or community property or as separate or nonmarital property. Consider, for example, spouses who first live in a common law (or community property) state that treats income from separate property as marital property and later move to a state that treats such income as nonmarital property. Courts in most common law property states have held that the state's own laws governing characterization as well as division should apply, which eliminates problems of relating inconsistent laws of different jurisdictions. William A. Reppy, Jr., Major Events in the Evolution of American Community Property Law and Their Import to Equitable Distribution States, 23 Fam. L.Q. 163, 191 (1989).

Other articles dealing with these choice-of-law issues include J. Thomas Oldham, What If the Beckhams Move to L.A. and Divorce? Marital Property Rights of Mobile Spouses When They Divorce in the United States, 42 Fam. L.Q. 263 (2008); Eugene F. Scoles, Choice of Law in Family Property Transactions, Hague Academy, 209 Recueil des Cours 13 (1988-II); Russell J. Weintraub, Obstacles to Sensible Choice of Law for Determining Marital Rights on Divorce or in Probate: *Hanau* and the Situs Rule, 25 Hous. L. Rev. 1113 (1988).

For a discussion of jurisdiction to award property located in another state and enforcement of such orders, see Chapter 12.

5. Dividing Debts

Most divorcing people do not have much property to divide. In 2021, the median net value of household assets was $140,800. Donald Hays & Briana Sullivan, The Wealth of Households: 2020 (U.S. Census Bureau, Current Population Reports P70BR-181, 2022). The Census

Bureau reported that in 1989 two-thirds of divorced women received no property settlement.[6] For many families, divorce is at least as much a matter of dividing up the obligation to pay bills as it is dividing assets. Even though many property division statutes do not address division of debts, most courts have assumed that they have authority to allocate responsibility for paying debts.

Geldmeier v. Geldmeier
669 S.W.2d 33 (Mo. App. 1984)

REINHARD, J. . . . Husband and wife married in 1963. Their two children, Mark and Kelly, were born in 1964 and 1968, respectively. Husband, a bottler at Anheuser-Busch for the past fifteen years, was the principal breadwinner. His gross income during 1981 was $36,465.00, which included substantial overtime. Husband had worked overtime in each of the past ten years, and testified that he regularly refused overtime work offered to him.

Wife was primarily a homemaker, although she had worked as a secretary at one point during the marriage. Wife completed her master's degree in clinical psychology shortly before the parties' dissolution. Although she was seeking employment in both her chosen profession and other fields, her job search had not proven fruitful at the time of trial.

In its order, the court divided the marital property and awarded wife custody of the two children and support of $80.00 per week, per child. Maintenance was set at $100.00 per month.

On appeal, husband contends that the court "divided the marital property and debts in such a disproportionate manner that the effect of the division of the property was to award property to wife while awarding more debts than property to the husband."

The disposition of marital property is governed by §452.330 RSMo. 1982:

> The court shall set aside to each spouse his property and shall divide the marital property in such proportions as the court deems just after considering all relevant factors. . . .

The court possesses broad discretion in the division of marital property. Its division must be just and equitable, but an equitable division need not be equal. Moreover, in reviewing this matter, we are bound to sustain the trial court's order unless there is no substantial evidence to support it or it is against the weight of the evidence.

Clearly, the court in its distribution of marital property was aware of the statutory framework within which it was required to act. The marital home, valued at approximately $40,000.00, was the major asset and was encumbered by two separate notes, secured by deeds of trust, for $16,400.00 and $15,000.00. ($16,400.00 was the amount still owed on the parties' original home mortgage; the latter $15,000 was borrowed to pay marital debts.) The court awarded the marital home to wife, who had custody of the minor children. In turn, the court ordered:

> petitioner [wife] [to] execute a note and deed of trust in favor of Respondent [husband] in the amount of Seven Thousand Five Hundred ($7500.00) Dollars, with no interest, payable on the earliest happening of one of the following events: (1) The emancipation of the minor child, Kelly Ann Geldmeier. (2) The marriage of petitioner. (3) The sale of the house by petitioner.

---

6. Bureau of the Census, Child Support and Alimony: 1989 (Current Population Reports, Series P-60, No. 173), at 2 (1991). The earliest to make this point was William J. Goode, After Divorce 217 (1956). Other studies reporting similar results include Marsha Garrison, Good Intentions Gone Awry: The Impact of New York's Equitable Distribution Law upon Divorce Outcomes, 57 Brook. L. Rev. 621, 660, tbl. 9 (1991) (summarizing several studies).

In its decree the court recognized that this note represented husband's interest in the marital home.

As to the other marital property, the court awarded wife the 1973 Cutlass automobile, valued at $800.00; household furniture worth $500.00 and personal property in her possession. Husband received, in addition to his interest in the marital home, a 1974 Chevelle automobile, valued at $450.00; a $500.00 boat; his interest in the Anheuser-Busch pension plan, worth approximately $2,000.00 and including insurance plans connected with the plan; his $1,100.00 interest in a life insurance policy, with directions that the children be named as beneficiaries until their emancipation; $2,500.00 from the recent sale of stock, and the remaining value of his Anheuser-Busch stock fund, worth approximately $3,000.00.

As to the parties' outstanding debts, the court ordered wife to pay the debt to her parents; husband to pay the debt to his parents. Wife was ordered to pay the first note for $16,400.00, secured by a deed of trust, and husband the second note of $15,000.00. By implication, husband is responsible for signature and student loans totaling approximately $6,500.00, for which payments are withheld from his weekly salary. Husband was also ordered to discharge all other debts, which amounted to $600.00, and hold wife harmless.

According to husband, the net result of the property division was that he received no assets, since the debts he was ordered to pay exceeded the property he received. We recognize that, were we to total the balance sheets of each party, husband winds up with a negative balance. However, a balance sheet approach is not necessarily the just approach to distribute marital assets. Here, the court was confronted with a difficult financial situation. By its order, it sought to divide the property in such a manner that the children, placed in wife's custody, would not be wrenched from the security of the family home during their minority. The court's order that husband assume responsibility for the lion's share of outstanding marital debts is supported by the evidence, since only husband at that time possessed the ability to assume those obligations. Moreover, its order concerning the debts does not alter the fact that, consistent with §452.330, RSMo. Supp. 1982, the court set aside to husband portions of the marital property. Therefore, we can find no abuse of discretion in the court's property division.

(The concurring opinion of Karohl, P.J., is omitted.)

NOTES AND QUESTIONS

1. Most state statutes are silent on how to allocate debts at divorce, but most courts conclude that they have jurisdiction to address the issue as part of equitable distribution. Margaret M. Mahoney, The Equitable Distribution of Marital Debts, 79 UMKC L. Rev. 445, 451-452 (2010).

Among the methods discussed in the case law for dividing debts are these:

a. Equitable division of all — treat as distinct issues the division of assets and the division of debts, dividing each "equitably." Relevant factors include ability to pay, which spouse was the principal financial manager or incurred the debt, and so forth.

b. Divide debts proportionately to division of assets — treat division of assets and debts as distinct issues but allocate responsibility for debts in the same proportion that assets are awarded.

c. Total netting out — from the total value of the divisible assets subtract the total amount of divisible debts. Divide the remainder (if any).

d. Netting out of specific assets — when an asset is specifically encumbered, value the asset at the difference between its market value and the debt (sometimes expressed by saying that until the debt is paid, the asset is not yet fully acquired; at the time of divorce the asset is acquired only to the extent that it is free of debt). Some courts extend this method to include debts traceable to the acquisition of a specific asset. Other assets and debts are divided equitably. Some courts say that if an asset is worth less than the amount of the debt incurred in acquiring it, the value of that item is simply reduced to zero; the balance of the debt is not used to reduce the net value of any other item.

Which method is more consistent with a contribution theory of property division? With a need-based theory? Should the choice of theory for purposes of property division govern division of debts? *See* In re Marriage of Fonstein, 552 P.2d 1169, 1175 (Cal. 1976); *see also* Cal. Fam. Code §2622 (2022) (equal division of community debts is not required when community debts exceed community assets).

2. In most states that permit division only of marital property, only marital debts are divisible at divorce. Separate debts are the responsibility of the spouse who incurred them. However, courts that allocate marital debts on an "equitable" basis may take separate debts into account in determining ability to pay. The court in *Geldmeier* seems to have assumed that all of the debts were marital.

Rules for characterizing debts as community or separate were first developed in community property states to determine what assets creditors could reach. Generally, each spouse's separate property is liable for his or her debts, and community property is liable for community debts. The states vary in their treatment of the liability of separate property for community debts and the liability of community property for separate debts. *See* James L. Musselman, Rights of Creditors to Collect Marital Debts after Divorce in Community Property Jurisdictions, 39 Pace L. Rev. 309 (2018).

Ordinarily, a debt is marital if it was incurred for the joint benefit of the parties or in acquiring a marital asset. Some courts have applied this test to characterize debts incurred during periods of separation as marital if they were incurred to pay family living expenses. *Cf.* Alford v. Alford, 120 S.W.3d 810 (Tenn. 2003), rejecting the "joint benefit" test as confusing and difficult; marital debt defined consistently with the definition of marital property, that is, "all debts incurred by either or both spouses during the course of the marriage up to the date of the final divorce hearing." *See also* In re Marriage of Scoffield, 852 P.2d 664 (Mont. 1993); In re Marriage of Welch, 795 S.W.2d 640 (Mo. App. 1990).

3. The *Geldmeier* court allocated to each spouse debts owing to his or her parents without discussing their amount. Why?

4. An order or agreement between spouses regarding the allocation of debts does not bind creditors. Why not? *See, e.g.,* Srock v. Srock, 466 P.2d 34, 35-36 (Ariz. App. 1970). For consideration of the consequences to one spouse if the other files bankruptcy, *see* Chapter 8.

PROBLEM

Ginger and Harley have no substantial debts and have the following marital assets: equity in home — $8000, 1998 Chevrolet — $550, 2005 Dodge — $1000, furniture — $500, boat — $500, pension plan — $2000, stock and cash — $5500. Ginger's attorney proposes that Harley, the custodian of three young children, be awarded the equity in the home, the Chevrolet, and the furniture, for a total of $9050; and that Ginger receive the Dodge, the boat, the pension plan, and the stock and cash, for a total of $9000. Ginger works full time and earns $40,000 per year. Harley has a part-time job and earns approximately $600 per month. As attorney for Harley, would you accept this proposal, which gives each spouse property of substantially equal dollar value?

6. The Marital Home

The major asset in *Geldmeier* was the family home. It could have been sold to satisfy the debts, but then the children would have been displaced. Even if the parties have no substantial debts, a similar problem arises if their only significant asset is the marital home and an equitable or equal division precludes awarding full ownership of the house to the custodial parent. The *Geldmeier* court sanctioned the common practice of ordering a division of the house but not requiring its immediate sale. Courts and legislatures in some states, however, have significantly limited the authority of trial courts to delay the sale of the family home for a long period of time because of the limitations such an order places on the ability of the spouse not occupying the home to make use of his or her share.

The *Geldmeier* trial court specifically said that the husband, who did not occupy the house, was not entitled to interest on the amount representing his share of the house. Was this fair? If instead of fixing a dollar amount for the spouse who does not occupy the home, a court orders the proceeds of the future sale of the home to be divided according to some formula, the nonoccupying spouse is not ordinarily guaranteed any return.

Instead of awarding ownership of the home to one spouse, with the obligation to pay the other some amount on sale, some courts order continued joint ownership of the house with sale ordered at some future date and permit the custodial parent to remain in the house until the sale. In such cases, the court should allocate responsibility for the mortgage payments until the house is sold. If the nonoccupying spouse is ordered to pay the mortgage, half the payments might be characterized as spousal or child support.

Of course, if the spouse who receives the home does not have enough income to pay the mortgage, taxes, and upkeep, the home will have to be sold anyway.

C. SPOUSAL SUPPORT AT DIVORCE

Spousal support, maintenance, or alimony, as it was traditionally known, is politically and emotionally significant but is much less important practically. Relatively few divorced people, who historically have been women, have ever been awarded alimony, much less received it. According to Census data collected between 1887 and 1922, only 9 percent to 15 percent of divorced women were awarded alimony.[7] In 1989, the last year in which these data were collected, only 15.5 percent of divorced or separated women were awarded spousal support.[8] In 2013 the Census Bureau found that only 1.8 million people were paying support to a former spouse, up from 106,000 in 2010.[9] A major reason is many soon-to-be ex-spouses simply do not have enough income to pay spousal support.

The law of alimony was originally developed by the ecclesiastical courts as an incident of legal separation, and that law was transferred wholesale to alimony following absolute divorce. Since divorce was based on a finding of fault and only the party at fault could ordinarily be ordered to pay, traditional alimony was often described as being similar to tort or contract damages. The shift from fault-based to no-fault divorce originally left alimony in conceptual limbo.

The influential Uniform Marriage and Divorce Act, which was promulgated only three years after California adopted no-fault divorce, brought a new approach to spousal support. In general, the UMDA divorce provisions were based on the ideal of providing the parties with a clean break and a new start on life.

---

7. Lenore J. Weitzman & Ruth B. Dixon, The Alimony Myth: Does No-Fault Divorce Make a Difference?, 14 Fam. L.Q. 141, 180 (1980), citing P. Jacobson, American Marriage and Divorce 126 (1959).

8. Bureau of the Census, Child Support and Alimony: 1989 (Current Population Reports, Series P-60, No. 173) tbl. L (1991).

9. Bureau of the Census, Support Providers: 2010 tbl. 10 (June 2012); Bureau of the Census, Support Providers: 2013 2 (Dec. 2018).

Uniform Marriage and Divorce Act §308 (1973)

(a) In a proceeding for dissolution of marriage . . . the court may grant a maintenance order for either spouse only if it finds that the spouse seeking maintenance:

(1) lacks sufficient property to provide for his reasonable needs; and

(2) is unable to support himself through appropriate employment or is the custodian of a child whose condition or circumstances make it appropriate that the custodian not be required to seek employment outside the home.

(b) The maintenance order shall be in amounts and for periods of time the court deems just, without regard to marital misconduct, and after considering all relevant factors including:

(1) the financial resources of the party seeking maintenance, including marital property apportioned to him, his ability to meet his needs independently, and the extent to which a provision for support of a child living with the party includes a sum for that party as custodian;

(2) the time necessary to acquire sufficient education or training to enable the party seeking maintenance to find appropriate employment;

(3) the standard of living established during the marriage;

(4) the duration of the marriage;

(5) the age and the physical and emotional condition of the spouse seeking maintenance; and

(6) the ability of the spouse from whom maintenance is sought to meet his needs while meeting those of the spouse seeking maintenance.

Consistent with the clean break philosophy, the UMDA favored ending spousal obligations at divorce. Its preference for using property division, rather than periodic payments of spousal support, as the primary vehicle for financial settlement between spouses furthered this goal. Property division awards are final, eliminating subsequent modification problems. They do not present continuing enforcement problems (if the award calls for only one lump sum payment or transfer), and they provide financial certainty and ability to plan to both parties. However, most states do not expressly prefer property division over spousal support to satisfy the need of one spouse. Instead, like paragraph (b) of the UMDA, their spousal support statutes typically grant judges discretion in light of a list of factors. The factors vary greatly from state to state, and no state ranks the factors in order of priority. Mary Kay Kisthardt, Re-Thinking Alimony: The AAML's Considerations for Calculating Alimony, Spousal Support, or Maintenance, 21 J. Am. Acad. Matrimonial L. 61 (2008). For a survey of current judicial approaches to alimony, *see* J. Thomas Oldham, An Overview of the Rules in the USA Regarding the Award of Post-Divorce Spousal Support in 2019, 41 Houston J. Internat'l L. 525 (2019).

In the first decades after the no-fault revolution, many state courts and legislatures took the view that the purpose of a spousal support award was to enable the recipient to become self-sufficient, a goal that is, again, consistent with the clean break philosophy. Often these rules included provisions that limited the duration of support awards. *E.g.*, Robinson v. Robinson, 366 So. 2d 1210 (Fla. App. 1979); Lumsden v. Lumsden, 603 P.2d 564 (Haw. 1979); Otis v. Otis, 299 N.W.2d 114 (Minn. 1980); Turner v. Turner, 385 A.2d 1280 (N.J. App. 1978); Hedin v. Hedin, 370 N.W.2d 544 (N.D. 1985); Booth v. Booth, 354 N.W.2d 924 (S.D. 1984); Ind. Code Ann. §31-15-7-2(3) (2022) (limit of three years unless spouse or child in custody of spouse is physically or mentally incapacitated); Kan. Stat. Ann. §23-2904 (2017) (limit of 121 months, subject to reinstatement).

The clean break philosophy still dominates spousal support awards for marriages of short duration, and half of all marriages ending in divorce last less than eight years. Rose M. Kreider & Renee Ellis, Number, Timing, and Duration of Marriages and Divorces: 2009, at 15 (Current Population Reports, P70-125, U.S. Census Bureau 2011).

However, experience with the early no-fault rules showed that most divorcing people do not have enough property to provide support for dependent spouses and children, and therefore courts, commentators, and legislators revisited dividing post-divorce income between spouses, particularly at the end of a marriage that lasted 15 to 20 years or more. A California appellate court colorfully expressed this view, saying "A woman is not a breeding cow to be nurtured during her years of fecundity, then conveniently and economically converted to cheap steaks when past her prime. If a woman is able to do so, she certainly should support herself. If, however, she has spent her productive years as a housewife and mother and has missed the opportunity to compete in the job market and improve her job skills, quite often she becomes, when divorced, simply a 'displaced homemaker.'" In re Marriage of Brantner, 136 Cal. Rptr. 635, 637 (Cal. App. 1977).

This does not mean, however, that indefinite spousal support for the long-term homemaker (whose former spouse can afford to pay) is accepted without question. The following commentators discuss competing approaches to this issue.

Paula England & George Farkas

Households, Employment and Gender
44-45, 55-56 (1986)

By "human capital" economists refer to the stock of attributes in a person that can be put to use in serving some end. When that end is productivity on the job, attributes such as intelligence, strength, education, and skills are relevant. Similarly, we can think of those qualities helpful in person-to-person interaction as a form of human capital as well. These include the ability to provide empathy, companionship, sexual and intellectual pleasure, social status, or earnings. Individuals "invest" in human capital whenever they forgo something desirable in the present to develop a personal attribute which will pay off in the future, whether in a job or household relationship.

. . . [M]any of the highest-return investments within the household sector are to relationship-specific rather than general human capital. To call an investment relationship-specific means that it has value only within the current relationship, and would be of no benefit in a different one. . . . Of course, investments may be anywhere along a continuum from those useless in a new relationship to those whose benefits are completely transferable to a new relationship. . . .

Marital investments that transfer poorly to a new relationship include learning what shared leisure activities both partners enjoy, learning what division of labor is most efficient with this partner, decorating the house in a style both partners like, learning to fight and make up with this partner, learning this partner's sexual preferences, and developing relationships with in-laws. In addition, the tremendous investments of time, caring and money that parents make in children bear fruit not only in the children's futures, but also in the satisfaction parents derive from the relationship. Investment in children with one partner contributes relatively little to improving one's relationship with a new partner. . . .

. . . [M]en typically make fewer relationship-specific investments than women, accumulating instead resources which are as useful outside as within their current relationship. Thus, while both men and women work at the relationship-specific issues of learning to get along with the other person, women are usually the expressive-emotional specialists, focusing heavily on personal relationships and empathic understanding. Of course, some of these efforts are potentially useful in future relationships as well — examples include skills at listening, pleasing, and compromising. Yet much of the investment in these emotional skills is by its very nature specific to the particular relationship. In addition, women typically take the major responsibility for child rearing, heavily investing their own time for the future benefit of the children, but also for the benefit of the particular marriage. Thus women's effort is skewed toward investments which are most valuable within the particular relationship.

. . . Of course, the earnings of employed women are something they can transfer out of the relationship. . . . Yet, even women with earnings seldom earn as much as their partners. . . . Thus, whether employed outside the home or not, wives tend to accumulate fewer resources that are of value outside the current relationship.

Herma Hill Kay

Equality and Difference: A Perspective on No-Fault Divorce and Its Aftermath
56 U. Cin. L. Rev. 1, 79-85 (1987)

I asked earlier whether, in order to implement equality between the sexes, legal significance should be accorded at the dissolution of the family unit to the consequences of choices made concerning sex roles during the existence of the family relationship. It seems clear that, at least in the short run, the answer to that question must be an affirmative one. It is necessary to take steps to alleviate the situation of those women who are trapped in circumstances neither they nor their husbands anticipated, and that they cannot now avoid. . . .

In the long run, however, I do not believe that we should encourage future couples entering marriage to make choices that will be economically disabling for women, thereby perpetuating their traditional financial dependence upon men and contributing to their inequality with men at divorce. I do not mean to suggest that these choices are unjustified. For most couples, they are based on the presence of children in the family. The infant's claim to love and nurturance is a compelling one both on moral and developmental grounds. Throughout history, the choice of the mother as the primary nurturing parent has been the most common response to the infant's claim. . . . But other choices are possible. . . . Serious discussion of the possibility of shared parenting for children, and for infants in particular, as a way of achieving equality between women and men is very recent. . . .

I do not propose that the state attempt to implement this view of family life by enacting laws requiring mothers to work or mandating that fathers spend time at home with their children. But since, as I noted earlier, Anglo-American family law has traditionally reflected the social division of function by sex within marriage, it will be necessary to withdraw existing legal supports for that arrangement as a cultural norm. No sweeping new legal reforms of marriage and divorce will be required, however, to achieve this end. It will be enough, I think, to continue the present trend begun in the nineteenth century toward the emancipation of married women, and implemented more recently by gender-neutral family laws, as well as the current emphasis on sharing principles in marital property law.

Ira Mark Ellman

The Theory of Alimony
77 Cal. L. Rev. 1, 49-52 (1989)

[Alimony is intended to compensate for] the "residual" loss in earning capacity that arises from . . . economically rational marital sharing behavior. . . . This is a residual loss in the sense that it survives the marriage. . . . Nonetheless, spouses are not necessarily liable for every loss their former mate incurs. . . . The function of alimony is . . . to reallocate the postdivorce financial consequences of marriage in order to prevent distorting incentives. Because its purpose is to reallocate, it is necessarily a remedy by one spouse against the other. . . . [B]y eliminating any financial incentives or penalties that might otherwise flow from different marital lifestyles, this theory maximizes the parties' freedom to shape their marriage in accordance with their nonfinancial preferences. . . .

A system of alimony that compensates the wife who has disproportionate postmarriage losses arising from her marital investment protects marital decision-making from the potentially destructive pressures of a market that does not value marital investment as much as it values career enhancement.

J. Thomas Oldham

Putting Asunder in the 1990s
80 Cal. L. Rev. 1091, 1110-1111 (1992)

Men and women have different earning capacities for many reasons. Although some of these reasons, such as discrimination, education levels, and career choice, are not directly related to roles assumed during marriage, a general argument could be made that all of these factors indirectly stem from society's assumption that women will bear primary child care responsibilities. Discrimination based on this assumption can place women at a considerable economic disadvantage. Employers might be concerned about pregnancy or other leave time, parents might provide less encouragement or education for daughters, and women themselves might choose less "desirable" careers that can more easily accommodate child care responsibilities. . . .

Even if one accepts the view that almost all of the wage gap stems from actual or potential child care responsibilities, it does not follow that the full cost of these employment disabilities should be borne by the divorcing husband. I believe it is fair only to ask the divorcing husband to share the costs of decisions in which he participated and that some mechanism should be found that isolates the effects of decisions made during marriage. It is not fair to ask the husband to compensate the wife for all career damage she incurred on the expectation that one day she would assume child care responsibilities. Even if the husband should be responsible for such damage, a goal of post-divorce equal living standards is not justified by compensation for career damage. Individual spouses have different levels of intelligence and education and have different career interests at the time of marriage; these all would cause income inequalities for reasons largely unrelated to sex. Thus, even a very broad concept of career damage due to child care responsibilities does not justify a goal of post-divorce equal living standards.

Joan Williams

Is Coverture Dead? Beyond a New Theory of Alimony
82 Geo. L.J. 2227, 2255-2258 (1994)

Ellman's exclusive focus on reimbursing the wife for losses in her earning capacity presents two separate problems. First, his model for measuring a wife's losses omits the losses typically experienced by lower-status wives. A service-sector or pink-collar worker does not suffer the same direct decrease in earnings as the attorney who leaves the partnership track, but she may well lose opportunities and other employment benefits. Sociological studies show that working-class women who start out in "women's work" often respond to attractive job opportunities; thus, a wife who started out as a clerical worker might have ended up a machinist. Moreover, even working-class wives who reenter the workforce after divorce doing the same job they did before may have sacrificed subtler benefits. For example, informal seniority and flexibility often are granted to valued, long-term workers; these informal benefits can prove extremely important for a mother with a sick child.

Ellman's exclusive focus on *detriment* to the wife also presents a deeper problem: it ignores the *benefits* conferred upon husbands by the dominant family ecology. A wife who shoulders childrearing and other domestic responsibilities allows her husband *both* to perform as an ideal worker *and* to have his children raised according to norms of parental care that Ellman himself explicitly embraces. Husbands receive this benefit regardless of whether or not the wife has received the kind of detriment Ellman is willing to recognize.

Ellman, like other commentators, also overlooks the important fact that divorcing fathers *retain the primary benefit they garner from the domestic ecology even after the marriage has ended.* In the 90 percent of divorces in which mothers are awarded sole physical and legal custody—and even in states such as California where joint custody is favored—mothers typically remain the child's primary caretaker. Thus, even after divorce, noncustodial fathers continue to receive the benefits of the dominant family ecology: they can continue to perform as ideal workers while their children are raised according to norms of parental care. . . .

My analysis of the dominant family ecology suggests an approach to post-divorce entitlements very different from Ellman's. Ellman perpetuates the "he who earns it" rule; I consider it a holdover from coverture. Although the husband clearly owns "his" wage vis-à-vis his *employer*, this does not necessarily determine the issue of whether he owns it vis-à-vis his *family.* My analysis of the dominant family ecology suggests that the wages of the family should be jointly owned. . . . I will argue that the way to accomplish this is by equalizing the incomes of the two post-divorce households.

Twila Perry

Alimony: Race, Privilege, and Dependency in the Search for Theory
82 Geo. L.J. 2481, 2483-2484, 2513 (1994)

Statistics indicate that Black women are awarded alimony at a significantly lower rate than white women. . . . It also appears that women in higher income marriages are more likely to receive alimony than women in lower income marriages. . . .

. . . [T]he marriage paradigm that has, to a great extent, shaped the discourse on developing a theory of alimony . . . has little relevance to the realities faced by most poor women of color and . . . , accordingly, most of the approaches to alimony based on it have little practical relevance to the lives of these women. I define the issue, however, as more than one of mere irrelevance or exclusion—I argue that the search to develop a theory of alimony may have serious negative implications for poor women of color, especially Black women. Specifically, the paradigmatic model of marriage and divorce has the potential to reinforce the subordination and marginalization of Black women in two ways: first by reinforcing privilege or an image of privilege for middle- and upper-middle class white women in both marriage and divorce, and second, by reinforcing a hierarchy among women in which their value is determined by the presence or absence of legal ties to men, particularly affluent men. . . .

Although no-fault divorce has been appropriately criticized for its failure to protect women economically, it has generated one positive result. To some degree, no-fault divorce has served as an equalizer among women. In calling off the bargain that formerly ensured some women compensation for giving up their careers to care for their home, the law, since no-fault, has been sending a similar message to all women: it is not wise to depend on a man for your lifelong economic survival. The privilege of choice, that many middle- or upper-middle class women once may have taken for granted is, more than ever, in jeopardy.

Indeed, it can be said that in some ways the lives of white mothers, either as a result of divorce or because they were never married, are becoming more similar to those of Black mothers. . . . The way that no-fault divorce has pulled the rug out from under women at some of the more comfortable levels of society can be seen as an opportunity for women from different social and economic backgrounds to consider their commonalities. . . . There may be increased connection and cooperation among women of diverse backgrounds if they all see themselves as having to play the multiple roles of parent and worker, without assuming economic dependence on a man.

In re Marriage of Pazhoor
971 N.W.2d 530 (Iowa 2022)

WATERMAN, Justice. . . . Suraj George Pazhoor and Hancy Chennikkara were married in India in 2002. Hancy had graduated from medical school in India and was completing her internship. She is a registered physician in India. Suraj had graduated from medical school in Russia and completed his internship in India. He was working and volunteering in the medical field in India when they married. After about a year of living with Suraj's parents in India, the couple relocated to Naperville, Illinois, to live with Hancy's parents. The couple later moved to their own residence. At the time, Hancy worked in a bookstore and Suraj worked day shifts at a college library and night shifts at a retailer.

Both Hancy and Suraj began studying to become licensed physicians in the United States. Suraj ultimately obtained his medical license; Hancy did not. Licensure requires completion of the United States Medical Licensing Exam: a four-part test, commonly known as "the Boards." Passing the first three parts is required for residency. The fourth part is completed during residency. Upon passing part of the exam, the examinee has a limited amount of time to pass the remaining parts. Neither Suraj nor Hancy were successful on the first attempt. Suraj ultimately passed the third part and entered residency. Hancy never passed the third part. Their daughter was born in 2008. Hancy was preparing for her second attempt at the third part of the exam when she learned her father had been diagnosed with cancer. She continued to study "[b]ut the fear of failing again was overwhelming," and she never retook the exam.

Hancy used her medical degree to research and coauthor several published articles with a cardiologist, most recently in 2010. In 2012, after Suraj completed a three-year residency program at Loyola University Chicago, the couple agreed Suraj would accept a hospitalist position in Wisconsin and Hancy would care for their children and home. Their son was born in 2013 while they lived in Wisconsin. Suraj was promoted that year to serve as a director of a hospitalist fellowship program, which added to his responsibilities without an increase in his pay.

In 2016, Suraj accepted a position as a hospitalist and medical director at the Grand River Medical Group (GRMG) in Dubuque, Iowa. While Suraj focused on his career, Hancy ran the household, facilitated their moves, managed their finances, provided childcare, and focused on the children's development, education, medical care, and extracurricular activities. From 2008 to 2017, Hancy earned no income. In 2017, she began volunteering as a religious education teacher on Wednesday and Sunday nights during the school year. Suraj's income in 2018 was $500,742. The family's lifestyle in Dubuque during the marriage was largely unbudgeted and reflected Suraj's substantial income.

Suraj petitioned for divorce on August 31, 2018. In response, Hancy began earning $12 an hour, or $918 annually, as a religious education teacher (instead of volunteering). She also began working part-time, up to twenty hours a week, as a barista at a local coffee shop for $8 an hour, or $8,320 annually. After Suraj filed for divorce, Hancy interviewed for a patient advocacy position at a local hospital. She was denied that employment because her foreign medical degree did not satisfy the requirement for a nursing degree. She earns passive income from a 10% interest in two commercial real estate holding companies ($13,387 average annual income over three years) and rental income from the Naperville condo ($490 annual net income). Her total annual income from these sources is $23,115.

The court conducted a two-day trial in August of 2019. The parties agreed that Hancy should receive spousal support but disagreed on its duration and amount. . . .

Suraj was age forty-three at trial. His parents still lived in India. Suraj had earned $252,172 by August and was on track to earn $415,152 in 2019. He testified that after paying 46.5% of his income in taxes, his after-tax income is approximately $232,500 annually or $19,375 a month. Hancy was age forty at trial. Her father died ten years earlier but her mother still lived in Illinois. Because too much time had passed, Hancy would essentially have to start over the process to become licensed to practice medicine in the United States. Suraj agreed that it was too late for Hancy to take the Boards again. Hancy testified she is interested in earning a master's degree in public health, which would take two to three years to complete if she attended school full-time, assuming her credits from medical school transferred. If her credits do not transfer, she would need to complete additional undergraduate coursework. Hancy estimated she will earn up to $80,000 a year after she earns her master's. Suraj asserted that Hancy does not need additional education and could immediately return to a nonclinical role earning $100,000 to $200,000 a year. His assertions were not supported by expert testimony or other evidence.

Hancy estimated her monthly expenses to be $10,244, which included tuition for a master's program. According to Hancy's counsel, this estimate omitted "variable purchases for the children, including clothing, club membership dues, incidentals, personal grooming, laundry, allowances, life insurance, babysitting, church donations, gifts, or the ability to save for herself." Suraj testified that he overstated his monthly expenses in his financial affidavit but estimates his monthly expenses to be at least $13,118, including allocations for vacations, clothing, and other incidentals, but not including contributions to his savings. In a brief filed with the district court during trial, Suraj discussed transitional alimony citing court of appeals decisions and advocated for a transitional award.

On October 18, the district court entered its decree dissolving the seventeen-year marriage. The court ordered shared custody and physical care of their children and divided their property. Each was awarded marital property valued at $337,754, and Hancy was able to retain premarital assets totaling $136,565. Hancy retained the Naperville condo, her vehicle, some bank accounts, and a portion of the marital debt as well as her premarital investment accounts and jewelry. The court ordered Suraj to pay Hancy $143,977 as an equalization payment from the property division, $643 a month in child support, and $7,500 monthly in spousal support for five years totaling $450,000. The court found Hancy "is more than a minimum wage employee" and "is, at the very least, capable of working full time at the hourly rate of $12.00, if she chooses to do so." The court imputed income of $40,000 to Hancy, which included $24,960 in estimated wages and her passive business income, the rental income, and child support. Pursuant to the dissolution decree, a Qualified Domestic Relations Order was filed awarding Hancy a 50% interest in the balance of Suraj's GRMG retirement plan as of October 18, 2019.

Hancy filed a motion to reconsider, enlarge, or amend the district court's order. . . . The court denied her motion, and Hancy appealed.

. . . The court of appeals reversed the district court's decision to impute income to Hancy, assigned Hancy an income of $23,115, and increased the spousal support awarded to $9,000 monthly for seven years, $8,000 monthly for another three years, and $7,000 monthly for two more years, totaling $1,212,000. The decision further provided, "[If] Hancy remarries after the first seven-year period, but before expiration or satisfaction of the twelve-year spousal-support obligation, the support obligation shall terminate so long as Suraj is current on his obligations for support. In the event of the death of either party, the spousal support obligation shall terminate." . . .

Suraj sought further review of the court of appeals award of spousal support. . . . We granted Suraj's application. . . .

Our review of alimony awards is de novo. We give the district court considerable latitude and will only disturb the award "when there has been a failure to do equity." "We give weight to the factual determinations made by the district court; however, their findings are not binding upon [this Court]."

III. Analysis

We first address whether to formally recognize transitional alimony. . . . We begin with an overview of alimony law, including the governing statute and the different types of spousal support. We conclude that it is time to formally recognize transitional alimony and proceed to determine the appropriate award in this case.

"The question of whether to award alimony is a matter of discretion and not a matter of right." The decision to award alimony depends on the particular facts and circumstances of each case. ("Our prior cases are of little value in determining the appropriate alimony award, and we must decide each case on its own peculiar circumstances.") "The legislature has not authorized Iowa courts to employ any fixed or mathematical formula in applying spousal support." Instead, courts are instructed "to equitably award spousal support by considering" the criteria listed in Iowa Code section 598.21A(1) (2018) [which] provides:

> Upon every judgment of annulment, dissolution, or separate maintenance, the court may grant an order requiring support payments to either party for a limited or indefinite length of time after considering all of the following:
>   a. The length of the marriage.
>   b. The age and physical and emotional health of the parties.
>   c. The distribution of property made pursuant to section 598.21.
>   d. The educational level of each party at the time of marriage and at the time the action is commenced.
>   e. The earning capacity of the party seeking maintenance, including educational background, training, employment skills, work experience, length of absence from the job market, responsibilities for children under either an award of custody or physical care, and the time and expense necessary to acquire sufficient education or training to enable the party to find appropriate employment.
>   f. The feasibility of the party seeking maintenance becoming self-supporting at a standard of living reasonably comparable to that enjoyed during the marriage, and the length of time necessary to achieve this goal.
>   g. The tax consequences to each party.
>   h. Any mutual agreement made by the parties concerning financial or service contributions by one party with the expectation of future reciprocation or compensation by the other party.
>   i. The provisions of an antenuptial agreement.
>   j. Other factors the court may determine to be relevant in an individual case.

Our review "need only mention those criteria relevant to the particular case." Our cases supplement "the statutory mandate to consider each criterion . . . by "establish[ing] the comparative weight or importance of certain statutory criteria relative to others."

We have recognized three types of alimony: rehabilitative, reimbursement, and traditional. "Each type of spousal support has a different goal."

> *Rehabilitative alimony* serves to support an economically dependent spouse through a limited period of education and retraining. Its objective is self-sufficiency. An award of *reimbursement alimony* is predicated upon economic sacrifices made by one spouse during the marriage that directly enhance the future earning capacity of the other. *Traditional alimony* is payable for life or for so long as a dependent spouse is incapable of self-support. The amount of alimony awarded and its duration will differ according to the purpose it is designed to serve.

We allow hybrid awards designed to accomplish more than one of the foregoing goals.

A. RECOGNIZING TRANSITIONAL ALIMONY

. . . Iowa cases have neither consistently defined nor formally recognized transitional alimony. . . .

The term "transitional" has been used interchangeably with "rehabilitative."

In *In re Marriage of Hansen*, the concurring opinion urged the adoption of an alternative interpretation of transitional alimony as a "distinct fourth category of spousal support." In this view, "transitional support applies where the recipient spouse may already have the capacity for self-support at the time of dissolution but needs short-term assistance in transitioning from married status to single status due to the economic and situational consequences of dissolution." For transitional alimony, "[t]he critical consideration is whether the recipient party has sufficient income and/or liquid assets to transition from married life to single life without undue hardship." Transitional alimony is not centered on retraining and the growth of human capital, which is the focus of rehabilitative alimony. . . .

Other states recognize transitional alimony as a distinct justification for spousal support. *See, e.g., Silvan v. Alcina*, 105 P.3d 117, 124 (Alaska 2005) ("Reorientation support 'is essentially transitional and may be awarded for brief periods to provide support pending the sale of marital property or to enable a spouse to get a job appropriate to the spouse's existing skills'"); *Evtimov v. Milanova*, 300 S.W.3d 110, 117 (Ark. App. 2009) (holding alimony can be awarded as "a 'bridge-the-gap' measure to aid the recipient spouse in making the transition from married life to being single"); *Bell v. Bell*, 68 So. 3d 321, 327 (Fla. Dist. Ct. App. 2011) (concluding bridge-the-gap alimony "should be used to assist a spouse with legitimate, identifiable, short-term needs" and "is most appropriately awarded in instances where the receiving spouse is already employed, possesses adequate employment skills, and requires no further rehabilitation other than a brief time to ease the transition to single life"); *Murphy v. Murphy*, 816 A.2d 814, 818 (Me. 2003) (holding one of the reasons courts may award transitional spousal support is to address "short-term needs resulting from financial dislocations associated with the dissolution of the marriage"); *Zaleski v. Zaleski*, 13 N.E.3d 967, 971 n.9 (Mass. 2014) (defining transitional alimony as "the periodic or one-time payment of support to a recipient spouse after a marriage of not more than [five] years to transition the recipient spouse to an adjusted lifestyle or location as a result of the divorce"); *Galassi v. Galassi*, 203 P.3d 161, 164 (N.M. App. 2009) (holding rehabilitative spousal support is used to increase the earning capacity of the recipient and "may be conditioned on compliance with a rehabilitation plan" while transitional support "supplement[s] the receiving spouse's income for a stated period" without requiring a rehabilitation plan); *Mayfield v. Mayfield*, 395 S.W.3d 108, 115 (Tenn. 2012) ("Where economic rehabilitation is unnecessary, transitional alimony may be awarded. . . . '[T]ransitional alimony is designed to aid a spouse who already possesses the capacity for self-sufficiency but needs financial assistance in adjusting to the economic consequences of establishing and maintaining a household without the benefit of the other spouse's income.'").

The court of appeals has also addressed transitional alimony in recent decisions. . . .

We conclude that formal recognition of transitional alimony will assist the bench and bar. . . . Transitional alimony can ameliorate inequity unaddressed by the other recognized categories of support. Divorcing spouses must adjust to single life. If one is better equipped for that adjustment and the other will face hardship, then transitional alimony can be awarded to address that inequity and bridge the gap. We now formally recognize transitional alimony as another tool to do equity.

B. The Spousal Support Award

We next review the spousal support awarded to Hancy. We begin our analysis by applying the statutory factors within Iowa Code section 598.21A(1). Then, we address each type of alimony before determining the amount and duration of an equitable hybrid alimony award in this case.

1. *Statutory factors.* Seventeen years is by no means a short marriage and weighs in favor of a substantial alimony award. Both parties are in good physical and emotional health and do not have conditions that impede their ability to hold a full-time job and share physical care of their children. Neither Hancy nor Suraj is near retirement. While Hancy is employable, Suraj will undoubtedly have a much higher income than Hancy for the remainder of their working years. We agree with the court of appeals that this factor weighs in favor of spousal support. Each has assets of roughly equal value in the property division, while Hancy retained her premarital property. Hancy's property award does not overshadow Suraj's comparatively large earning capacity.

While both parties earned medical degrees prior to marriage, only Suraj has been licensed to practice medicine in the United States. This weighs heavily in favor of support.

As for Hancy's earning capacity, we agree with both the district court and the court of appeals that the record does not support a finding that Hancy could earn a six-figure salary if she were to immediately return to the medical field. The court of appeals correctly measured Hancy's earning capacity at $23,115 because "[n]o evidence was presented concerning any full-time employment Hancy could obtain while sharing care for two young children and pursuing her master's degree." She has a foreign medical degree and is a licensed physician in India but lacks the qualifications to be a physician in the United States. She had been out of the workforce for nearly a decade before Suraj filed for divorce. Because Hancy and Suraj will share physical care of their children, Hancy needs time and financial resources to complete her master's degree. This factor weighs heavily in favor of support.

During their marriage, the family's lifestyle reflected Suraj's substantial income. Hancy cannot support herself at a standard of living comparable to the lifestyle she enjoyed while married to him. This factor weighs in favor of alimony.

Alimony payments are no longer tax-deductible, enhancing the burden on the payor, and alimony is no longer considered taxable income to the recipient, enhancing the value of the award. Suraj's after-tax annual income is approximately $232,500, or $19,375 a month.

The parties agree alimony is warranted, but they disagree over the amount and duration. The statutory factors favor an award of substantial alimony. We next consider the types of alimony.

2. *Traditional alimony.* "The purpose of a traditional or permanent alimony award is to provide the receiving spouse with support comparable to what he or she would receive if the marriage continued." "[A]n award of traditional spousal support is normally payable until the death of either party, the payee's remarriage, or until the dependent is capable of self-support at the lifestyle to which the party was accustomed during the marriage."

"[D]uration of the marriage is an important factor" to consider when awarding traditional alimony. It is "often used in long-term marriages where life patterns have been largely set and 'the earning potential of both spouses can be predicted with some reliability.'" "[P]articularly in a traditional marriage, when the parties agree a spouse should stay home to raise children, the economic consequences of absence from the workplace can be substantial." Marriages lasting twenty years or more are generally considered long-term, however, that is not required.

The award and duration of a traditional alimony award "is primarily predicated on need and ability." A determination that a spouse needs alimony is based on "the ability of a spouse to become self-sufficient at 'a standard of living reasonably comparable to that enjoyed during the marriage.'" We focus on the earning capacity of the spouses, not their actual income. "With respect to ability to pay, we have noted that '[f]ollowing a marriage of long duration, we have affirmed awards both of alimony and substantially equal property distribution, especially where the disparity in earning capacity has been great.'" If "a spouse does not have the ability to pay traditional spousal support, however, none will be awarded." "Ideally, the support should be fixed so the continuation of both parties' standard of living can continue, if possible."

Hancy and Suraj assumed different roles. Hancy took care of the children and the home. Suraj earned the income to support the family. The economic consequences of their shared decision warrant an alimony award. Hancy's prospective earning capacity is dwarfed by Suraj's. Yet with her property award, additional education, and substantial alimony, she can become self-sufficient.

Next, Suraj has the ability to pay. Suraj currently earns approximately $19,300 monthly after taxes, which is adequate to support a substantial award. With the expected retraining, Hancy's earning capacity will likely increase as she becomes self-sufficient. Hancy is not entitled to lifetime alimony given her age, health, potential earnings, and the seventeen-year duration of their marriage. Indeed, a purely traditional award would require Suraj to pay alimony for a longer period than he was married to Hancy. But we give weight to the factors supporting traditional alimony in modifying the hybrid award.

3. *Rehabilitative alimony.* "Rehabilitative spousal support is 'a way of supporting an economically dependent spouse through a limited period of re-education or retraining following divorce, thereby creating incentive and opportunity for that spouse to become self-supporting.'" It is awarded to help the recipient spouse become self-sufficient "and for that reason 'such an award may be limited or extended depending on the realistic needs of the economically dependent spouse.'" . . .

Here, the parties made the joint decision to have Hancy assume primary responsibility for the house and children while Suraj focused on his career. As a result of that decision, Hancy took a nearly decade-long break from the workforce and never started her career in the medical field. Suraj and Hancy agree it is more realistic for her to pursue a master's program instead of attempting to become a licensed physician. This path could require undergraduate coursework, up to three years of study, and the financial ability to take unpaid opportunities — as Suraj did — to advance her career. The alimony award should reflect Hancy's desire to pursue a master's degree in public health. We conclude Hancy is entitled to rehabilitative alimony.

4. *Reimbursement alimony.* Reimbursement alimony "is predicated upon economic sacrifices made by one spouse during the marriage that directly enhance the future earning capacity of the other." Such award "should not be subject to modification or termination until full compensation is achieved. Similar to a property award, but based on future earning capacity rather than a division of tangible assets, it should be fixed at the time of the decree." It is distinguishable from rehabilitative or traditional alimony because reimbursement alimony "is designed to give the 'supporting' spouse a stake in the 'student' spouse's future earning

capacity, in exchange for recognizable contributions to the source of that income — the student's advanced education."

Reimbursement alimony is most appropriate when a spouse contributed to the other's earning capacity and cannot otherwise be compensated for their contributions. . . .

Suraj had already completed medical school before they married. Both Suraj and Hancy worked part-time while studying for the Boards. Suraj was successful. Hancy was not. Hancy testified she used her premarital assets to pay for the family's living expenses, including childcare so that she could study — not Suraj — for the third part of the licensing exam. When the family moved for Suraj's career, Hancy made no contemporaneous economic sacrifice because she did not have paid employment. . . . Hancy and Suraj divorced well after he completed his residency. To the extent that Hancy provided homemaker services and financial support during the marriage that directly enhanced Suraj's earnings capacity, she was compensated by the division of the marital property that accumulated from Suraj's earnings. We conclude Hancy is not entitled to reimbursement alimony.

5. *Transitional alimony.* As we now recognize, transitional alimony is appropriate when a party capable of self-support nevertheless needs short-term financial assistance to transition from married to single life. Transitional alimony is not needed when the recipient has sufficient income or liquid assets to facilitate the change to single life. We decline to require a showing of undue hardship and instead rely on district courts to do equity when awarding transitional alimony to "bridge the gap" from married to single life.

Hancy is pursuing a master's degree while she is transitioning from married life to single life. She was not awarded the marital home and must find a new residence, obtain her own health insurance, and the like. However, Hancy was awarded approximately $475,000 in marital and nonmarital property in the dissolution decree, with an estimated $300,000 in cash, including the equalization payment. We conclude Hancy is not entitled to transitional alimony.

6. *The duration and amount of her alimony award.* The district court awarded $7,500 monthly in spousal support for five years, or $450,000 total. We agree with the court of appeals that the district court award is inequitable given the parties' disparity in income and the time it will take Hancy to obtain her master's degree to enhance her earning capacity while working part-time and sharing physical care of the two children. The district court's award would not allow Hancy "to maintain the same standard of living she enjoyed during the marriage throughout the period of time it will take her to become self-sufficient at her maximum earning capacity." Equity requires an award of substantial duration and amount. The parties agree that Hancy will never obtain an earning capacity approaching Suraj's. He can afford to pay substantial alimony, the disparity in the parties' earning capacity is great, and the marriage lasted seventeen years.

The court of appeals awarded Hancy hybrid alimony of $9,000 monthly for seven years, $8,000 monthly for another three years, and $7,000 monthly for two more years for a total span of twelve years and $1,212,000. We consider its modified award too long in duration. Seven years should be sufficient for Hancy to complete her master's degree and enhance her earning capacity while working part-time and sharing physical care of their children. At that time, their children will be teenagers, facilitating Hancy's ability to work full-time. The child support paid by Suraj will increase substantially when his alimony ends. We also consider $9,000 monthly too generous.

After considering the factors in section 598.21A(1) and the goals of hybrid traditional and rehabilitative alimony, we retroactively modify the alimony award to $8,500 monthly for seven years commencing with the date of the decree entered October 18, 2019. We vacate the court of appeals alimony award for years eight through twelve. This modification requires a recalculation of child support, which the district court shall determine on remand. . . .

NOTES AND QUESTIONS

1. What does it mean to need support beyond having enough money for the basics of life? This case, like others from many states, expresses the goal of permitting both spouses to continue to live at the marital standard of living. What justifies this goal, since the parties are, by definition, no longer married? How realistic is this goal? An alternate formulation from the Maryland courts is that the parties' standard of living cannot be "unconscionably disparate." Kaplan v. Kaplan, 241 A.3d 960 (Md. App. 2020). What does this mean?

2. What does it mean for a spouse to be rehabilitated, i.e., capable of self-support?

3. Typically, whatever the standard for awarding alimony, the parties submit detailed budgets to prove their needs. In Simmons v. Simmons, 409 N.E.2d 321 (Ill. App. 1980), the wife claimed needs for food and transportation higher than actual costs during marriage. She explained that she ate out four or five nights a week because she did not like to eat alone at home and that she took a cab to work. On what basis would a judge validly determine whether these were "needs"?

If the spouses lived frugally during their marriage, saving a substantial portion of their income, does a spouse who is entitled to spousal support because she has a much lower income and is the primary caretaker of children need to be able to continue adding to her savings? Boemio v. Boemio, 994 A.2d 911 (Md. App. 2010); Kampf v. Kampf, 732 N.W.2d 630 (Minn. App. 2007); Lombardi v. Lombardi, 145 A.3d 709 (N.J. App. 2016).

4. Even assuming that Hancy Pazhoor needs support, does the court explain why Suraj is responsible for satisfying that need after they are no longer married? How would Professors England and Farkas (above) answer that question? What would Professor Ellman say? How would Professor Williams respond?

5. If spousal support is justified by the contributions of one spouse to the career development of the other spouse, how is this measured?

6. If the justification for spousal support is compensating a spouse who forgoes development of a career to care for children and the home, how do we measure the compensation? Does the reason that the spouse made this choice matter? The ALI Family Dissolution Principles propose that "compensatory spousal payments" be ordered to compensate a spouse for financial losses occasioned by the marriage, rather than to relieve need. ALI, Principles of the Law of Family Dissolution §5.02 Comment, at 789 (2002). Section 5.03(2) provides for awards to compensate for loss of living standard in long-term marriages and loss of earning capacity caused by undertaking the care of dependents. Section 5.03(3) adds that awards may be made to compensate for "an unfairly disproportionate disparity between the spouses in their respective abilities to recover their pre-marital living standard" after a short marriage.

PROBLEMS

1. Britt and Jaime are divorcing following an 18-year marriage. Both are 45. Before the marriage and for the first two years after the wedding, Britt taught school but quit when they adopted their first child. The marital property was divided equally. The trial court awarded Britt sufficient spousal support for two years to enable her to renew her teaching certificate without having to work; at that point the award was to be reduced by 50 percent and was to continue for an indefinite duration. The judge justified this award as encouraging Britt to become self-supporting while recognizing that she was unlikely ever to be able to earn enough to enable her to live at the marital standard of living. Britt has appealed, arguing that this award amounts to a prospective modification of indefinite spousal support without requiring proof of changed circumstances. Can the award be defended?

Two months before the initial two-year period of the award is over, Britt moves to modify it on the ground that she has not completed the training necessary to renew her teaching certificate and so is not able to be self-supporting at the level expected at the time of divorce. She has been working part time and looking unsuccessfully for full-time work. A vocational expert called by Jaime testifies that she has been "minimally involved" in preparing for a career. Jaime moves to dismiss Britt's petition on the basis of *res judicata*. What arguments should the parties make? If Jaime loses the *res judicata* argument, what additional arguments can be made, and how should Britt respond?

2. Hank and Wendy were married for 15 years. Both worked throughout the marriage. During the marriage Hank invented a process to produce wooden parts for curved windows and started his own business based on the invention. By the time of the divorce the business had sales of more than $1 million a year. Wendy was awarded 40 percent of the total marital assets (mostly stock in Hank's company), worth $283,465, as her share of the property. Hank and Wendy did not change their standard of living much when Hank's invention began to pay off, and Wendy earns enough to live at nearly the marital standard of living.

Has Wendy sacrificed education or career opportunities so as to entitle her to spousal support? Does her employment prove that she did not sacrifice? Has a homemaker necessarily made such a sacrifice? Did she contribute to Hank's success, justifying an award of support? If she receives an award on this basis, has she been compensated twice for her contributions, since she received a share of the stock in his company? What if instead of living frugally, Hank and Wendy had had a lavish lifestyle, financed largely by the income from Hank's business?

3. The Emergence of Alimony Guidelines

The widespread adoption of child support guidelines (see Chapter 7) has inspired numerous law reformers and commentators to propose spousal support guidelines to increase consistency in orders, make settlement easier, and reduce the costs of divorce.

However, developing guidelines has been difficult because of lack of agreement on the purposes of spousal support and the large number of factors considered relevant. Soon after the ALI proposal, which would base spousal support on the principle of compensation, the American Academy of Matrimonial Lawyers proposed its own formula, rejecting the compensation principle and based on the income of the spouses and the duration of the marriage. The formula is described in Mary Kay Kisthardt, Re-Thinking Alimony: The AAML's Considerations for Calculating Alimony, Spousal Support, or Maintenance, 21 J. Am. Acad. Matrimonial Law. 61 (2008).

In 2011 the Massachusetts legislature enacted legislation that limits the duration of alimony obligations based on the length of the marriage. In the next case the court addresses the statutory provisions that distinguish between rehabilitative and long-term support.

Zaleski v. Zaleski
13 N.E.3d 967 (Mass. 2014)

Duffly, J. . . . We are asked to decide in this case of first impression whether a Probate and Family Court judge abused her discretion in determining that rehabilitative alimony, with its presumptive five-year payment period, was the appropriate form of alimony to be ordered, rather than general term alimony, which, based on the length of the parties' marriage, would have permitted alimony payments to continue for thirteen years. . . .

. . . The parties were married on October 15, 1994, in Massachusetts. At the time of trial, the wife was forty-five years old and the husband was forty-eight years old. They have two children, both of whom attend private schools; at the time of trial, their daughter was a sophomore in high school and their son was in the eighth grade. The parties are in agreement that their son should also attend a private high school. . . . The complaint for divorce was served on the husband in February, 2011.

The judgment of divorce ordered the husband to pay the wife rehabilitative alimony in the amount of $11,667 per month for five years; this amount is thirty-five per cent of the husband's annual base salary of $400,000. A stipulation of the parties that provided for shared legal and physical custody of the children was incorporated in the judgment; the judge ordered that neither was to pay child support "at this time." The judgment further provided that the husband shall be solely responsible for the children's private school tuition and expenses, and that the parties shall share equally the cost of the children's extracurricular and enrichment activities and their uninsured medical and dental costs. In addition, the judgment required both parties to maintain life insurance coverage as it existed at the time of trial as security for their obligations; allocated responsibility for certain joint indebtedness; ordered that each party will have responsibility for liabilities standing in his or her own name; and provided for a division of assets, including a payment from the husband to the wife in the amount of $27,466, "[i]n order to equalize the division."

. . . The courts' authority to grant alimony has been set forth in G.L. c. 208, §34. As noted, the alimony reform act of 2011 added new provisions to c. 208, creating four categories of alimony; only rehabilitative and general term alimony are at issue here.[10]

Both require that a judge consider the factors set forth in G.L. c. 208, §53, in deciding the appropriate form of alimony:

> "the length of the marriage; age of the parties; health of the parties; income, employment and employability of both parties, including employability through reasonable diligence and additional training, if necessary; economic and non-economic contribution of both parties to the marriage; marital lifestyle; ability of each party to maintain the marital lifestyle; lost economic opportunity as a result of the marriage; and such other factors as the court considers relevant and material."

These factors also are to be considered in determining the amount of alimony to be awarded. In sum, the primary differences between rehabilitative and general alimony relate to the initial term limits set forth in the act and the standard by which the term of alimony may be extended.

Rehabilitative alimony is defined as "the periodic payment of support to a recipient spouse who is expected to become economically self-sufficient by a predicted time, such as, without limitation, reemployment; completion of job training; or receipt of a sum due from the payor spouse under a

---

10. The other two forms of alimony are reimbursement and transitional alimony. Reimbursement alimony is defined as

> "the periodic or one-time payment of support to a recipient spouse after a marriage of not more than [five] years to compensate the recipient spouse for economic or noneconomic contribution to the financial resources of the payor spouse, such as enabling the payor spouse to complete an education or job training."

Reimbursement alimony terminates on the death of the recipient or on a date certain; once ordered, modification of reimbursement alimony is prohibited and income guidelines, applicable to all other forms of alimony, do not apply.

Transitional alimony is defined as:

> "the periodic or one-time payment of support to a recipient spouse after a marriage of not more than [five] years to transition the recipient spouse to an adjusted lifestyle or location as a result of the divorce."

Transitional alimony terminates on the death of the recipient or a date certain "that is not longer than [three] years from the date of the parties' divorce." The statute prohibits modification or extension of transitional alimony, which, once ordered, may not be replaced with another form of alimony.

judgment." The alimony reform act provides, among other things, that "[r]ehabilitative alimony shall terminate upon . . . the occurrence of a specific event in the future," but also that the alimony term shall not exceed five years. Extension of the term is authorized, however, on a showing of compelling circumstances that "unforeseen events prevent the recipient spouse from being self-supporting at the end of the term with due consideration to the length of the marriage, [and] the court finds that the recipient tried to become self-supporting." The amount of alimony may be modified during the term "upon material change of circumstance." By contrast, general term alimony is defined as "the periodic payment of support to a recipient spouse who is economically dependent." Payments continue, subject to durational time limits established by the act that depend upon the length of the marriage; here, general alimony would have entitled the wife to support payments of up to approximately thirteen years. General term alimony can be extended for "good cause" if there has been a material change in circumstances and the reasons are supported by "clear and convincing evidence."

We turn to a consideration whether the judge's findings in this case reflect that she considered the mandatory factors when determining the appropriate form of alimony, and whether those findings support her conclusion that the wife should receive rehabilitative alimony. We then consider whether the findings support the judge's determination regarding the amount of the alimony award. . . .

A judge has discretion in deciding whether to award rehabilitative alimony rather than general term alimony, so long as she has given appropriate consideration to the factors identified in G.L. c. 208, §53 (a).[11] Where the determination is made that rehabilitative alimony, with its shorter durational limits, is the most appropriate form, findings based on those factors must support the conclusion that a recipient spouse's economic dependence is temporary, and that, at a predictable date, the dependent spouse can become self-sufficient by undertaking reasonable efforts.

Here, the judge made comprehensive findings of fact in conjunction with her conclusion that the appropriate form of alimony in this case was rehabilitative. . . . According to those findings, this was a marriage of approximately sixteen years and four months; at the time of trial the wife was forty-five years old and the husband was forty-eight years old; both parties enjoyed good health, as did their children. During most of the marriage, both parties were employed full time outside the home and contributed their earnings to the marital enterprise. The marriage was a "true partnership in every aspect," from the financial contributions that each made "to child rearing[, and] to homemaking."

The husband, who holds a bachelor of arts degree in political science, initially worked as a real estate appraiser and then as an analyst and executive in real estate investment firms. The husband's income, as reported on his Internal Revenue Service W-2 forms, was $302,442 in 2004. It increased annually until it reached $1,024,555 in 2008, and was in excess of $900,000 in 2009 and 2010. In 2011, the husband's income as reported on his W-2 forms was $741,958. Since 2008, the husband's income has consisted of base salary in the amount of approximately $400,000, and bonuses that are paid annually in the year after they are earned. In 2011, the husband also received $286,625 in nonrecurring deferred compensation from a prior employer. The husband's income during the marriage was always greater than that of the wife. The husband was found to be self-supporting and fully employed commensurate with his training, skills, and experience.

---

11. There is nothing in the statutory scheme to suggest that, even where there is evidence of conditions supporting rehabilitative alimony, a judge must in every case award rehabilitative and not general term alimony; indeed, a fine line may distinguish the two in some circumstances.

The wife holds a bachelor of science degree in business; beginning early in the marriage, she was employed as a sales representative and, starting in 1990, as a pharmaceutical sales representative for several companies. In 2003, the wife was promoted to the position of sales district manager, a job from which she was terminated in 2007. At that time, her base salary was in the range of $127,000 to $130,000 annually, with a bonus of up to $40,000; she also had use of the company car.

The judge found that the wife, who has not been employed outside the home since 2008, is not presently self-supporting, but has the ability and the desire to work. The judge found credible the wife's testimony that she wants to work and plans to work outside the home, but found also that her job search efforts have been sporadic and superficial, and that she had not used her best efforts to secure employment. . . . The judge did not credit the opinion of the husband's expert that the wife was highly employable as a sales manager or marketing manager and in those jobs could earn an annual salary of $160,000 to $170,000, but did find that the wife had skills that were transferrable across many fields beyond pharmaceutical and medical device sales.

Also according to the findings, "[t]he parties lived an upper middle class lifestyle during the marriage. They dined out, vacationed, joined a yacht club," and owned boats, luxury vehicles, and a second home, which the parties sold by agreement during the litigation. The children attended private schools. The husband held membership in a fish and game club, while the wife was a member of a tennis club. The judge also found that the husband and wife "spent beyond their means" and that, despite the husband's significant income and the wife's "meaningful salary," their only assets at the time of trial consisted of the equity in their home and their retirement accounts.

The judge determined that the wife was in need of rehabilitative alimony and that it was "anticipated that [the w]ife will return to the workforce on a full time basis" within a predictable period of time, and that until such time she "is in need of alimony." The judge further found that, with reasonable effort, the wife "can be employed within five years. At such time, the parties will need to review each of their respective financial circumstances and the need for continued alimony and/or child support."

These factors reflect that the judge gave consideration to all the factors identified in G.L. c. 208, §53 (a). We turn now to the wife's claim that the findings do not support the judge's determination that the wife will become self-sufficient by a predictable date in the future.

The wife argues that the judge abused her discretion in awarding rehabilitative rather than general term alimony, because there is no specific event upon which termination was based. . . .

. . . The reference to a "specific event" is found only in G.L. c. 208, §50 (a), which establishes the durational limits for rehabilitative alimony. The meaning of "specific event" must be considered in light of other provisions in the alimony reform act that define rehabilitative alimony and list the factors a judge must consider when determining the form of the alimony award.

General Laws c. 208, §48, defines rehabilitative alimony as support paid to "a recipient spouse who is expected to become economically self-sufficient by a predicted time, such as, without limitation, reemployment; completion of job training; or receipt of a sum due from the payor spouse under a judgment." Although the wife makes no direct reference to this provision, it is implicit in her argument that she views the term "reemployment" to mean a specific, identifiable job that is expected to materialize on a date certain. But future employment is also among the factors a judge must consider in determining the form of alimony to be awarded.

As set forth in G.L. c. 208, §3 (a), a judge must consider the "employment and employability of both parties, including employability through reasonable diligence and additional training, if necessary." . . . "Employability" in this context means that a party has the capability of being employed. As the act suggests, to become employable may require that a party undertake "reasonable diligence and additional training." Thus, although a party may not be employed or employable at the time of entry of the alimony award, that party still could have predictable prospects of future employment in a specific type of work or position. In such circumstances, if a party's employability in the near future is a realistic prospect, rehabilitative alimony might, with other considerations, be appropriate.

The act itself sheds no further light on the specific circumstances in which a spouse might be deemed capable of economic independence at some predictable date that is five years or less in the future. Our decisional law, however, through which the concept of rehabilitative alimony has developed, provides some guidance. The purpose of an award of rehabilitative alimony is "to protect, for a limited time, a spouse whose earning capacity has suffered (or become nonexistent) while that spouse prepares to reenter the work force." The award of rehabilitative alimony is appropriate when a spouse's anticipated self-sufficiency is based on the predictable occurrence of a future event, such as reemployment. In accordance with these cases, the prospect of future employment, when based on a past history of commensurate employment followed by a brief hiatus, may be sufficiently predictable, even in the absence of an available, specifically identifiable job.

Rehabilitative alimony is the appropriate form of alimony if "a recipient spouse . . . is expected to become economically self-sufficient by a predicted time." Thus, the alimony reform act permits a judge to determine that rehabilitative alimony based on expected employment is appropriate where there is sufficient evidence for a judge to find, with a reasonable degree of certainty, that the recipient spouse can obtain employment through reasonable efforts, and thereby can gain economic self-sufficiency, in the near future.

Here, the judge found that both parties are educated professionals, experienced in their respective fields. The wife had been employed outside the home until 2008, fewer than four years before the end of the marriage; at that time, her income was approximately $170,000. After losing her job, the wife pursued her interest in interior design, attending classes in 2009 and 2010, and started a business that failed through no fault of her own. The judge found also that the wife wished to work, that she was highly employable in the area of sales, that her skills were transferrable, and that she could with reasonable diligence find employment at a level permitting self-sufficiency. These findings support the judge's determination that the wife can be "expected to become economically self-sufficient by a predicted time." Thus, the judge did not abuse her discretion in deciding that the wife was not entitled to general term alimony under the specific facts of this case. . . .

NOTES AND QUESTIONS

1. Mass. Gen. Laws Ann. ch. 208 §49 (2022) provides durational limits for general term alimony based on the length of the marriage. If the marriage lasted 20 years or less, the limit starts at half the length of the marriage and increases to 80 percent. There is no time limit for marriages of more than 20 years. As *Zaleski* discusses, the term limit for rehabilitative alimony is five years, and the limits on reimbursement and transitional alimony are set out in footnote 10, p. 287.

The guidelines also provide that except for reimbursement alimony, the amount of alimony "should generally not exceed . . . 30 to 35 per cent of the difference between the parties' gross incomes established at the time of the order being issued." They also permit deviation from this limit for reasons that include:

(1) advanced age; chronic illness; or unusual health circumstances of either party;
(2) tax considerations applicable to the parties;

(3) whether the payor spouse is providing health insurance and the cost of health insurance for the recipient spouse;

(4) whether the payor spouse has been ordered to secure life insurance for the benefit of the recipient spouse and the cost of such insurance;

(5) sources and amounts of unearned income, including capital gains, interest and dividends, annuity and investment income from assets that were not allocated in the parties' divorce;

(6) significant premarital cohabitation that included economic partnership or marital separation of significant duration, each of which the court may consider in determining the length of the marriage;

(7) a party's inability to provide for that party's own support by reason of physical or mental abuse by the payor;

(8) a party's inability to provide for that party's own support by reason of that party's deficiency of property, maintenance or employment opportunity; and

(9) upon written findings, any other factor that the court deems relevant and material.

2. Under the Massachusetts guidelines, what is the difference between rehabilitative and general alimony? Is it the same as the difference between rehabilitative and traditional alimony as discussed in *Pazhoor*?

As interpreted in *Zaleski*, what determines whether a spouse receives rehabilitative or general alimony? Would Hancy Pazhoor have received alimony? If so, of which kind, how much, and for how long? How would the problems following *Pazhoor*, on pages 285–86, be analyzed? Would Mrs. Zaleski have received alimony under *Pazhoor*? If so, what kind?

3. Many jurisdictions still have statutes that list factors for judges to consider in determining whether to award alimony without more guidance, and many courts in those states have not developed case law as complex as that in *Pazhoor*. Nevertheless, most recognize at least implicitly the categories of rehabilitative, reimbursement, and indefinite alimony. This does not mean, however, that courts in different states reach similar results because of the significant amount of discretion that judges have.

4. Do the Massachusetts guidelines appear to reduce the risk of irrational differences among awards of alimony? Do you think they make settlement easier?

5. The length of a marriage can be quite important in determining the type of alimony for which a person is eligible under most states' laws, as well as the amount. In Duff-Kareores v. Kareores, 52 N.E.3d 115 (Mass. 2016), the court held that a period of cohabitation preceding a marriage can be considered in determining the total length of the marriage for purposes of applying the guidelines. The parties were married in 1995 and divorced in 2004. In 2007 they started living together again, and they remarried in 2012. Six months later the wife filed for divorce again. The trial court treated the marriage as lasting 18 years, from 1995 until the second divorce petition, citing a statute allowing a court to "increase the length of the marriage if there is evidence that the parties' economic marital partnership began during their cohabitation period prior to marriage." The Supreme Judicial Court reversed, concluding that the period from 2004-2007 should be excluded, since the parties did not share a common household and did not share an economic partnership then. *See generally* Mark Strasser, Determining Marriage Length in Support Calculations: Should Cohabitation Count?, 30 J. L. & Pol'y 396 (2022).

6. A Boston Globe report on the Massachusetts alimony guidelines law described its purpose as "replacing an old system marred by inequities and abuses, including, in some cases, alimony payments for life, even for short-term marriages. Critics said the old law discouraged recipients, most of them women, from supporting themselves, and from remarrying." Bella English, New Mass. Alimony Law "Model"—But Is It Working?, Bos. Globe, Oct. 20, 2013. *See also* Stephen Hitner, New Law Stops Injustice of Paying Alimony Forever, CNN, Mar. 11, 2012. These articles, like others about alimony reform efforts in other states, emphasize stories of men required to pay indefinite spousal support for long periods of time and say that requiring termination of support obligations at definite points is a primary reform goal. *See, e.g.*, Maddie Hanna, New Jersey Bill Would Set Guidelines for Alimony, Phil. Inquirer, Dec. 2, 2013; Colleen O'Connor, New Law Changes Alimony Landscape for Divorcing Colorado Couples, Denv. Post, Oct. 18, 2013; Kathleen Haughney & Lisa Huriash, Alimony Law in Florida Changes Drastically Under New Bill, Sun Sentinel, Apr. 18, 2013.

7. Other statutes that create some kind of formula for spousal support include Colo. Rev. Stat. Ann. §14-10-114 (2022) (presumptive amounts and durational limits based on length of marriage and parties' incomes); 750 Ill. Comp. Stat. Ann. 5/504 (2022) (amount and duration based on income disparity and length of marriage); Me. Rev. Stat. Ann. §951-A (2022) (eligibility and duration based on duration of marriage); N.H. Rev. Stat. Ann. §458:19-a (2022); N.Y. Dom. Rel. Law §236 (2022); Tex. Fam. Code §8.054 (2022) (duration limits based on length of marriage); Utah Code Ann. §30-3-5 (2022) (duration limits based on length of marriage).

4. Fault Revisited

In the era of fault-based divorce a wife's misconduct could either bar her from receiving alimony or limit the amount, and in some places the husband's fault could be a factor in increasing the amount. As of 2020 the following states did not permit consideration of marital fault in spousal support awards: Arkansas, Colorado, Delaware, Hawaii, Illinois, Indiana, Iowa, Kansas, Kentucky, Maine, Massachusetts, Minnesota, Montana, Nebraska, Nevada, New Mexico, Oklahoma, Ohio, Oregon, South Dakota, Vermont, Washington, Wisconsin, and Wyoming. Family Law Quarterly Editorial Staff, Charts 2020: Family Law in the Fifty States, D.C., and Puerto Rico, Part 1, 54 Fam. L.Q. 341, 345 Chart 1 (2021). Many more states allow courts to consider marital fault in making decisions about alimony or spousal support than about property division. What explains this difference? Even if general fault is not a factor, economic misconduct may be, although some courts reject this approach as well.

In a few jurisdictions a person against whom a fault-based divorce is awarded cannot be awarded support, and in some others fault is a factor courts may consider. One of the states that makes fault an absolute bar is North Carolina, as the state court of appeals observed in Romulus v. Romulus, 715 S.E.2d 308, 311 (N.C. App. 2011) ("Our legislature has decreed that even one fleeting incident of 'illicit sexual behavior' by a dependent spouse automatically bars her from an alimony award, even if the supporting spouse has committed serious, indeed criminal, physical abuse against his wife and children throughout the marriage, and we have no authority to question the legislature's wisdom in adopting this rule.").

5. Spousal Support for the Caregiving Parent?

PROBLEM

Parker has filed for divorce from Louie, alleging incompatibility. They have two children, ages 3 and 6 years old. Parker was employed as a teacher until the older child was born; since then Parker has been the children's primary caregiver. Parker has requested spousal support at a level that will not require a return to work until the children are school-age. Louie opposes any award of permanent alimony and offers evidence that Parker can obtain employment as a teacher earning $30,000 per year. Louie offers to pay day-care costs for the children, the total cost of which will be $10,000 per year for both children. What arguments should each party make at the hearing on Parker's request for spousal support? In addition to the materials you have already read, consider the following.

EMPIRICAL DATA ON WORKING PARENTS

In 2021, in 62.3 percent of all families with children headed by a married couple, both parents were employed. Another way of looking at this phenomenon is by the labor force participation of mothers. In 2021, about 71 percent of mothers with children under age 18 were in the labor force, meaning that they were working or looking for work. In comparison, 93 percent of fathers were in the labor force. Employment is more common among unmarried mothers than married mothers and among mothers of older than younger children. About 76 percent of unmarried mothers were in the work force, compared with 69 percent of married mothers. Of mothers with children younger than 6, about 66 percent were in the labor force, compared to about 76 percent with children 6 to 17 years old. Bureau of Labor Statistics, Employment Characteristics of Families—2021 (Apr. 20, 2022).

OVERVIEW OF GOVERNING LEGAL PRINCIPLES AND PRACTICAL REALITIES

As we have seen, UMDA Section 308(a)(2) provides that a caretaker of children who is otherwise capable of self-support may be eligible for spousal support, and cases have certainly held that custodial parents of young children should receive spousal support to enable them to remain at home with the children. However, because of the emphasis on post-divorce self-sufficiency following short- to medium-term marriages, courts rarely approve long-term spousal support for the caretaking parent of young children. Instead, when spousal support is awarded because the recipient has custody of the children, it usually terminates at the latest when the youngest child attains the age of majority. As a practical matter, spousal and child support are often insufficient to provide for the needs of the children and the custodial parent, and so the parent must work anyway.

THE POLITICS AND SOCIAL VALUE OF CAREGIVING

Ann Laquer Estin, *Maintenance, Alimony, and the Rehabilitation of Family Care*, 71 N.C. L. Rev. 729-738 (1993): In an earlier era, although family care was not compensated, and usually not legally recognized, it was clearly understood to be central to the family's functioning and it was structurally supported through a variety of legal and social devices—devices which have eroded over the past generation. Caregiving is even less recognized today. Despite the language of modern divorce statutes, caregiving is perceived not as an independent contribution to the family, but only as one half of a traditional gender-structured marriage pattern. . . .

Despite our often polarized and politicized view of the family, there should be little dispute that caregiving is an essential attribute of family life, worthy of recognition in the law of divorce. . . . Support payments to caregivers would have two benefits: facilitating the care of children in the difficult period after divorce, and allocating to both parents the costs of putting children first *during* marriage. The literature in this area of family law suggests only one disadvantage to caregiver support remedies: the risk that they will foster traditional family roles, economic dependence, and the corresponding gender roles that many men and women find oppressive.

Cynthia Lee Starnes, *Lovers, Parents, and Partners: Disentangling Spousal and Co-Parenting Commitments*, 54 Ariz. L. Rev. 197, 232-236 (2012): A married parent is not simply a participant in two independent relationships, one with the other spouse and another with the child. From both a normative and a practical perspective, children add another dimension to marriage, as adults who are legally committed to each other as spouses undertake a new mutual commitment as parents. This parental commitment runs not only to the child, to whom each parent owes an independent state-imposed obligation, but also to the other parent, both spouses understanding that they will share the physical and financial costs of parenting. The result is a second layer of commitment between married parents — a co-parenting partnership that supplements the marital partnership. The co-parenting partnership builds on each parent's individual obligation to the child.

Although the co-parenting commitment may be express, more often it is implied, both spouses understanding that the addition of children to their family means a shared commitment to raise those children. The child benefits from the stability of the co-parenting partnership and from the mutuality of the parents' commitment, which at least as a normative matter, makes childcare more dependable, more bountiful, more efficient, and more manageable for parents. . . .

When parents divorce during their child's minority, the marital partnership terminates, but divorce does not so swiftly terminate the co-parenting partnership, which endures at least until its work is complete, i.e., until the couple's children reach majority. Continuation of the co-parenting partnership does not depend on love, intimacy, or friendship between former spouses, but rather on the parents' mutual commitment to take on the economic support and physical labor required to raise shared children.

Divorced parents may coordinate their care for the child or they may refuse to speak to each other. Whatever their inclination toward cooperation, each divorced parent benefits from the other's physical labor on behalf of the child, because what one parent does for the child the other parent need not do. As the ALI observes, while parents "can allocate that responsibility [for children] . . . they cannot avoid it, and the spouse who assumes it discharges a legal obligation of both parents." Simply put, if one parent provides the child with breakfast, the other parent need not; if one parent shops for a winter coat or shoes or crayons, the other need not; if one parent tutors the child, washes her pajamas, transports her to school or soccer practice, the other need not. The point is that labor expended on behalf of the child by one parent frees the other parent from the legal and moral obligation to perform it. While parenting may be pleasant work, it is work nonetheless — a point paid babysitters understand well enough.

As divorced co-parents continue to raise their children, the co-parenting commitment provides a conceptual basis for income sharing between them, and for new default rules that recognize, for the first time, a non-custodial parent's affirmative responsibility to share income not only with his or her child, but also with the other parent who is undertaking the lion's share of the daily labor required to raise joint children. Disentangled from the marital commitment, the co-parenting commitment stands as a distinct undertaking — one the law should encourage parents to honor, and one whose termination the law should police with an exit price. Current law, however, does just the opposite, ignoring the co-parenting commitment and encouraging divorcing partners to assume divorce signals the end of all commitments between them, whether or not they share children. The default rules that produce this result are sticky, nudging spouses to believe this is an appropriate divorce outcome. It is not. Divorce law must be reconceptualized to reflect policy goals more consistent with the best interests of children, their caretakers, and society at large.

Some may object to income sharing for primary caretakers on the grounds that these parents already reap a huge reward in the form of psychic joy stemming from their extensive time with children. This argument is unpersuasive. Most fundamentally, psychic joy is simply not possible of measurement and so cannot be quantified and then offset against a monetary award. Measurement is made more challenging by the fact that time spent with children is a poor proxy for psychic joy. A primary caretaker may spend much time tending to daily chores that produce little joy — cleaning the macaroni and cheese off the floor, laundering, shopping, cooking, and cleaning. The parent who spends less time with children may actually experience more psychic joy than the other parent, especially if that time is devoted more exclusively to child-intensive endeavors—time perhaps at the zoo, the soccer field, the ice cream shop, or the library. Time is a poor proxy for psychic joy. Moreover, the suggestion that psychic joy is time dependent raises uncomfortable questions about the children themselves and their tendency to inspire joy rather than sorrow or worry or frustration or any of the other psychic costs of parenting that are likely to fall disproportionately on the parent with primary residential responsibility.

The partnership metaphor provides an interesting perspective on the argument that income sharing would overcompensate a primary caretaker. Imagine the following exchange between equal partners:

"Did you enjoy your day—working at the office [or the shop, the restaurant, the car wash]?"

"Yes, very much . . ."

"Well then, you have reaped your reward and we will reduce your share of partnership income accordingly."

Psychic joy is a dubious basis for keeping primary caretakers and their children at a lower standard of living than the lesser-time parent.

The co-parenting partnership model I advocate in this Article provides a rationale for new laws that require divorced parents to share the full costs of parenting. Income sharing between parents may assume many forms and levels, and will raise many old and a few new questions, some of them tough ones. So there must be a next conversation, one that builds on the conceptual foundation for income sharing offered here.

D. DIVORCE AND NEW PROPERTY

1. Basic Principles

Traditionally, interests that may broadly be characterized as "new property," such as pensions and other employment benefits, goodwill in small businesses, professional licenses, and educational degrees were not considered divisible property but as potential sources of income from which spousal support could be paid. Over the last half century lawyers have successfully argued that these forms of wealth should be treated as property subject to division,[12] and legislatures have agreed.

As we have seen, former spouses who can be self-supporting often are not entitled to spousal support and so cannot share in employment-related interests through alimony. However, capacity for self-support does not bar property division. In addition, to the extent that an equal division of community or marital property is required or favored, courts that want to award one spouse the family home have often been able to find that the other spouse's interests in pension plans or business goodwill are intangible assets that offset such awards.[13] These circumstances have spurred efforts to expand the pot of interests called "property" for purposes of distribution at divorce.

---

12. In addition to the reasons discussed in the text, a well-known California decision on lawyer malpractice liability has probably motivated lawyers to press these claims as well. In Smith v. Lewis, 530 P.2d 589 (Cal. 1975) (en banc), the court held that an attorney had committed malpractice when he assumed that the husband's retirement benefits were separate property without researching the issue, at a time when the law was not entirely clear. The court awarded damages of $100,000.

13. Professor Herma Hill Kay has suggested that the California cases treating professional goodwill as divisible community property may be merely an effort to raise the total value of the community property to the point that the wife can receive the house as her half and the husband the goodwill as his half. Mary Ann Glendon, The New Family and the New Property 81 n.114 (1981).

On the other hand, if wealth associated with employment is treated as divisible property, distributions of pension benefits or professional goodwill will not be modifiable. Sometimes spouses want to characterize these interests as property precisely so that the court orders will not be changeable. However, some courts have been reluctant to deal with the interests in such a final fashion and have for that reason refused to call them "property."

If these interests are to be treated as property, courts ordinarily must assign a present value to them in the course of determining the total property division. However, because these interests typically take the form of a stream of payments of money payable over time, valuing them is difficult. If there were established markets in these interests, valuation could be determined by looking at market price. Often, though, there is no such market, and courts must use other techniques for assigning value. The following explains basic techniques that can be used.

NOTE: VALUING STREAMS OF PAYMENTS

Let's say that you have a goose that lays a golden egg every two weeks. What is it worth? The goose is surely worth more than what its meat and feathers would bring after its death. The meat and feathers constitute the goose's *salvage value*. Assets that produce income are almost always going to be worth more than their salvage value, although their total value includes their salvage value. Most of the assets we will discuss in this chapter are intangibles anyway.

We might try to value the goose by asking how much we paid for it, but what if we paid 59 cents because no one realized that it would lay golden eggs when it grew up? The goose's *book value* would be 59 cents, but this value is historical. It tells us nothing about the changes that have occurred in the goose or in the market for geese and thus has no necessary relationship to the goose's present market value. Besides, some of the assets we will discuss have no book value.

Since we expect that the goose will continue laying a golden egg every two weeks for some indefinite period of time, we are really trying to measure how much that stream of eggs is worth now. If we knew for sure how long the goose would continue to lay eggs and what the price of gold would be, we could easily calculate the total worth of the eggs that the goose will lay. But this sum would not be the value today of those eggs because of the *time value of money*. For example, let's say that the constant profit on one golden egg is $10 (the price we can get for the egg minus the costs of food and other expenses of producing it). A buyer would not pay $10 today for an egg to be delivered in one year because the buyer could invest the same $10 in an interest-bearing account and at the end of the year have $10 plus the interest it earned. Thus, the price today of one egg to be delivered in a year should be an amount that, when invested, will produce $10 in a year. Assuming an interest rate of 8 percent, the amount that must be invested today to earn $10 in one year is $10 divided by 1 plus the interest rate (here, 1.08), or $9.26. (The general formula is Present Value = Future Value divided by 1 + the interest rate. Fortunately, present-value tables are widely available.) This method of determining value is called the *discounted cash flow method*.

The critical choice in determining the present value is deciding what interest rate we assume. The higher the interest rate, the lower the present value will be. The interest rate depends on the current value of money and how uncertain our estimate is of the value of a thing. Valuing the goose is uncertain because we do not and cannot know for certain such critical facts as how long the goose will live, how long it will lay eggs, whether it will continue to lay regularly, and what the price of gold will be. Generally speaking, the more uncertain, or riskier, an investment is, the higher the interest rate will be, since people demand higher rates of return for risky investments. The discussion of assets in this chapter will include how interest rates, or rates of return, are chosen for purposes of valuing them. To the extent that the calculations take into account future uncertainties, they are based on actuarial assumptions for the hypothetical person, which almost always turn out to be inaccurate when applied to the real people involved.

2. Pensions and Other Employment-Related Benefits

Employment-related benefits, provided either by the employer or through public programs such as Social Security, are for many people the most important elements of economic security. Until the 1970s, though, these benefits hardly figured in economic settlements accompanying divorce. Employees' pension rights and other benefits were often very ephemeral; many plans provided that an employee had no absolute right to a pension unless he or she worked for the employer for many years and was employed by that employer at the time of retirement. Courts tended to hold that, under these conditions, pension rights could not be considered property.

Pension rights became more substantial and more common after 1975, the year in which the Employee Retirement Income Security Act (ERISA), 29 U.S.C. §§1001 et seq., became effective. Pension plans that are "qualified" under ERISA and related provisions of the Internal Revenue Code provide employers and employees with substantial federal income tax advantages. (The employer's contributions to the plan are deductible as a business expense, and the contributions to the plan and the income they produce are not income to an employee until retirement benefits are paid.) Most important for our purposes, employees covered by qualified plans are guaranteed that even after relatively short periods of employment, their interests in the plan will vest — that is, they will eventually be entitled to receive benefits through the plan. ERISA has made pension rights more substantial and thus more important at divorce, though they are not universal.

Disability payments and workers' compensation are other forms of wage-replacement benefits. Some forms of these benefits may be combined with retirement benefits, as in the next case, which concerns whether to treat these assets as property for purposes of divorce.

Mickey v. Mickey
974 A.2d 641 (Conn. 2009)

ZARELLA, J. . . . The marriage of the parties was dissolved on September 21, 2001. At the time of dissolution, the defendant had been employed by the state of Connecticut as a correction officer for approximately fourteen years. Pursuant to his employment with the state, the defendant was enrolled in tier II of the state employees retirement system. Due to the nature of his job, the defendant potentially was eligible for hazardous duty retirement under General Statutes §5-192n, and, as with all other state employees enrolled in tier II, also was eligible for normal retirement benefits under General Statutes §5-192*l*, and disability retirement benefits under §5-192p in the event that he became disabled during the course of his employment.

In its memorandum of decision issued in conjunction with the dissolution of the parties' marriage, the trial court, DYER, J., ordered that "[t]he plaintiff shall be entitled to, and the defendant's . . . pension plan shall pay to her, 40 percent of the defendant's monthly retirement benefit payment. It is the court's intention that the plaintiff receive 40 percent of the defendant's monthly retirement benefit payment under the contributory hazardous duty retirement plan should he qualify for [the] same, or 40 percent of the defendant's monthly retirement benefit payment under the noncontributory tier II plan should he fail to qualify for a hazardous duty pension." Despite specifically distributing the defendant's potential hazardous duty retirement benefits, however, the trial court did not mention any potential disability benefits that the defendant may have subsequently become entitled to under the plan.

Following the dissolution of the parties' marriage, the defendant suffered an injury in the course of his employment on February 28, 2002, which rendered him disabled and eventually forced him to retire. The defendant began receiving retirement benefits under the state employees retirement system in June, 2005, which was made retroactive to July 1, 2003, in the amount of $990 per month. The defendant's monthly benefit subsequently was increased to $2382.30 in November, 2005, in recognition of the enhanced benefit that he was entitled to receive as a result of the state's certification of his disability under §5-192p. The plaintiff thereafter continued to receive 40 percent of the defendant's entire monthly benefit payment, including that portion attributable to the defendant's disability benefits.

The defendant subsequently filed a motion for clarification on January 13, 2006, requesting that the trial court clarify that (1) it did not intend to distribute the defendant's disability benefits as part of its original financial orders, and (2) regardless of its intent, the trial court did not have the statutory authority to distribute those benefits because they were acquired after dissolution. . . . [T]he trial court, DYER, J., subsequently denied the defendant's motion for clarification, concluding, . . . that, because retirement benefits are properly distributable under §46b-81, the court had the authority to distribute those retirement benefits attributable to the defendant's disability, and that the defendant, therefore, was not entitled to any relief. This appeal followed. . . .

. . . [W]e now address the defendant's principal claim on appeal, namely, that his disability benefits do not constitute distributable marital property and, therefore, that the trial court lacked authority to distribute those benefits under §46b-81. . . .

With respect to §46b-81, we previously have determined that the purpose of postdissolution "property division is to unscramble the ownership of property, giving to each spouse what is equitably his." While undertaking this task, we have considered the nature of the marital relationship: "[M]arriage is, among other things, a shared enterprise or joint undertaking in the nature of a partnership to which both spouses contribute—directly and indirectly, financially and nonfinancially—*the fruits of which* are distributable at divorce." To this end, we generally have taken a liberal view of the term "property," while declaring that "the theme running through this area of our jurisprudence . . . pays mindful consideration to the equitable purpose of our statutory distribution scheme, rather than to mechanically applied rules of property law. In order to achieve justice, equity looks to substance, and not to mere form."

Placing each spouse in an equitable postdissolution position, however, requires a court to consider more than merely how to divide the marital property. Through General Statutes §46b-82, the legislature has empowered courts to create in either or both spouses an obligation to provide future financial support to the other through continuing alimony payments. We also must examine this companion statute, therefore, in order to understand more completely the interrelationship between §§46b-81 and 46b-82. These two statutes, working together, provide the courts of this state with their primary tools for apportioning the property and income of spouses when a marriage dissolves. . . . Despite their close relationship, however, the purposes and operation of §§46b-81 and 46b-82 are distinct and, to an extent, complementary, applying under different circumstances for different reasons. Although the purpose of §46b-81 is to "unscramble" the spouses' *current* property interests; the purpose of §46b-82 is to recognize "the obligation of support that spouses assume toward each other by virtue of the marriage." Thus, using both statutes, a court can consider the individual circumstances of each marriage to fashion a fair distribution of *presently* existing marital property as well as ensuring the *future* support of a dependent spouse.

Under §46b-81, a court has the authority to divide only the *presently* existing property interests of the parties at the time of dissolution, and such division, once made, cannot be altered. An alimony award made at the time of dissolution, on the other hand, *can* be subsequently modified at any time to account for any significant changes in the circumstances of the parties. . . .

In order to address fully the defendant's claim that his disability benefits are not subject to equitable distribution, it also is important to understand the nature of the disability and retirement plan under which those benefits were granted. General Statutes §§5-192e through 5-192x define the state employee tier II retirement plan of which the defendant was a member. The plan is a noncontributory, comprehensive scheme including provisions for normal retirement; hazardous duty retirement; and disability retirement. An employee's eligibility and amount of benefits under the normal retirement plan are based on (1) years of state employment, which are defined as "vesting service"; and (2) various qualified periods of nonstate employment, which together with years of state employment are defined as "credited service. . . ." An employee may retire voluntarily with a retirement benefit upon reaching a certain age with a defined number of years of accrued vesting service. Upon retiring under the normal retirement plan, the eligible employee's actual benefit is computed using formulas that primarily account for the employee's amount of credited service and his average annual earnings.

The disability retirement plan is distinct from, and complementary to, the normal retirement plan. If an employee under this plan is disabled prior to applying for retirement, the formula remains the same, except that §5-192p(c) provides the employee the benefit of an additional number of years of credited service that "he would have at age sixty-five if he continued to work until that age, but limited to a maximum of thirty years," unless his actual credited service as of his disability retirement date is greater, in which case the formula works exactly the same as in normal retirement. In this way, the acceleration clause of §5-192p(c) serves to reimburse a disabled employee for those years of compensation forgone due to disability, whereas the amount determined under §5-192l on the basis of the employee's actual years of credited service operates as a standard pension benefit, representing deferred compensation for those years of service actually completed.

With this background of the relevant statutes in mind, we now turn to a more specific examination of the meaning of the term "property" in §46b-81. The legislature has not seen fit to define this critical term, leaving it to the courts to determine its meaning through application on a case-by-case basis. . . . As we noted previously, this court has generally taken a rather "broad and comprehensive" view of the meaning of the term "property" for purposes of equitable distribution. We have not erased altogether, however, the limitations inherent in the term. We continue to recognize that "the marital estate divisible pursuant to §46b-81 refers to interests already acquired, not to expected or unvested interests, or to interests that the court has not quantified."

For instance, in *Krafick* [v. Krafick, 663 A.2d 872 (Conn. 1995)], we addressed the issue of whether a vested[14] but unmatured pension could be classified as marital property subject to equitable distribution pursuant to §46b-81. The plaintiff in *Krafick* was contesting the trial court's refusal to consider the defendant's pension benefits alongside other assets in distributing the marital estate. The defendant's pension vested at twenty years of service, and

---

14. Black's Law Dictionary defines "vested" as "[h]aving become a completed, consummated right for present or future enjoyment; not contingent; unconditional; absolute. . . ." Black's Law Dictionary (8th ed. 2004). The most important aspect of vesting in the context of pensions is that it immunizes the employee's interest from being unilaterally altered or abolished by the employer. For instance, in the context of statutory pensions, an employee who has a vested pension would be unaffected by legislative changes to the pension plan occurring *after* he has obtained a vested interest in a particular benefit.

A vested interest "matures" when the holder of that interest obtains a right to *present* possession or payment without further precondition.

the benefit, calculated pursuant to a formula based on the employee's total years of service and an average of the employee's three highest years of earnings, was payable, or matured, upon retirement. At the time of the trial, the defendant in *Krafick* was eligible to retire and represented that he intended to do so in approximately two years.

Analyzing the plaintiff's claim, we first described the nature of the interest in dispute: "Pension benefits represent a form of deferred compensation for services rendered. . . . [T]he employee receives a lesser present compensation plus the contractual right to the future benefits payable under the pension plan." . . . We concluded that vested pension benefits are "an economic resource acquired with the fruits of the wage earner spouse's labors which would otherwise have been utilized by the parties during the marriage to purchase other deferred income assets"; and, thus, distributable as marital property.

We next had to determine whether treating the defendant's vested, but unmatured, pension as property under §46b-81 violated our understanding of the limitations of the reach of the statute. Recognizing that §46b-81 "applies only to presently existing property interests, [and] not mere expectancies"; we concluded that *vested* pension benefits are appropriately characterized as a presently existing property interest because they "represent an employee's right to receive payment in the future, subject ordinarily to his or her living until the age of retirement." . . .

There also is a line of cases, at the other end of the spectrum, recognizing that the definition of property interests subject to distribution under §46b-81, although broad, is not without limits. For instance, in Simmons v. Simmons, 708 A.2d 949, we concluded that a spouse's medical degree is not property within the meaning of §46b-81. In so holding, we distinguished "presently existing property interest[s]," which are subject to distribution, from "mere expectanc[ies]," which are immune from such treatment; and declared that "the defining characteristic of property for purposes of §46b-81 is the present existence of the right and the ability to enforce that right." . . .

Our decision in Bender v. Bender, [785 A.2d 197 (2001),] updated this traditional, fairly rigid dichotomy by establishing a more nuanced approach to defining property interests under §46b-81. In *Bender*, this court "built [on the] foundation" of our prior cases in concluding that the unvested pension of the defendant in that case was property subject to equitable distribution. Consistent with our time-honored approach, we reiterated that presently enforceable rights, based on either property or contract principles, are *sufficient* to cause property to be divisible. Where *Bender* broke new ground was in its recognition that such rights are not the "sine qua non of 'property' under §46b-81." In building on our prior cases, we expanded our notion of property under §46b-81, recognizing that there is a spectrum of interests that do not fit comfortably into our traditional scheme and yet should be available in equity for courts to distribute.

If the acquisition of such an "unconventional" interest is contingent on a future event or circumstance, we now examine the contingency to determine if it is overly speculative. Thus, *Bender* created a two step framework that preserved the traditional definition of property while carving out a middle ground, encompassing some inchoate property interests that would have been excluded from the definition of distributable property under the older regime. These interests may now be considered on the basis of the likelihood that a contingency eventually would come to pass. Of course, in order to apply this analytical framework properly, it is critical to categorize the type of contingency being addressed. A contingency on which the mere *enjoyment* of a property interest depends differs from a contingency on which acquisition of the property interest *itself* hinges. The former — e.g., a vested but unmatured pension or an inchoate contractual right — would simply be classified as distributable property under the first step of the *Bender* analysis, whereas the latter would fail the classic test and therefore have to be addressed under *Bender*'s second step.

In *Bender*, we determined that the defendant's unvested pension benefits, although dependent on certain contingencies, were sufficiently certain to constitute divisible property because "these contingencies are susceptible to reasonably accurate quantification." In so concluding, we recognized that the various contingencies that may determine future property interests come in different degrees. Distinguishing the unvested pension benefits at issue in *Bender* from the inheritance interests in Rubin v. Rubin, and Krause v. Krause, we declared that "[u]nvested pension benefits . . . although dependent on certain future contingencies such as length of service and age [i.e., the mere passage of time], are simply not in [the] same *speculative category* [as a potential inheritance]. Moreover, unlike a potential inheritance, pension benefits represent a trade-off for potentially higher wages not earned during the marriage; they often represent . . . the only or principal material asset; and they are treated by employers and employees as property in the workplace."

We conclude that *Bender* stands for the proposition that, even in the absence of a presently enforceable right to property based on contractual principles or a statutory entitlement, a party's expectant interest in property still may fall under §46b-81 if the conditions precedent to the eventual acquisition of such a definitive right are not too speculative or unlikely. . . .

We turn finally to an application of the *Bender* analysis to the facts of the present case. First, it is clear that, whatever interest the defendant had in potential disability payments under §5-192p, that interest was not, at the time of dissolution, a presently existing, enforceable right to a future benefit. Although the defendant may have had an abstract statutory entitlement, in the event that he became disabled, to certain defined benefits, he had no concrete, enforceable right to those benefits unless and until an unfortunate accident befell him. Furthermore, the legislature could have modified or terminated the disability retirement program at any time before the defendant suffered a disability. Thus, unlike an interest in a vested pension or a granted but not yet matured stock option, the defendant's interest in his disability benefits was not enforceable prior to the occurrence of the disability. Presumably, the defendant actively was trying to avoid the occurrence of an event triggering an enforceable interest in his disability benefits. We can discern no distinction, for example, between the defendant's interest in his disability benefits and an employee's interest in a potential future workers' compensation claim. To consider these "interests" property in the sense that they could be construed as *presently existing, enforceable* rights to some future asset or income stream is simply to stretch the meaning of these words beyond the breaking point.

Our analysis cannot end here, however, as *Bender* instructs that a presently existing, enforceable right to property, although *sufficient* for purposes of §46b-81, is not *necessary*. As we noted previously, in light of *Bender*, analyzing an interest that does not become a "right," much less actual, possessory property, prior to the occurrence of some future event or events involves a second step. We must look at the nature of the contingency to determine whether it is so speculative as to be deemed a mere expectancy or, conversely, whether it is "sufficiently concrete, reasonable and justifiable as to constitute a presently existing property interest for equitable distribution purposes." . . .

In the present case, the defendant's receipt of disability benefits under §5-192p was contingent on his becoming sufficiently disabled prior to sixty-five years of age or completing twenty-five years of credited service. A potential disability is, by its very nature, an accidental event that every employee and employer strives to avoid. It is difficult to perceive how a property interest tied to such an occurrence is "sufficiently concrete, reasonable and justifiable"; to treat any benefits that *might* accrue, *if* the accident eventually occurs *and* is serious enough to cause permanent disability, as a presently existing property interest eligible for equitable distribution at the time of dissolution. We are persuaded that this eventuality is more speculative and far less predictable than the income expected to flow from a medical degree; or the property expected to be acquired through a bequest. As with a testamentary bequest, however, the disability benefits at issue in the present case were terminable at the state's discretion at any time before the defendant suffered a disability. We conclude, therefore, that, consistent with *Bender*, the defendant's interest in future disability benefits is far too speculative to be considered property subject to equitable distribution.

Furthermore, such an interest, even if it was sufficiently concrete to constitute distributable property, could not be classified as distributable under the facts of this case. A benefit derived from an injury occurring years after dissolution, meant solely to compensate for the loss of future wages, simply does not represent the "fruits" of the marital partnership that §46b-81 is designed to equitably parse. . . .

The difficulty with the present case is that the defendant's "retirement disability" is, in effect, a hybrid of two conceptually distinct interests. We conclude that, as of the date of the parties' dissolution, the portion of the defendant's retirement benefit attributable to his actual years of service—and, therefore, properly characterized as deferred compensation—is distributable as marital property. This conclusion is consistent with our reasoning in *Bender*, as the receipt of regular pension benefits represents, at least in part, deferred compensation earned during the marriage, the value of which is quantifiable at the time of dissolution to a reasonable degree of certainty. On the other hand, we conclude that the portion of the defendant's benefit attributable to the additional amount that he receives as a consequence of being disabled was too speculative at the time of dissolution to be considered distributable property under §46b-81, and was in no way earned during the course of the marriage. . . .

In the present case, the record indicates that the defendant was entitled to receive $990 per month in regular retirement benefits at the time of his injury. Once his application for disability retirement was approved, that amount increased to $2382.30 per month, reflecting the disability enhancement. Our precedents, together with the policy underlying §46b-81 and simple common sense, require us to treat the $990 as distributable property, and the difference, $1392.30, as nondistributable property. Therefore, pursuant to the judgment of dissolution, the plaintiff is entitled to 40 percent of the defendant's regular retirement benefits but is not entitled to a percentage of the defendant's disability benefits.

The judgment is reversed and the case is remanded with direction to render judgment granting the defendant's motion for clarification and to issue modified financial orders according to law.

NORCOTT, J., with whom KATZ, J., joins, concurring and dissenting. . . . In my view, . . . our prior precedents and the language of §5-192p make the defendant's interest in his disability benefits property under the first prong of *Bender* because the defendant had an enforceable and irrevocable right to those benefits as of the first day of his employment with the state, despite the fact that his receipt and future enjoyment of those benefits was contingent on him subsequently becoming disabled. Accordingly, I respectfully dissent.

As an initial matter, I note that I agree with the majority that, under the first prong of the *Bender* analysis, our cases generally have classified property interests by characterizing them as either presently existing and enforceable, and thus distributable, or as mere expectancies that are immune from distribution. My primary disagreement with the majority relates to the analysis that we employ to make that determination, as well as the application of that analysis to the benefits in the present case. Specifically, although our focus under the first prong of *Bender* is to determine whether the right to the benefit is presently existing and enforceable at the time of dissolution; that does not mean that the party must have the right to immediate *receipt* and *enjoyment* of the benefit, or even an unconditional guarantee that the benefit will be received at all. Rather, when the receipt of the benefit associated with a particular interest is contingent on the occurrence of a future event, that interest will nevertheless be considered marital property under our current case law if, at the time of dissolution, the party has an enforceable right to receive the benefit in the event that the condition *does* occur. . . .

Applying the analysis in these precedents to the present case, therefore, I would conclude that the defendant's interest in his disability benefits was distributable property. The language of §5-192p(a) expressly provides that "[i]f a member of tier II, while in state service, becomes . . . disabled as a result of any injury received while in the performance of his duty as a state employee, he is eligible for disability retirement, *regardless of his period of state service or his age.*" (Emphasis added.) Thus, from the moment the defendant began his employment with the state, he had an enforceable right to receive disability benefits in the event that he subsequently suffered a disabling injury within the scope of his employment. That right was both presently existing and enforceable from that time on, and, had the defendant become disabled on his first day of work, he would have been entitled to receive disability benefits without precondition. . . . Moreover, the fact that the contingency was unlikely to occur is not relevant to our analysis under the first prong of *Bender*, which focuses on whether he had a right to such benefits in the event that the contingency *did* occur. . . .

The majority also concludes that the defendant's interest was not marital property under the first prong of *Bender* because the disability benefit program could have been revoked by the legislature at any time prior to the defendant becoming disabled, implying that the defendant's interest in those benefits did not, and could not, vest until that time. In my view, however, the language of §5-192p indicates that the defendant's interest had in fact vested as of the first day of his employment with the state, and could not have been revoked by the legislature at any time thereafter. . . .

Finally, I briefly note my disagreement with the majority's conclusion that the defendant's interest in disability benefits did not constitute marital property because the injury occurred postdissolution and represents compensation for future lost wages. We have stated that whether an asset is marital property turns on the time at which an enforceable right to the particular benefit was obtained, and *not* on whether the benefits associated with the interest were received during the marriage. Moreover, we have recognized that "[e]xamining what an asset is intended to reflect is significant . . . only as it relates to whether [an enforceable right to the] asset was earned prior to or subsequent to the date of dissolution. Because in my view the defendant obtained an enforceable interest in his disability benefits under our current case law from the moment he began working for the state, I do not believe that the fact that those benefits were received after the marriage had been dissolved or that they represent, in part, compensation for future lost wages is relevant to our analysis. . . .

NOTES AND QUESTIONS

1. One argument against treating future rights to retirement and disability benefits as property is that they are contingent in many ways. In what ways may the right to receive a pension be contingent? In light of these contingencies, what problems are created if we treat them as property for purposes of divorce? Notwithstanding these problems, virtually all courts and many statutes now treat vested pension rights as property subject to division, and most treat nonvested rights in the same way. Can you see why? This does not mean that the contingencies are ignored; instead, they are addressed in the valuation and methodology of dividing pension rights, as discussed below.

The pension in *Mickey* was a *defined benefit* plan; in this kind of plan, an employee's benefits are determined on the basis of a formula, usually based on years of service and salary, which does not depend on the amount of contributions. Individual accounts are not maintained for each employee. In contrast, in *defined contribution* plans, each employee has a separate account that contains contributions to the plan, interest earned, and any other increase in value of the assets in the account. The amount of the employee's retirement benefit depends on how much is in the account when the employee begins to draw benefits.

Retirement plans can also be categorized according to who puts money into the plan. Both the employer and the employee contribute toward the cost of a *contributory* plan. Only the employer contributes to a *noncontributory* plan. If a plan is contributory, the employee's contributions are immediately vested, so the employee is entitled to them even if he or she quits participating in the plan before retirement. The employee's interest in the amount attributable to the employer's contributions may not vest until the employee has worked for a defined period of time, although ERISA limits how long the employer can delay vesting of pension rights. Both defined benefit and defined contribution plans can be contributory or noncontributory.

2. An employee is entitled to immediate payment of retirement benefits only if his or her interest is vested and matured. What is the difference between vesting and maturity?

If a pension is matured and paying benefits, should it still be treated as property if the employee and his or her spouse divorce? Or at this point should the pension belong to the employee and be treated as a source of income from which spousal support can be paid?

3. Are rights to a disability pension necessarily more contingent than rights to a retirement pension, as the majority in *Mickey* claims?

4. One way that courts divide retirement benefits is to give the entire benefit to the employee and, in lieu of his or her share, give the nonemployee spouse a greater share of other divisible assets. This is known as the "offset" approach and requires the court to determine the value at the time of divorce of the employee spouse's right to receive payments from the pension in the future.

Under the "if, as, and when" approach, each spouse receives a fractional share of each pension payment as it comes due. Originally, courts usually implemented this method by ordering the employee to pay the nonemployee his or her share of each payment as it came in.

What are the advantages and disadvantages of each of these approaches?

5. Many problems associated with the if, as, and when approach could be solved if a court could order the pension plan administrator to pay the nonemployee spouse his or her share of the benefits directly. However, as we saw in Chapter 2, pension plans subject to ERISA must provide that benefits are inalienable, and many other plans have the same rule. The Retirement Equity Act of 1984 (REA) solves this problem for pensions subject to ERISA by creating an exception to the inalienability requirement. It provides that a court may enter a qualified domestic relations order (QDRO), which directs the pension plan administrator to pay a portion of an employee's benefits to someone other than the employee. 29 U.S.C. §1056(d). The order can require that payments to the nonemployee begin before the employee actually retires, beginning on or after the earliest date on which the employee could retire. The nonemployees to whom these payments are made are called "alternate payees."

A QDRO must "relate[ ] to the provision of child support, alimony payments, or marital property rights to a spouse, former spouse, child, or other dependent" of the employee and thus can be used not only to divide a pension as property but also to use pension interests as a fund from which support payments are made. Some courts have held that a QDRO can be used to divide a pension between cohabitants, interpreting the statutory authorization to use these orders to divide "marital property" as including marital-property-like rights. Boulds v. Nielsen, 323 P.3d 58 (Alaska 2014) (set out in full at page 184, *supra*); Owens v. Auto Machinists Pension Trust, 551 F.3d 1138 (9th Cir. 2009). However, if there is no divorce or other family law matter pending, the anti-alienation clause of ERISA prevents the transfer of employee plan benefits to a spouse through the use of a QDRO. Jago v. Jago, 217 A.3d 289, 291 (Pa. Super. Ct. 2019).

REA imposes seven requirements that an order must meet to be a QDRO. If the order satisfies these requirements, the plan administrator must comply with it; if it does not, ERISA forbids the administrator to comply.

A QDRO divides a defined contribution plan by awarding the nonemployee an amount or percentage of the account balance. Because a defined benefit plan has no account balance, the QDRO uses a flat figure or a formula to designate how much will be paid to the nonemployee.

The Retirement Equity Act applies only to plans governed by ERISA; therefore, QDROs are available only for these plans. The largest group of plans not covered by ERISA are those for federal, state, and local government employees. Some states have legislation allowing QDROs to be used for state and local government pensions. QDROs are not required to transfer funds from one IRA to another; IRC §408 provides for a simpler process.

For more information, *see* Terrence Cain, A Primer on the History and Proper Drafting of Qualified Domestic Relations Orders, 28 T.M. Cooley L. Rev. 417 (2011).

6. Defined contribution and defined benefit plans are assigned present values in fundamentally different ways. Valuing an employee's interest in a defined contribution plan is in principle simple. Since each employee has a separate account, the employee's interest is worth the current fair market value of the assets in the account. If the assets are cash or its equivalent, the value will be the total amount of contributions plus any income they have earned. Valuation is more difficult if the assets are themselves more difficult to value, such as real estate.

Since defined benefit plans do not maintain separate accounts for each employee, valuation of interests in these is more difficult. The problem is similar to valuing the goose that laid the golden eggs. The valuator must estimate the stream of income that the pension will produce, making many assumptions, such as when it will begin and when it will end, and then calculate the value of that stream of income at the time of divorce, making still more assumptions about interest rates and other contingencies.

While a lawyer may well be able to determine the value of benefits in a defined contribution plan alone, most lawyers lack the expertise to value defined benefit plan benefits. Instead, they hire experts. The lawyer's responsibility here is to understand what kinds of analyses various experts perform so that an appropriate one can be chosen. In addition, a lawyer must understand generally the method that the expert uses to value a pension and, specifically, what assumptions about interest rates, mortality, and so on the expert made. These experts do not necessarily know family property law and so may not know that benefits earned after the divorce are not divisible or, in states that permit division only of property acquired during the marriage, that benefits attributable to premarital employment are not divisible. The lawyer must explain these rules to the expert and ensure that the calculations are consistent with them.

For more information, *see* Joshua G. Coyne et al., Tax Planning for Retirement Asset Division in Divorce, 44 Est. Plan. 28 (2017).

7. Employees may have a number of other kinds of benefits, which may or may not be intended to provide for retirement. Many of these are treated as defined contribution plans for purposes of property distribution at divorce. They include individual retirement accounts, Keogh plans, profit-sharing plans, stock option plans, employee stock ownership plans, and thrift and savings plans.

8. One of the most valuable employment-related benefits is the right to participate in group health or life insurance, because group insurance may not require proof of insurability and group rates are often substantially lower than the cost of similar coverage under an individual policy. Often an employee's dependents, including a spouse, can participate in the group plan, but those plans typically provide that coverage terminates when a person no longer qualifies as a dependent — for example, when a spouse becomes a divorced former spouse. Federal and state statutes now protect divorced spouses against loss of health insurance coverage. Under federal law, health insurance plans must permit divorced spouses to continue participating in their former spouses' plans for up to 36 months following a divorce. 26 U.S.C. §4980B (2014). Spouses must pay premiums to continue participating. In addition, some states have statutes, some of them pre-dating the federal law, that give divorced people the right to continue participating in group health insurance programs through their former spouses' employment for a limited time.

NOTE: DIVIDING BENEFITS INTO MARITAL AND NONMARITAL SHARES

In jurisdictions that permit only marital property to be divided at divorce, a pension earned in part before or after marriage and in part during marriage must be divided into marital and nonmarital shares. Most courts use the "time rule": the value of the pension rights is multiplied by a fraction whose numerator is the number of years the pension accrued during the marriage and whose denominator is the total number of years the pension accrued. Thus, if at the time of divorce the employee spouse has accrued rights for 20 years and if the spouses have been married for 15 of those years, 15/20, or three-quarters, of the pension rights are marital property.

If the employee spouse is still working at the time of divorce, two critical facts are unknown and unknowable: how long the employee will work until retirement and how much the retirement benefit will be. Together these raise the question of whether increases in the benefit at least partly attributable to the employee's work after divorce are divisible. The Utah Supreme Court discussed approaches to this issue in Johnson v. Johnson, 330 P.3d 704 (Utah 2014):

> At one end of the spectrum is the bright line approach—the approach advocated by Mr. Johnson. The bright line approach "likens post-divorce pension enhancements to post-divorce earnings and characterizes all such increases as the separate property of the employee spouse." Under this approach, "pension benefits accruing as compensation for services rendered after a divorce are not part of the [marital] estate . . . subject to division on divorce." This approach treats any subsequent advancement (and the resulting pay increase) as the separate property of the employee spouse because any such advances or increases result solely from the labors of the employee spouse. . . .
>
> At the other end of the spectrum is the marital foundation approach, which acknowledges that postdivorce *earnings* are separate property, but treats *all* postdivorce *increases* in pension benefits as marital property. The marital foundation approach is easy to apply, as a district court need only apply the time rule formula to the employee spouse's monthly pension benefit at retirement, with no need to "parse out the 'marital' portion of the post-dissolution enhancement from the 'separate' portion . . . attributable solely to the efforts of the employee spouse." Furthermore, the marital foundation approach seeks to offset the "risk of forfeiture, delay in receipt, and lack of control over the timing of the receipt of benefits" suffered by the nonemployee spouse by permitting the nonemployee spouse to share in postdivorce enhancements to benefits.
>
> The bright line and marital foundation approaches can be thought of as anchoring each end of a spectrum of approaches available to district courts. . . .
>
> . . . [W]e believe that a context-specific approach leads to the most equitable distribution of pension benefits. . . .
>
> When determining the most equitable distribution of the employee spouse's pension benefits, a district court should consider the pension benefits much like it does other marital property. That is, the district court should consider the extent to which the property was acquired during the marriage and the ultimate source of the property. In the context of pension benefits, this will require the district court to consider how the trajectory of the employee spouse's career intersected with the marriage and the extent to which the marriage contributed to the employee spouse's pay grade at retirement. For example, if the parties were married only briefly early in the employee

spouse's career, it is highly unlikely that the nonemployee spouse contributed significantly to the employee spouse's ultimate pay grade at retirement. In such a scenario, there would be no reason to award the nonemployee spouse the benefit of all of the employee spouse's subsequent pay raises, whether they result from promotions, renegotiations of union contracts, or job changes.

On the other hand, if the parties are married for a significant portion of the employee spouse's career, it is much more likely that the nonemployee spouse's contributions impacted the trajectory of the employee spouse's career in a way the court should credit. This would be especially true in circumstances in which the parties were married while the employee spouse underwent specialized training or schooling that would further his or her career. To the extent such training or education led to increases in rank or pay grade, the court could see fit to award the nonemployee spouse credit for the resulting increase in pension benefits. Even in this circumstance, however, it does not stand to reason that the nonemployee spouse would then be entitled to *all* subsequent increases. The district court should, in its discretion, determine what contribution the nonemployee spouse made to the subsequent increases, if any, and award credit only for those fairly attributable to that contribution.

330 P.3d at 713-716.

Why didn't *Mickey* treat disability benefits like pensions and classify them as marital or separate based on when they were earned? Why would the dissent use this methodology? In Holman v. Holman, 84 S.W.3d 903, 906-907 (Ky. 2002), the Kentucky Supreme Court discussed approaches to characterization of disability benefits as marital or separate:

> Those courts which hold that disability benefits constitute marital property have advanced several rationales for this conclusion. Under one approach, which has been referred to as the "mechanistic approach," courts consider whether disability benefits have been specifically excepted from the definition of marital property by statute. Disability benefits will be considered marital property unless there is a statutory provision specifically excluding disability benefits from the marital estate.
>
> Another rationale given in support of the mechanistic approach is that disability benefits should be considered marital property because the policy premiums were paid with marital funds or the marital estate acquired the benefits as a form of compensation for spousal labor during the marriage, much like a pension.
>
> However, the majority of courts considering the proper classification of disability benefits have adopted the analytical approach which focuses on the nature and purpose of the specific disability benefits at issue. Under this approach, benefits which actually compensate for disability are not classified as marital property because such benefits are personal to the spouse who receives them and compensate for loss of good health and replace lost earning capacity. However, where the facts warrant, courts utilizing the analytical approach will separate the benefits into a retirement component and a true disability component, with the retirement component being classified as marital property and the disability component being classified as separate property. This approach has been applied both to disability benefits paid in connection with insurance coverage maintained by the disabled spouse's employer and to disability benefits paid in connection with a private policy of disability insurance acquired with marital funds during the marriage.

A COMPARISON: SURVIVORSHIP RIGHTS AND DEATH BENEFITS

Both survivorship rights and death benefits provide money to an employee's successors after the employee dies. Survivorship rights typically give the successor a right to receive an annuity or to continue receiving the annuity that the employee was receiving before death. Most commonly, an employee takes retirement benefits in the form of a joint and survivor annuity, which provides for periodic payments to the retired employee and after the employee's death to the successor. Recall from Chapter 2 that if the pension plan is governed by ERISA and the employee is married at retirement, the employee must choose a joint and survivor annuity unless the spouse agrees in writing to another distribution. If an employee divorces before retirement, ERISA allows the nonemployee former spouse to retain joint and survivor annuity benefits, if the QDRO expressly so provides. A QDRO can also assign *only* survivor benefits to the nonemployee spouse, which means that the nonemployee will receive benefits only at the death of the employee. If the former spouse is the full survivor beneficiary, the employee cannot designate any future spouse as a beneficiary.

In contrast to survivorship rights, death benefits in an employee retirement plan are similar to life insurance benefits. The plan provides that at the employee's death, some amount of money will be paid to beneficiaries designated by the employee. Whether an employee's survivors will be entitled to any kind of death benefit if the employee dies before retiring depends on the terms of the plan. To the extent that the funds in the pension were contributed by the employee, there will be a death benefit, and often plans provide a death benefit as to the employee's vested rights based on the employer's contributions.

A number of states have enacted statutes that address the frequent failure of holders of life insurance policies and pension plans to change the designated death beneficiary of their plan or policy after divorce by providing that the designations are automatically revoked by divorce. In Egelhoff v. Egelhoff, 532 U.S. 141 (2001), the Supreme Court held that these statutes are preempted by ERISA. The Court said that the statutes conflict with ERISA because they require plan administrators to determine beneficiaries according to state law rather than the plan documents, which would affect the payment of benefits, a central ERISA concern.

In Kennedy v. Plan Administrator, 555 U.S. 285 (2009), the former wife of a pension plan participant had signed a document waiving any interest in the plan as part of a divorce settlement agreement, but the former husband did not file a change-of-beneficiary form, as required by the plan's governing documents. When he died, the executor of his estate claimed the death benefit, as did the former wife. The Supreme Court ruled that the former wife should prevail, relying on *Egelhoff*.

In contrast, Sveen v. Melin, 138 S. Ct. 1815 (2018), held that an automatic revision statute could constitutionally be applied to a life insurance policy not governed by ERISA. The former spouse, who had been designated as the primary beneficiary, claimed that the automatic revision provision unconstitutionally impaired a preexisting contract relationship. The Supreme Court rejected the claim. The Court held that the statute did not substantially impair a contractual relationship for three reasons:

> First, the statute is designed to reflect a policyholder's intent — and so to support, rather than impair, the contractual scheme. Second, the law is unlikely to disturb any policyholder's expectations because it does no more than a divorce court could always have done. And third, the statute supplies a mere default rule, which the policyholder can undo in a moment. Indeed, Minnesota's revocation statute stacks up well against laws that this Court upheld against Contracts Clause challenges as far back as the early 1800s.

138 S. Ct. at 1822.

NOTE: SOCIAL SECURITY, MILITARY, AND OTHER PENSIONS

Approximately 95 percent of all American workers are covered by Social Security. Workers may also be covered by other federal retirement programs, such as the Railroad Retirement Act or a military pension provision. Numerous cases, including several from the Supreme Court, have considered whether these retirement benefits should be treated like private pensions. Typically, state courts have treated federal pensions like other pensions and have applied their marital property law to them. However, the Supreme Court has held that statutory provisions that prevent covered employees from assigning or alienating their pension rights were intended to prevent courts from treating these rights as marital property, and, under the supremacy clause of the Constitution, this federal purpose controls.

The first of these cases was Hisquierdo v. Hisquierdo, 439 U.S. 572 (1979), which dealt with a husband's pension benefits under the federal Railroad Retirement Act. The Supreme Court concluded that the anti-assignment and anti-alienation provisions are intended to ensure that the benefits actually reach the beneficiary and that treating the benefits as divisible community property conflicts with this purpose. Congress later enacted legislation subjecting these benefits to state marital property law. The Railroad Retirement Act applies to relatively few people, but other federal pension statutes also contain anti-assignment and anti-alienation clauses like those in the Railroad Act.

Military Retirement Benefits   In McCarty v. McCarty, 453 U.S. 210 (1981), the Court held that states could not treat military retirement benefits as marital property, based on the statutes' anti-assignment and anti-alienation clauses. In 1982, in response to *McCarty*, Congress enacted the Uniformed Services Former Spouses' Protection Act (USFSPA), 10 U.S.C. §§1072, 1076, 1086, 1401, 1408, 1447, 1448, 1450, which provides that each state's divorce courts may treat disposable military retired pay or retainer pay according to the state law governing division of marital property.

USFSPA also allows former spouses of military personnel to obtain court-ordered payments of property settlements directly from the appropriate military finance center if while married the military spouse is credited with at least ten years of service toward earning retirement benefits. The former spouse can receive at most 50 percent of the service member's disposable retired or retainer pay through this direct payment method. If the ten-year test is not met, the divorce court can still treat the pension as divisible marital property, but the division can be enforced only by the offset method or by ordering the military spouse to pay a share of pension payments to the former spouse. Similarly, the divorce court can award the spouse who was not in the service more than 50 percent of the benefits, but amounts above 50 percent cannot be collected directly from the military finance center. Former spouses of military personnel may also receive direct payment of court-ordered spousal or child support, regardless of the length of the marriage.

Military personnel who are disabled may receive disability benefits instead of a corresponding amount of retirement pay, and it is often to their benefit to do so because disability payments are exempt from federal, state, and local income taxes, while retirement pay is not. In Mansell v. Mansell, 490 U.S. 581 (1989), the Supreme Court considered whether a wife who had been awarded a share of her former husband's military retirement benefits at divorce had any claim when the husband elected to take disability benefits instead. The Supreme Court held that military disability pay is not divisible marital property because the USFSPA definition of "disposable retired or retainer pay" excludes retirement pay waived to receive disability payments. The effect was that the former wife lost almost 30 percent of the monthly retirement income she would otherwise have received. In Howell v. Howell, 137 S. Ct. 1400 (2017), the Supreme Court held the federal rule also prevents divorce courts from ordering people receiving military disability pay in lieu of retirement pay to indemnify their former spouses for the share of the retirement pay that the ex-spouses lost. However, the Alaska Supreme Court has held that a property settlement agreement that required a husband to indemnify the wife if he "took any action" that reduced the wife's share of his military retirement pay was triggered when he converted his retirement to disability pay. The court distinguished *Howell* on the basis that the obligation here arose from a negotiated property settlement agreement. Jones v. Jones, 505 P.3d 224 (Alaska 2022). For more information, *see* Brentley Tanner, The Battle for the Biggest Assets: Dissolution of the Military Marriage and Postdivorce Considerations for Aging Clients, 50 Fam. L.Q. 49 (2016); Mark E. Sullivan, Family Support, Garnishment, and Military Retired Pay, 50 Fam. L.Q. 79 (2016).

CIVIL SERVICE PENSIONS   The Civil Service Act allows treatment of civil service benefits as marital property divisible at divorce, 5 U.S.C. §8345(j)(1).

SOCIAL SECURITY   Most courts have held that Social Security benefits are not property subject to division and that a court may not divide them indirectly by awarding the other spouse offsetting property of equal value. This conclusion is based on the anti-assignment and anti-alienation provisions of the Social Security Act, 42 U.S.C. §407. However, the Social Security Act explicitly allows courts to order the Social Security Administration to pay a person's legal obligations to support a spouse, former spouse, or children from his or her benefits. 42 U.S.C. §659. The courts are divided about whether the value of benefits may be "considered" in fashioning an equitable division of property, differing on whether this amounts to an offset or not. The Montana Supreme Court in Smith v. Smith, 358 P.3d 171 (Mont. 2015), reviewed case law from other states and found that almost all courts have held that courts may not give a property award to one spouse to offset the Social Security benefits of the other. However, in most states a court may "consider" the benefits as a relevant economic circumstance. *See, e.g.,* Jackson v. Sollie, 141 A.3d 1122 (Md. 2016); In re Marriage of Herald and Steadman, 322 P.3d 546 (Or. 2014) (en banc). *Contra* In re Marriage of Mueller, 34 N.E.3d 538 (Ill. 2015).

A surviving spouse is entitled to the amount of Social Security benefits that the deceased spouse was receiving or his/her own benefits, whichever is greater. A surviving spouse who marries again after age 60 does not lose benefits based on the account of the deceased spouse.

A divorced spouse is entitled to receive Social Security benefits on the account of a former spouse if the marriage lasted at least ten years. 42 U.S.C. §402(b)(1). The benefit payable to a divorced spouse does not reduce the benefit payable to the worker. 42 U.S.C. §403(a)(3). However, if the divorced spouse's own benefits are greater, the divorced spouse does not receive benefits on the account of the former spouse. A divorced spouse may apply for dependent benefits at age 62 if the former spouse is also at least 62, even though the latter is not yet collecting Social Security. The divorced spouse loses benefits upon remarriage before age 60, but not after that age.

A person who has been married and divorced more than once may draw benefits on the account of whichever former spouse will provide the greatest benefits. And more than one former spouse may be able to claim benefits on the account of the same earner. For example, assume that Q, a wage earner, and R, a homemaker, were married for 13 years and divorced. Q then married S, who was also a homemaker, and they were divorced after 11 years. R remarried T, another wage earner, and they divorced after 15 years. R, who is not independently entitled to Social Security, may draw benefits on the account of either Q or T, and both R and S may draw benefits on the account of Q.

In 2021 the U.S. Department of Justice and the Social Security Administration dropped appeals in two class-action suits in which lower courts held in favor of surviving same-sex partners who had not been married long enough to qualify for survivor benefits or who were not able to marry because their partners died before same-sex marriage was legalized. Tara Siegel Bernard, More Same-Sex Couples May Be Eligible for Social Security Survivor Benefits, N.Y. Times, Nov. 2, 2021.

PROBLEMS

1. Andy had pension rights through employment at the time of divorce. Andy received the pension and Max received other property as an offset. Andy's pension has matured, meaning that Andy is receiving monthly payments from it. Should these monthly payments be considered income to Andy in deciding if Max is entitled to spousal support, or would that allow Max to double-dip? If the pension was divided by awarding Max a fractional share of each payment, should these payments be treated as income to Max in determining spousal support issues?

2. When Beryl and Daye were divorced, Beryl was working as a high-level manager at Big Company. Six years later Beryl was offered an attractive early retirement package that included a significant increase in retirement benefits. If Daye had received an increased share of marital property in lieu of an interest in Beryl's pension, would Beryl have a claim to some portion of these benefits that were not anticipated when they divorced? If Beryl had been awarded a share in the pension retirement benefits in the form of an "if, as, and when" order, should the benefits Beryl receives include a portion of the enhanced package of benefits?

3. During her marriage to Gerald, Mary was awarded stock options. At the time that the options were to expire, the community did not have the funds to exercise the options, and so Mary used her separate funds to exercise the options and purchase the stocks. At the time, the options were worth $50,000, and the purchase price was $40,000. Mary and Gerald are divorcing. The stocks are worth $135,000. What portion of the stocks is community or marital property? What portion, if any, is Mary's separate property?

4. Val, a plaintiff's personal injury attorney, and Ann are divorcing. They disagree about whether contingent fees that Val hopes to recover for some pending cases are divisible marital property. Case 1 has been settled, but no payments have been made at the time of the divorce. In case 2, Val's client won a favorable jury verdict, but the case is on appeal. Case 3 is in the discovery stages. What arguments should Val and Ann make regarding the fees in each of these cases?

5. Hank inherited a Christmas tree farm from his parents during his marriage to Faye. He worked on the farm, which remained his separate property. Faye had a job in town. At the time of Hank and Faye's divorce they disagree about whether immature trees, which will be ready to harvest in ten years, are divisible marital property. What arguments should each side make?

6. Bobby's mother created a trust during Bobby's marriage to Alex. Bobby is entitled to one-sixth of the income for life. After Bobby's death, the interest goes to Bobby's children. When Bobby and Alex divorce, what portion of the trust, if any, is marital property subject to division?

3. Professional Practices and Other Closely Held Businesses

When one or both spouses own an interest in a small business, either as a sole proprietor, a partner, or a shareholder in a close corporation, dividing this interest may be the most important issue at divorce. Is the business interest divisible property at all? If so, how should this interest be valued (since there will probably not be a readily ascertainable market value) and divided?

When a spouse owns a personal service business, such as a professional practice, the problems are compounded. The practice likely owns some tangible assets — equipment, books, and accounts receivable — but, compared to a hardware store, these assets represent relatively little of the total value of the business. Expertise and services provided by the professional are relatively more important. Thus, there are real problems of defining what constitutes the property in the practice.

McReath v. McReath
800 N.W.2d 399 (Wis. 2011)

PATIENCE DRAKE ROGGENSACK, J. . . . Tracy and Tim were married on August 27, 1988. Three children, all of whom were minors at the time the divorce proceedings were initiated, were born of their marriage.[15]

In 1991, Tim received his dental degree, and in 1993, he received a master's degree in orthodontia. Accordingly, most of Tim's dental education was pursued during the marriage. Tim took out student loans to fund his education, all of which were repaid with marital funds.

Upon receiving his masters in orthodontia, Tim worked as an associate at Orthodontic Specialists for two years. Tim then purchased the Baraboo and Portage locations of Orthodontic Specialists from Dr. Grady.

Tim paid approximately $930,000 for the two locations of Orthodontic Specialists. A portion of this purchase price was attributed to a noncompete agreement that Dr. Grady signed and to transitional services that Dr. Grady provided Tim. Specifically, Tim testified that $100,000 was for the physical assets, corporate name, and corporate goodwill. The remaining $830,000 was for, as Tim described, "Dr. Grady's name, the noncompete clause, and the employment agreement that Dr. Grady would stay on to introduce me to his existing patients, [and] to counsel me through the process of learning how to do business."

With regard to the noncompete agreement, Tim testified that he would not have purchased Orthodontic Specialists for as high of a price as he did without a noncompete agreement because, "[Dr. Grady] could have just opened up a business just down the street and I'm assuming that he would have taken not only the majority of patients with him but the majority of the future patients in the area." Tim also testified that he was not aware of any transaction in the field of orthodontics, for any substantial value, that took place without a noncompete agreement. According to Tim, "the name of the practitioner is always weighted very heavily as opposed to the goodwill or the value of the name of the practice or corporation."

Tim has worked as the sole owner of Orthodontic Specialists since he purchased it from Dr. Grady. Tim has historically averaged a 60-hour work week. This is significantly more than the average orthodontist who works only 35 hours per week. Recently, Tim has reduced the number of hours he works to approximately 45 hours per week. Tim has no plans to sell or dispose of his practice.

Tim has been very successful in operating Orthodontic Specialists. His annual gross business revenues in the five years leading up to the divorce ranged from $1.6 million to in excess of $1.8 million. In the same five years, Tim received an average yearly net cash flow from Orthodontic Specialists of $697,522. Notably, Orthodontic Specialists maintains the only orthodontic offices in Baraboo and Portage.

The success of Orthodontic Specialists has resulted in a relatively high standard of living for the McReath family. They have significant assets and little, if any, personal debt.

Unlike Tim, Tracy does not have a professional degree. She is a high school graduate with some college credits, but no college degree. Tracy worked outside the home while Tim was attending dental school. Throughout much of their marriage, however, Tracy worked as a homemaker and the primary caretaker for the couple's children. Specifically, she was completely out of the workforce from 1993 to 2000. From 2000 to 2008, she performed some financial and clerical duties for Orthodontic Specialists. In this position, she was paid

---

15. The McReaths' eldest child has since reached the age of majority.

$15,000 to $16,000 per year. The circuit court found Tracy has a current earning capacity of $14.50 per hour, or $30,160 annually. . . .

Regarding the marital property division, with the exception of the value of Orthodontic Specialists, the parties stipulated to the value of their marital assets. They also stipulated to a division of assets with a balancing payment. Hearings were held on the appropriate fair market valuation of Orthodontic Specialists, and resulted in a valuation of $1,058,000. This was the value given by Tracy's expert, Craig Billings (Billings). The court rejected the $415,000 valuation of Tim's expert, Dennis Ksicinski (Ksicinski).

Having valued Orthodontic Specialists at $1,058,000, the court turned to dividing the assets. The court found that there was no reason to deviate from the presumption of equal property division in Wis. Stat. §767.61(3) (2009-10). It then combined the $1,058,000 valuation of Orthodontic Specialists with the other, stipulated-to, assets in the marital estate. Because, among other assets, Tim was the stipulated owner of Orthodontic Specialists, Tim's total assets exceeded Tracy's by $1,593,440. As such, to equalize the property division, the court awarded Tracy $796,720, to be paid at the rate of no less than $80,000 per year plus accrued interest.

Next, to set maintenance, the court used Tim's average annual earnings from Orthodontic Specialists over the preceding five years, i.e., $697,522. However, because the $697,522 salary was based on Tim working 50-70 hours per week, the court adjusted the figure to reflect a 40-hour work week. Consequently, the court set Tim's expected annual income from Orthodontic Specialists at $465,000 (rounded). Next, the court took its finding that Tracy had a current earning capacity of $14.50 per hour, or $30,160 annually. The court then added these income calculations to the other sources of income available to the parties, specifically rental and investment income, and found that Tim's total annual income was $535,806 (or $44,650/month) and Tracy's total annual income was $75,944 (or $6,328/month).

With these figures in hand, the court considered the statutory factors set forth in Wis. Stat. §767.56 in deciding whether to award maintenance. In considering these factors, the court found that it was unlikely that Tracy would ever have Tim's earning capacity or an income that would allow for a standard of living comparable to that enjoyed during the marriage. The court also underscored that Tracy had contributed to the dental education and increased earning capacity of Tim. Based on these findings, the court awarded Tracy maintenance in the amount of $16,000 per month for a period of 20 years.

Tim appealed and the court of appeals affirmed. . . .

In this case, the issue is whether the entire value of the salable professional goodwill in Orthodontic Specialists is included in the marital estate subject to division under Wis. Stat. §767.61. . . .

Defining professional goodwill is a necessary starting point. In 1967, we recognized a business's goodwill as a divisible marital asset. Spheeris v. Spheeris, 155 N.W.2d 130 (1967). In doing so, we underscored the difficulty in defining the concept, but set forth the following definition:

> In its broadest sense the intangible asset called good will may be said to be reputation; however, a better description would probably be that element of value which inheres in the fixed and favorable consideration of customers arising from an established and well-conducted business.

. . . As aforementioned, we recognized goodwill as part of the divisible marital estate as early as 1967. In *Spheeris*, in order to calculate Mr. Spheeris's net worth for the divorce judgment, the circuit court included the value of the goodwill attributable to the retail discount store owned by Mr. Spheeris. Mr. Spheeris did not challenge the inclusion of goodwill as a divisible marital asset; rather, he challenged the valuation of the goodwill by use of predictive formulas, absent a sale of the business. In other words, Mr. Spheeris argued that "the only way to establish [goodwill] is through a purchase price agreed upon in a voluntary arm's-length transaction."

We disagreed, holding that there need not be an actual sale in order to determine the existence and value of a business's goodwill. . . .

While *Spheeris* involved a commercial business, subsequent Wisconsin cases have recognized goodwill in professional practices. . . .

. . . [I]n *Peerenboom*, the court of appeals concluded that the goodwill in a divorcing spouse's dental practice could be a divisible marital asset. Peerenboom v. Peerenboom, 147 Wis. 2d 547, 552, 433 N.W.2d 282 (Ct. App. 1988). The court [said]:

> . . . [I] in this case the record shows no ethical or contractual barrier to [Dr. Peerenboom's] disposing of his interest in his dental practice. Accordingly, to the extent that the evidence shows that the goodwill exists, is marketable, and that its value is something over and above the value of the practice's assets and the professional's skills and services, it may be included as an asset in the marital estate and be subject to division.

. . . As aforementioned, the presumption of equal division recognizes the contributions of each spouse to the marriage, including a homemaker spouse's lost earning capacity from being out of the job market. Where the salable professional goodwill is developed during the marriage, it defies the presumption of equality to exclude it from the divisible marital estate. As one court has explained:

> [T]he wife, by virtue of her position of wife, made to that [goodwill] value the same contribution as does a wife to any of the husband's earnings and accumulations during the marriage. She is as much entitled to be recompensed for that contribution as if it were represented by the increased value of stock in a family business.

In sum, pursuant to Wis. Stat. §767.61, Wisconsin case law and the policy supporting the presumption of equality in the division of the marital estate, we hold that a circuit court shall include salable professional goodwill in the divisible marital estate when the business interest to which the goodwill is attendant is an asset subject to §767.61.

Tim urges us to require circuit courts to divide professional goodwill into two subgroups, "personal" goodwill and "enterprise" goodwill, and to create a presumption that personal goodwill is excluded from the marital estate. This is an approach taken by some courts and scholars.

When professional goodwill is so divided, enterprise goodwill is characterized as "[g]oodwill in a professional practice . . . attributable to the business enterprise itself by virtue of its existing arrangements with suppliers, customers or others, and its anticipated future customer base due to factors attributable to the business." Personal goodwill, on the other hand, is characterized as the goodwill that is "attributable to the individual owner's personal skill, training or reputation," i.e., it is "the goodwill that depends on the continued presence of a particular individual."

Some courts that divide professional goodwill into enterprise and personal goodwill have concluded that enterprise goodwill is included in the divisible marital estate, and personal goodwill is not. This conclusion is based in large part on the belief that enterprise goodwill is salable, while personal goodwill is not. . . .

After reviewing cases that distinguish between personal and enterprise goodwill, we choose not to require circuit courts to draw a distinction between personal and enterprise goodwill when dividing a marital estate that includes professional goodwill. This is so because the premise on which the distinction is grounded — that enterprise goodwill is salable and personal goodwill is not — is mistaken. As evidenced by the facts of the case at hand, Tim testified that when he bought Orthodontic Specialists for $930,000, nearly 90 percent of the sale price was for the professional goodwill. Tim described this goodwill as including elements of "personal" goodwill: "Dr. Grady's name, the noncompete clause, and the employment agreement that Dr. Grady would stay on to introduce me to his existing patients." Therefore, as this case demonstrates, in some situations, personal goodwill is salable. . . .

. . . The second issue presented is whether the circuit court double counted the value of Tim's professional goodwill by basing Tracy's maintenance award on Tim's expected future earnings when the future earnings will arise from Orthodontic Specialists. Under Tim's line of reasoning, the circuit court counted the goodwill once when it treated the goodwill as a divisible marital asset. Tim contends that the court then counted professional goodwill a second time when it awarded maintenance based on his past earnings from Orthodontic Specialists, given that professional goodwill increased those past earnings. . . .

There are two objectives that an award of maintenance seeks to meet. The first objective is support of the payee spouse. LaRocque v. LaRocque, 139 Wis. 2d 23, 33, 406 N.W.2d 736 (1987). This objective may not be met by merely maintaining the payee spouse at a subsistence level. Rather, maintenance should support the payee spouse at the pre-divorce standard. *Id.* This standard should be measured by "the lifestyle that the parties enjoyed in the years immediately before the divorce and could anticipate enjoying if they were to stay married." The second objective is fairness, which aims to "compensate the recipient spouse for contributions made to the marriage, give effect to the parties' financial arrangements, or prevent unjust enrichment of either party." . . .

As is the case here, concerns about double counting sometimes arise when awarding maintenance. . . .

. . . [I]n the typical property division case involving a pension, the trial court may determine the present value of the pension. When the present value of a pension plan is calculated, that present value is based, in part, on projected future benefit payments. Therefore, assuming the employee spouse is awarded the present value of the asset, he or she does not receive the value of the asset at the time of the property division. Rather, the spouse receives that value via future payments. Accordingly, . . . it would be double counting to count the present value of the pension as a divisible asset and also count the future payments as income, since the income, up to the valuation placed on the pension at the time of the division, are one and the same.

Contrarily, when an income earning asset is assigned to one spouse, . . . that spouse, generally, receives the full fair market value of that asset at the time of the property division. Stated otherwise, if the spouse was awarded income property, that spouse could turn around and sell the income property the next day and, thereby, attain the value of the property. The spouse could also elect to keep the property and earn income from it. As the spouse earns income, he or she does not lose the value of the property because he or she always has the option to sell the property for fair market value. Therefore, unlike pension benefit payments (up to the present value placed on the pension at the time of the division), the value of investment property is separate from the income it generates. Consequently, . . . counting income from income earning assets will typically not implicate double counting.

. . . [W]e opined that given the "infinite range of factual situations facing circuit courts in dividing property and determining maintenance and child support," it would be unwise to proscribe inflexible double-counting rules. Instead, we stressed that "the 'double-counting' rule serves to warn parties, counsel and the courts to avoid unfairness by carefully considering the division of income-producing and non-income-producing assets and the probable effects of that division on the need for maintenance and the availability of income to both parents for child support." In short, when analyzing whether there has been double counting, the focus should be on fairness, not rigid double-counting rules. . . .

We now apply the legal principles set forth above to the facts and circumstances of this case. . . .

Pursuant to our conclusion above, the entire amount of *salable* professional goodwill was appropriately included in the marital estate. Here, Tim has not shown that the $1,058,000 value placed on Orthodontic Specialists includes nonsalable goodwill. Rather, the facts indicate the contrary. In particular, Tim bought the practice, over a decade ago, for $930,000. Approximately 90 percent of this purchase price was paid for goodwill. Moreover, Tim testified that this goodwill included "Dr. Grady's name, the noncompete clause, and the employment agreement that Dr. Grady would stay on to introduce me to his existing patients, [and] to counsel me through the process of learning how to do business," much of which is included in what Tim classifies as personal goodwill. . . .

Tim argues that the circuit court double counted the value of his professional goodwill when it included the goodwill in the divisible marital estate, and then based Tracy's maintenance award on Tim's expected future earnings. According to Tim, the expected future earnings also included the value of the goodwill because it was calculated using Tim's average income over the preceding five years which was increased by the goodwill. We disagree.

We start by underscoring our directive . . . that the rule against double counting is advisory and not absolute. As set forth above, the double counting rule does not prohibit the inclusion of investment income from assets awarded to a spouse as part of property division when calculating maintenance. This is so because the value of the investment asset is separate from the income it produces. Contrarily, pension benefit payouts (until they reach the amount of the valuation given the pension as an asset at the time of the property division) do not create value separate from the pension as an asset at the time of the property division. Applying these principles to the case at hand, we conclude that the salable professional goodwill in Orthodontic Specialists is similar to an asset that produces income.

As with an income producing asset, the value of Orthodontic Specialists at the time of the property division had a set value, namely, $1,058,000. If Tim so chose, at the time of the property division, he could have sold Orthodontic Specialists and realized this value. Or, he could retain Orthodontic Specialists, earn income from it and sell it at a later time. Consequently, Tim has the option of continuing to generate substantial income from Orthodontic Specialists without diminishing its value. Specifically, the circuit court found that if Tim works 40 hours per week, Tim's income will be $465,000 annually. As with income from an income earning asset, this income is separate from the value of Orthodontic Specialists as it existed at the time of the property division. Consequently, the circuit court did not double count Orthodontic Specialists' professional goodwill and, therefore, did not erroneously exercise its discretion when it awarded Tracy $16,000 per month, for 20 years, in maintenance. . . .

The decision of the court of appeals is affirmed.

NOTES AND QUESTIONS

1. The tangible assets of a business, including a professional practice, may be divisible property, as may intangible assets, such as accounts receivable. In what ways is goodwill so different from these other types of assets that it should not be treated as divisible property? What arguments support treating it as property?

In some other legal contexts, goodwill is treated as property, but in others it is not. For example, under the Internal Revenue Code, goodwill is not subject to depreciation, loss of goodwill is not compensated for in eminent domain proceedings, and its loss does not produce an income tax deduction. However, since 1993 the Internal Revenue Code has provided that goodwill may be amortized over a 15-year period. IRC §197.

When professionals are associated in practice, their partnership agreement or corporate charter often includes provisions and formulas that permit the partner(s) continuing in the practice to buy out the interest of a partner who dies, resigns, etc. When the formula produces an amount greater than the withdrawing partner's fractional share of the tangible assets and accounts receivable, have the partners in effect acknowledged that the practice has goodwill? When a practice is sold or a partner withdraws, the selling or withdrawing practitioner often signs a covenant not to compete to prevent that partner from continuing to trade on his or her reputation in competition with that of his or her successors. Is this a device that requires the partner to leave his or her share of the goodwill in the business?

What is the relevance of the legal treatment of goodwill in other contexts to the question presented by *McReath*?

2. Some courts say that divisible goodwill can exist only in a partnership and not in a sole practice. *See, e.g.*, Nail v. Nail, 486 S.W.2d 761 (Tex. 1972); Sorensen v. Sorensen, 839 P.2d 774 (Utah 1992). What would be the basis for the distinction? This rule means that a person married to a professional who practices with others may share in goodwill at divorce, while one married to a sole practitioner will not.

3. What is the difference between "enterprise" and "professional" or "personal" goodwill? Why does the majority in *McReath* hold that both types of goodwill are divisible property? To the main case, compare the decision of the court in Moore v. Moore, 779 S.E.2d 533 (S.C. 2015):

> ... "Enterprise goodwill 'is based on the intangible, but generally marketable, existence in a business of established relations with employees, customers and suppliers.' " "[E]nterprise goodwill attaches to a business entity and is associated separately from the reputation of the owners. ... The asset has a determinable value because the enterprise goodwill of an ongoing business will transfer upon sale of the business to a willing buyer." Many courts have found "[e]nterprise goodwill is an asset of the business and accordingly is property that is divisible in a dissolution to the extent that it inheres in the business, independent of any single individual's personal efforts and will outlast any person's involvement in the business."
>
> "In contrast, [p]ersonal goodwill is associated with individuals." "It is that part of increased earning capacity that results from the reputation, knowledge and skills of individual people." "The implied assumption is that if the individual were not there, the clients would go elsewhere." ... "[A]ny value that attaches to a business as a result of this 'personal goodwill' represents nothing more than the future earning capacity of the individual and is not divisible [in a divorce proceeding]."

779 S.E.2d at 543.

4. *McReath* adopts the rule that goodwill must be salable for it to be treated as divisible property. In some states ethical rules forbid lawyers to sell their law practices. In those states a doctor, dentist, or accountant may have professional goodwill while a lawyer would not. Other professions may have ethical limitations that affect the salability of practices. This approach creates the anomaly that some professionals may have goodwill while others may not. What arguments support this position?

The ALI Family Dissolution Principles recommend that goodwill be treated as property, whether it is marketable or not. They also say that to the extent goodwill is not marketable, spousal earning capacity, labor, or skills should not be included in the value. ALI, Principles of the Law of Family Dissolution §4.07(3) (2002).

5. Where lawyers are ethically prohibited from selling their practices, the ban is based on a lawyer's obligation to preserve client confidences. Charles Wolfram, Modern Legal Ethics 879-880 (1986); EC 4-6 (a lawyer should not attempt to sell a law practice as a going business because to do so would involve the disclosure of confidences and secrets). In practice, however, this prohibition is sometimes circumvented by inflating the value of other assets or by having the buyer associate with the seller for a few months. Rule 1.17 of the ABA Model Rules of Professional Conduct allows the sale of law practices, including goodwill, but it requires that the seller give actual written notice to each client before the sale. Lawyers are also ethically prohibited from entering into partnership agreements that include covenants not to compete. Charles Wolfram, above, at 885; DR 2-108(A); ABA Model Rules of Professional Conduct, Rule 5.6.

6. If goodwill is divisible property, is it to be characterized as separate or marital, where that distinction matters? Is it separate if "brought into the marriage"? If so, are the profits it produces also separate? How do we distinguish profits attributable to the labor of the working spouse (which is marital property)? How should we account for the decrease in value over time of "old" goodwill while "new" goodwill is built up?

7. *McReath* cites prior cases holding that pension income cannot be the basis for spousal support if the nonemployee spouse received a share of the pension at divorce but says that the income that a former spouse earns can be considered available to pay spousal support even if his or her professional goodwill was treated as divisible property, analogizing the goodwill to tangible property. Does the fact that a professional practice and its goodwill can be sold justify this result? Consider that the *McReath* trial court ordered Dr. McReath to pay $80,000 per year in property division installment payments plus $16,000 per month ($192,000 per year) to his ex-wife, a total of $272,000 per year, and it estimated his total annual income to be more than $535,000 per year.

8. Valuation of goodwill (and small businesses generally) is notoriously difficult. If the same or a similar business has recently sold, valuation is not a problem because market value is widely accepted as the gold standard for this issue. Where there is not a ready market for the kind of business being valued, accounting methods are ordinarily used. These methods all look to the flow of income that the business produces and, using a "capitalization rate," calculate what amount of money would have to be invested at that rate of interest to produce the stream of income. The problems with these methods are obvious. Technical issues include how to calculate the income stream that is to be capitalized and what interest rate to choose. More generally, it can be argued that these methods produce figures that have no necessary relationship to what the businessperson would realize on sale or withdrawal from the business, to the extent that is important.

9. A popular way of dividing pensions is to use a QDRO to divide the pension into separate portions for each spouse. This solution is particularly useful when the spouses do not have enough other property to balance the pension or when valuing the pension is difficult. Since similar problems arise in valuing and dividing small businesses, can a similar solution be employed? That is, can the business be divided in kind by awarding each of the spouses a fraction of it? What problems would be created? Bowen v. Volz, 271 So.3d 1162 (Fla. App. 2019); Bowen v. Bowen, 473 A.2d 73 (N.J. 1984).

PROBLEMS

1. Robert started a State Farm Insurance Agency during his marriage to Bo. His agreement with State Farm provides that he may not sell any brand of insurance except State Farm and that all information about policyholders are trade secrets belonging to State Farm, as are the agency's computer system and business records. If Robert and State Farm ever terminate their relationship, Robert may keep the office and sell other companies' insurance, but he cannot solicit State Farm policyholders for one year. The agency has been the most profitable insurance agency in the state for the last ten years, and Robert works ten to eleven hours a day, seven days a week. The agency pays Robert considerably more than the industry average for insurance agents. Does Robert's agency have goodwill? Why or why not?

2. Vinny and Lynn are divorcing, and they dispute the value of the Green 'n' Tidy Landscape business, which Vinny founded during the marriage and has operated for 15 years. The business has six employees in addition to Vinny, all of whom do manual labor. Vinny is the only person who deals with clients. Lynn's expert included a value for goodwill in the calculation of the value of the business, based on the amount by which its earnings exceed a fair salary for Vinny and a fair rate of return on the tangible assets of the business. Vinny's expert's valuation did not include an amount for goodwill, based on the state supreme court's holding in an earlier case that a professional practice of a sole practitioner does not have a goodwill value for purposes of divorce. Should the court find that the business has divisible goodwill? Why or why not?

3. Would a well-known entertainer have professional goodwill that could be divisible marital property? *See* Piscopo v. Piscopo, 557 A.2d 1040 (N.J. Super. 1989) (entertainer Joe Piscopo), discussed in Jay E. Fishman, Celebrity as a Business and Its Role in Matrimonial Cases, 17 Am. J. Fam. L. 203 (2004).

4. Degrees, Licenses, Jobs, and Earning Capacity

Cases like *McReath* provide a remedy for a person who has helped a spouse establish a successful career if divorce comes after the career has been established. Even before courts confronted such cases, though, they faced cases involving divorces that occurred just as one spouse was finishing professional training, before the training had a chance to pay off — the "advanced degree, divorce decree problem," as the court described it in Francis v. Francis, 442 N.W.2d 59 (Iowa 1989). Typically, the couple had little property to divide, and the spouse who had not gone to school was not a good candidate for traditional forms of spousal support, since he or she had been supporting or at least contributing to the support of the family.

The economic value of education in general is clear. In 2022 the median weekly earnings of an adult with less than a high school diploma was $626, less than half of the earnings of a person with a bachelor's degree, and less than a third of someone with a professional degree or Ph.D. Median earnings for a high school graduate was $809. The median earnings of those who had attended college but did not earn degrees was $899 a week. The median for those with an associate's degree was $963, and for those with a bachelor's degree, $1,334. Graduate degrees increased earnings further. The median for those with master's degrees was $1,574; for professional degrees, $1,924; and for Ph.D.s, the median was $1,909. Bureau of Labor Statistics, Earnings and Unemployment Rates by Educational Attainment, 2021 (Sept. 8, 2022), https://www.bls.gov/emp/chart-unemployment-earnings-education.htm.

Today no state in the United States treats enhanced earning capacity as property, though a few experimented with doing so. In Oregon, the legislature enacted a statute treating enhanced earning capacity as divisible property but repealed this provision in favor of a spousal support remedy, as the next case discusses.

Marriage of Harris and Harris
244 P.3d 801 (Or. 2010)

DE MUNIZ, C.J. . . . [W]e set out here the statement of facts from the Court of Appeals opinion.

> "Wife and husband were married in March 1990. At that time, husband was a full-time college student, while wife worked full time for the State of Oregon and attended college classes part time. In 1992, husband completed his undergraduate degree and began dental school. Wife continued to work full time and to attend classes 'sporadically,' but stopped attending classes in 1993 after the parties' first child was born. Thereafter, the parties shared childcare and household responsibilities, with wife assuming the larger portion. Wife's job provided the family with financial support and health insurance. Husband also contributed to the family finances during dental school by way of student loans, money earned working occasionally in his father's dental office and at a few odd jobs, and, during one year, monthly $1,000 workers' compensation payments.

In 1996, husband graduated from dental school and joined his father's dental practice. He immediately began to earn more than $100,000 annually and became the family's primary wage-earner. After the parties' second child was born in 1997, wife left her employment and assumed primary childcare and household responsibilities.

In 1998, husband's father sold husband an interest in his practice at a substantially below-market price. Thereafter, husband's earned income increased dramatically, averaging slightly more than $355,000 per year from 2002 to 2005 and more than $407,000 in 2006, in addition to rental income in each of those years averaging $23,000. Among other things, husband's financial success enabled the parties to build a four-bedroom, 3,252 square foot home on 1.21 acres; lease luxury vehicles; purchase a high-speed motorboat and a time-share in Mexico; take several family vacations each year; and join a country club.

Sometime in 1999, wife began to work in husband's business approximately 10 hours each week planning office parties, making bank deposits, paying bills, completing data entry, mailing letters, and running errands. She continued to do so until the parties separated in February 2006, after approximately 16 years of marriage.

At the time of trial in April 2007, husband was 37 years old, and wife was 38 years old. Both parties were in good health. Wife testified that she intended to complete her undergraduate degree and to pursue a graduate degree in business, but that, even if she did not, she could earn between $30,000 and $40,000 per year as a state employee, at a job for which she is already qualified. The trial court awarded wife custody of the parties' children and divided the real and personal property equally; each party received assets valued at $720,402. The court further ordered that husband pay wife $1,087 per month in child support; $3,000 per month in transitional spousal support for four years; and $4,000 per month in maintenance spousal support for six years, stepped down to $2,500 per month for two years followed by $1,000 per month for one year."

As identified above, the issue in this case is whether wife is entitled to an award of compensatory spousal support and, if so, for how long. . . .

At the outset, we observe that compensatory spousal support is one of the three categories of spousal support set out in ORS 107.105(1). . . . Transitional spousal support provides support "as needed for a party to attain education and training necessary to allow the party to prepare for reentry into the job market or for advancement therein." Spousal maintenance is "a contribution by one spouse to the support of the other for either a specified or an indefinite period." Compensatory spousal support provides compensation to one of the parties to the marriage "when there has been a significant financial or other contribution by [that] party to the education, training, vocational skills, career or earning capacity of the other party and when such an order for compensatory support is otherwise just and equitable in all the circumstances." . . .

Wife contends that the compensatory spousal support provisions essentially incorporate much of what was formerly found in the enhanced earning capacity statute, *former* ORS 107.105(1)(f) (1993). Wife notes that the archetypal example of a spouse who qualified for a property distribution award under the enhanced earning capacity statute was the wife who supported the husband in medical school by working and keeping the home. Wife argues that she would have qualified for a property distribution based on her contributions to husband's enhanced earning capacity under the former statute, and that she should, therefore, qualify for an award of compensatory spousal support under the current statute, based on her contributions to husband's education, career, and earning capacity.

Husband contends that, for wife's contributions to be "significant" under the compensatory spousal support statute, those contributions must be significant in some aspect that is separate and apart from contributions that are typical of a healthy marital relationship. . . .

We reject husband's arguments. Although it is true that the compensatory spousal support statute provides that contributions from one spouse to another must be significant, as husband himself notes, "significant" is defined essentially as "having meaning." . . .

Oregon spousal support statutes have long taken into account the contribution of one spouse to the education and training of the other spouse. . . . In 1993, the legislature amended the spousal support statutes, retaining the provisions requiring consideration of the contribution of one spouse to the education, training, and earning capacity of the other spouse. The 1993 legislature, however, also added an "enhanced earning capacity" provision for the division of marital property . . . :

> "(f) . . . The present value of, and income resulting from, the future enhanced earning capacity of either party shall be considered as property. The presumption of equal contribution to the acquisition of marital property, however, shall not apply to enhanced earning capacity. A spouse asserting an interest in the income resulting from an enhancement of earning capacity of the other spouse must demonstrate that the spouse made a material contribution to the enhancement. Material contribution can be shown by, among other things, having contributed, financially or otherwise, to the education and training that resulted in the enhanced earning capacity. The contribution shall have been substantial and of prolonged duration."

In Denton and Denton, 951 P.2d 693 (Or. 1998), this court addressed the provisions of *former* ORS 107.105(1)(f) (1993). . . . The court then discussed the contributions that wife made to her husband's acquisition of his medical license and specialty:

> "During the period when husband was attempting to gain admission to medical school, and while husband was in medical school, wife worked full time, putting food on the family's table and a roof over their heads. Moreover, wife performed all domestic tasks during the entire period in which husband prepared himself for medical school, attended medical school, and performed his dermatology residency in Iowa. That freed husband to devote all his energy and concentration to his studies, which directly facilitated his acquisition of the medical degree as well as his dermatology specialty.
>
> "Wife also contributed directly to husband's educational expenses during medical school. The bulk of the financial aid that husband received during his attendance at OHSU was in the form of student loans that were later repaid with marital assets out of husband's salary after he graduated. However, those loans were lower than otherwise would have been the case, because wife supplied the income that kept the couple from having to borrow to pay living expenses while husband attended school. Additionally, . . . [wife's] continuing willingness to uproot, to relocate, and to find new employment constituted nonfinancial contributions to the enhancement."

In *Denton*, this court concluded that those contributions, "*when considered together*, as they must be, were both material and substantial." . . .

In 1999, the legislature revised the spousal support statutes and amended ORS 107.105 to its present form. Those amendments repealed the enhanced earning capacity statute and migrated some of the elements from the repealed enhanced earning capacity statute and the former spousal support provisions addressing compensatory-type awards into the new compensatory spousal support provision. . . .

. . . As a linguistic matter, the new compensatory spousal support provision has broadened the kinds of contributions that can be considered beyond those numerated under the former enhanced earning capacity statute. They also no longer require that the contributions all must be connected to enhanced earning capacity. . . .

The legislative history of the compensatory spousal support provision also supports our conclusion. . . .

The written testimony submitted before the House Civil Judiciary Committee by one of the chief proponents of the bill, Russell Lipetsky, also demonstrates that the bill was not intended to heighten the contribution required from spouses in order to qualify for support awards. In his written testimony on HB 2555, Lipetzky characterized the legislative proposal as follows:

"The enhanced earning capacity ('EEC') statute is found tucked into ORS 107.105(1)(f), which is a lengthy statute that provides the court with the general authority to divide property in a divorce. Since its inception, the EEC statute has been a continuing source of confusion and frustration for divorcing couples, family law attorneys, and the courts. That confusion stems mostly from the requirement of the statute that an intangible future economic benefit—a party's future enhanced earning capacity—be translated (somehow) into a present day dollar value and divided (somehow) by the court in a divorce proceeding. . . .

"In allowing a party's enhanced earning to be characterized as spousal support, the drafters of this bill believe the goals of the EEC statute can be fully met, and that those goals can be met with much greater ease and understanding by all participants in the legal process." . . .

. . . [W]e must now determine whether wife's contributions are "significant" as required under the compensatory support statute.

Husband characterizes wife's contributions as "typical" and "expected" household support activities in contrast to the "significant" contributions that he contends the statute requires. We disagree. The undisputed facts in this case show that wife contributed to husband's "education, training, vocational skills, career or earning capacity" by working full time while husband attended both undergraduate and dental school. Wife's work provided the family with financial support and health insurance. Once husband established his dental practice, wife assumed primary homemaking and childcare responsibilities. Wife also worked part time in husband's dental practice for a period of seven years. We conclude that wife's contributions were "significant contributions" to husband's education and career sufficient to trigger consideration of a compensatory spousal support award under the relevant statutory criteria. We now turn to consideration of the statutory criteria relevant to a determination of an appropriate compensatory spousal support award. . . .

A. Amount, Duration, and Nature of Contribution

The first factor to address under the statute includes the "amount, duration and nature of the contribution" of the contributing spouse. To a substantial degree, those factors mirror the kind of considerations that must be addressed in making the initial determination whether the contributions of the spouse are significant enough to warrant any award of compensatory spousal support. . . .

C. Relative Earning Capacity of the Parties

The third statutory factor addresses the earning capacities of the parties to the marriage. Here, the relative earning capacities of husband and wife contrast sharply. Husband averaged more than $350,000 per year in income from his dental practice from 2002 until the initiation of the marital dissolution in 2006. Husband also received rental income in each of those years averaging $23,000. . . . In contrast, wife's testimony established that her earning capacity is approximately $30,000 to $40,000 per year, based on her current training and prior job experience. . . .

D. Extent to Which the Marital Estate has Already Benefited

The fourth factor set out in ORS 107.105(1)(d)(B)(iv) is a legislative directive to consider the extent to which the marital estate has already benefited from the contribution made by the spouse seeking an award of compensatory spousal support. Not surprisingly, the parties view this requirement from different perspectives. . . .

In this case, during the period after husband began his dental practice until the marriage dissolved, the parties' lifestyle included a large home, luxury cars, expensive vacations, and a country club membership. In addition, wife received a substantial amount in the distribution of marital assets — *viz.*, assets valued at approximately $720,000. . . . As wife notes, if she and husband had married after he completed his dental degree (and consequently she had not made the contributions she did to help him through the years it took for him to obtain his dental degree), wife would almost certainly have received the same distribution of marital assets as she received here. We agree. Viewed in that manner and in light of husband's remaining 17- to 27-year highly productive earning career, we conclude that the significant asset distribution and comfortable lifestyle available to wife for the 10 years preceding the divorce does not offset completely the contributions wife made to husband's education, career, and enhanced earning capacity. . . .

F. Any Other Factors Court Deems Just and Equitable

Under ORS 107.105(1)(d)(B)(vi), the court may address any other factors that the court deems just and equitable. . . .

As discussed above, spousal support is divided into three categories of support: transitional spousal support, spousal maintenance, and compensatory spousal support. Those categories of spousal support are interrelated, and they also are cabined by the statutory directive to set the total spousal support award at "an amount of money for a period of time as may be just and equitable for one party to contribute to the other." Consequently, we conclude that the amounts of spousal support awarded under each of the spousal support categories are relevant considerations in determining the overall just and equitable amount of spousal support to award. . . .

. . . In determining the amount and the length of a compensatory spousal support award, we take into account the awards that wife has received as transitional support and as maintenance support, the comfortable lifestyle that the marital assets provided to wife during the marriage, and the substantial distribution of marital assets to wife. We have also considered the six years that wife contributed significantly to husband's ability to obtain his dental degree, that wife assumed primary childcare and household responsibilities when she left work, that wife frequently worked at husband's business for approximately seven years, and husband's ability to produce income from his dental practice of $350,000 to $400,000 per year over the next 17 to 27 years. Based on the foregoing, we conclude that a compensatory spousal support award of $2,000 per month for 10 years is just and equitable in all of the circumstances. Consequently, the decision of the Court of Appeals and the judgment of the circuit court must be modified to award compensatory spousal support to wife in that amount.

NOTES AND QUESTIONS

1. The Oregon statute that treated enhanced earning capacity as property followed a New York Court of Appeals decision, O'Brien v. O'Brien, 489 N.E.2d 712 (N.Y. 1985), which interpreted the New York property division statute as requiring the same result. Why did the Oregon legislature change to compensatory alimony?

The New York courts applied the principles of *O'Brien* broadly, treating as divisible property earned or developed during the marriage a teaching certificate, McGowan v. McGowan, 535 N.Y.S.2d 990 (App. Div. 1988); the career of an opera singer, Elkus v. Elkus, 572 N.Y.S.2d 901 (App. Div. 1991); and numerous other achievements. However, in 2016 the *O'Brien* era came to an end. The New York legislature enacted N.Y. Dom. Rel. Law §236(B)(5)(d)(7) (2017), which provides:

The court shall not consider as marital property subject to distribution the value of a spouse's enhanced earning capacity arising from a license, degree, celebrity goodwill, or career enhancement. However, in arriving at an equitable division of marital property, the court shall consider the direct or indirect contributions to the development during the marriage of the enhanced earning capacity of the other spouse. . . .

2. If the spouses divorce right after one earns an advanced degree, they probably will not have much in the way of accumulated assets. If one spouse's degree, earned during marriage, were treated as property, a court could not use the offset method to divide the value of an educational degree, but would instead likely require the degree holder to make periodic payments to the former spouse. Would these payments be modifiable or terminable? What remedy or remedies would the obligee have for nonpayment? Under a reimbursement or compensatory alimony theory, on what grounds should the payments be modifiable or terminable?

3. In *Harris*, the parties divorced years after Dr. Harris graduated and went into private practice. The divisible value of his practice might include goodwill, as we have seen. If the degree were property, would Mrs. Harris have been able to claim a share of his enhanced earning capacity as property as well? How does the *Harris* court handle this question, applying the compensatory alimony statute?

4. If the parties divorced years after Dr. Harris graduated, but he had never practiced dentistry, would his degree still have a divisible value if it were property? *Compare* Fanelli v. Fanelli, 740 N.Y.S.2d 823 (N.Y. Sup. 2002) (engineering degree that was never used did not enhance earning capacity), to Klutchko v. Baron, 768 N.Y.S.2d 217 (App. Div. 2003) (law license had value even though holder had not practiced for some years).

5. If a person who worked to put a spouse through school wanted to go back to school him- or herself when the parties divorced, would the spouse be entitled to rehabilitation alimony? If so, would the spouse also be entitled to reimbursement alimony, or would that be double-dipping?

6. Most states give some sort of reimbursement or compensation alimony to the spouse who is divorced at or near the end of the other spouse's education. However, the states are far from uniform in the relief they provide. The measure of reimbursement ranges from the amount the supporting spouse provided toward tuition, books, and laboratory fees of the other spouse (*see, e.g.*, Ind. Code §31-15-7-6 (2022)) to the present value of the supported spouse's enhanced future earnings and the supporting spouse's contribution to the capital needed to obtain the education and to support the family (*see, e.g.*, Francis v. Francis, 442 N.W.2d 59 (Iowa 1989)).

A California statute allows reimbursement to the pool of divisible community property for money spent on one spouse's education or training during the marriage. It reduces or eliminates this claim to the extent that the marital community "substantially benefitted from the education, training, or loan incurred for the education or training of the party. There is a rebuttable presumption, affecting the burden of proof, that the community has not substantially benefitted from community contributions to the education or training made less than 10 years before the commencement of the proceeding, and that the community has substantially benefitted from community contributions to the education or training made more than 10 years before the commencement of the proceeding." A claim under this statute can also be reduced or modified if the other spouse received education or training to which the community contributed or if the education or training that the person received enabled that person to work, substantially reducing the person's need for spousal support. Cal. Fam. Code §2641(c) (2022).

CHAPTER 7

PARENT-CHILD SUPPORT DUTIES

While continuation of spousal support duties after divorce may be controversial, everyone agrees that the parent-child relationship and the need for child support continue after divorce. Further, unmarried legal parents' child support duties are the same as those of divorcing parents. Nonetheless, child support orders directed to parents inevitably and significantly affect the shape of the household in which children live, and this circumstance raises its own theoretical and practical problems. The following excerpt explains the development of the parents' legal duty to support their children and introduces some of the complexities in implementing that duty.

Leslie Harris, Dennis Waldrop & Lori R. Waldrop

Making and Breaking Connections Between Parents' Duty to Support and Right to Control Their Children
69 Or. L. Rev. 689, 692-708 (1990)

At least from the early seventeenth century, the English Poor Laws imposed a legal duty on parents to support their poor children to minimize the financial burden on the community. Well into the nineteenth century, however, the English courts refused to hold parents legally responsible for the support of their children outside this context.

In contrast, during the nineteenth century American courts and legislatures established that under the private law, parents have a legal duty to support their children. The judicial path was not smooth, however. . . . Over the century, though, the judicial trend was to make parents' duty to support their children legally enforceable.

State legislatures also enacted statutes providing that parents had a duty to support their children. The final draft of the New York Field Draft Civil Code declared the existence of such a duty. . . .

The hesitation to make child support a legally enforceable duty did not reflect a belief that parents had no obligation. Blackstone, for example, discussed at length parents' moral duty to maintain and educate their children. Courts feared, however, that if this duty were legally enforceable, parents would lose control over their children to third parties or to the children themselves. . . .

When the courts did impose a legal support duty on parents, they protected parental control by structuring rules regarding the scope of the duty and the means of enforcing it which maximized parental discretion and made legal enforcement difficult. In addition, the expressed justification for requiring parents to support their children seems to have changed.

In the eighteenth century Blackstone based parents' moral duty to support their children on their having begotten the children and, by implication, voluntarily undertaken to care for them. In contrast, some nineteenth century courts began to justify requiring parents to support their children as a corollary to their right to custody. Nineteenth century code drafters also grounded the support duty in the parent's right to custody. Custody includes not only physical custody—living with and caring for a child day to day—but also legal custody—the authority to determine how children will live and behave. Thus, such codes effectively linked parents' support duty to their right to exercise control over their children. . . .

The nineteenth century jurists' linkage of support duties and control rights seems consistent with their general inclination to define human relations in contractarian terms. One nineteenth century family law author even conceived parental authority over children as part of a contract between parents and children:

> The parent shows himself ready, by the care and affection manifested to his child, to watch over him, and to supply all his wants, until he shall be able to provide them for himself. The child, on the other hand, receives these acts of kindness; a tacit compact between them is thus formed; the child engages, by acts equivalent to a positive undertaking to submit to the care and judgment of his parent so long as the parent, and the manifest order of nature, shall coincide in requiring assistance and advice on the one side, and acceptance of them, and obedience and gratitude on the other.[1]

While discussions of parent-child relationships today may not use such blunt language, they still are often perceived as being based on exchange. Consider, for example, the claim that one reason absent fathers do not pay child support is that their loss of contact with and control over their children attenuates their sense of responsibility to the children. This claim is partly empirical, but it also assumes that people's values and behavior are based on exchange. . . .

Current rationales for parental authority tend to justify it instrumentally as serving the best interests of children and society. Examples include claims that parents are in the best position to know and care about their children's needs, that giving parents authority encourages them to assume and discharge the responsibilities of parenthood, and that diffusing authority over how children will be raised promotes cultural and social diversity. . . .

Making parents' duty to support their children legally enforceable inherently limits the parents' control to some extent. However, in the intact family children cannot sue their parents to enforce this duty, for such suits would interfere too much with parental autonomy. The available common law and statutory enforcement mechanisms—the necessaries doctrine and family expense statutes—protect parental control by making enforcement difficult. In addition, the scope of the support duty is defined by parental choices about their lifestyle and their children's lifestyle.

In the nineteenth century the courts extended the necessaries doctrine, which was originally used to enforce a husband's duty to support his wife, to include parental support.[2] . . .

In approximately twenty states, legislatures have enacted family expense statutes,[3] which, like the necessaries doctrine, permit creditors to sue parents for goods and services supplied to their children without requiring a prior promise by the parents to pay. Parental liability under these statutes is usually broader than under the necessaries doctrine. For example, the creditor may not have to prove that an item was a "necessary." Nevertheless, the statutes preserve some control for parents, since liability exists only for family expenses. Further, the statutes permit only suits by creditors; they do not authorize one family member to sue another for support.

---

1. D. Hoffman, Legal Outlines (1836), quoted in Michael Grossberg, Governing the Hearth 235 (1985).
2. The necessaries doctrine is covered in Chapter 2.—Eds.
3. 1 Homer Clark, The Law of Domestic Relations in the United States, §7.1, at 433-434 (2d ed. 1987).

As a practical matter, neither the necessaries doctrine nor a family expense statute is a very effective means of enforcing support obligations. Third parties are likely to be reluctant to rely on these statutes in supplying goods or services to a child, because if a parent refuses to pay, the supplier must bring suit. Thus, both as a matter of substantive law and in practice, the necessaries doctrine and the family expense statute present relatively little threat to parental control. . . .

The most common situation in which courts require parents to support their children, even though they do not have physical or legal custody of them, is when the parents are separated or divorced.[4] An essential feature of such orders is that they impose a support duty on a person who no longer has legal authority to control the child.

During the nineteenth century as divorce became more common, the question of whether noncustodial fathers should be required to support their children arose increasingly. . . . Some noncustodial fathers argued that the legal duty to support arose from the right to custody, and that, therefore, they no longer had any such duty. Some fathers also argued that since they no longer had a right to their children's services, they should not be required to support them. Ultimately, courts usually rejected these blanket principles and ordered men who were at fault for the marital breakdown to pay child, as well as spousal, support. To the extent the noncustodial fathers' duty to support their children remained an open question, nineteenth century legislatures often resolved it by enacting separate maintenance and divorce statutes that empowered courts to award child support.

These judicial and statutory developments established that when parents divorce and children live with only one parent, the link between custody and support can be broken as well. Nevertheless, historical judicial reluctance to require divorced fathers to pay adequate sums for their children's support and to enforce support orders may be attributable in part to the lingering belief that support duties should coincide with custodial rights.

The first three parts of this chapter concern how the theoretical and principled issues discussed above play out in the determination of the amount of child support owed by a nonresidential parent. The last two parts consider the boundaries of intrafamilial support duties — when must parents support adult children, and when must adult children support their aging parents.

A. THE CURRENT CHILD SUPPORT MODEL

The extent to which judges' discretion should be limited by a formula or guideline was a recurring issue in the law of spousal support and property division. Not surprisingly, this issue has also arisen for child support. Federal legislation enacted during the 1980s mandates that all states use child support guidelines. 42 U.S.C. §667 (2022). A Senate report explained the reasons for requiring guidelines:

> Although the child support enforcement program has greatly strengthened the ability of children to have support orders established and collected, there remains a continuing problem that the amounts of support ordered are in many cases unrealistic. This frequently results in awards which are much lower than what is needed to provide reasonable funds for the needs of the child in the light of the absent parent's ability to pay. In some instances, however, there are also awards which are unrealistically high.

---

4. Today child support orders for nonmarital children are also very common. As discussed later in this chapter, child support is also ordered when parents share joint custody, meaning that both parents have some kind of legal authority over their children. — Eds.

Some States have established guidelines to be used by the courts in setting the amount of child support orders. Where these guidelines exist, overall award levels tend to be somewhat higher than where the amount of the order is entirely discretionary with each judge. Moreover, the existence of guidelines tends to assure that there is reasonable consideration given both to the needs of the child and the ability of the absent parent to pay. This provides some protection for both parties.

S. Rep. No. 387, 98th Cong., 2d Sess. 40, reprinted in 1984 U.S. Code Cong. & Admin. News 2397, 2436. Federal regulations provide that child support guidelines must "take into consideration all earnings and income of the [noncustodial] parent, be based on specific descriptive and numeric criteria and result in a computation of the support obligation." 45 C.F.R. §302.56. This amount must be rebuttably presumed to be the correct amount of child support, and a deviation must be supported by specific findings based on criteria specified by state law. "Such criteria must take into consideration the best interests of the child. Findings that rebut the guidelines shall state the amount of support that would have been required under the guidelines and include a justification of why the order varies from the guidelines." *Id.*

Early child support guidelines required parents to share the "costs" of raising a child. While this approach has substantial intuitive appeal, no state today bases its guidelines on this approach. The following excerpts explain the difficulties with the cost approach and describe the approaches used in the United States today.

Robert G. Williams

Guidelines for Setting Levels of Child Support Orders
21 Fam. L.Q. 281, 287-289, 290-293, 295 (1987)

Why has an equitable level of child support been so difficult to determine by the courts? The root of the problem is that most expenses related to child rearing are commingled with expenditures benefiting all household members. In a recent economic study, Espenshade estimates that over one-half of family expenditures on children fall into just three categories: food, housing and transportation.[5] It is apparent that, on an individual case basis, it is difficult to separate out a child's share of these major household expenses. . . .

. . . Since most expenditures made on behalf of children are intertwined with general household expenditures, it is not only virtually impossible to disentangle them reliably, but many costs of children become hidden in the larger pool of spending for the total household. Consequently, the full children's share of expenditures in those categories is generally not recognized, with the result that even parents may underestimate the true costs of bringing up their own children. . . .

. . . What are the costs of children above the minimum level needed for basic subsistence? Economists agree that, above the minimum level, there is no absolute "cost" of rearing a child. Studies of household expenditure patterns make it clear that parents with higher income spend more on their children because they can afford to do so. A more accurate way of posing this question, then, is: What are the normal levels of spending on children within households above the poverty level? Estimating these normal levels of spending is the only method that economists have of estimating costs of children in such households.

---

5. The reference is to T.J. Espenshade, Investing in Children: New Estimates of Parental Expenditures (1984), which was considered the most authoritative study then available. —Eds.

The best available evidence on this subject comes from the aforementioned Espenshade study. The study is based on data from 8,547 households drawn from the 1972-1973 Consumer Expenditure Survey, a national survey of household expenditure patterns conducted by the Bureau of Labor Statistics. . . .

As can be seen from Espenshade's estimates for three socioeconomic levels, amounts spent on children in intact households go up as family income increases. Based on Espenshade's figures, we have derived estimates for the proportion of net income expended for two children by income level of the parents. These estimates . . . show that spending on children can be validly described as proportions of household income, although the proportions decline as household income increases. Thus, spending on one child varies from 26.0 percent of net income at low-income levels to 19.2 percent at the upper end of the income range. Similarly, spending on two children decreases from 40.4 percent at low-income levels to 29.7 percent in high income households.

A third question relevant to determining levels of child support is: How is spending on children affected by the number of children in the family? From Espenshade's findings, we can develop estimates of the proportion of current family consumption devoted to one, two, and three children. . . . [E]stimates of expenditures on children as a proportion of current family consumption are 26.2 percent for one child, 40.7 percent for two children, 51.0 percent for three children, and 57.5 percent for four children. . . .

There is a common misperception that the declining increments primarily reflect economies of scale in rearing children. Instead, these figures seem to indicate a decreasing level of expenditures for each child as family size increases. Espenshade estimates, for example, that virtually equal amounts are spent on each child in a two-child family, but that the spending level for each represents only about three-fourths the amount that would have been spent on one child alone. . . .

A. FLAT PERCENTAGE GUIDELINE

This simplest type of guideline sets child support as a percentage of obligor income, with the percentage varying according to the number of children. Some percentage guidelines are based on gross income (before tax) while others are based on net income (after mandatory deductions). . . .

The Wisconsin percentage of income standard may be the most well-known example of a flat percentage guideline. Child support orders are determined only on the basis of the obligor's gross income and the number of children to be supported. The percentages of obligor gross income allocated to child support are 17 percent for one child, 25 percent for two children, 29 percent for three children, 31 percent for four children and 34 percent for five or more children. The percentage of income standard is designed to be comparable to a tax in simplicity of structure and ease of application. It is intended for use in conjunction with mandatory income withholding for all child support orders from the date a child support order is established. . . .

Under the percentage of income standard, the child support obligation is not adjusted for the income of the custodial parent. The standard assumes that each parent will expend the designated proportion of income on the child, with the custodial parent's proportion spent directly. There is no adjustment for other factors such as child care expenses, extraordinary medical expenses, or age of child. . . .

B. INCOME SHARES MODEL

. . . The income shares model is based upon the precept that the child should receive the same proportion of parental income that would have been received if the parents lived together. Thus, the income shares model calculates child support as the share of each parent's income estimated to have been allocated to the child if the parents and child were living in an intact household. . . .

Computing child support under the income shares model involves three basic steps:

1. Income of the parents is determined and added together.

2. A basic child support obligation is computed based on the combined income of the parents. This obligation represents the amount estimated to have been spent on the children jointly by the parents if the household were intact. The estimated amount, in turn, is derived from economic data on household expenditures on children. A total child support obligation is computed by adding actual expenditures for work-related child care expenses and extraordinary medical expenses.

3. The total obligation is then pro-rated between each parent based on their proportionate shares of income. The obligor's computed obligation is payable as child support. The obligee's computed obligation is retained and is presumed to be spent directly on the child. This procedure simulates spending patterns in an intact household in which the proportion of income allocated to children depends on total family income.

The income shares model has been specified in both net income and gross income versions. It incorporates a self-support reserve for the obligor, under which the formula is not applied in determining child support until an obligor's income exceeds the poverty level (although a minimum order is set on a case-by-case basis).

C. Delaware Melson Formula

The Delaware Child Support Formula was developed by Judge Elwood F. Melson and was adopted by the Delaware Family Court for statewide use beginning in January 1979. As stated in a recent report of the Delaware Family Court, the basic principles of the Melson child support formula are as follows:

Parents are entitled to keep sufficient income for their most basic needs to facilitate continued employment.

Until the basic needs of children are met, parents should not be permitted to retain any more income than required to provide the bare necessities for their own self-support.

Where income is sufficient to cover the basic needs of the parents and all dependents, children are entitled to share in any additional income so that they can benefit from the absent parent's higher standard of living.

Jane C. Venohr

Child Support Guidelines and Guidelines Reviews: State Differences and Common Issues
47 Fam. L.Q. 327, 332-336 (2013)

By 1990, thirty-one states had implemented the Income Shares Model, fifteen states had implemented the Percentage of Obligor Income Model, three states had implemented the Melson Formula, and two states had implemented another guidelines model that is no longer in use. Since 1990, nine states have switched guidelines models.[6] With the exception of

---

6. As of 2022, the great majority of the states and D.C. had adopted a version of the Income Shares formula. Only six states used a percentage of income formula, and three used the Melson formula. Family Law Quarterly Editorial Staff, Charts 2020: Family Law in the Fifty States, D.C., and Puerto Rico, Part 2, 55 Fam. L. Q. 211, 227 Chart 6 (2022).—Eds.

Montana, all of the states switched to the Income Shares Model. The most common switch was from the Percentage of Obligor Income Model to the Income Shares Model. Most states switched because the Income Shares Model can more readily factor in and address a larger variety of case circumstances than can the traditional Percentage of Obligor Income Model. This includes circumstances in which the custodial parent has more income than the noncustodial parent, shared-parenting time, and other circumstances.

Guidelines award amounts among states using the same guidelines model rarely produce identical amounts. As a consequence, one guidelines model does not consistently result in lower or higher support awards than another guidelines model.

Some Percentage of Obligor Income guidelines apply the same percentage to all obligor incomes, whereas other Percentage of Obligor Income guidelines use a sliding scale. Only about half of state guidelines categorized as Income Shares guidelines resemble the prototype Income Shares Model developed in the 1980s. Several states have developed their own version of the Income Shares Model. . . .

The numbers underlying state guidelines using the same model differ for several reasons. The most obvious difference is that states rely on different measurements of child-rearing expenditures. There are at least eight different studies of child-rearing expenditures that form the basis of current state guidelines. These studies vary in data years, and some of the studies rely on different methodologies to measure child-rearing expenditures. Some consider expenditures made by families surveyed in the early 1970s, whereas others consider expenditures from families surveyed as recently as 2009. When initially developing their guidelines, most states considered one of two economic studies that were available at the time. Since then, new studies that are based on more current expenditure data have become available. Many states have updated their guidelines formulas/schedules based on the new studies. Some of the studies currently used by states during their guidelines reviews are discussed in more detail later in this article.

There are several other economic assumptions made in the development of guidelines, such as assumptions concerning tax rates, price levels, and some types of child-rearing expenditures. . . . Nonetheless, the classification of a guidelines income basis as gross or net income is not always definitive because some states develop their own definitions of income available for child support. . . .

Many states with gross-income guidelines also incorporate assumptions about tax filing status and federal and state income tax rates from the year the state last updated its guidelines. In all, the year that the state last updated its guidelines can exacerbate differences because, over time, tax rates change, prices change, and new economic studies on the cost of child rearing become available. . . .

There are several other differences underlying state guidelines formulas/schedules. Some states with relatively high or low incomes or housing costs make additional adjustments to account for their particular state's economic circumstances. Many state guidelines factor in the actual cost of the child's health insurance and out-of-pocket medical expenses on a case-by-case basis so the core formulas/schedules in these states exclude some or all of these healthcare-related expenses. Many states make a similar adjustment for work-related childcare expenses. In contrast, other states guidelines do not contain similar exclusions to their core formulas/schedules.

The following example of the operation of the Percentage of Obligor Income formula and a generic Income Shares formula, based on parents' gross income, is adapted from Robert G. Williams, Development of Guidelines for Child Support Orders: Advisory

Panel Recommendations and Final Report II-106 through II-108 (Office of Child Support Enforcement 1987).

Parent 1 lives alone, and the two children live with Parent 2. The gross monthly income of Parent 1 is $1,600. Parent 2, the custodial parent, has a gross monthly income of $1,200 and spends $150 per month on work-related childcare. The children's health insurance and uninsured care cost $200 per month.

INCOME SHARES FORMULA

a) Calculate the parents' total monthly income and each parent's proportionate share of the total:

$$\text{Total} = \$1,600 + \$1,200 = \$2,800$$

$$\text{Parent 1 share} = 1,600/2,800 = 57.14\%$$

$$\text{Parent 2 share} = 1,200/2,800 = 42.86\%$$

b) Calculate the total child support obligation by adding the basic obligations (read applicable tables) to childcare costs, cost of medical insurance, and extraordinary medical expenses. Here, assume that the applicable table says that the basic support obligation for two children for parents earning a total of $2,800 per month is $646. Recall that the mother spends $150 in work-related childcare and the child's health insurance costs $200.

$$\text{Total} = \$646 + \$150 + \$200 = \$996$$

c) Calculate noncustodial parent's share by multiplying total child support obligation by his or her proportion from step a.

$$57.14\% \text{ of } \$996 = \$569.10$$

WISCONSIN FORMULA

a. Percent of Obligor's gross income for 2 children = 25%
b. 25% of $1,600 = $400.

NOTES AND QUESTIONS

1. The Percentage of Obligor Income approach is less sensitive to variations in the situations of individual families than the Income Shares approach. Why might a state nevertheless choose it?

2. Noncustodial parents often justify their resistance to paying child support by their claim that the money "isn't really going to the kids." Such a claim raises at least two issues. The first is deciding which expenditures really "go to the kids" and which benefit the custodial parent. The second issue is the form of child support orders. The typical order requires the obligor to pay a fixed sum to the other parent rather than pay specific expenses. Further, if the obligor supplies goods or services directly to the child, the obligor usually does not get an offset for them against the child support ordered. Should courts require the obligor to pay expenses directly rather than bundling everything into a lump sum? Should courts require recipients of child support to account for the money? Or are these kinds of limitations inconsistent with the custodial parents' prerogatives? *See* Krampen v. Krampen, 997 N.E.2d 73 (Ind. App. 2013), reversing an order requiring a mother to account for weekly child support payments of $3000 per week when the father claimed she was diverting some to her start-up veterinary hospital. The father admitted that the children's food, clothing, and housing were adequate, and the mother testified that she was financing the business with loans; the court, therefore, concluded that the evidence did not show that the mother had misappropriated the child support.

3. The Income Shares and Percentage of Obligor Income child support guidelines are based on the principle that parents should share their income with their children, and the size of that share is determined by how much an average intact family (both parents and all children living together) would spend on the children. What arguments support this model, the "continuity of expenditure" approach, as the most appropriate measure of the duty of parents when the family is not intact? Does the Income Shares or the Percentage of Obligor Income formula, both of which base the child support obligation on the extra amount that parents spend when a child is added to the family, include all the family expenditures that benefit the children? Do they require either parent to contribute more to the child's support than that parent would spend if the family were intact?

4. A 2022 survey found that half of U.S. parents spend more than 20 percent of their household income on childcare. Maryalene LaPonsie, How Much Does It Cost to Raise a Child? (U.S. News & World Report, Sept. 7, 2022). On average, 16 percent of the amount that middle-income married parents spend on their children is for child care, but expenses vary with household income level, the child's age, and the part of the country in which the family lives. Most single parents were in the lowest income group, and they spent about the same as married parents with the lowest incomes. Mark Lino et al., Expenditures on Children by Families, 2015 (U.S. Dept. of Agriculture, Jan. 2017). Because of this great variation, most child support formulas do not fold child care costs into the basic formula but allocate responsibility for this expense independently of the formula. *See* Family Law Quarterly Editorial Staff, Charts 2020: Family Law in the Fifty States, D.C., and Puerto Rico, Part 2, 55 Fam. L. Q. 211, 227 Chart 6 (2022).

5. Children's medical expenses also vary dramatically, and child support formulas generally do not fold them into the basic obligation but deal with them separately. Federal and state laws require that child support decrees specifically address how children's medical expenses will be paid. For employed parents this can usually be done most economically by ordering a parent whose employer provides insurance to include the children in his or her plan.

B. CHALLENGES TO THE CONTINUITY OF EXPENDITURES MODEL

States must review their child support guidelines at least once every four years to ensure that they produce "appropriate" orders. In conducting these reviews, the states must consider "economic data on the cost of raising children," and they must analyze case data to determine the extent to which orders deviate from the guidelines. 45 C.F.R. §302.56(e) (2022). As states have gone through this process, and as more information about the operation of guidelines has become available, critics have challenged both the theoretical assumptions and empirical foundations of existing guidelines. The two most widely discussed alternatives are those proposed by the American Law Institute's Principles of the Law of Family Dissolution and by proponents of the cost-shares approach.

Leslie Joan Harris

The Proposed ALI Child Support Principles
35 Willamette L. Rev. 717, 727-733 (1999)

In a memorandum introducing the *Principles*, the reporter explained that existing child support guidelines, "unlike the earlier need-based discretionary rubric, . . . are neither intended nor designed to register and reflect the need of the child in the residential household. They do not, in any meaningful manner, consider the resources independently available to the residential household." Therefore, the combined amount that the parents spent or would spend on the child if all lived in the same household has little directly to do with how much should be spent on the child living with only one parent.

Perhaps the most essential fact the marginal expenditures model fails to take into account is that the costs of the two households together are greater than one household alone because of loss of economies of scale. How this economic burden should be distributed, particularly with regard to its impact on the child, is a critical question that the marginal expenditures model simply does not address.

As it turns out, if the child's parents have equal amounts of income before child support is paid, the marginal expenditures model spreads the loss of economies of scale equally between the households. However, when the parents' incomes are unequal, child support guidelines based on the marginal expenditures model perpetuate, and can exacerbate, the difference in the two households' standards of living. . . .

As in first generation child support formulas, the *Principles* provide that parents will share income with their child or children. Unlike many first generation formulas, the ALI version explicitly acknowledges that each parent's interests sometimes diverge from those of the child, as well as from each other's. It seeks a balance among these interests that can be defended on principle. The *Principles* evaluate the need for and adequacy of child support awards by comparing the economic standard of living in the households of the parents, rather than looking only at the relative income of the parents. Where the household of the residential parent has a lower standard of living, the *Principles* call for increased child support to narrow the gap; where the residential parent's household has a higher standard of living, child support is lower. . . .

1. THE INTERESTS OF THE CHILD

A common aspiration expressed in judicial opinions and popular discussions concerning child support is that the child should not suffer economically because the parents are not living together. However, the *Principles* do not attempt to achieve this goal because doing so would infringe too greatly on the rights of the nonresidential parent. For the same reason, the *Principles* do not adopt the modest-sounding goal that the child should not suffer disproportionately as compared to other family members. The *Principles* argue that to achieve even this goal, it would be necessary to use an equal living standards formula for child support. The *Principles* reject this formula because of its intrusion on the nonresidential parent's interests. . . .

To avoid this, the *Principles* compromise the child's interests and provide instead that the goals of the child support formula should be to: (1) allow the child to "enjoy a minimum decent standard of living when the resources of both parents together are sufficient to achieve such result without impoverishing either parent"; (2) allow the child to "enjoy a standard of living not grossly inferior to that of the child's higher income parent"; and (3) prevent the child from suffering "loss of important life opportunities that the parents are economically able to provide without undue hardship to themselves or their other dependents."

2. THE INTERESTS OF THE RESIDENTIAL PARENT

The most fundamental interest of the residential parent recognized by the *Principles* is not to bear disproportionately the direct and indirect costs of child rearing. . . .

3. THE INTERESTS OF THE NONRESIDENTIAL PARENT

The *Principles* argue that the marginal expenditure principle, which, as discussed above, is the basis for most child support formulas today, fundamentally expresses a principle of justice for the nonresidential parent: to contribute no more to the support of the children than if the parent were living with the children in a two-parent household. The *Principles* accept this measure as a starting point but do not allow it to prevail in all situations.

> At bottom, the marginal expenditure principle reflects a strong cultural belief in the primacy of the earner's claim to his earnings. . . . It is true that any transfer of income to the child's residential household may also be enjoyed by other members of the household, including the residential parent. This is an inevitable and unavoidable effect of any child support transfer, and is not itself an adequate reason for limiting or disapproving child support. Nevertheless, the payor parent has an interest in limiting the measure of his child support obligation to his relationship to the child, rather than to the residential household. . . .
>
> [T]his notion of justice arguably overstates the nonresidential parent's claim. The continuity of marginal expenditure measure may be understood to be predicated on the notion that, insofar as he is the dominant earner, the nonresidential parent should be held harmless by divorce, that is, he should be no worse off economically after divorce than he was during marriage. Yet being no worse off suggests, in the alternative, that he should not be heard to complain so long as he does not suffer a decline in his standard of living. To the extent that he will not suffer a decline in his standard of living (using household equivalence measures), there is no persuasive reason he should not pay more than what he would have spent on the children were he living with him. This does not imply equalization of household standards of living. In view of the lost economies of scale, the standard of living in the child's residential household will necessarily drop well below the preseparation standard if the standard of living of the higher income nonresidential parent is held constant.

Although the *Principles* do not use "maintenance of the support obligor's marital standard of living" as the basis for any part of the child support obligation, they use this standard as a touchstone for determining whether the obligor is being treated fairly in particular circumstances. Indeed, to evaluate the fairness of proposed orders, the *Principles* consistently compare the standard of living of each household after payment of child support to the standard of living that the parties would enjoy if they all lived in the same household.

[The Principles begin by establishing a "base amount" of child support, which is the amount that would be required under a well-constructed marginal expenditure formula. When the residential parent's income is lower than the nonresidential parent's, as is true in most cases, a supplement is added to the base amount, so as to make the standards of living in the two households closer, though not equal. As the income of the residential parent approaches that of the nonresidential parent, the amount of the supplement decreases. When the two parents' households have equal incomes, the supplement is completely eliminated, leaving the base alone as the amount of child support owed. When the income of the residential parent's household is greater than the nonresidential parent's, the ALI Principles call for the child support obligation to be decreased below the base amount.]

The following article describes the cost-shares approach to child support guidelines, which was strongly supported by some critics in the 1990s and early 2000s but which has not been adopted anywhere.

Jo Michell Beld & Len Biernat

Federal Intent for State Child Support Guidelines: Income Shares, Cost Shares, and the Realities of Shared Parenting
37 Fam. L.Q. 165, 173-174, 177-180 (2003)

. . . The cost shares alternative was developed in the mid-1990s by affiliates of the Children's Rights Council (CRC), a non-profit organization with both national and state chapters "that works to assure children meaningful and continuing contact with both their parents and extended family regardless of the parents' marital status." Its proponents argue that cost shares guidelines are fundamentally different from income shares guidelines, principally in the estimation of child costs and the allocation of these estimated costs between the parents. These differences, in their view, make the model superior to income shares.

While it is true that there are important differences between the prevailing income shares model for child support guidelines and the cost shares model, there are some fundamental similarities as well. Both approaches attempt to establish a clear relationship between child support guidelines and expenditures on children by parents, although the underlying estimates for those expenditures are indeed quite different in the two models. Both approaches base support on the incomes of both parents, with the cost shares model reflecting a Melson-style method of determining each parent's income available for child support. But the cost shares model makes assumptions about expenditure patterns and cost offsets in separated families that income shares models do not routinely make. . . .

The cost shares model borrows several principles from existing income shares guidelines but reflects a very different set of economic assumptions about expenditures on children in separated families. Cost shares guidelines use a Melson formula approach to the determination of income; rely on estimates of expenditures on children in single-parent families after offsets for "tax benefits attributable to the children"; and apply a joint physical custody cross-credit approach to the calculation of the final support obligation. A cost shares order for support is calculated as follows:

(1) Determine each parent's share of their combined income available for child support. As in all three Melson formula states, a cost shares guideline subtracts a self-support reserve from a parent's net income to arrive at his or her income available for child support. The calculation of net income under cost shares includes "an imputed child support order for other biological or adopted children residing with the parent," which is not present in any of the Melson formula states. In addition, the self-support reserve under cost shares is slightly higher than the highest reserve under existing Melson guidelines. . . .

(2) Determine the parents' combined "basic" expenditures on the children. Cost shares guidelines estimate expenditures on the children quite differently than do income shares guidelines. First, cost shares uses estimated single-parent spending as the standard for spending by separated parents. Where the income shares approach adds together the incomes of the parents and estimates what two-parent families with that level of income spend for children's share of housing, food, transportation, and other pooled expenses, the cost shares approach averages the parents' incomes and estimates what a single-parent family with that level of income spends for these needs. Effectively, this means that the children will be allocated a

share of only half the combined income of the parents. Second, "fixed expenses" incurred by either parent (i.e., expenses that do not move with the children between households) are then subtracted from this estimate of single-parent spending on the children. The exact categories of expense in the "fixed expense" component vary with different versions of the cost shares model, but may include expenditures by each parent for housing for the children, medical insurance premiums, and court-ordered life insurance premiums. The remaining amount is considered the "basic child cost" subject to apportionment between the parents.

(3) Determine each parent's "total incurred child cost." The cost shares model also makes very strong assumptions about the way in which children's expenses are distributed between parents who live in separate households. The model assumes that each parent's spending on the children is determined solely by the amount of time the children spend in each household. There is no assumption that custodial parents incur a larger share of the costs by virtue of their status as custodial parents. Consequently, each parent's "total incurred child cost" is calculated as follows:

a. Apportion the basic child cost between the parents according to each parent's percentage of parenting time. The resulting amount is presumed to be the parent's "incurred basic child costs."

b. Add to each parent's incurred basic child costs any other actual expenditures for the children by each parent. Such expenditures include the "fixed expenses" previously subtracted from the estimates of total basic costs (e.g., life insurance premiums, medical insurance premiums, housing), as well as expenses not included in the table of "basic child costs" (e.g., child care, education). The resulting amount for each parent is presumed to be that parent's total expenditures for the children.

c. Calculate the "tax benefit attributable to the children" for each parent and subtract this benefit from the parent's total expenditures for the children to arrive at the parent's "total incurred child costs." Like the definition of "fixed expenses," the definition of "tax benefit attributable to the children" may vary with different versions of the model, but the authors generally describe it as the difference between the after-tax income of the parent after receiving his or her actual child-related tax benefits, and the after-tax income of the parent assuming single taxpayer/no dependents status.

(4) Determine the final order for support through a cross-credit calculation. This step resembles the formula used in some states to establish support for extended parenting time, but without the multiplier that is typically applied to child costs to reflect the increased cost of caring for children in separate households. Each parent's obligation to the other parent is calculated by multiplying the parent's share of their combined monthly income available for child support by the other parent's total incurred child costs. The parent who owes the higher amount to the other parent is the obligor, and pays the difference between the two obligations to the other parent.

NOTES AND QUESTIONS

1. All child support formulas use some kind of standardized measure to determine how much money parents at various levels of income "should" spend on their children. Parents and their attorneys regularly question where these amounts come from, and even experts who understand the economic analysis upon which the measures are founded debate the validity of various methodologies. Since no methodology for determining child support is value-neutral,

Professor Ellman argues that drafters of child support guidelines must directly confront these value choices rather than leaving them to the technical experts who have developed the various measures. Ira Mark Ellman, Fudging Failure: The Economic Analysis Used to Construct Child Support Guidelines, 2004 U. Chi. Legal F. 167. What are these choices? How would drafters go about balancing the interests of children and their parents? Would it be desirable to return to the preguideline days when judges decided child support based on individualized assessments of children's needs and parents' ability to pay?

2. Ellman participated in a major effort to revise Arizona's guidelines based on reassessment of these policy choices. The work group's proposal attempted to ameliorate three problems with existing guidelines, which were based on the Income Shares Model:

> First, they specify payment amounts that have very little effect on the child's living standard. If the custodial parent is poor, the custodial household remains poor after receiving the child support payment, even when the support obligor's income is high. Second, children whose parents have the same combined income can find themselves in dramatically different financial circumstances after divorce, if one lives primarily with the higher-earning parent and the other with the lower-earning parent. Third, low-income obligors are expected to pay unreasonably high support amounts to high-income custodial parents, given that in these cases the child enjoys a much higher living standard than the obligor even before any support is paid.

Ira Mark Ellman, A Case Study in Failed Family Law Reform: Arizona's Child Support Guidelines, 54 Ariz. L. Rev. 137, 151-152 (2012). The proposal, like the ALI Principles, focused on the standards of living in the two parents' households after child support was paid, rather than on the additional money that hypothetically would have been spent had the parents and children lived in the same household, which is the basis of the Income Shares Model. However, fathers' rights activists successfully opposed the changes, and the legislature ultimately enacted a law prohibiting adoption of the model that the study committee developed. *Id.* at 155.

3. Other critics of the continuity of expenditure approach also focus on the post-judgment standard of living and advocate for the equal living standards model. This approach was proposed in Judith Cassetty et al., The ELS (Equal Living Standards) Model for Child Support Awards, *in* Essentials of Child Support Guidelines Development: Economic Issues and Policy Considerations 329 (Women's Legal Defense Fund staff eds., 1986). It provides that the judge should order sufficient child support to equalize the living standards in the households of the child's two parents and clearly links the nonresidential parent's obligation both to the income of the residential parent and to the living standard in the residential parent's household. *See* Marsha Garrison, The Economic Consequences of Divorce: Would Adoption of the ALI Principles Improve Current Outcomes?, 8 Duke J. Gender L. & Pol'y 119 (2001); Marsha Garrison, An Evaluation of Two Models of Parental Obligation, 86 Cal. L. Rev. 41 (1998). However, the ELS model has been adopted in no state, and the Massachusetts Supreme Judicial Court reversed a trial court's child support order equalizing the incomes of the mother's and father's (high-income) households where their child spent equal amounts of time in each home because that approach was inconsistent with the state guidelines. M.C. v. T.K., 973 N.E.2d 130 (Mass. 2012). What problems do you see that might explain this approach's lack of political acceptance?

4. A group of researchers, including Professor Ellman, conducted a large-scale study of public opinion about child support, using members of Pima County, Arizona, jury pools. A series of experiments strongly supports the finding that lay people generally do not intuitively find either the Percentage of Obligor Income or the Income Shares approach to determining child support to be the fairest way of setting support. Instead, they choose a method in which the dollar amount of a noncustodial parent's obligation increases with his or her income but the percentage of net income that he or she owes does not vary. They also believed that the lower the custodial parent's income, the more rapidly the noncustodial parent's obligation should increase. This pattern held true for all demographic groups, even while those groups' judgments varied in other respects (*e.g.*, women generally favored overall higher child support obligations than men). In general, the respondents also believed that the amount of the obligor's child support obligation should be lower if the parents had never married and that an unmarried obligor's child support payment should increase less rapidly as income increased than would a married or formerly married obligor's payment. The studies are discussed in Sanford L. Braver et al., Public Intuitions About Fair Child Support Obligations: Converging Evidence for a "Fair Shares Rule" 20 Psychol. Pub. Pol'y & L. 146 (2014). *See also* Ira M. Ellman & Sanford L. Braver, Lay Intuitions About Child Support and Marital Status, 23 Child & Fam. L.Q. 465 (2011); Ira Mark Ellman et al., Abstract Principles and Concrete Cases in Intuitive Lawmaking, 36 Law & Hum. Behav. 96 (2012).

C. APPLYING CHILD SUPPORT FORMULAS

Tuckman v. Tuckman
61 A.3d 449 (Conn. 2013)

EVELEIGH, J. . . . The defendant and the plaintiff . . . were married on November 3, 1990. They have two children, a son, born in 1994, and a daughter, born in 1996. Both parties have substantial income and assets available to them. In 2005 and 2006, the defendant had an income of $530,000 and $945,000, respectively. The defendant's assets included a one-third stake in BJK Partners (BJK), an investment partnership with her two older brothers, and a one-third ownership interest in Offices Limited, Inc., a family office furniture business. According to the parties' financial affidavits, at the time of trial, the defendant's share of BJK was valued at approximately $2.7 million, while her share of Offices Limited, Inc., was valued at $1.25 million. The defendant also earned well over $2 million through her BJK investment partnership between 1996 and 2007. In 2006 and 2007, the plaintiff, who worked in the commodities division at Merrill Lynch, each year earned a base compensation of $200,000 with a bonus of $1.5 million. In 2008, the plaintiff was set to begin employment at Citicorp, where he was to receive base pay along with a bonus of $1.25 million in 2009 and 2010.

"On September 13, 2006, the plaintiff brought this dissolution action by complaint in which he sought a dissolution of the marriage. . . ."

In its memorandum of decision in the present case, the trial court entered the following order regarding child support: "As a contribution [toward] expenses related to the children when they are with [the defendant], the [plaintiff] shall pay child support to the [defendant] in the amount of $250 per week for each child." The trial court also stated in its memorandum of decision that it "considered the gross and net income of the parties."

Thereafter, the defendant filed a motion for articulation in which, inter alia, she requested that the trial court "articulate and clarify . . . [f]or purposes of the [trial] court's child support orders . . . did the [trial] court accept either parties' child support calculation worksheet and what did the [trial] court find to be the net income of each party." Although the trial court articulated and clarified some issues in its memorandum of decision, it did not address this request. In reviewing the trial court's memorandum of decision, the Appellate Court concluded as follows: "Based on the record before us and the court's memorandum of decision, we cannot conclude that the court properly fashioned its child support order. The court's order failed to follow the guideline's tables, and, more importantly, its memorandum of decision failed to make any reference to the guidelines. . . ."

In Maturo v. Maturo, supra, 296 Conn. at 89-90, 995 A.2d 1, this court considered the impact of the child support statutes, regulations and guidelines on high income families. In doing so, this court recognized that "[t]he legislature has enacted several statutes to assist courts in fashioning child support orders. Section 46b-84 provides in relevant part: (a) Upon or subsequent to the annulment or dissolution of any marriage or the entry of a decree of legal separation or divorce, the parents of a minor child of the marriage, shall maintain the child according to their respective abilities, if the child is in need of maintenance. . . .

"'(d) In determining whether a child is in need of maintenance and, if in need, the respective abilities of the parents to provide such maintenance and the amount thereof, the court shall consider the age, health, station, occupation, earning capacity, amount and sources of income, estate, vocational skills and employability of each of the parents, and the age, health, station, occupation, educational status and expectation, amount and sources of income, vocational skills, employability, estate and needs of the child.'" . . .

"The guidelines include a schedule for calculating 'the basic child support obligation' for families that have two minor children and a combined net weekly income ranging from $310 to $4000. The guidelines provide in relevant part that, '[w]hen the parents' combined net weekly income exceeds [$4000], child support awards shall be determined on a case-by-case basis, and the current support prescribed at the [$4000] net weekly income level shall be the minimum presumptive amount.' . . . [T]he guidelines emphasize that the support amounts calculated thereunder are the correct amounts to be ordered by the court unless rebutted by a specific finding on the record that such an amount would be inequitable or inappropriate. Any such finding shall include the amount required under the guidelines and the court's justification for the deviation, which must be based on the guidelines' '[c]riteria for deviation. . . .'

"In sum, the applicable statutes, as well as the guidelines, provide that all child support awards must be made in accordance with the principles established therein to ensure that such awards promote 'equity,' 'uniformity' and 'consistency' for children 'at all income levels.' . . . Although the guidelines grant courts discretion to make awards on a 'case-by-case' basis above the amount prescribed for a family at the upper limit of the schedule when the combined net weekly income of the parents exceeds that limit, which is presently $4000; the guidelines also indicate that such awards should follow the principle expressly acknowledged in the preamble and reflected in the schedule that the child support obligation as a percentage of the combined net weekly income should decline as the income level rises. Thus, an award of child support based on a combined net weekly income of $8000 must be governed by the same principles that govern a child support award based on a combined net weekly income of $4000, even though the former does not fall within the guidelines' schedule. Finally, although courts may, in the exercise of their discretion, determine the correct percentage of the combined net weekly income assigned to child support in light of the circumstances in each particular case, including a consideration of other, additional obligations imposed on the noncustodial parent, any deviation from the schedule or the principles on which the guidelines are based must be accompanied by the court's explanation as to why the guidelines are inequitable or inappropriate and why the deviation is necessary to meet the needs of the child."

. . . Although the trial court in the present case stated that it considered the gross and net income of the parties, it never determined the net income of the parties in its memorandum of decision. Without a determination of the net income of the parties, the trial court could not, as required by the guidelines, determine the presumptive amount of support required by the guidelines. . . .

Accordingly, we conclude that the Appellate Court properly determined that the trial court abused its discretion when it awarded $250 per child per week to the defendant without determining the net income of the parties, mentioning or applying the guidelines, or making a specific finding on the record as to why it was deviating from the guidelines.

We next address the defendant's claim that the trial court improperly determined that her subchapter S allocated income should be included in her annual net income. Specifically, the defendant asserts that the trial court improperly relied on her personal tax returns showing the taxable income of an S corporation of which she is a shareholder. The defendant claims that the trial court improperly relied on that income in determining alimony and child support, despite the fact that it was not available to her. In response, the plaintiff claims that the trial court did not improperly consider the defendant's gross income and that it properly considered the defendant's subchapter S allocated income under the facts of the present case. We agree with the defendant.

"It is well settled that a court must base child support and alimony orders on the available net income of the parties, not gross income."

In the present case, the trial court stated in its memorandum of decision as follows: "It should be noted that an examination of [the defendant's] tax returns shows that in 2006 her income was approximately $945,000 and the year before approximately $580,000." The trial court further stated in its memorandum of decision, as clarified by a subsequent rectification, "[the defendant] has substantial income available to her (at least $500,000 per annum)."

An examination of the defendant's tax returns demonstrates that a substantial portion of her taxable income for the years 2005 and 2006 was income from her share of the S corporation, Offices Limited, Inc. Because Offices Limited, Inc., is organized as an S corporation, all of its capital gains and losses, for federal income tax purposes, pass through Offices Limited, Inc., to the individual shareholders, and any federal income tax liability on capital gains is the responsibility of the individual shareholder. . . . The trial court did not, however, make any finding as to what portion of the income reported on her tax returns was actually available to the defendant and what portion was merely "[pass] through earnings" of the S corporation. In fact, the defendant's testimony at trial indicated that none of the shareholder taxable income was available to her, but was retained by the corporation for investment. She testified that only her salary of approximately $85,000 was available income.

Although this court has not directly addressed how to treat, for purposes of determining a parent's financial obligations, undistributed earnings of an S corporation that for income tax purposes are attributable to the parent-shareholder, we are persuaded by the Massachusetts Supreme Judicial Court, which addressed this issue in J.S. v. C.C., 912 N.E.2d 933 (Mass. 2009). The Massachusetts Supreme Judicial Court while recognizing that courts in a number of other jurisdictions have considered how to treat the retained earnings of an S corporation that are passed through to a shareholder for purposes of measuring and imposing a child support obligation, concluded as follows: "[T]he better reasoned decisions require a case-specific, factual inquiry and determination. . . . Such a fact-based inquiry is necessary to balance, inter alia, the considerations that a well-managed corporation may be required to retain a portion of its earnings to maintain corporate operations and survive fluctuations in income, but corporate structures should not be used to shield available income that could and should serve as available sources of child support funds."

The Massachusetts Supreme Judicial Court noted some relevant factors that a trial court judge should weigh in determining what portion of undistributed corporate earnings may be available to a shareholder for a child support obligation, "[f]irst, a shareholder's level of control over corporate distributions—as measured by the shareholder's ownership interest—is a factor of substantial importance. A minority shareholder lacking the power unilaterally to order a distribution may be relatively unlikely to have access to retained income of the corporation. . . . A majority shareholder may be relatively more likely to have access to retained funds and ability to manipulate pass-through income, and a sole shareholder even more so. . . . Second, the judge should evaluate the legitimate business interests justifying retained corporate earnings. . . . Third, the judge should weigh affirmative evidence of an attempt to shield income by means of retained earnings. . . . In that regard, the corporation's history of retained earnings and distributions may be relevant. . . . Finally, it is important to consider the allocation of burden of proof in relation to the treatment of an S corporation's undistributed earnings for purposes of determining income available for child support; this is an issue on which courts in other jurisdictions are split. Some courts shift the burden of proof depending on the shareholder's level of control over the corporation: a minority shareholder is presumed not to have access to retained income and therefore does not carry the burden of proof, while a majority or sole shareholder is presumed to have access to retained income and does carry the burden of proof. . . . Other courts place the burden on the shareholder to present evidence that he or she does not have access to retained income regardless of the shareholder's ownership percentage in the corporation; they reason that the shareholder is the party with greater access to the evidence. . . . We are persuaded that the second approach is more appropriate, because we agree that regardless of the percentage of his or her ownership interest, the shareholder is likely to have greater access to relevant information about the corporation than a party who is not connected to it."

In considering the same issue, the Florida's District Court of Appeal concluded that a majority shareholder's pass through income from an S corporation should not be included in available income for the purposes of determining alimony and child support. Zold v. Zold, 880 So. 2d 779, 781 (Fla. App. 2004). In doing so, it recognized as follows: "When a corporation has more than one shareholder, an officer/shareholder has a fiduciary duty to all shareholders. The corporation is not the personal piggy bank for any one shareholder simply because that shareholder may have a controlling interest in the corporation and is also the chief executive officer. Financial responsibilities to creditors and employees must be satisfied before distributions to shareholders take place if a corporation is to remain viable. Once the distributions are found to be possible, the distributions must be pro-rata in accordance with the percentage ownership of the capital stock of the corporation. Court ordered obligations in marital litigation should not place an ex-marital partner in the position of having to breach a corporate fiduciary obligation in order to avoid the possibility of a court finding that partner contemptuous."

. . . [T]he record in the present case demonstrates that the trial court looked to the defendant's entire income as measured for income tax purposes as available income for determining the alimony and child support order. The trial court did not make any findings as to the particular facts or circumstances of the S corporation of which the defendant was a shareholder. Accordingly, we conclude that remand is appropriate in the present case for a determination of what portion of the defendant's income was available income for purposes of fashioning alimony and child support orders. . . .

The judgment of the Appellate Court is affirmed and the case is remanded to that court with direction to reverse the judgment of the trial court as to the financial orders in their entirety and to remand the case to that court for a new trial in accordance with this opinion.

NOTES AND QUESTIONS

1. A major issue in *Tuckman* is how to set child support when the income of one or both parents is higher than the top amount on the child support scale. By what method did the *Tuckman* trial court resolve this problem? On remand, what will the trial court be required to do? What does the court mean when it says that the guidelines "indicate that such awards should follow the principle expressly acknowledged in the preamble and reflected in the schedule that the child support obligation as a percentage of the combined net weekly income should decline as the income level rises"? In high-income cases, most courts do not simply extrapolate the percentages in the scale to the parents' actual income. Why not? On the other hand, some states' guidelines include a percentage formula that courts must follow in high-income cases. For example, in Florida, if the parents' combined income is more than $10,000 per month, the child support is the highest amount on the scale plus 5 percent for one child, 7.5 percent for two children, 9.5 percent for three children, 11 percent for four children, 12 percent for five children, and 12.5 percent for six children. Fla. Stat. Ann. §61.30(6)(b) (2022).

2. Several courts have remarked that "no child needs three ponies" to explain limits on child support in high-income cases. Downing v. Downing, 45 S.W.3d 449 (Ky. App. 2001); Isaacson v. Isaacson, 792 A.2d 525 (N.J. App. Div.), *cert. denied*, 807 A.2d 195 (N.J. 2002); Pearson v. Pearson, 751 N.E.2d 921 (Mass. App. 2001). The origin of the phrase seems to be In re Patterson, 920 P.2d 450, 455 (Kan. App. 1996). What does it mean?

In some states the guidelines simply do not apply in very-high-income cases, and courts have discretion to set support under preguideline law. Dyas v. Dyas, 683 So. 2d 971 (Ala. Civ. App. 1995); In re Marriage of Krone, 530 N.W.2d 469 (Iowa App. 1995); Battersby v. Battersby, 590 A.2d 427 (Conn. 1991). In a number of states courts begin with the guideline amount that would apply if the parents' income were equal to the guideline maximum and then determine whether the facts warrant deviating upward. *See, e.g.*, Ga. Code Ann. §19-6-15(i)(2)(A) (2022).

State child support laws show some of the greatest variation in treatment of child support obligations of high-income parents. Linda D. Elrod & Robert G. Spector, A Review of the Year in Family Law: Working Toward More Uniformity in Laws Relating to Families, 44 Fam. L.Q. 469, 470 (2011); *see also* Charles J. Meyer et al., Child Support Determinations in High Income Families—A Survey of the Fifty States, 28 J. Am. Acad. Matrimonial Law. 483 (2016).

3. In several high-income cases, including a number involving professional athletes, in which the parent was likely to receive a very high income for only a short time, courts have permitted orders that contemplate or even require that some current child support be saved to provide for the child after the parent's income goes down. *See, e.g.*, Henry v. Beacham, 686 S.E.2d 892 (Ga. App. 2009); Passemato v. Passemato, 691 N.E.2d 549 (Mass. 1998); Mary L.O. v. Tommy R.B., 544 N.W.2d 417 (Wis. 1996) (allowing a court to order the establishment of an educational trust fund). This approach is not permitted in other states, which allow child support to be ordered only to provide for the child's current needs.

4. The other major issue in *Tuckman* is how to treat earnings of a subchapter S corporation that are allocated to a parent for purposes of the federal income tax but that are not actually paid out to the parent as a dividend. What arguments generally support including such income in the child support formula calculation? What arguments support a decision not to include it? Should it matter whether the parent is a sole proprietor, a majority shareholder, or a minority shareholder?

The Minnesota Supreme Court interpreted its child support guidelines as requiring inclusion of a parent's share of a subchapter S corporation's income after expenses, regardless of whether it is distributed to or available to parent. However, the court pointed out, a deviation from the formula amount may be justified if the income is not available to the parent. Haefele v. Haefele, 837 N.W.2d 703 (Minn. 2013). How is this approach different from that in *Tuckman*? Does the difference matter?

For a survey of the treatment of subchapter S corporation earnings and other assets where a support obligor receives no cash in hand but may be regarded as having income for tax or accounting purposes, *see* Timothy M. Todd, Phantom Income and Domestic Support Obligations, 67 Buff. L. Rev. 365, 365-405 (2019).

5. The *Tuckman* majority concluded that some income the mother had to report for purposes of the federal income tax was not income for purposes of the child support guidelines. Generally, courts have held that whether an item is includible or deductible from income for purposes of the federal income tax does not determine how it will be treated in calculating child support. For example, In re Marriage of Hein, 266 Cal.Rptr.3d 150, 158 (Cal. App. 2020), held that depreciation of business assets, which is deductible when calculating income tax liability, is not deductible for purposes of determining a parent's child support obligation. The court said, "depreciation is a fictional loss that, in the real world represents tax savings and, therefore, additional cash available to the parent to meet child support obligations." 266 Cal. Rptr.3d at 158. *See also* Jefferson v. Jefferson, 327 So.3d 1085 (Miss. App. 2021); Asfaw v. Woldberhan, 55 Cal. Rptr. 3d 323 (Cal. App. 2007); Fisher v. Fisher, 171 P.3d 917 (Okla. 2007); Eagley v. Eagley, 849 P.2d 777 (Alaska 1993); Turner v. Turner, 586 A.2d 1182 (Del. 1991); In re Marriage of Sullivan, 794 P.2d 687 (Mont. 1990). *But see* In re Marriage of Stevenson, 765 N.W.2d 811 (Wis. App. 2009) (under Wisconsin percentage of income formula, if beneficiary of trust must pay taxes on undistributed income, income must be included in child support calculation). Should income and expenses be treated the same for purposes of both income taxes and child support? Why or why not?

6. Child support guideline definitions of income are usually very inclusive, and courts have construed them broadly. Retirement income, lottery winnings, personal injury settlements, stock options, and spousal support have been treated as income. *See, e.g.*, Matter of Greenberg, 261 A.3d 293 (N.H. 2021); Wood v. Wood, 403 S.E.2d 761 (W. Va. 1991); In re Micaletti, 796 P.2d 54 (Colo. App. 1990). The states are divided in their treatment of gifts and inheritances. In some, the total amount of the inheritance is treated as income, while in others only the income that the inheritance generates is counted. *See* Charles J. Meyer et al., above, 28 J. Am. Acad. Matrimonial Law. at 490-496, for a discussion of this and other issues regarding what counts as income.

7. On the deduction side, legitimate business expenses are generally deductible for owners of small businesses. Employees cannot deduct their expenses because average costs of living are included in parents' self-support reserves.

8. In most states, the statutory criteria for deviating from the formula amount of child support are not exclusive, and a court may deviate for other reasons, provided that it states reasons on the record. *See, e.g.*, In re Marriage of Selley, 359 P.3d 891 (Wash. App. 2015). However, the majority of courts have held that parental agreement alone is not a sufficient reason to deviate downward from the formula amount. *See, e.g.*, Cox v. Cox, 776 P.2d 1045 (Alaska 1989); Ching v. Ching, 751 P.2d 93 (Haw. App. 1988); Peerenboom v. Peerenboom, 433 N.W.2d 282 (Wis. App. 1988). On the other hand, parents may enter into enforceable contracts for more child support than a court could order or for a longer term, and, if the parents agree, courts ordinarily may incorporate such agreements into their orders. *See, e.g.*, Short v. Short, 131 So. 3d 1149 (Miss. 2014).

PROBLEMS

1. Gale's employer pays for an apartment and a company car for him. Should the fair market value of these fringe benefits be treated as income for purposes of calculating child support? Does it matter whether Gale is a federal employee and under federal law these payments are not taxable? What about contributions that the employer makes to Gale's retirement account?

In a jurisdiction that bases child support on net income, should Gale be able to deduct mandatory amounts withheld from his pay to fund his pension? How about extra amounts that he contributes voluntarily to the pension? What if Gale is self-employed and regularly contributes to a retirement plan over which he has sole control?

2. Madison and Freddie are the parents of two children. Madison, a certified public accountant, is a minority shareholder in a closely held accounting firm; the other shareholders are Madison's father and two brothers. Freddie, a medical doctor, is a sole practitioner whose practice is incorporated. Last year each business retained some of its earnings rather than paying them out as dividends. Should the retained earnings of each parent's business be included as income to the parent?

3. Frank and Molly dated briefly in college but broke up when Molly learned she was pregnant. Molly dropped out of school when the baby was born; now, eight years later, she works as a secretary earning $3000 per month. Frank graduated from law school four years ago and has just been hired by a major law firm after having completed a prestigious clerkship. At his new firm he earns $14,000 per month. Molly has successfully argued that Frank's new job justifies modifying child support, which had been set at $1290. The highest amount on the child support scale is $1437 for one child whose parents' combined income is $10,000 per month. Following *Tuckman*, the court has ordered Frank to pay $2500 per month in child support. Frank appeals. What arguments should the parties make?

All states' child support rules provided for adjustments for shared parenting time. Thirty-five states permit courts to use a formula that allows for an offset based on time spent with each parent; other states treat shared parenting as a deviation factor. Family Law Quarterly Editorial Staff, Charts 2020: Family Law in the Fifty States, D.C., and Puerto Rico, Part 2, 55 Fam. L. Q. 211, 227 Chart 6 (2022). For a detailed analysis of the variations among states, *see* J. Thomas Oldham & Jane Venohr, The Relationship Between Child Support and Parenting Time, 54 Fam. L. Q. 141(2020).

The differences among the states may reflect differences in the political power of various constituencies in the different states, as well as empirical uncertainty about how much additional expense parents without primary custody incur, how much primary residential parents save when the child is with the other parent, and how parents' expenses vary with variations in the way the children's time is divided between the parents. Sanford L. Braver et al., Public Sentiments About the Parenting Time Adjustment in Child Support Awards, 49 Fam. L.Q. 433, 435-437 (2015).

In the common case where the primary residential parent's income is lower than the other parent's, the result of adjusting for shared parenting time is a reduced child support award to the primary household. To alleviate this, the Income Shares model recommends increasing the total amount to be shared to recognize the increased costs of the child living in two households. For examples based on the child support guidelines of Maryland, New Jersey, and California, *see* Karen Syma Czapanskiy, The Shared Custody Child Support Adjustment: Not Worth the Candle, 49 Fam. L.Q. 409 (2015).

While the argument favoring a closer link between parenting time and child support was originally made in support of lowering the support payments of nonresident parents, the next case explores how this principle should be employed when the residential parent's income is substantially higher than that of the nonresidential parent.

In re Marriage of Turk
12 N.E.3d 40 (Ill. 2014)

Justice KARMEIER delivered the judgment of the court, with opinion. . . . Iris and Steven Turk were married in October of 1993 and have two sons, Nathaniel, born in 1997, and Jacob, born in 1999. In 2004, Iris filed a petition in the circuit court of Cook County seeking dissolution of the marriage, division of the property, sole custody of the boys, and an award of maintenance and child support. Steven, in turn, filed a counter petition for dissolution requesting, among other things, that the award of custody be joint.

Following various developments not relevant here, the court entered an agreed judgment dissolving the marriage. Among the provisions of the judgment, filed July 25, 2005, was that

Steven would pay Iris $4,000 per month in unallocated maintenance and child support for 42 months, that the parties would have joint custody of the children, that the children would reside with Iris, and that Steven would provide the medical insurance for the children and cover 50% of their out-of-pocket medical and dental costs.

Over the years, Steven and Iris frequently returned to court to contest matters related to the custody and education of the children. . . .

On July 28, 2012, the circuit court entered an agreed "custody judgment and parenting order" which specified that Steven was to have "the sole care, custody, control and education" of the boys and gave him authority to make "[m]ajor decisions in connection with [their] education, health, care and religious training," subject to various conditions involving communication and cooperation. Iris was granted regular visitation with Nathan once a week, for dinner on Wednesdays. Her regular visitation with Jacob was substantially longer, with weekly visits from Monday to Wednesday mornings, plus alternating weekends, a system which gave her nearly equal time with him. In addition, a separate schedule was set up to insure that each parent would have equal time with both boys during holidays, spring break and summer vacations.

When the court signed the foregoing agreed order, it also entered a separate order disposing of Steven's remaining request to completely terminate his obligation to make child support payments to Iris. Based upon the provisions of the agreed order and a determination that Steven earned approximately $150,000 per year while Iris' earnings were less than $10,000 per year, the court ordered Steven to pay Iris child support of $600 per month and made him "solely responsible for all uncovered medical, dental, orthodontia, psychological and optical expenses for the children."

Steven appealed, arguing that because he has been designated as the custodial parent, the circuit court had no authority under section 505 of the Illinois Marriage and Dissolution of Marriage Act to order him to pay child support to Iris, a noncustodial parent. . . .

. . . [T]he appellate court rejected the contention that section 505 does not authorize a circuit court to order custodial parents to pay child support to noncustodial parents. . . . Steven filed a petition for leave to appeal from the appellate court's judgment. . . . We granted Steven's petition. . . .

Steven interprets section 505 to mean that the obligation to pay child support may be imposed only on noncustodial parents and that a custodial parent may never be ordered to pay child support to a noncustodial parent. The terms of the statute do not support such a view. In contrast to the child support laws of some states which single out noncustodial parents for payment of child support (see, *e.g.*, Rubin v. Salla, 964 N.Y.S.2d 41, 47 (App. Div. 2013) (applying New York law); Daigrepont v. Daigrepont, 458 So. 2d 637, 638-39 (La. Ct. App. 1984) (applying the law of Louisiana)), section 505 expressly confers on courts the option to "order *either or both parents* owing a duty of support to a child of the marriage to pay an amount reasonable and necessary for the support of the child, without regard to marital misconduct." (Emphasis added.) The statute further provides that in addition to support, the court may, in its discretion, "order *either or both parents* owing a duty of support to a child of the marriage to contribute to [various] expenses, if determined by the court to be reasonable," including health needs not covered by insurance. (Emphasis added.) . . .

Sometimes, as under the agreed custody judgment entered in this case, a parent who is technically noncustodial may have visitation rights which place the child in that parent's care for periods that rival those of the custodial parent and at commensurate cost. If Steven were correct and status as the custodial parent automatically precluded one from having to make any child support payments to the other parent, the noncustodial parent could end up having to pay a significant portion of the costs of raising the child without any regard to that parent's financial resources and needs or how they compared to the financial resources and needs of the custodial parent. That may not be problematic where the noncustodial parent happens to be the wealthier of the two, but where, as here, the noncustodial parent appears to have significantly fewer resources to meet the substantial support costs which are sure to arise from the extensive visitation schedule, disqualifying the poorer parent from obtaining any financial assistance for child care from the wealthier parent based solely on the poorer parent's classification as noncustodial would not only place an unfair burden on the poorer parent, it could also leave that parent with insufficient resources to care for the child in a manner even minimally comparable to that of the wealthier parent.

Section 505(a) was intended to protect the rights of children to be supported by their parents in an amount commensurate with the parents' income. Under Steven's approach, a child could well end up living commensurate with the parents' income only half the time, when he or she was staying with the wealthier parent. If custodial parents were categorically exempt from child support obligations, the wealthier parent's resources would be beyond the court's consideration and reach even though the visitation schedule resulted in the child actually residing with the poorer parent for a substantial period each week. This could be detrimental to the child psychologically as well as economically, for the instability resulting from having to "live a dual life in order to conform to the differing socio-economic classes of his or her parents" may cause the child to experience distress or other damaging emotional responses. Such an outcome would plainly not serve the child's best interest. Steven's approach therefore undermines rather than advances the purposes of the law. . . .

[Other courts have reached the same conclusion, including Williamson v. Williamson, 293 Ga. 721, 748 S.E.2d 679 (2013); Grant v. Hager, 868 N.E.2d 801, 804 (Ind. 2007); Colonna v. Colonna, 581 Pa. 1, 855 A.2d 648 (2004). In *Colonna*] the Supreme Court of Pennsylvania recognized that where the parent who does not have primary custody has a less significant income than the custodial parent, it is likely that he or she will not be able to provide an environment that resembles the one in which the children are accustomed to living with the custodial parent. "While a downward adjustment in lifestyle is a frequent consequence of divorce that affects both adults and children," the court observed,

> "we would be remiss in failing to ignore the reality of what happens when children are required to live vastly different lives depending upon which parent has custody on any given day. To expect that quality of the contact between the non-custodial parent and the children will not be negatively impacted by that parent's comparative penury vis-à-vis the custodial parent is not realistic. Issuing a support order that allows such a situation to exist clearly is not in the best interests of the children. . . ."

While obviously not binding on our court, we believe that the foregoing authorities are consistent with the principles set forth in section 505 of the Illinois Marriage and Dissolution of Marriage Act and further support our conclusion that under section 505, a trial court may order the custodial parent to pay child support to the noncustodial parent where circumstances and the best interest of the child warrant it.

The concern has been expressed that if we sanction awards of child support to noncustodial parents, we open the door to abuse by spouses who will use requests for modification of child support as a subterfuge for obtaining additional maintenance. We note, however, that the criteria for awarding and modifying child support are clearly set out in the statute. If those criteria are applied properly by the lower courts, and we must assume they will be, any abuse should be preventable. . . .

For the foregoing reasons, we affirm that portion of the appellate court's judgment which upheld the authority of the circuit court to order Steven to pay child support and remanded to the circuit court for an evidentiary hearing regarding the amount of child support Steven should be required to pay. . . .

[The concurring opinion of Justice Theis is omitted.]

NOTES AND QUESTIONS

1. In *Turk*, if the mother had been awarded custody and the timesharing arrangement had been the same, the father would have been ordered to pay child support. What difference, if any, does it make that one parent is designated as having "custody" or as being the "primary residential parent"?

At some point, does a parent spend so little time with the children that that parent should not be awarded child support, regardless of the income disparity? Why or why not? Should the amount of child support that a parent pays be reduced based on how much time the parent spends with the children? Why or why not?

2. In *Turk*, the father's income was 15 times that of the mother. If his income had only been twice hers, should the court have ordered him to pay support to her? By how much must the parents' incomes differ before a court enters an order as in *Turk*?

3. In split custody cases, where one child lives primarily with one parent and the other(s) primarily with the other parent, would the same principles apply that govern cases of shared custody?

4. Braver and his colleagues found substantial public support for varying the amount of child support even with small changes in parenting time. However, people did not favor large variations in the amount of support. The researchers concluded that the people in the study were focused on compensating for the amount of money the primary custodial parent saved when the children were with the other parent, rather than on the additional expenses that the other parent incurred. Sanford L. Braver et al., Public Sentiments About the Parenting Time Adjustment in Child Support Awards, 49 Fam. L.Q. 433, 445-447 (2015).

5. In many families, actual custodial arrangements change over time, and when shared custody falls apart, the children tend to move to the home of one parent, usually the mother. Given this fluidity, does it make sense to calibrate child support to small changes in how the children's time is divided?

NOTE: CHILD SUPPORT OBLIGATIONS OF LOW-INCOME PARENTS

When a parent has little or no income, the first issue that must be considered is whether additional income should be imputed to the parent on the theory that he or she could reasonably be expected to earn more. The question of when income should be imputed to a parent is similar to the question of when a support obligation should be reduced because the obligor's income has decreased. Both depend on a judgment about whether the obligor parent should be expected to earn more than he or she does. Modification of support based on reduced income is covered in Chapter 8.

Parents with very low incomes who cannot earn more are generally not totally exempt from child support. *See, e.g.,* McClure v. Haisha, 51 N.E.3d 831 (Ill. App. 2016), requiring a mother who earned $929 a month to pay child support of $10 per month to the father, who earned $21,000 a month. Many guidelines provide for a minimum child support obligation, since all parents are obligated to support their children. However, the courts in In re Marriage of Gilbert, 945 P.2d 238 (Wash. App. 1997), and Rose ex rel. Clancy v. Moody, 629 N.E.2d 378, 380 (N.Y. 1993), held that a rule that provided for a minimum monthly order violated the federal requirement that amounts determined by a child support formula must be treated as creating a rebuttable presumption. *Contra* A.M.S. ex rel. Farthing v. Stoppleworth, 694 N.W.2d 8 (N.D. 2005).

Most guidelines and courts that have considered the issue have held that public assistance payments, from either Supplemental Security Income (based on disability or old age) or

Temporary Assistance to Needy Families, are not "income" from which a parent may be ordered to pay child support. *See* Burns v. Edwards, 842 A.2d 186 (N.J. Super. App. Div. 2004) (discussing cases from around the country); Laura W. Morgan, Supplemental Security Income and Child Support, 16(4) Divorce Litig. 71 (2004). In comparison, most guidelines and courts include Social Security Disability payments received by a parent or a child in the calculation of child support, though the states vary in their approaches. *See* Tori R. A. Kricken, Child Support and Social Security Dependent Benefits: A Comprehensive Analysis and Proposal for Wyoming, 2 Wyo. L. Rev. 39 (2002).

While most states consider a parent's incarceration as grounds for modifying a child support order, they vary in whether they allow support orders to be entered against such parents, even though the parents have no ability to pay while in prison, and when states do allow orders, how the amount of support is calculated. Lauren Ruth, Note, Deadbeat, Deadbroke or Just Dead Wrong?: An Argument in Favor of a Mandated "Totality of the Circumstances" Test in the Modification of Child Support Orders for Parents Incarcerated for Crime Against Their Children, 72 Rutgers U. L. Rev. 907 (2020). A 2016 rule issued by the federal Office of Child Support Enforcement prohibits states from treating incarceration as voluntary unemployment. 5 C.F.R. §302.56(c)(3) (2022).

D. POST-MAJORITY CHILD SUPPORT

Leslie Harris, Dennis Waldrop & Lori R. Waldrop

Making and Breaking Connections Between Parents' Duty to Support and Right to Control Their Children
69 Or. L. Rev. 689, 717-720 (1990)

Today we ordinarily think of parents' support duty as terminating when a child attains the age of majority. However, in the nineteenth and into the twentieth century the determination of when parents were no longer required to support their children depended on the child's actual capacity for self-support and submission to parental control.

Older adolescents, especially boys, were considered capable of at least partial self-support and often worked for wages. So long as a minor child lived with or was supported by the parents and had not been emancipated, the father was entitled to the child's earnings. By the same token, a parent was obligated to support a minor child so long as the child remained under the parent's control. A parent might discharge, at least partially, the duty to support a minor child capable of earning wages by giving the child the right to retain the wages. Some authorities went so far as to say that a parent was not required to support a child to the extent that the child could earn money. Further, a parent was not required to support a minor child capable of self-support who left the parent and struck out on his or her own. Some courts expressed this idea by saying that parents were not obligated to support minor children who were emancipated. "Emancipation" is a term with multiple meanings, depending on the context in which it is used. In a formal sense, emancipation means the termination of some or all of the mutual rights and duties of the parent-child relationship, and it could occur by mutual agreement or when one party acted wrongfully, as when a father abandoned or forced a child out. In the latter situation the father was not entitled to the child's earnings. . . .

These rules were formulated in a time when children, especially boys, often attained functional adulthood in late adolescence, even though they were still legally minors. Parents were probably less worried about children remaining dependent for unreasonably long periods than they were that the children would strike out on their own when the parents felt they were still needed at home to work. In this context, the rules can be understood primarily as giving legal effect to circumstances as they actually existed. To some extent the rules also suggested that minors should remain subject to parental authority unless the parents acquiesced in their independence.

In the early 1970s most states lowered the age of majority to 18, the age at which most children are just finishing high school. However, social conditions have changed so that many young people continue in school well into their twenties, remaining economically, and to some extent personally, dependent on their parents. Many parents voluntarily support older children, but the question is whether parents are or should be legally obligated to continue to support them.

McLeod v. Starnes
723 S.E.2d 198 (S.C. 2012)

Justice HEARN. Less than two years ago, this Court decided Webb v. Sowell, 692 S.E.2d 543 (S.C. 2010), which held that ordering a non-custodial parent to pay college expenses violates equal protection, thus overruling thirty years of precedent flowing from Risinger v. Risinger, 253 S.E.2d 652 (S.C. 1979). . . . Today, we hold that Webb was wrongly decided and remand this matter for reconsideration in light of the law as it existed prior to Webb.

Kristi McLeod (Mother) and Robert Starnes (Father) divorced in 1993 following five years of marriage. Mother received custody of their two minor children, and Father was required to pay child support in the amount of $212 per week, which was later reduced to $175 per week by agreement, in addition to thirty-five percent of his annual bonus. At the time, Father earned approximately $29,000 per year plus a $2,500 bonus. However, his salary steadily increased to over $120,000 per year and his bonus to nearly $30,000 by 2007. In 2008, his salary was almost $250,000. During the same time period, Mother's income increased and fluctuated from less than $12,000 per year to a peak of approximately $40,000 per year. Despite the rather sizable increases in Father's income, Mother never sought modification of his child support obligation because, as Father admitted, she had no way of knowing about them.

In August 2006, the parties' older child, Collin, reached the age of majority and enrolled as a student at Newberry College.[7] To help take advantage of this opportunity, he sought all scholarships, loans, and grants that he could. Father wholly supported Collin's decision to attend Newberry. Indeed, Father wrote an e-mail in March 2006 agreeing to repay all of Collin's student loans upon graduation. He even co-signed a promissory note for Collin's student loans. Furthermore, in an August 2006 letter, Father agreed to pick up "odd expenses from [Collin]'s education" and told Collin to call him whenever he "needs a little help." Interestingly, Father took it upon himself in that same letter to unilaterally decrease his weekly child support from $175 to $100. Mother later acquiesced in this reduction, apparently in consideration of Father's assurances that he would support Collin while he was in college. However, Father did not uphold his end of the bargain, nor did he regularly pay the percentage of his bonus as required.

Mother brought the instant action in March 2007 seeking an award of college expenses, an increase in child support for Jamie, and attorney's fees and costs. Father counterclaimed, asking that the court terminate: (1) his child support for Collin because he had attained the age of

---

7. Their younger son, Jamie, has autism; although he attained the age of majority in 2008, he is not expected to graduate from high school until he is twenty-one.

majority and graduated from high school; (2) his support for Jamie upon graduation from high school; (3) and the requirement that he pay a percentage of his annual bonus as child support. He also denied that he should be required to pay any college expenses for Collin. . . .

. . . The court dismissed Mother's claim for college expenses on the ground that it violated the Equal Protection Clause of the United States Constitution.[8] . . .

In *Webb*, we held that requiring a parent to contribute toward an adult child's college expenses violated the Equal Protection Clause. We are not unmindful of the imprimatur of correctness which stare decisis lends to that decision. However, stare decisis is not an inexorable command: "There is no virtue in sinning against light or persisting in palpable error, for nothing is settled until it is settled right. . . . There should be no blind adherence to a precedent which, if it is wrong, should be corrected at the first practical moment." . . .

In *Webb*, we were asked to determine whether requiring a non-custodial parent to pay college expenses was a violation of equal protection. "The *sine qua non* of an equal protection claim is a showing that similarly situated persons received disparate treatment." Absent an allegation that the classification resulting in different treatment is suspect, a classification will survive an equal protection challenge so long as it rests on some rational basis. Under the rational basis test, a classification is presumed reasonable and will remain valid unless and until the party challenging it proves beyond a reasonable doubt that there "is no admissible hypothesis upon which it can be justified." . . .

In *Webb*, the majority viewed the classification created by *Risinger* for equal protection purposes as those parents subject to a child support order at the time the child is emancipated. Without any elaboration, the majority concluded that there is no rational basis for treating parents subject to such an order different than those not subject to one with respect to the payment of college expenses. Upon further reflection, we now believe that we abandoned our long-held rational basis rule that the party challenging a classification must prove there is no conceivable basis upon which it can rest and inverted the burden of proof. By not investigating whether there is any basis to support the alleged classification or refuting the bases argued, we effectively presumed *Risinger*'s reading of what is now section 63-3-530(A)(17) unconstitutional. Our treatment of this issue thus essentially reviewed *Risinger* under the lens of strict scrutiny as opposed to rational basis. . . .

As with any equal protection challenge, we begin by addressing the class *Risinger* created under section 63-3-530(A)(17). Mother argues that the appropriate classification is divorced parents versus non-divorced parents. . . . We accordingly review *Risinger* through the same lens used by the family court: whether it improperly treats divorced parents differently than non-divorced parents.

This State has a strong interest in the outcome of disputes where the welfare of our young citizens is at stake. As can hardly be contested, the State also has a strong interest in ensuring that our youth are educated such that they can become more productive members of our society. It is entirely possible "that most parents who remain married to each other support their children through college years. On the other hand, even well-intentioned parents, when deprived of the custody of their children, sometimes react by refusing to support them as they would if the family unit had been preserved." Therefore, it may very well be that *Risinger* sought to alleviate this harm by "minimiz[ing] any economic and educational disadvantages to children of divorced parents." There is no absolute right to a college education, and section 63-3-530(A)(17), as interpreted by *Risinger* and its progeny, does not impose a moral obligation on all divorced parents with children. Instead, the factors identified by *Risinger* and

8. *Webb* had not yet been decided at this time.

expounded upon in later cases seek to identify those children whose parents would *otherwise* have paid for their college education, but for the divorce, and provide them with that benefit.

We accordingly hold that requiring a parent to pay, as an incident of child support, for post-secondary education under the appropriate and limited circumstances outlined by *Risinger* is rationally related to the State's interest. While it is certainly true that not all married couples send their children to college, that does not detract from the State's interest in having college-educated citizens and attempting to alleviate the potential disadvantages placed upon children of divorced parents. Although the decision to send a child to college may be a personal one, it is not one we wish to foreclose to a child simply because his parents are divorced. It is of no moment that not every married parent sends his children to college or that not every divorced parent refuses to do so. The tenants (sic) of rational basis review under equal protection do not require such exacting precision in the decision to create a classification and its effect.

Indeed, Father's refusal to contribute towards Collin's college expenses under the facts of this case proves the very ill which *Risinger* attempted to alleviate, for Father articulated no defensible reason for his refusal other than the shield erected by *Webb.* What other reason could there be for a father with more than adequate means and a son who truly desires to attend college to skirt the obligation the father almost certainly would have assumed had he not divorced the child's mother? Had Father and Mother remained married, we believe Father undoubtedly would have contributed towards Collin's education. Collin has therefore fallen victim to the precise harm that prompted . . . *Risinger* to hold that a non-custodial parent could be ordered to contribute towards a child's college education. Thus, this case amply demonstrates what we failed to recognize in *Webb*: sometimes the acrimony of marital litigation impacts a parent's normal sense of obligation towards his or her children. While this is a harsh and unfortunate reality, it is a reality nonetheless that *Risinger* sought to address. . . .

We now hold *Risinger* does not violate the Equal Protection Clause because there is a rational basis to support any disparate treatment *Risinger* and its progeny created. In fact, the case before us particularly demonstrates the need for a rule permitting an award of college expenses in certain circumstances in order to ensure children of divorce have the benefit of the college education they would have received had their parents remained together. Accordingly, we reverse the order of the family court and remand this matter for a determination of whether and in what amount Father is required to contribute to Collin's college education under the law as it existed prior to *Webb*. . . .

Children's economic prospects are much improved if they receive advanced education, as the data on the economic value of education in Chapter 6 at page 319 confirm.

> The data are clear: adults with postsecondary credentials are, in fact, more likely to be employed and to earn more than individuals who did not attend college. In 2018, 83% of adults with bachelor's degrees or higher were employed, compared with 69% of adults with a high school diploma. . . . The benefits of a college education extend beyond financial gains. More educated citizens have greater access to health care and retirement plans. They are more likely to engage in healthy behaviors, be active and engaged citizens, and be in a position to provide better opportunities for their children . . . Over the course of a lifetime, and accounting for the costs of obtaining a degree, individuals with a bachelor's degree earn about $400,000 more than individuals with a high school degree. The financial benefits of an associate degree are roughly half as large.

Jennifer Ma, Matea Pender & Meredith Welch, Education Pays 2019: The Benefits of Higher Education for Individuals and Society 8 (CollegeBoard Trends in Higher Education 2019), available at https://research.collegeboard.org/media/pdf/education-pays-2019-full-report.pdf.

A study published in 2011 concludes that married parents provide much more financial assistance to their undergraduate children than do divorced or divorced and remarried parents. The study examined the financial information of 2400 undergraduate students drawn from a nationally representative sample of post-secondary students, including supplementary interviews with the parent with whom each child spent the most time. (The researchers excluded children of never-married and widowed parents because they believed that these parents are significantly different from married and divorced parents.) The findings are summarized here.

Ruth N. Lopez Turley & Matthew Desmond

Contributions to College Costs by Married, Divorced, and Remarried Parents
32 J. Fam. Issues 762, 776-778, 784 (2011)

Divorced or separated parents contributed significantly less toward their children's college costs than married parents. Compared with married parents, divorced parents contributed only about a third as many dollars toward college costs ($1,500 vs. $4,700 per year). Of course, this was partly because divorced parents tend to have significantly lower incomes. The median income of married parents was about twice as much as the median income of divorced or separated parents ($57,724 vs. $30,546). Remarried parents, however, earned about the same amount as married parents ($57,788 vs. $57,724, a statistically insignificant difference) but contributed considerably less than the latter ($2,490 vs. $4,700). As a proportion of their income, married parents contributed about 8%, divorced parents contributed about 6%, and remarried parents contributed only 5%. All these differences were statistically significant.

But these proportions do not account for students' financial need, which may be lower for children of divorced parents than children of married or remarried parents for the reasons described earlier, including attending lower-cost institutions and qualifying for more financial aid. If the children of divorced parents have less financial need than the children of married or remarried parents, divorced parents may be covering a larger proportion of their children's financial need. . . . [F]inancial need was indeed lower for the children of divorced parents ($4,909) than for the children of married ($6,873) or remarried parents ($5,875). However, despite their children's lower needs, divorced parents covered a significantly smaller proportion of their children's financial need (42%), compared with married parents (77%). The same was true for remarried parents, who covered just a hair above half (53%) of their children's college costs. Divorced or separated parents contributed significantly less than married parents—in absolute dollars, as a proportion of their income, and as a proportion of their children's financial need—and the same was true for remarried parents, even though they had incomes similar to those of married parents. . . .

. . . In aggregate, children whose parents are married must cover about 23% of college expenses themselves, but children with remarried parents must shoulder 47% themselves, and those from divorced households need to come up with a full 58% of the cost. We should stress that these estimates are quite conservative. Because we included loans not only in our measure of financial aid but also in our measure of parental contributions, our measure of unmet financial need does not take into account money that must be repaid, along with interest or loan fees. When we excluded loans from our measure of financial aid, the median student's financial need increased by $1,072. Moreover, the difference between these two measures of need (with and without loans) was smaller among high-income students because they do not take out as many loans as students from low-income families. These findings are troubling for college-bound students with divorced, separated, or remarried parents, especially given the fact that recent shifts in financial aid policy are making it harder for students to qualify for aid and are requiring families to contribute more money toward the cost of college.

NOTES AND QUESTIONS

1. More recent studies confirm the results that Turley and Desmond report. *See* Paula Fomby & Nicole Kravitz-Wirtz, Family Systems and Parents' Financial Support for Education in Early Adulthood, 56(5) Demography 1875 (2019), available at https://www.ncbi.nlm.nih.gov/pmc/articles/PMC6892702/ (discussing prior studies and reporting results of their own).

2. The constitutional challenge in McLeod v. Starnes is based on the different legal treatment of married and divorced parents. The data seem to support the conclusion that these groups of parents respond differently to claims for contribution to their children's post-secondary education. What might explain the difference? Why did the South Carolina Supreme Court do an about-face on the constitutional question after only two years?

In contrast to *McLeod* and the decisions of other state supreme courts, in Curtis v. Kline, 666 A.2d 265, 274–275 (Pa. 1995), the Pennsylvania Supreme Court held that a statute allowing courts to order divorced parents to pay support for adult children attending school violates the equal protection clause:

> It will not do to argue that this classification is rationally related to the legitimate governmental purpose of obviating difficulties encountered by those in non-intact families who want parental financial assistance for post-secondary education, because such a statement of the governmental purpose assumes the validity of the classification. Recognizing that within the category of young adults in need of financial help to attend college there are some having a parent or parents unwilling to provide such help, the question remains whether the authority of the state may be selectively applied to empower only those from non-intact families to compel such help. We hold that it may not. In the absence of an entitlement on the part of any individual to post-secondary education, or a generally applicable requirement that parents assist their adult children in obtaining such an education, we perceive no rational basis for the state government to provide only certain adult citizens with legal means to overcome the difficulties they encounter in pursuing that end.

3. Should courts ever order parents in "intact families," that is, those in which both parents live with their children, to pay for advanced education?

4. In states that authorize courts to award post-majority support, the court must still find that the child will benefit from the award and that the parents can afford to pay. How should a court go about determining when a child is benefiting from post–high school education? Whether and how much parents can afford to pay?

5. Requiring parents to help pay for post-secondary education is a politically charged issue, and in recent years the number of states imposing this duty has declined. In 2006 a law review article reported that about half the states allowed courts to order post-majority educational support. Leah duCharme, The Cost of Higher Education: Post-Minority Child Support in North Dakota, 82 N.D. L. Rev. 235, 236 (2006). In 2017, 16 states and the District of Columbia gave courts authority to order post-majority support for education. Leslie Joan Harris, Child Support for Post-Secondary Education: Empirical and Historical Perspectives, 29 J. Am. Acad. Matrimonial Law. 299 (2017).

At a minimum most states require support for children older than 18 who are still dependent in the sense of living at home and going to high school. Verna v. Verna, 432 A.2d 630 (Pa. Super. 1981); Ariz. Rev. Stat. §25-320(XV)(D) (2022); Tenn. Code Ann.

§34-1-102(b) (2022); Tex. Fam. Code §151.001(b) (2022). Some states require child support to continue until a child is 19 or finishes high school or its equivalent, whichever occurs first. Cal. Fam. Code §3901 (2022); Iowa Code §252A.3(2) (2022); S.D. Codified Laws Ann. §25-5-18.1 (2022).

6. Today the costs of higher education are rising, and more adult children are living at home and going to school. In 2020, during the coronavirus pandemic, 52 percent of young adults aged 18-29 lived with their parents. In contrast, in 2010, 44 percent lived with one or both parents. In 2020 young people in this age group were more likely than other employees to lose their jobs or take a pay cut, and the percentage of 16- to 24-year-olds who were not in school or employed doubled between February and June of 2020. Richard Fry, Jeffrey S. Passel & D'Vera Cohn, A Majority of Young Adults in the U.S. Live with Their Parents for the First Time Since the Great Depression (Pew Research Sept. 4, 2020), available at https://www.pewresearch.org/fact-tank/2020/09/04/a-majority-of-young-adults-in-the-u-s-live-with-their-parents-for-the-first-time-since-the-great-depression/. Of what significance are these changes to the question of whether parents should have a legal duty to help pay for their children's post-secondary education?

7. The efficacy of court orders to support children pursuing advanced education is called into question by the Turley and Desmond study excerpted above. The study concluded, "Among divorced/separated parents, living in a state that requires child support for college (postmajority state) did not seem to increase the amount they contributed toward their children's college expenses. And among remarried parents, living in a postmajority state was associated with slightly larger contributions, but these contributions represented neither a higher proportion of their income nor a higher proportion of their children's financial need (since parents in postmajority states had slightly higher incomes and their children had slightly higher financial needs)." 32 J. Fam. Issues at 780.

On the other hand, a recent empirical analysis of the relationship between the existence of a statute allowing child support orders for post-secondary school and the educational attainments of young people found a small but statistically significant positive correlation; that is, the study found higher college participation rates in the states that authorized child support orders for post-secondary education. Harris, above, 29 J. Am. Acad. Matrimonial Law. at 302-304.

8. Child support guidelines in 15 states allow courts to order parents to contribute to post-secondary educational expenses. Family Law Quarterly Editorial Staff, Charts 2020: Family Law in the Fifty States, D.C., and Puerto Rico, Part 2, 55 Fam. L. Q. 211, 227 Chart 6 (2022).

9. Assuming that divorcing parents agree to provide in their separation agreement that they will help pay for their children's post-secondary education, how would you advise them to choose between (a) continued child support, (b) creation of a college account funded through payment over the course of a child's minority, and (c) payments designated specifically for tuition and other expenses? What are the pros and cons of each approach?

10. In all but nine states parents have a statutory or common law duty to support a disabled child after the age of majority. In 23 of these states, the disability must have arisen before the child reached the age of majority, and in 19 others a disability that occurs after the age of majority can revive the support duty. Erica Fumagalli, A Survey of Post-Majority Child Support for Adults with Impairments, 29 J. Am. Acad. Matrimonial Law. 433 (2017); Molly A. Costanzo, States' Child Support Guidelines for Children with Disabilities 18-22 (Univ. of Wisc., Institute for Research on Poverty, Apr. 2021).

Weston v. Weston, 40 A.3d 934 (Me. 2012), discussed one aspect of the relationship between adult children's eligibility for public benefits and parental support duties. The father moved to terminate his child support obligation, arguing that because his 27-year-old son, who had been disabled from infancy, received Supplemental Security Income benefits, he was no longer principally dependent on his parents for support. The court rejected the argument because the son, who lived with his mother, was and would remain dependent on her both financially and for personal care. *See also* Lewis v. Dep't of Soc. Serv., 61 S.W.3d 248 (Mo. App. 2001), holding that a child's SSI benefits should not be considered in calculating child support because they are intended to defray some of the extraordinary expenses associated with caring for a disabled adult.

If child support is or can be used to pay for the child's basic expenses, such as housing and food, it may render the child ineligible for those benefits. Supplemental Security Income (SSI), like Temporary Assistance for Needy Families, is means-tested, and any money that can be used to pay a would-be recipient's basic living expenses is considered in that calculation. The solution is to put some of the funds into a special needs trust. The trust documents provide that the money cannot be used for these basic expenses and can only be used for extras that SSI will not provide. Complex federal and state statutes and regulations govern special needs trusts, and the trusts should be drafted by attorneys familiar with those rules. For a general discussion, *see* J.B. v. W.B., 73 A.3d 405 (N.J. 2013. Volume 42 No. 3 of the ABA Family Advocate (Winter 2020) is devoted to special needs trusts.

11. With some frequency, parents who have been ordered to pay support for older children attending school seek reduction or elimination of their obligation because the children are not behaving as the parents think they should. These cases raise starkly the issue of the extent to which child support and control should be linked. Some courts hold that, at least if the parent's commands are "reasonable," the child who disobeys has been "emancipated," meaning that the parent is no longer obliged to pay support. *See, e.g.,* Koontz v. Scott, 60 N.E.3d 1080 (Ind. App. 2016) (parent is not required to support adult child who refuses to participate in relationship with parent); Sexton v. Sexton, 970 N.E.2d 707 (Ind. App. 2012); Roe v. Doe, 272 N.E.2d 567 (N.Y. 1971). In New Jersey, children older than 18 are emancipated unless they carry the burden of proving that they are still subject to the parents' supervision and control. J.B. v. W.B., 73 A.3d 405 (N.J. 2013). In Mississippi, a child whose conduct was clear and extreme forfeits support from the parent. Copeland v. Copeland, 235 So. 3d 91, (Miss. 2017). Other courts hold that parents obligated to support their adult children may not condition their payments on their children's behavior. *See, e.g.,* Steele v. Neeman, 206 P.3d 384 (Wyo. 2009); In re Marriage of Miller, 660 P.2d 205 (Or. App. 1983). What are the relative advantages and disadvantages of each of these approaches?

PROBLEMS

1. Molly and Frank's divorce decree requires Frank to pay $450 per month as child support for their two children, Ollie and Terry. The decree is silent about what happens when Ollie, the older child, becomes 18, which is the age of majority in this jurisdiction. You are Frank's attorney. He has asked you whether he may cut his child support check in half in the month after Ollie becomes 18 without going to court. Molly claims that he cannot reduce his child support until he successfully moves to modify the decree because of Ollie's having attained the age of majority. What advice would you give Frank and why? What course of action would you advise and why?

2. If child support continues for an adult child attending school, should it be paid to the child or to the former custodial parent? Should child support continue during the summer and at other times when school is not in session?

3. Susan's parents' divorce decree requires her father to pay for her tuition, room and board and books while she is in school until age 22 so long as she maintains passing grades. Susan, who is now 19 and who has passing grades, recently moved out of the dorm into an apartment against her father's wishes. Her father, who does not deny that he has the financial ability to pay for Susan's schooling, has moved to terminate his support obligation because of her refusal to live where he believes that she should and because of her general lifestyle, which he regards as irresponsible and immoral. Should his motion be granted?

4. If an adolescent child in the legal custody of one parent moves to the other parent's house following a series of fights with the custodial parent, has the child forfeited a right to child support? Does it matter whether the parent with legal custody "threw the child out"? What if, after leaving, the child refuses to visit or speak to the parent with legal custody? Would the situation be different if the child went to live with a friend's parents?

E. ADULT CHILDREN'S LEGAL OBLIGATION TO SUPPORT PARENTS

Families provide a great deal of support to their adult members. In 2020, 47.9 million U.S. adults provided unpaid care to adults with disabilities, mostly relatives, at some time during the year. Greenwald & Associates, 2020 Report: Caregiving in the U.S. 4 (AARP & Nat'l Alliance for Caregiving May 2020). Three years earlier the economic value of unpaid family care was estimated to be $470 billion. Susan Reinhard et al., Valuing the Invaluable 2019 Update: Charting a Path Forward 1(AARP Public Pol'y Inst. 2019). Families also contribute billions of dollars to the financial support of their adult relatives not living in the same household. In 2013 people paid $12.7 billion to support their parents and $10.6 billion to support other relatives, not including adult children. The average annual payment to a parent was $2,888, and the average amount paid to other relatives was $4,906. Bureau of the Census, Support Providers: 2013 2-3 (Dec. 2018). Does it follow that because adult children often provide support for their parents, they generally should be required to do so?

American Healthcare Center v. Randall
513 N.W.2d 566 (S.D. 1994)

AMUNDSON, J. . . . . Appellant Robert Randall (Robert) is the only child of Harry and Juanita Randall. Although he grew up in Aberdeen, Robert has not resided in South Dakota since 1954. Robert is now a resident of the District of Columbia.

Following an accident which required Juanita's hospitalization, Robert came back to Aberdeen and checked into various nursing homes to place his mother. In the fall of 1990, Juanita was admitted to the Arcadia Unit of Americana Healthcare Center (Americana) in Aberdeen, South Dakota. The Arcadia Unit is specifically designed to deal with individuals who possess mental problems such as Alzheimer's disease. . . .

At that time, in view of Juanita's limited income, Robert discussed the possibility of financial assistance from Medicaid with various Americana personnel. Later that month, Robert completed an application for long-term care medical assistance for Juanita. In November, the South Dakota Department of Social Services (DSS) denied this application because Juanita had not exhausted all of her assets. At the time, Juanita's only assets were [the house and mutual funds that had been conveyed to a trust].

Juanita's bill was two months delinquent at the time Americana learned of the rejected Medicaid application. Americana then contacted Robert about his mother's unpaid bills. Because of Juanita's financial position, Robert, as her legal guardian, filed . . . a Chapter 7 bankruptcy petition . . . and discharged the Americana bill for Juanita individually and

Robert, as her guardian, on October 30, 1991. Meanwhile, Americana filed this suit to collect the unpaid bills. . . .

In June of 1991, Robert was requested to remove his mother from Americana because of the unpaid bills. Despite this request, Juanita remained at Americana until her death on December 8, 1991. At the time of Juanita's death, the unpaid balance for her care was $36,772.30. . . .

Prior to trial, the court granted Robert's motion for summary judgment as to Robert Randall as guardian of the person and estate of Juanita because of the discharge in bankruptcy, but denied summary judgment to Robert Randall individually. . . . At the summary judgment hearing, Americana raised its claim under SDCL 25-7-27 for the first time.[9]

On September 3, 1992, Robert renewed his motion for summary judgment on the additional ground that SDCL 25-7-27 was unconstitutional and requested a continuance. . . . The trial court stated that it was premature to rule on the constitutionality of the statute at that time and denied the continuance.

A court trial was held September 22, 1992. At the conclusion of Americana's case, Robert moved for directed verdict on the grounds that Americana had failed to establish either an oral or written contract to act as guarantor for his mother's nursing home bills. . . . The trial court granted Robert's motion for directed verdict on Americana's claims for liability based on an oral or written contract of guarantee. . . . The trial court found in favor of Americana on its SDCL 25-7-27 claim. This appeal followed. . . .

At common law, an adult child was not required to support a parent. Such an obligation could only be created by statute. Such statutes trace their beginnings from the Elizabethan Poor Law of 1601 in England. Swoap v. Superior Court, 516 P.2d 840, 848 (Cal. 1973). South Dakota adopted the current version of SDCL 25-7-27 in 1963. . . .

Robert claims SDCL 25-7-27 violates equal protection because it discriminates against adult children of indigent parents. The trial court held that it did not. Any legislative act is accorded a presumption in favor of constitutionality and that presumption is not overcome until the act is clearly and unmistakably shown beyond a reasonable doubt to violate fundamental constitutional principles. Since Robert challenges the constitutionality of the statute, he bears the burden of proving the act unconstitutional.

. . . No quasi-suspect classification or fundamental right has been implicated in this case, thus, a rational basis analysis will be applied to this support statute. . . .

Under the rational basis test, South Dakota uses a two-pronged analysis when determining whether a statute violates the constitutional right to equal protection under the laws. Lyons v. Lederle Laboratories, 440 N.W.2d 769, 771 (S.D. 1989). First, does the statute setup arbitrary classifications among various persons subject to it and, second, whether there is a rational relationship between the classification and some legitimate legislative purpose.

When applying the first prong of the Lyons test, it is clear that SDCL 25-7-27 does not make an arbitrary classification. Rather, "it is the moral as well as the legal duty in this state, of every child, whether minor or adult, to assist in the support of their indigent aged parents." An adult child is liable under SDCL 25-7-27 upon the same principle that a parent is liable for necessary support furnished to their child.

Much like the plaintiffs in Swoap v. Superior Court of Sacramento County, Robert argues that the only support obligations which are rational are those arising out of a relationship

---

9. SDCL 25-7-27 states:

Every adult child, having the financial ability so to do shall provide necessary food, clothing, shelter or medical attendance for a parent who is unable to provide for himself; provided that no claim shall be made against such adult child until notice has been given such adult child that his parent is unable to provide for himself, and such adult child shall have refused to provide for his parent.

voluntarily entered into. For instance, the obligation to support a child or spouse is at least initially voluntary, therefore, it is rationally based. Robert argues that, since children do not voluntarily enter into the relationship with their parents, it is arbitrary to force this obligation upon them. The fact that a child has no choice in the creation of a relationship with its parents does not per se make this an arbitrary classification. The fact that an indigent parent has supported and cared for a child during that child's minority provides an adequate basis for imposing a duty on the child to support that parent. . . .

It is certainly reasonable to place a duty to support an indigent parent on that parent's adult child because they are direct lineal descendants who have received the support, care, comfort and guidance of that parent during their minority. If a parent does not qualify for public assistance, who is best suited to meet that parent's needs? It can reasonably be concluded that no other person has received a greater benefit from a parent than that parent's child and it logically follows that the adult child should bear the burden of reciprocating on that benefit in the event a parent needs support in their later years. Consequently, this statute does not establish an arbitrary classification.

The second prong of the test requires a rational relationship between this classification and some legitimate state interest. Clearly, this state has a legitimate interest in providing for the welfare and care of elderly citizens. SDCL 25-7-27 prevents a parent from being thrown out on the street when in need of specialized care. Placing this obligation for support on an adult child is as legitimate as those interests recognized by this court in the past when applying the rational basis test. . . .

The primary purpose of this statute is to place financial responsibility for indigent parents on their adult children when a parent requires such assistance. Although the legislature repealed similar laws in the past, SDCL 25-7-27 has survived. Therefore, SDCL 25-7-27 serves a legitimate legislative interest, especially under the facts of this case, where indigency was voluntarily created by the trust and there would have been sufficient assets to pay for the parent's care had the trust not been created. Robert has not been denied his right to equal protection under the law. . . .

In conclusion, we affirm the trial court's decision in all respects.

Swoap v. Superior Court
516 P.2d 840 (Cal. 1973)

[Children held liable to reimburse the state for public assistance provided to their indigent parents' support argued that the statute imposing the duty on the children was unconstitutional on several grounds. Employing reasoning much like that in *Randall*, the California Supreme Court rejected the challenge.]

TOBRINER, J., dissenting. The majority propose, by the instant opinion, to establish a new constitutional standard for determining when the state may compel some of its citizens to pay for benefits which the state, in its wisdom, decides to provide to other citizens. Under the test proposed by the majority, a state can charge one class of citizens with the costs of providing public programs to another class whenever there is simply some "rational relationship" between the group of benefitted individuals and those who must pay the bill. Applying this "minimal rationality" test in the instant case, the majority hold that since the class of children have generally benefitted from parents, the state can require those children whose parents happen to be poor to reimburse the state for the cost of public old age assistance, regardless of whether a particular child is otherwise legally obligated to provide such support to his parent. . . .

Under the majority's newly propounded "rationality" test, a government intent on reducing the general tax burden could single out insulated minority classes to bear a disproportionate share of the tax burden of a whole range of public services. Thus, for example, the "mere rationality" standard would permit the state not only to charge adult children with the costs of old age benefits but would authorize public savings by charging such children for the costs of subsidized housing projects, medical care, recreational centers, reduced public transportation fares and the various other social programs the state decides to make available to its senior citizens. Although the children of the recipients of such benefits may have had no preexisting obligation to pay for such services, the majority's constitutional test would presumably sanction such charges on the ground that children as a whole have benefitted from parents. Moreover, since the circumstances of the individual case are assertedly irrelevant, the state presumably could require even a child who had been abandoned by his parents to pay the costs of these varied public programs. . . .

It might be possible to understand the reasons for the majority's uprooting of a consistent line of precedent and creation of a novel constitutional ruling if the legislation challenged in the instant case offered the promise of unquestionably beneficial social consequences; under such circumstances one might expect to find the court questioning past decisions that impeded the salutary result. The statutes in question here, however, offer no such beneficent social consequences.

On the contrary, almost all observers agree that the social effects of the challenged relative responsibility provisions are harsh and self-defeating. "[A] large body of social work opinion [has long maintained] that liability of relatives creates and increases family dissension and controversy, weakens and destroys family ties at the very time and in the very circumstances when they are most needed, imposes an undue burden upon the poor . . . and is therefore socially undesirable, financially unproductive, and administratively infeasible." As Justice Friedman, writing for the Court of Appeal in the instant case, observed: "[The challenged provisions] strike most aggressively and harshly at adult children occupying the lower end of the income scale. The enforced shift of subsistence funds from one generation to the other distributes economic desolation between the generations. It galls family relationships. It injects guilt and shame into elderly citizens who have made their contributions to society and have become dependent through life's vicissitudes."

Jenny Baxter, a 75-year-old Californian receiving Old Age Security benefits, eloquently summarized the true effect of the relative responsibility laws: "No one is born into this world with a debt to their parents for their birth and contributions until their maturity. That is the parents' contribution to life and society. When the child reaches maturity, he starts a new separate unit and in turn makes his contribution to life and society as did his parents, carrying on the generation cycle on through eternity. The children should not be saddled with unjust demands that keep them at or near poverty level with no hope to escape it, just because a parent still breathes. And aged parents should not have to live their remaining lives facing the heartbreaking experience of being such a burden to their children. Many would prefer death but are afraid of retribution for taking their own lives. Their grief—a living death."

NOTES AND QUESTIONS

1. Does it follow that, because parents support their children when young, children should support their parents when needy? Is there a general duty of reciprocity, as the court in *Randall* assumes? Are the parents providing some good or service without benefiting themselves? Is there an expectation of reciprocity by parents and children? Do parents generally expect that their children will use their resources to support them?

The view expressed by Jenny Baxter, quoted in Justice Tobriner's dissent, seems to be widely shared. Jane Gross, Adult Children, Aging Parents and the Law, N.Y. Times, Nov. 20, 2008.

2. Are family responsibility laws explained by the notion of the family as an economic unit? Is the family such a unit at the time that support by children is sought? *See* Lee E. Teitelbaum, Intergenerational Responsibility and Family Obligation: On Sharing, 1992 Utah L. Rev. 765, 776-777.

3. At one time 45 states had filial support laws; as of 2021, 12 states had statutes imposing criminal liability for failure to support indigent parents, and 24 states had statutes that imposed civil liability for failure to support. Karen L. Sheng, Note, Kinder Solutions to an Unkind Approach: Supporting Impoverished and Ill Parents Under North Carolina's Filial Responsibility Law, 71 Duke L. J. 209 (2021). Most of these states have little or no reported appellate case law within the last 30 or more years that applies the statutes. The exceptions are Pennsylvania and South Dakota.

4. Five years before she entered the nursing home, the mother in *Randall* transferred most of her assets into an irrevocable trust, which named her as the income beneficiary but prevented the trustee from using the corpus of the trust for her benefit. Her son Robert, the appellant in *Randall*, was both trustee and residual beneficiary of the trust. As his mother's guardian, Robert used the income from the trust and his mother's Social Security benefits to pay legal fees incurred by forming the guardianship, the bankruptcy proceedings, and an unsuccessful pursuit of Medicaid benefits instead of paying for her care in the nursing home. While Robert's actions were not illegal or a breach of fiduciary duty, the court expressed its disapproval of his choices and was distinctly untroubled that he would have to pay his mother's bill from the trust assets that he received. 513 N.W.2d at 574.

Presbyterian Medical Center v. Budd, 832 A.2d 1066 (Pa. Super. 2003), involved similar facts. A daughter had used her power of attorney to transfer her mother's assets to herself, rather than spending them on her mother's care, resulting in the mother neither having the money to pay for her own care nor being eligible for Medicaid (because of the transfer of assets to the daughter). The nursing home sued the daughter for these costs, and the court rejected the claims that the daughter was liable based on contract or fraud, finding that the facts did not support these claims. However, the court held that the daughter was liable under the state relative responsibility statute.

In each case, if the child had not received assets from the parent during the parent's lifetime, would the child still have been liable under the relative responsibility laws? Why or why not?

More recently a Pennsylvania case upheld an order requiring a son to pay his mother's nursing home bill of $93,000, even though he had played no role in accruing the debt and received no money from his mother, who was still alive and living in Greece. Health Care & Retirement Corp. of America v. Pittas, 46 A.3d 719 (Pa. Super. 2012). Professor Pearson says that the case is one of a larger group in which commercial entities use filial support laws to recover the costs of providing long-term care. In 2008 she found 15 cases pending in Pennsylvania trial courts in which third parties sued children and spouses under the relative responsibility law. Katherine C. Pearson, Filial Support Laws in the Modern Era: Domestic and International Comparison of Enforcement Practices for Laws Requiring Adult Children to Support Indigent Parents, 20 Elder L.J. 269, 293-294, 298 (2013). The practice of long-term care facilities pursuing adult children to recover the costs of their parents' long-term care was unsuccessfully challenged as violating the federal Fair Debt Collection Act and Nursing Home Reform Act. Eades v. Kennedy, PC Law Offices, 799 F.3d 161 (2d Cir. 2015).

While most of the recent cases invoking relative responsibility laws have been brought by long-term care facilities, a Pennsylvania man who provided care for his mother and who held his mother's power of attorney successfully invoked the law on behalf of his mother to require his brother to contribute to her care. Eori ex rel. Eori v. Eori, 2015 WL 6736193 (Pa. Super. 2015).

5. In both *Randall* and *Budd* the children attempted to obtain Medicaid benefits to pay for their mothers' custodial care. Medicaid is a public assistance program only for people whose assets and income fall below poverty levels. Federal law provides that if a person gratuitously transfers assets to another outright or in trust within five years of applying for Medicaid, the applicant is disqualified from eligibility for a period of time, as in *Budd*. 42 U.S.C. §1396p (2022)

On the other hand, federal law prohibits nursing homes from requiring third parties to guarantee payment as a condition for admitting new residents. 42 U.S.C. §§ 1395i-3(c)(5)(A)(ii), 1396r(c)(5)(A)(ii) (2022). Nevertheless, sometimes nursing homes quietly continue to seek third-party guarantees of payment.

6. In determining an unmarried person's eligibility for Medicaid, generally all the applicant's income, including gifts of cash or its equivalent, is considered available to pay for care. This rule limits the ability of a person's children or others to make voluntary contributions to the care of a person. However, trusts created by a Medicaid applicant or by a third party for the benefit of the applicant that provide that none of the money can be used for food, clothing, or shelter but can only be used for other needs, such as transportation, entertainment, and so on, are not considered resources and so do not disqualify the beneficiary from receiving Medicaid. The trusts are called special needs or supplemental needs trusts.

7. For additional perspectives, *see* Amy Ziettlow & Naomi Cahn, The Honor Commandment: Law, Religion, and the Challenge of Elder Care, 30 J.L. & Religion 229 (2015); Donna Harkness, What Are Families For? Re-Evaluating Return to Filial Responsibility Laws, 21 Elder L. J. 305 (2014).

CHAPTER 8

MODIFICATION, TERMINATION, ENFORCEMENT, AND TAX AND BANKRUPTCY TREATMENT OF ORDERS

This chapter examines the policies and rules relating to modification and enforcement of orders and to taxation and bankruptcy treatment of property transfers and obligations imposed incident to family break-up. As we saw in earlier chapters, it is often difficult to distinguish clearly between awards dividing property and those providing for spousal support. The same is true of spousal and child support obligations. However, the classification of an order as property division, spousal support, or child support is centrally important in the issues considered in this chapter.

A. MODIFICATION AND TERMINATION OF SUPPORT

Traditionally and still today in most jurisdictions, support duties terminate at the death of the obligor or the recipient. However, in some states, a court may order the obligor's estate to continue to pay spousal support, or the parties may agree in writing to such an extension. In some states, statutes or case law permit child support liability to be imposed on a parent's estate under some circumstances. *See, e.g.*, 750 Ill. Comp. Stat. Ann. 5/510(d) (2022); Nev. Rev. Stat. §125B.130 (2022); Kiken v. Kiken, 694 A.2d 557 (N.J. 19997); L.W.K. v. E.R.C., 735 N.E.2d 359 (Mass. 2000). *Contra* Benson ex rel. Patterson v. Patterson, 830 A.2d 966 (Pa. 2003). The ALI Principles recommend that state law should not provide for automatic termination of child support upon the death of the obligor; instead, the court should have discretion to modify or terminate the order or commute the obligation to a lump sum. ALI Principles of the Law of Family Dissolution §325, §5.07, and commentary (2000). This proposal is derived from the Model Marriage and Divorce Act, which was adopted in Arizona, Colorado, Illinois, Kentucky, Minnesota, Missouri, Montana and Washington.

The traditional rule is that, unlike property awards, spousal support and child support are modifiable. However, in some states limited-term alimony, often including reimbursement alimony, is not modifiable. *See, e.g.*, Self v. Self, 861 S.W.2d 360 (Tenn. 1993). In other states limited-term rehabilitative support awards may be modified if a spouse is not able to become self-supporting by the end of the support period. *See, e.g.*, In re Marriage of Deboer, 157 P.3d 1279 (Or. App. 2007); Bentz v. Bentz, 435 N.W.2d 293 (Wis. 1988). When support is modifiable, the usual basis is that there has been a "substantial (or material) change of circumstances." This standard gives judges considerable discretion to alter previously established support obligations. This section considers generally how courts and legislatures have given meaning to this phrase and the extent to which judicial discretion is narrowed by statute or case law.

As you consider these materials, think about how the problems raised in the cases relate to what you have already learned about the justifications and criteria for imposing support duties in the first place. Are the policies reflected in initial awards carried forward to solve modification problems? Are post-decree changes in circumstances treated the same when spousal support and child support are at stake?

1. "Foreseeable" Changes in Circumstances

In many cases a major issue is the tension between the value of rules that promote stability in orders and those that allow courts to respond to changes in individual circumstances. Sometimes courts deal with the tension between stability and flexibility by saying that a change that was "foreseeable" is not a ground for modification. This test cannot be taken literally, however. Many changes that are widely regarded as sufficient for modifying a support order are also entirely foreseeable. Indeed, some of these "foreseeable" changes are so predictable that courts and commentators have sought ways to adjust support orders for them automatically. Before widespread use of child support guidelines, cost-of-living adjustments (COLAs) in support orders to adjust for inflation were often proposed. While many courts approved inclusion of COLA provisions, others rejected them because they fail to account for actual changes in income and other factors relevant to need and ability to pay.

On the other hand, while it is predictable that parents will spend more to support older children than young ones, courts rarely approve orders automatically increasing child support as children grow older. Instead, they ordinarily require motions to modify previous orders to permit individualized determination of needs and ability to pay. However, the Mississippi Supreme Court in a preguidelines case observed:

> James and Marie, like so many couples who divorce, have been at each other's throat almost from the day of the divorce. . . . We add this recurring situation to what we have noted above — and what anyone can reasonably anticipate: That children's expenses generally will increase as they get older, that the father and mother's earning *capacity* will generally increase from year to year, and that inflation will continue at some level and will partially affect both the children's expenses and the parents' earning capacity.
>
> James would have us hold here that, because these things were reasonably foreseeable back in May of 1979 and because the separation agreement makes no reference to them, Marie has "waived" the claims she now makes. Surely, that cannot be the law. By the same token, because we "know" these things, we know that the chancery courts of this state will be swamped more than they already are if every increase in the father's salary, every increase in the inflation rate were to generate a modification hearing (where, to be sure, the first question will always be whether the "change" is enough of a change to be classified as a "material change").
>
> . . . Had James and Marie included in their separation agreement an escalation clause to provide for increases in children's expenses and parents' earning capacities, the agonies of the instant litigation likely could have been avoided. . . . In the child support provisions of their separation agreements, the parties generally ought to be required to include escalation clauses tied to the parents' earnings or to the annual inflation rate or to some factored combination of the two.

Tedford v. Dempsey, 437 So. 2d 410, 419 (Miss. 1983). In 2014 the court reaffirmed this endorsement of escalator clauses. Short v. Short, 131 So. 3d 1149 (Miss. 2014).

The advent of child support guidelines produced a clear difference between modification of child support and alimony. Federal legislation requires states to implement a regular review process that will ensure that child support orders are updated at least every four years.

42 U.S.C. §667(a) (2022). That requirement effectively abrogates the traditional approach under which a child support order, like an alimony order, could be modified only on the initiative of the party who proved a substantial change of circumstances. Despite this requirement of automatic updating, motions to modify based on changed circumstances remain common for both spousal and child support.

2. "Voluntary" Versus "Involuntary" Decreases in the Payor's Income

A decrease in an obligor's ability to pay is a commonly asserted ground for modifying support. Involuntary decreases, such as when the obligor is laid off from work, are generally treated as a sufficient reason to decrease support. However, treatment of "voluntary" reductions in income is more complex, as the next case illustrates.

Sharpe v. Sharpe
366 P.3d 66 (Alaska 2016)

BOLGER, J. . . . Jolene Lyon and Jyzyk Sharpe divorced in July 2012. The superior court awarded Jyzyk primary physical custody of the parties' only child and ordered Jolene to pay Jyzyk $1,507.00 per month in child support.

Jolene is a Yup'ik Eskimo who was raised in Nome and has family ties to the native village of Stebbins. When the child support order was issued, Jolene was "living in Anchorage, working at Alyeska Pipeline Service Company, and earning approximately [$]120,000 a year." In April 2013, she left Anchorage and took up a subsistence lifestyle in Stebbins.

Soon after relocating to Stebbins, Jolene moved to modify the child support order. She alleged that she was "no longer employed," that she was "a full time stay at home mother,"[1] and that her only income was her annual Permanent Fund Dividend. These developments, she argued, constituted a material change in circumstances warranting a modification of the child support order. She requested that the court reduce her monthly child support payment to $50 per month, the minimum allowed under Alaska Civil Rule 90.3(c)(3).

Jyzyk opposed the motion, arguing that modification of the child support order was not warranted because Jolene was "voluntarily and unreasonabl[y] unemployed." Although he acknowledged that Jolene was entitled to quit her job and move to a remote community, he argued that the parties' "ten year old daughter . . . should not be required to fund [Jolene's] lifestyle choice."

The superior court held a motion hearing in July 2013. During the hearing, Jolene testified about her life in Stebbins and the benefits she derived from her subsistence lifestyle. She expressed her desire to expose the parties' child to traditional life in Stebbins. And she said that living in Stebbins, a dry community, provided reprieve from an alcohol abuse issue she had experienced during her marriage.

Jyzyk also testified at the hearing. He expressed his belief that the parties' child would benefit from receiving child support from Jolene at its existing amount and noted that these monthly payments "helped with everything [including] rent, groceries, [and] clothes." Jyzyk testified that "[i]n a dream world [he] would bring [the parties' child] to Kotzebue [in the area where he was raised] and raise her on the river," but he recognized that financial constraints prevented him from prudently fulfilling this dream.

---

1. Although Jolene did not have primary custody of the parties' daughter when she moved to modify the child support order, Jolene was caring for another child from a separate relationship.

After the hearing the superior court denied Jolene's motion. . . . Jolene appeals. . . .

Jolene conceded that she was voluntarily unemployed. Therefore, the only issue at the hearing was whether her decision to be unemployed was unreasonable. . . .

In determining whether a parent is "unreasonably" unemployed, the superior court must look to the totality of the circumstances, including "such factors as whether the obligor's reduced income is temporary, whether the change is the result of economic factors or of purely personal choices, the children's needs, and the parents' needs and financial abilities." But "[b]ecause of the significance of a parent's duty to meet his or her child support obligations, we prioritize fulfillment of that duty over even legitimate decisions to be voluntarily unemployed or underemployed." And we have consistently recognized that, when a child support obligor makes a career change for personal reasons, the superior court should consider the financial impact of this decision on the child.

In *Pattee v. Pattee*, our first case considering imputed income, . . . [w]e rejected the notion that a voluntary career change should require an automatic reduction in child support:

> On the one hand, we do not believe that an obligor-parent should be "locked in" to a particular job or field during the minority of his or her children when accepting a lower-paying position may ultimately result in personal or professional advancement. On the other hand, the children of the marriage and the custodial parent should not be forced to finance the noncustodial parent's career change. We believe that the better rule is that stated by the Montana Supreme Court: "[T]he judge [is] to consider the nature of the changes and the reasons for the changes, and then to determine whether, under all the circumstances, a modification is warranted." . . .

The foregoing quote recognizes that a child support obligor should not be "locked in" to a particular career. But this language is in a sentence that implies that a career change must be supported by a "lower-paying position" that will "ultimately result in personal or professional advancement." And this sentiment is immediately followed by the observation that "the children . . . and the custodial parent should not be forced to finance the noncustodial parent's career change." Thus the financial impact of a career change on the obligor's children has always been regarded as an important factor when a trial court examines whether voluntary unemployment is reasonable. . . .

In this case, Jolene moved to Stebbins and adopted a subsistence lifestyle without any intention of seeking employment to meet her child support obligation. In support of her request for reduction of her child support obligation, she specifically stated that she had "no intention to return to the work force." The record thus supports the superior court's conclusion that Jolene's decision to leave her employment and move to Stebbins would have an unreasonable financial impact on the resources available to care for her daughter.

The dissent argues that when a court imputes income after an obligor relocates, the reasonableness of the obligor's decision to relocate must be analyzed prior to and separately from the reasonableness of the obligor's unemployment. It contends that once the decision to relocate is found reasonable, imputed income must be based on the obligor's new place of residence rather than former residence. The dissent concludes that the trial court should have found Jolene's decision to move to Stebbins reasonable and erred in imputing Jolene's income based on her former job in Anchorage rather than her employment opportunities in Stebbins.

As the dissent recognizes, neither Rule 90.3(a)(4) nor Child Support Services Division regulations say anything "about considering the reasonableness of a parent's decision to relocate" prior to and separately from the reasonableness of the obligor's unemployment. And the cases upon which the dissent relies also do not provide support for this contention. Rather these cases demonstrate that the obligor's reason for moving is simply one of the several factors courts may consider in deciding whether an obligor is unreasonably unemployed.

In *Richardson v. Kohlin*, contrary to the dissent's claim, we did not separately analyze the reasonableness of the obligor's move from the reasonableness of his underemployment. . . . Moreover, unlike the present case, the obligor in *Richardson* actively sought employment in the Pacific Northwest after he was laid off from his job in Anchorage, a fact we found particularly salient.

In declining to impute income based on the obligor's income in Alaska, we repeatedly emphasized the obligor's "diligen[t]" and "extensive attempts to find high-paying work in [his new location]." . . . No such diligent efforts to find work are present in the case now before us. In contrast, as Jolene testified, she has not applied for any jobs in Stebbins and "ha[s] no intention to return to the workforce." . . .

The dissent also argues that imputing income based on a non-custodial parent's job in a prior place of residence produces an asymmetry with the custodial parent's "absolute right to change careers, take a lower-paying job, . . . quit work altogether[, or] perhaps even . . . move to another geographic location with the children." But this "absolute right" of the custodial parent exists only in theory, as demonstrated by Jyzyk's testimony that "in a dream world" he would move back to his Native village with his daughter but "finances" prevented him from doing so. Contrary to the dissent's claim, custodial parents do not possess any such "absolute freedom"—their child's needs constrain their actions. . . .

Jolene argues that the superior court "direct[ed] nearly total focus on [her] past income history" and gave short shrift to Jolene's religious and cultural needs. It is true that "the parents' needs" is one of the factors the superior court must consider in evaluating the totality of the circumstances. But the superior court did adequately consider Jolene's needs, and after considering these needs it found that they did not outweigh other concerns, including her daughter's need for financial support:

> [Jolene] finds that [living in Stebbins] is sort of rehabilitative for her from the standpoint of her eliminating . . . some of the poisons of urban life. . . . She is finding sort of a spiritual reawakening or reconnecting with Native dance, Native culture, subsistence lifestyle, all of which is . . . admirable in an abstract sense.
>
> Then again . . . she effectively is . . . taking a vacation from the financial responsibilities that she assumed when she had a child, and the result of her not working and providing financial assistance is that it's going to impose . . . a greater burden on [Jyzyk], but, more importantly, it's going to have an impact over time on the opportunities . . . and resources that are available to take care of [the parties' daughter].
>
> Now, I don't know whether it's realistic to continue child support at [$]120,000 a year, . . . but given her background and her previous earnings I do not agree that it should be that she does not have any income capacity simply because she chose to relocate to the village of Stebbins and earn nothing. . . .
>
> . . . I do find it a difficult choice in this case because [Jolene] does seem to derive some very valid benefits from being in Stebbins, and I'm sure that for the summers [her daughter] derives some benefits there, too, but then there's the other nine months of the year when [the parties' daughter] lives in Anchorage and she'd be getting $50 a month, if that, instead of . . . $1500 a month, which could go a long way toward providing for necessities and also toward . . . providing for her future needs, educational needs, and to help give her a good start in life.

The record thus reflects that the superior court adequately considered Jolene's personal needs when it determined that her voluntary unemployment was unreasonable.

Despite this consideration, the dissent worries that the superior court "trivialize[s] Alaska Natives' way of life" and "devalues Alaska Natives' cultural, spiritual, and religious connections to their villages and their subsistence lifestyle." Yet in reality the dissent's desired outcome would have enormous financial implications for Alaska Native children. "The primary purpose of Rule 90.3 is to ensure that child support orders are adequate to meet the needs of children, subject to the ability of parents to pay." Granting either parent absolute freedom to exit the workforce would undermine this purpose. . . .

The judgment of the superior court is affirmed.

WINFREE, J., dissenting. I respectfully disagree with today's decision affirming the superior court's denial of Jolene Lyon's motion to modify her child support obligation. . . . The reasons behind Jolene's move to Stebbins are far more compelling—certainly not less compelling—than parental moves found reasonable in prior cases, and in those prior cases the parent" imputed income, if any, was determined by employment opportunities in the new location, not the old location. Accordingly the superior court should have focused on Jolene's employment opportunities in Stebbins. I would remand for further proceedings to determine whether Jolene is unreasonably unemployed based on her overall circumstances in Stebbins. . . .

At the hearing Jolene testified at some length about her cultural, religious, and spiritual ties to Stebbins. As noted above, Jolene's mother is a Yup'ik Eskimo born and raised in Stebbins; Jolene is half Yup'ik Eskimo and was raised in Nome and Stebbins. Like Jolene, her daughter is an enrolled tribal member of Stebbins Community Association. B.J. [Jolene's new partner] also is from Stebbins, and Jolene and B.J. want their son to grow up in the village and "know[ ] where he comes from and who his people are." Jolene always dreamed of living in the area, and she and Jyzyk had purchased the lot in Nome with that intent. Jolene stated that her "roots" brought her back to Stebbins and that Stebbins "is the cornerstone of [her] spiritual connection, [her] cultural connection, [and her] subsistence lifestyle." Her "family history[ ] and [her] relatives [are] all from [Stebbins]." Jolene reconnected with these roots in 2004 when she brought her daughter there and participated in her "first traditional dance with [her] daughter, [her] mom, and [her] brother and his son" and returned in later years for the "yuraq" (Eskimo dancing) and Yup'ik Eskimo lifestyle. Jolene wanted her daughter to be brought up in Alaska Native culture and experience village life. . . .

During its own questioning of Jolene, the superior court stated: "I've heard your testimony and I don't question . . . your sincerity and . . . the value you place in reconnecting with [your] . . . Native and historical cultural . . . roots. . . ." But when it came time to determine whether Jolene's move to Stebbins was for a legitimate purpose, the court characterized her decision as only "admirable in an abstract sense," "essentially taking a retreat from reality," and "a lovely dream." The court posited the following hypothetical:

> [I]f we change the facts in this case, just hypothetically, and I had a person who—non-Indian, non-Native, but had decided that—one of the obligor parents had decided they wanted to join an ashram in India because it reawakened them spiritually and reconnected them and they wanted to go to a mountainous retreat, live a basic normal lifestyle and do this, and essentially withdraw from providing financial support, I would have a hard time in that hypothetical situation simply approving it, and I have the same difficulty in this case.

This hypothetical and the court's other unfortunate comparisons to joining a monastery or going to a "Tibetan retreat" serve only to trivialize Alaska Natives' way of life. Contrary to the superior court's analogy, Alaska Natives' cultural, religious, and spiritual connection to their tribes, their lands, and their subsistence activities are a normal way of life, not an escape from normal life. Our legislature has recognized the spiritual nature of subsistence living, and we likewise have recognized the importance of subsistence activities to Alaska Native cultural and social identity. . . .

Our case law is clear that moves outside of Alaska to be near other family members and to decrease conflict over custody issues are legitimate for purposes of modifying child support. How can it not be legitimate for an Alaska Native living in an urban center and having difficulty with sobriety to relocate to her own dry tribal village where she has family, cultural, religious, and spiritual roots; where she can more easily maintain sobriety; where she has property interests; where she can raise her children in their tribal culture; and where, incidentally, she can reduce conflict with her former spouse over custody and visitation issues? Our case law also is clear that children may benefit from being exposed to extended family members and decreased custodial conflict between parents. How would Alaska Native children not similarly benefit from living, even part of the time, in their own tribal villages with extended family members, and from the ensuing decreased custodial conflict between parents? . . .

Today's decision not only flies in the face of these considerations, it suggests that when setting a child support obligation neither a Native Alaskan's return to her village nor a traditional Native Alaska subsistence lifestyle has a valid role. The court's decision means that once a non-custodial Native Alaska parent participates in the cash economy of urban Alaska that parent may be unable to voluntarily return to a rural tribal community and live either a local cash-economy lifestyle, a culturally and religiously based subsistence, non-cash, lifestyle, or even something in between. And as a more general matter, why should a parent with primary physical custody have an absolute right to change careers, take a lower-paying job, or quit work altogether—perhaps even have the right to move to another geographic location with the children—while a non-custodial parent with a child support obligation does not have those rights even if the actions are legitimate and provide benefits to the child? Why do we "take seriously" an alleged infringement only on a custodial parent's right to relocate, but not a non-custodial parent's right to relocate? In my view a court has no right to effectively order where a non-custodial parent must live and what specific job that parent must hold. . . .

I dissent.

NOTES AND QUESTIONS

1. In 2014, two years after the parties divorced and before the appellate decision in this case, Jyzyk Sharpe was charged with murder and manslaughter for the death of a different child who was unrelated to Jolene Lyon. Lyon regained custody of the child who was the subject of this case. Lisa Demer, *Court Rules Against Yup'ik Mother in Case that Pits Subsistence Against Cash Jobs*, Anchorage Daily News (Sept. 30, 2016), https://www.adn.com/rural-alaska/article/court-rules-against-yupik-mother-case-pits-native-culture-against-cash-jobs/2016/01/09/. Jyzyk pled guilty to manslaughter in 2022. KTUU, Alaska News Source, Sept. 26, 2022.

2. In intact marriages, an income-earning spouse may reduce his or her income. The other spouse may strongly object because of the adverse impact on their lifestyle and future options. However, courts will not ordinarily entertain a suit to require a current spouse not to reduce his or her income. How are such disputes resolved? Does the fact that the parties no longer live in the same household justify the different approach to justiciability of the dispute?

3. Is the majority more concerned that Jolene moved to Stebbins from the big city or that, having moved, she made no effort to find any kind of employment? If Jolene had taken a job in Stebbins paying minimum wage and that was the only job she could find, would the majority have been willing to reduce her child support obligation? (Apparently Jolene did not argue that her childcare obligations were the reason she was not working. We will take up this issue later in this chapter.)

4. The first issue in a loss of income case may be whether the loss was voluntary. The court in *Sharpe* assumes that Jolene's loss of income was voluntary. What if she quit her job and returned to her home village because her doctor told her that would be the best way to deal with health and alcohol problems?

5. Few courts hold that a voluntary loss of income can never be the basis for a reduction in support because of the harsh impact on obligors, and they use various tests for determining when a voluntary reduction can support a reduced order. Some courts require that the obligor have acted in good faith, which may mean simply that the obligor had reasons other than reducing the support obligation. Under this test, would Jolene's reduction in income be a basis for modifying child support? What test did the *Sharpe* court adopt?

Other tests that balance the interests of the child and the parent focus on the parent's diligence and concern for the child. *See, e.g.*, Busche v. Busche, 272 P.3d 748 (Utah App. 2012) (reduction in child support rejected because underemployed obligor did not make reasonable efforts to earn more income); Andrews v. Andrews, 719 S.E.2d 128 (N.C. App. 2011) (voluntary loss of income evidencing indifference to or a bad faith disregard for one's child support obligations cannot be the basis for reducing obligation). The Connecticut courts hold that a voluntary loss of income demonstrating extravagance, neglect, misconduct, or other fault cannot be the basis for a reduction. Olson v. Mohammadu, 81 A.3d 215 (Conn. 2013). Under these tests would the *Sharpe* court have found a basis for modification? To what extent should the test emphasize whether the parent's decision will benefit the child in the long run? *See, e.g.*, Edwin K. v. Bonnie W., 805 S.E.2d 416 (W. Va. 2017) (if parent is pursuing educational program, court should determine whether it will result in economic benefit to children).

If you had been Jolene's lawyer, how would you have argued that her decision adequately took into account her child's interests?

How does the fact that Jolene was an Alaska Native returning to a traditional lifestyle bear on the analysis of this problem? Should her choice be constrained in the same way as that of an American parent who wanted to move to an Indian ashram? Marcia Zug, Your Money or Your Life: Indian Parents and Child Support Modifications, 9 J. Am. Acad. Matrimonial Law. 409 (2017).

6. Many of the loss of income cases involve the obligor's retirement. Is this a voluntary loss of income that should be analyzed under the usual rules? In In re Marriage of Swing, 194 P.3d 498 (Colo. App. 2008), the court held that retirement or cutting back on employment at a "normal" age is not the kind of voluntary underemployment or unemployment that precludes modification of spousal support. The opinion says that this is the majority rule, citing cases from Minnesota, New Hampshire, North Dakota, and Tennessee. "Retirement is a unique circumstance in support modification cases. . . . Because retirement is somewhat of an entitlement, the foreseeability or voluntariness of the retirement decision does not affect the support modification analysis, and the weight given to various considerations is not precisely the same as that given under different circumstances. So long as the retirement is objectively reasonable and taken in good faith, we will not look to the potential income of the retired obligor, and we will give the reduced ability of the retired obligor to pay support at least equal consideration with the need of the receiving spouse." Bogan v. Bogan, 60 S.W.3d 721, 733-734 (Tenn. 2001).

In Pierce v. Pierce, 916 N.E.2d 3310 (Mass. 2009), the court held that there is no presumption that an obligation to pay alimony would terminate upon the payor's reaching full Social Security retirement age. This was a major impetus for the Massachusetts alimony reform legislation of 2011, which does create such a presumption. Charles P. Kindregan, Jr., Reforming Alimony: Massachusetts Reconsiders Postdivorce Spousal Support, 46 Suffolk U. L. Rev. 13 (2013).

7. When a parent is unemployed or underemployed, child support guidelines typically require that income be imputed to the parent upon a finding that the parent could reasonably be expected to earn more, and courts may interpret spousal support statutes as requiring a similar analysis. This analysis is closely related to the analysis of whether a loss of income justifies a reduction in support, but it may be required when the initial order is made, as well as during a modification proceeding. Support awards are not supposed to be based on "speculative" estimates of earning ability, but rather on actual earning ability. Where the obligor has the qualifications for jobs that are readily available, determining earning ability is not so difficult, but as the match between the obligor's skills and the requirements of available jobs decreases, the line between speculating and legitimate imputation of income is harder to discern. For example, in Hutchinson v. Hutchinson, 69 P.3d 815 (Or. App. 2003) (en banc), at the time of the modification hearing, the husband, who earlier had earned $240,000 per year, had been unemployed for a year. His efforts to find work at a comparable salary had been unsuccessful because of downturns in the economy, his age, and the specialized nature of his experience. He sought a reduction in spousal support from $6000 per month to $250 per month. An expert witness for his former wife testified that the husband was qualified for jobs with actual openings that paid $50,000 to $60,000 per year and that he could probably find work paying $120,000 within a year. The trial court modified the spousal support obligation, based on the assumption that the husband could earn $120,000 per year. The appellate court reversed, characterizing the finding as "speculative" but concluding that he could earn $60,000 per year. Why was the higher figure "speculative"? Because jobs paying that much are scarcer? Because the expert testified that the husband would probably have to look longer to find such a job?

8. When loss of income is involuntary because the obligor becomes disabled, the obligor's children may be eligible for Social Security or other benefits on the account of the obligor/parent. Most courts give the obligor a dollar-for-dollar credit for the benefits a child receives. In re Marriage of Belger, 654 N.W.2d 902 (Iowa 2002), summarizes case law from other jurisdictions. A minority of courts merely consider the child's receipt of benefits as a change in circumstances that may but does not necessarily justify modification of the child support duty. The New York Court of Appeals in Graby v. Graby, 664 N.E.2d 488 (N.Y. 1996), took this approach, analogizing the child's Social Security benefits to other government benefits such as welfare, which parents do not purchase. The court noted, "In many cases, granting the noncustodial parent a credit for Social Security disability benefits earmarked for dependent children might effectively abolish the child support obligation of that parent, who has regular and consistent income, and at the same time disproportionately reduce the resources available to the children." 664 N.E.2d at 491.

PROBLEMS

1. When Marty and Fred were divorced, Fred was awarded custody of their child, and Marty was ordered to pay child support. At the time Marty was an untenured teacher in the local school system who had been laid off because of budget cuts. Marty could get a job as a secretary, earning half as much as a teacher. However, Marty expects that the school system will be rehiring in a year or so and has decided to go back to school to get a master's degree, which will move her higher on the rehire list and increase her pay if she is rehired as a teacher. She has moved to eliminate her child support obligation temporarily, until she is rehired. Under the tests discussed in the notes above, how would her motion be analyzed? If the court finds that her motion should be denied, should the court impute income to her at the rate that a secretary would make, or that a teacher would make?

2. Assume instead that Marty decided to go to law school, and that she was not employed during the school year so that she could study hard and make good grades and also spend time with her children. She was a very well-paid summer associate between her first and second and her second and third years of law school at a firm where she had good prospects of being hired after she graduated. If the court modifies her child support obligation, should it impute additional income to her for the months when she is not employed, or should her obligation be based only on the income she actually earns during the summer?

3. When he was divorced two years ago, Joe Hill was ordered to pay support for his two children, who are in their mother's custody. Joe works in a manufacturing plant, and his union has called a strike because wage negotiations with the employer have been stalled for six months. The union does not have a strike fund, so that if Joe goes on strike he will have no income. If he does participate in the strike and then moves to reduce his child support obligation because of his loss in income, should the court grant the motion under the tests discussed above?

4. Ali and Carol were divorced three years ago, and their divorce decree provided that Carol would contribute to their daughter's support by paying Ali $475 per week in child support and by paying for the child's enrollment in a private elementary school through the end of fifth grade at a cost of $50,000 per year. The child completed fifth grade last year and is now enrolled in public middle school. Ali has filed a motion to modify child support upward, alleging that the change in schooling constitutes a substantial change in circumstances. Carol has counterclaimed, arguing that Ali's income has gone up 80 percent, which constitutes a substantial change in circumstances. Carol, whose net income has not changed since the divorce, also opposes Ali's motion, arguing that child support should be based on the parties' net incomes. How should the court rule on these motions and why?

3. New Families — Spousal Support, Remarriage, and Cohabitation

Traditionally, as we have seen, alimony was considered a continuation of the support duty imposed by marriage. Therefore, it terminated when the recipient remarried because her new spouse's support duty replaced the former spouse's support obligation. Traditional legal principles had little to say about the effect of cohabitation on alimony because open cohabitation without marriage was not socially acceptable. The following materials consider the impact on spousal support duties of two important changes — the changing justifications and criteria for requiring someone to support a former spouse following divorce, and the high incidence of unmarried cohabitation.

Peterson v. Peterson
434 N.W.2d 732 (S.D. 1989)

BRADSHAW, C.J. . . . Janey Peterson (Janey) appeals from a judgment terminating her right to receive alimony from Gregory A. Peterson (Gregory). . . .

Finally, the court decree provided the following language: (Gregory) is ordered to pay to (Janey) as alimony the sum of $1,000 per month for a seven-year period starting with the first month after the entry of judgment herein, . . . after said seven-year period, (Gregory) shall pay to (Janey) $500 per month, . . . for an additional 10 years unless during this last 10-year period (Janey) dies or *remarries*, at which time this portion of the alimony shall cease. (emphasis supplied)

Gregory petitioned the trial court to amend its divorce judgment and extinguish his duty to provide alimony when he learned that Janey had remarried on August 1, 1987. Janey resisted. . . .

The trial judge granted [the motion]. . . . [P]ursuant to our ruling in Marquardt v. Marquardt by Rempfer, 396 N.W.2d 753 (S.D. 1986), his obligation to pay alimony was cancelled.

[Janey appeals.]

Janey seeks an affirmative resolution of this issue by advancing three alternative assertions: (1) That the language of the trial court's alimony award indicates by implication that Gregory's duty to pay alimony would not cease if Janey remarried during the initial seven years following the parties' divorce; (2) That the alimony award was an integral part of the property settlement segment of the divorce decree; and (3) That extraordinary circumstances exist, i.e., Janey's new husband is unable to support her, which require the perpetuation of her alimony payments. These contentions will be addressed seriatim.

In *Marquardt*, supra, we opined that "[p]roof that the spouse receiving spousal support payments has remarried establishes a prima facie case requiring the court to terminate the support payments unless [the recipient of the support payments can show] extraordinary circumstances which justify continuation of the payments." By adopting this stance, we rejected the automatic termination rule espoused in Voyles v. Voyles, 644 P.2d 847 (Alaska 1982), and other cases. These automatic termination jurisdictions have allowed alimony to continue, despite remarriage, if the parties' agreement or the decree of the court expressly provided that the flow of alimony was to remain unimpeded by the recipient spouse's remarriage. Janey urges us to adopt this exception in this case.

We must repeat, in order to fully comprehend the gist of Janey's argument, the succeeding pertinent language of the alimony award: (Gregory) is ordered to pay to (Janey) as alimony the sum of $1,000 per month for a seven-year period starting with the first month after the entry of judgment herein. . . . After said seven-year period, (Gregory) shall pay to (Janey) $500 per month . . . for an additional 10 years unless during this last 10-year period (Janey) dies or remarries, at which time this portion of the alimony shall cease.

Since this language fails to provide that alimony payments will end if Janey remarries during the first seven years, Janey maintains that "it clearly implies that remarriage does not operate to terminate alimony during the first seven years." This assertion is without merit.

Janey's reliance on the *Voyles* exception is misplaced because the *Voyles* exception, by its terms, applies only where there is an express statement that alimony is to survive notwithstanding the remarriage of the recipient spouse. Silence in a divorce decree or a voluntary agreement, as to the occurrence of remarriage, falls short of a specific declaration that alimony will endure in the event the recipient spouse remarries. Thus, the parties to a divorce must, to avail themselves of the *Voyles* deviation, point to either a statement in an agreement or divorce decree which provides that the payor spouse will pay alimony, irrespective of the recipient spouse's remarriage, or evidence that the parties intended that the alimonial obligation would survive past the date of the payee spouse's remarriage. Here, since Janey has shown neither the amount of evidence required nor an agreement that alimony would continue after her remarriage, her argument must collapse.

Next, Janey argues that the alimony award was an intrinsic part of the property settlement segment of the divorce decree. . . . We refuse to countenance this contention on the basis of the facts before us.

In Lien v. Lien, 420 N.W.2d 26 (S.D. 1988) (*Lien II*), we held that payments, though denominated as "support," were, in fact, part of a property division between the parties. As such, they were not terminable under *Marquardt*. We reached that conclusion due to the husband's insistence, at trial, that the payments be labeled "support" so that he could avoid the adverse tax consequences attendant to a total cash award of property.

It is apparent from a reading of *Lien II*, supra, that when deciding whether an award of alimony is, in reality, a portion of a property settlement, a court must scrutinize the language of the divorce decree, the circumstances encompassing it, and the end sought to be achieved by the parties. After conducting this examination in the present case, we are left with the conviction that the alimony award was not a disguised property settlement.

Here, the divorce decree provided that Janey receive the parties' right, title, and interest in and to Karen's, Inc. (a retail store), the family residence, the personal property situated within the home, a 1978 station wagon, and $115,063 to be paid in cash within six months of the date of the decree. This amounted to a total property award of $329,858. The cash award was, in the trial judge's words, necessary to "effectuate the property division."

Based on this language, it is obvious that this money, not the periodically paid alimony, was an integral part of the property settlement necessary to accomplish an equitable division of property. The wording of the divorce decree, coupled with the circumstances of the divorce, indicates that the monthly payments made by Gregory to Janey were for her support and were not meant to accomplish an equitable property division. Thus, this contention of Janey's must also fail. . . .

Janey's final position under this alimony issue is that extraordinary circumstances exist which require the continuation of her alimony payments. Janey argues that since she has not profited economically from her second marriage, she needs the alimony to live in the style to which she had become accustomed prior to her divorce from Gregory. In one of her affidavits, Janey says that "I did marry Timothy W. Johnson on August 1, 1987; however, his income, together with my child support, is not sufficient to provide for me and my two minor children." The following passage, extracted from the opinion in Nugent v. Nugent, 152 N.W.2d 323, 329 (N.D. 1967), capsulizes our view of Janey's assertion:

> [W]e do not believe that such factors [that the husband's fault caused the divorce, that the wife contributed to the household while the husband obtained a medical degree, and that the wife's new husband was unable to provide for her in the same fashion as her previous mate] constitute extraordinary circumstances as would justify the continuation of the alimony payments in this case, [wife] having voluntarily elected to marry another, who now must assume the responsibility for her support.

Additionally, we have said "it is 'illogical and unreasonable' that a spouse should receive support from a present spouse and a former spouse at the same time."

Since Janey has shown no extraordinary circumstances to rebut the prima facie requirement that alimony should terminate, we hold that the trial court was correct and did not abuse its discretion in terminating Janey's alimony.

[The concurring opinions of Justice MORGAN and Justice HENDERSON are omitted.]

NOTES AND QUESTIONS

1. Janey first argued that the language of the decree on its face provided that the payments would not terminate during the first seven years after the divorce. What argument supports this construction of the language? Why do you think the court rejected the argument?

In Simpson v. Simpson, 352 S.W.3d 362 (Mo. 2011) (en banc), the court in a similar case reached the opposite conclusion. It held that an agreement providing that alimony would terminate "only in the event of the death of either party" expressed an agreement that it would not terminate upon the wife's remarriage. The court relied on the use of the word "only" as limiting the events that would terminate the obligation. Would the *Peterson* court have agreed?

Other cases requiring that language very specifically provide that spousal support will survive the recipient's remarriage to be enforceable include Moore v. Jacobsen, 817 A.2d 212 (Md. 2003); Hardesty v. Hardesty, 581 S.E.2d 213 (Va. App. 2003); Holm v. Holm, 678 N.W.2d 499 (Neb. 2004).

2. Janey's second argument was that the clause requiring Gregory to pay her $1000 a month for seven years was part of the property division and so not modifiable. Ambiguity about the character of an award is commonly found in divorce decrees (and separation agreements). Sometimes this ambiguity is the result of sloppy drafting, and sometimes it is created deliberately so that the obligation will be treated as property division for some purposes and as spousal support for other purposes. As you will see in the rest of this chapter, statutes and courts have created different tests to classify an award as property division or spousal support for purposes of modification and termination, for enforcement, and for bankruptcy. However, as *Peterson* illustrates, ambiguity about these issues often invites subsequent litigation. The alternative is for courts and lawyers to address collateral consequences explicitly.

If the agreement in *Petersen* had also provided, "The agreements of the parties as to the payment of alimony as set forth herein have been made and are given in reciprocal consideration for the agreements of the parties as to equitable distribution and property settlement of the parties," would the outcome of the case have been different? *See* Underwood v. Underwood, 720 S.E.2d 460 (N.C. 2011).

In the face of ambiguous language, the *Peterson* court, like most courts, uses a totality-of-the-circumstances test to determine whether the obligation is spousal support or property division. Which factors suggest that the $1000 a month duty was spousal support? Which suggest that it was property division?

3. Under *Peterson*, spousal support terminates on remarriage absent a showing of "exceptional circumstances." What circumstances did Janey allege, and why did the court find that they were not exceptional? How would the *Peterson* court define "exceptional circumstances"? What rationale today supports a rule that spousal support always terminates on the recipient's remarriage? What justifies the *Peterson* court's approach, which has been adopted in many jurisdictions?

The ALI Family Dissolution Principles provide that periodic payments to a former spouse should automatically terminate at the obligee's remarriage unless "the original decree provides otherwise" or "the court makes written findings establishing that termination of the award would work a substantial injustice because of facts not present in most cases. . . ." ALI, Principles of the Law of Family Dissolution §5.07 (2000).

4. The Oregon Supreme Court in Bates and Bates, 733 P.2d 1363 (Or. 1989) (en banc), adopted a different formulation for determining when spousal support should terminate on remarriage: when remarriage "supplants the purposes behind the initial award." 733 P.2d at 1366. If this standard had been applied in *Peterson*, would spousal support have been terminated? How does a court faced with a motion to modify ascertain what the purposes behind the initial award were?

In New Jersey, the state supreme court has held that the touchstone for determining the adequacy of a spousal support award is whether it assists "the supported spouse in achieving a lifestyle that is reasonably comparable to the one enjoyed while living with the supporting spouse during the marriage." Lepis v. Lepis, 416 A.2d 45 (N.J. 1980). In Crews v. Crews, 751 A.2d 524 (N.J. 2000), the court held that a motion to modify based on changed circumstances should be decided with reference to this standard. To facilitate that determination, it directed trial courts when setting initial awards to make findings establishing the standard of living during the marriage and evaluating whether the award will enable the parties to enjoy a lifestyle reasonably comparable to the marital standard. In Weishaus v. Weishaus, 849 A.2d 171 (N.J. 2004), the divorcing parties reached a financial settlement but could not agree whether the provisions would enable the former wife to maintain the marital standard of living, and they asked the court to enter a final order consistent with their agreement that did not include the findings that *Crews* calls for. The trial judge refused, and the wife appealed, arguing that the findings should not be required if they stood in the way of settlement. How should the case have been decided and why?

PROBLEMS

1. Wanda and Herbert divorced after a 30-year marriage. Wanda had quit work two years after the marriage to raise their four children, and she had never worked in the market after that. Herbert was the owner of a successful small business. The divorce court awarded Wanda more than half of the marital property other than the business and ordered Herbert to pay her $1500 per month indefinitely as spousal support. The judge said that the award was partially in recognition of Wanda's claim to an interest in the business. The judge explained that she thought spousal support, which is modifiable, was fairer than property division because it required the parties to share the risk that the business might fall on hard times. The judge said that Wanda's lost earning capacity and the length of the marriage justified the award. Two years later Wanda married Simon, who was disabled in a workplace accident and receives a small disability pension. Herbert has moved to terminate spousal support. Under the *Peterson* rule, how should a court rule on the motion and why? Under *Bates*?

2. When Willow and Harvey divorced, their separation agreement, incorporated into the divorce decree, provided that if Willow "shares a residence with an individual with whom she is having an intimate relationship for over a six-month period," her spousal support would terminate. It continued, "however, if such relationship shall cease, then six months after such cessation, the amount of maintenance will be reinstated." Three years later Willow married Joe, and Harvey quit making spousal support payments. However, the new marriage failed after six months, and Willow successfully sued to have it annulled. Under *Petersen*, would the provision in the separation agreement constitute an agreement that remarriage would not cause spousal support to terminate? If not, would the facts come within the terms of the agreement, so that Harvey's support obligation would be revived?

Absent a statute or agreement to the contrary, most courts hold that spousal support does not automatically terminate because the recipient is cohabiting with someone else. A formal reason is that cohabitation does not create automatic reciprocal support duties, and the rule may also reflect understanding of the relative impermanency of many cohabiting relationships. Proof of cohabitation might, however, be the basis for modification based on changed circumstances. Cynthia Lee Starnes, I'll Be Watching You: Alimony and the Cohabitation Rule, 50 Fam. L.Q. 261, 266-268 (2016). In states that have this rule, parties may agree to terminate support upon the recipient's cohabitation, and statutes in some states establish that recipients lose their alimony if they cohabit. Several of the statutes were enacted as part of broader alimony reforms discussed in Chapter 6. Starnes, 50 Fam. L.Q. at 264-266, 274-277.

Decisions interpreting such agreements and statutes vary greatly; some of the differences turn on language, but they also reflect different approaches to the underlying policy issues.

In the Matter of Raybeck
44 A.3d 551 (N.H. 2012)

LYNN, J. . . . The parties were divorced in Texas in August 2005 after a forty-two-year marriage. The respondent was awarded property in North Carolina and Texas, and the petitioner was awarded property in Laconia, New Hampshire. The divorce decree, based upon the parties' agreement, obligated the respondent to pay the petitioner alimony of $25,000 per year for ten years, in yearly installments. That obligation would cease, however, if the petitioner "cohabitates with an unrelated adult male."

Approximately three months before the January 2010 alimony payment was due, the petitioner moved out of her Laconia house and rented it to reduce her expenses. She moved into the upper level of a single family home in Plymouth owned by Paul Sansoucie, a man she had met through an online dating service. Sansoucie lived on the lower level and did not charge the petitioner for rent. She did, however, pay about $300 per month for food and often cooked for him. They also shared living space on the middle level of the house. When the respondent learned that the petitioner lived with another man, he stopped paying alimony. In response, the petitioner asked the family division to enforce the alimony agreement and require the respondent to resume his support payments.

After a hearing, the marital master recommended a finding that the petitioner was not cohabiting with Sansoucie under the terms of the divorce decree, and the family division approved the recommendation ordering the respondent to continue his alimony payments. This appeal followed. . . .

Neither the legislature nor this court has had occasion to define "cohabitation" as that term is often used in a divorce decree. Because the divorce decree here reflects the parties' agreement, we will interpret the cohabitation clause according to its common meaning. The trial court applied the following standard:

> [E]vidence of a sexual relationship is admissible, but not necessarily required, for a finding of cohabitation. . . . [T]here must be more to the relationship than just occupying the same living area or sharing some or all of the expenses incurred by both parties. The evidence should reflect a common and mutual purpose to manage expenses and make decisions together about common and personal goals, and a common purpose to make mutual financial and personal progress toward those goals.

Applying this definition, the court concluded that the petitioner and Sansoucie did not cohabit. In support of that decision, the court found, among other facts, that the petitioner was forced to relocate when the respondent first announced that he would discontinue the alimony payments; that she and Sansoucie sleep on different floors of the house although they do share a common living area; that she does not pay rent but pays for food; and that their financial relationship is limited to her paying for food in exchange for shelter. The court also found, however, evidence indicating that there was a personal component to their relationship. They had, for example, shared rooms during their travels together. In a letter to her children, the petitioner stated that she and Sansoucie had discussed marriage but did not marry for "personal and financial reasons." Specifically, the petitioner wrote that "neither of us is sure if we want to remarry. Financial matters become so complicated at our age. . . ." The record also reflected that the petitioner's son-in-law referred to Sansoucie as the petitioner's boyfriend in a Christmas letter. Notwithstanding the evidence of a personal connection, the trial court ruled that the petitioner and Sansoucie did not cohabit in light of their financial situation.

Our common law lacks a definition of cohabitation as that term is used in divorce decrees and separation agreements. Dictionary definitions confirm the trial court's conclusion that to qualify a living arrangement as one of cohabitation there must be a personal connection beyond that of roommates or casual bedfellows. *Black's Law Dictionary*, for example, defines cohabitation as "[t]he fact or state of living together, esp[ecially] as partners in life, usu[ally] with the suggestion of sexual relations." *The Oxford English Dictionary* defines it as "liv[ing] together as husband and wife, esp[ecially] without legal marriage." *Ballentine's Law Dictionary* defines it as "a dwelling together of a man and a woman in the same place in the manner of husband and wife"; see also *The New Oxford American Dictionary* ("live together and have a sexual relationship without being married"); *Webster's Third New International Dictionary* ("[T]o live together as or as if as husband and wife. The mutual assumption of those marital rights, duties and obligations which are usually manifested by married people, including but not necessarily dependent on sexual relations.").

Common law standards from other jurisdictions contain similar articulations. *See, e.g.,* State v. Arroyo, 435 A.2d 967, 970 (1980) ("[Cohabitation] is the mutual assumption of those marital rights, duties and obligations which are usually manifested by married people, including but not necessarily dependent on sexual relations."); Cook v. Cook, 798 S.W.2d 955, 957 (Ky. 1990) (cohabitation is "mutually assum[ing] the duties and obligations normally assumed by married persons"); Fisher v. Fisher, 540 A.2d 1165, 1169 (1988) (cohabitation "envisions at least the normally accepted attributes of a marriage"); Frey v. Frey, 416 S.E.2d 40, 43 (1992) (cohabitation "has been consistently interpreted by courts as encompassing both a permanency or continuity element and an assumption of marital duties"); *see also* Gordon v. Gordon, 675 A.2d 540, 546 n.8 (1996) (rejecting proposition that cohabitation is synonymous with common residence). Similarly, *Corpus Juris Secundum* states: "Generally, where alimony is sought to be modified on the basis of cohabitation with another by the recipient spouse, cohabitation is an arrangement in which the couple reside together on a continuing conjugal basis or hold themselves out as man and wife." The notes of that treatise elaborate: "Where the term 'cohabitation' is used in a divorce decree . . . , court must look to whether the parties have assumed obligations, including support, equivalent to those arising from a ceremonial marriage."

After carefully reviewing these authorities, we follow them in defining cohabitation as a relationship between persons resembling that of a marriage. As such, cohabitation encompasses both an element of continuity or permanency as well as an assumption of marital obligations. As the trial court recognized, whether two people are cohabiting will depend on the facts and circumstances of each particular case. Beyond living together on a continual basis, many factors are relevant to the inquiry. Primary among them are the financial arrangements between the two people, such as shared expenses, whether and to what extent one person is supporting the other, the existence and use of joint bank accounts or shared investment or retirement plans, a life insurance policy carried by one or both parties benefiting the other, and similar financial entanglements.

We observe, however, that, in considering the financial arrangements, the age of the putative couple may be an important consideration. Where, as here, the individuals are senior citizens, support of one by the other may have less significance than with younger people not only because older individuals may be more financially secure than their younger counterparts, but also because older individuals may have estate plans in place to benefit children of prior relationships.

Also important is the extent of the personal relationship, including evidence of an intimate connection, how the people hold themselves out to others, the presence of common friends or acquaintances, vacations spent together, and similar signs of an ongoing personal commitment. Evidence of a sexual relationship should also be considered, but is not dispositive. Here too, the age of the couple may be relevant in weighing this factor; for older people, a sexual component to intimacy may not be as significant as it would be for younger couples.

In addition, the shared use and enjoyment of personal property is an indication of cohabitation, such as common use of household rooms, appliances, furniture, vehicles, and whether one person maintains personal items, such as toiletries or clothing, at the residence of the other. So, too, are indications that family members and friends view the relationship as one involving an intimate personal commitment. Taken together, these factors will support a finding of cohabitation if they indicate that two people are so closely involved that their relationship resembles that of marriage.

Because the trial court did not have the benefit of the standard we articulate here for determining whether the relationship between the petitioner and Sansoucie amounted to cohabitation, we vacate and remand the case for the master to reconsider the matter in light of the standard we have established.

Vacated and remanded.

NOTES AND QUESTIONS

1. Assuming that cohabitation does not give rise to a support duty, what arguments support the interpretation of the court in *Raybeck*? If you represented the former husband, what test would you propose, and how would you argue in support of it?

To the main case, *compare* Paul v. Paul, 60 A.3d 1080 (Del. 2012) (statute defining cohabitation as "regularly residing with another adult . . . if the parties hold themselves out as a couple" satisfied where the parties maintained separate residences, spent two to four nights a week together and pursued different activities during the day).

2. Should spousal support be reduced or eliminated when the recipient becomes platonic roommates with someone else? Should this situation be distinguished from *Raybeck*?

3. The definition of cohabitation in statutes that provide for modification or termination of spousal support on this basis also varies. *E.g.*, Cal. Fam. Code §4323(a)(1) (2022) ("cohabiting with a nonmarital partner" creates a rebuttable presumption of decreased need for support); Ga. Code Ann. §19-6-19 (2022) (voluntary cohabitation, defined as "dwelling together continuously and openly in a meretricious relationship with another person, regardless of the sex of the other person"); N.Y. Dom. Rel. Law §248 (2022) ("payee is habitually living with another person and holding himself or herself out as the spouse of such other person"); 43 Okla. Stat. §134(C) (2022) ("voluntary cohabitation . . . with a person of the opposite sex," defined as "dwelling together continuously and habitually of a man and a woman who are in a private conjugal relationship not solemnized as a marriage according to law, or not necessarily meeting all the standards of a common-law marriage"); Fla. Stat. §61.14(1)(b) (2022) (recipient is in a "supportive relationship" with another person; statute provides a nonexclusive list of 11 factors to be considered in determining whether a "supportive relationship" exists: public reputation, length of cohabitation, pooled assets, mutual support, performance of services for one another, performance of services for one another's business or employer, common enterprises, joint contribution to purchase real property, express agreements about property or support, implied agreements about same, and support of one another's children regardless of legal duty). *See generally* Cynthia Lee Starnes, I'll Be Watching You: Alimony and the Cohabitation Rule, 50 Fam. L.Q. 261, 278-292 (2016).

Are statutes that require termination of alimony only for opposite-sex cohabitation (or marriage) constitutional after Obergefell v. Hodges (excerpted in Chapters 1 and 3)?

4. If state law provides that spousal support does not automatically terminate upon cohabitation or remarriage, but instead may be a change in circumstances, is it contrary to public policy to enforce an agreement providing for automatic termination? Consider the view of Justice O'Hern, dissenting from a decision upholding the enforceability of such an agreement in Konzelman v. Konzelman, 729 A.2d 7, 17-21 (N.J. 1999):

> When viewed through the Gaussian filter employed by the Court, the anti-cohabitation clause appears as a pleasant piece of bargaining between equals. Although the Court properly declines to presume that all women are passive players in this arena, it fails to afford proper weight to the uneven economic playing field upon which the contest takes place. . . .
>
> The majority downplays the woman's loss of freedom or autonomy by asserting that the case is not about sex, but that it is about money, the freedom of contract, and whether the anti-cohabitation provision entered into was "voluntary, knowing and consensual," and based upon "mutuality, voluntariness and fairness." It offends our intelligence for defendant to suggest that the anti-cohabitation clause in this case is not about sex. If the clause were not about sex, why then is cohabitation with another person of the same sex permitted without a reduction in support? For reasons rooted in our past, "social conventions [still seek to] . . . deny women the same chance of sexual happiness as men. . . ." There is a double standard at play here that views women as having a lesser need than men for companionship of the opposite sex, "yet . . . universally punishe[s] [women] if they display evidence to the contrary. . . ."

The danger against which courts have guarded in the past concerns "the numerous ways in which a spouse can use [economic power associated with spousal support] to exert unjust and inappropriate control over the recipient's personal life." . . .

Mrs. Konzelman is punished for her choice of companionship while Mr. Konzelman is relieved of the burden to demonstrate that his former partner's financial status is any better because of her new relationship. That approach ignores the economic needs and dependency test that underpins an alimony obligation. The trial court found that Mrs. Konzelman's financial status had improved only to the extent of $170 per week because of her relationship.

Mrs. Konzelman was married for twenty-seven years. The record does not disclose whether she left work to raise her children, thereby decreasing her potential for earnings. That is often the case. . . .

Dependency acquired during the marriage based on the marital roles assumed by the parties is at the heart of an alimony obligation. It is manifestly unfair to relieve Mr. Konzelman of all alimony obligations based upon Mrs. Konzelman's choice of companionship with another man, when economic need is the true measure of alimony. The law is casting this partner of twenty-seven years into poverty for what, a sin? If her relationship ends, she will not even have, from the partners' once-shared earning capacity, a dollar a week to live on while Mr. Konzelman will be permitted to reap the benefits of an increased earning capacity built up during the marriage. . . .

In *Melletz*, supra, Judge Dreier punctured the hypocrisy attendant to anti-cohabitation clauses by asking the rhetorical question: could a divorced wife obtain a similar promise from her husband in return for less alimony? . . .

Finally, the enforcement of anti-cohabitation clauses imposes a needless burden on the judiciary and the matrimonial bar. This trial consumed thirteen days over three months and included twenty-six witnesses. The evidence included the reports and testimony of several private investigators, one of whom watched Mrs. Konzelman's home seven days a week for 127 days. It would not have taken thirteen days or a spy in her yard to determine that Mrs. Konzelman's companion contributed $170 a week to the household. As a result of the Court's ruling, each Konzelman hearing hereinafter will result in an exhaustive (and exhausting) inquiry into whether the situation involved something more than "a mere, romantic, casual or social relationship. . . ." (Does this mean that there is a platonic defense to anti-cohabitation clauses?) Such tasteless inquiries into the private lives of divorced women, when unnecessary, are beneath the dignity of the judiciary.

In addition, by approving anti-cohabitation clauses, the Court will force attorneys and parties to bargain over the fair value of the clause. The Court's holding invites husbands to seek such clauses, perhaps as a bargaining chip. There are only two purposes for the clause, either to eliminate the need to examine changed economic circumstances or to retain control over the divorced spouse. Either way, there will be a price. Wives will not wish lightly to contemplate the kind of surveillance this woman endured. It is regrettably the way of the world that only the wealthy will want to or will be able to buy the clause. I would not add to the already emotionally charged denouement of a marriage this unseemly bit of bargaining. . . .

I would reverse the judgment of the Appellate Division and reinstate that of the trial court reducing Mrs. Konzelman's alimony by $170 per week.

PROBLEM

Helen and Martin were divorced in 2015 after a 31-year marriage. Helen had a GED and had not worked outside the home. Martin was a very successful optometrist. Helen was awarded permanent spousal support because the court found that her employment opportunities were limited to minimum-wage jobs. Martin has filed a motion to terminate spousal support because Helen has been living with Vic for almost three years in the home that she received in the divorce from Martin. The evidence shows that neither Helen nor Vic maintains another residence, that they share household expenses more or less evenly, that they have an exclusive sexual relationship, and that they are open about their relationship and socialize with friends and family as a couple. Vic and Helen do not intend to marry, neither has provided for the other by will, and each has arranged for his or her oldest child to manage things if he or she becomes incompetent. They do not have joint bank accounts, their car titles are not held jointly, and Helen has not put Vic's name on the title to the house. Helen has no income aside from the spousal support she receives from Martin, although she could earn $700 a month if she worked full time at a minimum wage job.

Under the approach in *Raybeck*, how should the court rule on Martin's motion and why? Under the statutes cited in note 3 above?

4. New Families — Child Support

One way of understanding cases and statutes that terminate spousal support when the recipient remarries or cohabits is that the appropriate family unit for allocating economic responsibility is the one that functions as a day-to-day household. On the other hand, rules that do not make termination of spousal support automatic express the view that the economic consequences of a previous marriage are so important that they should continue to have an impact despite the reconfiguring of the family. This section considers the similar, but even more complicated, problems in determining how decisions by parents to remarry or assume financial responsibility for children from a new marriage should affect their child support obligations.

Most divorced adults, including parents with custody, remarry, and never-married parents often marry as well. And, of course, many parents form new intimate partnerships outside marriage. The estimated number of children living with a stepparent varies among surveys because of differences in data collection. A study using data from the 2010 census and the 2016 Current Population Survey estimated that 9 percent of American children lived in stepfamilies. Of those children, 55 percent lived in married stepparent families, and 45 percent lived with a parent and that parent's cohabiting partner. Kasey J. Eickmeyer, American Children's Family Structure: Stepparent Families (Nat'l Ctr. For Fam. & Marr. Res., Fam. Profile No. 17, 2017), available at https://www.bgsu.edu/content/dam/BGSU/college-of-arts-and-sciences/NCFMR/documents/FP/eickmeyer-stepparent-families-fp-17-16.pdf.

When a parent has children from several relationships, the presumptive child support obligation is calculated separately for each group of full siblings, raising the question of how the parent's obligation to his or her other children is taken into account, if at all.

Harte v. Hand
81 A.3d 667 (N.J. Super. 2013)

KOBLITZ, J.A.D. This appeal raises the issue of how to properly calculate child support for multiple families. Defendant David Richard Hand appeals from two separate child support orders entered on November 7, 2011. . . .

Defendant has three children, each of whom has a different mother. Defendant's oldest son lives with defendant and his current wife. This child's mother lives in Florida and does not contribute to his support. Defendant's younger son lives with his mother, plaintiff T.B. His youngest child, a girl, lives with defendant's former wife, Harte. Defendant was employed as a concrete layer and finisher before he was seriously injured in a 2003 garage collapse at the Tropicana Casino Hotel in Atlantic City. As a result of this injury, he received a settlement of $1.2 million in 2007. He claims to have netted $533,822 after paying several "obligations."

At the time of his personal injury settlement, defendant was married to Harte and paying child support to T.B.

After the settlement, defendant agreed to an imputation of $57,200 in annual income when recalculating child support for T.B. Harte and defendant were divorced in 2008 and defendant again consented to an imputation of $57,200 in annual income as part of their January 2009 final judgment of divorce. In 2011, after a history of enforcement motions by both plaintiffs, defendant unsuccessfully moved to reduce child support for both children, claiming he was unable to obtain through wages and investments the agreed-upon imputed income. The motion judge denied his application, but suggested that if he presented a vocational expert who could demonstrate his lack of ability to earn the imputed income, the judge would consider his application again.

Defendant, representing himself for his re-application, moved again to reduce his support, this time supplying the judge with a vocational expert's report that had been prepared prior to his previous motion, but not provided by his counsel to the judge. Defendant stated on the record at oral argument that his wife supported him. . . .

The judge calculated child support for the two children not living with defendant based on the individual financial circumstances of the mothers as provided in the Child Support Guidelines. In both calculations, the judge entered the undisputed dependent deduction of $177 for the child living with defendant on line 2(d). She determined that it would be unfair to the mothers to designate either order as the initial order, thereby deducting that amount from defendant's available income when calculating the support order for the other child. The judge therefore calculated both support obligations using defendant's imputed annual income of $57,200 as if the only other child defendant supported was the oldest son living with him.

We do not approve the child support calculation method utilized by the motion judge. Equality in treatment for the mothers should not be obtained by requiring the father to pay an inappropriately high level of support for both children. According to Rule 5:6A, the Child Support Guidelines "shall be applied" when a court is calculating or modifying child support. The "guidelines may be modified or disregarded by the court only where good cause is shown. . . ." Although we agree with the judge's concern that the two mothers should not be treated unequally, we do not approve of the method used to achieve equality.

The Guidelines require the court to consider multiple family obligations to obtain an equitable resolution that does not favor any family. The Guidelines also anticipate an adjustment when an obligor must support more than one family. Pursuant to the Guidelines, prior child support orders must be deducted from an obligor's weekly income because such an obligation "represents income that is not available for determining the current child support obligation. . . ." Thus, "the amount of such orders must be deducted from the obligor's total weekly Adjusted Gross Taxable Income." By leaving line 2(b) blank on both the Harte and T.B. worksheets, the judge misapplied the Guidelines.

A later-born child should not be penalized by reducing the obligor's available income by the prior child support obligation. To achieve parity among the children of defendant, we suggest the use of the "prior order" adjustment under the child support guidelines must be modified. For example, here, Guidelines support should be calculated for Harte, first considering her child as having the prior order and listing T.B.'s child as the recipient of the second order; then flipping these positions so the T.B. child is considered the first order and Harte's child considered the recipient of the second order. Similar calculations would be performed in T.B.'s matter, first considering her order as the first entered, then as the second entered. In each calculation, the party receiving the "second" order would have the amount calculated for the "first" order entered on line 2(b) of the worksheet. Then, after the four calculations are prepared, all including defendant's oldest child as another dependent deduction of $177 on line 2(d), the two resulting T.B. worksheet obligations, located at line 27, would be averaged and the two Harte worksheet calculations averaged. Defendant would then be ordered to pay the average of the two support calculations to each plaintiff. This method would ensure that the children were treated fairly regardless of birth order, while not disregarding the father's obligation to pay for all three children. This may well not be the only way to equitably calculate support for multiple families, but we suggest it as one workable method of doing so that is consistent with the Guidelines. We therefore remand for a recalculation of support for the two families. . . .

NOTES AND QUESTIONS

1. What arguments justify a rule that attempts to equalize the support a parent pays for all of his or her children, regardless of when they were born or which household they live in? What arguments would support the dominant approach, which provides that the support for children born earlier is not reduced because of afterborn children (the first family first approach)? *See* Adrienne Jennings Lockie, Multiple Families, Multiple Goals, Multiple Failures: The Need for "Limited Equalization" as a Theory of Child Support, 32 Harv. J.L. & Gender 109 (2009).

2. Why shouldn't a parent with children with multiple partners be required to support each set of children as if none of the other children existed, as the trial court in *Harte* decreed?

3. Other jurisdictions have struggled with how to equalize support among different families of children. The Vermont legislature enacted the following statute:

(a) As used in this section, "additional dependents" means any natural and adopted children and stepchildren for whom the parent has a duty of support.

(b) In any proceeding to establish or modify child support, the total child support obligation for the children who are the subject of the support order shall be adjusted if a parent is also responsible for the support of additional dependents who are not the subject of the support order. The adjustments shall be made by calculating an amount under the guidelines to represent the support obligation for additional dependents based only upon the responsible parent's available income, without any other adjustments. This amount shall be subtracted from that parent's available income prior to calculating the total child support obligation based on both parents' available income. . . .

(c) The adjustment for additional dependents shall not be made to the extent that it contributes to the calculation of a support order lower than a previously existing support order for the children who are the subject of the modification hearing at which the adjustment is sought.

15 Vt. Stat. Ann. §656a (2022). Under this section, would Mr. Hand have received a deduction for the support he provided the child who lived with him? How would his obligations to his two sets of noncustodial children have been calculated?

The ALI Family Dissolution Principles provide for a deduction from the obligor's income of child support actually paid under a prior order or agreement. If the prior child lives with the obligor, the obligor gets a deduction for the amount of support that the parent would pay if the child lived with the other parent. ALI, Principles of the Law of Family Dissolution §3.14(3) (2000). The Principles give the fact finder discretion to grant a deduction when the obligor has subsequently born children. *Id.* §3.16(1)(c).

4. A number of state child support guidelines list obligations to support other dependents as a reason that may justify deviating from the basic support obligation produced by the guideline formula.

5. Mary Ann Glendon in The New Family and the New Property 71-72 (1981) notes that much of the problem with child support is that persons of limited means divorce, remarry, and produce new families, incurring more obligations than they can fulfill. She discusses "other, more experienced, polygamous societies," that is, Muslim countries, but suggests that they have not been more successful in dealing with the economic consequences of multiple families:

> In countries where Muslims are still legally permitted to have more than one wife at a time, they are admonished by religious law not to take more wives than they can afford. At least this is a common interpretation of 4 Koran, Verse 4: "[M]arry of the women who seem good to you, two, or three or four; and if ye fear that you cannot do justice, then one only. . . ." Yet this counsel, like much traditional Western marriage law, seems merely the expression of a moral ideal, with little or no legal sanction.

6. Constitutional challenges to child support schemes that give financial preference to prior children have generally been rejected. In Gallaher v. Elam, 104 S.W.3d 455 (Tenn. 2003), a father argued that the Tennessee child support guidelines, which give obligors a deduction for child support paid pursuant to a court order but not for support paid without an order, including for children living with the obligor, violate equal protection. The state supreme court rejected the argument that strict or heightened scrutiny should be applied to the rule, holding that it did not infringe upon the father's right to be a parent or his right to have a relationship with the children and that the classification made by the statute among children did not justify enhanced scrutiny. The court found the distinction drawn by the rule to be rational. *See also* Kimbrough v. Kentucky Child Support Div. ex rel. Belmar, 215 S.W.3d 69 (Ky. App. 2006); Child Support Enforcement Agency v. Doe, 91 P.3d 1092 (Haw. 2004); Pohlmann v. Pohlmann, 703 So. 2d 1121 (Fla. App. 1997); Feltman v. Feltman, 434 N.W.2d 590 (S.D. 1989).

7. Most states adhere to the common law rule that stepparents have no duty to support their stepchildren based on their status alone. A number of states' statutes impose a support duty on stepparents when the child lives in the stepparent's home. *See, e.g.,* N.D. Cent. Code §14-09-09 (2022); Or. Rev. Stat. §108.045 (2022); S.D.C.L. §25-7-8 (2022). Empirical studies show that custodial stepparents almost always support their stepchildren. David Chambers, Stepparents, Biologic Parents, and the Law's Perceptions of "Family" After Divorce, *in* Divorce Reform at the Crossroads 102, at 105 (Stephen D. Sugarman & Herma Hill Kay eds., 1990). Should the fact that a stepparent does support a stepchild be a ground for deviating from the amount calculated under the guidelines formula?

Chapter 13 considers the circumstances under which courts impose support duties on stepparents after a marriage between a parent and stepparent ends.

8. Most child support guidelines provide that the income of a parent's new spouse is not income for purposes of calculating the basic obligation. In some community property states, courts have held that half of the earnings of the new spouse, which are community property, belong to the obligated parent and are to that extent considered in calculating the child support obligation. DeTevis v. Aragon, 727 P.2d 558 (N.M. App. 1986).

On the other hand, the California code provides that income of a parent's new spouse or nonmarital partner "shall not be considered when determining or modifying child support, except in an extraordinary case where excluding that income would lead to extreme and severe hardship to any child subject to the child support award, in which case the court shall also consider whether including that income would lead to extreme and severe hardship to any child" supported by the parent or the parent's new spouse or nonmarital partner, Cal. Fam. Code §4057.5(a)(1) (2022). Courts in other community property states as well as common law property states have interpreted statutes providing that spouses are not liable for each other's premarital debts to mean that a noncustodial stepparent's income cannot be considered in calculating his or her spouse's child support obligation. Hines v. Hines, 707 P.2d 969 (Ariz. App. 1985); Duffey v. Duffey, 631 P.2d 697 (Mont. 1981). *See also* Van Dyke v. Thompson, 630 P.2d 420 (Wash. 1981) (en banc), and Abitz v. Abitz, 455 N.W.2d 609 (Wis. 1990).

Even though a stepparent's income cannot be considered in calculating the basic support obligation, many cases decided before and after the advent of guidelines have held that courts may consider the extent to which the new spouse's income increases the parent's ability to pay and so may justify an increase in an award. *E.g.*, J.P.D. v. W.E.D., 114 A.3d 887 (Pa. Super. 2015) (upholding upward deviation to more than twice the formula amount because father testified that his wealthy new wife paid for everything and that he did not rely on his income to support himself or his wife).

A number of courts have also held that a custodial parent's remarriage can reduce the needs of the children, leading to reduced support from the noncustodial parent. *See, e.g.*, Gardner v. Perry, 405 A.2d 721 (Me. 1979); Beverly v. Beverly, 317 N.W.2d 213 (Mich. App. 1981); Abitz v. Abitz, 455 N.W.2d 609 (Wis. 1990).

What is the practical difference between including a stepparent's income in calculating the basic child support obligation and finding that the custodial parent's ability to pay has increased because of his or her new spouse's income?

PROBLEMS

1. When Tam and Joe were divorced five years ago, Tam was awarded custody of their child, and Joe was ordered to pay child support. Joe has remarried and has moved with his new spouse to another state, where the spouse was offered a new job paying $30,000 a year more. Joe has accepted a job paying $14,000 less per year than he was making, and he has moved to modify his child support downward as a result. Tam argues that Joe's loss of income is voluntary and cannot be the basis for a downward modification. How should Joe respond? If the court holds that a modification is justified, should the court impute income to Joe? How should it handle Joe's new spouse's income?

2. When Mary and Fred were divorced, she received sole custody of their child, Carl. Mary married Sam a year ago, and they now have a new baby. Mary has decided to quit work and stay home to care for Carl, the baby, and Amy, Sam's child from a former relationship. Carl goes to kindergarten three hours a day, and Amy is in school six hours a day. Before she quit work, Mary earned $35,000 a year. Fred has asked the court to impute this much income to Mary when it recalculates child support for Carl. What arguments can be made in support of this request? How should Mary respond?

B. ENFORCEMENT

Timothy Grall

Custodial Mothers and Fathers and Their Child Support: 2017
Current Population Reports P60-269 (U.S. Census Bureau May 2020)

In April of 2018, 12.9 million parents (who are referred to as custodial parents in this report) lived with 21.9 million children under 21 years of age, while the child's other parent lived somewhere else. The 21.9 million children living with their custodial parent represented over one-fourth (26.5 percent) of all 82.6 million children under the age of 21 living in families.

Approximately half (48.8 percent) of all Black children lived in families with their custodial parent, while their other parent lived outside their household, more than twice as large as the proportion of White children (22.7 percent). Among children of other races—including

American Indian and Alaska Native, Asian, or Native Hawaiian and Other Pacific Islander—13.6 percent lived in custodial-parent families. Over one-quarter (28.7 percent) of Hispanic children, who may be any race, lived with their custodial parent in 2018.

In 2018, about 4 of every 5 (79.9 percent) of the 12.9 million custodial parents were mothers. One of every five custodial parents were fathers (20.1 percent). . . .

The distribution of custodial parents by marital status differed between mothers and fathers. Custodial mothers were more likely to have never married (40.4 percent) than to have been divorced (30.1 percent) or be currently married (16.3 percent), separated (11.9 percent), or widowed (1.3 percent). Custodial fathers were more likely than mothers to be divorced (39.1 percent) and less likely to be never married (29.3 percent). . . .

Less than half (44.2 percent) of custodial mothers were non-Hispanic White, 28.1 percent were Black, and 24.1 percent were of Hispanic origin. Custodial fathers were more likely than custodial mothers to be non-Hispanic White (62.9 percent) and less likely to be Black (15.1 percent). The proportion of custodial fathers who were Hispanic (18.4 percent) was not statistically different from the proportion of custodial mothers who were Hispanic (24.1 percent). . . .

One-half (49.4 percent) of all 12.9 million custodial parents had a court order, child support award, or some other type of agreement to receive financial support from the noncustodial parent(s) in 2018. Of the 6.4 million custodial parents with child support agreements, 88.2 percent reported that these agreements were formal legal orders—established by a court or other government entity—while 11.8 percent reported informal agreements or understandings. . . .

Child support order or agreement rates varied by the characteristics of the custodial parents. For example, 56.5 percent of non-Hispanic White custodial parents had child support orders or agreements, higher than the rate for Black custodial parents, 40.1 percent. Custodial parents whose child(ren) had contact with their other parent had child support order or agreement rates of 53.1 percent, higher than the rate for parents whose child(ren) did not have contact with their other parent, 42.3 percent.

Of the 6.4 million custodial parents who had some type of order or agreement for child support in 2018, 50.0 percent of noncustodial parents had visitation privileges with their children but did not have shared legal or physical custody. An additional 30.6 percent of noncustodial parents had some type of joint-custody arrangement (physical and/or legal), and 19.4 percent had neither noncustodial parental visitation nor any type of joint custody. . . .

In 2017, about 7 in 10 custodial parents who were supposed to receive child support from noncustodial parents received either full or partial child support payments. Approximately 45.9 percent of custodial parents received all payments they were supposed to receive, while 24.0 percent received some, but not all, payments. The remaining 30.2 percent of custodial parents who were supposed to receive child support in 2017 received no payments.

There was no statistical difference between the proportions of custodial mothers who received full child support payments in 2017 (46.4 percent) and custodial fathers (43.1 percent). However, a larger proportion of custodial fathers (38.4 percent) compared with custodial mothers (28.7 percent) did not receive any child support payments in 2017. . . .

In 2017, custodial parents with legal orders or informal agreements for child support were supposed to receive, on average, $5,519, or approximately $460 per month. The median amount of child support supposed to be received in 2017 was $4,356, meaning half of custodial parents were supposed to receive less than that amount and half were supposed to receive more. Among custodial parents who had agreements for child support, a total of $30.0 billion in child support payments was supposed to be received in 2017.

The mean annual amount received by custodial parents with legal or informal child support agreements in 2017 was $3,431 or $286 per month. However, the median annual amount of child support received was lower at $1,800.

A total of $18.6 billion of child support was reported as received by custodial parents, amounting to 62.2 percent of the $30.0 billion that was supposed to be received in 2017.

In 2017, custodial mothers received $16.1 billion of the $25.7 billion in support that was supposed to be received (62.8 percent), and custodial fathers received $2.5 billion of the $4.3 billion that was supposed to be received (58.4 percent). . . .

1. Private Enforcement Mechanisms — Liens, Trusts, and Insurance

Under some circumstances judges (and lawyers drafting separation and other agreements) can do much to eliminate or minimize enforcement problems. For example, if a transfer of property is to take effect at the time the decree or agreement is signed, all the necessary documents should be available at the time of execution so that the transfer can be completed immediately. For executory terms, the decree or agreement should establish definite time limits and procedures for carrying out obligations.

The decree or agreement can also employ devices that preclude or discourage noncompliance and make enforcement easier, such as liens and trusts to secure payment of future money obligations. In some states statutes explicitly authorize courts to order that trusts for dependents be established incident to divorce.

To protect a dependent person against the premature death of a supporting former spouse or parent, some states allow courts to order the obligor to maintain life insurance for the benefit of the obligee in a sufficient amount to provide the ordered support. *E.g.*, Fla. Stat. §61.08(3) (2022); Or. Rev. Stat. §§107.810-107.830 (2022). In other states, though, such an order is considered postmortem alimony and can only be entered with the agreement of the parties. If a marital separation agreement requires a parent to maintain life insurance to secure child support and that parent commits suicide, has the parent breached the agreement? The New Jersey Supreme Court held that this constituted a breach, resulting in the assets of the parent's estate being paid to the children. Woytas v. Greenwood Tree Experts, Inc., 206 A.3d 386 (N.J. 2019).

Federal law provides that if a parent can opt to provide medical insurance to his or her children through an employment-based plan, the employers must allow employees to enroll their children who do not live with them, as well as those who do, and regardless of whether the parent may claim the child as a dependent for income tax purposes. The insurance plan must allow the child to be enrolled outside limited enrollment seasons, and if the noncustodial parent does not enroll the child, the plan must allow the custodial parent to enroll the child. The insurance plan must provide the child the same documents about the plan that it gives participants, and it must permit the custodial parent to submit claims without the approval of the noncustodial parent. It cannot eliminate coverage for the child unless it receives written evidence that a court order requiring coverage is no longer in effect or that the child is covered by other, comparable health insurance. 42 U.S.C. §1396g-1 (2022).

ERISA requires covered group health plans to honor a qualified medical child support order (QMCSO). 29 U.S.C. §1169 (2022). This order creates or recognizes the right of a child to benefits from a parent's group health care plan. QMCSOs, which bear an obvious resemblance to the QDROs (discussed in Chapter 6), must include the following information:

- The name and last known mailing address of the plan participant and each "alternate recipient" covered by the order (an "alternate recipient" is a child entitled by the court order to enroll in the plan);
- A reasonable description of the type of coverage to be provided by the plan, or the method by which coverage is to be determined;
- The period to which the order applies; and
- Each plan to which the order applies.

The QMCSO cannot require the plan to provide a type or form of benefit that it does not otherwise provide. Insurance plans must have procedures for determining the validity of QMCSOs and communicating the decisions to affected parties promptly. Since the QMCSO applies only to the plan named in the order, if the parent employee changes jobs, a new QMCSO must be obtained. The rest of this section considers mechanisms for enforcing duties to transfer property or to pay support when the original decree or agreement did not include enforcement mechanisms or the mechanisms were ineffective.

2. Jailing "Deadbeat" Parents

Both federal and state law provide that in some circumstances failure to pay child support is a crime, and obligors who fail to pay court-ordered support for their dependents may be held in contempt of court and jailed in all states. (The use of contempt to enforce custody and parenting time orders is considered in Chapter 9.)

Both remedies can be imposed only if the obligor knew of the support duty and willfully refused to pay while having the ability to do so. The following case considers whether an indigent obligor is entitled to a court-appointed attorney in a civil contempt proceeding for failure to pay child support.

Turner v. Rogers
564 U.S. 431 (2011)

Justice BREYER delivered the opinion of the Court. . . . South Carolina family courts enforce their child support orders in part through civil contempt proceedings. Each month the family court clerk reviews outstanding child support orders, identifies those in which the supporting parent has fallen more than five days behind, and sends that parent an order to "show cause" why he should not be held in contempt. The "show cause" order and attached affidavit refer to the relevant child support order, identify the amount of the arrearage, and set a date for a court hearing. At the hearing that parent may demonstrate that he is not in contempt, say, by showing that he is not able to make the required payments. If he fails to make the required showing, the court may hold him in civil contempt. And it may require that he be imprisoned unless and until he purges himself of contempt by making the required child support payments (but not for more than one year regardless).

In June 2003 a South Carolina family court entered an order, which (as amended) required petitioner, Michael Turner, to pay $51.73 per week to respondent, Rebecca Rogers, to help support their child. (Rogers' father, Larry Price, currently has custody of the child and is also a respondent before this Court.) Over the next three years, Turner repeatedly failed to pay the amount due and was held in contempt on five occasions. The first four times he was sentenced to 90 days' imprisonment, but he ultimately paid the amount due (twice without being jailed, twice after spending two or three days in custody). The fifth time he did not pay but completed a 6-month sentence.

After his release in 2006 Turner remained in arrears. On March 27, 2006, the clerk issued a new "show cause" order. And after an initial postponement due to Turner's failure to appear, Turner's civil contempt hearing took place on January 3, 2008. Turner and Rogers were present, each without representation by counsel.

The hearing was brief. The court clerk said that Turner was $5,728.76 behind in his payments. The judge asked Turner if there was "anything you want to say." Turner replied,

> "Well, when I first got out, I got back on dope. I done meth, smoked pot and everything else, and I paid a little bit here and there. And, when I finally did get to working, I broke my back, back in September. I filed for disability and SSI. And, I didn't get straightened out off the dope until

I broke my back and laid up for two months. And, now I'm off the dope and everything. I just hope that you give me a chance. I don't know what else to say. I mean, I know I done wrong, and I should have been paying and helping her, and I'm sorry. I mean, dope had a hold to me."

The judge then said, "[o]kay," and asked Rogers if she had anything to say. After a brief discussion of federal benefits, the judge stated,

"If there's nothing else, this will be the Order of the Court. I find the Defendant in willful contempt. I'm [going to] sentence him to twelve months in the Oconee County Detention Center. He may purge himself of the contempt and avoid the sentence by having a zero balance on or before his release. I've also placed a lien on any SSI or other benefits." . . .

The court made no express finding concerning Turner's ability to pay his arrearage (though Turner's wife had voluntarily submitted a copy of Turner's application for disability benefits). Nor did the judge ask any followup questions or otherwise address the ability-to-pay issue. . . .

While serving his 12-month sentence, Turner, with the help of *pro bono* counsel, appealed. He claimed that the Federal Constitution entitled him to counsel at his contempt hearing. The South Carolina Supreme Court decided Turner's appeal after he had completed his sentence. And it rejected his "right to counsel" claim. The court pointed out that civil contempt differs significantly from criminal contempt. The former does not require all the "constitutional safeguards" applicable in criminal proceedings. And the right to government-paid counsel, the Supreme Court held, was one of the "safeguards" not required.

Turner sought certiorari. In light of differences among state courts (and some federal courts) on the applicability of a "right to counsel" in civil contempt proceedings enforcing child support orders, we granted the writ. . . .

We must decide whether the Due Process Clause grants an indigent defendant, such as Turner, a right to state-appointed counsel at a civil contempt proceeding, which may lead to his incarceration. This Court's precedents provide no definitive answer to that question. This Court has long held that the Sixth Amendment grants an indigent defendant the right to state-appointed counsel in a *criminal* case. And we have held that this same rule applies to *criminal contempt* proceedings (other than summary proceedings).

But the Sixth Amendment does not govern civil cases. Civil contempt differs from criminal contempt in that it seeks only to "coerc[e] the defendant to do" what a court had previously ordered him to do. A court may not impose punishment "in a civil contempt proceeding when it is clearly established that the alleged contemnor is unable to comply with the terms of the order." Hicks v. Feiock, 485 U.S. 624, 638, n.9 (1988). And once a civil contemnor complies with the underlying order, he is purged of the contempt and is free. *Id.*, at 633 (he "carr[ies] the keys of [his] prison in [his] own pockets" (internal quotation marks omitted)).

Consequently, the Court has made clear (in a case not involving the right to counsel) that, where civil contempt is at issue, the Fourteenth Amendment's Due Process Clause allows a State to provide fewer procedural protections than in a criminal case. *Id.*, at 637-641 (State may place the burden of proving inability to pay on the defendant). . . .

Civil contempt proceedings in child support cases constitute one part of a highly complex system designed to assure a noncustodial parent's regular payment of funds typically necessary for the support of his children. Often the family receives welfare support from a state-administered federal program, and the State then seeks reimbursement from the noncustodial parent. Other times the custodial parent (often the mother, but sometimes the father, a grandparent, or another person with custody) does not receive government benefits and is entitled to receive the support payments herself.

The Federal Government has created an elaborate procedural mechanism designed to help both the government and custodial parents to secure the payments to which they are entitled. These systems often rely upon wage withholding, expedited procedures for modifying and enforcing child support orders, and automated data processing. But sometimes States will use contempt orders to ensure that the custodial parent receives support payments or the government receives reimbursement. Although some experts have criticized this last-mentioned procedure, and the Federal Government believes that "the routine use of contempt for nonpayment of child support is likely to be an ineffective strategy," the Government also tells us that "coercive enforcement remedies, such as contempt, have a role to play." South Carolina, which relies heavily on contempt proceedings, agrees that they are an important tool.

We here consider an indigent's right to paid counsel at such a contempt proceeding. It is a civil proceeding. And we consequently determine the "specific dictates of due process" by examining the "distinct factors" that this Court has previously found useful in deciding what specific safeguards the Constitution's Due Process Clause requires in order to make a civil proceeding fundamentally fair. Mathews v. Eldridge, 424 U.S. 319, 335 (1976). As relevant here those factors include (1) the nature of "the private interest that will be affected," (2) the comparative "risk" of an "erroneous deprivation" of that interest with and without "additional or substitute procedural safeguards," and (3) the nature and magnitude of any countervailing interest in not providing "additional or substitute procedural requirement[s]."

The "private interest that will be affected" argues strongly for the right to counsel that Turner advocates. That interest consists of an indigent defendant's loss of personal liberty through imprisonment. The interest in securing that freedom, the freedom "from bodily restraint," lies "at the core of the liberty protected by the Due Process Clause." And we have made clear that its threatened loss through legal proceedings demands "due process protection."

Given the importance of the interest at stake, it is obviously important to assure accurate decisionmaking in respect to the key "ability to pay" question. Moreover, the fact that ability to comply marks a dividing line between civil and criminal contempt reinforces the need for accuracy. That is because an incorrect decision (wrongly classifying the contempt proceeding as civil) can increase the risk of wrongful incarceration by depriving the defendant of the procedural protections (including counsel) that the Constitution would demand in a criminal proceeding. And since 70% of child support arrears nationwide are owed by parents with either no reported income or income of $10,000 per year or less, the issue of ability to pay may arise fairly often.

On the other hand, the Due Process Clause does not always require the provision of counsel in civil proceedings where incarceration is threatened. And in determining whether the Clause requires a right to counsel here, we must take account of opposing interests, as well as consider the probable value of "additional or substitute procedural safeguards."

Doing so, we find three related considerations that, when taken together, argue strongly against the Due Process Clause requiring the State to provide indigents with counsel in every proceeding of the kind before us.

First, the critical question likely at issue in these cases concerns, as we have said, the defendant's ability to pay. That question is often closely related to the question of the defendant's indigence. But when the right procedures are in place, indigence can be a question that in many — but not all — cases is sufficiently straightforward to warrant determination *prior* to providing a defendant with counsel, even in a criminal case. Federal law, for example, requires a criminal defendant to provide information showing that he is indigent, and therefore entitled to state-funded counsel, *before* he can receive that assistance.

Second, sometimes, as here, the person opposing the defendant at the hearing is not the government represented by counsel but the custodial parent *un*represented by counsel. The custodial parent, perhaps a woman with custody of one or more children, may be relatively poor, unemployed, and unable to afford counsel. . . .

A requirement that the State provide counsel to the noncustodial parent in these cases could create an asymmetry of representation that would "alter significantly the nature of the proceeding." Doing so could mean a degree of formality or delay that would unduly slow payment to those immediately in need. And, perhaps more important for present purposes, doing so could make the proceedings *less* fair overall, increasing the risk of a decision that would erroneously deprive a family of the support it is entitled to receive. The needs of such families play an important role in our analysis.

Third, as the Solicitor General points out, there is available a set of "substitute procedural safeguards" which, if employed together, can significantly reduce the risk of an erroneous deprivation of liberty. They can do so, moreover, without incurring some of the drawbacks inherent in recognizing an automatic right to counsel. Those safeguards include (1) notice to the defendant that his "ability to pay" is a critical issue in the contempt proceeding; (2) the use of a form (or the equivalent) to elicit relevant financial information; (3) an opportunity at the hearing for the defendant to respond to statements and questions about his financial status, (*e.g.*, those triggered by his responses on the form); and (4) an express finding by the court that the defendant has the ability to pay. In presenting these alternatives, the Government draws upon considerable experience in helping to manage statutorily mandated federal-state efforts to enforce child support orders. It does not claim that they are the only possible alternatives, and this Court's cases suggest, for example, that sometimes assistance other than purely legal assistance (here, say, that of a neutral social worker) can prove constitutionally sufficient. But the Government does claim that these alternatives can assure the "fundamental fairness" of the proceeding even where the State does not pay for counsel for an indigent defendant.

While recognizing the strength of Turner's arguments, we ultimately believe that the three considerations we have just discussed must carry the day. In our view, a categorical right to counsel in proceedings of the kind before us would carry with it disadvantages (in the form of unfairness and delay) that, in terms of ultimate fairness, would deprive it of significant superiority over the alternatives that we have mentioned. We consequently hold that the Due Process Clause does not *automatically* require the provision of counsel at civil contempt proceedings to an indigent individual who is subject to a child support order, even if that individual faces incarceration (for up to a year). In particular, that Clause does not require the provision of counsel where the opposing parent or other custodian (to whom support funds are owed) is not represented by counsel and the State provides alternative procedural safeguards equivalent to those we have mentioned (adequate notice of the importance of ability to pay, fair opportunity to present, and to dispute, relevant information, and court findings).

We do not address civil contempt proceedings where the underlying child support payment is owed to the State, for example, for reimbursement of welfare funds paid to the parent with custody. Those proceedings more closely resemble debt-collection proceedings. The government is likely to have counsel or some other competent representative. And this kind of proceeding is not before us. Neither do we address what due process requires in an unusually complex case where a defendant "can fairly be represented only by a trained advocate."

The record indicates that Turner received neither counsel nor the benefit of alternative procedures like those we have described. He did not receive clear notice that his ability to pay would constitute the critical question in his civil contempt proceeding. No one provided him with a form (or the equivalent) designed to elicit information about his financial circumstances. The court did not find that Turner was able to pay his arrearage, but instead left the relevant "finding" section of the contempt order blank. The court nonetheless found Turner in contempt and ordered him incarcerated. Under these circumstances Turner's incarceration violated the Due Process Clause.

We vacate the judgment of the South Carolina Supreme Court and remand the case for further proceedings not inconsistent with this opinion.

[The dissenting opinion of Justice SCALIA, joined by Justice SCALIA and joined in part by The Chief JUSTICE and Justice ALITO, is omitted.]

NOTES AND QUESTIONS

1. Do the alternate procedural safeguards that *Turner* says states must provide to unrepresented obligors adequately protect against erroneous findings that obligors have the ability to pay the amount of support ordered?

In 2016 the Department of Health and Human Services issued final regulations requiring states to establish guidelines for the use of civil contempt to enforce child support obligations through the federal system. The guidelines must require that the state

    (i) Screen the case for information regarding the noncustodial parent's ability to pay or otherwise comply with the order;

    (ii) Provide the court with such information regarding the noncustodial parent's ability to pay, or otherwise comply with the order, which may assist the court in making a factual determination regarding the noncustodial parent's ability to pay the purge amount or comply with the purge conditions; and

    (iii) Provide clear notice to the noncustodial parent that his or her ability to pay constitutes the critical question in the civil contempt action.

45 C.F.R. §303.6(c) (2022). In Dept. of Rev. Child Supp. Enf. v. Grullon, 147 N.E.3d 1066 (Mass. 2020), the court held that a contempt defendant was denied due process when he was not provided with the *Turner* safeguards and the state guidelines, which complied with the federal rule, were not followed.

2. If an obligor moves to reduce a child support obligation because he or she lost a job and is unable to find work, we have seen that a court will very likely grant the motion. However, many people do not seek downward modifications of support orders as soon as they have grounds. Instead, they stop paying and wait. Until the mid-1980s, in some states a court could have retroactively decreased a child support obligation in recognition of these changes. Federal law now requires states to provide that overdue child support is a final judgment by operation of law, foreclosing retroactive modification. 42 U.S.C. §666(a)(9) (2022).

3. If a parent who becomes involuntarily unemployed does not seek an immediate modification but also quits paying court-ordered child support, can he or she successfully claim inability to pay in a contempt action? The answer is often no. "Inability to pay" for purposes of a contempt proceeding has a very strict meaning. The obligor must be truly unable to pay in the sense that he or she not only has no money but also has not been able to find work. When an obligor falls behind on support obligations because of loss of employment, courts today typically issue "seek work" orders, which, as their name suggests, require the obligor to look for work and to report on those efforts to the court.

Did Michael Turner appear to know that if he was "unable" to pay he would have a defense? If the trial judge had told him this, do you think he would have known how to prove his inability to pay?

4. As *Turner* says, due process does not require the petitioner in a civil contempt proceeding to prove that the defendant was able to pay, and many states put the burden of proof on the defendant. In a jurisdiction that treats ability to pay as an element of nonsupport that must be proven by the petitioner, what kind of evidence would be sufficient to establish that an obligor was able to pay? In State v. Nuzman, 95 P.3d 252 (Or. App. 2004), the mother testified that when the order was entered, the father was capable of working as a bartender. Over the next 17 years, however, she received small support payments from him on only two occasions, and she had no contact with him or even knowledge of his whereabouts. A clerk who worked for the attorney handling the case testified that the file did not contain any information indicating that the father had a criminal record or that he was receiving disability payments. The clerk also testified that in the usual course of business the office checks criminal records and disability rolls for the names of delinquent obligors every three months. From this, the attorney argued, it should be inferred that the father was not incarcerated or disabled during the time he had not paid support. Would this be enough evidence to prove beyond a reasonable doubt that the father had the ability to pay? Would it make any difference if the file contained 17 years' worth of printouts showing that the father was not incarcerated or receiving disability payments?

5. How important to the decision in *Turner* is the possibility that the petitioner in a civil contempt proceeding may also be unrepresented? Why isn't the solution to this imbalance to provide an attorney to both parties?

The *Turner* opinion suggests that a defendant in a civil contempt action brought by the state child support enforcement agency might be entitled to a court-appointed attorney. The few courts that have addressed the issue are divided. *Compare* State v. Currier, 295 P.3d 837 (Wyo. 2013); Miller v. Deal, 761 S.E.2d 274 (Ga. 2014) (both holding no right to counsel); *with* Crain v. Crain, 2012 WL 6737836 (Ohio App. 2012) (due process requires counsel).

Some anticipated that *Turner* might be the "civil *Gideon*," *i.e.*, the case holding that a person facing the threat of jail, whether the proceeding is civil or criminal, has a constitutional right to counsel. The unanimous opinion finding no such a right provoked mixed responses. Supporters of the Court's alternative solution doubted whether a constitutional right to a lawyer would provide much protection, considering the poor quality of representation provided to many criminal defendants who have overworked public defenders with caseloads much too large to allow them to do consistently thorough work. From this perspective, the Court's invitation to make contempt proceedings more accessible to lay people could be a much more successful means of providing access to justice. Commentary includes Stephanos Bibas, Shrinking *Gideon* and Expanding Alternatives to Lawyers, 70 Wash. & Lee L. Rev. 1287 (2013); Russell Engler, Turner v. Rogers and the Essential Role of the Courts in Delivering Access to Justice, 7 Harv. L. & Pol'y Rev. 31 (2013).

6. Defendants in child support contempt proceedings have argued that jailing them for nonpayment violates the Thirteenth Amendment ban on involuntary servitude, state constitutional rules against debtor's prison, or both, but these claims fail. For example, in Moss v. Superior Court, 950 P.2d 59 (Cal. 1998), the court said:

In its decisions applying the Thirteenth Amendment, the United States Supreme Court has recognized that many fundamental societal obligations involving compelled labor do not violate the proscription of involuntary servitude. It has never held that employment undertaken to comply with a judicially imposed requirement that a party seek and accept employment when necessary to meet a parent's fundamental obligation to support a child is involuntary servitude.

In those decisions in which a Thirteenth Amendment violation has been found on the basis of involuntary servitude, the court has equated the employment condition to peonage, under which a person is bound to the service of a particular employer or master until an obligation to that person is satisfied. A court order that a parent support a child, compliance with which may require that the parent seek and accept employment, does not bind the parent to any particular employer or form of employment or otherwise affect the freedom of the parent. The parent is free to elect the type of employment and the employer, subject only to an expectation that to the extent necessary to meet the familial support obligation, the employment will be commensurate with the education, training, and abilities of the parent. . . .

A parent's obligation to support a minor child is a social obligation that is no less important than compulsory military service, road building, jury service and other constitutionally permissible enforced labor. Even if the necessity of accepting employment in order to meet this obligation were somehow analogous to those forms of compelled labor, we have no doubt that this form of labor would be recognized as an exception to the ban on involuntary servitude found in the Thirteenth Amendment. . . .

Family support obligations are not ordinary debts subject to the constitutional prohibition of imprisonment for debt. It is held that the obligation to make such payments is not a "debt" within the meaning of the constitutional guaranty against imprisonment for debt.

. . . [A] parent who knows that support is due, has the ability to earn money to pay that support, and still willfully refuses to seek and accept available employment to enable the parent to meet the support obligation acts against fundamental societal norms and fair dealing, and necessarily intentionally does an act which prejudices the rights of his children. This conduct would fall within the fraud exception to the constitutional prohibition of imprisonment for debt.

950 P.2d at 66–76.

Is the court's argument convincing? Is a parent free to decline work that he does not enjoy? Could a parent who left a high-paying job for one that provided lower pay and more job satisfaction successfully claim inability to pay child support at a level based on the original job?

7. Since Elizabethan times, willful failure to support a dependent has been a crime, and many states have criminal nonsupport statutes on the books. *See, e.g.*, Model Penal Code §230.5. These statutes have fallen into disuse in many places, though they are being used more frequently as a result of current interest in child support enforcement. People v. Likine, 823 N.W.2d 50 (Mich. 2012), held that the Michigan criminal nonsupport statute imposes strict liability and that the traditional claim of inability to pay is not a defense. However, it also concluded that if it was truly impossible for the defendant to pay, he or she had not acted voluntarily and should be acquitted on the basis that the state had not proven the actus reus of the crime. The court explained, "[W]e hold that to establish an impossibility defense for felony nonsupport, a defendant must show that he or she acted in good faith and made *all reasonable efforts* to comply with the family court order, but could not do so through no fault of his or her own." 823 N.W.2d at 70.

8. Failure to pay child support may be a crime under the federal Child Support Recovery Act. The criminal provision, also known as the Deadbeat Parents Punishment Act, 18 U.S.C. §228 (2022), authorizes imprisonment for six months for willful failure to pay support for more than a year for a child who lives in another state; it authorizes up to two years' imprisonment for traveling in interstate commerce with intent to evade a support obligation or for willfully failing to pay support for more than two years for a child in another state. Ability to pay is an element of the crime, but it is rebuttably presumed from proof that a support obligation was in effect at the time of the failure to pay. 18 U.S.C. §228(b) (2022). If this presumption is construed as shifting the burden of persuasion on the issue of ability to pay to the defendant, it is unconstitutional. United States v. Grigsby, 85 F. Supp. 2d 100 (D.R.I. 2000). However, the presumption may be constitutional if it is construed so that the prosecution bears the burden of persuasion on this issue.

9. The people jailed for nonpayment of support are disproportionately African-American; in large U.S. cities 15 percent of African-American fathers are incarcerated at some point for failing to pay child support. Noah D. Zatz, A New Peonage?: Pay, Work, or Go to Jail in Contemporary Child Support Enforcement and Beyond, 39 Seattle U. L. Rev. 927 (2016); Noah D. Zatz et al., Get to Work or Go to Jail 8, n. 34 (2016). *See also* Tonya L. Brito, Fathers Behind Bars: Rethinking Child Support Policy Toward Low-Income Noncustodial Fathers and Their Families, 15 J. Gender Race & Just. 617 (2012).

10. Some courts have tried more unusual means of getting child support obligors to pay up. For example, a Wisconsin judge, in addition to a prison sentence, placed David Oakley on probation on condition that he not have any more children unless he could demonstrate that he was supporting his existing children and had the ability to support another child. Oakley had nine children and had repeatedly been convicted of nonsupport. Oakley sought postconviction relief, arguing that the condition unconstitutionally limited his right to procreate, citing Skinner v. Oklahoma, 316 U.S. 535 (1942), and Zablocki v. Redhail, 434 U.S. 374 (1978).

The divided Wisconsin Supreme Court affirmed in State v. Oakley, 629 N.W.2d 200 (Wis. 2001). The majority, emphasizing that Oakley was convicted of felony intentional refusal to support, scrutinized the probation condition for reasonableness. It found that the condition was not overly broad because it did not eliminate his right to procreate and that it was reasonably related to the goal of rehabilitation. The dissenting justices argued that the means chosen to achieve the state goals here were, as in *Zablocki*, not sufficiently closely tailored to the state goals. In State v. Chapman, 170 N.E.3d 6 (Ohio 2020), the trial court ordered a man who was convicted of criminal nonsupport to make all reasonable efforts to avoid impregnating a woman while he was on community control or until he could prove that he was current on all his child support obligations. The Ohio Supreme Court held that the order was unconstitutional because it was not rationally related to the goals of community control.

11. Sometimes an obligor who fails to pay support attempts to justify this action on the basis that he or she is not receiving access to the child as required by a court order because of the actions of the residential parent, the child or both. Ordinarily, access and child support are independent in the sense that a residential parent's failure to allow the other parent access does not excuse the nonresidential parent from paying child support.

Some courts distinguish visitation interference, which is not a defense to nonpayment of support, from active concealment of a child, which is. The leading case is Damico v. Damico, 872 P.2d 126 (Cal. 1994). The bases for the distinction are that a parent whose child is actively concealed cannot invoke other remedies to gain access and that if the payor does not know where the child is, he or she cannot make payments and the purpose of the order, to provide for the child, is defeated. In Comer v. Comer, 927 P.2d 265 (Cal. 1996), the California Supreme Court limited *Damico*, holding that even if a child has been "actively concealed," the parent deprived of visitation may be required to pay child support arrearages that accrued during the concealment if the concealment ends while the child is still a minor because the child can still benefit from payment of the arrearages.

12. Courts are divided about whether contempt proceedings can be used to enforce nonmodifiable property division orders. Some courts say that the constitutional prohibition of debtors' prison precludes this use of contempt. *E.g.*, Stone v. Stidham, 393 P.2d 923 (Ariz. 1964); Bradley v. Superior Court, 310 P.2d 634 (Cal. 1957); McAlear v. McAlear, 469 A.2d 1256 (Md. 1984). Other courts have found no constitutional impediment to the use of the contempt power to enforce property division orders. *E.g.*, Sickler v. Sickler, 878 N.W.2d 549 (Neb. 2016), holding that jailing a person who failed to comply with a property division order for contempt does not violate the state constitutional ban on imprisonment for debt, and discussing cases from other states.

NOTE: CIVIL OR CRIMINAL CONTEMPT?

A defendant facing a criminal contempt action for failure to pay child support is entitled to the constitutional protections generally afforded defendants in criminal proceedings, including the right to have the facts constituting the contempt proven by the prosecution beyond a reasonable doubt, the privilege against self-incrimination, and the right to jury trial. Hicks v. Feiock, 485 U.S. 624, 629 (1988); United Mine Workers of America v. Bagwell, 512 U.S. 821, 826-827 (1994).

In its first case dealing with the distinction between civil and criminal contempt, the U.S. Supreme Court observed, "It may not be always easy to classify a particular act as belonging to either of these two classes." Bessette v. W.B. Conkey Co., 194 U.S. 324, 329 (1904). The problem arises because neither the nature of the proceeding nor the kind of behavior leading to the sanction provides a basis for categorizing. An individual may be held in civil contempt for acts arising out of a criminal case. For example, a witness's refusal to testify may be treated as a civil contempt, even in a murder prosecution. An individual may also be held in criminal contempt for acts arising in a civil matter, as where a plaintiff or her lawyer curses the judge. Nor is the contemnor's behavior a clear indicator of the kind of contempt. Nonpayment of child support may be civil or criminal.

In Hicks v. Feiock, above, an appeal from a California decision holding a child support obligor in contempt for nonpayment, the Supreme Court discussed the test for distinguishing civil from criminal contempt:

> The question of how a court determines whether to classify the relief imposed in a given proceeding as civil or criminal in nature, for the purposes of applying the Due Process Clause and other provisions of the Constitution, is one of long standing, and its principles have been settled at least in their broad outlines for many decades. . . . [T]he labels affixed either to the proceeding or to the relief imposed under state law are not controlling and will not be allowed to defeat the applicable protections of federal constitutional law. This is particularly so in the codified laws of contempt, where the "civil" and "criminal" labels of the law have become increasingly blurred.
>
> Instead, the critical features are the substance of the proceeding and the character of the relief that the proceeding will afford. . . . The character of the relief imposed is thus ascertainable by applying a few straightforward rules. If the relief provided is a sentence of imprisonment, it is remedial if "the defendant stands committed unless and until he performs the affirmative act required by the court's order," and is punitive if "the sentence is limited to imprisonment for a definite period." If the relief provided is a fine, it is remedial when it is paid to the complainant, and punitive when it is paid to the court, though a fine that would be payable to the court is also remedial when the defendant can avoid paying the fine simply by performing the affirmative act required by the court's order. . . .
>
> In repeatedly stating and following the rules set out above, the Court has eschewed any alternative formulation that would make the classification of the relief imposed in a State's proceedings turn simply on what their underlying purposes are perceived to be. Although the purposes that lie behind particular kinds of relief are germane to understanding their character, this Court has never undertaken to psychoanalyze the subjective intent of a State's laws and its courts, not only because that effort would be unseemly and improper, but also because it would be misguided. In contempt cases, both civil and criminal relief have aspects that can be seen as either remedial or punitive or both: when a court imposes fines and punishments on a contemnor, it is not only vindicating its legal authority to enter the initial court order, but it also is seeking to give effect to the law's purpose of modifying the contemnor's behavior to conform to the terms required in the order. . . . For these reasons, this Court has judged that conclusions about the purposes for which relief is imposed are properly drawn from an examination of the character of the relief itself.

485 U.S. at 631-635.

PROBLEM

Oliver faithfully complied with an order requiring him to pay $500 per month to his former wife, Paula, for the support of their child, Carlo, until he lost his job as a skilled worker in a plywood mill when the mill closed. While he received unemployment compensation, Oliver looked for work and continued to pay child support. He could not find another mill job, however, and since his unemployment compensation ran out, Oliver has only worked sporadically at odd jobs. He stopped paying child support. Because Oliver was at home much of the time, Carlo, now four, began to spend most of his time at Oliver's house.

A month ago Paula, whose hours at work had just been cut, demanded that Oliver pay her the amounts he owes her for the last five months. She says that she cannot afford to maintain the house for herself and Carlo without this money, and she believes that Oliver could get steady work if he only tried harder. When Oliver refused, Paula angrily told him he could not see Carlo anymore unless he paid up. Oliver has not seen Carlo since, even though the divorce degree provides that he is entitled to visit for eight hours every Saturday.

Two weeks ago Oliver was served with a motion to show cause why he should not be held in (civil) contempt for failing to comply with the child support order. What defenses should his attorney assert on his behalf? How should Paula's attorney respond?

3. The State-Federal Child Support Enforcement Program

Support orders enforced by levying on an obligor's property or by using contempt powers suffer from limitations in addition to the legal ones that we have been examining. As a practical matter, obligees ordinarily need attorneys to draft the appropriate documents and shepherd cases through court. And both kinds of devices are available only to enforce past-due support; neither operates prospectively.

Responding to mounting evidence of problems in child support enforcement, in 1975 Congress enacted Title IV-D of the Social Security Act, which created the federal Office of Child Support Enforcement. The legislation requires each state to establish a child support enforcement agency, also called a IV-D agency. Additional requirements have been imposed since then. Major provisions are codified at 42 U.S.C. §§651-662, 666 (2022). A state that does not comply with these requirements loses substantial federal funding for its welfare program. In addition, the federal government pays a percentage of the costs of the states' enforcement programs and provides other financial incentives, which are based in part on the amount of support money collected.

The state IV-D agency must provide certain services, including establishment of support duties, establishment of paternity, and location of absent parents. States cannot charge custodial parents receiving welfare benefits for these services, although they may charge parents who are not receiving welfare a modest application fee. In most states the agency attorney who provides these services does not represent the residential parent; instead, like criminal prosecutors, they are said to represent the state. IV-D agencies play a role in 50 to 60 percent of all child support cases in the country. Stacy Brustin & Lisa Martin, Bridging the Justice Gap in Family Law: Repurposing Federal IV-D Funding to Expand Community-Based Legal and Social Services for Parents, 67 Hastings L.J. 1265, 1269 (2016). For a discussion of the complex practical and ethical issues that this role presents for attorneys, *see* Barbara Glesner Fines, From Representing "Clients" to Serving "Recipients": Transforming the Role of the IV-D Child Support Enforcement Attorney, 67 Fordham L. Rev. 2155 (1999).

EXPEDITED PROCESSES To expedite the collection of child support, states must have an administrative or quasi-judicial process for obtaining and enforcing support orders in IV-D cases. Some states also handle non-IV-D cases through their administrative processes. Most states that use an administrative process give their courts concurrent original jurisdiction in support cases and provide for appellate judicial review of administrative orders. Federal regulations require that states provide obligors with due process safeguards. Administrative orders must have the same force and effect as court orders, each party must receive a copy of the order, and the state must have written procedures for ensuring that the presiding officers are qualified. 45 C.F.R. §303.101(c) (2022).

ENFORCEMENT BY WAGE WITHHOLDING Perhaps the most important enforcement devices are those that allow wage withholding. States must require wage withholding in all child support cases unless a court or administrative agency hearing officer finds good cause, put in writing, not to implement withholding immediately, or the parties agree not to implement withholding immediately. A delinquency equal to one month's amount of support that occurs after an exception takes effect results in mandatory income withholding, regardless of the good cause finding or parties' agreement.

Where income withholding is triggered by an alleged arrearage, the obligor is entitled to prior notice and a hearing. The exact procedures for giving notice and allowing contests vary from state to state. The Federal Consumer Credit Protection Act, 15 U.S.C. §§1671-1677 (2022), limits how much of a person's wages may be withheld. The basic limit is 50 percent of disposable earnings for a noncustodial parent who is not supporting a second family. This amount is much higher than the amount of an obligor's wages that can be withheld to enforce other debts.

OTHER ENFORCEMENT DEVICES States must provide a number of other ways to enforce child support, including judicial authority to impose liens against real and personal property for amounts of overdue support; judicial authority to require obligors to post a bond or give some other guarantee to secure payment of overdue support; allowing failure to pay child support to be reported to consumer credit bureaus; withholding state tax refunds payable to a parent of a child receiving child support services, if the parent is delinquent in making payments; and suspending the driver's licenses and professional, occupational, and recreational licenses of delinquent obligors. In addition, the IRS must withhold federal tax refunds due to delinquent child support obligors, and parents who owe child support may be denied federal loans.

EFFORTS TO LOCATE PARENTS Federal legislation requires the establishment of a national directory of new hires, which contains employment information about everyone hired in the United States, and of similar state directories. The legislation also requires creation of national and state registries of child support orders. These databases will be linked so that orders can be matched with obligors quickly. States must also have automated, centralized systems for recording the payment and dispersal of child support.

4. The Continuing Challenge of Childhood Poverty

Timothy Grall

Custodial Mothers and Fathers and Their Child Support: 2017
Current Population Reports P60-269 (U.S. Census Bureau May 2020)

The poverty rate in 2017 of all custodial-parent families with children under 21 years of age was 24.1 percent, 10.5 percentage points higher than the poverty rate of all families with children under 21 years old (13.6 percent). Approximately 6.6 million (30.1 percent) of all children in custodial-parent families lived in poverty in 2017.

Poverty rates vary greatly among types of custodial-parent families. The poverty rate of custodial-mother families in 2017 (27.3 percent) was statistically higher than the poverty rate for custodial-father families (11.2 percent). . . .

For the 1.2 million custodial parents below poverty who were supposed to receive child support in 2017, 40.0 percent received full payments, 28.7 percent received partial payments, and 31.2 percent received none—proportions that were not statistically different from each other. . . .

Among the 5.4 million custodial parents who were supposed to receive child support in 2017, 1.2 million or 22.2 percent had family incomes below the poverty threshold. If all of these custodial parents had received the full amount of child support they were supposed to receive, 1.1 million custodial parents would be in poverty (not statistically different from the current 1.2 million), and their poverty rate would be 20.1 percent (not statistically different from the current 22.2 percent). . . .

In 2017, 69.8 percent of custodial parents who were supposed to receive child support received either full or partial payments. This was a decrease from 1993, when 75.8 percent of custodial parents who were supposed to receive support received at least some payment. The proportion of custodial parents who were to receive child support, but received none, increased from 24.2 percent in 1993 to 30.2 percent in 2017. . . .

A comparative study of the child support enforcement systems of the United States and Australia found that though the two countries use quite different systems, neither was very successful at improving child support compliance between 1995 and 2015. J. Thomas Oldham & Bruce M. Smyth, Child Support Compliance in the USA and Australia: To Persuade or Punish? 52 Fam. L. Q. 325, 330 (2018); *see also* Margaret F. Brinig & Marsha Garrison, Getting Blood from Stones: Results and Policy Implications of an Empirical Investigation of Child Support Practice in St. Joseph County, Indiana Paternity Actions, 56 Fam. Ct. Rev. 521 (2018). Moreover, the amount of child support in arrears in the United States grew from more than $60 billion in 2002 to $117 billion in February 2020. Office of Child Support Enforcement, The Story Behind the Numbers: Major Change in Who Is Owed Child Support Arrears 1 (Mar. 13, 2014); Elaine Sorensen, Certified Child Support Arrears Shows Sharp Decline (OCSE May 11, 2021). About 88 percent of the arrears in 2021 was submitted to the Office of Child Support Enforcement more than five years ago, and nearly 30 percent was submitted more than 20 years ago. Elaine Sorensen, Most Arrears Were Submitted to OCSE More Than Five Years Ago (OCSE Sept. 2, 2021). "Most arrears are owed by parents who owe substantial amounts of arrears, have little or no income, and have owed arrears for some time. These characteristics make it difficult to collect arrears." Story Behind the Numbers, *supra.*

Leslie Joan Harris

Questioning Child Support Enforcement Policy for Poor Families
45 Fam. L.Q. 157, 164-165 (2011)

. . . A very significant reason that very poor mothers and their children receive so much less formal child support is, of course, that often the children's fathers themselves are also very poor. . . . This does not mean, however, that very poor fathers generally are not contributing to the household economies of their children's mothers. . . .

According to the Census Bureau, more than 57% of custodial parents received noncash support from noncustodial parents, compared to 40% who received cash payments. Data from the *Fragile Families* study[2] shows that poor, unmarried mothers are especially likely to benefit from informal and in-kind support. The study also found that efforts to establish and collect formal child support tends to result in these voluntary informal forms of support being shut off. . . .

---

2. The Fragile Families and Child Wellbeing Study is a longitudinal study of about 5000 children born in urban areas with a population over 200,000 and their families. For more information, *see* Sara McLanahan et al., The Fragile Families and Child Wellbeing Study: Baseline National Report (2003) http://www.fragilefamilies.princeton. edu/documents/nationalreport.pdf. — Eds.

The researchers also found that almost all custodial mothers received only formal support or only informal support. Only 6% received both. Mothers without child support orders were much more likely than those with them to receive in-kind and informal support, and they received a much higher amount of informal support. . . .

The *Fragile Families* study concluded that when formal child support enforcement efforts were undertaken on behalf of mothers receiving informal and in-kind support, the voluntary contributions tended to stop and were not replaced by equal amounts of formal support. Other researchers have also found that strong efforts to establish and enforce formal child-support obligations result in informal support drying up, leaving the mothers and children who had been receiving informal support worse off. A Department of Health and Human Services report about paternity establishment, published in 2000, found that many mothers receiving public assistance are unable or unwilling to assist with paternity establishment. This is because they want to protect fathers from collection or believe that their identifying the father will result in their loss of informal support, leaving them worse off if the state cannot collect anything. Researchers Esther Wattenberg and Kathryn Edin reached similar conclusions. . . .

Between February and October 2020, the amount of child support arrears fell by $4 billion, an unprecedented drop in such a short time. "This significant drop in arrears was driven in large part by the Economic Impact Payments of $1,200 per adult and $500 per child issued to most Americans as part of the 2020 CARES Act. The CARES Act did not exempt these payments from the Treasury Offset Program, and thus they were handled the same as a tax refund offset. Noncustodial parents who were eligible for a tax refund offset had their payments intercepted. While other factors may have also played a role in the decline of child support arrears in 2020, the offsets from Economic Impact Payments were probably the largest contributing factor." Child Support Arrears Shows Sharp Decline, *supra*.

The impact of the pandemic benefits was greater than even these figures suggest. The Census Bureau estimated that the federal aid reduced the poverty rate in 2021 to 7.8 percent, the lowest rate on record, down 9.2 percent from the previous rate. The number of poor children shrank 4.5 percent, down to 4.2 percent, also a record low. These rates were calculated using the Supplemental Poverty Measure, which includes wages, taxes, and all government aid. The expanded child tax credit, which temporarily provided a guaranteed income to families with children, contributed the most to changes. In comparison, the official poverty rate, which does not take into account much federal assistance, did not change significantly from 2020. The pandemic payments were temporary and have largely expired, and families are again facing economic distress. Lydia DePillis & Jason DeParle, Pandemic Aid Cut U.S. Poverty to New Low in 2021, Census Bureau Reports (N.Y. Times Sept. 13, 2022).

C. TAXES

The relationship of federal tax policy to family groups, however defined, has posed fundamental questions for both tax policy and family law. The most basic is whether the appropriate unit for imposing taxes is the individual or the family. The other is whether state variations in family law should affect federal tax liability.

The extent to which the tax code treats taxpayers differently, depending on their marital and parental status, has varied. Originally, the income tax code implicitly assumed that the individual was the tax-paying unit, and married and unmarried people were taxed at the same rates. However, until recently the trend was to treat people differently based on their marital status. For purposes of tax issues state law controls whether people are married.

Partly in response to the controversy during the 2000s over the legal treatment of same-sex relationships, a number of legal scholars challenged the policy that family membership should affect a person's federal tax liability, arguing that the individual should be the unit for taxation regardless of his or her family status. Stephanie Hunter McMahon, To Have and to Hold: What Does Love (of Money) Have to Do with Joint Tax Filing?, 11 Nev. L.J. 718 (2011), discusses these arguments but cautions that in the past when individuals were the unit of taxation, wealthy people developed many strategies to avoid taxes. The policy issue is not simply whether marriage should be the basis for different tax treatment. Professor Anne Alstott argues that tax law should continue to make distinctions based on familial relationships but that marriage should no longer be used as the basis for determining when people are members of a family for three reasons: the decline of marriage generally and the rise of cohabitation, increasing variety in the nature of economic arrangements within marriage, and increasing class-based variations in who marries. Anne L. Alstott, Updating the Welfare State: Marriage, the Income Tax, and Social Security in the Age of Individualism, 66 Tax L. Rev. 695 (2013). On the current tax treatment of unmarried cohabitants, *see* Pat Cain, Taxation of Unmarried Partners, 99 Wash. U. L. Rev. 1931 (2022).

In 2017 Congress amended the Internal Revenue Code to shift the tax rules back toward treating people as individuals regardless of their marital status for purposes of the income tax, as the next section describes.

1. Taxation of the Ongoing Family

Because tax rates are progressive — that is, the rates increase as income goes up — a system that is marriage neutral, *i.e.*, one that treats the individual as the taxing unit, is likely to extract a different amount of tax from a family with two income earners than a family earning the same amount with one income earner. To illustrate, imagine two families, the Joneses and the Smiths. Mr. Jones is employed in the marketplace, earning $60,000 per year, and Mrs. Jones is a homemaker. Both Mr. and Mrs. Smith work in the marketplace, each earning $30,000 per year. Further, assume that the income tax rate is 10 percent on the first $20,000 of income, 15 percent on income between $20,000 and $50,000, and 33 percent on income over $50,000. The tax owed by the Joneses (ignoring exemptions, deductions, and the like) is 10 percent of $20,000 ($2000), 15 percent of $30,000 ($4500), and 33 percent of $10,000 ($3300), for a total of $9800. The Smiths owe 10 percent of $20,000 ($2000) each, plus 15 percent of $10,000 ($1500) each, for a total of $7000.

In comparison, a system that taxes couples equally results in couples with equal amounts of household income paying the same taxes. This outcome can be achieved by taxing the combined incomes of a couple at the same rate that would be imposed on a single taxpayer. In such a system, the Joneses' tax would be the same as above, that is, $9800. The Smiths will also pay $9800 because their combined incomes of $60,000 is taxed at the single individual rate. The Smiths would pay a "marriage penalty" of $2800. To avoid the marriage penalty, married couples could still be taxed on their combined incomes, but their tax brackets would be twice as wide as the bracket for individual taxpayers. In this system the Joneses, who have taxable income of $60,000, would pay 10 percent on the first $40,000 ($4000) and 15 percent on the next $20,000 ($3000), for a total of $7000. The Smiths, who also have a combined taxable income of $60,000 would pay the same. The marriage penalty on the Smiths is eliminated, but the Joneses have a marriage bonus of $2800.

As noted above, the federal income tax was originally marriage neutral. Applying this system in Poe v. Seaborn, 282 U.S. 101 (1930), the Supreme Court held that a married couple of one wage-earner and one homemaker who lived in a community property state and who each owned half the wage-earner's income under state law would be taxed as two individuals, each at the lower tax rate applicable to half the income. As word of the tax advantages of living in community property states got out, six common law property jurisdictions enacted community property legislation between 1939 and 1949. Carolyn C. Jones, Split Income and Separate Spheres: Tax Law and Gender Roles in the 1940s, 6 Law & Hist. Rev. 259, 266-274 (1988); Stephanie Hunter McMahon, To Save State Residents: States' Use of Community Property for Federal Tax Reduction, 1939-1947, 27 Law & Hist. Rev. 585 (2009).[3] Congress eliminated the advantage enjoyed by residents of community property states in 1948 by amending the Internal Revenue Code to provide for joint returns and thus for income splitting between married couples, regardless of the underlying marital property regimes.[4] Married and single people were taxed at the same rates, resulting in marriage penalties for two-earner couples.

In 2017 Congress amended the Internal Revenue Code to eliminate the marriage penalty for all couples earning up to $600,000 by making the tax rate brackets for joint returns twice as wide as the rate brackets for single taxpayers. This change also increased the opportunities for single-earner couples to enjoy marriage bonuses. For details on the history of the income tax and family status as well as the 2017 reforms *see* Mark W. Cochran, Back to the Future: Marriage and Divorce Under the 2017 Tax Act, 51 St. Mary's L.J. 1 (2019).

Besides the joint return rules, other tax rules create marriage penalties and bonuses, particularly the earned income tax credit. If two parents receiving earned income tax credit payments marry, their joint income may disqualify them from the credit or reduce it. Further, combining households may reduce the credit. Marriage might also increase the credit, as when one parent with a low income and children marries someone who has no children and a higher income. Employer-provided health insurance for family members of their employees is not taxable income if the recipients are the spouses or legal children of the employees. Since the last quarter of the twentieth century, a number of employers have also provided such benefits to the domestic partners of employees and to those partners' children. These benefits are typically taxable income to the employees.

2. Taxation of the Family After Divorce

Until the 2017 amendments to the Internal Revenue Code, lawyers for families earning enough income to make tax planning important could structure post-divorce financial obligations to reduce the amount of taxes that the former spouses collectively paid. Two basic principles of tax law were at the heart of divorce tax planning: (1) As previously discussed, the income tax is progressive, so that people with higher incomes pay tax at a higher rate; (2) property division and child support payments had no income tax consequences, but spousal support was a deduction for the payor and income for the recipient. Taken together, these principles generally made it more desirable, from the perspective of income taxes, for payments to be treated as alimony if the payor's income was significantly higher than the recipient's. In return for taking on the tax burden that spousal support imposed, the recipient could be given a greater absolute number of support dollars.

The 2017 legislation eliminated this tax planning strategy by providing that all transfers between ex-spouses imposed after the legislation took effect—property division, alimony, and child support—have no income tax consequences. For more information *see* Nancy Chausow Shafer, Changing Tax Laws and Support: Keeping Up as the Ground Shifts, 33 J. Am. Acad.

---

3. The states were Michigan, Nebraska, Oklahoma, Oregon, Pennsylvania, and the territory of Hawaii. Colorado, Illinois, Kansas, Massachusetts, New Jersey, New York, South Dakota, and Wyoming considered but did not enact such legislation. Jones, 6 Law & Hist. Rev. at 268-269.

4. The same legislation also introduced the marital deduction and splitting of estates and gifts for purposes of the federal estate and gift tax. These changes introduced treatment of married people as an economic unit into the tax code. Today, this process has been completed; under IRC §§2056 and 2523, spouses can now transfer unlimited amounts of property to each other without federal gift or estate tax consequences.

Matrimonial Lawy. 159 (2020); Anne Bryson Bauer, We Can Do It? How the Tax Cuts and Jobs Act Perpetuates Implicit Gender Bias in the Code, 43 Harv. J. L. & Gender 1, 8-26 (2020).

a. Property Division—IRC §1041

IRC §1041 provides that, just as spouses may transfer unlimited amounts of property to each other during marriage and at death without estate or gift tax consequences, their property may also be divided at divorce without income tax consequences.

More specifically, IRC §1041 eliminates income tax consequences for property transfers "incident to divorce." A transfer falls in this category if it occurs within one year of the termination of the marriage, or within six years of termination of the marriage if made pursuant to a divorce decree or separation agreement. Other transfers are presumed not to be incident to divorce, but the taxpayer can rebut the presumption.

Section 1041 also provides for no income tax consequences if one spouse transfers property to a third party for the benefit of a former spouse if (1) the transfer is required by the decree or separation agreement, (2) the transfer is made pursuant to a written request from the former spouse, or (3) the transferor receives written consent or ratification from the former spouse.

Property transfers between former spouses incident to divorce are also free from gift tax under IRC §2516.

Property transfers between unmarried couples are not covered by IRC §1041, though they may in some circumstances be gifts not subject to the income tax, though they would be taxable under the federal estate and gift tax law.

TRANSFERS OF PENSIONS AND RELATED ASSETS As you recall from earlier chapters, if an employee's pension rights are covered by the Employee Retirement Income Security Act (ERISA), some or all of those rights can be transferred to a former spouse by a Qualified Domestic Relations Order (QDRO). An alternate payee under a QDRO is treated as the recipient of benefits under the plan for tax purposes. This means that the alternate payee pays any income taxes owing on benefits as they are paid. The payments have no tax consequences for the employee; they are not income, and they are not deductible. IRC §402. The code also permits transfers of Individual Retirement Accounts (IRAs) between former spouses under a divorce decree or written separation agreement without tax consequences. IRC §408(d)(6). When such a transfer is made, the IRA becomes the IRA of the transferee.

b. Spousal Support—Former IRC §§71 and 215

While alimony payments no longer have tax consequences, alimony obligations created before the 2017 IRC amendments went into effect continue to be deductible to the payor and includable as income to the recipient. The character of payments under state law does not determine whether they are alimony for purposes of the income tax. Instead, payments must satisfy the objective test that was set out in IRC §§71 and 215 to receive tax treatment as alimony. The requirements of the test are:

   (1) Payments must be in cash or cash equivalent to or for the benefit of a former spouse.
   (2) Payments must be required by a
        a. written separation agreement, or
        b. divorce or separate maintenance decree, or
        c. other support decree such as an order of temporary support.
   (3) If the payments are made after a final decree of divorce or legal separation, the payor and payee cannot live in the same household. The parties have a one-month grace period to establish separate households.

(4) Payments must end at the payee's death, and the payor cannot be required to make substitute payments to the payee's estate or third parties after the payee's death.

(5) The payments may not be treated as child support.

Lump sum as well as periodic payments may be treated as alimony.

If the size of payments treated as alimony declines precipitously in the first three years, the payor will owe income taxes under the "recapture rule." The recapture rule discourages front-end loading of payments. If recapture is required, the party who paid alimony must declare the recaptured amount as income and pay taxes on it. The recipient is entitled to a corresponding deduction.[5]

Even if payments are originally set up so that no amounts will be recaptured, the calculations are based on actual payments, not obligations. Thus, if a payor falls into arrears in the first or second year and then catches up in the third year, a recapture may be created that would reverse the intended tax consequences of the payments. The risk of recapture also makes modification of payments tricky within the first three years.

In some circumstances amounts will not be recaptured, even though the calculation discussed here apparently calls for recapture:

(1) If the payments cease within the three years because of the death of either party or the remarriage of the payee.

(2) If payments are made under temporary support orders.

(3) If the payments are to be made for at least three years and the amount is a fixed portion of the income from a business or property or from employment rather than a fixed dollar amount.

See generally Stephen P. Comeau, An Overview of the Federal Income Tax Provisions Related to Alimony Payments, 38 Fam. L.Q. 111 (2004).

c. *Child Support, Child Tax Credits, Child Care Credits, Earned Income Credits, and Children's Medical Expenses*

Child support payments are tax-free to the payee and not deductible to the payor.

The parent who has custody may claim the child tax credit of $2000 per child. IRC §§151, 152, 24. To qualify, the child must be younger than 17, the parent must have paid more than half the child's support, and the child must have lived with the parent more than half the time during the year. If the child spends an equal amount of time with both parents, the parent with the higher adjusted gross income receives the exemption. The majority of courts have held that a domestic relations court may order that the custodial parent assign the dependency exemption

---

5. A recapture calculation must be done only once, in the third year after payments begin. The recapture formula requires comparison of the total amount paid during the second year to the total paid in the third year and then comparison of the amount paid in the first year to the amounts paid in the second and third years in the following way:

    (I) Subtract [the amount paid in Year 3 plus $15,000] from the amount paid in Year 2 to get R1.

    (II) Average [the amount paid in Year 2 plus the amount paid in Year 3 minus R1]. Add $15,000 to this amount, and subtract all from the amount paid in Year 1. This is R2.

    (III) Total R1 and R2 to get the amount to be recaptured, if any.

For example, say that *A* pays *B* alimony of $30,000 in Year 1, $30,000 in Year 2, and $5000 in Year 3. The amount of recapture is calculated this way:

    (I) 30,000 − (5000 + 15,000) = 10,000 = R1.

    (II) 30,000 − [(30,000 + 5000 − 10,000)/2 + 15,000] = 30,000 − [12,500 + 15,000] = 2500 = R2.

    (III) $10,000 + $2500 = Amount to be recaptured in Year 3.

If either R1 or R2 is negative, it is treated as 0 for purposes of the rest of the calculations, so one negative number does not fully or partially cancel a positive number.

to the other parent. Leseberg v. Taylor, 78 P.3d 201 (Wyo. 2003). However, a court order is not effective to shift the exemption to the noncustodial parent; only a written document signed by the custodial parent is. The child credit is partially refundable for low-income families.

The custodial parent alone is entitled to claim two other kinds of credits, both of which are phased out for higher-income taxpayers: the child care credit and the earned income credit. Neither of these credits can be assigned to the other parent, and if the parents have joint custody, the parent with physical custody for a longer time gets the credits. The child care credit reduces taxes for parents with earned income who must pay for child care to enable themselves to work. IRC §21. Low-income custodial parents are also entitled to the earned income credit if they have earned income.

Allocation of one tax benefit associated with children — the deduction for medical expenses — depends only upon who pays. Regardless of who has custody, whichever parent pays a child's medical expenses may deduct them. IRC §213(d)(5).

D. BANKRUPTCY

When Senator Elizabeth Warren was a professor at Harvard Law School, she and her colleagues conducted an empirical study of families who filed for bankruptcy. "Our study showed that married couples with children are more than twice as likely to file for bankruptcy as their childless counterparts. A divorced woman raising a youngster is nearly three times more likely to file for bankruptcy than her single friend who has no children." Elizabeth Warren, The Growing Threat to Middle Class Families, 69 Brook. L. Rev. 401, 402 (2004); *see also* Elizabeth Warren, The New Economics of the American Family, 12 Am. Bankr. Inst. L. Rev. 1 (2004).

> Personal bankruptcy often follows a serious economic reversal. About two-thirds of all bankruptcies occur after one or both adults in a household have had a serious interruption in income, such as a layoff, cutback in hours, downsizing, outsourcing, or some other euphemism that means income has been cut sharply. Nearly half of all families file for bankruptcy in the aftermath of a serious medical problem. Divorce has hit more than one in five families in bankruptcy. In the 2001 sample, nearly nine out of ten filers listed at least one of these three reasons in explaining their bankruptcy petitions.

Elizabeth Warren, Bankrupt Children, 86 Minn. L. Rev. 1003, 1022 (2002). The financial strains that lead to bankruptcy may undermine the marriage too, or the costs of divorce may force either or both former spouses into bankruptcy shortly after the divorce is final.

The fundamental purpose of bankruptcy law is to give debtors a fresh start by freeing them from pre-bankruptcy debts while equitably dividing their assets among creditors. Individuals may undergo either of two kinds of bankruptcy proceedings. In a Chapter 7 proceeding, the debtor's nonexempt assets are liquidated under the supervision of a trustee to pay off creditors to the extent possible. People with a regular income may instead go through Chapter 13 proceedings, which allow the debtor to remain in control of his or her assets and to set up a reorganization plan to pay off some or all of the debts over three or five years. In other words, a Chapter 13 proceeding allows the debtor to rehabilitate him- or herself and repay at least some debts.

For purposes of a Chapter 7 proceeding, spousal and child support and property division obligations are all nondischargeable in bankruptcy. 11 U.S.C. §523(a)(15), (c). However, for actions brought under Chapter 13, only "domestic support obligations" (DSOs) — that is, orders for spousal or child support, obligations in lieu of a support order, and obligations assigned to the government, as in welfare recovery cases — are not dischargeable. 11 U.S.C. §§101(14A), 523(a)(5), (c). Property division orders are dischargeable. 11 U.S.C. §1328(a)(2). "If the debtor manages to propose and complete a Chapter 13 plan, the debtor could successfully discharge a divorce-related, non-domestic support obligation. This, indeed, remains the debtor's only pawn to play to renegotiate the terms of a divorce decree or separation agreement in a bankruptcy case. The ability of the debtor to discharge the non-DSO in Chapter 13 is the reason why clearly differentiating between support and non-support obligations in a divorce decree or separation agreement is still necessary." Shayna M. Steinfeld, The Impact of Changes Under the Bankruptcy Abuse Prevention and Consumer Protection Act of 2005 on Family Obligations, 20 J. Am. Acad. Matrimonial Law. 251, 278 (2007). *See also* Jennifer L. Bjurling, Vermont Content: Bringing a Lamb to Slaughter: How Family Law Attorneys Unknowingly Lead Clients to Financial Disaster in the Negotiation of a Divorce Stipulation, 40 Vt. L. Rev. 939 (2016) (emphasizing protecting against the risk of property division discharges in Chapter 13 proceedings).

In re Chamberlain
721 Fed.Appx. 826 (10th Cir. 2018)

Robert E. Bacharach, Circuit Judge. . . . Stephen and Judith Chamberlain were divorced in 2009 after a 21-year marriage. During their marriage, Stephen worked for Southwest Airlines and his wife stayed home to care for their three children, Sarah, Kate, and John.

The divorce decree incorporated a marital settlement agreement signed by Stephen and Judith. This agreement included a "College Education" provision, which stated that following exhaustion of their college savings accounts, "Husband shall pay the costs of tuition, room and board, books, registration fees, and reasonable application fees incident to providing each Child with an undergraduate college education for four consecutive years of college."

Stephen did not meet his obligations under the college education provision, which led Judith to file a motion in Maryland state court to enforce the marital settlement agreement. This motion was resolved in 2011 through a consent order. In the order, Stephen reaffirmed his obligation to pay his children's college expenses under the marital settlement agreement, including repayment of student loans to the two oldest children.

Stephen later failed to pay John's college expenses, and Judith filed another action in state court to enforce the marital settlement agreement and the 2011 consent order. This action was resolved by a second consent order. There Stephen agreed to contribute up to $14,000 per academic year toward John's college expenses. After Stephen again failed to comply, the state court found him in contempt and awarded judgment to Judith for $14,000 (Stephen's share of the first year of John's college tuition) and the attorney fees incurred by Judith to enforce the marital settlement agreement. When Judith initiated collection efforts, Stephen filed bankruptcy.

Judith filed a proof of claim, which included

- the amounts still owed on Sarah and Kate's undergraduate student loans and
- the amount that Stephen had agreed to pay toward John's college expenses.

According to Judith, these amounts constituted "domestic support obligations" under 11 U.S.C. § 101(14A), creating priority claims that must be fully repaid. Stephen objected, arguing that his obligation to pay the children's college expenses did not constitute a domestic support obligation . . .

After an evidentiary hearing, the bankruptcy court

- sustained Stephen's objection to $8,632.85 of the amount claimed by Judith and
- found that $108,085.08 of the debt constituted a domestic support obligation and created a priority claim.

Stephen appealed in district court, which affirmed. He now appeals to our court. . . .

The primary question is whether Stephen's obligation to pay his children's college expenses qualifies as a "domestic support obligation." The bankruptcy court answered "yes," and we uphold this determination.

The requirements of a domestic support obligation. A debt constitutes a "domestic support obligation" if it meets four requirements:

1. It is "owed to or recoverable by . . . a spouse, former spouse, or child of the debtor or such child's parent, legal guardian, or responsible relative" or a governmental unit.
2. It is "in the nature of alimony, maintenance, or support . . . of such spouse, former spouse, or child of the debtor or such child's parent, without regard to whether such debt is expressly so designated."
3. It arises from "a separation agreement, divorce decree, or property settlement agreement," "an order of a court of record," or a lawful determination by a governmental unit.
4. It has not been assigned to a nongovernmental entity unless for collection purposes.

11 U.S.C. § 101(14A). As the party challenging discharge, Judith bore the burden of proving that the debt entailed a domestic support obligation.

The arguments in bankruptcy court and the court's finding. In bankruptcy court, Stephen argued that his obligation to pay his children's college expenses did not constitute a domestic support obligation because it was not "in the nature of alimony, maintenance, or support" (the second requirement). . . . We conclude that the bankruptcy court did not commit clear error. The court properly conducted a dual inquiry to determine whether these obligations involved support, "looking first to the intent of the parties at the time they entered into their agreement, and then to the substance of the obligation."

Intent of the parties when entering into the agreement. With respect to the initial issue of intent, the court appropriately considered

- the language and structure of the college expense obligation in the marital settlement agreement and
- the parties' testimony regarding surrounding circumstances, including the disparity in Stephen and Judith's financial circumstances at the time of the divorce.

The bankruptcy court found that the parties had intended Stephen's college expense obligation to constitute support because

- this obligation was located in the part of the marital settlement agreement that addressed child support, alimony, and related matters,
- the evidence established that Stephen and Judith had viewed a college education as an important part of their children's upbringing,
- the couple had long intended to provide for the children's education, and
- this intent could not be carried out at the time of the divorce, given the couple's relative financial capabilities, without Stephen assuming this obligation.

These considerations support the bankruptcy court's finding that the parties had intended Stephen's college expense obligation to constitute support.

Stephen disputes the bankruptcy court's conclusions, relying on his testimony and consent to a modification of the marital settlement agreement. This reliance is misguided.

The bankruptcy court considered Stephen's testimony but "[did not] give [it] much credence" in light of the other evidence of the parties' intent at the time of the divorce. This assessment of credibility fell within the bankruptcy court's purview because the intent determination "does not turn on one party's post hoc explanation as to his or her state of mind at the time of the agreement, even if uncontradicted."

Stephen also argues that his obligation originated in the 2011 and 2014 consent orders rather than the marital settlement agreement. For this argument, Stephen points out that he consented to a modification of terms between entry into the marital settlement agreement and the consent orders. For example, in the consent orders, he agreed to pay Sarah and Kate's college loans and then cap his obligation to pay John's college expenses at $14,000 per year. As a result, Stephen argues, the bankruptcy court should have assessed his intent at the time of the consent orders rather than at the time of divorce.

We are not persuaded. Stephen's obligation had already been established by the college expense provision in the marital settlement agreement, which was then included in the two consent orders. The bankruptcy court therefore properly considered the parties' intent as of their entry into the marital settlement agreement.

The substance of the obligation. In determining whether Stephen's obligation involved support, the bankruptcy court also considered the substance of Stephen's obligation. "The critical question in determining whether the obligation is, in substance, support is the function served by the obligation at the time of the divorce." In turn, the function of the obligation is affected by the parties' relative financial circumstances at the time of the divorce.

Here, the bankruptcy court reasonably determined that Stephen was the only parent financially able to pay for the children's college education. Thus, the court was justified in regarding Stephen's obligation, in substance, as support.

For the foregoing reasons, we affirm the bankruptcy court's conclusion that Stephen's college expense obligation was "in the nature of support" as required for a domestic support obligation under the Bankruptcy Code. . . .

Affirmed.

NOTES AND QUESTIONS

1. Most bankruptcy courts examine the parties' or the court's intent at the time of divorce to determine whether an order is in the nature of support. For a discussion of the intent test, *see* Shayna M. Steinfeld & Bruce R. Steinfeld, A Brief Overview of Bankruptcy and Alimony/Support Issues, 38 Fam. L.Q. 127 (2004). What facts led the court in *Chamberlain* to conclude that Stephen's obligation to pay his children's college expenses was in the nature of support? If you had represented him, how would you have argued that the expenses were not in the nature of support?

2. If the court had found that Stephen's obligation was not in the nature of support, and if the bankruptcy proceeding was brought under section 7 of the bankruptcy code rather than section 13, Judith still could have argued that the debt was nondischargeable under §523(a)(15). This section provides that a bankruptcy court may deny a debtor a discharge for a debt

> to a spouse, former spouse, or child of the debtor and not [in the nature of support] that is incurred by the debtor in the course of a divorce or separation or in connection with a separation agreement, divorce decree or other order of a court of record, or a determination made in accordance with State or territorial law by a governmental unit.

Would Stephen have had a defense to this claim?

Under older versions of the bankruptcy law, property division obligations were often dischargeable. These obligations became nondischargeable when the bankruptcy code was revised in 2005. Courts have explained that Congress "was concerned with the dependent spouse who, as part of the divorce agreement, negotiated a lower support payment in exchange for the nondependent spouse shouldering more of the marital debt." In re Taylor, 737 F.3d 670, 681 (10th Cir. 2013).

3. When a bankruptcy proceeding is filed, all creditors' efforts to collect against the debtor are automatically stayed. 11 U.S.C. §362(a). A creditor may move to lift the stay, and the motion will be granted if lifting the stay will not be detrimental to the debtor's estate and if the creditor's rights are not otherwise adequately protected. When the bankrupt person's assets are distributed in the bankruptcy, secured creditors generally are preferred to unsecured ones, though by statute certain unsecured creditors have priority over other unsecured creditors. Once the bankruptcy proceeding is concluded, the debtor starts anew with the exempt property that he or she retained, and any debts that were not paid from the bankruptcy estate are discharged. *See generally* Steinfeld & Steinfeld, above.

The automatic stay applies to property division and measures to enforce judgments against property that is in the bankruptcy estate. Almost all other family law–related actions are exempt from the stay. Therefore, even if a bankruptcy petition has been filed, a court can proceed with domestic violence matters and with actions to grant a divorce; establish paternity; establish or modify a support order; and establish, modify, or enforce custody and related rights. 11 U.S.C. §362(b)(2)(A). The stay also does not apply to various types of child support enforcement actions, including income withholding, driver's license suspensions, tax intercepts, and credit reporting, or to enforcement of medical support obligations. 11 U.S.C. §362(b)(2).

4. Some assets, such as a homestead interest in real property, may be exempt from bankruptcy and will not be taken to satisfy the debtor's creditors. 11 U.S.C. §522. In addition, if exempt assets are encumbered by judicial liens, under certain circumstances the liens will be avoided (that is, eliminated) as well. Most important for our purposes, a lien on exempt property that secures an obligation characterized as part of the property division and that attaches to property that the debtor owned before the lien was created is avoided by the bankruptcy proceeding. However, if the underlying debt secures a duty to pay support, the lien is not avoided. 11 U.S.C. §522(f).

This rule creates a risk for obligees of property division debts, as illustrated in Farrey v. Sanderfoot, 500 U.S. 291 (1991). Gerald and Jeanne Sanderfoot were divorced in Wisconsin. Gerald was awarded the family home, and he was ordered to pay his former wife an equalizing judgment. To secure this award, the decree also gave Jeanne a lien against the property to secure the debt. Less than a year after the divorce, Gerald filed for Chapter 7 bankruptcy and claimed the home as exempt property. He also moved under §522 to avoid Jeanne's lien on the ground that it was a judicial lien that impaired his exemption. Jeanne ultimately prevailed in the Supreme Court.

The Court interpreted §522 as avoiding only those judicial liens that attach to property interests that the debtor owns before the lien attaches. 500 U.S. at 296. Gerald had conceded for purposes of argument that the divorce decree gave him a wholly new interest in the home rather than adding his former wife's share to his pre-existing share. 500 U.S. at 294. The Court therefore held that §522 did not apply and that Jeanne's lien survived Gerald's bankruptcy. If Gerald had not made this concession, though, would Gerald's interest in the property have been characterized as pre-existing the divorce decree or as newly created by the decree? This is a question of state law, which differs from state to state.

5. If a former spouse successfully discharges obligations under a divorce decree by declaring bankruptcy, may the domestic relations court modify its decree to provide relief to the other spouse? In such cases, the obligee is often successful in modifying support obligations in the family law court, though it is improper for the domestic relations court to reinstate the discharged obligation in effect. Alyson F. Finkelstein, A Tug of War: State Divorce Courts Versus Federal Bankruptcy Courts Regarding Debts Resulting from Divorce, 18 Bankr. Dev. J. 169 (2001).

CHAPTER 9

CHILD CUSTODY

A. INTRODUCTION

During the colonial period in this country, and in England during the same time, custody disputes rarely came before the courts. Common law doctrine assigned sole custody of legitimate children to their fathers. A father not only had the sole right to custody while he lived, he could determine custody after death by appointing a testamentary guardian. The following excerpt describes the transition from a clear rule of paternal custody to judicial superintendence in the United States.

Michael Grossberg

Governing the Hearth: Law and the Family in Nineteenth Century America
235-239 (1985)

Prerepublican Anglo-American law granted fathers an almost unlimited right to the custody of their minor legitimate children. Moored in the medieval equation of legal rights with property ownership, it assumed that the interests of children were best protected by making the father the natural guardian and by using a property-based standard of parental fitness. Custody law held children to be dependent, subordinate beings, assets of estates in which fathers had a vested right. Their services, earnings, and the like became the property of their paternal masters in exchange for life and maintenance. Literary critic Jay Fliegelman summarized the stark reality of the traditional law of parent and child: "[T]he debt is owed nature not nurture." These assumptions lingered on in the new republic. The influential University of Maryland law professor David Hoffman explained the dual nature of paternal authority in his 1836 Legal Outlines. First was "the injunction imposed on parents by nature, of rearing, and carefully watching over the moral, religious, and physical education of their progeny, and the impracticality of advantageously discharging that duty, unless children yield implicit obedience to the dictates of parental concern, seeing that they are not of sufficient age and discretion to limit the measure of their submission or obedience." Second was "the presumed consent of the offspring." . . .

Professor Hoffman also emphasized that these parental rights conferred authority primarily on the father:

> If parental power arose not in truth from these principles, but from some fancied property given to the parent in his offspring, by the act of propagation, it would seem to follow . . . that this authority would appertain in the largest degree to the mother, since she not

only has the pains and deprivations incident to gestation and parturition, but is the principal sharer in the cares which succeed the birth. Yet it is the father who holds and exercises the principal authority. . . .

In 1809 a South Carolina equity court heard Jennette Prather's demand for a separation from her husband and the custody of her children. She charged her mate with living openly in adultery. The judges easily complied with her first request but hesitated in granting the second. Chancellor Henry De Saussure was mindful, he said, of the father being the children's "natural guardian, invested by God and the law of the country with reasonable power over them. Unless his parental power has been monstrously and cruelly abused, this court would be very cautious in interfering with the execution of it." The court finally denied the errant husband his full parental rights. It gave the custody of an infant daughter, though not of the older children, to Jennette. In doing so, the judges acknowledged that they were treading on uncertain legal ground.

The ambivalence of the South Carolina court reveals the conflicting pressures on the post-Revolutionary bench generated by custody disputes between mothers and fathers. Traditional male authority over the family remained a fundamental tenet of family law. But a growing concern with child nurture and the acceptance of women as more legally distinct individuals, ones with a special capacity for moral and religious leadership and for child rearing, undermined the primacy of paternal custody rights. . . .

The judicial disposition to emphasize child welfare in determining custody began to refashion the preferences of the common law. The "best interests of the child" became a judicial yardstick used to measure all claims for children. Its dramatic impact is most apparent in the resolution of disputes between the natural parents for their children.

B. STANDARDS FOR CUSTODY DETERMINATION

1. An Introduction to the "Best Interests" Standard

Professor Grossberg describes the transition in the American law of custody as a movement from paternal patriarchy to judicial patriarchy, by which he means (at least in part) the replacement of virtually unbounded paternal authority by virtually unbounded judicial authority (exercised, of course, by male judges). The doctrinal vehicle conveying that judicial power was the "best interests" doctrine. In many situations family law uses "standards" rather than rules to govern the exercise of official authority, and, plainly, the "best interests" doctrine falls in the "standards" category.

Although moving from a nearly absolute and therefore clear rule of paternal custody to a best-interest standard enhanced judicial authority over child custody decisions, the breadth of the latter standard creates problems of management for judges and parties alike. The difference between rules and standards is between an approach to legal decision making that employs apparently mechanical formulae (rules) and one that proceeds by the individualized application of generally stated social policies (standards).

The tension between rules and standards runs throughout the law of custody, but the fault lines change with each generation. When the best-interest standard first took hold, the courts were convinced that custody needed to be awarded to one, and only one, parent. Under the best-interest rubric, the determination of which parent gradually changed from a preference for fathers to a presumption, at least for children of "tender years," in favor of mothers. Under either approach, the participation of the other parent then depended on the cooperation of the custodial parent. Certainty in parental decision-making authority was considered essential.

More recently, with greater acceptance of joint parenting and more egalitarian gender roles, legislatures and courts have authorized shared custody awards that acknowledge both parents' importance to child rearing. In some jurisdictions, the preference for the continuing involvement of both parents has become a rule creating a legal presumption in favor of shared custody; in all jurisdictions, the law favors the continuing inclusion of both parents in the child's life and makes it difficult to deny a parent access to a child altogether.

The presumption of both parents' continuing involvement, in turn, places greater emphasis on the definition of who counts as a legal parent and on disqualifying conduct, including determinations of unfitness. The U.S. Constitution recognizes "fit parents" as having a fundamental liberty interest in the care, custody, and management of their children, limiting the courts' discretion to award custody or visitation to others. *See* Troxel v. Granville, 530 U.S. 57 (2000). Chapters 13 and 14 explore the increasingly contentious law regarding how legal parenthood is determined. The materials in this chapter assume that legal parenthood has been decided and address custody and visitation disputes between a child's legal parents or between a legal parent and an increasingly broad group of third parties, such as grandparents, stepparents and unmarried partners who may have standing to seek visitation. The first part of this section introduces the meanings and application of the "best interests" standard, and the second examines shared custody. As we will see, custody standards permit and sometimes even require courts to judge parents' conduct to determine their "fitness" to parent. The remainder of this section concerns the legal issues that arise from this inquiry.

Painter v. Bannister
140 N.W.2d 152 (Iowa), *cert. denied*, 385 U.S. 949 (1966)

STUART, J. . . . The custody dispute before us in this habeas corpus action is between the father, Harold Painter, and the maternal grandparents, Dwight and Margaret Bannister. Mark's mother and younger sister were killed in an automobile accident on December 6, 1962 near Pullman, Washington. The father, after other arrangements for Mark's care had proved unsatisfactory, asked the Bannisters to take care of Mark. They went to California and brought Mark to their farm home near Ames in July, 1963. Mr. Painter remarried in November, 1964 and about that time indicated he wanted to take Mark back. The Bannisters refused to let him leave and this action was filed in June 1965. Since July 1965 he has continued to remain in the Bannister home under an order of this court staying execution of the judgment of the trial court awarding custody to the father until the matter could be determined on appeal. For reasons hereinafter stated, we conclude Mark's better interests will be served if he remains with the Bannisters.

Mark's parents came from highly contrasting backgrounds. His mother was born, raised and educated in rural Iowa. Her parents are college graduates. Her father is agricultural information editor for the Iowa State University Extension Service. The Bannister home is in the Gilbert Community and is well kept, roomy and comfortable. The Bannisters are highly respected members of the community. Mr. Bannister has served on the school board and regularly teaches a Sunday school class at the Gilbert Congregational Church. Mark's mother graduated from Grinnell College. She then went to work for a newspaper in Anchorage, Alaska, where she met Harold Painter.

Mark's father was born in California. When he was 2-1/2 years old, his parents were divorced and he was placed in a foster home. Although he has kept in contact with his natural parents, he considers his foster parents, the McNelly's, as his family. He flunked out of a high school and a trade school because of a lack of interest in academic subjects, rather than any lack of ability. He joined the navy at 17. He did not like it. After receiving an honorable discharge, he took examinations and obtained his high school diploma. He lived with the McNelly's and went to college for 2-1/2 years under the G.I. bill. He quit college to take a job on a small newspaper in Ephrata, Washington in November 1955. In May 1956, he went to work for the newspaper in Anchorage which employed Jeanne Bannister. . . .

We are not confronted with a situation where one of the contesting parties is not a fit or proper person. There is no criticism of either the Bannisters or their home. There is no suggestion in the record that Mr. Painter is morally unfit. It is obvious the Bannisters did not approve of their daughter's marriage to Harold Painter and do not want their grandchild raised under his guidance. The philosophies of life are entirely different. As stated by the psychiatrist who examined Mr. Painter at the request of the Bannisters' attorneys: "It is evident that there exists a large difference in ways of life and value systems between the Bannisters and Mr. Painter, but in this case, there is no evidence that psychiatric instability is involved. Rather, these divergent life patterns seem to represent alternative normal adaptations." . . .

The Bannister home provides Mark with a stable, dependable, conventional, middle-class, middle-west background and an opportunity for a college education and profession, if he desires it. It provides a solid foundation and secure atmosphere. In the Painter home, Mark would have more freedom of conduct and thought with an opportunity to develop his individual talents. It would be more exciting and challenging in many respects, but romantic, impractical and unstable. . . .

Our conclusion as to the type of home Mr. Painter would offer is based upon his Bohemian approach to finances and life in general. We feel there is much evidence which supports this conclusion. His main ambition is to be a free lance writer and photographer. He has had some articles and picture stories published, but the income from these efforts has been negligible. At the time of the accident, Jeanne was willingly working to support the family so Harold could devote more time to his writing and photography. In the 10 years since he left college, he has changed jobs seven times. . . .

There is general agreement that Mr. Painter needs help with his finances. Both Jeanne and Marilyn, his present wife, handled most of them. Purchases and sales of books, boats, photographic equipment and houses indicate poor financial judgment and an easy come easy go attitude. He dissipated his wife's estate of about $4300, most of which was a gift from her parents and which she had hoped would be used for the children's education.

The psychiatrist classifies him as "a romantic and somewhat of a dreamer." An apt example is the plan he related for himself and Mark in February 1963: "My thought now is to settle Mark and myself in Sausalito, near San Francisco; this is a retreat for wealthy artists, writers, and such aspiring artists and writers as can fork up the rent money. My plan is to do expensive portraits ($150 and up), sell prints ($15 and up) to the tourists who flock in from all over the world. . . ."

The house in which Mr. Painter and his present wife live, compared with the well kept Bannister home, exemplifies the contrasting ways of life. In his words, "it is a very old and beat up and lovely home. . . ." They live in the rear part. The interior is inexpensively but tastefully decorated. The large yard on a hill in the business district of Walnut Creek, California, is of uncut weeds and wild oats. The house "is not painted on the outside because I do not want it painted. I am very fond of the wood on the outside of the house."

The present Mrs. Painter has her master's degree in cinema design and apparently likes and has had considerable contact with children. She is anxious to have Mark in her home. Everything indicates she would provide a leveling influence on Mr. Painter and could ably care for Mark.

Mr. Painter is either an agnostic or atheist and has no concern for formal religious training. He has read a lot of Zen Buddhism and "has been very much influenced by it."

Mrs. Painter is Roman Catholic. They plan to send Mark to a Congregational Church near the Catholic Church, on an irregular schedule. . . .

Were the question simply which household would be the most suitable in which to raise a child, we would have unhesitatingly chosen the Bannister home. We believe security and stability in the home are more important than intellectual stimulation in the proper development of a child. There are, however, several factors which have made us pause.

First, there is the presumption of parental preference, which though weakened in the past several years, exists by statute. We have a great deal of sympathy for a father, who in the difficult period of adjustment following his wife's death, turns to the maternal grandparents for their help and then finds them unwilling to return the child. There is no merit in the Bannister claim that Mr. Painter permanently relinquished custody. It was intended to be a temporary arrangement. A father should be encouraged to look for help with the children from those who love them without the risk of thereby losing the custody of the children permanently. This fact must receive consideration in cases of this kind. However, as always, the primary consideration is the best interest of the child, and if the return of custody to the father is likely to have a seriously disrupting and disturbing effect upon the child's development, this fact must prevail.

Second, Jeanne's will named her husband guardian of her children and if he failed to qualify or ceased to act, named her mother. The parent's wishes are entitled to consideration.

Third, the Bannisters are 60 years old. By the time Mark graduates from high school they will be over 70 years old. Care of young children is a strain on grandparents and Mrs. Bannister's letters indicate as much.

We have considered all of these factors and have concluded that Mark's best interest demands that his custody remain with the Bannisters. Mark was five when he came to their home. The evidence clearly shows he was not well adjusted at that time. He did not distinguish fact from fiction and was inclined to tell "tall tales" emphasizing the big "I." He was very aggressive toward smaller children, cruel to animals, not liked by his classmates and did not seem to know what was acceptable conduct. As stated by one witness: "Mark knew where his freedom was and he didn't know where his boundaries were." In two years he made a great deal of improvement. He now appears to be well disciplined, happy, relatively secure and popular with his classmates, although still subject to more than normal anxiety.

We place a great deal of reliance on the testimony of Dr. Glenn R. Hawks, a child psychologist. The trial court, in effect, disregarded Dr. Hawks' opinions stating: "The court has given full consideration to the good doctor's testimony, but cannot accept it at full face value because of exaggerated statements and the witness's attitude on the stand." We, of course, do not have the advantage of viewing the witness's conduct on the stand, but we have carefully reviewed his testimony and find nothing in the written record to justify such a summary dismissal of the opinions of this eminent child psychologist.

Dr. Hawks is head of the Department of Child Development at Iowa State University. However, there is nothing in the record which suggests that his relationship with the Bannisters is such that his professional opinion would be influenced thereby. Child development is his specialty and he has written many articles and a textbook on the subject. He is recognized nationally, having served on the staff of the 1960 White House Conference on Children and Youth and as consultant on a Ford Foundation program concerning youth in India. He is now education consultant on the project "Head Start." He has taught and lectured at many universities and belongs to many professional associations. He works with the Iowa Children's Home Society in placement problems. Further detailing of his qualifications is unnecessary.

Between June 15th and the time of trial, he spent approximately 25 hours acquiring information about Mark and the Bannisters, including appropriate testing of and "depth interviews" with Mark. Dr. Hawks' testimony covers 70 pages of the record and it is difficult to pinpoint any bit of testimony which precisely summarizes his opinion. He places great emphasis on the "father figure" and discounts the importance of the "biological father." "The father figure is a figure that the child sees as an authority figure, as a helper, he is a nurturant figure, and one who typifies maleness and stands as maleness as far as the child is concerned."

His investigation revealed: ". . . the strength of the father figure before Mark came to the Bannisters is very unclear. Mark is confused about the father figure prior to his contact with Mr. Bannister." Now, "Mark used Mr. Bannister as his father figure. This is very evident. It shows up in the depth interview, and it shows up in the description of Mark's life given by Mark. He has a very warm feeling for Mr. Bannister."

Dr. Hawks concluded that it was not for Mark's best interest to be removed from the Bannister home. He is criticized for reaching this conclusion without investigating the Painter home or finding out more about Mr. Painter's character. He answered: "I was most concerned about the welfare of the child, not the welfare of Mr. Painter, not about the welfare of the Bannisters. In as much as Mark has already made an adjustment and sees the Bannisters as his parental figures in his psychological makeup, to me this is the most critical factor. . . ."

It was Dr. Hawks' opinion "the chances are very high (Mark) will go wrong if he is returned to his father." This is based on adoption studies which "establish that the majority of adoptions in children who are changed, from ages six to eight, will go bad, if they have had a prior history of instability, some history of prior movement. When I refer to instability I am referring to where there has been no attempt to establish a strong relationship." . . .

Mark has established a father-son relationship with Mr. Bannister, which he apparently had never had with his natural father. He is happy, well adjusted and progressing nicely in his development. We do not believe it is for Mark's best interest to take him out of this stable atmosphere in the face of warnings of dire consequences from an eminent child psychologist and send him to an uncertain future in his father's home. Regardless of our appreciation of the father's love for his child and his desire to have him with him, we do not believe we have the moral right to gamble with this child's future. He should be encouraged in every way possible to know his father. We are sure there are many ways in which Mr. Painter can enrich Mark's life.

For the reasons stated, we reverse the trial court and remand the case for judgment in accordance herewith.

Anna Freud

Painter v. Bannister: *Postscript by a Psychoanalyst*
7 The Writings of Anna Freud 247, 247-255 (1966-1970)

I can imagine plaintiff and defendants, father and grandparents of Mark, in spite of their tug of war, being sufficiently united in their concern for the child to seek expert advice concerning him instead of bringing the matter to the court. If the clinic to which they turned were the Hampstead one (or the Yale Child Study Center), the advice given would be based on psychoanalytic reasoning. The main difference between the legal and the clinical situation then would be that in the first instance the warring partners would have a solution imposed on them, while in the second instance they would be left free either to adopt or to reject the solution with which they are presented.

MARK'S PROBLEM

I do not think that we would find Mark's problem easier to handle than either the trial judge or Mr. Justice Stuart. . . . Mark was lucky enough to live in normal family circumstances until he was five. There is no reason to suspect that during these decisive years his father did not play the usual important role for him. This "normal" life came to an end only with the disastrous accident which, for reason of their deaths, deprived him of mother and sister and, for other reasons, soon thereafter deprived him of the presence of his father.

Disturbing as the accident was, it does not alter the fact that Mark grew up with parents of his own. We take it for granted that the sudden loss of mother and sibling coupled with the separation from his father, was deeply upsetting for him. There is no evidence to show how his relations with mother, father, and sister had developed, or how his personality had been shaped before the traumatic moment intervened. That he showed signs of maladjustment after the events, i.e., when he arrived at the grandparents, is not surprising, nor is this necessarily connected with mismanagement on the part of the father or other influences derived from the father's personality. Children frequently react with overt behavior problems to shocks, upsets, and disruptions in their lives, i.e., to events following which adults withdraw into a lengthy mourning process.

MARK'S PAST

In the absence of any other surviving member of the immediate family, the clinic would have to enlist the father's help for clarifying questions concerning Mark's past. We would want to know whether developmental progress was satisfactory or unsatisfactory until age five; whether Mark was in good affectionate contact with his mother, or his father, or with both; whether they considered him a clinging or an independent child; whether before losing his mother, he had reached the stage of obvious preference for her, accompanied by rivalry with and jealousy of his father; whether at this time he had impressed people as a manly or as an unmanly little boy; whether the parents considered him to be a "good" child, age adequately in control of his impulses, or whether they found him self-indulgent and difficult to manage. Data of this kind would give a clue whether or not the disruption of the family had caused him to undergo a change of personality.

Other relevant information concerning Mark would have to be elicited in the clinic's usual manner from the boy himself. The investigator would have to piece together in particular the residues of his infantile love life. What methods did Mark adopt to cope with his losses? Has he forgotten, denied, or repressed all memories of events before the accident? How far is the image of his dead mother still alive in his mind? Does it or does it not play an important role in his conscious fantasies or, perhaps inaccessible to consciousness, in his unconscious? To what extent has he transferred the feelings for his mother to his grandmother? If he has done so in an intense way, how would he react to a further separation, this time from her? Are there signs to be noted that he would be able to shift his affections, this time to a stepmother who is, so far, unknown to him? . . .

As regards Mark, we have no evidence so far to show what happened in his case. There is the contention that the boy's allegiance to his father has been transferred in its entirety to the grandfather. If this were proved to be true, inquiry would still be needed whether this shift was a wholly positive one or whether it was prompted, at least in part, by the boy's anger with the absent father, an anger which may well be smoldering under the surface and may burst out some time to the detriment of his development.

The Warring Adults

Since in the clinical situation both parties in the dispute have consulted us of their own free will, we can also count on their cooperation in investigating their own respective attitudes toward the child. . . .

With Mark's father and grandparents it is difficult to foresee the result of our investigations. In the father, there are signs of obvious, object-directed feelings for the child, alternating with periods of detachment, which may or may not be attributable to the man's immediate reaction to his tragic losses. On the other hand, there are also indications that, as a father, he is not disinclined to use his son selfishly, i.e., for his own aggrandizement as an author, a figure on TV, etc.

As for the grandparents, we are prepared to find that for them Mark represents the daughter whom they have lost and mourn. There is also the suspicion that in claiming Mark, they reclaim symbolically their daughter from the son-in-law, who from the start was unwelcome to them for many reasons. There also is little doubt that the grandparents love Mark himself, are attentive to his needs, and sacrifice for him some of the peace and quiet of their home life to which every elderly couple is entitled.

The weight and truth of any of these pronouncements remain tentative until they are confirmed or disputed by probing interviews with the three adults in question.

Legal v. Psychoanalytic Aspects

Unlike the two courts, we are in the lucky position not to have to pronounce judgment. We merely formulate advice. When doing so, we disregard or minimize the importance of some of the facts which swayed the courts.

In disagreement with the trial judge, and in agreement with his expert, Dr. Hawks, we discount the importance of the "biological father" as such. The "blood ties" between parent and child as well as the alleged paternal and maternal "instincts" are biological concepts which, only too often, prove vague and unreliable when transferred to the field of psychology. Psychologically speaking, the child's "father" is the adult man to whom the child attaches a particular, psychologically distinctive set of feelings. When this type of emotional tie is disrupted, the child's feelings suffer. When such separations occur during phases of development in which the child is particularly vulnerable, the whole foundation of his personality may be shaken. The presence of or the reunion with a biological father to whom no such ties exist will not recompense the child for the loss which he has suffered. Conversely, the biological father's or mother's unselfish love for their child is by no means to be taken for granted. It happens often enough that biological parents fail in their duty to the child, while other adults who are less closely related to him, i.e., who have no "instinctive" basis for their feelings, successfully take over the parental role.

We place less emphasis than Mr. Justice Stuart on benefits such as a "stable, dependable background" with educational and professional opportunities. Important as such external advantages are, we have seen too often that they can be wasted unless they are accompanied by the internal emotional constellations which enable the children to profit from them. Children are known to thrive in socially and financially unstable situations if they are firmly attached to their parents, and to come to grief under the best social conditions when such emotional security is missing. . . .

FORMULATION OF ADVICE

It is not possible at this point to foretell whether, after investigation, our advice will be in line with the judgment of the trial court or with Mr. Justice Stuart. What can be promised is that it will be based not on external facts but on internal data. We shall advise that Mark had better stay with his grandparents provided that the following facts can be ascertained:

> that the transfer of his attachment from the parents to the grandparents is fairly complete and promises to be permanent during his childhood; i.e., that they have become the central figures toward whom his feelings are directed and around whom his emotional life revolves . . . that, given this new attachment, a further change is not advisable . . . ; that the grandparents, on their part, cherish Mark for his own sake, not only as a replacement for the daughter who was killed, nor as a pawn in the battle with their son-in-law.

Conversely, we shall advise that Mark had better be returned to his father if the following facts emerge:

> that Mr. Painter still retains his place as "father" in Mark's mind and that in spite of separation and new experiences the child's feelings and fantasies continue to revolve around him; that anger about the "desertion" (and perhaps blame for the mother's death) have not succeeded in turning this relationship into a predominantly hostile one; that the father cherishes Mark for his own sake; that it can be shown that Mr. Painter's using the child for publicity purposes was not due to lack of paternal consideration on his part but happened owing to the bitterness and resentment caused by the fight for possession of his son.

Provided that Mr. Painter, Mr. and Mrs. Bannister, and Mark would allow the clinic two or three weeks' time for investigation, I am confident that we should be able to guide them toward a potentially helpful solution of their difficult problem.

NOTES AND QUESTIONS

1. The court in *Painter* notes the existence of a presumption favoring custody by a child's parents against all others. Who bore the burden of overcoming that presumption? What kind of factual showing did the court require to overcome the presumption? Did the court's use of the best-interest standard effectively eliminate the parental presumption? The *Painter* court noted that the presumption of parental preference had been "weakened in the past several years." In 2000, however, in Troxel v. Granville, 530 U.S. 57 (2000) (*see* Chapter 13), the U.S. Supreme Court found court-ordered grandparent visitation to be an unconstitutional infringement of a parent's fundamental right to make decisions concerning the custody, care, and control of the child. Subsequent decisions have added teeth to the presumption in favor of parents' custody and visitation preferences, and a number of courts require either a showing of parental unfitness or detriment to the child to overcome the presumption that parents will act in their children's best interests. If Painter v. Bannister were decided today, do you think the case would come out differently? Do you think constitutional protection is necessary to protect parents from the type of subjective judgments made in *Painter*? If you represented the Bannisters in an action today, is there additional evidence you would try to present? Would you characterize the existing evidence differently?

2. The *Painter* court treated the custody determination as a de novo proceeding although Mark had lived with his grandparents, with his father's consent, for almost two years when the action was filed. Had the grandparents secured a custody award when Mark initially moved in with them, in most states, the father would have had to establish a substantial change in circumstances to justify a custody transfer. Such a change would ordinarily need to involve something that detrimentally affected Mark, rather than merely an improvement in the father's circumstances. *See* Rennels v. Rennels, 257 P.3d 396 (Nev. 2011) (finding that when parent consented to grandparent visitation order, acrimony grew, and parent changed his mind, presumption in favor of deference to parental views no longer controls, and parent was required to show a substantial change in circumstances that justified modification or termination of the order); Lovlace v. Copley, 418 S.W.3d 1 (Tenn. 2013) (ruling that custodial parents seeking modification or termination of a grandparent visitation order must show a material change in circumstances); In re Marriage of Epler, 633, 341 P.3d 742, 748 (Or. 2014) (en banc) (deference to parental preferences does not apply in modification proceeding). *But see* Hunter v. Hunter, 771 N.W.2d 694 (Mich. 2009) (stating that even where parents consented to a guardianship by the children's uncle and aunt because of the parents' drug abuse, the parental presumption still prevails over the presumption in favor of an established custodial environment, and the parental presumption can be rebutted only by clear and convincing evidence that custody with the natural parent is not in the best interests of the child); In re K.I., 903 N.E.2d 453 (Ind. 2009) (asserting that although a parent must show a significant change of circumstances to change an initial custody award from a grandparent to a parent, the necessary showing was a "modest" one because the presumption in favor of custody with the parent over a third party did not end with the initial order). The characterization of the existing custody arrangement and the differing burdens of proof come up as potential issues in most of the cases in this chapter. Consider whether you think the characterization changes the outcome of these cases.

3. Judgments regarding a child's best interests inevitably involve social scientific propositions. It is not surprising, therefore, that expert witnesses commonly play an important role in contested custody matters, as Dr. Hawks did in Painter v. Bannister. Their role is the subject of much controversy. Must the trier of fact give any weight to expert testimony? If one party produces expert evidence and the other does not, does it follow that the former will succeed? If not, why not? Could the grandparents have overcome a presumption in favor of the parent in a case like this without expert testimony? Should the courts appoint an independent expert, and if so, who should be expected to pay for the expert?

4. Mark later chose to return to his father. Is this fact instructive in any way?

5. An extensive literature addresses children's adjustment to divorce. This literature can inform evaluation of the adults' parenting capacity and the children's adjustment. It finds that:

Divorce is a process: Joan Wexler emphasized that divorce "is not a single stressful event confined to a certain moment," but rather something that changes over time, beginning prior to the formal divorce with a state of family dissolution and ending some time as the parties experiment with ways to cope and adjust over time. She notes that:

> during that first year [following the divorce], family conflict escalates rather than declines. . . . The authors described a cycle of negative parent-child interaction, with the most notable effect on the mother-son relationship. Only after that first year of heightened tension did an increased sense of well-being begin to emerge. At the two-year follow-up, the most debilitating effects of the divorce on both parents and children had abated.

Joan G. Wexler, Rethinking the Modification of Child Custody Decrees, 94 Yale L.J. 757, 784-788 (1985).

Conflict harms children in all families: Sociologist Paul Amato found that children in high-conflict marriages show signs of distress even before a divorce occurs, and the children in the highest-conflict marriages do better if their parents divorce even though children generally do better if their parents stay together. Paul R. Amato, Good Enough Marriages: Parental Discord, Divorce, and Children's Long Term Well-Being, 9 Va. J. Soc. Pol'y & L. 71, 71-94

(2001); Solangel Maldonado, Facilitating Forgiveness and Reconciliation in "Good Enough" Marriages, 13 Pepp. Disp. Resol. L.J. 105 (2013). Children exposed to high levels of parental conflict are at greater risk for developing problems such as depression, anxiety, social and behavioral problems, and difficulties developing relationships in later life. Karen Oehme et al., Trauma-Informed Co-Parenting: How a Shift in Compulsory Divorce Education to Reflect New Brain Development Research Can Promote Both Parents' and Children's Best Interests, 39 U. Haw. L. Rev. 37, 42-43 (2016).

Resources matter. Two parents typically have both more money and more time to spend on their children. "Courts recognize, albeit reluctantly, that financial deprivation and its attendant harms—including frequent moves, foreclosures, material deprivation, and parental stress—can undermine a parent's ability to provide children with a sufficiently safe and stable environment for them to prosper and thrive as they develop into adults." Sarah Abramowicz, Beyond Family Law, 63 Case W. Res. L. Rev. 293, 316 (2012).

Two parents are better than one—when they reinforce each other's parenting. Children generally benefit from the involvement of both parents, and divorce typically involves a substantial loss of contact with the noncustodial parent. Joan B. Kelly & Robert E. Emery, Children's Adjustment Following Divorce: Risk and Resiliency Perspectives, 52 Fam. Rel. 352-362 (2003). Moreover, the loss of parental contact following divorce may have an especially large impact on young children. R. Chris Fraley & Marie E. Heffernan, Attachment and Parental Divorce: A Test of the Diffusion and Sensitive Period Hypotheses, 39 Pers. Soc. Psychol. Bull. 1199 (2013). Other studies show, however, that it is the quality of parental involvement, not the amount of time that a parent spends with a child, that matters most. Paul R. Amato & Joan G. Gilbreth, Nonresident Fathers and Children's Well-being: A Meta-analysis, 61 J. Marriage & Fam. 557 (1999). For a compilation of social science research related to custody, *see* Jennifer E. Lansford, Parental Divorce and Children's Adjustment, 4 Persp. on Psych. Sci. 140 (2015).

Consider how these factors can and should influence judicial decisionmaking. Should the courts seek to protect the children's affective relationships at the time of the divorce? If so, how should the courts evaluate conflict between caretakers that may harm children? How should the courts assess changes over time in caretaking relationships? How should they take into account the resources available to address children's needs? These issues will recur in discussion of the legal standards courts apply to custody decisionmaking.

In the sections below, consider how the best-interest-of-the-child standard interacts with other custody presumptions.

2. Shared Custody

We have already considered a number of areas of substantial change in family law doctrine and procedure. The grounds for divorce, the theory of alimony, the principles of property distribution at divorce, and the process for dissolving families have all changed dramatically over the last several decades. The shift from recognition of a sole parent with decision-making power to encouragement of the continuing involvement of all parents in the child's life may also be counted as a significant development.

Until relatively recently, courts generally agreed that all children of a family should be placed with a single custodial parent. Shared custody arrangements were disfavored or simply rejected on several grounds, including the notion that a single parent with primary responsibility provided consistency in discipline and moral education. Joint legal custody also seemed to threaten a continuation of the spousal conflict leading to divorce—a conflict that would now directly involve the children. Rejection of joint custodial arrangements was so strong that courts were reluctant to award joint custody even where the parents agreed to it. *See* J. Herbie DiFonzo, From the Rule of One to Shared Custody, 52 Fam. Ct. Rev. 213 (2014).

Over the last 40 years, however, attitudes and legal rules concerning joint custody have changed. Central among the changes is the conviction, in an era of greater family instability, that children's interests are best served by custody orders that facilitate continuing contact with both parents, and that designation of one parent as the "custodian" and the other as a "visitor" contributes to acrimony underlying custodial disputes and the weakening of the children's ties to the noncustodial parent. As we will see, some states now articulate a preference for joint custody, and most permit shared custody in appropriate cases. The most contentious remaining issue is not whether joint custody should be allowed, but when, and to what extent the courts use it to avoid having to choose between two otherwise fit parents.

In the case that follows, consider how the court deals with the conclusion that the two parents should continue to be involved in the child's life even if they cannot deal with each other.

J.R. v. M.S.
55 N.Y.S.3d 873 (N.Y. Sup. 2017)

Matthew F. Cooper, J. One of the more encouraging developments that I have observed as a judge sitting in a matrimonial part in New York County is an increased willingness on the part of divorcing parents to attempt to work together to cooperatively raise their children. And even if real cooperation is not possible, there is often recognition by the parties and their attorneys that provisions should be made to allow both parents to participate in the child's upbringing to the greatest extent possible.

This trend towards the inclusion of both parents in the parenting process might be attributable to the changing views of what it means to be a parent—fatherhood no longer relegated to an inferior position to motherhood. Or it might be reflective of what has become the almost universally held belief that children are generally disserved by having either parent—be it a mother or a father—playing only a peripheral role in their young lives.

Whatever the reason, the result is that the vast majority of custody disputes that come before me are ultimately resolved . . . by the parties agreeing to a parenting plan. In almost every instance, the parenting plan provides for some form of shared decision-making. This arrangement, which is commonly referred to as "joint custody" or "joint legal custody," enables both parents to have a real say as to what happens in their child's life. . . .

This is a custody dispute that one would think could readily be resolved by the parties agreeing to a form of shared decision-making. None of the factors that militate against co-parenting are present. In almost all respects, the situation appears ideal for it to work. For example, both parties are intelligent, educated, involved, loving parents, each of whom has more than adequate parenting skills. Their child is a healthy and well-adjusted 10-year-old boy who is happy at the prestigious private school he attends, and although more closely bonded with the mother, certainly wants the father to be part of his life. Both parents' households are located in close proximity to each other, and there are more than ample financial resources with which to pay for family therapists, parent coordinators and other professionals to assist in the process. Despite all the factors favoring a co-parenting arrangement, there is one flaw, at least from the mother's perspective, that calls into question whether shared decision-making is feasible in this instance: the father's vexatious personality. According to the mother—and others in the father's professional and personal life—he can be argumentative, contentious and rigid. It is the mother's position that because the father can be so difficult to co-parent with, she should be awarded sole decision-making authority over all spheres, and by implication, be deemed to have sole custody of their child. The father, while conceding that joint decision-making is not viable, argues that he and the mother should each have final decision-making authority over specified zones, and by implication, they both should be deemed to have joint custody of their son. . . .

The parties were married in 1999. Their only child, a son, was born in 2007. Although the parties, both of whom received an MBA at Wharton, attained great professional success and together lived a privileged Manhattan lifestyle, never seemed to have enjoyed being married to one another. The tensions in the relationship only intensified after the birth of the child in 2007, and neither marital therapy, nor the services of a parent coordinator, proved to be helpful. In 2013, the father revealed he had been engaged in another relationship and that he was seeking a different type of life than the one he could have with the mother. After this announcement, the parties decided to separate.

In January 2014, the father commenced this divorce action. In September 2014, the parties entered into an agreement setting forth an interim parental access schedule. Shortly thereafter, the father moved to his own apartment. For the next two years, the parties attempted to agree on a parenting plan. There were countless settlement conferences, both in court and out, and numerous draft agreements exchanged and redlined. Unfortunately, this effort was to no avail, and the parties were unable to reach a compromise.

Notably however, there have been relatively few problems with either the interim access schedule or decision-making during the course of this litigation. In fact, the only disputes that I am aware of concerned which sports programs the child was going to be enrolled and how many weeks he would attend summer day camp. There have been no problems with the child's education, as he is thriving at a school that he will be able to attend through 12th grade, and there are no issues concerning his medical care, as he is doing well under the care of a mutually agreed-upon pediatrician and child therapist. In short, the parents, while fixating on relatively inconsequential matters in their child's life, have somehow managed, despite their differences, to successfully raise him to this point.

The trial that ensued took place over a number of days in the late summer and fall of 2016, with post-trial briefs submitted at the end of the year. The witnesses were the parties, the person who briefly served as a parent coordinator and later as a consultant to the father, and the psychiatrist appointed by the court to conduct the forensic custody evaluation. Following the conclusion of testimony, I met with the child, accompanied by the attorney for the child, in an *in camera* proceeding known as a Lincoln Hearing[1]

The key witness was the forensic psychiatrist. In his forensic report, prepared in the fall of 2015, and in his testimony, he provided examples of the father's rigidity and idiosyncrasies, and articulated how making decisions jointly would be an ordeal for the mother because of the father's difficult, often combative, personality. The forensic psychiatrist, however, was clear that both parents possess the "basic skills and knowledge to be more than competent parents," and that, although the father was "rigid about his beliefs," his "parenting skills are nevertheless well within the range of normal."

Although the forensic psychiatrist largely focused on the father's various personality deficiencies, he identified flaws on the part of the mother as well. For instance, he pointed out that, at times, she too can be rigid, has a tendency to be "somewhat overprotective" of the

---

1. This commonly referred to moniker is derived from the Court of Appeals case Lincoln v. Lincoln, 247 N.E.2d 659 (N.Y. 1969), which approved a procedure for a judge to hear directly from the child with the record sealed and the child's statements, unless he or she specifies otherwise, kept confidential.

child, and is "angry and resentful" towards the father. Nevertheless, he concluded that because the mother is more sensitive to the child's needs, more able to give consideration to the other parent's views, and because the parents cannot "work together," the mother should have final decision-making authority in all areas. In his report, he did not address the question of zones of decision-making, but in his testimony he stated that while employing zones might "incentivize" both sides to be inclusive in the decision-making process and prevent a parent from being marginalized, he felt that it would give rise to problems because "one could be handled in radically different ways than the other" and because decisions do not always fall neatly into one zone or another.

The former parent coordinator testified as a witness for the father. He was apparently called to express his view that the parent coordination process would have worked had the mother been willing to continue with it and had she been less angry with the father. The testimony was of limited value in that the parent coordinator was clearly aligned with the father, whom he later worked with on an individual basis without notifying the mother. He also admitted on cross-examination that during the eight months he worked with the parties, the father, at times, lost his temper and exhibited disrespect for the mother.

Both parents testified on their own behalf. Predictably, they each sought to blame the other for their inability to work together. The mother focused on how contentious and uncompromising the father could be and just how exhausting it was trying to make a decision with him. She introduced the father's employment evaluations to show that the people he worked with had the same problems dealing with him that she did. And she stressed that the father's rigidity and idiosyncratic tendencies—which included a wide array of food-related beliefs and a strict adherence to rules and schedules—impacted negatively on his relationship with the child.

The father, in turn, attempted to attribute the parenting problems to the mother's anger and dislike of him, and what he saw as her willingness to give in to the child's wishes rather than exert appropriate parental authority. On a more positive note, he acknowledged that he had become increasingly aware of how difficult he could be to deal with, and explained that he was working with a therapist to address the less attractive aspects of his personality.

The odd thing about the parties' testimony—and that of the other witnesses—is that despite the fixation on how these parents cannot co-parent, and the mother's difficulty dealing with the father, the evidence shows that when needed, the parties have somehow managed to collectively make major parenting decisions for their child, such as education and medical treatment. What they have been unable to do is make the minor parenting decisions. . . .

The same way that the arrangements by which divorced parents raise their children have changed over recent years, the language employed to describe those arrangements has begun to change as well. The terms "legal custody," "physical custody," and "visitation"—all deeply ingrained components of the process by which we determine what role each parent will play in the child's life—are gradually giving way to new terms. These new terms are reflective of the greater emphasis that is now being placed on co-parenting.

A. Legal Custody and Decision-Making

The word "custody" itself—whether in the context of legal custody or physical custody—is fraught with implications. Because the word is defined as the "care and control" of another, the granting of custody to one parent can be seen as a declaration that the other parent has no role, or at best, a decidedly secondary role, in raising the child. Thus, it makes sense, wherever possible, to avoid using the word in favor of more neutral terms that do not give rise to the negative associations that come with being designated the non-custodial parent. This is why many family law attorneys now craft parenting agreements without using perceivably divisive labels. Instead, they merely set forth the agreed upon method by which the parties will make parental decisions for their child. Alternatively, parenting agreements that do contain a custodial designation almost always provide for the parents to have joint custody, even in cases where there is little expectation that the parties will work together cooperatively or engage in real shared decision-making. This reflects the recognition that joint custody is basically just a title, as are all custodial designations, with decision-making being the mechanism that actually guides the parenting process.

So far, courts, when determining custody matters, have been slow to join practitioners in jettisoning the traditional custody-centric model in favor of one that is centered on decision-making. This is evidenced by a series of recent Appellate Division decisions, all of which treat parental decision-making as a function that is tied to legal custody. . . .

. . . Accordingly, in addition to determining how the parties will handle decision-making, I will decide what form legal custody will take. In particular, I will determine if the custodial designation should be joint custody to both parties or sole custody to the mother.

Nationally, joint custody is increasingly becoming the favored custodial designation. Statutes in 18 states and the District of Columbia create a presumption that joint custody is in the best interests of the child, and those in three other states list it as the preferred option. Not only does New York not have a statutory presumption or preference, but case law has traditionally looked somewhat skeptically at the notion of joint custody. . . .

Now, almost four decades [later] . . . appellate courts still tend to be reluctant to order joint custody absent an agreement by the parties or a showing that they can work well together. . . .

This case presents a good example of why, even in a situation where hostility and poor-communication abound, courts, when called upon to designate legal custody, should opt, if at all possible, for designating both parents joint custodial parents, rather than making one the custodial and the other the non-custodial parent. Whatever the father's idiosyncrasies and personality flaws, he is undeniably a loving, capable, and devoted parent. Moreover, he is the type of involved father who coaches the child's soccer team and is highly active in the child's school's parent association. To designate him a non-custodial parent would, in effect, label him—to the child and the rest of the world—as being somehow defective and inferior to the mother, who, in turn, would wear the crown of custodial parent. Under the circumstances presented here, it is difficult to see how it could be in the child's best interests to have his father's parental standing denigrated in this manner. Consequently, I find that the parties should be designated joint custodial parents.

This brings us then to the question of decision-making, the true essence of the parenting process. Here, too, I find that the child's interests would be better served if there is a form of shared decision-making. To this end, as set forth below, there will be certain zones where each party, after full consultation with the other, will have final decision-making authority. There will be other zones where a hybrid format will apply, meaning that certain decisions that come within the ambit of that zone will be subject to the tie-breaking vote of a parent coordinator or other designated professional.

In making my decision to employ zones, I am aware that the forensic psychiatrist recommended that the mother have across-the-board final decision-making authority. Although I have fully considered the concerns he articulated about utilizing zones, I find that they are outweighed by the risks that come with power being vested in the mother alone. One is that the father will be marginalized. The other is that a complete power imbalance will remove any incentive for the parties to be more inclusive in the decision-making process. . . .

Having concluded that the meaningful involvement of both parents in the child's life is best realized here by awarding each of them zones of decision-making—along with permitting each of them to claim the title of being a joint custodial parent—I now turn to defining which zone each parent will have. Generally, the two most important zones are education and medical. Ironically, in this case, these are the two areas over which there has been the least disagreement. Because the child is happily attending his top-tier private school and can look forward to staying there until he graduates from 12th grade, there should be little need for educational decisions to be made outside of the extras, like tutoring and SAT preparation. Based on the father serving on the parent association at the son's school and his being a trustee of the college he attended, I find that he is well-suited to be the final decision-maker in this zone. The one exception will be in the unlikely event the child needs to change from his current school. If consensus cannot be reached by the parents as to the new school that the child will attend, then a parent coordinator will cast the tie-breaking vote.

Happily, the child is healthy and, despite his parents' acrimonious divorce, relatively well-adjusted. Almost as importantly for our purposes here, both parents are pleased with the pediatrician and the child-therapist whom they selected together to attend to their child's physical and mental-health needs. In light of the mother's attention to the child's needs and the child's greater willingness to share his feelings with her than with the father, I find that she should have final decision-making authority as to medical issues. As with education, there will be one carve-out. That is, a provision requiring mutual agreement to change either the pediatrician or the therapist. Absent such an agreement, a parent coordinator will be empowered to break the deadlock by voting with one side or the other.

The remaining zones will not be subject to the hybrid provision of a tie-breaker vote. . . .

With regards to summer camp, which has been a source of continual conflict, I find that the mother shall have final-decision making as to both what camp the child attends and how long he attends. Unlike the father, who strikes me as being intent on having the child emulate his experience as a youngster—or at least what he would like to believe was his experience—the mother appears to be focused more on the child's needs and preferences. . . .

As concerning extracurricular activities, I am troubled that the father is inordinately invested in what sports the child plays. While organized sports play an important role in promoting physical fitness, teaching the importance of team work, and other interpersonal skills, the parental strife it generates can be disproportional to its value. Such is the case here. As with camp, the father, who in no way strikes me as being particularly athletic, seems more focused on the experiences he had playing a particular sport—or again, what his gauzy view of his youth leads him to believe that experience was—than what sports the child himself wants to play. Accordingly, the mother will have final decision-making authority with regard to weekly organized sports activities, which by their nature take place on both parent's parenting time. Naturally, each parent will be free to select extracurricular activities, athletic or otherwise, that take place during his or her individual parenting time, but that do not conflict with sports programs selected by the mother.

The final zone to be assigned is religion. The mother is a non-practicing Christian. The father is a lightly-practicing Jew. Because the evidence establishes that the parties intended to raise the child Jewish and sent him to a Jewish pre-school, the father will have final decision-making with regard to the child's religious upbringing. This authority, however, will not be unfettered. Rather, it will extend to little more than arranging for the necessary training and preparation for the child to have a Bar Mitzvah in a reform synagogue. One encouraging note is that the parents have agreed that they will share Jewish holidays—so that the mother can also partake in the child's Jewish heritage—while at the same time having the child partake in Christian traditions. Thus, the child is assured of having the type of rich multi-denominational experience that benefits so many children in this city.

While a parent coordinator was not terribly helpful to the parties in the past, I am convinced that one can be helpful going forward. Even if one parent has final decision-making in a particular zone, that parent is still required to have meaningful consultation with the other parent and seriously consider his or her views. A strong parent coordinator will be able to set up and supervise the process by which that happens and, if necessary, rein in the father when he becomes too overbearing. If the parents are unable to jointly select a parent coordinator, I will appoint one on their behalf.

B. Physical Custody

. . . In this case, it is agreed that the child will spend the majority of overnights with the mother. Thus, the mother will be entitled to receive child support from the father without the need to designate her the custodial parent or otherwise make a finding as to physical custody. Under these circumstances, the judgment need only provide that the child shall reside primarily with the mother.

C. Parenting Time

At one time, a non-custodial parent — or stated in more contemporary terms, the parent with whom the child does not primarily reside — was considered to have visitation with his or her child. The term "visitation" seems more applicable to what takes place in a hospital or a prison, rather than what should be substantial and meaningful time spent between a parent and a child. As a result, what we used to refer to as visitation is now more often called parenting time or parental access. These more expansive terms reflect the notion that both parents have the right, and the child the reciprocal right, to a real relationship where actual parenting, not merely visiting, takes place.

For more than two years, the parties here have been abiding by an interim schedule. . . . Under this schedule, the father has five overnights and one two-and-a-quarter-hour long dinner with the child every 14 days. . . .

Although the current school year schedule may not be entirely satisfactory to either party, or even to the child, it nevertheless successfully fulfills the important and long-recognized mission of allowing the child to have regular and meaningful access with both his parents. . . .

NOTES AND QUESTIONS

1. What difference does terminology make? The New York court in J.R. v. M.S. objects to the terms "custody" and "visitation." What terms does it use instead? Could the parenting arrangement in J.R. v. M.S. be termed primary custody to one parent and visitation to the other? If so, which parent would have "primary custody"? How would such an arrangement differ, if at all, from the arrangement the court adopts in *J.R.*?

2. Courts that use the term "joint custody" generally distinguish between joint physical custody (or parenting time) and joint legal custody (or decision-making power). Jurisdictions differ in how they treat each term. Iowa, for example, defines joint physical care to mean that "both parents have rights to and responsibilities toward the child including, but not limited to, shared parenting time with the child, maintaining homes for the child, [and] providing routine care for the child." This definition does not tie joint physical custody to a particular allocation of time, but rather to joint assumption of responsibility for the child. *See* In re Marriage of Hansen, 733 N.W.2d 683 (Iowa 2007). Other states specify a minimum amount of time that each parent must have the children for the arrangement to be called joint custody. This minimum amount varies from 30 percent of the overnights to a 50-50 division. *See, e.g.,* N.H. Rev. Stat. Ann. §461-A:20 (2022) (unless the parties had agreed that they would each have 50 percent of the residential responsibility, only one of them could be the "custodial parent"); Tenn. Code Ann. §36-6-402(4) (2022) ("primary residential parent" means "the parent with whom the child resides more than fifty percent (50%) of the time," reserving joint physical custody only for those cases with an equal division of parenting time); Utah Code Ann. §78B-12-102(15) (2022) ("joint physical custody" means "the child stays with each parent overnight for more than 30% of the year").

In *J.R.*, the father had five overnights and one two-and-a-quarter-hour long dinner with the child every 14 days. Would that be joint physical custody or visitation in Iowa? New Hampshire? Tennessee? Utah? What implications does the court in *J.R.* see as arising from the amount of time the child spends with each parent?

3. The term "joint legal custody" refers to decision-making power. In many jurisdictions, courts routinely award joint legal custody even if the child primarily resides with one of the parents. If a court awarded joint legal custody and the parents differed about matters such as whether the child plays soccer or baseball, the court could approach the dispute in one of three ways. First, since the parents share joint decision-making authority, the court could take the position that the child could not play either sport unless both parents agreed; in other words, neither parent would have the unilateral power to authorize the child's participation. Second, the court could decide on its own whether it was in the child's best interest to play soccer or baseball, issuing a court order addressing the choice of soccer or baseball. Third, the court could defer to the preferences of the party with primary physical custody. How does the court's approach in J.R. v. M.S. differ from these more traditional determinations? Is the court's approach likely to provide a better way of resolving disputes? What difficulties do you foresee in implementing the court's approach?

4. The court characterized the disputes in J.R. v. M.S. as relatively trivial. More serious conflicts between parents often involve the choice of which school the child is to attend. The choice of a school can be particularly contentious if the parents do not live close to each other. In such a case, the school choice is likely to require that one parent rather than the other have more time with the child. The Michigan Supreme Court, in a case involving the choice of which school a child should attend, suggested that the courts should apply a two-step analysis:

> To summarize, when considering an important decision affecting the welfare of the child, the trial court must first determine whether the proposed change would modify the established custodial environment of that child. In making this determination, it is the child's standpoint, rather than that of the parents, that is controlling. If the proposed change would modify the established custodial environment of the child, then the burden is on the parent proposing the change to establish, by clear and convincing evidence, that the change is in the child's best interests. Under such circumstances, the trial court must consider all the best-interest factors because a case in which the proposed change would modify the custodial environment is essentially a change-of-custody case. On the other hand, if the proposed change would not modify the established custodial environment of the child, the burden is on the parent proposing the change to establish, by a preponderance of the evidence, that the change is in the child's best interests.

Pierron v. Pierron, 782 N.W.2d 480, 487 (Mich. 2010). How does this approach differ from the approach in J.R. v. M.S. on the question of school choice?

5. Split physical custody occurs when each parent has physical care of at least one child. Many states recognize a presumption that siblings should not be separated on the ground that such an arrangement "deprives children of the benefit of constant association with one another." In re Marriage of Pundt, 547 N.W.2d 243, 245 (Iowa App. 1996); Sickels v. Sickels, 221 So. 3d 778 (Fla. App. 2017). As is true of most custody rules, however, disapproval of split custody is not ironclad, and "circumstances may arise which demonstrate that separation may better promote the long-range best interests of children. Good and compelling reasons must exist for a departure." In re Marriage of Pundt, 547 N.W.2d 243, 245 (Iowa App. 1996); Brouillet v. Brouillet, 875 N.W.2d 485 (N.D. 2016); JCLK v. ZHB, 353 P.3d 720 (Wyo. 2015); McCarty v. McCarty, 867 N.W.2d 355 (S.D. 2015). *See also* Johns v. Cioci, 865 A.2d 931, 943 (Pa. Super. 2004) (refusing to apply presumption in favor of keeping siblings together to half-siblings because it would be "blatantly unfair" to parent who is not related to both children). For a comprehensive review of the law's failure to protect sibling ties, *see* Jill Elaine Hasday, Siblings in Law, 65 Vand. L. Rev. 897 (2012).

NOTE: SHARED CUSTODY PRESUMPTIONS

The court in *J.R.* resolved the custody dispute in that case in accordance with the best-interests-of-the-child standard. Does it apply any presumptions about what is in the best interests of the child?

The court observes that "[n]ationally, joint custody is increasingly becoming the favored custodial designation. Statutes in 18 states and the District of Columbia create a presumption that joint custody is in the best interests of the child, and those in three other states list it as the preferred option." In these states, the presumption is rebuttable through a showing that it is not in the child's best interests.

A primary factor in rebutting the presumption that joint custody is in the best interests of the child is the inability of the parents to cooperate. Indeed, the court in *J.R.* stated that in New York, which does not recognize a presumption in favor of joint custody, the "appellate courts still tend to be reluctant to order joint custody absent an agreement by the parties or a showing that they can work well together." The court in *J.R.* described at some length how the parents in that case had a difficult time communicating with each other. Should these difficulties have disqualified the parents from a joint custody arrangement in a state that otherwise favors such arrangements? In In re Marriage of Harris, 877 N.W.2d 434, 444 (Iowa 2016), the Iowa Supreme Court reversed the trial court, finding that a joint physical care award had not worked because of the acrimony between the parties. It ordered a change from joint to sole physical care because of "the parents' failure to cooperate in addressing the behavioral and medical issues of the children and in promoting the extracurricular interests of the children." It nonetheless left the joint legal custody provisions in place. Where parents cannot cooperate, what does it mean to designate a primary physical custodian, but continue to give the parents joint decision-making authority?

Some fathers' rights groups argue for a presumption favoring not only joint physical custody, but also equal shares of the child's time for both parents. Is such a presumption practical? *See* Margaret F. Brinig, Penalty Defaults in Family Law: The Case of Child Custody, 33 Fla. St. U. L. Rev. 779 (2006); David D. Meyer, The Constitutional Rights of Non-Custodial Parents, 34 Hofstra L. Rev. 1461 (2006); Milfred Dale, "Still the One": Defending the Individualized Best Interests of the Child Standard Against Equal Parenting Time Presumptions, 34 J. Am. Acad. Matrim. Law. 307 (2022) (evaluating the empirical evidence supporting joint custody and equal time presumptions and concluding the evidence shows that individualized determinations are more appropriate than blanket presumptions). Arkansas enacted such a statute in 2013, favoring joint custody and defining joint custody to mean "the approximate and reasonable equal division of time with the child by both parents individually." Ark. Code §9-13-101(a)(1)(A), (5) (2022). Arizona has also adopted a preference for shared parenting, providing that "the court shall adopt a parenting plan that provides for both parents to share legal decision-making regarding their child and that maximizes their respective parenting time." Ariz. Rev. Stat. §25-403.02(B) (2022). In 2018, Kentucky enacted a rebuttable presumption "that joint custody and equally shared parenting time is in the best interest of the child" and that, "[i]f a deviation from equal parenting time is warranted, the court shall construct a parenting time schedule which maximizes the time each parent or de facto custodian has with the child." Ky. Rev. Stat. Ann. §403.270 (2022).

What does it mean to "maximize" each parent's respective parenting time? How do the Arkansas, Arizona, and Kentucky statutes differ from the statutes discussed in note 2 above?

Many states, without necessarily adopting a presumption in favor of joint physical custody, presume that it is in the child's best interest to have frequent and continuing contact with both parents. How does such a presumption affect the choice between joint custody and other custody arrangements?

Joint custody has been the subject of ongoing social science research for the last four decades. This research finds that shared parenting has benefits for children when the parents cooperate and support each other. For a summary of the most recent findings, *see* Linda Nielsen, Shared Physical Custody: Does It Benefit Most Children?, 28 J. Am. Acad. Matrimonial Law. 79 (2015) (concluding that children overwhelmingly benefit from shared parenting); Marsha Kline Pruett & J. Herbie DiFonzo, Closing the Gap: Research, Policy, Practice, and Shared Parenting, 52 Fam. Ct. Rev. 152 (2014) (finding that the impact of shared parenting is necessarily case specific).

NOTE: CHILDREN'S PREFERENCES

Most presumptions that inform best-interest determinations involve children's presumed interest in a relationship with their parents. Children have other interests as well, including a right to express their own preferences about custody outcomes.

The court in J.R. v. M.S., for example, conducted what it termed a "Lincoln hearing" to determine the views of the child, and the court considered those views in fashioning the parenting arrangements. In Dugama v. Ayatew, 145 A.3d 517 (D.C. 2016), the District of Columbia's highest court held that trial courts must consider the custody preferences of older children. In that case, the children were 14, 9, and 7 when the mother petitioned to modify the custody arrangements. The Court of Appeals held that the trial judge must receive "evidence relating to the children's wishes," given the children's ages and ability to express their opinions about the matter. *Id.* at 521. The appellate court, while finding that the trial court's failure to do so constituted "reversible error," left the determination of the best way to do so to the trial judge's discretion. *Id.* at 522. Can you think of circumstances where the trial court might not want to ask the child directly about what outcome the child prefers? In such a case, what methods might the trial court use to determine the child's views?

Article 12 of the United Nations Convention on the Rights of Children, which has been ratified by every United Nations member except the United States, provides that children capable of forming their own views should be allowed to express those views on all matters affecting them, and due weight should be given to those views in accordance with the age and maturity of the child. Kim Hai Pearson, Children Are Human, 8 Tex. A&M L. Rev. 495, 520 (2021).

NOTE: PARENTAL ALIENATION AND JOINT CUSTODY

As the *J.R.* case indicates, many parents cannot communicate effectively with each other or cooperate in the care of the child, even if each adult is otherwise a competent parent. Indeed, many custody conflicts involve intense bickering between parents with allegations of disrespectful language, failure to inform the other parent of medical issues or vacation travel with the children, tardiness in showing up for transfers in custody, and lack of cooperation in facilitating the other parent's relationship with the child. The most serious cases, as we will see below, involve accusations of domestic violence or child abuse.

In response, many states have a custody preference for the parent who will facilitate a positive relationship and the child's continuing contact with the other parent. These statutory provisions are often called "friendly parent" provisions. *See, e.g.*, Cal. Fam. Code §3040(a)(1) (2022) ("the court shall consider, among other factors, which parent is more likely to allow the child frequent and continuing contact with the non-custodial parent"); Va. Code Ann. §20-124.3(6) (2022) (directing the courts to consider, in determining the child's best interests, "[t]he propensity of each parent to actively support the child's contact and relationship with the other parent, including whether a parent has unreasonably denied the other parent access to or visitation with the child"). The Arkansas custody statutes state that when "in the best interest of a child, custody shall be awarded in such a way so as to assure the frequent and continuing contact of the child with both parents" and "[i]f, at any time, the circuit court finds by a preponderance of the evidence that one (1) parent demonstrates a pattern of willfully creating conflict in an attempt to disrupt a current or pending joint-custody arrangement, the circuit court may deem such behavior as a material change of circumstances and may change a joint custody order to an order of primary custody to the nondisruptive parent." Ark. Code Ann. §9-13-101(b)(1)(A)(i), (iii) (2022).

These statutes encourage the courts to determine whether one parent is more responsible than the other for the ongoing conflict. In the early 1990s, psychologist Richard Gardner argued that "parental alienation syndrome" should be recognized as a divorce phenomenon in which one parent, typically the mother, attempts to maintain the psychological bond with the child by undermining the child's relationship with the other parent. He recommended a transfer of custody to the non-alienating parent in egregious cases. The Parental Alienation Syndrome: A Guide for Mental Health and Legal Professionals (1992, 2d ed. 1998). Critics have noted that parental alienation syndrome is not a recognized diagnosis in the Diagnostic and Statistical Manual IV and that Gardner's work did not appear in peer-reviewed journals. Courts, however, can consider parental willingness to cooperate without a formal diagnosis of a psychiatric "syndrome." *See, e.g.*, C.J.L. v. M.W.B., 879 So. 2d 1169 (Ala. 2003), discussing the distinction between expert testimony establishing parental alienation syndrome and a custody evaluation documenting the mother's efforts to undermine the children's relationship with their father through, among other things, false accusations of child abuse. Today, many courts use the term "parental alienation" to describe such conduct without reference to a "syndrome" or other psychological diagnosis. *See* Joan S. Meier, A Historical Perspective on Parental Alienation Syndrome and Parental Alienation, 6 J. Child Custody 232, 237-238 (2009); Joan S. Meier, Denial of Family Violence in Court: An Empirical Analysis and Path Forward for Family Law, 110 Geo. L.J. 835, 838 (2022).

The usual indicia of willingness to foster post-divorce relationships between a parent and the child include willingness to permit visitation; provide information about the child's health, education, and activities; and avoid unfounded allegations and other negative comments regarding the other parent. *See, e.g.*, Bingham v. Bingham, 167 P.3d 14 (Wyo. 2007); Puddicombe v. Dreka, 167 P.3d 73 (Alaska 2007). The unwillingness to allow a parent's relatives to visit with the child can be regarded as a sign of "unfriendliness" even though other cases recognize parents as having a constitutional right to deference with respect to visitation. *See* Nancy M. v. John M., 308 P.3d 1130 (Alaska 2013).

Consider the application of the Arkansas standard to the facts of a case such as *J.R.*, in which the parents cannot get along with each other, but where there are no allegations of abuse. Evidence at trial indicated that the father was combative, sometimes lost his temper, and expressed disrespect for the mother. The father introduced evidence that the parenting problems arose from the mother's anger and dislike of him. Does any of this amount to demonstrating "a pattern of willfully creating conflict in an attempt to disrupt a current or pending joint-custody arrangement"? Arkansas law strongly favors joint custody awards. Does this affect the interpretation of the statute addressing the change of custody? What weight should the court give to the children's views in such a case?

Parental alienation and friendly parent provisions can apply during an initial custody determination or can be the basis for a motion to modify custody. How should a child's established relationships with each parent be taken into account in such determinations? In K.T.D. v. K.W.P., 119 So. 3d 418 (Ala. Civ. App. 2012), for example, the mother was 16 and the father was 21 at the child's birth. The father established paternity and received visitation when the child was nine months old. Four years later, the parents, who could not communicate and agreed on little, both moved to modify custody, with the mother seeking to restrict the father's visitation rights and the father seeking a larger share of the child's time. The father had been convicted of assault involving the mother's family around the time of the birth, and menacing in a traffic dispute unrelated to the mother or her family, and he admitted that he had an anger management problem for which he was receiving psychiatric care. The mother has refused to respond to the fathers' calls, tried to micromanage the fathers' visits with the child, and had belittled his parenting in front of the child. Finding that the mother had shown poor judgment toward the father and his family and sought to undermine his relationship with the child, the court changed the mother's sole custody award to joint legal and physical custody of the child and provided that the child would spend approximately half of his time with the father. The dissenting judge argued that the mother's conduct should be dealt with through contempt, rather than a change of custody. Cf. T.N.S.R. v. N.P.W., 170 So. 3d 684 (Ala. Civ. App. 2014) (reversing transfer of 4-year-old to father on the basis of parental alienation because the court did not give sufficient weight to the mother's role as primary caretaker and the child's interest in remaining in the home, with his half siblings, where he had spent his entire life).

Do "friendly parenting" provisions invite courts to use custody awards as a sanction for parental failure to support the other parent's relationship with the child? How much weight should be given to "friendly parenting" as opposed to other factors that go into a best interest determination? Is joint custody appropriate where parents have such poor relationships with each other?

NOTE: PARENTING PLANS AND PARENTING COORDINATORS

Some states, in an effort to avoid labelling parenting time, have switched to the use of parenting plans. Parenting plans give parents greater flexibility in crafting solutions that meet their individual needs. Such plans may provide for dispute resolution procedures as well as substantive provisions governing the child's schedule, dividing holidays between the parents, and specifying decision-making responsibility in accordance with the type of detailed provisions the court adopted in *J.R.* N.H. Rev. Stat. Ann. §461-A:4 (2022), for example, states that:

> In any proceeding to establish or modify a judgment providing for parenting time with a child, . . . the parents shall develop and file with the court a parenting plan to be included in the court's decree. If the parents are unable to develop a parenting plan, the court may develop it. In developing a parenting plan under this section, the court shall consider only the best interests of the child . . . and the safety of the parties.

These plans may provide for the appointment of a "parenting coordinator" to help resolve disputes. The coordinators serve as case managers who can mediate parental disputes, refer the parties for counselling or other assistance, or work with the family court judge to resolve individual disputes without relitigating the custody determination. *See* Christine A. Coates,

The Parenting Coordinator as Peacemaker and Peacebuilder, 53 Fam. Ct. Rev. 398 (2015). The Nevada Supreme Court, however, has held that a lower court could not delegate its decision-making authority to a parent coordinator in making substantive changes to the custody plan. Bautista v. Picone, 419 P.3d 157 (Nev. 2018).

American Law Institute

Principles of the Law of Family Dissolution
§2.05 Parenting Plan: Proposed, Temporary, and Final (2002)

(1) An individual seeking a judicial allocation of custodial responsibility or decision making responsibility . . . should be required to file with the court a proposed parenting plan. . . .

(2) Each parenting plan filed under Paragraph (1) should be required to be supported by an affidavit containing . . . [the names and addresses of involved individuals, a description of the past allocation of caretaking and other parenting functions, the child's and caretakers' schedules, a description of the known areas of agreement and disagreement, and other relevant information].

(5) . . . [T]he court should order a parenting plan that is consistent with the custody provisions of §§2.08-2.12 [favoring continuation of the division of responsibility that existed during the marriage] and contains the following provisions:

(a) a provision for the child's living arrangements and for each parent's custodial responsibility, which should include either

(i) a custodial schedule that designates in which parent's home each minor child will reside on given days of the year; or

(ii) a formula or method for determining such a schedule in sufficient detail that, if necessary, the schedule can be enforced in a subsequent proceeding.

(b) an allocation of decision making responsibility as to significant matters reasonably likely to arise with respect to the child; and

(c) a provision . . . for resolution of disputes that arise under the plan, and a provision establishing remedies for violations of the plan.

NOTES AND QUESTIONS

1. Like the court in *J.R.*, the ALI approach moves away from the use of labels (*e.g.*, "sole custody," "joint custody," and "visitation") to allocate decision-making power in favor of more detailed plans that define the respective responsibilities of each parent. A parenting plan might specify, for example, that the parent, who coaches the child's soccer team, shall have physical custody on the days of every soccer game and practice, and sole decision-making power over team-related issues, whereas the other parent shall attend parent-teacher conferences and have primary decision-making responsibility for homework disputes. Are more detailed plans likely to generate conflict as circumstances change (*e.g.*, the child joins a more competitive team that practices more frequently and travels during the period the other parent is supposed to have custody) or prevent conflict by eliminating some of the ambiguity and discretion in more traditional awards?

2. The ALI Principles provide that "a court may modify a court-ordered parenting plan if it finds, on the basis of facts that were not known or have arisen since the entry of the prior order and were not anticipated therein, that a substantial change has occurred in the circumstances of the child or of one or both parents and that a modification is necessary to the child's welfare." §2.15(1). The Principles also permit modifications in the child's best interest if the parents agree, the modification reflects a de facto change already in place for at least six months, the change is necessary to accommodate an older child's preferences, and other circumstances. §2.16.

PROBLEMS

1. Andy and Bo have joint legal custody, but Andy is the physical custodian. Their separation agreement defined "joint custody" as "mutual cooperation and decision making regarding the child's health, education, and welfare." The agreement also provided for equal sharing of unreimbursed medical expenses and barred both parents from incurring non-emergency major medical expenses without the other's knowledge and consent.

After a bicycle accident, a doctor recommended elective surgery to correct an obstruction to their daughter's nose. Bo secured two "second opinions" concluding that surgery at that time was not necessary and risky. The surgery will not be covered by insurance, and Bo has refused to consent to it. Andy has confidence in the doctor who recommended the surgery and would like him to perform it. Andy seeks an order permitting arrangements for the surgery to be made and to compel Bo to pay half the cost. What result? How might the outcome differ in J.R. v. M.S.?

2. Dale and Terry share joint legal and physical custody. With the court's permission, Dale has moved 45 minutes away, and the two children attend a school near Dale's residence. Terry enjoys custodial time with the children on weekends and during the summer. Terry has become concerned that the younger child's reading and math scores are poor, and the child has not been doing well in school. The school near Terry's residence is a much better school, with smaller classes and more support for struggling students. Terry enrolls the child in a summer school class and a tutoring program, and the child's test scores jump. The gains dissipate over the course of the following year when the child returns to the school near Dale. Terry petitions the court for permission to change the child's school. This will require that the child live with Terry during the school year, with Dale enjoying custodial time on weekends and during the summer. Dale objects that this is in effect a change in custody from Dale to Terry, and Terry must therefore meet the more stringent test requiring clear and convincing evidence of changed circumstances and of a benefit to the child to prevail. Terry argues that this is not a change in custody, and therefore a change can be made based on a preponderance of the evidence that the switch in schools is in the child's best interest. Who has the stronger argument?

3. The court awards Gene and Nicky joint legal and physical custody of three children, who are 14, 12, and 9. The marriage broke up when Gene had an affair, and the 14-year-old actively dislikes and blames Gene for the divorce. In addition, the 14-year-old would like to spend more time with his friends. The 14-year-old persuades the younger children that they do not want to spend time with Gene either. The last time Gene was supposed to spend time with the children, Nicky called to say that the children just didn't want to go. The next time this happened, Gene showed up with the police. The children remained defiant and told the police that they do not want to spend time with Gene. Nicky petitions the court to change the custody arrangement from joint custody to sole custody. Gene alleges that Nicky has turned the children against him and asks the court to switch custody to him. The children tell the judge in a "Lincoln hearing" that they dislike Gene and do not wish to spend time with him. The jurisdiction has a presumption favoring joint custody or in the alternative sole custody to the parent who will best promote the involvement of the other parent. Gene has testified that he welcomes Nicky's involvement with the children; Nicky has testified about efforts to encourage the children to spend time with Gene. How should the court respond in a jurisdiction that presumes that joint custody is in the best interests of the children? In a jurisdiction that favors the award of custody to the parent who best promotes the involvement of the other parent?

4. Consider how you would draft a parenting plan in the following case: Donny would ideally like joint legal decision-making power and equal time with the two children, ages 7 and 9. Donny also prefers to have parenting time on weekends and one day during the week, preferably on the evening when the children have their piano lessons. Marty prefers an award of sole decision-making power, and visitation for Donny every other weekend and on rotating days during the week that change with Marty's work schedule. If you represented Donny, what kind of plan would you propose, and how might you try to persuade Marty to accept it? How would use of a parenting plan differ from an award of sole legal or physical custody to Marty, with visitation for Donny, giving each the same amount of time promised in the parenting plan?

3. Primary Caretaker

If the court does not award joint physical and legal custody or use a parenting plan that allocates custodial responsibilities without using labels such as "primary residential custody," then the court must choose between the two parents. Legislators typically list a series of factors to guide the judge. A particularly important consideration is the identification of the parent who has been the child's "primary caretaker." At one time, courts usually presumed that it was in the child's best interests to remain with the primary caretaker. Today, jurisdictions differ substantially in how they define what it means to be a primary caretaker, and how much weight is to be given to this consideration. The case below illustrates the dispute.

Deyle v. Deyle
825 N.W.2d 245 (N. Dak. 2012)

CROTHERS, Justice. . . . Christina Deyle and Eric Deyle were married on September 8, 2007 and have two children together: H.F.D. born in 2004 and C.E.D. born in 2008. The parties separated in June 2010 when Eric Deyle left the marital home and moved into an apartment. Christina Deyle and the children remained in the marital home in Milnor, North Dakota until December 2011 when a foreclosure action was commenced after Eric Deyle ceased making mortgage payments. Christina Deyle and the children moved in with Christina Deyle's parents in Milnor. Christina Deyle was the primary caretaker of the children throughout the parties' separation.

Christina Deyle commenced a divorce action and sought primary residential responsibility, spousal support and child support. Following trial, the district court awarded Eric Deyle primary residential responsibility and granted Christina Deyle parenting time. . . .

Christina Deyle argues granting Eric Deyle primary residential responsibility was clearly erroneous. . . .

"District courts must award primary residential responsibility of children to the party who will best promote the children's best interests and welfare." *Morris*, 2012 ND 74, 815 N.W.2d 266. "A district court has broad discretion in awarding primary residential responsibility, but the court must consider all of the relevant factors under N.D.C.C. §14-09-06.2(1)." . . .

Christina Deyle argues the district court erred in finding factor (d) favored Eric Deyle. Under factor (d) the court considers "[t]he sufficiency and stability of each parent's home environment, the impact of extended family, the length of time the child has lived in each parent's home, and the desirability of maintaining continuity in the child's home and community." The district court found that "it is in the children's best interest to stay in Milnor to be near Christina's family (for both children) and to maintain continuity in community activities and school (at this time for the older child)." The district court explained:

> "Christina's living situation is likely going to change at least two and perhaps three times in the foreseeable future; moving out of her parent's home into another home in Milnor, possibly moving to Wahpeton for school, and then moving to find work as a hygienist. While I commend her for continuing her education, stability and continuity is what is best for these children."

Christina Deyle argues the district court erred as a matter of law by speculating about future events and by making findings that were not supported by any evidence.

The district court did not misapply the law in its analysis regarding factor (d) by examining the effects of a potential future relocation by Christina Deyle. Traditionally, "[f]actor (d) require[d] consideration of the stability and quality of the child's *past* environment." "[F]actor (e) use[d] a forward-looking approach to the stability of the family unit, its interrelations and environment, versus the backward-looking factor (d)." Section 14-09-06.2(1), N.D.C.C., was amended in 2009. . . .

Pre-2009 factor (d) directed consideration of "[t]he length of time the child has lived in a stable satisfactory environment and the desirability of maintaining continuity." Pre-2009 factor (e) directed consideration of "[t]he permanence, as a family unit, of the existing or proposed custodial home." Current factor (d) incorporates consideration both of the length of time the child has lived in a stable home as well as the permanence or stability of the home environment and adds the forward-looking consideration of "the desirability of maintaining continuity in the child's home and community."

Factor (d) no longer restricts the district court's analysis to past events. The district court found granting Eric Deyle primary residential responsibility would provide greater continuity and stability because of Christina Deyle's potential relocations. This finding was supported by the record. The district court's finding factor (d) favored Eric Deyle is not clearly erroneous both because it is a correct application of law and because it is supported by the evidence.

Christina Deyle argues the district court erred in finding factor (e) favored neither party. Courts applying factor (e) consider "[t]he willingness and ability of each parent to facilitate and encourage a close and continuing relationship between the other parent and the child." The district court found "the parties are both willing and able to foster the parental relationship of the other" and both parties recognized the importance of the other parent's role in the children's lives. . . .

Christina Deyle argues the district court erred by speculating as to Christina Deyle's future.

Factor (h) expressly requires that the court consider the potential effects of change. The court must look forward under this factor to determine whether foreseeable changes could impact a child's life in the home, school and community. Here, the district court noted the reasonable possibility of future relocation by Christina Deyle due to her anticipated education and employment in the dental field and the lack of those jobs in the Milnor area. From that evidence, the district court found Christina Deyle's likely move would have an adverse impact on the children. The district court also found Eric Deyle actively involved the older child in community activities. These findings are supported by the record. . . .

Christina Deyle argues the district court erred in finding factor (k) favored neither party because the district court did not consider the close bond the children have with their maternal grandparents. Under factor (k) the court considers:

"The interaction and interrelationship, or the potential for interaction and interrelationship, of the child with any person who resides in, is present, or frequents the household of a parent and who may significantly affect the child's best interests. The court shall consider that person's history of inflicting, or tendency to inflict, physical harm, bodily injury, assault, or the fear of physical harm, bodily injury, or assault, on other persons."

We have explained that factor (k) addresses the negative influence of third parties, not the positive influence of extended family. The district court properly considered the children's close bond with their maternal grandparents in its factor (m) analysis. . . .

Christina Deyle argues the district court erred in finding factor (m) favored Eric Deyle. Under factor (m) the court considers "[a]ny other factors considered by the court to be relevant to a particular parental rights and responsibilities dispute." The district court found that the children's maternal grandparents played a significant role in their lives and that Eric Deyle fostered the children's relationship with their maternal grandparents. The district court was concerned with the possibility of Christina Deyle's relocation and the potential negative impact a move would have on the children. Eric Deyle testified he intended to remain in the Milnor area, and Christina Deyle testified about her intent to become a dental hygienist and the possibility of a future move to find work. The record supports the district court's findings. . . .

MARING, Justice, dissenting. . . . I believe Christina Deyle's role as primary caretaker, the trial court's improper speculation of where Christina Deyle will reside two years post-divorce, and Eric Deyle's failure to financially support his children resulted in findings unsupported by the record and a misapplication of factors (d), (h), and (m).

1. Primary Caretaker

In 2009, the legislature amended N.D.C.C. §14-09-06.2(1), the best interest factors. . . .

The amendment was intended to combine and clarify the factors, but not to change the meaning or application of either factor. *See* Hearing on S.B.2042 Before the Senate Judiciary Comm., 61st N.D. Legis. Sess. (Jan. 19, 2009) (testimony of Attorney Sherry Mills Moore, State Bar Assoc. of N.D., lobbyist). Moore explained:

> Proposed paragraph (d) requires the court to look at the sufficiency and stability of each parent's home environment, the length of time the child has lived in each home and the desirability of maintaining continuity in the child's home and community. The amendments are not intended to eliminate the court's ability to consider the permanence of the family unit.

Therefore, this Court's interpretation of the new factor (d) should be consistent with this Court's interpretation of the pre-amended factors (d) and (e).

Although this Court does not presume custody in favor of the primary caretaker, the concept of the primary caretaker "inheres in the statutory factors" and deserves recognition. While a trial court may not rely upon the primary caretaker status to the exclusion of all other factors, it certainly should consider which parent served as the primary caretaker. Established patterns of care and nurture are relevant factors. "Continuity in a child's relationship with the closest, nurturing parent is . . . a very important aspect of stability." If factors (d) and (e) are properly construed, "they go to the overriding importance of the stability, continuity, and permanence embodied in a primary caretaker's relationship with the children."

Here, the trial court found Christina Deyle to be the primary caretaker. However, the trial court erred when it found this to weigh in her favor only under N.D.C.C. §14-09-06.2(1)(b). A primary caretaker can be given consideration under factor (b); however, to reduce the primary caretaker to consideration of whether a person provides "adequate food, clothing, shelter, medical care, and a safe environment" undermines the psychological relationship shared by a child and the primary caretaker. A primary caretaker has intimate interactions with the child creating a vital bond. Consideration of this social and emotional bond must be given weight under N.D.C.C. §14-09-06.2(1)(d). The trial court's findings under factor (d) completely ignored Christina Deyle's role as primary caretaker and is, therefore, clearly erroneous.

Further, factor (d) focuses on the emotional stability as well as the physical environment of a child's past and future home. The pre-amended version of N.D.C.C. §14-09-06.2(1)(d) "addresses past stability of [the] environment, including a consideration of place or physical setting, as well as a consideration of the prior family unit and its lifestyle as part of that setting. It also addresses the quality of that past environment, and the desirability of maintaining continuity." A prior custodial arrangement should be considered when examining factor (d).

To decide factor (d) solely based on the children remaining in a location wrongfully places the emphasis on geography rather than parental relations. . . . I continue to be troubled by the emphasis on the continuity of the child's physical setting over the importance of the continuity of the parent-child relationship under factor (d).

2. SPECULATION OF MOVE

Unsupported speculation of where Christina Deyle will be two years post-divorce pervade the trial court's findings that factors (d), (h), and (m), N.D.C.C. §14-09-06.2(1), favored Eric Deyle and are, therefore, clearly erroneous.

. . . Any reliance on Christina Deyle's move from her parents' home is misplaced as a basis to find against her under factors (d), (h), or (m). The record establishes that Eric Deyle did not provide a stable home for the children in the interim, and he failed to pay the mortgage forcing the children and Christina Deyle out of their home. Christina Deyle took the children with her to her parents' home. Any move from her parents' home is a direct result of Eric Deyle's actions and should not be weighed against Christina Deyle.

Any reliance on subsequent moves is not supported by the record. The trial court found Christina Deyle is likely to move for school. However, the record is completely void of any reference to her moving for school. Further, Christina Deyle testified that she is applying to the dental hygienist program, but has not yet been accepted [although she testified that she hoped to be]. . . . Based on this testimony, the trial court found Christina Deyle was likely moving to Wahpeton for school, yet she has not been accepted into the program. Further, Christina Deyle currently attends classes in Wahpeton while living with her parents in Milnor.[2] There is no basis for the trial court to speculate such an arrangement would be different if she attended the dental hygienist program.

The trial court also found Christina Deyle would likely move out of the area after she finishes school. However, Christina Deyle testified she would like to remain in the Milnor area after she finishes school. . . .

The trial court speculated, based on the fact Christina Deyle was unaware of dental hygienist jobs in the Milnor area, that she would move away from Milnor. However, her testimony does not support such a finding.

The trial court found Christina Deyle to be the primary caretaker, yet found factor (d) to weigh in favor of Eric Deyle because of its speculation that Christina Deyle "may move." I agree with the majority in holding that a trial court may look into the future to determine whether factor (d) favors one parent. However, the trial court may not speculate as to future events, when such is not supported by the record. I am of the opinion that the trial court went

---

2. Travel time is 40 to 45 minutes. — Eds.

beyond the forward-looking approach discussed in Lindberg v. Lindberg, 2009 ND 136, 770 N.W.2d 252, and engaged in speculation unsubstantiated by facts in the record. . . .

Under factor (h), the trial court found the potential effect of any change to home, school, and community weighed "slightly" in favor of Eric Deyle. However, again, this finding is premised on speculation that Christina Deyle "may move." . . .

Under factor (m), the trial court found Eric Deyle was able to provide a more stable physical and emotional environment. This is again premised on the trial court's speculation that Christina Deyle "may move." . . .

3. FINANCIAL SUPPORT

The trial court further erred in its findings under factor (m) when it ignores its findings under factor (b). In its analysis of N.D.C.C. §14-09-06.2(1)(b), "[t]he ability of each parent to assure that the child receives adequate food, clothing, shelter, medical care, and a safe environment," the trial court found that Eric Deyle has done little to financially support his children since the parties' separation. Specifically, the trial court found:

> These children have been without meaningful financial support from Eric since June 2010. Eric earns considerably more than Christina but has provided very little financial support for the children's needs since their separation. Eric allowed the home that his children were living in go into foreclosure.
>
> The fact that Eric failed to support his children during the separation and that he allowed the home in which they were living to go into foreclosure during the parties' separation *weigh heavily against him in this court's consideration of residential responsibility.* (Emphasis added.)

The trial court specifically found Christina Deyle "has been the children's primary caregiver during the marriage and separation," and, therefore, concluded factor (b) "strongly favors" Christina Deyle. Those findings are supported by the evidence in the record. And yet, after finding Eric Deyle's failure to financially support his children "weigh heavily against him" and finding Christina Deyle was the children's primary caretaker in its analysis under factor (b), the trial court then found Eric Deyle would provide a more stable physical and emotional setting for the children under factor (m).

The evidence in this record supports that Eric Deyle allowed the home in which his children lived to go into foreclosure; he has not provided a stable environment for the children; he essentially caused his children to become homeless; and he has failed to pay child support since June of 2010.

Therefore, I am of the opinion that the trial court's finding that Eric Deyle is able to provide a more stable physical and emotional environment than Christine Deyle and, therefore, N.D.C.C. §14-09-06.2(1)(m), favors him is clearly erroneous.

NOTES AND QUESTIONS

1. How would *Deyle* have been decided in a state with a presumption for joint physical and legal custody? Could a court have awarded joint physical custody to the parents if the mother chose to attend a school 40 miles away? How would *Deyle* have been decided in a state that uses parenting plans that do not necessarily include a custodial designation?

2. *Deyle* involves an initial award of custody. In the next section of this chapter, we will consider relocations as justification for a modification of a custody award. In some states, there is a presumption that a parent with primary residential custody of a child may move without triggering reconsideration of the custody order. Might such a presumption influence the initial designation of custody in a case like this where the court believes that a parent might move?

3. The majority and the dissent disagree about how to define the primary caretaker factor and about how much weight to give it. How much importance does each opinion accord to past acts of caretaking, such as making meals, managing medical appointments, or supervising homework? How much weight does each opinion accord to psychological bonding? To the continuity of relationships with schools, community activities, friends, and extended family? To what degree is consideration of future caretaking a factor in *Deyle*? Is that an appropriate part of a primary caretaker analysis? In defining what caretaking means, how does each opinion tie its position to its interpretation of the state custody statute and the best-interests standard?

4. Professor Katherine Bartlett, a reporter for the ALI Principles on Family Dissolution, has observed that:

> Substantively, past caretaking is a reasonable proxy for the less determinate factors that are generally thought to be related to a child's best interests. Past caretaking will tend to correspond with the child's emotional bonds to the parents, parental abilities, and the child's need for stability and continuity. Past caretaking also takes into account the individual circumstances of the child. When a court approximates past caretaking patterns, a child who has had a primary caretaker will maintain that primary caretaker after the parents' separation, whereas a child who has enjoyed equal caretaking from each parent can expect that arrangement to continue to the extent practicable. An additional advantage is that past caretaking arrangements reflect the lived expectations of the parents themselves.

Katharine T. Bartlett, Prioritizing Past Caretaking in Child-Custody Decisionmaking, 77 Law & Contemp. Probs. 29, 33 (2014). ALI Principles §2.08 proposed that:

> (1) Unless otherwise resolved by agreement of the parents . . ., the court should allocate custodial responsibility so that the proportion of custodial time the child spends with each parent approximates the proportion of time each parent spent performing caretaking functions for the child prior to the parents' separation.

The approach that Bartlett and the ALI Principles propose looks backward at the assumption of responsibility for caretaking before the parents' separation. How does such an approach differ from that adopted in *Deyle*? Why does the majority consider only caretaking after the separation while the dissent observes that the mother was a primary caretaker during the marriage as well? What are the advantages and disadvantages of each approach?

5. The courts have declared explicitly gendered custody standards, such as a maternal preference, unconstitutional. *See, e.g.*, Pusey v. Pusey, 728 P.2d 117 (Utah 1986). Is the primary caretaker preference a socially acceptable strategy for reaching the same result produced by the maternal preference or "tender years" doctrine? The primary caretaker standard gives a preference to the parent who has assumed primary responsibility for the child before the custodial dispute arose. Robert Mnookin observes that, based on time-allocation surveys going back to 1965, fathers have nearly tripled the amount of time they spend with their children living in the same household as the father. A large gender gap in time spent with children nonetheless remains, with mothers spending "about twice as much time with their children as fathers do. (In 2011, mothers spent about 13.5 hours per week, compared with 7.3 hours for fathers)." Robert Mnookin, Child Custody Revisited, 77 Law & Contemp. Probs. 249, 257-258 (2014). This means that a custody standard that favors an award of sole physical custody to the primary caretaker is likely to favor mothers. Is that objectionable as a violation of equal protection?

The ALI proposes, as an alternative, that custodial rights be awarded in proportion to the amount of time the parents spent on caretaking activities while the relationship was intact.

Mnookin estimates that this would result, on average, in a two-to-one allocation of custodial time in favor of mothers. Is this also objectionable as a violation of equal protection?

6. Most states use the primary caretaker factor as one of a number of unweighted factors that contribute to a holistic best-interests determination. *See, e.g.*, M.J.M. v. M.L.G., 63 A.3d 331, 337-338 (Pa. Super. 2013). A primary caretaker *presumption*, in contrast, assumes that the child's best interests lie with an award of custody to the primary caretaker, absent a demonstration to the contrary. The presumption makes the primary caretaker role central to the definition of the child's best interests, giving it precedence over other considerations. Does the dissent in *Deyle* argue for such a result explicitly or implicitly?

7. To what extent should child care arrangements influence custody determinations? In W.C.F. v. M.G., 115 A.3d 323, 329-330 (Pa. Super. 2015), the maternal grandmother had been caring for the child while the mother worked; the father would have to rely on paid child-care if he received custody. The trial court found that "a change in primary custody would be disruptive for the child, particularly because it would mean placement in child-care rather than with a family member during the week." *Id.* at 330. The appellate majority objected to this analysis because the grandmother had not supported the father's involvement with the child and because the trial court had found that it "will be beneficial for the child to be in contact with other children on a regular basis and to be among adults other than Mother's family members." *Id.* at 331. The observation about contact with other children conflicts with other cases favoring care by a custodial parent, *see, e.g.*, Reed v. Pieper, 713 S.E.2d 309, 313 (S.C. App. 2011), but leaves open the question of whether grandparent care should be part of the primary caretaker factor. Child-care arrangements often reflect the parties' respective resources. For a discussion of the ways that socioeconomic status influences custody decision-making, *see* Michele Benedetto Neitz, Socioeconomic Bias in the Judiciary, 61 Clev. St. L. Rev. 137, 158-161 (2013).

What role did the maternal grandparents' ability to provide care play in *Deyle*? Should it have been considered at all? Should it have played a greater role in the decision?

8. Where the parents did not live together before the custody proceeding, the child will typically have resided with the mother. If a custody action is not filed until some time after the child's birth, what weight should be given to the child's established relationship with the custodial parent? *Compare* Clare Huntington, Postmarital Family Law: A Legal Structure for Nonmarital Families, 67 Stan. L. Rev. 167 (2015) (arguing for legal reforms that would give unmarried mothers and fathers more equal custodial rights starting at birth) *with* Pamela Laufer-Ukeles, The Children of Nonmarriage: Towards a Child-First Family Law, 40 Yale L. & Pol'y Rev. 384, 425-426 (2022) ("[t]he push to joint parenthood can make nonmarried parenthood even more difficult for single mothers than it already is. . . . A casual sexual encounter may not justify the interference in autonomy that joint parenthood would entail over the parent who is more able and willing to provide needed care.").

In Harrison v. Tauheed, 256 P.3d 851 (Kan. 2011), the father argued that the trial court's emphasis on the mother's role as the child's primary caretaker amounted to "a demand that he demonstrate a compelling reason to have [his son's] living arrangement changed" and that such a standard was inappropriate in an initial custody determination. The Kansas Supreme Court agreed with the mother, however, that the trial court's choice to "place great weight" on the length of time the child had spent with each parent and his successful adjustment to the mother's home, the school she chose, and the community in which she was living with the son were appropriate parts of a multi-factor best-interests determination.

In light of these standards, how would you advise the father of a newborn, when the father is not living with the mother and child, to preserve his ability to secure custodial rights?

PROBLEMS

1. Bryan and Shannan were married and had two young children. After the birth of their youngest child, Shannan became depressed and began taking medication and drinking heavily. Shannan entered a rehabilitation program and remained there for four and a half months. While Shannon was still in the rehabilitation program, Bryan filed for dissolution of the marriage. The trial court awarded Bryan sole physical custody. Five months later, Shannan asked for and received alternating weekend and holiday visitation.

A year after the initial custody award, Shannan moved to modify the custody award to grant her physical custody. Because Bryan worked long hours, the children were spending many hours with day care providers and Bryan's parents. Shannan had remarried and had another child. She was a full-time homemaker who could care for the children in her home during the day, and she argued that being with her would be in the child's best interests.

The trial court found that Shannan's recovery efforts had been successful and that she had been sober for more than a year. The judge ruled that it would be in the children's best interests to live with Shannan, since she could provide personal care for them. Bryan was granted visitation.

Bryan appeals, emphasizing his role as a primary caretaker. What arguments should the parties make?

2. Jennifer gave birth to her daughter when she was 15 years of age. The child's unmarried father, Steve, was three months older. He acknowledged paternity immediately. The child is now three, and Steve seeks sole custody.

Jennifer has been raising the child in her mother's house. Since the child's birth, Jennifer has assumed primary responsibility for the child with her mother and sister providing most of the care as Jennifer completed high school. The mother and sister have also supplied almost all of the child's necessities, since neither parent has the earning capacity to provide support.

Jennifer, a talented student, has received a scholarship from the University of Michigan. She plans to live in resident housing during the period required for a bachelor's and, perhaps, a master's degree. She contemplates living at the university and placing the child in appropriate day care or schooling. In off-school times she and the child would return to her mother's home.

Steve resides with his parents and, in the early days, exercised visitation with his mother participating in caring for the child, though the parties have never formalized the arrangement through a court order. He has a good relationship with his daughter. He is currently a student at the local community college in California and maintains part-time employment. Steve's mother, who is in good health and 39 years old, is not employed outside the home and would welcome the opportunity to care for the child when Steve is at school or work. What custodial order should be entered?

3. After Molly and Amy were married, Amy bore a daughter, Jill, who was conceived by artificial insemination. Since Molly had a more flexible schedule, she became the primary caretaker, but both women supported and cared for the child. The following year, Molly became pregnant using the same sperm donor Amy had used, but the couple separated before the child's birth. After the separation, Molly continued to care for Jill. Three months later, when Jill was 15 months old, Amy moved to Oregon and took Jill with her, cutting off all contact with Molly. Molly gave birth to a daughter, Mia, and then sued for divorce and for primary custody of both children. Amy has not sought any relationship with Mia and seeks sole physical and legal custody of Jill. The court has recognized both women as legal parents of both children. Who should be viewed as the primary caretaker of each child? What custodial order should the court issue? How should custody be allocated under the primary caretaker preference?

4. Managing Shared Parenting

With increased emphasis on shared parenting, managing parental conflicts has become more important and more difficult. The most frequent source of dispute is a type of changed circumstance that may not be the fault of either parent — relocation. A move of a significant distance often disrupts shared parenting arrangements. Yet the ability to move — to take advantage of new job opportunities, relationships, or extended family support — is often critical to one parent's well-being. Such issues often pit each parent's interests against the other's, with uncertain consequences for the child. This section examines how the courts deal with such parents' changing needs.

The section then considers allegations of parental misbehavior that raise questions about suitability for custody. Allegations of sexual abuse, parental alienation, and domestic violence all potentially disqualify a parent from assuming a custodial role. On the other hand, the allegations are often hard to prove, and the fact of such allegations can undermine parental relationships.

Finally, the section considers circumstances when the parents may simply have different preferences, such as different religious convictions and different views about appropriate new relationships that require a choice among competing parental interests.

a. Relocation and Changed Circumstances

Arnott v. Arnott
293 P.3d 440 (Wyo. 2012)

Burke, J. . . . . The parties were married in 2001 and lived together in Jackson, Wyoming until their divorce in 2010. Their first daughter, AGA, was born on June 6, 2003, and their second daughter, ALA, was born on June 30, 2005. At the time of their divorce, the parties agreed that they would share joint legal custody of the children, and that Mother would have primary physical custody, subject to Father's reasonable visitation. The parties agreed to "consult with each other regarding major decisions involving the children, including but not limited to their education, health, and other issues involving the children's welfare." The parties agreed that Father would have visitation every other weekend, as well as on alternating Thursdays. They also agreed to Father's visitation on alternating holidays and during two two-week periods in the summer. The decree of divorce required Mother to provide notice if she intended to relocate.

On July 8, 2011, Mother filed a notice of intent to relocate, indicating that she intended to move with the children to Mechanicsville, Virginia on August 13, 2011. Ten days later, Father filed a petition for modification of custody alleging that Mother's anticipated move constituted a material change in circumstances with respect to custody and visitation. . . .

Mother moved to dismiss the petition to modify custody and visitation, asserting that under this Court's decision in Watt v. Watt, 971 P.2d 608, 614 (Wyo. 1999), relocation by a custodial parent, by itself, is not a material change in circumstances sufficient to justify a modification of child custody. . . .

The court found that the children had "an outstanding set of parents" and "an incredibly involved father whose life revolves around his relationship with his children." The court noted that both Mother and Father were exemplary parents, that the children were "thriving" in their current environment, and that the "arrangement here in Jackson has worked incredibly well." The court further commented that "If I had my wish it would be that Ms. Arnott would find some way to stay here or nearer so that the extraordinary relationship that

Mr. Arnott has with his children could continue to blossom in a similar fashion." But the court again noted that Wyoming precedent had created a "strong presumption in favor of allowing the custodial parent to move with [the] children" and had placed a "difficult burden" on the noncustodial parent to show a material change in circumstances based on the custodial parent's relocation.

Following the criteria set forth in *Watt*, the district court determined that Mother's motives for the relocation were legitimate, sincere, and in good faith. The court also found that Mother's relocation would still permit Father's reasonable visitation if visitation was expanded. The court concluded that Father had not established that Mother's relocation constituted a material change of circumstances sufficient to warrant consideration of a change in custody. . . . Father appeals from the district court's order.

Discussion

Disputes arising from the relocation of a custodial parent "present some of the knottiest and most disturbing problems that our courts are called upon to resolve." As one commentator has noted,

> Relocation cases are "intractable problems" and the "San Andreas fault" of family law. When one parent attempts to move a child a significant distance from the other parent, the child's relationship with each parent changes in quality and quantity. These "no-win" cases are occurring with increasing frequency, create enormous tensions for parents and their children, and burden the legal system and the judges who have to decide them. A potential relocation can generate conflict in cases where there had been none before, reopen old wounds in others, or exacerbate an already highly-conflicted situation.

Elrod, Linda D., *National and International Momentum Builds for More Child Focus in Relocation Disputes*, 44 Fam. L.Q. 341, 341-42 (2010). Unfortunately, such cases are increasingly common. . . .[3]

The present case relates to the threshold inquiry under Wyo. Stat. Ann. §20-2-204(c): whether relocation of a custodial parent may constitute a material change in circumstances sufficient to warrant consideration of whether modification of custody is in the best interests of the children. . . .

This Court's first occasion to consider modification of child custody based on the possible relocation of a custodial parent arose in Martin v. Martin, 798 P.2d 321 (Wyo. 1990). In that case, both parents remained in Laramie at the time of their divorce, and the divorce decree specified that each parent would have physical custody of the children for six months of the year. The divorce decree further specified, however, that if either parent relocated from Laramie, the relocating parent would have custody for three months, and the remaining parent would have custody for nine months. On appeal, this Court held that inclusion of the provision for automatic future modification of child custody was an abuse of discretion, noting that child custody determinations are based on the best interests of the children, and that such a determination cannot be made absent "all facts necessary to make such a determination." . . .

The Court's next opportunity to consider a modification of custody based on relocation was presented in Love v. Love, 851 P.2d 1283 (Wyo. 1993). In that case, the . . . divorce decree

---

3. "According to the U.S. Census Bureau, about 1 in 6 Americans moves each year. Approximately 7 million people a year move from state to state. The 'average American' makes 11.7 moves in a lifetime. Because of the ordinary needs of both parents after a marital dissolution to secure or retain employment, pursue educational or career opportunities, or reside in the same location as a new spouse or other family or friends, it is unrealistic to assume that divorced parents will permanently remain in the same location." In re Marriage of Ciesluk, 113 P.3d 135, 147 (Colo. 2005) (internal citations omitted).

incorporated a stipulation of the parties that "the residence of the children will not be changed to a place beyond the radius of 100 miles from the City of Sheridan, Wyoming, unless both parents consent thereto or unless an order . . . has been entered approving such change." Mother subsequently sought an order to show cause as to why she should not be allowed to change her residence and that of her children to Sioux Falls, South Dakota. . . .

On appeal, this Court affirmed the district court's decision with respect to the parties' daughter [permitting the move]:

> . . . The test we will utilize in relocation cases is most similar to that espoused in *Arquilla*. We agree:
>
>> It would be incongruous for a court, when presented with a custodial order originally based upon the best interests of the child, to refuse to support the efforts of the custodial parent to maintain and enhance *their* standard of living, albeit in another jurisdiction. So long as the court is satisfied with the motives of the custodial parent in seeking the move and reasonable visitation is available to the remaining parent, removal should be granted. . . .

The Court took Wyoming's relocation jurisprudence a step further in *Watt*. . . . On appeal, this Court began [observing] that, "So long as the court is satisfied with the motives of the custodial parent in seeking the move and reasonable visitation is available to the remaining parent, removal should be granted." The Court pronounced that "Relocation as a substantial and material change in circumstances was foreclosed by the decision in *Love. Our decision established a strong presumption in favor of the right of a custodial parent to relocate with her children . . .*" (emphasis added). In determining that the trial court abused its discretion in finding a material change in circumstances based on mother's relocation, *Watt* held that "a relocation, by itself, is not a substantial or material change in circumstances sufficient to justify a change in custody order." The decision focused heavily on the custodial parent's right to travel, reasoning as follows:

> . . . The right of travel enjoyed by a citizen carries with it the right of a custodial parent to have the children move with that parent. This right is not to be denied, impaired, or disparaged unless clear evidence before the court demonstrates another substantial and material change of circumstance and establishes the detrimental effect of the move upon the children. While relocation certainly may be stressful to a child, the normal anxieties of a change of residence and the inherent difficulties that the increase in geographical distance between parents imposes are not considered to be "detrimental" factors. . . .
>
> An inhibition upon the right to travel is never imposed upon the non-custodial parent who is free to move at will despite the location of the children. The motives of the non-custodial parent will not be questioned by the court with respect to such relocation, and the custodial parent has no power to inhibit it. The inherent inequities of such a situation stand as an additional reason that courts have concluded that custodial parents should be permitted to move with their children. . . .

Against this background, we turn to a discussion of the issues presented in this appeal. . . .

We begin our analysis by identifying the competing rights and interests at stake. . . . First, as this Court properly recognized in *Watt*, the custodial parent has a right of travel worthy of protection. Importantly, however, the custodial parent's right to travel is not the only interest deserving of protection in relocation cases. The minority time parent in a shared custody arrangement has an equally important fundamental right of familial association. . . . Further, just as parents have a fundamental right to associate with their children, "Children have as fundamental a right to familial association [with their] parents." . . .

In Basolo v. Basolo, 907 P.2d 348, 354 (Wyo. 1995), we . . . emphasized that the best interests of the children are of overriding importance, and that they take precedence over the fundamental rights of parents:

In the wreckage of any marriage, . . . vindication of parental rights shall not be lavished at the expense of the "paramount purpose" of serving the welfare and best interests of the child. Recognition that parental rights are fundamental does not alter the cardinal rule that when the rights of a parent and the rights of a child collide, it is the rights of the parent which must yield. . . . On further examination of *Watt*, we find that its exclusive focus on the custodial parent's right to travel is not supported by our earlier precedent, and that the decision, in holding that a relocation, by itself, cannot constitute a material change in circumstances, unjustifiably elevates the custodial parent's right to travel over the competing interests of the minority time parent and the state's concern for the best interests of the child. . . .

We note that our conclusion that a relocation may constitute a material change in circumstances does not conflict with the proper application of res judicata in determining whether modification of custody is warranted. Clearly, a move by a custodial parent, especially when the distance from the remaining parent is significant, may create "new issues framed by facts differing from those existing when the original decree was entered," which preclude the application of res judicata. These new facts may include a change in the ability of the parties to maintain the existing parenting agreement, a change in the ability of the children to maintain a close relationship with the remaining parent, factors affecting quality of life in the new location, the child's geographic preference, and the relative merits of available social and educational opportunities in the new location. . . .

. . . With this decision, we explicitly recognize that a relocation by the primary physical custodian, as well as "factors that are derivative of the relocation" — including "the inherent difficulties that the increase in geographical distance between parents imposes" — may constitute a material change in circumstances sufficient to warrant consideration of the best interests of the children. To the extent this conflicts with this Court's holding in *Watt*, we hereby overrule *Watt*.

Further, based on the facts of the present case, we find that Mother's relocation to Virginia, over 2,000 miles away from Father, constitutes a material change in circumstances. As we have previously noted, however, "a material change of circumstance does not automatically equate with a change in custody." We note that the district court was able to consider a great deal of evidence bearing on the best interests of the children in addressing the issue of whether there had been a material change in circumstances. . . . Accordingly, we remand for further consideration of this issue with instructions that the district court consider all relevant facts and circumstances in determining a proper custodial arrangement that is in the best interests of the children. Because Father is the party seeking the modification of the custodial arrangement, he has the evidentiary burden of establishing that a modification of custody is in the best interests of the children. . . .

NOTES AND QUESTIONS

1. The court in *Arnott*, quoting Professor Elrod, observes that "[r]elocation cases are 'intractable problems' and the 'San Andreas fault' of family law." Given the intrinsically difficult nature of these decisions, state courts vary considerably in their articulation of the standards to be applied to relocation cases.

At one time, most states had presumptions against moves, and some still do. *See, e.g.*, Ala. Code §30-3-169.4 (2022) (creating a rebuttable presumption that relocating is not in the best interest of the child). Such a standard generally requires the custodial parent who wishes to move with the children to prove that the move is justified and in the children's best interests, even if the move involves relatively short distances; otherwise, the relocating parent risks a transfer of custody to the other parent. Courts in many states considered this type of standard as too restrictive and biased against women, who were more likely to be custodial parents. A series of judicial decisions including Tropea v. Tropea, 665 N.E.2d 145, 148 (N.Y. 1996), In re Marriage of Burgess, 913 P.2d 473, 480 (Cal. 1996), and *Watt* in Wyoming (1999) liberalized the standards, making it easier for custodial parents to relocate (although they did not necessarily adopt identical approaches in doing so).

The California Supreme Court in *Burgess* explained that:

> [O]urs is an increasingly mobile society. Amici curiae point out that approximately one American in five changes residences each year. Economic necessity and remarriage account for the bulk of relocations. Because of the ordinary needs for *both* parents after a marital dissolution to secure or retain employment, pursue educational or career opportunities, or reside in the same location as a new spouse or other family or friends, it is unrealistic to assume that divorced parents will permanently remain in the same location after dissolution or to exert pressure on them to do so. It would also undermine the interest in minimizing costly litigation over custody and require the trial courts to "micromanage" family decisionmaking by second-guessing reasons for everyday decisions about career and family.

In re Marriage of Burgess, 913 P.2d at 480-481 (emphasis in original).

As shared custody has become more common, and states place greater emphasis on the importance to the child of continuing contact with both parents, a number of courts have reconsidered the standard to be applied to relocation cases, adopting a case-by-case approach. In addition, many courts have come to distinguish between shorter moves that need not necessarily limit visitation and longer moves that may make it substantially more difficult. *Compare*, for example, *Burgess*, involving a move of 40 miles, *with* In re Marriage of LaMusga, 88 P.3d 81 (Cal. 2004), a case that involved a cross-country move and the conclusion that relocation would undermine the children's already tenuous relationship with their father.

How would you describe the standard the court adopts in *Arnott*? How does it differ from the standard in *Watt*?

2. Under either *Watt* or *Arnott*, the parent in *Arnott* who wished to challenge the move had the burden of showing "changed circumstances" justifying a modification of the custody decree. What arguments did the mother make that her proposed move did not constitute changed circumstances? If the mother had primary physical custody in *Deyle* and chose to go to a school 40 miles away, would that be "changed circumstances" sufficient to justify modification of the custody order?

Would the arguments in *Arnott* have been substantially different if the original custody order had provided for joint physical and legal custody or if the parents had roughly equal time with the children? Would the arguments have been substantially different if the custody order provided for a parenting plan such as the one in J.R. v. M.S. without using the labels "joint" or "primary" custody? In Singletary v. Singletary, 431 S.W.3d 234 (Ark. 2013), the initial custody order specified that mother and father would have "joint custody," named the mother as the "primary physical custodian," and gave the parents approximately equal time with the child. When the mother proposed to move from Arkansas to Texas, the trial court ruled that the original custody order was a joint custody award and therefore that the mother's proposed move constituted "changed circumstances" that justified a change in custody to the father. The appellate court affirmed.

3. The father in *Arnott* made two arguments: first, that the move constituted a change in circumstances justifying reconsideration of the original custody order, and second, that the children's best interests lay with a change in primary custody from the mother to the father. Assuming that the mother's proposed relocation in fact justifies reconsideration of the original custody order, how should the court evaluate the children's best interests? How should the court undertake such an inquiry if the mother indicates that she will not move if the result would be a transfer of custody to the father?

For empirical studies evaluating the impact of decisions not to move on mothers and children, *see* Patrick Parkinson & Judy Cashmore, When Mothers Stay: Adjusting to Loss After Relocation Disputes, 47 Fam. L.Q. 65 (2013); Megan Gollop & Nicola J. Taylor, New Zealand Children and Young People's Perspectives on Relocation Following Parental Separation, in 14 Law and Childhood Studies: Current Legal Issues 219 (Michael Freeman ed., 2012).

4. Under *Watt* or *Arnott*, approving the move would require a change in the father's visitation schedule. If you represented the father, what changes would you suggest that he propose? How might the possible changes in visitation affect the determination of whether the move constitutes a change in circumstances and whether it justifies a change in primary custody from the mother to the father? In *Deyle* the court expanded the mother's parenting time over the summer and on weekends. Might that be appropriate in *Arnott*?

5. Parenting plans often adopt provisions addressing relocation. If you were drafting a parenting plan in the *J.R.* case on behalf of the father, what provision would you recommend that the plan include addressing relocations in light of the *Arnott* decision?

PROBLEMS

1. Alma is the custodial parent for three children, ages 4, 6, and 9. She is a sales executive. Her employer has decided to close its Atlanta office, where Alma has worked for the past several years, and has offered to promote Alma to a more senior position, with a substantial raise, in San Francisco. Alma has looked and found nothing comparable to her current job in Atlanta. Her former husband, Ralph, is employed at a job that does not allow him to make lengthy trips. He is very much opposed to any arrangement that will interfere with his continuing visitation (which he has carried out faithfully). Alma plans to accept the transfer and seeks your advice regarding her custodial situation. Advise Alma what arguments she should make in opposition if Ralph seeks a change in custody in response to her plans to move and the arguments Ralph is likely to make in response.

2. Suppose that Alma is not currently employed but has decided to enroll in law school. She has been accepted at an ABA-accredited law school in her home state of Georgia and at Stanford. Alma would greatly prefer to study at Stanford. Ralph, who has visited the children regularly, seeks an order prohibiting Alma from moving with the children to any location more than 180 miles from Atlanta. Should that order be granted?

3. In problem 2, Ralph also offers the testimony of a psychologist that the children's best interests would be served by continuing regular contact with him. Should this affect the outcome?

4. Does the availability of other relatives to assist with child-care affect the result? Suppose that in problem 1, Alma grew up in the Bay Area, and her sisters and their children still live there. Suppose as well that Ralph's elderly parents, who are close to the children, live in Atlanta. How might these factors affect the analysis?

b. Unfriendly Co-Parenting: Domestic Violence, Abuse, and Alienation

Niemann v. Niemann
746 N.W.2d 3 (N.D. 2008)

VANDEWALLE, C.J. . . . In 1998, Lyle Niemann and Heidi Wolf divorced and Heidi Wolf was granted custody of their son and daughter. Both remarried. By agreement in June 2004, their daughter moved in with Lyle Niemann. In August 2005, Lyle Niemann brought a motion to gain custody of their son and the district court ordered an evidentiary hearing.

. . . The parties, prior to the hearing, stipulated to the physical change in custody of their daughter from Heidi Wolf to Lyle Niemann. However, the parties could not agree on a custodial arrangement for their son. . . .

A custody investigator was appointed and interviewed Lyle Niemann, Heidi Wolf, their spouses, the two children and several friends and family members of both parties. The custody investigator recommended in her affidavit and at the hearing that custody of the son be awarded to Lyle Niemann, citing concerns about domestic violence, alcohol abuse, lack of structure and arguments with vulgar, inappropriate language in front of the children at the Wolf home.

The domestic violence concerns stem from two alleged incidents. First, in June 2002, the daughter spoke with a social worker at her school about a fight between her mother and stepfather. According to the daughter, after Heidi Wolf locked her keys in her car, her husband yelled and swore at her in front of the children, then "trashed" the house when they arrived home. The daughter stated she wanted to call the police and her stepfather chased them when they left the house.

The second incident occurred in May 2005, when the children indicated to their school social worker that their stepfather came home drunk, yelled, swore and pushed their mother. A report was filed with Social Services. The custody investigator interviewed several of the Wolfs' friends regarding the incident. Two friends said Heidi Wolf and her husband were "in each other's faces" and yelling but saw no physical violence. A third friend said he took his child and Heidi Wolf's son out of the house and was told by Heidi Wolf's husband to leave. The parties' daughter said she saw her stepfather yell, swear and push her mother. She said she grabbed her half-brother and snuck out of the house through a construction area.

Heidi Wolf admits she left with the children that night and her husband admitted to yelling, swearing and name-calling when angry. Heidi Wolf said she left the confrontation rather than dealing with it. She denied any domestic violence but admitted to the involvement of Social Services. A Social Services note indicates the case was closed after Heidi Wolf said she was leaving her husband and would obtain counseling for herself and the children. Heidi Wolf never obtained such counseling and disputes Social Services' note.

. . . The judge, ruling from the bench, found no material change of circumstances and denied Lyle Niemann's motion.

II.

A court may modify a prior custody order after the two-year period following the date of entry of an order establishing custody if the court finds either a) on the basis of facts that have arisen since the prior order or which were unknown to the court at the time of the prior order, a material change has occurred in the circumstances of the child or the parties, and b) modification is necessary to serve the best interest of the child. . . .

A material change of circumstances includes important new facts unknown at the time of the prior custodial decree. A material change of circumstances can occur if a child's present environment may endanger the child's physical or emotional health or impair the child's emotional development. Improvements in a non-custodial parent's situation, coupled by a general decline in the condition of the children with the custodial parent over the same period may constitute a significant change in circumstances. The party seeking to modify the custody order bears the burden of proof.

Lyle Niemann argues the incident in May of 2005 was domestic violence and constitutes a material change of circumstances. Section 14-07.1-01, N.D.C.C., defines domestic violence to include "physical harm, bodily injury, sexual activity compelled by physical force, assault, or the infliction of fear of imminent physical harm, bodily injury, sexual activity compelled by physical force, or assault, not committed in self-defense." The district court stated, "The court does not find that credible domestic violence or a pattern of domestic violence exists." But the language used by the district court suggests the domestic violence must rise to the level of the standard used to invoke the domestic violence presumption in N.D.C.C. §14-09-06.2(1)(j) for purposes of determining whether a material change of circumstances occurred. Under that section the presumption is invoked if the court finds credible evidence that domestic violence has occurred and there exists one incident of domestic violence resulting in serious bodily injury, or "there exists a pattern of domestic violence within a reasonable time proximate to the proceeding."

. . . Insofar as the district court believed there must be serious bodily injury or a pattern of domestic violence to justify a change in custody, we conclude the district court made a mistake of law by applying the standard necessary to invoke the domestic violence presumption to determine whether a change in circumstances justifying a change in custody occurred.

The incident in May 2005 comports with the definition of domestic violence. . . . Domestic violence is not confined to instances where the parent is the direct victim of the violence. Even if Heidi Wolf did not fear imminent physical harm during the fight with her husband, it is obvious the children were afraid. The parties' son was removed from the house by his step-father's friend. Their daughter's fear of imminent physical harm is evident in her testimony regarding that night and in her current refusal to have contact with her stepfather.

The new split-custody arrangement also appears to be a material change in circumstances. After living together with Heidi Wolf since the divorce in 1998, the children were separated when the daughter went to live with Lyle Niemann in 2005. Although split custody is not flatly prohibited, as a general rule we do not look favorably upon separating siblings in custody cases. . . .

Lyle Niemann argues the language of the district court order suggests the district court went through the best interest analysis and found in favor of him. The judge stated in his ruling from the bench, "If this was first round, Lyle would get custody." However, in a best interest analysis, the trial court's findings of fact should be stated with sufficient specificity to enable us to understand the factual basis for the court's decision. There are not sufficient findings of fact in the record regarding the best interest analysis to conclude the district court found in favor of Lyle Niemann on this part of the test. . . .

We reverse and remand for further proceedings in accordance with this opinion.

MARING, J., dissenting in part and concurring in part. I respectfully dissent from parts I and IIA. I would affirm the order of the trial court in its entirety. . . .

I disagree with the majority's statement of the "two-step" test. The statute specifically requires a material change in the circumstances of the child or the parties and that "modification is *necessary* to serve the best interest of the child." I also disagree with the majority's implication that the trial court misapplied or misapprehended the law with regard to domestic violence. The trial court considered the mother Heidi Wolf's version of what happened in May 2005 and the minor daughter's version and found the mother's explanation credible. In the trial court's September 20, 2006, Order Denying Motion for Reconsideration, the court stated:

> This incident did not rise to the level of domestic violence but rather is an isolated domestic disagreement. While such disagreements and conduct should be avoided, it surely is not the basis for a material change of circumstances.

In the parties' Stipulation to Correct and Supplement the Record, the trial court's findings included a sentence left out by the majority:

If there is no domestic violence, and only strong words, that is not good, but the incidents in 2002 and then in 2005 don't rise to the level of domestic violence as we recognize it. The court does not find that credible domestic violence or a pattern of domestic violence exists.

(Emphasis added.) This Court has never held that loud words or domestic disagreements amount to domestic violence.

The trial court did not find any credible evidence of domestic violence. It did not find "physical harm, bodily injury, sexual activity compelled by physical force, assault, or the infliction of fear of imminent physical harm, bodily injury, sexual activity compelled by physical force, or assault, not committed in self-defense, on the complaining family or household members."

The majority makes a finding that the testimony of the daughter is evidence of the daughter's fear of imminent physical harm. The daughter said in her affidavit about the incident in May 2005, "It was really scary." In her testimony, she said she was afraid of Vance Wolf and when asked why she said, "[h]e just scares me." There is no evidence she was in fear of imminent physical harm, and the trial court did not make any such finding. The majority is reweighing the evidence, thereby ignoring precedent and applying a de novo standard of review. This Court has held that when two parties present conflicting testimony on issues of fact, we will not redetermine the trial court's findings based upon that testimony. Here, the trial court found the mother's version of what occurred credible and impliedly did not find the testimony of the daughter that there was physical violence credible.

Although the majority is correct that we have held that domestic violence does not need to be directed to a child to have a harmful effect on the child, there is no finding of domestic violence in this case, only a loud and strongly worded domestic disagreement. Such a finding is not a material change in circumstances necessitating a modification of custody in the best interest of the minor son, who was the only child left at issue.

The majority, at P 16, goes on to find "the new split-custody arrangement also appears to be a material change in circumstances" as a matter of law. The parties stipulated to this split after the parties' minor daughter stated a preference to live with her father. If this amounts to a material change as a matter of law, it will discourage parties from settling custody disputes such as this. There is little, if any, evidence in this record about the relationship between the minor daughter and the minor son. What is there is lacking in detail and substance. There is no evidence they spend a substantial amount of time together or share any activities or interests. . . .

NOTES AND QUESTIONS

1. In considering a request to change an existing custody order, a "two-step" process requires consideration, first, of whether there has been "a material change of circumstances," and, second, whether a best interests of the child analysis favors the party seeking the change. In *Arnott*, the court applied such a two-step analysis to relocations and in *Niemann*, the court applied a similar analysis to domestic violence. Is the "two-step" rule in *Arnott* the same as the one in *Niemann*? If so, how do they differ? In *Niemann*, do the majority and dissent differ in their approach to a two-step rule?

2. Substantial empirical evidence shows that children may be harmed by exposure to domestic violence even when that violence is directed against other family members and the children themselves are not at risk of physical abuse:

The effects of intimate partner violence on children's adjustment have also been well documented. . . . Violence has an independent effect on children's adjustment and is significantly more potent than high levels of marital conflict. . . . Behavioral, cognitive, and emotional problems include aggression, conduct disorders, delinquency, truancy, school failure, anger, depression, anxiety, and low self-esteem. Interpersonal problems include poor social skills, peer rejection, problems with authority figures and parents, and an inability to empathize with others. Preschool children traumatized by the earlier battering of their mothers had pervasive negative effects on their development, including significant delays and insecure or disorganized attachments. School-age children repeatedly exposed to violence are more likely to develop posttraumatic stress disorders, particularly when combined with other risk factors of child abuse, poverty, and the psychiatric illness of one or both parents. . . .

Joan B. Kelly & Michael P. Johnson, Domestic Violence: Differentiation Among Types of Intimate Partner Violence: Research Update and Implications for Interventions, 46 Fam. Ct. Rev. 476, 489-490 (2008). *See also* Gregory K. Moffatt & Savannah L. Smith, Childhood Exposure to Conjugal Violence: Consequences for Behavioral and Neural Development, 56 De Paul L. Rev. 879 (2007) (exposure to domestic violence during childhood may have life-long impact on children's developing brains); Debra Pogrund Stark et al., Properly Accounting for Domestic Violence in Child Custody Cases: An Evidence-Based Analysis and Reform, 26 Mich. J. Gender & L. 1, 11 (2019) (summarizing evidence).

In a little less than a decade, the courts shifted from viewing domestic violence as a private matter between the parents to seeing it as a critical consideration in child custody decisions. Today, all jurisdictions mandate consideration of domestic violence as a factor in custody decisionmaking, and many have enacted presumptions against an award of custody to a parent who has engaged in domestic violence. For a summary of the different state approaches, *see* Erin Bajackson, Best Interests of the Child—A Legislative Journey Still in Motion, 25 J. Am. Acad. Matrimonial Law. 311, 330-339 (2013). For an assessment of these changes, *see* Leigh Goodmark, A Troubled Marriage: Domestic Violence and the Legal System (2012); Leslie Joan Harris, Failure to Protect from Exposure to Domestic Violence in Private Custody Contests, 44 Fam. L.Q. 169 (2010); Suzanne Reynolds & Ralph Peeples, When Petitioners Seek Custody in Domestic Violence Court and Why We Should Take Them Seriously, 47 Wake Forest L. Rev. 935 (2012). Despite the legal changes, some scholars find that courts vary in their willingness to take such charges seriously. *See* Joan S. Meier, Denial of Family Violence in Court: An Empirical Analysis and Path Forward for Family Law, 110 Geo. L.J. 835, 838 (2022).

Is the domestic violence alleged to have occurred in *Niemann* likely to have a negative effect on the children involved? Should the negative effect on children be assumed?

3. The ALI defines domestic violence as "the infliction of physical injury, or the creation of a reasonable fear thereof, by a parent or a present or former member of the child's household, against the child or another member of the household. Reasonable action taken by an individual for self-protection, or the protection of another individual, is not domestic violence." Principles of the Law of Family Dissolution §2.03(7). How does this definition compare to the definition in *Niemann*? Would use of the ALI definition have affected the approach of either the majority or the dissent?

4. ALI Principles §2.11(3) provides that if a parent is found to have engaged in domestic violence, "the court should not allocate custodial responsibility or decisionmaking responsibility to that parent without making special written findings . . . that the child, other parent, or other household member can be adequately protected from harm. . . ." A parent found to have engaged in domestic violence "should have the burden of proving that an allocation of custodial responsibility or decisionmaking responsibility to that parent will not endanger the child, other parent, or other household member." Protecting family members from harm may involve a range of measures from supervised visitation to anger management classes to denial of custodial or decision-making responsibility. North Dakota, in contrast, creates a statutory presumption against granting custody to a parent who has committed acts of domestic violence:

> If the court finds credible evidence that domestic violence has occurred, and there exists one incident of domestic violence which resulted in serious bodily injury or involved the use of a dangerous weapon or there exists a pattern of domestic violence within a reasonable time proximate to the proceeding, this combination creates a rebuttable presumption that a parent who has perpetrated domestic violence may not be awarded residential responsibility for the child. This presumption may be overcome only by clear and convincing evidence that the best interests of the child require that parent have residential responsibility.

N.D. Cent. Code §14-09-06.2(1)(j) (2022). The North Dakota statute accordingly combines a stricter definition of domestic violence with a strong presumption against an award of custody, while the ALI has a broader definition of domestic violence and a range of possible consequences that follow from such a finding. Which approach do you prefer? Would the analysis in *Niemann* have been different under the ALI standards?

Would the result be different in an initial award of custody? In Law v. Whittet, 844 N.W.2d 885 (N.D. 2014), the mother had been arrested for hitting her own mother in front of the children on an evening in which she was heavily intoxicated, and later escaped from a police car. She eventually pled guilty to disorderly conduct and escape. The trial court awarded the unmarried mother and father joint residential responsibility for the child, but the North Dakota Supreme Court reversed and awarded primary residential responsibility for the child to the father. The court opined:

> Even if the evidence of domestic violence does not trigger the statutory presumption under N.D.C.C. §14-09-06.2(1)(j), the violence must still be considered as one of the factors in deciding primary residential responsibility, and when credible evidence of domestic violence exists it "dominates the hierarchy of factors to be considered" when determining the best interests of the child.

Is this consistent with the approach in *Niemann?*

5. Chapter 2 describes research defining different types of domestic violence and comparing them in terms of severity. Researchers emphasize that the studies documenting the harmful effects of domestic violence on children do not necessarily distinguish among these types of violence. Jaffe et al. suggest that whether or not domestic violence should preclude shared custody depends on the nature of the violence involved, and that mild incidents of domestic violence (*e.g.*, separation-related violence involving isolated incidents uncharacteristic of the relationship) need not prevent development of a parenting plan in which parents share continued involvement with the child. They describe a continuum of shared parenting measures any of which might be appropriate depending on the level of violence. These measures include:

- Co-parenting, generally involving joint custody in which both parents are involved in making cooperative decisions about the child's welfare;
- Parallel parenting with both parents involved, but including arrangements designed to minimize contact and conflict between the parents;
- Supervised exchanges of the child from parent to parent in a manner that minimizes the potential for parental conflict or violence;
- Supervised access, when one or both parents pose a temporary danger to the child, provided under direct supervision in specialized centers and/or by trained personnel with the hope that the conditions that led to supervised access will be resolved and the parent can proceed to a more normal relationship with the child.
- Prohibition of all contact with the child, in the most serious cases, in which a parent poses an ongoing risk to the child.

Peter G. Jaffe et al., Custody Disputes Involving Allegations of Domestic Violence: Toward a Differentiated Approach to Parenting Plans, 46 Fam. Ct. Rev. 500, 516 (2008). Under what circumstances would each measure they propose be appropriate? Once an incidence of domestic violence has been substantiated, are there measures the parent who committed the violence can take to regain custody? *See* Zoe Garvin, The Unintended Consequences of Rebuttable Presumptions to Determine Child Custody in Domestic Violence Cases, 50 Fam. L.Q. 173, 179 (2016) (California allows the presumption against an award of custody to be rebutted by completion of a domestic violence prevention course).

6. How should the court deal with a case in which credible evidence existed that both parents had engaged in domestic violence? The Alaska Supreme Court wrote:

> When both parents have a history of perpetrating domestic violence the superior court must either: (1) award custody "to the parent who is less likely to continue to perpetrate the violence and require that the custodial parent complete a treatment program"; or (2) if necessary to protect the child's welfare, award custody "to a suitable third person if the person would not allow access to a violent parent except as ordered by the court." If both parents have a history of domestic violence, but the court "finds that neither parent is more likely than the other to continue to perpetrate the violence," the court may in its discretion determine that [the] presumption against custody applies to neither parent, in which case the court "should consider the remaining best-interests factors in making its custody decision."

Sarah D. v. John D., 352 P.3d 419, 430 (Alaska 2015). *See* Leigh Goodmark, When Is a Battered Woman Not a Battered Woman? When She Fights Back, 20 Yale J.L. & Feminism 75, 96-113 (2008). How should a court deal with a case in which one parent engaged in domestic violence and the second parent, after the first relationship ended, entered in a new relationship where domestic violence occurred?

7. If a parent alleges that the other parent has committed domestic violence and the allegations are not substantiated, what effect should this have on the custody determination? Should the response be the same as the response to unsubstantiated allegations of child abuse? *See, e.g.,* 23 Pa. Stat. and Cons. Stat. Ann. §5328 (2022), which requires consideration of:

> (a)(8) The attempts of a parent to turn the child against the other parent, except in cases of domestic violence where reasonable safety measures are necessary to protect the child from harm . . .
>
> (a)(13) The level of conflict between the parties and the willingness and ability of the parties to cooperate with one another. A party's effort to protect a child from abuse by another party is not evidence of unwillingness or inability to cooperate with that party.

How do you interpret the Pennsylvania standards? How is Section (a)(8) different from Section (a)(13)? How do these standards apply to *Niemann*?

8. For a discussion of the use of mediation in cases involving domestic violence, *see* Chapter 11.

PROBLEMS

1. Sandra and Jerome are in their mid-20s and have a 4-year-old son. On several occasions, neighbors called the police when they heard screams and shouts coming from their house. On other occasions, Jerome initiated the calls, alleging that Sandra had attacked him. Each time, Jerome told police his version of the events, but Sandra refused to talk to them. She was arrested as the perpetrator more than once and was charged with resisting arrest, even though the police report stated that Jerome had assaulted Sandra and that she was injured and bleeding at the time of the arrest. Prosecutors eventually dropped the charges against her without explanation. Sandra sought legal protection from Jerome for the first time after they had broken up and he was arrested for assaulting her outside a shopping mall — an incident that resulted in his conviction for battery. After the incident, Sandra went to family court and asked for an award of sole physical and legal custody, and a civil restraining order limiting his contact with her and the child. Jerome responded by also seeking sole legal and physical custody and asking the court to limit Sandra's contact with their son to supervised visitation. At the family court hearing, Sandra testified that Jerome had assaulted her at least once a month over the five years they were together, but that she was too afraid of him to tell the police. Jerome testified that they often quarreled when they were together and that Sandra had initiated most of the violence by cursing, pushing, or slapping him.

What arguments might Sandra and Jerome raise if the case is heard in North Dakota? Would your answer change under the ALI Principles? Is the continuing involvement of both parents with the child appropriate in this case? If so, what measures should be taken to protect the child from exposure to violence? If so, in what way? *See* Elizabeth L. MacDowell, Theorizing from Particularity: Perpetrators and Intersectional Theory on Domestic Violence, 16 J. Gender Race & Just. 531, 537-538 (2012) (describing a case involving similar facts).

2. Chris and Logan lived together for a short time after their son was born. When the child was 5, Chris and the child moved to another town to live with a new partner, Mackenzie. Four years later, Chris left Mackenzie and moved back in with Logan. Shortly thereafter, Chris reconciled with Mackenzie and filed for custody.

At trial, Logan argued that Chris should not have custody because of domestic violence that had occurred between Chris and Mackenzie in the presence of the child. The testimony included descriptions of two occasions when Chris had fled with the child because of fear of Mackenzie's behavior and other occasions when Mackenzie pushed the child or exposed him to marijuana use. Chris minimized the violence and denied that the child had been exposed to it. Chris also testified that Logan had been convicted of assaulting Chris when they were together. The 9-year-old child testified that he wanted to live with Chris, but Logan argued that the boy's views reflected the fact that Chris had continually denigrated Logan to the boy and interfered with their relationship.

The trial court awarded primary physical custody to Logan and visitation to Chris, finding that Chris, who was still living with Mackenzie, had failed to protect their son from exposure to domestic violence. What arguments would you make on Chris's behalf on appeal? What alternatives were available to the trial judge if she concluded that the boy would be better off remaining with Chris, but that Chris's relationship with Mackenzie posed a risk of exposure to domestic violence?

3. Susan and Walter married ten years ago, shortly after graduating from college. They have a 7-year-old and a 9-year-old. Susan has been the primary caretaker, but Walter has been actively involved with the children. One day, shortly after he returned home from work, Susan told Walter she was leaving him for his best friend, Arthur. Susan moved out the next day, taking the children with her. Walter, who had no idea that Susan was dissatisfied with their relationship, was devastated. He tried to talk Susan into returning, but to no avail. Several weeks later, Susan came by unexpectedly to pick up some of her belongings. She and Walter quarreled. Walter, who had been drinking, struck her, knocking her across the room and breaking her nose. Susan quickly obtained a restraining order keeping Walter away from her and the children. He has not seen the children in six months. At trial, Susan testifies that Walter had been controlling and verbally abusive during the marriage and that she is afraid of him. The guardian ad litem for the children testified that Walter was actively involved with the children's homework and extracurricular activities, but he was moody and inconsistent, sometimes berating them and other times surprising them with gifts or spur-of-the-moment activities. She also testified that the children are deeply distressed about the conflict between their parents; they were often present when they quarreled. How should custody be allocated under the principles set out in *Niemann* and the ALI Principles? Under what circumstances should Walter be allowed visitation?

In the Matter of Miller
20 A.3d 854 (N.H. 2011)

Hicks, J. . . . Miller and Todd met in 1999 over the internet and established a relationship. At that time, Miller lived in Michigan and Todd lived in New Hampshire. Although they never married, their relationship produced two daughters, Laurel born in 2002 and Lindsay born in 2003. During 2002 and 2003, the parties spent some time living together in Michigan, Todd and the children spent some time alone in New Hampshire living with Todd's parents, and the parties all spent some time together at Todd's parents' house in New Hampshire.

Toward the end of 2003, the parties' relationship broke down. On December 23, 2003, Miller obtained an *ex parte* order in the circuit court in Michigan granting him sole temporary legal and physical custody of his daughters. That same day, Todd took the children to her parents' home in Hampton, New Hampshire. On January 6, 2004, Todd was served with the Michigan custody order. . . .

Sometime in January, Todd's mother told her that, four months earlier, she saw Miller molest Laurel by inserting his forefinger into her. On January 27, on the advice of her attorney, Todd took the children to the emergency department at Exeter Hospital and requested a "well baby check." The physician's report states: "[P]atient here for well child check-up; told by Lawyer to have evaluated for custody issue." There is no evidence in the record that Todd notified the hospital staff of any concerns regarding sexual abuse. The physical exam indicated the children's condition was good. Todd then transferred the children to Miller's custody.

On February 5, 2004, a report was filed with the Family Independence Agency of Michigan, Child Protective Services, alleging that maternal grandparents recalled an incident that occurred in New Hampshire between 10/03/03 and 10/05/03 when father was rubbing diaper cream on Laurel because she had a diaper rash. Maternal grandmother states she did not have [a] diaper rash. Maternal grandmother stated father inserted his forefinger inside of Laurel. This was never reported to anyone. The agency investigated the report, including having pelvic examinations of both children administered. No indications of sexual abuse of either child was found and the investigation was closed.

In November 2004, the Rockingham County Superior Court issued a temporary decree awarding the parties joint legal custody of the children. In that order, the trial court questioned the credibility of both parties. Regarding Todd, the court found "most troubling" the allegations of sexual abuse raised by her. As the court stated, "It is simply far too convenient to believe the testimony put forth by [Todd]: that her mother [chose] not to reveal the allegations of [Miller's] alleged sexual assault until custody of the minor children was awarded to [Miller]." The court noted that neither party "appears to care to whom they lie so long as they achieve favorable results."

In June 2005, Todd's father reported to the Hampton police that while he was lying in bed with Lindsay and Laurel watching a movie, Laurel tried to "straddle" him on his chest and stated, "I'm f——— you." When the grandfather asked Laurel where she heard that she said nothing. When the grandfather then asked, "from your father," Laurel said "yes." The police noted the report as a "possible disclosure" of sexual abuse, but took no action.

In September 2005, a friend of Todd's made a statement to the police that Laurel had reported that Miller had spanked her in the groin area. Todd filed an *ex parte* petition for temporary stay of visitation between Miller and the children alleging that the children reported being spanked by Miller and a third party in the groin area and that Laurel had displayed "other alarming behavior of a sexual nature," referring to the grandfather's report to the police in June. As a result of these allegations, the court issued an order prohibiting Miller from having any contact with the children "until this matter is duly investigated and any and all allegations of abuse are deemed unfounded." After an investigation that included a second pelvic examination of Laurel, the New Hampshire Division for Children, Youth, and Families (DCYF) closed the matter as unfounded. . . .

In November 2005, Todd and the children's therapist reported to DCYF that Laurel had stated that Miller took "pictures of her with her clothes off," made her "eat his pee pee" and "panks her in the front." On January 30, 2006, DCYF sent a letter to Miller stating that it had determined that he was "the individual responsible for the abuse" and that his name would be entered "on its central registry of founded child abuse and neglect reports." Miller appealed the finding and, on February 24, 2006, DCYF rescinded its initial determination. In a letter to Todd, DCYF informed her that new evidence had come to its attention and that "the assessment regarding your children has been closed unfounded." DCYF stated that "[t]here has been a concern that Laurel has been coached with the information that she has been disclosing. Please understand that this . . . type of coaching, if proven, is equally as abusive to a child as if the abuse had actually occurred." . . .

In July 2006, the parties agreed to be evaluated by psychologist Peggie Ward. . . . On December 18, 2007, Dr. Ward issued an eighty-eight page report in which she considered several hypotheses. First, Dr. Ward posed the hypothesis that "Laurel was not sexually abused by her father or anyone else." Dr. Ward noted that both children were subjected to multiple examinations and questioning and that Laurel's statements to the Child Advocacy Center "do not appear to be consistent with her initial statement nor do they have a good deal of context." Dr. Ward opined that "this hypothesis may be supported by the data" in that "Laurel's presentation is less consistent with a child who has been repeatedly sexually abused."

Second, Dr. Ward posed the hypothesis that "Laurel was sexually abused or inappropriately touched by Mr. Miller." Dr. Ward noted that "Laurel's statements and behaviors are less consistent with child sexual abuse than they are of premature focus on the genital area followed by a good deal of anxiety and distress about sexual abuse from both Janet Todd as well as [Todd's mother]." Due to the "lack of context and the lack of memory regarding abusive behavior, combined with multiple physical exams and multiple interviews," it was "impossible to determine whether Laurel was sexually abused by her father." Dr. Ward's opinion was that "Laurel's presentation is less consistent with a child sexually abused by her father and more consistent with other hypotheses."

Third, Dr. Ward posed the hypothesis that Todd "has deliberately coached the children in what to say and scripted their responses." It was Dr. Ward's opinion that "this hypothesis is not the hypothesis best supported by the data."

Fourth, Dr. Ward posed the hypothesis that "Todd came to believe that Laurel, not Lindsay, was sexually abused by Mr. Miller." It was Dr. Ward's opinion that this hypothesis "is the most likely hypothesis supported by the data. That is, that Ms. Todd, after experiencing her parent's concerns about Mr. Miller and after having experienced her own negative interactions with Mr. Miller, became increasingly convinced that Mr. Miller was harming Laurel." Referring to a psychological report on Todd that was prepared in August 2007 by Dr. David Medoff, Dr. Ward noted that

> [p]sychological testing shows that Ms. Todd has a "serious impairment in her ability to accurately process the information she takes in from her surroundings and the degree of misperception she demonstrates has major implications for her adaptive functioning. . . . These data

indicate that Ms. Todd will not only fail to recognize or foresee the consequences of her actions at times, but that she will also become confused at times in separating fantasy from reality."

As Dr. Ward explained,

Ms. Todd has the liability of distortion of information and failure to accurately identify intentions, motivations and behavior of others. Ms. Todd's emotional state placed her at risk for misinterpreting information that she gained from her environment, adamantly believing that Laurel was sexually abused, and acting with full force on this information.

Dr. Ward thus concluded that "the hypothesis that Ms. Todd unintentionally but clearly caused Laurel to come to believe that she has been sexually abused by her father is the hypothesis best supported by the data."

In making her recommendations, Dr. Ward cautioned that "[w]hile it is unlikely that Mr. Miller has sexually abused Laurel, it is not possible to say with an absolute certainty that he did not." She concluded, however, that while it is "likely that Janet Todd did influence her children with her negative beliefs about Mr. Miller, from her psychological profile, it is most likely that her feelings colored her perceptions and that she not only came to see Mr. Miller as harmful to Laurel but also did not protect the children from her feelings." In addition, Dr. Ward noted that "Ms. Todd's parents appear to have wholly and adamantly accepted that Mr. Miller is a pervasive negative influence on his children. Mrs. Todd in particular is active in helping her daughter prove that Mr. Miller sexually abused the children." Finally, Dr. Ward noted that "Laurel's therapist is convinced that Laurel has been sexually abused, and may have inadvertently reinforced the abuse by making a 'book' with Laurel about her abuse." . . .

On January 7, 2008, the trial court . . . expressed its intent

to set a course for the immediate *therapeutic* reunification of the children with their father. Too much time has already passed and too much opportunity has been lost. The children certainly deserve better. [Todd] asserts that she accepts the goal of reunification, but wants it to proceed at a slow pace. The court is convinced that [Todd's] pace for reunification is far too slow and is premised on assertions which may not be true.

. . . The court found "that the children's best interests require that they 'normalize' their relationship with their father. It is extraordinarily harmful to them to deprive them of a relationship with one parent, especially when the reasons for doing so appear to be wholly unjustified." . . .

[Over the next 16 months, the court issued numerous additional orders, and found fault with both parties. The father refused to cooperate with the reunification therapists, with two therapists the father had chosen withdrawing because of his belligerence. The mother alleged additional instances of abuse, and Laurel's first grade teacher reported that she had started crying in school, stating that the father had threatened to harm the mother. At the final hearing on custody, the master found that the children had nonetheless reestablished a healthy bond with their father, and enjoyed visiting him and his family in New York. He concluded, though, that the children had lived with their mother in New Hampshire for nearly five years, and that a move to New York would be a drastic change requiring them to leave most of what they have known during their formative years and would not be in their best interest.]

. . . "When determining matters of child custody, a trial court's overriding concern is the best interest of the child." RSA chapter 461-A, the Parental Rights and Responsibilities Act, states that "children do best when both parents have a stable and meaningful involvement in their lives." Accordingly, it is the policy of this state to "[s]upport frequent and continuing contact between each child and both parents" and to "[e]ncourage parents to share in the rights and responsibilities of raising their children." The Act codifies the "best interests of the child" criteria, setting forth twelve factors that the court must consider, including:

(e) The ability and disposition of each parent to foster a positive relationship and frequent and continuing physical, written and telephonic contact with the other parent, except where contact will result in harm to the child or to a parent.

(f) The support of each parent for the child's contact with the other parent as shown by allowing and promoting such contact.

(g) The support of each parent for the child's relationship with the other parent.

"Across the country, the great weight of authority holds that conduct by one parent that tends to alienate the child's affections from the other is so inimical to the child's welfare as to be grounds for a denial of custody to, or a change of custody from, the parent guilty of such conduct." . . .

In addition, many courts have held that unfounded allegations of sexual abuse made by one parent can be grounds for granting custody to the other parent.

In Beekman v. Beekman, 96 Ohio App. 3d 783, 645 N.E.2d 1332, 1336 (1994), the court reasoned:

> Although a court grants one parent custody and the other visitation, the children need to know that they are loved by both parents regardless of the antagonism the parents might feel for each other. It is the duty of each parent to foster and encourage the child's love and respect for the other parent, and the failure from that duty is as harmful to the child as is the failure to provide food, clothing, or shelter. Perhaps it is more harmful because no matter how well fed or well clothed, a child cannot be happy if he or she feels unloved by one parent.
>
> When a court makes a custodial decision, it makes a presumption that the circumstances are such that the residential parent will promote both maternal and paternal affection. The residential parent implicitly agrees to foster such affection, not out of any good feeling toward the nonresidential parent, but out of the need of the child for both parent's love. Where the evidence shows that after the initial decree the residential parent is not living up to the court's presumption and is attempting to poison the relationship between the ex-spouse and the child, this is a change of circumstances that warrants a modification of the prior custody decree. Unsubstantiated allegations of abuse are the worst kind of poisoning of the relationship. . . .

Based upon the record before us, the negative ramifications of Todd's unfounded belief that Miller has sexually abused his children, and continues to do so, are several and serious. First and foremost, the false allegations of abuse significantly interfered with Miller's visitation and deprived him of any relationship with his children for years. Further, as a result of the false allegations, both children have been subjected repeatedly to invasive physical examinations, they have been interviewed by DCYF and law enforcement, they have been evaluated by Dr. Ward, they have had two guardians ad litem and they have twice participated in reunification therapy. These actions were not in the children's best interests. . . .

The trial court awarded custody to Todd primarily because the children have spent the majority of their lives with her and that is where they are most comfortable. However, it was because of the unfounded allegations of sexual abuse that Miller was denied *any* contact with his children for over two years and had little opportunity to establish a home life with them between 2004 and 2009. This raises the question whether Todd has benefitted from her misbehavior. In Begins v. Begins, 168 Vt. 298, 721 A.2d 469, 470-71 (1998), the children's relationship with their mother deteriorated following the parents' separation due to the fact that the father unfairly blamed her for the parties' marital problems and made disparaging remarks about her lifestyle. The trial court concluded that the boys' hostility toward their mother, encouraged and fueled by their father, precluded an award of custody to mother. Although the court found that father did not "deserve to win custody," it concluded that it had no choice but to award custody to him. The Vermont Supreme Court rejected such reasoning. As the court stated:

Although obviously well intended, the court's decision effectively condoned a parent's willful alienation of a child from the other parent. Its ruling sends the unacceptable message that others might, with impunity, engage in similar misconduct. Left undisturbed, the court's decision would nullify the principle that the best interests of the child are furthered through a healthy and loving relationship with both parents.

Dr. Ward's report, characterized by the master as "thorough and extraordinarily perceptive," contains several conclusions particularly relevant to Todd's inability to foster a positive relationship with Miller and to support the children's contact with him. . . .

We conclude that the award of parental rights and responsibilities must be vacated and the case remanded for reconsideration in light of this opinion.

NOTES AND QUESTIONS

1. In *Miller*, the New Hampshire Supreme Court chided the trial court for its failure to cite the state's "friendly parent" statute and to apply "the statutory factors to the specific facts" of the case. How would you expect the trial court to rule on remand? If the court wished to keep its previous parenting plan in place, what additional findings would you recommend that the court make?

2. False charges of spousal or child abuse are perhaps the most dramatic instances of bad relations between parents, and they pose a particularly intense dilemma for the courts and the parents. Compare the approach of the trial court in *Miller* with that of a Missouri court in Holmes v. Holmes, 436 S.W.3d 599 (Mo. App. 2014). The dissent in that case observed:

> Acknowledging the deference that is due the trial court in one of the most disturbing dissolution cases that I have reviewed, I believe the trial court erred in awarding Father sole custody of the four-year-old child. I note that, at the end of the evidence, the guardian ad litem ("GAL") who represented the child suggested that a neutral therapist meet with all of the parties. That never happened. Instead, the trial court decided that Father had not sexually abused the child and, by inference, that Mother was at fault for the allegations. That decision stemmed from the work of a licensed psychologist, Dr. Frederick Nolen. Although the court claimed it "rejected other parts of the [trial] testimony as not credible" and referred to Dr. Nolen's report twice in its judgment as the "flawed report by Fred Nol[e]n . . .," it is clear in reviewing the evidence that it was not possible to separate Dr. Nolen's influence . . . in the trial.
>
> Dr. Nolen did something that no reputable therapist would do. He stated with absolute certainty that the child's statements were false. Then, . . . he came to the conclusion that there was absolutely no possibility that Father had abused the child. That is an important conclusion and one that is disturbing. But more disturbing is the manner in which Dr. Nolen arrived at his conclusions. He reasoned that if the child's statements were false, then Mother must have been at fault for the child making the statements. Dr. Nolen indicated, in an absolutely bizarre report, that he must "rule out for factitious disorder of [Mother] in [his] report of her." As a result of his conclusions in his report to the juvenile office, the child was taken into foster care. . . .
>
> Despite the overwhelming probative evidence contrary to the proposition that Mother coached the child into making allegations that she had been sexually abused by her father, the judgment awarded Father sole legal [and physical] custody. I believe the judgment is against the weight of the evidence and should not stand.

The differences between these two cases illustrate the difficult issues at the core of sexual abuse cases.

First, can sexual abuse be *disproven* with certainty? The overwhelmingly answer is no. Proving sexual abuse occurred in accordance with criminal or civil standards of proof can be difficult. Proving that it did *not* occur is substantially harder. Reputable experts, who will confidently testify that allegations of abuse cannot be substantiated, may be more reluctant to say that abuse did not happen. Yet, finding that the abuse did not happen or could not be reasonably alleged may be important to the custody determination. In *Miller*, the court observed that none of the investigations validated the charges, but neither could they establish that the abuse had not occurred. In contrast, in *Holmes*, the court stated categorically that the abuse did not happen and that the mother's allegations suggested that she was not trustworthy. How do these determinations affect the custody decision in the two cases?

Second, irrespective of the strength of the corroborating evidence, the child and the custodial parent may believe the allegations. How should that affect the custodial ruling? In *Miller*, the court relies on expert testimony that "Ms. Todd, after experiencing her parent's concerns about Mr. Miller and after having experienced her own negative interactions with Mr. Miller, became increasingly convinced that Mr. Miller was harming Laurel." The court accordingly concluded both that Ms. Todd's allegations were probably false *and* that it was likely that she sincerely believed them and that the child's statements were not necessarily the product of coaching. In contrast, in *Holmes*, once the expert concluded that the abuse had not happened, he also concluded that the child's allegations were the result of coaching. The trial court stated that the mother's insistence on pursuing the unsubstantiated allegations "raise[d] questions as to her ability to properly raise the minor child," in part because it raised doubt about the mother's ability to distinguish fact from fiction. Can you identify circumstances when it can be simultaneously true that the abuse was unlikely to have occurred and that the custodial parent genuinely believes that it occurred? How do such circumstances affect the determination of the child's best interests?

Third, how should the court address the best interests of the child in these cases? In *Miller*, the trial court placed considerable emphasis on the children's ties to the mother and the community in which the mother was living. Yet, the appellate court suggests that if the children's ties to the mother, as opposed to the father, were the result of unfounded allegations, the court should switch custody. In *Holmes*, the trial court did precisely that, first putting the 4-year-old in foster care and then transferring custody from the mother to the father because of the mother's persistent allegations of sexual abuse. If the child bonds more closely with one parent than the other because of unfounded allegations of abuse, how should the courts evaluate the child's best interests?

Fourth, how can the courts resolve individual cases without creating incentives that will negatively affect other cases? If the courts allow parents to influence custody decisions through unfounded accusations, they will create incentives to make such allegations. In *Miller*, for example, the abuse allegations were the primary basis for changing the child's custody from the father to the mother in the early proceedings. On the other hand, once a parent reports a child's statements that indicate abuse to a doctor, teacher, or other professional, that professional is bound to report them, triggering an investigation. Should a custodial parent not report such statements, particularly if there does not seem to be evidence sufficient to corroborate a finding of abuse, for fear of undermining the child's relationship with the other parent? How would you advise a parent in such a case when the parent is unsure of the accuracy of the child's statements and has no corroboration of them?

Research indicates that a parent who raises hard-to-prove allegations of child abuse is at increased risk of losing custody. *See* Joan S. Meier, U.S. Child Custody Outcomes in Cases Involving Parental Alienation and Abuse Allegations: What Do the Data Show?, 42 J. Soc. Welfare & Fam. L. 1, 6-8 (2020) (showing that when mothers alleged abuse and fathers alleged alienation, fathers prevailed by a significant percentage over mothers in custody determinations). Other research indicates that custodial parents often believe that their behavior toward the other parent or even their compliance with court orders may not necessarily trigger repercussions. Richard Warshak, Parental Alienation: Overview, Management, Intervention, and Practice Tips, 28 J. Am. Acad. Matrimonial Law. 181, 209 (2015). Could both findings be true?

3. One solution to abuse allegations is to make a therapist, rather than a custodial parent or the court, the gatekeeper for reunification efforts with an estranged parent. In Allen v. Farrow, for example, actress Mia Farrow alleged that film director Woody Allen had abused their daughter, Dylan. The court conditioned Allen's continued visitation rights with Dylan on participation in therapy after finding that the allegations had not been unsubstantiated. Dylan objected to seeing her father because of his relationship with her adopted sister Soon Yi (whom Allen subsequently married), and in a subsequent proceeding, the court denied Allen's request for therapeutic visitation. Neither the court nor the therapist based the denial of visitation on the abuse allegations, relying instead on Dylan's preferences and the potential impact of visitation on her well-being. The order was upheld on appeal. Allen v. Farrow, 215 A.D.2d 137, 626 N.Y.S.2d 125 (1995). What roles did the various therapists play in *Miller*?

June Carbone

From Partners to Parents: The Second Revolution in Family Law
193-194 (2000)

Custody battles have become ground zero in the gender wars because they are among the few remaining family law disputes where courts judge adult behavior. . . . Maintaining parental ties is the new sine qua non of responsible parenthood—and a possible lever in the effort to exact revenge on the other spouse. The emphasis on parental cooperation then increases the importance of potentially disqualifying conduct: domestic violence, child abuse, and parental alienation carry greater significance as they become the limited exceptions to the principle of shared parenting. And, in this context, the courts still pass judgment. While neither the *Allen* nor the *Renaud*[4] courts considered the fathers' infidelity to their partners, they ruled that Woody's behavior with Soon Yi . . . had harmed his children, and that Gail Renaud's baseless allegations against her faithless ex-husband were bad parenting. Custody decisions—and the connections between parents and children—hold the new moral center of family law.

NOTE: VISITATION AND PARENTING PLANS

A court that awards primary custody to one parent may still allocate substantial parenting time to the other parent, even if the court changes custody because of a relocation, unsubstantiated abuse allegations, or domestic violence. Denial of visitation is an extreme remedy, and in the past has rarely been approved. Visitation may be regarded as a basic human right. In 2008 the House of Lords in the United Kingdom held, in EM (Lebanon) v. Secretary of State for the Home Department, [2008] UKHL 64, that a Lebanese woman should have been granted asylum in England because deporting her to Lebanon would infringe the right to respect for family life under Article 8 of the European Convention on Human Rights. She was

---

4. Renaud v. Renaud, 168 Vt. 306, 312, 721 A.2d 463 (1998) (upholding custody award to mother in spite of allegations that the mother persisted in making unfounded allegations of abuse against the father, conditioned on her cooperation in repairing the child's relationship with the father).—Eds.

divorced from her husband, and Sharia law provides that he is entitled to custody and has the absolute right to decide whether the mother will have any contact with the child, despite the fact that the father had seen the child only once, on the day of his birth.

States may nevertheless restrict visitation, particularly by a party who has been convicted of child abuse or, depending on the jurisdiction, any number of similar offenses. 23 Pa. Cons. Stat. Ann. §5329(a) (2022), for example, lists 30 different offenses from murder to having sex with an animal to drug offenses that give rise to a presumption against an award of custody to anyone in a household where any member of that household has been convicted of such an offense. *See also* Cannon v. Cannon, 280 S.W.3d 79 (Mo. 2009), which upholds the constitutionality of a statute restricting custody against a challenge from a father who had been convicted of sexually abusing his stepdaughter, and as a result was limited to supervised visitation with his biological children when he was released from prison. The Arkansas courts have also limited a father to supervised visitation of a young child where the father admitted that he was sexually attracted to teenage girls and had sent disturbing text messages to the mother. Martin v. Martin, 455 S.W.3d 360, 362 (2015). However, courts have generally required a showing of harm to restrict visitation. *Compare* Sharp v. Keeler, 256 S.W.3d 528 (Ark. App. 2007) (overturning order limiting mother to supervised visitation because of her lack of support for father's parenting) *with* Phillips v. Phillips, 442 S.W.3d 901, 906 (Ark. App. 2014) (upholding supervised visitation order where mother continued to badmouth father and his family).

PROBLEMS

1. Sharon's marriage with her husband Eric broke up when Sharon discovered that Eric was having an affair. She has not trusted him since then but has supported his relationship with their child, Heather. When Heather was three, Sharon learned that Eric had been accused of sexually abusing another child. Sharon asked Heather about her visits with Eric and the child, who had been coming back from visits with Eric throwing tantrums, complained that her "bottom hurts," and described taking showers with Eric and playing with his "boy thing." Sharon shared her concerns with Heather's doctor, who reported them to child protective services. The court suspended Eric's visitation with Heather while the investigation was pending. The investigators concluded that there was reason to believe that Heather has been abused, but insufficient evidence to find that Eric committed the abuse. Heather, who by the time of the next court hearing was 5, was adamant that she did not want to see her father. A psychiatrist who interviewed Heather testified that Heather is terrified of Eric and traumatized by the prospect of spending time with him. At the time of the hearing, Eric had not seen Heather for the preceding year because of the allegations. He testified that he and Heather had a strong relationship before the allegations surfaced, that he believes that Sharon has coached Heather based on the allegations in the other case, and that she had been trying to undermine his relationship with Heather even before the allegations of abuse arose.

The judge asks you for suggestions about how to handle this case. The judge informs you that she sees no grounds on which to conclude that Eric has abused Heather. She also believes the psychiatrist's testimony that visitation with Eric may traumatize Heather. She asks you to discuss what options she has in designing appropriate parenting provisions in this case.

2. Cyndall and M.J. were in their teens when their son, Corbin, was born. They were not married, and they never lived together. They have never gotten along. When Corbin was a year old, the court awarded Cyndall sole custody with visitation for M.J. The order specified that neither parent was to badmouth the other, and that whenever Cyndall needed a babysitter, M.J. should be given the opportunity to care for Corbin.

After the court issued the order, Corbin developed a rare blood disorder, needed surgery to remove a tumor from his arm, and underwent chemotherapy. Cyndall became more reluctant to allow Corbin to visit M.J., and when Corbin was with M.J., Cyndall texted incessantly to check on Corbin's health.

Five months after the court issued the initial custody order, M.J. alleged that Cyndall had failed to comply with the order and asked the court to grant M.J. sole custody. M.J.'s motion alleged that Cyndall did not have Corbin ready for visitation, failed to provide timely information about Corbin's health and medical treatments, and criticized and belittled M.J. in Corbin's presence. In addition, when Corbin had another surgery, M.J. found out about it in an away message from Cyndall's email, and Cyndall refused to allow M.J.'s mother to visit Corbin in the hospital. Cyndall responded that M.J.'s mother had threatened her and that M.J. had hung up several times when she tried to call with information about the surgery. Cyndall maintains that Corbin's condition made visitation difficult because he was sleeping more and needed greater continuity of care.

The trial court is inclined to find that Cyndall has undermined M.J.'s relationship with Corbin and violated the initial court order. At the time of the hearing, Corbin is 18 months old and has never had an overnight visit with M.J.

What arguments would you make on behalf of each party? If the judge determines that Cyndall has violated the court order, what should be the judge's response?

c. Choosing Between Parents: Religion, Race, and Caretaking

Weisberger v. Weisberger
60 N.Y.S.3d 265. (N.Y. Sup. 2017)

Per Curiam. The parties were married on March 5, 2002. In 2005, the mother told the father that she could not tolerate having sexual relations with men, and that she was sexually attracted to women. The parties were divorced by a judgment of divorce dated March 6, 2009. They have three children together, a son and two daughters. At the time of the divorce, the parties' older daughter was five years old, their son was three years old, and their younger daughter was two years old. In a stipulation of settlement . . ., the parties agreed to joint legal custody of the children with the mother having primary residential custody. . . . Central to the issues raised on appeal, the stipulation contained the following religious upbringing clause:

> Parties agree to give the children a Hasidic upbringing in all details, in home or outside of home, compatible with that of their families'. Father shall decide which school the children attend. Mother to insure that the children arrive in school in a timely manner and have all their needs provided.

The stipulation of settlement further provided that each party "shall be free from interference, authority and control, direct or indirect, by the other."

On November 29, 2012, more than three years after the divorce, at which time the children were nine, seven, and five years old, respectively, the father moved, by order to show cause: (1) to modify the stipulation of settlement so as to award him sole legal and residential custody of the children . . . ; (2) to modify the stipulation of settlement so as to award the mother only supervised therapeutic visitation with the children; (3) to enforce the religious upbringing clause so as to require the mother to direct the children to practice full religious observance in accordance with the Jewish Hasidic practices of ultra Orthodoxy at all times and require her to practice full religious observance in accordance with the Hasidic practices of ultra Orthodoxy during any period in which she has physical custody of the children and at any appearance at the children's schools. . . .

In support of the motion, the father alleged that the mother had radically changed her lifestyle in a way that conflicted with the parties' religious upbringing clause. . . . The father alleged that since the parties had entered into the stipulation of settlement the mother had, among other things, come out publicly as a lesbian, disparaged the basic tenets of Hasidic Judaism in front of the children, allowed the children to wear non-Hasidic clothes, permitted them to violate the Sabbath and kosher dietary laws, and referred to them by names that were not traditionally used in the Hasidic community. The father further alleged that the mother had dressed immodestly, dyed her hair, and permitted a transgender man to reside in her home with the children.

Pending the hearing and determination of the father's motion, the Supreme Court awarded him temporary residential custody of the children. . . .

The mother opposed the father's motion and separately . . . proposed that the religious upbringing clause be modified to provide as follows:

> "Mother agrees to provide the children with a conservative or progressive modern orthodox Jewish upbringing compatible in all details, in home or outside of home, with a conservative or progressive modern orthodox Jewish community that is inclusive of gay individuals. Such community shall be as near to Borough Park, Brooklyn, New York, as possible, and in [sic] under no circumstances outside of the Borough of Brooklyn. The children will attend a conservative or progressive modern orthodox Jewish school that is similarly inclusive. Mother and Father shall consult with one another on selecting the Children's schools. Father shall continue to teach the Children all aspects of a Hasidic upbringing, and in furtherance of this shall have visitation rights with the children every Shabbos, beginning Friday night one hour before sundown through Sunday morning at 10 am. Mother will keep a [k]osher home and shall only provide the Children kosher food outside of her home." . . .

The Supreme Court held a hearing for the purpose of deciding both motions. . . . The father testified that his and the mother's extended families were integrally involved in the founding of the Emunas Yisroel branch of Orthodox Hasidic Judaism, and their families were neighbors in Monsey, New York. When the parties were both 19 years old, they were introduced through a shadchan (matchmaker). Shortly thereafter, they became engaged and, in 2002, they were married.

After marrying, the parties moved to Boro Park, Brooklyn, so that the father could pursue religious studies. They had three children, and raised them according to traditional Hasidic practices and beliefs. During the marriage, the father left the house in the morning and generally returned after the children were in bed. The mother was primarily responsible for taking care of the children's needs, and the father was satisfied with her care of them. The parties kept a strictly kosher home, spoke Yiddish, observed the Sabbath, and always wore traditional clothing. According to the father, Hasidic children never wear T-shirts, jeans, or shorts, boys do not have their hair cut until the age of three, and there is no television or Internet in the home.

. . . The parties were divorced on March 6, 2009, and the father married a different woman later that same month. At the time of his testimony, the father and his new wife had two children together. Despite the parties' agreement that the father would have visitation with the children every other Shabbos, the father testified that during the first 18 months of his new marriage he would not permit the children to come over to his house, he did not fully exercise his biweekly right to visitation during Shabbos, and he did not take their son for Yom Kippur in 2009 through 2011. The father testified that when he did visit with the parties' children, he did so at his parents' house.

The father learned that in fall 2012 a transgender man (hereinafter "O.") moved into the mother's home, and that a curtain was installed to separate the adult bedrooms from the children's bedrooms. According to the father, his children informed him that O. assisted in bathing them and told them about sexual parts of the human body. In October 2012, the mother began dressing the children in secular clothes and cut their son's payos (sidelocks). The father testified that the children began speaking English in school, stopped saying blessings at meals and nighttime prayers, and were eating non-kosher food. Further, the father testified that the mother had allowed the children to ride a train and use light switches on the Sabbath. The father also testified that the mother allowed the children to watch movies, including a movie about Christmas, and participate in an egg hunt at a Purim party. The father testified that in March 2013, the younger daughter told him that she had read a book about children with two fathers and other books about homosexuality.

The father denied that the mother's sexual orientation was the motivation behind his request for a change in custody; however, he had expected the mother to keep her sexual orientation a secret from the children. The father testified that he sought custody of the children so that he could give them a traditional upbringing according to his religion without interference from the mother. The father objected to the children being exposed to anyone who was openly non-religious, or to any intimate relationship that was not sanctioned by Jewish law. The father believed that homosexuality violated the Torah. The father also believed that the mother's visits with the children should be limited to one or two hours per week and supervised by a family member. When asked whether he could reach a compromise, the father testified: "[T]here's no place for compromising in our religion."

The mother testified that the parties' move to Boro Park was difficult for her because she did not have a community network. Approximately one year into their marriage, at a time before the mother identified as gay, the mother began seeing a therapist regarding her attraction to women. After several attempts at marriage counseling, the mother eventually came to the conclusion that she wanted a divorce. She never spoke with a lawyer during the divorce process. Her father-in-law gave her an agreement to review and make notes. She met with a rabbi, who guided her as to which issues she should negotiate. She negotiated the financial aspects of the agreement and, according to her testimony, Rabbi Glassman—the parties' designated mediator—was supposed to incorporate her changes into the agreement. When she appeared at the Beth Din to sign the agreement, it did not include her changes. She inquired why the agreement did not include the changes and the mediator said he would take care of it, so she signed the agreement. The stipulation of settlement provided that the father would pay the mother $600 per month in child support. The mother waived her right to, among other things, maintenance and to the distribution of marital property. The mother testified that she believed the custody arrangement provided for in the stipulation of settlement was good for the children. However, the mother noted that the father had not made a single child support payment to her since their separation, notwithstanding the explicit terms of the stipulation of settlement.

. . . The mother testified that even while married she was never as strict as the father regarding blessings, washing rituals, prayers, and exposure to secular books and ideas. For a number of years, the mother never told the children about her sexual orientation. However, the mother testified that, in 2012, she learned that the older daughter was beginning to suspect the mother was gay. The mother testified that she consulted with the older daughter's therapist about the issue, and then told the older daughter that she was gay, which she believed deepened the child's level of trust and openness with her. In September 2012, the mother's friend, O., came to live with her. The children and O. got along well with each other. However, in October 2012, after the older daughter returned from a visit with the father, she was confused and upset because the father's family had teased her about her level of religious observance and had told her that O. was really a woman. After the December 5, 2012, temporary order of visitation was entered, and the children began spending half of the week with the father, the mother found the children would often be upset and confused. The mother testified that she carefully obeyed the order's provision requiring her to behave religiously with the children and in Boro Park, but felt hypocritical for doing so and for hiding parts of herself. She believed the father's custody proposal was devastating, as she had been the most present parent in the children's lives since they were born, and she worried about the children's emotional well-being while in the father's custody. In connection with her motion to modify the religious upbringing clause, the mother believed the children would be better served by attending a school that was more accepting of diversity, and she offered to continue to keep a kosher home and let the children spend religious holidays with the father. . . .

In the order appealed from, the Supreme Court determined that there had been a change of circumstances caused by the mother's transition from an ultra Orthodox Hasidic lifestyle to a "more progressive, albeit Jewish, secular world." The court noted that the mother's conduct was in conflict with the parties' agreement, which "forbade living a secular way of life in front of the children or while at their schools." The court posited that had there been no agreement it might have considered the parties' arguments differently; however, "given the existence of the Agreement's very clear directives, [the] Court was obligated to consider the religious upbringing of the children as a *paramount factor* in any custody determination" (emphasis added).

The Supreme Court granted that branch of the father's motion which was to modify the stipulation of settlement so as to award him sole legal and residential custody of the children, as well as final decision-making authority. . . .

"Factors to be considered include the quality of the home environment and the parental guidance the custodial parent provides for the child[ren], the ability of each parent to provide for the child[ren]'s emotional and intellectual development, the financial status and ability of each parent to provide for the child[ren], the relative fitness of the respective parents, and the effect an award of custody to one parent might have on the child[ren]'s relationship with the other parent" (Mohen v. Mohen, 53 AD3d 471, 473). Additionally, to the extent the mother's sexual orientation was raised at the hearing, we note that courts must remain neutral toward such matters, such that the focus remains on the continued best interests and welfare of the children. . . .

Here, both parties contend that there has been a change in circumstances warranting modification of the stipulation of settlement. . . .

However, the Supreme Court's determination to modify the stipulation of settlement so as to award the father sole legal and residential custody of the children, as well as final decision-making authority over medical and dental issues, and issues of mental health, with supervised therapeutic visitation to the mother, lacked a sound and substantial basis in the record. In pertinent part, the court gave undue weight to the parties' religious upbringing clause, finding it to be a "paramount factor" in its custody determination. . . . "New York courts will consider religion in a custody dispute when a child has developed actual religious ties to a specific religion and those needs can be served better by one parent than the other." However, clauses in custody agreements that provide for a specific religious upbringing for the children will only be enforced so long as the agreement is in the best interests of the children. . . .

Considering all of the facts and circumstances of this case, the father failed to demonstrate that it is in the children's best interests to award him sole legal and residential custody of the children, as well as final decision-making authority over medical and dental issues, and issues of mental health. The mother has been the children's primary caretaker since birth, and their emotional and intellectual development is closely tied to their relationship with her. The record overwhelmingly demonstrates that the mother took care of the children's physical and emotional needs both during and after the marriage, while it is undisputed that the father consistently failed to fully exercise his visitation rights or fulfill his most basic financial obligations to the children after the parties' separation. Indeed, aside from objecting to her decision to expose the children to views to which he personally objects, the father expressed no doubts whatsoever about the mother's ability to care and provide for the children. The weight of the evidence established that awarding the father full legal and residential custody of the children with limited visitation to the mother would be harmful to the children's relationship with her. Furthermore, "[s]upervised visitation is appropriately required only where it is established that unsupervised visitation would be detrimental to the child[ren]." Here, there was no showing that unsupervised visitation was detrimental to the children and, as discussed more fully below, it was wholly inappropriate to use supervised visitation as a tool to compel the mother to comport herself in a particular religious manner.

Furthermore, the Supreme Court improperly directed that enforcement of the parties' stipulation of settlement required the mother to practice full religious observance in accordance with the Hasidic practices of ultra Orthodoxy during any period in which she has physical custody of the children and at any appearance at the children's schools. Although the court accepted the father's argument that the religious upbringing clause "forb[ids] [the mother from] living a secular way of life in front of the children or while at their schools," the plain language of the parties' agreement was "to give *the children* a Hasidic upbringing" (emphasis added). The parties' agreement does not require the mother to practice any type of religion, to dress in any particular way, or to hide her views or identity from the children. Nor may the courts compel any person to adopt any particular religious lifestyle. To the contrary, "[i]t is beyond dispute that, at a minimum, the Constitution guarantees that government may not coerce anyone to support or participate in religion or its exercise." Thus, a religious upbringing clause should not, and cannot, be enforced to the extent that it violates a parent's legitimate due process right to express oneself and live freely. Indeed, the parties themselves agreed in the stipulation of settlement that they "shall [each] be free from interference, authority and control, *direct or indirect*, by the other" (emphasis added). While we respect the parties' right to agree to raise their children in a chosen religion and to seek judicial relief to enforce that right, given the change in circumstances here, the weight of the evidence does not support the conclusion that it is in the children's best interests to have their mother categorically conceal the true nature of her feelings and beliefs from them at all times and in all respects, or to otherwise force her to adhere to practices and beliefs that she no longer shares. There is no indication or allegation that the mother's feelings and beliefs are not sincerely held, or that they were adopted for the purpose of subverting the religious upbringing clause, and there has been no showing that they are inherently harmful to the children's well-being.

This is not to say that it would be in the children's best interests to become completely unmoored from the faith into which they were born and raised. Indeed, we conclude that the children's best interests would be better served by a more limited modification of the religious upbringing clause than that proposed by the mother. The evidence at the hearing established that the children have spent their entire lives in the Hasidic community, they attend Hasidic schools, and their extended families are Hasidic. . . . Contrary to the mother's contention, the weight of the evidence demonstrates that it is in the children's best interests to continue to permit the father to exercise final decision-making authority over the children's education and to continue to permit him to require the children to practice full religious observance in accordance with the Hasidic practices of ultra Orthodoxy while they are in his custody, or in the custody of a school that requires adherence to such practices. To this end, the children's interests will be best served if their parents work together to surmount the challenges the children will face as they continue on their current educational path. As such, we deem it appropriate to direct the mother to make all reasonable efforts to ensure that the children's appearance and conduct comply with the Hasidic religious requirements of the father and of the children's schools while the children are in the physical custody of their father or their respective schools. Further, in light of the mother's proposal, made in both her motion papers and her testimony, to keep a kosher home and to provide the children exclusively with kosher food, we find that it would be in their best interests for her to do so, and in a manner consistent with Hasidic practices. Except for these specified matters, we otherwise modify the religious upbringing clause to allow each parent to exercise his or her discretion while the children are in his or her care or custody. . . .

[T]he parties' religious, moral, and ethical beliefs and values with respect to raising their children, while once compatible, have now become incompatible in many important respects. . . . We are confident that both parties will exercise their best judgment in these matters in a manner that furthers the best interests of their children.

Finally, the parties' stipulation provided, inter alia, that the parties shall "encourage the child[ren] to honor, respect and love the other party," shall not "attempt to alienate or destroy the affection of the child[ren] for the other party," and shall not "speak idly about the other party in front of the children." This provision applies equally to both parties and, therefore, neither party may, directly or indirectly, denigrate the other to or before the children for any reason, including their disagreement with the other party's identity or beliefs. . . .

Ordered that the order is modified . . . (1) by modifying the stipulation of settlement so as to award [the father] additional visitation every other weekend from Thursday after school until Sunday at 11:00 A.M. . . ., (2) by modify[ing] the religious upbringing clause contained in the stipulation of settlement . . . by: (a) permitting the father to require the children to practice full religious observance in accordance with the Hasidic practices of ultra Orthodoxy only when they are in the father's custody, or in the custody of a school that requires adherence to such practices, (b) directing the mother to make all reasonable efforts to ensure the children's compliance with the religious requirements of the father and of the children's schools, if any, to the extent that such requirements pertain to the children's appearance and conduct while they are in the physical custody of the father or their respective schools, (c) directing that the mother shall keep a kosher home and shall provide the children exclusively with kosher food in a manner consistent with Hasidic practices, and (d) permitting each parent to exercise his or her discretion while the children are in his or her care or custody, (3) . . . [modifying the agreement to] award the father visitation during all Jewish holidays and for two weeks during summer vacation, and to award the mother visitation during all non-religious school vacations. . . .

NOTES AND QUESTIONS

1. The parties' settlement agreement framed the issues in *Weisberger*. If there had been no agreement at the time of the divorce, and each party requested the approach they advocated above, how do you think that the court would have ruled? If this case arose in a jurisdiction that has adopted a presumption that joint physical and legal custody was in the best of the interest of the children, yet each of the parties sought sole physical and legal custody, how do you think the court would have responded? How might the court in *J.R.* above have crafted a parenting plan that took into account both parties' religious preferences?

2. Professor Brian Bix observes that:

Doctrinally, courts are supposed to treat terms relating to the purely financial obligations between the parties (*e.g.*, property division and alimony) more deferentially than they treat terms relating to children (*e.g.*, custody and child support), but by most accounts, judges tend to simply rubber stamp their approval of separation agreements without significant scrutiny of any of the provisions. Invalidation of a previously entered separation agreement on grounds of unfair terms or unfair process is rare, but it does occur.

Brian Bix, Marriage Agreements and Religion, 2016 U. Ill. L. Rev. 1665, 1973. If the court had reviewed the settlement agreement in this case at the time it was entered, what issues should it have considered? How should the court have approached the question of the best interests of the children at the time the agreement was entered? How might such an inquiry have differed from the court's consideration of the children's best interests in the request for modification above?

Professor Margaret Brinig finds that couples who enter into such agreements differ from those who do not. Based on a study of parenting plans in Arizona and Indiana, she reported that "divorcing couples specifying religious upbringing in their parenting plans tend to be more affluent, have fewer reports of domestic violence, settle cases before litigation more often, share custody more equally, and come from lengthier marriages. These couples were also more likely to divorce alleging substance abuse and were more likely to seek reductions of the noncustodial parent's time with the children." Margaret F. Brinig, Religion and Child Custody, 2016 U. Ill. L. Rev. 1369. Should any of these factors affect the enforceability of such agreements? Settlement agreements are considered in greater depth in Chapter 10.

3. In *J.R.*, a case also decided in accordance with New York law, the court held a "Lincoln hearing" to determine the views of the child in that case. There is little mention of the children's views in *Weisberger*, although they were 9, 7, and 5 at the time that the motions for modification were filed in November 2012 and considerably older by the time of decision above in 2017. Was that appropriate? What might explain the court's failure to determine the views of the children?

4. The *Weisberger* court observes that "[t]he parties' religious, moral, and ethical beliefs and values with respect to raising their children, while once compatible, have now become incompatible in many important respects." How does the court deal with the parties' conflicting "religious, moral, and ethical beliefs"? How does it determine what is in the children's best interests?

NOTE: FREE EXERCISE OF RELIGION AND CUSTODY DECISIONMAKING

Where parents' religious preferences conflict, the courts must balance each parent's First Amendment right to exercise the religious practices of his or her choosing against the other parent's similar right and the best interests of the children. If the parents have mutually exclusive preferences, the challenge can be daunting. In In re Marriage of Hadeen, 619 P.2d 374 (Wash. App. 1980), for example, the mother belonged to the First Community Churches of America. The court found that the "First Community Church is a fundamentalist Christian sect which demands much of its members' time, their total loyalty, and a subservience to the teachings of the church. . . ." At trial, witnesses had "testified that the church teaches . . . that there are essentially two classes of people: 'natural people' and 'spirit filled people' who have repented, been baptized and received the Holy Spirit. There was testimony that children were taught to use foul language when speaking to other children who were 'natural people' and that there was nothing wrong with lying to 'natural people.'" The father, who had originally belonged to the church along with the mother, no longer did so. One of the couples' five children, Lisa, did not want to attend church. The mother had spanked her for two hours with a Ping-Ping paddle while the other children held her down because of her refusal to go to church. The other four children, however, were church members and doing well, and wished to remain with their mother. The trial court found, among other things:

e) That the Petitioner, Judith Hadeen, is in complete submission to the First Community Church of America, to the exclusion of other reasonable relationships. . . .

f) That the Petitioner's first fidelity is to the church, as is evidences [sic] by the Petitioner's rejection of the parties' minor child Lisa. . . .

h) To award custody to the Petitioner, Judith Hadeen, would effectively cut Glen Hadeen off from his involvement with the children, and that the children need to have continued contact with both parents.

The trial court accordingly transferred custody of all the children except for the oldest child to the father. The mother appealed, arguing that the order was a violation of her First Amendment rights. The appellate court stated that:

We glean from . . . [prior] cases that religious decisions and acts may be considered in a custody decision only to the extent that those decisions or acts will jeopardize the temporal mental health or physical safety of the child. The question remains whether jeopardy to a child must be one of actual present impairment of the child's physical and/or mental well-being or a reasonable and substantial likelihood of impairment. We conclude that the . . . requirement of actual impairment is improvident and could lead a trial court to ignore a child's present welfare. We hold that the requirement of a reasonable and substantial likelihood of immediate or future impairment best accommodates the general welfare of the child and the free exercise of religion by the parents.

The trial court's finding that Mrs. Hadeen is in complete submission to the church to the exclusion of other "reasonable" relationships is a subjective conclusion which should have played no part in the trial court's decision unless Mrs. Hadeen's submission posed a substantial threat of endangering the children's mental or physical welfare. . . .

The appellate court accordingly reversed and remanded for a new determination. What determination would be necessary to show "a substantial threat of endangering the children's mental or physical welfare"? Would paddling a child in accordance with church teachings that encouraged the use of physical punishment be sufficient? Would alienation of the children from the parent who is not a church member be enough?

PROBLEMS

1. Frank and Irene Jones are divorcing. They have two children, who are 4 and 6. Irene is a devout member of a religious sect led by her father. Among this sect's principal tenets, shared by Irene, are beliefs that government is a manifestation of Satan and that all persons who are not members of the sect are God's enemies. Sect members also believe that they may ignore all acts of government, including tax laws and hunting and fishing regulations. There is no evidence that the children have been harmed, and they maintain a close bond with their mother. During the marriage, Frank participated in church activities, but the divorce occurred in part because of Frank's growing skepticism about the sect's teachings, and since the separation, Frank has not attended any church and has been critical of Irene's father, calling him a con man who fleeces his congregants. Both Frank and Irene have asked for sole legal custody. Frank objects to raising the children with the sect, and Irene objects to exposing the children to any other religion.

What arguments should Frank and Irene make? To what extent, if any, should the court consider the religious views of the sect and Irene? Would it be appropriate in this case to award joint physical or legal custody? What provisions would you recommend that the court include in a parenting plan?

2. Juan and Anita are seeking a divorce. Both identify as Roman Catholics. Juan is highly observant, has participated in church-related activities, and believes that the children should attend parochial school. Anita is less observant and attends church infrequently, has no interest in church-related activities, and prefers that the children go to public school. Both wish primary custody of their children. May and should the trial judge take the relative religious commitments of the parents into account? If so, in what way? If Juan asks for custody of the children on all major religious holidays including Christmas and Easter so that he can ensure that they attend services, how should the judge respond?

3. How, if at all, would your answer to each of the preceding problems change if two of the children were 8 and 10, the 10-year-old strongly preferred that the nonreligious parent receive custody, and the 8-year-old believed that he would go to hell if he did not follow the observances of the more religious parent? Would it matter if the two children had been very close, but were now fighting with each other over religious issues?

4. Cheryl and Elsey lived in a committed relationship for 11 years. They adopted a child from China; after being informed by a social worker that same-sex couples were not permitted to adopt in China, they filed the adoption proceedings in Cheryl's name alone. Nonetheless, both women went to China together to pick up the 6-month-old, and both participated equally in her upbringing. Six years after the adoption, the couple separated. The court awarded Cheryl primary physical custody and recognized Elsey as a psychological parent who was entitled to substantial visitation. After the separation, Cheryl became more religious, and she and her daughter now regularly attend a church that teaches that same-sex relationships are sinful. The trial court specified in the custody award that Cheryl "make sure that there is nothing in the religious upbringing or teaching that the minor child is exposed to that can be considered homophobic." Upon what grounds could Cheryl challenge the condition?

5. Burch and Lipscomb are both devout Christians with two children. When they divorced, Burch received primary custody at a time when Lipscomb was deployed overseas with the military. When COVID-19 vaccines became available, both parents opposed having the children vaccinated on religious grounds because they believed that the vaccines were produced using fetal tissue. After returning from the deployment, Lipscomb had a change of heart, and now wishes to have the children vaccinated. Burch continues to oppose vaccination even though the children's school will not allow them to return in the fall unless they are vaccinated. Burch proposes to home school the children if they are not allowed to attend the public school they had been attending. Lipscomb seeks a court order requiring that the children be vaccinated. How should the court rule?

6. Jessie and Quinn have two children, ages 9 and 11. When they divorce, they enter into a custody agreement that specifies that the two parents will share custody equally and that they will raise their children as Catholics and observe Catholic values in the home. Jessie remarries. Jessie, who appeared to be visibly pregnant, takes a trip out of state while the children are with Quinn and returns no longer looking pregnant. Quinn hears from Jessie's friends that Jessie had an abortion. Jessie and Quinn live in a state that has banned abortion, except when necessary to save the life of the mother. Does Quinn have grounds to seek a modification of the custody order?

NOTE: NEW PARTNERS

In 1980, custody law did not vary widely across the United States in its attitude toward nonmarital cohabitation. In that year, a Utah court cited a New York case in holding that overnight visitation should be conditioned on a prohibition on nonmarital cohabitation in the presence of the child. *See* Kallas v. Kallas, 614 P.2d 641, 645 (Utah 1980). Today, courts in some parts of the country reject requests for non-cohabitation orders out of hand (*see* Logan v. Logan, 763 A.2d 587, 589 (R.I. 2000)), while courts in other parts of the country still grant them. Arkansas courts, for example, have repeatedly stated that it is "the long-standing public policy of the courts of this state that a parent's extramarital cohabitation with a romantic partner in the presence of the children, or a parent's promiscuous conduct or lifestyle, has never been condoned." Jeffers v. Wibbing, 2021 Ark. App. 239, 12 (2021).

Nonmarital cohabitation continues to influence custody determinations in two circumstances. The first is where the presence of another adult in the home is a source of potential harm to the child in ways that go beyond the mere fact of cohabitation itself. In 2005, for example, the Arkansas Supreme Court, in Alphin v. Alphin, 219 S.W.3d 160 (Ark. 2005), observed that while the trial court changed custody from the mother to the father because of the mother's nonmarital relationships, it could have also based the change of custody on the mother's lack of stability and multiple nonmarital partners. The dissent attacked the court's double standard because the father had married his current wife when she was three months pregnant, and his lack of support had left the mother dependent on her new partners.

Second, non-cohabitation clauses in separation agreements may affect custody determinations, particularly where they reflect a commitment to raise the children in accordance with religious beliefs that preclude nonmarital cohabitation. In *Weisberger*, for example, the father sought modification of the custody arrangement only after he learned that a transgender man moved into the mother's home.

In Moix v. Moix, 430 S.W.3d 680 (Ark. 2013), the parties' settlement agreement provided that neither party was to have overnight guests of the opposite sex. After the mother learned that the father had "a romantic relationship with a live-in male companion" and that the father and the male companion had engaged in a physical altercation in which the father was injured, the mother sought a change in custody that involved no overnight visitation. The Arkansas Supreme Court, without reaching the constitutional questions, concluded that it was inappropriate to bar the presence of the father's partner without a finding that doing so was in the best interests of the child. Similarly, in Beckman v. Beckman, 870 S.E.2d 66 (Ga. App. 2022), the parents' marriage ended in divorce after the husband had an affair with his brother-in-law's wife. At the time of the divorce, the affair had ended, and the parents agreed that the sister-in-law would not be allowed to be alone with the child. The father, however, later discovered that the sister-in-law was pregnant with his child and married her. The Georgia Court of Appeals held that the trial court abused its discretion by imposing an absolute prohibition on all contact between the father's child and his new wife when there was no evidence that exposure to her would adversely affect the child's best interests.

NOTE: RACE

In *Weisberger*, the court took pains to distinguish the parents' agreement to give the children a Hasidic upbringing from disapproval of the mother's sexual orientation. The father denied that the mother's sexual orientation motivated his motion for a change in custody and the court stated expressly that "to the extent the mother's sexual orientation was raised at the hearing, we note that courts must remain neutral toward such matters, such that the focus remains on the continued best interests and welfare of the children." 60 N.Y.S.3d at 273. The court nonetheless found that it was in the children's interest to receive a Hasidic upbringing even if Hasidic teachings disapproved of the mother's sexual orientation.

How do courts deal with similar issues that arise with respect to race? In Palmore v. Sidoti, 466 U.S. 429 (1984), the U.S. Supreme Court addressed the question of whether courts could consider race in custody decision making. In that case, the white mother and father divorced, and the mother received custody of the couple's 3-year-old daughter. After the divorce, the mother moved in with and then married a Black man. The Supreme Court described the proceedings in the trial court:

> [The trial court] noted the counselor's recommendation for a change in custody because "[t]he wife [petitioner] has chosen for herself and for her child, a lifestyle unacceptable to the father and to society. . . . The child . . . is, or at school age will be, subject to environmental pressures not of choice."
>
> The court then concluded that the best interests of the child would be served by awarding custody to the father. The court's rationale is contained in the following: "The father's evident resentment of the mother's choice of a black partner is not sufficient to wrest custody from the mother. It is of some significance, however, that the mother did see fit to bring a man into her home and carry on a sexual relationship with him without being married to him. Such action tended to place gratification of her own desires ahead of her concern for the child's future welfare. This Court feels that despite the strides that have been made in bettering relations between the races in this country, it is inevitable that Melanie will, if allowed to remain in her present situation and attains school age and thus becomes more vulnerable to peer pressures, suffer from the social stigmatization that is sure to come."

The Supreme Court reversed the transfer of custody, stating that:

> It would ignore reality to suggest that racial and ethnic prejudices do not exist or that all manifestations of those prejudices have been eliminated. There is a risk that a child living with a stepparent of a different race may be subject to a variety of pressures and stresses not present if the child were living with parents of the same racial or ethnic origin.
>
> The question, however, is whether the reality of private biases and the possible injury they might inflict are permissible considerations for removal of an infant child from the custody of its natural mother. We have little difficulty concluding that they are not. The Constitution cannot control such prejudices but neither can it tolerate them. Private biases may be outside the reach of the law, but the law cannot, directly or indirectly, give them effect. . . .

How does the court address the biases that may exist in *Weisberger*? Does it matter that the Hasidic community may tease the children because of their mother's behavior? What weight should the court give to the fact that the oldest daughter returned from visits with her father "confused and upset" because of comments that the mother's transgender friend who lived with them was really a woman?

Palmore v. Sidoti has been distinguished in a number of cases. In Jones v. Jones, 542 N.W.2d 119 (S.D. 1996), the father was an enrolled member of the Sisseton-Wahpeton Dakota Nation who was adopted at age 7; the mother was white. The father was employed on a family farm and earned about $22,000 per year, and the mother was a homemaker and nursing student. The father was a recovering alcoholic, and the mother suffered from depression and low self-esteem. They had three children, all of whom have Native American features. In its findings, the trial court noted the father's arguments that the children would be discriminated against if they moved from their home and the family farm and that he wished to continue to make the children aware of their culture and heritage. The trial court indicated that this was an example of the father's concern for "the totality of the upbringing of his children," but also stated that its decision had to be "made on a racially neutral basis." On appeal, this decision was affirmed against the mother's claim that race was impermissibly taken into account:

> While the trial court was not blind to the racial backgrounds of the children, we are satisfied that it did not impermissibly award custody on the basis of race. As noted, [the father] showed

a sensitivity to the need for his children to be exposed to their ethnic heritage. All of us form our own personal identities, based in part, on our religious, racial and cultural backgrounds. To say, as [the mother] argues, that a court should never consider whether a parent is willing and able to expose to and educate children on their heritage, is to say that society is not interested in whether children ever learn who they are. *Palmore* does not require this. . . .

See also David D. Meyer, *Palmore* Comes of Age: The Place of Race in the Placement of Children, 18 U. Fla. J.L. & Pub. Pol'y 183 (2007); Solangel Maldonado, Bias in the Family: Race, Ethnicity, and Culture in Custody Disputes, 55 Fam. Ct. Rev. 213 (2017).

PROBLEMS

1. Judith received custody of her son, Reynard, age 7, after a bitterly contested divorce. She has married a Latino, and they are the only ethnically mixed couple in the neighborhood in which they reside. Reynard's father Allen has sought custody and has offered evidence from school teachers and school children that Reynard has been teased unmercifully by the Anglo children in the school and that he is not invited to birthday parties by their parents. Is this evidence relevant to the assignment of custody? Would the testimony of a psychologist that the child faces a significant risk of emotional distress as a result of the behavior of other children and parents in the community be relevant? Is it in a child's best interest to grow up without conflict or unusual discomfort?

2. Marie and Pierre married when they were both 22. They separated shortly after their only child, Claude, turned 6. The separation occurred after Pierre told Marie that her entire life she has thought of herself as a woman, and now wants to live as one. Pierre and Marie are both devout Catholics, and Pierre explained to Marie that she tried to dismiss these feelings, and she has always loved Marie and Claude. Marie feels betrayed that Pierre never said anything before they were married. She is also worried about the effect on Claude. He is shy, has a slight build, and has been a target for bullies for as long as she can remember. The bullying got worse when he started school, but over the last year, Pierre signed Claude up for a soccer team, which Pierre helped coach. Claude is very fast and has gained confidence since joining the team. After the separation, Marie insisted that Pierre stop coaching the team, and Pierre agreed, though she has continued to attend Claude's games. Claude and Pierre have always been very close.

Pierre has recently told Marie that she has changed her name to Pauline, prefers to be addressed as "she," and will soon have gender reassignment surgery. Marie responded by cutting off all contact between Pauline and Claude. Marie believes that Claude will be confused by what has happened, and that it will make him the subject of even more bullying. Marie thinks that if Pauline is awarded custodial time with Claude it should be conducted in a way where none of Claude's classmates find out about it, or she will have to move and have Claude attend a different school with classmates who have never met Pauline. Marie is reluctant to move, however, because Claude has been doing well academically and the other schools in the area are not as strong.

Pauline would like Claude to know the truth as soon as possible but has put off telling Claude at Marie's request. A psychological report finds that Claude had been deeply affected by the bullying he experienced earlier and is just beginning to be able to feel he can trust other children. The report concludes that Claude is still fragile, and it is hard to predict how he will respond to Pauline or to the response of other children if they find out about what has happened. The psychologist is concerned that Claude will be compelled to choose between a relationship with Pauline and his relationships with his friends, particularly if Marie is not supportive.

In the meantime, Pauline has become increasingly frustrated with Marie's unwillingness to let her spend time with Claude. During the marriage, Pauline had arranged her schedule to pick Claude up from school every day, supervised his homework, and made dinner for the family. Pauline asks for primary physical custody as Claude's primary caretaker or, in the alternative, joint physical custody with shared time on an equal basis with Marie. Marie in turn asks that she be awarded sole physical and legal custody of Claude and that Pauline be limited to supervised visitation.

If you were the judge in the case, what evidence would you want to hear before deciding the custody matter? How would you deal with Marie's insistence that Pauline present herself as a man as a condition of exercising custodial rights with Claude? If Marie believes that it is essential to move to a new school if Pauline is to spend time with Claude as a woman, how would you address such concerns? If Marie is unwilling to support Pauline's relationship with Claude, how would that affect your determination?

C. VISITATION AND ITS ENFORCEMENT

Morgan v. Foretich
546 A.2d 407 (D.C. Cir. 1988)

STEADMAN, J. The formal parties to this appeal are the divorced parents of a daughter, *H*, the ultimate real party in interest. She was born in 1982. On November 8, 1984, appellant Morgan was awarded custody of *H* and appellee Foretich was given liberal visitation. Almost continuously since that date, the parties have been in litigation on these issues. . . . Now before us is an appeal from an order of August 19, 1987, granting Foretich a two-week summer visitation with *H* and a subsequent order of civil contempt and imprisonment of Morgan for refusal to comply with the August 19 order.

. . . In January 1985, within two months of the custody and visitation order of November 8, 1984, Morgan began to make accusations that Foretich was sexually abusing *H* during visitation. . . .

Matters first came to a head in February 1986, when Morgan refused to allow *H* to visit Foretich in accordance with the court-ordered visitation schedule. Hearings were held in June and July of 1986 on several motions, including Foretich's motions to hold Morgan in contempt and for change of custody and Morgan's motions for temporary suspension of visitation and to compel discovery. On July 17, 1986, Judge Dixon orally announced his finding that Morgan had failed to prove by a preponderance of the evidence that Foretich had abused *H*, and that Morgan had disobeyed the visitation orders without lawful justification or excuse. A series of further hearings and orders then ensued, resulting in a finding of contempt and order of incarceration in August 1986. . . . On appeal, we upheld the closure of the contempt hearings and affirmed the judgment of contempt.

Meanwhile, Judge Dixon had ordered that visitation be resumed. When Morgan again failed to comply, Judge Dixon found her in contempt and ordered her incarcerated on February 17, 1987. Morgan was released from jail on February 19, 1987, and on February 24, 1987, visitations resumed for the first time in over a year. From February 24 through April 1, 1987, the visits were supervised and lasted one hour. On April 1, Judge Dixon ordered that the visits be extended to four hours.

On April 6, 1987, Judge Dixon began a series of hearings on a motion by Foretich for a change of custody and termination of Morgan's parental rights and on Morgan's cross motion to suspend visitation, or, in the alternative, to require supervised visitation. . . .

During the course of the hearings on the motions, Judge Dixon entered several orders continuing to gradually expand the visitation schedule. On April 21, 1987, he ordered the first overnight unsupervised weekend visitations. Pursuant to further orders, *H* spent nine or ten weekends with Foretich. Several emergency stays of the weekend visitation orders sought by Morgan and *H*'s guardian were denied by this court. *H*'s guardian played some part in most of these weekend visits and submitted reports of her observations to Judge Dixon.

Then on August 19, 1987, with the hearings still not completed, Judge Dixon entered an order providing for an extended visitation from August 22 through September 6, 1987. In his six-page order, he noted, inter alia, that since *H* was scheduled to return to school on September 8, "[w]hatever the court's ultimate ruling may be on the pending motions, to further delay the defendant-father's entitlement to summer visitation with his child until that ultimate ruling results in a denial of said summer visitation by default."

Morgan appealed this visitation order that same day. Her emergency motion for stay pending appeal filed the following day was denied by this court on August 21. Morgan failed to comply with the visitation order. She secreted the child and refused to reveal her whereabouts. (To this day, *H* remains hidden.) On August 24, Judge Dixon issued an order to show cause why Morgan should not be held in contempt. . . .

After a hearing held on August 26, Judge Dixon held Morgan in contempt and ordered her incarcerated, effective August 28. He also ordered that the security posted one year earlier pursuant to this court's order be forfeited at the rate of $5,000 per day. On August 27, Morgan appealed the contempt judgment and sought a stay pending appeal. The stay was denied and Morgan was incarcerated on August 28, where she remains.

A principal issue before us is whether the record supports the trial court's action in ordering a two-week summer visitation. Our standard of review is well established. Trial court decisions as to visitation rights are reversible only for clear abuse of discretion. . . . [A] trial court judgment may not be set aside except for errors of law, unless it appears the judgment is "plainly wrong or without evidence to support it." Thus, to the extent that such decisions rest on factual foundations, such findings are binding unless clearly erroneous. Such is particularly the case where, as here, the findings rest in significant part on considerations of credibility. . . .

The critical factual determination challenged by Morgan was that sexual abuse of *H* by her father had not been proven, or, as the court put it, the evidence was "in equipoise." That finding, asserts Morgan, was "plainly wrong." . . .

A review of the record shows that there was probative evidence on both sides of the issue of abuse. The ultimate question, however, is not how we weigh the evidence but rather whether a finder of fact, fully and personally knowledgeable of not only the evidence presented in the April to August hearings but also the entire history of these proceedings from November 1985 forward, would be clearly erroneous in concluding that the alleged sexual abuse had not been proven and would commit a clear abuse of discretion in allowing a two-week visitation. We cannot so conclude. . . .

In this litigation, neither party can conclusively speak for *H*. She has her own champion, a court-appointed guardian. Although the guardian states that she is in clear disagreement with the trial court's order for the extended summer visitation, we think correct her assessment that she "cannot argue that the order was without evidence to support it or an abuse of Judge Dixon's discretion." . . .

Probably neither our courts nor any courts anywhere in the world can deal in a perfect way with matters so intimately linked to a family unit formed and dissolved. We can but try. The little girl *H* grows older day by day. It is she, first and foremost, to whom the courts must seek to render justice as the process moves on.

. . . [T]he orders appealed from are affirmed.

NOTES AND QUESTIONS

1. Contempt proceedings are not unusual in high-conflict custody disputes. In the *Morgan* case, what alternatives did the court have once it determined that Morgan would defy an order to cooperate with unsupervised visitation for Foretich? Once her parents fled with the child and she refused to reveal their location? Did the court have any tools it could have used to defuse the conflict between the parents at an earlier point in the proceeding?

2. What weight should trial judges give to the child's expressed preference regarding visitation? Should that preference be given more or less weight in a contempt proceeding than in the determination of custody? Although interference with visitation often is attributed to hostile custodial parents, children themselves may be unwilling to cooperate in visitation arrangements. A study of 59 children between the ages of 5 and 12 in Toronto, Ontario, who were involved in custody or visitation disputes, reports that some 60 percent of the children held generally negative attitudes toward visitation, but only 10 percent completely refused to see a parent. Older children more often held negative attitudes toward visitation, and a history of parental violence was often present. Negative feelings were related to the quality of their own interactions with the parents (such as punitive or restrictive parenting) and to negative personality traits they associated with parents (lying, selfishness). Since the sample for this study came from high-conflict families, it is quite plausible that attitudes were influenced by stories from the custodial parent or by interparental behavior. Helen Radovanovic et al., Child and Family Characteristics of Children's Post-Separation Visitation Refusal, 25 J. Psychiatry & L. 33 (1997). Courts often hold custodial parents responsible for failure to comply with a visitation order even when the child is older and does not want to see the other parent. In In re Marriage of Marez and Marshall, 340 P.3d 520, 524-25 (Mont. 2014), the 14-year-old daughter indicated in an in camera proceeding that she did not wish to see her father. The Montana Supreme Court nonetheless found that use of the contempt power was appropriate "where a parent fails to make reasonable efforts to require a recalcitrant child to attend visitation." 340 P.3d at 527. In a Michigan case, however, the judge held three children, ages 14, 11, and 9, in contempt for their repeated refusals to spend time with their father and ordered their transfer to a juvenile detention center. The Supreme Court of Michigan censured the judge for her actions. In re Honorable Lisa O. Gorcyca, Judge, Sixth Circuit Court, No. 152831, 2017 WL 3221073 (Mich. July 28, 2017).

3. Dr. Morgan arranged for her parents to take the child abroad, convinced that if the U.S. courts regained jurisdiction, they would not just insist on unsupervised visitation, but would transfer custody to Dr. Foretich. *See* June Carbone & Leslie J. Harris, Family Law Armageddon: The Story of Morgan v. Foretich, *in* Family Law Stories (Carol Sanger ed., 2007). Indeed, that is the most common result in a case in which parents have fled with their children in order to prevent court-ordered visitation. *See, e.g.*, D.C. v. D.C., 988 So. 2d 359 (Miss. 2008). *Cf.* Schultz v. Schultz, 187 P.3d 1234 (Idaho 2008) (reversing a lower court order requiring that the mother return from Oregon, where she had fled immediately following a physical assault, on the ground that the trial court had not made specific findings about the child's best interests).

4. The court in *Morgan* used the contempt sanction in an effort to secure compliance with its visitation order. Dr. Morgan remained in jail for just over two years and was released only when President George H. W. Bush signed a bill limiting the period of incarceration for contempt to one year. Congress passed the bill expressly to deal with Elizabeth Morgan's situation.

Eric Foretich continued to search for Hilary (i.e., *H*). He finally located her in New Zealand, living with her maternal grandparents, and sought custody there. However, the New

Zealand courts ruled that it was in Hilary's best interests to remain with her grandparents rather than being put in the custody of a father she feared and had not seen in two years.

In September 1996, Congress passed the Elizabeth Morgan Act, which allowed Dr. Morgan to return with Hilary to the United States without being subject to the outstanding visitation order, and without the possibility of a new order being entered without Hilary's consent. In December 2003, the Act was declared to be an unconstitutional bill of attainder that applied to only one person. By then, however, Hilary had reached the age of majority. *See* Foretich v. United States, 351 F.3d 1198 (2003). (For a fuller account of Hilary's flight to New Zealand and the aftermath of the trial, *see* Carbone and Harris, above.)

Was Congress right to intervene in this case at any time? Is there some sanction other than incarceration that might have been effective in dealing with Morgan's refusal to comply with the court order? Is it appropriate to use coercive civil contempt beyond the point where it is likely to produce compliance with a court order? For a review of the use of contempt sanctions in the context of custody and visitation disputes, *see* Margaret M. Mahoney, The Enforcement of Child Custody Orders by Contempt Remedies, 68 U. Pitt. L. Rev. 835 (2007); Laurie S. Kohn, The False Promise of Custody in Domestic Violence Protection Orders, 65 DePaul L. Rev. 1001, 1018 (2016).

In the majority of cases that involve child abductions, fathers take the children. The abductions typically take place when a noncustodial parent has visitation and leaves the area with the child. These cases are highly correlated with a history of family violence. As in the *Morgan* case, they tend to involve younger children, typically between the ages of 2 and 6. *See* Jane K. Stoever, Parental Abduction and the State Intervention Paradox, 92 Wash. L. Rev. 861, 881 (2017).

5. Dr. Morgan's father had been in the OSS (the forerunner to the CIA) during World War II, and he orchestrated the departure from Virginia of himself, his wife, and Hilary. The family traveled on their own passports, largely using their own names. *See* Carbone and Harris, above. Such a flight would be harder today. A much larger number of countries, including the United States (1988) and New Zealand (1991), have ratified the Hague Convention on International Child Abduction, which would have required Hilary's return to Washington, D.C. The Hague Convention is discussed in Chapter 12. Moreover, in 1993 Congress passed the International Parental Kidnapping Crime Act, 18 U.S.C. §1204 (2022), which makes it a federal offense wrongfully to take a child outside of the United States. If the Act had been in effect when Morgan's parents took Hilary to New Zealand, they could have been prosecuted upon their return, whether or not New Zealand recognized the Hague Convention. In addition, the U.S. State Department has tightened passport controls; minors under 14 must apply for a passport in person, and issuance may be conditioned on both parents' consent. The airlines have also become stricter about allowing children to travel without both parents' consent.

PROBLEM

You represent Sharon, in the problem at page 463, above. While the sexual abuse allegations are being investigated, Sharon has arranged for Heather to see a therapist, who tells Sharon that Heather is displaying behavior consistent with having been abused. She also tells her that when she (the therapist) raised the possibility of seeing her father, Heather was inconsolable and displayed signs of post-traumatic stress disorder. The therapist believes that unsupervised visitation with Eric will be psychologically devastating for Heather.

In the meantime, the court, frustrated by the inconclusive report from the sexual abuse investigators, arranges for an evaluation by an independent expert. At the most recent hearing, that expert, on whom the judge has relied heavily in the past, presents a report concluding that no abuse has occurred, that Heather has given inconsistent statements that undermine her credibility, and that the only way to repair her relationship with her father is for Heather to spend extended time with him. The court proposes that the two lawyers draft a plan to repair Heather's relationship with her father, preferably as soon as possible.

Before the hearing, Sharon told you that she was taking Heather to visit her grandmother in Moldovia (a former Soviet Socialist Republic). When you call to report on the results of the hearing, Sharon tells you that she has not decided when she and Heather will return. She also asks you not to tell anyone where she is.

A few days later, Eric's lawyer calls to coordinate the response to the court's request for a plan to facilitate Eric's reunification with Heather. The court has asked for information including Heather's current address, and plans for the school year that will start in a couple of weeks. You suspect that Sharon is unlikely to return from Moldovia. If Eric's lawyer asks you directly where Heather is, what should you say to him? How should you respond to the court's request for an address? If Sharon decides not to return with Heather, what, if any, information can you disclose to the court?

NOTE: ATTORNEY-CLIENT CONFIDENTIALITY AND DUTIES TO DISCLOSE

Attorney-client confidentiality involves two related issues. One has to do with the scope of the lawyer-client privilege, which is defined by local rules of evidence. Many states have adopted Proposed Rule 503 of the Federal Rules of Evidence, which provides in subsection d(1) that there is "no privilege under this rule . . . [i]f the services of the lawyer were sought or obtained to enable or aid anyone to commit or plan to commit what the client knew or reasonably should have known to be a crime or fraud."

The most obvious instance occurs when a client engages a lawyer to provide legal assistance in connection with contemplated illegal activity. People v. Chappell, 927 P.2d 829 (Colo. 1996), involved the disbarment of an attorney who helped her client flee after the attorney learned that a custody evaluator was going to recommend that the husband receive custody of their son and as-yet-unborn baby, and that the court was likely to follow the recommendation. The client stated that the attorney advised her "as her attorney to stay, but as a mother to run." The lawyer also informed her client about a network of safe houses for people in her situation and helped her to liquidate her assets and empty her bank accounts. The lawyer contacted a friend of the client, asked the friend to pack her client's belongings from the marital home and to put them into storage, let the friend into the home with a key, gave the friend money from the client to pay for moving and storage, and retained the storage locker key. The client fled in violation of a court order that had awarded her temporary custody but prohibited either parent from taking the child from Colorado. After the client left the jurisdiction, but before the husband realized that she had fled, the attorney appeared in court and accepted the husband's offer to continue paying support and maintenance without informing him or the court of the client's actions, which under the court's existing order would produce a change in custody. The Colorado courts concluded that the attorney's conduct contributed to a fraud, violating R.P.C. 1.2(d) (a lawyer "shall not counsel a client to engage, or assist a client, in conduct that the lawyer knows is criminal or fraudulent"), R.P.C. 3.3(a)(2) (a lawyer shall not knowingly fail to disclose a material fact to a tribunal when disclosure is necessary to avoid assisting a criminal or fraudulent act by the client), R.P.C. 8.4(b) (it is professional misconduct for a lawyer to commit a criminal act by aiding the lawyer's client to commit a crime), and R.P.C. 8.4(c) (it is professional misconduct for a lawyer to engage in conduct involving dishonesty, fraud, deceit, or misrepresentation). When the client later returned to Colorado, she was charged with a felony for violation of the court order, and the husband obtained custody of both children.

The second issue concerns the reach of rules of professional conduct. Model Rule 1.6 provides that:

> A lawyer shall not reveal information relating to representation of a client unless the client consents after consultation. . . . A lawyer may reveal such information to the extent the lawyer reasonably believes necessary . . . to prevent the client from committing a criminal act that the lawyer believes is likely to result in imminent death or substantial bodily harm. . . .

The language of this Rule does not make explicit the relationship between the evidentiary privilege and ethical requirements. If information received by the lawyer *is* subject to the attorney-client evidentiary privilege, its disclosure over the objection of the client cannot be ordered. If, however, the information is not subject to the lawyer-client privilege, it may still be confidential as an ethical matter. Indeed, all information received by an attorney that relates to representation is subject to the general expectation of confidentiality set out in Rule 1.6. However, if confidential information is not privileged, it is subject to *involuntary* disclosure when ordered by a court. *See* Comment to Rule 1.6.

See generally Leigh Goodmark, Going Underground: The Ethics of Advising a Battered Woman Fleeing an Abusive Relationship, 75 UMKC L. Rev. 999 (2007); Julie Saffren, Professional Responsibility in Civil Domestic Violence Matters, 24 Hastings Women's L.J. 3 (2013).

CHAPTER 10

FAMILY CONTRACTS

The expression *family contracts* may refer to a wide variety of agreements. In addition to an agreement to marry, contracts affecting family relationships may include agreements between spouses regarding religious upbringing of children, ownership of wealth during the marriage, and settlements in contemplation of divorce. A contract can also be an important vehicle for analyzing the rights and duties of unmarried cohabitants (Chapter 4), or in establishing parentage in surrogacy arrangements (Chapter 14). This chapter will focus on contracts between intimate partners before marriage, during marriage, and at separation.

As we noted in Chapter 5, those who most embrace the idea of marriage as a covenant, that is, as a bond not just between the spouses, but between the spouses and God, the state or the community, tend to be the most distrustful of contract language. The philosopher Georg Hegel, for example, embracing such views, denounced the idea of marriage as a contract as "shameful" and insisted that, if marriage were to be treated as a contract, it was as "a contract to transcend the standpoint of contract." Georg W.F. Hegel, Philosophy of Right ¶ 163 112 (1821) (T.M. Knox trans., Oxford Univ. Press 1952). On the other hand, those who see marriage as a product of the couples' self-expression, *see, e.g.,* the discussion of *Obergefell* in Chapter 1, view marital contacting as an appropriate act of self-definition. That self-definition may extend to the enforceable contracts ordering the spouses' financial affairs or to a more personal expression of values that may not necessarily be enforceable in court.

Thus, contracts are important for reasons that go beyond economic transactions. We talk routinely about the social contract or church covenants. The *idea* of contract (or promise or agreement) is not the same as a legal contract a court enforces. Surrogacy contracts, for example, often contain clauses addressing abortion, even though the parties may recognize that such clauses are unlikely to be enforceable. The word *contract*, then, also may be understood as referring to an image, a metaphor, or a piece of paper useful in framing the expectations of the parties.

Yet, for many decades, family law doctrines precluded spouses from contracting with each other or prohibited certain agreements between family members for reasons of public policy. Law tended to enforce contracts that served marital purposes and disfavored those at odds with the public purpose of marriage. But as these public purposes change, so too has the enforceability of particular types of agreements. Contracts between married and soon-to-be divorced people are widely acceptable, though, as illustrated below, courts will not enforce agreements if they appear too one-sided (at execution and sometimes at enforcement) or if they undermine particular spousal and parental duties established by statute or at common law.

Contracts form a crucial part of parents' and spouses' understandings of their rights and responsibilities—before, during, and after their relationships. Indeed, as the last part on settlement agreements makes clear and as Chapter 11 on out-of-court processes explains, more and more family members privately order their affairs and resolve their conflicts without court management. As you read the following materials, keep in mind the competing considerations of fairness and freedom of contract as courts decide when and how to enforce family agreements.

A. PREMARITAL AGREEMENTS

At least since the sixteenth century, spouses have used premarital agreements to alter the legal regimes for marital property ownership and management. The English Statute of Frauds of 1677 dealt with such contracts, requiring them to be in writing to be enforceable. Today, in the United States, they are still with us, but their popularity waxes and wanes. As marital regimes ossify, contract offers a more flexible way to order individual relationships. Yet, while marriage laws seek to protect the vulnerable; premarital contracts have become more associated with the rich and powerful. The headlines belong to the famous; the premarital agreements of a baseball player or a technology billionaire receive disproportionate attention. While premarital agreements have always been more common among those with assets to protect, premarital agreements have become more common, particularly among two groups: educated couples who have accumulated assets before marriage and increasingly represent the population of people marrying today, and parties entering second marriages who seek to keep assets of a first marriage separate or to avoid responsibility for their spouse's debt. *See* Michael Waters, Prenups Aren't Just for Rich People Anymore, The New Yorker, July 22, 2022.

To be enforceable, premarital agreements must satisfy the usual contract requirements. They must be entered into voluntarily, be supported by consideration, and satisfy the statute of frauds. Traditionally, and still today in most states, premarital agreements must also satisfy additional procedural requirements and are subject to greater judicial supervision of their substantive terms than are commercial contracts. The following materials consider three approaches to the enforceability of prenuptial agreements: first, the Uniform Premarital Agreement Act (UPAA) and a number of state court decisions such as Simeone v. Simeone proceed from the belief that the parties should be relatively free to reach whatever agreements they like and to rely on the enforceability of such contracts at separation or divorce. Second, the ALI Principles and the decisions in other states place greater weight on the fairness of the result at the time of enforcement, even if that makes the result less predictable. Finally, the Uniform Premarital and Marital Agreement Act (UPMAA), approved in 2012, is the middle ground between the UPAA and ALI. The following materials first consider a common law decision, rooted in contract doctrine, and then compare the UPAA, ALI Principles, and the UPMAA. As you study these materials, consider whether the resolution of specific issues, such as the importance of representation by counsel, reflects different approaches to the enforceability of these agreements, and whether the justifications for treating these agreements differently from commercial contracts still ring true.

Simeone v. Simeone
581 A.2d 162 (Pa. 1990)

FLAHERTY, J. At issue in this appeal is the validity of a prenuptial agreement executed between the appellant, Catherine E. Walsh Simeone, and the appellee, Frederick A. Simeone. At the time of their marriage, in 1975, appellant was a twenty-three year old nurse and appellee was a thirty-nine year old neurosurgeon. Appellee had an income of approximately $90,000 per year, and appellant was unemployed. Appellee also had assets worth approximately $300,000. On the eve of the parties' wedding, appellee's attorney presented appellant with a prenuptial agreement to be signed. Appellant, without the benefit of counsel, signed the agreement.

Appellee's attorney had not advised appellant regarding any legal rights that the agreement surrendered. The parties are in disagreement as to whether appellant knew in advance of that date that such an agreement would be presented for signature. Appellant denies having had such knowledge and claims to have signed under adverse circumstances, which, she contends, provide a basis for declaring it void.

The agreement limited appellant to support payments of $200 per week in the event of separation or divorce, subject to a maximum total payment of $25,000. The parties separated in 1982, and, in 1984, divorce proceedings were commenced. Between 1982 and 1984 appellee made payments which satisfied the $25,000 limit. In 1985, appellant filed a claim for alimony pendente lite. A master's report upheld the validity of the prenuptial agreement and denied this claim. . . .

There is no longer validity in the implicit presumption that supplied the basis for Estate of Geyer, 533 A.2d 423 (Pa. 1987) and similar earlier decisions. Such decisions rested upon a belief that spouses are of unequal status and that women are not knowledgeable enough to understand the nature of contracts that they enter. Society has advanced, however, to the point where women are no longer regarded as the "weaker" party in marriage, or in society generally. Indeed, the stereotype that women serve as homemakers while men work as bread-winners is no longer viable. Quite often today both spouses are income earners. Nor is there viability in the presumption that women are uninformed, uneducated, and readily subjected to unfair advantage in marital agreements. Indeed, women nowadays quite often have sub-stantial education, financial awareness, income, and assets.

Accordingly, the law has advanced to recognize the equal status of men and women in our society. Paternalistic presumptions and protections that arose to shelter women from the inferiorities and incapacities which they were perceived as having in earlier times have, appropriately, been discarded. . . . It would be inconsistent, therefore, to perpetuate the standards governing prenuptial agreements that were described in *Geyer* and similar decisions, as these reflected a paternalistic approach that is now insupportable.

Further, *Geyer* and its predecessors embodied substantial departures from traditional rules of contract law, to the extent that they allowed consideration of the knowledge of the con-tracting parties and reasonableness of their bargain as factors governing whether to uphold an agreement. Traditional principles of contract law provide perfectly adequate remedies where contracts are procured through fraud, misrepresentation, or duress. Consideration of other factors, such as the knowledge of the parties and the reasonableness of their bargain, is inap-propriate. . . . Prenuptial agreements are contracts, and, as such, should be evaluated under the same criteria as are applicable to other types of contracts. . . . Absent fraud, misrepresenta-tion, or duress, spouses should be bound by the terms of their agreements.

Contracting parties are normally bound by their agreements, without regard to whether the terms thereof were read and fully understood and irrespective of whether the agreements embodied reasonable or good bargains. Based upon these principles, the terms of the present prenuptial agreement must be regarded as binding, without regard to whether the terms were fully understood by appellant. *Ignorantia non excusat.*

Accordingly, we find no merit in a contention raised by appellant that the agreement should be declared void on the ground that she did not consult with independent legal coun-sel. To impose a per se requirement that parties entering a prenuptial agreement must obtain independent legal counsel would be contrary to traditional principles of contract law, and would constitute a paternalistic and unwarranted interference with the parties' freedom to enter contracts.

Further, the reasonableness of a prenuptial bargain is not a proper subject for judicial review. *Geyer* and earlier decisions required that, at least where there had been an inadequate disclosure made by the parties, the bargain must have been reasonable at its inception. *See*

Geyer, 516 Pa. at 503, 533 A.2d at 428. Some have even suggested that prenuptial agreements should be examined with regard to whether their terms remain reasonable at the time of dissolution of the parties' marriage.

By invoking inquiries into reasonableness, however, the functioning and reliability of prenuptial agreements is severely undermined. Parties would not have entered such agreements, and, indeed, might not have entered their marriages, if they did not expect their agreements to be strictly enforced. If parties viewed an agreement as reasonable at the time of its inception, as evidenced by their having signed the agreement, they should be foreclosed from later trying to evade its terms by asserting that it was not in fact reasonable. . . .

Further, everyone who enters a long-term agreement knows that circumstances can change during its term, so that what initially appeared desirable might prove to be an unfavorable bargain. Such are the risks that contracting parties routinely assume. Certainly, the possibilities of illness, birth of children, reliance upon a spouse, career change, financial gain or loss, and numerous other events that can occur in the course of a marriage cannot be regarded as unforeseeable. If parties choose not to address such matters in their prenuptial agreements, they must be regarded as having contracted to bear the risk of events that alter the value of their bargains. . . .

The present agreement recited that full disclosure had been made, and included a list of appellee's assets totaling approximately $300,000. Appellant contends that this list understated by roughly $183,000 the value of a classic car collection which appellee had included at a value of $200,000. The master, reviewing the parties' conflicting testimony regarding the value of the car collection, found that appellant failed to prove by clear and convincing evidence that the value of the collection had been understated. The courts below affirmed that finding. . . . Appellant's contention is plainly without merit.

Appellant's final contention is that the agreement was executed under conditions of duress in that it was presented to her at 5 P.M. on the eve of her wedding, a time when she could not seek counsel without the trauma, expense, and embarrassment of postponing the wedding. The master found this claim not credible. The courts below affirmed that finding, upon an ample evidentiary basis.

Although appellant testified that she did not discover until the eve of her wedding that there was going to be a prenuptial agreement, testimony from a number of other witnesses was to the contrary. . . . And the legal counsel who prepared the agreement for appellee testified that, prior to the eve of the wedding, changes were made in the agreement to increase the sums payable to appellant in the event of separation or divorce. He also stated that he was present when the agreement was signed and that appellant expressed absolutely no reluctance about signing. It should be noted, too, that during the months when the agreement was being discussed appellant had more than sufficient time to consult with independent legal counsel if she had so desired. Under these circumstances, there was plainly no error in finding that appellant failed to prove duress.

Hence, the courts below properly held that the present agreement is valid and enforceable. Appellant is barred, therefore, from receiving alimony pendente lite.

Order affirmed.

PAPADAKOS, J., concurring. . . . I cannot join the opinion authored by Mr. Justice FLAHERTY, because, it must be clear to all readers, it contains a number of unnecessary and unwarranted declarations regarding the "equality" of women. Mr. Justice FLAHERTY believes that, with the hard-fought victory of the Equal Rights Amendment in Pennsylvania, all vestiges of inequality between the sexes have been erased and women are now treated equally under the law. I fear my colleague does not live in the real world. If I did not know him better I would think that his statements smack of male chauvinism, an attitude that "you women asked for it, now live with it." If you want to know about equality of women, just ask them about comparable wages for comparable work. Just ask them about sexual harassment in the workplace. Just ask them about the sexual discrimination in the Executive Suites of big business. And the list of discrimination based on sex goes on and on.

I view prenuptial agreements as being in the nature of contracts of adhesion with one party generally having greater authority than the other who deals in a subservient role. I believe the law protects the subservient party, regardless of that party's sex, to insure equal protection and treatment under the law.

McDermott, J., dissenting. Let me begin by setting forth a common ground between my position in this matter and that of the majority. There can be no question that, in the law and in society, men and women must be accorded equal status. I am in full agreement with the majority's observation that "women nowadays quite often have substantial education, financial awareness, income, and assets." However, the plurality decision I authored in Estate of Geyer, 516 Pa. 492, 533 A.2d 423 (1987), as well as the Dissenting Opinion I offer today, have little to do with the equality of the sexes, but everything to do with the solemnity of the matrimonial union. . . .

The subject of the validity of pre-nuptial agreements is not a new issue for this Court. A pre-nuptial agreement is the reservation of ownership over land, money and any other property, acquired in the past, present or future, from the most unique of human bargains. A pre-nuptial agreement may also prove an intention to get the best out of a marriage without incurring any obligation to do more than be there so long as it suits a purpose. Certainly, a prenuptial agreement may serve many purposes consistent with love and affection in life. It may answer obligations incurred prior to present intentions, obligations to children, parents, relatives, friends and those not yet born. . . . Moreover, society has an interest in protecting the right of its citizens to contract, and in seeing the reduction, in the event of a dissolution of the marriage, of the necessity of lengthy, complicated, and costly litigation. Thus, while I acknowledge the long-standing rule of law that pre-nuptial agreements are presumptively valid and binding upon the parties, I am unwilling to go as far as the majority to protect the right to contract at the expense of the institution of marriage. Were a contract of marriage, the most intimate relationship between two people, not the surrender of freedom, an offering of self in love, sacrifice, hope for better or for worse, the begetting of children and the offer of effort, labor, precious time and care for the safety and prosperity of their union, then the majority would find me among them.

In my view, one seeking to avoid the operation of an executed pre-nuptial agreement must first establish, by clear and convincing evidence, that a full and fair disclosure of the worth of the intended spouse was not made at the time of the execution of the agreement. This Court has recognized that full and fair disclosure is needed because, at the time of the execution of a pre-nuptial agreement, the parties do not stand in the usual arm's length posture attendant to most other types of contractual undertakings, but "stand in a relation of mutual confidence and trust that calls for the highest degree of good faith. . . ." In addition to a full and fair disclosure of the general financial pictures of the parties, I would find a pre-nuptial agreement voidable where it is established that the parties were not aware, at the time of contracting, of existing statutory rights which they were relinquishing upon the signing of the agreement. It is here, with a finding of full and fair disclosure, that the majority would end its analysis of the validity of a pre-nuptial agreement. I would not. An analysis of the fairness and equity of a pre-nuptial agreement has long been an important part of the law of this state. . . .

At the time of dissolution of the marriage, a spouse should be able to avoid the operation of a pre-nuptial agreement upon clear and convincing proof that, despite the existence of full and fair disclosure at the time of the execution of the agreement, the agreement is nevertheless so inequitable and unfair that it should not be enforced in a court of this state. . . . The majority holds to the view, without waiver, that parties, having contracted with full and fair disclosure, should be made to suffer the consequences of their bargains. In so holding, the majority has given no weight to the other side of the scales: the state's paramount interest in the preservation of marriage and the family relationship, and the protection of parties to a marriage who may be rendered wards of the state, unable to provide for their own reasonable needs. . . .

It is also apparent that, although a pre-nuptial agreement is quite valid when drafted, the passage of time accompanied by the intervening events of a marriage, may render the terms of the agreement completely unfair and inequitable. While parties to a pre-nuptial agreement may indeed foresee, generally, the events which may come to pass during their marriage, one spouse should not be made to suffer for failing to foresee all of the surrounding circumstances which may attend the dissolution of the marriage. Although it should not be the role of the courts to void pre-nuptial agreements merely because one spouse may receive a better result in an action under the Divorce Code to recover alimony or equitable distribution, it should be the role of the courts to guard against the enforcement of pre-nuptial agreements where such enforcement will bring about only inequity and hardship. It borders on cruelty to accept that after years of living together, yielding their separate opportunities in life to each other, that two individuals emerge the same as the day they began their marriage.

At the time of the dissolution of marriage, what are the circumstances which would serve to invalidate a pre-nuptial agreement? This is a question that should only be answered on a case-by-case basis. However, it is not unrealistic to imagine that in a given situation, one spouse, although trained in the workforce at the time of marriage, may, over many years, have become economically dependent upon the other spouse. In reliance upon the permanence of marriage and in order to provide a stable home for a family, a spouse may choose, even at the suggestion of the other spouse, not to work during the marriage. As a result, at the point of dissolution of the marriage, the spouse's employability has diminished to such an extent that to enforce the support provisions of the pre-nuptial agreement will cause the spouse to become a public charge, or will provide a standard of living far below that which was enjoyed before and during marriage. In such a situation, a court may properly decide to render void all or some of the provisions of the pre-nuptial agreement.

I can likewise conceive of a situation where, after a long marriage, the value of property may have increased through the direct efforts of the spouse who agreed not to claim it upon divorce or death. In such a situation, the court should be able to decide whether it is against the public policy of the state, and thus inequitable and unfair, for a spouse to be precluded from receiving that increase in the value of property which he or she had, at least in part, directly induced. I marvel at the majority's apparent willingness to enforce a pre-nuptial agreement in the interest of freedom to contract at any cost, even where unforeseen and untoward illness has rendered one spouse unable, despite his own best efforts, to provide reasonable support for himself. I would further recognize that a spouse should be given the opportunity to prove, through clear and convincing evidence, that the amount of time and energy necessary for that spouse to shelter and care for the children of the marriage has rendered the terms of a pre-nuptial agreement inequitable, and unjust and thus, avoidable.

NOTES AND QUESTIONS

1. The landmark case of Posner v. Posner, 233 So. 2d 381 (Fla. 1970), *rev'd on other grounds*, 257 So. 2d 530 (1972), held that contracts concerning property division and spousal support at divorce are not inherently contrary to public policy. Most courts faced with the issue since then have taken the same view, concluding that no-fault divorce laws express a legislative policy of neutrality toward divorce and that, in an era of frequent divorce, public policy favors settling disputes amicably. Only a few jurisdictions hold that agreements waiving spousal support are contrary to public policy. *See* In re Marriage of Erpelding, 917 N.W.2d 235, 242 n.5 (Iowa 2018). *Simeone* remains one of the watershed cases embracing the right of married couples to reach their own agreements. Part of the reasoning of the case stems from its declaration that "the law has advanced to recognize the equal status of men and women in our society." What does the court mean by "equal status," and how do the concurrence and dissent differ in their consideration of gender equality?

2. The majority, concurring, and dissenting opinions in the case associate the historical reluctance to enforce premarital agreements with the historic role of gender in the assignment of marital roles and women's dependence (and weaker bargaining power) because of their gender. How do the various opinions describe women's roles today? What relationship does each opinion see between the status of women and the enforceability of the *Simeone* agreement? How do they view the nature of marriage? Would the justices come to the same conclusions if the roles of husband and wife were reversed?

3. What role should unequal bargaining power play in shaping family contracts? Tess Wilkinson-Ryan and Deborah Small note:

> Family law has become increasingly dependent on private contracts to determine the allocation of entitlements before, during, and after marriage. Ideally, prenuptial contracts, divorce settlements, and child custody agreements each require the parties involved to negotiate effectively in order to maximize the joint welfare of the spouses, ex-spouses, and children. Evidence suggests, however, that this contractarian ideal is not borne out by the current reality in which women are at a financial disadvantage to their male counterparts after divorce. . . . The first trend we review is the increasing preference for private, face-to-face negotiations rather than judge-made settlements. We review literature suggesting that women and men may bring different goals to the bargaining table, which may produce different behavior and outcomes for men and women in these negotiations.

Tess Wilkinson-Ryan & Deborah Small, Negotiating Divorce: Gender and the Behavioral Economics of Divorce Bargaining, 26 Law & Ineq. 109, 111-112 (2008). *See also* Emily Rothkin, How to Create Better Mediation: Using Divorce Mediation Outcomes to Assess Gender's Effect on Mediation, 102 B. U. L. Rev. 631 (2022) (factors such as income, education, self-esteem, and social resources shape mediation outcomes in gendered ways); Morial Shah, Negotiation: Women's Voices, 20 Pepp. Disp. Resol. L.J. 167, 170 (2020) ("Women negotiators are more likely to accept equal splits even when they have stronger negotiating positions.").

Amy Cohen, however, notes design problems with the research on gendered negotiations that Wilkinson-Ryan and Small summarize:

> [G]lorification of feminine values has met with several persistent critiques: (1) it essentializes and reinforces stereotypes that have traditionally disempowered women, with little regard to class, race, or situational power; (2) it extols and idealizes qualities arising from women's subordination and thus serves to further entrench their oppression; (3) it ignores or even contradicts "empirical" evidence to the contrary; and (4) it maintains a structural system of (heterosexual) masculine and feminine identity that ultimately perpetuates rather than subverts the status quo.

Amy Cohen, Gender: An (Un)Useful Category of Prescriptive Negotiation Analysis?, 13 Tex. J. Women & L. 169, 171 (2003). For further discussion, *see* Chapter 11, Section D, on alternative dispute resolution.

4. The Pennsylvania cases prior to *Simeone* required full disclosure or fair and adequate provision before a court would enforce a premarital agreement. What is the relationship between disclosure, a matter of the bargaining process, and fair and adequate provision, which pertains to the substance of the agreement? The Supreme Court of Tennessee explained its reasoning this way:

> At least three principles support our interpretation of the [disclosure] rule. First, . . . an agreement to marry gives rise to a confidential relationship. As a result, the parties to an antenuptial agreement do not deal at arm's length and must exercise candor and good faith in all matters bearing upon the contract.
>
> Secondly, parties to an antenuptial agreement are very often ill-matched in terms of bargaining power. As one court put it, "candor compels us to raise to a conscious level the fact that, as in this case, prenuptial agreements will almost always be entered into between people with property or an income potential to protect on one side and people who are impecunious on the other." Gant v. Gant, 329 S.E.2d 106, 114 (W. Va. 1985). Thus, a rule requiring full disclosure or independent knowledge serves to level the bargaining field for the party in the weaker position.
>
> Finally, unlike other private commercial contracts, the State has an interest and is a party to every marriage. . . . In the absence of antenuptial agreements, state laws govern the division of marital property and the awarding of alimony in the event of divorce. Often, antenuptial agreements alter the rights parties otherwise would have under those state laws. Consequently, it is altogether appropriate that parties entering into antenuptial agreements do so with knowledge of the holdings to which they are waiving any claim under state law. . . .

Randolph v. Randolph, 937 S.W.2d 815 (Tenn. 1996).

None of these requirements applies to ordinary contracts. Why should they apply to agreements between people about to be married? Should parties who are engaged to be married have fiduciary obligations to each other? Many states agree with *Randolph*, but California and Georgia, for example, distinguish between spouses, who do have such fiduciary obligations, and those contemplating marriage, who do not. In re Bonds, 5 P.3d 815 (Cal. 2000); Mallen v. Mallen, 622 S.E.2d 812, 815 (Ga. 2005). Consider these questions as you read Lane v. Lane and the materials that follow, which challenge and confirm traditional ideas about who signs premarital agreements.

5. While empirical data about the content of premarital agreements have been relatively scarce, Professor Elizabeth Carter conducted a 2019 study that challenges the commonly expressed belief that premarital agreements are inherently unfair against women. Examining premarital agreements drafted in Louisiana, Carter analyzed the demographics of the population of signatories, the length of the waiting period between drafting and signing, and various substantive terms. She concluded that thoughtfully crafted premarital agreements can result in fairness at divorce. Elizabeth Carter, Are Premarital Agreements Really Unfair?: An Empirical Study, 48 Hofstra L. Rev. 387 (2019).

Lane v. Lane
202 S.W.3d 577 (Ky. 2006)

LAMBERT, C.J. Three days before their marriage on November 24, 1990, Appellant, Paula O. Lane, and Appellee, David L. Lane, entered into an antenuptial agreement. Appropriate asset disclosures were made and the underlying validity of the agreement is not at issue herein. What is at issue is whether events subsequent to the nine and a half year marriage and the birth of two children render enforcement of the agreement unconscionable. . . .

At the time of their marriage, Appellant was working as a night desk clerk in a hotel earning $19,000 a year. She was twenty-nine years of age. Despite his youthful age of twenty-six, Appellee was already a successful stockbroker at Edward D. Jones and Company, earning

$166,000 per year. Appellee was a college graduate while Appellant had only a high school education. Two children were born of the marriage, after which Appellant did not work outside the home as she was the primary caregiver for the children. By the time the marriage was dissolved, Appellee had achieved great financial success. He was earning approximately one million dollars per year and he was a partner in a regional brokerage firm.

According to the agreement, the parties waived their rights under the law to claim maintenance in the event the marriage was dissolved. The parties further agreed that the separate property of each would be deemed nonmarital in the event of divorce. The agreement explicitly identified certain items as Appellee's separate property. These items were two parcels of real estate (not relevant here), a partnership interest in Edward D. Jones, and Appellee's pension plan, profit sharing plan and voluntary profit sharing plan through Edward D. Jones. The agreement further provided that should either party default in or breach any obligations contained therein, the defaulting party would be responsible for attorney's fees, court costs, costs of depositions, transportation, lodging, and other related expenses. As there was a dramatic difference in the parties' economic circumstances when enforcement of the agreement was sought, we must determine whether the doctrine of unconscionability allows relief to Appellant. . . .

This Court has embraced the view that antenuptial agreements are not per se invalid as against public policy. However, courts retain the right to analyze such agreements for unconscionability at the time of enforcement. . . .

From the time this Court first recognized the validity and enforceability of antenuptial agreements, we have included the following qualification:

> The ingenuity of persons contemplating marriage to fashion unusual agreements, particularly with the assistance of counsel, cannot be overestimated. We will observe the tradition whereby the law develops on a case by case basis. It should be recognized, however, that trial courts have been vested with broad discretion to modify or invalidate ante-nuptial agreements.

Thus, it is beyond reasonable dispute that a trial court may modify or invalidate all or part of an ante-nuptial agreement where enforcement is unconscionable in its application. This includes cases where "the facts and circumstances changed since the agreement was executed so as to make its enforcement unfair and unreasonable." On this basis, the trial court modified the agreement and ordered Appellee to pay maintenance of $12,000.00 per month for three years. . . .

In the case at bar, this was the first marriage for both Appellant and Appellee and both parties were in their twenties. Two children were born of the marriage and Appellant quit her job to care for the children while Appellee rapidly progressed in his career. While a significant disparity in the parties' incomes existed at the time of the marriage, this disparity grew exponentially during the marriage in large part because the husband was able to concentrate on his career while the wife stayed home to care for the children and the home. Contrary to the dissent's contention, Appellant's discontinuance of employment to rear the children and maintain the household is not of nominal value and should in fairness be considered a substantial factor in this case, along with the affluent lifestyle maintained during their marriage, towards rendering the maintenance waiver provision unconscionable.

Parties who contemplate entering into antenuptial agreements have a duty to appropriately consider their circumstances and whether such an agreement is right for them. The more one-sided an agreement appears at the time it is made, the more likely courts are to invalidate the agreement at the time enforcement is sought. Bare-knuckle bargaining is not an appropriate practice. As this was a first marriage between younger persons, it is curious that these parties even wanted an antenuptial agreement. Their situation differed vastly from the customary and proper antenuptial agreement circumstances where parties desire to preserve their assets for their children and grandchildren. But they made their agreement and it will be enforced, subject to judicial scrutiny for unconscionability.

. . . [O]n the maintenance issue, we reinstate the judgment of the trial court. . . .

GRAVES, J., concurring. I concur with the majority but write separately to express some additional thoughts in this case. Entering such an antenuptial agreement during the period of excitement on the eve of a wedding evokes questions about the sufficiency of the parties' consent and indicates that Appellee likely had serious mental reservations about marriage. . . . Perhaps, an *anti*-nuptial agreement would be a more apt description as KRS 402.005 defines marriage as a union for life.

The intimate partnership of life and love which constitutes the married state is rooted in the conjugal covenant of irrevocable personal consent. In the eyes of society, marriage receives its stability from the human act by which the partners mutually surrender themselves to each other without any hesitation or reservation whatsoever. While there is no single definitive explanation for the breakdown of the sacred institution of marriage, the casual attitude expressed in this antenuptial agreement is no doubt a facilitating factor contributing to a disturbing trend.

. . . Since 1916, it was the declared public policy of this Commonwealth that antenuptial agreements contemplating divorce and separation were void as they tended to promote (or at least predict) marital instability. Yet, the . . . Court nonetheless overruled [the 1916 decision] explaining that the policy declared therein was no longer necessary or pertinent as it was designed primarily to protect women, who were "decidedly second class" citizens at the time. *Edwardson v. Edwardson*, 798 S.W.2d 941, 944 (Ky. 1990). Unfortunately, the great strides made by both women and children, as a class, have done nothing to validate the majority's reasoning in *Edwardson, supra.*

While anecdotal, but sadly not surprising, it was the husband and not the wife who scored the commercial deal of the century in this fateful contract. Perhaps the wife felt lucky to receive the scraps she did obtain, as she was granted the ultimate privilege of being this man's wife and bearing his children for at least the duration of her youth. Or perhaps as behavioral studies have continually demonstrated, the wife never believed that her incredibly bad bargain would ever come to fruition. *See* Reviewing Premarital Agreements to Protect the State's Interest in Marriage, 91 Va. L. Rev. 535, 543 (2005) (citing one study demonstrating "that although most people accurately estimated the country's overall divorce rate at fifty percent, they assessed their own chances of divorce at zero").

Our current case law nevertheless mandates that brides and grooms-to-be must be held to their bad bargains, no matter how foolish, last minute, or ill-conceived they may be, unless such bargains rise to the level of being unconscionable. . . .

It is indeed chauvinistic for one to contend that the agreement in this case is somehow fair since the wife was merely some lowly hotel clerk[1] while the husband was a youthful and successful stockbroker. Perceiving these positions as vastly disparate on life's socioeconomic ladder, some would suggest that the wife's nine and a half years of living beyond her assigned socioeconomic rung with her stockbroker husband was more than enough consideration for her (1) discontinuance of employment; (2) her bearing of two children; (3) her caring for those two children; (4) her maintenance of the household; and (5) her role as her husband's consort, hostess, and social liaison. Indeed, the record demonstrates that the wife held numerous and lavish parties for her husband's associates and held positions in several high-profile

---

1. Who, apparently, was past her prime at the ripe old age of 29.

community organizations for the purpose of benefiting her husband's reputation and promoting his career.

Yet, as the majority rightly acknowledges, the varied contributions of a homemaker is not of nominal value in this Commonwealth. . . . [Kentucky statutes reflect the concept that] marriage is a partnership that both spouses contribute to in equal, yet differing ways, and that children and the accumulation of financial assets is a corresponding result or byproduct of that partnership.

In the case of homemaker spouses, the division of labor in a family is compartmentalized. One spouse focuses time, talents, and experience to the marketplace while the other spouse focuses equal time, talents, and experience to the family. In such a system, the partnership strives to achieve maximum output and return in two essential areas of life—one spouse will have more time and energy to develop greater skill and earnings potential in the marketplace while the other will have more time and energy to ensure that the children and the household thrive and grow. This system is nothing new and has always been valued as a meaningful and successful model for maintaining both a marriage and a family.[2]

However, when homemaker spouses find themselves in the midst of family breakdown through either separation or divorce, they are prematurely forced to abandon their chosen callings and start anew in the marketplace. These spouses are understandably ill-equipped to compete in such an arena as they are frequently impaired by the loss of youth and lack of skills. Years spent homemaking are viewed by potential employers as years of "unemployment." Contacts and relevant experience are almost always lacking on a homemaker's resume and many are simply regarded as too old for entry-level employment. Rehabilitative alimony for homemaker spouses is therefore not a gift, but something these hardworking spouses have earned after years of toiling outside the marketplace on behalf of their families. This is analogous to an on-the-job anatomical injury in workers' compensation and the resulting functional impairment.

The antenuptial agreement in this case is fundamentally unfair in large part because it accords almost no consideration for the wife's contributions as a homemaker in this marriage. Were we to hold as the dissent suggests it would be foolish, indeed, to continue investing in a marriage through the role of a homemaker as such a contribution would be accorded diminished status under the laws of Kentucky and hence, this Court would be contributing to the feminization of poverty.

Fortunately for the children and families in this Commonwealth, the majority continues to respect and protect the partnership theory of marriage, the sanctity of the family, and the important contributions of homemaker spouses as such concepts are codified in our statutory law.

McANAULTY, J., dissenting. Respectfully, I dissent from that portion of the Majority's Opinion affirming the trial court's determination that the provision of the agreement regarding waiver of maintenance was unconscionable. . . . I believe that the trial court, and now a Majority of this Court, set aside the provisions of the waiver of maintenance clause because it constituted a bad—not unconscionable—bargain for Paula at the time of divorce. I agree with the reasoning of the Court of Appeals that considered the lack of evidence to suggest that the marriage caused Paula to forego the completion of her education so that now her decision to forego joining the work force to pursue her education somehow makes the agreement unfair and unreasonable.

---

2. This division of labor concept has also been very successful in our modern industrial society, to wit: the assembly line.

The highest number that Paula agrees that she received in the trial court's division of marital property is $233,593.12. I do not disagree that David is in a significantly better financial position with his monthly income, as found by the trial court, of $95,728.33, but I cannot agree with Paula that the amount that she received will not support her while she sensibly and responsibly pursues her career interests. Nor can I agree that an affluent lifestyle as opposed to a comfortable lifestyle (which I believe Paula and her children can enjoy with her property award plus $3,000.00 per month child support) should necessarily render the maintenance provision unconscionable.

I believe the trial court abused its discretion in declaring the waiver of maintenance provision unconscionable when David and Paula had disparate incomes from the start of the marriage; they signed the antenuptial agreement; they signed the agreement with the assistance and advice of independent counsel and with full knowledge that the agreement substantially altered their marital and property rights, claims, or interests that they would have had but for the execution of the agreement; and they were married for 9-1/2 years.

NOTES AND QUESTIONS

1. *Lane* was decided 16 years after *Simeone*. How would you describe the differences between *Lane* and *Simeone* in their evaluation of the status of women, their identification of the purposes of marriage, and their articulation of the reasons for validating or invalidating the respective agreements? Has the passage of time changed the justices' evaluation of the homemaking role? What views do the justices in *Simeone* and *Lane* express about the purposes of marriage and the relationship between those purposes and their willingness to enforce a premarital agreement? Are those views inclusive of different family forms and relationships beyond women-men dyads?

While the courts traditionally permitted at least some contracts addressing financial obligations within marriage, family law has historically been far more hostile to contracts that establish parentage or alter parental rights and responsibilities. As with adult relationships, however, parent-child relationships are increasingly seen as a product of the individual undertakings rather than state-mandated responsibilities. Pamela Laufer-Ukeles suggests that instead of focusing on the horizontal relationship between adults, family law, as well as contracts, should focus on the vertical parent-child relationship. Agreements between parents, argues Laufer-Ukeles, could allow multiple "parent like" caregivers instead of applying "marriage like" obligations to join parents. The Children of Nonmarriage: Towards a Child-First Family Law, 40 Yale L. & Pol'y Rev. 384 (2022). Still, to a much greater degree than with respect to financial agreements, family law generally holds that parentage cannot be established or negated solely by contract. For extensive discussion of how parentage is established, see Chapter 13.

2. What is the relationship between "equal status" and equal bargaining power? Barbara Atwood and Brian Bix report that:

> Notwithstanding the persistence of economic inequality along gender lines, the relative value of marriage for men and women has been shifting since the original UPAA was enacted. Women have exceeded men in education and income growth over the last four decades and have almost reached parity as a percentage of the workforce. In almost a quarter of marriages, wives are now the higher wage earners, and in a majority of marriages, wives have an equal or higher education level than their husbands. If these trends continue, marriage will carry greater economic value for men than for women, giving women new leverage in this form of intimate contract.

Barbara A. Atwood & Brian H. Bix, A New Uniform Law for Premarital and Marital Agreements, 46 Fam. L.Q. 313, 316 (2012). How does same-sex marriage, as Atwood and Bix argued, "render assumptions about gender dynamics in marital contracting somewhat dated"? *Id.* How should the courts take such changes into account?

In 1975, at the time of the marriage in *Simeone*, it was not unusual for a man to marry a spouse who had less education and income than he did. Since then, sociologists find that couples have become much more likely to marry someone with similar education and income and that both men and women place greater emphasis on a prospective spouse's income than they did a half-century ago. Sociologists call this "assortative mating." Christine R. Schwartz & Robert D. Mare, Trends in Educational Assortative Marriage from 1940 to 2003, 43 Demography 621-646 (2011); Philip Cohen, College Graduates Marry Other College Graduates Most of the Time, The Atlantic, Apr. 4, 2013, http://www.theatlantic.com/sexes/archive/2013/04/college-graduates-marry-other-college-graduates-most-of-the-time/274654/.

Yet although the differences in income between men and women who work full time have narrowed overall since 1990, the gap has *grown* for those with the highest incomes and, indeed, for college graduates overall. So while gender wage differentials for high school graduates have narrowed, the gender gap in income for college graduates has widened. Elise Gould & Jori Kandra, State of Working America 2021, Economic Policy Institute, available at https://www.epi.org/publication/swa-wages-2021/. In short, men's income is most likely to exceed women's among couples with the highest incomes — the couples most likely to have premarital agreements.

In an empirical study of over 2000 premarital agreements litigated between 1985 and 2013, Peter Leeson and Joshua Pierson found similar gaps in income between parties as well as other inequalities. Prenups, 45 J. Legal Stud. 367, 368 (2016). Leeson and Pierson explained their findings in comparison with income, age, and education statistics for the general population of married couples:

> First, prenup users tend to be older at marriage. Prenup-using husbands' median age at marriage is 51 years and wives' is 39 years. In contrast, median age at marriage among husbands and wives in general is only 28 years and 25 years, respectively. Moreover, the difference in median age at marriage between prenup-using husbands and wives, 12 years, is substantially larger than between husbands and wives in general, which is only 3 years.
>
> Second, prenup users tend to be well educated at marriage. A large majority of both prenup-using husbands and wives are college educated when they marry. In contrast, husbands and wives in general tend to have considerably less education at marriage. For example, nearly 90 percent of prenup-using husbands are college educated at marriage compared with only 30 percent of husbands in general.
>
> Third, prenup-using husbands tend to have considerable wealth at marriage. Median net assets owned by such husbands when they marry are worth (in 1990 dollars) over $900,000. We do not have data on wealth at marriage among husbands in general. However, we do have data on their income, and, perhaps unsurprisingly, median annual income at marriage of husbands in general is nearly 15 percent lower than that of prenup-using husbands.
>
> Finally, and most striking, economic inequality between prenup-using spouses at marriage tends to be substantial. Prenup-using husbands' median net worth at marriage is more than 21 times wives', and wives' median annual income at marriage is less than 39 percent of husbands'. Similarly, while both prenup-using husbands and wives tend to be well educated at marriage, there is a large education gap between them. The percentage of prenup-using husbands with a college education at marriage is 20 points higher than the percentage of prenup-using wives with a college education. In contrast, economic and educational inequality at marriage among husbands and wives in general is modest. In this group, wives' median annual income at marriage is more than 76 percent of husbands', and the percentage of husbands with a college education at marriage is nearly identical to that of wives.

Id. at 374-375. *See also* Judith T. Younger, Lovers' Contracts in the Courts: Forsaking the Minimum Decencies, 13 Wm. & Mary J. Women & L. 349 (2007) surveying appellate cases from 2000 to 2007 and finding that premarital agreements are most (common in second marriages, which frequently involve men older and wealthier than the women they are marrying).

How should these disparities affect the validity and enforcement of premarital agreements? If disparities become less common over time, should that make premarital agreements more likely or less likely to be enforced?

3. Courts and commentators disagree as to whether courts should police the contracting process (*e.g.*, by mandating disclosure, requiring legal representation for each party, and ensuring voluntariness), review the substantive fairness of the agreement, or both. Courts differ in their approaches in a number of ways, with some holding that:

   a. if the parties reached their agreement through an appropriate process, the court will not review the substantive fairness of the agreement at all;
   b. the court will invalidate an unconscionable agreement only if the parties did not have (and did not waive) full disclosure at the time it was signed;
   c. the court will determine unconscionability only in terms of the facts that existed at the time the contract was signed;
   d. the court will consider the fairness of the agreement in light of the facts that exist at the time of enforcement even if the agreement was otherwise fair and enforceable at the time it was signed.

See Gail F. Brod, Premarital Agreements and Gender Justice, 6 Yale J.L. & Feminism 229, 283-284, 286 (1994). What approach does each of the *Simeone* and *Lane* opinions take in determining the enforceability of the agreement?

4. Another issue that affects the evaluation of the fairness of premarital agreements is the change in the parties' position after the marriage. The single most common change is the birth of children, particularly when one spouse decreases workforce participation in response to children's needs. The assumption of child care responsibilities continues to affect women disproportionately, though such responsibilities affect men to a greater degree today than in the past. *See, e.g.*, Jessica Schieder & Elise Gould, Economic Policy Institute, "Women's Work" and the Gender Pay Gap: How Discrimination, Societal Norms, and Other Forces Affect Women's Occupational Choices — and Their Pay 6-7 (2016). *See also* Richard Fry, Some Gender Disparities Widened in the U.S. Workforce during the Pandemic, Pew Research Center, Jan. 14, 2022 (women generally took on greater child care responsibilities during the COVID-19 pandemic, and women without college degrees have suffered the greatest losses in workforce participation).

For couples who plan to have children, these changes may be predictable, and when the disparities between the two spouses are as great as they are in *Lane*, it might also be predictable that the lower-earning spouse will be the one who cuts back workforce participation more. Should such changes always be grounds to refuse to enforce a premarital agreement? Or only when the parties could not reasonably foresee the changes? *See* Kelcourse v. Kelcourse, 23 N.E.3d 124, 127-128 (Mass. App. 2015) (invalidating a prenuptial agreement because, "upon taking a second look," enforcement would leave the wife, who was the primary custodian of three children, living on $300 per week in the dilapidated marital residence too costly for her to repair). *But see* Grabe v. Hokin, 267A.3d 145, 152 (Conn. 2021) (marriages are by nature subject to changing circumstances, and so to render the agreement unenforceable the circumstances must be "so far beyond contemplation at the time of signing" that enforcement would "work an injustice").

A factor that can affect the evaluation of an agreement is the impact on children. Courts sometimes note that a child support award may provide the custodial parent with a substantial sum that contributes to expenses such as housing. Courts also may consider the impact of large disparities in parents' incomes as a factor in invalidating an agreement. *See* Ware v. Ware, 748 A.2d 1031, 1047 (Md. App. 2000) (citing the substantial effect that large income disparities have on the children of a marriage, the court stated that "[t]here is a child involved, who will undoubtedly go back and forth between the father, who can afford to live in luxury, and the mother, who cannot"). Should courts address such considerations by invalidating the agreement rather than by awarding higher amounts of child support?

5. The other set of issues that affects the validity of premarital agreements involves the bargaining process. In *Simeone*, for example, the wife claimed that the husband first presented her with the premarital agreement on the eve of the wedding and therefore she entered into it under duress. Why does the court reject the wife's argument in *Simeone*? *Compare* In re Yannalfo, 794 A.2d 795 (N.H. 2002) (refusing to adopt a per se rule that a premarital agreement presented one day before the wedding is unenforceable), *with* In re Estate of Hollett, 834 A.2d 348 (N.H. 2003) (invalidating an agreement presented two days before the wedding in a case in which the wife had rejected a similar agreement two years earlier).

In In re Bonds, 5 P.3d 815 (Cal. 2000), Barry Bonds and his fiancée had rushed to the lawyer's office to complete an antenuptial agreement in time to make a flight to Las Vegas, where the wedding was scheduled for the following day. Despite the fact that Sun Bonds saw the agreement for the first time that afternoon, the California Supreme Court upheld the trial court's finding that "the temporal proximity of the wedding to the signing of the agreement was not coercive, because under the particular circumstances of the case, including the small number of guests and the informality of the wedding arrangements, little embarrassment would have followed from postponement of the wedding." 5 P.3d at 825-836 (superseded by statute; *see* below).

6. If spouses are required to make full disclosure to each other, what must be disclosed? Must each spouse know the details of the other's holdings, or is having a general idea sufficient? In Randolph v. Randolph, 937 S.W.2d 815 (1996), the court required that "the spouse seeking to enforce an antenuptial agreement must prove, by a preponderance of the evidence, either that a full and fair disclosure of the nature, extent, and value of his or her holdings was provided to the spouse seeking to avoid the agreement, or that disclosure was unnecessary because the spouse seeking to avoid the agreement had independent knowledge of the full nature, extent, and value of the proponent spouse's holdings." 937 S.W.2d at 821. The *Randolph* court put the burden of proof on the party seeking enforcement. In California, by contrast, the burden of proof is placed on the party challenging the premarital agreement. In re Marriage of Caldwell-Faso, 119 Cal. Rptr.3d 818 (Cal. Dist. Ct. App. 2011).

If you were advising a party on how to ensure sufficient disclosure to validate an agreement in a state following *Randolph*, what would you suggest? How would your answer differ in a state following *Simeone*?

Connecticut courts have held that disclosure need not be tailored to the capacity of the spouse to understand the significance of the disclosure provided. Friezo v. Friezo, 914 A.2d 533, 551 (Conn. 2007). *See also* Silverman v. Silverman 206 A.3d 825, 833 (Del. 2019) ("Absent fraud or overreaching, the inadvertent failure to disclose an asset or the unintentional undervaluation of an asset will not invalidate a prenuptial agreement as long as the disclosure provides an essentially accurate understanding of the party's financial holdings.").

In Georgia, the extent of disclosure required by a party seems based, in part, on how much a spouse knew or could have known of the other's finances at the time of marriage. In Mallen v. Mallen, 622 S.E.2d 812 (Ga. 2005), the wife alleged that, although the husband revealed his holdings in an attachment to the premarital agreement, the agreement said nothing about his income, which was over $500,000 per year. The Georgia Supreme Court upheld the agreement, observing that the couple lived together before the marriage, and the wife should have been aware of her husband's income and substantial resources. Three years later, the Georgia Supreme Court invalidated a premarital agreement in which the husband, a truck driver with a relatively modest income, did not disclose that he had saved $150,000 to build a house on the land that was subject to the premarital contract. The court reasoned that the wife, who had not lived with the husband before marriage, could not have known of the $150,000, Blige v. Blige, 656 S.E.2d 822 (Ga. 2008). *See also* Brantley v. Brantley, 814 S.E.2d 787 (Ga. App. 2018) (finding a trial court erred in confining its analysis of full disclosure to the text of the prenuptial agreement); Dodson v. Dodson, 779 S.E.2d 638, 640 (Ga. 2015) (distinguishing *Mallen* because "the disclosure was neither full, because Wife had no real knowledge of the value of Husband's bank accounts, nor fair, because Husband never allowed Wife to have reasonable access to those accounts"). How relevant should a party's knowledge of the other's wealth be in enforcing a premarital contract?

7. Must each party's legal rights absent an agreement be disclosed, as the wife in *Simeone* argued? If so, does this mean as a practical matter that each person must have independent legal advice? Many courts suggest that independent legal advice is the best means of ensuring that an agreement is enforceable, but no statutes impose a requirement of counsel in all cases. California, in response to the *Bonds* case described above, enacted one of the strictest statutes in the country. It provides, inter alia, that:

(c) . . . it shall be deemed that a premarital agreement was not executed voluntarily unless the court finds in writing or on the record all of the following:

(1) The party against whom enforcement is sought was represented by independent legal counsel at the time of signing the agreement or, after being advised to seek independent legal counsel, expressly waived, in a separate writing, representation by independent legal counsel. The advisement to seek independent legal counsel shall be made at least seven calendar days before the final agreement is signed.

(2) One of the following:

(A) For an agreement executed between January 1, 2002, and January 1, 2020, the party against whom enforcement is sought had not less than seven calendar days between the time that party was first presented with the final agreement and advised to seek independent legal counsel and the time the agreement was signed. This requirement does not apply to nonsubstantive amendments that do not change the terms of the agreement.

(B) For an agreement executed on or after January 1, 2020, the party against whom enforcement is sought had not less than seven calendar days between the time that party was first presented with the final agreement and the time the agreement was signed, regardless of whether the party is represented by legal counsel. This requirement does not apply to nonsubstantive amendments that do not change the terms of the agreement.

(3) The party against whom enforcement is sought, if unrepresented by legal counsel, was fully informed of the terms and basic effect of the agreement as well as the rights and obligations the party was giving up by signing the agreement, and was proficient in the language in which the explanation of the party's rights was conducted and in which the agreement was written. The explanation of the rights and obligations relinquished shall be memorialized in writing and delivered to the party prior to signing the agreement. The unrepresented party shall, on or before the signing of the premarital agreement, execute a document declaring that the party received the information required by this paragraph and indicating who provided that information.

Cal. Fam. Code §1615 (2022). As a lawyer drafting a premarital agreement for one party, would you advise the other party to seek independent counsel? If the other party has representation, the agreement is more likely to be upheld. Some lawyers, concerned about malpractice charges if an agreement is invalidated, routinely recommend that counsel be provided for the other party.

If you were asked to represent the wife in a case like *Simeone* or *Lane*, what would you do if you concluded that the only impact your participation would have was to make it more likely that the agreement would be upheld? What is your obligation in a case in which you believe that the agreement is one-sided or unfair but the client intends to sign the agreement over your objections?

Brian Bix

Bargaining in the Shadow of Love: The Enforcement of Premarital Agreements and How We Think About Marriage
40 Wm. & Mary L. Rev. 145, 182, 188 (1998)

When the court in *Simeone* and certain commentators advocated applying the standards from contract law to premarital agreements, they intended the agreements to be subject to minimal scrutiny. That perspective seems to depend, however, on a view of contract law that is decades behind the developments in contractual doctrine and commentary. A modern approach to contract law might reach results that, by enforcing some premarital agreements but not others, better reflect the intuitions of most people regarding the fair result in different cases. . . .

The court in *Simeone*, when it relegated premarital agreements to a contractual approach, seemed to have in mind some classical conception of contract encompassing caveat emptor, naïve "plain meaning" enforcement, and little attention to the relationship between the parties or the larger context within which the agreement was signed. If one could apply "contract principles" to premarital agreements, why not apply, by analogy, the quite different principles underlying Article 2 of the U.C.C.?

The U.C.C. obligates parties to exercise good faith in performing and enforcing the obligation of an agreement, construes contractual terms in light of the parties' course of performance and course of dealing and in light of trade usage, and implies various warranties unless they are expressly excluded. For contracts of indefinite duration, a party may terminate only after reasonable notice, and courts sometimes have held actions apparently authorized by the express wording of a contract to be bad faith actions in breach of the agreement. These changes from classical contract thinking are by no means limited to U.C.C. cases.

If courts apply *these* types of contract principles to premarital agreements, there will be far less reason for complaint. Perhaps courts could interpret the terms of premarital agreements that appear to be one-sided in more reasonable ways by using the tools of modern contract law, or by disallowing the strict enforcement of the express terms of some agreements as contrary to "good faith." . . .

Although both the traditional theories justifying contract law and the ideas underlying the influential economic analysis of law assume that people act rationally to protect their own interests, recent work in psychology has begun to question that assumption. There are particular situations and circumstances in which parties are particularly unlikely to act in a rational way, and the law—especially contract law—should respond to that reality.

Premarital agreements are good examples of contracts that illustrate problems with rational judgment, as they involve long-term planning and the consideration of possible negative outcomes at a time when the parties are most likely to be optimistic that no such negative outcomes will occur. Parties need protection in this situation because they are unlikely to be able to think clearly for themselves regarding the consequences of divorce at any time, and certainly not immediately before marriage. . . . [E]ven those who are well educated in such matters, e.g., law students in a family law course, carry an unduly optimistic view about the chances that their marriage will last. More general studies in psychology have confirmed that people tend to evaluate causal theories in a self-serving manner; though people may know that fifty percent of marriages end in divorce, they convince themselves—with little grounding for their conclusions—that they have characteristics that will put them in the portion that will endure. People who assume that they will not divorce will not work hard to maintain a fair deal contingent on divorce occurring, just as parties do not bargain for reasonable terms on the failure of installment payments, as they do not expect to ever fail in their payments. Additionally, parties may have some sense of the consequences of failure one year from now, but it may be harder to foresee and plan for the consequences of failure fifteen years from now—after one or both partners have made sacrifices in their careers and perhaps after children have been born.

In her study of appellate decisions on premarital agreement enforcement, Professor Judith Younger argued that courts increasingly upheld agreements despite one party being at a clear advantage over the other. She argued that "increased enforcement would be tolerable as long as courts respected 'minimum decencies' in the process. Three disconcerting trends suggest that courts are not meeting these standards: conflicting decisions on similar facts within the same jurisdiction, and other judicial errors in resolving these cases; removal of substance from substantive fairness reviews at both execution and enforcement with [ ] disregard for dependent spouses; and mythifying procedural fairness by upholding agreements entered under subtle coercion, without independent representation or concern for legal ethics or proper disclosure." Judith T. Younger, Lovers' Contracts in the Courts: Forsaking the Minimum Decencies, 13 Wm. & Mary J. Women & L. 349, 420 (2007). How do Professor Younger's concerns about the willingness of courts to enforce one-sided agreements sit with Professor Bix's description of contract law's assumption that parties' bargain rationally and consistent with evolving standards under Article 2 of the UCC?

The National Conference of Commissioners on Uniform State Laws (NCCUSL) drafts proposed uniform acts in an effort to promote more consistent state legislation. These acts become law if enacted by the individual state legislatures. NCCUSL accordingly attempts to draft acts of broad applicability and acceptability. The Uniform Premarital Agreement Act (UPAA) was adopted by roughly half the states between the mid-1980s and the late 1990s. In 2012, NCCUSL approved a new Uniform Premarital and Marital Agreement Act (UPMAA) intended to replace the UPAA and address marital as well as premarital agreements. Two states (Colorado and North Dakota) have adopted the UPMAA. NCCUSL, Legislative Fact Sheet (2022), available at http://www.uniformlaws.org/Act.aspx?title=Premarital%20and%20 Marital%20Agreements%20Act. The UPAA and UPMAA are discussed below. The ALI Principles that address premarital agreements follow, with commentary that will help you to recognize the differences among the ALI, UPAA, and UPMAA.

UNIFORM PREMARITAL AND MARITAL AGREEMENTS ACT (UPMAA)

Section 9. Enforcement.

(a) A premarital agreement or marital agreement is unenforceable if a party against whom enforcement is sought proves:

(1) the party's consent to the agreement was involuntary or the result of duress;

(2) the party did not have access to independent legal representation under subsection (b);

(3) unless the party had independent legal representation at the time the agreement was signed, the agreement did not include a notice of waiver of rights under subsection (c) or an explanation in plain language of the marital rights or obligations being modified or waived by the agreement; or

(4) before signing the agreement, the party did not receive adequate financial disclosure under subsection (d).

(b) A party has access to independent legal representation if:

(1) before signing a premarital or marital agreement, the party has a reasonable time to:

(A) decide whether to retain a lawyer to provide independent legal representation; and

(B) locate a lawyer to provide independent legal representation, obtain the lawyer's advice, and consider the advice provided; and

(2) the other party is represented by a lawyer and the party has the financial ability to retain a lawyer or the other party agrees to pay the reasonable fees and expenses of independent legal representation.

(c) A notice of waiver of rights under this section requires language, conspicuously displayed, substantially similar to the following, as applicable to the premarital agreement or marital agreement:

"If you sign this agreement, you may be:

Giving up your right to be supported by the person you are marrying or to whom you are married.

Giving up your right to ownership or control of money and property.

Agreeing to pay bills and debts of the person you are marrying or to whom you are married.

Giving up your right to money and property if your marriage ends or the person to whom you are married dies.

Giving up your right to have your legal fees paid."

(d) A party has adequate financial disclosure under this section if the party:

(1) receives a reasonably accurate description and good-faith estimate of value of the property, liabilities, and income of the other party;

(2) expressly waives, in a separate signed record, the right to financial disclosure beyond the disclosure provided; or

(3) has adequate knowledge or a reasonable basis for having adequate knowledge of the information described in paragraph (1).

(e) If a premarital agreement or marital agreement modifies or eliminates spousal support and the modification or elimination causes a party to the agreement to be eligible for support under a program of public assistance at the time of separation or marital dissolution, a court, on request of that party, may require the other party to provide support to the extent necessary to avoid that eligibility.

(f) A court may refuse to enforce a term of a premarital agreement or marital agreement if, in the context of the agreement taken as a whole[:]

(1) the term was unconscionable at the time of signing[; or

(2) enforcement of the term would result in substantial hardship for a party because of a material change in circumstances arising after the agreement was signed].

(g) The court shall decide a question of unconscionability [or substantial hardship] under subsection (f) as a matter of law.

Section 10. Unenforceable Terms.

(a) In this section, "custodial responsibility" means physical or legal custody, parenting time, access, visitation, or other custodial right or duty with respect to a child.

(b) A term in a premarital agreement or marital agreement is not enforceable to the extent that it:

(1) adversely affects a child's right to support;

(2) limits or restricts a remedy available to a victim of domestic violence under law of this state other than this [act];

(3) purports to modify the grounds for a court-decreed separation or marital dissolution available under law of this state other than this [act]; or

(4) penalizes a party for initiating a legal proceeding leading to a court-decreed separation or marital dissolution.

(c) A term in a premarital agreement or marital agreement which defines the rights or duties of the parties regarding custodial responsibility is not binding on the court.

UNIFORM PREMARITAL AGREEMENT ACT (UPAA)

§3. Content

(a) Parties to a premarital agreement may contract with respect to:

(1) the rights and obligations of each of the parties in any of the property of either or both of them whenever and wherever acquired or located; . . .

(4) the modification or elimination of spousal support; . . .

(8) any other matter, including their personal rights and obligations, not in violation of public policy or a statute imposing a criminal penalty.

(b) The right of a child to support may not be adversely affected by a premarital agreement. . . .

§5. Amendment, Revocation

After marriage, a premarital agreement may be amended or revoked only by a written agreement signed by the parties. The amended agreement or the revocation is enforceable without consideration.

§6. Enforcement

(a) A premarital agreement is not enforceable if the party against whom enforcement is sought proves that:

(1) that party did not execute the agreement voluntarily; or

(2) the agreement was unconscionable when it was executed and, before execution of the agreement, that party:

(i) was not provided a fair and reasonable disclosure of the property or financial obligations of the other party;

(ii) did not voluntarily and expressly waive, in writing, any right to disclosure of the property or financial obligations of the other party beyond the disclosure provided; and

(iii) did not have, or reasonably could not have had, an adequate knowledge of the property or financial obligations of the other party.

(b) If a provision of a premarital agreement modifies or eliminates spousal support and that modification or elimination causes one party to the agreement to be eligible for support under a program of public assistance at the time of separation or marital dissolution, a court, notwithstanding the terms of the agreement, may require the other party to provide support to the extent necessary to avoid that eligibility.

(c) An issue of unconscionability of a premarital agreement shall be decided by the court as a matter of law.

Professors Barbara Atwood and Brian Bix, the reporters for the UPMAA, summarize their approach and the comparison with the UPAA as follows:

> The enforcement standards for premarital and marital agreements, set out in Section 9 of the Act, reflect the Committee's goals of protecting vulnerable parties and promoting informed decision-making without placing all agreements under a cloud of uncertainty. Like the UPAA, the Act starts from a presumption of validity, placing the burden of proof on the party seeking to avoid enforcement. The standards for enforceability, however, diverge significantly from the UPAA. Under UPMAA's Section 9, an agreement is unenforceable if a party proves any one of four independent showings: that the agreement was involuntary or the result of duress; that the party lacked access to independent legal representation; that the party, if unrepresented by counsel, received neither an explanation of the rights being waived nor a safe-harbor warning in the agreement; or that adequate financial disclosure was not made. Each of these showings represents an independent requirement for validity; two are newly-formulated versions of similar requirements in the UPAA, and two are new requirements. Importantly, a court may refuse to enforce an agreement if it finds a term to have been unconscionable at the time of signing or, as a bracketed alternative, if enforcement would result in substantial hardship because of a material change in circumstance since the signing of the agreement.

Barbara A. Atwood & Brian H. Bix, A New Uniform Law for Premarital and Marital Agreements, 46 Fam. L.Q. 313, 339 (2012).

NOTES AND QUESTIONS

1. Under the UPAA, what is the relationship between disclosure (or the lack thereof) and the fairness of the terms? How does this differ, if it does, from a traditional approach? From the approach adopted in *Simeone*? From the approach under the UPMAA? Under the UPAA, what is the relationship between voluntariness and disclosure? *See* Penhallow v. Penhallow, 649 A.2d 1016, 1021 (R.I. 1994). What do Professors Atwood and Bix mean when they describe the four showings the UPMAA requires as "independent" requirements?

In 2005, the Pennsylvania legislature enacted a statute that combined the approaches of Section 6(a) of the UPAA and the reasoning of *Simeone*. 23 Pa. Cons. Stat. Ann. §3106 (2022). The Pennsylvania statute differs from the UPAA §6(a) in two areas: "While embracing the voluntary execution and disclosure provisions of the Uniform Act, subsection (a) does not adopt the unconscionability or public assistance provisions. Note that under the Uniform Act, lack of disclosure would render an agreement unenforceable only if the agreement were also unconscionable when executed. Under subsection (a), the party seeking to set aside the agreement must prove that either the agreement was not executed voluntarily (paragraph (1)) or all the elements of paragraph (2) are met." Pa. Joint St. Gov't Comm. Comment (2004). How might the omission of language governing unconscionability under the UPAA affect the enforcement of premarital agreements?

2. Most interpretations of the UPAA reject any requirement of independent counsel. *See, e.g.,* Penhallow, 649 A.2d at 1022. How does the UPMAA differ? What does it mean to have access to legal representation under the UPMAA? Are there circumstances in which an agreement will be enforceable even without legal representation? If the UPMAA applied and you represented the husband in *Simeone*, what would you suggest he do to make sure that the agreement is enforceable under the UPMAA?

3. The UPAA, like a number of recent cases, provides that under certain circumstances an agreement is unenforceable if it is "unconscionable." This term is borrowed from the commercial context. Both the Uniform Commercial Code (UCC) and the Restatement of the Law of Contracts 2d provide that unconscionable contracts are not enforceable.[3]

The UCC uses the term without defining it. What does it mean? Does it implicate substantive as well as procedural fairness? Consider an explanation offered by a contract law scholar:

> When the concept of unconscionability was first made explicit by the Uniform Commercial Code, the initial effort was to reconcile it with the bargain principle . . . distinction, drawn in 1967 by Arthur Leff, between "procedural" and "substantive" unconscionability. Leff defined procedural unconscionability as fault or unfairness in the bargaining *process*; substantive unconscionability as fault or unfairness in the bargaining *outcome*—that is, unfairness of terms. The effect (if not the purpose) of this distinction, which influenced much of the later analysis, was to domesticate unconscionability by accepting the concept insofar as it could be made harmonious with the bargain principle (that is, insofar as it was "procedural"), while rejecting its wider implication that in appropriate cases the courts might review bargains for fairness of terms. Correspondingly, much of the scholarly literature and case law concerning unconscionability has emphasized the element of unfair surprise, in which a major underpinning of the bargain principle—knowing assent—is absent by hypothesis.
>
> Over the last fifteen years, however, there have been strong indications that the principle of unconscionability authorizes a review of elements well beyond unfair surprise, including, in appropriate cases, fairness of terms.

Melvin A. Eisenberg, The Bargain Principle and Its Limits, 95 Harv. L. Rev. 741, 752 (1982). Compare the different approaches to unconscionability in the UPMAA and the UPAA. Some commentators have argued that the UPAA made it easier to enforce a premarital agreement than a commercial contract. One of the purposes of the UPMAA was to address that anomaly. Under the UPMAA, is the standard for unconscionability the same as the standard that applied to commercial contracts, or does it make premarital agreements harder or easier to enforce?

4. What does Section 3(b) of the UPAA, pertaining to child support, mean? How does it differ from Section 10 of the UPMAA? What latitude for bargaining do the two Acts give the parties? Traditionally, parties' agreements regarding arrangements for children have not been enforceable on the theory that the court must always have authority to act in the best interests of children. What does this principle suppose about the way parents negotiate agreements? About the capacity of courts?

---

3. UCC §2-302. Unconscionable Contract or Clause: If the court as a matter of law finds the contract or any clause of the contract to have been unconscionable at the time it was made, the court may refuse to enforce the contract, or it may enforce the remainder of the contract without the unconscionable clause, or it may so limit the application of any unconscionable clause as to avoid any unconscionable result.

When it is claimed or appears to the court that the contract or any clause thereof may be unconscionable the parties shall be afforded a reasonable opportunity to present evidence as to its commercial setting, purpose and effect to aid the court in making the determination.

Restatement of the Law of Contracts 2d §208, Unconscionable Contract or Term: If a contract or term thereof is unconscionable at the time the contract is made, a court may refuse to enforce the contract, or may enforce the remainder of the contract without the unconscionable term, or may so limit the application of any unconscionable term as to avoid any unconscionable result.

Compare the treatment of substantive and procedural fairness under the UPAA and the UMPAA with the ALI's requirement that agreements do not "work a substantial injustice."

AMERICAN LAW INSTITUTE PRINCIPLES OF THE LAW OF FAMILY DISSOLUTION (2002)

§7.04 Procedural Requirements

(1) An agreement is not enforceable if it is not set forth in a writing signed by both parties.

(2) A party seeking to enforce an agreement must show that the other party's consent to it was informed and not obtained under duress.

(3) A premarital agreement is rebuttably presumed to satisfy the requirements of Paragraph (2) when the party seeking to enforce the agreement shows that

(a) it was executed at least 30 days before the parties' marriage;

(b) both parties were advised to obtain independent legal counsel, and had reasonable opportunity to do so, before the agreement's execution; and

(c) in the case of agreements concluded without the assistance of independent legal counsel for each party, the agreement states, in language easily understandable by an adult of ordinary intelligence with no legal training,

(i) the nature of any rights or claims otherwise arising at dissolution that are altered by the contract, and the nature of that alteration, and

(ii) that the interests of the spouses with respect to the agreement may be adverse.

§7.05 When Enforcement Would Work a Substantial Injustice

(1) A court should not enforce a term in an agreement if, pursuant to Paragraphs (2) and (3) of this section,

(a) the circumstances require it to consider whether enforcement would work a substantial injustice; and

(b) the court finds that enforcement would work a substantial injustice.

(2) A court should consider whether enforcement of an agreement would work a substantial injustice if, and only if, the party resisting its enforcement shows that one or more of the following have occurred since the time of the agreement's execution:

(a) more than a fixed number of years have passed, that number being set in a rule of statewide application;

(b) a child was born to, or adopted by, the parties, who at the time of execution had no children in common;

(c) there has been a change in circumstances that has a substantial impact on the parties or their children, but when they executed the agreement the parties probably did not anticipate either the change, or its impact.

(3) The party claiming that enforcement of an agreement would work a substantial injustice has the burden of proof on that question. In deciding whether the agreement's application to the parties' circumstances at dissolution would work a substantial injustice, a court should consider all of the following:

(a) the magnitude of the disparity between the outcome under the agreement and the outcome under otherwise prevailing legal principles;

(b) for those marriages of limited duration in which it is practical to ascertain, the difference between the circumstances of the objecting party if the agreement is enforced, and that party's likely circumstances had the marriage never taken place;

(c) whether the purpose of the agreement was to benefit or protect the interests of third parties (such as children from a prior relationship), whether that purpose is still relevant, and whether the agreement's terms were reasonably designed to serve it;

(d) the impact of the agreement's enforcement upon the children of the parties.

NOTES AND QUESTIONS

1. As noted, many attorneys are wary of drafting premarital agreements because of potential liability for malpractice in the event that the agreements are found to be unenforceable. Would adoption of the ALI Principles make such attorneys more or less willing to draft premarital agreements?

2. Contract law and the UPAA determine unconscionability at the time the agreement is signed. The ALI Principles and a number of non-UPAA state court rulings determine validity at the time of enforcement. *See* Judith T. Younger, A Minnesota Comparative Family Law Symposium: Antenuptial Agreements, 28 Wm. Mitchell L. Rev. 697, 716-720 (2001) (emphasizing the ALI's limited review of a contract's substance at signing and far more extensive review at enforcement, which "tread[s] a middle ground between those who would refuse to enforce antenuptial agreements altogether and those who would enforce them as ordinary business contracts"). Which approach makes more sense? What does this mean for the validity of an agreement that clearly favors one party over another? Is it possible for a contract to be valid when signed, but not enforceable 20 years later?

3. The ALI Principles also emphasize procedural requirements such as "a signed writing, financial disclosure and a showing of informed consent not obtained under duress," which were already required by a number of states. Is the approach of the ALI to financial disclosure and a showing of informed consent similar to or different from the UPAA's? How does it compare to the UPMAA?

The ALI's procedural requirements refer to the "reasonable opportunity" to "obtain independent legal counsel." In Friezo v. Friezo, 914 A.2d 533 (Conn. 2007), the trial court concluded that the wife did not have such an opportunity, as required by Connecticut law, because the wife consulted an attorney, suggested by her husband's sister, who charged her no fee, met with her only briefly, and did not explain the agreement to her or provide her with significant advice. The Connecticut Supreme Court reversed the trial court decision, finding that she had the opportunity to meet with any attorney she chose, signed a conflict-of-interest waiver permitting the attorney to represent her, and never sought additional representation or legal advice. 914 A.2d at 557-558. *See also* Carter v. Fairchild-Carter, 159 A.D.3d 1315 (N.Y. App. Div. 2018) (facts sufficient to strike down a prenuptial agreement when a party was given a new agreement while standing outside the County Clerk's office and did not have time to read the document or consult an attorney before marrying).

4. Courts have held that a premarital agreement that waives a party's right to spousal support does not abrogate a U.S. citizen's obligation to provide for a spouse that immigrated to this country. For immigration rules governing fiancés and non-U.S. spouses, *see* Chapter 3. Citizens who sponsor a spouse in the immigration process must sign an affidavit of support, which pledges to provide financial support for the noncitizen party, even after divorce. That duty continues, courts have held, even if parties have signed premarital agreements barring the payment of alimony. *See* Erler v. Erler, 824 F.3d 1173 (9th Cir. 2016); Liu v. Mund, 686 F.3d 418 (7th Cir. 2012); Golipour v. Moghaddam. 438 F. Supp. 3d 1290 (Utah D. Ct. 2020) (holding that neither an agreement nor payment of a dowry relieved the obligation to provide financial support so long as the affidavit of support was enforceable). *Compare*

Backman v. Backman, 875 S.E.2d 510 (Ga. App. 2022) (finding that the sponsoring spouse is not required to provide additional support when the sponsored immigrant spouse's income exceeds the required 125 percent of the federal poverty guideline required by the immigration rules).

5. Note that this chapter concerns contracts within marriage, and Chapter 4 contemplates contracts between unmarried partners. Without default rules defining rights and duties between married couples, cohabiting individuals have limited protection upon separation. Though the number of unmarried, cohabiting couples has increased, as noted in Chapters 1 and 4, the number of individuals who would consider entering a cohabitation agreement remains low. Margaret Ryznar, The Unpopularity of Cohabitation Agreements, Fam. Ct. Rev. (forthcoming). *See* Courtney G. Joslin, A Symposium on Nonmarriage and the Law: Family Choices, 51 Ariz. St. L.J. 1285 (2019) (discussing the need to rethink the legal default of treating nonmarried families as legal strangers given the increasing cohabitation rates and the contrasting decline in marriage rates).

PROBLEMS

1. On the day of Hank and Wanda's wedding they signed a premarital agreement providing that if they divorced, Hank would give Wanda a house and $500,000 or half his assets, whichever value was greater. Hank and Wanda divorced eight months later. Hank has attacked the agreement as violating public policy because it encourages divorce. How should the court rule and why? If you learned that Hank and Wanda are immigrants and that such agreements are common in the country of their births, would you change your answer?

2. When Carl and Jill were married, Jill was 18, pregnant, and unemployed. Carl, who was 25, had graduated from college and worked on his family's farm. Their premarital agreement, drafted by Carl's family attorney, provided that if the parties divorced, neither would be entitled to the property of the other, and neither would be entitled to spousal or child support. Carl told Jill that if she would not sign the agreement, he would not marry her. Jill, who was not represented by counsel, reluctantly agreed. Their baby was born six months after the wedding, and ten months later Carl moved out of the house. Jill filed for divorce and sought spousal and child support. Carl responded with the premarital agreement. In a jurisdiction that has adopted the UPAA, what arguments should Jill's attorney make in support of her position that the agreement is not enforceable? How should Carl's attorney respond? How would the analysis change if the parties live in a jurisdiction that follows traditional principles about the enforceability of premarital agreements? In a jurisdiction that followed the ALI Principles? In a jurisdiction that adopted the UPMAA?

3. Harriet and Wynona were married 10 years ago. At the time of their wedding, Harriet, then 32 years old, was part owner of her family's successful business. Wynona, who was 27, worked as a secretary in the business. When they married, Wynona owned property worth $5000, and Harriet's interest in the family business was worth $550,000. After fully disclosing their assets and income to each other, they signed a premarital agreement, which provided that all of the property Harriet owned before marriage, along with increases in value and income from it, would remain her separate property. The agreement also limited Wynona's claim to spousal support to $200 per month for ten years. During their marriage Harriet gave birth to another child, using Wynona's egg and sperm from an anonymous donor. After the child's birth, Wynona did not work outside the home, and Harriet continued to work in the family business, which grew rapidly. At the time of divorce Harriet's interest in the business was worth $8 million, and her income was $250,000 per year. Wynona's property had tripled in value (to $15,000), but she had no income and only decades-old skills as a secretary. Under traditional rules, would the agreement be enforceable? Under *Simeone*? Under *Lane*? Under the UPMAA? Under the UPAA? Under the ALI Principles?

4. Susan was 50, and John was 78, when they married four years ago. Susan, who was divorced and had two children and three grandchildren, owned her own home and worked as a real estate agent. John lived on his 30-acre farm. He had never married before and had no children or living siblings. On the day of their wedding, they signed a premarital agreement drafted by Susan's attorney. The agreement did not include a written disclosure of their assets, but the attorney explained the agreement in detail to both parties and asked if they had any questions. Neither did, and both affirmed that they wanted to sign the agreement. The agreement provided that all Susan's property would remain her separate property, that John would transfer all his real property into tenancy by the entireties, and that he would transfer all his cash and personal property into joint tenancy with Susan. The agreement also said that if Susan initiated a divorce, she would have to return to John all property she had acquired under the agreement, but that if he initiated a divorce, Susan would retain the property she had acquired. After the wedding the couple lived on John's farm.

Three months ago Susan filed a domestic violence complaint against John and obtained a restraining order requiring him to move out and to stay away from her. He went to stay with neighbors, who filed a complaint with the local senior services agency alleging that Susan was abusing and financially exploiting John. A state social worker investigated the complaint and made a written report that it was "founded," but no further action was taken.

John has now filed a petition for divorce, which requests that the premarital agreement be invalidated. Under *Simeone*, would the agreement be enforceable? Under the UPAA? Under the ALI Principles? Under the UPMAA?

5. Carol was 55, and Martha was 50 when they married two years ago. Martha had a teenage daughter she had adopted with a former partner, for whom she received child support, and Carol had no children. Before the wedding, Carol and Martha signed a premarital agreement providing that "neither one shall have or acquire any right, title or claim to the property of the other" and that "neither party, in the case of a divorce, shall have a right to division of property or support from the other." Neither was represented by an attorney, but both knew the nature and extent of the other's property. At the time of the wedding, Carol owned little property, had taken early retirement, and received pension income of $1247 per month. Martha owned a home worth $60,000 and other assets worth $5500. Martha was employed and earned $30,000 per year, but during the marriage she became permanently and severely disabled and had to quit her job. She cannot work and has no source of income, though she may be eligible for Social Security Disability benefits. She still owns the home, which together with other assets is now worth $70,000. Carol has petitioned for divorce and asked the court to enforce the premarital agreement. Should the agreement be enforced under the UPAA?

B. SPOUSAL CONTRACTS DURING MARRIAGE

Borelli v. Brusseau
16 Cal. Rptr. 2d 16 (Cal. App. 1993)

PERLEY, J. . . . On April 24, 1980, appellant and decedent entered into an antenuptial contract. On April 25, 1980, they were married. Appellant remained married to decedent until the death of the latter on January 25, 1989.

In March 1983, February 1984, and January 1987, decedent was admitted to a hospital due to heart problems. As a result, "decedent became concerned and frightened about his health and longevity." He discussed these fears and concerns with appellant and told her that he intended to "leave" the following property to her.

(1) "An interest" in a lot in Sacramento, California.
(2) A life estate for the use of a condominium in Hawaii.
(3) A 25 percent interest in Borelli Meat Co.
(4) All cash remaining in all existing bank accounts at the time of his death.
(5) The costs of educating decedent's stepdaughter, Monique Lee.
(6) Decedent's entire interest in a residence in Kensington, California.
(7) All furniture located in the residence.
(8) Decedent's interest in a partnership.
(9) Health insurance for appellant and Monique Lee.

In August 1988, decedent suffered a stroke while in the hospital. "Throughout the decedent's August, 1988 hospital stay and subsequent treatment at a rehabilitation center, he repeatedly told [appellant] that he was uncomfortable in the hospital and that he disliked being away from home. The decedent repeatedly told [appellant] that he did not want to be admitted to a nursing home, even though it meant he would need round-the-clock care, and rehabilitative modifications to the house, in order for him to live at home."

"In or about October, 1988, [appellant] and the decedent entered an oral agreement whereby the decedent promised to leave to [appellant] the property listed [above]. . . . In exchange for the decedent's promise to leave her the property . . . [appellant] agreed to care for the decedent in his home, for the duration of his illness, thereby avoiding the need for him to move to a rest home or convalescent hospital as his doctors recommended. . . ."

Appellant performed her promise but the decedent did not perform his. Instead his will bequeathed her the sum of $100,000 and his interest in the residence they owned as joint tenants. The bulk of decedent's estate passed to respondent, who is decedent's daughter.

DISCUSSION

"It is fundamental that a marriage contract differs from other contractual relations in that there exists a definite and vital public interest in reference to the marriage relation. . . ."

"The laws relating to marriage and divorce have been enacted because of the profound concern of our organized society for the dignity and stability of the marriage relationship. This concern relates primarily to the status of the parties as husband and wife. The concern of society as to the property rights of the parties is secondary and incidental to its concern as to their status." . . .

In accordance with these concerns the following pertinent legislation has been enacted: Civil Code section 242 — "Every individual shall support his or her spouse. . . ." Civil Code section 4802 — "[A] husband and wife cannot, by any contract with each other, alter their legal relations, except as to property. . . ." Civil Code section 5100 — "Husband and wife contract toward each other obligations of mutual respect, fidelity, and support." Civil Code section 5103 — "[E]ither husband or wife may enter into any transaction with the other . . . respecting property, which either might if unmarried." Civil Code section 5132 — "[A] married person shall support the person's spouse while they are living together."

The courts have stringently enforced and explained the statutory language. "Although most of the cases, both in California and elsewhere, deal with a wife's right to support from the husband, in this state a wife also has certain obligations to support the husband."

"Indeed, husband and wife assume mutual obligations of support upon marriage. These obligations are not conditioned on the existence of community property or income." "In entering the marital state, by which a contract is created, it must be assumed that the parties voluntarily entered therein with knowledge that they have the moral and legal obligation to support the other."

Moreover, interspousal mutual obligations have been broadly defined. "[Husband's] duties and obligations to [wife] included more than mere cohabitation with her. It was his duty to offer [wife] his sympathy, confidence [citation], and fidelity." When necessary, spouses must "provide uncompensated protective supervision services for" each other.

Estate of Sonnicksen (1937) [73 P.2d 643] and Brooks v. Brooks (1941) [119 P.2d 970] each hold that under the above statutes and in accordance with the above policy a wife is obligated by the marriage contract to provide nursing-type care to an ill husband. Therefore, contracts whereby the wife is to receive compensation for providing such services are void as against public policy; and there is no consideration for the husband's promise.

Appellant argues that *Sonnicksen* and *Brooks* are no longer valid precedents because they are based on outdated views of the role of women and marriage. She further argues that the rule of those cases denies her equal protection because husbands only have a financial obligation toward their wives, while wives have to provide actual nursing services for free. We disagree. The rule and policy of *Sonnicksen* and *Brooks* have been applied to both spouses in several recent cases arising in different areas of the law. . . .

Vincent v. State of California (1971) [99 Cal. Rptr. 410], held that for purposes of benefit payments spouses caring for each other must be treated identically under similar assistance programs. In reaching such conclusion the court held: "Appellants suggest that one reason justifying denial of payment for services rendered by ATD attendants who reside with their recipient spouses is that, by virtue of the marriage contract, one spouse is obligated to care for the other without remuneration. Such preexisting duty provides a constitutionally sound basis for a classification which denies compensation for care rendered by a husband or wife to his spouse who is receiving welfare assistance. . . . But insofar as one spouse has a duty created by the marriage contract to care for the other without compensation when they are living together, recipients of aid to the aged, aid to the blind and aid to the disabled are similarly situated."

These cases indicate that the marital duty of support under Civil Code sections 242, 5100, and 5132 includes caring for a spouse who is ill. They also establish that support in a marriage means more than the physical care someone could be hired to provide. Such support also encompasses sympathy, comfort, love, companionship and affection. Thus, the duty of support can no more be "delegated" to a third party than the statutory duties of fidelity and mutual respect. Marital duties are owed by the spouses personally. This is implicit in the definition of marriage as "a personal relation arising out of a civil contract between a man and a woman." (Civ. Code, sec. 4100).

We therefore adhere to the long-standing rule that a spouse is not entitled to compensation for support, apart from rights to community property and the like that arise from the marital relation itself. Personal performance of a personal duty created by the contract of marriage does not constitute a new consideration supporting the indebtedness, alleged in this case. . . .

Speculating that appellant might have left her husband but for the agreement she alleges, the dissent suggests that marriages will break up if such agreements are not enforced. While we do not believe that marriages would be fostered by a rule that encouraged sickbed bargaining, the question is not whether such negotiations may be more useful than unseemly. The issue is whether such negotiations are antithetical to the institution of marriage as the Legislature has defined it. We believe that they are.

The dissent maintains that mores have changed to the point that spouses can be treated just like any other parties haggling at arm's length. Whether or not the modern marriage has become like a business, and regardless of whatever else it may have become, it continues to be defined by statute as a personal relationship of mutual support. Thus, even if few things are left that cannot command a price, marital support remains one of them. . . .

POCHE, J., dissenting. A very ill person wishes to be cared for at home personally by his spouse rather than by nurses at a health care facility. The ill person offers to pay his spouse for such personal care by transferring property to her. The offer is accepted, the services are rendered and the ill spouse dies. Affirming a judgment of dismissal rendered after a general demurrer was sustained, this court holds that the contract was not enforceable because — as a matter of law — the spouse who rendered services gave no consideration. Apparently, in the majority's view she had a preexisting or precontract nondelegable duty to clean the bedpans herself. Because I do not believe she did, I respectfully dissent.

The majority correctly read Estate of Sonnicksen (1937) [73 P.2d 643] and Brooks v. Brooks (1941) [119 P.2d 970] as holding that a wife cannot enter into a binding contract with her husband to provide "nursing-type care" for compensation. . . . It reasons that the wife, by reason of the marital relationship, already has a duty to provide such care, thus she offers no new consideration to support an independent contract to the same effect. The logic of these decisions is ripe for reexamination.

Sonnicksen and *Brooks* are the California Court of Appeal versions of a national theme. Excerpts from several of these decisions reveal the ethos and mores of the era which produced them.

"It would operate disastrously upon domestic life and breed discord and mischief if the wife could contract with her husband for the payment of services to be rendered for him in his home; if she could exact compensation for services, disagreeable or otherwise, rendered to members of his family; if she could sue him upon such contracts and establish them upon the disputed and conflicting testimony of the members of the household. To allow such contracts would degrade the wife by making her a menial and a servant in the home where she should discharge marital duties in loving and devoted ministrations, and frauds upon creditors would be greatly facilitated, as the wife could frequently absorb all her husband's property in the payment of her services, rendered under such secret, unknown contracts."

"A man cannot be entitled to the services of his wife for nothing, by virtue of a uniform and unchangeable marriage contract, and at the same time be under obligation to pay her for those services. . . . She cannot be his wife and his hired servant at the same time. . . . That would be inconsistent with the marriage relation, and disturb the reciprocal duties of the parties." . . .

Statements in two of these cases to the effect that a husband has an entitlement to his wife's "services" smack of the common law doctrine of coverture which treated a wife as scarcely more than an appendage to her husband. . . . One of the characteristics of coverture was that it deemed the wife economically helpless and governed by an implicit exchange: "The husband, as head of the family, is charged with its support and maintenance in return for which he is entitled to the wife's services in all those domestic affairs which pertain to the comfort, care, and well-being of the family. Her labors are her contribution to the family support and care." But coverture has been discarded in California, where both husband and wife owe each other the duty of support.

Not only has this doctrinal base for the authority underpinning the majority opinion been discarded long ago, but modern attitudes toward marriage have changed almost as rapidly as the economic realities of modern society. The assumption that only the rare wife can make a financial contribution to her family has become badly outdated in this age in which many married women have paying employment outside the home. A two-income family can no longer be dismissed as a statistically insignificant aberration. Moreover today husbands are increasingly involved in the domestic chores that make a house a home. Insofar as marital duties and property rights are not governed by positive law, they may be the result of informal accommodation or formal agreement. If spouses cannot work things out, there is always the no longer infrequently used option of divorce. For better or worse, we have to a great extent left behind the comfortable and familiar gender-based roles evoked by Norman Rockwell paintings. No longer can the marital relationship be regarded as "uniform and unchangeable." . . .

No one doubts that spouses owe each other a duty of support or that this encompasses "the obligation to provide medical care." There is nothing found in *Sonnicksen* and *Brooks*, or cited by the majority, which requires that this obligation be *personally* discharged by a spouse except the decisions themselves. However, at the time *Sonnicksen* and *Brooks* were decided — before World War II — it made sense for those courts to say that a wife could perform her duty of care only by doing so personally. That was an accurate reflection of the real world for women years before the exigency of war produced substantial employment opportunities for them. . . .

However the real world has changed in the 56 years since *Sonnicksen* was decided. Just a few years later with the advent of World War II Rosie the Riveter became not only a war jingle but a salute to hundreds of thousands of women working on the war effort outside the home. We know what happened thereafter. Presumably, in the present day husbands and wives who work outside the home have alternative methods of meeting this duty of care to an ill spouse. Among the choices would be: (1) paying for professional help; (2) paying for nonprofessional assistance; (3) seeking help from relatives or friends; and (4) quitting one's job and doing the work personally.

A fair reading of the complaint indicates that Mrs. Borelli initially chose the first of these options, and that this was not acceptable to Mr. Borelli, who then offered compensation if Mrs. Borelli would agree to personally care for him at home. To contend in 1993 that such a contract is without consideration means that if Mrs. Clinton becomes ill, President Clinton must drop everything and personally care for her.

According to the majority, Mrs. Borelli had nothing to bargain with so long as she remained in the marriage. This assumes that an intrinsic component of the marital relationship is the *personal* services of the spouse, an obligation that cannot be delegated or performed by others. The preceding discussion has attempted to demonstrate many ways in which what the majority terms "nursing-type care" can be provided without either husband or wife being required to empty a single bedpan. It follows that, because Mrs. Borelli agreed to supply this personal involvement, she was providing something over and above what would fully satisfy her duty of support. That personal something — precisely because it was something she was not required to do — qualifies as valid consideration sufficient to make enforceable Mr. Borelli's reciprocal promise to convey certain of his separate property.

Not only does the majority's position substantially impinge upon couples' freedom to come to a working arrangement of marital responsibilities, it may also foster the very opposite result of that intended. For example, nothing compelled Mr. Borelli and plaintiff to continue living together after his physical afflictions became known. Moral considerations notwithstanding, no legal force could have stopped plaintiff from leaving her husband in his hour of need. Had she done so, and had Mr. Borelli promised to give her some of his separate property should she come back, a valid contract would have arisen upon her return. Deeming them contracts promoting reconciliation and the resumption of marital relations, California courts have long enforced such agreements as supported by consideration. Here so far as we can tell from the face of the complaint, Mr. Borelli and plaintiff reached largely the same result without having to endure a separation. There is no sound reason why their contract, which clearly facilitated continuation of their marriage, should be any less valid. . . .

NOTES AND QUESTIONS

1. Contracts by married women were generally unenforceable at common law. As the opinions in *Borelli* indicate, several grounds have been advanced to support that view. For Blackstone, the myth of marital unity was a sufficient bar to recognition of agreements between spouses: "A man cannot grant any thing to his wife, or enter into covenant with her: for the grant would be to suppose her separate existence; and to covenant with her, would be only to covenant with himself." 1 William Blackstone, Commentaries on the Laws of England 430. The author of the first treatise on marital relations in the United States took a second, more sophisticated, view: "The law considers the wife to be in the power of the husband; it would not, therefore, be reasonable that she should be bound by any contract she makes during the coverture. . . ." Moreover, execution upon contracts included arrest and confinement in prison; these remedies imposed upon a wife would deprive the husband of her household and other services. Tapping Reeve, Baron and Femme 98 (1846). Marylynn Salmon provides a third explanation:

> In one way or another, everything women owned before marriage became their husbands' afterwards. A significant result of this social policy was the inability of femes coverts to contract. No agreement a woman made could be enforced against her because she owned nothing the court could seize to meet a judgment. Even a woman's contract to provide services was unenforceable. According to common law rules, a woman's services belonged to her husband. They could not be given to another unless he consented.

Marylynn Salmon, Women and the Law of Property in Early America 41 (1986).

A fourth, perhaps more modern, rationale for the refusal of courts to enforce spousal agreements is rooted in judicial economy, as exampled in the classic English case of Balfour v. Balfour, L.R. 2 K.B. 571 (C.A. 1919). Plaintiff wife sued her husband for money she claimed to be due from an agreed allowance of £30 a month. They made the agreement while on a visit to England from their home in Ceylon. The wife was unable for medical reasons to return with her husband, and she testified that Mr. Balfour agreed to send her £30 per month until she returned. Subsequently, she decided not to return, and her husband said he would send her £30 a month for maintenance until he returned. Mrs. Balfour later sued for divorce, and the court order enforced the support agreement. Mr. Balfour appealed, and the Court of Appeals reversed. The court held that the wife failed to prove that the promise was intended to carry legal consequences, and reasoned that courts are poorly equipped to enforce during-marriage agreements:

> . . . [I]t is necessary to remember that there are agreements between parties which do not result in contracts within the meaning of that term in our law. The ordinary example is when two people agree to take a walk together. . . . [O]ne of the most usual forms of agreement which does not constitute a contract appears to me to be the arrangements which are made between husband and wife. It is quite common, and it is the natural and inevitable result of the relationship of husband and wife, that the two spouses should make arrangements between themselves—agreements such as are in dispute in this action—agreements for allowances, by which the husband agrees that he will pay to his wife a certain sum of money per week, or per month,

or per year, to cover either her own expenses or the necessary expenses of the household and of the children of the marriage. . . .

To my mind it would be the worst possible example to hold that agreements such as this resulted in legal obligations which could be enforced in the Courts. . . . All I can say is that the small Courts of this country would have to be multiplied one hundredfold if these arrangements were held to result in legal obligations. They are not sued upon, not because the parties are reluctant to enforce their legal rights when the agreement is broken, but because the parties, in the inception of their arrangement, never intended that they should be sued upon. . . . The terms may be repudiated, varied or renewed as performance proceeds or as disagreements develop, and the principles of the common law as to exoneration and discharge and accord and satisfaction are such as find no place in the domestic code. The parties themselves are advocates, judges, Courts, sheriff's officer and reporter. In respect of these promises each house is a domain into which the King's writ does not seek to run, and to which his officers do not seek to be admitted.

2. The *Borelli* court applied the contractual doctrine of preexisting duty to bar enforcement of the agreement. Contract rules apply to postnuptial agreements as they do to premarital agreements. During-marriage contracts must be entered into voluntarily and cannot be the product of duress or fraud, for example. How do courts view duress if one party threatens to divorce the other unless a during-marriage agreement is signed? *See* Hall v. Hall, 27 N.E.3d 281 (Ind. App. 2015), upholding an agreement drafted by the wife who reconciled with her incarcerated husband on the condition that he sign the contract and divorced him eight years later. The husband's claim that his incarceration created conditions of duress failed. 27 N.E.3d at 286. In In re Marriage of Labuz, 54 N.E.3d 886, 898 (Ill. App. Ct. 2016), the court rejected a husband's claim that duress made a postnuptial agreement unenforceable because his wife threatened to leave the marriage and relocate with the parties' child unless he signed the agreement. *Compare* Pacelli v. Pacelli, 725 A.2d 56, 59 (N.J. Super. App. Div. 1999) (holding that husband's ultimatum that wife sign an agreement or he would pursue divorce was a fabricated marital crisis and "was inherently coercive;" wife's "decision was dictated not by a consideration of her legal rights, but by her desire to preserve the family"); Lewis v. Lewis, 234 A.3d 706 (Pa. Super. Ct. 2020) (finding coersion because of husband's longstanding mental and physical abuse of the wife and his threat to withhold access to their child if she did not sign agreement). Although many states subject postmarital agreements to stricter scrutiny, courts differ in assessing parties' claims of unconscionability. The *Labuz* court, cited above, also held that although the postmarital agreement significantly favored the wife, an agreement benefiting one party is not necessarily unenforceable. *Labuz*, 54 N.E.3d at 902.

3. It might seem that Mrs. Borelli would have had a greater chance of success in enforcing her contract if she had not been married to Mr. Borelli and thus not subject to the assumption that her services were duties of her marriage. Consider, however, the other traditional contract doctrines that might have been at issue in the case: the statute of frauds ordinarily applies to contracts to make a will, Mr. Borelli's capacity to contract might have been questioned on the basis of the stroke he suffered, and, if he had changed his will, his daughter might have questioned the result on the basis of undue influence. Indeed, American courts have generally regarded with suspicion contractual efforts to induce or acknowledge support by non–family members. They may impose heightened evidentiary standards for enforcement, such as the requirement of writing for any recovery beyond quantum meruit. *See, e.g.,* Uniform Probate Code §2-514 (requiring written evidence of contract to devise) and Frances H. Foster, The Family Paradigm of Inheritance Law, 80 N.C. L. Rev. 199, 215-216 (2001). Even if evidentiary requirements for proving the contract are met, contractual caregiving provisions may be challenged by "natural" objects of a decedent's bounty on grounds of fraud, duress, and undue influence. If nonmarital sexual relations with the caregiver were also involved, courts may occasionally invalidate the contract on the ground that it rests on "illegal consideration." *See* Foster, above, at 217.

5. For further analysis of the scope and legal recognition of agreements made during marriage, *see* Linda Ravdin, Postmarital Agreements: Validity and Enforceability, 52 Fam. L. Q. 245, 246-249 (2018).

Bedrick v. Bedrick
17 A.3d 17 (Conn. 2011)

McLachlan, J. This appeal involves a dissolution of marriage action in which the defendant, Bruce L. Bedrick, seeks to enforce a postnuptial agreement.[4] Today we are presented for the first time with the issue of whether a postnuptial agreement is valid and enforceable in Connecticut.

The defendant appeals from the trial court's judgment in favor of the plaintiff, Deborah Bedrick. . . . We conclude that postnuptial agreements are valid and enforceable and generally must comply with contract principles. We also conclude, however, that the terms of such agreements must be both fair and equitable at the time of execution and not unconscionable at the time of dissolution. Because the terms of the present agreement were unconscionable at the time of dissolution, we affirm the judgment of the trial court. . . .

. . . We begin our analysis of postnuptial agreements by considering the public policies served by the recognition of agreements regarding the dissolution of marriage, including prenuptial, postnuptial and separation agreements. . . .

Postnuptial agreements are consistent with public policy; they realistically acknowledge the high incidence of divorce and its effect upon our population. . . . "[R]ecent statistics on divorce have forced people to deal with the reality that many marriages do not last a lifetime. As desirable as it may seem for couples to embark upon marriage in a state of optimism and hope, the reality is that many marriages end in divorce. There is a growing trend toward serial marriage; more people expect to have more than one spouse during their lifetime." T. Perry, Dissolution Planning in Family Law: A Critique of Current Analyses and a Look toward the Future, 24 Fam. L.Q. 77, 82 (1990). "[B]oth the realities of our society and policy reasons favor judicial recognition of prenuptial agreements. Rather than inducing divorce, such agreements simply acknowledge its ordinariness. With divorce as likely an outcome of marriage as permanence, we see no logical or compelling reason why public policy should not allow two mature adults to handle their own financial affairs. . . . The reasoning that once found them contrary to public policy has no place in today's matrimonial law." Brooks v. Brooks, 733 P.2d 1044, 1050-51 (Alaska 1987). Postnuptial agreements are no different than prenuptial agreements in this regard.

Having determined that postnuptial agreements are consistent with public policy, we now must consider what standards govern their enforcement. Neither the legislature nor this court

---

4. A postnuptial agreement is distinguishable from both a prenuptial agreement and a separation agreement. Like a prenuptial agreement, a postnuptial agreement may determine, inter alia, each spouse's legal rights and obligations upon dissolution of the marriage. As the name suggests, however, a postnuptial agreement is entered into during marriage — after a couple weds, but before they separate, when the spouses "plan to continue their marriage"; A.L.I., Principles of the Law of Family Dissolution: Analysis and Recommendations (2002) §7.01(1)(b), p. 1052; and when "separation or divorce is not imminent." Black's Law Dictionary (9th Ed. 2009).

has addressed this question. To aid in our analysis of the enforceability of postnuptial agreements, we review our law on the enforceability of prenuptial agreements.[5] . . .

Prenuptial agreements entered into on or after October 1, 1995, are governed by the Connecticut Premarital Agreement Act, General Statutes §46b-66a et seq. The statutory scheme provides that a prenuptial agreement is unenforceable when: (1) the challenger did not enter the agreement voluntarily; (2) the agreement was unconscionable when executed or enforced; (3) the challenger did not receive "a fair and reasonable disclosure of the amount, character and value of property, financial obligations and income of the other party" before execution of the agreement; or (4) the challenger did not have "a reasonable opportunity to consult with independent counsel." . . .

Although we view postnuptial agreements as encouraging the private resolution of family issues, we also recognize that spouses do not contract under the same conditions as either prospective spouses or spouses who have determined to dissolve their marriage. The Supreme Judicial Court of Massachusetts has noted that a postnuptial "agreement stands on a different footing from both a [prenuptial agreement] and a separation agreement. Before marriage, the parties have greater freedom to reject an unsatisfactory [prenuptial] contract. . . .

"A separation agreement, in turn, is negotiated when a marriage has failed and the spouses intend a permanent separation or marital dissolution. . . . The circumstances surrounding [postnuptial] agreements in contrast are pregnant with the opportunity for one party to use the threat of dissolution to bargain themselves into positions of advantage. . . .

"For these reasons, we join many other [s]tates in concluding that [postnuptial] agreements must be carefully scrutinized." Ansin v. Craven-Ansin, supra, 457 Mass. at 289-90, 929 N.E.2d 955. The Appellate Division of the New Jersey Superior Court has also recognized this "contextual difference" and has noted that a wife "face[s] a more difficult choice than [a] bride who is presented with a demand for a pre-nuptial agreement. The cost to [a wife is] . . . the destruction of a family and the stigma of a failed marriage." Pacelli v. Pacelli, 319 N.J. Super. 185, 190, 725 A.2d 56 (App. Div.), cert. denied, 161 N.J. 147, 735 A.2d 572 (1999). A spouse who bargains a settlement agreement, on the other hand, "recogniz[es] that the marriage is over, can look to his or her economic rights; the relationship is adversarial." Thus, a spouse enters a postnuptial agreement under different conditions than a party entering either a prenuptial or a separation agreement.

Other state courts have not only observed that spouses contract under different conditions; they have also observed that postnuptial agreements "should not be treated as mere 'business deals.'" Stoner v. Stoner, 572 Pa. 665, 672-73, 819 A.2d 529 (2003). They recognize that, just like prospective spouses, "parties to these agreements do not quite deal at arm's length, but rather at the time the contract is entered into stand in a relation of mutual confidence and trust. . . ."

Because of the nature of the marital relationship, the spouses to a postnuptial agreement may not be as cautious in contracting with one another as they would be with prospective spouses, and they are certainly less cautious than they would be with an ordinary contracting party. With lessened caution comes greater potential for one spouse to take advantage of the other. This leads us to conclude that postnuptial agreements require stricter scrutiny than prenuptial agreements. In applying special scrutiny, a court may enforce a postnuptial

---

5. We do not review our law on the enforceability of separation agreements, which are distinct from both prenuptial and postnuptial agreements and are entered into when spouses have determined to dissolve their marriage. We merely note that their enforcement is governed by General Statutes §46b-66(a), which provides in relevant part that "where the parties have submitted to the court an agreement concerning . . . alimony or the disposition of property, the court shall . . . determine whether the agreement of the spouses is fair and equitable under all the circumstances. . . ."

agreement only if it complies with applicable contract principles,[6] and the terms of the agreement are both fair and equitable at the time of execution and not unconscionable at the time of dissolution.

We further hold that the terms of a postnuptial agreement are fair and equitable at the time of execution if the agreement is made voluntarily, and without any undue influence, fraud, coercion, duress or similar defect. Moreover, each spouse must be given full, fair and reasonable disclosure of the amount, character and value of property, both jointly and separately held, and all of the financial obligations and income of the other spouse. This mandatory disclosure requirement is a result of the deeply personal marital relationship.

Just as "[t]he validity of a [prenuptial] contract depends upon the circumstances of the particular case"; McHugh v. McHugh, supra, 436 A.2d 8; in determining whether a particular postnuptial agreement is fair and equitable at the time of execution, a court should consider the totality of the circumstances surrounding execution. A court may consider various factors, including "the nature and complexity of the agreement's terms, the extent of and disparity in assets brought to the marriage by each spouse, the parties' respective age, sophistication, education, employment, experience, prior marriages, or other traits potentially affecting the ability to read and understand an agreement's provisions, and the amount of time available to each spouse to reflect upon the agreement after first seeing its specific terms . . . [and] access to independent counsel prior to consenting to the contract terms." Annot., 53 A.L.R.4th 85, 92-93, §2[a] (1987). . . .

Unfairness or inequality alone does not render a postnuptial agreement unconscionable; spouses may agree on an unequal distribution of assets at dissolution. . . . Unforeseen changes in the relationship, such as having a child, loss of employment or moving to another state, may render enforcement of the agreement unconscionable.

. . . [W]e turn to the present case and address the question of whether the trial court properly concluded that the parties' postnuptial agreement should not be enforced. . . .

Although the value of the parties combined assets is $927,123, the last addendum to the agreement, dated May 18, 1989, provides that the plaintiff will receive a cash settlement of only $75,000. This addendum was written prior to the initial success of the car wash business in the early 1990s, the birth of the parties' son in 1991, when the parties were forty-one years old, and the subsequent deterioration of the business in the 2000s. At the time of trial, the parties were both fifty-seven years old. Neither had a college degree. The defendant had been steadily employed by the car wash business since 1973. The plaintiff had worked for that business for thirty-five years, providing administrative and bookkeeping support, and since

---

6. The defendant also argues that the trial court improperly concluded that the postnuptial agreement at issue failed to comply with contract principles because it lacked adequate consideration. Because we conclude that the trial court properly found that the present agreement was unenforceable, we need not address whether the agreement also could have failed for lack of consideration.

General Statutes §46b-66c, however, expressly provides that prenuptial agreements are enforceable without consideration. Because no similar statute exists for postnuptial agreements, and because such agreements generally must comply with contract principles, the present agreement would require adequate consideration to be enforceable.

. . . In the present case, the plaintiff released, *inter alia*, her right to alimony and her interest in the defendant's car wash business, in exchange for, *inter alia*, the defendant's right to alimony and his release of the plaintiff's liability for the defendant's personal and business loans. Although the trial court found that the present agreement lacked adequate consideration, the agreement would not fail for lack of consideration.

In the present case, the defendant does not argue that a promise to remain married constitutes adequate consideration, and the postnuptial agreement does not refer to any promise to remain married or right to dissolution of marriage. Thus, for purposes of the present dispute, it is irrelevant whether a spouse's forbearance from bringing a claimed dissolution action and the continuation of the marriage provides adequate consideration for a postnuptial agreement.

approximately 2001, when the business began to deteriorate, the plaintiff had managed all business operations excluding maintenance. In 2004, the plaintiff also had worked outside of the business in order to provide the family with additional income. Since approximately 2007, when the plaintiff stopped working for the business, the defendant had not been able to complete administrative or bookkeeping tasks, and had not filed taxes.

The trial court found that "[t]he economic circumstances of the parties had changed dramatically since the execution of the agreement" and that "enforcement of the postnuptial agreement would have worked injustice." It, therefore, concluded that the agreement was unenforceable. Although the trial court did not have guidance on the applicable legal standards for postnuptial agreements, which we set forth today, we previously have determined that the question of whether enforcement of a prenuptial agreement would be unconscionable is analogous to determining whether enforcement would work an injustice. Thus, the trial court's finding that enforcement of the postnuptial agreement would work an injustice was tantamount to a finding that the agreement was unconscionable at the time the defendant sought to enforce it. We review the question of unconscionability as a matter of law. The facts and circumstances of the present case clearly support the findings of the trial court that, as a matter of law, enforcement of the agreement would be unconscionable. . . .

NOTES AND QUESTIONS

1. Would the postmarital agreement in *Borelli* have been enforced under the standards adopted in *Bedrick*? Under the UPMAA?

2. In *Bedrick*, the Connecticut Supreme Court emphasized that agreements entered during marriage are different from ones entered into before marriage and should be subject to stricter review. What differences did the Connecticut court see between the two types of agreements? Does the UPMAA also draw a distinction between the enforceability of the two types of agreements?

For an example of a statutory scheme with different requirements for premarital and marital agreements, *compare* Minn. Stat. §519.11, Subd. 1 (2022) (Antenuptial contract) *with id.*, Subd. 1a (Postnuptial contract). Under Minnesota law, a postnuptial agreement must meet all the requirements of premarital agreements, both parties must be represented by counsel, and the contract is presumed unenforceable if either party seeks a divorce within two years of its signing (subject to the party seeking enforcement showing the agreement to be fair). Ohio is even stricter, suggesting that contracts that alter the terms of marriage are not enforceable at all. Ohio Rev. Code Ann. §3103.06 (West 2022). In other states, premarital agreements and postmarital agreements are treated the same by statute. *See* Va. Code Ann. §20-155 (West 2022) ("Married persons may enter into agreements with each other for the purpose of settling the rights and obligations of either or both of them, to the same extent, with the same effect, and subject to the same conditions, as . . . agreements between prospective spouses."). Many states have no statutes or case law that expressly govern postnuptial contracts.

3. In Bratton v. Bratton, 136 S.W.3d 595 (Tenn. 2004), the court held that a postnuptial agreement entered into while the husband was in medical school lacked consideration and was unenforceable. The wife requested the agreement soon after the marriage, while she was supporting the husband through medical school; it provided that she was entitled to half his salary for the rest of her life. When the wife sought to enforce the agreement at the time of the divorce 17 years later, the court held that the wife's promise to forgo dental school was illusory because she had made the decision before the agreement was signed. Professors Atwood and Bix, the UPMAA reporters, observe that:

The issue of consideration, however, is not a dead letter in the context of marital agreements, with some state courts requiring a showing that agreements between spouses rest on valid consideration. An inquiry into the adequacy of consideration may engage courts in an assessment of the mutuality of the spouses' exchanges, or a determination of whether a delay in filing for divorce constitutes valid consideration. The Committee chose to avoid such inquiries, . . . in holding that marital agreements cannot be invalidated on the basis of an absence of consideration. As elsewhere in contract law, questions about consideration often serve as a vehicle for effectuating general policies of fair dealing. Rather than requiring a showing of consideration, the Act provides such protections more directly through other provisions.

Barbara A. Atwood & Brian H. Bix, A New Uniform Law for Premarital and Marital Agreements, 46 Fam. L.Q. 313, 338 (2012).

3. Chapter 9 explored agreements defined by religion and the implications for custody; some couples of Jewish or Muslim faiths, for example, enter agreements about the duties they owe each other based on their religious faiths. *See* Brian H. Bix, Marriage Agreements and Religion, 2016 U. Ill. L. Rev. 1665, 1672. Often people enter those agreements as part of or before a wedding but after civil ceremonies. Courts in a number of states enforce those agreements as postmarital contracts. For instance, a New York court held that a mahr agreement, governing payment of dower upon Islamic divorce (referenced in Chapter 11, Section D) was a postnuptial agreement under the laws of the state and applied the secular principles governing marital contracts to award the wife her mahr payment. S.B. v. W.A., 959 N.Y.S.2d 802, 819-820 (N.Y. Sup. 2012). Maryland courts will recognize mahr "as secular contracts if they are enforceable under neutral principles of contract law[.]" Chaudry v. Chaudry, 2021 Md. App. LEXIS 615 (Md. Ct. Spec. App. 2021). In *Chaudry*, unlike the New York case, the court found "the mahr agreement between the parties did not constitute a valid, enforceable prenuptial agreement by which [the wife] relinquished her right to an equitable division of marital property in exchange for $10,000." 2021 Md. App. LEXIS 615 at 22-23.

4. Half of the attorney members of the American Academy of Matrimonial Lawyers (AAML) reported in a 2015 survey that an increasing number of clients asked for draft postnuptial contracts; only 2 percent of survey participants said they were drafting fewer agreements. The most common topics covered by postnuptial agreements included property division (90 percent), alimony (73 percent), and retirement accounts (45 percent). The next most common issues covered by postnuptial agreements were "occupancy of the marital residence" (30 percent), payment of legal fees in future litigation (14 percent), and the consequences of infidelity (7 percent). AAML, Big Increase in Spouses Seeking Postnuptial Agreements, Oct. 28, 2015, available at https://www.prnewswire.com/news-releases/big-increase-in-spouses-seeking-postnuptial-agreements-300167901.html. How effective do you think postnuptial agreements are in keeping couples together? If research shows that most couples who sign postnuptial agreements ultimately get divorced, what are the benefits of during-marriage contracting? *See* M. Neil Browne & Katherine S. Fister, The Intriguing Potential of Postnuptial Contract Modifications, 23 Hastings Women's L.J. 187 (2012) (arguing that postnuptial contracts promote more amicable and less contentious divorce proceedings).

5. How is a contract that settles the parties' affairs upon divorce, the subject of the next section, different from a postnuptial agreement in contemplation of the couple's separation? In In re Marriage of Traster, 339 P.3d 778 (Kan. 2014), the Supreme Court of Kansas held that even though parties characterized an agreement as postnuptial, the contract should be treated as a separation agreement, subject to the relevant state statute. In the absence of legislative definitions of postmarital agreements, the court "include[d] all agreements entered during marriage that provide for a spouse's property rights in the event of divorce or separation within the meaning of 'separation agreement,' regardless of whether the parties intend to remain married at the time of execution." 339 P.3d at 789 (citation omitted).

Consider the differences between premarital, postmarital, and settlement agreements as you read the following section.

C. AGREEMENTS AT THE END OF RELATIONSHIPS

In contrast to the relative rarity of premarital agreements, separation agreements are the norm. The great majority of divorce cases are uncontested, and a high percentage of divorces are settled by agreement and not by litigation. Marlene M. Browne, The Divorce Process: Empowerment Through Knowledge (2001) (95 percent of all divorces are uncontested); Tess Wilkinson-Ryan & Jonathan Baron, The Effect of Conflicting Moral and Legal Rules on Bargaining Behavior: The Case of No-Fault Divorce, 37 J. Legal Stud. 315, 316 (2008) ("In a typical divorce, couples negotiate a financial agreement detailing how they will divide their property, and a judge signs off on the agreement, usually with minimal, if any, oversight.").

Like the other types of contracts reviewed in this chapter, separation agreements must satisfy basic contract law requirements to be enforceable. They sometimes raise issues under the statute of frauds because they concern real property or their terms cannot be performed within one year, although judicial approaches limit the significance of the stationary requirement of a writing.

1. The Permissible Scope of Settlement Agreements

Just as the law of premarital agreements has evolved from a position that officially limited the parties' ability to determine by contract the legal consequences of marriage, the law of separation agreements has also moved toward a model of contractual freedom. Agreements routinely address issues of property division and spousal support as well as child support and child custody. However, traditionally, and still officially in most states, parties may not enter into binding contracts with regard to child support, custody, and visitation that tie the hands of the court. The following UMDA and ALI Principles seek to bring uniformity to how divorcing couples and courts approach settlement agreements. The commentary and notes that follow highlight the decreasing oversight of courts and the increasing importance of private ordering in family law.

UNIFORM MARRIAGE AND DIVORCE ACT (UMDA) §306

(a) To promote amicable settlement of disputes between parties to a marriage attendant upon their separation or the dissolution of their marriage, the parties may enter into a written separation agreement containing provisions for disposition of any property owned by either of them, maintenance of either of them, and support, custody, and visitation of their children.

(b) In a proceeding for dissolution of marriage or for legal separation, the terms of the separation agreement, except those providing for the support, custody, and visitation of children, are binding upon the court unless it finds, after considering the economic circumstances of the parties and any other relevant evidence produced by the parties, on their own motion or on request of the court, that the separation agreement is unconscionable.

(c) If the court finds the separation agreement unconscionable, it may request the parties to submit a revised separation agreement or may make orders for the disposition of property, maintenance, and support.

AMERICAN LAW INSTITUTE PRINCIPLES OF THE LAW OF FAMILY DISSOLUTION §7.09 (2002)

(2) Except as provided in the last sentence of this Paragraph, the terms of a separation agreement providing for the disposition of property or for compensatory payments are unenforceable if they substantially limit or augment property rights or compensatory payments otherwise due under law, and enforcement of those terms would substantially impair the economic well-being of a party who has or will have

    (a) primary or dual residential responsibility for a child or

    (b) substantially fewer economic resources than the other party. Nevertheless, the court may enforce such terms if it finds, under the particular circumstances of the case, that enforcement of the terms would not work an injustice.

Robert H. Mnookin & Lewis Kornhauser

Bargaining in the Shadow of the Law: The Case of Divorce
88 Yale L.J. 950, 954-956 (1979)

In families with minor children, existing law imposes substantial doctrinal constraints. For those allocational decisions that directly affect children—that is, child support, custody, and visitation—parents lack the formal power to make their own law. Judges, exercising the state's parens patriae power, are said to have responsibility to determine who should have custody and on what conditions. Private agreements concerning these matters are possible and common, but agreements cannot bind the court, which, as a matter of official dogma, is said to have an independent responsibility for determining what arrangement best serves the child's welfare. . . .

On the other hand, available evidence on how the legal system processes undisputed divorce cases involving minor children suggest that parents actually have broad powers to make their own deals. Typically, separation agreements are rubber stamped even in cases involving children. . . .

The parents' broad discretion is not surprising for several reasons. First, getting information is difficult when there is no dispute. The state usually has very limited resources for a thorough and independent investigation of the family's circumstances. Furthermore, parents may be unwilling to provide damaging information that may upset their agreed arrangements. Second, the applicable legal standards are extremely vague and give judges very little guidance as to what circumstances justify overriding a parental decision. Finally, there are obvious limitations on a court's practical power to control the parents once they leave the courtroom. For all these reasons, it is not surprising that most courts behave as if their function in the divorce process is dispute settlement, not child protection. When there is no dispute, busy judges or registrars are typically quite willing to rubber stamp a private agreement, in order to conserve resources for disputed cases.

Huss v. Weaver
134 A.3d 449 (Pa. Super. 2016) (en banc)

BENDER, P.J.E. In October 2008, Huss and Weaver, who were involved in a romantic relationship, entered into a contract ("Agreement") in which they agreed that if their relationship resulted in the birth of a child, Huss would have primary physical custody and Weaver would have specified visitation rights, and that if Weaver sought court modification of these terms he would pay Huss $10,000 for each such attempt. The parties had a son in November 2010 and Weaver filed a complaint for custody in December 2010. Huss then filed a complaint alleging that Weaver had failed to abide by his contractual promise to make the required $10,000 payments.

. . . On September 25, 2013, the trial court entered the order now on appeal and an accompanying opinion, sustaining Weaver's preliminary objections and dismissing Huss' amended complaint with prejudice.

In her amended complaint, Huss alleged that the parties entered into the Agreement on October 17, 2008, that at that time Weaver was a practicing attorney with the law firm of Buchanan Ingersoll & Rooney in Pittsburgh, and that he had provided Huss with "legal representation in various legal matters." Huss further alleged that Weaver, along with a colleague at the Buchanan Ingersoll & Rooney law firm, drafted the Agreement. The relevant provisions of the Agreement state as follows:

> WHEREAS, currently [Huss] is a real estate agent capable of earning large commissions if she works excessive hours and [Weaver] is an attorney capable of earning a large salary; and
>
> WHEREAS, in the event that [Huss] has a child or children of [Weaver] and the parties' relationship is ended by either party, whether or not the parties are married at the time of the termination of the relationship, the parties desire to set forth their agreement as to the custody of such child or children.
>
> NOW THEREFORE the parties for and in consideration of the covenants contained in the Agreement, and intending to be legally bound thereby, agree as follows:
>
> 1. Custody. In the event that either [Weaver] or [Huss] terminates the relationship with the other, whether or not they are married at the time of such termination, the legal custody of any child by this Agreement shall be shared by [Weaver] and [Huss] shall have primary physical custody of such children. In the event such termination of the relationship occurs, [Weaver] agrees that he will not pursue full physical custody of any child by this agreement and further agrees that he will not attempt to use the fact that [Huss] must work excessive hours selling real estate in order to earn large commissions to pursue custody of such child or children.
>
> 2. Visitation. In the event that either [Weaver] or [Huss] terminates the relationship with the other, whether they are married at the time of such termination, [Weaver] shall be entitled to unsupervised visitation with any child by this Agreement as follows
>
>> a. So long as the parties reside within 50 miles of one another, [Weaver] shall be entitled to every other weekend beginning at 7 P.M. Friday evening and ending 4 P.M. Sunday evening. [Weaver] agrees to be responsible for transportation.
>> b. In the event that the parties reside more than 50 miles from one another, [Weaver] shall be entitled to one month during the summer as agreed to by the parties.
>> c. [Huss] has the right to relocate out of state if she desires.
>
> 3. Support. [Weaver] agrees that, regardless of any custody arrangement between the parties, [Weaver] waives any rights to pursue [Huss] for child support for any child. [Weaver] further agrees to pay [Huss] child support for any child or children to be agreed upon by the parties or determined by Domestic Relations.
>
> 4. Modification of Agreement. This Agreement may only be modified or amended by the parties by a written instrument signed by both [Weaver] and [Huss]. The parties acknowledge that this Agreement may be modified or superseded by a court of competent jurisdiction. *In the event that [Weaver] files a complaint, motion, petition or similar pleading seeking the modification or amendment of the custody and/or visitation provisions set forth herein, [Weaver] agrees to pay [Huss] $10,000 for each modification or amendment sought.*
>
> 5. Voluntary Agreement. Each party understands that in the absence of this Agreement, as a matter of law, that he or she might be entitled to a greater level of custody or more visitation than is provided herein. Both parties acknowledge that they have read this Agreement carefully

and thoroughly, and each considers the provisions of this Agreement to be fair, just and reasonable, and that they fully understand each of its provisions and are executing the same freely and voluntarily, without coercion or other compulsion. (emphasis added).

Huss also alleged in her amended complaint that Weaver had breached the highlighted portion of paragraph 4 of the Agreement. She noted that, since the birth of their son, the parties have been "embroiled in litigation" regarding custody and visitation issues, that Weaver filed numerous "complaints, motions, petitions, and/or similar pleadings," and that he failed and refused to pay her $10,000 for each such filing. Finally, Huss contended that Weaver, as her legal advisor, either negligently or intentionally misrepresented to her that she should enter into the Agreement, which "she in fact did not wish to enter," and that he never indicated to her that he believed any of its provisions to be against public policy.

The trial court dismissed Huss' complaint, ruling that the provision for the $10,000 payments was void as against public policy. In its written opinion in support of its sustaining of Weaver's preliminary objections, the trial court first cited cases holding that parents may not bargain away their child's right to receive child support (citing Knorr v. Knorr, 527 Pa. 83, 588 A.2d 503, 505 (1991)). The trial court then noted that custody agreements between parents are subject to court modification in the best interests of the child. Based on these tenets, the trial court reasoned as follows:

> Imposing a fee upon [Weaver] to pay $10,000 if he decides to file a modification of child custody is against the public policy of assuring continuing contact between child and parent. It substantially impairs the Court's power and the Commonwealth's duty to determine what is in a child's best interest. "Our paramount concern in child custody matters is the best interests of the children." Yates v. Yates, 963 A.2d 535, 539 (Pa. Super. 2008). It is against public policy to impose a fee on one party in order to determine the best interests of the child.[7]

Huss filed a notice of appeal and the case was assigned to a three-judge panel of this Court. Following the panel's review, it determined that the trial court's ruling with respect to the $10,000 clause was in error, i.e., the Agreement was not unenforceable as against public policy. Thus, the trial court's sustaining of Weaver's preliminary objections was overturned. See Huss v. Weaver, 2014 PA Super 238 (Pa. Super. filed October 21, 2014). Weaver then filed a timely application for reargument before the court en banc, which was granted by per curiam order, dated December 12, 2014. Thus, the panel decision was withdrawn on December 12, 2014. . . .

Huss raises the following issues for our review:

(1) Did the lower court err in concluding that the parties' Agreement was not enforceable as a matter of public policy?

(2) Whether [Weaver, an attorney] who drafted a contract should be estopped from asserting the contract is unenforceable when he advised [Huss] the contract was legal and enforceable?[8]

---

7. The trial court also indicated that the provision in paragraph 3 of the Agreement preventing Weaver from filing for child support from Huss if he is ever awarded custody violates public policy. In her present action, however, Huss is not attempting to enforce this provision and thus its enforceability is not at issue here. Moreover, its enforceability should have no effect on the issues currently ripe for resolution, since the Agreement contains a severability clause providing that if any of its provisions are determined to conflict with Pennsylvania law, "the remaining terms of this Agreement shall remain in full force and effect."

8. In a deleted footnote, the majority held that the court need not resolve the issue of estoppel, having found that the contract term was enforceable per the first issue. For the conflicts of interest implicated by Weaver drafting his own agreement and advising Huss in prior matters, see Chapter 11, Section C on lawyering. — Eds.

Contrary to the decision reached by the trial court, we have not identified any "dominant public policy" grounded in governmental practice, statutory enactments, or violations of obvious ethical or moral standards, which provides a basis for declaring the "$10,000 clause" in the Agreement to be unenforceable as against public policy. The trial court grounded its analysis on *Knorr*, in which our Supreme Court held that parents have no power to "bargain away the rights of their children," and that if an agreement between parents for child support provides "less than required or less than can be given," courts may ignore the agreement and require a satisfactory level of support. *Knorr*, 588 A.2d at 505. Subsequent to *Knorr*, this Court has routinely held that a child's right to adequate support payments cannot be bargained away and that any release or compromise on child support obligations is invalid if it prejudices the child's welfare. (citation omitted).

However, no similar appellate authority exists with respect to agreements between parents regarding custody and visitation. While custody and visitation agreements are always subject to modification by the courts in the best interests of the child, *Mumma*, 550 A.2d at 1343, we are unaware of any cases in which Pennsylvania courts have declared such contracts to be unenforceable as against public policy. The reason for this distinction would appear to be obvious, since the right to child support *belongs to the child*, and thus cannot be "bargained away" by the parents. (emphasis in the original). *See* Kesler v. Weniger, 744 A.2d 794, 796 (Pa. Super. 2000) ("[T]he right to support is a right of the child, not the mother or father. . . ."). Accordingly, when the parents agree among themselves to provide an inadequate level of child support, the child's rights have been violated and thus the agreement may be declared void as against public policy. . . .

Rights to custody and visitation, on the other hand, belong to the parents (or guardians). 23 Pa. C. S. §5322; Pa. R. C. P. 1915.1(b). Because children are not mere chattel, agreements regarding custody and visitation are always subject to court review and adjustment in the best interests of the child. . . . In no way, however, do custody and visitation agreements involve the bargaining away of the rights of the children, and accordingly they are not unenforceable as against public policy on the same basis as are agreements regarding child support. . . .

The trial court nevertheless concluded that the "$10,000 clause" is unenforceable as against public policy because it "substantially impairs the Court's power and the Commonwealth's duty to determine what is in a child's best interests." To this end, in its written opinion, the trial court refers to the "10,000 clause" as a "fee," an "impediment," an "impairment," and would have a "chilling effect" on the filing of custody complaints or modification petitions. In support of this position, in his appellate brief Weaver cites this Court's decision in Kraisinger v. Kraisinger, 928 A.2d 333 (Pa. Super. 2007), a case in which we struck down as invalid a provision in a child support agreement requiring the mother to pay the father's legal fees if she challenged the amount of child support set forth in their agreement. The parties' agreement specifically provided that the attorneys' fees provision was included to "discourage frivolous filings." *Id.* at 337. In accord with the rationale employed in the above-discussed child support cases, we concluded that "[w]e cannot tolerate a provision which penalizes a parent for pursuing her children's rights." *Id.* at 345.

The issue of whether a provision in a custody/visitation contract that places a serious impediment on either party's ability to seek court modification in the best interests of the child is not presently before this Court. No language in the Agreement at issue here provides either that the "$10,000 clause" is intended to discourage Weaver from seeking court intervention, or evidences that the payment would act as an impediment to his ability to do so. Whether the "$10,000 clause" would act as an impediment would depend, first and foremost, upon Weaver's financial ability to pay it. In the Agreement, however, Weaver plainly acknowledged that he "is an attorney capable of earning a large salary." He also straightforwardly recognized that all of the terms of the Agreement (including the "$10,000 clause" in the immediately preceding paragraph) are "fair, just and reasonable." Finally, Weaver agreed that he fully understood each of the Agreement's provisions and executed it "freely and voluntarily, without coercion or other compulsion."

As set forth above, our standard of review in this circumstance provides that the salient facts must be derived solely from Huss' amended complaint (including the attached Agreement), and that we must treat all well-pleaded material facts in the amended complaint, and all inferences reasonably deduced therefrom, as true. . . . No facts of record support a finding that the "$10,000 clause" constituted an impediment to Weaver's ability to seek court modification of any of the terms of the Agreement.

Huss contends that the "$10,000 clause" was intended as a "defense fund" in the event of litigation regarding the Agreement. While we agree with the trial court that the Agreement contains no specific language to support this suggestion, we cannot also agree that the parol evidence rule would bar her from testifying about her understanding of the parties' intentions with respect to this payment. *See, e.g.*, Steuart v. McChesney, 498 Pa. 45, 444 A.2d 659, 663 (1982) (explaining that parol evidence is admissible to explain, clarify, and resolve ambiguities). Whether the parties intended to provide Huss with a "defense fund" to assist with the cost of any future litigation may depend upon the parties' relative abilities to afford the expense of any such future litigation. In this regard, the first "WHEREAS" clause in the Agreement is ambiguous, as it leaves their relative financial capabilities unclear. Weaver is described as an attorney "capable of earning a large salary," while Huss is a real estate agent "capable of earning large commissions *if she works excessive hours*." (emphasis in the original). Without parol evidence, we cannot ascertain whether this provision intended to convey that the parties have approximately the same capabilities to earn large salaries/commissions, or alternatively if Weaver is best able to earn more money (since he apparently can do so without working excessive hours, which arguably would be difficult for Huss to do after the birth of their child). (footnote omitted). In short, whether the parties recognized Weaver's superior ability to finance the cost of future litigation, and thus provided for a "defense fund" in the Agreement, is not clear.

For these reasons, we conclude that the trial court erred in ruling that the "$10,000 clause" in the Agreement is unenforceable as against public policy. The record does not reflect that this provision constitutes any limitation on Weaver's ability to seek court intervention to modify the custody and/or visitation provisions in the Agreement between these parties in the best interests of the child.

. . . Order reversed. Case remanded. Jurisdiction relinquished.

BOWLES, J., concurring. . . . Stated plainly, I agree that the agreement is not contrary to public policy *per se*. I write separately, however, because I believe that, while Mother's amended complaint is legally sufficient to survive preliminary objections, it is premature to opine as to whether the provision is enforceable in this case. . . .

Instantly, the four corners of the custody accord do not establish whether the $10,000 payments were intended either as penalties or a defense fund. The agreement simply does not disclose the intended purpose of the payments. Moreover, nothing in the amended complaint or custody accord revealed, much less suggested, that the fee provision was crafted as a penalty or as an impediment to Father's ability to litigate custody arrangements. Rather, the amended pleading and attached exhibit indicated that Father, a lawyer, both participated in drafting the provision that established the fee and had sufficient financial resources to pay it. Accordingly, mindful that the correct analysis is limited to Mother's amended complaint and the attached exhibit . . . , it does not appear with certainty that the law would preclude Mother from recovery based upon the facts averred.

The current facts and procedural posture of this case supply an inadequate basis for either the trial court's determination that this type of provision is fundamentally contrary to public policy or the majority's suggestion that the $10,000 fee is enforceable. Several factors exist that the trial court was unable to contemplate in this case due to the procedural posture of the matter and the fact that its review was limited to Mother's pleadings. Prior to reaching the ultimate decision regarding enforceability, a determination must first be made in consideration of the dynamics of this precise agreement vis-à-vis the parties' intentions and each person's relative financial status. Only then, after full deliberation, should the trial court determine the provision's enforceability.

Accordingly, for the foregoing reasons, I concur with the majority's decision to reverse the trial court order that sustained Father's preliminary objections to Mother's amended complaint. However, in my view, it is premature to confront the ultimate determination regarding whether the fee provision is, in fact, enforceable under the procedural posture of this case. Unlike my esteemed colleagues, I would unambiguously limit the holding in this case to the record before the trial court at this time.

JENKINS, J., dissenting. I respectfully dissent. I would affirm the trial court's order sustaining James P. Weaver's preliminary objections and dismissing Amy Huss's complaint seeking enforcement of the parties' agreement. Although rights involving child custody and visitation belong to the parents, these rights are limited to those which serve the best interest of the child. A child has a right to a custody arrangement that meets his or her best interests. In my view, a contractual provision that potentially hinders or chills an interested party's ability to ensure a custody arrangement that is in the child's best interest is against public policy and unenforceable. . . .

In Knorr v. Knorr, the Pennsylvania Supreme Court held:

> Parties to a divorce action may bargain between themselves and structure their agreement as best serves their interests, [Brown v. Hall, 495 Pa. 635, 435 A.2d 859 (1981)]. They have no power, however, to bargain away the rights of their children, [Sonder v. Sonder, 378 Pa. Super. 474, 549 A.2d 155 (1988)].

527 Pa. 83, 588 A.2d 503, 505 (1991). (footnotes omitted). In *Knorr*, the Court found it was not bound by the parties' agreement regarding child support payments. *Id.* at 505.

Equally as important to a child as monetary support, if not more so, is a custody arrangement that meets his or her best interests. Parents are free to enter into agreements regarding custody and visitation.[9] Miller v. Miller, 423 Pa. Super. 162, 620 A.2d 1161, 1165-66 (1993). However, a court is not bound by, and may set aside, such agreements. *Id.* In child custody proceedings, courts are charged with the task of designing a custody arrangement that is in the child's best interest. 23 Pa. C. S. §5328(a) ("[i]n ordering any form of custody, the court shall

---

9. This Court has described the usefulness of private custody arrangements as follows: "First, most parents genuinely love their children, and it is reasonable to assume that the children's welfare is a vital consideration in the parents' decision to resolve their dispute by agreement. One major reason that parents agree on custody is to spare their children the trauma inherent in an adversarial hearing. Second, parents have a better informational base upon which to make a decision about custody. The adversarial process is an inadequate means to assemble sufficient 'facts' to resolve custodial disputes satisfactorily. Third, it is difficult to protect a child from the painful pull of divided loyalties when his parents fail to agree. Parental agreements help to preserve an atmosphere of at least superficial peace between parents and thereby facilitate a much easier and more meaningful future relationship between the child and the non-custodial parent." *Miller*, 620 A.2d at 1164 (quoting Witmayer v. Witmayer, 320 Pa. Super. 372, 467 A.2d 371, 374-75 (1983)). Accordingly, the policy reasons that courts promote private agreements regarding custody include that the parents are likely to act in the best interests of the child and that it is in the best interests of the child to have an amicable resolution.

determine the best interests of the child by considering all relevant factors, giving weighted consideration to those factors which affect the safety of the child"). The focus is on the child, not the parent. . . .

A contractual provision that impedes the trial court's ability to review a custody or visitation arrangement is against public policy and unenforceable. *Cf.* Kraisinger v. Kraisinger, 928 A.2d 333, 345 (Pa. Super. 2007) (contract provision invalid where it "penalizes mother for, and therefore would act to discourage her from, seeking a court's review of the parties' agreement as to child support"). . . .

The majority attempts to distinguish *Knorr.* It reasons that *Knorr* addressed a child' right to adequate child support payments and, unlike child support payments, any right to custody and visitation belong to a parent, not a child. However, as stated above, the right of parents to craft a custody arrangement is always subject to the child's right to a custody plan that serves the child's best interests. There is no reason to treat custody actions differently than child support actions, as the goal of both is to ensure that a child's best interests are met. . . .

The majority asserts the "issue of whether a provision in a custody/visitation contract that places a serious impediment on either party's ability to seek court modification in the best interest of the child is not presently before this Court." It reasons the contract does not provide that the provision is intended to discourage Weaver from seeking intervention or that the payment would act as an impediment to his ability to do so. The majority claims whether it would be an impediment would depend on Weaver's ability to pay the $10,000.00 fee. The majority notes the contract states Weaver is "an attorney capable of earning a large salary," Weaver recognized the Agreement's terms were "fair, just, and reasonable," and he agreed that he voluntarily executed the agreement. *Id.* The majority further notes that it is unclear whether the parties intended to provide Huss with a defense fund. (footnote omitted).

The circumstances surrounding the drafting of the provision requiring a $10,000.00 payment are irrelevant to the analysis. Rather, any provision that requires payment to the other party for filing actions or motions to ensure that a child's best interests are met, is unenforceable. Regardless of Weaver's income or his ability to make a "large salary," a provision that would potentially prevent him from filing, or make him question his ability to file, an action to ensure a child's best interests, is against public policy.[10]

I believe the child's right to a custody arrangement that provides for his or her best interests is paramount, and therefore the contract provision requiring payment of $10,000.00 for any "modification or amendment" to custody or visitation sought is against public policy and unenforceable.

---

10. That this case is at the preliminary objection stage does not affect my analysis. I believe we must grant prospective relief from a contract provision requiring payment for seeking custody modification. That a party may, at some future date, receive relief from the contractual fee provision, does not alter that the fee provision could deter a person from seeking a custody arrangement that meets a child's best interests. Under the majority's rationale, if Weaver did not have the $10,000.00, he would be faced with a choice: (1) file a petition, knowing he could not abide by the contract terms, and then be forced to expend additional funds in a breach of contract action to establish that enforcement of the provision acted as an impediment to seeking custody modification in the best interests of the child; or (2) not file a petition to modify custody or visitation because he did not have the funds to pay the fee knowing that the custody arrangement was falling short of meeting the child's best interest. Therefore, such a provision could prevent court review of custody arrangements and allow a child to remain in a custody arrangement that does not meet his or her best interests.

NOTES AND QUESTIONS

1. *Huss* presents an example of a somewhat unusual agreement between unmarried parents, but showcases how courts think about what contract terms may include. The majority and dissent in *Huss* disagree about if and why a contract term with implications for custody modification offended public policy. How much latitude should courts give parties in drafting provisions on child custody in settlement agreements? Sarah Abramowicz summarized states' approaches to custody provisions in settlement agreements:

> There are two main approaches to considering [custody] agreements. Under the more prevalent approach, followed by the majority of the states, courts will enforce custody agreements made by divorced or separated parents only if to do so is consistent with the child's interests. Here, an agreement may be a factor to consider in assessing children's interests, but is given no deference. A substantial minority of states, on the other hand, require courts to enforce such agreements unless they find that to do so is adverse to the child's interests. Under this approach, the parental determination is given greater deference. A number of states, moreover, have found that courts can agree with the parents regarding custody without holding a full hearing about the child's interests, which increases the likelihood that the courts will not have the information or inclination to review the agreement carefully. But courts in all of these states nonetheless retain the authority to refuse enforcement of the parents' agreement on the basis that the child's interests require a different custodial arrangement.

Sarah Abramowicz, Contractualizing Custody, 83 Fordham L. Rev. 67, 82 (2014). Both the UMDA and the ALI Principles carve out protection for children's interests but do so in different ways. For instance, the ALI Principles provide that terms governing child support or custodial responsibilities are not enforceable unless such agreements are approved and adopted by the court. *Compare* §7.09(5) *with* §§2.06 and 3.13. What are the advantages and disadvantages for close court scrutiny of contract terms on custody?

2. Notice in the first footnote of *Huss* that the majority opinion distinguished the contract provision at issue from the contract term barring Huss from paying Weaver child support should the custodial arrangement change. Would such a term be enforceable? When prohibiting parties from contracting for lower amounts of child support than would be required under state guidelines, courts reason that the support award belongs to the child and not a parent. The *Huss* majority distinguished custody from support because custodial rights belong to the parent, not the child. The dissent disagreed with the majority's characterization. Do you think the distinction drawn by the majority opinion is persuasive? Why or why not?

3. The *Huss* majority, concurrence, and dissent also disagreed about whether the contract term at issue created an impediment for Weaver to pursue modification of custody. The majority opinion cites Kraisinger v. Kraisinger, 928 A.2d 333, 345 (Pa. Super. 2007), in which the court struck down a provision requiring a mother to pay attorney's fees were she to pursue custody modification. *Id.* ("A child's right to adequate support cannot be bargained away by either parent and any release or compromise is invalid to the extent it prejudices a child's welfare."). With which opinion in *Huss* on the effect and purpose of the $10,000 payment did you agree? Why?

4. Courts generally allow parties to agree to more extensive obligations than a court would impose on them. For example, in a jurisdiction that does not allow courts to order parents to support their children after the age of majority, an agreement to support an adult child attending school is usually enforceable. *See, e.g.,* Shortt v. Damron, 649 S.E.2d 283 (W. Va. 2007). In the same vein, parents may contract for covering children's expenses in greater amounts than child support formulas provide. Should the parties be able to agree to child support below the presumptive amount calculated under the child support guidelines but agree to a correspondingly greater amount of spousal support? What problems can you see with parents agreeing to support below the guidelines, even if that reduction is offset by higher alimony payments?

Parties might desire such an agreement for the purposes of tax deductions or for the purpose of future modifications. In most jurisdictions, if a court does not award spousal support at the time of the decree, it does not have jurisdiction to award it later. Therefore, in some jurisdictions parties may agree that a separation agreement that would not otherwise provide for spousal support will include a requirement that one spouse pay the other $1 per year. The idea is that if spousal support is needed later, the court can "modify" this provision. In other states, though, this tactic is not permitted.

5. If the parties have agreed to no spousal support or to spousal support for a limited term, should a court have authority to order support beyond that provided for in the agreement if the dependent spouse will otherwise become a "public charge"? *See, e.g.*, O'Brien v. O'Brien, 623 N.E.2d 485 (1993). *Compare* the UMDA *with* the ALI Principles. Note that the UMDA and ALI Principles differ in regard to the fairness of a settlement agreement, with the UMDA incorporating language on unconscionability and the ALI Principles on contract terms that "substantially impair the economic well-being of a party." Rarely do courts set aside a settlement agreement, even if the terms favor one party over another and even if one party did not have the advice of counsel. *See, e.g.*, Brennan-Duffy v. Duffy, 804 N.Y.S.2d 399, 400 (N.Y. App. Div. 2005) (holding that a settlement agreement will not be vacated because one party was unrepresented by counsel or because "some of its provisions were improvident or one-sided").

An example of an unconscionable agreement is In re Marriage of Thornhill, 200 P.3d 1083, 1084 (Colo. App. 2008), in which the court set aside the property settlement of a couple married for 27 years. The husband owned a substantial share of a profitable energy company he founded, and the wife worked low-wage jobs and cared for the couple's children:

> After considering the totality of the circumstances, we conclude the property disposition is not fair, just, or reasonable and we set it aside and remand for a new permanent orders hearing. The following facts support our conclusion that the agreement is unconscionable:
>
> - Importantly, despite the fact that the parties had more than one million dollars in marital assets, wife was not represented by counsel at the time the separation agreement was negotiated and signed. Although in recent years she earned a graduate degree in occupational therapy, the record does not indicate she is sophisticated in legal or financial matters.
> - Wife's father, who was chief financial officer of the [husband's] business, had assisted in negotiating the separation agreement. . . . However, purely by virtue of his role as chief financial officer, the father was required to attempt preservation of the business assets, which necessarily resulted in dual loyalties under the circumstances presented here.
> - Wife testified to her lack of mathematical ability, her need to rely on her father to explain financial details of the settlement, her repeated statements that she did not understand the details, and the fact that she was never presented with the promissory note referenced in the agreement concerning payment of husband's obligation to her.
>
> Thus, even accepting the [trial] court's implicit finding that there was no fraud, overreaching, concealment of assets, or sharp dealing, we conclude that the agreement is unconscionable. To accomplish the parties' avowed purpose of dividing equally the marital assets that existed at the time of the agreement, it provided that husband would pay wife $752,692, half of what was represented to be the marital assets at the time the agreement was entered into. However, he was not required to pay that sum to wife immediately. Rather, the parties' agreement called for him to pay it in equal monthly installments of $6,272 over ten years,

and failed to require him to pay her interest on the total sum or to secure the obligation. Accordingly, wife lost the ability to obtain the full use and enjoyment, as well as the investment value, of the entire sum, while husband, whose income is substantially greater than wife's, obtained the considerable benefit of retaining the use, enjoyment, and investment value of the unpaid balance. Thus, the present value of the payments to wife was considerably less than $756,692. As wife testified, "[husband] wants me to be [his] bank." Even applying a modest interest rate, the accumulated interest on $752,692 over ten years would be a considerable sum (citations omitted).

On appeal, the Supreme Court of Colorado did not reach the issue of whether the separation agreement was unconscionable and decided the case on other grounds. In re Marriage of Thornhill, 232 P.3d 782, 783 (2010). Does the Court of Appeals indicate which of the factors listed proved determinative of its finding of unconscionability? Would any of those factors standing alone make a case for vacating the settlement agreement at issue? *See* Van Orden v. Van Orden, 515 P.3d 119 (Idaho 2022) (settlement agreement was not substantively unconscionable because "wife received a $30,000 vehicle, payment of her student loans, avoiding disclosure of sensitive personal information, and release from all marital debt associated with parties' ranch, and given wife's other concerns, such as expediting divorce, making custody negotiations more amiable, and exiting the marriage debt-free, a similarly situated reasonable person might have agreed to the [settlement]").

As you read the next section, compare the arguments parties make when they seek to defeat enforcement of settlement agreements versus contesting enforcement of premarital or during-marriage contracts.

6. Often custody agreements take the form of parenting plans. Chapter 9 explored the ALI Principles that govern parenting plans, which seek to enable parties to solve their own problems and select their own means for resolving disputes (*e.g.*, arbitration, which is described in Chapter 12). Professor Abramowicz describes various approaches of state courts to parenting plans:

> Only one state, West Virginia, follows the recommendation of the ALI to give greater deference to parental custody agreements reached at separation or divorce. The West Virginia/ALI approach provides for the enforcement of such agreements—termed "parenting plans"—unless a court finds that an agreement was not knowing or voluntary or that enforcement will impose harm on the child. Even under the more deferential West Virginia/ALI approach to parental custody agreements, however, this deference seems limited to situations where parents have agreed to a parenting plan and then jointly asked the court to incorporate the plan into a court order. The West Virginia statute, following the ALI, indicates that a "prior agreement" regarding custody—an agreement to which one of the parents presumably no longer wants to adhere—is not enforceable, but instead only a factor for courts to consider in the event that the parents cannot agree on custody.
>
> Indeed, a court's decision to reject the parents' custody agreement often occurs when one of the parents has contested the arrangement that he or she formerly agreed to. Sometimes, a court may reject an earlier agreement on the basis that it has proved "unworkable," as courts have done, for instance, where parents initially agreed to offer each other the option to babysit for their child before making any other caretaking arrangements, but one of the parents found this arrangement too cumbersome to carry out, or, more typically, where parents have agreed to share decision-making authority but have not been able to do so without generating conflict.

Sarah Abramowicz, Contractualizing Custody, 83 Fordham L. Rev. 67, 82 (2014). *See also* Katharine T. Bartlett, Prioritizing Past Caretaking in Child-Custody Decisionmaking, 77 Law & Contemp. Probs. 29, 34, n.27 (2014) (describing the trend toward drafting parenting plans and the passage of the ALI Principles).

2. Post-Decree Attacks on Separation Agreements

Courts often do not scrutinize the terms of separation agreements closely at the time of divorce. Some time after the divorce decree has been entered, however, one of the parties may find fault with the agreement and the negotiating process that produced it. A successful attack at this point requires setting aside not only the agreement but also the decree.

Hresko v. Hresko
574 A.2d 24 (Md. App. 1990)

ALPERT, J. . . . During the spring or early summer of 1985, James and Marie Hresko decided to terminate their 24-year marriage. The parties agreed to and signed a separation and property settlement agreement on July 10, 1985. According to terms of the settlement agreement, James (appellant) agreed to pay $400 per month in child support, to pay the total costs of the minor child's college education, and to assume payment of certain family consumer debts. The agreement further provided that Marie (appellee) had the option of buying out appellant's interest in the family home three years from the date of the settlement agreement.

On August 4, 1987, appellee filed a Complaint for Absolute Divorce against appellant in the Circuit Court for Anne Arundel County. On October 5, 1987, appellant filed an answer to the complaint which did not contest the divorce. A hearing before Master Malcolm M. Smith was held on December 7, 1987, with only appellee and her counsel present. Based on the master's findings, the Honorable James A. Cawood, Jr. entered an order of divorce *a vinculo matrimonii* on December 23, 1987. A voluntary separation agreement that the parties had executed two years earlier was incorporated but not merged into the order.

In the summer of 1988, appellee exercised her option to buy out appellant's interest in the family home and on the day of settlement, August 4, 1988, paid appellant $30,000 in cash for his one-half interest. Appellant had assumed that appellee would require a mortgage to purchase his interest in the house and claimed that he was "stunned" when she fulfilled her obligation with cash. He then became convinced that a fraud had been perpetrated against him during the 1985 negotiations that led to the property settlement. This alleged fraud involved the concealment, by appellee, of at least $30,000 in cash at the time of the agreement. As a result of this belief, appellant filed a Motion to Revise Judgment and to Rescind Separation and Property Settlement Agreement, together with a memorandum of law and an affidavit. Appellee responded by filing a motion to dismiss appellant's motion. Judge Cawood held a hearing on appellee's motion on June 7, 1989. After briefly holding the matter sub curia, the judge issued a written opinion on June 13, 1989, granting appellee's motion to dismiss appellant's motion to revise judgment. . . .

In an action to set aside an enrolled judgment or decree, the moving party must initially produce evidence sufficient to show that the judgment in question was the product of fraud, mistake or irregularity. Furthermore, it has long been black letter law in Maryland that the type of fraud which is required to authorize the reopening of an enrolled judgment is extrinsic fraud and not fraud which is intrinsic to the trial itself.

Appellant contends that appellee concealed from him an unknown, but apparently sizable, sum of money at the time the two parties were negotiating the subject separation and property settlement agreement. In an affidavit accompanying his motion, appellant alleges that during negotiations between the parties prior to the agreement, appellee represented and constantly reiterated to him that she had no money in any account or investment except for a small reserve account used for her expenses during the summer when she was not working or receiving a salary from her public school teaching job. . . . Appellant claims that, based on

532 Part II Family Dissolution

these incidents and appellee's frequent assertions that she was not hiding money, he entered into the subject agreement.

Assuming without deciding that appellant has produced facts and circumstances sufficient to establish fraud, we will address whether this alleged fraud is extrinsic or intrinsic to the trial itself. We hold, based on appellant's claims and verified statements, that appellee's alleged concealment of funds is an example of, at most, intrinsic fraud.

Intrinsic fraud is defined as "[t]hat which pertains to issues involved in the original action or where acts constituting fraud were, or could have been, litigated therein." Black's Law Dictionary (5th ed. 1979). Extrinsic fraud, on the other hand, is "[f]raud which is collateral to the issues tried in the case where the judgment is rendered." *Id.*

Fraud is extrinsic when it actually prevents an adversarial trial. *Fleisher*, 483 A.2d 1312. In determining whether or not extrinsic fraud exists, the question is not whether the fraud operated to cause the trier of fact to reach an unjust conclusion, but whether the fraud prevented the actual dispute from being submitted to the fact finder at all. *Id.* In Schwartz v. Merchants Mortgage Co., 322 A.2d 544 (1974), the Court of Appeals, quoting from United States v. Throckmorton, 98 U.S. 61 (1878), provided examples of what would be considered extrinsic fraud:

> Where the unsuccessful party has been prevented from exhibiting fully his case, by fraud or deception practiced on him by his opponent, as by keeping him away from court, a false promise of a compromise; or where the defendant never had knowledge of the suit, being kept in ignorance by the acts of the plaintiff; or where an attorney fraudulently or without authority assumes to represent a party and connives at his defeat; . . . or where the attorney regularly employed corruptly sells out his client's interest in the other side — these, and similar cases which show that there has never been a real contest in the trial or hearing of the case, are reasons for which a new suit may be sustained to set aside and annul the former judgment or decree, and open the case for a new and a fair hearing.

Schwartz, 322 A.2d 544.

Appellant contends that appellee's alleged fraudulent representations were extrinsic to the subsequent divorce action because they took place over two years before its inception and served to prevent appellant from taking advantage of his right to an adversarial proceeding. He argues that appellee's concealment is a "fraud or deception practiced upon the unsuccessful party by his opponent as by keeping him away from court or making a false promise of a compromise."

As stated above, the issue of whether appellee's alleged fraudulent concealment of assets during pre-separation agreement negotiations is intrinsic or extrinsic to the divorce litigation is one of first impression in Maryland courts. Upon looking to other jurisdictions for guidance, we find conflict among our sister states.

California courts have uniformly recognized that the failure of one spouse to disclose the existence of community property assets constitutes extrinsic fraud. In re Marriage of Modnick, 663 P.2d 187 (Cal. 1983). The principle underlying these cases is that each spouse has an obligation to inform the other spouse of the existence of community property assets. This duty stems in part from the confidential nature of the marital relationship and from the fiduciary relationship that exists between spouses with respect to the control of community property. . . .

Other courts have found extrinsic fraud holding, as appellant would have us do, that a spouse's concealment or misrepresentation of assets can be classified as an intentional act by which the one spouse has prevented the other spouse from having a fair submission of the controversy and thus amounts to extrinsic fraud. Pilati v. Pilati, 592 P.2d 1374, 1380 (Mont. 1979).

Other jurisdictions have reached the opposite result, determining that the fraudulent concealment of assets by one spouse during a property settlement agreement is intrinsic to the divorce litigation. Recently, in Altman v. Altman, 150 A.D.2d 304, 542 N.Y.S.2d 7, 9 (1989), the New York Supreme Court, Appellate Division, held that alleged fraud in the negotiations of the separation agreement involves the issue in controversy and is not a deprivation of the opportunity to make a full and fair defense. The court reasoned that the alleged misrepresentations of financial status are in essence no different from any other type of perjury committed in the course of litigation and thus constitute intrinsic fraud.

Similarly, in Chapman v. Chapman, 591 S.W.2d 574, 577 (Tex. Civ. App. 1979), the Texas court refused to overturn on the basis of fraud a property settlement agreement incorporated into a divorce decree. The court stated that the fraud alleged at most related to untruths which misled the wife into acquiescence and approval of an unjust division of property. Because these misrepresentations bore only on issues in the trial (or which could have been at issue in the trial), they, therefore, amounted to no more than intrinsic fraud. . . .

We are persuaded that these latter cases are the better reasoned ones. Misrepresentations or concealment of assets made in negotiations leading to a voluntary separation and property settlement agreement later incorporated into a divorce decree represent matters intrinsic to the trial itself. In fact, a determination of each party's respective assets, far from being a collateral issue, would seem to be a central issue in a property settlement agreement. . . .

No "extrinsic fraud" prevented appellant from seeking trial and this court will not, therefore, reopen the decree in the present case. To rule otherwise would be to subject every enrolled divorce decree that includes a property settlement to revision upon discovery of alleged fraud in the inducement of the settlement. Public policy of this state demands an end to litigation once the parties have had an opportunity to present in court a matter for determination, the decision has been rendered, and the litigants afforded every opportunity for review.

NOTES AND QUESTIONS

1. For purposes of attacks made on an agreement after the parties have signed it, what difference does it make that the agreement has been the basis for a divorce decree? Should it make a difference? Why or why not? Should a decree that was based on a separation agreement be given the same amount of protection from collateral attack that a decree entered at the close of a trial has?

2. Are parties negotiating a divorce in a confidential relationship so that they have a duty of full disclosure to each other? Is this situation distinguishable from that of engaged people negotiating a premarital agreement? If each party is represented by counsel, are they in a confidential relationship? What duties of disclosure do the parties have then? *See* In re Marriage of Roepenack, 966 N.E.2d 1024, 1032 (2012) (husband's misreporting income on a child support form and failure to disclose marital assets in the business he owned constituted unconscionable and fraud because "it is likely that the marriage settlement agreement would not have been approved had the trial court been furnished with complete information").

Courts have historically been reluctant to reopen litigated judgments because of their desire to promote finality, and a number of cases hold, for example, that perjury constitutes intrinsic fraud that will not support a collateral attack on the judgment. *See, e.g.,* Shih Ping Li v. Tzu Lee, 62 A.3d 212, 237 (Md. App. 2013). In some jurisdictions, however, the courts have become more willing to provide relief from judgments procured through an intentional effort to conceal assets. *See, e.g.,* Ray v. Ray, 647 S.E.2d 237 (S.C. 2007). In *Ray*, the husband

and wife sold a pharmacy they jointly owned to CVS. The wife, however, arranged separately to sign an agreement not to compete with CVS for an additional $130,000, but delayed the payment until after the divorce became final and concealed the agreement from her husband. The majority found that the deliberate effort to structure the agreement to take effect only after the divorce constituted "extrinsic" fraud while the dissent characterized it as a classic case of "intrinsic" fraud. Would the *Ray* majority have reached the same conclusion if, instead of going to trial, the husband had reached a settlement incorporated into the divorce decree without knowledge of the contract with CVS?

3. As a matter of contract law, would Mrs. Hresko's concealment of assets (assuming for these purposes that she did hide them) be a basis for setting aside the agreement? On what ground? *See* McNeil v. Hoskyns, 337 P.3d 46, 49-50 (2014) (holding that a court may modify alimony, otherwise not subject to modification according to the parties' agreement, if a party defrauds the court by knowing of but failing to disclose accidental overpayment of alimony). *See* In Re Marriage of Hutchinson, 974 N.W.2d 466 (Iowa 2022) (rejecting a wife's request to vacate a divorce decree that released wife's right to retirement accounts because failure to disclose an asset is intrinsic, not extrinsic fraud and because she could have reasonably discovered the pension prior to the decree's approval).

4. How can a lawyer ensure that the other spouse is not hiding assets? Would you as a lawyer rely on the opposing party's representations about value? *See, e.g.*, Gainey v. Gainey, 675 S.E.2d 792 (S.C. App. 2009); In re Marriage of Conrad, 81 P.3d 749, 751 (Or. App. 2003); In re Kasner 437 P.3d 1149 (Or. App. 2019).

PROBLEMS

1. Jack and Marian separated five years ago, and they have lived in different cities since then. During their marriage Jack purchased a business, and their original plan was that Marian and their two children would join him once the business was well established. However, Jack always reported that the business was struggling, and Marian and the children never made the move. When Jack moved away, Marian went back to work, since the children were in school, and she has been self-supporting since Jack left. Jack has sent Marian $400 per month as support for the children. Last year Jack and Marian agreed to divorce, and they negotiated a separation agreement by themselves without a lawyer. Jack told Marian that his business was nearly bankrupt and that he could not afford to pay spousal support but would continue to pay the same amount of child support. He offered to let Marian take the house (and its mortgage payments) and told her there was not much else to share. Jack then took the agreement to a lawyer, who drafted a petition for divorce. Marian consented to entry of a decree consistent with the terms of the agreement. After the time for appeal had passed, Marian learned that in fact Jack's business has been very successful and that he has become a wealthy man. Under the approach of *Hresko*, can Marian successfully reopen the divorce on the grounds of fraud? In a jurisdiction that presumes that married people are in a confidential relationship, will Marian have greater success? Why or why not?

2. Hal and Hank live in a state in which the appreciation in value of premarital property is marital property unless the increase is attributable purely to market factors or inflation. Hank purchased a house before marriage, and he never added Hal's name to the title of the house during the marriage. During the marriage they made mortgage payments on the house, paying an additional $3500 in principal. They also did some remodeling, at a cost of $4500, which increased the house's value by $11,000. During the marriage the housing market was rising as well. At the end of the marriage the fair market value of the house was $24,000 greater than it had been at the beginning of the marriage. Hank was the family bookkeeper, and only he knew this information during the marriage. If Hal and Hank live in a jurisdiction that imposes a duty of disclosure on spouses who are negotiating a separation agreement without attorneys, how much of the information about the house must Hank disclose and why?

3. Modification of Settlement Agreements

Support awards are ordinarily modifiable; property awards are not. If a divorce agreement provides that a support award is not modifiable, does the agreement supersede the power of the court to modify the agreement? In child support cases, the answer is no because the right belongs to the child, who is not a party to the agreement. In spousal support cases, jurisdictions have taken varying approaches. The following case summarizes these approaches, although the majority and dissent interpret cases that support these approaches differently. At the heart of the differences between the majority and the dissent is the role of courts in policing the fairness of agreements for the protection of vulnerable parties.

Toni v. Toni
636 N.W.2d 396 (N.D. 2001)

VANDE WALLE, C.J. . . . Conrad and Sheila Toni were married from July 9, 1971, until May 10, 1999. The couple had three children during the marriage, and one of them was a minor at the time of the divorce. Both parties are employed in Fargo: Conrad as a urologist, and Sheila as a clerk at Barnes & Noble Bookstore.

Before their divorce was granted, the parties entered into a "Custody and Property Settlement Agreement" which comprehensively addressed all divorce issues. The agreement stated that, although Conrad had been represented by counsel, Sheila "has not been represented by counsel and has been informed that Maureen Holman does not represent her interests in this matter but has not sought such independent counsel and enters into this custody and property settlement agreement of her own free will." The agreement also stated, "both parties agree that each has made a full disclosure to the other of all assets and liabilities and is satisfied that this custody and property settlement agreement is fair and equitable," and "each party has entered into this custody and property settlement agreement intending it to be a full and final settlement of all claims of every kind, nature, and description which either party may have or claim to have, now or in the future, against the other and, except as is expressly provided herein to the contrary, each is released from all further liability of any kind, nature or description whatsoever to the other."

The agreement provided for "joint physical custody" of the couple's minor daughter, who was expected to graduate from high school in May 1999. The agreement divided the parties' real property, stocks and retirement accounts, but did not disclose the value of those assets. The agreement also contained the following provision on spousal support:

> Commencing May 1, 1999, Conrad shall pay to Sheila the sum of $5,000 per month as and for spousal support. Said payments will continue on the first day of each month thereafter until the death of either party, Sheila's remarriage, or until the payment due on April 1, 2002 has been made. It is intended that the spousal support payable to Sheila shall be included in Sheila's gross income for income tax purposes and shall be deductible by Conrad. The court shall be divested of jurisdiction to modify in any manner whatsoever the amount and term of the spousal support awarded to Sheila immediately upon entry of the judgment and decree herein. The court shall retain jurisdiction to enforce Conrad's obligation to pay spousal support to Sheila.

At the divorce hearing, Conrad appeared with his attorney, but Sheila . . . did not personally appear. The trial court granted the divorce and, finding the parties' agreement to be "a fair, just and equitable settlement," incorporated its provisions into the divorce decree.

In November 2000, Sheila moved under N.D.C.C. §14-05-24 to modify the spousal support award. Sheila claimed in an affidavit that Conrad earned $14,000 per month in "take-home pay" when they married and she believed he continued to earn a "similar" amount per month, while she earns $1,000 per month working full-time as a clerk at Barnes & Noble Bookstore. Sheila further alleged, although income from assets she received in the divorce had paid her about $2,700 per month, the "return on those assets this year has been almost nothing." Sheila estimated her monthly expenses to be $5,340, and said her accountant informed her she could convert a retirement account into an annuity producing $2,000 per month in additional income, but she is "afraid to convert this to an annuity because I believe I need it for my retirement." Sheila claimed she has a "neurological condition" that causes her trouble sleeping, and she stayed home with the children during her marriage to Conrad rather than pursuing her own career. Sheila also stated:

> I met Bob Boman after I separated from my husband. I had agreed to a reduced three-year term for spousal support because Dr. Boman was in his residency following medical school. Once he finished, we had agreed that he would pay the family expenses. Conrad and I had decided to divorce in August and I met Bob in October. Bob and I planned to marry after the divorce. Bob and I are no longer together and I do not receive any money from him.

The parties agreed to submit to the trial court the sole issue whether the provision of the parties' agreement divesting the court of jurisdiction to modify spousal support was valid under North Dakota law. . . . The trial court dismissed Sheila's motion, ruling "the parties entered into a binding contract which was incorporated into the judgment and . . . the court now lacks jurisdiction to modify spousal support."

We assume, for purposes of argument only, that Sheila's claims of lowered investment yields and a failed relationship are sufficient to constitute a material change of circumstances to support a motion to modify spousal support. . . . The legal question in this case is whether the parties' divorce stipulation regarding spousal support can divest the trial court of its statutory authority to modify the amount and duration of support. . . .

. . . Under N.D.C.C. §14-05-24, the trial court generally retains continuing jurisdiction to modify spousal support, child support, and child custody upon a showing of changed circumstances. This Court has construed the statute, however, to not allow a trial court continuing jurisdiction to modify a final property distribution, and we have held when a trial court makes no initial award of spousal support and fails to expressly reserve jurisdiction over the issue, the court subsequently lacks jurisdiction to award spousal support. Sheila argues N.D.C.C. §14-05-24 gives a trial court the unconditional right to modify a spousal support award, regardless of any agreement by divorcing parties purporting to divest the court of that power.

We encourage peaceful settlements of disputes in divorce matters. . . . It is the promotion of the strong public policy favoring prompt and peaceful resolution of divorce disputes that generates a judicial bias in favor of the adoption of a stipulated agreement of the parties. We have also noted a person may waive "all rights and privileges to which a person is legally entitled, whether secured by contract, conferred by statute, or guaranteed by the constitution, provided such rights and privileges rest in the individual who has waived them and are intended for his benefit."

In line with these principles, this Court has held a trial court has continuing jurisdiction to modify child support notwithstanding parental divorce settlement agreements prohibiting or limiting the court's modification powers, because the right to child support belongs to the child rather than to the parent, rendering such agreements violative of public policy and invalid. On the other hand, we have encouraged spousal support awards based on agreements between the divorcing parties, and noted those agreements "should be changed only with great reluctance by the trial court." Although this Court has often said a spousal support award based on an agreement between the parties can be modified upon a showing of material change of circumstances, we have not been confronted with a contractual settlement clause, adopted by the trial court and incorporated into the divorce decree, attempting to divest the court of its continuing jurisdiction to modify the amount and term of the spousal support award.

Jurisdictions differ over their treatment of agreements between divorcing couples seeking to limit a court's ability to modify spousal support arrangements. Some jurisdictions, by statute, specifically allow parties to enter into nonmodifiable spousal support agreements. (citations omitted.)

Several jurisdictions, by judicial decision, have allowed contractual waivers of the right to seek spousal support modification. (citations omitted.)

We think the reasoning of the current trend of jurisdictions which allow divorcing couples to agree to make spousal support nonmodifiable is persuasive.

This result is consistent with our prior caselaw on spousal support. In *Becker*, 262 N.W.2d at 484, this Court held, unless a trial court makes an initial award of spousal support or expressly reserves jurisdiction over the issue, the court lacks jurisdiction under N.D.C.C. §14-05-24 to subsequently modify its decision and award spousal support. The original divorce decree in *Becker* stated, "'neither party shall pay alimony to the other,'" and that language was incorporated from the parties' stipulation and property settlement agreement found to be "fair and equitable" by the trial court. This Court ruled the contract provision was unambiguous, and the "parties are bound by their contract provision for no alimony even if the court is not." We see no valid distinction between a stipulation to waive all spousal support at the time of the initial divorce decree and a waiver of future modification. If a spouse can waive all right to spousal support, it logically follows that a spouse can waive the right to modification.

In response to the argument that contracting parties cannot divest a court of its jurisdiction under a statute similar to N.D.C.C. §14-05-24, the court in *Karon*, 435 N.W.2d at 503, reasoned:

> It is not the parties to the stipulation who have divested the court of ability to relitigate the issue of maintenance. The court had the authority to refuse to accept the terms of the stipulation in part or *in toto*. The trial court stands in place and on behalf of the citizens of the state as a third party to dissolution actions. It has a duty to protect the interests of both parties and all the citizens of the state to ensure that the stipulation is fair and reasonable to all. The court did so here and approved the stipulation and incorporated the terms therein in its decree. Thus, the decree is final absent fraud. . . .

Our caselaw invalidating parental divorce stipulations prohibiting or limiting a court's modification powers over child support is governed by public policy principles entirely different from those present when reviewing an agreement concerning spousal support. While a spousal support agreement "serves primarily to determine the interests of the contracting parties themselves," a child support agreement "directly affects the interests of the children of the marriage, who have the most at stake as a result of such an agreement but who have the least ability to protect their interests." "Put simply, the parties to a [spousal support] agreement are both grown-ups, free to bargain with their own legal rights." Freedom to contract on terms not specifically prohibited by statute, is the major public policy question presented here.

Permitting parties to determine the future modifiability of their spousal support agreements maximizes the advantages of careful future planning and eliminates uncertainties based on the fear of subsequent motions to increase or decrease the obligations of the parties. In *Staple*, 616 N.W.2d at 228, the court relied on public policy reasons identified by the American Academy of Matrimonial Lawyers (AAML) for validating agreements to waive future modification of spousal support awards:

> The AAML comments that "recognizing and enforcing" the parties' waiver of modification "does no violence to public policy, and is consistent with the reasonable expectancy interests of the parties." The AAML also offers five public policy reasons why courts should enforce duly executed nonmodifiable alimony arrangements: (1) Nonmodifiable agreements enable parties to structure package settlements, in which alimony, asset divisions, attorney fees, postsecondary tuition for children, and related matters are all coordinated in a single, mutually acceptable agreement; (2) finality of divorce provisions allows predictability for parties planning their postdivorce lives; (3) finality fosters judicial economy; (4) finality and predictability lower the cost of divorce for both parties; (5) enforcing agreed-upon provisions for alimony will encourage increased compliance with agreements by parties who know that their agreements can and will be enforced by the court.

(footnote omitted). . . . It has been noted that honoring and enforcing nonmodification agreements will "discourage former spouses from using the modification process 'repeatedly for vexatious purposes only.'" In *Karon*, 435 N.W.2d at 504, the court also found "compelling" amicus curiae's argument that setting aside the parties' spousal support agreement incorporated into the divorce decree would be "insulting and demeaning to women," because it would mean "the state must protect them in the manner it protects children in the role of parens patriae," resulting "in chaos in the family law field and declining respect for binding agreements as well." . . .

The divorce court found the agreement to be "a fair, just and equitable settlement" of the parties' divorce action and incorporated the provisions of the agreement into the divorce decree. We conclude the trial court correctly ruled it had no jurisdiction under N.D.C.C. §14-05-24 to entertain Sheila's motion to modify the spousal support award. . . .

The trial court's order is affirmed.

MARING, J., dissenting. . . . We have consistently concluded trial courts have the power to modify spousal support awards regardless of what the parties may have agreed to in their stipulation. . . . The majority opinion deviates from these holdings today. The principle of finality has never applied to spousal support or child support. If parties need finality and freedom to agree to a definitive spousal support, then we should not modify their agreement for any reason. Parties, however, should not be able to bind themselves in advance to an amount and duration regardless of what circumstances arise because the right to seek modification of a judgment for spousal support is not only given for the protection of persons obligated to pay and the persons who are entitled to support, but also for the benefit of society. If a spouse becomes destitute, then society will bear the burden of support.

We are not dealing with contract law in these cases; we are dealing with family law matters. When, as in this case, a trial court wholly incorporates a settlement agreement into a divorce judgment, the settlement agreement merges with the judgment and "ceases to be independently viable or enforceable." "Consequently, when a stipulation is incorporated into a divorce judgment, we are concerned only with interpretation and enforcement of the judgment, not with the underlying contract." "As such, the court retains management and control over the incorporated stipulation, and remedies can be sought in the divorce action rather than starting afresh with another lawsuit based on the stipulation as a contract." A court dealing with family law matters and exercising powers granted by the Legislature cannot divest itself of the power to modify a judgment contrary to legislative will. . . .

The majority . . . instead abrogates the will of the Legislature and concludes a court can divest itself of the power conferred by statute to modify decrees of spousal support. However, a number of the decisions relied on by the majority are distinguishable from the case at hand and directly conflict with our statutes and prior case law.

In Beasley v. Beasley, 707 So. 2d 1107, 1108 (Ala. Civ. App. 1997), the parties' agreement stated it could not be modified unless the parties consented in writing. However, the decision in *Beasley* turned on whether the property rights and the alimony rights were integrated in the agreement. *Id.* The court never even addressed the portion of the agreement regarding modification. . . .

The next decision cited by the majority is Rockwell v. Rockwell, 681 A.2d 1017 (Del. 1996). *Rockwell* is distinguishable from the case at hand in that the parties never stipulated to divest the court of jurisdiction at all. At issue in *Rockwell* was whether the statutory standard for modification of alimony applied when parties stipulated to an alimony award. In concluding that it did not apply, the court reasoned "with regard to alimony awards, the stipulation, merger, or incorporation of the parties' voluntary agreement into a court order does not divest that agreement of its contractual nature." Thus, the court held "unlike a prior judicial determination of alimony, the Family Court cannot modify an agreement between the parties regarding alimony, pursuant to the 'real and substantial change' statutory standard." *Id.* In contrast, we have stated "once the settlement agreement is merged into the divorce decree, it is interpreted and enforced as a final judgment of the court, not as a separate contract between the parties." *Sullivan*, 506 N.W.2d at 399. . . .

Relying on Voigt v. Voigt, 670 N.E.2d 1271, 1279 (Ind. 1996), the majority lists Indiana as a jurisdiction which, by judicial decision, has allowed contractual waivers of the right to seek spousal support modification. However, the decision in *Voigt* turned on a statute which provided: "The disposition of property settled by such an agreement and incorporated and merged into the decree shall not be subject to subsequent modification by the court except as the agreement itself may prescribe or the parties may subsequently consent." *Id.* at 1278 (quoting Ind. Code Ann. §31-1-11.5-10(c) (West 1979)). . . .

In *Karon*, the stipulation at issue expressly stated: "Except for the aforesaid maintenance, each party waives and is forever barred from receiving any spousal maintenance whatsoever from one another, and this court is divested from having any jurisdiction whatsoever to award temporary or permanent spousal maintenance to either of the parties." 35 N.W.2d at 502. Unlike the stipulation in *Karon*, the stipulation at issue in this case contained no express waiver of the statutory right to modification. . . . Furthermore, *Karon*, which was a four to three decision, has been superseded by statute. . . . Under the current Minnesota statute, non-modifiable spousal support agreements are only enforceable "if the court makes specific findings that the stipulation is fair and equitable, is supported by consideration described in the findings, and that full disclosure of each party's financial circumstances has occurred." Minn. Stat. §518.552, subd. 5 (1996).

The decision of the Supreme Court of Wisconsin in Nichols v. Nichols, 162 Wis. 2d 96, 469 N.W.2d 619 (Wis. 1991), can also be distinguished. The Wisconsin Supreme Court decided to recognize an exception to its general rule that maintenance is always subject to modification. It concluded a party is estopped from seeking modification if:

> both parties entered into the stipulation freely and knowingly, . . . the overall settlement is fair and equitable and not illegal or against public policy, and . . . one party subsequently seeks to be released from the terms of the court order on the grounds that the court could not have entered the order it did without the parties' agreement.

Therefore, the Wisconsin Supreme Court will enforce a waiver of modification only if the requirements of the doctrine of estoppel are established.

. . . The majority reasons, "If a spouse can waive all right to spousal support, it logically follows that a spouse can waive the right to modification." I do not agree with this logic. When a trial court orders spousal support, it does so to accomplish a variety of objectives; i.e., rehabilitation, economic parity, equalization of the burden of divorce, etc. It logically follows that if spousal support is not ordered, the need to attain these objectives did not exist. If the need did not exist, modification under N.D.C.C. §14-05-24 is not necessary because there is no objective the modification would further. However, when spousal support is ordered initially, trial courts must have the power to modify the spousal support award in order to accomplish the objective for which it was originally ordered.

Like this Court, Oregon courts recognize that "when no spousal support was awarded in the original decree, the court cannot modify the decree to provide spousal support." At the same time, however, Oregon courts recognize the rule that "specific language in the decree or in an underlying property settlement incorporated in the decree does not bar the court from modifying the decree as it relates to spousal support." . . . The reason for this rule and the reason we should not travel down the path taken by the majority opinion was well summarized by the Supreme Court of Oregon in Prime v. Prime, 172 Or. 34, 139 P.2d 550 (Or. 1943).

> The right to alimony is, therefore, based upon the statute and not upon any contractual obligations. The law is designed for the protection of the parties and to promote the welfare of society. How, then, can parties, by any private agreement, oust the court of jurisdiction to regulate the payment of alimony when the status of the parties justifies a modification? Any agreement of the parties in reference to the payment of alimony was made in view of the statute authorizing the court to modify the same. The mere fact that the court incorporated in the decree the stipulation concerning alimony is immaterial. It is entirely possible that, while the court undoubtedly considered the stipulation of the parties fair and equitable at the time the decree was rendered, it might, upon a showing of subsequent changed conditions, deem it unjust. To hold otherwise would defeat the very purpose and spirit of the statute.

Prime, at 554-55 (quoting Warrington v. Warrington, 160 Or. 77, 83 P.2d 479 (Or. 1938)).

Sheila also argues that, even if nonmodifiable spousal support agreements are enforceable, the particular spousal support agreement at issue in this case does not prevent a trial court from modifying the spousal support award under N.D.C.C. §14-05-24. . . .

The parties to this agreement were married for 28 years. They had three children, one of whom was a minor at the time of the divorce. Conrad was 53 years old at the time of the divorce and employed as a urologist making $14,000 per month in take home pay. Sheila was 51 years old and is employed as clerk at a bookstore making $1,000 per month. The property division did not reveal any valuations of the assets of the parties. On these facts, the trial court found the agreement to be "fair, just, and equitable."

Although we favor prompt and peaceful settlements of divorces, we must not sacrifice our responsibility to ensure they are fair and equitable. . . .

. . . Our statutes and case law certainly set the stage for permanent spousal support under the facts of this case, which include a long-term marriage, forgone career opportunities, and a huge disparity in earning capacity and standard of living.

The majority argues a person can waive their statutory right to seek modification of spousal support. However, "for a waiver to be effective, it must be a voluntary and intentional relinquishment and abandonment of a known existing right, advantage, benefit, claim or privilege which, except for such waiver, the party would have enjoyed." . . . Nowhere in this agreement does Sheila acknowledge she is voluntarily and intentionally waiving that right. Furthermore, Sheila was not represented by counsel according to the agreement. Under these circumstances, I am of the opinion Sheila did not effectively waive her right to seek modification of spousal support.

. . . Unfortunately, the trial court's mere recitation that the agreement is "a fair, just and equitable settlement" is a far cry from the Uniform Marriage and Divorce Act's requirement that the trial court make a finding whether the agreement is unconscionable, a standard which "includes protection against overreaching, concealment of assets, and sharp dealing" and inquiry into "the conditions under which the agreement was made, including the knowledge of the other party." *Id.* The risk of overreaching in divorce stipulations where one party is unrepresented is significant, and without a requirement that the trial court actively engage in determining the conditions under which the agreement was entered, the risk increases tremendously. The decision reached by the majority today provides no protection whatsoever against these risks.

I am also concerned that there is nothing in the record of this case to indicate the trial court took an active role in determining the stipulation was fair and equitable. The Minnesota Supreme Court has stated the trial court "stands in place and on behalf of the citizens of the state as a third party to dissolution actions . . . to protect the interests of both parties and all the citizens of the state to ensure that the stipulation is fair and reasonable to all."

I, therefore, respectfully dissent and would reverse and remand.

NOTES AND QUESTIONS

1. *Toni* discusses the substantive issue of whether North Dakota law permits the parties to agree to limit the courts' jurisdiction to modify support awards. Other cases, including some of those discussed in *Toni*, turn on the technical issue of whether the agreement has been "merged" into the decree, making it part of a judicial order, or whether the court merely "approved," "ratified," or "incorporated" the agreement into the decree, making it enforceable as a contract. The court in In re Hereford, 756 P.2d 30 (Or. 1988), explained:

A great deal of incomprehensible domestic relations law in the State of West Virginia hinges upon the technicality of whether a property settlement has been "ratified and confirmed" by a court, in which case the parties are left to contract remedies for the enforcement of the settlement or, alternatively, whether provisions of a property settlement are "merged" into the divorce decree. If the provisions are "merged" they become subject to the continuing jurisdiction of the court which may extinguish or enlarge rights to periodic payments (alimony) initially provided by the property settlement agreement.

We have held that where a property settlement agreement is merely "ratified and confirmed" the property settlement agreement does not become part of the decree and any periodic payments (alimony) provided for in such property settlement agreement can be neither enlarged nor diminished by the circuit court. Where, however, a property settlement agreement providing for alimony or periodic payments is merged or made a part of the decree, we have held that the circuit court may increase or decrease the amount of payments in subsequent proceedings in the same way that it could if it had awarded alimony after a contest without any property settlement agreement.

In *Hereford*, the wife, who was in a nursing home and dependent on support payments, survived the husband. If the support award were merged into the divorce decree, the court could order support only until the death of the payor. On the other hand, the agreement provided that support was to continue until the wife's death or remarriage, and as a contract term, it could be enforced against the payor's estate. The court mused, "We dream today of inaugurating a system of domestic relations law in this State which is not dependent upon the use of words of art." The opinion speculated that the lawyers who drafted the agreement used the "so-called 'words of art' . . . without intending or implying any particular legal consequences," and it concluded that the one clear (and equitable) intent was to have the support continue until the wife's death. For a review of the aftermath of *Hereford* and of the abundant and confusing case law in this area, *see* Doris Del Tosto Brogan, Divorce Settlement Agreements: The Problem of Merger or Incorporation and the Status of the Agreement in Relation to the Decree, 67 Neb. L. Rev. 235 (1988).

2. In *Toni*, would the distinction between merger into the decree versus ratification and confirmation by the court make any difference to the outcome of the case? The dissent observes, "We are not dealing with contract law in these cases; we are dealing with family law matters. When, as in this case, a trial court wholly incorporates a settlement agreement into a divorce judgment, the settlement agreement merges with the judgment and 'ceases to be independently viable or enforceable.'" If the trial court had ratified and confirmed the agreement, but not incorporated it into the decree, would the dissent reach a different conclusion about its modifiability? Does the dissent suggest that substantially different policies underlie the exercise of judicial authority from those addressing enforcement of private agreements? If so, is the distinction between merger into the decree and ratification and confirmation a substantive policy matter? Or is the real problem the failure of trial courts to police agreements more carefully?

3. If the court ratifies but does not incorporate the separation agreement into the divorce decree, may either party be held in contempt for failing to comply with the terms of the agreement? Why or why not?

4. States vary substantially in their treatment of a court's ability to modify an order based on a separation agreement. For example, in Rockwell v. Rockwell, 681 A.2d 1017 (Del. 1996), the court rejected the distinction between incorporation and merger and concluded that the underlying agreement retains its nature as a contract, and, therefore, that a court cannot modify an agreement regarding support according to the standard normally used for court-ordered support. Note, however, that the Supreme Court of Delaware did not apply *Rockwell*'s holding to a custody matter. Morrisey v. Morrisey, 45 A.3d 102, 107 (2012) ("*Rockwell* is not applicable to custody and visitation agreements. . . . Because alimony does not directly affect the children, we decline to extend *Rockwell*'s contract principles analysis to parental agreements involving child visitation.").

In contrast, in Massachusetts, even if the agreement survives the decree as an independently enforceable contract, the court has power to modify the spousal support terms in the decree, though in deciding whether to do so a court is to consider the parties' expressed desire that the support terms not be modifiable. Bercume v. Bercume, 704 N.E.2d 177 (Mass. 1998). In Idaho, if the agreement is merged into the decree, support terms may be modified without consent of the parties unless the court finds that the agreement is integrated. This means that the parties agreed that the property division and support terms were "reciprocal consideration" and thus that the support provisions are "necessarily part and parcel of a division of property." Keeler v. Keeler, 958 P.2d 599 (Idaho App. 1998).

5. The distinction between a contract and a decree may affect the power of the court to grant relief. In Alabama, for example, the court does not have the authority to order alimony payments to a party who remarries. The couple, however, may agree contractually to provide for such payments. In Ex parte Murphy, 886 So. 2d 90 (Ala. 2003), the Supreme Court of Alabama accordingly held that when the parties petitioned the court to incorporate an alimony agreement into the decree in light of one of the parties' remarriage, the court lost the authority to order continuing alimony payments. *See* ALI Principles of Family Dissolution §7.10, which provides that contract terms unenforceable as terms of a decree survive as independent contracts even if the rest of the agreement is incorporated into the decree.

6. If a court incorporates a separation agreement into a divorce decree and the agreement and decree allow for modification of spousal support after certain events, if the parties agree to reduce support but do not move the court to modify the decree, is the payor obligated to pay the amount in the decree or the amount in the modified agreement?

7. If a court incorporates a separation agreement into a divorce decree, and the agreement and the decree do not provide for modification of spousal support, are there any circumstances in which the court can nonetheless modify the award? In Richardson v. Richardson, 218 S.W.3d 426 (Mo. 2007), the Missouri Supreme Court held that where the separation agreement had been incorporated into the divorce decree and expressly provided for nonmodifiable alimony, the court had no discretion to modify the payments even when the ex-husband alleged that his former wife had attempted to have him murdered.

8. Uniform Marriage and Divorce Act (UMDA) Section 306 deals with the relationship between the agreement and the decree in the following way:

> (d) If the court finds that the separation agreement is not unconscionable as to disposition of property or maintenance, and not unsatisfactory as to support:
> (1) unless the separation agreement provides to the contrary, its terms shall be set forth in the decree of dissolution or legal separation and the parties shall be ordered to perform them, or
> (2) if the separation agreement provides that its terms shall not be set forth in the decree, the decree shall identify the separation agreement and state that the court has found the terms not unconscionable.
> (e) Terms of the agreement set forth in the decree are enforceable by all remedies available for enforcement of a judgment, including contempt, and are enforceable as contract terms.
> (f) Except for terms concerning the support, custody, or visitation of children, the decree may expressly preclude or limit modification of terms set forth in the decree if the separation agreement so provides. Otherwise, terms of a separation agreement set forth in the decree are automatically modified by modification of the decree.

If an agreement is incorporated into the divorce decree, can one of the parties later challenge it as unconscionable? *Compare* In re Marriage of Nilles, 955 N.E.2d 611 (Ill. App. 2011) (rejecting unconscionability challenge to nonmodifiable support award on the grounds that the agreement must be determined to be unconscionable when signed, not in light of financial circumstances ten years later), *with* Stewart v. Stewart, 41 A.3d 401 (Del. 2012) (holding that a lifetime award that was not modifiable even in the event of the wife's marriage or cohabitation was unconscionable). *See also* In re Marriage of Callahan, 984 N.E.2d 531 (Ill. App. 2013) (permitting post-judgment attack on settlement as unconscionable and procured through fraud because unrepresented wife relied on husband's attorney's inaccurate description of the implications of the agreement).

PROBLEM

When Judy and Richard were divorced in 1995, Richard was a surgeon earning $100,000 per year, and he had unearned income of $15,000 per year and property worth $600,000. Judy was a homemaker who received property worth $400,000, consisting mostly of the marital home. Their separation agreement provided that Richard will pay Judy one-third of his annual gross earned income until his death, her death, or her remarriage. The agreement also provided that the parties intended it to survive entry of a divorce decree and that it would not be modifiable "even though future events might occur that would alter the position of either party as it exists [at the time of the divorce]." Richard, who is now 55 years old, has recently retired. He has no earned income and is living on unearned income of $50,000, and his property has increased in value to $1 million. Judy, who is 57, earns $97 per week as a museum tour guide, and she has unearned income of $104 per month. Richard has stopped paying Judy spousal support, saying that he no longer has any earned income. Judy has filed a petition to modify the decree, seeking one-third of Richard's gross unearned income, notwithstanding the separation agreement. What arguments should each side make? How should the court rule and why?

Would your answer change if Richard had been represented by counsel and Judy had not been? What if Judy testified further that Richard's counsel told her that the agreement ensured that she would be taken care of "for life"? If you were Richard's counsel and believed that the settlement agreement you had negotiated was a good one for your client, what steps might you take to protect the settlement from a later claim of unconscionability?

CHAPTER 11

LAWYERS AND FAMILY DISPUTE RESOLUTION

In the aftermath of divorce liberalization, the courts were overwhelmed. Jessica Pearson and Nancy Thoennes reported in the 1980s that "[o]ver half of the cases filed in all trial courts are concerned with matrimonial actions." Mediation and Litigating Custody Disputes: A Longitudinal Evaluation, 17 Fam. L.Q. 497, 497-498 (1984). Since then, family dispute resolution has become even more complex, with an expansion in the range of services family courts provide or require and a change in the characteristics of the litigants and the complexity of the issues they present. John Lande, The Revolution in Family Law Dispute Resolution, 24 J. Am. Acad. Matrimonial Law. 411, 415 (2012).

Moreover, with the growth in the sheer number of cases came the growing conviction that the process itself escalated conflict. The result has been what Jana Singer has termed a "paradigm shift" from "the law-oriented and judge-focused adversary model" to "a more collaborative, interdisciplinary, and forward-looking family dispute resolution regime." This shift "has also transformed the practice of family law and fundamentally altered the way in which disputing families interact with the legal system." Jana B. Singer, Dispute Resolution and the Post-divorce Family: Implications of a Paradigm Shift, 47 Fam. Ct. Rev. 363 (2009). *See also* Jane C. Murphy & Jana B. Singer, Divorced from Reality: Rethinking Family Dispute Resolution 1 (2015). This has led to a redefinition of the role of lawyers and the family law litigation process.

This chapter addresses that paradigm shift. The first two sections deal with aspects of the lawyer-client relationship that present special issues in family law cases. The last part of the chapter considers proposals to change the method by which family disputes are resolved and the role of lawyers in alternative approaches to dispute resolution.

A. LAWYERS' DUTIES TO CLIENTS AND THE COURT

In re the Discipline of Ortner
699 N.W.2d 865 (S.D. 2005)

GILBERTSON, B.V. . . . Throughout their marriage David and Jami Reaser lived on David's family ranch where he worked. For twenty years Ortner helped the family with branding. When David initiated divorce proceedings in 1999 he retained Ortner to represent him. Jami did not have a lawyer. Ortner was aware that Jami's mother and stepfather were South Dakota lawyers and he assumed that they were assisting her.

Ortner prepared a stipulation regarding child custody, child support, alimony and property division which David and Jami signed. Pursuant to this stipulation David received custody of the children and relieved Jami of any child support obligation. Jami waived alimony. Ortner was aware of Circuit Judge Kern's policy to require child support in divorce decrees because when he presented the stipulation and decree of divorce to Judge Kern, he specifically "advised her there was something unusual about this particular stipulation for this divorce and that was that there was no provision in it for child support." Judge Kern refused to grant the divorce due to the omission of any provision for child support.

Ortner advised David that whoever did not have primary custody of the children would have to pay child support. Since David was receiving custody, Ortner advised him that he could simply tear up any checks he received for child support. David discussed the proposal with Jami who, according to Ortner, definitely wanted something in writing.

Ortner revised the stipulation to include a provision for child support:

> [Jami] is required to pay child support for the minor children in the total amount of $250.00 per month, except during those summer months when she has the children for visitation. During those summer months, [David] shall pay $250.00 per month for support of the minor children. Said support shall continue until the younger child graduates from high school or turns 19 years of age, whichever is earlier.

The judgment decreeing dissolution of marriage that Ortner drafted incorporated the stipulation, "it being the intention of this court that all of the terms and conditions of said Stipulation be made an express part of this Decree of Dissolution."

At the time Ortner drafted these documents he also drafted a "Private Contractual Agreement Between Parties" which provided:

> It is hereby stipulated and agreed by and between David R. Reaser, the Plaintiff, and Jami D. Reaser, the Defendant, subject to the approval of the above-named Court, that in the event the Court does see fit to grant [David] hereto a dissolution as prayed for in his Complaint, the same shall be upon the terms and conditions as set forth in the Stipulation and Agreement, except that the parties further privately stipulate and agree between themselves as follows:
>
> I. That [David] agrees that he will not seek to collect the Two Hundred Fifty Dollars ($250.00) per month child support ordered to be paid by [Jami].
>
> II. [Jami] stipulates and agrees that during those times when she has custody of the minor children for visitation purposes in the summer for one month or longer that she will not seek to collect child support from [David].
>
> III. Both parties stipulate and agree and contract as set forth above even though the Court itself has ordered payment of child support. The basis of the agreement for the dissolution of the marriage was that no child support be paid and this agreement carries out that earlier agreement reached by the parties.

On March 29, 1999, Jami came to Ortner's office and signed the revised stipulation and the private contractual agreement. David signed the documents the next day. Judge Kern signed the judgment decreeing dissolution of marriage which incorporated the revised stipulation on April 1. It was filed on April 6, 1999. At no time did Ortner advise Judge Kern of the private contractual agreement.

In May 2002 Jami moved for a change in custody and sought child support. Circuit Judge Thomas Trimble heard the motions and learned of the existence of the private contractual agreement. He denied the motion for a change of custody and advised David that he was free to seek child support from Jami.

In the fall of 2002 David initiated a child support action against Jami. The child support referee's recommendations that Jami pay current child support and arrearages were adopted by the circuit court. Jami's motions to set aside the interim order of support and eliminate the arrearages were heard by Judge John J. Delaney. Judge Delaney learned about the private contractual agreement and expressed serious concerns about the deception created by it. During this proceeding Ortner filed an "Affidavit Regarding Motion to Deny Claim for Arrears" which was dated April 1, 2003.

[Ortner's affidavit described what took place, including that "Affiant informed [Ms. Twiss] that even though the private agreement should be binding on the parties themselves it would not be binding upon the Court."] Judge Delaney filed findings of fact, conclusions of law and an order vacating judgment in regard to child custody, visitation, alimony and property settlement on November 18, 2003. Judge Delaney did so essentially sua sponte, because of the private contractual agreement and the court's findings of fraud upon the court.

[David appealed.] In Reaser v. Reaser we examined Ortner's conduct in light of Judge Delaney's findings:

> Here, under Judge Delaney's findings, the actions of these parties and the attorney are egregious conduct involving corruption of the judicial process itself. Considering those findings, this fraudulent conduct may have violated a criminal statute, and it certainly violated the Rules of Professional Conduct for attorneys. . . .

This Court's opinion in Reaser v. Reaser was handed down on October 13, 2004. Six days later, on October 19, 2004, Ortner wrote to Judge Kern:

Dear Judge Kern:

> As hollow as it may seem at this late date, I cannot adequately express how deeply I apologize to you for the way I mishandled the Reaser divorce five and one-half years ago.
>
> My heart and emotions totally got in the way of my brain and legal training. I had been going to brandings with David Reaser and his father for nearly twenty years at that time, and David was so adamant about not accepting any child support from his wife that I went ahead and prepared the private agreement for them to sign. I had no intent to defraud the Court or violate any laws. While trying to help a client I have totally jeopardized twenty-six years of law practice and nearly forty years of public service and service to the public.
>
> You had always treated me with total honesty and fairness and that is what makes me so sick and ashamed about the way I handled this matter.
>
> When this came to light in April 2003, I did an affidavit admitting to everything that had occurred. Since that date I have not had a decent night of sleep.
>
> In twenty-six years there has been one private reprimand from the Disciplinary Board and two investigations in criminal cases which were found to be frivolous and were sealed.
>
> What I did in this case clearly violated the Rules of Professional Responsibility, and I am ready to accept whatever action is recommended by the Disciplinary Board.

Respectfully submitted,

/s/

MICHAEL P. ORTNER
LAWYER

. . . On February 15, 2005 the Disciplinary Board entered its findings of fact, conclusions of law, recommendations, and formal accusation. The Board . . . recommended, in part:

1. Michael Ortner be censured for his violation of the Rules of Professional Conduct.

. . . The purpose of the disciplinary process is to protect the public from fraudulent, unethical or incompetent practices by attorneys. It is also intended to deter like conduct by other attorneys. The disciplinary process is not conducted to punish the lawyer. . . .

. . . As the Disciplinary Board found, "Ortner did not advise Judge Kern of the parties' intent to not actually collect child support from each other, nor did he inform her of the existence of their written agreement to that effect." Moreover, Ortner admitted at the Disciplinary Board hearing that in one other case he had prepared a similar type of secret agreement in an attempt to avoid paying child support. . . .

. . . Without question Ortner has led a life of public service. His disciplinary history is minimal. Custer and Fall River County attorneys have found him honest and ethical in legal matters. The judge he deceived views his deception as an isolated act that will not be repeated. Weighing against this, however, is that Ortner's conduct in this matter was a direct fraud on the court which corrupted the delicate balance of judicial fact finding, went to the heart of legal decision making and constituted egregious conduct by an officer of the court that corrupted the judicial process. . . .

. . . This was an issue involving child support. While Jami and David protected their respective interests, the trial court which properly protected the best interests of the children by refusing to waive child support at the outset, was ultimately duped by Ortner's actions. This made the trial court's already difficult duty to provide for the interests of the children, now impossible. . . .

In some cases we have examined an attorney's misrepresentation and have determined that public censure was the appropriate discipline. . . . We warned, however, "public censure in this type of case has been the penalty of the past, but whether it will be in the future is debatable and the whole Bar should take note of this." . . .

The Disciplinary Board concluded that "no public interest or professional purpose would be served by suspending Ortner's privilege to practice law." Its recommendation of a public censure cannot be accepted by this Court. . . .

It is difficult to conceive of a more blatant act of fraud than that committed in Ortner's drafting of the private contractual agreement and his participation in its execution which were directly contrary to the trial court's express direction after reviewing the first stipulation. This cannot be viewed as accidental or an honest mistake as Ortner has conceded that he knew prior to this case that it was Judge Kern's policy to require child support in divorce cases involving minor children. This private agreement did exactly what the trial court refused to approve after Ortner previously called the proposed no-support provision to the court's attention. The subsequent execution of the decree of dissolution was predicated on the revised stipulation's provision providing for meaningful child support. Ortner failed to self report for approximately six years. It was only after Judges Trimble and Delaney discovered the private contractual agreement that Ortner admitted his conduct. His apology to Judge Kern came only after the release of our decision in Reaser v. Reaser where his conduct became public. Moreover, he admitted he prepared a similar "secret agreement" on another occasion.

Lawyers must guard against conduct that diminishes public confidence in the legal system. . . . It is clear from the frequency of this type of misconduct that public censure is not providing sufficient deterrence to adequately protect the public in the future.

Had there been a history of violations by Ortner or if we suspected he was likely to repeat such acts in the future, for the protection of the public our only appropriate course of action would be to enter an order of disbarment. . . . Our review of the record indicates that such does not appear to be the case.

. . . After reviewing this record we conclude that Ortner's conduct was of such egregious professional nature that it is in the best interests of the public and the legal profession to suspend him from the practice of law for a period of nine months. . . .

Prior to any application for reinstatement Ortner must take and pass the Multistate Professional Responsibility Examination. He must also reimburse the State Bar of South Dakota and the Unified Judicial System for expenses allowed under SDCL 16-19-70.2. . . .

NOTES AND QUESTIONS

1. The secret agreement Ortner drafted was clearly a fraud on the court. Can you think of other ways to reach a resolution that would have satisfied the parties in this case but would not have subjected the attorney to disciplinary proceedings?

2. The court articulates two types of harm arising from Ortner's deception. The first is that it undermines confidence in the bar and the judiciary. The second is that it interferes with the court's ability to protect the interests of the children, who were not represented in this litigation. What do you think the court had in mind when it observed that the parties' actions "made the trial court's already difficult duty to provide for the interests of the children, now impossible . . ."?

3. Ortner represented David in the divorce while Jami acted pro se. Did Ortner have any obligations to Jami? Did she have a basis for objecting to David's actions in drafting the agreement and presenting it to her? ABA Model Rule of Professional Conduct 4.3 states:

> In dealing on behalf of a client with a person who is not represented by counsel, a lawyer shall not state or imply that the lawyer is disinterested. When the lawyer knows or reasonably should know that the unrepresented person misunderstands the lawyer's role in the matter, the lawyer shall make reasonable efforts to correct the misunderstanding. The lawyer shall not give legal advice to an unrepresented person, other than the advice to secure counsel, if the lawyer knows or reasonably should know that the interests of such a person are or have a reasonable possibility of being in conflict with the interests of the client.

What arguments might Jami make that Ortner violated this obligation to her in this case?

B. CONFLICTS OF INTEREST

As recounted by the *Ortner* opinion, "[t]hroughout their marriage David and Jami Reaser lived on David's family ranch where he worked. For twenty years Ortner helped the family with branding." Could Ortner's personal relationship with the Reasers have given rise to a conflict of interest that made his representation of David inappropriate? Does it matter that Ortner had never previously represented either David or Jami? Would your answer change if Jami had spoken to Ortner about the possibility of hiring him to represent her, but then decided not to do so? This section addresses how lawyers address conflicts of interest raised by these types of questions, beginning with the relevant ABA rule.

ABA MODEL RULE OF PROFESSIONAL CONDUCT 1.7, CONFLICT OF INTEREST: CURRENT CLIENTS

(a) Except as provided in paragraph (b), a lawyer shall not represent a client if the representation involves a concurrent conflict of interest. A concurrent conflict of interest exists if:

(1) the representation of one client will be directly adverse to another client; or

(2) there is a significant risk that the representation of one or more clients will be materially limited by the lawyer's responsibilities to another client, a former client or a third person or by a personal interest of the lawyer.

(b) Notwithstanding the existence of a concurrent conflict of interest under paragraph (a), a lawyer may represent a client if:

(1) the lawyer reasonably believes that the lawyer will be able to provide competent and diligent representation to each affected client;

(2) the representation is not prohibited by law;

(3) the representation does not involve the assertion of a claim by one client against another client represented by the lawyer in the same litigation or other proceeding before a tribunal; and

(4) each affected client gives informed consent, confirmed in writing.

NOTES AND QUESTIONS

1. In *Ortner*, David and Jami appear to have agreed on the divorce settlement, and both wanted the side agreement that Ortner drafted for them. Yet Ortner represented only David while Jami did not have legal counsel. Could Ortner have represented both of them? Clients with a common purpose (such as establishing a partnership or concluding a real estate transaction) often retain a single lawyer to carry out that purpose. Could an attorney ever represent both parties in a divorce? Rule 1.7 above was modified in 2002 to add Section (b)(3). How does this addition affect the possibility of joint representation in a divorce?

In Klemm v. Superior Court, 142 Cal. Rptr. 509 (Cal. App. 1977), an attorney who knew the husband and the wife agreed to represent them both, without fee, in an uncontested dissolution. Neither party could afford an attorney, both consented in writing to the joint representation, and the consent was filed with the court. The wife, however, was receiving Aid for Dependent Children payments from the county, and the county recommended that the husband be required to pay child support to reimburse the county for the payments. The attorney objected in writing to the recommendation on behalf of the wife (who had custody of the children in accordance with the divorce agreement), but appeared at the hearing on behalf of the husband. Even after the attorney appeared with both the husband and wife and their written consent to the joint representation, the trial court refused to permit the attorney to represent both parties in opposing the county's recommendation. The court of appeal disagreed and explained:

> As a matter of law a purported consent to dual representation of litigants with adverse interests at a contested hearing would be neither intelligent nor informed. . . .
>
> However, if the conflict is merely potential, there being no existing dispute or contest between the parties represented as to any point in litigation, then with full disclosure to and informed consent of both clients there may be dual representation at a hearing or trial.
>
> In our view the case at bench clearly falls within the latter category. The conflict of interest was strictly potential and not present. The parties had settled their differences by agreement. There was no point of difference to be litigated. The position of each inter se was totally consistent throughout the proceedings. The wife did not want child support from the husband, and the husband did not want to pay support for the children. The actual conflict that existed on the issue of support was between the county on the one hand, which argued that support should be ordered, and the husband and wife on the other, who consistently maintained the husband should not be ordered to pay support.
>
> While on the face of the matter it may appear foolhardy for the wife to waive child support,[1] other values could very well have been more important to her than such support — such as maintaining a good relationship between the husband and the children and between the husband and herself despite the marital problems — thus avoiding the backbiting, acrimony and ill will which the Family Relations Act of 1970 was, insofar as possible, designed to eliminate. It could well have been if the wife was forced to choose between A.F.D.C. payments to be reimbursed to the county by the husband and no A.F.D.C. payments she would have made the latter choice. . . .

---

1. It is to be noted that the parties' agreement that the children should not receive support would not prevent the court from awarding child support either at the hearing or at some time subsequent thereto. Therefore, the children's rights are not in issue nor are they jeopardized.

The conclusion we arrive at is particularly congruent with dissolution proceedings under the Family Law Act of 1970, the purpose of which was to discard the concept of fault in dissolution of marriage actions, to minimize the adversary nature of such proceedings and to eliminate conflicts created only to secure a divorce. It is contrary to the philosophy of that act to create controversy between the parties where none exists in reality. . . .

142 Cal. Rptr. at 512-513. The attorney in *Klemm*, like Michael Ortner, was involved in a case where neither parent sought to have the other pay child support, and both wished to oppose a different result. The courts treat the two cases very differently. At least part of the reason is that the attorney in *Klemm* did not in any way conceal the attorney's or the clients' actions. Is that the only difference?

2. What are the circumstances in which joint representation might be appropriate? In Olson v. Olson, 139 So. 3d 539 (La. App. 2014), a Louisiana Court of Appeals upheld a postnuptial agreement, approved by the trial court, where a single attorney represented both spouses. The couple later divorced, and the husband challenged the validity of the agreement on the grounds that the joint representation violated the Rules of Professional Conduct. The Court of Appeals disagreed, emphasizing that the attorney had informed the couple at the time that their interests might be adverse, and the husband had signed a verification certifying to the court that the matrimonial agreement was in his best interest and that he understood the principles involved. Would the result have been different if the agreement had not been presented to a court with such verifications?

3. Many jurisdictions prohibit joint representation in family law proceedings altogether. The American Academy of Matrimonial Lawyers (AAML) takes the position in Goal 3.1 that "[a]n attorney should not represent both husband and wife even if they do not wish to obtain independent representation." The comments observe that "[e]ven a seemingly amicable separation or divorce may result in bitter litigation over financial matters or custody. A matrimonial lawyer should not attempt to represent both husband and wife, even with the consent of both." In Ware v. Ware, 687 S.E.2d 382, 389 (W. Va. 2009), the West Virginia Court of Appeals held that the "likelihood of prejudice is so great with dual representation so as to make adequate representation of both spouses impossible, even where the separation is 'friendly' and the divorce uncontested." The court further extended the per se rule against joint representation to premarital agreements, observing that "the parties' interests are fundamentally antagonistic to one another" and that the very purpose of a prenuptial agreement is to prevent a spouse "from obtaining that to which he or she might otherwise be legally entitled."

4. In re Gamino, 753 N.W.2d 521 (Wis. 2008), provides a catalogue of the things that can go wrong with joint representation. In *Gamino*, the attorney claimed that the parties had come to him to finalize a settlement agreement that they had reached while represented by other attorneys. The disciplinary proceedings against the lawyer, however, included allegations that:

- The parties were confused about when the attorney began and ended his representation of each party.
- He failed to communicate the same information at the same time to each of the parties, including information about scheduled hearings.
- He prepared a financial statement without independently ascertaining the value or accuracy of the assets listed to the disadvantage of one of the parties.
- He failed to turn over records on a timely basis to a new attorney for one of the parties because of the other party's lack of consent.
- He did not address the unequal status between the two parties in a case in which one of the spouses had been a victim of domestic violence, was in poor health, and had less education and financial experience than the other spouse.

- He drafted a settlement that was later determined to be patently unfair to one of the parties and did so without a knowing waiver, undermining the ability of the other party to enforce it.
- He failed to inquire about a possible claim with respect to dissipation of assets.

Wisconsin suspended Gamino's license to practice law for 18 months. *See also Klemm*, above, observing that:

> Attorneys who undertake to represent parties with divergent interests owe the highest duty to each to make a full disclosure of all facts and circumstances which are necessary to enable the parties to make a fully informed decision regarding the subject matter of the litigation, including the areas of potential conflict and the possibility and desirability of seeking independent legal advice. Failing such disclosure, the attorney is civilly liable to the client who suffers loss caused by lack of disclosure. In addition, the lawyer lays himself open to charges, whether well founded or not, of unethical and unprofessional conduct. Moreover, the validity of any agreement negotiated without independent representation of each of the parties is vulnerable to easy attack as having been procured by misrepresentation, fraud and overreaching. It thus behooves counsel to cogitate carefully and proceed cautiously before placing himself/herself in such a position.

142 Cal. Rptr. at 514. For a defense of joint representation, *see* Rebecca Aviel, Counsel for the Divorce, 55 B.C. L. Rev. 1099, 1106 (2014), arguing "that commitment to client-centered representation, respect for client autonomy, and humility about the legal profession's competence to pre-judge the actual interests of divorcing families militate in favor of the transparent, responsible, and regulated practice of joint representation."

5. Gamino claimed to play a "scrivener's role" in representing the parties to the divorce. That is, he attempted to limit his representation to drafting a final settlement agreement and presenting it to the court. In characterizing his representation this way, he argued that he should be held responsible only for a limited scope of representation (the drafting of the settlement to which the parties had already agreed) rather than a full duty to investigate his clients' circumstances and look out for their best interests, particularly when the clients had not asked him to do so. Gamino, however, had no written understanding with the clients, not even an oral agreement in which he explained the implications of such limited representation, and he did not secure a waiver of the clients' rights. The Wisconsin Supreme Court accordingly held him responsible for his failure to recognize the conflicts between the parties' respective positions and to consider their broader interests.

6. *Gamino* is an example of one common situation in which the propriety of limited representation arises, and the opinion left open the question of whether attorneys can ever agree to limited representation of their clients' interests. For example, what if the spouses reach an agreement and then ask the mediator (who is also an attorney) to set forth their agreement in writing. Is the mediator permitted to do so? Does it matter if the attorney-mediator who drafts the agreement does not sign the papers and does not enter an appearance for either of the parties, each of whom appears pro se in the divorce proceeding? The Illinois State Bar says no. The State Bar concluded that it would violate Rule 1.7(a) above for a mediator to represent both sides in a divorce because the proceeding involves parties with adverse interests and that preparing a proposed dissolution agreement constitutes representation even if the mediator does not enter an appearance in the case. Illinois State Bar Ass'n Comm. on Professional Ethics, Op. 04-03, 4/05, 31 Fam. L. Rptr. 1319 (2005). *See also* Utah State Bar Ethics Advisory Op. Comm., Op 05-03, 5/6/05, 31 Fam. L. Rptr. 1321 (2005). The Wisconsin Supreme Court, to the contrary, issued an order that allowed lawyers to serve in a mediator role by drafting and filing documents for couples. Lawyer-mediators must maintain their neutrality throughout the process, and both parties must give informed consent to the lawyer's role. Wis. Sup. Ct. R. Ch. 20 R. 20:2.4(C) (2018). *See* Mark B. Baer,

The Amplification of Bias in Family Law and Its Impact, 32 J. Am. Acad. Matrim. Law. 305, 315 (2020) (noting that the general public assumes that divorce is litigated by adversarial lawyers and does not understand the importance of dispute resolution techniques). California, which as noted above, permits lawyers to represent both sides in an uncontested divorce, and Virginia, which defines the scrivener's role (in which a mediator simply writes down those terms to which the parties have agreed) as outside of the practice of law, would appear to permit the practice.

The ABA Model Rules of Professional Conduct recognize the lawyer's role in alternative dispute resolution as a "third-party neutral," whether as mediator, arbitrator, conciliator, or evaluator. Model Rule 2.4 states that a lawyer serves that role when assisting two or more persons *who are not clients of the lawyer* to reach a resolution of some dispute or issue between them. Rule 2.4(b) requires a lawyer in this capacity to inform unrepresented parties that the lawyer is not representing them and, if it appears necessary, to explain the difference between a lawyer's role as a third-party neutral and the role of a lawyer who represents a client. *See* Calvin Lee, Note, May Mediators Draft Settlement Agreements?, 54 Fam. Ct. Rev. 501, 503 (2016).

7. The propriety of limited representation also arises when a lawyer purports to provide "unbundled" legal services. Divorcing parties who cannot afford to hire an attorney to handle the entire proceeding might nonetheless want to retain an attorney to advise them about a particular issue (*e.g.*, the tax aspects of a settlement) or to draft a particular pleading or agreement. May an attorney provide such limited representation without investigating the rest of the client's case or considering other arguments the client might raise? An Illinois ethics opinion initially said no. It concluded that the mediator could not limit the scope of representation to preparation of the proposed documents. But Illinois, like many states, has since altered its position to permit some forms of limited scope representation, including the preparation of documents. Ill. Rule of Professional Conduct 1.2(c) (2022); Supreme Court Rule 137 (2022); ABA Standing Committee on the Delivery of Legal Services, An Analysis of Rules that Enable Lawyers to Serve Self-Represented Litigants: A White Paper (2014). The Illinois changes do not address the issue of dual representation, and some jurisdictions that allow representation to review a proposed settlement may limit the representation to one of the parties. *See* Michael Millemann, Reporter, ABA Handbook on Limited Scope Legal Assistance (2003), available at https://www.americanbar.org/content/dam/aba/administrative/legal_aid_indigent_defendants/ls_sclaid_handbook_on_limited_scope_legal_assistance.pdf.

8. Limited scope representation has gained increasing use in family law practice more generally. Clients may wish to consult an attorney with respect to a particularly complex legal matter, such as division of the value of a closely held business, or with respect to specific language in an agreement without retaining the lawyer to handle the case as a whole. Aviel, above, 55 B.C. L. Rev. at 1103. Companies offer a different business model by selling Internet-based assistance to divorcing couples. In making available computerized forms by topic, and providing assistance in filling out forms, websites attempt to tailor their services to a couple's needs. Similarly, states increasingly are experimenting with licensing programs for non-lawyer professionals that can provide discrete legal services and skills. This trend follows a 2014 report of the ABA Task Force on the Future of Legal Education, which called on states to license "persons other than holders of a JD to deliver limited legal services." *See* Krista A. Hess, The Broad Reach of Limited Scope Representation: A Pathway to Access to Justice, 39 W. New Eng. L. Rev. 263 (2017). The growth of limited scope representation through online platforms has increased since the onset of the COVID-19 pandemic. *See* Dalton Courson, Limited-Scope Representation: Preparing for the COVID-19 Influx of Cases, American Bar Association

(2021); *see also* Tracey Wiltgen, Providing Access to Justice Through Mediation During a Pandemic, 24 Haw. B.J. 1, 11 (2020).

Use of limited scope representation presents other issues. While some individuals do not hire attorneys because they wish to keep control of their own divorces, many cannot afford attorneys. This raises questions about effectiveness. Empirical studies tend to find that limited scope representation is not as effective as full representation in protecting the client's interests. Others have been concerned about attorney accountability, particularly when attorneys engage in "ghostwriting" and help clients prepare documents to be filed in court that do not bear the attorney's name or signature. *See* Michele N. Struffolino, Taking Limited Representation to the Limits: The Efficacy of Using Unbundled Legal Services in Domestic-Relations Matters Involving Litigation, 2 St. Mary's J. Legal Mal. & Ethics 166 (2012); Jessica K. Steinberg, In Pursuit of Justice? Case Outcomes and the Delivery of Unbundled Legal Services, 18 Geo. J. on Poverty L. & Pol'y 453 (2011); Colleen F. Shanahan et al., Can a Little Representation Be a Dangerous Thing?, 67 Hastings L. J. 1367, 1385 (2016).

ABA MODEL RULE OF PROFESSIONAL CONDUCT RULE 1.9, DUTIES TO FORMER CLIENTS

(a) A lawyer who has formerly represented a client in a matter shall not thereafter represent another person in the same or a substantially related matter in which that person's interests are materially adverse to the interests of the former client unless the former client gives informed consent, confirmed in writing. . . .

(c) A lawyer who has formerly represented a client in a matter or whose present or former firm has formerly represented a client in a matter shall not thereafter:

(1) use information relating to the representation to the disadvantage of the former client except as these Rules would permit or require with respect to a client, or when the information has become generally known; or

(2) reveal information relating to the representation except as these Rules would permit or require with respect to a client.

NOTES AND QUESTIONS

1. Conflicts of interest are troublesome because they create concerns about the loyalty of the lawyer to a client. These concerns in turn arise from two sources. One has to do with whether a lawyer will fully advise or zealously represent a party if that same lawyer owes an identical duty to an opposing party. The other source of concern is the lawyer's duty to preserve a client's confidences.

Simultaneous representation of two clients in a common matter as in *Klemm* and *Gamino* presents both of these sets of concerns. However, a conflict reflecting the second concern may also arise when a lawyer clearly represents only one party but that lawyer *has previously* represented the other party. The critical question is whether there is reason to believe that that lawyer acquired confidential information during the first representation that would be relevant to the present matter. If it appears that the lawyer may have done so and the former client has not consented to the lawyer's current representation, the lawyer may be disqualified on motion of the former client. *See* Rule 1.9 of the ABA Model Rules of Professional Conduct; Bergeron v. Mackler, 623 A.2d 489 (Conn. 1993).

Rule 1.9 uses the "substantial relationship" test, which focuses on whether the scope of the prior representation is such that information relating to the current case would have been pertinent to the earlier representation. Courts differ on the specificity with which they examine similarities between the former and current matters, but most require a particularized inquiry into scope of representation, as opposed to information actually transmitted:

> Essentially, then, disqualification questions require three levels of inquiry. Initially, the trial judge must make a factual reconstruction of the scope of the prior legal representation. Second, it must be determined whether it is reasonable to infer that the confidential information allegedly given would have been given to a lawyer representing a client in those matters. Finally, it must be determined whether that information is relevant to the issues raised in the pending case against the former client.

Westinghouse Electric Corp. v. Gulf Oil Corp., 588 F.2d 221, 225 (7th Cir. 1978).

Courts have held that "[d]oubts should be resolved in favor of disqualification." In re Kennedy, 2008 Bankr. LEXIS 1108. Thus, where lawyers in the same firm as an attorney who represented the wife in a divorce proceeding later represented the husband in a bankruptcy action, the court disqualified the law firm. Even though the wife was not an adverse party in the bankruptcy and no confidential information appeared to be involved, the court observed that the bankruptcy addressed the dischargeability of the husband's obligations in the divorce decree and thus might adversely affect the wife. In Gabel v. Gabel, 955 N.Y.S.2d 171 (N.Y. App. Div. 2012), the attorney had previously represented the wife in the formation of a corporation, but the appellate division nonetheless reversed the trial court's disqualification on the ground that the attorney did not have any information about the corporation other than that contained in the public filings about the business. How can the court be sure that no confidential communications were involved?

2. Model Rule 1.18(c) provides that "[a] lawyer . . . shall not represent a client with interests materially adverse to those of a prospective client in the same or a substantially related matter if the lawyer received information from the prospective client that could be significantly harmful to that person in the matter. . . ." "Prospective clients" include those who discuss the possibility of forming an attorney-client relationship with the lawyer even if no such relationship ever comes into existence. In In re Z.N.H., 280 S.W.3d 481 (Tex. App. 2009), a prospective client had a 35- to 40-minute consultation with an attorney but did not hire him. The attorney later agreed to represent the prospective client's ex-wife, a custodial parent who wished to move over the ex-husband's objections. The attorney did not remember that he had met the ex-husband, nor did he remember anything about the interview. The trial court concluded that no conflict existed and a multi-day trial ensued. The Texas appellate court reversed and remanded for a new trial with another attorney. It held that under the Texas Rules of Evidence, the term *client* includes one "who consults a lawyer with a view to obtaining professional legal services from that lawyer," Tex. R. Evid. 503(a)(1) (2022), and thus the husband was entitled to a conclusive presumption that he had imparted confidential information to the lawyer. *See also* In re Conduct of Knappenberger, 108 P.3d 1161 (Or. 2005) (attorney-client relationship existed on the basis of a two-hour interview because the attorney provided advice, billed client for the interview, and led him to believe the interview was confidential). The conclusive presumption applies even if the movant cannot establish that the current matter is substantially related to the former representation. In re Thetford, 574 S.W.3d 362 (Tex. 2019) (overruling a principle upon which In re Z.N.H., cited above, was decided, that the prospective client must first prove that representation violates Rule 109(a)(3) because the current matter is substantially related to the former).

In other jurisdictions, however, the courts do not use the term *client* to include those who consult with an attorney for the purpose of deciding whether to retain that attorney. Instead, they place the burden on the party seeking disqualification to show that the attorney had access to confidential information adverse to the consulting party. When the party cannot establish the transmission of confidential information, the attorney can represent another party in the same litigation. In In re Marriage of Perry, 293 P.3d 170 (Mont. 2013), for example, the court allowed the attorney to represent the husband, even though the wife testified that she had revealed confidential information during a number of phone calls with the attorney. The attorney testified that it was her practice not to engage in confidential communications over the phone before an attorney-client relationship had been established and that her notes of the communications and office records did not contain any indication that the wife had transmitted confidential information.

Model Rule 1.18 cannot be used by one party to "conflict out" potential opposing attorneys in bad faith. A New York court held that an attorney is disqualified if the attorney received confidential information that could be "significantly harmful" to a party in the matter; the moving party must describe the information with specificity rather than simply claiming it was "confidential." Thus, Model Rule 1.18 incorporates an element of good faith. In Bernacki v. Bernacki, 1 N.Y.S.3d 761 (N.Y. Sup. Ct. 2015), the court held that the husband at issue had acted in bad faith by purposefully attempting to "conflict . . . out" a list of divorce attorneys that he advised his wife to hire. *See also* State ex rel. Thompson, 346 S.W.3d 390, 396 (Mo. App. 2011) (husband's attempt to disqualify a lawyer from representing his wife failed because the husband did not seek or receive any legal advice).

3. In general, any conflict of interest affecting a member of a firm and any confidential information received by a firm member are imputed to all members of the firm. Thus, in In re Kennedy, cited above, lawyers from the law firm that represented the wife in a divorce were barred from representing the husband in a bankruptcy even though there did not appear to be confidential communications at issue.

Some courts have disqualified firms even when the family members they represented in earlier litigation were not the same family members as those involved in the new litigation. In Kennedy v. Eldridge, 135 Cal. Rptr. 3d 545 (Cal. App. 2011), for example, the litigation involved unmarried parents disputing custody and support. The father in the case retained his own father (the child's grandfather) to represent him. The attorney and his wife (the child's grandmother), who were in practice together, had represented the mother's father in an earlier divorce action. The trial court disqualified the firm, and the court of appeal affirmed. The grandfather/attorney, who doted on the grandchild, had many interactions with the mother of the child apart from the firm's earlier representation of her father. Would the courts have disqualified him solely because of those interactions had his firm not been involved in the earlier divorce action? *See* Halberstam v. Halberstam, 995 N.Y.S.2d 738 (App. Div. 2014) (wife's counsel was disqualified because the attorney was the parties' brother-in-law and husband had shared confidential information with attorney before husband was aware of attorney's representation of wife).

The ABA Model Rules of Professional Conduct suggest that lawyers employed in the same unit of a legal services organization constitute a firm, but the same is not necessarily true of lawyers employed in separate units. What constitutes a separate unit apparently depends on "the particular rule that is involved, and on the specific facts of the situation." Comment 2 to Rule 1.10. If the lawyers are in the same unit, whatever that means, the categorical rule of disqualification set out in Rule 1.10(a) seemingly applies.

Perhaps the most rapidly growing group of conflict of interest cases between lawyers and clients are those involving sexual relationships. This issue is discussed below in note 8, page 566.

PROBLEMS

1. Alma and Gustav Mahler have been married for ten years and now have agreed to divorce. Gustav is employed as a mechanic by an aircraft company, making about $90,000 a year; Alma has not worked outside the home for several years. They have been discussing matters for some time and have agreed that Alma will have custody of their two children (ages 2 and 5). Gustav will have visitation for one day each weekend and will pay child support according to the state child support guidelines. Alma will seek employment. Their real and personal property consists of a house, in which they have $88,000 equity, two cars worth approximately $8000 each, and about $20,000 in personal property (mostly household furnishings). Alma will keep the house, the furnishings, and one car.

Alma and Gustav have both come to your office for assistance in securing the divorce. They want you to represent both of them, and they do not want a second attorney, who would, in their view, add unnecessarily to the expense of the divorce and perhaps create problems. Would you and should you represent Alma and Gustav?

2. Assume Alma comes to you two years after receiving a divorce. She and her former husband, Gustav, had reached an agreement between themselves, identical with the agreement described in problem 1. Arnold Becker, an experienced divorce lawyer, represented both. Last week, however, Alma was talking with a friend of hers, also divorced, who mentioned that she has received an interest in her ex-husband's pension plan. Alma was not aware that she might have some interest in Gustav's pension plan and wants to know if she can still receive something for it. How would you advise her?

3. Jean and Taylor are divorcing. Taylor is represented by Haddock & Carp, a law firm that has previously represented Taylor in connection with her business interests. The firm also represented both Jean and Taylor when they challenged a lien on their home initiated by an electrician who charged what they considered, and the court agreed, to be an exorbitant amount for replacing the house's wiring. Jean now seeks to disqualify Haddock & Carp from representing Taylor. Should she succeed?

4. Suppose that, in problem 3, Taylor's lawyer had previously represented Taylor in a bankruptcy proceeding. Would that affect your analysis?

5. Harold schedules a consultation for the purpose of deciding whether to retain you with respect to a custody dispute he is having with his ex-spouse. You discover that another person with the same last name as Harold already has an appointment to see you, also about a custody matter. You have never met or spoken to either party. What steps should you take to avoid any conflicts of interest and to keep open the possibility that at least one of the parties can hire you if they are in fact involved in the same dispute?

NOTE: FEE ARRANGEMENTS

Most courts take the view that contingent fees are not allowed in domestic relations cases. The court in Meyers v. Handlon, 479 N.E.2d 106 (Ind. App. 1985), summarizes the usual justifications for this prohibition:

> . . . [W]e discern at least five reasons for the traditional disapproval of contingent fee contracts. They are: 1) the public policy favoring marriage; 2) disapproval of giving attorneys a financial incentive to promote divorce; 3) the statutory availability of attorney fee awards making contingent fees unnecessary; 4) the potential for overreaching or undue influence in a highly emotional situation; and 5) a need for the court to make an informed distribution of property which includes the obligation of attorney fees. . . .
>
> The reason cited in virtually every case dealing with this issue is the State's interest in preserving the marital relationship and discouraging divorce. It is thought that a contingent fee contract in contemplation of divorce gives an attorney some incentive to actually promote the divorce or hinder possible reconciliation. Such a financial interest in derogation of marriage offends public policy. . . .
>
> . . . The evolution away from restrictive divorce laws occurred, in our opinion, not because of a diminished societal interest in preserving the marriage relationship but in recognition that

society's interest was rarely served by prolonging the agonies of a dying marriage. This does not, however, lessen the impropriety of an attorney having a financial stake in promoting a hostile, adversarial atmosphere between the parties. . . .

The fourth reason . . . is potential for overreaching and undue influence. . . . Divorce and the resulting division of the marital property creates an emotional atmosphere in which distraught parties are especially vulnerable to agreeing to a contract which turns out to be oppressive. . . .

The final reason . . . is the concern that the trial court's duty to provide an equitable property settlement and establish support for minor children or a disabled spouse may be thwarted by the existence of a contingent fee arrangement — especially where the court has not been informed of its existence. . . .

479 N.E.2d at 109-111. *See also* Maxwell Schuman & Co. v. Edwards, 663 S.E.2d 329 (N.C. App. 2008) (finding contingent fee agreement with Canadian law firm in child custody and support action to be void as against public policy); Olszewski v. Jordan, 109 A.3d 910, 920 (Conn. 2015) ("attorneys are not entitled by operation of law to equitable charging liens on marital assets for fees and expenses incurred in obtaining judgments for their clients in marital dissolution proceedings in Connecticut").

Rule 1.5(d)(1) of the ABA Model Rules of Professional Conduct also prohibits "any fee in a domestic relations matter, the payment of which is contingent upon the securing of a divorce or upon the amount of alimony or support, or property settlement in lieu thereof. . . ." Comment [6] of Section 1.5 provides that the prohibition does not apply to "legal representation in connection with the recovery of post-judgment balances due under support, alimony, or financial orders because such contracts do not implicate the same policy concerns." The Comments provide no explanation for the prohibition generally. Why are the policy concerns present in the initial divorce proceeding not also present in post-judgment actions? For a discussion of this issue, *see* Ethics Opinion: How Far Can You Go in a Divorce?, 29 Mont. Law. (2004) (allowing a contingent fee agreement for a lawyer investigating the possibility that one of the parties to a divorce concealed assets).

As noted above, courts often shift responsibility for fees in divorce cases from one party to another. Such awards are usually entered and/or upheld when the party lacks sufficient funds to pay the agreed (reasonable) fee in whole or in part, or when the spouse seeking relief will have substantially fewer resources than the other. An allowance of attorneys' fees will be overturned only when there is an abuse of discretion, that is, when it appears that the trial court could not reasonably concluded as it did. *Compare* In re Marriage of Robinson and Thiel, 35 P.3d 89 (Ariz. App. 2001) (abuse of discretion for a spouse with far fewer resources), *with* In re Marriage of Duncan, 108 Cal. Rptr. 2d 833 (Cal. App. 2001) (no abuse of discretion when both parties had sufficient financial resources to pay for their litigation, even though husband had substantial earned income and wife had none).

"Performance" or "value-added" fees — fees that reflect the outcome reached rather than the amount or kind of work done — have become common in many legal settings. A New York court has considered the extent to which such fees are "contingent" and therefore improper where contingent fees are prohibited in domestic relations cases. The wife had agreed to pay her attorney a "bonus" of $2 million in light of the favorable results achieved in the divorce action — an agreement by the husband to pay her $15 million in property and alimony after his initial offer of $750,000. The wife sought to avoid paying the lawyer $1 million and to rescind the performance agreement because it was executed 24 hours before the husband signed the separation agreement, which provided for an uncontested divorce. The trial court entered summary judgment in favor of the client, finding the agreement amounted to a contingent fee on the property and alimony arrangement and violated the disciplinary rule barring such arrangements. The Appellate Division reversed the summary judgment and remanded, noting that the separation agreement was complete at the time the fee agreement was made and that the issue was whether any contingency remained after that point. Weinstein v. Barnett, 640 N.Y.S.2d 103 (App. Div. 1996). *See* Denise Fields, Risky Business or Clever Thinking? An Examination of the Ethical Considerations of Disguised Contingent Fee Agreements in Domestic Relations Matters, 75 UMKC L. Rev. 1065 (2007).

Given the difficulty of financing divorces, some third-party lenders have begun to help divorcing parties cover the costs of their divorce. They provide loans that can be used to pay for expenses during the litigation, with repayment tied to a judgment or settlement. The loans are designed, in particular, for lower-earning parties who stand to gain a sizeable share of a marital estate. There is almost no regulation of these practices. *See* Bibeane Metsch-Garcia, Note, Eliminating Financiers from the Equation: A Call for Court-Mandated Fee Shifting, 113 Mich. L. Rev. 1271 (2015); Cyn Haueter, "I Can't Afford to Leave Him:" Divorcing a Spouse with Superior Financial Resources, 31 Hastings Women's L.J. 237, 241-246 (2020).

PROBLEMS

1. Martha visits your office to discuss her divorce action, which has been in negotiation for some time. She has been married for 18 years, and a considerable amount of property is involved. Her husband's attorney is a well-known, aggressive divorce lawyer. Martha has lost confidence in her current attorney because "he just doesn't seem interested in my problems and isn't willing to take on my husband's lawyer." She tells you that she has heard good things about you but wants to be quite sure that you are really committed to her success. Accordingly, she would prefer a fee arrangement in which you receive an initial retainer of $15,000, a fee of $100 per hour (substantially less than your normal hourly rate) for any work you perform after the first 100 hours on the case, a bonus of $10,000 if she receives spousal support for a period longer than two years (she is currently employed and self-supporting, and her prior attorney told her she is unlikely to receive more than minimal support), 20 percent of any amount her husband agrees to provide toward the children's college education (a contribution the court has no power to award in this jurisdiction), and one-third of any property she receives greater than a 50 percent interest in the house, car, and bank accounts jointly titled in her and her husband's names. May you enter into the proposed fee arrangement? Would you?

2. In the same situation as that in problem 1, Martha tells you that she settled the divorce action and the final decree was entered two years ago. She received relatively little property because most of what the court identified was tied up in her husband's law practice and was not subject to division at divorce. In addition, the court decided that she did not need alimony because she had a good job, which she has held for the last several years. Martha has recently heard, however, that her ex-husband concealed extensive assets that should have been part of the property division. She also tells you that she believes her last lawyer took her for a ride, collecting large fees while doing very little to assist her, and that she does not have much in the way of savings because of the divorce and she is supporting two children in college without much assistance from her husband. She would like to enter into a contingent fee agreement in which you receive a percentage of any assets you are able to obtain. May you enter into the proposed fee arrangement? Would you?

C. COUNSELING, NEGOTIATION, AND CLIENT RELATIONS

The allocation of authority between lawyers and their clients is both important and complex. Rule 1.2(a) of the ABA Model Rules of Professional Conduct provides as follows:

(a) Subject to paragraphs (c) and (d), a lawyer shall abide by a client's decisions concerning the objectives of representation and, as required by Rule 1.4, shall consult with the client as to the means by which they are to be pursued. A lawyer may take such action on behalf of the client as is impliedly authorized to carry out the representation. A lawyer shall abide by a client's decision whether to settle a matter. . . .

In principle, it seems that the client should have the authority to decide whether to pursue a potentially available legal remedy, whether to propose a settlement, and whether to accept an offered settlement. At the same time, clients should ordinarily "defer to the special knowledge and skill of their lawyer with respect to the means to be used to accomplish their objectives, particularly with respect to technical, legal, and tactical matters." Comment to Rule 1.2.

The practical difficulty in distinguishing between the responsibilities of clients and lawyers, however, is reflected in longstanding, theoretical disagreement regarding the role of the lawyer. One view maintains that the primary duty of lawyers is to support their clients' expressions of their own dignity and autonomy, rather than deciding for the client what is good and wise. *E.g.*, Charles J. Fried, The Lawyer as Friend: The Moral Foundations of the Lawyer-Client Relationship, 85 Yale L.J. 1060, 1071 (1976); Monroe H. Freedman, Client-Centered Lawyering—What It Isn't, 40 Hofstra L. Rev. 349 (2011). The other urges lawyers to take responsibility on behalf of clients and be guided by their own senses of both client interests and just conduct. *E.g.*, David Luban, Lawyers and Justice: An Ethical Study (1988); William W. Simon, Ethical Discretion in Lawyering, 101 Harv. L. Rev. 1083, 1113-1119 (1988).

What is not disputed is that lawyers act as advisors to their clients, however their respective responsibilities are defined and allocated. A broader counseling role has been increasingly recognized over the last several decades. Model Rule 2.1 provides that "[i]n representing a client, a lawyer shall exercise independent professional judgment and render candid advice. In rendering advice, a lawyer may refer not only to law but to other considerations such as moral, economic, social, and political factors that may be relevant to the client's situation."

American Academy of Matrimonial Lawyers (AAML)

Bounds of Advocacy: Goals for Family Lawyers, Preliminary Statement
§§1, 6 (2000)

Family law disputes occur in a volatile and emotional atmosphere. It is difficult for matrimonial lawyers to represent the interests of their clients without addressing the interests of other family members. Unlike most other concluded disputes in which the parties may harbor substantial animosity without practical effect, the parties in matrimonial disputes may interact for years to come. In addition, many matrimonial lawyers consider themselves obligated to consider the best interest of children, regardless of which family member they represent. . . .

Matrimonial lawyers should recognize the effect that their words and actions have on their client's attitudes about the justice system, not just on the "legal outcome" of their cases. As a counselor, a problem-solving lawyer encourages problem solving in the client. Effective advocacy for a client means considering with the client what is in the client's best interest and determining the most effective means to achieve that result. The client's best interests include the well being of children, family peace, and economic stability. Clients looks to attorneys' words and deeds for how they should behave while involved with the legal system. Even when involved in a highly contested matter, divorce attorneys should strive to promote civility and good behavior by the client toward the parties, the lawyers and the court. . . .

1. COMPETENCE AND ADVICE

. . .

1.2 An attorney should advise the client of the emotional and economic impact of divorce and explore the feasibility of reconciliation.

1.3 An attorney should refuse to assist in vindictive conduct and should strive to lower the emotional level of a family dispute by treating all other participants with respect.

1.4 An attorney should be knowledgeable about different ways to resolve marital disputes, including negotiation, mediation, arbitration and litigation.

1.5 An attorney should attempt to resolve matrimonial disputes by agreement and should consider alternative means of achieving resolution.

COMMENT

The litigation process is expensive and emotionally draining. Settlement may not be appropriate or workable in some cases due to the nature of the dispute or the animosity of the parties. Litigation is the best course in those cases.

In matrimonial matters, a cooperative resolution is highly desirable. Matrimonial law is not a matter of winning or losing. At its best, matrimonial law should result in disputes being solved fairly for all parties, including children. Major tasks of the matrimonial lawyer include helping the client develop realistic objectives and attempting to attain them with the least injury to the family. The vast majority of cases should be resolved by lawyers negotiating settlements on behalf of their clients.

Parties are more likely to abide by their own promises than by an outcome imposed on them by a court. When resolution requires complex trade-offs, the parties may be better able than the court to forge a resolution that addresses their individual values and needs. An agreement that meets the reasonable objectives of the parties maximizes their autonomy and their own priorities. A court-imposed resolution may, instead, maximize legal principles that may seem arbitrary or unfair within the context of the parties' family. An agreement may establish a positive tone for continuing post-divorce family relations by avoiding the animosity and pain of court battles. It may also be less costly financially than a litigated outcome. Parents who litigate their custody disputes are much more likely to believe that the process had a detrimental effect on relations with the divorcing spouse than parents whose custody or support disputes are settled. These issues should be discussed with the client. . . .

6. CHILDREN

One of the most troubling issues in family law is determining a lawyer's obligations to children. The lawyer must competently represent the interests of the client, but not at the expense of the children. The parents' fiduciary obligations for the well being of a child provide a basis for the attorney's consideration of the child's best interests consistent with traditional advocacy and client loyalty principles. It is accepted doctrine that the attorney for a trustee or other fiduciary has an ethical obligation to the beneficiaries for whom the fiduciary's obligations run. Statutory law and decisional law in most jurisdictions imposes a fiduciary duty on parents to act in their children's interests. For this analysis to be of benefit to practitioners, however, a clearer mandate must be adopted as part of the ethical code or its interpretations.

6.1 An attorney representing a parent should consider the welfare of, and seek to minimize the adverse impact of the divorce on, the minor children.

6.2 An attorney should not permit a client to contest child custody, contact or access for either financial leverage or vindictiveness. . . .

NOTES AND QUESTIONS

1. Does a lawyer's role as counselor conflict with the lawyer's traditional role as litigator? Do the principles in the AAML Bounds of Advocacy conflict with your understanding of the attorney's role in other disputes? If so, how would you manage these conflicts? How do you understand the obligation of a lawyer to settle in a routine divorce case? Does it matter whether there are children involved? Is this obligation different from the obligation of a lawyer in a torts action? Why? For discussion of the Bounds of Advocacy, *see* John M. Burman, Ethics in Child Custody Proceedings: Changing from Client-Centered to Family-Centered Representation, 33 Wyo. Law. 40 (2010); In re T.S., 192 A.3d 1080 (Pa. 2018) (holding there is no conflict when an attorney guardian ad litem seeks to represent the best interests of the child regarding parental rights as well as the child's legal interests so long as no conflict exists between the child's legal interests and best interests).

2. In a classic study of family law negotiations, Austin Sarat & William B. Felstiner, Law and Strategy in the Divorce Lawyer's Office, 20 Law & Soc'y Rev. 93 (1986), the authors observed one side of family law negotiations in 40 divorce cases in Massachusetts and California, attended court proceedings, recorded lawyer-client sessions, and interviewed the participants about their perception of the events. While many of the clients tended to view the legal system as a formal, rule bound, relatively predictable process, the lawyers emphasized uncertainty — the outcome might depend on the judge, the persuasiveness of witnesses who might be nervous or uncertain of their recollections, or the occurrence of events the lawyers might not be able to foresee, such as a change in a child's school performance.

The study focused in particular on how lawyers deal with clients' emotions in conducting negotiations. The authors described in detail a divorce case that turned on the division of the couples' one major asset: their house. Although the parties had initially indicated a willingness to try mediation, that ended when the husband secured an ex parte restraining order that barred the wife from setting foot on the property. In the negotiations, the wife's first priority was rescinding the restraining order, but her lawyer tried to persuade her to focus instead on a global settlement resolving the divorce. She wanted vindication; she described the lawyer as her "knight in shining armor." She saw him as someone who would protect her and do battle for her. The lawyer tried to shift her attention from the restraining order to her objectives in the property settlement, where compromise was possible. The negotiation between lawyer and client was as, if not more, complex than the negotiation between the two sides. The lawyer had to retain the client's trust, even as he counseled compromise, and to defend himself against "a kind of emotional transference" in which "the client makes the lawyer into a kind of husband substitute." The authors emphasized the importance for both lawyer and client of separating the "legal self" and the "emotional self" and describe the lawyer's role in assisting the client in maintaining the separation between the two. In this particular example, these demands, including the need to establish trust with someone who has experienced betrayal from an intimate and the need to police lawyer-client boundaries, "typify the kind of environment in which divorce lawyers work."

Consider how you would handle such a client and whether the AAML Bounds of Advocacy suggest principles that would be helpful in doing so. How does a lawyer persuade a client to negotiate who wants vindication more than a particular outcome? Would your answer change if the issue involved child custody rather than a property division? Does the answer depend on what legal outcome you would predict from litigation or on your assessment of the clients' long-term interests? How should you proceed if your view of the clients' interests is different from their view? For an alternative view of the lawyers' role that places weight on the importance of empathy, *see* Douglas O. Linder & Nancy Levit, The Good Lawyer: Seeking Quality in the Practice of Law (2014).

PROBLEM

Fred's softball team wins the division championships and has a wild party to celebrate. His teammates hire prostitutes for the celebration and Fred indulges. His wife Maria finds out about it, and she is furious. She tells him she wants a divorce. A couple of weeks later, Fred stops by the house to apologize. He had been drinking earlier in the evening. He and Maria argue, and Fred grabs Maria and shakes her in an effort to stop her from yelling at him. Maria calls the police. Although their two young children had been asleep during the argument, Maria obtains an ex parte order barring Fred from the residence and limiting his contact to the children to supervised visitation.

Fred is your client. He is convinced that the marriage is over, and his first priority is to protect his relationship with the children, as he is very involved with them. His argument with Maria had been the first time anything like this had happened between them, and Fred says he never intended to hurt Maria but just get her attention. Fred wants you to do everything you can to remove the restraining order. He would also like to fight for as much time as he can with the children. He feels he has been the more involved parent and Maria's response to the party and to subsequent events, which Fred didn't organize and didn't know about in advance, was entirely disproportionate to what really happened.

You believe that the best way to approach the restraining order is to ignore it for now. If the judge sees that Fred is cooperative, no further incidents occur, and you reach a settlement on custody, the court will lift the order anyway. You also wonder if reconciliation is possible, though Fred rejected the idea when you mentioned it.

What obligations do you have under the AAML Bounds of Advocacy to promote reconciliation between Fred and Maria? To what extent should you accept Fred's insistence on trying to lift the restraining order before trying to settle the custody issue? If Maria were to propose lifting the order in exchange for a custody order giving her sole legal and physical custody with once a week visitation for Fred, how would you respond? If you are convinced you could do better in court, but Fred wants to accept the proposal, how would you advise him?

Timothy Hedeen & Peter Salem

What Should Family Lawyers Know? Results of a Survey of Practitioners and Students
44 Fam. Ct. Rev. 601, 605-606, 608-611 (2006)

Presented with a list of twenty-two skills, . . . the respondent pool was asked to rank each skill as "extremely important," "moderately important," or "not important at all." Fully ninety-seven percent (97.0%) indicated that listening was extremely important, while more than nine in ten identified setting realistic expectations for clients (93.6%), involving clients in decision making (93.1%), and identifying clients' interests (91.3%) as extremely important. These responses suggest that today's family law practitioner should be equipped with strong interpersonal, collaborative, and negotiation skills. While some of the most frequently identified skills reflect traditional expectations of lawyers as drivers of cases—setting expectations, keeping clients informed, client counseling—the preponderance of interactive, joint decision-making skills indicates the need for training in other areas as well. The interpersonal skills of listening, working with clients in emotional crisis, and conveying empathy are important for contemporary practice. . . .

We examined whether students placed the same level of importance on the skills, knowledge, and attributes of family lawyers as did law professors and practicing lawyers.

There was considerable agreement as to what skills, knowledge, and attributes were considered extremely important, including listening (law professors 100%; lawyers 100%; law students 97.1%), identifying clients' interests (law professors 96.3%; lawyers 95.4%; law students 94.1%), family court procedure (law professors 96.2%; lawyers 78.8%; law students 88.2%), governing law (law professors 92.3%; lawyers 86.2%; law students 91.2%), and preparedness (law professors 88.5%; lawyers 91.2%; law students 87.9%). It is interesting to note that family court procedure was ranked higher among both law professors and law students than it was among practicing lawyers.

There were also some noteworthy differences. Of the skills considered extremely important, law students tended to place a greater emphasis than their professors, lawyers, and indeed, virtually all of those surveyed, on the traditional legal skills of courtroom advocacy (law students 61.8%; lawyers 52.3%; law professors 33.3%), ability to question witnesses (law students 55.9%; lawyers 44.0%; law professors 44.4%), and persuasive writing (law students 44.1%; lawyers 39.8%; law professors 33.3%). . . .

Moreover, fewer law students (79.4%) than professors (100%) and lawyers (94%) responded that involving clients in decision making was extremely important, and fewer students (67.6%) than professors (88.9%) and lawyers (80.3%) considered the ability to work with clients in emotional crisis to be an extremely important skill.

Law students in this survey were not as concerned with the ethics of family law practice as were the lawyers and law professors who responded to the survey. Knowledge of the ethical dimensions of family law was extremely important for 88.5% of law professors, 80.7% of lawyers, and 67.6% of law students. Consistent with these findings, ethical behavior was extremely important for 100% of law professors, 90% of lawyers, and 72.7% of law students. Further, while 88.9% of law professors and 75.7% of lawyers responded that recognizing and resolving ethical dilemmas was extremely important, this was the case with only 55.9% of law students. Finally, 76.0% of law professors, 64.5% of lawyers, and 54.5% of law students reported that they believed fair-mindedness to be extremely important.

NOTES AND QUESTIONS

1. How does the lawyer's role as described in the AAML Bounds of Advocacy compare with the lawyer's role described in the Hedeen and Salem surveys? Do the surveys suggest that lawyers will need new skills and perhaps a different type of training to live up to the roles described in the AAML Bounds of Advocacy? How would you expect family law practice to change in accordance with these prescriptions? What are the implications for legal education? What are the implications for the structure of law practice? Do websites such as Wevorce, which provide online financial counseling and channel clients into self-guided mediation, offer a better way to address clients' needs?

2. The Hedeen and Salem survey asked the participants to describe the skills that are important to family law practice. What do you think accounts for the differences among lawyers, law professors, and students? When these groups differed about the importance of ethical knowledge and behavior, do you think they were making a positive statement (*i.e.*, describing what was important to being a successful lawyer) or a normative statement (*i.e.*, stating what they thought successful lawyers *should* be)? *See* Mark B. Baer, The Amplification of Bias in Family Law and Its Impact, 32 J. Am. Acad. Matrim. L. 305, 315 (2020).

3. A 2006 study of family law attorneys by Andrea Kupfer Schneider and Nancy Mills concluded that "[t]he proportion of family lawyers rated as adversarial (including both ethical and unethical) is higher than that of any other practice group." Andrea Kupfer Schneider &

Nancy Mills, What Family Lawyers Are Really Doing When They Negotiate, 44 Fam. Ct. Rev. 612 (2006). Would it surprise you to learn that divorce attorneys are more adversarial than attorneys specializing in other areas of civil litigation? Why or why not? Professor Linda McClain argues that the Kupfer Schneider and Mills study, which found that family lawyers are disproportionately adversarial, is inaccurate. Assessing the rise of alternative dispute resolution, she argues that family law practitioners have increasingly shunned adversarial styles and adopted collaborative and cooperative approaches:

> In *Divorce Lawyers at Work*, Lynn Mather and her colleagues found that divorce attorneys understand advocacy by reference to a model of the "reasonable lawyer," which, although it differs by community of practice, generally finds the zealous advocacy model inapt for family law disputes. Their research confirms prior work finding that "divorce lawyers dampen legal conflict far more than they exacerbate it and generally try to avoid adversarial actions." . . . If a family lawyer in a high-stakes divorce, with lots of assets or contested custody and lots of resources with which to wage battle, faces an opponent with a winner-take-all or zero-sum mentality or is negotiating with a very aggressive opponent, then that lawyer will "play the game," but it may not be the game the lawyer prefers. Apart from such high-stakes cases, family lawyers practice mindful of the fact that the parties will be dealing with each other on an ongoing basis concerning children.

Linda C. McClain, Is There a Way Forward in the "War Over the Family"?, 93 Tex. L. Rev. 705, 736 (2015).

4. Margo Melli, Howard Erlanger, and Elizabeth Chambliss emphasize that settlement is not the same thing as agreement. They write:

> . . . Divorcing couples are usually in a major life crisis and one or both are bitter; the resulting "settlement" does not represent genuine agreement but a "best I can get" solution. In other words, true agreement between the parties is much less common than the frequency of settlements might indicate. We have data on satisfaction with the settlement for 41 of the 44 parties interviewed. Twenty of these were satisfied; six said they were satisfied but nonetheless felt that the settlement was unfair to them, while 15 were very dissatisfied. The following are typical comments from the latter 21 parties, who constituted half the group for which we have data; clearly their settlements do not represent consensual agreements.
>
> > Well, I was worn down. . . . I cried through the whole thing, I could hardly say yes, I could hardly sign. [But I did and] I walked out of there and cried for probably two weeks straight. . . .
>
> This characteristic of divorce negotiation — that it often results in settlements which are not agreeable to one or both of the parties — may help explain a current problem in the divorce courts: the high volume of post-divorce litigation.

The Process of Negotiation: An Exploratory Investigation in the Context of No-Fault Divorce, 40 Rutgers L. Rev. 1133, 1142 (1988). Other countries have experimented with dispute resolution forums for family law matters. Australia has responded to these concerns by creating Family Relationship Centres in which parents with children are encouraged to provide for their children in a nonadversarial way with no lawyers permitted. The goal is to encourage greater shared parenting after a break-up. *See* Joan B. Kelly, Getting It Right for Families in Australia: Commentary on the April 2013 Special Issue on Family Relationship Centres, 51 Fam. Ct. Rev. 278 (2013); Patrick Parkinson, The Idea of Family Relationship Centres in Australia, 51 Fam. Ct. Rev. 195 (2013). Why might Australia conclude that the inclusion of lawyers exacerbates conflict?

5. Family law mediation is discussed below, and mediators have a different view of the role of lawyers in family law disputes than the lawyers do of themselves. A study of mediators' views of the obstacles they face included dealing with lawyers. The study found that:

Family law attorneys may have conflicting thoughts about the value of mediation, particularly mandatory mediation, and may feel "caught in the crossfire" when they must "suddenly shift out of a litigation mindset and into the delicate role of conciliator; a role, which some otherwise competent litigants are ill equipped and/or loath to play." They may have a win-lose or zero-sum view of the matrimonial case and project that bias onto the client in advance of the mandatory mediation process. Further, if the parties come to a successful mediated child custody or visitation agreement, the parties' attorneys may believe they cannot properly advise their clients whether the agreement is fair and therefore cannot provide proper protection because the attorneys have not "witness[ed] the give-and-take of the negotiations that created them and lack access to the information needed to evaluate properly alternatives to settlement."

Sandra J. Perry, Tanya M. Marcum & Charles R. Stoner, Stumbling Down the Courthouse Steps: Mediators' Perceptions of the Stumbling Blocks to Successful Mandated Mediation in Child Custody and Visitation, 11 Pepp. Disp. Resol. L.J. 441, 450-451 (2011). How do you reconcile these views with those of the other studies cited in this section?

6. In principle, the client is entitled to make the substantive decisions about how to conduct the case. The client may decide whether to seek, or to accept, sole or joint custody; what to seek by way of property distribution; whether to ask for or forgo alimony. If, after advising the client, the lawyer is profoundly dissatisfied with the client's position, the lawyer may withdraw *if* that can be accomplished without a materially adverse effect on the client's interests or if, among other things, the client insists on a criminal or fraudulent course of action or one that the lawyer considers repugnant or with which the lawyer fundamentally disagrees. Model Rule 1.16(b). How ready should a lawyer be to withdraw? Some lawyers try to anticipate conflicts with the client by establishing a reputation for a certain type of lawyering or by describing to a client at the beginning of the representation how they plan to handle the divorce. For example, some lawyers clearly state a belief that the continuing involvement of both parents is in the children's interest and that the law creates a presumption in favor of such involvement absent egregious conduct. How should a lawyer respond if the client later insists on seeking sole legal and physical custody and excluding the other parent from the child's life without a legally adequate justification?

7. The common law of fraud, of course, applies to lawyers and imposes a minimum standard of conduct for negotiations. *See* Russell Korobkin, Michael Moffitt & Nancy Welsh, The Law of Bargaining, 87 Marq. L. Rev. 839 (2004). Similarly, Rule 4.1 of the ABA Model Rules of Professional Conduct provides that "[i]n the course of representing a client a lawyer shall not knowingly: (a) make a false statement of material fact or law to a third person." Model Rule 8.4 has language that suggests an even broader set of restrictions. These obligations may become particularly difficult to apply when the other party is not represented by counsel. Rule 4.3(b) provides that a lawyer "shall not give legal advice to an unrepresented person, other than the advice to secure counsel, if the lawyer knows or reasonably should know that the interests of such a person are or have a reasonable possibility of being in conflict with the interests of the client." Applying Rule 4.3(b), in In re Robinson, 209 A.3d 570 (Vt. 2019), a lawyer was disbarred for an ongoing pattern of misconduct, including his failure to advise an unrepresented person that she should seek independent counsel and encouraging her to sign a document waiving her right to assert certain claims in the future. How can attorneys in cases in which the other party is unrepresented by a lawyer protect themselves from alleged violations of this rule?

8. Is an intimate relationship between a lawyer and the lawyer's client permitted? ABA Model Rule 1.8(j) prohibits a lawyer from having sex with a client unless a consensual sexual relationship existed prior to the beginning of professional representation. Standard 3.4 of the AAML Standards of Conduct sets out the same rule as the ABA Model Rule 1.8(j). Other provisions of the Standards of Conduct clarify that "[a]n attorney should never have a sexual relationship with a client or opposing counsel during the time of the representation" and that "[a]n attorney should not simultaneously represent both a client and a person with whom the client is sexually involved." Standard 2.16.

To take a state ethics rule, Rule 3-120(B) of the California Rules of Professional Conduct previously provided that a lawyer shall not "(1) Require or demand sexual relations with a client incident to or as a condition of any professional representation; or (2) Employ coercion, intimidation, or undue influence in entering into sexual relations; or (3) Continue representation of a client with whom the member has had sexual relations if such sexual relations cause the member to perform legal services incompetently. . . ." The California State Bar updated Rule 3-120(B) in 2018. Rule 1.8.10: Sexual Relations with Current Client states,

(a) A lawyer shall not engage in sexual relations with a current client who is not the lawyer's spouse or registered domestic partner, unless a consensual sexual relationship existed between them when the lawyer-client relationship commenced.

(b) For purposes of this rule, "sexual relations" means sexual intercourse or the touching of an intimate part of another person for the purpose of sexual arousal, gratification, or abuse.

(c) If a person other than the client alleges a violation of this rule, no Notice of Disciplinary Charges may be filed by the State Bar against a lawyer under this rule until the State Bar has attempted to obtain the client's statement regarding, and has considered, whether the client would be unduly burdened by further investigation or a charge.

See also Attorney Grievance Comm'n of Maryland v. O'Leary, 69 A.3d 1121 (Md. App. 2013); In re Fuerst, 157 So. 3d 569 (La. 2014) (attorney suspended for having a sexual relationship with a current client).

9. The changing nature of family court and the increasing awareness of mental health issues has also forced family lawyers to confront complex legal, ethical, and practical issues. Changes in family court procedure, such as mandated mediation, and statutory changes encouraging shared care and custody of children, coupled with the rise of pro se representation in family law matters require significant engagement and competence on the part of litigants. Family law attorneys may find themselves representing a potentially impaired client or facing a potentially impaired "adversary" who has chosen self-representation. Either can raise significant ethical issues for the attorney's ability to negotiate, contract, and meaningfully engage with a party. *See* Lynda E. Frost & Connie J. A. Beck, Meeting the Increasing Demands on Family Attorneys Representing Clients with Mental Health Challenges, 54 Fam. Ct. Rev. 39 (2016).

PROBLEMS

1. During a hotly contested custody litigation, you realize that you, the other attorney, and the parents are not going to reach any interim or permanent settlement. You are also convinced that the children are undergoing terrible emotional strain because of the conduct of their parents. You feel the best recourse is to ask the court to appoint a guardian ad litem for the children. Must you discuss this step with your client? If your client directs you not to seek such an appointment, may you do so anyway? Are there any other actions you might take? Is there any action you could have taken at the beginning of your representation of the client to lay the foundation for the resolution of this type of dispute with a client?

2. You represent an ex-wife in a petition for an increase in child support. You have negotiated a deal for an amount above the state child support guidelines and feel you will not do any better in court. You so inform your client, but she still wants more and refuses to settle. Can you accept the offer on your client's behalf? If not, should you seek to withdraw, and can you properly do so?

3. Your client has told you that he feels very guilty about the end of his marriage, and he is willing to give his wife all the marital property except for one automobile and is willing to pay her substantial alimony, even though she has been employed throughout the marriage. You have advised him that, under the circumstances, a court is unlikely to require more than an equal distribution of marital property and would almost surely not award spousal maintenance. Nonetheless, your client does not want any contest with his wife and instructs you to accept any offer that leaves him an automobile and provides alimony of not more than $1000 per month.

Opposing counsel opens negotiations by saying, "My client wants to be reasonable. She thinks that 80 percent of the marital property will suffice. But she really does not want to fight about this, and there is some flexibility. Will your client give her the 80 percent?" How do you answer?

D. ALTERNATIVE DISPUTE RESOLUTION

Jana B. Singer

Dispute Resolution and the Post-divorce Family: Implications of a Paradigm Shift
47 Fam. Ct. Rev. 363 (2009)

Over the past two decades, there has been a paradigm shift in the way the legal system handles most family disputes—particularly disputes involving children. This paradigm shift has replaced the law-oriented and judge-focused adversary model with a more collaborative, interdisciplinary, and forward-looking family dispute resolution regime. It has also transformed the practice of family law and fundamentally altered the way in which disputing families interact with the legal system. . . .

The paradigm shift in family dispute resolution encompasses a number of related components. The first component is a profound skepticism about the value of traditional adversary procedures. An overriding theme of recent divorce reform efforts is that adversary processes are ill suited for resolving disputes involving children. Relatedly, social science suggests that children's adjustment to divorce and separation depends significantly on their parents' behavior during and after the separation process: the higher the levels of parental conflict to which children are exposed, the more negative the effects of family dissolution. Armed with these social science findings, academics and court reformers have argued that family courts should abandon the adversary paradigm, in favor of approaches that help parents manage their conflict and encourage them to develop positive post-divorce co-parenting relationships. . . .

A second element of the paradigm shift in family dispute resolution is the belief that most family disputes are not discrete legal events, but ongoing social and emotional processes. This de-legalization of family disputes began with the shift from fault-based to no-fault divorce; more recently, it has become one of the basic tenets of the movement for unified family courts. Thus recharacterized, family disputes call *not* for zealous legal approaches, but for interventions that are collaborative, holistic, and interdisciplinary, because these are the types of interventions most likely to address the family's underlying dysfunction and emotional needs. Understanding family conflict as primarily a social and emotional process, rather than a legal event, also reduces the primacy of lawyers in handling these disputes and enhances the role of nonlegal professionals in the family court system.

Third, this new understanding of family disputes has led to a reformulation of the goal of legal intervention in the family. Traditionally, legal intervention was a backward-looking process, designed primarily to assign blame and allocate rights; under the new paradigm, by contrast, judges assume the forward-looking task of supervising a process of family reorganization. As Andrew Schepard has noted, family court judges no longer function primarily as fault finders or rights adjudicators, but rather as ongoing conflict managers. . . .

Fourth, to achieve these therapeutic goals, family courts have adopted systems that deemphasize third-party dispute resolution in favor of capacity-building processes that seek to empower families to resolve their own conflicts. Consistent with this philosophy, jurisdictions across the country have instituted mandatory divorce-related parenting education and other programs designed to enhance litigants' communication and problem-solving skills. Similarly, the American Law Institute's (ALI) Principles of the Law of Family Dissolution endorses individualized parenting plans as an alternative to judicial custody rulings and urges the adoption of court-based programs that facilitate these voluntary agreements. . . . More recently, a number of family courts have added parenting coordinators to their staffs; these quasi-judicial officials assist high-conflict families to develop concrete parenting plans and to resolve ongoing parenting disputes that arise under these plans.

A fifth component of the paradigm shift is an increased emphasis on predispute planning and preventive law. Familiar examples include the increased acceptance and enforceability of prenuptial agreements and domestic partnership contracts. Parenting plans that include a mechanism for periodic review or a process for resolving future disagreements are similarly designed to minimize the need for future court intervention. More recently, a number of commentators have advocated a similar, preventive approach to determining, prior to a child's birth, the parental status of a non–biologically related adult who anticipates caring for the child. Perhaps more ambitiously, a few states have considered broad-based premarriage education requirements as a prerequisite for obtaining a marriage license, and the federal government has invested substantial resources in public and private marriage education programs aimed especially at low-income partners. More generally, scholars and advocates of preventive law have urged individuals to use legal mechanisms to anticipate and plan for family transitions such as the formation and dissolution of intimate partnerships. . . .

Interest in alternative dispute resolution arises from a variety of sources: academic commentary, the legal and other "helping" professions, and the popular media. Jane C. Murphy & Jana B. Singer, Divorced from Reality: Rethinking Family Dispute Resolution 1 (2015). In its 1991 Standards of Conduct, the AAML added its support through Standard 1.4, which provides that "[a]n attorney should be knowledgeable about alternate ways to resolve matrimonial disputes." The comment has been revised since then to suggest that many clients favor a problem-solving model over litigation. It is essential that family law lawyers have sufficient knowledge about alternative dispute resolution to understand the advantages and disadvantages for a particular client and to counsel the client appropriately concerning the particular dispute resolution mechanism selected.

The phrase "alternative dispute resolution" or "ADR" refers to a variety of methods of handling disputes that are considered alternatives to adversarial litigation. Negotiation, which as noted above has always been part of litigation, is one alternative. So is arbitration, a long-established practice in a number of fields. As perceptions of the costs, dangers, and ineffectiveness of litigation have become more acute, increasing attention has turned to mediation and collaborative practice. The rest of the chapter will consider the ability of arbitration, mediation, and collaborative practice to defuse the tensions and to reduce the costs that litigation appears to exacerbate.

1. Arbitration

Arbitration typically involves a contractual agreement to designate a third party to resolve a dispute without the formality and expense of litigation. The agreement to submit a dispute to arbitration can be set forth in a premarital agreement, as part of a divorce settlement, or at any time the dispute arises. Arbitration allows the parties to choose a decision maker who shares their values. It also allows the parties to control the timing and the form of the hearing. Arbitration is typically much faster than litigation, and the arbitrator's decision is final. The speed and informality of the process make it much less expensive than litigation. On the other hand, arbitration generally does not involve discovery, it lacks the procedural protections of formal litigation, and the arbitrator's decision may be subject to greater review in many jurisdictions if it affects children's interests. Rochelle Grossman, Choosing Your Approach to Resolution, 43 Fam. Advoc. 8 (2020); Audrey J. Beeson, Arbitration. A Promising Avenue for Resolving Family Law Cases?, 18 Pepp. Disp. Resol. L.J. 211 (2018) (discussing trends in arbitration, including the adoption of Family Law Arbitration Statutes, and how they have changed since the 1990s).

Fawzy v. Fawzy
973 A.2d 347 (N.J. 2009)

LONG, J. . . . Plaintiff, Christine Saba Fawzy, and defendant, Samih M. Fawzy, were married on September 28, 1991, and have two children born in 1996 and 1997, respectively. On September 13, 2005, Mrs. Fawzy filed a complaint for divorce. . . .

On January 22, 2007, the day on which the trial on all issues was to take place, the parties apparently notified the judge that they had agreed to arbitrate in place of proceeding to trial. . . . The judge stated that he would delay issuing the judgment of divorce until March 5, 2007, which would give the parties six weeks to complete the arbitration proceedings.

During the same proceeding, . . . the attorney for Mr. Fawzy asked that the parties be sworn and place on the record their agreement to submit the case to arbitration. The following colloquy ensued:

[The Court:]   Both of you need and want closure as do your children. Arbitration is unappealable. . . . You can never — neither you nor she can ever return to court, except in one or two circumstances. And here's how you can return.

If there's a change of circumstances, you can return. Now, a change of circumstances is a legal term of art. . . .

. . . If down the road, you or your wife believe that — that circumstances have changed and that the best interests of your children will be served by a modification of Mr. Busch's order, which again as the arbitrator he's — he'll be deciding parenting time, not recommending it. He'll be deciding it. . . .

Let's assume there's a child support obligation, and I assume there will be. If someone's financial circumstances change, you can return to court. Child support can always be revisited. . . .

I think the incomes are, again, about $80,000.00 and $40,000.00. If, hypothetically, someone's income doubles . . . or if someone loses their job, someone can say we need a modification of the financial obligations.

> Here's what you can't do. You can't come back to me and say I
> don't like the award or I think Mr. Busch was partial or I think he was
> unbalanced. Neither side could do that.
>
> . . . There's one other instance in which you can return to court.
> To enforce the award. If Mr. Busch's award says X dollars in child support
> and someone's not paying it, you can come back to court to enforce that.
> But you can't come back to court because you've said I don't like Mr.
> Busch's decision.
>
> Okay. Now, before either side is questioned by their attorney, Mrs.
> Fawzy, do you understand and agree to everything I just said?

Mrs. Fawzy:	Yes, I do.
The Court:	Sir, do you?
Mr. Fawzy:	Yes, I do.
The Court:	Okay. Thank you. . . .

On March 6, 2007, judgment of divorce was entered, including reference to the agreement to arbitrate. . . .

[The arbitrator] issued a custody and parenting-time award on April 4, 2007, which granted the parties joint legal custody with primary physical custody to Mrs. Fawzy; designated Mrs. Fawzy as the parent of primary residence; and granted Mr. Fawzy weekday, weekend, vacation, and holiday parenting time. . . .

Mr. Fawzy appealed. . . .

We begin with some brief observations regarding arbitration, which is " 'a method of dispute resolution involving one or more neutral third parties who are usu[ally] agreed to by the disputing parties and whose decision is binding.' " . . .

"Although arbitration is traditionally described as a favored remedy, it is, at its heart, a creature of contract." It is for that reason that binding arbitration cannot be imposed by judicial fiat . . . .

In 2003, the Legislature adopted the Arbitration Act, which in most respects mirrors the Uniform Arbitration Act. L. 2003, c. 95. Under the Act, a court will vacate an arbitration award only if:

(1)   the award was procured by corruption, fraud, or other undue means;

(2)   the court finds evident partiality by an arbitrator; corruption by an arbitrator; or misconduct by an arbitrator prejudicing the rights of a party to the arbitration proceeding;

(3)   an arbitrator refused to postpone the hearing upon showing of sufficient cause for postponement, refused to consider evidence material to the controversy, or otherwise conducted the hearing contrary to section 15 of this act, so as to substantially prejudice the rights of a party to the arbitration proceeding;

(4)   an arbitrator exceeded the arbitrator's powers;

(5)   there was no agreement to arbitrate, unless the person participated in the arbitration proceeding without raising the objection pursuant to subsection c. of section 15 of this act not later than the beginning of the arbitration hearing; or

(6)   the arbitration was conducted without proper notice of the initiation of an arbitration as required in section 9 of this act so as to substantially prejudice the rights of a party to the arbitration proceeding. . . .

As can be seen from those provisions and, as might be expected, the scope of review of an arbitration award is narrow. Otherwise, the purpose of the arbitration contract, which is to provide an effective, expedient, and fair resolution of disputes, would be severely undermined.

We note that there is no express bar to the arbitration of family law matters in the Arbitration Act. Further, in Faherty v. Faherty, we long ago approved the arbitration of some family law issues, alimony and child support in particular. 97 N.J. 99, 108-09, 477 A.2d 1257 (1984). There we reserved decision on the issue of arbitration of child-custody questions. . . . Today, the issue left open in *Faherty*—whether child-custody and parenting-time issues can be resolved by arbitration—is before us.

The legal landscape across the country has changed in the quarter century since *Faherty*, which was decided at a time when few, if any, jurisdictions allowed arbitration of child-custody disputes. Indeed, the majority of our sister states that have addressed the issue have concluded that parents are empowered to submit child-custody and parenting-time issues to arbitration in the exercise of their parental autonomy.

We note as well that that conclusion has been urged by the bulk of scholarly writing on the subject.

Such scholarly support for child-custody arbitration recognizes that it has the potential to minimize the harmful effects of divorce litigation on both children and parents. As Professor Linda Elrod explained:

> Unlike a tort action where the issue is liability and the litigants may never cross paths again, a divorce legally ends a relationship between people who may not have separated emotionally and who must continue to interact as long as there are minor children. . . . The win/lose framework [of child-custody litigation] encourages parents to find fault with each other rather than to cooperate. . . .
>
> In addition, unlike tort cases that end with a money judgment, issues regarding children remain modifiable throughout a child's minority, giving parents more opportunities to carry on a dispute. . . . The entire process becomes negative and expensive.

[Linda D. Elrod, Reforming the System to Protect Children in High Conflict Custody Cases, 28 Wm. Mitchell L. Rev. 495, 501-502 (2001).]

On the other hand, "arbitration conducted in a less formal atmosphere, often in a shorter time span than a trial, and always with a fact-finder of the parties' own choosing, is often far less antagonistic and nasty than typical courthouse litigation." In sum, the benefits of arbitration in the family law setting appear to be well established. . . .

As the arguments of the parties make clear, although the stated issue before us is whether we should permit arbitration of child-custody issues, the case is really about the intersection between parents' fundamental liberty interest in the care, custody, and control of their children, and the state's interest in the protection of those children. . . .

The question then becomes whether the right to parental autonomy subsumes the right to submit issues of child custody and parenting time to an arbitrator for disposition. We think it does. As we have said, the entitlement to autonomous family privacy includes the fundamental right of parents to make decisions regarding custody, parenting time, health, education, and other child-welfare issues between themselves, without state interference. That right does not evaporate when an intact marriage breaks down. It is for that reason, as the parties conceded, that when matrimonial litigants reach a settlement on issues regarding child custody, support, and parenting time, as a practical matter the court does not inquire into the merits of the agreement. It is only when the parents cannot agree that the court becomes the default decision maker.

Indeed, Mr. Fawzy does not suggest otherwise. He recognizes that parental autonomy subsumes all child-custody and parenting-time questions and that so long as the parties agree, they can make decisions on those subjects between themselves without state interference. The only decision that he appears to carve out of that right to parental autonomy is the decision to submit child-custody and parenting-time matters to arbitration.

We see no basis for that exception. For us, the bundle of rights that the notion of parental autonomy sweeps in includes the right to decide how issues of custody and parenting time will be resolved. Indeed, we have no hesitation in concluding that, just as parents "choose" to decide issues of custody and parenting time among themselves without court intervention, they may opt to sidestep the judicial process and submit their dispute to an arbitrator whom they have chosen. . . .

Under *Faherty*, the review of an arbitration award is to take place within the confines of the Arbitration Act, unless there is a claim of adverse impact or harm to the child. . . .

Mere disagreement with the arbitrator's decision obviously will not satisfy the harm standard. The threat of harm is a significantly higher burden than a best-interests analysis. Although each case is unique and fact intensive, by way of example, in a case of two fit parents, a party's challenge to an arbitrator's custody award because she would be "better" is not a claim of harm. Nor will the contention that a particular parenting-time schedule did not include enough summer vacation time be sufficient to pass muster. To the contrary, a party's claim that the arbitrator granted custody to a parent with serious substance abuse issues or a debilitating mental illness could raise the specter of harm. Obviously, evidential support establishing a prima facie case of harm will be required in order to trigger a hearing. Where the hearing yields a finding of harm, the court must set aside the arbitration award and decide the case anew, using the best-interests test.

We recognize that some other jurisdictions have approached the standard of review issue differently. For example, Pennsylvania has adopted a pure best-interests test for judicial review of an arbitrated custody award. We decline to adopt that model, which allows a court to substitute its judgment regarding the child's best interests for that of the arbitrator chosen by the parents and fails to accord the constitutionally required deference to the notion of parental autonomy. . . .

In our view, the hybrid model we have adopted at once advances the purposes of arbitration by providing a final, speedy, and inexpensive resolution of the dispute; affords deference to parental decision making by allowing the parents to choose the person who will resolve the matter; and leaves open the availability of court intervention where it is necessary to prevent harm to the child.

We therefore direct that . . . in respect of child-custody and parenting-time issues only, a record of all documentary evidence shall be kept; all testimony shall be recorded verbatim; and the arbitrator shall state in writing or otherwise record his or her findings of fact and conclusions of law with a focus on the best-interests standard. It is only upon such a record that an evaluation of the threat of harm can take place without an entirely new trial. Any arbitration award regarding child-custody and parenting-time issues that results from procedures other than those that we have mandated will be subject to vacation upon motion. . . .

We turn finally to the question of how parents may exercise their rights and bind themselves to arbitrate a child-custody dispute. . . . The [Arbitration] Act defines a record necessary to establish an agreement to arbitrate as "information that is inscribed on a tangible medium or that is stored in an electronic or other medium and is retrievable in perceivable form." N.J.S.A. 2A:23B-1. . . . In addition, it must state in clear and unmistakable language: (1) that the parties understand their entitlement to a judicial adjudication of their dispute and are willing to waive that right; (2) that the parties are aware of the limited circumstances under which a challenge to the arbitration award may be advanced and agree to those limitations; (3) that the parties have had sufficient time to consider the implications of their decision to arbitrate; and (4) that the parties have entered into the arbitration agreement freely and voluntarily, after due consideration of the consequences of doing so.

It goes without saying that parties are not bound to arbitrate on an all-or-nothing basis, but may choose to submit discrete issues to the arbitrator. The arbitration agreement should reflect, with specificity, which issues are to be subject to an arbitrator's decision. . . .

Applying the standards we have enunciated to the facts of this case, we are satisfied that the agreement to arbitrate was insufficient to bind the parties. Although both Mr. and Mrs. Fawzy responded affirmatively to questions regarding their agreement, the nature of what was spread upon the record was inadequate to assure that they fully understood the consequences of removing their custody dispute from the judicial arena and into binding arbitration.

. . . Although the judge fully explained "changed circumstances," . . . he did not as fully explain the parties' statutorily limited ability to challenge the award without such a change. Nor did he allude to the particular standards under which modification or vacation of the award would be allowed, or what other standards would warrant judicial intervention. Further, he erred in suggesting that bias on the part of the arbitrator would not be a basis for challenge under the Arbitration Act.

To be fair, the judge, who did not have the benefit of this opinion, most likely thought that all the details of the arbitration had been worked out and explained by the lawyers, and indeed, they might have been. We simply cannot tell from the record whether that is so. Thus, lacking a basis on which to conclude that the Fawzys understood what they were relinquishing by opting for arbitration, we cannot say that they agreed to arbitrate their custody dispute. . . .

NOTES AND QUESTIONS

1. Judicial enforcement of arbitration clauses and acceptance of arbitration decisions have varied widely, particularly regarding child custody. Compare *Fawzy* with Kelm v. Kelm, 749 N.E.2d 299 (Ohio 2001), which held that "[t]he trial court has a continuing responsibility . . . to protect the best interests of the children. . . . [T]he parties' agreement to arbitrate custody and visitation disputes impermissibly interferes with the court's ability to carry out this responsibility." The Ohio court acknowledged that the decisions from other states permit arbitration of custody and visitation, but noted:

> Typically, these decisions protect the courts' role as *parens patriae* by making the arbitrator's decision subject to *de novo* review and modification by the courts. . . . While this approach preserves the court's role as *parens patriae*, we believe that, ultimately, it advances neither the children's best interests nor the basic goals underlying arbitration.
>
> A two-stage procedure consisting of an arbitrator's decision followed by *de novo* judicial review "is certain to be wasteful of time and expense and result in a duplication of effort." Clearly, it does not seem advantageous to the best interests of children that questions of custody be postponed " 'while a rehearsal of the decisive inquiry is held.' "
>
> The protracted two-stage process adopted by some courts also frustrates the very goals underlying arbitration. "Arbitration is favored because it provides the parties thereto with a relatively expeditious and economical means of resolving a dispute . . . [and] '. . . has the additional advantage of unburdening crowded court dockets.' " A two-stage process consisting of both arbitration and judicial review achieves none of these goals.
>
> Furthermore, "if an issue is to be arbitrated, the expectation [of the parties] is that an award will not be disturbed." *De novo* review destroys this expectation. Thus, there is an inevitable tension between the court's traditional responsibility to protect the best interests of children and the parties' expectation that an arbitration award will be final.

749 N.E.2d at 302. *See also* Tuetken v. Tuetken, 320 S.W.3d 262 (Tenn. 2010). Does *Fawzy* address the Ohio court's concerns about duplicative proceedings?

2. *Fawzy*'s discussion of divorce contrasted the idea of marriage as a contract, that is, an expression of the agreement of the parties, and as a covenant, that is, a status determined by the relationship between the couple, the state, and the community. In determining the enforceability of arbitration agreements, the *Fawzy* and *Kelm* courts also disagree about the extent to which custody should be resolved by the parties, and the extent to which the state has an independent duty to determine children's well-being.[2] The courts both use the term *parens patriae* as part of their analysis of the proper allocation of decision-making responsibility. In the *Fawzy* opinion, the court defines *parens patriae* from Black's Law Dictionary as "'parent of his or her country,' and refers to 'the state in its capacity as provider of protection to those unable to care for themselves,' such as children." 973 A.2d 347, n.2. Do the two courts use it to mean the same thing? What are the implications of their use of the phrase for the enforceability of arbitration agreements?

3. The New Jersey court refers to an article on arbitration by Professor Gary Spitko, which argues that couples who fear that judges may reflect majoritarian values hostile to their own may wish to use arbitration to select decision makers who share their values. E. Gary Spitko, Gone but Not Conforming: Protecting the Abhorrent Testator from Majoritarian Cultural Norms Through Minority-Culture Arbitration, 49 Case W. Res. L. Rev. 275 (1999). He develops his analysis in the context of will contests, but the same principles could be applied to divorce or custody disputes. A same-sex couple, for example, raising children together could specify that any dispute over custody, visitation, or child support will be subject to mandatory arbitration, with the arbitrators to be chosen from a group of arbitrators with track records of serving LGBTQ clients.

Professor Ayelet Shachar explored the practice of some couples using arbitration to select decision makers who share their values because they fear that judges may reflect majoritarian values hostile to their own. Professor Shachar questions the practice to the extent it is intended to result in decision makers who are not just more in sync with the parties' values or cultural perspectives, but expected to apply different legal standards. She asks:

> [S]hould a court be permitted to enforce a civil divorce contract that also has a religious aspect, namely a promise by a Jewish husband to remove all barriers to remarriage by granting his wife the religious *get* (Jewish divorce decree)? Is it legitimate to establish private religious tribunals — as alternative dispute resolution (ADR) forums — in which consenting adults arbitrate family law disputes according to the parties' religious personal laws in lieu of the state's secular family laws? And, is there room for considerations of culture, religion, national-origin, or linguistic identity in determining a child's best interests in cases of custody, visitation, education, and so on? None of these examples are hypothetical. They represent real-life legal challenges raised in recent years by individuals and families who are seeking to redefine the place of culture and religion in their own private ordering, and, indirectly, in the larger polity as well.

Ayelet Shachar, Privatizing Diversity: A Cautionary Tale from Religious Arbitration in Family Law, 9 Theoretical Inquiries L. 573, 576 (2008). Professor Shachar notes, for example, the uproar over an announcement by the Canadian Society of Muslims (a small, relatively conservative religious group) that it intended to rely on the Canadian Arbitration Act to establish a Sharia tribunal that "would have permitted consenting parties not only to enter a less adversarial, out-of-court, dispute resolution process, but also to use the Act's *choice of law* provisions to apply religious norms to resolve family disputes, according to the 'laws (*fiqh*) of any [Islamic] school, *e.g.* Shiah or Sunni (Hanafi, Shafi'i, Hambali, or Maliki).'" *Id.* at 577-578. Canada has since amended the Act to preclude the application of religious principles in conflict with secular law. *See* Arbitration Act, 2006 S.O., ch. 1, §1(2) (incorporated into Section 2.2 of the 1991 Arbitration Act).

What would happen if a couple in the United States stipulated in a premarital agreement that any dispute between them was to be resolved through mandatory arbitration, and the

---

2. A similar tension exists in deciding how much latitude to accord to provisions of settlement and marital agreements that govern child custody, as explained in Chapter 10.

arbitrator was to be chosen from a list of arbitrators who had agreed to decide the dispute in accordance with Islamic or Judaic laws and customs? Would New Jersey and Ohio differ in their approaches to child custody arbitration in such circumstances? *See, e.g.*, Schechter v. Schechter, 881 N.Y.S.2d 151 (N.Y. App. Div. 2009) (rejecting child custody arbitration by religious tribunal); Evan M. Lowry, Note, Where Angels Fear to Tread: Islamic Arbitration in Probate and Family Law: A Practical Perspective, 46 Suffolk U. L. Rev. 159 (2013).

4. Suppose the parties include a provision in their separation agreement stating that the noncustodial spouse need not pay child support if visitation provisions are violated. The agreement also includes an arbitration provision. State court decisions hold that noncompliance with visitation orders does not affect the child support obligation. What should the result be if an arbitrator finds repeated interference with the noncustodial parent's visitation rights? Would judicial review be effective?

5. Although arbitration of custody disputes remains unusual, use of another third party to aid decisionmaking is not; the child custody evaluator often plays a significant role in custody decision making. (The next section on mediation notes the role of parenting coordinators.) Professors Kelly and Ramsay explain that the child custody evaluator may take one of three forms:

> *Source 1: Court-Appointed Private-Sector Forensic Evaluator*, the judge orders an evaluation unilaterally or as part of a stipulation agreed to by the parties and appoints the evaluator from the pool of available private mental health professionals.
>
> *Source 2: Court-Appointed Public-Sector Forensic Evaluator* is the same as Source 1, with the exception that the evaluator comes from a publicly financed agency or program, which normally, but not always, is associated with the court.
>
> *Source 3: Party-Paid Mental Health Expert Testimony* has fallen into disfavor. Under this model, one or both parties unilaterally commission a custody investigation with the implicit expectation that the report will favor the commissioning party.

Robert F. Kelly & Sarah H. Ramsay, Child Custody Evaluations: The Need for Systems-Level Outcome Assessments, 47 Fam. Ct. Rev. 286 (2009). In each case, the evaluation is submitted to the court, and the judge remains the ultimate decision maker. Nonetheless, the recommendations, particularly in situations where the judge appoints the evaluator, tend to be influential. This process is similar to arbitration in that a neutral third party evaluates the circumstances, and does so in accordance with a less formal, less adversarial process. It differs from arbitration in the following respects:

- Although in some cases the parties initiate the evaluation and jointly choose an evaluator, the court typically initiates the process and may select a professional without input from the parties.
- The judge remains the ultimate decision maker in accordance with the best-interest-of-the-child standard.
- The evaluator's recommendations are not ordinarily binding on the court or the parties (although the parties can agree to follow the evaluator's recommendations).
- The standards behind the evaluators' recommendations generally reflect mental health practices rather than legal rules, with the court bearing the ultimate responsibility for determining how the evaluation adheres to the best-interest-of-the-child legal standard.

Kelly and Ramsay emphasize that while there is an extensive literature on the substance of child custody evaluations, there is relatively little empirical research assessing their use, influence, or effectiveness — not only on judicial decisions, but also on parties' negotiations and resolution of custody disputes. *See also* Association of Family and Conciliation Courts, Model Standards of Practice for Child Custody Evaluation, 45 Fam. Ct. Rev. 70 (2007); Robert E. Emery, Randy K. Otto & William T. O'Donohue, A Critical Assessment of Child Custody Evaluations:

Limited Science and a Flawed System, 6 Psychol. Sci. Pub. Int. 16 (2005); T.M. Tippins & J.P. Wittmann, Empirical and Ethical Problems with Custody Recommendations: A Call for Clinical Humility and Judicial Vigilance, 43 Fam. Ct. Rev. 45 193 (2005).

6. In 2016, the Uniform Law Commission enacted the Uniform Family Law Arbitration Act. National Conference of Commissioners of Uniform State Laws, Uniform Family Law Arbitration Act (2016), available at http://www.uniformlaws.org/. The purpose of the Act is to create a comprehensive arbitration system for the states. It is based in part on the Revised Uniform Arbitration Act, applicable to arbitration across various areas of law, and tailored to the family law issues that differ from commercial arbitration. The issues covered by the Act include matters relating to children, arbitrator qualifications and powers, and protections for victims of domestic violence and child abuse.

The Act also sets out the grounds for arbitrator disqualification and for vacating an arbitration award. Arbitrators must disclose any impediment to making a timely award and any partiality, "including bias, a financial or personal interest in the outcome of the arbitration, or an existing or past relationship with a party, attorney representing a party, or witness." *Id.* §9(a)(1)(2). Courts may vacate awards if a moving party establishes that the award was "procured by corruption, fraud, or other undue means;" that there was partiality or corruption by the arbitrator; that the arbitrator exceeded his or her powers; that the arbitrator refused to postpone a hearing on showing sufficient cause; or that a party failed to provide proper notice to the other party. *Id.* §19(a)(1)-(7). Courts may vacate awards under the Act that are "contrary to the best interests of the child" or do not comply with the law of the state. *Id.* §19(b)(1). Only four states have passed legislation adopting the Act, with four more introducing the Act, but not passing it, as of 2022.

PROBLEM

You are a law clerk to Judge Wilson, who sits on the Family Court of your county. Pending before her is the case of an orthodox Jewish couple with six children. The couple decided to divorce and voluntarily submitted their custody dispute for arbitration to a Beth Din (a religious court). The Beth Din divided custody between the parents, with the three oldest placed with the father and the three youngest with the mother. The father has filed a divorce petition in Judge Wilson's court. The petition seeks incorporation of the religious court's decree in the civil order, relying on a state statute providing generally for judicial enforcement of decisions reached by an arbitrator to whom a dispute has been submitted by the parties. Judge Wilson asks for your analysis of the father's request.

2. Mediation

The most widespread institutionalized form of alternative dispute resolution is mediation. The Model Standards of Practice for Family and Divorce Mediation define mediation as:

> a process in which a mediator, an impartial third party, facilitates the resolution of family disputes by promoting the participants' voluntary agreement. The family mediator assists communication, encourages understanding and focuses the participants on their individual and common interests. The family mediator works with the participants to explore options, make decisions and reach their own agreements.[3]

---

3. Model Standards of Practice for Family and Divorce Mediation, Overview and Definitions (2000), available at https://cdn.ymaws.com/acrnet.org/resource/resmgr/docs/Model_Standards_of_Practice_.pdf (last visited July 18, 2022).

The increase in divorce rates increased interest in alternative mechanisms that could resolve disputes more quickly, less expensively, and with less judicial involvement. At the same time, the move away from fault-based decision making increased the need for an alternative foundation for resolving disagreements. Professor Jay Folberg, an early advocate of mediation, argued that:

> Mediation can help the parties learn how to solve problems together . . . and recognize that cooperation can be of mutual advantage. Mediation is bound neither by rules of procedure and substantive law nor by other assumptions that dominate the adversary process. The ultimate authority in mediation belongs to the parties. . . . The emphasis is not on who is right and who is wrong . . . but on establishing a workable resolution that best meets the needs of the participants.

Jay Folberg, Mediation of Child Custody Disputes, 19 Colum. J.L. & Soc. Probs. 413, 414-418 (1985).

The cornerstone of mediation is self-determination. The parties negotiate and resolve disputes on their own, and the mediator serves as a third-party neutral who guides the process of negotiation. Several decades of research have produced impressive arguments for the value of mediation. Psychologist Robert Emery, for example, persuaded the court in Charlottesville, Virginia, to assign divorcing couples randomly to either mediation or litigation groups. Emery and his colleagues then tracked the families for 15 years. They found that those assigned to the mediation group were more likely to settle their disputes, and to do so earlier in the process. They reported some evidence of greater compliance with child support orders, and greater satisfaction with the process. The increase in satisfaction was particularly striking for fathers, while some mothers were happier with the results of litigation. In a follow-up study, Emery and his colleagues found that:

> . . . [B]eing randomly assigned to mediation versus adversary settlement did indeed make a substantial difference in nonresidential parent-child contact twelve years later. Thirty percent of nonresidential parents who mediated saw their children once a week or more twelve years after the initial dispute in comparison to only 9% of parents in the adversary group. At the opposite extreme, 39% of nonresidential parents in the adversary group had seen their children only once or not at all in the last year compared to 15% in the mediation group. These differences are both substantively important and statistically significant.

Robert E. Emery, David Sbarra & Tara Grover, Divorce Mediation: Research and Reflections, 43 Fam. Ct. Rev. 22, 30 (2005). The study also reported no increase in conflict between parents despite greater contact. Instead, the researchers found that "when parents mediated rather than continuing with the legal action over their children, twelve years later the residential parent reported that the nonresidential parent was (statistically and substantively) significantly more likely to discuss problems with the residential parent" and "the nonresidential parent had a greater influence on childrearing decisions, and was more involved in the children's discipline, grooming, moral training, errands, holidays, significant events, school or church functions, recreational activities, and vacations." *Id.* at 31. These improvements, with long-lasting effects, came after an average mediation session of five hours.

Mediation has its critics. Professor Grillo argued that mediation does not necessarily bring in "the woman-identified values of intimacy, nurturance, and care into a legal system" but rather "deliver[s] something coercive in its place." For instance, "[i]f two parties are forced to engage with one another, and one has a more relational sense of self than the other, that party may feel compelled to maintain her connection with the other, even to her own detriment. For this reason, the party with the more relational sense of self will be at a disadvantage in a mediated negotiation." Trina Grillo, The Mediation Alternative: Process Dangers for Women, 100 Yale L.J. 1545, 1551-1555 (1991).

Professor Suzanne Reynolds and her co-authors explained the custody-related feminist critiques of mediation:

[O]pponents feared that mandatory mediation created artificial incentives for parties to agree to joint physical custody, or the significant sharing of parenting time by both parents. While commentators generally applauded joint physical custody for parents committed to it, opponents of routine use of mediation argued that it would force equal parenting on parents in inappropriate cases. Circumstances might advise against joint physical custody, for example, for parents whose high conflict made it difficult to coordinate the child's living arrangements in two households. Also, for parents whose approaches to discipline varied dramatically, joint physical custody might confuse an already troubled child. Most dramatically, domestic violence might make joint custody not only ill-advised but dangerous. For any number of reasons, joint physical custody might be inappropriate in a particular case.

Suzanne Reynolds, Catherine T. Harris & Ralph A. Peeples, Back to the Future: An Empirical Study of Child Custody Outcomes, 85 N.C. L. Rev. 1629, 1631 (2007). For a summary of critiques of mediation, *see* Amy Cohen, The Family, the Market, and ADR, 1 J. Disp. Resol. 91, 118-122 (2011).

In re Lee
411 S.W.3d 445, 447-467 (Tex. 2013)

JUSTICE LEHRMANN announced the Court's decision and delivered the opinion of the Court with respect to Parts I, II, III, V, and VII, in which JUSTICE JOHNSON, JUSTICE WILLETT, JUSTICE GUZMAN, and JUSTICE BOYD joined, and delivered an opinion with respect to Parts IV and VI, in which JUSTICE JOHNSON, JUSTICE WILLETT, and JUSTICE BOYD joined. . . . Relator Stephanie Lee and Real Party in Interest Benjamin Redus are the parents . . . of their minor daughter. Stephanie has the exclusive right to designate the child's primary residence under a 2007 order adjudicating parentage. Benjamin petitioned the court of continuing jurisdiction to modify that order, alleging that the circumstances had materially and substantially changed because Stephanie had relinquished primary care and possession of the child to him for at least six months. Benjamin sought the exclusive right to determine the child's primary residence and requested modification of the terms and conditions of Stephanie's access to and possession of the child, alleging that Stephanie's "poor parenting decisions" had placed the child in danger. He also sought an order requiring that Stephanie's periods of access be supervised on the basis that she "has a history or pattern of child neglect directed against" the child. Additionally, Benjamin sought an order enjoining Stephanie from allowing the child within twenty miles of Stephanie's husband, Scott Lee, a registered sex offender, and requiring Stephanie to provide Benjamin with information on her whereabouts during her periods of access so that Benjamin could verify her compliance with the twenty-mile restriction.

Before proceeding to trial, the parties attended mediation at which they were both represented by counsel. The mediation ended successfully with the parties executing a mediated settlement agreement modifying the 2007 order. The MSA gives Benjamin the exclusive right to establish the child's primary residence, and it gives Stephanie periodic access to and possession of the child. Among the terms and conditions of Stephanie's access and possession, the MSA contains the following restriction concerning Scott:

> At all times[,] Scott Lee is enjoined from being within 5 miles of [the child]. During [Stephanie]'s periods of possession with [the child,] Scott Lee shall notify [Benjamin] through Stephanie Lee by e-mail or other mail where he will be staying . . . [a]nd the make and model of the vehicle he will be driving. This shall be done at least 5 days prior to any visits. [Benjamin] shall have the right to have an agent or himself monitor Mr. Lee's location by either calling or driving by the location at reasonable times.

The introductory paragraph of the MSA explains that "[t]he parties wish to avoid potentially protracted and costly litigation, and agree and stipulate that they have carefully considered the needs of the child[ ] . . . and the best interest of the child." The MSA also contains the following language in boldfaced, capitalized, and underlined letters:

THE PARTIES ALSO AGREE THAT THIS MEDIATION AGREEMENT IS BINDING ON BOTH OF THEM AND IS NOT SUBJECT TO REVOCATION BY EITHER OF THEM.

The MSA was signed by both Stephanie and Benjamin, as well as their attorneys.

Benjamin appeared before an associate judge to present and prove up the MSA. During Benjamin's testimony in support of the MSA, the associate judge inquired about the injunction regarding Scott. Benjamin informed the judge that Scott was a registered sex offender, and he testified that Scott "violated conditions of his probation with [Benjamin's] daughter in th[e] house" and that he "sle[pt] naked in bed with [Benjamin's] daughter between [Scott and Stephanie]." Stephanie did not attend the hearing and therefore was not able to respond to these allegations. Based on this testimony, the associate judge refused to enter judgment on the MSA. . . .

II. THE NEED FOR MEDIATION IN HIGH-CONFLICT CUSTODY DISPUTES

Encouragement of mediation as an alternative form of dispute resolution is critically important to the emotional and psychological well-being of children involved in high-conflict custody disputes. Indeed, the Texas Legislature has recognized that it is "the policy of this state to encourage the peaceable resolution of disputes, *with special consideration given to disputes involving the parent-child relationship, including the mediation of issues involving conservatorship, possession, and support of children*, and the early settlement of pending litigation through voluntary settlement procedures." Tex. Civ. Prac. & Rem. Code §154.002 (emphasis added). This policy is well-supported by, *inter alia*, literature discussing the enormous emotional and financial costs of high-conflict custody litigation, including its harmful effect on children. Children involved in these disputes—tellingly, referred to as "custody battles"—can face perpetual emotional turmoil, alienation from one or both parents, and increased risk of developing psychological problems. All the while, most of these families have two adequate parents who merely act out of fear of losing their child. For the children themselves, the conflict associated with the litigation itself is often much greater than the conflict that led to a divorce or custody dispute. The Legislature has thus recognized that, because children suffer needlessly from traditional litigation, the amicable resolution of child-related disputes should be promoted forcefully. With the Legislature's stated policy in mind, we turn to the statute in question.

III. STATUTORY INTERPRETATION

The sole issue before us today is whether a trial court presented with a request for entry of judgment on a validly executed MSA may deny a motion to enter judgment based on a best interest inquiry. . . .

B. SECTION 153.0071

Consistent with the legislative policy discussed above regarding the encouragement of the peaceable resolution of disputes involving the parent-child relationship, the Legislature enacted section 153.0071 of the Family Code, which provides in pertinent part as follows: . . .

(c) On the written agreement of the parties or on the court's own motion, the court may refer a suit affecting the parent-child relationship to mediation.

(d) A mediated settlement agreement is binding on the parties if the agreement:

(1) provides, in a prominently displayed statement that is in boldfaced type or capital letters or underlined, that the agreement is not subject to revocation;

(2) is signed by each party to the agreement; and

(3) is signed by the party's attorney, if any, who is present at the time the agreement is signed.

(e) If a mediated settlement agreement meets the requirements of Subsection (d), a party is entitled to judgment on the mediated settlement notwithstanding Rule 11, Texas Rules of Civil Procedure, or another rule of law.

(e-1) Notwithstanding Subsections (d) and (e), a court may decline to enter a judgment on a mediated settlement agreement if the court finds that:

(1) a party to the agreement was a victim of family violence, and that circumstance impaired the party's ability to make decisions; and

(2) the agreement is not in the child's best interest.

Tex. Fam. Code §153.0071(a)-(e-1). . . .

D. ANALYSIS OF SECTION 153.0071

Section 153.0071(e) unambiguously states that a party is "entitled to judgment" on an MSA that meets the statutory requirements "notwithstanding Rule 11, Texas Rules of Civil Procedure, or another rule of law." Subsection (e-1) provides a narrow exception, allowing a trial court to decline to enter judgment on an MSA when three requirements are all met: (1) a party to the agreement was a victim of family violence, *and* (2) the court finds the family violence impaired the party's ability to make decisions, *and* (3) the agreement is not in the child's best interest. By its plain language, section 153.0071 authorizes a court to refuse to enter judgment on a statutorily compliant MSA on best interest grounds *only* when the court also finds the family violence elements are met. Stated another way, "[t]he statute does not authorize the trial court to substitute its judgment for the mediated settlement agreement entered by the parties unless the requirements of subsection 153.0071(e-1) are met." . . .

Section 153.0071(b), governing arbitration of child-related disputes, is also instructive. In stark contrast with subsection (e), subsection (b) explicitly gives trial courts authority to decline an arbitrator's award when it is not in the best interest of the child. This distinction between arbitration and mediation makes sense because the two processes are very different. Mediation encourages parents to work together to settle their child-related disputes, and shields the child from many of the adverse effects of traditional litigation. On the other hand, arbitration simply moves the fight from the courtroom to the arbitration room. If the Legislature had intended to authorize courts to inquire into the child's best interest when determining whether to render judgment on validly executed MSAs, as it did in section 153.0071(b) with respect to judgments on arbitration awards, it certainly knew how to do so.

Benjamin argues that, despite section 153.0071's plain language, "[n]othing precludes the court from considering the best interests of the child, including a request for entry on a mediated settlement agreement." Benjamin and the State are correct that the Family Code provides that "[t]he best interest of the child shall always be the primary consideration of the court in determining the issues of conservatorship and possession of and access to the child." However, section 153.0071(e) reflects the Legislature's determination that it is appropriate for parents to determine what is best for their children within the context of the parents' collaborative effort to reach and properly execute an MSA. This makes sense not only because parents are in a position to know what is best for their children, but also because successful mediation of child-custody disputes, conducted within statutory parameters, furthers a child's best interest by putting a halt to potentially lengthy and destructive custody litigation. . . .

IV. A Trial Court's Duty to Take Protective Action

. . . [W]e hold today that a trial court may not deny a motion to enter judgment on a properly executed MSA [mediated settlement agreement] . . . based on a broad best interest inquiry. But we certainly do not hold that a child's welfare may be ignored. Rather, we recognize that [the] mandatory duty to report abuse or neglect [under state law], the numerous other statutes authorizing protective action by the trial court, and the safeguards inherent in the mediation process fulfill the need to ensure that children are protected. And they do so without subjecting MSAs to an impermissible level of scrutiny that threatens to undermine the benefits of mediation. The trial court's authority to continue an MSA hearing and to take protective action under the various statutes discussed above is triggered not by a determination that an MSA is not in a child's best interest, but by evidence that a child's welfare is in jeopardy. Thus, the mediation process and its benefits are preserved, and, most importantly, children are protected.

Guzman, J., concurring. . . . Despite discord on other issues, the opinions make several matters apparent. First, the Court holds that section 153.0071 of the Family Code prohibits a trial court from conducting a broad best-interest inquiry at a hearing for the purpose of entering judgment on a properly executed MSA. Second, a different majority of the Court would hold that a trial court does not abuse its discretion by refusing to enter judgment on an MSA that could endanger the safety and welfare of a child—an issue on which the remaining four justices express no opinion. Third, no Justice disputes that trial courts possess a number of mechanisms to protect children from endangerment, such as issuing temporary orders and contacting the Texas Department of Family and Protective Services. Finally, a majority of the Court agrees that if there is evidence of endangerment, an additional mechanism the trial court possesses to protect the child is to refuse to enter judgment on the MSA.

I write separately because although I agree with Court that section 153.0071 precludes a broad best-interest inquiry, I also believe that it does not preclude an endangerment inquiry. . . . The trial court sustained a hearsay objection to the only statement at the hearing that could have demonstrated the mother might not comply with the MSA (a statement from the father that the mother informed him after signing the MSA that she did not have to inform him of her and her husband's whereabouts). Thus, this record is sparse and does not establish the threshold I believe must be met before a trial court may disregard legislative policy concerning the deference to which MSAs are entitled. . . . If on remand the trial court considers evidence and finds that entry of judgment on the MSA could endanger the child, I am certain the trial court will take appropriate action.

Green, J. joined by Chief Justice Jefferson, Justice Hecht, and Justice Devine, dissenting. . . . Although the Court tries to distinguish between this case—in which the trial court stated on the record that it was not in the best interest of the child to approve the MSA—and a case in which modification pursuant to an MSA could endanger a child, here it is a distinction without a difference. Whether the trial court calls its grounds "best interest" or "endangerment," the bottom line is the same—the trial court, having heard testimony of the parties, refused to adopt the parents' agreed modification that it believed would subject the child to exposure to a registered sex offender. The Legislature has made the policy of this state clear: "The best interest of the child *shall always be the primary consideration* of the court in determining the issues of conservatorship and possession of and access to the child." (emphasis added). I would hold that a trial court has discretion to refuse to enter judgment on a modification pursuant to an MSA that could endanger the child's safety and welfare and is, therefore, not in the child's best interest. To suggest that the Legislature intended otherwise is, I believe, absurd. I respectfully dissent.

NOTES AND QUESTIONS

1. Professor Reynolds and her colleagues conducted an empirical study of the criticisms of mediation in custody disputes in one district in North Carolina and found that:

> the comparison of the three types of custody resolution events — mediation, settlement, and litigation — reveals that in this mandatory mediation jurisdiction, mothers did not receive less physical custody in mediation. On the contrary, in our study, in a comparison of those three types of custody resolution events, mothers received primary physical custody more often in mediation than they did in either settlements or litigation.
>
> The findings belie another widely-held belief about the prevalence of joint physical custody. . . . Again, to the contrary, in our study, custody disputes ended in joint physical custody in less than 16% of the cases. Moreover, joint physical custody appeared more often in lawyer-negotiated settlements than it did either in mediation or litigation.

Reynolds et al., above, 85 N.C. L. Rev. at 1633. The authors emphasize that mediation is no longer a single process. The North Carolina study found that representation by counsel and the ability to resort to litigation in the absence of a satisfactory proposal helped resist pressures to settle. Is the role of custody lawyers in the North Carolina study consistent with or different from the role of lawyers under the ABA Model Rules or AAML Bounds of Advocacy? Is the adversarial nature of litigation, with the ability to present the case for each side, a protection for less powerful family members or a source of victimization? Or do the results have more to do with the substantive law?

2. The most controversial aspect of mediation, especially mandatory mediation in custody disputes, is how domestic violence, mental illness, and substance abuse affect the process. William Howe and Hugh McIsaac insist that:

> Whenever there is significant or persistent domestic violence and significant issues of mental health on the part of one or both parties, or significant levels of chemical abuse, generally the adversarial model is preferable because of procedural and other safeguards it provides to the victim or less capable party. Essentially, non-adversarial decision-making models presuppose rational actors, that is, parties who are generally capable of accurately perceiving their self-interest and acting upon it. Most jurisdictions using alternative means in dispute resolution, such as mediation, private arbitration or any of the models discussed above, have developed elaborate safeguards to filter inappropriate cases, assuring that those requiring the control and muscle of the court are directed to the conventional litigation track.

William Howe & Hugh McIsaac, Finding the Balance: Ethical Challenges and Best Practices for Lawyers Representing Parents When the Interests of Children Are at Stake, 46 Fam. Ct. Rev. 78, 84 (2008). Judge Mary Ann Grilli, who was a family law judge on the California Superior Court, County of Santa Clara, saw a clearer role for mediation in cases involving domestic violence:

> After years of experience in cases involving parents, domestic violence, and child custody, I have concluded that if properly designed and operated, mediation provides a safe, effective way of resolving these custody disputes. What many people forget is that the court process does not offer a better environment for the resolution of these cases. The parties have to appear together in the same courtroom, and there is much less time for the judge to hear evidence and understand the family dynamics. Moreover, in the courtroom there will be no opportunity for the parties to exchange proposals and to have some level of control over what happens to their children.

Leonard Edwards, Comments on the Miller Commission Report: A California Perspective, 27 Pace L. Rev. 627, 663-664 (2007). Professor Nancy Ver Steegh offers factors for deciding when mediation might be appropriate and means by which lawyers can help protect client safety:

> In order to make informed decisions about participation in mediation, families should consider factors such as the following: the pattern of domestic violence; the frequency and severity of the

violence; the health and mental health status of the parties; the likely response of the primary perpetrator; the quality of the mediation process actually available; whether the parties are represented; the presence of children; relative financial resources; and preferred decision making approach. If it occurs, mediation should be conducted by an experienced and specially trained mediator who institutes tailored safety precautions and procedures. At a minimum, these should include written ground rules, inclusion of lawyers and support persons; separate arrivals and departures, and use of separate caucusing.

Nancy Ver Steegh, Family Court Reform and ADR: Shifting Values and Expectations Transform the Divorce Process, 42 Fam. L.Q. 659, 665-666 (2008). *See also* Nancy Ver Steegh et al., Look Before You Leap: Court System Triage of Family Law Cases Involving Intimate Partner Violence, 95 Marq. L. Rev. 955, 956 (2012); Margaret Drew, Collaboration and Intention: Making the Collaborative Family Law Process Safe(r), 32 Ohio St. J. Disp. Resol. 373 (2017) (describing how lawyers can identify signs of abuse or coercion and alter their mediation and lawyering practices accordingly).

Can you reconcile these perspectives? Ver Steegh, like the North Carolina researchers, emphasizes the inclusion of lawyers in the process. What role should lawyers be expected to play in a case in which domestic violence is an issue and the state mandates custody mediation as a precondition to litigation? How should lawyers define domestic violence in vetting clients for mediation?

3. To provide protection from the concerns raised about domestic violence, the Texas statute in *Lee* authorized courts to review mediated agreements reached where domestic violence — and only domestic violence — was a concern. Should the statute have authorized the courts to consider the interests of children more broadly, as the dissent in *Lee* suggests?

4. In *Lee*, the father, who had agreed to the MSA, raised issues before the court about the adequacy of the agreement in a proceeding that the wife may not have expected to be adversarial and did not attend. How should a court respond to such issues? In In the Interest of K.D., 471 S.W.3d 147 (Tex. 2015), the Texas Supreme Court held that *Lee* did not apply to MSAs in which parties agreed to terminate one parent's rights. A trial court may, under the Texas statute governing termination of parental rights, set aside the agreement based on the child's best interests.

5. Should children or their representatives be included in child custody mediation? Can parents involved in mediation be expected to take the children's interests into account? How do assumptions about the parents' ability and willingness to do so influence the different opinions in *Lee*? *See* Jennifer E. McIntosh et al., Child-Focused and Child-Inclusive Divorce Mediation: Comparative Outcomes from a Prospective Study of Postseparation Adjustment, 46 Fam. Ct. Rev. 105, 105 (2008).

6. Parenting coordinators, who typically are not trained as lawyers but as social workers or clinical counselors, can help parents settle disputes over custody and other issues related to their children. While most courts will not order the involvement of a parenting coordinator, settlement agreements may provide for the appointment of a coordinator, typically with the consent of both parties. The agreement defines the coordinator's role, and may include power to oversee the resolution of parenting issues, such as a change in the time or place for picking up a child or the choice of the child's extracurricular activities. The coordinator ideally tries to encourage the parents to agree and resolve conflicts over parenting decisions, but may also have the power to decide disputes. Many collaborative practices, discussed below, incorporate the work of parenting coordinators, and settlement agreements can contemplate various roles for a parenting coordinator.

7. The majority opinion in *Lee* contrasts the statutory approach to arbitration, which expressly gives the court the power to consider the best interest of the child, with the approach to mediation, which limits judicial review to a greater degree. Do you find the distinction persuasive? Should the form of alternative dispute resuolution matter to courts' willingness to review it?

8. Mediation may take different forms. It may be voluntary or mandatory. Mandatory mediation may be subject to certain limitations in order to protect the parties' rights. For example, an appellate court in Massachusetts reversed a lower court decision imposing out-of-court mediation as a prerequisite to either party filing a subsequent action in a court and at the parties' own expense. The court said that imposition of mediation by the lower court interfered with a state right of free access to courts and discouraged parties from seeking modification. Ventrice v. Ventrice, 26 N.E.3d 1128 (Mass. App. 2015). Mediation may be comprehensive or limited to a single issue, such as custody. The parties may be represented by lawyers who provide advice before, during, or after the sessions, or they may be acting pro se. They may (or may not) have "coaches" who help them to prepare. The mediator may be a lawyer, a professional with multi-disciplinary training, or none of the above. Depending on the jurisdiction, the mediator may be able to report to the court if the mediation fails or may be precluded from disclosing any part of the mediation sessions or any recommendation for a resolution. *See* Russell M. Coombs, Noncourt-Connected Mediation and Counseling in Child-Custody Disputes, 17 Fam. L.Q. 469 (1984).

A compilation of new state legislation related to ADR for the 2019-2020 legislative session focuses on mediation and child care and the rise in mediation for familial disputes. Most of this legislation was introduced before the COVID-19 pandemic but nevertheless shows increasing use of mediation in family law. Austin Davis, Eli Dodge, Kevin Johnston & Seth Christensen, State Legislative Update, 2021, J. Disp. Resol. 161, 161-189 (2021).

9. While mediation once served as the primary alternative to litigation, some courts now offer greater assistance to struggling litigants. Mediator Peter Salem writes:

> The proliferation of services for separating and divorcing families since the early 1970s has been nothing short of remarkable. . . . Over the years this movement—combined with the growing number of challenges families bring with them to the court—has unleashed the creativity of professionals worldwide, resulting in literally dozens of distinct dispute resolution processes for separating and divorcing parents. These include multiple models of mediation; psycho-educational programs; collaborative law; interdisciplinary arbitration panels; parenting coordination; and early neutral custody evaluation to name just a few. . . . Many jurisdictions have court-connected family court service agencies and offer a continuum of services, e.g., parent education, mediation, custody evaluation, judicially moderated settlement conference and high conflict interventions. These services are traditionally offered in a linear or tiered fashion, where families begin with the least intrusive and least time consuming service and, if the dispute is not resolved, proceed to the next available process, which is typically more intrusive and directive than the one preceding it. Under a tiered service model, virtually all parents participate in mediation and in many jurisdictions are required by statute or administrative rule to do so.
>
> In recent years, a handful of family court service agencies, including those in Connecticut, Arizona and British Columbia, have begun to explore variations of triage, or differentiated case management, as an alternative service delivery model. Triage proponents suggest a departure from the common practice of referring all parents to mediation. Instead, they contend that identifying the most the appropriate service on the front end may result in a reduced burden on families, more effective provision of services, and more efficient use of scarce court resources.

Peter Salem, The Emergence of Triage in Family Court Services: The Beginning of the End for Mandatory Mediation?, 47 Fam. Ct. Rev. 371 (2009). How are Salem's suggestions likely to be implemented in an era of budget cuts that affect the services courts are able to offer?

Jane Murphy and Jana Singer have highlighted how the costs of some ADR processes, such as collaborative divorce (described below) are burdensome for low-income families and have called for experimentation with community-based services. They recommend different types of dispute resolution processes, like "evaluative mediation," and argue for training in mediation and collaboration for lawyers who serve low-income clients. Jane C. Murphy & Jana B. Singer, Divorced from Reality: Rethinking Family Dispute Resolution 130-132, 137-139 (2015). Murphy and Singer, for example, described a clinic at the University of Denver Law School in which legal professionals and law students provide intensive mediation, counseling, and integrated clinic services at affordable rates.

For alternative approaches that combine mediation and arbitration under the guidance of a single professional, compare Allan Barsky, "Med-Arb": Behind the Closed Doors of a Hybrid Process, 51 Fam. Ct. Rev. 637 (2013), with Yishai Boyarin, Court-Connected ADR—A Time of Crisis, a Time of Change, 95 Marq. L. Rev. 993 (2012). Would a "med-arb" approach provide more or less protection for victims of domestic violence? Would the adoption of a "triage" approach help deal with issues such as domestic violence? With protection of the child in *Lee*? How do changes in the variety of available services change the lawyer's role? Should basic definitions of competence include an obligation to:

- know what services are available in each court in which the attorney appears?
- have the training to advise the client which services may be appropriate for that client's personality, circumstances, and needs?
- recognize the warning signs of domestic violence or mental illness?
- discourage the client from pursuing alternatives for which the client may not be suited even if they save the client money or reduce the attorneys' fees?

For discussion of the complex ethical issues underlying family representation, *see* Barbara Glesner-Fines, Ethical Issues in Family Representation (2009).

10. For many years, family law scholars and practitioners have suggested that family law mediation can occur online. *See* Rebecca Brenna, Mismatch.com: On-Line Dispute Resolution and Divorce, 13 Cardozo J. Conflict Resol. 197 (2011). Online mediation may be more cost-effective and thus more accessible to a broader range of people. Relying on housing court as her primary example, Ellen Waldman argued that technology can help reduce disparities between mediating parties, particularly those who are low income and enter mediation without representation. Ellen Waldman, How Mediation Contributes to the "Justice Gap" and Possible Technological Fixes, 88 Fordham L. Rev. 2425 (2020).

Over the course of the COVID-19 pandemic, commentators documented the turn to online dispute resolution (ODR) and the consequences of its uptake. *See, e.g.*, Laura A. Wasser, Design Challenges in Applying Online Dispute Resolution to Divorce, 59 Fam. Ct. Rev. 268 (2021) (arguing that ODR has the potential to radically democratize access to the legal system but potentially at a cost to the quality of service). Mediators addressed new issues related to the COVID-19 pandemic: "the work of mediators during the pandemic has not only shifted to providing services through online platforms, it has also quickly adapted to addressing new, pressing COVID-19 generated issues. These issues range from parental disputes over previously agreed upon time-sharing arrangements that one parent no longer supports, [and] family conflicts regarding whether an elder family member can safely interact with other family members. . . ." Tracey Wiltgen, Providing Access to Justice Through Mediation During a Pandemic, 24 Haw. B.J. 1, 11 (2020). *See also* Madison McBratney, How to Stay-at-Home When You Have Two Homes: COVID-19's Effect on Co-Parenting and Child Custody, 33 J. Am. Acad. Matrim. L. 225 (2020) (suggesting online mediations as a potential solution to custody disputes during the pandemic). ODR, some have argued, may be able to offer victims of domestic violence a way of resolving their marital or family problems while remaining safe. Fernanda S. Rossi et al., Shuttle and Online Mediation: A Review of Available Research and Implications for Separating Couples Reporting Intimate Partner Violence or Abuse, 55 Fam. Ct. Rev. 390 (2017) (discussing the possibilities of applying shuttle and online mediation to intimate partner violence and abuse cases). Parties need not be in the same room, limiting further physical contact or potential psychological abuse. Laura A. Wasser, Design Challenges in Applying Online Dispute Resolution to Divorce, 59 Family Court Rev. 268 (Apr. 29, 2021), https://onlinelibrary-wiley-com.libproxy.temple.edu/doi/epdf/10.1111/fcre.12573. *See* Brad Boserup et al., Alarming Trends in US Domestic Violence During the COVID-19 Pandemic, 38 Am. J. Emergency Med. 2753 (2020) (noting a rise in reports of domestic violence during the pandemic).

11. Can ODR processes produce the same quality of outcomes as traditional dispute resolution? ODR is gaining popularity because of its ease of access and faster time to resolution, but neither of those factors necessarily contributes to a fair and just outcome. And with the wider introduction of ODR, lawyers and clients will confront new issues and technologies. For instance, mediation conducted over the Internet could raise privacy concerns. Additionally, ODR could evolve into a process that does not require much human interaction with some disputes settled by computer algorithms or artificial intelligence designed to determine an equitable outcome. *See* Colin Rule, Online Dispute Resolution and the Future of Justice, 16 Ann. Rev. Law. Soc. Sci. 277 (2020); Meredith McBride, ODR in the Era of COVID-19, American Bar Association (2022), https://www.americanbar.org/groups/family_law/committees/alternative-dispute-resolution/odr/.

PROBLEMS

1. Michael and Sue are ending their 20-year marriage. Both express resistance to hiring individual lawyers for all of the usual reasons. During the interview, Michael does most of the talking; Sue speaks only when spoken to and always agrees with her husband. Michael is a salesman for a computer company; Sue has not been employed since their youngest child (now age 8) was born. She was previously a secretary in the company for which Michael then worked. Michael thinks that each should keep his or her own separate property, which accounts for most of the parties' wealth in this case. He has inherited a substantial amount of money; his wife has inherited none. Sue wants custody of their two children; Michael wants joint legal custody. (His travel schedule makes physical custody impossible.) Michael is willing to pay child support according to the state guidelines and is opposed to alimony that will discourage Sue from finding employment. Sue does not want to find employment outside the home until the children are out of high school. Accordingly, she thinks alimony is necessary. How will you approach this mediation?

Would your answer change if, in the course of discussions, Sue tells you that she will give up on her alimony claim and seek work if Michael abandons any claim to joint custody?

2. You are a lay leader in your local church as well as a prominent attorney. Your church strongly discourages divorce. Two members of that church come to you for counseling and assistance in connection with their marriage, which has been weak for some time. They know you as a religious leader and as a leader at the bar, where you have specialized in trusts and estates for many years. Is there any reason why you should not serve as an intermediary?

3. Collaborative Practice

As Professors Murphy and Singer explained, alternative dispute resolution, with its emphasis on family conflict as a social and emotional process rather than a legal event, "reduces the primacy of lawyers in handling these disputes and enhances the role of nonlegal professionals in the family court system." Murphy & Singer, Divorced from Reality at 14. Many lawyers, however, have sought to redefine their roles rather than cede the field to other professionals. Notable among these efforts has been the advent of collaborative practice. Like mediation and arbitration, collaborative divorce is client-centered and focused on clients' negotiation and the resolution of their disputes. But unlike mediation or arbitration, collaboration occurs *before* either party has filed for divorce so that it is an entirely "out-of-court" process governed by a self-enforced participation agreement among the parties and professionals involved.

Collaborative divorce, in this way, relies on a "team approach" and seeks to integrate the lawyer's role and the work of experts and non-lawyer professionals:

> Most collaborative materials begin with the well-known premise that divorce litigation, and the conflict it entails, is costly, time consuming, and, most importantly, destructive for parties and their children. . . . [U]nlike mediation, collaborative divorce promises an "interdisciplinary team approach that . . . offer[s] divorcing couples a consistent, positive, supportive, contained system for working with mental health and financial professionals on divorce-related issues."
>
> In establishing a team approach, everyone who participates in collaboration — the clients, lawyers, and neutral professionals — must sign a participation agreement. The non-lawyer professionals on a team can include a licensed mental health professional or "divorce coach" (usually a psychologist or clinical social worker), a child specialist or parenting coordinator (also typically a psychologist), and a neutral financial specialist or accountant. With the advice of attorneys, parties pick the professionals they need, and specialists work with the lawyers who explain the legal framework to their clients. Because collaboration happens entirely out of court, however, the team urges parties to reach a settlement fitted to their particular needs and not shaped only or primarily by the state's divorce laws. . . .
>
> The participation agreement governs how collaborative negotiations will operate. The process consists of a series of meetings: the parties and their lawyers meet, each party meets individually with each expert, and the entire group meets once or twice (or more, as needed). . . . A participation agreement requires parties to provide full disclosure of material information, actively participate in settlement conferences and team meetings, keep communications and documents confidential, and negotiate in good faith. Collaborative guidelines and rules describe the concept of "good faith" in terms of the conduct clients' must avoid, such as threatening litigation, misleading the other party, or failing to disclose pertinent information. Specifically, the parties pledge to provide complete and accurate financial information and agree to its review by a financial neutral.
>
> . . . If the process breaks down, both attorneys, and all neutral professionals, agree to withdraw from the case and refrain from further representation of either party against the other. The financial and emotional costs of starting over with new representation are usually significant. . . .

Rachel Rebouché, A Case Against Collaboration, 76 Md. L. Rev. 547, 554-557 (2017).

Collaborative practice arose in response to demand from both lawyers and clients, and there is evidence that it is gaining momentum. Some long-time family law practitioners wanted to reshape adversarial practices, and some clients in turn wished to maintain an amicable post-divorce relationship and avoid the expense, hostility, and invasion of privacy that litigation might encourage. Professor Ertman states that collaborative divorce "honors the role of emotions in disputes by including mental health professionals as necessary to help divorcing spouses work through any fear, anger, or other fiery emotions that get in the way of resolving the financial and legal disputes." Martha M. Ertman, Love's Promises: How Formal and Informal Contracts Shape All Kinds of Families 169 (2015). Professor Rebouché noted how proponents of collaborative divorce describe its benefits:

> When faced with criticisms of steep price or a prolonged process, supporters of collaborative divorce respond that the appeal of collaboration is not just speed and cost savings. The reward of collaborative divorce is its transformative potential for clients and attorneys. Extolling the benefits for lawyers, Marsha Baucom asked and answered of collaborative law, "Why do it? To save yourself!" Stuart Webb similarly proclaimed, "I can testify to the fact that it has also transformed the quality of my life!" This transformation is, in part, the result of collaboration's therapeutic component: lawyers shed their disillusion with divorce litigation and "embrace an

identity as a member of a 'helping profession'" that assists parties in navigating the emotional trauma of divorce. . . .

. . . One goal of collaborative divorce is to limit the conflict between divorcing couples by producing "an atmosphere of honesty, cooperation, integrity, and professionalism geared toward the future well-being of the family." But collaborative divorce promises more than just professionalism; the process also addresses disagreements that gave rise to the marital split as well as conflicts that might persist after the divorce. Writings on collaboration proclaim the process's transformative potential—from "restructuring of highly significant intimate personal relationships" to pursuing "ethical or religious beliefs about fairness, appropriate dispute-resolution procedures, forgiveness, and personal accountability" and "preserv[ing] the most positive post-divorce relationship." Collaboration looks both to the past and to the future, resolving conflicts in order to build a better relationship for the benefit of the parties and their children. To meet these goals, parties to a collaborative divorce are expected to develop communication and coping skills.

Rebouché, above, 76 Md. L. Rev. at 563-564.

A number of groups have established ethical and legal principles to guide the development of collaborative practice. These principles begin with the issue of whether collaborative agreements can be reconciled with attorneys' more general ethical obligations. A 2007 ABA ethics opinion finds collaborative practice to be an acceptable form of limited scope representation. The ethics commission explained:

When a client has given informed consent to a representation limited to collaborative negotiation toward settlement, the lawyer's agreement to withdraw if the collaboration fails is not an agreement that impairs her ability to represent the client, but rather is consistent with the client's limited goals for the representation. A client's agreement to a limited scope representation does not exempt the lawyer from the duties of competence and diligence, notwithstanding that the contours of the requisite competence and diligence are limited in accordance with the overall scope of the representation. Thus, there is no basis to conclude that the lawyer's representation of the client will be materially limited by the lawyer's obligation to withdraw if settlement cannot be accomplished. In the absence of a significant risk of such a material limitation, no conflict arises between the lawyer and her client under Rule 1.7(a)(2).

ABA Comm'n on Ethics and Professional Responsibility, Formal Op. 07447 (2007). The opinion underscores the importance of clear communication to the client about the nature of collaborative practice and the client's knowing consent to the terms of the agreement.

In 2009, the Uniform Law Commission approved the first Uniform Collaborative Law Act. In 2010, the Uniform Law Commission adopted amendments that created an explicit mechanism for the Act to be adopted by rule rather than by statute and included an option for states to limit collaborative law to family law matters. The Act would not take the place of state bar ethics oversight, but it establishes some benchmarks for ethical conduct. Among them are screening requirements. Given that a collaborative agreement "fails" if the parties cannot negotiate a settlement, screening out those for whom such an approach is inappropriate is an important component to its success. As of 2022, 23 states and the District of Columbia have enacted the Uniform Collaborative Law Act, and one state, Missouri, has introduced the Act in its legislature. Collaborative Law Act, Uniform Law Commission, available at https://www. uniformlaws.org/committees/community-home?CommunityKey=fdd1de2f-baea-42d3-bc16-a33d74438eaf#LegBillTrackingAnchor (last visited July 18, 2022).

Collaborative law also depends on establishing trust between the parties and their attorneys. Accordingly, confidence that both parties have disclosed relevant information and that the information cannot be used to the detriment of either party in subsequent litigation is critical to the process. Section 12 of the Uniform Collaborative Practice Act provides that each party "shall make timely, full, candid, and informal disclosure of information related to the collaborative matter without formal discovery, and shall update promptly information that has materially changed." The Act also states that collaborative law communications are confidential and privileged from disclosure in subsequent litigation. *See also* David A. Hoffman et al., To Disclose or Not to Disclose? That is the Question in Collaborative Law, 58 Fam. Ct. Rev. 83 (2020) (arguing that transparency is integral to collaborative lawyering; lawyers should assume an affirmative duty to disclose material information to the other parties).

NOTES AND QUESTIONS

1. An increasing number of states have statutes expressly regulating collaborative law. Ohio defines a "collaborative family law process" as "a procedure intended to resolve a matter without intervention by a court in which parties sign a collaborative family law participation agreement and are represented by collaborative family lawyers." Ohio Rev. Code §3105.41(C) (2022). *See also* D.C. Code Ann. §16-4002(3) (2022) (a procedure intended to resolve a collaborative matter without intervention by a tribunal); Ala. Code 1975 §6-6-26.01(2022) (same); Cal Fam. Code §2013 (2022) (a "process in which the parties and any professionals engaged by the parties to assist them agree in writing to use their best efforts and to make a good faith attempt to resolve disputes . . . on an agreed basis without resorting to adversary judicial intervention"); N.C. Gen. Stat. §50-72 (2022) ("A collaborative law agreement must be in writing, signed by all the parties to the agreement and their attorneys, and must include provisions for the withdrawal of all attorneys involved in the collaborative law procedure if the collaborative law procedure does not result in settlement of the dispute."); Tex. Fam. Code Ann. §15 (2022) (setting out the state's regulation of collaborative practice in a Collaborative Family Law Act).

2. For empirical studies of collaborative practice, and commentary on the effectiveness of collaborative divorce, *see* Luke Salava, Collaborative Divorce: The Unexpectedly Underwhelming Advance of a Promising Solution in Marriage Dissolution, 48 Fam. L.Q. 179, 184-185 (2014); Forrest S. Mosten, Collaborative Divorce Handbook: Helping Families Without Going to Court 64 (2009) ("there appears to be no data showing [collaborative divorce] is less expensive than traditional lawyer-negotiated settlements . . . and no data comparing the cost of collaborative divorce to mediation, even with consulting attorneys"); Gregg Herman, Why Are There Fewer Collaborative Divorce Filings?, Wis. L.J., June 8, 2011, available at http://wislawjournal.com/2011/06/08/why-are-there-fewer-collaborative-divorce-filings/.

John Lande compares collaborative lawyers with "cooperative" lawyers, who commit themselves to cooperative practices without the agreement to withdraw if the case does not settle. John Lande, Practical Insights from an Empirical Study of Cooperative Lawyers in Wisconsin, 2008 J. Disp. Resol. 203.

3. All collaborative professionals recognize that some people will be poor candidates for the process, such as individuals with severe mental health problems or untreated substance abuse issues. And most writings on collaborative divorce conclude that parties with a history of abuse should not choose collaboration. How should attorneys assess whether a client has an abusive or violent relationship with another party if the client does not disclose the information? Should the duty to screen clients to determine an appropriate approach to family dispute resolution be limited to collaborative law? For a discussion of the importance of such screening and the tools available to lawyers, *see* Nancy Ver Steegh, Differentiating Types of Domestic Violence: Implications for Child Custody, 65 La. L. Rev. 1379 (2005); *see also* Rachel L. Virk, When Is Collaboration the Most Appropriate Method of Dispute Resolution in Divorce, and Why Is It Beneficial to Collaborate?, 31 Fam. L. News 1, 3 (2011).

Some commentators worry that many attorneys are not prepared to screen adequately for domestic violence (as well as its cycle of coercion and control) and that the collaborative process is uniquely vulnerable to manipulation. For discussion of the particular dangers, *see* Margaret B. Drew, Collaboration and Coercion, 24 Hastings Women's L.J. 79 (2013). Others have argued that personality disorders or abusive behavior are not insurmountable obstacles to parties' collaboration. *See* Nancy K. Brodzki, Reaching a Successful Outcome Through Collaborative Family Law, in Understanding Collaborative Family Law: Leading Lawyers on Navigating the Collaborative Process, Working with Clients, and Analyzing the Latest Trends 197 (2011).

4. For further discussion of these ethics of collaborative practice, *see* Larry R. Spain, Collaborative Law: A Critical Reflection on Whether a Collaborative Orientation Can Be Ethically Incorporated into the Practice of Law, 56 Baylor L. Rev. 141, 148-149 (2004); Christopher M. Fairman, Growing Pains: Changes in Collaborative Law and the Challenge of Legal Ethics, 30 Campbell L. Rev. 237 (2008); Rebecca Aviel, Counsel for the Divorce, 55 B.C. L. Rev. 1099, 1108 (2014); Marina Tolou-Shams, Collaborative Divorce: An Oxymoron?, 31 Child & Adolescent Behav. 1 (2015).

5. While traditionally used in domestic relations proceedings, collaborative law has been offered as an option for resolving disputes between family members who operate family businesses together. Whether the dispute is between divorcing partners, siblings, or parents and their children, collaborative law may be an option to preserve the relationship while resolving family business disputes. Collaborative law lends itself to resolving family business disputes because the collaborative practice is structured so that both the business environment and the family relationships can be maintained and strengthened through the use of shared experts. The collaborative law process offers an opportunity for more creative resolutions that would not necessarily burn bridges as is often the case with litigation. Hayley R. Goodman, Note: Divorcing Partners and Fighting Siblings: Using the Collaborative Model to Resolve Disputes in Family Businesses, 30 U. Miami Bus. L. Rev. 1 (2021).

PROBLEMS

1. Paul and Maria are divorcing. Maria accused Paul of sexually abusing their 2-year-old daughter, Amy, but the court-ordered evaluation found no evidence of abuse, and the judge has threatened to switch custody to Paul if Maria persists in the allegations. Maria, who does not want Paul to be alone with Amy, is very frustrated with the judicial proceedings; and Paul, who has exhausted most of his savings defending the abuse allegations, feels that he cannot afford continued litigation. Maria's parents have helped pay her legal fees, and she has recently hired a new lawyer, who has suggested a collaborative approach. Paul has come to you for a consultation about representing him in a collaborative proceeding. What problems do you foresee? How would you go about determining whether Paul is a suitable client for a collaborative approach? If you enter into discussions with Paul, Maria, and Maria's attorney about a collaborative practice arrangement, but the discussions fall through without signing a collaborative practice agreement, are you free to represent Paul in subsequent litigation? Does it matter that Paul communicated confidential information to you? Does it matter that Maria's attorney also communicated confidential information to you during the initial meetings? *See* Mandell v. Mandell, 949 N.Y.S.2d 580 (N.Y. Sup. Ct. 2012).

2. You, Paul, Maria, and Maria's attorney sign a collaborative practice agreement. During the negotiations you learn that Paul had a brief affair during the marriage that Maria never knew about. Since the separation, Paul and the girlfriend have become closer, and Paul recently moved in with her. She earns considerably more than Paul does. In the jurisdiction in which Paul and Maria live, the girlfriend's income would not affect any determination of spousal or child support unless she and Paul marry. Soon after the separation Paul fell behind in his child support payments and told Maria that it was because all of his money had been going toward rent and legal fees. Maria has not pressed him to make up the arrears. Do you have any obligation to inform Maria of the relationship or to encourage Paul to do so? *See* H.K. v. A.K., 950 N.Y.S.2d 723 (N.Y. Sup. Ct. 2012) (the fact that the husband, without the wife's knowledge, had entered into a new relationship during the collaborative negotiations did not in and of itself void the agreement).

3. Maria continues to insist that Paul be limited to supervised visitation with Amy. Paul, who claims that he has been wrongly accused of sexual abuse, is incensed. The negotiations break up over the issue, and Maria—who has since moved a short distance away, but across the state line—decides to discontinue the collaborative process. Maria would like the attorney who participated in the collaborative agreement to continue to represent her. He is also licensed in the other state. Paul has told you and Maria that he doesn't care, and that he doesn't have enough money to hire another attorney, so he will appear in any continuing litigation on a pro se basis. You would like to oppose Maria's attorney's continuing participation in the case. Do you have standing to do so? By virtue of the four-way collaborative agreement the four of you signed, can you claim that the attorney breached his contractual obligations to you? If you cannot do so on behalf of yourself, can you do so on Paul's behalf?

4. During the collaborative sessions, Paul shared with Maria the results of a psychological evaluation prepared by a psychiatrist Paul had consulted. The report indicates that after Maria accused Paul of sexually abusing Amy, he became deeply depressed and took an overdose of sleeping pills. Paul's girlfriend found him and rushed him to the hospital in time to revive him. The psychiatrist concluded that while Paul suffered from clinical depression at the time of the incident, he had since overcome the depression and did not constitute a threat to himself or others. No one but Paul, Paul's girlfriend, the psychiatrist, and the parties to the collaborative practice session know about the overdose of sleeping pills. If Maria ultimately litigates the custody issue, will she be able to introduce the psychiatrist's report or call the psychiatrist as a witness?

5. What, if any, of the foregoing interactions or sessions between Paul and Maria could have been conducted online and for what benefit to the parties?

CHAPTER 12

JURISDICTION

John and Harriet Haddock were married in New York in the summer of 1868. The marriage was never consummated, however, because John—feeling that he had been tricked into the marriage—left New York the same day. Harriet remained in New York, while John drifted about the country, finally settling in Connecticut nine years later. Thirteen years after the wedding, in 1881, John sought a divorce from Harriet, mailing notice to her last known address in New York and publishing it in the local Connecticut newspaper. John obtained his divorce and remarried.

In 1891, 23 years after the wedding and 10 years after the divorce action, John inherited considerable property from his father. Harriet, from whom John had not heard since their wedding day, sued John for a legal separation in New York. She received a default separation decree and an award of alimony but could not recover because of lack of personal service on John. Five years later, John returned to New York. Harriet obtained personal service in New York and refiled her suit for legal separation and alimony.

John's defense to Harriet's suit, of course, was his prior Connecticut divorce. The New York court refused to recognize the sister-state decree because Harriet had not been subject to the jurisdiction of the Connecticut court when the decree was rendered. Holding that, as far as New York courts were concerned, John and Harriet were still married, the court awarded Harriet her legal separation and $780 a year in maintenance.

Variations of this story provide the basis for a vexing set of jurisdictional problems peculiar to matrimonial issues. The case itself arises out of desertion, in this case, the husband's, which was the primary ground for divorce in nineteenth-century America. Norma Basch, The Victorian Compromise: Divorce in New York City, 1787-1870, at 20 (unpublished paper delivered at the 1985 Annual Meeting of the Organization of American Historians), quoted in Neal R. Feigenson, Extraterritorial Recognition of Divorce Decrees in the Nineteenth Century, 34 Am. J. Legal Hist. 119, 123 (1990). Because desertion was the most common basis for divorce, most nineteenth-century suits, like John Haddock's Connecticut action, were uncontested (although it would have been more usual for the deserted spouse to prosecute the suit). As a practical matter, service of process did not notify defendants of the pending divorce because their whereabouts were usually unknown at the time of the suit. And a decree issued by one state, even though relied on by the plaintiff, was often refused recognition by a sister state.

There are many questions presented by this situation, which is based on the facts of Haddock v. Haddock, 201 U.S. 562 (1906). Could Harriet, had she wished, have sought a divorce from John in New York? Was John's Connecticut divorce valid? If the Connecticut divorce was invalid, was John a bigamist? If either Harriet or John could secure a divorce without the presence of the other, would that mean that the defendant could be required to pay or lose any entitlement to property or support he or she might have claimed had he or she participated?

The answers to these questions depend on whether a court in one state would, or would be required to, recognize a divorce decree issued in another state. And the answer to that question, in turn, depends on when and to what extent a state court has jurisdiction to enter a decree of divorce. The first section of this chapter discusses this question. The following two sections look at jurisdiction to award support and to divide property and interjurisdictional enforcement of those orders. The fourth section considers jurisdiction over child custody disputes, and the final section concludes with materials on federal court jurisdiction over domestic relations litigation.

A. DIVORCE JURISDICTION

A principal benefit of absolute divorce is the possibility of remarriage. A party seeking a divorce wants assurance that any future alliance will be immune from attack on the ground that it is invalid because of a prior subsisting marriage. Jurisdiction is the key to any such assurance.

The basis for saying so lies in two principles: *res judicata* and full faith and credit. *Res judicata* provides that a matter that has been, or could have been, litigated in an action brought before a court and decided on the merits cannot be relitigated in a subsequent action, at least between the same parties. This is a rule seeking finality of judgments, designed to establish stable relations by denying endless opportunities for harassment and to protect courts from repeated litigation of the same matter. However, a court that lacks jurisdiction over a defendant cannot issue a binding decision. Absent jurisdiction, the defendant would be free to ignore the decision and, if need be, could litigate the issues in a second case if the plaintiff were to bring another action. In short, there can be no *res judicata* if there was no jurisdiction.

Full faith and credit becomes important when two or more states deal with issues related to a divorce. Suppose, for example, that Arthur sues Bernice in Florida for breach of contract, and both are present at the time of the suit. Bernice loses and then moves to New York. Arthur writes Bernice asking her to pay up, and Bernice replies, "Nuts" (or words to that effect). Arthur sues Bernice in New York based on the judgment entered in Florida. Bernice says in the New York court, "I shouldn't have to pay this. I have a good defense, and the Florida judge was wrong and silly." Bernice's claim will not be heard because the Florida judgment, which would be *res judicata* in that state, is entitled to recognition in New York under the full faith and credit clause of Article IV, §1 of the federal constitution. That clause states:

> Full Faith and Credit shall be given in each State to the public acts, Records, and judicial Proceedings of every other State.

By virtue of the full faith and credit clause, the New York court must recognize Arthur's valid final judgment against Bernice, which entitles him to recover on the basis of the Florida judgment, without retrying the case here.

Matters would be different if Florida did not have jurisdiction over Bernice. Full faith and credit must be given only to orders that the court had power to enter. If Florida did not have jurisdiction, the court in New York can refuse to recognize the Florida order. Indeed, New York *cannot* enforce the Florida order. To do so would violate Bernice's right to due process because she did not participate voluntarily in the Florida litigation, and Florida had no authority to require her participation.

Thus far, we have been talking about jurisdiction in actions to determine personal liability. But jurisdiction is not the same in all actions. Actions to determine personal liability are called "transitory" precisely because jurisdiction depends on the location of the parties rather than on any other fact. There are some cases, however, where it is not enough that the parties are before the court. When land, for example, is involved, a different jurisdictional requirement appears.

Suppose Arthur sues Bernice over title to a piece of land located in New York. The suit is brought in Florida, where Arthur has served Bernice with process during one of her business trips to that state. Presumably, the Florida court would decline jurisdiction. Although service of process on Bernice creates personal jurisdiction over her as the defendant, the court does not have jurisdiction over the subject matter of this action, the land. And because the court does not have jurisdiction over the subject matter, it cannot enter an order touching the land. Jurisdiction over land depends not on the location of the parties but on the location of the land. This power over land is called *in rem* jurisdiction—jurisdiction over things. An *in rem* order speaks not simply to the relationships between the parties, but to the world at large.

What is jurisdiction for purposes of divorce? Courts sometimes talk of marriage as a "civil contract," and if it were only that, the answer would be simple. Personal jurisdiction over the parties would be both necessary and sufficient. It would be necessary in the sense that, generally speaking, a court cannot make a binding determination without jurisdiction over the person of the defendant. It would be sufficient in that, if both parties were actually before the court, that circumstance alone would allow the court to render a binding decision concerning the marriage. In practice, this would mean that divorces could be rendered wherever both parties are present. If Arthur wished to sue Bernice, he would have to find her and sue her there. Similarly, if Bernice had moved from the state where Arthur lived and wished to get a divorce, she would have to go back to the state of Arthur's residence, or to any state where Arthur might be found, and bring the divorce action there. (Long-arm statutes can, of course, change this scheme.)

Here, as elsewhere, however, marriage is not viewed as a simple matter of contract. The relationship is the concern not solely of the two parties but, so it is said, of the state. The *status* aspect of marriage (or better, the public aspect) is important, and courts sometimes seem to take the same view concerning marriage as they do regarding land—that is, they tend to view it as an *in rem* action. Accordingly, one looks for a forum that has some interest in the marriage relationship, not simply for a court that happens to have power over the litigants. This is done by reifying the marital status into a fictional situs. What is such a situs? In many cases, the answer is simple. If the parties have always lived in State X, were married there, raised their children there, and seek to get divorced there, surely State X is the forum with an interest in determining whether the marriage should come to an end. Moreover, it is the only state with such an interest and therefore with jurisdiction to end the marriage. No other state may take jurisdiction to divorce the parties. If another state purports to do so, its decree is not entitled to recognition under the full faith and credit clause.

To this point, determining the jurisdiction with authority over the *res*—the marital status—has been easy enough. Suppose, however, that one spouse is physically abusive to the other spouse. If the abused spouse leaves the state and seeks a divorce, can she bring a divorce action in the new state of residence?

The answer depends on whether the domicile of one spouse (but not the other) is sufficient to give that state jurisdiction over that spouse's marital status. This issue was much disputed during the nineteenth century but was resolved for some time in Haddock v. Haddock. Although some courts had taken the view that, where the parties were domiciled in different jurisdictions, each state had sufficient interest in the subject matter of the relationship to issue a divorce, *Haddock* decided otherwise. An ex parte divorce (that is, one in which only one spouse participates) could be obtained only in the state of the "matrimonial domicile," meaning the last state in which both parties were domiciled as husband and wife. Accordingly, John Haddock's Connecticut decree, which we know was obtained ex parte with service by mail and publication, was not entitled to recognition in New York.

In 1942, however, the Supreme Court overruled *Haddock* in Williams v. North Carolina, 317 U.S. 287 (1942) (*Williams I*). After some 20 years of marriage to their respective spouses in North Carolina, Mr. Williams and Mrs. Hendrix decamped together to Las Vegas, Nevada, where they each obtained divorces and then married each other. The North Carolina spouses received notice of the divorce proceedings but were not served with process in Nevada, nor did they appear in the divorce proceedings. Upon their return from Nevada, the newlyweds were prosecuted for bigamy. They were convicted on the basis that their Nevada divorces were not entitled to recognition in North Carolina.

Although this conclusion would follow from *Haddock*, the Supreme Court held that every state has a "rightful and legitimate concern" in the marital status of persons domiciled in that state, which is sufficient to justify termination of the marital status even though the other spouse is not present. Moreover, such an assertion of jurisdiction is entitled to full faith and credit by other states. Thus, if Nevada were the domicile of Mr. Williams and Mrs. Hendrix, North Carolina must recognize their divorces. North Carolina's interest in the integrity of its divorce laws, of great concern in *Haddock*, was now dismissed as "part of the price of our federal system." 317 U.S. at 302. Left-at-home spouses have argued, without success, that permitting a state to grant a divorce or legal separation based on the domicile of the spouse who left violates procedural due process, relying on the minimum contacts test of International Shoe Co. v. Washington, 326 U.S. 310 (1945). *See, e.g.*, Henderson v. Henderson, 818 A.2d 669 (R.I. 2003).

Williams I held that Nevada could exercise divorce jurisdiction *over its domiciliaries*. In the first prosecution, there was no need to determine the domicile of Mr. Williams and Mrs. Hendrix. The persistent North Carolina prosecutor retried the defendants for bigamy, claiming that they had never intended to reside indefinitely in Nevada and therefore had never been domiciliaries of that state. The defendants were again convicted and again appealed to the Supreme Court. This time the Court upheld the conviction, holding that, under the full faith and credit clause, the Nevada finding of the jurisdictional fact of domicile incorporated in the original divorce decree did not bind North Carolina (which did not participate in the Nevada proceeding). That finding, therefore, was subject to reexamination by the North Carolina court. Williams v. North Carolina, 325 U.S. 226 (1945) (*Williams II*).

One of the implications of *Williams II* is that domicile is not only a sufficient, but a necessary, condition for full faith and credit recognition of divorce decrees. Another is that Mrs. Williams could also have challenged the ex parte divorce decree for lack of jurisdiction. If she had never appeared in the foreign divorce action, she did not have the opportunity to be heard on the jurisdictional issue and thus was not precluded from challenging that jurisdictional basis at a later time. But that is all that she could challenge. If a second court determines that the court issuing the divorce decree had jurisdiction because the plaintiff was a domiciliary of the forum state at the time the decree was entered, the spouse left behind cannot then litigate the existence of adequate grounds for the divorce. And while those spouses can attack the jurisdictional finding if they did not participate, they will carry the burden of proving the absence of domicile. *See* Homer H. Clark, Jr., Domestic Relations 718-719 (2d ed. 1987). Of course, if they prevail on the jurisdictional issue, then the divorce is invalid and has no effect.

Professor Ann Estin places the *Williams* cases in the context of a national debate about whether divorce laws should be relaxed and argues that when differences among the states could not be resolved through the political process, the Court "was eventually unwilling to allow the policies of a few states to block a more workable national compromise. . . . In the process of this transition, the Supreme Court set family law on a new course. After these cases, marital fault was no longer relevant to the determination of divorce jurisdiction, and states were free to grant unilateral ex parte divorces. Married couples gained a greater measure of freedom to come to terms together for the dissolution of their marriages. And while these developments spelled the end of strict controls over the grounds for divorce, they also ushered in a new era of greater attention to its custodial and financial incidents." Ann Laquer Estin, Family Law Federalism: Divorce and the Constitution, 16 Wm. & Mary Bill Rts. J. 381, 431-432 (2007). The following case considers the consequences if both spouses participate in the divorce action.

Sherrer v. Sherrer
334 U.S. 343 (1948)

Vinson, C.J. [Mr. and Mrs. Sherrer lived in Massachusetts during their marriage. In April 1944, Mrs. Sherrer went to Florida, ostensibly for vacation. In July, she filed for divorce on the ground of extreme cruelty, alleging that she was domiciled in Florida. Mr. Sherrer was notified by mail of the proceedings and appeared generally through counsel. He denied his wife's jurisdictional allegations and the grounds for divorce, but the Florida court granted Mrs. Sherrer a divorce, specifically finding that she was domiciled there. Mr. Sherrer did not appeal. In December, Mrs. Sherrer married Mr. Phelps. They lived together in Florida for two months and then returned to Massachusetts. In June 1945, Mr. Sherrer filed an action in Massachusetts predicated on the claim that he was still married to (the former) Mrs. Sherrer. She defended on the grounds that the Florida divorce was valid and that the parties were no longer married. The Massachusetts court reexamined the Florida court's basis for asserting jurisdiction, found that Mrs. Sherrer had not been domiciled there, and granted Mr. Sherrer the relief he sought.]

At the outset, it should be observed that the proceedings in the Florida court prior to the entry of the decree of divorce were in no way inconsistent with the requirements of procedural due process. We do not understand the respondent to urge the contrary. . . . It is clear that respondent was afforded his day in court with respect to every issue involved in the litigation, including the jurisdictional issue of petitioner's domicile. Under such circumstances, there is nothing in the concept of due process which demands that a defendant be afforded a second opportunity to litigate the existence of jurisdictional facts. . . .

That the jurisdiction of the Florida court to enter a valid decree of divorce was dependent upon petitioner's domicile in that State is not disputed. . . . But whether or not petitioner was domiciled in Florida at the time the divorce was granted was a matter to be resolved by judicial determination. Here, unlike the situation presented in Williams v. North Carolina, 325 U.S. 226 (1945), the finding of the requisite jurisdictional facts was made in proceedings in which the defendant appeared and participated. The question with which we are confronted, therefore, is whether such a finding . . . may be subjected to collateral attack in the courts of a sister State. . . .

The question of what effect is to be given to an adjudication by a court that it possesses requisite jurisdiction in a case, where the judgment of that court is subsequently subjected to collateral attack on jurisdictional grounds has been given frequent consideration by this Court over a period of many years. Insofar as cases originating in the federal courts are concerned, the rule has evolved that the doctrine of *res judicata* applies to adjudications relating either to jurisdiction of the person or of the subject matter where such adjudications have been made in proceedings in which those questions were in issue and in which the parties were given full opportunity to litigate. . . .

This Court has also held that the doctrine of *res judicata* must be applied to questions of jurisdiction arising in state courts involving the application of the Full Faith and Credit Clause where, under the law of the state in which the original judgment was rendered, such adjudications are not susceptible to collateral attack. . . .

Applying these principles to this case, we hold that the Massachusetts courts erred in permitting the Florida divorce decree to be subjected to attack on the ground that petitioner was not domiciled in Florida at the time the decree was entered. . . . It has not been contended that respondent was given less than a full opportunity to contest the issue of petitioner's domicile or any other issue relevant to the litigation. There is nothing to indicate that the Florida court would not have evaluated fairly and in good faith all relevant evidence submitted to it. . . . If respondent failed to take advantage of the opportunities afforded him, the responsibility is his own. . . .

It is urged . . . however, that because we are dealing with litigation involving the dissolution of the marital relation, a different result is demanded from that which might properly be reached if this case were concerned with other types of litigation. It is pointed out that under the Constitution the regulation and control of marital and family relationships are reserved to the States. . . .

But the recognition of the importance of a State's power to determine the incidents of basic social relationships into which its domiciliaries enter does not resolve the issues of this case. This is not a situation in which a State has merely sought to exert such power over a domiciliary. This is, rather, a case involving inconsistent assertions of power by courts of two States in the Federal Union and thus presents considerations which go beyond the interests of local policy, however vital. In resolving the issues here presented, we do not conceive it to be a part of our function to weigh the relative merits of the policies of Florida and Massachusetts with respect to divorce and related matters. . . .

It is one thing to recognize as permissible the judicial reexamination of findings of jurisdictional facts where such findings have been made by a court of a sister State which has entered a divorce decree in ex parte proceedings. It is quite another thing to hold that the vital rights and interests involved in divorce litigation may be held in suspense pending the scrutiny by courts of sister States of findings of jurisdictional fact made by a competent court in proceedings conducted in a manner consistent with the highest requirements of due process and in which the defendant has participated. . . . That vital interests are involved in divorce litigation indicates to us that it is a matter of greater rather than lesser importance that there should be a place to end such a litigation. And where a decree of divorce is rendered by a competent court under the circumstances of this case, the obligation of full faith and credit requires that such litigation should end in the courts of the State in which the judgment was rendered.

NOTES AND QUESTIONS

1. The practical effect of *Sherrer* is that a bilateral divorce — one in which both parties appear — cannot be attacked collaterally. Justice Frankfurter dissented vigorously, arguing that the Court's decision largely vitiates the domicile requirement, since it prevents attack on the decree where the defendant appeared and the court makes a finding of domicile, even though subsequent events plainly establish that the finding was erroneous. Is this problem more severe in divorce than in other kinds of litigation?

2. The Court emphasizes that principles of *res judicata* and full faith and credit require that sister states give a decree as much finality as the forum state provides. It follows that no state is required to give greater finality to a decree than does the rendering state and that challenges that would be available to the jurisdictional finding in the forum might be available in a collateral attack brought in a sister state. The requirement of full faith and credit thus depends on the rules of *res judicata* and collateral attack of the state granting the divorce.

This approach provides part of the answer to an issue left unresolved by *Sherrer* — the position of third parties who might wish to challenge the validity of the divorce. Suppose that Mr. and Mrs. Lear marry in New York and have two children. The husband receives an ex parte Nevada divorce. He then marries a second wife, who is also a divorcee with three children and a great deal of money. The second wife dies intestate. Can the children of the second Mrs. Lear attack the validity of their stepfather's divorce on the grounds that he was not domiciled in Nevada, and argue therefore that his marriage to their mother was invalid because he was still married? In Johnson v. Muelberger, 340 U.S. 581 (1951), the Court held that where the law of the forum did not permit a child to collaterally attack her parent's divorce decree, the full faith and credit clause prevented such an attack in any other state. To the same effect is Cook v. Cook, 342 U.S. 126 (1951) (second husband cannot attack wife's divorce from her first husband). *See* Note, Stranger Attacks on Sister-State Decrees of Divorce, 24 U. Chi. L. Rev. 376 (1957).

3. In today's increasingly mobile society, does it make sense to base divorce jurisdiction on the domicile of one of the parties? How does one even determine domicile if a person moves frequently? *See* Black v. Black, 968 N.Y.S.2d 722 (N.Y. App. Div. 2013), holding that a woman who grew up, was married, and lived in New York until she was 38 and then relocated with her husband 6 times over 16 years retained her domicile in New York (even though the parties lived for 7 years in France). *See also* Dean v. Dean, 51 Misc. 3d 1229(A) (N.Y. Sup. Ct. 2016). Professor Kerry Abrams and Kathryn Barber argue that domicile, as traditionally defined, is increasingly difficult to establish for two reasons:

> Domicile has always been a legal fiction; it has never perfectly described how people actually live. But . . . in the last fifty years, the legal fiction of domicile has become increasingly unmoored from the reality of people's lives. This change has less to do with increased mobility—although for some social classes, mobility has increased—and more to do with two factors that we think have been unappreciated in legal scholarship. The first is the rise of gender equality. As women entered the workforce in increasing numbers and gained access to higher education, their mobility and autonomy increased. Simultaneously, they began to delay marriage, or to forego marriage altogether, and those who were married were less likely to reflexively adopt their husband's domicile and were more inclined to make domiciliary choices for themselves and their families. . . . The second is the increasingly long time it takes young adults to become financially and emotionally self-sufficient and independent from their parents. This so-called phenomenon of "emerging adulthood," identified by psychologists as a new phase of life that sometimes lasts into a person's thirties, has made it more difficult for young adults to establish a new domicile.

Kerry Abrams & Kathryn Barber, Domicile Dismantled, 92 Ind. L.J. 387, 390 (2017). For contemporary challenges in establishing state domicile for divorce, *see* Mark Strasser, Divorce, Domicile, and the Constitution, 108 Ky. L.J. 301, 302-334 (2019). Professor Strasser highlights the difficulties for couples in the military and in same-sex marriages in states that do not have a domicile requirement.

4. Obergefell v. Hodges, excerpted in Chapters 1 and 3, extends the rules that govern domicile in marriage and divorce to couples of the same sex across all states. Obergefell v. Hodges, 576 U.S. 644, 670 (2015) (granting same-sex couples "the constellation" of "rights, benefits, and responsibilities" that "the states have linked to marriage"). The First Circuit Court of Appeals held that *Obergefell* required the U.S. territory of Puerto Rico to recognize same-sex marriages under the Fourteenth and Fifth Amendments. Conde-Vidal v. Rius-Armendariz, No. 14-2184, 2015 WL 10574261, at *1 (1st Cir. July 8, 2015).

Before *Obergefell* and with the piecemeal legalization of same-sex marriage across states, divorce jurisdiction re-emerged as a hotly contested issue. Much of the analysis of divorce jurisdiction dwelled on alternative approaches to divorce and domicile. Professor Courtney Joslin discussed the problem same-sex couples faced when their marriages ended and they were domiciled in a state that did not recognize their marriage from another state. Modernizing Divorce Jurisdiction: Same-Sex Couples and Minimum Contacts, 91 B.U. L. Rev. 1669 (2011). She argued that the domicile rule should be replaced by the typical minimum contacts rule and recommended that states amend their long-arm statutes to provide that, by marrying in the state, parties submit to the state's jurisdiction over their divorce, requiring parties who marry in the state to consent to jurisdiction over a later dissolution. *Id.* at 1716-1717. *See also* Susan Frelich Appleton, Domicile and Inequality by Design: The Case of Destination

Weddings, 2013 Mich. St. L. Rev. 1449. Do you think a minimum contacts approach is preferable to a domicile test for divorce? Why or why not?

Jurisdictional questions also arise when couples seek the dissolution of civil unions, which confer the same rights but not the status of marriage. In some states, courts have jurisdiction to apply the state's divorce laws to couples in civil unions that were entered into before marriage rights extended to same-sex couples. *See, e.g.,* Neyman v. Buckley, 153 A.3d 1010 (Pa. Super. 2016). *See also* Solomon v. Guidry, 155 A.3d 1218 (Vt. 2016) (for a couple who had entered a civil union in Vermont, the state law governing civil unions permitted dissolution for nonresidents without first attempting to dissolve the union in the couple's current resident state).

5. When restrictive divorce laws were prevalent in the United States, some foreign countries — most notably Mexico — conducted a substantial business in matrimonial dissolutions. "Mail-order" Mexican divorces, which could be obtained without the presence of either party in Mexico at any time, were among the most notorious strategies, particularly favored in New York at one time. The validity of foreign divorces is not governed by the full faith and credit clause, which speaks only to the judicial acts of other states. Rather, recognition is a matter of comity. Although there is no constitutional obligation to grant comity recognition to a foreign decree, it is regarded as a matter of international duty that should be discharged as long as the foreign court had jurisdiction of the subject matter and the judgment will not offend domestic public policy. *See, e.g.,* Kugler v. Haitian Tours, Inc., 293 A.2d 706, 709 (N.J. Super. 1972).

What issues are relevant to determining whether an American jurisdiction should recognize a unilateral foreign divorce? A bilateral divorce? *Compare* Rosenstiel v. Rosenstiel, 209 N.E.2d 709 (N.Y. 1965), *cert. denied,* 384 U.S. 971 (1966), *and* Hyde v. Hyde, 562 S.W.2d 194 (Tenn. 1978) (recognizing bilateral Dominican Republic divorce), *with* Warrender v. Warrender, 190 A.2d 684 (N.J. App. 1963) (bilateral Mexico divorce "absolutely void on its face"), *and* Everett v. Everett, 345 So. 2d 586 (La. App. 1977).

6. The doctrine of equitable estoppel may prevent attack on divorces that would otherwise be subject to collateral challenge. This doctrine prevents a party from challenging a decree that one has obtained or has led another to rely on. The most obvious case of estoppel arises when the party who obtained the divorce later claims that it is invalid. Parties may also be estopped if they participated collusively in securing the divorce, or if they acquiesce for a long time in the divorce, knowing of its jurisdictional defect. Acceptance of benefits associated with the divorce may have the same result. Third parties may also be subject to estoppel if they actively participate in securing a defective divorce for another. Analysis and rationalization of estoppel in divorce is one of the many contributions of Professor Clark's treatise on Domestic Relations. *See* 1 Homer H. Clark, Jr., Domestic Relations §13.3, at 732-755 (2d ed. 1987).

PROBLEMS

1. Casey and Glenn were domiciled in State *A.* Casey went to State *B* on vacation and sought and was granted a divorce. The State *B* court erroneously found that Casey was domiciled there. Glenn in no way participated in the State *B* proceedings. Casey then returned to State *A.* Glenn collaterally attacked the State *B* divorce in a State *A* court. Casey claimed that State *A* must give the State *B* decree full faith and credit. Must it?

2. Harper and Jesse were domiciled in State *A.* Harper moved to State *B* to go to college. Six months later, Harper sued Jesse for a divorce in State *B,* relying on a State *B* statute that says that State *B* has jurisdiction to grant a divorce if either spouse has been resident there for six months. Jesse, who remained in State *A,* was served by mail but did not appear or participate in any way in the State *B* action. The State *B* court granted the divorce. Jesse collaterally attacked the decree in State *A*. Harper claimed that State *A* must give the State *B* decree full faith and credit. Must it?

3. Pat and Sydney were domiciled in State *A*. Pat went to State *B* and sued Sydney for divorce. Pat served Sydney in State *B*, and Sydney entered an appearance by attorney. The divorce was granted. Sydney collaterally attacked the State *B* divorce in State *A*, claiming that State *B* lacked jurisdiction to grant the divorce since neither Pat nor Sydney was domiciled there. What should Pat argue in response? What if Sydney was personally served in State *B* but elected not to appear? If the court were to adopt a minimum contacts test, would that test be satisfied?

4. Tatum and Alex were domiciled in State *A*. Tatum went to Mexico and sued Alex for divorce. Tatum served Alex in State *A*, but Alex did not appear or participate in any way in the Mexican proceedings. The divorce was granted, and Tatum returned to State *A*. Alex, who remained in State *A*, remarried. Alex's new spouse died, and Alex claimed the rights of a surviving spouse in the spouse's estate. The estate's executor rejected Alex's claim on the basis that the divorce from Tatum was not valid and that therefore Alex was not the surviving spouse. What are the arguments of Alex and the executor? If instead Alex claimed rights as Tatum's surviving spouse, what arguments should the executor of Tatum's estate make in opposition to Alex's claim?

B. DIVISIBLE DIVORCE

We have seen that jurisdiction to grant a divorce or legal separation is viewed, after *Williams I* and *Williams II*, as an *in rem* matter. The *res* is the marriage relationship itself, embodied in the domicile of one of the parties to the marriage. Accordingly, the state in which one of the parties is domiciled has jurisdiction to adjudicate the divorce action.

The *Williams* cases held not only that the state of domicile of one party may adjudicate the marital status of its domiciliary but also that the state's judgment, even if ex parte, is entitled to extraterritorial effect through the full faith and credit clause. However, the Supreme Court expressly reserved judgment regarding the extraterritorial effect of ex parte orders about the parties' financial interests. The Supreme Court addressed that issue in Estin v. Estin, 334 U.S. 541 (1948), and in the next case.

Vanderbilt v. Vanderbilt
354 U.S. 416 (1957)

BLACK, J. Cornelius Vanderbilt, Jr., petitioner, and Patricia Vanderbilt, respondent, were married in 1948. They separated in 1952 while living in California. The wife moved to New York, where she has resided since February 1953. In March of that year the husband filed suit for divorce in Nevada. This proceeding culminated, in June 1953, with a decree of final divorce which provided that both husband and wife were "freed and released from the bonds of matrimony and all the duties and obligations thereof. . . ."[1] The wife was not served with process in Nevada and did not appear before the divorce court.

In April 1954, Mrs. Vanderbilt instituted an action in a New York court praying for separation from petitioner and for alimony. The New York court did not have personal

---

1. It seems clear that in Nevada the effect of this decree was to put an end to the husband's duty to support the wife—provided, of course, that the Nevada courts had power to do this. Sweeney v. Sweeney, 42 Nev. 431, 438-439, 179 P. 638, 639-640; Herrick v. Herrick, 55 Nev. 59, 68, 25 P.2d 378, 380. *See* Estin v. Estin, 334 U.S. 541, 547.

jurisdiction over him, but in order to satisfy his obligations, if any, to Mrs. Vanderbilt, it sequestered his property within the State. He appeared specially and, among other defenses to the action, contended that the Full Faith and Credit Clause of the United States Constitution compelled the New York court to treat the Nevada divorce as having ended the marriage and as having destroyed any duty of support which he owed the respondent. While the New York court found the Nevada decree valid and held that it had effectively dissolved the marriage, it nevertheless entered an order, under Section 1170-b of the New York Civil Practice Act, directing petitioner to make designated support payments to respondent. The New York Court of Appeals upheld the support order. Petitioner then applied to this Court for certiorari contending that Section 1170-b, as applied, is unconstitutional because it contravenes the Full Faith and Credit Clause.

In Estin v. Estin, 334 U.S. 541, this Court decided that a Nevada divorce court, which had no personal jurisdiction over the wife, had no power to terminate a husband's obligation to provide her support as required in a pre-existing New York separation decree. . . . Since the wife was not subject to its jurisdiction, the Nevada divorce court had no power to extinguish any right which she had under the law of New York to financial support from her husband. It has long been the constitutional rule that a court cannot adjudicate a personal claim or obligation unless it has jurisdiction over the person of the defendant. Here, the Nevada divorce court was as powerless to cut off the wife's support right as it would have been to order the husband to pay alimony if the wife had brought the divorce action and he had not been subject to the divorce court's jurisdiction. Therefore, the Nevada decree, to the extent it purported to affect the wife's right to support, was void and the Full Faith and Credit Clause did not obligate New York to give it recognition. . . .

Affirmed.

[The dissenting opinion of Justice FRANKFURTER is omitted.]

NOTES AND QUESTIONS

1. Is the majority's primary concern the rights of the states or the due process interests of the parties?

2. Suppose New York law did *not* allow Mrs. Vanderbilt to prosecute a suit for support if her marital status had been validly terminated. Would this mean that Mrs. Vanderbilt could not pursue a right to spousal maintenance following a valid ex parte divorce in Nevada? Would such a rule be constitutional?

3. In Simons v. Miami Beach First National Bank, 381 U.S. 81 (1965), the Court indicated that there is at least one situation in which a spouse's economic interests can be affected by an ex parte divorce. The husband, who had lived with his wife in New York, went to Florida and secured an ex parte Florida divorce with constructive service. He continued to pay support to her under a New York judicial separation order until his death. After he died, his ex-wife appeared in probate proceedings in Florida, claiming dower rights under Florida law. The respondent bank opposed the dower claim. The ex-wife brought an action to set aside the divorce decree and to obtain a declaration that the divorce, even if valid with regard to her marital status, did not affect her claim to dower. The Florida courts dismissed her action. The Supreme Court affirmed, rejecting her argument that Florida could not extinguish her dower right without personal jurisdiction:

> Insofar as petitioner argues that since she was not subject to the jurisdiction of the Florida divorce court its decree could not extinguish any dower right existing under Florida law, Vanderbilt v. Vanderbilt, 354 U.S. 416, 418, the answer is that under Florida law no dower right survived the decree. The Supreme Court of Florida has said that dower rights in Florida

property, being inchoate, are extinguished by a divorce decree predicated upon substituted or constructive service.

It follows that the Florida courts transgressed no constitutional bounds in denying petitioner dower in her ex-husband's Florida estate.

381 U.S. at 85.

The majority assumed that its decision is consistent with *Estin* and *Vanderbilt.* Is this because dower rights are in some way different from the kinds of rights the Court had previously protected? For a consideration of this explanation, *see* Note, Divorce ex Parte Style, 33 U. Chi. L. Rev. 837 (1966). If *Simons* is consistent with prior decisions, is it because the property interest asserted here arose under the law of the divorcing state rather than the nonparticipating spouse's domicile? What if New York law eliminated dower interests upon divorce?

In 1975, Florida replaced dower with a forced spousal share upon death. Would that be extinguished as well by an ex parte divorce? If a forced share can be thus terminated, what about the wife's interest in property that she might receive through an "equitable distribution"?

4. The principle underlying *Estin* and *Vanderbilt,* that there are different jurisdictional bases for divorce and for support orders, is commonly called "divisible divorce." As you will see in the remainder of the chapter, the principle goes even further, as still different criteria are used to establish jurisdiction to decide property division and custody.

NOTE: PROPERTY DIVISION—JURISDICTION AND FULL FAITH AND CREDIT

As discussed earlier, only a court in the state in which real property is located has *in rem* jurisdiction to determine its ownership and thus to enter property division orders. The Supreme Court applied this principle in Fall v. Eastin, 215 U.S. 1 (1909), holding that a Washington divorce decree awarding real property in Nebraska to a wife was not entitled to full faith and credit. However, many courts today will recognize property division orders from courts in states in which the property is not located if the court validly asserted *in personam* jurisdiction over the parties. *E.g.,* Weesner v. Weesner, 95 N.W.2d 682 (Neb. 1959); McElreath v. McElreath, 345 S.W.2d 722 (Tex. 1961); Ivey v. Ivey, 439 A.2d 425 (Conn. 1981); Russo v. Russo, 714 A.2d 466 (Pa. Super. 1998); Roberts v. Locke, 304 P.3d 116 (Wyo. 2013); Pathak v. Bhardwaj, 2015 WL 1516596, at *2 (Ariz. App. 2015) (a "California family court had authority to compel Husband to sell marital property at divorce even though it lacked authority to directly affect title to property lying outside its jurisdiction").

A concomitant of the traditional rule is that a court in a state in which real property is located may constitutionally assert jurisdiction to divide the property even though the defendant has no other contact with the state. Homer H. Clark, Jr., Domestic Relations §13.4, at 763-764, discussing Shaffer v. Heitner, 433 U.S. 186, 207-208 (1977); In re Ramsey's Marriage, 526 P.2d 319 (Colo. App. 1974); Harrod v. Harrod, 526 P.2d 666 (Colo. App. 1974); Hodge v. Hodge, 422 A.2d 280 (Conn. 1979); Gelkop v. Gelkop, 384 So. 2d 195 (Fla. App. 1980).

PROBLEMS

1. Brook and Cam were domiciled in State *A.* Cam moved to State *B,* established a domicile, and sued Brook for divorce. Cam served Brook in State *A,* but Brook did not appear or in any way participate in the State *B* proceedings. The State *B* court granted Cam a divorce, ordered Brook to pay Cam $200 per month in spousal support, and found that Brook was not entitled to spousal support from Cam. Cam took the decree to State *A* and asked the State *A* court to enforce the spousal support order. Brook cross-claimed for spousal support from Cam. Cam argued that the State *A* court must give full faith and credit to the State *B* decree. What should Brook argue in response? Who wins and why?

2. Honor and Spencer were domiciled in State *A*. Honor moved to State *B*, established domicile there, and sued Spencer for divorce. Honor served Spencer in State *A*, but Spencer did not appear or in any way participate in the State *B* proceedings. The State *B* court granted Honor a divorce. The decree was silent on the issue of spousal support. Honor returned to State *A*, where Spencer sued for spousal support, serving Honor personally in State *A*. Under the law of State *A*, if a divorce decree makes no provision for spousal support, a court cannot later grant it. How should the court rule on Spencer's motion for support?

3. Rory and Sage were divorced in State *A*, where they are both domiciled. The State *A* court awarded their vacation home, located in State *B*, to Sage. After the order was entered, Rory did nothing to comply with the decree, and the State *B* title continued to show that Rory and Sage owned the vacation home as joint tenants with right of survivorship. Sage died. The executor of Sage's estate claimed that Sage owned the State *B* vacation home, relying on the divorce decree. Rory claimed the home because the title had never been changed from joint tenancy with right of survivorship. If this dispute were litigated in State *B*, would the State *B* court have to give full faith and credit to the State *A* order?

NOTE: JURISDICTION TO ENTER DOMESTIC VIOLENCE PROTECTIVE ORDERS

May a court issue a domestic violence protective order even though it lacks *in personam* jurisdiction over the respondent? In several cases, victims of domestic violence left home and fled to another state, where they sought a protective order. The people accused of abuse moved to dismiss for lack of jurisdiction because they had had no contacts with the forum state. In Caplan v. Donovan, 879 N.E.2d 117 (Mass. 2008), the court rejected the respondent's argument, analogizing the case to ones involving divorce. The court, therefore, concluded that a trial court could properly exercise jurisdiction to prohibit the respondent from abusing or approaching the plaintiff so long as it was not ordering an affirmative act of the respondent. *See also* Rios v. Ferguson, 978 A.2d 592 (Conn. 2008) (man living in North Carolina who posted a video on YouTube threatening his girlfriend in Connecticut committed a tortious act in Connecticut, supporting jurisdiction to issue protective order); Bartsch v. Bartsch, 636 N.W.2d 3 (Iowa 2001); Spencer v. Spencer, 191 S.W.3d 14 (Ky. App. 2006); Hemenway v. Hemenway, 992 A.2d 575 (N.H. 2010); Shah v. Shah, 875 A.2d 931 (N.J. 2005). *Contra*, T.L. v. W.L., 820 A.2d 506 (Del. Fam. Ct. 2003); Becker v. Johnson, 937 So. 2d 1128 (Fla. App. 2006); Anderson v. Deas, 632 S.E.2d 682 (Ga. App. 2006). Examples of "affirmative action" by the respondent, which state courts agree requires *in personam* jurisdiction, include paying child support or not possessing a firearm. *E.g.*, Fox v. Fox, 106 A.3d 919, 926 (2014). For further discussion, *see* Jessica Miles, We Are Never Ever Getting Back Together: Domestic Violence Victims, Defendants, and Due Process, 35 Cardozo L. Rev. 141 (2013); Cody Jacobs, The Stream of Violence: A New Approach to Domestic Violence Personal Jurisdiction, 64 UCLA L. Rev. 684 (2017).

The federal Violence Against Women Act requires states to give full faith and credit to and enforce domestic violence restraining orders from other states. 18 U.S.C. §2265 (2022). An order that is valid according to the law of the state that issued it must be enforced, even if it includes terms or applies to parties that the law of the forum state would not permit. *See* Emily J. Sack, Domestic Violence Across State Lines: The Full Faith and Credit Clause, Congressional Power, and Interstate Enforcement of Protection Orders, 98 Nw. U. L. Rev. 827 (2004). In 2022, the Violence Against Women Act was reauthorized as part of the Consolidated Appropriations Act, 2022, H.R. 2471, 117th Cong. (2022). This Act includes an expansion of special criminal jurisdiction for Native courts to address sexual assault, child abuse, stalking, and sex trafficking.

C. JURISDICTION AND FULL FAITH AND CREDIT FOR SUPPORT DUTIES

Estin and *Vanderbilt* confirm that *in personam* jurisdiction is required for orders that establish parties' rights and duties regarding spousal and child support. In other words, jurisdiction to decide these rights must satisfy the minimum-contacts test of International Shoe Co. v. Washington, 326 U.S. 310, 316 (1945), and its successors. In Burnham v. Superior Court, 495 U.S. 604 (1990), the Supreme Court addressed the constitutional sufficiency of "tag jurisdiction"—that is, jurisdiction asserted over a defendant who is served while physically present in the state but has no other substantial connection to the state. Burnham, a New Jersey resident, was served with process in a suit for divorce and determination of support and property issues while he was in California to take care of business and visit his children. The Court unanimously agreed that the defendant was subject to California's jurisdiction, although the Justices differed significantly as to the theory supporting jurisdiction.

The next case considers the extent to which courts may assert jurisdiction over obligors or obligees who are not physically present in the jurisdiction. *Estin* and *Vanderbilt* were, of course, cases concerning interstate enforceability of support orders under the full faith and credit clause, but since the lower courts' assertion of jurisdiction violated due process, the cases do not actually address when courts must recognize and enforce support orders from other jurisdictions. The second part of this section addresses these issues.

1. Long-Arm Jurisdiction in Support Cases

Kulko v. Superior Court
436 U.S. 84 (1978)

[Ezra and Sharon Kulko, then both New York domiciliaries, were married in 1959 in California during Ezra's three-day stopover while he was en route to overseas military duty. After the wedding, Sharon returned to New York, as did Ezra following his tour of duty. In 1961 and 1962 a son and daughter were born in New York. The family lived together in New York until March 1972, when Ezra and Sharon separated. Sharon moved to California. The spouses entered into a separation agreement in New York, which provided that the children would live with Ezra during the school year and visit Sharon in California during specified vacations. Ezra agreed to pay Sharon $3000 per year in child support for the periods when the children were with her. Sharon obtained a divorce in Haiti, which incorporated the terms of the separation agreement, and returned to California. In December 1973, the daughter asked to move to California to live with her mother. Ezra consented. Without Ezra's consent, Sharon arranged for the son to join her in California about two years later. Sharon then sued Ezra in California to establish the Haitian divorce decree as a California judgment, to modify the judgment to award her full custody of the children, and to increase

Ezra's child support obligation. Ezra, resisting the claim for increased support, appeared specially, claiming that he lacked sufficient "minimum contacts" with California under International Shoe Co. v. Washington, 326 U.S. 310, 316 (1945), to warrant the state's assertion of personal jurisdiction over him. The California Supreme Court upheld lower-court determinations adverse to Ezra.]

MARSHALL, J. The issue before us is whether, in this action for child support, the California state courts may exercise *in personam* jurisdiction over a nonresident, nondomiciliary parent of minor children domiciled within the State. For reasons set forth below, we hold that the exercise of such jurisdiction would violate the Due Process Clause of the Fourteenth Amendment. . . .

The Due Process Clause of the Fourteenth Amendment operates as a limitation on the jurisdiction of state courts to enter judgments affecting rights or interests of nonresident defendants. *See* Shaffer v. Heitner, 433 U.S. 186, 198-200 (1977). It has long been the rule that a valid judgment imposing a personal obligation or duty in favor of the plaintiff may be entered only by a court having jurisdiction over the person of the defendant. Pennoyer v. Neff, 95 U.S. 714, 732-733 (1878); International Shoe Co. v. Washington, 326 U.S., at 316. The existence of personal jurisdiction, in turn, depends upon the presence of reasonable notice to the defendant that an action has been brought, Mullane v. Central Hanover Trust Co., 339 U.S. 306, 313-314 (1950), and a sufficient connection between the defendant and the forum State to make it fair to require defense of the action in the forum. In this case, appellant does not dispute the adequacy of the notice that he received, but contends that his connection with the State of California is too attenuated, under the standards implicit in the Due Process Clause of the Constitution, to justify imposing upon him the burden and inconvenience of defense in California.

The parties are in agreement that the constitutional standard for determining whether the State may enter a binding judgment against appellant here is that set forth in this Court's opinion in International Shoe Co. v. Washington, supra: that a defendant "have certain minimum contacts with [the forum State] such that the maintenance of the suit does not offend 'traditional notions of fair play and substantial justice.' " . . . [A]n essential criterion in all cases is whether the "quality and nature" of the defendant's activity is such that it is "reasonable" and "fair" to require him to conduct his defense in that State. . . .

In reaching its result, the California Supreme Court did not rely on appellant's glancing presence in the State some 13 years before the events that led to this controversy, nor could it have. . . . To hold such temporary visits to a State a basis for the assertion of *in personam* jurisdiction over unrelated actions arising in the future would make a mockery of the limitations on state jurisdiction imposed by the Fourteenth Amendment. Nor did the California court rely on the fact that appellant was actually married in California on one of his two brief visits. We agree that where two New York domiciliaries, for reasons of convenience, marry in the State of California and thereafter spend their entire married life in New York, the fact of their California marriage by itself cannot support a California court's exercise of jurisdiction over a spouse who remains a New York resident in an action relating to child support.

Finally, in holding that personal jurisdiction existed, the court below carefully disclaimed reliance on the fact that appellant had agreed at the time of separation to allow his children to live with their mother three months a year and that he had sent them to California each year pursuant to this agreement. . . . [T]o find personal jurisdiction in a State on this basis, merely because the mother was residing there, would discourage parents from entering into reasonable visitation agreements. Moreover, it could arbitrarily subject one parent to suit in any State of the Union where the other parent chose to spend time while having custody of their offspring pursuant to a separation agreement. As we have emphasized: "The unilateral activity of those who claim some relationship with a nonresident defendant cannot satisfy the requirement of contact with the forum State. . . . [It] is essential in each case that there be some act by which the defendant purposefully avails [him]self of the privilege of conducting activities within the forum State. . . ." Hanson v. Denckla, 357 U.S. 235 (1958).

The "purposeful act" that the California Supreme Court believed did warrant the exercise of personal jurisdiction over appellant in California was his "actively and fully [consenting] to Ilsa living in California for the school year . . . and . . . [sending] her to California for that purpose." We cannot accept the proposition that appellant's acquiescence in Ilsa's desire to live with her mother conferred jurisdiction over appellant in the California courts in this action. A father who agrees, in the interests of family harmony and his children's preferences, to allow them to spend more time in California than was required under a separation agreement can hardly be said to have "purposefully availed himself" of the "benefits and protections" of California's laws.

Nor can we agree with the assertion of the court below that the exercise of *in personam* jurisdiction here was warranted by the financial benefit appellant derived from his daughter's presence in California for nine months of the year. This argument rests on the premise that, while appellant's liability for support payments remained unchanged, his yearly expenses for supporting the child in New York decreased. But this circumstance, even if true, does not support California's assertion of jurisdiction here. Any diminution in appellant's household costs resulted, not from the child's presence in California, but rather from her absence from appellant's home. . . .

The circumstances in this case clearly render "unreasonable" California's assertion of personal jurisdiction. . . . The cause of action herein asserted arises, not from the defendant's commercial transactions in interstate commerce, but rather from his personal, domestic relations. It thus cannot be said that appellant has sought a commercial benefit from solicitation of business from a resident of California that could reasonably render him liable to suit in state court; appellant's activities cannot fairly be analogized to an insurer's sending an insurance contract and premium notices into the State to an insured resident of the State. Furthermore, the controversy between the parties arises from a separation that occurred in the State of New York; appellee Horn seeks modification of a contract that was negotiated in New York and that she flew to New York to sign. As in Hanson v. Denckla, the instant action involves an agreement that was entered into with virtually no connection with the forum State.

Finally, basic considerations of fairness point decisively in favor of appellant's State of domicile as the proper forum for adjudication of this case, whatever the merits of appellee's underlying claim. It is appellant who has remained in the State of the marital domicile, whereas it is appellee who has moved across the continent. . . . Appellant has at all times resided in New York State, and, until the separation and appellee's move to California, his entire family resided there as well. As noted above, appellant did no more than acquiesce in the stated preference of one of his children to live with her mother in California. This single act is surely not one that a reasonable parent would expect to result in the substantial financial burden and personal strain of litigating a child-support suit in a forum 3,000 miles away, and we therefore see no basis on which it can be said that appellant could reasonably have anticipated being "haled before a [California] court." To make jurisdiction in a case such as this turn on whether appellant bought his daughter her ticket or instead unsuccessfully sought to prevent her departure would impose an unreasonable burden on family relations, and one wholly unjustified by the "quality and nature" of appellant's activities in or relating to the State of California.

Reversed.

NOTES AND QUESTIONS

1. One standard for determining the permissible extent of state court jurisdiction asks whether the defendant purposely took advantage of the protection and benefits of California law. Didn't the defendant in *Kulko* do so? Justice Brennan, joined by Justice Powell and Justice White, wrote a dissent arguing that the "appellant's connection with the State of California was not too attenuated under the standards of reasonableness and fairness implicit in the Due Process Clause, to require him to conduct his defense in the California courts." 436 US at 102. The dissenting justices, however, did not address the nature of the legal relationships in a family law context. The majority seems to distinguish between commercial undertakings (for example, where an insurance company sends a policy to a California insured) and the father's sending his daughter to California. Doesn't that distinction mean that commercial agreements will be more easily enforced than child support obligations? Why shouldn't the agreement between the parties in *Kulko* be viewed as any other interstate contract between two parties? *See* Mary-Beth Moylan & Katherine Macfarlane, Kulko v. Superior Court in Feminist Judgments: Family Law Opinions Rewritten 141-161 (Rachel Rebouché ed., 2020) (rewriting *Kulko* to emphasize "purposeful acts that invoke the benefits and protections of California law in the form of the relationship between the nonresident father and his children, and the ongoing negotiations about care and support of the children between the parties").

2. The court also addresses the question of whether it is fair to require Kulko to participate in a California adjudication. Is fairness a categorical question? For example, is asking a defendant to participate in a proceeding in another state with which the person does not have minimal contacts always unfair? Suppose in *Kulko* that the wife and children were living in New Jersey. What factors influence the meaning of "fairness" and "inconvenience"? *See* Terry S. Kogan, Geography and Due Process: The Social Meaning of Adjudicative Jurisdiction, 22 Rutgers L.J. 627 (1991).

3. The Uniform Interstate Family Support Act (UIFSA), which did not exist at the time of *Kulko* but which all states have now adopted in some form, deals with all aspects of interstate support orders, including personal jurisdiction. Section 201 is a long-arm statute providing that a court may exercise personal jurisdiction over a nonresident to establish, enforce, or modify a support order or to determine parentage if

1) the individual is personally served with [citation, summons, notice] within this State;
2) the individual submits to the jurisdiction of this State by consent in a record, by entering a general appearance, or by filing a responsive document having the effect of waiving any contest to personal jurisdiction;
3) the individual resided with the child in this State;
4) the individual resided in this State and provided prenatal expenses or support for the child;
5) the child resides in this State as a result of the acts or directives of the individual;
6) the individual engaged in sexual intercourse in this State and the child may have been conceived by that act of intercourse;
7) the individual asserted parentage of a child in the [putative father registry] maintained in this State by the [appropriate agency]; or
8) there is any other basis consistent with the constitutions of this State and the United States for the exercise of personal jurisdiction.

As described further below, UIFSA creates special procedures that a court may use to invoke the assistance of courts in other states to obtain evidence and discovery in those states. UIFSA §§316, 318.

4. Statutes and case law in many states provide that a court that validly asserts personal jurisdiction to determine a person's support duties has continuing jurisdiction for purposes of modification, even after the person has moved from the state. *See* Annot., E. H. Schopler, Necessity of Personal Service Within State upon Nonresident Spouse as Prerequisite of Court's Power to Modify Its Decree as to Alimony or Child Support in Matrimonial Action, 62 A.L.R.2d 544, 546 (1958 with weekly updates). What are the outer constitutional limits on such an assertion of jurisdiction? A number of courts have upheld claims of continuing jurisdiction even after *both* parties have moved away. Compare the continuing-jurisdiction provisions of UIFSA, which are discussed in the next section.

PROBLEMS

1. Jordan and Kelly were married and lived in State *A* for the first years of their marriage. Four years ago they separated, and Kelly moved to State *B*, where the couple together purchased a condo, titled in Kelly's name only. Jordan has paid the mortgage but has never been to the condo. Jordan has also leased a car for Kelly in State *B*. Kelly has filed for divorce in State *B* and asks the court for an award of the condo and for an order for Jordan to pay spousal support. State *B*'s long-arm statute allows its courts to assert *in personam* jurisdiction over a person outside the state who has transacted business within the state; made a contract within the state; committed a tort within the state; owns, uses, or possesses real estate within the state; or has "lived in lawful marriage" within the state. Under this statute, may a State *B* court assert jurisdiction to determine ownership of the condo and to award Kelly spousal support? Would such assertions of jurisdiction be consistent with due process?

2. Mackenzie and Val were married in New York, and their children were born there. After 15 years of marriage, they separated, and Mackenzie moved to California. Val brought a divorce action 18 months later, seeking child support. Would New York have jurisdiction to order child support under UIFSA? Would it be constitutional for New York to assert this jurisdiction? What if it were five years later?

3. Drew and Jules were married and had two children in California. Ten years later they moved to New York, where they lived for three months before moving overseas. They lived in Mali for three years, and then Jules returned to California with the children. Could California assert jurisdiction under UIFSA to determine Drew's child support obligation? If Jules and the children returned to New York instead, would New York have jurisdiction under UIFSA over Drew to decide child support?

4. Fran and Cori were married in Texas. Fran abused Cori physically and mentally. Fran eventually threatened to kill Cori, and Cori left that night, moving in with a friend. Fran stalked Cori at work and at home. On the recommendation of police, Cori moved to a shelter for victims of intimate violence. Fran continued to stalk Cori, and friends saw Fran with guns at the house where Cori had lived. Fran also called Cori's father in Colorado to threaten Cori. Cori fled to Colorado and sued Fran for divorce and child support. Fran moved to dismiss the child support action on the basis that UIFSA does not support jurisdiction on these facts and that if a Colorado court tried to assert jurisdiction to award child support, due process would be violated. Should the court grant Fran's motion?

2. Interstate Modification and Enforcement of Support

Sharon Horn could have pursued her action for child support against Ezra Kulko by traveling to New York and filing suit there. For many people, though, the costs of such a suit would be prohibitive. Further, even if a New York court had ordered Ezra to pay child support, if he refused to pay, Sharon might have had to return to New York or at least retain New York counsel to enforce the order.

If Ezra moved to a third state and refused to pay, Sharon would have had still more difficulties. Besides the practical ones, under traditional legal principles, the third state might not have recognized her New York order because states did not have to give full faith and credit to modifiable support orders. Sistare v. Sistare, 218 U.S. 1 (1910); Barber v. Barber, 62 U.S. (21 How.) 582 (1858). While other states might have enforced nonfinal orders as a matter of comity, the practical difficulties of interstate enforcement of support remained. Worthley v. Worthley, 283 P.2d 19 (Cal. 1955); Restatement (Second) of Conflicts §109 (1971). Moreover, due process requires that obligors be given an opportunity to present defenses and arguments for modification in such cases. Griffin v. Griffin, 327 U.S. 220 (1946). The Uniform Reciprocal Enforcement of Support Act (URESA), in place at the time of *Kulko*, was intended to solve the practical and legal problems of interstate support enforcement. Most American jurisdictions adopted one version or another of the Act, but state law was never uniform because of inconsistencies in the versions adopted by the various states.

UIFSA, which was amended most recently in 2008, replaced URESA and creates a uniform set of laws. In compliance with federal legislation, all states have enacted the UIFSA 2008 Amendments. Interstate Family Support Act Enactment History, available at http://www.uniformlaws.org.

To complement UIFSA, Congress enacted the Full Faith and Credit for Child Support Orders Act (FFCCSOA), 28 U.S.C. §1738B (2022), which implements the full faith and credit clause and requires states to recognize, enforce, and not modify child support orders from other states. Its principles track those of UIFSA.

UIFSA applies to orders to establish, modify, or enforce child or spousal support, including income withholding, and to proceedings to determine parentage. UIFSA §301. Its fundamental concept is simple: only one state at a time may exercise jurisdiction to determine the amount of support owed, and all other states must enforce—without modification—a support order issued by the state exercising jurisdiction consistent with the Act. UIFSA §§205, 603. Under UIFSA, a support order issued in one state may be enforced in other states through state agency administrative processes, which obligees can invoke personally without having to go through their home state agencies. Interstate judicial enforcement is also governed by the Act and is initiated by registering a support order from one state in the state where enforcement is sought. UIFSA §§601-608. Procedures for contesting the validity or enforceability of a registered order are provided in UIFSA §§605-607. A registered order continues to be the order of the issuing state but can be enforced in the same way that an order from a court in the registering state would be enforced. A party seeking to modify an order from one state in the court of another must register it and petition to modify it, but the court in the second state may assert jurisdiction to modify only if the conditions of UIFSA §611 or §613 are satisfied. UIFSA §§609, 610. If these conditions are not satisfied, the court does not have jurisdiction to modify and may only enforce the order. The next case discusses a potentially complex issue—the difference between orders that modify prior support orders and new orders.

OCS/Pappas v. O'Brien
67 A.3d 916 (Vt. 2013)

DOOLEY, J. . . . Mother and father were married in Oklahoma in 1979. They had two sons, P.P. and A.P. The couple moved to New York in 1983, where they lived until they separated in 1985. The parties were divorced in Los Angeles County, California, in October 1986. Pursuant to the California divorce order, the parties were awarded joint legal custody of the children, then ages three and five. Primary physical custody was awarded to mother, and father was ordered to pay child support in the amount of $237 per month for each child. Eventually, father returned to Oklahoma, and mother moved with the children to Atlanta, Georgia. In October 1994, the Superior Court of Gwinnett County, Georgia, issued an order domesticating the California divorce order and modifying the child support obligation. Finding that father's financial condition had improved and that the needs of the children had increased, the court ordered father to pay $350 per month for each child, as well as a percentage of any bonuses father should receive in addition to his salary. This order stated that child support would cease if "custody is changed by a Court of competent jurisdiction." In 1996, mother moved with the children to New York.

Beginning in July 1998, the younger child, P.P., moved from his mother's home in New York to his father's home in Oklahoma. In November 1998, the older child, A.P. turned eighteen years of age. In April 1999, father filed documents to initiate a child custody proceeding in Oklahoma under the Uniform Child Custody Jurisdiction and Enforcement Act (UCCJEA). Father initially petitioned to have custody of P.P. transferred to him and to have his child support obligation for both children ended — for A.P. because he had attained the age of majority and for P.P. because he was residing with father. Mother moved to bifurcate the issues of custody and child support. A hearing was held in October 1999, at which mother attempted to make a limited appearance for the purposes of the child custody determination. During the hearing, father requested an order obligating mother to pay him child support for P.P. in addition to changing the child's custody. The Oklahoma court awarded custody to father and retroactively relieved him of any child support obligation as of April 22, 1999, the date he moved for a change of custody. Furthermore, the court ordered mother to pay child support to father in the amount of $338.50 per month, retroactive to April 22, including an arrearage of $2724.00. Mother made two motions for new trials in the Oklahoma court raising jurisdictional concerns. The court denied the first, and mother withdrew the second, after P.P. returned to her custody. She did not appeal either the initial Oklahoma order or the denial of her motion for a new trial.

In early July 2000, P.P. returned to live with mother in Georgia. At that time, father sought enforcement of the child support judgment for the time when P.P. had been in his custody. On July 18, 2000, an Oklahoma Administrative Law Judge issued an administrative order awarding judgment to father in the amount of $2369.50 for child support for the period from January through July of 2000. When this amount was added to the previous judgment, the total arrearage became $5093.50. . . .

Mother is now a resident of Vermont; father continues to reside in Oklahoma. In 2008, the Oklahoma Department of Human Services sought to collect the outstanding child support from mother. These enforcement efforts were transferred to Vermont, and, on September 4, 2009, Vermont's Office of Child Support (OCS) filed a petition to register the Oklahoma support order in Vermont, pursuant to UIFSA. Mother responded on October 16, 2009, by filing a motion to set aside the Oklahoma order, contesting inter alia the subject matter jurisdiction . . . in the Oklahoma proceedings. After three days of hearings, a magistrate issued an order registering the Oklahoma support order and granting judgment against mother in the amount of $7611.30. Mother appealed the magistrate's order to the Chittenden Superior Court, Family Division, pursuant to Vermont Rule for Family Proceedings 8(g). On September 15, 2010, the superior court affirmed, concluding that collateral estoppel barred mother from challenging the Oklahoma court's subject matter jurisdiction. . . .

Mother also responded to father's enforcement action by pursuing her own enforcement. She filed three documents simultaneously on April 21, 2010, within thirty days from the date of the magistrate's decision: (1) an appeal of the magistrate's decision to the family court; (2) a request for a stay of the magistrate's decision; and (3) an application to register and enforce the Georgia child support order to collect support owed by father to mother under that order. The stay request argued that father owed back child support to mother and it would be inequitable for father to collect back child support owed to him, without paying the child support he owed to mother. The application to enforce the Georgia order was to have the Vermont court determine the amount of back support owed to mother. She claimed that the amount due under the Georgia order, with interest, amounted to $34,093.50. On May 12, before the application was accepted as a separate case, the court denied the stay saying: "If [mother] is entitled to collect past due child support from [father], she may seek appropriate enforcement."

Mother served father with the application, and, in addition, the court notified OCS of the filing. OCS intervened and moved to dismiss. On August 11, 2010, the magistrate granted OCS's motion and dismissed mother's petition, concluding that Vermont courts lacked personal jurisdiction over father under UIFSA. . . .

Mother appeals from both adverse decisions—one allowing registration of the Oklahoma order and one denying her attempt to register and enforce the Georgia order. We have consolidated these matters on appeal. In both cases, the primary question is whether Vermont has the authority under UIFSA to register and enforce an out-of-state child support order. . . .

Before we address the legal issues, we make one observation to explain, in part, the length and coverage of this opinion. Although the facts may seem commonplace at first, they are not when understood in the context of the applicable law. The combination of three factual elements complicates the analysis of the legal issues: (1) at the time that father sought child support, neither he nor mother nor either of the children resided in the state in which the original child support order was created—California—or in the state in which it was domesticated and modified—Georgia; (2) one of the children moved from the custody of one parent to the custody of the other; and (3) each party alleges that the other party owes back child support. . . .

The three elements of factual complexity are combined with an element of particular legal complexity. There are two legal regimes governing interstate enforcement and modification of child support orders and each, read in isolation from the other, would not likely produce the same result on some of the legal issues in this case. The two are UIFSA, 15B V.S.A. §§101-904, and the Full Faith and Credit for Child Support Orders Act (FFCCSOA), 28 U.S.C. §1738B. . . .

We begin by considering the validity of the Oklahoma child support order, which mother contests on several grounds under UIFSA. In considering mother's arguments, we focus primarily on UIFSA, only occasionally touching upon the application of FFCCSOA,[2]

---

2. There is a significant question concerning whether FFCCSOA preempts UIFSA, which we note here, but do not decide. FFCCSOA has many of the same purposes as UIFSA, particularly "to establish national standards under which the courts of the various States shall determine their jurisdiction to issue a child support order and the effect to be given by each State to child support orders issued by the courts of other States," and "to avoid jurisdictional competition and conflict among State courts in the establishment of child support orders." FFCCSOA and UIFSA "are for the most part 'complementary or duplicative and not contradictory.' " . . . [H]owever, that where it applies, FFCCSOA "preempts any inconsistent provision of state law."

In this case, the UIFSA prohibition on modifying the Georgia child support order on motion of a resident of Oklahoma, see 43 Okla. Stat. Ann. §601-611A (describing requirements for modifying child support order from another state including either nonresidence of the petitioner or residence of the child and consent of all parties); see also U.L.A. Unif. Interstate Family Support Act, Refs & Annos, Prefatory Note II.D.2 (1996) ("Except for modification by agreement or when the parties have all moved to the same new state, the party petitioning for modification must submit himself or herself to the forum state where the respondent resides."), is arguably in tension with FFCCSOA, 28 U.S.C. §1738B. The UIFSA section provides that the forum court "may modify" the foreign order only if the petitioner is a nonresident of the forum state or obtains written consent. FFCCSOA has a provision that covers the same subject, listing three requirements for when "a State may modify" a child support order from another state, none of which require nonresidency of the petitioner. In short, FFCCSOA does not require the same preconditions for modification as UIFSA—in particular, it does not include the nonresidency requirement that mother argues father failed to meet in the Oklahoma court.

A number of courts have addressed this tension and have split on its consequence. Some courts have refused to find preemption on the grounds that Congress almost certainly did not intend that FFCCSOA preempt UIFSA. See Hamilton v. Hamilton, 914 N.E.2d 747, 751 (Ind. 2009); Basileh v. Alghusain, 912 N.E.2d 814, 818-20 (Ind. 2009); LeTellier v. LeTellier, 40 S.W.3d 490, 497 (Tenn. 2001). Other courts have found preemption, concluding that the nonresidency requirement is inconsistent with the purposes of FFCCSOA and the FFCCSOA cannot be read to accommodate it. See Draper v. Burke, 450 Mass. 676, 881 N.E.2d 122 (2008); Bowman v. Bowman, 82 A.D.3d 144, 917 N.Y.S.2d 379 (2011). This issue was not raised or briefed by either party and we do not decide it here.

because this is how the parties framed the issues. Mother's first and major argument is that the Oklahoma court lacked subject matter jurisdiction to issue the order. . . .

Father, through OCS, responds that the Georgia order "terminated automatically" when custody was changed due to language in the order stating that "monthly payments shall be made on the first (1st) day of each consecutive month thereafter until . . . custody is changed by a Court of competent jurisdiction." It is the position of father and OCS, therefore, that there was no longer anything to modify—that the Georgia order had expired. . . .

Nevertheless, we reject mother's attempt to contest the validity of the Oklahoma order on the basis that the Oklahoma court lacked subject matter jurisdiction. Her argument fails for two reasons. First, we conclude that mother is precluded from challenging subject matter jurisdiction because she thoroughly litigated that issue in the Oklahoma proceeding. Second, mother's argument fails on the merits insofar as we conclude that the Oklahoma court's child support order was not a modification for the purposes of UIFSA.

The superior court concluded that mother is collaterally estopped from raising subject matter jurisdiction. We affirm the court's conclusion. Because the issue of subject matter jurisdiction was decided by the Oklahoma court after having been litigated there, we must give that determination full faith and credit. . . .

Even if we were to conclude that mother could renew her jurisdictional challenge in this Court, we are not convinced that the UIFSA jurisdictional requirements were violated in this case. The UIFSA requirement that the petitioner not reside in the forum state applies only to modifications of prior [support] orders. Thus, mother's contention that the Oklahoma court lacked subject matter jurisdiction to issue its support order is premised on the notion that father was seeking a modification of the prior Georgia support order. We conclude that the Oklahoma order was not a modification of the preexisting Georgia order for the purposes of UIFSA.

As noted, the Georgia order explicitly stated that child support would cease if "custody is changed by a Court of competent jurisdiction." Here, there is no dispute that custody was changed by a court of competent jurisdiction. As a result, father's ongoing support obligation expired. This does not mean that the Georgia support order no longer exists or cannot form the basis for an arrearage or other claim. But though the Georgia order still governs the parties' support obligations from before the change of custody, it has expired in the sense that it has no prospective effect with respect to support obligations. Once the Oklahoma court, a court of competent jurisdiction, entered an order transferring custody of the only remaining minor child from mother to father, father's support obligation expired under the terms of the Georgia support order. Having modified custody, and with the Georgia support obligation no longer in effect by its own terms, the Oklahoma court had jurisdiction to address father's new and independent request for child support.

In short, by its own terms, the Georgia order expired when father obtained custody of P.P., thereby ending both parents' prospective child support obligations under the order. Absent the automatic termination provision of the Georgia order, father's obligation to pay mother child support would have continued—even after he was awarded custody of the child—until the Georgia order was modified by court decision. Thus, without a provision automatically terminating child support upon change of custody, an award of child support to the new custodian would have been a modified order necessarily terminating the former custodian's right to child support under the preexisting order and would therefore have been subject to the jurisdictional requirements for modification under UIFSA. This case is different, however, because, for the reasons stated above, the Georgia support order expired when the Oklahoma court transferred custody to father.

. . . [T]he Oklahoma order in this case was entirely consistent with the expired Georgia order, which, by its own terms, ended father's ongoing child support obligations upon a change of custody, which occurred before the Oklahoma court issued its support order. . . .

[T]he Oklahoma court's order was a new and independent order rather than a modification of the expired Georgia order.

We do not consider this result to be at odds with UIFSA's one-order philosophy. The primary aim of UIFSA is to ensure that states do not second-guess the support orders of other states, thereby opening the door to forum shopping and the proliferation of conflicting orders. That is not what occurred in this case.

Allowing father to proceed in Oklahoma also makes practical sense. Having obtained custody of P.P., father was in no different position than a custodial parent who was seeking a support order for the first time against the other parent residing in another state. In general, if there is no child support order in place, then the custodial parent can initiate a proceeding in his or her state of residence—assuming the custodian has personal jurisdiction over the noncustodial parent under UIFSA's liberal personal jurisdiction rules—and then seek an enforcement order in the state of the noncustodial parent. In the present case, when father obtained custody of P.P., there was no order in effect providing child support for the ongoing costs of P.P.'s living expenses. If we define the Oklahoma court's action as a modification of the Georgia order in this case, father is denied the normal UIFSA avenue to obtain child support through the courts of his home state. Father would have fewer options for obtaining child support essentially because he was previously a noncustodial parent.

This additional hurdle may have practical significance for parents like father. Given the age of the child and the temporary nature of father's custody, the cost of pursuing establishment and enforcement of a support order in Vermont, or Georgia if jurisdiction there is still available, is likely prohibitive in relation to the amount of support to be obtained. Thus, the consequence of accepting mother's argument is very likely no support order at all for a period in which the child is undeniably entitled to support from the noncustodial parent. While we have become consumed by jurisdictional challenges, mother has no apparent defense to a claim that she should pay some amount of child support during the period father was the custodial parent.[3] We cannot view there being no support order for that period as consistent with the intent of UIFSA. . . .

We turn now to mother's appeal from the superior court's denial of her separate attempt to register and enforce the Georgia child support order. Mother contends that, if father is able to register and enforce the Oklahoma order against her in Vermont, then she should be able to register and enforce the Georgia order against him in Vermont. OCS responded on father's behalf, arguing that Vermont lacks personal jurisdiction over father for the purposes of collecting child support. The magistrate accepted this assessment, and the superior court affirmed the magistrate.

As we understand mother's petition, there are three components to her child support claim. First, mother alleges that father failed to pay child support under the Georgia order for the period when P.P. was living with father but before father moved to modify custody. Second, mother alleges that father failed to pay support under the order from the date when P.P. moved back to live with mother until he reached the age of majority. Third, mother alleges that father failed to pay the child support amount with respect to the oldest son, A.P., in part of 1996 and for one month in 1998.

Mother's central argument is that, by choosing to register the Oklahoma order in Vermont, father thereby subjected himself to the personal jurisdiction of Vermont. She contends that

---

3. Indeed, to the extent we can determine why this conflict has escalated over a relatively small amount of money, it is because mother believes she is owed child support in an amount at least as great as the amount claimed by father. As we hold *infra*, the reasonable response is to allow mother to litigate all her claims against father at the same time his are litigated against her in the hope that the whole dispute can finally be resolved.

the Oklahoma order incorporates the Georgia order, that father therefore necessarily registered the Georgia order alongside the Oklahoma order, and that he has therefore waived any objection to personal jurisdiction. Father's argument is that, under UIFSA, mother is required to bring an enforcement action not in her home state but in his home state. The superior court concluded that father was entitled to a limited immunity under UIFSA affording him the ability to petition to enforce child support without submitting to personal jurisdiction "in another proceeding." . . .

We conclude the trial court erred in ruling that mother's application could not go further because of lack of personal jurisdiction over father. Two provisions of Vermont's UIFSA potentially establish personal jurisdiction. Section 201 grants personal jurisdiction over a nonresident where "the individual submits to the jurisdiction of this state by consent or by filing with the tribunal a responsive document having the effect of waiving any contest to personal jurisdiction," and also where "there is any other basis consistent with the constitutions of this state and the United States for the exercise of personal jurisdiction." It is well established that initiating a legal proceeding in a state is sufficient to waive any challenge to personal jurisdiction for the purposes of a countersuit. . . .

The waiver of personal jurisdiction here is somewhat complicated by the fact that Vermont OCS has been litigating this case on father's behalf. It was OCS, not father, who filed the request to register the Oklahoma order. UIFSA explicitly fails to resolve whether the relationship between a state enforcement agency and a petitioner constitutes legal representation.

We need not decide this question. Irrespective of whether the relationship between OCS and a nonresident obligee is one of attorney and client, we hold that father's initiation of the present enforcement action is sufficient to constitute a waiver of personal jurisdiction. Technically, father is the plaintiff in the present action. Furthermore, UIFSA authorizes OCS involvement only "upon request." In this sense, the rationale for finding waiver in the traditional context—namely, that a petitioner has deliberately availed himself of the forum state's courts—applies just as well when litigation is carried out by an enforcement agency that is acting at the request of the petitioner. Finally, UIFSA's limited immunity provision grants immunity for "[p]articipation by a petitioner in a proceeding before a responding tribunal, whether in person, by private attorney, or *through services provided by the support enforcement agency*," presupposing that participation through OCS would waive personal jurisdiction normally.

Implicitly accepting that there would otherwise be personal jurisdiction over father, the superior court held that the UIFSA immunity provision prevented finding personal jurisdiction in this case. UIFSA's immunity provision entitles father to appear specially for the purpose of enforcing child support without submitting to personal jurisdiction "in another proceeding." Father's initiation of this UIFSA proceeding would not, for example, create personal jurisdiction in an unrelated dispute about marital property—the marital property dispute is "another proceeding." Nor would it create jurisdiction over a dispute over child custody or jurisdiction. . . . The superior court ruled that mother's attempt to raise father's alleged child support arrearage was similarly barred.

We conclude that this determination was incorrect. We hold that the UIFSA immunity provision does not operate to prevent personal jurisdiction over a claim of outstanding child support between the same parties. That is, we read UIFSA's grant of immunity "in another proceeding" as not including immunity regarding claims of child support that are sufficiently connected with the proceeding initiated by the petitioner. This includes, as here, not only claims involving the same parents and the same child, but also claims involving the same parents and a different child. This reading is based on the understanding that a dispute concerning outstanding support obligations is not a collateral issue, which the official comment describes as "[t]he primary object of this prohibition."

For two reasons, we conclude that mother's claim in this case is not collateral and therefore that adjudicating it would not involve the kind of proceeding cognized by the immunity provision. First, the child support obligation ultimately exists for the benefit of the child, not the obligee. Even in a case like this where the children have long ago reached the age of majority and only an arrearage is involved, it is important to create the expectation for parents who share an unfair burden of the costs of supporting children that they will be able eventually to obtain reimbursement for the other parent's share of those costs. That expectation inures to the benefit of the children.

In this light, father's obligations under the Georgia order and mother's obligations under the Oklahoma order both relate to the parents' joint duty to ensure that the needs of their children are met. That is, both orders established ways to discharge partially the overarching shared duty to the children. Mother has not paid her share of what was allocated under the Oklahoma order. Mother is entitled to have this failure balanced against previous or later stretches during which father allegedly failed to pay his share and she was forced to pick up the financial slack. This is because, in the broader picture, any dispute over arrearages is a dispute over equitably allocating the burdens of a shared obligation to the child. . . .

Second, at least in a case where the only amounts in issue are arrearages, it is in everyone's interest to resolve all related claims in one proceeding in one location. The underlying purpose of UIFSA is "to cure the problem of conflicting support orders entered by multiple courts." It is wholly inconsistent with this purpose for father to pursue his arrearage in one jurisdiction while mother pursues her arrearage in another jurisdiction. In a controversy where it is likely that the transactional costs have already greatly exceeded the amount in controversy, the need for an efficient, final, and complete resolution is compelling. Thus, the policy considerations behind the limited immunity provision of §314 are entirely different when we are dealing with disputes over child support arrearages involving the same parents. Introducing other issues into a child support proceeding interferes with the compelling purpose that the children have the protection of a child support order and it is enforced. There is no interference when all issues involve child support. . . .

NOTES AND QUESTIONS

1. UIFSA and the FFCCSOA *forbid* a state court from modifying a support order from another state if the issuing state has continuing, exclusive jurisdiction. *Pappas* holds that the Oklahoma child support order was not a modification but a new order. What distinguishes the two?

2. The mother in *Pappas* argued that this case was similar to the New York case, Spencer v. Spencer, 882 N.E.2d 886 (N.Y. 2008). In *Spencer*, the court held that if a child support obligation terminates because the child attains the age of majority under the law of the state that issued the initial order, New York courts cannot issue new orders requiring payment of child support until the child reaches the age of 21, which is the New York age of majority. *Spencer* said that such orders are modifications, not new orders. The *Pappas* court wrote: "This case is plainly distinguishable. In the cases governed by *Spencer*, the New York orders were inconsistent with, and therefore a modification of, the original issuing courts' support orders. In contrast, the Oklahoma order in this case was entirely consistent with the expired Georgia order, which, by its own terms, ended father's ongoing child support obligations upon a change of custody, which occurred before the Oklahoma court issued its support order. This is not a situation in which one court extended the duration of the original child support obligation. In this case, the support obligation no longer had any prospective effect based on the original order's own terms following a change of custody." Do you agree with how the *Pappas* court distinguished *Spencer*?

UIFSA §303 provides that the tribunal ordinarily will use forum law rather than the law of another jurisdiction. Important exceptions are set out in §604, which provides that if a support order from one state is registered in another, the law of the issuing state governs the nature, extent, amount, and duration of current payments, and other obligations of support and the payment of arrearages for so long as the issuing state remains the residence of the obligor, the obligee, or the child for whose benefit the support is ordered. However, the applicable statute of limitations is that of the statute providing the longer time period.

3. A court that issues an initial order but then loses jurisdiction to modify continues to be able to assert enforcement jurisdiction. Sometimes parties dispute whether an action by a court that did not issue the initial order is a modification or an enforcement. For example, in Philipp v. Stahl, 798 A.2d 83 (N.J. 2002), after Georgia issued the initial child support order, New Jersey courts issued orders changing who had responsibility to pay for the children's medical expenses and the travel costs when the children visited their father, who remained in Georgia, as well as changing the father's monthly obligation. Reversing the intermediate appellate court, the New Jersey Supreme Court held that these changes were not modifications but were requirements for implementing and enforcing custody changes. *See also* Morgan v. Pfau, 2014 WL 6861277, at *4 (N.J. Super. App. Div. 2014) (under *Philipp*, "even if the parties had consented to transfer jurisdiction over support, such consent would have been ineffective").

4. Ordinarily, a court with personal jurisdiction over an obligor must enforce a valid support order from another state, but in Sidell v. Sidell, 18 A.3d 499 (R.I. 2011), the court held that this jurisdiction is permissive and that a trial court could decline to enforce a support order that was part of a larger case involving possible modification of custody and visitation orders and that had to be tried in another state. *Cf.* Hogan v. McAndrew, 131 A.3d 717, 726 (R.I. 2016) (distinguishing a case in which the court had clear subject matter jurisdiction).

5. If the state that issued a child support order no longer has continuing, exclusive jurisdiction to modify, another state may acquire jurisdiction to modify the order under the provisions of UIFSA §611 or §613.

SECTION 611. MODIFICATION OF CHILD-SUPPORT ORDER OF ANOTHER STATE

(a) If Section 613 does not apply, upon [petition] a tribunal of this state may modify a child-support order issued in another state which is registered in this state if, after notice and hearing, the tribunal finds that:

(1) the following requirements are met:

(A) neither the child, nor the obligee who is an individual, nor the obligor resides in the issuing State;

(B) a [petitioner] who is a nonresident of this State seeks modification; and

(C) the [respondent] is subject to the personal jurisdiction of the tribunal of this State; or

(2) this State is the residence of the child, or a party who is an individual is subject to the personal jurisdiction of the tribunal of this State, and all of the parties who are individuals have filed consents in a record in the issuing tribunal for a tribunal of this State to modify the support order and assume continuing, exclusive jurisdiction. . . .

SECTION 613. JURISDICTION TO MODIFY CHILD-SUPPORT ORDER OF ANOTHER STATE WHEN INDIVIDUAL PARTIES RESIDE IN THIS STATE

(a) If all of the parties who are individuals reside in this State and the child does not reside in the issuing State, a tribunal of this State has jurisdiction to enforce and to modify the issuing state's child-support order in a proceeding to register that order. . . .

Could Oklahoma properly have asserted jurisdiction over a motion to modify under either of these provisions?

As footnote 3 in *Pappas* discusses, the FFCCSOA provision on this issue is slightly different. 28 U.S.C. §1738B(i) provides: "If there is no individual contestant or child residing in the issuing State, the party or support enforcement agency seeking to modify, or to modify and enforce, a child support order issued in another State shall register that order in a State *with jurisdiction over the nonmovant* for the purpose of modification" (emphasis added). Some courts hold that the FFCCSOA language refers to personal and subject matter jurisdiction, making it consistent with UIFSA. Others say that it refers only to personal jurisdiction, and that, therefore, the FFCCSOA may sometimes authorize the state to assert jurisdiction even though the petitioner resided in the state. The FFCCSOA provision thus would prevail under the supremacy clause. In addition to the cases cited in the footnote above, *see* Pulkkinen v. Pulkkinen, 127 So. 3d 738 (Fla. App. 2013).

6. UIFSA provides that the state that issued a spousal support order has "continuing, exclusive jurisdiction over a spousal-support order *throughout the existence of the support obligation.*" UIFSA §211. That section further provides, "A tribunal of this State may not modify a spousal-support order issued by a tribunal of another State or a foreign country having continuing, exclusive jurisdiction over that order under the law of that State or foreign country." The commentary explains this difference in treatment on the basis that laws regarding spousal support orders vary from state to state much more than laws regarding child support. Recent cases enforcing this provision, even though neither party still lived in the issuing state, include Midyett v. Midyett, 2013 Ark. App. 291 (2013); O'Neil v. O'Neil, 724 S.E.2d 247 (Va. App. 2012); In re Marriage of Purganan, 2017 WL 836601, at *1 (Cal. App. 2017).

7. UIFSA §204 governs simultaneous proceedings in two states and provides that if either state is the home state, *i.e.*, the state in which the child has resided for at least six months, the action in its court should proceed and the action in the other court should be stayed. If neither state is the home state, the first action filed should proceed, and the other court should stay its proceeding. The purpose of this rule is to ensure that conflicting orders will not be issued, and the rule requires courts to seek information to determine whether support actions have been filed in other states and to cooperate with each other in determining which action has priority. Section 311 imposes pleading and related requirements so that courts will have the necessary information.

8. UIFSA §305(d) provides that visitation interference cannot be raised as a defense to child support enforcement.

9. Each state and the federal government have parent locator services to facilitate interstate support enforcement. 42 U.S.C. §§653, 654(8) (2022). The federal Parent Locator Service also maintains a national directory of new hires and a registry of child support orders, which will contain an abstract of every child support order that is part of the IV-D system (collecting support payments for parents receiving government assistance and discussed in Chapter 7). The goal of these provisions is to enable the federal Parent Locator Service to match orders in the registry with information in the new hires directory to track down parents quickly.

PROBLEMS

1. Morgan and Jamie were domiciled in and divorced in State *A*. Their divorce decree provides that Morgan must pay Jamie $250 per month in child support and $150 per month in spousal support. Morgan moved to State *B* and stopped paying. Jamie registered the State *A* decree in State *B* and asked the State *B* court to order Morgan to pay the past-due amounts and to enforce the decree without modifying as to future payments. Morgan asked the State *B* court to modify downward both the past-due amounts and the future award. States *A* and *B* have enacted UIFSA. May the State *B* court take jurisdiction to modify the State *A* order?

2. In addition to the facts in problem 1, assume that Jamie and the children moved from State *A* to State *C* and that Morgan again quit paying support. Jamie registered the State *A* decree in State *C* and asked the court to enforce the overdue amounts and to modify the decree to increase the amount of child and spousal support Morgan owes in the future. State *C* has also enacted UIFSA. May the State *C* court take jurisdiction to modify the State *A* order?

3. Chris and Lane were divorced in State *A*; the divorce decree provided that Chris would pay Lane child support of $750 per month. Lane and the children moved to State *B*, and Chris moved to State *C*. Lane registered the support order in State *C* and asked the court to modify the amount of child support upward, alleging changed circumstances under the law of State *C*. Chris responded that the court should use the law of the issuing state, State *A*, to determine the amount of child support. Should the court use the law of State *A* or State *C*? Why?

NOTE: INTERNATIONAL SUPPORT ENFORCEMENT

Negotiations to establish the Hague Convention on the Recovery of Child Support and Other Forms of Family Maintenance were completed in 2007. The full text and an official explanatory document are available at http://www.hcch.net/en/instruments/conventions/specialised-sections/child-support. As was true of earlier treaties on the subject, the Convention does not propose uniform rules regarding assertion of jurisdiction. Some countries permit jurisdiction to be asserted in the state in which the creditor is located, and others, including the United States, require that a state have minimum contacts with the obligor to assert jurisdiction.

The United States signed the Convention in 2007, and the Convention took effect in 2017. The U.S. Office of Child Support Enforcement explained the process of implementing the Convention in this way: "The United States actively participated in the development of the Convention from the beginning of negotiations in 2003. The United States was the first country to sign on to the approved Convention in 2007 under the previous Administration. The Senate gave its advice and consent to the Convention in 2010, and—with bipartisan support—the Congress passed needed federal legislation in 2014. The National Conference of Commissioners on Uniform State Laws immediately drafted amendments to the Uniform Interstate Family Support Act (UIFSA) to implement the Convention at the state level. By the spring of [2016], all states had enacted UIFSA, the last step before the President could sign the Instrument of Ratification." U.S. Ratification of Hague Child Support Convention, DCL 16-11, Aug. 30, 2016, available at https://www.acf.hhs.gov/css/resource/us-ratification-of-hague-child-support-convention.

The federal legislation implementing the Convention is the Preventing Sex Trafficking and Strengthening Families Act. As discussed above, the Act incorporates the 2008 UIFSA Amendments and requires all states to enact the 2008 UIFSA Amendments in order to receive federal funds for state child support programs. The Convention, as incorporated by the Act, limits the circumstances under which a court can review or object to a foreign order, requires recognition of U.S. orders by Convention countries, provides for free legal assistance in child support cases, limits available objections to enforcement, and allows a court to refuse recognition of a foreign order if it is manifestly incompatible with public policy. Most of these requirements were already part of U.S. law. The Act also includes a reservation against enforcing orders that do not comply with U.S. due process principles. For additional information, *see* U.S. Dep't of State Press Release, United States Deposits Its Instrument of Ratification for the Hague Convention on the International Recovery of Child Support and Other Forms of Family Maintenance (Sept. 7, 2016), at https://2009-2017.state.gov/secretary/remarks/2016/09/261631.htm.

D. CHILD CUSTODY JURISDICTION

Determining which state may decide a custody dispute is perhaps the most difficult jurisdictional issue of all. The traditional view was that only the state where the child was domiciled had jurisdiction to grant a custody order. Restatement, Conflict of Laws §117 (1934). Custody was regarded as a status, and only the state of the child's domicile had sufficient interest to regulate that status. *Id.* §§119, 144. The benefit of that approach is simplicity: only one state can have custody jurisdiction at any given time. However, the rule was sharply criticized on the ground that it was too simple, because it failed to recognize that states other than that of domicile may have substantial interests in the child's care and welfare and may be in a better position than the state of domicile to determine what action would serve the child's interests. Over time, the rigidity of the Restatement view was replaced by a more flexible approach, recognizing that several states may have significant interests in determining the child's custody. In the only Supreme Court case that addresses constitutional limits on custody jurisdiction, May v. Anderson, 345 U.S. 528 (1953), the Court held that Ohio did not have to give full faith and credit to a Wisconsin custody order that was issued ex parte by a court that did not have personal jurisdiction over the mother, who lived in Ohio. The Court said:

> . . . [W]e have before us the elemental question whether a court of a state, where a mother is neither domiciled, resident nor present, may cut off her immediate right to the care, custody, management and companionship of her minor children without having jurisdiction over her *in personam.* Rights far more precious to appellant than property rights will be cut off if she is to be bound by the Wisconsin award of custody. "It is now too well settled to be open to further dispute that the 'full faith and credit' clause and the act of Congress passed pursuant to it do not entitle a judgment *in personam* to extra-territorial effect if it be made to appear that it was rendered without jurisdiction over the person sought to be bound." Baker v. Baker, Eccles & Co., 242 U.S. 394.

345 U.S. at 533.

Justice Frankfurter concurred in the judgment, interpreting the lead opinion as not requiring Ohio to recognize the decree but also as not holding that Wisconsin's assertion of jurisdiction to decide custody violated due process.

At the time May v. Anderson was decided, custody disputes between parents living in different states were comparatively rare. By the mid-1960s, however, the number of cases had increased significantly and continued to grow through the 1970s. Parents dissatisfied with unfavorable custody decisions were tempted to take their children and run to other states to seek modification of the decrees. The flexible law of child custody jurisdiction combined with other factors to facilitate interstate child snatching. Once states other than that of a child's domicile could claim an interest in regulating custody, the only substantial obstacle to awards favoring the petitioning (and often relocating) parent was the obligation to give full faith and credit to a prior custody decree. However, as we have seen, courts of one state are required to give judgments of another state only such finality as the rendering forum grants. Child custody orders, as we know, are routinely considered modifiable on a showing of changed circumstances and thus were not traditionally considered to be entitled to full faith and credit. *Cf.* Kovacs v. Brewer, 356 U.S. 604 (1958); Halvey v. Halvey, 330 U.S. 610 (1947).

By the mid-1960s the indeterminacy of child custody jurisdiction law prompted the National Conference of Commissioners on Uniform State Laws to develop the Uniform Child Custody Jurisdiction Act (UCCJA), which was adopted, sometimes with modifications, by all 50 states and the District of Columbia. The National Conference recommended replacement of the UCCJA with the Uniform Child Custody Jurisdiction and Enforcement Act (UCCJEA) in 1997. The UCCJEA is available on the website of the Uniform Law Commission, http://www.uniformlaws.org. As of 2017, the UCCJEA had been enacted in all states except Massachusetts, which introduced a bill to enact the UCCJEA in the 2022 legislative session. Legislative Fact Sheet—Child Custody Jurisdiction and Enforcement Act, available at http://www.uniformlaws.org.

The UCCJEA, which applies to a broad range of custody proceedings, including actions regarding visitation, see UCCJEA §102(3)–(4), prescribes when a state may take jurisdiction in the first instance to decide a custody dispute, when a state must enforce custody orders from other states, and when a state may and may not take jurisdiction to modify a custody order from another state. Under the UCCJEA, only one state at a time has jurisdiction to decide custody disputes, and once a state obtains jurisdiction, it retains exclusive jurisdiction to modify until statutory conditions for losing that jurisdiction occur.

Just as the UIFSA is complemented by the federal FFCCSOA, the UCCJEA is complemented by the federal Parental Kidnapping Prevention Act (PKPA), which was enacted in 1980. The PKPA implements the full faith and credit clause and prescribes when states must recognize and enforce custody and visitation decrees from other states and when they must refuse to modify such decrees. Most courts hold that the PKPA does not itself grant jurisdiction; instead, state law does that.

The first part of this section deals with subject matter jurisdiction to make an initial custody order, and the second considers interstate enforcement and modification. The third part addresses jurisdiction in adoption cases, and the last part deals with international custody disputes.

1. Initial Jurisdiction

Ex parte Siderius
144 So. 3d 319 (Ala. 2013)

Moore, Chief Justice. . . . From September 2006 to July 2009, [Caroline M. Siderius and Kenneth V.] Fordham lived together as husband and wife in Mobile with their minor children, L.F. and M.F. Siderius worked as a prosecutor in Mobile. Fordham is a retired Coast Guard officer and is involved in several business enterprises. In June 2009, Siderius accepted an appointment with the Social Security Administration's Office of Disability Adjudication and Review ("ODAR") to serve as an administrative law judge in the Portland, Oregon, ODAR office. In July 2009, Siderius moved with L.F. and M.F. to Portland to begin her new job. Fordham thereafter joined the family in Portland.

The family lived in Portland until March 2010. . . . In February 2010, Siderius sought a hardship transfer to the Spokane, Washington, ODAR office. The hardship transfer was approved, and in March 2010 the whole family relocated to Washington. . . .

In May 2011, the parties retained a court-approved mediator to assist with the dissolution of their marriage and custody of the minor children. . . . Fordham does not dispute that the parties agreed that M.F. would be in Alabama from June 17 to July 7 or 8, 2011, and would then return to Washington. Likewise, Fordham does not dispute that the parties agreed that L.F. would be in Alabama from July 21 to August 6, and would then return to Washington. M.F. and L.F. traveled to Alabama as planned, and remained there with Fordham.

. . . Siderius purchased a plane ticket for M.F. to return to Spokane on August 11, 2011. However, on September 6 and 7, Fordham transferred the school registration of both children, who had remained in Alabama, from Spokane to schools in Mobile.

On August 11, 2011, Fordham filed a child-custody petition and complaint for divorce in the Mobile Circuit Court. Fordham also filed an emergency motion seeking immediate custody of the children. The next day, the Mobile Circuit Court signed an order granting Fordham's emergency motion and awarding him custody of the children pendente lite. On August 15, 2011, Siderius filed a petition in Spokane seeking dissolution of the marriage and custody of the minor children. The same day, the Spokane trial court issued an ex parte restraining order ordering Fordham to return the minor children to Washington. The Spokane trial court also scheduled initial divorce, custody, contempt hearings, and a telephone conference with the Mobile Circuit Court pursuant to the Uniform Child Custody Jurisdiction and Enforcement Act, §30-3B-101, et seq., Ala. Code 1975 ("the UCCJEA"). Also on August 15, 2011, Siderius filed a limited appearance in Fordham's Mobile proceeding to challenge personal and subject-matter jurisdiction.

On August 30, 2011, the Spokane and Mobile courts held a telephone conference as required by the UCCJEA. The Mobile court also held an evidentiary hearing on that day on the question of which state had jurisdiction and held a follow-up hearing on October 4, 2011. . . .

On October 7, 2011, the Mobile court issued an order finding that it had jurisdiction over Siderius on the basis of her minimum contacts with Alabama. The court did not rule on the applicability of the UCCJEA to the proceeding. . . .

On February 10, 2012, the Spokane court issued an order awarding custody of the children to Siderius and finding, among other things, that Washington had jurisdiction under the UCCJEA because the minor children had lived with their parents in Washington for 17 months before the commencement of the child-custody proceeding in Alabama. . . . On February 24, 2012, Siderius registered the Spokane court's custody determination and a motion for enforcement with the Mobile court. In March 2012, the Mobile court held a hearing on Siderius's motion. On July 12, 2012, the Mobile court issued a brief order denying Siderius's motion to enforce the Spokane court's custody determination.

Siderius again petitioned the Court of Civil of Appeals for a writ of mandamus, seeking review of the Mobile court's July 2012 order. The Court of Civil Appeals denied Siderius's petition on January 11, 2013. . . .

Siderius thereafter filed this petition with this Court, together with the transcript of the Alabama trial court's September and October 2011 hearings and relevant supporting evidence. . . .

For this Court to issue a writ of mandamus, Siderius must demonstrate that she has a clear legal right to an order dismissing Fordham's custody proceeding in Alabama. The controlling issue is which state—Alabama or Washington—has jurisdiction to make an initial child-custody and visitation determination under §30-3B-201, Ala. Code 1975.

A. Home-State Jurisdiction Under the UCCJEA

Alabama and Washington have both adopted the UCCJEA.

The relevant parts of Washington's and Alabama's respective versions of the UCCJEA are substantially the same. Section 30-3B-201 governs jurisdiction of Alabama courts to make an initial child-custody determination:

> (a) Except as otherwise provided in Section 30-3B-204, a court of this state has jurisdiction to make an initial child custody determination only if:
>> (1) This state is the home state of the child on the date of the commencement of the proceeding, or was the home state of the child within six months before the

commencement of the proceeding and the child is absent from this state but a parent or person acting as a parent continues to live in this state;

. . .

(b) Subsection (a) is the exclusive jurisdictional basis for making a child custody determination by a court of this state.

(c) Physical presence of a child is not necessary or sufficient to make a child custody determination.

The UCCJEA defines the term "home state" as follows:

> The state in which a child lived with a parent or a person acting as a parent for at least six consecutive months immediately before the commencement of a child custody proceeding. In the case of a child less than six months of age, the term means the state in which the child lived from birth with any of the persons mentioned. A period of temporary absence of the child or any of the mentioned persons is part of the period.

B. Two Definitions of "Home State" in the UCCJEA

Section 30-3B-201(a)(1) provides that a state has jurisdiction in a child-custody matter if the state "was the home state of the child *within six months before*" the commencement of the child-custody proceeding. Section 30-3B-102(7), Ala. Code 1975, defines "home state" as "[t]he state in which a child lived with a parent . . . for at least *six consecutive months immediately before*" the proceeding commenced (emphasis added). On their face, it appears that §30-3B-201(a)(1) and the definition of "home state" in §30-3B-102(7) are in conflict.

In this case the children had lived in Washington for 17 months, nearly a year beyond the required "six consecutive months," before Fordham filed the child-custody proceeding in Alabama. The children's stay in Washington, however, was interrupted in June 2011, as to M.F., and in July 2011, as to L.F., when the children went to Alabama temporarily for either vacation or visitation. On August 11, 2011, Fordham filed his petition for divorce and custody in Alabama. On August 15, 2011, Siderius filed her petition in Washington.

It is undisputed that the children did not live in Alabama for "six consecutive months immediately before" Fordham filed his custody proceeding in Alabama. Thus, Alabama cannot be the "home state" under §30-3B-102(7). The children also did not live in Washington in the "six consecutive months *immediately before*" the mother filed for divorce and custody. Thus, Washington cannot be the "home state" under §30-3B-102(7). However, under §30-3B-201(a)(1), Washington was the home state of the children "within six months before" Fordham's August 11 filing for divorce and custody in Mobile.

Because the description of "home state" in §30-3B-201(a)(1) is broader than the definition in §30-3B-102(7), we resolve the apparent conflict between the two sections, in keeping with the purposes of the UCCJEA, by applying the construction that finds the existence of a home state, rather than the one that finds that the children had no home state. We interpret the UCCJEA in order to "[a]void jurisdictional competition and conflict with courts of other states in matters of child custody which in the past resulted in the shifting of children from state to state with harmful effects on their well-being." Official Comment to §30-3B-101, Ala. Code 1975. There are two ways to resolve the apparent lack of "home state" jurisdiction under §30-3B-201(a)(1), which is the "exclusive jurisdictional basis for making a child custody determination."

1. Temporary Absences are Included in Calculating the Six-Month Period

First, "[a] period of temporary absence of the child or any of the mentioned persons is part of the period" of six consecutive months immediately before the custody proceeding commences. §30-3B-102(7), Ala. Code 1975. . . .

In addition, "[c]ourts have found that 'temporary absences include court-ordered visitations, and *vacations* and business trips.'" "[W]here both parents intend a child's absence from a state to be temporary, the duration of that absence must be counted toward the establishment of a home state pursuant to the UCCJEA. . . ." 175 Wash. App. at 489-90, 307 P.3d at 728. "[T]emporary absences do not interrupt the six-month pre-complaint residency period necessary to establish home state jurisdiction." Ogawa v. Ogawa, 125 Nev. 660, 662, 221 P.3d 699, 700 (2009). . . .

Based on the facts before us, the children's absence from Spokane appears to have been only temporary, i.e., for the purpose of vacation or visitation. This temporary absence from Spokane is thus part of the "six consecutive months immediately before" the custody proceeding commenced. When the children's temporary absences are factored in, therefore, the Spokane court clearly has home-state jurisdiction to make an initial child-custody and visitation determination under the UCCJEA. Conversely, Alabama does not.

2. THE SIX-MONTH "EXTENDED HOME STATE PROVISION"

Second, Washington's home-state jurisdiction continued for an extended period of up to six months *after* the children had been removed to Alabama by Fordham, because Siderius continued to reside in Washington, the home state. In determining the legislative intent of the UCCJEA, "we must examine the statute as a whole and, if possible, give effect to each section." . . .

One purpose of the UCCJEA is to "[p]romote cooperation with the courts of other States to the end that a custody decree is rendered in that State which can best decide the case in the interest of the child." Official Comment to §30-3B-101, ¶2. The UCCJEA "prioritizes home state jurisdiction" "over other jurisdictional bases," such as personal jurisdiction obtained through sufficient minimum contacts. The Official Comment to Section 30-3B-201 provides:

> "The six-month *extended home state provision* of subsection (a)(1) has been modified slightly from the UCCJA [Uniform Child Custody Jurisdiction Act]. The UCCJA provided that home state jurisdiction continued for six months when the child had been removed by a person seeking the child's custody or for other reasons and a parent or a person acting as a parent continues to reside in the home state. Under this Act, it is no longer necessary to determine why the child has been removed. The only inquiry relates to the status of the person left behind."

(Emphasis added.) The comment to the model Uniform Child Custody Jurisdiction Act, the predecessor to the UCCJEA, explained the six-month extended home-state provision:

> Subparagraph (ii) of paragraph (1) extends the home state rule *for an additional six-month period in order to permit suit in the home state after the child's departure.* The main objective is to protect a parent who has been left by his spouse taking the child along.

In order to give effect to the legislative purpose of the UCCJEA, §30-3B-201(a)(1) must be construed to extend home-state jurisdiction under §30-3B-102(7) for an additional six months. Thus, the "home state" is not limited to *only* the "six consecutive months *immediately before*" the custody proceeding commences. The applicable six-consecutive-month period may also be determined "within" an extended or additional six-month period before the commencement of the proceeding under the second prong of §30-3B-201(a)(1).

This construction of the UCCJEA avoids the absurd result here of the minor children's having no home state because they did not live in Washington, the home state, for the full six months "immediately before" the proceeding commenced. This construction prioritizes home-state jurisdiction "over other jurisdictional bases," and carries forward the clear intent of the UCCJEA that expressly incorporated the "six-month extended home state provision" from the UCCJA.

Finally, our construction of this apparent conflict in the UCCJEA comports with the construction given the UCCJEA by other state courts (citations omitted). Thus, the

Washington trial court in this case properly exercised jurisdiction under the UCCJEA because it was the "home state" of the children *within six months before* the commencement of the child-custody proceeding under the "six-month extended home state provision" of §30-3B-201(a)(1). Because Washington is the home state under the "extended home state provision" of the UCCJEA, the Alabama trial court lacks home-state jurisdiction over Fordham's custody proceeding. . . .

Siderius's petition for a writ of mandamus is granted and we direct the Mobile Circuit Court to dismiss Fordham's child-custody proceeding.

NOTES AND QUESTIONS

1. Many of the cases involving disputes over initial jurisdiction under the UCCJEA arise when a parent files for custody in the midst of or shortly after a major move, as in *Siderius*. The practical issue is whether the custody litigation will occur in the state from which the children moved or in the state of their new residence. The starting point of the analysis is determining which state, if either, has home state or extended home state jurisdiction. In *Siderius* the court concluded that Washington had jurisdiction under both criteria by applying the rule that temporary absence from a state does not disrupt the required six months. What would have happened if the home state and extended home state analyses conflicted?

Should the intent of the parents to remain in a state matter? *Compare* Ocegueda v. Perreira, 181 Cal. Rptr. 3d 845 (Cal. App. 2015) (parental intent is irrelevant to the determination of where the child has lived for home state determination) *with* Chick v. Chick, 596 S.E.2d 303 (N.C. App. 2004) (holding that a "totality of the circumstances" approach is "the most appropriate" way to determine a child's residence); Marriage of McDermott, 307 P.3d 717 (Wash. App. 2013) (parents' intent is relevant in determining if a period of absence was temporary or permanent).

In a Texas case, the never-married father and the mother of a child lived in Georgia before ending their relationship. The father married another woman and moved with her and the child (from the first relationship) from Georgia to Texas in late May. After about two weeks in Texas, the family returned to Georgia. The child remained in Georgia until late July, spending several days at the mother's house, when the father moved the child back to Texas. The child's mother at all times lived in Georgia. In November (six months after the first trip to Texas), the father filed for custody in Texas after the mother visited Texas and returned to Georgia with the child. Did Texas have home state jurisdiction? Was the time that the child spent in Georgia over the summer a temporary absence? *See* In re Walker, 428 S.W.3d 212 (Tex. App. 2014) (holding that Texas was not the child's home state and Georgia was the child's home state within six months before commencement of the initial custody proceeding in Texas). If the child's mother filed for custody in Georgia in January (six months after the July move), would Georgia still have had extended home state jurisdiction?

2. For a state to have extended home state jurisdiction, a parent or person acting as parent must still live in the state. UCCJEA §201(a)(1). If this condition is not satisfied, or if a child has simply moved around a great deal, the child may not have a home state. In that case, a state may claim jurisdiction if "the child and the child's parents, or the child and at least one parent or a person acting as a parent, have a significant connection . . . other than mere physical presence" with the state, and "substantial evidence is available concerning the child's care, protection, training, and personal relationships" in the state. UCCJEA §201(a)(2). In the rare case where no state has home state, extended home state, or significant connection jurisdiction, another state may take jurisdiction. UCCJEA §201(a)(4).

3. The UCCJEA provides that if a child is less than six months old, the state in which the child has lived from birth is the home state. UCCJEA §102(7). Courts have consistently held that the UCCJEA does not provide jurisdiction over a custody proceeding involving a fetus. Gray v. Gray, 139 So. 3d 802 (Ala. Civ. App. 2013); Arnold v. Price, 365 S.W.3d 455, 461 (Tex. App. 2012); Fleckles v. Diamond, 35 N.E.3d 176 (Ill. App. 2015); In re Sarah Ashton McK. v. Samuel Bode M., 974 N.Y.S.2d 434 (App. Div. 2013). This area of law may shift, however, as states enact laws that recognize legal personhood at conception. For instance, Georgia's Living Infants Fairness and Equality (LIFE) Act redefines natural person as "any human being including an unborn child." The law had been enjoined in 2020 as unconstitutional; with Roe v. Wade overturned—*see* Chapter 2 on Dobbs v. Jackson Women's Health Organization—the U.S. Court of Appeals for the Eleventh Circuit reinstated the Act in 2022. Sistersong v. Kemp, 472 F.Supp. 3d 1297 (11th Cir. 2022).

4. UCCJEA §204 provides that a court may take emergency jurisdiction if the child has been abandoned in the state or if action is necessary to protect the child or the child's sibling or parent from mistreatment or abuse, regardless of whether a prior custody order exists or not. The section also makes explicit that the orders of a court acting on this jurisdictional basis last only until a court with jurisdiction under other provisions of the UCCJEA takes charge. *See, e.g.,* In re T.N.G., 781 S.E.2d 92 (N.C. App. 2015). The emergency jurisdiction provision of UCCJEA has generally been interpreted narrowly, allowing a court to enter temporary custody orders only to protect the child until a court with jurisdiction under another provision of the statute can step in.

5. The commentary to UCCJA §13, which, as noted, was replaced by the UCCJEA, indicates that the Act's drafters assumed that Justice Frankfurter's concurrence in May v. Anderson, above, employs the due process test to determine when a state may assert personal jurisdiction over an absent parent or other person claiming rights to custody. Based on this assumption, the UCCJEA does not require that the state have minimum-contacts jurisdiction over all the parties, though notice "reasonably calculated to give actual notice" is required. UCCJEA §108. But a party need not be personally served. In a case in which a mother fled to Puerto Rico from Maryland, and the trial court ruled that Maryland was the home state, an e-mail and letter from the Maryland court provided sufficient notice and service. Cabrera v. Mercado, 146 A.3d 567 (Md. App. 2016). Participation in a custody suit, however, does not in and of itself give a court jurisdiction over a person with regard to other matters. UCCJEA §109.

Professor Coombs has argued that in some extreme circumstances, a state's assertion of jurisdiction to determine the custody rights of a person with no contacts with the state would violate due process. Russell M. Coombs, Interstate Child Custody: Jurisdiction, Recognition and Enforcement, 66 Minn. L. Rev. 711 (1982).

6. The jurisdictional provisions of the UCCJEA in many cases enhance the chances that the same state will have jurisdiction over both custody and child support. However, jurisdiction under UIFSA and the UCCJEA is not always consolidated. For example, under the UCCJEA, a court in a state that is the child's home state has exclusive jurisdiction to determine custody, but it may not have jurisdiction to award child support if the defendant parent does not have sufficient contacts with the state to satisfy due process, as interpreted in *Kulko. See, e.g.,* Coleman v. Coleman, 864 So. 2d 371 (Ala. Civ. App. 2003).

PROBLEM

Pat and Kris were married and then moved to Virginia for Kris's job as a college basketball coach; six months later, twin boys were born to Kris and Pat. Kris lost the coaching job five years after the twins' birth, and Pat moved to Ohio to prepare an apartment for the family on property owned by Pat's mother. The family subsequently began the process of moving their belongings from Virginia to Ohio. Though the family planned to make a permanent move to Ohio, Kris continued to live with the children in Virginia, where the children attended preschool through the end of the year. At the end of the year, Kris and the children joined Pat in Ohio. The family lived together in Ohio until April 2012, at which time Kris and the children visited Virginia. The children were re-enrolled and attended school in Virginia starting the following spring. Kris stated an intention to stay in Virginia only temporarily and visited Ohio with the children over May and June. In June, the couple's relationship fell apart, and Pat filed a complaint for divorce and a motion for temporary custody in Ohio. Kris and the children continued to live in Virginia, and Kris filed a motion to dismiss the complaint for lack of jurisdiction.

What state — Ohio or Virginia — may exercise jurisdiction over this custody matter under the UCCJEA? Why? If you are a lawyer for Pat, what arguments would you make to pursue custody in an Ohio court?

2. Interstate Enforcement and Modification Jurisdiction

The UCCJEA provides that a court must enforce a custody order from another state if the first state exercised jurisdiction "in substantial conformity with this [Act] or the determination was made under factual circumstances meeting the jurisdiction standards of this [Act]." UCCJEA §303; *see also* PKPA 28 U.S.C. §1738A(a) ("appropriate authorities of every State shall enforce according to its terms, and shall not modify any custody determination made consistently with the provisions of this section"). A custody order is made consistently with the PKPA or the UCCJEA if the court issuing the order had jurisdiction under its own state laws. 28 U.S.C. §1738A(c)(1). In addition, one of five conditions enumerated in PKPA §1738A(c)(2) must be met. They are:

(A) such State (i) is the home State of the child on the date of the commencement of the proceeding, or (ii) had been the child's home State within six months before the date of the commencement of the proceeding and the child is absent from such State because of his removal or retention by a contestant or for other reasons, and a contestant continues to live in such State;

(B) (i) it appears that no other State would have jurisdiction under subparagraph (A), and (ii) it is in the best interest of the child that a court of such State assume jurisdiction because (I) the child and his parents, or the child and at least one contestant, have a significant connection with such State other than mere physical presence in such State, and (II) there is available in such State substantial evidence concerning the child's present or future care, protection, training, and personal relationships;

(C) the child is physically present in such State and (i) the child has been abandoned, or (ii) it is necessary in an emergency to protect the child because he has been subjected to or threatened with mistreatment or abuse;

(D) (i) it appears that no other State would have jurisdiction under subparagraph (A), (B), (C), or (E), or another State has declined to exercise jurisdiction on the ground that the State whose jurisdiction is in issue is the more appropriate forum to determine the custody of the child, and (ii) it is in the best interest of the child that such court assume jurisdiction; or

(E) the court has continuing jurisdiction pursuant to subsection (d) of this section.

The UCCJEA provides that the mechanism for obtaining enforcement of a custody order from another state is by registration. A court receiving an order for registration must give notice to the parties, give them an opportunity to contest on the basis that the court lacked jurisdiction or that the order has been modified, or that the person contesting did not receive notice. If the registration is not contested or if objections are overruled, the order is to be enforced to the same extent as custody orders issued by courts in the state. UCCJEA §305.

The UCCJEA and the PKPA strictly limit the jurisdiction of a court to modify a custody order from another state. The statutory provisions are, for the most part, quite unambiguous. UCCJEA §202 provides that a court that has validly asserted jurisdiction has exclusive, continuing jurisdiction until a court in that state "determines that neither the child, the child and one parent, nor the child and a person acting as a parent have a significant connection with this State and that substantial evidence is no longer available in this State concerning the child's care, protection, training and personal relationships," or until "the child, the child's parents, and any person acting as a parent do not presently reside in this State."

Brandt v. Brandt
268 P.3d 406 (Colo. 2012) (en banc)

Justice HOBBS delivered the Opinion of the Court. . . . Petitioner Christine Brandt and Respondent George Brandt were divorced in Montgomery County, Maryland on May 25, 2006. At that time, the terms of the parties' Voluntary Separation and Property Settlement Agreement were incorporated into the divorce decree. The agreement provided that the couple would have joint custody of their child, C.B., with Christine Brandt having primary physical custody. . . .

In 2008, the Army transferred George Brandt to Fort Carson, Colorado Springs, Colorado. The parties divided time with C.B. equally during the summer of 2008, and C.B. returned to Maryland for the 2008-09 school year. George Brandt served at Fort Carson until 2010 when he retired, re-married, and settled with his new wife in Littleton, Colorado.

Christine Brandt was commissioned into the Army in 2009, serving in the Nursing Corps. Following training, she was stationed at Fort Hood, Texas, where she moved with C.B. from Maryland in March of that year. C.B.'s 2009 summer was also split between his parents. Christine Brandt was deployed to Iraq on active duty in April 2010. The parties mutually agreed that, while she was in Iraq, C.B. would live with George Brandt in Colorado. Christine Brandt returned from Iraq on October 10, 2010, and was reassigned to Fort Hood, Texas. She and George Brandt agreed to let C.B. complete the remainder of the 2010-11 school year in Colorado at which point George Brandt would return C.B. to Christine Brandt.

On April 26, 2011, Christine Brandt received military orders to return to Maryland and finish her active duty in a non-deployable position at Fort Meade. Her orders required her to report there no later than August 1, 2011, and authorized her to report there on July 15, 2011. As previously agreed between the parties, C.B. returned on May 22, 2011, to live with Christine Brandt, who was still at Fort Hood.

Meanwhile, on May 6, 2011, George Brandt filed a petition in [Colorado's] Arapahoe County district court to register the Maryland custody order pursuant to section 14-13-305, C.R.S. (2011), and to request that the court assume jurisdiction to modify the custody order pursuant to section 14-13-203, C.R.S. (2011) ("May 6 Petition"). Christine Brandt was served in Texas on May 18 with the May 6 Petition and a Notice of the Registration of the Maryland decree. On May 25, the district court entered its order registering the Maryland decree and assuming jurisdiction to modify it ("May 25 Order"). The court based its assumption of modification jurisdiction on the fact that C.B. had resided in Colorado for more than one year and neither Christine Brandt nor George Brandt nor their child "currently reside[d]" in Maryland.

On June 1, within the time allowed to contest the petition following service upon her, Christine Brandt filed a pro se motion to dismiss the petition George Brandt had filed. On June 8, Christine Brandt and C.B. returned to her home in Maryland pursuant to her military orders. On June 13, George Brandt simultaneously filed a petition to modify parenting time in the Arapahoe County District Court, together with an emergency motion for issuance of a writ of habeas corpus and writ of assistance in order to secure the return of C.B. In the latter motion, George Brandt claimed that Christine Brandt abducted C.B. to Maryland without his consent because he and Christine Brandt had previously agreed that C.B. would spend the second half of the summer (commencing on June 25) with him in Colorado. The district court issued both requested writs on June 16.

On June 20, Christine Brandt traveled back to Texas to out-process from Fort Hood, during which time she left C.B. in Maryland with his maternal grandmother. At some point during the next week, C.B. and his grandmother traveled to Pennsylvania. George Brandt, with the help of local law enforcement, exercised the Colorado writ, taking C.B. into his physical custody and returning to Colorado, where C.B. has resided with him since June 26.

In the meantime, Christine Brandt obtained counsel in Colorado and, on June 22, filed a motion for reconsideration and motion to dismiss the May 25 Order. She also filed an emergency motion for a telephone conference in Maryland, pursuant to which Judge Quirk in Montgomery County, Maryland held three teleconferences with Judge Russell in Arapahoe County during which both parties were represented by counsel.

On July 29, during the final teleconference, our district court said that: (1) Maryland had lost exclusive continuing jurisdiction due to Christine Brandt's presence in Texas, not Maryland; (2) under the UCCJEA, the preferred forum is where a child has lived for six months; and (3) Colorado was the most convenient forum to hear this case. Judge Quirk explicitly disagreed and reiterated his position from earlier teleconferences that Maryland retained exclusive continuing jurisdiction over the custody order:

> [I]t would still be my decision that continuing exclusive jurisdiction is proper here because residence, quite frankly, within the meaning of our Maryland law, of Ms. Brandt has never been anywhere but Maryland, and has continued here, and there is a connection. That connection exists, as well as the connection of the child to Maryland.

The Maryland judge lamented that both states were now asserting jurisdiction, the very result the legislatures in both states had intended to avoid in enacting the uniform statute.

Christine Brandt petitioned us for a rule to show cause, which we issued. She claims that the district court erred in finding that she no longer resided in Maryland for purposes of determining modification jurisdiction under the UCCJEA. . . .

2. EXCLUSIVE CONTINUING JURISDICTION

Once a state enters an initial child custody determination, that state has exclusive jurisdiction to modify the determination provided that initial jurisdiction was proper. Exclusive jurisdiction continues until:

> (a) A court of [the issuing] state determines that the child, the child's parents, and any person acting as a parent do not have a significant connection with [the issuing] state and that substantial evidence is no longer available in [the issuing] state concerning the child's care, protection, training, and personal relationships; or
> (b) A court of [the issuing] state or a court of another state determines that the child, the child's parents, and any person acting as a parent *do not presently reside* in [the issuing] state.

§14-13-202(1)(a)–(b) (emphasis added).

It is clear from the statute that only a court of the issuing state can decide that it has lost jurisdiction due to erosion of a "significant connection" between the child and the state. However, it is equally clear that a court in either the issuing state or any other state may divest the issuing state of jurisdiction by making a determination that the child and both parents do not "presently reside" there.

Thus, although a child's home state may change within the meaning of the UCCJEA provision regarding jurisdiction to enter an initial custody order, the issuing state nevertheless may not be divested of exclusive continuing jurisdiction by any other state unless no party presently resides in the issuing state. This provision tracks the PKPA and helps ensure that parents do not have an incentive to take their child out-of-state in order to re-litigate the issue of custody.

3. MODIFICATION

A state may modify the custody order of another state only if it would have jurisdiction to make an initial determination, and either:

(a) The court of the [issuing] state determines that it no longer has exclusive, continuing jurisdiction under [section 14-13-202] . . . or that a court of the [new] state would be a more convenient forum . . . ; *or*

(b) A court of the [issuing] state or a court of the [new] state determines that the child, the child's parents, and any person acting as a parent *do not presently reside* in the [issuing] state.

The issue of modification thus tracks the issue of exclusive continuing jurisdiction: the new state may modify only if it has jurisdiction to make an initial custody order, *and* if the issuing state decides that it has lost exclusive continuing jurisdiction pursuant to section 14-13-202 or either state determines that no party presently resides in the issuing state. The issuing state may also decline to exercise its jurisdiction on the grounds that the new state would be a more convenient forum to hear a modification proceeding. If a new state enters a modification order, that state then assumes exclusive continuing jurisdiction over determinations of child custody.

4. THE APPROPRIATE PROCEDURE FOR DETERMINING WHERE THE PARENTS AND THE CHILD "PRESENTLY RESIDE"

Although there is no Colorado case on point, cases from other jurisdictions strongly suggest that more than a perfunctory determination of residence is required to divest an issuing state of jurisdiction. In a 2006 New Mexico case, the court affirmed that the UCCJEA "specifically requires action" by the state of potential modification before exclusive continuing jurisdiction in the issuing state ceases. State of N.M. ex rel. CYFD v. Donna J., 139 N.M. 131, 129 P.3d 167, 171 (2006). The court held that "[a]n automatic loss of jurisdiction, without any factual determination, would add uncertainty, diminish oversight ability of the courts, and increase conflicts between the states." . . .

The UCCJEA requires a "clear end-point to the decree state's jurisdiction." Only a state that has made a child custody decree "consistent" with §14-13-201 (the provision for initial jurisdiction) or -203 (the provision for modification jurisdiction) is entitled to exclusive continuing jurisdiction. Therefore, it is imperative that an out-of-state court tasked with enforcing a custody order has a clear factual record, either by stipulation or from the taking of evidence, on which to assess whether jurisdiction was properly asserted by the court which entered the order.

A plaintiff typically "bears the burden of proving that the trial court has jurisdiction to hear the case." Because, under the UCCJEA, a new state may not modify an out-of-state child custody order unless it properly finds that the issuing state has been divested of jurisdiction (or declined to exercise it), the parent petitioning the new state to assume jurisdiction bears the burden of proving, not only that the new state would have jurisdiction to enter an initial child custody order, but that the issuing state has lost or declined to exercise jurisdiction as well.

Communication between the courts as authorized in sections 14-13-110 to -112 is exceedingly beneficial in this type of proceeding. Inter-court communication facilitates an understanding between sister states regarding whether the issuing state has lost jurisdiction pursuant to section 14-13-202(1)(a)–(b) or -203(1)(a)–(b), or declined to exercise jurisdiction in favor of a more convenient forum pursuant to section 14-13-207. Such communication alerts the issuing state to a potential loss of exclusive continuing jurisdiction, based on residence, before the new state assumes jurisdiction to modify the issuing state's child custody order. It also alerts the new state to any pending actions in the issuing state and helps to develop a factual record in the matter of jurisdiction.

We therefore determine that, before a court of this state may assume jurisdiction to modify an out-of-state custody order, the court must communicate with the issuing state pursuant to sections 14-13-110 to -112, conduct a hearing at which both sides are allowed to present evidence if there is a factual dispute on the residency issue, with the burden of proof being on the parent who has petitioned for the court to assume jurisdiction, following which the district court in our state makes its findings of fact, conclusions of law, and order.

5. Totality of Circumstances Test for "Presently Reside"

We interpret sections 14-13-202 and -203, the provisions of the UCCJEA upon which the court below will determine whether it has jurisdiction to modify the Maryland child custody order. . . .

. . . [W]hile the UCCJEA for some purposes does prioritize the "home state"—the state where the child lived for the six months prior to the custody determination—this preference pertains only to jurisdiction to enter an initial child custody order, not jurisdiction to modify an order that has already been entered by another state. "Home state" preference at the modification stage would defeat the purposes of exclusive continuing jurisdiction, which are to ensure that custody orders, once entered, are as stable as possible and to discourage parents from establishing new "home states" for their children so as to re-litigate the issue of custody in a friendlier forum.

Absent action by Maryland disclaiming exclusive continuing jurisdiction or declining to exercise it, the only basis for Colorado to divest Maryland of jurisdiction is to determine that "the child, the child's parents, and any person acting as a parent do not presently reside" there.

Unfortunately, comment 2 to section 14-13-202 has confused construction of the operative statutory term "presently reside" and has led to a split among states in applying the act. This comment states, in part:

> Continuing jurisdiction is lost when the child, the child's parents, and any person acting as a parent no longer reside in the original decree State. . . . It is the intention of this Act that [the phrase, "do not presently reside"] means that the named persons *no longer continue to actually live within the State.* . . . [W]hen the child, the parents, and all persons acting as parents *physically leave the state to live elsewhere,* the exclusive continuing jurisdiction ceases.
>
> The phrase "do not presently reside" is *not used in the sense of technical domicile.* The fact that the original determination State still considers one parent a domiciliary does not prevent it from losing exclusive, continuing jurisdiction after the child, the parents, and all persons acting as parents have moved from the state.

§14-13-202, cmt. 2 (emphasis added). Based on this commentary, some states take the view that a person resides only where physically present when a petition for assumption of modification jurisdiction is filed. In Staats v. McKinnon, the Tennessee court of appeals concluded that the "sole question is whether the relevant individuals 'continue to actually live within the state' or have 'physically left the state to live elsewhere.'" 206 S.W.3d 532, 549 (Tenn. Ct. App. 2006). Relying on the same language, the Tennessee court also held in a separate case that, although one of the litigants maintained a residence, nursing license, driver's license, and voting registration in Arkansas and paid Arkansas state taxes, she nonetheless did not "presently reside" in Arkansas because she was, albeit temporarily, physically residing in Tennessee on the date the action commenced. Highfill v. Moody, 2010 WL 2075698, at *12 (Tenn. Ct. App. May 25, 2010).

A Pennsylvania court has defined "residence" as "living in a particular place, requiring only physical presence." Wagner v. Wagner, 887 A.2d 282, 287 (Pa. Super. Ct. 2005). The court held that, for UCCJEA purposes, a parent presently resided in New Jersey, where she had been assigned by the Army, notwithstanding that she retained a Florida mailing address, driver's license, and voter registration.

However, cases from other jurisdictions disagree that "presently reside" means only physical presence. In 2009, a California court of appeal found that the relevant question under the UCCJEA was "not whether Husband 'resided' in Pakistan, but whether he *stopped* residing in California." In re Marriage of Nurie, 98 Cal. Rptr. 3d at 219. Additionally, the court rejected the wife's construction of the word "presently":

> Wife insists that the term "presently" must be given effect in the statute, and that it means continuing jurisdiction may be lost based on where the parties are "actually living" regardless of their volition or intent. *We perceive a different significance to the word "presently,"* namely that the determination of relocation must be made during the period of nonresidence in the decree state.

The court concluded that, because it is well established that a party may have more than one residence, the husband could have "presently resided" in Pakistan at the time the Pakistan court asserted jurisdiction while "still maintaining a 'present residence' in California." The court held that, since the husband maintained a functioning home, car, telephones, and fax in California and was employed there, he continued to "presently reside" there. Thus, California (the issuing state) retained jurisdiction.

Similarly, in Russell v. Cox, a South Carolina court was tasked with determining whether South Carolina had jurisdiction to modify a Georgia custody decree where the mother resided in Florida and the father and child resided in South Carolina. 383 S.C. 215, 678 S.E.2d 460 (App. 2009). The court concluded that Georgia had not lost jurisdiction because the father, "notwithstanding significant evidence that he currently resided in South Carolina, was still a resident of Georgia as well." Underlying the court's reasoning was evidence that the father owned real estate in Georgia, was registered to vote there, held a Georgia driver's license, was paid as a Georgia resident, and paid Georgia state taxes.

We agree that, for UCCJEA purposes, the term "presently reside" does not equal "technical domicile." The reference to "technical" domicile suggests that "presently reside" means something other than meeting the technical requirements of domicile for specific purposes, including, for example, the obligation to pay state taxes. Instead, "presently reside" necessitates a broader inquiry into the totality of the circumstances that make up domicile—that is, a person's permanent home to which he or she intends to return to and remain. *Black's Law Dictionary* at 558 (9th ed. 2009).

Residency provisions contained in other Colorado statutes provide guidance for what factors should be considered in making the totality of the circumstances determination. . . . While those statutes do not specifically address the term "presently reside" in section 14-13-202(1)(b), which itself contains no definition, we conclude that factors to be weighed in making the residency determination under section 14-13-202(1)(b) and -203(1)(b), a mixed question of fact and law, include but are not limited to the length and reasons for the parents' and the child's absence from the issuing state; their intent in departing from the state and returning to it; reserve and active military assignments affecting one or both parents; where they maintain a home, car, driver's license, job, professional licensure, and voting registration;

where they pay state taxes; the issuing state's determination of residency based on the facts and the issuing state's law; and any other circumstances demonstrated by evidence in the case.

The statutory language of sections 14-13-202(1)(b) and -203(1)(b) is clear that, before a new state can divest the issuing state of jurisdiction, the new state must "*determine[ ]* that the child, the child's parents, and any person acting as a parent *do not presently reside*" in the issuing state. (Emphasis added). This statutory requirement for determination is consistent with the UCCJEA's emphasis on the primacy of exclusive continuing jurisdiction as a means to ensure the stability of custody orders and to discourage parental kidnapping. To hold that the term "presently reside" means only physical presence would undercut the actual statutory language and purpose that centers on exclusive continuing jurisdiction remaining in the issuing state unless that jurisdiction has been clearly divested, enabling the new state to assume jurisdiction.

In addition, such a construction of the statute would allow Parent A to move out of the issuing state with the child, establish a new home state for the child, and engage in a "race to the courthouse" by simply filing a petition for the new state to assume jurisdiction as soon as Parent B leaves the issuing state to physically live elsewhere for any length of time. Under this construction, the issuing state would lose jurisdiction if Parent B were temporarily out-of-state on vacation, in a hospital, or on military assignment. . . .

In the case before us, residency is a hotly contested issue. Christine Brandt alleges that she has constantly maintained a home, driver's license, nursing license, and voting registration in Maryland and pays Maryland state taxes. Indeed, under both federal and Colorado law, she cannot gain or lose residence for purposes of taxation and voting registration by virtue of her service in the armed forces. Moreover, she received her orders to transfer back to Maryland on April 26, ten days *before* George Brandt filed the May 6 Petition. At that point, she contends, her return to Maryland was not just a matter of her intention; it was certain to occur.

The portion of the May 25 Order divesting Maryland of jurisdiction reads, in its entirety, as follows: "the Court finds that neither the child nor the child's parents currently reside in Maryland and the child has resided in Colorado for more than a year before the filing of the petition. As a result, this Court assumes jurisdiction for purposes of modifying the Maryland child-custody determination."

While George Brandt argues that he and the child have significant contacts with Colorado, it is clear that the district court did not have the benefit of the legal test we articulate in this opinion. Its order assuming jurisdiction to modify Maryland's custody decree cannot stand because that order appears to be based solely on Christine Brandt being out of Maryland on military assignment. . . .

. . . On remand, as the petitioning party, George Brandt bears the burden of proving that Maryland has lost exclusive continuing jurisdiction and that Colorado may assume it. If the facts are still in dispute, the district court should afford the parties an opportunity to present additional evidence and argument in light of our decision, and engage in additional consultation with the Maryland court regarding the factual and legal issues concerning Maryland residency and the Maryland court's jurisdiction. . . .

NOTES AND QUESTIONS

1. As we have seen, in determining whether a state has home state jurisdiction for an initial order, most courts' interpretations tend to send the case back to the state from which a child came if a parent remains there. Do the same arguments support expansive findings on the issue of whether a parent still "resides" in the issuing state for purposes of determining whether that state has lost jurisdiction to modify? Would a test that looked exclusively to where the parent maintained a physical residence be more or less favorable to a parent who wanted the court to find that the issuing state had not lost jurisdiction? How about a test based on the parent's intent? The parent's physical presence? Can a person have more than one residence?

2. Recall that, for purposes of initial jurisdiction, if no state has home state jurisdiction, the next choice is a state with a "significant connection" to the case and in which "substantial evidence is available concerning the child's care, protection, training, and personal relationships." UCCJEA §201(a)(2). Should interpretations of this language from initial jurisdiction cases be used when the issue is continuing jurisdiction, and vice versa? Even if a child or parent still resides in the issuing state, a court in that state may find that it no longer has continuing jurisdiction because the case no longer has a significant connection with the state and because substantial evidence is no longer available in the state. UCCJEA §202.

Section 203 complements this section, providing that a court may not modify a child custody determination made by a court of another state unless the court in the state determines it no longer has exclusive, continuing jurisdiction. The meaning of this provision is typically contested when the children moved away from the original state some time ago and return infrequently for visits, if at all. The fundamental question is whether the "significant connection" provision should be interpreted broadly, which favors retention of jurisdiction in the issuing state, or narrowly. Should the fact that one parent continues to reside in the state that issued the initial custody order create a "significant connection"? *See* Ex parte Collins, 184 So. 3d 1036 (Ala. Civ. App. 2015) (residence of parent is not enough to demonstrate significant connection).

3. In *Brandt*, the mother was in the military. Federal legislation and rules address the rights of military parents. *See* U.S. Department of Defense, Military on Source, Child Custody Considerations for Service Members and MilSpouses, https://www.militaryonesource.mil/relationships/separation-divorce/. In July 2012, the Uniform Law Commission gave final approval to the Uniform Deployed Parents Custody and Visitation Act (UDPCVA), which attempts to standardize custody rights for deployed servicemembers. Section 104 of the UDPCVA integrates the UCCJEA and the Act by stating that "the residence of the deploying parent is not changed by reason of the deployment for the purposes of [the UCCJEA] during the deployment." Section 104 applies to temporary, permanent, and foreign custody orders. Section 104 does not, however, alter the UCCJEA, and it does not attempt to create or alter rules for initial or subsequent custody jurisdiction. As of 2022, 16 states had enacted the UDPCVA. Uniform Law Commission, Deployed Parents Custody and Visitation Act Enactment History, http://www.uniformlaws.org.

How would application of UDPCVA affect the outcome in *Brandt*? Would it have made it easier to resolve the dispute?

4. A court that validly asserts initial jurisdiction or jurisdiction to modify has discretion to decline to exercise it on the ground that a court in another state would be a more convenient forum. Under the UCCJEA §207, in deciding whether to grant a motion to decline jurisdiction on the basis of *forum non conveniens*, the court should consider:

a) Whether domestic violence has occurred and is likely to continue in the future and which state could best protect the parties and the child;

b) The length of time that the child has resided outside this state;

c) The distance between the court in this state and the court in the state that would assume jurisdiction;

d) The relative financial circumstances of the parties;

e) Any agreement of the parties as to which state should assume jurisdiction;

f) The nature and location of the evidence required to resolve the pending litigation, including testimony of the child;

g) The ability of the court of each state to decide the issue expeditiously and the procedures necessary to present the evidence; and

h) The familiarity of the court of each state with the facts and issues in the pending litigation.

5. UCCJEA §208 says that a court with initial or modifying jurisdiction shall decline to exercise that authority on the basis that the petitioner "has engaged in unjustifiable conduct" unless the parties agree to the court's exercise of jurisdiction, the court with jurisdiction determines that the state is a more appropriate forum, or no other state has jurisdiction. The commentary to the UCCJEA section notes:

> Most of the jurisdictional problems generated by abducting parents should be solved by the prioritization of home State in Section 201; the exclusive, continuing jurisdiction provisions of Section 202; and the ban on modification in Section 203. . . . Nonetheless, there are still a number of cases where parents, or their surrogates, act in a reprehensible manner, such as removing, secreting, retaining, or restraining the child. This section ensures that abducting parents will not receive an advantage for their unjustifiable conduct. If the conduct that creates the jurisdiction is unjustified, courts must decline to exercise jurisdiction that is inappropriately invoked by one of the parties.

If a court learns that another custody proceeding regarding the child is ongoing, UCCJEA §206 provides that the court may not exercise its jurisdiction if the other court's assumption of jurisdiction is "substantially in conformity with this Act, unless the proceeding has been terminated or is stayed by the court or the other State because a court of this State is a more convenient forum under Section 207."

6. Several sections of the UCCJEA provide that a court may find that it lacks jurisdiction or that it will not exercise jurisdiction on the assumption that a court in another state will have and will take jurisdiction. The sections presuppose a high degree of cooperation among courts in the various states, and the Act includes several sections that facilitate this cooperation. First, the parties must state, under oath in the first pleading, "the child's present address or whereabouts, the places where the child has lived during the last five years, and the names and present addresses of the persons with whom the child has lived during that period." Each party must also provide information about prior custody proceedings affecting the child and whether anyone not already named has physical custody of the child or claims rights to legal custody of the child. UCCJEA §209(a). Courts may communicate with each other and ask that courts in other states take testimony and hold hearings, forward the records to the state in which litigation is occurring, order custody evaluations, and forward records. UCCJEA §§110-112. Judges from different states are encouraged to confer with each other before deciding whether to accept jurisdiction in particular cases.

7. Custody orders from foreign countries are to be treated like orders from other states if they were made "under factual circumstances in substantial conformity with the jurisdictional standards of the Act." UCCJEA §105. UCCJEA §104 is a similar provision that applies to custody determinations made by Native American tribal courts. The Indian Child Welfare Act (ICWA) provides for tribal court jurisdiction in child welfare and adoption cases and requires state recognition of tribal decrees. (ICWA does not apply to custody disputes at divorce. 25 U.S.C. §§1903, 1911(d)). In a case involving the intersection of ICWA and the UCCJEA, a state appellate court held that the juvenile court properly applied the UCCJEA and dismissed the dependency action after finding ICWA inapplicable. In re A.T., 277 Cal. Rptr. 3d 573 (Cal. Ct. App. 2021). ICWA is considered in Chapter 14 and, at the time of writing, is the subject of cases challenging its constitutionality before the Supreme Court. *See* Haaland v. Brackeen, 142 S. Ct. 1205 (2022) (challenging ICWA's placement preferences for "other Indian families" and for "Indian foster home[s]").

8. The same legislation that created the PKPA provides that the federal Parent Locator Service, established to facilitate interstate child support enforcement, may also be used to search for people who have taken children in violation of custody decrees in some circumstances. 42 U.S.C. §663 (2022). The PKPA also amended the Federal Fugitive Felony

Act, 18 U.S.C. §1073 (2022), to allow its use in cases of parent child snatching. The Act previously had been interpreted to exclude these cases. The effect is to allow FBI involvement in cases of interstate child snatching if a state statute makes parental kidnapping a felony.

NOTE: DOMESTIC VIOLENCE CASES AND THE UCCJEA

A number of interstate custody cases involve claims that custodial parents left the state in which they and the children were living to escape domestic violence. This circumstance may affect determinations under the UCCJEA, particularly the application of the home state preference and the *forum non conveniens* analysis. Note that Chapter 9 looks at the role of intimate partner abuse in custody determinations and examines the legal treatment of an abused, custodial parent's relocation to another state.

In one of the best-known examples, Stoneman v. Drollinger, 64 P.3d 997 (Mont. 2003), the mother obtained several domestic abuse restraining orders against the father in Montana, but he repeatedly violated them. The parties were divorced in Montana in 1998, and the mother then moved to Washington. The Montana trial court ordered her to return the children to Montana every other weekend for unsupervised visits with their father, despite the recommendations of a GAL that unsupervised visits not be allowed; the Montana Supreme Court reversed, holding that it was an abuse of discretion to order unsupervised visitation. The mother then asked the Montana court to decline to exercise its continuing jurisdiction over custody on the basis that Washington was a more convenient forum. The trial court denied her motion, and the Montana Supreme Court again reversed. It explained,

> The UCCJEA places domestic violence at the top of the list of factors that courts are required to evaluate when determining whether to decline jurisdiction as an inconvenient forum for child custody proceedings. Since domestic violence was not raised by the now-repealed UCCJA as a factor for court consideration, the NCCUSL, which drafted the UCCJEA, offered the following guidance to assist courts in applying this factor:
>
>> For this purpose, the court should determine whether the parties are located in different States because one party is a victim of domestic violence or child abuse. If domestic violence or child abuse has occurred, this factor authorizes the court to consider which State can best protect the victim from further violence or abuse. 9 U.L.A. 683.
>
>> The NCCUSL explicitly recognized that past abuse or a continuing threat of violence might compel a battered spouse or parent of an abused child to relocate to another state. The NCCUSL further directed courts to proceed with an evaluation of which forum can provide the greater safety whenever domestic violence or child abuse has occurred. . . .
>> Given the high propensity for recidivism in domestic violence, we hold that when a court finds intimate partner violence or abuse of a child has occurred or that a party has fled Montana to avoid further violence or abuse, the court is authorized to consider whether the party and the child might be better protected if further custody proceedings were held in another state. While this factor alone is not dispositive under §40-7-108, MCA, we urge district courts to give priority to the safety of victims of domestic violence when considering jurisdictional issues under the UCCJEA.

The court held that the trial court abused its discretion when it failed to consider which forum could better protect the mother and children, given the well-documented history of domestic violence in the case. *See* Huege v. Huege, 2013 WL 2286102 (Ariz. App. 2013) (upholding inconvenient forum finding where mother testified that she would not have a safe place to stay if required to return to Arizona to litigate custody); *compare* Foster v. Foster, 664 S.E.2d 525 (Va. App. 2008) (trial court did not abuse discretion in declining to make inconvenient forum finding despite evidence of domestic violence).

New York courts have held that when a parent takes a child from the forum to escape domestic violence, the general rule that a wrongful removal is treated as a temporary absence for purposes of the home state analysis does not apply. Felty v. Felty, 882 N.Y.S.2d 504 (App. Div. 2009).

PROBLEMS

1. Cass and Gale, an unmarried couple, had a child, Cynthia, while they were living in State *X*. When Cynthia was three months old, Cass left Gale and moved to State *Y*, where Cass's mother lived. Cass then refused to let Gale visit Cynthia. Gale sued Cass in State *X*, seeking custody or visitation. Cass moved to dismiss, alleging that State *X* lacked jurisdiction under the UCCJEA. How should the court rule and why?

2. Dana and Jan lived with their two children in State *A*. They were divorced three years ago and were awarded joint physical and legal custody. Two years ago Jan took the children and left the state without telling Dana. Jan moved to State *B* and obtained an order for full legal and physical custody of the children. To obtain the order Jan falsely denied knowing where Dana was, and Dana was served only by publication in a small newspaper in State *B*. Eight months ago Jan and the children moved to State *C*. Dana recently found Jan and the children in State *C* and brought the State *A* custody order to a State *C* court, asking the State *C* court to recognize the State *A* order and modify it to give Dana full custody. Jan has asked the State *C* court to enforce the State *B* order and argues that State *C* does not have jurisdiction to hear the motion to modify. Dana continues to live in State *A*. Under the UCCJEA, must the court in State *C* enforce either of the prior orders? May it take jurisdiction to decide the motion to modify custody?

3. Kit and Terry lived in State *A* with their son, Bob. When Bob was two years old, a court in State *A* granted Terry a divorce and custody of Bob. Kit moved to State *B* shortly after the divorce. Terry and Bob moved to State *C* four months ago. Terry sent Bob to visit Kit in State *B* for two weeks, and Kit has refused to return Bob. Terry went to State *B* and registered the custody order, asking State *B* to enforce it. Kit counterclaimed, asking the State *B* court to modify the order, giving Kit custody. Terry moved the court to dismiss the counterclaim, alleging that State *B* lacks jurisdiction to modify the order. How should the court rule and why?

4. Lynn and Zia were divorced in State *A*; the divorce decree awarded custody to Lynn, with visitation to Zia. Shortly thereafter, Lynn, the children, and Lynn's mother Dorothy, who lived with them, moved to State *B*. Four years later Dorothy, believing that Lynn was abusing the children, left home with the children over Lynn's objection and moved across town. Dorothy then filed a motion in State *B*, seeking sole custody of the children. Zia was served but did not enter an appearance. Lynn moved to dismiss, arguing that under the UCCJEA State *B* does not have jurisdiction. How should the court rule and why?

If instead Dorothy had returned to State *A* and asked the court to find that it had no jurisdiction or that it should decline to exercise its jurisdiction, what arguments should she make? How should the court rule? (Assume again that Zia is served but does not appear.)

3. Adoption Jurisdiction

The UCCJEA applies to cases of neglect, abuse, dependency, wardship, guardianship, termination of parental rights, and protection from domestic violence. UCCJEA §102(4). It does not apply to adoption cases but instead defers to the Uniform Adoption Act (UAA). UCCJEA §103. The jurisdictional provisions of the UAA are fundamentally consistent with those of the UCCJEA and the PKPA, but they are modified to fit the adoption context. UAA §3-101(a)(1) includes "prospective adoptive parents" among those people whose relationship with a child may give rise to a basis for jurisdiction. The following alternative criteria for asserting jurisdiction over an adoption matter are provided by UAA §§3-101(a)(1)–(c)(2):

(a) (1) immediately before commencement of the proceeding, the minor lived in this State with a parent, a guardian, a prospective adoptive parent, or another person acting as parent, for at least six consecutive months, excluding periods of temporary absence, or, in the case of a minor under six months of age, lived in this State from soon after birth with any of those individuals and there is available in this State substantial evidence concerning the minor's present or future care;

(2) immediately before commencement of the proceeding, the prospective adoptive parent lived in this State for at least six consecutive months, excluding periods of temporary absence, and there is available in this State substantial evidence concerning the minor's present or future care;

(3) the agency that placed the minor for adoption is located in this State and it is in the best interest of the minor that a court of this State assume jurisdiction because:

(i) the minor and the minor's parents, or the minor and the prospective adoptive parent, have a significant connection with this State; and

(ii) there is available in this State substantial evidence concerning the minor's present or future care;

(4) the minor and the prospective adoptive parent are physically present in this State and the minor has been abandoned or it is necessary in an emergency to protect the minor because the minor has been subjected to or threatened with mistreatment or abuse or is otherwise neglected; or

(5) it appears that no other State would have jurisdiction under prerequisites substantially in accordance with paragraphs (1) through (4), or another State has declined to exercise jurisdiction on the ground that this State is the more appropriate forum to hear a petition for adoption of the minor, and it is in the best interest of the minor that a court of this State assume jurisdiction.

(b) A court of this State may not exercise jurisdiction over a proceeding for adoption of a minor if at the time the petition for adoption is filed a proceeding concerning the custody or adoption of the minor is pending in a court of another State exercising jurisdiction substantially in conformity with [the UCCJA] or this [act] unless the proceeding is stayed by the court of the other State.

(c) If a court of another State has issued a decree or order concerning the custody of a minor who may be the subject of a proceeding for adoption in this State, a court of this State may not exercise jurisdiction over a proceeding for adoption of the minor unless:

(1) the court of this State finds that the court of the State which issued the decree or order:

(i) does not have continuing jurisdiction to modify the decree or order under jurisdictional prerequisites substantially in accordance with [the Uniform Child Custody Jurisdiction Act] or has declined to assume jurisdiction to modify the decree or order; or

(ii) does not have jurisdiction over a proceeding for adoption substantially in conformity with subsection (a)(1) through (4) or has declined to assume jurisdiction over a proceeding for adoption; and

(2) the court of this State has jurisdiction over the proceeding.

In several termination of parental rights cases, parents have argued minimum-contacts jurisdiction is necessary for these proceedings, with mixed results. Cases that require minimum contacts include In the Interest of Doe, 926 P.2d 1290, 1296 (Haw. 1996);

Matter of Laurie R., 760 P.2d 1295, 1297 (N.M. App. 1988). Other courts have found that the "status exception" based on May v. Anderson, above, applies to terminations. *See* J.D. v. Tuscaloosa County Dep't of Human Resources, 923 So. 2d 303 (Ala. Civ. App. 2005); S.B. v. State, 61 P.3d 6 (Alaska 2002); Matter of Interest of M.L.K., 768 P.2d 316, 319 (Kan. App. 1989); Div. Youth & Fam. Serv. v. M.Y.J.P., 823 A.2d 817 (N.J. Super. App. Div. 2003); In re Williams, 563 S.E.2d 202, 205 (N.C. App. 2002); In re Adoption of Copeland, 43 S.W.3d 483, 487 (Tenn. App. 2000); In the Interest of M.S.B., 611 S.W.2d 704, 706 (Tex. App. 1980); State ex rel. W.A., 63 P.3d 100 (Utah 2002); In re Thomas J.R., 663 N.W.2d 734 (Wis. 2003); In re R.W., 39 A.3d 682 (Vt. 2011). For a summary of these two positions, *see* Robert E. Oliphant, Essay: Jurisdiction in Family Law Matters, 30 Wm. Mitchell L. Rev. 557, 572-575 (2003).

In addition, under some circumstances interstate adoptions are subject to the requirements of the Interstate Compact on the Placement of Children. The Compact applies to interstate placements of children for foster care or "preliminary to a possible adoption" except for placements of children made by their parents, stepparents, grandparents, adult brothers, sisters, uncles, aunts, or guardians. Interstate Compact Art. III, VIII(a). The Compact requires that interstate placements be coordinated through public authorities. A revised version of the Compact, which will, among other changes, apply to some placements by parents, will go into effect as soon as 35 states have adopted it. As of September 2022, only 12 states had adopted the Compact. The American Public Human Services Association cites difficulties in securing state funding for the Interstate Commission that the Compact would establish. APHSA, The Interstate Compact for the Placement of Children, https://aphsa.org/AAICPC/ICPC.aspx.

4. International Enforcement of Custodial Rights

Child abduction is an international problem as well. The Hague Convention on the Civil Aspects of International Child Abduction is an international treaty intended to solve these problems. The Convention does not grant or withhold jurisdiction to determine custody disputes. Therefore, jurisdiction continues to be determined by state law. However, the Convention limits the application of state law because it requires that children wrongfully removed from the country of their "habitual residence" be returned to that country. If the Convention applies, the responding country is supposed to order return of the child without addressing the merits of the custody dispute and without making value judgments about the culture of and conditions in the child's country of habitual residence. The following case considers the meaning of some of the core provisions of the Convention.

Monasky v. Taglieri
140 S. Ct. 719 (2020)

Justice GINSBURG delivered the opinion of the Court.

Under the Hague Convention on the Civil Aspects of International Child Abduction (Hague Convention or Convention), Oct. 25, 1980, T. I. A. S. No. 11670, S. Treaty Doc. No. 99–11 (Treaty Doc.), a child wrongfully removed from her country of "habitual residence" ordinarily must be returned to that country. This case concerns the standard for determining a child's "habitual residence" and the standard for reviewing that determination on appeal. The petitioner, Michelle Monasky, is a U.S. citizen who brought her infant daughter, A.M.T., to the United States from Italy after her Italian husband, Domenico Taglieri, became abusive to Monasky. Taglieri successfully petitioned the District Court for A.M.T.'s return to Italy under the Convention, and the Court of Appeals affirmed the District Court's order.

Monasky assails the District Court's determination that Italy was A.M.T.'s habitual residence. First of the questions presented: Could Italy qualify as A.M.T.'s "habitual residence" in the absence of an actual agreement by her parents to raise her there? . . . In accord with decisions of the courts of other countries party to the Convention, we hold that a child's habitual residence depends on the totality of the circumstances specific to the case. An actual agreement between the parents is not necessary to establish an infant's habitual residence . . . .

I

A

The Hague Conference on Private International Law adopted the Hague Convention in 1980 "[t]o address the problem of international child abductions during domestic disputes." Lozano v. Montoya Alvarez, 572 U.S. 1, 4, 134 S.Ct. 1224, 188 L.Ed.2d 200 (2014) (internal quotation marks omitted). One hundred one countries, including the United States and Italy, are Convention signatories. Hague Conference on Private Int'l Law, Convention of 25 Oct. 1980 on the Civil Aspects of Int'l Child Abduction, Status Table, https://www.hcch.net/en/instruments/conventions/status-table/?cid=24. The International Child Abduction Remedies Act (ICARA), 102 Stat. 437, as amended, 22 U.S.C. § 9001 et seq., implements our Nation's obligations under the Convention. It is the Convention's core premise that "the interests of children . . . in matters relating to their custody" are best served when custody decisions are made in the child's country of "habitual residence." Convention Preamble, Treaty Doc., at 7; see Abbott v. Abbott, 560 U.S. 1, 20, 130 S.Ct. 1983, 176 L.Ed.2d 789 (2010).

To that end, the Convention ordinarily requires the prompt return of a child wrongfully removed or retained away from the country in which she habitually resides. Art. 12, Treaty Doc., at 9 (cross-referencing Art. 3, *id.*, at 7). The removal or retention is wrongful if done in violation of the custody laws of the child's habitual residence. Art. 3, *ibid.* The Convention recognizes certain exceptions to the return obligation. Prime among them, a child's return is not in order if the return would place her at a "grave risk" of harm or otherwise in "an intolerable situation." Art. 13(b), *id.*, at 10.

The Convention's return requirement is a "provisional" remedy that fixes the forum for custody proceedings. Silberman, Interpreting the Hague Abduction Convention: In Search of a Global Jurisprudence, 38 U. C. D. L. Rev. 1049, 1054 (2005). Upon the child's return, the custody adjudication will proceed in that forum. See *ibid.* To avoid delaying the custody proceeding, the Convention instructs contracting states to "use the most expeditious procedures available" to return the child to her habitual residence. Art. 2, Treaty Doc., at 7. See also Art. 11, id., at 9 (prescribing six weeks as normal time for return-order decisions).

B

In 2011, Monasky and Taglieri were married in the United States. Two years later, they relocated to Italy, where they both found work. Neither then had definite plans to return to the United States. During their first year in Italy, Monasky and Taglieri lived together in Milan. But the marriage soon deteriorated. Taglieri became physically abusive, Monasky asserts, and "forced himself upon [her] multiple times." 907 F.3d 404, 406 (CA6 2018) (en banc).

About a year after their move to Italy, in May 2014, Monasky became pregnant. Taglieri thereafter took up new employment in the town of Lugo, while Monasky, who did not speak Italian, remained about three hours away in Milan. The long-distance separation and a difficult pregnancy further strained their marriage. Monasky looked into returning to the United States. She applied for jobs there, asked about U.S. divorce lawyers, and obtained cost information from moving companies. At the same time, though, she and Taglieri made preparations to care for their expected child in Italy. They inquired about childcare options there, made purchases needed for their baby to live in Italy, and found a larger apartment in a Milan suburb.

Their daughter, A.M.T., was born in February 2015. Shortly thereafter, Monasky told Taglieri that she wanted to divorce him, a matter they had previously broached, and that she anticipated returning to the United States. Later, however, she agreed to join Taglieri, together with A.M.T., in Lugo. The parties dispute whether they reconciled while together in that town.

On March 31, 2015, after yet another heated argument, Monasky fled with her daughter to the Italian police and sought shelter in a safe house. In a written statement to the police, Monasky alleged that Taglieri had abused her and that she feared for her life. Two weeks later, in April 2015, Monasky and two-month-old A.M.T. left Italy for Ohio, where they moved in with Monasky's parents.

Taglieri sought recourse in the courts. With Monasky absent from the proceedings, an Italian court granted Taglieri's request to terminate Monasky's parental rights, discrediting her statement to the Italian police. In the United States, on May 15, 2015, Taglieri petitioned the U.S. District Court for the Northern District of Ohio for the return of A.M.T. to Italy under the Hague Convention, pursuant to 22 U.S.C. § 9003(b), on the ground that Italy was her habitual residence.

The District Court granted Taglieri's petition after a four-day bench trial. Sixth Circuit precedent at the time, the District Court observed, instructed courts that a child habitually resides where the child has become "acclimatiz[ed]" to her surroundings. An infant, however, is "too young" to acclimate to her surroundings. The District Court therefore proceeded on the assumption that "the shared intent of the [parents] is relevant in determining the habitual residence of an infant," though "particular facts and circumstances . . . might necessitate the consideration [of] other factors." The shared intention of A.M.T.'s parents, the District Court found, was for their daughter to live in Italy, where the parents had established a marital home "with no definitive plan to return to the United States." Even if Monasky could change A.M.T.'s habitual residence unilaterally by making plans to raise A.M.T. away from Italy, the District Court added, the evidence on that score indicated that, until the day she fled her husband, Monasky had "no definitive plans" to raise A.M.T. in the United States. In line with its findings, the District Court ordered A.M.T.'s prompt return to Italy.

The Sixth Circuit and this Court denied Monasky's requests for a stay of the return order pending appeal. In December 2016, A.M.T., nearly two years old, was returned to Italy and placed in her father's care.

In the United States, Monasky's appeal of the District Court's return order proceeded. A divided three-judge panel of the Sixth Circuit affirmed the District Court's order, and a divided en banc court adhered to that disposition.

The en banc majority noted first that, after the District Court's decision, a precedential Sixth Circuit opinion, Ahmed v. Ahmed, 867 F.3d 682 (2017), established that, as the District Court had assumed, an infant's habitual residence depends on "shared parental intent." The en banc majority then reviewed the District Court's habitual-residence determination for clear error and found none. Sustaining the District Court's determination that A.M.T.'s habitual residence was Italy, the majority rejected Monasky's argument that the District Court erred because "she and Taglieri never had a 'meeting of the minds' about their child's future home."

No member of the en banc court disagreed with the majority's rejection of Monasky's proposed actual-agreement requirement. Nor did any judge maintain that Italy was not A.M.T.'s habitual residence. . . .

We granted certiorari to clarify the standard for habitual residence, an important question of federal and international law, in view of differences in emphasis among the Courts of Appeals. . . .

II

The first question presented concerns the standard for habitual residence: Is an actual agreement between the parents on where to raise their child categorically necessary to establish an infant's habitual residence? We hold that the determination of habitual residence does not turn on the existence of an actual agreement.

A

We begin with "the text of the treaty and the context in which the written words are used." The Hague Convention does not define the term "habitual residence." A child "resides" where she lives. See Black's Law Dictionary 1176 (5th ed. 1979). Her residence in a particular country can be deemed "habitual," however, only when her residence there is more than transitory. "Habitual" implies "[c]ustomary, usual, of the nature of a habit." Id., at 640. The Hague Convention's text alone does not definitively tell us what makes a child's residence sufficiently enduring to be deemed "habitual." It surely does not say that habitual residence depends on an actual agreement between a child's parents. But the term "habitual" does suggest a fact-sensitive inquiry, not a categorical one.

The Convention's explanatory report confirms what the Convention's text suggests. . . . The report refers to a child's habitual residence in fact-focused terms: "the family and social environment in which [the child's] life has developed." What makes a child's residence "habitual" is therefore "some degree of integration by the child in a social and family environment." Accordingly, while Federal Courts of Appeals have diverged, if only in emphasis, in the standards they use to locate a child's habitual residence, they share a "common" understanding: The place where a child is at home, at the time of removal or retention, ranks as the child's habitual residence. (citations omitted).

Because locating a child's home is a fact-driven inquiry, courts must be "sensitive to the unique circumstances of the case and informed by common sense." For older children capable of acclimating to their surroundings, courts have long recognized, facts indicating acclimatization will be highly relevant. Because children, especially those too young or otherwise unable to acclimate, depend on their parents as caregivers, the intentions and circumstances of caregiving parents are relevant considerations. No single fact, however, is dispositive across all cases. Common sense suggests that some cases will be straightforward: Where a child has lived in one place with her family indefinitely, that place is likely to be her habitual residence. But suppose, for instance, that an infant lived in a country only because a caregiving parent had been coerced into remaining there. . . .

The treaty's "negotiation and drafting history" corroborates that a child's habitual residence depends on the specific circumstances of the particular case. Medellín v. Texas, 552 U.S. 491, 507 (2008) (noting that such history may aid treaty interpretation). The Convention's explanatory report states that the Hague Conference regarded habitual residence as "a question of pure fact, differing in that respect from domicile." . . .

The bottom line: There are no categorical requirements for establishing a child's habitual residence — least of all an actual-agreement requirement for infants. Monasky's proposed actual-agreement requirement is not only unsupported by the Convention's text and inconsistent with the leeway and international harmony the Convention demands; her proposal would thwart the Convention's "objects and purposes." An actual-agreement requirement would enable a parent, by withholding agreement, unilaterally to block any finding of habitual residence for an infant. If adopted, the requirement would undermine the Convention's aim to stop unilateral decisions to remove children across international borders. Moreover, when parents' relations are acrimonious, as is often the case in controversies arising under the Convention, agreement can hardly be expected. In short, as the Court of Appeals observed below, "Monasky's approach would create a presumption of no habitual residence for infants, leaving the population most vulnerable to abduction the least protected."

B

Monasky counters that an actual-agreement requirement is necessary to ensure "that an infant's mere physical presence in a country has a sufficiently settled quality to be deemed 'habitual.'" An infant's "mere physical presence," we agree, is not a dispositive indicator of an infant's habitual residence. But a wide range of facts other than an actual agreement, including facts indicating that the parents have made their home in a particular place, can enable a trier to determine whether an infant's residence in that place has the quality of being "habitual."

Monasky also argues that a bright-line rule like her proposed actual-agreement requirement would promote prompt returns of abducted children and deter would-be abductors from "tak[ing] their chances" in the first place. Adjudicating a winner-takes-all evidentiary dispute over whether an agreement existed, however, is scarcely more expeditious than providing courts with leeway to make "a quick impression gained on a panoramic view of the evidence." When all the circumstances are in play, would-be abductors should find it more, not less, difficult to manipulate the reality on the ground, thus impeding them from forging "artificial jurisdictional links . . . with a view to obtaining custody of a child."

Finally, Monasky and amici curiae raise a troublesome matter: An actual-agreement requirement, they say, is necessary to protect children born into domestic violence. Domestic violence poses an "intractable" problem in Hague Convention cases involving caregiving parents fleeing with their children from abuse. We doubt, however, that imposing a categorical actual-agreement requirement is an appropriate solution, for it would leave many infants without a habitual residence, and therefore outside the Convention's domain. Settling the forum for adjudication of a dispute over a child's custody, of course, does not dispose of the merits of the controversy over custody. Domestic violence should be an issue fully explored in the custody adjudication upon the child's return. . . .

III

[The Court determined the correct standard of appellate review to be a "clear-error review standard deferential to the factfinding courts," as the habitual-residence determination is a mixed question of law and fact.]

IV

. . . A remand would consume time when swift resolution is the Convention's objective. The instant return-order proceedings began a few months after A.M.T.'s birth. She is now five years old. The more than four-and-a-half-year duration of this litigation dwarfs the six-week target time for resolving a return-order petition. . . . Given the exhaustive record before the District Court, the absence of any reason to anticipate that the District Court's judgment would change on a remand that neither party seeks, and the protraction of proceedings thus far, final judgment on A.M.T.'s return is in order.

• • •

For the reasons stated, the judgment of the Court of Appeals for the Sixth Circuit is Affirmed.

NOTES AND QUESTIONS

1. A person is entitled to the return of a child under the Hague Convention only if they were exercising rights of custody, an issue decided under the law of the habitual residence. A parent who does not have custody but who has visitation rights is not entitled to the remedy of return of the child, but the Convention protects visitation rights without specifying a particular remedy. Hague Convention Arts. 12, 21.

Sometimes a court couples an order granting custody or visitation with an order prohibiting a parent from taking the child out of the jurisdiction without the consent of the other parent or a court; the latter provision is called a *ne exeat* clause in international law. The Supreme Court held in Abbott v. Abbott, 560 U.S. 1 (2010), that a parent with visitation rights protected by a *ne exeat* clause has a form of joint custody for purposes of the Hague Convention. Therefore, if the child is taken from the country without that parent's permission, the parent may claim the return remedy under the Convention. Most foreign courts have held that a right to visitation protected by a *ne exeat* clause is a custody right under the Hague Convention. *Abbott*, 560 U.S. at 16.

2. Article 12 of the Hague Convention creates an exception to the obligation to return a child who was wrongfully removed or retained. It applies only if the proceedings for return of the child were commenced more than one year after the wrongful removal or retention and grants the court discretion to deny the petition if the child is "well settled" in the new environment. How is this analysis different from consideration of whether the child has become "acclimatized" to the new environment, which bears on the finding of habitual residence? *See* Hoffman v. Sender, 716 F.3d 282, 294 n.5 (2d Cir. 2013) ("We note that the second prong of the [habitual residence] analysis seems to address the same concerns as the 'now-settled' defense found in Article 12 of the Hague Convention. Hypothetically, these ostensibly parallel analyses could allow for a finding that a child has become well settled in its new country before the one year time limit in Article 12 has elapsed.").

In Lozano v. Montoya Alvarez, 134 S. Ct. 1224 (2014), the Supreme Court held that the one-year period for the well-settled exception begins even if the abductor conceals the child from the person entitled to custody. The unanimous Court concluded that tolling was inconsistent with the intent of the drafters of the Convention and that the well-settled provision allows a court to consider the child's interests.

3. The Convention provides affirmative defenses to return of a child who has been wrongfully removed. The first, created by Article 13b, says that a child should not be returned if there is a grave risk of harm to the child. Hirst v. Tiberghien, 947 F. Supp. 2d 578, 595 (D.S.C. 2013), summarizes the courts' interpretation of this clause:

> Some courts have held that demonstrating grave risk requires a showing that the child would be returned to an environment in which the child would experience war, famine or disease, or that there exists the serious threat of abuse where the court in the country of habitual residence could not protect the child. *See Friedrich II*, 78 F.3d at 1060. Other cases have held that a respondent must establish by clear and convincing evidence a pattern of sexual or physical abuse of child or parent in order to invoke the Article 13(b) grave risk exception. *See, e.g.*, Danaipour v. McLarey, 386 F.3d 289 (1st Cir. 2004). The Third Circuit Court of Appeals has held the grave risk exception applies only if the respondent shows "that the alleged physical or psychological harm is a great deal more than minimal [and] something more than would normally be expected on taking a child away from one parent and passing him to another." Baxter v. Baxter, 423 F.3d 363, 373 n.8 (3d Cir. 2005). All courts agree that an Article 13(b) defense "may not be used as a vehicle to litigate (or relitigate) the child's best interests." Danaipour v. McLarey, 286 F.3d 1, 14 (1st Cir. 2002) (quoting Hague International Child Abduction Convention: Text and Legal Analysis, 51 F.R. 10,494, 10,510 (Dep't of State Mar. 26, 1986)).

In *Miller*, the Fourth Circuit held that the grave risk exception was not applicable where the "courts in the abducted-from country are as ready and able as we are to protect children." The court further stated:

> If return to a country, or to the custody of a parent in that country, is dangerous, we can expect that country's courts to respond accordingly. . . . When we trust the court system in the abducted-from country, the vast majority of claims of harm — those that do not rise to the level of gravity required by the Convention — evaporate.

Miller, 240 F.3d at 402 (quoting *Friedrich*, 78 F.3d at 1068).

In addition, a state may also refuse to return the child if doing so would contravene "fundamental principles . . . relating to the protection of human rights and fundamental freedoms." Art. 20. For analyses of this provision and how it relates to "grave risk," *see* Merle Weiner, Strengthening Article 20, 38 U.S.F. L. Rev. 701 (2004); Jane K. Stoever, Parental Abduction and the State Intervention Paradox, 92 Wash. L. Rev. 861 (2017). Does a court have to enforce a custody order from another country in which one parent claims deprivation of due process in contravention of fundamental or human rights? In a case at the intersection of the UCCJEA and the Hague Convention, the Supreme Court of New Hampshire granted enforcement of a father's Convention petition and rejected the mother's claim that the state is not obligated to enforce a Turkish custody order under the UCCJEA because she was denied due process in the Turkish proceeding or because Turkish custody law lacked provision for joint custody. In re Yaman, 105 A.3d 600 (N.H. 2014).

4. Another affirmative defense arising under Article 13 of the Hague Convention, the child's objection clause, allows a court to consider the objection of a child of sufficient age and maturity to being returned to the country of habitual residence. American courts rarely refuse to order return based on the child's objection alone, however. For a discussion of the clause, *see* Linda D. Elrod, "Please Let Me Stay": Hearing the Voice of the Child in Hague Abduction Cases, 63 Okla. L. Rev. 663 (2011).

5. A final affirmative defense is that the person seeking the child's return consented or acquiesced in the child's removal to the jurisdiction where the child is alleged to be wrongfully held. Art. 13(b). *See* Darín v. Olivero-Huffman, 746 F.3d 1 (1st Cir, 2014); Mota v. Castillo, 692 F.3d 108 (2d Cir. 2012) (conditional consent does not bar return if condition does not occur); Hoffman v. Sender, 716 F.3d 282 (2d Cir. 2013) (same); Nicholson v. Pappalaardo, 605 F.3d 100 (1st Cir. 2010) (applying law to close facts). In instances in which a party claims that the other parent agreed to change the habitual residence, there must be shared intent to leave the former habitual residence. *See, e.g.*, Velasquez v. Funes de Velasquez, 102 F. Supp. 3d 796 (E.D. Va. 2015).

6. In 2021, 147 abducted children whose habitual residence was in the United States returned to the United States; 118 returned from Convention countries, and 29 returned from non-Convention countries. In the same year, the U.S. Department of State worked on 175 abduction cases that were unresolved. By far the largest number of cases involved Native American residents. U.S. Dep't of State, Bureau of Consular Affairs, Annual Report on International Child Abduction 2022. Reports are available at https://travel.state.gov/content/travel/en/International-Parental-Child-Abduction/for-providers/legal-reports-and-data/reported-cases.html.

7. If a Hague claim was raised in state court litigation regarding a child's custody, a federal court is expressly barred from relitigating the issue. 22 U.S.C. §9003(g) (2022). What if the Hague claim is not raised in the state court? Should a parent be barred by principles of *res judicata* or principles of abstention from later seeking return of the child in federal court? In Holder v. Holder, 305 F.3d 854 (9th Cir. 2002), the Ninth Circuit held that *res judicata* should not be applied to bar the federal court litigation, saying that to apply preclusion would undermine the purposes of the Hague Convention. Further, the court said, the issues in a Hague petition are not substantially similar to the issues in state custody litigation, even though there might be some overlap between the Hague "habitual residence" and the state court "home state" issues.

Article 16 of the Hague Convention provides that if a Hague proceeding is pending, other proceedings regarding the child's custody should be stayed until the Hague issue is resolved. Thus, if the issue is raised in federal court, state court proceedings should be stayed. However, the petitioner may choose to raise the Hague issue in state court; in such a situation, any federal proceeding should be stayed. Yang v. Tsui, 416 F.3d 199 (3d Cir. 2005).

8. Removing a child from the United States or retaining a child who has been in the United States outside the United States with intent to obstruct the lawful exercise of parental rights is a federal felony punishable by up to three years in prison. 18 U.S.C. §1204 (2022). The statute creates three affirmative defenses: (1) the defendant had been granted custody or visitation by a court acting pursuant to the UCCJA or the UCCJEA; (2) the "defendant was fleeing from an incident or pattern of domestic violence"; and (3) the defendant had "physical custody of the child pursuant to a court order granting legal custody or visitation rights and failed to return the child as a result of circumstances beyond the defendant's control, and the defendant notified or made reasonable attempts to notify the other parent or lawful custodian of the child of such circumstances within 24 hours after the visitation period had expired and returned the child as soon as possible." *Id.*

Golan v. Saada
142 S. Ct. 1880 (2022)

Justice SOTOMAYOR delivered the opinion of the Court.

Under the Hague Convention on the Civil Aspects of International Child Abduction, if a court finds that a child was wrongfully removed from the child's country of habitual residence, the court ordinarily must order the child's return. There are, however, exceptions to that rule. As relevant here, a court is not bound to order a child's return if it finds that return would put the child at a grave risk of physical or psychological harm. In such a circumstance, a court has discretion to determine whether to deny return.

In exercising this discretion, courts often consider whether any "ameliorative measures," undertaken either "by the parents" or "by the authorities of the state having jurisdiction over the question of custody," could "reduce whatever risk might otherwise be associated with a child's repatriation." The Second Circuit has made such consideration a requirement, mandating that district courts independently "examine the full range of options that might make possible the safe return of a child" before denying return due to grave risk, even if the party petitioning for the child's return has not identified or argued for imposition of ameliorative measures.

The Second Circuit's categorical requirement to consider all ameliorative measures is inconsistent with the text and other express requirements of the Hague Convention.

I

A

The Hague Convention "was adopted in 1980 in response to the problem of international child abductions during domestic disputes." One hundred and one countries, including the United States and Italy, are signatories.

The Convention's "core premise" is that " 'the interests of children . . . in matters relating to their custody' are best served when custody decisions are made in the child's country of 'habitual residence.' " Accordingly, the Convention generally requires the "prompt return" of a child to the child's country of habitual residence when the child has been wrongfully removed to or retained in another country. . . .

Return of the child is, however, a general rule, and there are exceptions. As relevant here, the Convention provides that return is not required if "[t]here is a grave risk that . . . return would expose the child to physical or psychological harm or otherwise place the child in an intolerable situation." Art. 13(b), *id.*, at 10. . . .

B

Petitioner Narkis Golan is a citizen of the United States. She met respondent Isacco Saada, an Italian citizen, while attending a wedding in Milan, Italy, in 2014. Golan soon moved to Milan, and the two wed in August 2015. Their son, B. A. S., was born the next summer in Milan, where the family lived for the first two years of B. A. S.' life.

The following facts, as found by the District Court, are not in dispute. Saada and Golan's relationship was characterized by violence from the beginning. The two fought on an almost daily basis and, during their arguments, Saada would sometimes push, slap, and grab Golan and pull her hair. Saada also yelled and swore at Golan and frequently insulted her and called her names, often in front of other people. Saada once told Golan's family that he would kill her. Much of Saada's abuse of Golan occurred in front of his son.

In July 2018, Golan flew with B. A. S. to the United States to attend her brother's wedding. Rather than return as scheduled in August, however, Golan moved into a domestic violence shelter with B. A. S. In September, Saada filed in Italy a criminal complaint for kidnapping and initiated a civil proceeding seeking sole custody of B. A. S.

. . . The District Court granted Saada's petition after a 9-day bench trial. As a threshold matter, the court determined that Italy was B. A. S.' habitual residence and that Golan had wrongfully retained B. A. S. in the United States in violation of Saada's rights of custody. The court concluded, however, that returning B. A. S. to Italy would expose him to a grave risk of harm. The court observed that there was "no dispute" that Saada was "violent — physically, psychologically, emotionally, and verbally — to" Golan and that "B. A. S. was present for much of it." The court described some of the incidents B. A. S. had witnessed as "chilling." While B. A. S. was not "the target of violence," undisputed expert testimony established that "domestic violence disrupts a child's cognitive and social-emotional development, and affects the structure and organization of the child's brain." Records indicated that Italian social services, who had been involved with the couple while they lived in Italy, had also concluded that " 'the family situation entails a developmental danger' for B. A. S." The court found that Saada had demonstrated no "capacity to change his behavior," explaining that Saada "minimized or tried to excuse his violent conduct" during his testimony and that Saada's "own expert said . . . that [Saada] could not control his anger or take responsibility for his behavior."

The court nonetheless ordered B. A. S.' return to Italy based on Second Circuit precedent obligating it to " 'examine the full range of options that might make possible the safe return of a child to the home country' " before it could " 'deny repatriation on the ground that a grave risk of harm exists.' " The Second Circuit based this rule on its view that the Convention requires return "if at all possible." To comply with these precedents, the District Court had required the parties to propose " 'ameliorative measures' " that could enable B. A. S.' safe return. Saada had proposed that he would provide Golan with $30,000 for expenses pending a decision in Italian courts as to financial support, stay away from Golan until the custody dispute was resolved, pursue dismissal of the criminal charges he had filed against Golan, begin cognitive behavioral therapy, and waive any right to legal fees or expenses under the Convention. The court concluded that these measures, combined with the fact that Saada and Golan would be living separately, would "reduce the occasions for violence," thereby ameliorating the grave risk to B. A. S. sufficiently to require his return.

On Golan's appeal of this return order, the Second Circuit vacated the order, finding the District Court's measures insufficient to mitigate the risk of harm to B. A. S. . . . Because the record did "not support the conclusion that there exist *no* protective measures sufficient to ameliorate the grave risk of harm B. A. S. faces if repatriated," the court remanded for the District Court to "consider whether there exist alternative ameliorative measures that are either enforceable by the District Court or supported by other sufficient guarantees of performance." *Id.*, at 543 (emphasis added).

To comply with the Second Circuit's directive, . . . the parties petitioned the Italian courts for a protective order, and the Italian court overseeing the underlying custody dispute issued a protective order barring Saada from approaching Golan for one year. In addition, the Italian court ordered that an Italian social services agency oversee Saada's parenting classes and therapy and that visits between Saada and B. A. S. be supervised.

The District Court concluded that these measures were sufficient to ameliorate the harm to B. A. S. and again granted Saada's petition for B. A. S.' return. . . . The Second Circuit affirmed. . . .

II

A

"The interpretation of a treaty, like the interpretation of a statute, begins with its text." As described above, when "a child has been wrongfully removed or retained" from his country of habitual residence, Article 12 of the Hague Convention generally requires the deciding authority (here, a district court) to "order the return of the child." Treaty Doc., at 9. Under Article 13(b) of the Convention, however, a court "is not bound to order the return of the child" if the court finds that the party opposing return has established that return would expose the child to a "grave risk" of physical or psychological harm. By providing that a court "is not bound" to order return upon making a grave-risk finding, Article 13(b) lifts the Convention's return requirement, leaving a court with the discretion to grant or deny return.

Nothing in the Convention's text either forbids or requires consideration of ameliorative measures in exercising this discretion. The Convention itself nowhere mentions ameliorative measures. . . . The longstanding interpretation of the Department of State offers further support for the view that the Convention vests a court with discretion to determine whether to order return if an exception to the return mandate applies.

Unable to point to any explicit textual mandate that courts consider ameliorative measures, Saada's primary argument is that this requirement is implicit in the Convention's command that the court make a determination as to whether a grave risk of harm exists. Essentially, Saada argues that determining whether a grave risk of harm exists necessarily requires considering whether any ameliorative measures are available.

The question whether there is a grave risk, however, is separate from the question whether there are ameliorative measures that could mitigate that risk. That said, the question whether ameliorative measures would be appropriate or effective will often overlap considerably with the inquiry into whether a grave risk exists. In many instances, a court may find it appropriate to consider both questions at once. For example, a finding of grave risk as to a part of a country where an epidemic rage may naturally lead a court simultaneously to consider whether return to another part of the country is feasible. The fact that a court may consider ameliorative measures concurrent with the grave-risk determination, however, does not mean that the Convention imposes a categorical requirement on a court to consider any or all ameliorative measures before denying return once it finds that a grave risk exists.

. . . The Second Circuit's rule, "in practice, rewrite[s] the treaty," by imposing an atextual, categorical requirement that courts consider all possible ameliorative measures in exercising this discretion, regardless of whether such consideration is consistent with the Convention's objectives (and, seemingly, regardless of whether the parties offered them for the court's consideration in the first place).

B

. . . While a district court has no obligation under the Convention to consider ameliorative measures that have not been raised by the parties, it ordinarily should address ameliorative measures raised by the parties or obviously suggested by the circumstances of the case, such as in the example of the localized epidemic.

. . . The Second Circuit's rule, by instructing district courts to order return "if at all possible," improperly elevated return above the Convention's other objectives. The Convention does not pursue return exclusively or at all costs. Rather, the Convention "is designed to protect the interests of children and their parents," and children's interests may point against return in some circumstances. Courts must remain conscious of this purpose, as well as the Convention's other objectives and requirements, which constrain courts' discretion to consider ameliorative measures in at least three ways.

First, any consideration of ameliorative measures must prioritize the child's physical and psychological safety. . . . A court may therefore decline to consider imposing ameliorative measures where it is clear that they would not work because the risk is so grave. Sexual abuse of a child is one example of an intolerable situation. . . .

Second, consideration of ameliorative measures should abide by the Convention's requirement that courts addressing return petitions do not usurp the role of the court that will adjudicate the underlying custody dispute. Accordingly, a court ordering ameliorative measures in making a return determination should limit those measures in time and scope to conditions that would permit safe return, without purporting to decide subsequent custody matters or weighing in on permanent arrangements.

Third, any consideration of ameliorative measures must accord with the Convention's requirement that courts "act expeditiously in proceedings for the return of children." . . . A requirement to "examine the full range of options that might make possible the safe return of a child," is in tension with this focus on expeditious resolution. In this case, for example, it took the District Court nine months to comply with the Second Circuit's directive on remand. . . . Consideration of ameliorative measures should not cause undue delay in resolution of return petitions.

To summarize, although nothing in the Convention prohibits a district court from considering ameliorative measures, and such consideration often may be appropriate, a district court reasonably may decline to consider ameliorative measures that have not been raised by the parties, are unworkable, draw the court into determinations properly resolved in custodial proceedings, or risk overly prolonging return proceedings. The court may also find the grave risk so unequivocal, or the potential harm so severe, that ameliorative measures would be inappropriate. . . . A district court's compliance with these requirements is subject to review under an ordinary abuse-of-discretion standard.

NOTES AND QUESTIONS

1. Studies have long showed that many international abductors of children leave relationships that were marked by domestic violence. Geoffrey L. Freig & Rebecca L. Hega, When Parents Kidnap 18-19 (1993); Lord Chancellor's Dep't, Child Abduction Unit, Report on the Third Meeting of the Special Commission to Discuss the Operation of the Hague Convention on the Civil Aspects of International Child Abduction, Apr. 8, 1997, at 1.

2. Before *Golan*, the Sixth Circuit in Simcox v. Simcox, 511 F.3d 594 (6th Cir. 2007), discussed how to analyze a claim that domestic violence directed toward the abducting parent constitutes a grave risk of physical or psychological injury to the children so that return is not required:

> First, there are cases in which the abuse is relatively minor. In such cases it is unlikely that the risk of harm caused by return of the child will rise to the level of a "grave risk" or otherwise place the child in an "intolerable situation" under Article 13b. In these cases, undertakings designed to protect the child are largely irrelevant; since the Article 13b threshold has not been met, the court has no discretion to refuse to order return, with or without undertakings. Second, at the other end of the spectrum, there are cases in which the risk of harm is clearly grave, such as where there is credible evidence of sexual abuse, other similarly grave physical or psychological abuse, death threats, or serious neglect. [citation omitted.] In these cases, undertakings will likely be insufficient to ameliorate the risk of harm, given the difficulty of enforcement and the likelihood that a serially abusive petitioner will not be deterred by a foreign court's orders. Consequently, unless "the rendering court [can] satisfy itself that the children will in fact, and not just in legal theory, be protected if returned to their abuser's custody," the court should refuse to grant the petition. Third, there are those cases that fall somewhere in the middle, where the abuse is substantially more than minor, but is less obviously intolerable. Whether, in these cases, the return of the child would subject it to a "grave risk" of harm or otherwise place it in an "intolerable situation" is a fact-intensive inquiry that depends on careful consideration of several factors, including the nature and frequency of the abuse, the likelihood of its recurrence, and whether there are any enforceable undertakings that would sufficiently ameliorate the risk of harm to the child caused by its return. Even in this middle category, undertakings should be adopted only where the court satisfies itself that the parties are likely to obey them. Thus, undertakings would be particularly inappropriate, for example, in cases where the petitioner has a history of ignoring court orders. Where a grave risk of harm has been established, ordering return with feckless undertakings is worse than not ordering it at all. . . .

511 F.3d at 607-608.

E. FEDERAL COURT JURISDICTION OVER DOMESTIC RELATIONS

Ankenbrandt v. Richards
504 U.S. 689 (1992)

WHITE, J. . . . Petitioner Carol Ankenbrandt, a citizen of Missouri, brought this lawsuit on September 26, 1989, on behalf of her daughters L. R. and S. R. against respondents Jon A. Richards and Debra Kesler, citizens of Louisiana, in the United States District Court for the Eastern District of Louisiana. Alleging federal jurisdiction based on the diversity of citizenship provision of §1332, Ankenbrandt's complaint sought monetary damages for alleged sexual and physical abuse of the children committed by Richards and Kesler. Richards is the divorced father of the children and Kesler his female companion. On December 10, 1990, the District Court granted respondents' motion to dismiss this lawsuit. Citing In re Burrus, 136 U.S. 586, 593-594 (1890), for the proposition that "[t]he whole subject of the domestic relations of husband and wife, parent and child, belongs to the laws of the States and not to the laws of the United States," the court concluded that this case fell within what has become known as the "domestic relations" exception to diversity jurisdiction, and that it lacked jurisdiction over the case. . . .

We granted certiorari limited to the following questions: (1) Is there a domestic relations exception to federal jurisdiction? (2) If so, does it permit a district court to abstain from exercising diversity jurisdiction over a tort action for damages? . . .

The domestic relations exception upon which the courts below relied to decline jurisdiction has been invoked often by the lower federal courts. The seeming authority for doing so originally stemmed from the announcement in Barber v. Barber, 21 How. 582 (1859), that the federal courts have no jurisdiction over suits for divorce or the allowance of alimony. In that case, the Court heard a suit in equity brought by a wife (by her next friend) in Federal District Court pursuant to diversity jurisdiction against her former husband. She sought to enforce a decree from a New York state court, which had granted a divorce and awarded her alimony. The former husband thereupon moved to Wisconsin to place himself beyond the New York courts' jurisdiction so that the divorce decree there could not be enforced against him; he then sued for divorce in a Wisconsin court, representing to that court that his wife had abandoned him and failing to disclose the existence of the New York decree. In a suit brought by the former wife in Wisconsin Federal District Court, the former husband alleged that the court lacked jurisdiction. The court accepted jurisdiction and gave judgment for the divorced wife.

On appeal, it was argued that the District Court lacked jurisdiction on two grounds: first, that there was no diversity of citizenship because although divorced, the wife's citizenship necessarily remained that of her former husband; and second, that the whole subject of divorce and alimony, including a suit to enforce an alimony decree, was exclusively ecclesiastical at the time of the adoption of the Constitution and that the Constitution therefore placed the whole subject of divorce and alimony beyond the jurisdiction of the United States courts. Over the dissent of three Justices, the Court rejected both arguments. After an exhaustive survey of the authorities, the Court concluded that a divorced wife could acquire a citizenship separate from that of her former husband and that a suit to enforce an alimony decree rested within the federal courts' equity jurisdiction. . . . [T]he Court also announced the following limitation on federal jurisdiction:

> Our first remark is—and we wish it to be remembered—that this is not a suit asking the court for the allowance of alimony. That has been done by a court of competent jurisdiction. The court in Wisconsin was asked to interfere to prevent that decree from being defeated by fraud.
>
> We disclaim altogether any jurisdiction in the courts of the United States upon the subject of divorce, or for the allowance of alimony, either as an original proceeding in chancery or as an incident to divorce a vinculo, or to one from bed and board. . . .

The statements disclaiming jurisdiction over divorce and alimony decree suits, though technically dicta, formed the basis for excluding "domestic relations" cases from the jurisdiction of the lower federal courts, a jurisdictional limitation those courts have recognized ever since. . . .

Counsel argued in *Barber* that the Constitution prohibited federal courts from exercising jurisdiction over domestic relations cases. An examination of Article III, *Barber* itself, and our cases since *Barber* makes clear that the Constitution does not exclude domestic relations cases from the jurisdiction otherwise granted by statute to the federal courts. . . .

Subsequent decisions confirm that *Barber* was not relying on constitutional limits in justifying the exception. . . .

The Judiciary Act of 1789 provided that "the circuit courts shall have original cognizance, concurrent with the courts of the several States, *of all suits of a civil nature at common law or in equity, where the matter in dispute exceeds*, exclusive of costs, the sum or value of *five hundred dollars*, and . . . an alien is a party, or the suit is *between a citizen of the State where the suit is brought, and a citizen of another State*." Act of Sept. 24, 1789, §11,1 Stat. 73, 78. (Emphasis added.) The defining phrase, "all suits of a civil nature at common law or in equity," remained a key element of statutory provisions demarcating the terms of diversity jurisdiction until 1948, when Congress amended the diversity jurisdiction provision to eliminate this phrase and replace in its stead the term "all civil actions."

The *Barber* majority itself did not expressly refer to the diversity statute's use of the limitation on "suits of a civil nature at common law or in equity." The dissenters in *Barber*, however, implicitly made such a reference, for they suggested that the federal courts had no power over certain domestic relations actions because the court of chancery lacked authority to issue divorce and alimony decrees. . . .

We have no occasion here to join the historical debate over whether the English court of chancery had jurisdiction to handle certain domestic relations matters. . . . We thus are content to rest our conclusion that a domestic relations exception exists as a matter of statutory construction not on the accuracy of the historical justifications on which it was seemingly based, but rather on Congress's apparent acceptance of this construction of the diversity jurisdiction provisions in the years prior to 1948, when the statute limited jurisdiction to "suits of a civil nature at common law or in equity." . . . Considerations *of stare decisis* have particular strength in this context, where "the legislative power is implicated, and Congress remains free to alter what we have done." . . .

In the more than 100 years since this Court laid the seeds for the development of the domestic relations exception, the lower federal courts have applied it in a variety of circumstances. Many of these applications go well beyond the circumscribed situations posed by *Barber* and its progeny. *Barber* itself disclaimed federal jurisdiction over a narrow range of domestic relations issues involving the granting of a divorce and a decree of alimony, and stated the limits on federal-court power to intervene prior to the rendering of such orders:

> It is, that when a court of competent jurisdiction over the subject-matter and the parties decrees a divorce, and alimony to the wife as its incident, and is unable of itself to enforce the decree summarily upon the husband, that courts of equity will interfere to prevent the decree from being defeated by fraud. The interference, however, is limited to cases in which alimony has been decreed; then only to the extent of what is due, and always to cases in which no appeal is pending from the decree for the divorce or for alimony. Id., at 591.

The *Barber* Court thus did not intend to strip the federal courts of authority to hear cases arising from the domestic relations of persons unless they seek the granting or modification of a divorce or alimony decree. The holding of the case itself sanctioned the exercise of federal jurisdiction over the enforcement of an alimony decree that had been properly obtained in a state court of competent jurisdiction. . . .

Subsequently, this Court expanded the domestic relations exception to include decrees in child custody cases. . . .

Not only is our conclusion rooted in respect for this long-held understanding, it is also supported by sound policy considerations. Issuance of decrees of this type not infrequently involves retention of jurisdiction by the court and deployment of social workers to monitor compliance. As a matter of judicial economy, state courts are more eminently suited to work of this type than are federal courts, which lack the close association with state and local government organizations dedicated to handling issues that arise out of conflicts over divorce, alimony, and child custody decrees. Moreover, as a matter of judicial expertise, it makes far more sense to retain the rule that federal courts lack power to issue these types of decrees because of the special proficiency developed by state tribunals over the past century and a half in handling issues that arise in the granting of such decrees.

By concluding, as we do, that the domestic relations exception encompasses only cases involving the issuance of a divorce, alimony, or child custody decree, we necessarily find that the Court of Appeals erred by affirming the District Court's invocation of this exception. This lawsuit in no way seeks such a decree; rather, it alleges that respondents Richards and Kesler committed torts against L. R. and S. R., Ankenbrandt's children by Richards. Federal subject-matter jurisdiction pursuant to §1332 thus is proper in this case. . . .

Judith Resnik

"Naturally" Without Gender: Women, Jurisdiction, and the Federal Courts
66 N.Y.U. L. Rev. 1682, 1742-1744, 1750-1757 (1991)

The assumption of lack of federal judicial power over personal relations has been eroded by litigation over the course of this century about reproduction and federal benefits, both of which structure relations "among different members of private families in their domestic intercourse." Further, that assertion ignored nineteenth century federal efforts to control polygamy and sexual relations, which in turn affect family relations, albeit nontraditional ones. In 1862, 1882, and 1887, Congress outlawed polygamy. Fragments of these laws still remain. While this legislation was directed at federal governance of the territories and was implemented by the federal courts in their capacity as "territorial courts" (thus acting as "state courts" for these purposes), other federal legislation did bring the federal courts into the governance of multiple marriages in the states. The "Mann Act"—involving federal regulation of sexual activity—was used in prosecutions of individuals who transported women in "interstate commerce." In one of the cases prosecuted under the Mann Act, the Court expressly endorsed Congress's authority to "defeat what are deemed to be immoral practices; the fact that the means used may have the 'quality of police regulations' is not consequential." Despite a claim of noninvolvement in interpersonal relations (some of which might bear the title "family"), federal law and federal courts have, on selected occasions, taken on these issues. . . .

Pointing out links between federal law and families raises a question, traditional for federal courts scholars. While not discussed by federal courts jurisprudence, a complex mosaic of federal regulation of economic and social relations now overlays state laws on divorce, alimony, and child support. What is to be made of this fact of joint governance of the field? Because I hope scholars of federal courts will take seriously the topic of federal family law, it is appropriate to consider how doctrinal developments—shaped by different images of what is on the national agenda that federal courts implement and adjudicate—might take federal courts' authority over family life into account. The central question is what "business is the federal business," and it is time to answer this question by recognizing that there already is joint federal and state governance of an array of issues, from land use and torts to families. Once understood as a joint endeavor, the next issue is how to allocate authority.

A first possibility is that federal court involvement in family life is bad, per se, at a structural level. This claim takes seriously the arguments made in the many cases espousing (slight pun intended) state control over family life and fearing that the federal courts would become hopelessly "enmeshed" in family disputes. Under this vision, the states (and Indian tribes) as smaller units of government are closer to "the people" and thus a more appropriate level of government to determine matters affecting intimate life.

Possible justifications for this view exist. Contemporary invocations of the domestic relations exception discard arguments based on ecclesiastical authority, the alleged lack of jurisdictional diversity between married couples, and the claim that divorces lack monetary value—all in favor of a "modern view that state courts have historically decided these matters and have developed both a well-known expertise in these cases and a strong interest in disposing of them." . . . Holding aside the ever-present question of boundaries, doctrine might shift in a variety of ways when ideological claims about the relationship between federal courts and family are revised.

First, one could insist that, despite recognition of federal laws of the family, the claim of deference to state governance remains strong and, as a matter of doctrine, complete abstention (a form of reverse preemption) is desirable. To the extent recent federal law in bankruptcy, pensions, and benefits law points in the other direction, that erosion should be stopped—by legislation or judicial interpretation. But were one to really press this claim—that states are specially situated and should be controlling family life—one would not seek only to cabin the federal courts. This position would also require urging Congress and agencies to avoid defining families by rewriting statutes and regulations to incorporate state law, so as to permit state governance of interpersonal relations. An array of federal statutes would have to incorporate state definitions of families, and what would be lost in uniformity and national norms would be gained in recognition of the special relationship of states in defining family life. . . .

Yet a problem remains. The current hierarchy stipulates the federal courts as most powerful; the supremacy clause confirms that sense of authority. Further, federal courts theorists might affirmatively argue that federal courts are needed in this area—either because of their special capacity to protect the politically disfavored or because federal sovereign and administrative interests are at stake. While neither the appeal to the community envisioned by the claim of closeness of the state to the family nor the concern about attitudes and knowledge of federal judges should be discounted, the "inevitability of federal involvement" in family life remains, as does a sense that the rejection of that role by federal courts reconfirms the marginalization of women and families from national life.

Federal involvement emerges here, as it does in torts, land use, health regulation, criminal law, and other areas, because of the wealth of interactions that make the imagined coherence of the very categories "federal" and "state" themselves problematic. Whether looking at the problem from the top down, and seeing "joint governance" or considering the issue from the perspective of individuals and speaking of "membership in multiple communities," the point is the same: an interlocking, enmeshed regulatory structure covers the host of human activity in the United States. There is not a priori line one can invoke to separate legal regulation into two bounded boxes "state" and "federal." Uniform state laws demonstrate the limits of state court borders and the need for regulatory structures that bridge them. State and federal court interpretations of "family" are unavoidable.

NOTES AND QUESTIONS

1. As *Barber* and *Ankenbrandt* both make clear, and as Professor Resnik also emphasizes, the domestic relations exception does not preclude federal courts from hearing all cases involving family law issues. For example, courts have held that tort suits based on interference with custody and visitation are not within the exception. *See, e.g.*, Drewes v. Ilnicki, 863 F.2d 469 (6th Cir. 1988); MacIntyre v. MacIntyre, 771 F.2d 1316 (9th Cir. 1985); Bennett v. Bennett, 682 F.2d 1039 (D.C. Cir. 1982).

In Lannan v. Maul, 979 F.2d 627 (8th Cir. 1992), the court held that a child's suit to enforce a separation agreement term for her benefit was not within the exception either. However, framing a claim in terms of breach of contract or tort does not automatically mean that the domestic relations exception does not apply:

> The proper inquiry focuses on the type of determination the federal court must make in order to resolve the claim. If the federal court is called upon to decide those issues regularly decided in state court domestic relations actions such as divorce, alimony, child custody, or the support obligations of a spouse or parent, then the domestic relations exception is applicable.

Vaughan v. Smithson, 883 F.2d 63, 65 (10th Cir. 1989). In 2014, a federal district court described the application of *Ankenbrandt* in just one circuit:

> The scope of the domestic relations exception has been the subject of conflicting interpretations in the Sixth Circuit. In Catz v. Chalker, 142 F.3d 279 (6th Cir. 1998), *overruled on other*

grounds as stated in Coles v. Granville, 448 F.3d 853, 859 n.1 (6th Cir. 2006), a former husband brought civil rights actions against his former wife and her attorneys alleging that the procedures in the state divorce trial violated his due process rights. The Sixth Circuit narrowly construed *Ankenbrandt* as holding that the domestic relations exception applies "only where a plaintiff positively sues in federal court for divorce, alimony, or child custody." *Id.* at 292; *see also* Callahan v. Callahan, 247 F. Supp. 2d 935, 944 (S.D. Ohio 2002) (post-divorce action brought by ex-wife seeking to hold ex-husband in contempt of divorce decree due to his failure to transfer all of his interest in his ERISA pension plan to her was not an action specifically for divorce and domestic relations exception did not apply).

However, a year later, another panel of the Sixth Circuit took a broader view of the domestic relations exception in McLaughlin v. Cotner, 193 F.3d 410 (6th Cir. 1999). That case involved a former wife's claim for breach of a separation agreement for the sale of real estate. This agreement had been incorporated into the divorce decree, and was also the subject of a pending state court action. Plaintiff argued that the domestic relations exception did not apply because she was merely suing for breach of contract and tortious interference with contract. The court rejected this argument, noting that plaintiff was "attempting to disguise the true nature of the action by claiming that she is merely making a claim for damages based on a breach of contract." The court concluded that because the alleged contract was incorporated into the divorce decree, the case "involve[d] issues arising out of conflict over a divorce decree" and fell within the domestic relations exception. The court went on to hold that the federal court lacked jurisdiction, "as this case is not a tort or contract suit that merely has domestic relations overtones, but is one seeking a declaration of rights and obligations arising from marital status."

The Sixth Circuit in *McLaughlin* noted that the case before it was similar to Allen v. Allen, 518 F. Supp. 1234 (E.D. Pa. 1981), where, despite the pendency of divorce proceedings and other state court actions concerning the marital property at issue, the husband filed another state court action for breach of monetary obligations contained in a separation agreement, which the wife removed to federal court. Although the husband pleaded claims for breach of contract and fraud, the court in *Allen* noted that these claims and the pending state court actions "contain overlapping factual and legal matrices" with "a multiplicity of intertwined suits, the dominant theme of which is a dispute over the ownership of marital property." The *Allen* court also stated that the case before it was one in which "the parties are attempting to play one court system off against the other." The *Allen* court granted the husband's motions to dismiss and for remand, concluding that "this is a clear case for the application of the domestic relations exception." The *McLaughlin* court observed that a similar rationale applied to the case before it, as the property at issue was also the subject of a pending state court action.

. . .

In United States v. MacPhail, 149 Fed. Appx. 449, 455-56 (6th Cir. 2005), the Sixth Circuit concluded that cross-claims filed by ex-spouses seeking to recover the amount of a refund erroneously paid to the husband by the Internal Revenue Service for the tax year immediately preceding the year their divorce decree became final fell within the domestic relations exception. The court noted that resolution of the indemnification cross-claims required allocation of the refund into some combination of separate or marital property in accordance with Ohio domestic relations law. *Id.* The court concluded that the "division of property as either separate or marital raises exactly the kind of 'delicate issue[ ]' that is more 'appropriate for the federal courts to leave . . . to the state courts.' " *Id.* at 456 (quoting Elk Grove Unified Sch. Dist. v. Newdow, 542 U.S. 1, 13 (2004)).

Chevalier v. Barnhart, 992 F.Supp.2d 810 (S.D. Ohio 2014). How would you draw the line between federal and non-federal jurisdiction? Or should the domestic relations exception simply be abandoned? In addition to Professor Resnik's analysis, *see* Naomi R. Cahn, Family Law, Federalism, and the Federal Courts, 79 Iowa L. Rev. 1073 (1994); Emily J. Sack, The Domestic Relations Exception, Domestic Violence, and Equal Access to Federal Courts, 84 Wash. U. L. Rev. 1441 (2006); Courtney G. Joslin, The Perils of Family Law Localism, 48 U.C. Davis L. Rev. 623, 628-629 (2014).

2. If the domestic relations exception is difficult to justify on a purely historical basis, why is it retained in *Ankenbrandt*? Is there any inconsistency between the result in *Ankenbrandt* and the constitutional review of marriage restrictions or the adoption of federal legislation governing child support and child custody awards?

3. In Marshall v. Marshall, 547 U.S. 293 (2006), the Supreme Court clarified the circumstances in which federal courts that would otherwise have jurisdiction must decline to exercise it under the "probate exception" to federal jurisdiction, a judicially created doctrine closely related to the domestic relations exception. In *Marshall*, the scope of the exception determined whether a federal bankruptcy court could resolve a conflict between a bankrupt person, Anna Nicole Smith (whose real name was Vickie Lynn Marshall), and her creditor (Pierce Marshall, son of Anna Nicole's octogenarian deceased husband, J. Howard Marshall). J. Howard, who died after 14 months of marriage to the 1993 Playmate of the Year, left a will and trust that gave the entire estate to Pierce. Vickie asserted that he had intended to take care of her by amending the living trust, in fulfillment of his promise to give her half his estate if she would marry him. J. Howard did not make these amendments, and a Texas probate court jury found that he had not made that promise to her. While the Texas probate was pending, Vickie, who was facing an unrelated tort judgment, filed for bankruptcy in California. Pierce Marshall filed a proof of claim in the bankruptcy proceeding stating that Vickie had defamed him by alleging he had engaged in forgery, fraud, and overreaching to gain control of his father's assets. He wanted a declaration that the claim was not dischargeable in bankruptcy. Vickie counterclaimed for tortious interference with an expectancy. The bankruptcy court granted Vickie summary judgment with regard to Pierce's claims against her and, after a trial on the merits, entered judgment for her on her counterclaim. Vickie promptly voluntarily dismissed her claims in the Texas probate proceeding. The bankruptcy court awarded her more than $449 million in compensatory damages and $25 million in punitive damages. Pierce appealed. When the case reached the Supreme Court, it interpreted the probate exception narrowly, as it had narrowed the domestic relations exception in *Ankenbrandt*. The Court held that the exception prevents federal courts only from taking jurisdiction over "the probate or annulment of a will and the administration of a decedent's estate" and from "endeavoring to dispose of property that is in the custody of a state probate court." 547 U.S. at 312. Because Vickie sought a tort judgment that would impose personal liability on Pierce, the Court said that the case was not within the probate exception to federal jurisdiction. In the end, and after another Supreme Court decision, Vickie did not recover the $449 million in compensatory damages and $25 million in punitive damages. Stern v. Marshall, 564 U.S. 462 (2011) (holding that the bankruptcy court did not have constitutional authority to decide Vickie's tort claim).

4. Since *Ankenbrandt* was decided, the Fourth, Fifth, and Ninth Circuits have held that the domestic relations exception does not apply when federal jurisdiction is based on a federal question rather than on diversity of the parties. United States v. Bailey, 115 F.3d 1222 (5th Cir. 1997); United States v. Johnson, 114 F.3d 476 (4th Cir. 1997); Atwood v. Fort Peck Tribal Court Assiniboine, 513 F.3d 943 (9th Cir. 2008). *See also* Elk Grove Unified School Dist. v. Newdow, 542 U.S. 1, 13 (2004) ("Thus, while rare instances arise in which it is necessary to answer a substantial federal question that transcends or exists apart from the family law issue, *see, e.g.*, Palmore v. Sidoti, 466 U.S. 429, 432-434 (1984), in general it is appropriate for the federal courts to leave delicate issues of domestic relations to the state courts."). *But see* Jones v. Brennan, 465 F.3d 304 (7th Cir. 2006) (probate exception to federal jurisdiction applies in federal question cases). For discussion of this issue, *see* Meredith Johnson Harbach, Is the Family a Federal Question?, 66 Wash. & Lee L. Rev. 131 (2009).

5. A party may also be barred from seeking relief in federal court if the relief sought is "unnecessary" or "inappropriate" because an adequate remedy exists within the state divorce proceedings, or if the federal claim is inconsistent with a claim asserted in the state court.

For example, in Atwood v. Fort Peck Tribal Court Assiniboine and Sioux Tribes, cited in the paragraph above, the court dismissed Atwood's federal claim because he had failed to exhaust his remedies in tribal court. *See also* Mooney v. Mooney, 471 F.3d 246 (1st Cir. 2006) (federal district court properly abstained because plaintiff husband's claim in state court seeking modification of a divorce decree either made the requested federal relief unnecessary or was inconsistent with that relief, depending on interpretation of the claim).

6. In Thompson v. Thompson, 484 U.S. 174 (1988), the Supreme Court held that Congress did not intend to create an implied federal cause of action when it enacted the PKPA. Had the court ruled to the contrary, the effect would have been to open the federal courts to litigation over the validity of conflicting custody orders from different states. In California v. Superior Court, 482 U.S. 400 (1987), Louisiana asked California to extradite a father and grandfather who were charged with kidnapping. The men took the father's children from Louisiana in violation of a Louisiana custody order. They argued, in effect, that Louisiana had not charged them with a crime because the Louisiana order violated the PKPA. The Supreme Court held, however, that, in an extradition proceeding, California could not inquire into the merits of a jurisdictional dispute.

PART III

CHILDREN, PARENTS, AND THE STATE

CHAPTER 13

DETERMINING LEGAL PARENTHOOD: MARRIAGE, BIOLOGY, AND FUNCTION

Parenthood may be the least settled part of family law. The leading candidates for determining legal parenthood are biological relationships, functional parent-child relationships, and the marital relationship of a child's mother. For most of American history, biological relationship determined legal maternity, and legal paternity was established almost exclusively by marriage. As recently as the 1970s, about 90 percent of all children were born to married mothers. A married woman's spouse was (and still is) presumed to be the legal parent of her children. Children born to unmarried mothers usually did not have a second parent, legally or socially. Fathers rarely established paternity outside of marriage, and most single mothers did not live with the biological fathers of their children.

Today, roughly 40 percent of births occur outside of marriage, and those children's legal paternity is established on bases other than marriage. Unmarried mothers have become much more likely to be living with a partner who assumes a parental relationship to the children. Between 2002 and 2010, the percentage of births to unmarried mothers who were in cohabitations, primarily with the father of their children, increased from 41 percent to 58 percent.[1] Cohabitations, however, are less stable than marriages, and parents—once married or never married—have become more likely to enter into multiple relationships with adults who play parental roles during the child's minority.

Moreover, in the last 50 years, major advances in genetic testing, the development of an aggressive national child support program, recognition of the legal status of same-sex couples, as well as dramatic changes in adults' marriage, divorce, and cohabitation practices have shaken the traditional law of parent-child relationships to its foundations. In 2021, 16.395 million children lived with single mothers, compared to 7.452 million in 1970, and 3.565 million lived with single fathers in 2021, compared to 748,000 in 1970.[2] In 2015,

---

1. The Changing Profile of Unmarried Parents, Pew Research Center, April 19, 2018, available at https://www.pewresearch.org/social-trends/2018/04/25/the-changing-profile-of-unmarried-parents/ (indicating that approximately 40 percent of births are nonmarital; Sally C. Curtin et al., Recent Declines in Nonmarital Childbearing in the United States, Center for Disease Control, NCHS Data Brief No. 162, August 2014, available at https://www.cdc.gov/nchs/data/databriefs/db162.htm (showing increase in births to cohabiting couple through 2010). The percentage of unmarried births to cohabiting couples increased further between 2010 and 2015, while births to single women declined. Key Statistics from the National Survey of Family Growth—B Listing, Center for Disease Control, July 7, 2017, https://www.cdc.gov/nchs/nsfg/key_statistics/b.htm#martialmothers.

2. U.S. Bureau of the Census, Living Arrangements of Children Under 18 Years Old: 1960 to Present, Ch-1 through Ch-5 (2021). Last revised: November 22, 2021.

40.3 percent of all births in the United States were nonmarital, down from a peak of 41 percent in 2009.[3] Unmarried parents on average are younger, poorer, and more likely to be members of a minority group than married parents. Over the last decade, however, the number of children living with two parents has remained steady at approximately 70 percent of the total because unmarried parents have become more likely to cohabit, at least in the early years of a child's life, and children living with single parents have become more likely to be living with never married rather than divorced parents.[4]

With the increased recognition of LGBT couples, there is also more accurate data on LGBT parenting. Gary Gates of the Williams Institute at UCLA reports that "[a]n estimated 37% of LGBT-identified adults have had a child at some time in their lives."[5]

These couples tend to be poorer than non-LGBT families. Gates observes that "[s]ingle LGBT adults raising children are three times more likely than comparable non-LGBT individuals to report household incomes near the poverty threshold" and that "[m]arried or partnered LGBT individuals living in two-adult households with children are twice as likely as comparable non-LGBT individuals to report household incomes near the poverty threshold."[6] Same-sex couples are more likely than different-sex couples to be raising children who are not the biological or stepchildren of the partners. These children include adopted and foster children and other relatives.

More diverse families, together with greater family instability, have increased the occasions for questions about a child's biological paternity to arise. In the 1980s, the federal-state child support enforcement program began to emphasize identifying the fathers of nonmarital children as the first step in establishing and collecting child support. Between 1992 and 2016, paternity establishment increased from 516,000 to more than 1.5 million children per year, though the numbers have been declining over the last five years as birth rates have fallen.[7] Still, many men today are identified as legal fathers and are required to support children with whom they may never have lived or developed a parent-child relationship.

When someone becomes suspicious that a child's legal father may not be the biological father, genetic testing can readily resolve the question. By the 1990s, the science of genetic testing had advanced to the point that in most cases a test can not only exclude a man falsely identified as the biological father but can also positively identify a biological father to near-certainty. Home paternity testing kits, which may not even require a sample from the mother, are readily available and can cost under $100.

All these changes create complex issues as to which adults should be regarded as children's legal parents, both for purposes of having rights of access to the children and duties to support them. Legal parenthood is thus ready for redefinition, with a persistent question of whether definitions of parenthood for purposes of determining support may differ from the definitions used to establish standing to seek custodial rights. Further, an increasing number of states recognize that more than two adults may be entitled to claim the legal status of "parent."

---

3. Joyce A. Martin et al., Births: Final Data for 2016, Nat'l Vital Stat. Rep., Jan. 5, 2017, at 8, available at https://www.cdc.gov/nchs/data/nvsr/nvsr66/nvsr66_01.pdf.

4. U.S. Bureau of the Census, Living Arrangements of Children Under 18 Years Old: 1960 to Present, Fig. Ch-1 (2021). Child Trends, Births to Unmarried Women: Indicators on Children and Youth 2, 4 (2013), available at http://www.childtrends.org/wp-content/uploads/2012/11/75_Births_to_Unmarried_Women.pdf (showing characteristics of unmarried parents).

5. Gary Gates, LGBT Parenting in the United States, The Williams Institute (February 2013), http://williamsinstitute.law.ucla.edu/wp-content/uploads/LGBT-Parenting.pdf.

6. *Id.* at 1.

7. Child Support Enforcement FY 2016 Preliminary Report tbl. P-71, Off. Child Support Enforcement (2020), https://www.acf.hhs.gov/sites/default/files/programs/css/2020_preliminary_report.pdf.

This chapter first examines the constitutional rights of those designated as legal parents in relationship to others who might play a parental role. The rest of the chapter explores the legal designation of parenthood, examining its relationship to marriage, biological ties, step-parent status, and same-sex partnership. It concludes with proposals to divide parental rights and responsibilities among more than two parents. Chapter 14 considers alternative means of establishing parental status, including adoption and assisted reproduction.

A. THE CONSTITUTIONAL RIGHTS OF PARENTS

One way of approaching the definition of family is to ask what difference the definition makes. The issue in the following case is what degree of deference the Constitution guarantees for parental decision making. In reading the following case, consider how the Supreme Court's decision might affect the importance of who fits the definition of a legal parent and who does not in other cases. Consider as well how the definition of "parent" may affect the extent of constitutional protection afforded to "families."

Troxel v. Granville
530 U.S. 57 (2000)

Justice O'CONNOR announced the judgment of the Court and delivered an opinion, in which THE CHIEF JUSTICE, Justice GINSBURG, and Justice BREYER join. . . . Tommie Granville and Brad Troxel shared a relationship that ended in June 1991. The two never married, but they had two daughters, Isabelle and Natalie. Jenifer and Gary Troxel are Brad's parents, and thus the paternal grandparents of Isabelle and Natalie. After Tommie and Brad separated in 1991, Brad lived with his parents and regularly brought his daughters to his parents' home for week-end visitation. Brad committed suicide in May 1993. Although the Troxels at first continued to see Isabelle and Natalie on a regular basis after their son's death, Tommie Granville informed the Troxels in October 1993 that she wished to limit their visitation with her daughters to one short visit per month.

In December 1993, the Troxels . . . [petitioned for visitation under Washington law]. Section 26.10.160(3) [of the Wash. Rev. Code] provides: "Any person may petition the court for visitation rights at any time including, but not limited to, custody proceedings. The court may order visitation rights for any person when visitation may serve the best interest of the child whether or not there has been any change of circumstances." . . . In 1995, the Superior Court issued an oral ruling and entered a visitation decree ordering visitation one weekend per month, one week during the summer, and four hours on both of the petitioning grand-parents' birthdays.

Granville appealed, during which time she married Kelly Wynn. . . . The Washington Supreme Court granted the Troxels' petition for review and, after consolidating their case with two other visitation cases, affirmed. . . .

The demographic changes of the past century make it difficult to speak of an average American family. The composition of families varies greatly from household to household. While many children may have two married parents and grandparents who visit regularly, many other children are raised in single-parent households. In 1996, children living with only one parent accounted for 28 percent of all children under age 18 in the United States. . . . Understandably, in these single-parent households, persons outside the nuclear family are called upon with increasing frequency to assist in the everyday tasks of child rearing. In many cases, grandparents play an important role. For example, in 1998, approximately 4 million children — or 5.6 percent of all children under age 18 — lived in the household of their grandparents.

The nationwide enactment of nonparental visitation statutes is assuredly due, in some part, to the States' recognition of these changing realities of the American family. Because grandparents and other relatives undertake duties of a parental nature in many households, States have sought to ensure the welfare of the children therein by protecting the relationships those children form with such third parties. The States' nonparental visitation statutes are further supported by a recognition, which varies from State to State, that children should have the opportunity to benefit from relationships with statutorily specified persons — for example, their grandparents. The extension of statutory rights in this area to persons other than a child's parents, however, comes with an obvious cost. For example, the State's recognition of an independent third-party interest in a child can place a substantial burden on the traditional parent-child relationship. . . .

The liberty interest at issue in this case — the interest of parents in the care, custody, and control of their children — is perhaps the oldest of the fundamental liberty interests recognized by this Court. More than 75 years ago, in Meyer v. Nebraska, we held that the "liberty" protected by the Due Process Clause includes the right of parents to "establish a home and bring up children" and "to control the education of their own." Two years later, in Pierce v. Society of Sisters, we again held that the "liberty of parents and guardians" includes the right "to direct the upbringing and education of children under their control." We explained in Pierce that "[t]he child is not the mere creature of the State; those who nurture him and direct his destiny have the right, coupled with the high duty, to recognize and prepare him for additional obligations." . . .

Section 26.10.160(3), as applied to Granville and her family in this case, unconstitutionally infringes on that fundamental parental right. The Washington nonparental visitation statute is breathtakingly broad. According to the statute's text, "[a]ny person may petition the court for visitation rights *at any time*," and the court may grant such visitation rights whenever "visitation may serve *the best interest of the child*." §26.10.160(3) (emphases added). That language effectively permits any third party seeking visitation to subject any decision by a parent concerning visitation of the parent's children to state-court review. Once the visitation petition has been filed in court and the matter is placed before a judge, a parent's decision that visitation would not be in the child's best interest is accorded no deference. Section 26.10.160(3) contains no requirement that a court accord the parent's decision any presumption of validity or any weight whatsoever. Instead, the Washington statute places the best-interest determination solely in the hands of the judge. Should the judge disagree with the parent's estimation of the child's best interests, the judge's view necessarily prevails. Thus, in practical effect, in the State of Washington a court can disregard and overturn any decision by a fit custodial parent concerning visitation whenever a third party affected by the decision files a visitation petition, based solely on the judge's determination of the child's best interests. . . .

Turning to the facts of this case, the record reveals that the Superior Court's order was based on precisely the type of mere disagreement we have just described and nothing more. The Superior Court's order was not founded on any special factors that might justify the State's interference with Granville's fundamental right to make decisions concerning the rearing of her two daughters. To be sure, this case involves a visitation petition filed by grandparents soon after the death of their son — the father of Isabelle and Natalie — but the combination of several factors here compels our conclusion that §26.10.160(3), as applied, exceeded the bounds of the Due Process Clause.

First, the Troxels did not allege, and no court has found, that Granville was an unfit parent. That aspect of the case is important, for there is a presumption that fit parents act in the best interests of their children. . . .

Accordingly, so long as a parent adequately cares for his or her children (i.e., is fit), there will normally be no reason for the State to inject itself into the private realm of the family to further question the ability of that parent to make the best decisions concerning the rearing of that parent's children.

The problem here is not that the Washington Superior Court intervened, but that when it did so, it gave no special weight at all to Granville's determination of her daughters' best interests. More importantly, it appears that the Superior Court applied exactly the opposite presumption. In reciting its oral ruling after the conclusion of closing arguments, the Superior Court judge explained:

> "The burden is to show that it is in the best interest of the children to have some visitation and some quality time with their grandparents. I think in most situations a commonsensical approach [is that] it is normally in the best interest of the children to spend quality time with the grandparent, unless the grandparent, [sic] there are some issues or problems involved wherein the grandparents, their lifestyles are going to impact adversely upon the children. That certainly isn't the case here from what I can tell."

The judge's comments suggest that he presumed the grandparents' request should be granted unless the children would be "impact[ed] adversely." In effect, the judge placed on Granville, the fit custodial parent, the burden of disproving that visitation would be in the best interest of her daughters. The judge reiterated moments later: "I think [visitation with the Troxels] would be in the best interest of the children and I haven't been shown it is not in [the] best interest of the children."

The decisional framework employed by the Superior Court directly contravened the traditional presumption that a fit parent will act in the best interest of his or her child. In that respect, the court's presumption failed to provide any protection for Granville's fundamental constitutional right to make decisions concerning the rearing of her own daughters. . . . In an ideal world, parents might always seek to cultivate the bonds between grandparents and their grandchildren. Needless to say, however, our world is far from perfect, and in it the decision whether such an intergenerational relationship would be beneficial in any specific case is for the parent to make in the first instance. And, if a fit parent's decision of the kind at issue here becomes subject to judicial review, the court must accord at least some special weight to the parent's own determination.

Finally, we note that there is no allegation that Granville ever sought to cut off visitation entirely. Rather, the present dispute originated when Granville informed the Troxels that she would prefer to restrict their visitation with Isabelle and Natalie to one short visit per month and special holidays. In the Superior Court proceedings Granville did not oppose visitation but instead asked that the duration of any visitation order be shorter than that requested by the Troxels. . . .

Considered together with the Superior Court's reasons for awarding visitation to the Troxels, the combination of these factors demonstrates that the visitation order in this case was an unconstitutional infringement on Granville's fundamental right to make decisions concerning the care, custody, and control of her two daughters. The Washington Superior Court failed to accord the determination of Granville, a fit custodial parent, any material weight. . . . As we have explained, the Due Process Clause does not permit a State to infringe on the fundamental right of parents to make childrearing decisions simply because a state judge believes a "better" decision could be made. Neither the Washington nonparental visitation statute generally—which places no limits on either the persons who may petition for visitation or the circumstances in which such a petition may be granted—nor the Superior Court in this specific case required anything more. Accordingly, we hold that §26.10.160(3), as applied in this case, is unconstitutional. . . .

Justice SOUTER, concurring in the judgment. I concur in the judgment affirming the decision of the Supreme Court of Washington, whose facial invalidation of its own state statute is consistent with this Court's prior cases addressing the substantive interests at stake. I would say no more. The issues that might well be presented by reviewing a decision addressing the specific application of the state statute by the trial court, are not before us and do not call for turning any fresh furrows in the "treacherous field" of substantive due process.

Justice THOMAS, concurring in the judgment. . . . I agree with the plurality that this Court's recognition of a fundamental right of parents to direct the upbringing of their children resolves this case. . . . I would apply strict scrutiny to infringements of fundamental rights. Here, the State of Washington lacks even a legitimate governmental interest — to say nothing of a compelling one — in second-guessing a fit parent's decision regarding visitation with third parties. On this basis, I would affirm the judgment below.

Justice STEVENS, dissenting. . . . In response to Tommie Granville's federal constitutional challenge, the State Supreme Court broadly held that Wash. Rev. Code §26.10.160(3) (Supp. 1996) was invalid on its face under the Federal Constitution. Despite the nature of this judgment, Justice O'CONNOR would hold that the Washington visitation statute violated the Due Process Clause of the Fourteenth Amendment only as applied. I agree with Justice SOUTER that this approach is untenable.

We are . . . presented with the unconstrued terms of a state statute and a State Supreme Court opinion that, in my view, significantly misstates the effect of the Federal Constitution upon any construction of that statute. . . .

In my view, the State Supreme Court erred in its federal constitutional analysis because neither the provision granting "any person" the right to petition the court for visitation, nor the absence of a provision requiring a "threshold . . . finding of harm to the child," provides a sufficient basis for holding that the statute is invalid in all its applications. I believe that a facial challenge should fail whenever a statute has "a 'plainly legitimate sweep.' " Under the Washington statute, there are plainly any number of cases — indeed, one suspects, the most common to arise — in which the "person" among "any" seeking visitation is a once-custodial caregiver, an intimate relation, or even a genetic parent. Even the Court would seem to agree that in many circumstances, it would be constitutionally permissible for a court to award some visitation of a child to a parent or previous caregiver in cases of parental separation or divorce, cases of disputed custody, cases involving temporary foster care or guardianship, and so forth. As the statute plainly sweeps in a great deal of the permissible, the State Supreme Court majority incorrectly concluded that a statute authorizing "any person" to file a petition seeking visitation privileges would invariably run afoul of the Fourteenth Amendment.

The second key aspect of the Washington Supreme Court's holding — that the Federal Constitution requires a showing of actual or potential "harm" to the child before a court may order visitation continued over a parent's objections — finds no support in this Court's case law. While, as the Court recognizes, the Federal Constitution certainly protects the parent-child relationship from arbitrary impairment by the State, we have never held that the parent's liberty interest in this relationship is so inflexible as to establish a rigid constitutional shield, protecting every arbitrary parental decision from any challenge absent a threshold finding of harm. The presumption that parental decisions generally serve the best interests of their children is sound, and clearly in the normal case the parent's interest is paramount. But even a fit parent is capable of treating a child like a mere possession.

Cases like this do not present a bipolar struggle between the parents and the State over who has final authority to determine what is in a child's best interests. There is at a minimum a third individual, whose interests are implicated in every case to which the statute applies—the child. . . .

. . . A parent's rights with respect to her child have thus never been regarded as absolute, but rather are limited by the existence of an actual, developed relationship with a child, and are tied to the presence or absence of some embodiment of family. These limitations have arisen, not simply out of the definition of parenthood itself, but because of this Court's assumption that a parent's interests in a child must be balanced against the State's long-recognized interests as parens patriae, and, critically, the child's own complementary interest in preserving relationships that serve her welfare and protection. . . .

. . . [P]resumptions notwithstanding, we should recognize that there may be circumstances in which a child has a stronger interest at stake than mere protection from serious harm caused by the termination of visitation by a "person" other than a parent. The almost infinite variety of family relationships that pervade our ever-changing society strongly counsel against the creation by this Court of a constitutional rule that treats a biological parent's liberty interest in the care and supervision of her child as an isolated right that may be exercised arbitrarily. . . . It seems clear to me that the Due Process Clause of the Fourteenth Amendment leaves room for States to consider the impact on a child of possibly arbitrary parental decisions that neither serve nor are motivated by the best interests of the child.

Accordingly, I respectfully dissent.

Justice SCALIA, dissenting. In my view, a right of parents to direct the upbringing of their children is among the "unalienable Rights" with which the Declaration of Independence proclaims "all Men . . . are endowed by their Creator." And in my view that right is also among the "othe[r] [rights] retained by the people" which the Ninth Amendment says the Constitution's enumeration of rights "shall not be construed to deny or disparage." The Declaration of Independence, however, is not a legal prescription conferring powers upon the courts; and the Constitution's refusal to "deny or disparage" other rights is far removed from affirming any one of them, and even farther removed from authorizing judges to identify what they might be, and to enforce the judges' list against laws duly enacted by the people. Consequently, while I would think it entirely compatible with the commitment to representative democracy set forth in the founding documents to argue, in legislative chambers or in electoral campaigns, that the state has no power to interfere with parents' authority over the rearing of their children, I do not believe that the power which the Constitution confers upon me as a judge entitles me to deny legal effect to laws that (in my view) infringe upon what is (in my view) that unenumerated right. . . .

Judicial vindication of "parental rights" under a Constitution that does not even mention them requires (as Justice KENNEDY's opinion rightly points out) not only a judicially crafted definition of parents, but also—unless, as no one believes, the parental rights are to be absolute—judicially approved assessments of "harm to the child" and judicially defined gradations of other persons (grandparents, extended family, adoptive family in an adoption later found to be invalid, long-term guardians, etc.) who may have some claim against the wishes of the parents. If we embrace this unenumerated right, I think it obvious—whether we affirm or reverse the judgment here . . . —that we will be ushering in a new regime of judicially prescribed, and federally prescribed, family law. . . .

Justice KENNEDY, dissenting. . . . The first flaw the State Supreme Court found in the statute is that it allows an award of visitation to a non-parent without a finding that harm to the child would result if visitation were withheld; and the second is that the statute allows any person to seek visitation at any time. In my view the first theory is too broad to be correct, as it appears to contemplate that the best interests of the child standard may not be applied in any visitation case. I acknowledge the distinct possibility that visitation cases may arise where, considering the absence of other protection for the parent under state laws and procedures, the best interests of the child standard would give insufficient protection to the parent's constitutional right to raise the child without undue intervention by the state; but it is quite a different matter to say, as I understand the Supreme Court of Washington to have said, that a harm to the child standard is required in every instance.

Given the error I see in the State Supreme Court's central conclusion that the best interests of the child standard is never appropriate in third-party visitation cases, that court should have the first opportunity to reconsider this case. I would remand the case to the state court for further proceedings. . . .

My principal concern is that the holding seems to proceed from the assumption that the parent or parents who resist visitation have always been the child's primary caregivers and that the third parties who seek visitation have no legitimate and established relationship with the child. That idea, in turn, appears influenced by the concept that the conventional nuclear family ought to establish the visitation standard for every domestic relations case. . . . As we all know, this is simply not the structure or prevailing condition in many households. For many boys and girls a traditional family with two or even one permanent and caring parent is simply not the reality of their childhood. This may be so whether their childhood has been marked by tragedy or filled with considerable happiness and fulfillment. . . .

NOTES AND QUESTIONS

1. Troxel v. Granville produced a fractured decision with a plurality opinion by Justice O'Connor in which three other Justices joined. What differences do you see among the Justices? Are there any principles that can be said to command a majority of the Court?

2. At the time that *Troxel* was decided, all 50 states had statutes that permitted grandparent visitation in at least some circumstances. The *Troxel* decision generated a wave of litigation, with some cases upholding and other cases invalidating the state statutes. Professor Sonya Garza surveyed state court responses to *Troxel* in 2009:

After *Troxel*, the majority of states waited for the challenges to visitation statutes to play out in court. Either through appellate court or supreme court decisions, twenty-one states found their third-party visitation statutes to be constitutional. Only six states found their third-party statutes facially unconstitutional. Nine states found their third-party statutes unconstitutional as applied, and fourteen states made no court determination regarding their third-party visitation statutes. Even in those instances where courts found third-party visitation statutes to be unconstitutional on their face, state legislatures did not always subsequently respond.

The variety among the individual third-party visitation statutes is even more apparent after *Troxel*. While most states limit third-party visitation to grandparents, many include great-grandparents, stepparents, siblings, and third parties who have a significant relationship with the child. For those states that permit third-party visitation, only some states define what is necessary to establish the significant or existing relationship required. Further, some states do not rely on third-party visitation statutes to award visitation; instead, they use the common law doctrines of de facto parenthood, in loco parentis, or psychological parenthood. In addition, even though part of the ultimate holding in *Troxel* articulated a longstanding constitutional presumption that a parent is fit and acts in a child's best interests, twenty-one states do not have such a presumption via statute or common law. Most statutes use a "best interests of the child" standard in third-party visitation cases, but only some states provide factors to be considered by the court, leaving the best interests standard open to interpretation by individual courts. In addition, only a few states require a showing of harm as discussed in *Troxel*.

Sonya C. Garza, The *Troxel* Aftermath: A Proposed Solution for State Courts and Legislatures, 69 La. L. Rev. 927, 940-942 (2009). *See also* Margaret Ryznar, A Curious Parental Right, 71 SMU L. Rev. 127, 128 (2018) (observing that the Supreme Court did not articulate a consistent level of scrutiny for judicial review of restrictions on parental rights and that the federal circuits and the states have varied in their approaches).

3. If third parties requesting visitation must overcome a presumption that the parent's decision is in the child's best interest, what kind of showing would they need to make? What kind of evidence would you advise the grandparents to develop in *Troxel*? In In re R.L.S., 844 N.E.2d 22 (Ill. 2006), the court found that the grandparents, with whom the mother and child had been living at the time of the mother's death in an automobile accident, lacked standing to sue for custody unless they overcame the presumption that the father was willing and able to make day-to-day child care decisions. The court in *R.L.S.* concluded that if the father, who had been living in another state, "is a fit person who is competent to transact his own business, he is entitled to custody." In contrast, the Ohio Supreme Court in Harrold v. Collier, 836 N.E.2d 1165 (Ohio 2005), *cert. denied*, 547 U.S. 1004 (2006), upheld visitation to the grandparents after giving "special weight" to the father's opposition in a case where the mother, who had been living with the 5-year-old and her own parents, died and the father claimed that the grandparents were undermining his relationship with the child. In Smith v. Martin, 222 So. 3d 255 (Miss. 2017), the Mississippi Supreme Court held that a Mississippi statute conferred standing on grandparents as a distinct class but that the trial court must still find that visitation is in the child's interest before awarding visitation. The Idaho Supreme Court, however, struck down the state's grandparent visitation statute on its face because the statute did "not limit standing or provide meaningful guidance for how to apply the best interests test." Nelson v. Evans, No. 49233 (Idaho Supreme Court, Sept. 16, 2022). Michigan upheld the constitutionality of the state's guardianship statute, which required that, for the grandparents to be appointed as the child's legal guardians over a parent's opposition, there must be a showing of permanent residency with the grandparents at the time of the petition. The court reasoned that while parents' are still owed deference in such proceedings, the case could not arise without parental consent or an earlier court ruling establishing the child's residency with the grandparents. In re Guardianship of Versalle, 963 N.W.2d 701 (Mich. App. 2020), *appeal denied*, 972 N.W.2d 846 (Mich. 2022).

4. The *Troxel* decision potentially affects not just grandparent visitation, but whether the courts can recognize the child's interest in a relationship with any nonparent over the parent's objection. *See* David D. Meyer, What Constitutional Law Can Learn from the ALI Principles of Family Dissolution, 2001 BYU L. Rev. 1075; Rebecca L. Scharf, Psychological Parentage, *Troxel*, and the Best Interests of the Child, 13 Geo. J. Gender & L. 615 (2012); Leslie Joan Harris, *Obergefell*'s Ambiguous Impact on Legal Parentage, 92 Chi.-Kent L. Rev. 55 (2017). Stepparents and unmarried partners will be discussed in more depth later in the chapter.

PROBLEMS

1. Consider the facts of Painter v. Bannister on page 413 in Chapter 9. On the facts of that case, would the ruling pass constitutional muster under *Troxel*? Why or why not?

2. Kira and Terry, who have never married, have a daughter, Dakota. Kira and Terry broke up after Terry was arrested and sent to prison while Dakota was still less than a year old. Terry's mother, Brenda, helped take care of Dakota during the period immediately after Dakota's birth when Kira was suffering from post-partum depression, and she has remained close to Dakota ever since. Dakota is now two. After one of her visits to Brenda's home,

Dakota broke out in hives. Kira believes that Brenda was not sufficiently attentive to Dakota's lactose intolerance and refuses to permit Dakota to stay at her grandmother's house, though she permits Brenda to visit Dakota at her house. Brenda, who states that Dakota did not receive milk products during the visit in which she broke out in hives, seeks a court order requiring visitation. She introduces evidence that she has had a close relationship with Dakota since her birth, that Kira's new husband has encouraged Kira to cut off visitation, and that numerous complaints have been filed about Kira's parenting skills with Social Services. What would be the result in a state that requires a showing of detriment to the child to award grandparent visitation? Parental unfitness? Extraordinary circumstances?

3. Sam and Lynn have been raising Sam's biological son, Jason, who is not biologically related to Lynn, together since Jason's birth. They have never married and Lynn has never adopted Jason. Jason's other biological parent has never been involved in his life. Sam and Lynn separate when Jason is 8 years old. If Sam and Lynn live in a state with a third-party visitation statute such as the one at issue in *Troxel*, would the court be able to award Lynn visitation over Sam's objection? If Sam and Lynn had married after Jason's birth, making Lynn a stepparent, would your answer change? If Lynn were recognized as a de facto parent, would your answer change? In each case, what constitutional rights would Sam have to prevent visitation?

B. DETERMINING PARENTAGE IN THE CONTEXT OF CUSTODIAL RIGHTS AND SUPPORT DUTIES

Leslie Joan Harris

Reforming Paternity Law to Eliminate Gender, Status and Class Inequality
2013 Mich. St. L. Rev. 1295, 1299-1302

From very early in English history, the law of paternity sharply distinguished between children born to married and unmarried women, strongly privileging father-child relationships within marriage. This pattern prevailed well into the twentieth century until the Supreme Court began using the Equal Protection Clause to dismantle the distinction. . . .

The husband of a married woman has long been presumed to be the father of her children, a presumption that at common law could be rebutted only by showing that the husband had been out of the kingdom of England for more than nine months.[8] This rule presumed the existence of a biological relationship between the legal father and child at a time when biological truth was often very uncertain, but it also excluded highly reliable evidence that no biological relationship existed (e.g., the mother's testimony), protecting the social relationship between a child and the functional father, as well as the integrity of the marriage. The marital presumption continues to be the law in all states, although in all states it is rebuttable, at least in some circumstances.

In contrast, at common law nonmarital children were bastards, the children of no one,[9] although by the early nineteenth century, these children were recognized as legally related to

---

8. 1 William Blackstone, Commentaries on the Laws of England 457 (Thomas M. Cooley ed., 2d ed. 1872). Lord Mansfield's Rule, first articulated in 1777, prevented either spouse from giving testimony that casts doubt on the husband's biological paternity. Goodright v. Moss, (1777) 98 Eng. Rep. 1257 (K.B.) 1258; 2 Cowp. 591, 592-94.

9. Blackstone at 454, 459.

their mothers in most American states.[10] During the twentieth century, many states revised their laws, allowing nonmarital children to inherit from their fathers in some circumstances, but many states clung to the old rule that nonmarital children had no right to inherit from their fathers, to receive other financial benefits at the deaths of their fathers, or to be supported during their fathers' lives.[11] And in many states unmarried fathers had no legal right to custody or visitation.

This regime began to change in the late 1960s . . . as the Supreme Court started applying the Equal Protection Clause to state statutes that discriminated against nonmarital children and their parents. The first cases held that nonmarital children could not be denied the right to inherit from their parents and receive other death benefits in circumstances when marital children would inherit and receive benefits.[12] Another early case held that if parents of a child born in marriage could sue for the wrongful death of their child, this right had to be extended to nonmarital parents too.[13] In 1972, the Court first considered the custodial rights of nonmarital fathers, ruling in Stanley v. Illinois that a biological father who had lived with his children and their mother over a period of years and acted as a father was entitled to be recognized as the children's legal father in a custody matter.[14]

* * *

Today, some states have eliminated all *legal* differences based on parents' marital status. For example, Section 202 of the Uniform Parentage Act (2017), excerpted below, provides: "A parent-child relationship extends equally to every child, regardless of the marital status of the parent." In addition, the Uniform Parentage Act seeks to make parentage determinations gender neutral, supporting recognition of two men or two women as legal parents of a child.

However, legal distinctions on the basis of marriage and biological parenthood continue to be made for varying purposes in almost all jurisdictions, as you will see. In addition, even in states that have eliminated legal distinctions based on marriage, marital and nonmarital children are still in significantly different positions as a matter of practicality. In all states, a child born to a married woman is at least rebuttably presumed to be the child of her spouse. This means that if no one challenges the presumption, the spouse is the legal parent of the child.

---

10. Michael Grossberg, Governing the Hearth: Law and the Family in Nineteenth-Century America 198-200, 207-15 (1985).

11. *See id.* at 228-33.

12. The Constitution does not bar all distinctions, but it does prohibit distinctions if there is no means by which a nonmarital child can become entitled to the rights of a child born in marriage. Levy v. Louisiana, 391 U.S. 68, 71-72 (1968) (statute limiting inheritance rights to legitimate children unconstitutional because it posed an insurmountable barrier to inheritance); Labine v. Vincent, 401 U.S. 532, 539-40 (1971) (statute denying nonmarital child right to inherit from father who had legitimated her violated equal protection); Weber v. Aetna Cas. & Sur. Co., 406 U.S. 164, 165, 175-76 (1972) (statute denying right of nonmarital children to receive worker's compensation benefits on death of their father violated equal protection); Trimble v. Gordon, 430 U.S. 762, 773-76 (1977) (state law denying nonmarital children right to inherit from father violated equal protection).

[While the Supreme Court in *Levy* did not mention race, Illinois law professor Harry Krause argued in an amicus brief in the case that the statute "discriminates on the basis of race." Brief for NAACP Legal Defense and Educational Fund as Amicus Curiae at 18, Levy v. Louisiana, 391 U.S. 68 (1967) (No. 508), 1968 WL 112827. The brief explained that the discrimination stemmed partly from the fact that disproportionately more Black than white children are born outside of marriage and partly from the fact that "a high percentage (70%) of white illegitimate children are adopted . . . whereas very few (3-5%)" Black children are. As a result, "95.8 percent of all persons affected by discrimination against illegitimates under the statute" are Black. *Id.* at 18-19. The brief concluded, "The classification of illegitimacy . . . is a euphemism" for racial discrimination. *Id.* at 20.—Eds.]

13. Glona v. Am. Guarantee & Liab. Ins. Co., 391 U.S. 73, 76 (1968).

14. 405 U.S. 645, 646, 658 (1972).

However, other processes are required to establish the parenthood of children born to unmarried women, and these processes include consideration of biological paternity. The first part of this section concerns procedures for establishing legal parentage. The second part examines the custodial and related rights of unmarried partners, as well as their duties to support their children.

1. Establishing Legal Parenthood

Despite the variety of ways to establish parentage, marriage is still the most common way to establish a child's second parent, as about 60 percent of children are born to married women whose spouses are presumed to be the legal parents of their children. In most cases, no one tries to rebut the presumption. Traditionally, and still in many states, if unmarried parents marry after their child's birth, the marital presumption also applies to that family. In addition, in many states the marital presumption covers children when a parent dies or the marriage is terminated during the pregnancy. For example, Section 204(a)(2) of the 2017 Uniform Parentage Act extends the marital presumption to births within 300 days of a divorce or the partner's death.

At common law, the only way that an unmarried father could establish his parental status (if he and the mother did not marry) was through a quasi-criminal judicial proceeding called a bastardy action. Its limited purpose was to establish the father's responsibility to support the child when the child would otherwise become dependent on the people of the parish.[15] Today, the modern successor of the bastardy action, called a paternity suit or a filiation suit, is an option in all states, but other procedures are much more commonly used.

In at least 19 states, a man who is not married to a child's mother may nevertheless be presumed to be the father when he has lived with and held out the child as his own.[16] These states are Alabama, California, Colorado, Delaware, Hawaii, Indiana, Massachusetts, Minnesota, Montana, Nevada, New Mexico, Oklahoma, North Dakota, New Hampshire, New Jersey, Pennsylvania, Texas, Washington, and Wyoming. These states vary as to whether they allow proof that the man is not the biological father to rebut the presumption, and whether they apply the holding out rule to same-sex couples. For details on the statutes, *see* Harris, above, 92 Chi.-Kent L. Rev. at 77-80.

However, even these provisions are much less important than they might seem because all states, in compliance with federal law, have statutes that allow mothers and alleged fathers to file signed documents with the state identifying the man as a child's legal father. 42 U.S.C. §666(a)(5) (2022). Once filed, a voluntary acknowledgment of paternity (VAP) becomes final unless one of the parties rescinds it within 60 days, and it must be given the legal effect of a judicial determination of paternity. 42 U.S.C. §666 (a)(5)(D)(ii) (2022). After 60 days, a VAP can be challenged only on the ground of fraud, duress, or material mistake of fact. *Id.* States may not require blood testing as a precondition to signing a VAP, and they must give full faith and credit to VAPs signed in other states. *Id.* §666 (a)(5)(C) (iv) (2022).

VAPs have become easily the most common way to establish the legal parentage of unmarried parents. In 2015, 1.07 of the 1.49 million cases in which paternity was established were

---

15. *See* R.H. Helmholz, Support Orders, Church Courts, and the Rule of Filius Nullius: A Reassessment of the Common Law, 63 Val. U. L. Rev. 431 (1977).

16. Sections 201 and 204 of the 2017 Uniform Parentage Act create such a presumption and require that the spouse have lived with the child during the first two years of the child's life.

done by a VAP.[17] VAPs are most commonly signed at the time of birth at the hospital or other birthing facility. The partner's name can appear on the birth certificate only if a VAP has been filed, or a court or administrative agency has ruled that the partner is a legal parent. 42 U.S.C. §666 (a)(5)(D)(i) (2022). Recent sociological studies show that most unmarried parents are emotionally committed to each other and are living together at birth and want to raise their child together; the high rate at which they sign VAPs at the time of birth reflects such attitudes. *See* Leslie Joan Harris, Voluntary Acknowledgments of Parentage for Same-Sex Couples, 20 Am. U. J. Gender Soc. Pol'y & L. 467, 476-478 (2012); Leslie Joan Harris, Questioning Child Support Enforcement Policy for Poor Families, 45 Fam. L.Q. 157, 166-171 (2011). The Uniform Parentage Act of 2017 makes VAPs gender neutral, allowing same-sex couples to use them to establish parenthood.

Paternity or filiation suits are usually brought as part of child support enforcement proceedings, which are by definition adversarial in form and very often are initiated because the mother and child are receiving public assistance. These suits depend on biological paternity. If a case is contested, the most important evidence, except in very unusual cases, is genetic testing evidence. State law must require that the results of a genetic test to establish paternity will be admitted into evidence if the test is "of a type generally acknowledged as reliable by accreditation bodies designated by the Secretary [of HHS]" and performed by an accredited laboratory. 42 U.S.C. §666(a)(5)(F) (2022). State law must create a rebuttable presumption, or, at the option of the state, a conclusive presumption of paternity "upon genetic testing results indicating a threshold probability that the alleged father is the father of the child." 42 U.S.C. §666(a)(5)(G) (2022).

Many paternity or filiation suits are resolved without genetic testing. In compliance with federal requirements, state laws allow paternity suits to be resolved by a default judgment, and, even if both parties appear, cases can be settled without genetic testing. Alleged fathers who believe that they are in fact biological fathers can be motivated by finances to forgo testing, since a state may recover the costs of testing from the man if paternity is established.

The complexity of parentage law creates many possibilities for uncertainty about the identity of a child's legal parents. Consider, for example, the possibilities under the provisions of the Uniform Parentage Act.

UNIFORM PARENTAGE ACT (2017)
Section 201. Establishment of Parent-Child Relationship

(a) The parent-child relationship is established between an individual and a child by:
. . .

(2) an unrebutted presumption of parentage under Section 204;

(3) an adjudication of the individual's parentage; [or] . . .

(5) an acknowledgment of paternity under [Article] 3, unless the acknowledgment has been rescinded or successfully challenged under Section 505;

. . .

Section 204. Presumption of Parentage

(a) An individual is presumed to be the parent of a child if:

(1) the individual and the woman who gave birth to the child are married to each other and the child is born during the marriage;

17. Off. Child Support Enforcement FY 2015 Preliminary Report, 7 tbl. P-2, http://www.acf.hhs.gov/sites/default/files/programs/css/fy2015_preliminary.pdf.

(2) the individual and the woman who gave birth to the child were married to each other and the child is born within 300 days after the marriage is terminated by death, annulment, declaration of invalidity, divorce, or dissolution[, or after a decree of separation];

(3) before the birth of the child, the individual and the woman who gave birth to the child married each other in apparent compliance with law, even if the attempted marriage is or could be declared invalid, and the child is born during the invalid marriage or within 300 days after its termination by death, annulment, declaration of invalidity, divorce, or dissolution[, or after a decree of separation];

(4) after the birth of the child, the individual and the woman who gave birth to the child married each other in apparent compliance with law, whether or not the marriage is or could be declared invalid, and the individual voluntarily asserted parentage of the child, and:

(A) the assertion is in a record filed with [state agency maintaining birth records];

(B) the individual agreed to be and is named as the child's parent on the child's birth certificate; or

(C) the individual promised in a record to support the child as the individuals; or

(5) for the first two years of the child's life, the individual resided in the same household with the child and openly held out the child as the individual's own. A period of temporary absence is part of the period.

Section 505. Genetic Testing Results; Challenge to Results

(a) Subject to a challenge under subsection (b), a man is identified as the genetic father of a child under this [Act] if the genetic testing complies with this [article] and the results disclose that:

(1) the man has at least a 99 percent probability of genetic paternity, using a prior probability of 0.50, as calculated by using the combined paternity index obtained in the testing; and

(2) a combined paternity index of at least 100 to 1.

(b) A man identified under subsection (a) as the genetic father of the child may challenge the genetic testing results only by other genetic testing satisfying the requirements of this [article] which:

(1) excludes the man as a genetic father of the child; or

(2) identifies another man as the possible genetic father of the child.

Greer ex rel. Farbo v. Greer
324 P.3d 310 (Kan. App. 2014)

ARNOLD-BURGER, J. . . . Jack and Dana married in 2009. After a time, the couple began to experience marital discord, and in August 2011 they separated. Dana moved in with her father, and Jack obtained a divorce attorney and filed for divorce in Missouri.

Shortly after the separation, Dana contacted her long-time acquaintance John and the two entered into a dating relationship. Although John discovered early in the relationship that Dana was married, Dana assured John that she and Jack planned on divorcing. As the relationship progressed, John and Dana discussed a variety of long-term plans, including living together as a family unit with Dana's daughter from a previous relationship. John moved from

Illinois to Kansas during this time. But in February 2012, Jack and Dana reconciled, and Dana ended her relationship with John.

A few weeks later, in March 2012, Dana contacted John and informed him that she was pregnant. John assumed the child was his and informed Dana that he wished to be part of the child's life and help support the child financially.

The child, Emily, was born in October 2012. John discovered the fact of Emily's birth a few weeks later, as his contact with Dana during her pregnancy was inconsistent and Dana had not informed him of Emily's birth. In January 2013, John, Dana, and Emily underwent genetic testing that determined there was a 99.99% probability that Emily was in fact John's biological child. Based on the genetic testing, John filed a paternity suit in Franklin County to establish Emily's legal paternity. In his petition, he asked the court, pursuant to In re Marriage of Ross, 245 Kan. 591, 783 P.2d 331 (1989), "for a hearing to determine it is in the best interests of the minor child to determine paternity [and] to make a finding that petitioner is the natural father." . . .

The *Ross* hearing occurred on June 3, 2013. John, Dana, and Jack each testified. . . . [A] brief overview of the hearing is as follows:

> John testified that, in the time between Emily's birth and the hearing, he had seen Emily approximately 22 times. These visits occurred during time periods in which Jack was temporarily living away from the Greer residence. John explained that during visits he had helped Dana and Dana's older daughter care for Emily and had attempted to establish a parental bond with the baby. John also testified that he had purchased a number of items for Emily and set up a room for Emily in his home. He gave Dana a few items, such as a stroller and car seat, to help her care for the baby. John further stated that he bought formula and diapers for Emily and paid for at least one doctor's visit, although he admitted he never sent Dana money.

Dana did not counter John's version of events in her testimony. However, Dana noted that she felt pressured by her family and John to involve John in Emily's life. Dana acknowledged that she blocked John's phone number because he continued to contact her even after she asked him to stop. Regarding her marriage to Jack, Dana testified that although she and Jack were estranged twice after Emily's birth, they had started seeing a marriage counselor to work on their relationship. Dana emphasized that Jack coparented Emily with her and that, since Emily's birth, Emily and Jack had formed a strong father-child bond. Dana also stated that although she believed Jack's relationship with Emily would not suffer if Emily knew her biological parentage, she worried that forcing a relationship between John and Emily might confuse Emily unnecessarily.

Jack briefly testified, explaining that most people in the community and his personal life understand Emily to be his child. Jack explained that he wanted Emily to grow up in his home as his child and that he wanted John to stop "interfering" with his family. However, he also acknowledged that his feelings about Emily would not change were John part of her life.

After John's attorney closed his argument, the district judge asked the following question:

> The briefs which I received, which were good, were on the issue of the *Ross* hearing, which we're having today, which is whether it's in the best interest of the child for the court to admit the evidence of the genetic testing. . . .

The attorneys appeared to agree that the district court first needed to determine whether consideration of the genetic testing was in Emily's best interests and then, if such consideration was in her best interests, decide which man should be adjudged her legal father.

When the district court reconvened on June 6, 2013, to issue its decision, it began by considering the factors traditionally applied to a *Ross* hearing. After determining that the factors balanced equally between Jack and John, the district judge explained:

. . . I would think that the overall best interest is that—the guardian ad litem I think had a good point that although if I would grant the petition for paternity and moving forward the child would have, Emily would have two fathers, that that might start out as a normal situation or that that would be her paradigm of being normal, that she doesn't really need to have two fathers, and I think I agree with that rationale. . . .

. . . [T]he district court ultimately found that, based on both the evidence and Kansas caselaw, considering the genetic test results was not in Emily's best interests. Based upon that finding, the district court went on to find that all the court was "left with is the presumption of paternity that this child was born of the marriage of Dana Greer and Jack Greer. So that will be the finding and order of the court." . . .

The *Ross* Hearing and Admission of Genetic Test Results

John contends that the district court erred in conducting a *Ross* hearing. John bases this contention on the premise that because the genetic test establishing him as Emily's biological father existed prior to the paternity action, it also established a presumption in his favor. John acknowledges that under the Kansas Parentage Act (KPA), K.S.A. 2013 Supp. 23-2201 *et seq.*, a presumption exists in Jack's favor as well however, John argues that the proper procedural mechanism was not to conduct a *Ross* hearing and exclude the genetic test results but rather to weigh the conflicting presumptions as provided in K.S.A. 2013 Supp. 23-2208(c). . . .

We Examine the Law Regarding Presumptions of Paternity

A paternity proceeding determines who a child's legal father is and, therefore, who will enjoy the rights and responsibilities of legal parenthood. Presumptions of paternity may simultaneously arise in favor of different men. In family law, "[t]here is a strong presumption that a woman's husband is the father of any child born during the marriage." This presumption exists both at common law and statutorily. . . . However, this presumption—also sometimes referred to as the presumption of legitimacy—can, like any other presumption, be rebutted.

But the presumption of legitimacy is not the only statutory presumption in Kansas. In fact, five other presumptions exist in Kansas, including those that arise when "[t]he man notoriously or in writing recognizes paternity of the child" and when "[g]enetic test results indicate a probability of 97% or greater that the man is the father of the child." Additionally, many of the criteria that tend to establish these presumptions overlap, meaning that "[m]ore than one man may be presumed to be the father." Therefore, in the case of conflicting presumptions, "the presumption which on the facts is founded on the weightier considerations of policy and logic, including the best interests of the child, shall control." K.S.A. 2013 Supp. 23-2208(c). A presumption "may be rebutted only by clear and convincing evidence, by a court decree establishing paternity of the child by another man," or as provided by the section of the statute regarding conflicting presumptions.

We Examine the *Ross* Case

Because the district court relied on the *Ross* case to find that admission of the genetic test establishing John as the biological father of Emily was not in Emily's best interests and, therefore, the only remaining presumption was the legitimacy presumption, it is important to review the *Ross* case.

During the marriage of Sylvia and Robert Ross, a child was born. When the couple subsequently divorced, Sylvia was given custody of the child, and Robert was given visitation rights and ordered to pay child support. . . . Sylvia subsequently remarried and was interested in her new husband adopting the child. Two years after her divorce from Robert, Sylvia filed a paternity action under the KPA claiming that Charles, a man she had a sexual relationship with around the time of the child's conception, was the father. Charles had no interest in parenting the child, and he and Sylvia had already discussed whether he would be amenable to relinquishing his parental rights and allowing Sylvia's new husband to adopt the child if it was determined that he was the father. . . .

The court subsequently conducted a hearing to determine paternity but only allowed evidence regarding the child's biological parentage. The court did not accept any evidence regarding the best interests of the child. Charles was determined, by clear and convincing evidence, to be the biological father of the child. Charles was ordered to pay child support, but the court maintained joint custody of the child between Sylvia and Robert, finding that Robert stood in loco parentis.

The Kansas Supreme Court found that the district court abused its discretion by admitting the blood test results without first having a hearing as to whether such testing was in the child's best interests. The court specifically rejected the notion that if blood testing proves the presumed father to be the biological father, the issue of parentage is closed and the necessity for extended evidence as to the child's best interests is precluded. The Supreme Court . . . ordered the district court to conduct a hearing purely based upon the best interests of the child and not to consider the blood tests "until such consideration is determined to be in [the child's] best interest."

A review of the statute in effect at the time of *Ross* is critical to understanding the court's analysis. . . .

Although genetic testing was allowed and could be offered into evidence at the time, it had not yet been elevated to the level of a presumption. The statutes did require a court, either on its own motion or on the motion of any party, to order blood tests "[w]henever the paternity of a child is in issue." But because the shifting of paternity from the presumed father [on the basis of the marital presumption] to the biological father [who did not enjoy a presumption of paternity] could easily be detrimental to the emotional and physical well-being of any child, the Kansas Supreme Court found that prior to ordering a paternity test the court must conduct a hearing to determine the best interests of the child, including the child's physical, mental, and emotional needs. *Ross*, 783 P.2d 331. . . .

WE EXAMINE THE STATUTORY SCHEME SINCE *ROSS*

The applicable provisions of the KPA have changed dramatically since *Ross* and, perhaps in part, in response to it. In 1994, the legislature elevated genetic test results to a presumption of paternity. It also included the "best interests of the child" as a consideration when weighing competing presumptions. The 1994 legislature also specifically provided that "[p]arties to an action may agree to conduct genetic tests prior to or during the pendency of any action for support of a child." . . .

Based upon the current statutes and caselaw, if there is not a genetic test in place at the time the action is filed and a party requests that one be performed, the order for genetic testing must be based on a determination, after a hearing, that such a test is in the best interests of the child. But if the testing is completed before the case is filed, the presumption is elevated to a legal, albeit rebuttable, presumption. . . .

In summary, our Supreme Court's mandate in *Ross* continues to be good law. But the caselaw and statutory changes since *Ross* make it clear that a *Ross* hearing is only required in two very specific situations: when (1) there is not a genetic test resulting in a presumption of paternity performed prior to the filing of the paternity action, or (2) a genetic test was completed prior to the filing of the paternity action but the result is inadmissible due to a proper statutory objection being lodged. In addition, *Ross* would only apply when one man's presumption is at risk of rebuttal; when "no credible evidence exists that child has a presumed father," a *Ross* hearing in advance of admitting a genetic test results is not required.

WE APPLY THE LAW TO THE FACTS

Under the current statutory scheme, . . . the district judge was faced with two competing presumptions: legitimacy and genetic. Both presumptions were in place prior to the filing of the paternity action. The court was required to admit and consider the genetic test results because no objection was lodged as required by K.S.A. 2013 Supp. 23-2212(c). In addition, . . . the parties agreed to genetic testing, and a copy of the report was filed with the court at the same time as the petition to determine paternity. During the hearing, no one disputed the test results and the fact that John was Emily's biological father. A *Ross* hearing to determine whether to *consider* the test results was not required because, given the posture of the case and the lack of objection, the court was required to consider the test results as one of the presumptions of paternity. The court did not disregard the test results due to any concerns about its validity; its validity was not in question. Instead, the court disregarded the test results totally on a *Ross* "best interests of the child" analysis. By not considering the genetic test results, the district court committed an error of law.

Additionally, the district court was required to weigh the competing presumptions and find in favor of the presumption "founded on the weightier considerations of policy and logic, including the best interests of the child." K.S.A. 2013 Supp. 23-2208(c). The district court failed to weigh competing presumptions because it refused to even consider one of the presumptions. This is also an error of law. . . .

At the conclusion of the *Ross* hearing, the district court found that upsetting Jack's presumption of legitimacy was not in Emily's best interests and, accordingly, dismissed the paternity action without considering the genetic test results. Although the court spoke to Emily's best interests, the judge's failure to recognize both competing presumptions, legitimacy and genetic, and then conduct the weighing of presumptions was the cause of the error we have found here.

Accordingly, we reverse the decision of the district court and remand the case for a hearing for the district court to weigh the two competing presumptions as required by K.S.A. 2013 Supp. 23-2208(c).

WE PROVIDE GUIDANCE IN WEIGHING THE CONFLICTING PRESUMPTIONS AND THE BEST INTERESTS OF THE CHILD . . . THE WEIGHTIER CONSIDERATIONS OF POLICY AND LOGIC

The KPA does not designate any one presumption as conclusive, and K.S.A. 2013 Supp. 23-2208(c) requires that when presumptions conflict, "the presumption which on the facts is founded on the *weightier considerations of policy and logic*, including the best interests of the child, shall control." (Emphasis added.)

A few courts around the country have tried to parse the *considerations of policy and logic* language. The Wyoming Supreme Court noted that this language is not only limited to legal policy but "clearly implies that a court should consider the broader sociological and psychological ramifications of its decision as to which man should be adjudicated the legal father." See GDK v. State, Dept. of Family Services, 92 P.3d 834, 839 (Wyo. 2004). The Minnesota Court of Appeals observed that the statutory language embraces "the policy of not unnecessarily impairing blood relationships" and requires that the outcome be "logically based on the facts." In re Paternity of B.J.H., 573 N.W.2d 99, 103 (Minn. App. 1998). Appropriately, the *policy and logic* portion of the inquiry appears in part to be heavily based on a state's individual caselaw and policy.

Several courts, including those in Kansas, have specifically referred to the strength of the presumption of legitimacy. The *Ross* court emphasized that if a blood test proves the presumed father is the biological father, the issue of parentage is not closed. "Though such reasoning promotes judicial economy, it is contrary to our longstanding public policy that a child born during a marriage should not be bastardized." The district court is still required to consider the best interests of the child.

Our Supreme Court has also recognized, in an adoption proceeding, the important rights of biological fathers who promptly assert their rights by taking affirmative steps to show they are fully committed to accepting parenting responsibilities.

> A natural parent's right to the companionship, care, custody, and management of his or her child is a liberty interest. The liberty interest of a natural parent has its origin in the biological connection between the parent and child, but a biological relationship does not guarantee the permanency of the parental rights of an unwed natural father. Rather, the significance of the biological connection is that it offers the natural father an opportunity that no other male possesses to develop a relationship with his offspring. The opportunity is lost, however, if the natural father does not come forward to demonstrate a full commitment to the responsibilities of parenthood.

The West Virginia Supreme Court noted that *both* marriage to the child's mother and "factual, biological parentage" are weighty factors. State ex rel. v. Michael George K., 207 W. Va. 290, 299, 531 S.E.2d 669 (2000). . . .

THE BEST INTERESTS OF THE CHILD

Over the years, courts have distilled the best interests of the child consideration present in paternity cases to include approximately 10 factors. These factors have been summarized as including: (1) whether the child thinks the presumed father is his or her father and has a relationship with him; (2) the nature of the relationship between the presumed father and child and whether the presumed father wants to continue to provide a father-child relationship; (3) the nature of the relationship between the alleged father and the child and whether the alleged father wants to establish a relationship and provide for the child's needs; (4) the possible emotional impact of establishing biological paternity; (5) whether a negative result regarding paternity in the presumed father would leave the child without a legal father; (6) the nature of the mother's relationships with the presumed and alleged fathers; (7) the motives of the party raising the paternity action; (8) the harm to the child, or medical need in identifying the biological father; (9) the relationship between the child and any siblings from either the presumed or alleged father; and (10) whether there have been previous opportunities to raise the issue of paternity.

"Time may be a major factor" in determining best interests, as well as "the notoriety of the child's situation in the community," the stability of the home in which the child will reside, the child's uncertainty regarding the paternity issue, "and any other factors that will maximize the child's opportunities for a successful life."

However, most courts also recognize that a best interests analysis is incredibly fact-specific and rarely limited to a narrow number of factors. In N.A.H. v. S.L.S., 9 P.3d at 363, the Colorado Supreme Court observed that "the whole paternity proceeding [is intended] to be about the best interests of the child." This focus is in part because "[t]he outcome of a paternity action irrevocably alters a child's current family situation and her future." Accordingly, it is clear that courts weighing two or more conflicting presumptions may consider a wide array of nonexclusive factors when deciding which presumption serves the child's best interests.

NOTES AND QUESTIONS

1. In *Greer*, the genetic testing that established biological paternity created a presumption of legal parenthood. What arguments support the biological father's claim that his genetic tie to the child should establish legal parenthood? Once paternity tests establish that someone else is the child's biological father, is that enough to rebut the marital presumption? If not, what policies support the husband's claim of legal parenthood in *Greer*? Do the same policies that underlie the marital presumption support a presumption of paternity based on living with a child and holding out the child as one's own? How, if at all, do these policies apply to same-sex couples in accordance with the Uniform Parentage Act (2017), above?

2. *Greer* holds that when two or more people are presumed to be a child's legal parent, based on conflicting presumptions, the trial court should "find in favor of the presumption founded on the weightier considerations of policy and logic, including the best interests of the child." In most jurisdictions, the usual rule for resolving the problem of conflicting presumptions is to prefer the one best supported by policy and logic; Kansas added "best interests of the child." How does a best-interest analysis differ from consideration of "policy and logic"? What policies are relevant to the determination of parenthood? Upon what basis should the court make the choice between the two possible fathers in *Greer*? If Dana and Jack Greer had divorced instead of reconciling, would the analysis in the case have been different?

3. Note that if the parties in *Greer* had not agreed to genetic testing and if the trial court had not ordered it, only the presumption favoring the mother's spouse would have been at play in the case. Under the *Ross* case, before ordering genetic testing, the trial court would have to have found that this was in the child's best interests. What arguments would support ordering the testing in *Greer*? What arguments would support denying tests?

Recognizing the overarching legal and human importance of genetic testing, Section 502(g) of the Uniform Parentage Act (2017) allows a court to deny an order for testing if the court determines it is not within the child's best interests based on the factors listed in Section 612(3), which include the age of the child, the length of time the presumed or genetic parents have assumed the role of parent, the nature of the relationship between the child and any presumed parent and the harm to the child if that relationship is not recognized, and other "equitable factors" arising from the disruption of the child's relationship with the presumed parent. Under these provisions, should a court have ordered genetic testing on the facts of *Greer*?

4. Until 1980, the California marital presumption was conclusive against all the world if the spouses were cohabiting and the husband was not impotent or sterile. In 1980, the California legislature amended the statute to permit the husband to introduce blood test evidence to rebut the presumption of parentage within two years of the child's birth and in 1981 amended it to give the mother the same opportunity, provided that the biological father files an affidavit acknowledging paternity. The amendments did not give the biological father standing to contest the marital presumption on his own. In Michael H. v. Gerald D., 491 U.S. 110 (1989), the Supreme Court upheld the amended statute against due process challenges brought by a child's undisputed biological father, Michael. He sought to establish paternity because the mother, Carole, and her husband, Gerald, had reconciled and cut off Michael's contact with the child. A majority of the Court rejected Michael's procedural and substantive due process claims. The plurality opinion by Justice Scalia denied that Michael had any constitutional right:

> Where . . . the child is born into an extant marital family, the natural father's unique oppor-
> tunity [to establish a parental relationship with the child] conflicts with the similarly unique
> opportunity of the husband of the marriage; and it is not unconstitutional for the State to give
> categorical preference to the latter. . . .
>
> We do not accept Justice Brennan's criticism that this result "squashes" the liberty that con-
> sists of "the freedom not to conform." It seems to us that reflects the erroneous view that there is
> only one side to this controversy — that one disposition can expand a "liberty" of sorts without
> contracting an equivalent "liberty" on the other side. Such a happy choice is rarely available.
> Here, to provide protection to an adulterous natural father is to deny protection to a marital
> father, and vice versa. If Michael has a "freedom not to conform" (whatever that means), Gerald
> must equivalently have a "freedom to conform." One of them will pay a price for asserting that
> "freedom" — Michael by being unable to act as father of the child he has adulterously begotten,
> or Gerald by being unable to preserve the integrity of the traditional family unit he and Victoria
> have established. Our disposition does not choose between these two "freedoms," but leaves
> that to the people of California.

491 U.S. at 128-130. Justice Brennan dissented for himself and two others, criticizing the
plurality for ignoring the premise "that marriage is not decisive in answering the question
whether the Constitution protects the parental relationship under consideration." *Id.* at 144.

As a practical matter, *Michael H.* left the continued validity of the marital presumption
to the states. At least two state supreme courts have held that their state constitutions, unlike
the federal constitution as interpreted in *Michael H.*, may protect an unwed father's interest in
establishing paternity even though the child's mother is married to another. In the Interest of
J.W.T., 872 S.W.2d 189 (Tex. 1994); Callender v. Skiles, 591 N.W.2d 182 (Iowa 1999) (finding denial of standing to biological father unconstitutional). Other states have done so on
statutory or common law grounds. *See, e.g.*, In C.C. v. A.B., 550 N.E.2d 365 (Mass. 1990).
The majority of states, like Kansas, give the biological father standing to bring a paternity
action, pursuant to a variety of standards. In doing so, some courts have observed that, as a
practical matter, upholding the marital presumption allows the mother to choose who the
father will be. Do you understand what the courts meant? How might that affect the result in
a case like *Greer*? Did the Kansas approach in *Greer* do a better job of recognizing the competing rights of the two men who sought parental status than a decision resolving the case on the
basis of constitutional considerations?

5. State approaches vary considerably. Leslie Harris emphasizes that despite their differences, most states protect the established relationship between a husband and child when the
husband wants the relationship to continue. Leslie Joan Harris, Reforming Paternity Law to
Eliminate Gender, Status and Class Inequality, 2013 Mich. St. L. Rev. 1295, 1312-1316.

Federal law requires that states have "procedures ensuring that the putative father has a
reasonable opportunity to initiate a paternity action." 42 U.S.C. §666(a)(5)(L). If a state subjects the request for a paternity test to a best-interest determination or uses estoppel to preclude rebuttal of the presumption, does this violate this requirement? Does the approach in
Greer solve the problem?

6. For more on the marital presumption, *see* Theresa Glennon, Somebody's Child: Evaluating the Erosion of the Marital Presumption of Paternity, 102 W. Va. L. Rev. 547 (2000);
June Carbone & Naomi Cahn, Marriage, Parentage and Child Support, 45 Fam. L.Q. 219
(2011); Melanie Jacobs, Overcoming the Marital Presumption, 50 Fam. Ct. Rev. 289 (2012);
Douglas NeJaime, Marriage Equality and the New Parenthood, 129 Harv. L. Rev. 1185, 1187
(2016); Jana Singer, Marriage, Biology, and Paternity: The Case for Revitalizing the Marital
Presumption, 65 Md. L. Rev. 246 (2006); Robin Fretwell Wilson, Evaluating Marriage: Does
Marriage Matter to the Nurturing of Children?, 42 San Diego L. Rev. (2005).

Pavan v. Smith
137 S.Ct. 2075 (2017)

Per Curiam. As this Court explained in Obergefell v. Hodges, 576 U.S. [644] (2015), the Constitution entitles same-sex couples to civil marriage "on the same terms and conditions as opposite-sex couples." . . .

The petitioners here are two married same-sex couples who conceived children through anonymous sperm donation. Leigh and Jana Jacobs were married in Iowa in 2010, and Terrah and Marisa Pavan were married in New Hampshire in 2011. Leigh and Terrah each gave birth to a child in Arkansas in 2015. When it came time to secure birth certificates for the newborns, each couple filled out paperwork listing both spouses as parents—Leigh and Jana in one case, Terrah and Marisa in the other. Both times, however, the Arkansas Department of Health issued certificates bearing only the birth mother's name.

The department's decision rested on a provision of Arkansas law, . . . "[i]f the mother was married at the time of either conception or birth," the statute instructs that "the name of [her] husband shall be entered on the certificate as the father of the child." §20-18-401(f)(1). There are some limited exceptions to the latter rule—for example, another man may appear on the birth certificate if the "mother" and "husband" and "putative father" all file affidavits vouching for the putative father's paternity. But as all parties agree, the requirement that a married woman's husband appear on her child's birth certificate applies in cases where the couple conceived by means of artificial insemination with the help of an anonymous sperm donor. . . .

[T]he State defends its birth-certificate law on the ground that being named on a child's birth certificate is not a benefit that attends marriage. Instead, the State insists, a birth certificate is simply a device for recording biological parentage—regardless of whether the child's parents are married. But Arkansas law makes birth certificates about more than just genetics. As already discussed, when an opposite-sex couple conceives a child by way of anonymous sperm donation—just as the petitioners did here—state law requires the placement of the birth mother's husband on the child's birth certificate. And that is so even though (as the State concedes) the husband "is definitely not the biological father" in those circumstances. Arkansas has thus chosen to make its birth certificates more than a mere marker of biological relationships: The State uses those certificates to give married parents a form of legal recognition that is not available to unmarried parents. Having made that choice, Arkansas may not, consistent with *Obergefell*, deny married same-sex couples that recognition.

Gorsuch, J. with whom Justice Thomas and Justice Alito join, dissenting.

Summary reversal is usually reserved for cases where "the law is settled and stable, the facts are not in dispute, and the decision below is clearly in error." Schweiker v. Hansen, 450 U.S. 785, 791 (1981) (Marshall, J., dissenting). Respectfully, I don't believe this case meets that standard.

To be sure, *Obergefell* addressed the question whether a State must recognize same-sex marriages. But nothing in *Obergefell* spoke (let alone clearly) to the question whether §20-18-401 of the Arkansas Code, or a state supreme court decision upholding it, must go. The statute in question establishes a set of rules designed to ensure that the biological parents of a child are listed on the child's birth certificate. Before the state supreme court, the State argued that rational reasons exist for a biology based birth registration regime, reasons that in no way offend *Obergefell*—like ensuring government officials can identify public health trends and helping individuals determine their biological lineage, citizenship, or susceptibility to genetic disorders. In an opinion that did not in any way seek to defy but rather earnestly engage *Obergefell*, the state supreme court agreed. And it is very hard to see what is wrong with this conclusion for, just as the state court recognized, nothing in *Obergefell* indicates that a birth registration regime based on biology, one no doubt with many analogues across the country and throughout history, offends the Constitution. To the contrary, to the extent they speak to the question at all, this Court's precedents suggest just the opposite conclusion. See, *e.g.*, Michael H. v. Gerald D., 491 U.S. 110, 124-125 (1989); Tuan Anh Nguyen v. INS, 533 U.S. 53, 73 (2001). Neither does anything in today's opinion purport to identify any constitutional problem with a biology based birth registration regime. So whatever else we might do with this case, summary reversal would not exactly seem the obvious course.

NOTES AND QUESTIONS

1. What is the purpose of a birth certificate? In *Pavan*, the Court observed that the document is "often used for important transactions like making medical decisions for a child or enrolling a child in school." Other courts have held that a birth certificate is prima facie, but not necessarily conclusive, proof of legal parenthood. *See, e.g.*, In re Raphael P., 118 Cal. Rptr.2d 610 (Cal. App. 2002). State statutes therefore typically tie the ability to list a person's name on a birth certificate to something that gives rise to a presumption of parenthood, such as marriage to the woman giving birth or the signing of a VAP. On what basis would the prima facie case of parenthood created by the birth certificate in *Pavan* be rebuttable in accordance with the majority and dissenting opinions?

2. States that recognize same-sex marriage, civil unions, or domestic partnerships generally extend the marital presumption to same-sex couples. *See, e.g.*, Hunter v. Rose, 975 N.E.2d 857 (Mass. 2012). Is there any basis, after *Pavan*, for any state to refuse to do so? What does the presumption mean in the context of two partners who could not possibly both be genetic parents? What grounds, if any, should be recognized as a basis for rebutting the presumption? Will two men who arrange for the birth of child, genetically related to one of the two men, through a surrogate be entitled to the marital presumption on the same terms as two women, where one of the two women gives birth? *See* Susan Frelich Appleton, Presuming Women: Revisiting the Presumption of Legitimacy in the Same-Sex Couples Era, 86 B.U. L. Rev. 227 (2006); Leslie Joan Harris, *Obergefell's* Ambiguous Impact on Legal Parentage, 92 Chi.-Kent L. Rev. 55, 74 (2017); Douglas NeJaime, The Nature of Parenthood, 126 Yale L.J. 2260, 2295 (2017); June Carbone & Naomi Cahn, Marriage and the Marital Presumption Post-*Obergefell*, 84 UMKC L. Rev. 663, 667 (2016).

Within opposite sex unions, is the marital presumption gender neutral? Consider the differences between application of the marital presumption where the wife conceived a child with a man to whom she was not married versus application of the presumption where the husband conceives a child with a woman to whom he is not married. The obvious difference is that in the case of the husband who conceives a child with a woman to whom he is not married, there is no doubt about the wife's lack of biological connection to the child. In addition, the genetic mother who gives birth may develop a closer tie to the child she bears than a biological father who is not living with the mother during the pregnancy. Should this matter? For discussion of this issue, *see* In re S.N.V., 284 P.3d 147, 151 (Colo. App. 2011).

3. The Arizona Supreme Court concluded that *Pavan* requires extension of the marital presumption to same-sex couples, at least in the circumstances where state law would recognize the husband as the father of a child born to his wife using artificial insemination with donor sperm. The court observed that a "primary purpose of the marital paternity presumption is to ensure children have financial support from two parents" and that extending the

presumption "would better ensure that all children—whether born to same-sex or oppo-site-sex spouses—are not impoverished." In addition, the court wrote that the "the marital paternity presumption also promotes the family unit" and allows "[c]hildren born to same-sex spouses . . . [to] know that they will have meaningful parenting time with both parents even in the event of a dissolution of marriage." McLaughlin v. Jones, 401 P.3d 492 (Ariz. 2017). *See also* LC v. MG & Child Support Enf't Agency, 430 P.3d 400, 418 (Haw. 2018) (holding that, pursuant to the Uniform Parentage Act, the wife of the biological mother is presumed to be the legal parent of a child born during the couple's marriage even though the spouses sep-arated before the child's birth); Treto v. Treto, 622 S.W.3d 397, 403 (Tex. App. 2020) (apply-ing the marital presumption to a same-sex couple). *Cf.* Gatsby v. Gatsby, 495 P.3d 996 (Idaho 2021) (holding that, while the Idaho legislature intended its assisted reproduction statute to apply to all married couples, the same-sex partner without a biological tie to the child could not qualify as a parent because she and her partner had not strictly complied with the statu-tory terms requiring, among other things, that a doctor conduct the insemination). *Gatsby* is discussed in Chapter 14.

PROBLEMS

1. Margaret was married to Frank and having an affair with Harry. When she was three months pregnant, she divorced Frank, and she and Harry were married a month before her child, Carol, was born. Throughout her marriage to Harry, Margaret told him that he was Carol's biological father. When Carol was six weeks old, blood tests were done to determine whether Harry was the biological father, but they were inconclusive. Harry was a loving father who actively cared for Carol. When Carol was 5, Margaret and Harry divorced. Margaret and Carol had nothing to do with Frank after Margaret divorced him.

(a) Seeking to avoid paying child support, Harry offers evidence to rebut the pre-sumption that he is Carol's biological father. In a state that follows the rule that the presumption can be rebutted only if it is in the child's best interest, should the court allow the presumption to be rebutted? How should the court rule in a state that has adopted the rule that says a person may be estopped from denying paternity?

(b) Margaret seeks to introduce evidence that Harry is not Carol's biological father because she does not want him to have parenting time with Carol. In a state that fol-lows the best-interest rule, should the evidence be admitted? Should it be admitted in a state that has adopted the estoppel doctrine?

(c) Would your answers to (a) or (b) change if Harry and Margaret separated when Carol was 5, Harry learned at that time that he was not Carol's biological father, the divorce hearing did not occur until two years later, and by that time Carol was 7 and had not seen Harry in the intervening two years? Would your answers change if Carol identifies Mike, a man with whom Carol had a brief affair around the time of Carol's conception, as the biological father and Mike has developed a relationship with the child and offers to provide support by the time of the hearing?

2. Brenda and Julie had been in an on again–off again relationship for several years when *Obergefell* was decided. They married soon afterwards, but separated two years after the wed-ding. During their separation, Brenda began a relationship with Mark. That relationship ended after Brenda filed domestic violence charges against him. Soon thereafter, Brenda dis-covered that she was pregnant. She told Julie, but not Mark, about the pregnancy. The two women reconciled, and Julie supported Brenda during the pregnancy, accompanied her to the hospital for the birth, selected the child's name (Jenny), and signed the birth certificate.

Brenda has let Mark see Jenny only twice; he initiated a paternity action when Jenny was 8 months old. Brenda has stipulated that she had sexual relations only with Mark during the period in which Jenny was conceived, and that she has never used artificial insemination. Brenda and Julie separated again shortly after Jenny's first birthday, but Julie, who has a close relationship with Jenny, has continued to see her and contribute to her support. Brenda regards Julie as Jenny's parent and has encouraged her continued involvement with the child.

If this action were filed in Kansas, who would be Jenny's presumed parents under the decision in *Greer*? If Mark asked the court to order genetic testing to establish paternity, what standard would apply to his request? If Mark were to introduce genetic tests establishing his paternity, what standard would apply to the determination of parenthood? What would be the "weightier considerations of policy and logic" in these circumstances? What would be in Jenny's "best interest" based on these facts? Would it matter if Julie had filed for divorce, listing Jenny as a child of the marriage?

2. Unmarried Parents' Rights—Adoption and Custody

Historically, unmarried fathers who did not marry the mother had no right to recognition as legal parents, whether or not the mothers were married to someone else. The U.S. Supreme Court held for the first time that the Constitution protects unmarried fathers' custodial rights, at least in some situations, in Stanley v. Illinois, 405 U.S. 645 (1972). In that case, Illinois law provided that, upon the death of an unmarried mother, her children became wards of the state and the state granted custody to a court-appointed guardian. The father, who had lived intermittently with the mother and children for 18 years, received no legal recognition. The Court declared the statute, which failed to accord any unwed father legal status as a parent however devoted to his children, an unconstitutional violation of due process. The Court did not determine, however, whether unmarried fathers, by virtue of the biological tie to the child alone, should acquire parental status.

Consider how the courts in the next two cases deal with that issue.

Lehr v. Robertson
463 U.S. 248 (1983)

STEVENS, J. . . . . Jessica M. was born out of wedlock on November 9, 1976. Her mother, Lorraine Robertson, married Richard Robertson eight months after Jessica's birth. On December 21, 1978, when Jessica was over two years old, the Robertsons filed an adoption petition in the Family Court of Ulster County, New York. The court heard their testimony and received a favorable report from the Ulster County Department of Social Services. On March 7, 1979, the court entered an order of adoption. In this proceeding, appellant contends that the adoption order is invalid because he, Jessica's putative father, was not given advance notice of the adoption proceeding.

The State of New York maintains a "putative father registry." A man who files with that registry demonstrates his intent to claim paternity of a child born out of wedlock and is therefore entitled to receive notice of any proceeding to adopt that child. Before entering Jessica's adoption order, the Ulster County Family Court had the putative father registry examined. Although appellant claims to be Jessica's natural father, he had not entered his name in the registry.

In addition to the persons whose names are listed on the putative father registry, New York law requires that notice of an adoption proceeding be given to several other classes of possible fathers of children born out of wedlock—those who have been adjudicated to be the father, those who have been identified as the father on the child's birth certificate, those who live openly with the child and the child's mother and who hold themselves out to be the father, those who have been identified as the father by the mother in a sworn written statement, and those who were married to the child's mother before the child was six months old. Appellant admittedly was not a member of any of those classes. He had lived with appellee prior to Jessica's birth and visited her in the hospital when Jessica was born, but his name does not appear on Jessica's birth certificate. He did not live with appellee or Jessica after Jessica's birth, he has never provided them with any financial support, and he has never offered to marry appellee. Nevertheless, he contends that the following special circumstances gave him a constitutional right to notice and a hearing before Jessica was adopted.

On January 30, 1979, one month after the adoption proceeding was commenced in Ulster County, appellant filed a "visitation and paternity petition" in the Westchester County Family Court. In that petition, he asked for a determination of paternity, an order of support, and reasonable visitation privileges with Jessica. Notice of that proceeding was served on appellee on February 22, 1979. Four days later appellee's attorney informed the Ulster County Court that appellant had commenced a paternity proceeding in Westchester County; the Ulster County judge then entered an order staying appellant's paternity proceeding until he could rule on a motion to change the venue of that proceeding to Ulster County. On March 3, 1979, appellant received notice of the change of venue motion and, for the first time, learned that an adoption proceeding was pending in Ulster County.

On March 7, 1979, appellant's attorney telephoned the Ulster County judge to inform him that he planned to seek a stay of the adoption proceeding pending the determination of the paternity petition. In that telephone conversation, the judge advised the lawyer that he had already signed the adoption order earlier that day. According to appellant's attorney, the judge stated that he was aware of the pending paternity petition but did not believe he was required to give notice to appellant prior to the entry of the order of adoption.

. . . On June 22, 1979, appellant filed a petition to vacate the order of adoption on the ground that it was obtained by fraud and in violation of his constitutional rights. The Ulster County Family Court . . . denied the petition. . . .

The Appellate Division of the Supreme Court affirmed. . . .

The New York Court of Appeals also affirmed by a divided vote. . . .

THE DUE PROCESS CLAIM

. . . This Court has examined the extent to which a natural father's biological relationship with his illegitimate child receives protection under the Due Process Clause in precisely three cases: Stanley v. Illinois, 405 U.S. 645 (1972), Quilloin v. Walcott, 434 U.S. 246 (1978), and Caban v. Mohammed, 441 U.S. 380 (1979).

Stanley involved the constitutionality of an Illinois statute that conclusively presumed every father of a child born out of wedlock to be an unfit person to have custody of his children. The father in that case had lived with his children all their lives and had lived with their mother for eighteen years. There was nothing in the record to indicate that Stanley had been a neglectful father who had not cared for his children. . . . [T]he Court held that the Due Process Clause was violated by the automatic destruction of the custodial relationship without giving the father any opportunity to present evidence regarding his fitness as a parent.

Quilloin involved the constitutionality of a Georgia statute that authorized the adoption of a child born out of wedlock over the objection of the natural father. The father in that case had never legitimated the child. It was only after the mother had remarried and her new husband had filed an adoption petition that the natural father sought visitation rights and filed a petition for legitimation. The trial court found adoption by the new husband to be in the child's best interests, and we unanimously held that action to be consistent with the Due Process Clause.

Caban involved the conflicting claims of two natural parents who had maintained joint custody of their children from the time of their birth until they were respectively two and four years old. The father challenged the validity of an order authorizing the mother's new husband to adopt the children; he relied on both the Equal Protection Clause and the Due Process Clause. Because this Court upheld his equal protection claim, the majority did not address his due process challenge. The comments on the latter claim by the four dissenting Justices are nevertheless instructive, because they identify the clear distinction between a mere biological relationship and an actual relationship of parental responsibility.

Justice STEWART correctly observed: "Even if it be assumed that each married parent after divorce has some substantive due process right to maintain his or her parental relationship, it by no means follows that each unwed parent has any such right. Parental rights do not spring full-blown from the biological connection between parent and child. They require relationships more enduring." 441 U.S., at 397.

In a similar vein, the other three dissenters in *Caban* were prepared to "assume that, if and when one develops, the relationship between a father and his natural child is entitled to protection against arbitrary state action as a matter of due process." Caban v. Mohammed, 441 U.S. 380, 414.

The difference between the developed parent-child relationship that was implicated in *Stanley* and *Caban*, and the potential relationship involved in *Quilloin* and this case, is both clear and significant. When an unwed father demonstrates a full commitment to the responsibilities of parenthood by "com[ing] forward to participate in the rearing of his child," *Caban*, 441 U.S., at 392, his interest in personal contact with his child acquires substantial protection under the due process clause. At that point it may be said that he "act[s] as a father toward his children." Id., at 389, n.7. But the mere existence of a biological link does not merit equivalent constitutional protection. The actions of judges neither create nor sever genetic bonds. "[T]he importance of the familial relationship, to the individuals involved and to the society, stems from the emotional attachments that derive from the intimacy of daily association, and from the role it plays in 'promot[ing] a way of life' through the instruction of children as well as from the fact of blood relationship." Smith v. Organization of Foster Families for Equality and Reform, 431 U.S. 816, 844 (1977) (quoting Wisconsin v. Yoder, 406 U.S. 205, 231-233 (1972)).

The significance of the biological connection is that it offers the natural father an opportunity that no other male possesses to develop a relationship with his offspring. If he grasps that opportunity and accepts some measure of responsibility for the child's future, he may enjoy the blessings of the parent-child relationship and make uniquely valuable contributions to the child's development. If he fails to do so, the Federal Constitution will not automatically compel a state to listen to his opinion of where the child's best interests lie.

In this case, we are not assessing the constitutional adequacy of New York's procedures for terminating a developed relationship. Appellant has never had any significant custodial, personal, or financial relationship with Jessica, and he did not seek to establish a legal tie until after she was two years old. We are concerned only with whether New York has adequately protected his opportunity to form such a relationship. . . .

After this Court's decision in *Stanley*, the New York Legislature appointed a special commission to recommend legislation that would accommodate both the interests of biological fathers in their children and the children's interest in prompt and certain adoption procedures. The commission recommended, and the legislature enacted, a statutory adoption scheme that automatically provides notice to seven categories of putative fathers who are likely to have assumed some responsibility for the care of their natural children. If this scheme were likely to omit many responsible fathers, and if qualification for notice were beyond the control of an interested putative father, it might be thought procedurally inadequate. Yet, as all of the New York courts that reviewed this matter observed, the right to receive notice was completely within appellant's control. By mailing a postcard to the putative father registry, he could have guaranteed that he would receive notice of any proceedings to adopt Jessica. The possibility that he may have failed to do so because of his ignorance of the law cannot be a sufficient reason for criticizing the law itself. The New York legislature concluded that a more open-ended notice requirement would merely complicate the adoption process, threaten the privacy interests of unwed mothers, create the risk of unnecessary controversy, and impair the desired finality of adoption decrees. Regardless of whether we would have done likewise if we were legislators instead of judges, we surely cannot characterize the state's conclusion as arbitrary.

THE EQUAL PROTECTION CLAIM

. . . The legislation at issue in this case . . . [is] designed to promote the best interests of the child, protect the rights of interested third parties, and ensure promptness and finality. To serve those ends, the legislation guarantees to certain people the right to veto an adoption and the right to prior notice of any adoption proceeding. The mother of an illegitimate child is always within that favored class, but only certain putative fathers are included. Appellant contends that the gender-based distinction is invidious.

As we noted above, the existence or nonexistence of a substantial relationship between parent and child is a relevant criterion in evaluating both the rights of the parent and the best interests of the child. In Quilloin v. Walcott, supra, we noted that the putative father, like appellant, "ha[d] never shouldered any significant responsibility with respect to the daily supervision, education, protection, or care of the child. Appellant does not complain of his exemption from these responsibilities. . . ." 434 U.S., at 256. We therefore found that a Georgia statute that always required a mother's consent to the adoption of a child born out of wedlock, but required the father's consent only if he had legitimated the child, did not violate the Equal Protection Clause. . . .

We have held that these statutes may not constitutionally be applied in that class of cases where the mother and father are in fact similarly situated with regard to their relationship with the child. In Caban v. Mohammed, 441 U.S. 380 (1979), the Court held that it violated the Equal Protection Clause to grant the mother a veto over the adoption of a four-year-old girl and a six-year-old boy, but not to grant a veto to their father, who had admitted paternity and had participated in the rearing of the children. . . .

Jessica's parents are not like the parents involved in *Caban*. Whereas appellee had a continuous custodial responsibility for Jessica, appellant never established any custodial, personal, or financial relationship with her. If one parent has an established custodial relationship with the child and the other parent has either abandoned or never established a relationship, the Equal Protection Clause does not prevent a state from according the two parents different legal rights.

The judgment of the New York Court of Appeals is affirmed.

WHITE, J., with whom MARSHALL, J., and BLACKMUN, J., join, dissenting. . . . It is axiomatic that "[t]he fundamental requirement of due process is the opportunity to be heard 'at a meaningful time and in a meaningful manner.'" As Jessica's biological father, Lehr either had an interest protected by the Constitution or he did not. If the entry of the adoption order in this case deprived Lehr of a constitutionally protected interest, he is entitled to notice and an opportunity to be heard before the order can be accorded finality.

According to Lehr, he and Jessica's mother met in 1971 and began living together in 1974. The couple cohabited for approximately 2 years, until Jessica's birth in 1976. Throughout the pregnancy and after the birth, Lorraine acknowledged to friends and relatives that Lehr was Jessica's father; Lorraine told Lehr that she had reported to the New York State Department of Social Services that he was the father. Lehr visited Lorraine and Jessica in the hospital every day during Lorraine's confinement. According to Lehr, from the time Lorraine was discharged from the hospital until August, 1978, she concealed her whereabouts from him. During this time Lehr never ceased his efforts to locate Lorraine and Jessica and achieved sporadic success until August, 1977, after which time he was unable to locate them at all. On those occasions when he did determine Lorraine's location, he visited with her and her children to the extent she was willing to permit it. When Lehr, with the aid of a detective agency, located Lorraine and Jessica in August, 1978, Lorraine was already married to Mr. Robertson. Lehr asserts that at this time he offered to provide financial assistance and to set up a trust fund for Jessica, but that Lorraine refused. Lorraine threatened Lehr with arrest unless he stayed away and refused to permit him to see Jessica. Thereafter Lehr retained counsel who wrote to Lorraine in early December, 1978, requesting that she permit Lehr to visit Jessica and threatening legal action on Lehr's behalf. On December 21, 1978, perhaps as a response to Lehr's threatened legal action, appellees commenced the adoption action at issue here. . . .

Lehr's version of the "facts" paints a far different picture than that portrayed by the majority. The majority's recitation, that "[a]ppellant has never had any significant custodial, personal, or financial relationship with Jessica, and he did not seek to establish a legal tie until after she was two years old," obviously does not tell the whole story. Appellant has never been afforded an opportunity to present his case. The legitimation proceeding he instituted was first stayed, and then dismissed, on appellees' motions. Nor could appellant establish his interest during the adoption proceedings, for it is the failure to provide Lehr notice and an opportunity to be heard there that is at issue here. We cannot fairly make a judgment based on the quality or substance of a relationship without a complete and developed factual record. This case requires us to assume that Lehr's allegations are true—that but for the actions of the child's mother there would have been the kind of significant relationship that the majority concedes is entitled to the full panoply of procedural due process protections.

I reject the peculiar notion that the only significance of the biological connection between father and child is that "it offers the natural father an opportunity that no other male possesses to develop a relationship with his offspring." A "mere biological relationship" is not as unimportant in determining the nature of liberty interests as the majority suggests.

"[T]he usual understanding of family implies biological relationships, and most decisions treating the relation between parent and child have stressed this element." Smith v. Organization of Foster Families, supra, 431 U.S., at 843. The "biological connection" is itself a relationship that creates a protected interest. Thus the "nature" of the interest is the parent-child relationship; how well developed that relationship has become goes to its "weight," not its "nature." Whether Lehr's interest is entitled to constitutional protection does not entail a searching inquiry into the quality of the relationship but a simple determination of the fact that the relationship exists—a fact that even the majority agrees must be assumed to be established.

Beyond that, however, because there is no established factual basis on which to proceed, it is quite untenable to conclude that a putative father's interest in his child is lacking in substance, that the father in effect has abandoned the child, or ultimately that the father's interest is not entitled to the same minimum procedural protections as the interests of other putative fathers. Any analysis of the adequacy of the notice in this case must be conducted on the assumption that the interest involved here is as strong as that of any putative father. That is not to say that due process requires actual notice to every putative father or that adoptive parents or the State must conduct an exhaustive search of records or an intensive investigation before a final adoption order may be entered. The procedures adopted by the State, however, must at least represent a reasonable effort to determine the identity of the putative father and to give him adequate notice.

II

In this case, of course, there was no question about either the identity or the location of the putative father. The mother knew exactly who he was and both she and the court entering the order of adoption knew precisely where he was and how to give him actual notice that his parental rights were about to be terminated by an adoption order. Lehr was entitled to due process, and the right to be heard is one of the fundamentals of that right, which "has little reality or worth unless one is informed that the matter is pending and can choose for himself whether to appear or default, acquiesce or contest."

. . . The State asserts that any problem [with the New York statute] is overcome by the seventh category of putative fathers to whom notice must be given, namely those fathers who have identified themselves in the putative father register maintained by the State. . . . I have difficulty with this position. First, it represents a grudging and crabbed approach to due process. The State is quite willing to give notice and a hearing to putative fathers who have made themselves known by resorting to the putative fathers' register. It makes little sense to me to deny notice and hearing to a father who has not placed his name in the register but who has unmistakably identified himself by filing suit to establish his paternity and has notified the adoption court of his action and his interest. I thus need not question the statutory scheme on its face. Even assuming that Lehr would have been foreclosed if his failure to utilize the register had somehow disadvantaged the State, he effectively made himself known by other means, and it is the sheerest formalism to deny him a hearing because he informed the State in the wrong manner. . . .

The State's undoubted interest in the finality of adoption orders likewise is not well served by a procedure that will deny notice and a hearing to a father whose identity and location are known. As this case well illustrates, denying notice and a hearing to such a father may result in years of additional litigation and threaten the reopening of adoption proceedings and the vacation of the adoption.

NOTES AND QUESTIONS

1. What was Lehr trying to accomplish by attempting to participate in the adoption proceeding? Was it important that this was a stepparent adoption? Should that matter?

2. What test does *Lehr* adopt for determining when an unmarried father has constitutionally protected custodial rights? What is the basis under this test for custodial rights? What interest of the child (if any) does this test protect? What interests (if any) are disserved?

3. Under the New York statute considered in *Lehr*, when was an unmarried father entitled to notice of an adoption proceeding and an opportunity to participate in it? Is this statute adequate to identify all biological fathers who are entitled to notice under the *Lehr* criteria? Is the statute intended to discover fathers who have developed a substantial relationship with their children as well as those who have not but might want to? Could there be some parents who have developed a relationship with their children who would not be entitled to notice under the statute?

4. Section 201 of the Uniform Parentage Act (2017), set out in part above at page 673, provides that an individual who is presumed to be a child's parent, who has been adjudicated to be a child's parent, or who has signed a voluntary acknowledgment of paternity with the child's mother is entitled to full parental rights, including, of course, notice of adoption and custody proceedings regarding the child. Under the Act, the rights of other putative parents to notice vary depending on the child's age. Sections 402 and 404 provide that if the child is less than a year old, such a putative parent is entitled to notice only if he has registered with the state putative father registry or has commenced a proceeding to adjudicate his paternity. If the child is older than one year, under Section 405, notice must be given to every "alleged father," regardless of whether he has registered. Section 102(3) defines "alleged father" as "a man who alleges himself to be, or is alleged to be, the genetic father or a possible genetic father of a child, but whose paternity has not been determined. The term does not include: (A) a presumed father."

The age-based distinction facilitates adoption of babies while protecting fathers who developed relationships with older children. How would *Lehr* have been decided under the Uniform Parentage Act?

5. Statutes of limitation in a number of states provide that an adoption decree may not be collaterally attacked for any reason, including jurisdictional defects, after the statutory period (often one year) expires. If the court applies such statutes of limitation in a case in which the father has not been notified of the adoption, is the result constitutional? *See* In re M.N.M., 605 A.2d 921 (D.C. App. 1992); In re S.L.F., 27 P.3d 583 (Utah App. 2001).

6. In *Caban* and *Lehr* the unmarried father claimed that the statute unconstitutionally discriminated between mothers and fathers. Why did this claim succeed in *Caban* but fail in *Lehr*?

7. *Lehr* dealt with the rights of the biological father of an older child who never took steps to protect his relationship with the child until adoption was proposed. It did not discuss the rights of fathers of newborns, which the next case considers.

In re Adoption of S.D.W.
758 S.E.2d 374 (N.C. 2014)

EDMUNDS, J. . . . Laura Marshburn Welker ("Welker") and [Gregory] Johns ["Johns"] acknowledge that they are the biological parents of the minor child "S.D.W." Although they neither married nor cohabited, Johns and Welker were involved in an intimate relationship from approximately May 2009 to February or March 2010. Johns described their involvement as "mostly physical," adding that the couple "had sex[ ] 10 to 20 times a week."

During this time, Johns was aware that Welker had given birth about three years previously to a son who was then living with Welker's mother. Understanding that Welker used a form of birth control that he characterized as an "IUD band," Johns did not wear condoms during intercourse with Welker. In the summer of 2009, Welker became pregnant and she and Johns decided that she would have an abortion. After that pregnancy was terminated, Welker told Johns that she was using another form of birth control. According to Johns: "It's either a shot or a patch. I know she wasn't taking pills every day, that I do know. I don't remember seeing a patch, but I remember we were talking about it, but I'm—I would say it was a shot, a birth control shot." Johns continued his practice of not wearing a condom.

At some time around the end of January 2010, Johns broke up with Welker. Even so, until early March 2010, they engaged in additional acts of sexual intercourse during three to five visits Welker made to Johns's home. Thereafter, Welker cut off all contact with Johns, and except for Johns's birthday on 26 November 2010 when Welker stopped by his home to mark the occasion with another act of sexual intercourse, there was no further communication between them until late April 2011.

In the interim, Welker gave birth to S.D.W. on 10 October 2010. The next day, 11 October, she executed an "Affidavit of Parentage" incorrectly naming "Gregory Thomas James" as the father and leaving blank the line for the father's last known address. At the same time, she executed a Department of Social Services form relinquishing custody of S.D.W. to adoption agency Christian Adoption Services, Inc. ("the agency") through its director, James M. Woodward. The agency identified Benjamin Allen Jones and Heather Pitts Jones ("the Joneses" or "petitioners") as prospective adoptive parents for S.D.W., and on 12 October, the infant was placed in their custody, where he has remained. On 27 October, Welker signed a form provided by the agency titled "Birth Father Information," in which she again misidentified the father as "Gregory Thomas James."

The Joneses filed a petition to adopt S.D.W. on 2 November 2010. The agency, relying on the false name provided by Welker, attempted to locate the biological father. On 16 November 2010, after failing to find "Gregory Thomas James," the agency filed a petition to terminate the parental rights of the absent father. . . .

In late April 2011, Johns first heard that Welker had given birth. After calling Welker on 25 April 2011 and confirming with her both that the child was his and that she had placed the child for adoption, Johns took steps to assert his intention to obtain custodial rights of S.D.W. and to prevent the adoption from proceeding. Welker also contacted the agency in late April to disclose Johns's correct identity. . . .

On 19 September 2011, petitioners . . . moved for summary judgment, contending that Johns had failed to carry his burden of showing his consent was required. . . . The . . . statute provides, in pertinent part regarding an agency placement:

> Unless consent is not required under G.S. 48-3-603, a petition to adopt a minor may be granted only if consent to the adoption has been executed by . . . [a]ny man who may or may not be the biological father of the minor but who . . . [b]efore the earlier of the filing of the petition or the date of a hearing under G.S. 48-2-206, has acknowledged his paternity of the minor and . . . [h]as provided, in accordance with his financial means, reasonable and consistent payments for the support of the biological mother during or after the term of pregnancy, or the support of the minor, or both, which may include the payment of medical expenses, living expenses, or other tangible means of support, and has regularly visited or communicated, or attempted to visit or communicate with the biological mother during or after the term of pregnancy, or with the minor, or with both. . . .

A hearing was held on 6 January 2012. . . . At the conclusion of the hearing, Judge Trosch in open court entered an order allowing the adoption to proceed without Johns's consent and denying all motions made by him. . . .

In its conclusions of law, the trial court stated that:

> A putative Father who engages in a sexual relationship with a woman multiple times without benefit of contraception is on notice that a child may result from the sexual relationship and must make diligent inquiry to discover the existence of his child in order to establish a Constitutional Parental Right regarding that Minor Child. . . .

Johns appealed to the Court of Appeals, which reversed. . . .

The initial question we must consider is "the extent to which a natural father's biological relationship with his child receives protection under the Due Process Clause." Lehr v. Robertson, 463 U.S. 248, 258, 103 (1983). . . .

. . . After acknowledging that "[t]he intangible fibers that connect parent and child . . . are sufficiently vital to merit constitutional protection in appropriate cases," the Court limited the reach of such protection because " 'it by no means follows that each unwed parent has any such right. *Parental rights do not spring full-blown from the biological connection between parent and child. They require relationships more enduring'* ". . . .

Against this backdrop, we now turn to Johns's case. Recognizing the concern for a biological father's interest identified in *Lehr*, which exists only in those men who have "grasp[ed] that opportunity [to develop a relationship with their offspring] and accept[ed] some measure of responsibility for the child's future," North Carolina has adopted a statutory framework designed to protect "both the interests of biological fathers in their children and the children's interest in prompt and certain adoption procedures." Like the New York statute, the North Carolina statute designates classes of biological fathers entitled to notice.

However, as the Supreme Court noted in *Lehr*, statutes that establish classes of biological fathers entitled to notice nevertheless may fail constitutional scrutiny . . . if the qualifications for notice are beyond the control of an interested putative father. Even though the question of Johns's rights as a biological father are raised in the context of consent under N.C.G.S. §48-3-601, while Lehr's rights were considered under a New York statute dealing with notice, that difference is insignificant because notice and consent are intertwined. A father who has not received notice cannot give or withhold consent. . . .

Johns's challenge arises under the second *Lehr* inquiry, whether the qualification for notice was beyond his control. Specifically, he argues that he was deprived of knowledge of S.D.W.'s birth and denied the opportunity to demonstrate his commitment as a parent within the time provided by the statute. As we consider this contention, we observe that Johns's case can be distinguished from *Lehr* on the grounds that Welker took steps to disguise Johns's identity and failed to advise Johns of the child's birth when given the opportunity. In contrast, the Supreme Court's recitation of the facts in *Lehr* noted that "[t]here is no suggestion in the record that [the mother] engaged in fraudulent practices that led [Lehr] not to protect his rights." Accordingly, we must consider whether, under the facts presented here, obtaining notice of S.D.W.'s birth was beyond Johns's control.

Johns contends that petitioners urge us to adopt a rule that an act of sex is by itself notice of a possible resulting pregnancy. We instead decide this case on the basis of the facts as applied to the statutes. Both parents demonstrated troubling behavior. Welker provided a false name for the father, both when S.D.W. was born and again later when she signed the adoption service's "Birth Father Information" form, obstructing official efforts to locate the father. When she visited Johns to celebrate his birthday less than two months after S.D.W. was born, she kept the news of the birth to herself.

Johns, on the other hand, demonstrated only incuriosity and disinterest. He knew that Welker was fertile because she already had a child when they met. He knew that, despite Welker's purported use of birth control, he had impregnated her once, leading to an abortion. He assumed that her subsequent birth control methods would be effective without making detailed inquiry. He and Welker continued an active sex life, even after they broke up. From Johns's perspective, the sex was unprotected and contraception was wholly Welker's responsibility. The burden on him to find out whether he had sired a child was minimal, for he knew how to contact Welker. All he had to do was ask, for when he finally did call her, she told him. All the while, S.D.W. continued to live and bond with his adoptive parents.

From this dreary record we conclude that, despite our concern over Welker's behavior, nothing she did or failed to do placed Johns in a position in which "qualification for notice" of the existence of S.D.W. was "beyond [his] control" during the relevant statutory time frame. Accordingly, we conclude both that Johns had the opportunity to be on notice of the pregnancy and that he failed to grasp that opportunity by taking any of the steps that would establish him as a responsible father. Because of his passivity in the face of ample evidence that Welker may have become pregnant with his child and given birth, Johns does not fall into the class of protected fathers who may claim a liberty interest in developing a relationship with a child, and thus he was not deprived of due process. We reverse the decision of the Court of Appeals.

JACKSON, J., dissenting. . . . Central to the majority's analysis is the conclusion that Johns does not have a claim based upon federal or state substantive due process because, "under the facts presented here, obtaining notice of S.D.W.'s birth was [not] beyond Johns's control." As the majority notes, the key precedent in this case is the United States Supreme Court's opinion in Lehr v. Robertson. The majority has correctly recounted the facts and procedural history in that case, with one significant exception. . . . What the majority discounts from its analysis . . . is that *Lehr* established that biological fathers possess at least an "inchoate" interest in their offspring, which is constitutionally entitled to at least some measure of protection. . . . [P]ursuant to *Lehr*, any statutory framework, on its face and as applied, must respect that inchoate interest by allowing biological fathers to "grasp[ ] th[e] opportunity" to develop that interest into a relationship more substantial and more enduring. The issue here, then, is whether the opportunities afforded to Johns in this case were adequate to protect that interest.

I conclude that they were not. While the majority also has accurately recounted the facts and circumstances that preceded S.D.W.'s birth and the filing of the petition for adoption, I think several of these facts do not support the majority's conclusion, and some likely undermine it. First, the majority notes that Welker told defendant that she was using birth control, specifically an intrauterine device, a hormonal patch, or a hormonal shot. However, despite this, the majority concludes that Johns should have been on notice, in part because he did not use condoms *in addition to* one of these other methods of birth control. In my view, it is unrealistic to require potential biological fathers to use multiple, redundant forms of contraception or risk losing any rights they might have to raise and care for any children that result from this (protected) sexual activity.

Second, the majority opines that defendant should have been aware of Welker's continued fertility because he previously had impregnated her, and they had decided together that she would get an abortion. My reading of the majority opinion suggests that this history should have urged Johns to remain in contact with Welker and affirmatively inquire whether she was pregnant with his child, even after their romantic relationship ended; however, in my view, this prior incident argues to the contrary. Because Welker previously informed Johns when she became pregnant, it was reasonable for him to believe that she would tell him if she became pregnant again.

Third, Welker declined to tell Johns about her pregnancy or the birth of S.D.W., despite having every opportunity to do so. Welker knew during the entire duration of the pregnancy that Johns was the biological father. She knew his address: Johns lived at the same apartment for several years, including at the time of S.D.W.'s birth and adoption, and Welker visited him there over one hundred times during the course of their relationship. She knew his home telephone number and his cell phone number, both of which remained unchanged for several years (though she changed her own). In short, if Welker had wanted to contact Johns, she easily could have done so.

Fourth, and perhaps most important, Welker actively concealed her pregnancy from Johns. Welker listed no father on the birth certificate, despite knowing that Johns is the biological father. Later, when asked by the adoption agency to provide the biological father's name on the "Affidavit of Parentage," she falsely put "Gregory Thomas James," rather than "Gregory Joseph Johns." She repeated that falsehood two weeks later when filling out the adoption agency's "Birth Father Information" form. Then, when Johns learned through rumor that Welker had been pregnant, she initially denied it to him as well. Only when he pressed her did she finally admit that he is, in fact, the biological father of S.D.W. In light of these facts, it is reasonable to doubt whether Welker would have told Johns about the pregnancy, even if he had questioned her about this subject following their breakup.

For these reasons I conclude that the majority's opinion allowing the adoption to proceed without Johns's consent is not in harmony with the Supreme Court's opinion in Lehr v. Robertson and imposes unrealistic requirements on potential biological fathers. . . . Accordingly, I respectfully dissent.

NOTES AND QUESTIONS

1. The judges in *S.D.W.* disagree about whether the biological father had a sufficient opportunity to establish a relationship with his child. How would you describe their disagreement? In accordance with the views of the majority, what should the father have done to preserve his parental status? In accordance with the views of the dissent, what opportunity should the father have been given to develop a relationship with the child in order to vindicate his constitutional rights?

2. If you represented a mother who wished to place her child for adoption in North Carolina, what obligations would you advise her that she has toward the biological father? Is she obligated to tell him about the pregnancy? About the birth? About her plans to place the child for adoption? How would you explain to her the consequences of lying about the father's identity? If the dissent in *S.D.W.* were the governing law, how would you answer these questions?

In a Missouri case, an attorney represented a woman who wished to place a child for adoption knowing that the biological father would not consent. He advised her to take a "passive strategy," in which he and the mother "would 'actively do nothing' to communicate with the expectant father or his counsel, and would not advise the expectant father or his counsel of adoption plans, the actual birth of the child, and the institution of any legal proceedings." The attorney and the mother followed this strategy even though the father's attorney clearly communicated to the mother's attorney that his client wished to seek custody of the child and would not consent to an adoption. The mother (who had given the father a due date later than the time of the actual birth) then accurately testified that the father had not contacted her after the birth nor made any effort to assert his parental rights without telling the court that she had never informed him of the birth.

Has the attorney committed any ethical violations in giving his client such advice? Did he have any obligation to inform the father's counsel, who called him during this period, of the child's birth? *See* In re Krigel, 480 S.W.3d 294, 306 (Mo. 2016). *See* Chapter 11, Section A on disciplining lawyers for ethics violations.

3. Would the father in *S.D.W.* have been entitled to notice of his baby's adoption under the Uniform Parentage Act, note 4, above?

States vary greatly in the extent to which they give unmarried fathers the right to prevent adoption of their children by withholding consent. A number of states have adopted tests that require the biological father to demonstrate a commitment to the child before he can prevent an adoption. *See, e.g.*, Racine v. Nelson, 378 S.W.3d 93, 103 (Ark. 2011); Adoption of Michael H., 898 P.2d 891 (Cal. 1995) (en banc); In re C.L.O., 41 A.3d 502, 520 (D.C. 2012); Matter of Adoption of Doe, 543 So. 2d 741 (Fla. 1989); In re Adoption of J.S., 358 P.3d 1009 (Utah 2014). Professor Mary Beck calls this "prenatal abandonment theory" and reports that 34 states have adopted some version of the theory. Mary M. Beck, Prenatal Abandonment: "Horton Hatches the Egg" in the Supreme Court and Thirty-Four States, 24 Mich. J. Gender & L. 53, 57 (2017).

In contrast, in some states, once the fact of paternity is established, the father's rights are the same as those of the mother. *See* Laura Oren, Unmarried Fathers and Adoption: "Perfecting" or "Abandoning" an Opportunity Interest, 36 Cap. U. L. Rev. 253 (2007); Jeffrey A. Parness, Adoption Notices to Genetic Fathers: No to Scarlet Letters, Yes to Good-Faith Cooperation, 36 Cumb. L. Rev. 63 (2006). If you practiced in a state with this rule, how would you advise the unmarried father? The would-be adoptive parents?

4. On unwed fathers' rights generally, *see* Nancy E. Dowd, Fathers and the Supreme Court: Founding Fathers and Nurturing Fathers, 54 Emory L.J. 1271 (2005); James G. Dwyer, A Constitutional Birthright: The State, Parentage, and the Rights of Newborn Persons, 56 UCLA L. Rev. 755 (2009); Leslie J. Harris, A New Paternity Law for the Twenty-first Century: Of Biology, Social Function, Children's Interests, and Betrayal, 44 Willamette L. Rev. 297 (2007); Jennifer S. Hendricks, Fathers and Feminism: The Case Against Genetic Entitlement, 91 Tul. L. Rev. 473 (2017); Clare Huntington, Postmarital Family Law: A Legal Structure for Nonmarital Families, 67 Stan. L. Rev. 167 (2015); Serena Mayeri, Foundling Fathers: (Non-)marriage and Parental Rights in the Age of Equality, 125 Yale L.J. 2292, 2368 (2016); Barbara B. Woodhouse, Hatching the Egg: A Child-Centered Perspective on Parents' Rights, 14 Cardozo L. Rev. 1747 (1993). For a discussion of these issues in child maltreatment cases, *see* Leslie Joan Harris, Involving Nonresident Fathers in Dependency Cases: New Efforts, New Problems, New Solutions, 9 J.L. Fam. Stud. 281 (2007).

5. The European Court of Human Rights has also recognized that the European Convention for the Protection of Human Rights and Fundamental Freedoms protects the relationship of the father and child. *See* Sahin v. Germany, No. 30943/96, Judgment 11/10/2001, Sommerfeld v. Germany, No. 31871/96, Judgment 11/10/2001, Hoffman v. Germany, No. 34045/96, Judgment 11/10/2001 (finding that a German law that gave mothers custody of children born outside marriage and the right to determine whether the father could visit violated the Convention). The judgments are available from the Court's website at http://www.echr.coe.int/Eng/Judgments.htm. In 1998, German law was amended to provide that the father and mother share parental rights and that they have joint custody with regard to children born outside marriage. *See also* Koychev v. Bulgaria, No. 32495/15, Judgment 13.10.2020. (holding that Bulgaria's failure to recognize paternity of biological father of child born into the mother's marriage to a different man violated the Convention).

The European Court of Human Rights has ruled that, under Article 8, children have a right to identity that includes a right to determine, though DNA testing, the identity of their deceased fathers even if the "child" is 60 years old (Jaggi v. Switzerland, No. 58757/00, Judgment July 13, 2006). Alleged fathers also have a right of access to DNA testing to disprove paternity established through the marital presumption (Tavli v. Turkey, No 11449/02, Judgment Nov. 9, 2006; Mizzi v. Malta, 26111/02 Judgment Dec. 1, 2006), and the statute of limitations cannot bar an action where the alleged father did not have reason to suspect he might not be a biological father until after the time period had elapsed (Shofman v. Russia, No. 74826/01, Judgment Nov. 24, 2005). Alleged fathers further have a corresponding right to establish paternity that cannot be limited to cases in which the mothers agree or state authorities choose to pursue a paternity action (Rozanski v. Poland, No. 55339/00, Judgment May 18, 2006). Fathers' rights to establish biological paternity cannot be terminated simply because another man has been recognized as a legal father. (L.D. and P.K. v. Bulgaria, Nos. 7949/11 and 45522/13, Judgment Aug. 12, 2016).

PROBLEMS

1. Madelyn and Frank were dating. Madelyn told Frank that she was pregnant, but he seemed indifferent. She told him that she intended to place the baby for adoption, and he was silent. After the baby was born, Frank visited Madelyn and the baby in the hospital once, but he did not provide any financial support to Madelyn or the baby during the pregnancy or after the birth. Madelyn placed the child with an adoption agency, relinquishing her parental rights, when the baby was three days old. Madelyn told the agency that Frank was the father, and a representative of the agency contacted him. He refused to sign a form consenting to the baby's adoption but said that he would not interfere. The agency placed the baby for adoption with the Patrick family. When the baby was seven months old, Frank filed a petition seeking custody or visitation of the baby. The Patricks and the adoption agency responded by filing an adoption petition, alleging that Frank's consent was not required. Under *S.D.W.*, is his consent required?

2. While Dawn was separated from her longtime partner, Morgan, she began living with Jerry and became pregnant by him. Three months later she moved back in with Morgan and gave birth to a son shortly after she and Morgan married. From the time Jerry first learned of the pregnancy, he took parenting classes, purchased items for the baby for his house, and took other steps to prepare himself for fatherhood. He tried unsuccessfully to see Dawn after she returned to Morgan and to persuade Dawn and Morgan to let him visit the baby. Jerry has now filed a paternity suit under the Uniform Parentage Act seeking a declaration of paternity and visitation rights. What arguments should Dawn and Morgan, who want to keep Jerry out of their lives, make? How should Jerry respond?

3. Biological Parenthood and Child Support

Legal parenthood is not always a voluntary status. A major impetus in the evolving law of parentage over the last quarter-century, particularly as the number and needs of nonmarital children have increased, has been the effort to establish duties of child support. While today we consider such rights to be the most important claim of a child against parents, the common law did not recognize a generally applicable, legally enforceable support duty for any parent. The modern efforts to enhance the effectiveness of child support enforcement coincided with the expansion of welfare benefits and the desire to protect the public fisc. *See generally* Leslie J. Harris, Dennis Waldrop & Lori R. Waldrop, Making and Breaking Connections Between Parents' Duty to Support and Right to Control Their Children, 60 Or. L. Rev. 691, 692-696 (1990). As recently as 1971 some states still imposed no generally applicable support duty on unmarried fathers. Harry Krause, Illegitimacy: Law and Social Policy 22 (1971). In Gomez v. Perez, 409 U.S. 535 (1973), however, the Supreme Court held that denying a nonmarital child the right to support from the father when marital children had such a right violates the equal protection clause.

Current policy trends contrast sharply with the common law reluctance to enforce parental support duties, including the duties of unmarried fathers. The general rule is that proof of biological parenthood is sufficient for imposing a support duty, and courts and legislatures are extremely reluctant to excuse this duty. The principle of holding biological fathers responsible for supporting their children has resulted in some extreme judicial holdings, perhaps the most well-known of which are the "statutory rape" rule and the "lie about contraception" rule. First, applying the statutory rape rule, a number of courts have held that teenage and even pre-teen boys, too young to consent legally to sexual intercourse, were liable for child support for their children born to older girls and adult women. One court reached this conclusion even though it expressly acknowledged that there was very little chance that any money would ever be collected. The courts in these cases have emphasized that the right to support is the right of the child. San Luis Obispo County v. Nathaniel J, 57 Cal. Rptr. 2d 843 (Cal. App. 1996) (15-year-old boy who had sex with a 34-year-old woman); *see also* Dep't of Revenue v. Miller, 688 So. 2d 1024 (Fla. App. 1997) (15-year-old boy and 20-year-old woman); Kansas ex rel. Hermesmann v. Seyer, 847 P.2d 1273, 1279 (Kan. 1993) (12-year-old boy held liable for support, even though the state welfare office conceded that there was very little chance any money would be collected). For a history of the policies underlying these cases, *see* Michele Goodwin, Law's Limits: Regulating Statutory Rape Law, 2013 Wis. L. Rev. 481.

Second, in a number of cases from around the country, biological fathers have argued that they should not be required to pay child support because the mother intentionally lied about using birth control. Courts do not find this to be fraud or say that, even if it is, excusing the man from the child support obligation is not the remedy. *See, e.g.*, Erwin L.D. v. Myla Jean L., 847 S.W.2d 45, 46 (Ark. App. 1993); Stephen K. v. Roni L., 164 Cal. Rptr. 618, 619-621 (Cal. App. 1980); Wallis v. Smith, 22 P.3d 682 (N.M. 2001); Hughes v. Hutt, 455 A.2d 623 (Pa. 1983).

In a more sophisticated attempt to avoid liability, the biological father in L. Pamela P. v. Frank S., 449 N.E.2d 713 (N.Y. 1983), argued that he had a constitutionally protected right to choose whether to be a parent and that finding him to be the child's legal father for purposes of the support duty unconstitutionally infringed upon that right. The New York Court of Appeals rejected the argument, saying that a man has a right to decide whether to be a *biological* parent, but that the Constitution only protects against governmental interference with private choice. The court said that in this case Pamela, a private individual, interfered with his choice, and that the Constitution provides no redress for that. The Sixth Circuit in Dubay v. Wells, 506 F.3d 422 (6th Cir. 2007), agreed with the father that the critical question in such a case is whether the man is the child's legal father, an issue determined by state law, not by the mother. However, the court also rejected the man's equal protection argument, finding that the statutory provision making him the child's legal father was rationally related to the state's interest in "ensur[ing] that the minor children born outside marriage are provided with support and education."

Alleged fathers who turn out not to be biologically related to the child have been somewhat more successful in recovering in tort for paternity fraud, though many states reject such causes of action. *See, e.g.*, Dier v. Peters, 815 N.W.2d 1, 4 (Iowa 2012); Hodge v. Craig, 382 S.W.3d 325 (Tenn. 2012) (awarding damages for paternity fraud). These and related issues are discussed in Donald C. Hubin, Daddy Dilemmas: Untangling the Puzzles of Paternity, 13 Cornell J.L. & Pub. Pol'y 29 (2003); Fernanda G. Nicola, Intimate Liability: Emotional Harm, Family Law, and Stereotyped Narratives in Interspousal Torts, 19 Wm. & Mary J. Women & L. 445, 449 (2013); Vanessa S. Browne-Barbour, "Mama's Baby, Papa's Maybe": Disestablishment of Paternity, 48 Akron L. Rev. 263, 303 (2015); Susan Ayres, Paternity Un(Certainty): How the Law Surrounding Paternity Challenges Negatively Impacts Family Relationships and Women's Sexuality, 20 J. Gender Race & Just. 237 (2017). For a comprehensive discussion of the role of deception in family relationships, *see* Jill Hasday, Intimate Lies and the Law (2019). For a discussion of the implications of surprise results from DNA testing on child support liability, *see* Sean Hannon Williams, DNA Dilemmas, 40 Yale L. & Pol'y Rev. 536 (2022).

In child support cases, as in custody and visitation cases, mothers have sometimes argued that a man should be estopped to deny paternity because he represented that he would act as the child's parent and the mother or child detrimentally relied on the representation. In other cases, mothers have argued that their partner stands in loco parentis to the child and so has a support duty. While some courts have held that these allegations state a claim for relief, they typically require a very strong showing of detrimental reliance on the man's representations that he would act as the father. *See, e.g.*, M.H.B. v. H.T.B., 498 A.2d 775 (N.J. 1985); A.S. v. I.S., 634 Pa. 629, 130 A.3d 763 (Pa. 2015); *see also* Margaret Mahoney, Support and Custody Aspects of the Stepparent-Child Relationship, 70 Cornell L. Rev. 38 (1984). For example, in Sheetz v. Sheetz, 63 N.E.3d 1077, 1078 (Ind. App. 2016) (finding that husband agreed to raise the child as his own, did so for 12 years, and told the wife not to contact the biological father, not to seek support from him, and not to institute paternity proceedings).

The legal issue linking legal paternity and child support duties that is most frequently litigated today is under what circumstances paternity can be disestablished. We have already examined an aspect of this issue above, considering challenges to presumptions of paternity, particularly the presumption based on marriage. Paternity determinations that are theoretically more conclusive, those based on judgments or voluntary acknowledgments, are also commonly the subject of disputes. The first issue in such challenges is often whether a court will order genetic testing.

McGee v. Gonyo
140 A.3d 162 (Vt. 2016)

EATON, J. . . . The facts may be summarized as follows. The child, a girl, was born on May 27, 2011. Shortly thereafter, on June 6, 2011, the child's mother and defendant filed a Voluntary Acknowledgment of Parentage (VAP) form with the Department of Health, Agency of Human Services. Both parties signed the form, which stated that they "voluntarily and without coercion, and of our own free will, hereby acknowledge that we are the biological parents of the child" and understand and accept "the legal rights and responsibilities that come with being a parent," including rights to custody, visitation, and notice before the child may be adopted. The child's birth certificate identified mother and defendant as the child's parents.

Mother and defendant separated in 2012. About a year later, in October 2013, the Office of Child Support (OCS) filed a Complaint for Support and Recovery of Debt, together with a "Motion for Genetic Testing Despite Parentage Presumption." The motion alleged that, despite the presumption of parentage arising from the VAP, there were grounds to believe that defendant was not the biological father based on mother's affidavit naming another individual as the biological father, and stating that she was already fourteen weeks pregnant when she and defendant got together. The following month, defendant filed a pro se pleading in which he opposed the motion for genetic testing and asked the court "to grant [him] a parentage order of the child." Defendant acknowledged that he was not the child's biological father and was aware of this when he signed the VAP, but claimed that there was "nothing wrong" with doing so, and that the time for rescinding it had expired. Defendant followed with a more formal motion to establish parentage in December 2013.

In the meantime, the family court granted the motion for genetic testing, which took place in early January 2014. The test excluded defendant as the child's biological father. . . .

Defendant appeared pro se at the hearing [to determine parentage] and testified in his own behalf. Defendant testified that he began living with mother when she was already fourteen weeks pregnant, was present at the child's birth, took an active role in the care of the child, and bought her clothes and gifts. Defendant stated that he moved out of the home in November 2012, when the child was about seventeen months old, but continued to visit with her until mother was granted a relief-from-abuse order in May 2014, barring him from contacting either mother or the child.

Mother also testified, acknowledging that she and defendant had knowingly signed the VAP, which falsely stated that defendant was the child's biological father. She admitted that defendant had been "good" with the child, but stated that he had recently been harassing and stalking her. Her reason for seeking to rescind the VAP, mother explained, was to afford the biological father an opportunity to become more involved with the child, an opportunity he had not thus far pursued. . . .

The family court . . . concluded that defendant lacked standing to bring a parentage action because he is not the "natural parent" of the child . . . , and further concluded that the VAP was ineffective to establish parentage because defendant is not a "biological" parent of the child. This pro se appeal by defendant followed.

We begin with the validity of the VAP, which we find to be dispositive. As explained below, we agree with OCS's assertion that, inasmuch as both signatories knowingly misrepresented defendant to be the child's biological father, the VAP in this case was a per se fraud upon the court, and properly set aside on that basis. . . .

The Act places considerable emphasis on the legal consequences of filing a signed VAP, providing that it establishes "a presumptive *legal determination* of parentage," (emphasis added), which may be subsequently rescinded only "within 60 days after signing the form" and thereafter "challenged only pursuant to Rule 60 of the Vermont Rules of Civil Procedure." . . .

It is not surprising, therefore, that courts have generally concluded that voluntary acknowledgments of paternity effectively "operate as judgments," a conclusion reinforced by the common statutory provision authorizing later challenges to VAPs solely by means of a motion for relief from judgment.

. . . Although in Vermont, as elsewhere, a motion for relief from judgment based on fraud or misrepresentation must be filed within one year of the proceeding, a motion brought under the general provision for "any other reason justifying relief" must "be filed within a reasonable time," and therefore may be brought outside the one-year limitation period. Thus, in Godin v. Godin, we recognized that a claim of fraud "upon the court" is "governed by the catch-all provision of Rule 60(b)(6)" and therefore is not subject to the one-year limitation period. . . .

Applying this rubric, a number of courts have set aside fraudulently obtained parentage determinations. . . .

The facts here present a close fit to these cases, and compel a similar conclusion. Both parties acknowledge that they knowingly filed the VAP falsely identifying defendant as the child's biological father, and mother conceded that until recently the child's biological father "didn't even know she existed." As OCS correctly observes, the effect of the parties' fraudulent conduct was thus to "employ the VAP as a *de facto* adoption process, side-stepping the requirements of [the Adoption Act], compliance with which would require notice to all interested persons and the filing of consents to adoption, absent which a hearing would be held" in which the court considered all of the relevant interests. This is a classic fraud on the court, depriving the interested parties — including the child, the biological father, and the State as parens patriae — their day in court.

Of course, like most courts elsewhere, we have also recognized that "the fraud-on-the-court doctrine must be narrowly applied" lest it "become indistinguishable from ordinary fraud, and undermine the important policy favoring finality of judgments." *Godin*, 725 A.2d at 907. Indeed, *Godin* itself involved an alleged misrepresentation of paternity — a post-divorce claim by the putative father that the mother had failed to inform him that he was not the biological father — but we concluded that "to the extent the mother's conduct was fraudulent, if at all, it constituted fraud upon *plaintiff*, not upon the *court*." *Id.* (emphases added). As we explained, there was "nothing fraudulent" in the mother's representation that the child was "born of the marriage" inasmuch as the law "supplied the presumption that plaintiff was the child's natural parent," and "the mere nondisclosure to an adverse party" or the court of facts pertinent to a controversy do not "add up to 'fraud upon the court' for purposes of vacating a judgment under Rule 60(b)."

This case, as the decisions cited above recognize, is different. Here, the fraud was not perpetrated by one party against another, but by both parties agreeing together to perpetrate a fraud on the court, and the judicial process, by falsely representing defendant to be the child's biological parent. This was not a case where a VAP was signed by the parties under a mistaken belief that they were the child's biological parents, or where one party was intentionally misled by the other. On the contrary, these parties knew at the time they signed the VAP that defendant was not what he was purporting himself to be. Nor is this a case where the record shows that a putative parent has neglected to challenge a parentage acknowledgment for such an unreasonable length of time that it would be unconscionable to set it aside. Defendant admittedly left the home in 2012, when the child was no more than sixteen or seventeen months old, and the VAP was challenged the following year. Thus, there are no facts here to support a finding of unreasonable delay.

We conclude, accordingly, that the undisputed facts support the motion to set aside the acknowledgment of paternity as a fraud on the court, and affirm the judgment of nonparentage as to defendant on that basis. . . .

Affirmed.

ROBINSON, J., dissenting.

In its elevation of biological connection between parent and child over our ordinary rules regarding the finality of judgments, the majority has adopted a legal rule that is at odds with our prior case law, and is squarely contrary to the best interests of Vermont's children.

Before addressing the majority's legal reasoning, I note two considerations relating to the framing of this case. First, it's unfortunate, but not surprising, that this case arises in the context of allegations by Ms. McGee (mother) against Mr. Gonyo (putative father) that paint putative father in an unfavorable light. It's not surprising, because a biological[18] mother, who has previously signed a voluntary acknowledgment of the parenthood of an individual about whom she has nothing bad to say, is far less likely to seek to cut off that individual's parental relationship with their child than one who has become disaffected with the other acknowledged parent.[19] It's unfortunate because I fear that the specific factual circumstances of this case might cloud the legal analysis.

The majority has apparently established a per se rule that two parents who sign a voluntary acknowledgment of parentage (VAP), knowing that one of them is not biologically related to the child, have committed a fraud upon the court such that the acknowledgment may be set aside by the court at any time; this rule will apply with equal force in a range of factual settings in which its application may seem far more inequitable to all concerned.[20] If putative father were a model parent, and had served for years as the child's primary caregiver and sole means of support, mother could nonetheless unilaterally take action to sever his parent-child

---

18. I use the term "biological" to describe mother's relationship to the child because that is the term that this Court, and many other courts, have commonly used. I acknowledge that the term is imprecise: it does not clearly signal whether the significant characteristic of the parent-child connection is that the parent bore the child or, rather, is that the child carries the parent's DNA.

19. See *Moreau*, 95 A.3d 416 (Robinson, J., dissenting) (noting that abuse allegations by mother against putative father are immaterial to parentage analysis, and that even if court legally recognized father as children's parent, it could deny him parental rights and responsibilities and even parent-child contact if facts warranted such ruling).

20. I don't mean to suggest that the consequences of the majority's analysis are not inequitable in *this* case. Given that the trial court resolved this case on the basis that putative father is not the child's biological father, I accept for purposes of this analysis father's testimony that: (1) mother and putative father held him out to each other, their child, and the world as the child's father; (2) putative father lived with mother and helped raise the child for nearly the first year and a half of the child's life; (3) after putative father and mother separated he maintained frequent contact with the child for the next year; (4) putative father is the only father child has ever known; (5) putative father has provided parental love and care for the child and stands ready to continue doing so; and (6) putative father has provided material support for the child and is prepared to financially support her as a parent. Given these assumptions, the loss to both putative father and child of legal protection for their established bond and the loss to child of the added security of having two parents responsible for her care and support is distressing.

relationship to accommodate a new partner in her life. Likewise, if putative father had held himself out to the world as the child's parent for years, but then sought to sever his legal obligations because he won the lottery and wanted to avoid paying increased child support, or he wanted to get out from under a child-support arrearage, he could do so. The majority's broad exception to our ordinary rules of finality leaves both parties to a VAP with the open-ended power to avoid the consequences of that commitment, and the accompanying legal judgment, when it serves their own self-interest, without regard to the best interests of the child for whom they had agreed to share responsibility.

Second, the status of the supposed biological father in this case is relevant. This is *not* a case in which the court is confronted with a claim by the supposed biological father seeking recognition of his parental status in lieu of or in addition to an already legally recognized parent. Instead, this is a case in which *mother*—who previously signed and filed with the Department of Health a VAP acknowledging putative father as the child's father—has decided that she now wants to disavow that prior acknowledgment. The distinction is significant. As set forth more fully below, if the supposed biological father sought to establish his parental rights, he would be entitled to do so to the extent that his claims of parentage enjoyed constitutional protection. But he has not. And mother does not have standing to assert the claims of the supposed biological father.

All we know about the supposed biological father is that: (1) mother alleges him to be the child's biological father; and (2) he has made no effort to pursue parental rights for this child even though several months before the hearing in this case mother sent him a letter, a text, and an email informing him that she believed him to be the child's biological father. Mother had this to say about the supposed biological father:

> [H]e is a good guy, what I knew of him. We were only dating maybe four months before I got pregnant. We did get in one fight, and the cops were called, and, you know, I haven't seen him since. You know, I never really pushed the matter, so he never—he doesn't—not till now didn't even know she existed.

At this stage, we cannot assume that a ruling denying putative father's parental status will clear the way for a ruling assigning parentage of this child to someone else. . . . All we know with confidence is that the trial court's ruling leaves this child, at least for now, and possibly indefinitely, with only one legally recognized parent—an outcome we should generally disfavor.

I.

With these considerations in mind, I turn to the critical flaws in the majority's reasoning. This is not simply another nonbiological parenting case. This case involves the finality of a final judgment of parentage in the face of a claim by one of the parties to the original proceeding, more than two years later, that an adjudicated parent shares no biological connection with the child. In considering this issue . . . the majority has dialed back this Court's established commitment to finality in a context in which that finality is *most*, not *least*, urgent.

I agree with the majority that a voluntary acknowledgment of parentage that is not rescinded within sixty days operates as a judgment that may be challenged only pursuant to Rule 60 of the Vermont Rules of Civil Procedure. 15 V.S.A. §307(f). In that sense, it has the same effect as a judicial determination of parentage in a parentage action, or a judgment of parentage intrinsic to a final divorce judgment. The Legislature has been clear about that. . . .

This Court offered the following analysis of the evolution of the "fraud on the court" doctrine following the [U.S. Supreme Court's] *Hazel-Atlas* decision:

> Since *Hazel-Atlas*, courts and commentators alike have observed that the fraud-on-the-court doctrine must be narrowly applied, or it would become indistinguishable from ordinary fraud,

and undermine the important policy favoring finality of judgments. "If fraud on the court were to be given a broad interpretation that encompassed virtually all forms of fraudulent misconduct between the parties, judgments would never be final and the time limitations of Rule 60(b) would be meaningless." . . .

Godin, 725 A.2d 904, 907-08 (citations omitted).

In *Godin*, we considered a motion to require genetic testing to determine the paternity of a child six years after the final divorce decree that deemed the child to be a child of the marriage. The husband invoked the fraud-on-the-court doctrine in seeking to set aside the paternity judgment implicit in the final divorce order, arguing that wife had committed fraud on the court, in addition to fraud against him, by representing in her divorce pleadings that he was the father of the child in question. Because "the mere nondisclosure to an adverse party and to the court of facts pertinent to a controversy before the court does not add up to 'fraud upon the court,' " . . . this Court rejected the husband's fraud-on-the-court argument. . . .

In analyzing the husband's claim . . . , this Court considered the policy implications of allowing belated challenges to parentage determinations predicated on the absence of a biological connection. . . . I quote the Court's discussion of these policy concerns at length because they are directly relevant to this case:

> [T]he State retains a strong and direct interest in ensuring that children born of a marriage do not suffer financially or psychologically merely because of a parent's belated and self-serving concern over a child's biological origins. These themes underlie the conclusion, reached by numerous courts, that the public interest in finality of paternity determinations is compelling, and that the doctrine of res judicata therefore bars subsequent attempts to disprove paternity. . . .

Although we understand the plaintiff's interest in ascertaining the true genetic makeup of the child, we agree with the many jurisdictions holding that the financial and emotional welfare of the child, and the preservation of an established parent-child relationship, must remain paramount. Where the presumptive father has held himself out as the child's parent, and engaged in an ongoing parent-child relationship for a period of years, he may not disavow that relationship and destroy a child's long-held assumptions, solely for his own self-interest. Whatever the interests of the presumed father in ascertaining the genetic "truth" of a child's origins, they remain subsidiary to the interests of the state, the family, and the child in maintaining the continuity, financial support, and psychological security of an established parent-child relationship. Therefore, absent a clear and convincing showing that it would serve the best interests of the child, a prior adjudication of paternity is conclusive.

. . . In addition, I cannot reconcile the majority's analysis here with our much more recent analysis in Columbia v. Lawton, 71 A.3d 1218 (2013). In that case, as in this case, a child's biological mother legally stipulated to a putative father's parentage. Subsequently, another man (Mr. Columbia) filed a parentage action claiming to be the child's actual biological father. The trial court concluded that Mr. Columbia lacked standing to seek an order recognizing his parentage since another individual was already legally adjudicated to be the child's parent. . . . We explained that an individual's status as a parent requires consideration of a host of factors, including but not limited to a child's genetic connection, or lack thereof. Given that Mr. Columbia had not had any contact or relationship with the child, he did not formally assert his parentage for more than two years after the child's birth, he had not assumed any responsibility for the child's emotional or material well-being, and another legally adjudicated father had lived in a family relationship with the child, we concluded that the case was not closed. The only indicia of parenthood Mr. Columbia could claim was a possible genetic connection to the child.

The upshot of our analysis in *Columbia* was that the judgment of parentage in favor of the child's first adjudicated father, who we assumed for the purposes of that motion was not, in fact, the child's biological parent, carried the day, even in the face of a claim by another man who was, in fact, the child's biological father. . . . *Columbia* was a much stronger case than this one for setting aside a final judgment of parentage because an actual alternative parent was seeking to displace the adjudicated parent. Yet in that case, we upheld the existing parentage judgment in favor of a father who we assumed was not in fact the child's biological father, and left the child's actual (alleged) biological father with no recourse. . . .

The primary question here involves the finality of parentage judgments. . . . Almost thirty percent of the children born in Vermont since 1997 have had their parenthood established by a VAP. That's tens of thousands of children whose parentage is established by a VAP. Families organize themselves in reliance on these VAPs. The Office of Child Support relies on them to ensure that children are getting the support they need, and parents are paying the support they should.

Even if only one percent of those cases are similar to this one in that both parents knew that one of them was not biologically related to the child, the majority's decision today leaves hundreds of children, and their parents, vulnerable to a change of heart by either parent — an outcome decidedly at odds with the best interests of the children our parentage statutes are designed to protect. A father who has signed and filed a VAP, and has stepped up to the plate and supported a child for years can back out, invoking Rule 60(b)(6) and the majority's decision in this case, leaving the other parent, or the Office of Child Support, with no alternative source of support for the child. A mother who no longer wishes to deal with the partner with whom she formerly parented a child can disavow the VAP, severing the longstanding parent-child bond with the other parent — even though she invited and legally agreed to the co-parenting arrangement long ago, and even if her actions leave that child with only one parent. Wholly apart from my views about the definition of a parent, I would not do violence to the goal of finality that runs through our case law — most especially when it comes to legally established parent-child relationships.

II.

. . . A factor that this Court and other courts have identified as among the most significant in determining whether an individual is a child's legal parent is the intentions and expectations of the putative parent and the established legal parent.

. . . [I]n this case, the parties could not have expressed their intentions and expectations with respect to their respective roles and status concerning this child any more clearly. Both putative father and mother signed and filed with the state a document acknowledging father's parentage. At the top, the document states:

> Parentage creates specific legal obligations. . . . You should seek legal advice before signing this form if you have any questions or if you are confused about your rights and responsibilities. Further, information about the legal rights and responsibilities of a parent is available on the back of this form. The legal rights and responsibilities of a parent are serious, and you should not sign this form unless you understand them.

The back of the page describes the consequences of the acknowledgment, including the fact that both parents have the right to seek parental rights and responsibilities and both are financially responsible for the child. Both parties signed this form within ten days of the child's birth. . . .

Mother clearly expressed her intention from the outset to recognize putative father as the child's legal father, and putative father clearly expressed his intention from the outset to accept that responsibility. Putative father actually exercised that responsibility and acted as a parent to this child for over two years. No other claimant has come forward seeking to assume the responsibilities of parentage. Given these factors, I believe that putative father is entitled to a hearing. . . .

NOTES AND QUESTIONS

1. The majority in *McGee* maintains that when both parties signing a VAP know that the putative father is not the biological father of the child, they are committing a fraud against the court, and the VAP cannot be used to establish paternity. In contrast, when the mother knows that the putative father is not the biological father, but the putative father does not know, she commits a fraud only against him, and the VAP may be valid. Does this distinction make sense?

2. In *McGee*, after the parties separated, the mother obtained a restraining order against the putative father. Does this influence the majority's decision? Do you think it should? How does the dissent address the issue? If the putative father were held to be a legal father, would he have a constitutional right to a relationship with the child? If so, what showing would be necessary to limit his contact with the child? How do the child's interests affect the reasoning of the majority? Of the dissent?

3. The mother states that she wrote to the biological father about the existence of the child but did not receive a reply. If the court had upheld the validity of the VAP, how would that have affected the ability of the biological father to establish a relationship with the child? How does the dissent deal with the biological father's right to a relationship with the child?

4. The states vary in the standards they apply to actions to rescind VAPs. In State ex rel. Sec'y of Dep't for Children & Families v. Smith, 392 P.3d 68, 79-81 (Kan. 2017), the Kansas Supreme Court expressly declined to adopt the reasoning in *McGee*. It explained:

> The VAP form sets up a situation by which an individual may become a legal parent even though not a biological or adoptive one. Neither the federal nor the Kansas VAP statutes limit the availability of the VAP procedure to those who are, or reasonably believe themselves to be, biological parents. And neither K.S.A. 2016 Supp. 23-2204 nor the Office of Vital Statistics form requires a person who signs the form to make a declaration of biological parenthood of the newborn child. Accordingly, under the VAP procedure enacted by the legislature, genetic testing would not void the VAP or automatically negate the responsibilities of a person who had signed a VAP. . . .
>
> That brings us back to the question of whether, under the facts of this case, the VAP procedure created a permanent parent and child relationship or merely created a rebuttable presumption of such a relationship. . . . [T]he Court of Appeals did not consider the effect of K.S.A. 2016 Supp. 23-2209, which defines the procedure for establishing a parent and child relationship and, in doing so, indicates a legislative intent for a VAP to permanently bind those who sign the document. It does so, in part, by limiting the parties who may bring an action to revoke the VAP to "the man named as the father [on the VAP form], the mother or the child" and by requiring the action to be filed within "one year after the child's date of birth" if the action is brought by the man or the mother. Clearly, the legislature intended to impose strict limitations on the two individuals who sign the VAP form. It seems contrary to this intent to allow either of those parties the ability to sidestep the VAP's terms—to effectively seek its revocation—by rebutting a presumption or raising a conflicting presumption, such as would arise through genetic testing. . . .

The Kansas Supreme Court accordingly concluded that Smith's effort to deny paternity was time barred, though it left open the possibility that others representing the child's interests might seek, on the basis of different statutory provisions, to establish competing presumptions of paternity. *Id.* at 80. In the *Smith* case, however, the child's biological father had died by the time of the proceeding, leaving Smith, the man who signed the VAP, as the child's only possible legal father.

Can *McGee* be distinguished from *Smith* on the basis that the VAP form in *McGee* required the parties to assert that they "voluntarily and without coercion, and of our own free will, hereby acknowledge that we are the *biological* parents of the child" (emphasis added)? How does the *McGee* majority treat a case in which paternity is established through the marital presumption, which does not require the married couple to do anything to establish the father's paternity? Under the *McGee* rationale, would it matter whether the husband and wife knew that the husband was not the biological father when his name was entered on the child's birth certificate or when a divorce decree identified the child as a "child of the marriage"?

5. Would *McGee* have come out differently if the putative father, instead of trying to assert paternity, were trying to escape responsibility for child support? In many states, a putative father who signs a VAP knowing or having reason to suspect that he is not the biological father cannot later rescind the VAP or vacate a child support order on the basis of the lack of a biological tie to the child. *See, e.g.*, Davis v. Wicomico County Bureau, 135 A.3d 419 (Md. App. 2016); Madison v. Osburn, 396 S.W.3d 264 (Ark. App. 2013), *overruled on other grounds by* Furr v. James, 2013 Ark. App. 181; Allison v. Medlock, 983 So. 2d 789 (Fla. App. 2008); Van Weelde v. Van Weelde, 110 So. 3d 918 (Fla. App. 2013); In re Paternity of H.H. v. Hughes, 879 N.E.2d 1175 (Ind. App. 2008); In re Paternity of Cheryl, 746 N.E.2d 488 (Mass. 2001); Demetrius H. v. Mikhaila C.M., 827 N.Y.S.2d 810 (App. Div. 2006).

Would the result in *McGee* have been different if the putative father mistakenly believed that he was the biological father? Would it matter whether his belief was reasonable?

Many states allow a putative parent to set aside a VAP if that parent can show that consent to the VAP was based on fraud, duress, or material mistake of fact. *See, e.g., Davis*, above. More than half the states, however, have enacted statutes that allow a legal determination of the paternity to be set aside based on evidence that the legal father is not the biological father without additional evidence of fraud, duress, mistake, or something equivalent. Of these states, 18 allow courts to refuse to set aside a judgment or a VAP based on estoppel or the child's best interests, or both, but the remainder do not. Thirteen states have statutes of limitations on motions to disestablish paternity in some or all cases; in the other states, a legal determination of paternity is vulnerable to challenge at least throughout the child's minority. And almost half of these statutes are not gender neutral but instead empower only the legal father to challenge paternity, at least in some situations. Leslie Joan Harris, Reforming Paternity Law to Eliminate Gender, Status and Class Inequality, 2013 Mich. St. L. Rev. 1295, 1320-1327. Moreover, even in states that allow paternity disestablishment without a showing of fraud, duress, or material mistake, the mother may be estopped from bringing such an action if she knew or suspected that the VAP signatory was not the biological father at the time she joined him in signing the VAP. *See* In re McQuillen v. Hufford, 466 P.3d 380, 385 (Ariz. App. 2020), *rev. denied* (Jan. 5, 2021) (concluding that a mother who had signed a VAP establishing the paternity of a man the mother knew was not the biological father was "precluded, as a matter of law, from seeking relief based on her own fraudulent misrepresentations"). Illinois has ruled that a guardian ad litem for the child has standing to challenge paternity, irrespective of the father's knowledge about the facts of biological paternity and without meeting a best-interest-of-the-child standard. In re A.A., 43 N.E.3d 947 (Ill. 2015).

6. In the 1990s, the federal government, eager to reduce federal welfare aid, sought to encourage the states to streamline paternity establishment. Before then, most policy makers believed that unmarried fathers had deserted the mothers. The Fragile Families research demonstrated, however, that the majority of unmarried mothers were in relationships with the fathers of their children and that the high point of the relationship often came at the time of the child's birth. At that point, the father is often happy to acknowledge the child as "his" even if it means responsibility for support.

Some authors have suggested that the men in these relationships do not inquire too closely into paternity so long as they wish the relationship with the mothers to last. *See* June Carbone & Naomi Cahn, Which Ties Bind? Redefining the Parent-Child Relationship in an Age of Genetic Certainty, 11 Wm. & Mary Bill Rts. J. 1011, 1066 (2003). Given the opportunity to have a paternity test done, most fathers refuse. Leslie Joan Harris, Voluntary Acknowledgements of Parentage for Same-Sex Couples, 20 Am. U. J. Gender Soc. Pol'y & L. 467, 477 (2012). Cases of disputed paternity then typically occur when the relationship ends and either the mother wishes to cut off the putative father's contact with the child or he wishes to avoid responsibility for support. At that point, more than 60 days is likely to have passed since he signed the VAP.

How does the *McGee* majority justify its ruling in terms of the purposes of VAPs? What are the child's interests in such cases? Some authors have suggested mandatory paternity testing at birth to create greater certainty. *See, e.g.*, Carbone & Cahn, above. What are the objections to such proposals?

7. Studies of the general population show that almost always the man identified as a child's legal father is the biological father. The most comprehensive data analysis concluded that in the United States, 98 percent of the men raising children they believe to be their biological children are correct. Kermyt G. Anderson, How Well Does Paternity Confidence Match Actual Paternity? Results from Worldwide Nonpaternity Rates, 47 Current Anthropology 513, 516 (2006). European studies have suggested that the numbers there may be above 99 percent. Barry Starr, New DNA Studies Debunk Misconceptions About Paternal Relationships, KQED Science, Nov. 25, 2013, https://ww2.kqed.org/science/2013/11/25/new-dna-studies-debunk-misconceptions-about-paternal-relationships/; Torstein Dahlén, et al., Jingcheng Zhao, Patrick K. E. Magnusson, Yudi Pawitan, Jakob Lavröd, Gustaf Edgren, Gustaf, The Frequency of Misattributed Paternity in Sweden is Low and Decreasing: A Nationwide Cohort Study, 291 J. Internal Med. 95 (2022) (placing historical rates at 1.7% and more recent figures below 1%). The percentage of cases with mistributed paternity is higher among men who seek blood tests to confirm paternity, but even among this group, only 30 percent of the men find out that they are not the biological fathers. Anderson, above.

8. For further discussion of voluntary acknowledgments and the legal status of unmarried parents, *see* Melanie B. Jacobs, When Daddy Doesn't Want to Be Daddy Anymore: An Argument Against Paternity Fraud Claims, 16 Yale J.L. & Feminism 193 (2004); Melanie B. Jacobs, Parental Parity: Intentional Parenthood's Promise, 64 Buff. L. Rev. 465, 496 (2016); Kerry Abrams & Brandon L. Garrett, DNA and Distrust, 91 Notre Dame L. Rev. 757, 801 (2015); Jeffrey A. Parness, Challenges in Handling Imprecise Parentage Matters, 28 J. Am. Acad. Matrimonial Law. 139, 158 (2015).

PROBLEM

When Jana was born, Sheldon, the baby's biological father, refused to acknowledge that the child might be his and provided the mother with no support or assistance during the period leading up to the child's birth. The mother and Leon, a friend of the mother, signed and filed a voluntary declaration of paternity so that the child would have someone to look after her should something happen to her mother. After the birth, blood tests confirmed Sheldon's paternity. Sheldon then moved in with Jana and her mother, and he contributed support to the household. After the child turned 3, Sheldon and Jana's mother separated. Sheldon has never taken any action to establish paternity, and Leon has never sought to challenge or revoke the VAP he signed. If Jana's mother seeks state support, and the state files a child support action against Leon, what will be the result? In an action against Sheldon for child support, what will be the result?

C. LEGAL RECOGNITION OF FUNCTIONAL PARENTS

Traditionally, the marital presumption served not just as a convenient presumption of biological paternity, but as a bright-line rule that provided legal recognition to functional parents. Pregnant women felt the pressure to marry someone, whether or not the biological father, to "give the child a name," and the courts often used estoppel principles to confirm the parental status of a man who held out the child as his own in the face of certain knowledge that he could not have fathered the child. *See, e.g.*, Clevenger v. Clevenger, 189 Cal. App. 2d 658 (1961). The same courts, however, would almost certainly refuse to recognize the parental status of a partner playing the same functional role who neither married the mother nor adopted the child. Moreover, if a legal parent divorced and remarried, or married a spouse who was not presumed to be a biological parent, the law, absent adoption, also did not recognize parental rights and duties between the legal parent's spouse and the child. *See* Cynthia Grant Bowman, The Legal Relationship Between Cohabitants and Their Partners' Children, 13 Theoretical Inquiries L. 127 (2012); Margaret M. Mahoney, Stepparents as Third Parties in Relation to Their Stepchildren, 40 Fam. L.Q. 81 (2006).

Today, many children live in families that include additional adults who play a parental role in the child's life. These adults are often the legal parent's new partner, but, as we discussed above, they may also include grandparents and other caregivers who lack a legal tie to the child. The following excerpts examine the varying nature of these relationships and suggest the difficulties in developing laws that afford greater recognition to relationships between children and these "functional" parents. Consider whether what Professor Chambers says of "stepparents" also applies to grandparents, unmarried partners, and other caregivers who play "parent-like" roles in children's lives, roles explored in the excerpt by Professors Joslin and NeJaime.

David Chambers

Stepparents, Biologic Parents, and the Law's Perceptions of "Family" After Divorce
Divorce Reform at the Crossroads 102, 104-108, 118-119
(Stephen D. Sugarman & Herma Hill Kay eds., 1990)

The stepparent relationship, by contrast [to the biologic parent relationship] lacks—and I would argue, cannot possibly obtain—a single paradigm or model of appropriate responsibilities. . . .

Even if we consider residential stepparents only, we still lack a single paradigm for the normal relationship of stepchild and stepparent. . . . The child who begins to live with a stepparent while still an infant is likely to develop a different relationship and bond with the stepparent than the child who begins the relationship as an adolescent.

In cases in which the biologic parents have been divorced (in contrast to cases in which one of the biologic parents has died), the course of the stepparent-child relationship is especially difficult to predict because of the very existence of the nonresidential parent and the variations in the frequency and quality of the visits between the child and the nonresidential parent. Indeed, the range of family compositions in the lives of children one or both of whose parents remarry is vast. . . .

It is thus unsurprising that . . . researchers have confirmed that stepparents and stepchildren come into these relationships uncertain what to expect and what is expected of them. As they begin a stepparent relationship, neither stepparents nor stepchildren have available to them a set of clear norms to guide their behaviors. . . .

. . . [T]he relationship between many stepparents and stepchildren remains unclear and uncomfortable well beyond the initial stages. In his study of children with a residential stepparent, Furstenberg found that children were much less likely to say they felt "quite close" to their stepparent than to say they felt "quite close" to their custodial parent and much less likely to say that they wanted to grow up to be like their stepparent than to say they wanted to be like their custodial parent. In fact, about a third of children living with a stepparent did not mention that person when asked to name the members of their family. Nearly all named their noncustodial parent, even when they saw him or her erratically.

By much the same token, about half the stepfathers in the Furstenberg study said that their stepchildren did not think of them as a "real" parent, about half said that the children were harder to love than their own children, and about half said that it was easier to think of themselves as a friend than as a parent to the stepchildren. Stepparents had difficulty figuring out their appropriate role in disciplining the child and determining how to show affection for the child. Many stepparents and children remain uninvolved or uncomfortable with each other throughout the years they live together. . . .

Part of the difficulty for stepparents, as Furstenberg's questions themselves may suggest, is that many may believe that they are expected to be seen as a true "parent," an equal at caretaking and counseling, even when they recognize that that role is unlikely to be attainable. To be sure, not all stepparents have difficult relations with their stepchildren. Some—many of those in the other half of Furstenberg's respondents—come to see themselves as a parent and are viewed by children as such. Many others attain a comfortable relationship with the child but not in the role of a parent, establishing themselves over time not as an adult authority figure but as an adult companion and adviser. Those stepparents who prove least comfortable in the stepparent role are often those who find themselves stuck in the role of "other mother" or "other father," seen by themselves and the child as being in a parent role, but competing with and compared unfavorably with the noncustodial parent. . . .

Perhaps it is psychologically inevitable that children will see a stepparent with whom they live as a person assigned to take the place of the absent parent. The least that can be said is that we as a society do not regard the advent of stepparenthood as we do the arrival of a new baby—as a treat that offers the opportunity for rich relationships. . . .

* * *

Part of the concern about the growth in the variety and instability of adult relationships that include children is that, as David Chambers suggests, families lack shared expectations about what the new adult roles involve. At the same time, other scholars have expressed concern about the lack of protection for children's affective relationships with their caregivers. They call for increased protection of "functional parenthood" alongside parental roles established by biology, marriage, and adoption. Courtney G. Joslin and Douglas NeJaime have surveyed the reported cases in the United States recognizing function as a basis for the assignment of parental rights and responsibilities and found that 34 states assign parental status on the basis of having functioned as a parent in some situations. These statuses exist in addition to the even larger group of states that extend standing to seek visitation to specified third parties such as stepparents and grandparents. The excerpt below reports their findings and how they relate to debate over the legal treatment of functional parents.

Courtney G. Joslin & Douglas NeJaime

How Parenthood Functions
123 Columbia L. Rev. __ (forthcoming 2023)

This article documents how functional parent doctrines operate in practice, examining when, how, and to whom they apply. It does so by providing an empirical account of functional parent case law. We have collected and coded all electronically reported judicial decisions from 1980 to 2021 in every U.S. jurisdiction that has what we categorize as a functional parent doctrine. By this we mean a doctrine that extends parental rights to an individual based on the conduct of forming a parental relationship with the child and parenting the child. . . .

In total, our data set includes 669 decisions. It includes cases decided under judicially created doctrines, like *in loco parentis* and psychological parenthood, and codified provisions, such as the "holding out" presumption and de facto custodian. It includes doctrines that treat functional parents as legal parents, as well as those that grant functional parents only some parental rights, such as standing to seek custody. Some jurisdictions have more than one relevant doctrine. . . .

Although our empirical study clearly has limitations, it provides a more clear-eyed and thorough assessment of functional parent doctrines and how they operate in litigation. In the overwhelming majority of cases in our data set, the functional parent has been the child's primary caregiver. In many cases in our study, the functional parent is the only person who has consistently cared for the child. Seeking to avoid disruption of this parent-child relationship, courts in our study routinely apply functional parent doctrines to protect children's relationships with the person who is in fact parenting them.

Our account looks different than those offered in extant treatments. Commentators and advocates typically assume a paradigmatic claimant — the nonbiological parent in a same-sex couple. On this view, the doctrines' primary beneficiaries are LGBTQ parents who had been excluded from protections under discriminatory parentage rules. Commentators and advocates also typically imagine a paradigmatic context — post-dissolution custody disputes — in which functional parent doctrines are at issue. In this vision, the doctrines primarily arise when a former intimate partner who had cared for the child alongside the legal parent seeks custody or visitation over the legal parent's objection. It is assumed that, but for the functional parent's claim, the state would otherwise not be involved in the lives of the legal parent or child. Because bitter custody disputes are not good for children, commentators and advocates worry that functional parenthood doctrines will create or exacerbate conflict and instability in children's lives.

These assumptions about who functional parent claimants are, how their claims arise, and what effects they have on children support normative arguments against using function as a basis for assigning parental rights and responsibilities. Based on these assumptions, critics claim that the doctrines are unnecessary, intrusive, unwieldy, unpredictable, and wrongheaded. Although framed as normative objections, these diverse criticisms rest on empirical claims or assumptions about what the doctrines do, or what they will do if adopted.

. . . Functional parent doctrines have long existed, offering ample evidence to collect and examine. . . . Rather than LGBTQ parents representing the dominant class of claimants, relatives constitute the largest share of functional parents in our data set. Rather than post-dissolution custody disputes overwhelmingly predominating, our data set includes a range of scenarios that give rise to functional parent claims, including cases involving parental death and child welfare intervention. Rather than find that functional parent doctrines are invoked in ways that disrupt and unsettle children's lives, our study finds that courts typically apply the doctrines in ways that secure children's relationships with the individuals who are in fact parenting them. In a large swath of cases in our data set, protection of the functional parent-child relationship does not fundamentally alter the existing dynamic between the biological or legal parent and the child. Instead, courts in our study routinely apply the doctrine in ways that preserve the child's existing living arrangement with the person who is serving as their primary caregiver.

* * *

Joslin and NeJaime find further that the largest number of cases come from Kentucky, Pennsylvania, and California, and that the number of cases has increased substantially over the last 15 years. In their data set, 36% of the functional parents are relatives, 17% are same-sex couples, 17% are stepparents, and another 17% are unmarried different sex partners. The criteria for invoking functional parenthood and the consequences of finding that a person is a functional parent vary substantially from state to state. According to Joslin and NeJaime, the most commonly cited functional parent doctrines involve the common law concepts of de facto parent, psychological parent, *in loco parentis*, equitable parent, and parent by estoppel. In addition, some states have interpreted parentage statutes, such as the Uniform Parentage Act, to create presumptions of parenthood that are no longer treated as presumptions of a biological tie. The two cases below provide illustrations of these doctrines.

Elisa B. v. Superior Court
117 P.3d 660 (Cal. 2005)

MORENO, J. . . . On June 7, 2001, the El Dorado County District Attorney filed a complaint in superior court to establish that Elisa B. is a parent of two-year-old twins Kaia B. and Ry B., who were born to Emily B., and to order Elisa to pay child support. Elisa filed an answer in which she denied being the children's parent.

A hearing was held at which Elisa testified that she entered into a lesbian relationship with Emily in 1993. They began living together six months later. Elisa obtained a tattoo that read "Emily, por vida," which in Spanish means Emily, for life. They introduced each other to friends as their "partner," exchanged rings, opened a joint bank account, and believed they were in a committed relationship.

Elisa and Emily discussed having children and decided that they both wished to give birth. Because Elisa earned more than twice as much money as Emily, they decided that Emily "would be the stay-at-home mother" and Elisa "would be the primary breadwinner for the family." At a sperm bank, they chose a donor they both would use so the children would "be biological brothers and sisters."

After several unsuccessful attempts, Elisa became pregnant in February, 1997. Emily was present when Elisa was inseminated. Emily began the insemination process in June of 1997 and became pregnant in August, 1997. Elisa was present when Emily was inseminated and, the next day, Elisa picked up additional sperm at the sperm bank and again inseminated Emily at their home to "make sure she got pregnant." They went to each other's medical appointments during pregnancy and attended childbirth classes together so that each could act as a "coach" for the other during birth, including cutting the children's umbilical cords.

Elisa gave birth to Chance in November, 1997, and Emily gave birth to Ry and Kaia prematurely in March, 1998. Ry had medical problems; he suffered from Down's Syndrome, and required heart surgery.

They jointly selected the children's names, joining their surnames with a hyphen to form the children's surname. They each breast-fed all of the children. Elisa claimed all three children as her dependents on her tax returns and obtained a life insurance policy on herself naming Emily as the beneficiary so that if "anything happened" to her, all three children would be "cared for." Elisa believed the children would be considered both of their children.

Elisa's parents referred to the twins as their grandchildren, and her sister referred to the twins as part of their family and referred to Elisa as the twins' mother. Elisa treated all of the children as hers and told a prospective employer that she had triplets. Elisa and Emily identified themselves as co-parents of Ry at an organization arranging care for his Down's Syndrome.

Elisa supported the household financially. Emily was not working. Emily testified that she would not have become pregnant if Elisa had not promised to support her financially, but Elisa denied that any financial arrangements were discussed before the birth of the children. Elisa later acknowledged in her testimony, however, that Emily "was going to be an at-home mom for maybe a couple of years and then the kids were going to go into day care and she was going to return to work."

They consulted an attorney regarding adopting "each other's child," but never did so. Nor did they register as domestic partners or execute a written agreement concerning the children. Elisa stated she later reconsidered adoption because she had misgivings about Emily adopting Chance.

Elisa and Emily separated in November, 1999. Elisa promised to support Emily and the twins "as much as I possibly could" and initially paid the mortgage payments of approximately $1,500 per month on the house in which Emily and the twins continued to live, as well as other expenses. Emily applied for aid. When they sold the house and Emily and the twins moved into an apartment in November, 2000, Elisa paid Emily $1,000 a month. In early 2001, Elisa stated she lost her position as a full-time employee and told Emily she no longer could support her and the twins. At the time of trial, Elisa was earning $95,000 a year.

The superior court rendered a written decision on July 11, 2002, finding that Elisa and Emily had rejected the option of using a private sperm donor because "[t]hey wanted the child to be raised *exclusively* by them as a couple." The court further found that they intended to create a child and "acted in all respects as a family," adding "that a person who uses reproductive technology is accountable as a de facto legal parent for the support of that child. Legal parentage is not determined exclusively by biology."

The court further found that Elisa was obligated to support the twins under the doctrine of equitable estoppel. . . .

Elisa petitioned the Court of Appeal for a writ of mandate, and the court directed the superior court to vacate its order and dismiss the action, concluding that Elisa had no obligation to pay child support because she was not a parent of the twins within the meaning of the Uniform Parentage Act (Fam. Code, §7600 et seq.). We granted review. . . .

. . . The UPA defines the " '[p]arent and child relationship' " as "the legal relationship existing between a child and the child's natural or adoptive parents. . . ." [T]he UPA provides that the parentage of a child does not depend upon " 'the marital status of the parents' " stating: "The parent and child relationship extends equally to every child and to every parent, regardless of the marital status of the parents." (§7602.) . . .

Section 7611 provides several circumstances in which "[a] man is presumed to be the natural father of a child," including: if he is the husband of the child's mother, is not impotent or sterile, and was cohabiting with her (§7540); if he signs a voluntary declaration of paternity stating he is the "biological father of the child" (§7574, subd. (a)(6)); and if "[h]e receives the child into his home and openly holds out the child as his natural child."

Although . . . the UPA contains separate provisions defining who is a mother and who is a father, it expressly provides that in determining the existence of a mother and child relationship, "[i]nsofar as practicable, the provisions of this part applicable to the father and child relationship apply." . . .

We perceive no reason why both parents of a child cannot be women. That result now is possible under the current version of the domestic partnership statutes, which took effect this year.

. . . [W]e proceed to examine the UPA to determine whether Elisa is a parent to the twins in addition to Emily. As noted above, section 7650 provides that provisions applicable to determining a father and child relationship shall be used to determine a mother and child relationship "insofar as practicable."

Subdivision (d) of section 7611 states that a man is presumed to be the natural father of a child if "[h]e receives the child into his home and openly holds out the child as his natural child." . . .

Applying section 7611, subdivision (d), we must determine whether Elisa received the twins into her home and openly held them out as her natural children. There is no doubt that Elisa satisfied the first part of this test; it is undisputed that Elisa received the twins into her home. Our inquiry focuses, therefore, on whether she openly held out the twins as her natural children.

The circumstance that Elisa has no genetic connection to the twins does not necessarily mean that she did not hold out the twins as her "natural" children under section 7611. We held in In re Nicholas H. (2002), 46 P.3d 932 that the presumption under section 7611, subdivision (d), that a man who receives a child into his home and openly holds the child out as his natural child is not necessarily rebutted when he admits he is not the child's biological father.

The presumed father in *Nicholas H.*, Thomas, met the child's mother, Kimberly, when she was pregnant with Nicholas. Nevertheless, Thomas was named as the child's father on his birth certificate and provided a home for the child and his mother for several years. Thomas did not marry Kimberly. When Nicholas was removed by the court from Kimberly's care, Thomas sought custody as the child's presumed father, although he admitted he was not Nicholas's biological father.

We held in *Nicholas H.* that Thomas was presumed to be Nicholas's father despite his admission that he was not Nicholas's biological father. The Court of Appeal had reached the opposite conclusion, observing that "the Legislature has used the term 'natural' to mean 'biological' " and concluding that the presumption under section 7611, subdivision (d) is rebutted under section 7612, subdivision (a) by clear and convincing evidence "that the man is not the child's natural, biological father." We noted, however, that the UPA does not state that the presumption under section 7611, subdivision (d), *is* rebutted by evidence that the presumed father is not the child's biological father, but rather that it *may* be rebutted *in an appropriate action* by such evidence. We held that *Nicholas H.* was not an appropriate action in which to rebut the presumption because no one had raised a conflicting claim to being the child's father. Applying the presumption, therefore, would produce the "harsh result" of leaving the child fatherless. . . .

We conclude that the present case . . . is not "an appropriate action" in which to rebut the presumption of presumed parenthood with proof that Elisa is not the twins' biological parent. This is generally a matter within the discretion of the superior court, because it would be an abuse of discretion to conclude that the presumption may be rebutted in the present case. It is undisputed that Elisa actively consented to, and participated in, the artificial insemination of her partner with the understanding that the resulting child or children would be raised by Emily and her as coparents, and they did act as coparents for a substantial period of time. Elisa received the twins into her home and held them out to the world as her natural children. She gave the twins and the child to whom she had given birth the same surname, which was formed by joining her surname to her partner's. The twins were half siblings to the child to whom Elisa had given birth. She breast-fed all three children, claimed all three children as her dependents on her tax returns, and told a prospective employer that she had triplets. Even at the hearing before the superior court, Elisa candidly testified that she considered herself to be the twins' mother.

Declaring that Elisa cannot be the twins' parent and, thus, has no obligation to support them because she is not biologically related to them would produce a result similar to the situation we sought to avoid in *Nicholas H.* of leaving the child fatherless. The twins in the present case have no father because they were conceived by means of artificial insemination using an anonymous semen donor. Rebutting the presumption that Elisa is the twin's parent would leave them with only one parent and would deprive them of the support of their second parent. Because Emily is financially unable to support the twins, the financial burden of supporting the twins would be borne by the county, rather than Elisa. . . .

We observed in dicta in *Nicholas H.* that it would be appropriate to rebut the section 7611 presumption of parentage if "a court decides that the legal rights and obligations of parenthood should devolve upon an unwilling candidate." But we decline to apply our dicta in *Nicholas H.* here, because we did not consider in *Nicholas H.* a situation like that in the present case.

Although Elisa presently is unwilling to accept the obligations of parenthood, this was not always so. She actively assisted Emily in becoming pregnant with the expressed intention of enjoying the rights and accepting the responsibilities of parenting the resulting children. She accepted those obligations and enjoyed those rights for years. Elisa's present unwillingness to accept her parental obligations does not affect her status as the children's mother based upon her conduct during the first years of their lives. . . .

We were careful in *Nicholas H.*, therefore, not to suggest that every man who begins living with a woman when she is pregnant and continues to do so after the child is born necessarily becomes a presumed father of the child, even against his wishes. The Legislature surely did not intend to punish a man like the one in *Nicholas H.* who voluntarily provides support for a child who was conceived before he met the mother, by transforming that act of kindness into a legal obligation.

But our observation in *Nicholas H.* loses its force in a case like the one at bar in which the presumed mother under section 7611, subdivision (d), acted together with the birth mother to cause the child to be conceived. . . .The judgment of the Court of Appeal is reversed.

[The concurring opinion of Justice KENNARD is omitted.]

NOTES AND QUESTIONS

1. The key precedents for *Elisa B.* are cases in which the California Supreme Court held that proof that a "holding out father" is not the biological father does not necessarily rebut the presumption that he is the legal father. What test does the court adopt for deciding when such evidence would rebut the presumption? How does this test differ from the test discussed in *Greer* at page 674 above for resolving which of two conflicting presumptions of paternity should prevail?

2. Two earlier California cases cited in *Elisa B.*, In re Nicholas H., 46 P.3d 932 (Cal. 2002), and In re Jesusa V., 85 P.3d 2 (Cal. 2004), were juvenile court child neglect cases in which, for different reasons, the mothers were unable to take care of the children and the fathers were unidentified and in prison, respectively. The children in the two cases had been living with their mothers and their mothers' partners. Those partners had assumed a parental role and were willing and suitable to care for the children. However, under California juvenile court law, the court could not place the children in the custody of the men if they were unrelated third parties. Characterizing them as legal fathers via the holding out presumption allowed the children to remain in the partners' care. *Elisa B.* and its companion cases, K.M. v. E.G., 117 P.3d 673 (Cal. 2005), and Kristine H. v. Lisa R., 117 P.3d 690 (Cal. 2005), all concerned children conceived by artificial insemination and born to lesbian co-parents who had raised the children. If the court had not recognized the biological mothers' partners as parents, the children would have had only one legal parent. How important are these facts in determining whether the presumption can be rebutted? For a discussion of these and related cases, *see* June Carbone, From Partners to Parents Revisited: How Will Ideas of Partnership Influence the Emerging Definition of California Parenthood?, 7 Whittier J. Child & Fam. Advoc. 3 (2007). In the Joslin and NeJaime study, above, 33 percent of the cases arose in state-initiated proceedings, most commonly because of abuse or neglect allegations against a legal parent. Are these cases substantially different from those which arise from the break-up of an intimate relationship?

3. A growing number of states recognize the holding out doctrine as establishing legal parenthood in the absence of a biological tie to the child. *See, e.g.*, In re the Parental Responsibilities of A.D., 240 P.3d 488, 490-492 (Colo. App. 2010); People in Interest of J.C.G., 318 P.3d 576 (Colo. App. 2013); Partanen v. Gallagher, 59 N.E.3d 1133 (Mass. 2016); Chatterjee v. King, 280 P.3d 283 (N.M. 2012). Kansas and New Hampshire have reached similar results based on other statutory provisions. *See* Frazier v. Goudschaal, 295 P.3d 542 (Kan. 2013); In re Guardianship of Madelyn B., 98 A.3d 494, 500-501 (N.H. 2014). *See* Leslie Joan Harris, above, 92 Chi.-Kent L. Rev. at 77-80 for a review of the different statutes. In In re S.N.V., 284 P.3d 147 (Colo. App. 2011), the court extended this principle to conclude that the wife of a biological father could rely on the holding out presumption to seek a declaration of parentage of a child born to another woman, when the birth mother claimed that the child was the product of an affair and the husband and wife claimed that they had a surrogacy arrangement with her.

In re Custody of B.M.H.
315 P.3d 470 (Wash. 2013) (en banc)

GONZÁLEZ, J. . . . Ms. Holt and Mr. Holt began a romantic relationship in 1993 and had a son, C.H., in 1995. The couple separated in 1998, without having married, and Ms. Holt soon became engaged to another man. Unfortunately, her fiancé died in an industrial accident in 1999 while she was three months pregnant with his biological child, B.M.H.

Mr. Holt provided significant emotional support to Ms. Holt during the pregnancy, was present at B.M.H.'s birth, and even cut B.M.H.'s umbilical cord. Mr. Holt and Ms. Holt married shortly after B.M.H.'s birth but divorced in 2001. The resulting parenting plan designated Ms. Holt as C.H.'s primary residential parent and gave Mr. Holt residential time every other weekend. The parenting plan did not include provisions for B.M.H., but the parties do not dispute that B.M.H. essentially followed the same visitation schedule as C.H.

Mr. Holt was actively involved in B.M.H.'s life. In 2002, Ms. Holt changed B.M.H.'s last name from the biological father's last name to Mr. Holt's last name. Ms. Holt and Mr. Holt discussed Mr. Holt's adopting B.M.H. in 2007, but according to the guardian ad litem (GAL), adoption was not pursued because of the effect it might have on the survivor benefits that B.M.H. receives by virtue of his biological father's death.

Ms. Holt married another man in 2007 but divorced in 2008. During that relationship, Mr. Holt claims that Ms. Holt started to separate B.M.H. from Mr. Holt's visitations with C.H. In the summer of 2009, C.H. moved in with Mr. Holt. The parties dispute the reason for the move.

In late 2009 or early 2010, Mr. Holt learned that Ms. Holt planned to move with B.M.H. from Vancouver, Washington, to her new boyfriend's home in Castle Rock, about 50 miles away. On February 23, 2010, Mr. Holt filed a nonparental custody petition, alleging that Ms. Holt was not a suitable custodian for B.M.H. He explained that Ms. Holt "is threatening to move [B.M.H.] out of the area and thus disrupt the close relationship that [he] and [B.M.H.] have together." Mr. Holt also asked the court to find that he was B.M.H.'s de facto parent. Mr. Holt alleged that "[Ms. Holt] held [him] out as the child's father in all respects"; that he and B.M.H. are "extremely bonded"; and that "[B.M.H.] refers to [him] as his father." . . .

On August 20, the trial court found that adequate cause existed to proceed to a show cause hearing. The adequate cause finding reads:

> The Guardian Ad Litem has testified that it is in the child's best interest to have a continued relationship with the petitioner, [Mr. Holt]. . . . The Court finds that if the Respondent/mother denies contact between Petitioner and minor child it would cause actual detriment to the minor child's growth and development if the relationship between the minor child and the Petitioner is not protected, and the Court has concerns that the mother may withhold visitation contact in the future. . . .

1. Adequate Cause on Third Party Custody Petition

Under chapter 26.10 RCW, a third party can petition for child custody, but the State cannot interfere with the liberty interest of parents in the custody of their children unless a parent is unfit or custody with a parent would result in "actual detriment to the child's growth and development." The law's concept of the family rests in part on a presumption that "natural bonds of affection lead parents to act in the best interests of their children," and only under " 'extraordinary circumstances' " does there exist a compelling state interest that justifies interference with the integrity of the family and with parental rights. . . .

Whether placement with a parent will result in actual detriment to a child's growth and development is a highly fact-specific inquiry, and " '[p]recisely what might [constitute actual detriment to] outweigh parental rights must be determined on a case-by-case basis.' " In *Shields*, we noted that when this heightened standard is properly applied, the requisite showing required by the nonparent is substantial and a nonparent will be able to meet this substantial standard in only " 'extraordinary circumstances.' " The actual detriment standard has been met, for example, when a deaf child needed a caregiver who could effectively communicate with the child and the father was unable to do so, when a suicidal child required extensive therapy and stability at a level the parents could not provide, and when a child who had been physically and sexually abused required extensive therapy and stability at a level the parent could not provide.

Facts that merely support a finding that nonparental custody is in the "best interests of the child" are insufficient to establish adequate cause.

Mr. Holt does not allege that Ms. Holt is unfit. Rather, he alleges that . . . the "[mother] intends to immediately relocate the child to a situation that is unstable." Mr. Holt's petitions and declarations stated that since Ms. Holt's 2008 divorce she has "started relationships and moved several different men in and out of her home in Vancouver" and that "[t]hese relationships have been confusing and disruptive to [B.M.H.].'' . . . According to Mr. Holt's declaration, "[B.M.H.] has expressed to [Mr. Holt] that he does not want to move to Castle Rock and he is missing his brother and it's all just happening too quickly for him." Mr. Holt's former wife stated in her declaration:

> I have observed over the years how Laurie jumps right into relationships head-on leaving very little time for the boys to adjust to the new man in her life. The constant shuffling of boyfriends in and out of the household I believe has taken its toll on both boys but especially on [B.M.H.] who sees Michael as his one and only father.

Ms. Holt's biological father stated in his declaration that "having watched the choices [Laurie] has made and the men come in and out of her life over the years, I feel strongly that the choices she is making now are detrimental to the boys."

. . . [H]ere without more extraordinary facts bearing on B.M.H.'s welfare, the prerequisites for a nonparental custody action have not been met. The concern that Ms. Holt might interfere with Mr. Holt and B.M.H.'s relationship is insufficient to show actual detriment. . . . This court has consistently held that the interests of parents yield to state interests only where "parental actions or decisions seriously conflict with the physical or mental health of the child." . . . We reverse the Court of Appeals and dismiss the nonparental custody petition without prejudice.

2. DE FACTO PARENTAGE

. . . De facto parentage is a flexible equitable remedy that complements legislative enactments where parent-child relationships arise in ways that are not contemplated in the statutory scheme. In *L.B.*, we identified a "statutory silence regarding the interests of children begotten by artificial insemination" and we granted equitable relief. Two women who had lived together in a long-term relationship decided to have a child. One of the women conceived using donor sperm. For six years, the women coparented the child. Some time after they separated, the biological mother terminated contact between her former partner and the child, and the former partner petitioned for recognition as the child's de facto parent. Because there was no statutory means by which the former partner could establish her parental status, we adopted the de facto parentage doctrine established by the Wisconsin courts.

Establishing de facto parentage requires a showing that (1) the natural or legal parent consented to and fostered the parent-like relationship; (2) the petitioner and child lived together in the same household; (3) the petitioner assumed obligations of parenthood without expectation of financial compensation; and (4) the petitioner has been in a parental role for a length of time sufficient to have established with the child a bonded, dependent relationship, parental in nature. De facto parent status is " 'limited to those adults who have fully and completely undertaken a permanent, unequivocal, committed, and responsible parental role in the child's life.' " The de facto parentage doctrine incorporates constitutionally required deference to parents by requiring that the biological or legal parent consent to and foster the parentlike relationship. Once a petitioner has made the threshold showing that the natural or legal parent consented to and fostered the parent-like relationship, the State is no longer "interfering on behalf of a third party in an insular family unit but is enforcing the rights and obligations of parenthood that attach to de facto parents." Under the test, attaining de facto parent status is "no easy task."

De facto parentage remains a viable equitable doctrine under Washington law. We respectfully disagree with the dissent's suggestion to the contrary. Since *L.B.*, legislative amendments have "clarif[ied] and expand[ed] the rights and obligations of state registered domestic partners and other couples related to parentage" but have not abrogated the common law doctrine of de facto parentage. . . . In *L.B.*, we chronicled the long standing history of Washington courts exercising equity powers "in spite of legislative enactments that may have spoken to [an] area of law, but did so incompletely," and we determined that our state's relevant statutes do not provide the exclusive means of obtaining parental rights and responsibilities. That pronouncement stands as true today as it was then. . . . Where the legislature remains silent with respect to determinations of parentage because it cannot anticipate every way that a parent-child relationship forms, we will continue to invoke our common law responsibility to "respond to the needs of children and families in the face of changing realities." We cannot say that legislative pronouncements on this subject preclude any redress to Mr. Holt or B.M.H., and it is our duty to apply the common law in a manner "consistent with our laws and stated legislative policy."[21]

Ms. Holt also argues that if de facto parentage remains a viable doctrine, our case law precludes a stepparent from becoming a de facto parent. In *M.F.*, we held that a former stepfather could not be his stepdaughter's de facto parent, but we did not preclude all stepparents as a class from being de facto parents. To do so would be contrary to legislative directive that children not be treated differently based on the marital status of their parents. Side by side, this case and *M.F.* illustrate that there is no single formula for all stepparents. M.F.'s biological parents separated shortly after her birth and shared parenting rights and responsibilities under a parenting plan. We found that the specific factual scenario in that case was contemplated by the legislature and addressed in chapter 26.10 RCW and that applying the equitable remedy would "infringe[ ] upon the rights and duties of M.F.'s existing parents." . . . Here, where it is alleged that an individual entered a child's life at birth following the death of that child's second biological parent, and undertook an unequivocal and permanent parental role with the consent of all existing parents but does not have a statutorily protected relationship, justice prompts us to apply the de facto parent test. . . .

Ms. Holt contends that as a former stepparent, Mr. Holt has a sufficient statutory remedy because he can file a nonparental custody petition under chapter 26.10 RCW. But that remedy was available in *L.B.* as well. Precluding *any* individual from petitioning for de facto parentage because he or she can file for nonparental custody would obliterate the de facto parentage doctrine because *any* person not recognized as a parent may seek nonparental custody. . . . Like the former partner in *L.B.*, Mr. Holt has no meaningful statutory means by which he can seek a determination of parentage, and nonparental custody is an inadequate remedy to protect his weighty interests relative to the child and its biological parent. . . . We affirm the Court of Appeals and remand to the trial court for further proceedings on Mr. Holt's de facto parent petition. . . .

MADSEN, C.J. (concurring/dissenting). . . . The majority's approach is impermissible because it allows a stepparent to seek custody in violation of a parent's fundamental constitutional rights in her child.

The majority believes, though, that the consent prong of the de facto parent test protects the parent's constitutional rights. As we pointed out in *M.F.*, the de facto parent test would be too-easily applied in the stepparent context, is ill-suited to the custody issue, and makes no meaningful distinctions in this context. We said about the consent prong: "in the vast

---

21. The UPA was amended in 2011 to specifically reference state-registered domestic partnerships in various provisions and to specify that the UPA applies to persons of the same sex who have children together to the same extent it applies to opposite sex couples who have children together. Gender-specific terms in the act were replaced with gender-neutral terms. Additionally, a new provision for the presumption of parentage was adopted. Now, a party is "presumed to be the parent of a child if, for the first two years of the child's life, the person resided in the same household with the child and openly held out the child as his or her own."

majority of cases a parent will encourage his or her spouse, the stepparent, to act like a parent in relationship to the child." Our concern is echoed by one noted author, who says in connection with the American Law Institute's treatment of de facto parents and its test that similarly includes consent:

> Because agreement may be implied, this [part of the test] is satisfied when a mother acquiesces to the partner's behavior — behavior that virtually any mother would welcome in her partner, such as taking the child to the doctor, reading to the child, helping the child get ready for bed, and making dinner for the family.

Robin Fretwell Wilson, *Trusting Mothers: A Critique of The American Law Institute's Treatment of De Facto Parents*, 38 Hofstra L. Rev. 1103, 1112 (2010).

Accordingly, satisfying the consent prong is meaningless in the stepparent context. Consent to coparent within the marriage and family unit is not the same as consent to a life-long, parent-child relationship on the part of the stepparent to continue no matter what happens to the marriage. Yet consent is precisely the hook upon which the majority hangs its catch.

The other prongs are not particularly probative in the stepparent context, either. We said in *M.F.*:

> [T]he second factor will nearly always be met — that "the petitioner and the child lived together in the same household." The third element is that the petitioner assumed obligations of parenthood without expectation of compensation, and one only has to envision the stepparent attending school functions, helping the child get dressed in the morning, or engaging in the other numerous events that together make up family life with a child to see how easily this factor might be satisfied. The only variable in most cases, it would appear, is the length of time the stepparent has been in a parental role, and generally this would be merely a matter of how long the relationship with the parent endures — hardly a basis for deciding parental status.

. . . Finally, I note that in *M.F.* there were two fit parents. This, of course, cannot be a viable distinction because our statutory and constitutional law plainly contemplates and protects the single parent just as it does two parents. A single parent's constitutional rights in her child must be safeguarded every bit as vigorously as the constitutional rights of two parents together.

The majority also believes that the present case is analogous to *L.B.*, and that just as the third party custody statutes were available to the same-sex nonbiological parent in *L.B.*, the de facto parent theory is applicable here.

L.B. is not like the present case. In *L.B.*, the same-sex partners could not marry, nor were rights equal to those of heterosexual parents recognized under state statutes at the time. The two parties had been in a long-term committed relationship and did everything they could do to create a child together. . . .

In *L.B.*, the de facto test was a necessary legal channel for attributing to the two partners the parenthood that they already shared. Because of the nature of the parties' relationship — as a same-sex couple — the parent who was not a biological parent could otherwise be cut off from parental rights under the heightened showing that applies when a nonparent seeks custody. The de facto status gave legal effect to a person who was and always had been the child's parent. . . .

The circumstances in a stepparent context are not the same. Parentage exists in the two biological parents who created the child and brought into existence the parent-child relationship. Here, Laurie's child was created by her and her fiance, who passed away before the child was born.

Without doubt, a stepparent may enter the picture and assume a role as a loving, caring parental figure. Our laws permit a stepparent to seek custody of a child under the third party custody statutes. Adoption is also a possibility. But a parent's constitutional rights must be given precedence over the stepparent and it takes a very strong showing to overcome a fit parent's rights. . . .

The majority's decision that de facto parent status is available to a stepparent means that the stepparent is a parent in every respect. This means that the stepparent will be able to proceed under the "best interests of the child" standard that applies under chapter 26.09 RCW when two parents dispute custody of their child, an easier showing that places the parent's and the stepparent's interests on a par.

This result is in tension with the common law view of stepparents and their obligations to their spouses' children. June Carbone, *The Legal Definition of Parenthood: Uncertainty at the Core of Family Identity*, 65 La. L. Rev. 1295, 1311-12 (2005). . . .

Under our state law "[t]he obligation to support stepchildren shall cease upon the entry of a decree of dissolution, decree of legal separation, or death." Thus, once the marriage ended without Michael having adopted the child, Laurie was unable to compel Michael to pay support. The statute supports the view that Michael is only in a parent-like relationship because of his marriage to Laurie and any rights and responsibilities vis-à-vis Laurie's child are derivative of that relationship. Once the relationship ends, so do these rights and responsibilities. . . .

However, if he were to obtain de facto parent status, he would have the rights and obligations of a parent, as we said in *L.B.* His relationship to the child would become primary and permanent, and he could seek custody under a "best interests of the child" standard. If he did not seek de facto parent status, however, Laurie herself cannot compel him to or make the argument herself, nor can she seek support for the child. This one-sided paradigm is fundamentally at odds with the constitutional rights she has in her child. . . .

The majority poses a threat to parents' constitutional rights that may be far-reaching because of the sheer number of stepparents and stepchildren potentially affected, the fact that the majority's analysis applies equally well to cohabiting partners of parents, and because the majority appears inclined to find statutory "gaps" that must be filled based solely on different factual circumstances, notwithstanding recent legislation. . . .

One author has described such potential for broad application of the de facto parent theory as "a thinned-out conception of parenthood" that is "primarily a function of co-residence" and that "would give former live-in partners access to a child" even when opposed by the legal parent, "nearly always a child's mother." Wilson, *supra*, at 1109. "Mothers are disproportionately affected by the extension of new parental rights to live-in partners because most non-marital children and children of divorce live with their mothers." *Id.* at 1109-10.

In short, the parents who are most likely to be affected by the majority's decision are mothers who will often be members of a minority race or group. Many women faced with custody disputes will have resources so limited that they are highly unlikely to be able to afford to hire legal assistance in private custody disputes. . . .

The majority excuses its constitutional violations by an analysis that can turn Michael into a parent, allowing him to proceed under the "best interests of the child" standard. Although he is not the child's natural, biological, or adoptive parent, as a de facto parent he can proceed without regard to Laurie's fitness as a parent and without having to show detriment to the child because Laurie's rights are no longer superior to his.

I do not ascribe to the majority's loosely reframed de facto parent standard for stepparents. Our cases are to the contrary, and the fundamental rights a parent has in the care, custody, and control of her child are too precious to cast aside as no longer of any moment. . . .

WIGGINS, J. (dissenting in part). . . . This court adopted the de facto parentage doctrine to address a very specific statutory deficiency: the respondent in *L.B.* acted as a parent in every way but could not be L.B.'s legal parent because she was in a same-sex relationship with L.B.'s biological mother. . . . However, we also acknowledged that "the legislature may eventually choose to enact differing standards than those recognized here today, and to do so would be within its province." . . .

In 2009, the legislature did just that, filling the legislative void we addressed in *L.B.* by granting state registered domestic partners all of the privileges and rights of married spouses. . . .

The question before us today is this: given that the reason for the de facto parentage doctrine no longer exists, should we defer to the legislature and follow the statutory scheme, or should we expand the de facto parentage doctrine to include other relationships that were never omitted from the statutory scheme? By needlessly enlarging the reach of the de facto parentage doctrine in this case, the majority places its judgments above the legislature's. . . .

NOTES AND QUESTIONS

1. Recall that Troxel v. Granville, above at page 663, concerned the constitutionality of the Washington state third-party visitation statute. After *Troxel*, the state amended its statute to the version discussed in *B.M.H.* What requirements does the new version of the statute impose on third parties who seek visitation? Are they required by *Troxel*? How do these requirements differ from the requirements for becoming a de facto parent? Since the version of the de facto parent doctrine adopted by Washington gives the successful claimant full legal parent status, it seems to be a greater intrusion on the parental rights of the original legal parent than a third-party visitation order. How, then, does the court in *B.M.H.* reach the conclusion that the stepfather could not satisfy the requirements of the visitation statute but could become a de facto parent?

Justice Madsen's concurring and dissenting opinion in *B.M.H.* objects to the recognition of de facto parentage in part because it imposes a second parent on the first. The opinion observes that "the parents who are most likely to be affected by the majority's decision are mothers who will often be members of a minority race or group" and that the majority opinion "can turn Michael into a parent" and allow him to "proceed without regard to Laurie's fitness as a parent and without having to show detriment to the child because Laurie's rights are no longer superior to his." How does the majority respond to his argument?

Joslin and NeJaime identify the prospect of "bitter custody disputes" between former partners as a reason some oppose recognizing functional parenthood. Does this case illustrate — or provide a basis for refuting — such concerns?

2. The majority opinion in *B.M.H.* observed that the "de facto parentage doctrine incorporates constitutionally-required deference to parents by requiring that the biological or legal parent consent to and foster the parentlike relationship" and that once such consent has occurred the state is no longer "interfering on behalf of a third party in an insular family unit but is enforcing the rights and obligations of parenthood that attach to de facto parents." For a more general discussion of the role of consent in defining parentage, *see* E. Gary Spitko, The Constitutional Function of Biological Paternity: Evidence of the Biological Mother's Consent to the Biological Father's Co-Parenting of Her Child, 48 Ariz. L. Rev. 97 (2006) (arguing that mothers ordinarily acquire parental status by giving birth and that recognition of a second parent depends on the mother's consent).

The dissent in *B.M.H.*, however, insists: "Consent to coparent within the marriage and family unit is not the same as consent to a life-long, parent-child relationship on the part of the stepparent to continue no matter what happens to the marriage." For a critique of what consent means in the context of de facto parent relationships, *see* Gregg Strauss, What Role Remains for De Facto Parenthood?, 46 Fla. St. U. L. Rev. 909 (2019).

Which view do you find more persuasive? Do these arguments also apply to the holding out doctrine in *Elisa B*?

3. De facto parenthood has been described as a form of "functional parenthood" that protects the relationships that children form with their caretakers. *See, e.g.,* Douglas NeJaime, Marriage Equality and the New Parenthood, 129 Harv. L. Rev. 1185, 1193 (2016). In *B.M.H.*, function and intent coincide, that is, the de facto father assumed a parental role with the consent of the mother. Can you think of cases in which a second adult functions as a parent without the consent of the legal parent? For an argument that intent and function do not always coincide, *see* June Carbone & Naomi Cahn, Jane the Virgin and Other Stories of Unintentional Parenthood, 7 UC Irvine L. Rev. 511, 529 (2017): Katharine K. Baker, Quacking Like a Duck? Functional Parenthood Doctrine and Same-Sex Parents, 92 Chi.-Kent L. Rev. 135, 159 (2017).

4. If the de facto parent doctrine applies to stepparents, who needs to consent to the formation of the stepparent relationship? *See* E.N. v. T.R., 255 A.3d 1, 6 (Md. 2021) (holding that for establishment of de facto parenthood, where there are two legal (biological or adoptive) parents, "a prospective *de facto* parent must demonstrate that both legal parents consented to and fostered a parent-like relationship with a child, or that a non-consenting legal parent is an unfit parent or exceptional circumstances exist"). What facts would be necessary to establish such consent?

5. In the earlier Washington stepparent case, *M.F.*, which is discussed in *B.M.H.*, the Washington Supreme Court held that the stepfather could not invoke the de facto parent doctrine and had to use the third-party visitation statute to assert his claim. Why? How does *B.M.H.* distinguish *M.F.*?

6. The Maine Supreme Court in Pitts v. Moore, 90 A.3d 1169 (Me. 2014), upheld earlier decisions recognizing the de facto parent doctrine, but articulated a different test. It held that a would-be de facto parent must prove by clear and convincing evidence that "1) he or she has undertaken a 'permanent, unequivocal, committed, and responsible parental role in the child's life,' and 2) there are exceptional circumstances sufficient to allow the court to interfere with the legal or adoptive parent's rights." *Id.* at 1179. The court further explained that the test requires proof that the claimant lived with the child, the claimant engaged in caretaking functions, the legal parent and co-parent intended the co-parent to act as a parent, and "the child's life would be substantially and negatively affected if the person" no longer is able to exercise these functions. *Id.* at 1181. How does this test differ from the *B.M.H.* test? Would the claimant in *B.M.H.* be recognized as a de facto parent under *Pitts*? Does the test address any of the concerns of the *B.M.H.* dissent?

7. Some states have refused to recognize de facto parentage. For example, in Moreau v. Sylvester, 95 A.3d 416 (Vt. 2014), the Vermont Supreme Court affirmed an earlier decision rejecting the doctrine. The unmarried mother of two children and her partner had been in an on again–off again relationship for eight to ten years. The partner, who was not the biological father of the children, had played a "significant, father-like role" while they lived together, and had shared responsibility for the children after the couple separated. When their relationship deteriorated, he began to harass the mother and eventually sought recognition as a de facto parent. The Vermont Supreme Court rejected the man's de facto parent claim, explaining:

> . . . [T]here are public-policy considerations that favor allowing third parties claiming a parent-like relationship to seek court-compelled parent-child contact. These considerations, however, are still not so persuasive as to compel recognition of a new cause of action, and matching equitable jurisdiction to entertain it, so that acquaintances and partners with less than adoptive or even stepparent status can seek court-compelled visitation with children of persons not legally related to them and against the wishes of their natural parents. . . . "[G]iven the complex

social and practical ramifications of expanding the classes of persons entitled to assert parental rights by seeking custody or visitation, the Legislature is better equipped" to address this issue.

Id. at 424. The *Moreau* court explained in a footnote that the implications of de facto parentage "could be far-reaching." It queried:

> Does recognition of a common law or equitable claim for parental contact by unrelated domestic partners include a corresponding right to claim child support from an unrelated but putative de facto parent? Can an unrelated but putative de facto parent then interfere with the biological parent's decision to move away with his or her children? Will every relief-from-abuse proceeding present an avenue for defendant partners to counterattack with de facto parentage complaints?

Id. at 424, n.12. *Cf.* Sinnott v. Peck, 180 A.3d 560, 564 (Vt. 2017) (finding that in a case "in which there is no competing claimant, parental status can flow from the mutual agreement and actions of the established legal parent and a putative second parent"). How would the majority in *B.M.H.* have responded to such questions? Would the dissent agree with the issues raised in *Moreau*? How would the court in *B.M.H.* have dealt with the assertion of de facto parentage if Mr. Holt had been harassing and threatening Ms. Holt? If Mr. Holt had sought recognition as a de facto parent only after Ms. Holt had decided to move to another state? *See also* LP v. LF, 338 P.3d 908, 919 (Wyo. 2014); Doty-Perez v. Doty-Perez, 388 P.3d 9, 12 (Ariz. App. 2016), *rev. denied* (Aug. 30, 2017) (rejecting de facto parentage doctrine); Cook v. Sullivan, 307 So.3d 1121 (La. App. Cir. 2020) (dismissing a former same-sex partner's petition for parentage because the legal parent's constitutional rights would be violated if the former same-sex partner were awarded joint custody).

8. As the *B.M.H.* opinions discuss, the fight for recognition of LGBT parenting led many states to adopt de facto parenthood provisions to address circumstances in which the adults could not marry or adopt each other's children. Now that marriage equality extends to all 50 states, the question arises whether de facto parentage provisions remain appropriate or necessary and, if so, to whom should they apply. Two cases overruled recent precedents insisting on bright line rules such as marriage, adoption, or biology for determining parentage after the adoption of marriage equality. *See* Conover v. Conover, 146 A.3d 433 (Md. 2016) (observing that a majority of states now recognize some form of de facto parentage); Brooke S.B. v. Elizabeth A.C.C., 61 N.E.3d 488 (N.Y. 2016) (holding that "where a partner shows by clear and convincing evidence that the parties agreed to conceive a child and to raise the child together, the non-biological, non-adoptive partner has standing, as a parent, to seek visitation and custody"). What does this indicate about the continuing importance of de facto parenthood?

9. The ALI Principles of the Law of Family Dissolution propose recognition of de facto parenthood, which gives some legal rights to a person "who, for a significant period of time not less than two years, lived with the child and, for reasons primarily other than financial compensation, and with the agreement of a legal parent to form a parent-child relationship, or as a result of a complete failure or inability of any legal parent to perform caretaking functions, (A) regularly performed a majority of the caretaking functions for the child, or (B) regularly performed a share of caretaking functions at least as great as that of the parent with whom the child primarily lived." ALI Principles of the Law of Family Dissolution §203(1)(c). The rights of a de facto parent are subordinate to those of a "parent by estoppel," who has full legal parental rights and responsibilities in most situations. Under the ALI, parent by estoppel (1) has lived with the child for at least two years and had a reasonable good faith belief that he was the child's biological father, and continued to make reasonable, good faith efforts to accept parental responsibilities even if the belief no longer existed; or (2) lived with the child since the child's birth or for at least two years and holds out and accepts full and permanent responsibility as a parent as the result of a co-parenting arrangement with the child's legal parent if recognition of the relationship is in the child's best interests; or (3) is liable for child support.

ALI Principles §2.03(1)(b). How do the ALI elements necessary to establish parenthood by estoppel differ from the elements necessary to establish de facto parenthood in *B.M.H.*?

The ALI indicates that being liable for support may be a basis for recognizing de facto parenthood but does not provide that de facto parents are liable for child support. The courts in some states, however, have held that once an adult seeks custody on a functional basis such as "psychological parent," they may also be liable for child support. *See, e.g.*, In re Moore v. McGillis, 408 P.3d 1196 (Alaska 2018) (involving stepparent); In re A.C.H., 440 P.3d 1266, 1270 (Colo. 2019) (finding unmarried partner who received custodial rights liable for support).

For a critique of the ALI approach and discussion of the different parental statuses in the ALI, *see* David D. Meyer, Partners, Care Givers, and the Constitutional Substance of Parenthood, Robin Fretwell Wilson, Undeserved Trust: Reflections on the ALI's Treatment of De Facto Parents, and Katharine K. Baker, Asymmetric Parenthood, all in Reconceiving the Family: Critical Reflections on the American Law Institute's Principles of the Law of Family Dissolution (Robin Fretwell Wilson ed., 2006).

NOTE: SECOND PARENT ADOPTION

Historically, the primary alternative to establishing parenthood through marriage was adoption. Legislatures crafted early adoption statutes to address "stranger adoption," that is, adoption by parents unrelated to (and often unknown to) the biological parents. These practices are addressed in greater length in Chapter 14. Over time, however, adoption procedures changed to incorporate stepparent adoption; that is, adoption by a spouse who, through adoption, acquired a legal parental status equivalent to that of the other spouse. Stepparent adoption differed from stranger adoption in that the initial legal parent retained parental status, whereas in stranger adoption, the adoption terminated the initial legal parent or parents' parental standing. In Marshall v. Marshall, 196 Cal. 761, 767 (1925), the California Supreme Court addressed the issue and "effectively read second parent adoption into the statutory scheme, by approving a type of second parent adoption, stepparent adoption, which at that time the adoption statutes did not expressly authorize. In so doing, we [the court] necessarily determined that relinquishment of the birth parent's rights was not essential to adoption." Sharon S. v. Superior Court, 73 P.3d 554 (Cal. 2003). Subsequent legislation distinguished between stranger adoption and stepparent adoption, generally allowing the latter to take place without the home study or other review by state agencies required for stranger adoption.

Same-sex couples who could not receive recognition of their parenting status through marriage began using adoption to do so. These adoptions typically involved an initial legal parent who had established a legal relationship to the child either through biology or adoption as a single parent. The adoptions are called "second parent adoptions" to indicate that they involve a second parent of the same sex, and to indicate that the first legal parent consented to the adoption by the second parent "without surrendering her [the initial legal parent's] rights and responsibilities." Emily Doskow, The Second Parent Trap, 20 J. Juv. L. 1, 5 (1999). The result is that "the child has two legal parents who have equal legal status in terms of their relationship with the child." Sharon S. v. Superior Court, above.

With marriage equality and recognition of de facto parenthood, parenthood by estoppel, and other judicial doctrines for recognizing functional parents, lawyers will need to consider what role adoption will continue to play in securing recognition of parenthood for partners who are not biologically related to the child. For married couples, adoption will presumably not be necessary for a child born into the marriage. *See Pavan*, above. Stepparent adoption will be available for married couples who wish to adopt a child born before the marriage. Adoption produces a judicial decree that is entitled to full faith and credit in all 50 states, and is therefore entitled to recognition even in a state that would not otherwise permit the couple to adopt. The Supreme Court unanimously upheld the obligation of the Alabama courts, for example, to grant full faith and credit to a Georgia adoption involving a same-sex couple. V.L. v. E.L., 136 S. Ct. 1017 (2016). The states have also been striking down legislation that prohibits same-sex couples from adopting. *See, e.g.*, Campaign for Southern Equality v. Mississippi Dep't of Human Servs., 175 F. Supp. 3d 691, 710 (D. Miss. 2016) (concluding that *Obergefell* recognized the right to adopt as a benefit of marriage); In re Adoption of Yasmin S., 956 N.W.2d 704 (Neb. 2021).

Couples who are not certain of their parental status may still wish to adopt. Some states do not recognize the functional parent doctrines, discussed above. In other cases, state law may not necessarily confer equal status on de facto parents. Moreover, litigation establishing functional parenthood can be expensive because of the need to go to court, and recognition is available only if, in hindsight, a court determines that the adult has become a functional parent. The latter feature alone means that unrelated adults who develop relationships with children cannot rely on these devices to protect those relationships, nor be certain that third parties will recognize their status. The fact that the doctrines are indeterminate and discretionary exacerbates this problem. In some states, however, unmarried couples still face greater obstacles in adopting than married couples – or outright prohibitions on their ability to adopt their partners' children. For a review of state laws, *see* Susan Hazeldean, Illegitimate Parents, 55 U.C. Davis L. Rev. 1583 (2022).

PROBLEMS

1. When Hank and Wanda were divorced, Hank agreed to pay child support for Bobby, their son born during the marriage, and for Ellie, Wanda's child from a former relationship who had lived with Hank and Wanda throughout their six-year marriage. The agreement was incorporated into Hank and Wanda's divorce decree. During the marriage Hank had signed an affidavit of paternity for Ellie and filed it with the Bureau of Vital Statistics, even though he was not in fact her biological father. He never formally adopted her, though. It is now two years since the divorce. Hank has remarried, and his new wife has just had twins. He has moved to terminate his duty to support Ellie on the basis that she is not his biological child. Ellie's biological father lives in an adjoining state. Wanda has had no contact with him since before Ellie's birth. What arguments should Wanda make? How should Hank respond?

2. Ross and Kathy were married when Kathy's child from her former marriage, Danny, was 6 months old. Ross knew that he was not Danny's biological father, but he treated him as his son in every way. Kathy died when Danny was seven years old. Until Kathy's death Danny had no contact with his biological father, Greg, who refused to visit. After Kathy's death Greg came forward, claiming the right to Danny's custody. Ross also seeks custody. As between Ross and Greg, to whom should the court award custody and why? As between Kathy's mother and Ross, to whom should the court award custody?

Would your answer change if Ross and Kathy divorced when Danny was six, Kathy had received primary custody, Ross had visitation one night a week, and Kathy and Danny lived with Kathy's mother?

3. Circe and Kelly had lived together for several years. Circe wanted children and she and Kelly decided to adopt. They approached international adoption agencies, who told them that, as an unmarried couple, they could not adopt together; one would need to adopt the child as a single individual and the other could enter into a second parent adoption once the child was in the United States. Circe filled out the forms, listing Kelly as a roommate. Before an adoption occurred, the two broke up though they remained in touch. About a year after their separation, the adoption agency contacted Circe, who had never withdrawn the application, about adopting Abush, an Ethiopian toddler. Circe excitedly told Kelly, who met the two of them at the airport in London on their way back from Ethiopia and accompanied them back to the United States. Although Circe and Kelly did not live together, Kelly regularly picked up Abush from school, took him to afterschool activities, and had him overnight. The two developed a close emotional bond. Circe and Kelly discussed Kelly's status and decided that Kelly would be a "godparent." Five years after Abush's adoption, Circe decides to move back to London, where she was raised, to be closer to relatives and to be able to take advantage of the National Health Service and better job opportunities. Kelly is devastated at the thought of losing contact with Abush. In jurisdictions such as California or Washington that recognize functional parenthood, what arguments can Kelly make for recognition as a parent? What basis does Circe have to rebut these arguments? Where do Abush's interests lie and how should his interests affect the outcome?

D. MORE THAN TWO PARENTS?

Traditional parentage law, particularly the strong marital presumption, protected the relationships that children form with their caretakers. Today, however, a significant number of children are raised by a changing cast of adults. It is no longer clear that an insistence on two—and only two—parents continues to makes sense. Moreover, with recognition of functional parent doctrines, multiple adults may satisfy the legal standards for parenthood. *See, e.g.*, Greer ex rel. Farbo v. Greer, 324 P.3d 310 (Kan. App. 2014) (above). In Michael H. v. Gerald D., above, the case in which the United States Supreme Court addressed the constitutionality of the marital presumption, a guardian ad litem was appointed to represent the interests of the child, Victoria. The guardian argued that Victoria's interests would best be served by allowing her to maintain a personal relationship with both men, her mother's husband who was raising her and the biological father she called "Daddy." Justice Scalia's plurality opinion rejected this argument out of hand, saying, "California law, like nature itself, makes no provision for dual fatherhood." The case might have been decided quite differently if the lower court had had the option of recognizing both Michael and Gerald as Victoria's fathers, and then deciding what role each would play on the basis of a best-interests determination. Today, as we will discuss below, California and 12 other states permit such a possibility. The Louisiana courts were among the first to do, recognizing the possibility of "dual paternity" under state law.

T.D. v. M.M.M.
730 So. 2d 873 (La. 1999)

TRAYLOR, J. . . .

The child's mother, T.D., and legal father, M.M.M., were married in October of 1984. In October of 1985, T.D. met P.W., who was also married at the time. T.D. and P.W. began having adulterous sexual relations in March or April of 1986. The affair spanned a period of approximately seven and one-half years. In March of 1988, T.D. conceived a child, C.M. T.D. informed P.W. that she suspected he was the father because she had not been intimate with her husband at the time of conception. T.D. also informed her husband that he was the father of the child.

T.D. and P.W. discontinued their sexual relations during the pregnancy, but continued with the affair shortly after the child's birth in December of 1988. P.W. testified that he regularly visited the mother and child throughout the affair and always suspected that he was the child's father. In November of 1992, T.D. and M.M.M. separated. At T.D.'s request, P.W. curbed his visits during most of the separation, but resumed them in March of 1993. In April of 1993, the child and P.W. underwent DNA paternity testing. In June of 1993, the DNA test results confirmed to a 99.5% probability that P.W. was the child's biological father. That same month, T.D. and M.M.M. were granted a divorce. In August of 1993, the trial court named T.D. as the domiciliary parent and granted M.M.M. visitation. T.D. ended the affair with P.W. in November 1993 and, thereafter, would not allow P.W. access to the child.

In December 1994, P.W. intervened in the legal parents' domestic proceedings seeking recognition of his biological paternity, joint custody, and visitation. The legal parents objected to this intervention. The court held that P.W.'s suit was not untimely because "his suspicions of parenthood were not confirmed until he received the results of the [DNA test]" and that visitation rights of any parent must be considered in light of the best interests of the child. The court recognized P.W. as the child's biological father, ordered a mental health evaluation of the child to assess possible effects of parentage information and visitation with the biological father, and, finding itself without sufficient evidence to determine the best interest of the child, the court ordered an evidentiary hearing to determine visitation rights and to assess income for potential child support issues.

The legal parents appealed from this ruling, arguing the biological father's action was untimely. . . .

In order for this court to decide the timeliness of the instant action, we must first set out the jurisprudential background of avowal. Louisiana courts have traditionally recognized a biological father's right to his illegitimate child[22] by means of an avowal action. This action is available despite the La. Civ. Code art. 184 presumption that the husband of the mother is the father of all children born or conceived during the marriage.[23]

In our view, several policy factors favor allowing a biological father to avow his child where such action will result in dual paternity. First, a biological father is susceptible to suit for child support until his child reaches nineteen years of age. La. Civ. Code art. 209. Second, a child who enjoys legitimacy as to his legal father may seek to filiate to his biological father in order to receive wrongful death benefits or inheritance rights. It seems only fair, in light of the obligations to which a biological father is susceptible and the multitude of benefits available to the biological child due to the biological link, that the biological father should be afforded at least an opportunity to prove his worthiness to participate in the child's life. Alternatively, a biological father who cannot meet the best-interest-of-the-child standard retains his obligation of support but cannot claim the privilege of parental rights. Finding that a biological father clearly has the right to avow his illegitimate child under the law of this state, we now turn to the issue of whether P.W. asserted his action in a timely manner. . . .

---

22. In this context, we use the term "illegitimate" to connote a child who is not born in the marriage of his biological father to his mother and/or is assumed to be the child of another man. A child who enjoys legitimacy as to his legal father may also be the illegitimate child of his biological parent. Our jurisprudence allowing dual paternity provides that such a child may filiate to his biological father or the biological father may avow the child.

23. Contrast this to the holding of the U.S. Supreme Court in Michael H. v. Gerald D., 491 U.S. 110 (1989). We find the instant case distinguishable from the former case because, unlike Louisiana law, a California statute specifically prohibits dual paternity and mandates that the husband of the mother of the child born during marriage is conclusively presumed to be the father. Such a finding is not tenable in Louisiana because the law of this State allows recognition of dual paternity and the Article 184 presumption of paternity is rebuttable.

The legal parents based their appeal on the argument that laches bars a biological father's avowal action where it is not promptly asserted. As a matter of law, the purpose of the doctrine is to prevent an injustice which might result from the enforcement of long neglected rights and to recognize the difficulty of ascertaining the truth as a result of that delay. However, this court has clearly established that the common law doctrine of laches does not prevail in Louisiana. Nevertheless, we have applied the doctrine in rare and extraordinary circumstances.

We will consider the elements of the doctrine as they apply to the instant case to determine if rare and extraordinary circumstances exist in the instant case which merit application of the doctrine of laches. Regarding the first element of prejudice, we find no proof of prejudice to the child nor to the defendants in intervention, the legal parents. To the contrary, the trial judge expressly limited his ruling to a finding of fact that P.W. is the child's father. The trial court passed on the issue of the best interest of the child because it was without sufficient evidence to make a knowledgeable finding. If evidence of the best interest of the child was lacking, certainly there is insufficient proof institution of this action has caused prejudice to the child. . . . The legal parents failed to prove the first element of laches. . . .

Regarding the second element of delay, we surmise that the delay in this case is not entirely the fault of the biological father. It is apparent that the actions of the mother have caused much of the delay. P.W. regularly visited his child when he was on good terms with the mother. This appears to be the reason why he did not file suit until after the affair ended and his attempts to visit his child were thwarted. P.W. filed his suit less than one year after it became apparent that he was not free to visit his child, and approximately six years from the child's birth. We find P.W. did not seek enforcement of long neglected rights because his filing was not unreasonable in light of circumstances which impute much of the delay to the mother. Thus, the legal parents failed to prove the second element of laches.

It is the province of the trial court to determine the nature and extent of a biological father's rights to his illegitimate child. For this reason, we remand this matter to the trial court for such a determination. Assuming arguendo that P.W. can convince the trial court that his involvement in C.M.'s life is in the best interest of C.M., he should not be precluded from participating in the child's life. . . .

KNOLL, J., concurring. I write separately to concur in the result only. In my view, since Louisiana law (our Civil Code and statutory law) fails to provide for an avowal action for an unwed biological father, the real focus of the majority opinion should be directed toward a consideration of the unwed biological father's constitutional rights, placed in balance with competing interests. . . .

If an unwed biological father's claim is supported by constitutionally based rights, a procedural bar cannot deny consideration of those claims based on state law or absence thereof, because state law is subordinate to the Constitution according to the supremacy clause. . . . Specifically, the majority should have addressed the unwed biological father's liberty interest in the relationship with his child and whether he may be deprived of his rights without due process of law. . . .

In the case *sub judice*, the biological father did develop a relationship with his natural child, particularly as the natural mother's marriage was drawing to a close. He should not be faulted for not coming forward during the time in which his child's mother was married to another man, because Louisiana's public policy favors protecting the marital unit. Given the presumption of paternity in La. Code Civ. P. art. 184 and the strong State interests in preserving the marital family unit that gave rise to the presumption, any efforts made during that marriage would have been properly thwarted.

The fact that a biological father is thwarted from exercising parental rights when the mother is married to another man is not constitutionally offensive, because the balance tips in favor of preserving the marital family over the biological father's individual rights. *See* Michael H. v. Gerald D., 491 U.S. 110 (1989). However, once the bonds of matrimony are dissolved *a vinculo matrimonii*, the State's interest in preserving the marital family disappears. This does not ignore the fact that some rights spring from the dissolution of a lawful marriage, but recognizes instead the policy behind the codal provision and the perspective of our times. Today's realities are that illegitimacy and "broken homes" have neither the rarity nor the stigma as in the past. When parenthood can be objectively determined by scientific evidence, and where illegitimacy is no longer stigmatized, presumptions regarding paternity are "out of place." . . . In this case, where we have conclusive scientific evidence of true paternity based on DNA testing, it is inappropriate not to address the biological father's substantive rights. . . .

For the reasons above, I respectfully concur in the results.

Calogero, C.J., dissenting. . . . I would hold that this biological father lacks standing to bring an avowal action, as no statutory or codal authority exists granting him standing to rebut the article 184 presumption of paternity. Rather, the Civil Code only permits the child to seek dual paternity. La. Civ. Code art. 209. Moreover, public policy dictates that the relationships among a legal father, child, and his or her mother remain protected, even though the marital relationship has dissolved. Accordingly, I respectfully dissent.

NOTES AND QUESTIONS

1. If Louisiana law did not allow "dual paternity," what arguments for being recognized as C.M.'s legal father might P.W. raise under the Uniform Parentage Act? What counterarguments could the mother, T.D., make? Could P.W. successfully argue that he was a de facto parent under *B.M.H.*?

2. California adopted the following statute, which it incorporated into the California Uniform Parentage Act:

> In an appropriate action, a court may find that more than two persons with a claim to parentage under this division are parents if the court finds that recognizing only two parents would be detrimental to the child. In determining detriment to the child, the court shall consider all relevant factors, including, but not limited to, the harm of removing the child from a stable placement with a parent who has fulfilled the child's physical needs and the child's psychological needs for care and affection, and who has assumed that role for a substantial period of time.

(Cal. Fam. Code §7612(c) (2016)) What showing would P.W. have to make to meet the requirements to be a third parent under California law?

3. Other Louisiana cases on dual paternity hold that an unmarried biological father whose paternity is established in Louisiana can be liable for child support, and his child may claim wrongful death benefits or inheritance rights at the father's death, but he is unlikely to prevail in an action for custody or visitation over the objection of the mother and her husband. Smith v. Cole, 553 So. 2d 847 (La. 1989); Smith v. Jones, 566 So. 2d 408 (La. App. 1990); Finnerty v. Boyett, 469 So. 2d 287 (La. 1985); Durr v. Blue, 454 So. 2d 315 (La. App. 1984). *Cf.* Geen v. Geen, 666 So. 2d 1192, 1193 (La. App. 1995), *writ denied,* 669 So. 2d

1224 (La. 1996) (awarding all three parents joint legal custody in a case where the biological father had married the mother and was living with the mother and child).

In 2015, the Louisiana Supreme Court considered the whether the biological father's income should be considered when calculating a divorced husband's child support obligation. State Dep't of Children and Fam. Servs. ex rel. A.L. v. Lowrie, 167 So. 3d 573 (La. 2015). The state had sued the husband for support. The husband responded that the biological father was living with the child and providing support at the time of the litigation, and should be joined as a party to the litigation. The court concluded that "[i]f it is proven that Mr. Wetzel is the biological father of A.L. and is, therefore, legally obliged to contribute to A.L.'s support, Mr. Lowrie [the legal father] should be entitled to a deviation in the calculation of the child support obligation to include in the calculation the income of Mr. Wetzel." *Id.* at 587.

What are the advantages of the Louisiana dual paternity approach, which allows more than two legal parents, over the other doctrines we have examined in this chapter? What problems does it create?

4. After *T.D.* was decided, the Louisiana legislature amended various statutes in 2005 so that now a husband who wishes to disavow his paternity must do so within one year of a child's birth, and a man claiming to be the biological father of a child presumed to be the child of another man must bring a filiation action within a year of birth unless the mother in bad faith deceived the biological father about his paternity. In the latter situation, the suit must be brought within one year from the day the father knew or should have known of his paternity, or within ten years from the birth of the child, whichever occurs first. La. Civ. Code art. 189, 198 (2022). For more information, *see* Katharine Shaw Spaht, Who's Your Momma, Who Are Your Daddies? Louisiana's New Law of Filiation, 67 La. L. Rev. 307 (2007).

5. In enacting the three-parent statute set out in note 2 above, the California legislature found that "[m]ost children have two parents, but in rare cases, children have more than two people who are that child's parent in every way. Separating a child from a parent has a devastating psychological and emotional impact on the child, and courts must have the power to protect children from this harm." Senate Bill No. 274, Section 1(a) (2014).

The statute's requirement of a showing of "detriment to the child" is the same standard California uses to justify an award of visitation over the objections of a parent to a third party such as a grandparent or stepparent. *See* In re Marriage of W., 7 Cal. Rptr. 3d 461 (Cal. App. 2003). Does designation of a person as a "parent" or, indeed, as a third parent, rather than as a stepparent or grandparent, have constitutional implications? For a summary of the constitutional debate, *see* David D. Meyer, Partners, Care Givers, and the Constitutional Substance of Parenthood, *in* Reconceiving the Family: Critical Reflections on the American Law Institute's Principles of the Law of Family Dissolution (Robin Fretwell Wilson ed., 2006).

In 2015, Maine adopted a statute that provided, "Consistent with the establishment of parentage under this chapter, a court may determine that a child has more than 2 parents." Me. Rev. Stat. tit. 19-A §1853 (2022). Unlike the California statute, the Maine statute does not require a showing of detriment to the child to recognize three parents. If the first two parents object to recognition of the third person, would they have a constitutional basis on which to invalidate the Maine statute?

Connecticut, which adopted the 2017 Uniform Parentage Act, effective in 2022, also recognizes the possibility of three parents. Conn. Gen. Stat. Ann. §46b (2022). Colorado, however, has concluded that its state version of the Uniform Parentage Act does not permit more than two. People In Int. of K.L.W., 492 P.3d 392, 395 (2021).

6. Other states have occasionally recognized three parents, particularly where all three parents were in agreement on the inclusion of the third person, though most of the decisions are unreported. A Pennsylvania case is one of the first reported decisions to recognize more than two legal parents. In Jacob v. Shultz-Jacob, 923 A.2d 473 (Pa. Super. 2007), a lesbian couple, who had entered into a civil union in Vermont, were jointly raising four children. The biological father of two of the children, who had acted as a sperm donor but never sought to sever his parental standing, provided support and saw the children on a regular basis. The trial court awarded partial custody to each of the two women, and partial custody of two of the children to their biological father but rejected the possibility of holding three parents liable for support. The appellate court, in the first reported case of its kind, vacated the support order and remanded, instructing the trial court to consider fractional support awards among the three parties. The Canadian courts have also recognized three parents, including two lesbian partners and a sperm donor in a case involving an ongoing family arrangement. *See* A.A. v. B.B., [2007] 278 D.L.R. (4th) 519, 522, 533-534 (Can.), *leave to appeal denied sub nom.* Alliance for Marriage & Family v. A.A., [2007] 3 S.C.R. 124.

In addition, a number of states recognize third-party visitation rights. *See, e.g.*, McAllister v. McAllister, 779 N.W.2d 652, 660-661 (N.D. 2010) (awarding visitation to stepparent in a case in which the mother had primary custody and the biological father had visitation). In addition, the ALI Principles recognizing de facto parenthood provide that "[t]he case for recognition of an additional parent is weaker if a child already has two (or more) parents, although this factor is not dispositive, particularly if one of the child's legal parents has formed no significant parental relationship with the child." ALI Principles of the Law of Family Dissolution: Analysis and Recommendations §2.03 (Ira M. Ellman et al. eds., 2002).

7. Can multiple-parent statutes be used to recognize polyamorous couples? In California, two married, biological parents raised a child together with their long-time intimate partner in a polyamorous relationship. The three adults sought to have the partner adopt the child without terminating the parental status of the biological parents. The trial court refused to grant the adoption petition, even though the home inspection found that it was in the best interests of the child, because the parties had not established that adoption would avoid a "detriment to the child." The Court of Appeal reversed on the ground that the trial court has applied the wrong standard: recognizing a third party under the California Uniform Parentage Act (set forth in Note 2) requires a showing of detriment but granting an adoption only requires a finding that it was in the child's best interests. Adoption of E.B., 76 Cal. App. 5th 359, 370 (2022). What arguments, if any, could be made on remand regarding the child's best interests? If, instead, the couple dissolved their relationship without an adoption and all three adults sought custodial rights, what standard should the court apply to their custody petitions?

8. Almost 40 years ago, Katharine Bartlett, the principal author of the ALI de facto parent and parent by estoppel provisions, first fully set out the argument for legal recognition of the roles multiple adults play in some children's lives. Katharine Bartlett, Rethinking Parenthood as an Exclusive Status: The Need for Legal Alternatives When the Premise of the Nuclear Family Has Failed, 70 Va. L. Rev. 879 (1984). More recent discussions include Susan Frelich Appleton, Parents by the Numbers, 37 Hofstra L. Rev. 11 (2008); Katharine K. Baker, Bionormativity and the Construction of Parenthood, 42 Ga. L. Rev. 649, 655 (2008); Cynthia Grant Bowman, The Legal Relationship Between Cohabitants and Their Partners' Children, 13 Theoretical Inquiries L. 127 (2012); Nancy E. Dowd, Multiple Parents/Multiple Fathers, 9 J.L. & Fam. Stud. 231 (2007); Leslie Joan Harris, The Basis for Legal Parentage and the Clash Between Custody and Child Support, 42 Ind. L. Rev. 611 (2009); Melanie B. Jacobs, Why Just Two? Disaggregating Traditional Parental Rights and Responsibilities to Recognize Multiple Parents, 9 J.L. & Fam. Stud. 209 (2007); Laura T. Kessler, Community Parenting, 24 Wash. U. J.L. & Pol'y 47, 49 (2007); Melissa Murray, The Networked Family: Reframing the Legal Understanding of Caregiving and Caregivers, 94 Va. L. Rev. 385 (2008); Myrisha S. Lewis, Biology, Genetics, Nurture, and the Law: The Expansion of the Legal Definition of Family to Include Three or More Parents, 16 Nev. L.J. 743, 744-745 (2016); June

Carbone & Naomi Cahn, Parents, Babies, and More Parents, 92 Chi.-Kent L. Rev. 9 (2017); Jacqueline V. Gaines, The Legal Quicksand 2+ Parents: The Need for a National Definition of a Legal Parent, 46 U. Dayton L. Rev. 105 (2021). Jessica Feinberg, The Boundaries of Multi-Parentage, 75 SMU L. Rev. 307 (2022). *See also* Shelly Ann Kamei, Comment, Partitioning Paternity: The German Approach to a Disjuncture Between Genetic and Legal Paternity with Implications for American Courts, 11 San Diego Int'l L.J. 509 (2010).

PROBLEMS

1. Donna and Emily were married in California. Emily supported Donna when Donna became pregnant and gave birth to a baby girl, Ingrid, named after Emily's mother. George and Harry also married in California, and they contributed sperm to Donna with the understanding that the two men would play an "uncle" role in the child's upbringing. George and Harry mixed their sperm before the insemination, and no one knows whether George or Harry is Ingrid's biological father. George and Harry see Ingrid at least once every two weeks, and they often contribute financially.

Donna and Emily divorced when Ingrid was a year old, and Emily moved to the East Coast. Her relationship with Donna remains amicable, and Emily sees Ingrid two to three times a year. A few months after the split with Emily, Donna entered into a new informal relationship with Francine. When Ingrid was 4, Francine and Donna separated. The separation was not amicable, and Donna refuses to let Francine continue to see Ingrid. Ingrid regards Donna and Francine as her two "mommies." She views George and Harry as her two uncles. Who should be regarded as Ingrid's parents and with what rights and obligations?

2. Melissa and Irene, who registered as domestic partners, had a tumultuous relationship. After a particularly intense conflict, Melissa moved out and obtained a restraining order against Irene, alleging physical and emotional abuse. Melissa entered into a relationship with Jesus and became pregnant. During the first few months of the pregnancy, she lived with Jesus and his family, and he supported her financially. Before the baby was born, however, Melissa left Jesus and reconciled with Irene. Melissa did not notify Jesus of her address or of the child's birth. Jesus, who had moved to Oklahoma, did not make any effort to contact Melissa. Melissa listed only her own name on the child's birth certificate, but she and Irene jointly cared for the child for about a month after the child's birth. Then Melissa moved out, and when the child was two months old, Irene filed for shared custody or visitation. Melissa contacted Jesus, who sent money on several occasions. At his request, Melissa regularly took the baby to visit his family.

Melissa then entered into a relationship with Jose. When the child was about six months old, Jose attacked Irene with a knife, stabbing her in the neck and causing severe injuries. Melissa admitted that she and Jose were using drugs at the time and that the attack was intended to scare Irene and keep her away from the baby. Melissa was arrested and charged with being an accessory to attempted murder. Jose fled and has had no contact with Melissa or the child since the attack.

Irene was badly injured in the attack. She has no means of support and has been living with friends. Melissa suffers from bipolar disorder and severe depression. Jesus has a stable job in Oklahoma and support from his fiancée and grandmother in caring for the child.

Who should receive recognition as the child's parents under the California statute above and how should custody be allotted? What would the result be under the Uniform Parentage Act in a state that limits recognition to two parents? Would the result change if Irene and Melissa, who could not marry at the time they entered into a domestic partnership, were married at the time of the child's conception or birth?

CHAPTER 14

ADOPTION AND ALTERNATIVE REPRODUCTIVE TECHNOLOGIES

In the previous chapter we examined basic principles used to determine who the legal parents of a child are—biology, marriage, and functioning in a parental role. We also looked at traditional premises regarding parenthood, such as the proposition that each child must have one and only one mother and father, and challenges to these premises. In the process, we considered the growing role of function and intent in establishing parenthood and the challenges to the notion that parenthood necessarily involves two and only two parents.

The topics of this chapter—adoption and parenthood by means of alternative reproductive technologies—continue our study of these issues. The adoption materials raise fundamental questions about the role of intention in defining parenthood, how society determines when parents can lose their legal status, and what role, if any, adults who are not legal parents should play in determining how a child will be raised. Alternative reproductive technologies— artificial insemination, in vitro fertilization, embryo transplantation, and others—also raise these issues and even challenge our understanding of what it means to be a biological parent.

Thus, although the issues covered in this chapter do not arise in practice nearly as often as do those in Chapter 13, they are very important for what they reveal about our understanding of legal parent-child relationships.

A. ADOPTION

Burton Z. Sokoloff

Antecedents of American Adoption
3(1) The Future of Children 17, 18, 21-22 (Spring 1993)[1]

Reference to adoption may be found in the Bible and in the ancient codes, laws, and writings of Babylonians, Chinese, Egyptians, Hebrews, and Hindus. It is believed that this practice was usually employed to provide male heirs to childless couples, to maintain family lines and estates, or to fulfill the requirements of specific religious practices such as ancestor worship. It is commonly stated that adoption law in the United States is based upon early Roman laws;

---

1. This journal is a publication of The Future of Children, a collaboration of the Woodrow Wilson School of Public and International Affairs at Princeton University and the Brookings Institution, formerly published by the David and Lucile Packard Foundation.—Eds.

however, as Presser points out: "In contrast with current adoption law, which has as its purpose the 'best interests of the child,' it appears that ancient adoption law . . . was clearly designed to benefit the *adopter*, and any benefits to the adoptee were secondary."[2] . . . Hollinger adds that the adoptees were all male and usually adults, not children, and concludes that the relationship between adoption as known by the Romans and adoption as practiced by Americans "is tenuous at best."[3]

Likewise, English common law cannot be cited as the precedent for American adoption law because the former makes no reference to adoption and because the first general adoption statute was not enacted in England until 1926, some 75 years after passage of the first adoption statute in the United States. Thus, as Hollinger states, American adoption is "purely a creature of the statutes which have been enacted in this country since the mid-nineteenth century."[4] . . .

During the nineteenth century, adoption laws developed in response to the desire both to give legal status to children whose care had been transferred and to encourage more available and better care for dependent children. . . .

The first comprehensive adoption statute was passed in Massachusetts in 1851.

. . . The Massachusetts statute is particularly notable in that, for the first time, the interests of the child were expressly emphasized and the adoption had to be approved by a judge.

. . . [B]y 1929 all states had enacted some form of adoption legislation. Virtually all statutes emphasized the "best interests of the child" as the basis for adoption. . . .

During the first half of the twentieth century, *secrecy, anonymity*, and the *sealing of records* became statutorily required and standard adoption practice. The Minnesota Act of 1917 is commonly credited with having initiated the secrecy and sealed records aspects of adoption. Actually, as Hollinger points out, these practices "were not designed to preserve anonymity between biological parents and adopters, but to shield the adoption proceedings from public scrutiny. These statutes barred all persons from inspecting the files and records on adoption except for the parties to the adoption and their attorneys."[5] Nevertheless, beginning in the 1920s and extending well into the 1940s, states progressively amended their statutes "to provide not only for the sealing of adoption records, but also for denial to everyone of access to these records except upon a judicial finding of 'good cause.'" In these statutes, the identities of the birthparents and the adoptive parents were to remain secret, even from each other. . . .

The movement toward secrecy is said to have been urged by social workers in child-placing agencies with the goal of removing the stigma of illegitimacy from children born out of wedlock. These workers believed that assuring the anonymity of the birth mothers and the privacy of the adoptive family would make the integration of the child into the adoptive family more secure. . . .

In addition to the passage of adoption legislation, the first half of the twentieth century is characterized by a dramatic increase in interest in adoption on the part of childless couples and in the steady trend toward adoption of infants. Prior to the 1920s very few legal adoptions of children actually took place when compared with the numbers of children in institutions, in foster care, or in situations created by informal transfers. . . .

---

2. Presser, S. B. The historical background of the American law of adoption, Journal of Family Law (1972) 11:446.

3. Hollinger, J. H. Introduction to adoption law and practice. In Adoption Law and Practice. J. H. Hollinger, ed. New York: Matthew Bender & Co., Inc. 1991, p.1-19.

4. *See id.*, p.1-18.

5. *Id.*, p.13-5.

World War I and the influenza epidemic that followed resulted in a sharp drop in the birth rate and an increased interest in infant adoption. . . . Major factors encouraging infant adoption were the development of successful formula feeding and the perception that environment, not heredity, was the major determinant of child development.

Hollinger describes the end of the first half of the twentieth century as follows:

> By the 1950s, a complete transition had occurred from the earlier interest in adopting older children to the present desire for adoptable babies. . . . A 1951 survey of 25 states indicated that nearly 70% of children being placed for adoption were under the age of one. . . . Well over half of the children were born out of wedlock, two-fifths of the mothers being under 18. The remaining children came primarily from "broken homes." . . . Fewer than 10% of the children were placed because both of their parents were dead.

For more on the history of American adoption law, in addition to the sources cited in this excerpt, *see* Jamil S. Zainaldin, The Emergence of a Modern American Family Law: Child Custody, Adoption, and the Courts, 1796-1851, 73 Nw. U. L. Rev. 1038 (1979); Michael Grossberg, Governing the Hearth 268-280 (1985); Naomi Cahn, Perfect Substitutes or the Real Thing?, 52 Duke L.J. 1077 (2003). *See also* The Adoption History Project, available at https://pages.uoregon.edu/adoption/ (last visited Sept. 7, 2022); Part I Adoption, Society and the Law: The Common Law Context, 41 IUS Gentium 2 (2015); Part II Developing International Benchmarks for Modern Adoption Law, 41 IUS Gentium 78 (2015).

The incidence of adoption today differs substantially from a half-century ago. In 2020, 1.4 million adopted children under the age of 18 lived in the United States, a drop from 1.5 million in 2010 and 1.6 million in 2000. Adopted children made up only 1.9 percent of all children under the age of 18. Bureau of the Census, 2020: American Community Survey 5-year Estimates, tbl. B09018 (2020).

In this country, children come into adoption through one of three primary routes. Some children are adopted from abroad, though by 2021, the number of international adoptions had fallen to approximately 2,000 children, less than 10 percent of the 2007 total. U.S. Department of State, Bureau of Consular Affairs, Adoption Statistics (2022), https//travel.state.gov/content/travel/en/Intercountry-Adoption/adopt_ref/adoption-statistics-esri.html?wcmmode=disabled. Some children are adopted out of foster care, with the numbers of adoptions from foster placements remaining more consistent, varying from approximately 52,000 in 2012 to 66,000 in 2019 and then falling modestly with the COVID pandemic. Children's Bureau, U.S. Department of Health and Human Services, Trends in Foster Care and Adoption: FY 2012 – 2021 (Nov. 1, 2022), https://www.acf.hhs.gov/cb/report/trends-foster-care-adoption. Some children are placed for adoption with private agencies at birth. Exact numbers for these adoptions are hard to come by, but they have been estimated at roughly 18,000 per year. Olga Khazan, The New Question Haunting Adoption, The Atlantic, Oct. 19, 2021. "As an option in cases of unintended pregnancy, adoption is surprisingly uncommon in the U.S. with less than 3% of white unmarried women and less than 2% of Black unmarried women deciding to place a child for adoption. These figures represent a marked decline from 50 years ago when 40% of unmarried white women placed for adoption." Priscilla K. Coleman & Debbie Garratt, From Birth Mothers to First Mothers: Toward a Compassionate Understanding of the Life-Long Act of Adoption Placement, 31 Issues L. & Med. 139, 141 (2016). Of the 64,000 children who were adopted from foster care in 2019, 52 percent were adopted by their foster parent(s) and 36 percent by a relative; 26 percent were age nine years or older.

Total adoptions in the United States sharply decreased from 115,535 in 2019 to 95,306 in 2020, in part because of COVID. The three most common countries of origin for international adoption in 2020 were China (202), South Korea (188), and Colombia (137).

Domestic adoptions of infants also fell during the pandemic, declining from 25,800 in 2019 to 19,800 in 2020. Adoption in the U.S.: How Many? How Much? How Long?, Creating a Family, https://creatingafamily.org/adoption-category/adoption-blog/adoption-cost-length-time (last accessed Sept. 1, 2022).

State law governs adoption, and statutory requirements vary significantly from state to state. Nevertheless, it is possible generally to describe adoption as a two-stage process. The first stage is the termination of the parent-child relationship between the child and any legal parent who is going to be "replaced." The second stage is creation of the new legal parent-child relationship between the adoptive parent and the child, which under most circumstances requires a judicial proceeding.[6]

The next two sections consider the adoption process; the third explores the role that a child's membership in a social group plays in determining whether a child will be adopted and, if so, by whom.

1. Terminating the First Parent-Child Relationship

Ordinarily, before a child with a legal parent may be adopted, that parent's relationship to the child must be terminated. A second parent's rights must be terminated before the child can be adopted if the second parent is entitled to substantive custodial rights under state law (*see* Section B of Chapter 13). In some circumstances, a legal parent's former unmarried partner, whether biologically related to the child or not, may also have custodial rights. *See, e.g.,* A.H. v. W.R.L., 482 S.W.3d 372 (Ky. 2016). A parent may voluntarily give up parental rights by consenting to the child's adoption, and all states also have enacted statutes that allow courts to terminate parents' rights without their consent.

a. Consent to Adopt

All states permit a parent to consent to the adoption of a child and require that consent be voluntary. Some statutes provide that a parent may not give legally effective consent to adopt before a child is born, and some say that effective consent cannot be given until several days (typically three to five) after the birth.

If a parent who gave apparent consent has a change of heart and can show that consent was obtained by duress or fraud or that procedural requirements were not satisfied, the adoption may be invalidated. However, some cases refuse this remedy on theories of estoppel or laches if the parent raises this claim long after the adoptive parents have assumed physical custody.

Physical placement of the child with a prospective adoptive family alone does not amount to consent to adoption. In most states, consent must be given to the court. In some states, the biological parents must personally appear in court to give their consent, while in other states a written document expressing consent is sufficient. If the adoption is being arranged by an agency, the biological parents relinquish physical custody of the child to the agency and give

---

6. The doctrine of "equitable adoption," which is based on estoppel principles, is recognized in some states. Under this doctrine, the would-be adoptive parents have agreed to adopt a child, but for some reason the adoption is never completed. Upon a showing of detrimental reliance on this agreement to adopt, the adoptive parents (and their successors) are estopped to deny that the child was adopted, and the child has the same rights that he or she would have if the adoption had been completed. Most of the equitable adoption cases arise in the context of probate of the "adoptive" parents' estates, and the effect of finding that a child was equitably adopted is to give the child inheritance rights. For purposes of Social Security survivors' benefits, equitably adopted children are considered a decedent's children. 20 C.F.R. §404.354(a). *See also* Cynthia Grant Bowman, The New Illegitimacy: Children of Cohabiting Couples and Stepchildren, 20 Am. U. J. Gender Soc. Pol'y & L. 437 (2012).

written consent to termination of their rights to the agency. After the agency has placed the child with the prospective adoptive parents, it gives the necessary consent during the judicial proceedings.

The next case concerns the meaning of consent to adoption in the context of the now-common practice of open adoption.

Monty S. v. Jason W.
863 N.W.2d 484 (Neb. 2015)

HEAVICAN, C.J. . . . The parties in this case were friends. Rebecca was unable to have children, and a foster child that had been placed with Rebecca and Jason had been moved to a placement with biological relatives. Teresa and Monty "felt sorry" for Rebecca and discussed the possibility that Teresa might serve as a surrogate for the couple. Rebecca and Jason ultimately agreed, and it was decided that Teresa and Monty would conceive a child and, at the time of its birth, give that child to Rebecca and Jason for private placement adoption.

The parties agree that from the beginning, and certainly throughout Teresa's pregnancy and the days immediately following the child's birth, the intent was that Teresa and Monty would be a part of the child's life. The parties mostly agree that no discussions beyond this general agreement took place; it was an understanding, and not a detailed plan, that a relationship would exist.

Teresa testified that in her view, an "open" adoption was one in which the "adoptive parents [were] open to allowing the biological parents to be a part of his life and that his records would never be sealed." The record suggests that this was the general definition of the term as understood by all the parties.

Monty testified that he and Teresa were not informed that "open" adoptions were essentially unenforceable in Nebraska. This was confirmed by the testimony of the attorney conducting the meeting, as well as by Rebecca and Jason. Teresa and Monty also testified that had they known that they would not be able to maintain contact with the child, they would not have signed the relinquishment forms.

Teresa gave birth to the child in July 2013. The child went to Rebecca and Jason's home from the hospital. Two days after the child's birth, both couples and the child rode together to a meeting at the office of Rebecca and Jason's attorney. During that meeting, Teresa and Monty each signed separate documents relinquishing their parental rights and consenting to the adoption by Rebecca and Jason. At this meeting, Rebecca tore up the nonconsent forms presented to Teresa and Monty and announced that they were unnecessary because the adoption was to be "open." Nonconsent forms are signed by biological parents to signify the intent that adoption records be sealed. Where the forms are not signed, such records are not sealed.

On May 12, 2014, Teresa and Monty filed a petition for habeas corpus, seeking return of the child. . . . Following a best interests hearing, custody of the child was placed with Teresa and Monty. Rebecca and Jason appeal. . . .

[The adoptive parents proffered evidence that they terminated the biological parents' visits because the mother's visits "became so frequent that they began to interfere with Rebecca and Jason's relationships with the child."]

We now turn to whether the relinquishments in this case were invalid. This case presents a private adoption. In this situation, the child is relinquished directly into the hands of the prospective adoptive parents without interference by the state or a private agency.

A natural parent who relinquishes his or her rights to a child by a valid written instrument gives up all rights to the child at the time of the relinquishment. A valid relinquishment is irrevocable. The only right retained by the natural parents is the "right to commence an action seeking . . . to be considered as a prospective parent if the best interests of the child so dictate. The natural parent's rights are no longer superior to those of the prospective adoptive family."

Where the relinquishment of rights by a natural parent is found to be invalid for any reason, a best interests hearing is nevertheless held: "The court shall not simply return the child to the natural parent upon a finding that the relinquishment was not a valid instrument."

Such relinquishments are generally upheld. We have held repeatedly that a change of attitude subsequent to signing a relinquishment is insufficient to invalidate the relinquishment. Rather . . . in the absence of threats, coercion, fraud, or duress, a properly executed relinquishment of parental rights and consent to adoption signed by a natural parent knowingly, intelligently, and voluntarily is valid.

Neb. Rev. Stat. §43-111 (Reissue 2008) provides that after a decree of adoption has been entered in a private adoption case, the natural parents of an adopted child shall be relieved of all parental duties and responsibilities for the child and shall have no rights over the child.

In this case, the district court explicitly found that there were no threats, fraud, or duress involved in the execution of Teresa and Monty's relinquishments. But the district court, relying on this court's decision in McCormick v. State, concluded that the relinquishments were conditioned upon the retention of some parental rights and were therefore invalid.

McCormick involved the parental rights of Richard and Joan McCormick to their son. The State had filed for termination of those rights. Just prior to the final hearing on the State's motion to terminate, a meeting took place between the McCormicks, their counsel, the guardian ad litem, and their caseworker. It was explained to the McCormicks that if they signed a relinquishment of their parental rights, there was a possibility that an "open" adoption could be arranged if cooperative adoptive parents were found. This idea was originally suggested by the caseworker. The McCormicks were told by their counsel that it was likely the court would terminate their parental rights if the hearing were held.

The McCormicks signed the relinquishments. Despite the conversation regarding the "open" adoption, the McCormicks were not permitted visitation with their son after they signed the relinquishments. The McCormicks filed a motion for a writ of habeas corpus, which was denied.

The McCormicks appealed. The court found that the McCormicks' relinquishments were coerced by the promise of the open adoption. We noted that "[a] relinquishment conditioned upon the retention of some parental rights is invalid." . . .

In this case, the record is clear, and the parties do not dispute, that an open adoption was planned. But this retention of parental rights, however slight, is sufficient to invalidate Teresa's and Monty's relinquishments.

We are not unsympathetic to the plight of adoptive and biological parents as they navigate through the highly emotional process of adoption. And it may be that in some situations, benefit could result from open arrangements such as those endorsed by the Legislature in the foster-adopt situation. At the same time, it is not this court's place to make such policy judgments. Until the Legislature acts to approve of these open adoption arrangements in a private adoption context, this court will not recognize them and will instead continue to hold that relinquishments signed with the promise of such an open adoption are invalid.

NOTES AND QUESTIONS

1. "Open adoption" means different things to different people. Sometimes it means only that birth parents choose the adoptive family from a pool generated by an adoption agency. Sometimes it connotes contact between the biological and adoptive parents before the adoption or after it on an ongoing basis. Birth parents' desire for more control over the placement of their children and for information about what happens to them and the negative experiences of some adults adopted as children in closed (anonymous and confidential) adoptions during the 1940s and 1950s have provided the impetus for opening adoptions from the outset.

After the *McCormick* decision, cited in *Monty S.*, the Nebraska legislature authorized open adoptions for children adopted from foster care, but *Monty S.*, in an omitted part of the opinion, concluded that this legislation does not apply to private adoptions. For a discussion of the circumstances of foster care adoptions, *see* Carol Sanger, Bargaining for Motherhood: Postadoption Visitation Agreements, 41 Hofstra L. Rev. 309 (2012). Monica Faulkner & Elissa E. Madden, in Open Adoption and Post-Adoption Birth Family Contact: A Comparison of Non-Relative Foster and Private Adoptions, 15 Adoption Q. 35 (2012), found that children adopted from foster care were less likely to experience post-adoption contact with their families of origin than children adopted privately, even though they were more likely to have lived with their families of origin.

2. In *Monty S.*, the Nebraska Supreme Court concludes that "the effect of an open adoption acts as the retention of some parental rights and . . . the retention of some parental rights renders a relinquishment invalid." Why does it render the relinquishment of the child invalid?

In contrast, some other states hold that while an agreement to permit postadoption visitation is unenforceable, the existence of such an agreement does not render consent to the adoption invalid. In other words, the adoption is valid, but the visitation provisions are not, allowing the adoptive parent or parents to cut off contact with the biological parents. *See, e.g.*, In re Petition of S.O., 795 P.2d 254 (Colo. 1990) (en banc). What arguments can you make for this result?

3. Suppose that the adoptive parents in *Monty S.* came to you before the pregnancy had occurred and informed you about their plans. They indicate that they are willing to allow their friends, the biological parents, to have contact with the child, but they want to make sure that they are recognized as the only legal parents. Assuming that Nebraska has no comprehensive surrogacy regulations, but would recognize the intended parents as legal parents pursuant to a valid adoption, would you advise them to enter into an agreement promising to allow such contact? How would you explain the potential implications of such an agreement?

Now suppose that the biological parents in *Monty S.* came to you before the pregnancy had occurred and informed you about their plans. They indicate that they are willing to allow their friends, the intended parents, to adopt the baby, but want to be able to make sure that they will have continued contact with the child. What would you advise them to do? If the biological parents in *Monty S.* had known at the time they agreed to the adoption that Nebraska does not recognize open adoptions, how would that have affected the result?

For discussion of the law governing surrogacy, *see* the discussion later in this chapter at p. 772.

4. Even consent validly given may be revocable. In some states, consent is revocable for a set period; in others, it is revocable until an adoption decree is entered. In some states, consent is revocable until the entry of the final decree for private adoptions; however, if consent is given to an agency, it is irrevocable. Uniform Adoption Act Section 2-404(a) provides that consent may be revoked within 192 hours (eight days) after the child's birth. If the consent is executed more than eight days after the child's birth, it is generally not revocable. The Act also requires that the biological parent have been informed about the meaning and consequences of adoption, the availability of personal and legal counseling, and procedures for release of identifying and nonidentifying information. *Id.*

The document of consent must be executed in the presence of a judicial official or attorney. Many states, however, have shorter time periods. *See* 1 Adoption Law and Practice § 2.11(1)(a) (2021).

5. Does the birth parent's ability to understand the adoption agreements affect the validity of consent? F.R. v. Adoption of Baby Boy Born November 2, 2010, 135 So.3d 301 (Fla. App. 2012) (finding that adoption agency's failure to translate documents into a language the birth mother could understand invalidated consent). For a discussion of potential grounds to challenge the validity of adoptions, including consent, fraud, and notice, *see* Justin Owens, Challenging Post-Adoption Decrees and the Convoluted Applications of State Courts, 31 J. Am. Acad. Matrim. Law. 209 (2018).

6. In many states, adoption of an older child requires that the child consent as well. If the adoptee is an adult, only the adoptee's consent may be required; consent of the biological parents is often dispensed with.

NOTE: OPEN ADOPTION AND OPEN RECORDS

Today almost all prospective domestic birth mothers (approximately 90 percent) choose to meet the adoptive parents of their children, and even the majority of those who do not meet them can choose the adoptive parents from profiles. Evan B. Donaldson Adoption Institute, Safeguarding the Rights and Well-Being of Birthparents in the Adoption Process (Jan. 2007), available at https://www.nationalcenteronadoptionandpermanency.net/post/safeguarding-the-rights-and-well-beingof-birthparents-in-the-adoption-process.

As of 2018, 29 states and the District of Columbia had statutes that allow enforceable agreements for contact after the finalization of an adoption. The written agreements specify the type and frequency of contact and are often incorporated into the adoption order. Contact can range from the adoptive and birth parents exchanging information about a child (*e.g.*, cards, letters, and photos via traditional or social media) to the child exchanging information or having visits with the birth parents or relatives. Judicial enforcement may involve use of the court's contempt power, fines, or jail time. In addition, enforcement may be subject to the child's best interest. Five more states have statutes that address open adoption without providing for judicial enforcement of agreements. Postadoption Contact Agreements Between Birth and Adoptive Families (2019), Child Welfare Information Gateway, Washington, DC: U.S. Department of Health and Human Services, Children's Bureau; Danny R. Veilleux, Postadoption Visitation by Natural Parent, 78 A.L.R.4th 218 (2011) (updated weekly).

In states that recognize the possibility of more than two adults having parental status or that allow third-party visitation, should the states also recognize the possibility of "non-exclusive adoption"? That is, could a state permit a third party to adopt without terminating the parental status of the birth parents? *See* Josh Gupta-Kagan, Non-Exclusive Adoption and Child Welfare, 66 Ala. L. Rev. 715, 724 (2015).

Researchers in Minnesota and Texas conducted the most extensive studies of open adoption. They followed 190 adoptive families and 169 birth mothers, beginning in the mid-1980s. The adoptions ranged from fully closed through fully disclosed. Among the most significant findings are (1) high percentages of the adoptive parents and adopted children who had ongoing contact with birth mothers were satisfied or very satisfied with the level of openness, (2) over time the level of openness generally remained the same, (3) relationships were dynamic and had to be renegotiated over time, (4) the extent to which adolescents did not have ongoing contact with their birth mothers varied but was not related to how satisfactory their relationships with their parents were, and (5) there was no relationship between the degree of openness and the children's socioemotional adjustment. Harold D. Grotevant & Ruth G. McRoy, Openness in Adoption: Outcomes for Adolescents Within Their Adoptive Kinships Networks (Nov. 2003), *chapter also in* Psychological Issues in Adoption: Theory, Research, and Application (D. Brodzinsky & J. Palacios eds., 2005). The lead researchers also conclude that no one type of adoption arrangement is best for all families and that the needs and desires of family members may well shift over time. For updates on the study, *see* Harold D. Grotevant, Ruth G. McRoy & Susan Ayers-Lopez, Contact Between Adoptive and Birth Families: Perspectives from the Minnesota/Texas Adoption Research Project, 7 Child Dev. Persp. 193-198 (2013).

For more information, *see* Priscilla K. Coleman & Debbie Garratt, From Birth Mothers to First Mothers: Toward a Compassionate Understanding of the Life-Long Act of Adoption Placement, 31 Issues L. & Med. 139, 141 (2016); Sophie Mashburn, Mediating a Family: The Use of Mediation in the Formation and Enforcement of Post-Adoption Contact Agreements, 2015 J. Disp. Resol. 383, 384; Annette Ruth Appell, Reflections on the Movement Toward a More Child-Centered Adoption, 32 W. New Eng. L. Rev. 1 (2010).

A second challenge to traditional adoption practice is the trend toward open records. While constitutional challenges to closed record laws by adopted children have generally not been successful, most states allow adult adoptees to have access to nonidentifying information about themselves from their adoption records, and all but 14 allow birth parents to access nonidentifying information about adoptive families. In most states, identifying information is available through mutual consent registries, and a few states have statutes allowing adult adoptees to gain access to their adoption records even in the absence of consent by the birth parents. Indeed, Kansas has never sealed its adoption records, and Alaska has allowed access since 1950. In the absence of such a statute, identifying information is available only by court order upon a showing of good cause. State-by-state information on access laws is available at Access to Adoption Records (2020), Child Welfare Information Gateway, U.S. Department of Health and Human Services, Children's Bureau, available at https://www.childwelfare.gov/pubPDFs/infoaccessap.pdf.

b. Adoption Without Consent

All states permit adoption without parental consent on proof of statutory grounds, most often serious neglect and some variation of desertion or abandonment. In addition, some states dispense with the requirement for the father's consent where the pregnancy was the result of rape. The states vary, however, in whether or not they require a criminal conviction for the rape before they dispense with consent. *Compare* Wash. Rev. Code §26.33.170(2) (2022) ("An alleged father's, birth parent's, or parent's consent to adoption [may] be dispensed with if the court finds that . . . the alleged father, birth parent, or parent has been found guilty of rape") *with* Wis. Stat. §48.415(9) (2022) (allowing the termination of parental rights upon a showing "indicating that the person who may be the father of the child committed, during a possible time of conception, a sexual assault . . . against the mother of the child"). *See* Karen Syma Czapanskiy, The Constitution, Paternity, Rape, and Coerced Intercourse: No Protection Required, 35 J. Am. Acad. Matrim. Law. 83, 94 (2022); Deirdre M. Smith, Termination of Parental Rights as a Private Remedy: Rationales, Realities, and Alternatives, 72 Syracuse L. Rev. 1173, 1175 (2022).

Generally, the legal principles for determining when a parent's rights can be terminated are the same for adoptions by both a relative and a stranger, but the most bitterly contested adoptions are probably stepparent and other in-family adoptions. Often such cases are prosecuted on the grounds that the noncustodial biological parent abandoned the child, as in the next case.

Rodgers v. Rodgers
519 S.W.3d 324 (Ark. 2017)

RHONDA K. WOOD, Associate Justice. . . . Chris Rodgers and Reanna Rodgers were married in 2002 and divorced in 2011. The divorce decree gave them joint custody of their four children. In May 2013, Chris married Destiny Rodgers. On September 6, 2013, the circuit court, following a hearing, entered a temporary custody order that awarded Chris sole custody of the children because Reanna had tested positive for amphetamine and methamphetamine. The court explained that the test showed she had used within 72 hours. It further suspended Reanna's visitation with the children. At the hearing, the circuit court stated, "So when I say that she is not to have any visitation at all with these children, I mean she is not to have any visitation at all with these children," and warned Chris that if he permitted any visitation between Reanna and the children that it would hold Chris in contempt of court. The circuit court also told Reanna,

> [A]nd when you decide that your children are more important to you than methamphetamine, then you can certainly come back and you can ask the Court to reverse this ruling and the Court will certainly look at it. But until that happens then there's not going to be even visitation with your children.

The circuit court's order stated "[t]hat the Plaintiff may petition this court for a review of the issue of child custody, or child visitation, at such time as the Plaintiff can pass a drug screen." In addition, the court's order specifically required her to submit to a hair-follicle test. The circuit court's order also stated that "no child support shall be ordered from the Plaintiff at this time."

Reanna filed two separate drug-test results with the circuit court in October 2013 and April 2014 showing that she was negative for methamphetamine and other controlled substances. She did not file a petition for visitation following the clean drug screens. She later admitted that she relapsed after the October drug screen, but she claimed that she has been drug free since approximately December 2013.

On September 19, 2014, Destiny, with Chris's consent, petitioned the circuit court to adopt the children. Destiny alleged that Reanna's consent was not required because Reanna, for a period of more than one year, had without justifiable cause failed to provide for the care and support of the children in a significant or meaningful fashion and because Reanna had failed to communicate with or maintain any significant contact with them. Reanna challenged the adoption and filed a petition for visitation in the divorce action on October 19, 2014.

At the hearing on the adoption petition, Reanna testified that she had not had visitation with her children since August 2013. She admitted that she continued to use drugs until December of 2013. In October 2014 she married Michael Eller with whom she has a five-month-old son. She conceded that she had not communicated with or provided support for the children between September 2013 and September 2014. She stated she attempted to pay child support in December 2014, after the petition for adoption had been filed. She believed that her failures were justified because the court had suspended her visitation and had not ordered her to pay any child support. She also stated that she did not file a negative hair follicle test until March 10, 2015, six months after the petition for adoption. After the hearing, the circuit court granted the petition for adoption, concluding that Reanna's consent was not required pursuant to Arkansas Code Annotated section 9-9-207(a)(2) (Repl. 2015) because she failed significantly and without justifiable cause for at least one year to communicate with her children or to provide for their care and support. . . .

Arkansas Code Annotated section 9-9-207(a)(2) provides that consent to an adoption is not required of "a parent of a child in the custody of another, if the parent for a period of at least (1) year has failed significantly and without justifiable cause (i) to communicate with the child or (ii) to provide for the care and support of the child as required by law or judicial decree." As we have previously held, "failed significantly" does not mean "failed totally." Rather, it means a failure that is meaningful or important. "Without justifiable cause" denotes a failure that is voluntary, willful, arbitrary, and without adequate excuse. . . .

The circuit court's findings were not clearly erroneous. Reanna does not dispute that she failed to significantly communicate with or provide support for her children for over a year. Rather, she claims that the court erred in concluding that she did not have justifiable cause for not contacting her children because at the September 2013 custody hearing the circuit court instructed that she was to have no visitation with the children. We disagree.

This court is unwilling to hold that when a parent cannot have visitation with her children, due to a court order, that gives the parent justifiable cause to make no effort in continuing a relationship with the children. The statute reads it's a parent's failure to "communicate with the child," not a failure to have visitation with the child that allows adoption to proceed without consent. Despite having her visitation suspended, Reanna could have communicated with the children other ways. She could have made telephone calls to the children, sent birthday or Christmas cards, letters, or emails, but she attempted to do none of these. She also did not attend any school, church, or sporting events involving her children. She failed to show an interest in their lives despite living approximately 150 feet from the children. Furthermore, once she was drug free, she failed to petition the court for a review of the temporary order that suspended the visitation until October 19, 2014, which was thirty days after the petition for adoption had been filed and more than one year after her first clean drug screen. While she claims she was unable to afford an attorney, she admitted that she was capable of working but did not work, and while she relied on her husband's income, she did not ask him or her parents for money to hire an attorney or file the petition. She gives no justifiable cause for failing to have any contact with her children, despite the father having sole custody. The court found that from September 6, 2013 until May 20, 2015, the date of the adoption hearing, Reanna had failed to make even one effort to contact her children. The circuit court did not err in finding that Reanna placed other interests in priority over communicating with her children.

This case is distinguishable from our recent decision in another stepparent adoption case. *See Martini*, 2016 Ark. 472, 507 S.W.3d 486. In *Martini*, we held that there was insufficient evidence to establish that the child's father had failed without justifiable cause to communicate with his child for a period of one year. The father was subject to two no-contact orders that barred him from contact with the child's mother, and he had no other means to contact the child except through the mother. The mother had moved to another state and not informed the father of the child's residence. We concluded that it was reasonable for the father to be concerned that contact aimed at the young child could constitute a violation of the no-contact order that would expose him to incarceration. Here, the court only terminated Reanna's visitation but did not issue a no-contact order, nor did it order her to refrain from communicating with her children or even their father. Nevertheless, she did not attempt any form of communication with the children, who lived down the road from her. More importantly, the circuit court had explicitly told Reanna that she could petition the court to review the suspension of visitation as soon as she could pass a drug screen. Thus, Reanna alone controlled when her visitation would be reinstated. Reanna alone controlled whether she communicated with her children through cards, letters, and phone calls. However, she did not avail herself of these opportunities to maintain contact with her children.

. . . We agree that Reanna significantly and unjustifiably failed to communicate with the children for at least one year. Thus, we affirm the circuit court's conclusion that her consent to the adoption was not required.

ROBIN F. WYNNE, Justice, concurring. I cannot agree with the majority that Reanna's failure to communicate with the children in the face of an order that would have punished her with contempt for having visitation with the children justifies a finding that her consent to a step-parent adoption is not required on that basis. Here, the trial court was quite emphatic that allowing visitation while the order was in place would be dealt with harshly. The majority concludes that a ban on visitation did not preclude Reanna from having contact with the children in other ways. As persons trained in the law, we know this. It is apparent from the record that Reanna did not. In fact, there is some indication in the record that both Reanna *and* Chris thought that the trial court's order meant that she could not have contact with the children while the order remained in effect. I do not believe that stripping a parent of her right to consent to the adoption of her children is warranted essentially because she does not understand the legal distinction between visitation and contact. . . .

However, in addition to alleging that Reanna had failed to maintain contact with the children, Destiny Rodgers alleged in the adoption petition that Reanna had failed to provide care and support for the children. . . . It is undisputed that Reanna provided no support for the children for at least one year prior to the filing of the adoption petition. Reanna admitted before the circuit court that she understood that she had a duty to support the children. Nonetheless, Reanna contends that her failure to provide support is justified by the fact that the trial court's order did not require her to pay child support. However, in Fonken v. Fonken, 334 Ark. 637, 976 S.W.2d 952 (1998), this court held that a parent has a legal and moral duty to support a minor child, regardless of the existence of an order of support. . . . Under these circumstances, I do not believe that the circuit court erred in finding that Reanna's failure to provide support was without justifiable cause. . . .

KAREN R. BAKER, Justice, dissenting. . . . Based on Reanna's reliance on the circuit court's admonitions and the amended temporary order in the divorce proceeding, Reanna's failure to communicate with her children and her failure to pay child support was not without justifiable cause. This case is even more compelling than our recent case, Martini v. Price, 2016 Ark. 472, 507 S.W.3d 486, where this court set aside a stepparent adoption. There, the "no contact" order was directed toward the father's contact with the mother. Here, the order restricted Reanna's visitation with the children. Further, the order specifically stated that Reanna was not required to pay child support, so there was a "judicial decree" setting out her responsibilities regarding support of the children. *Martini* supports the setting aside of the stepparent adoption. . . .

[The dissenting opinion of Justice WOMACK is omitted.]

NOTES AND QUESTIONS

1. Traditionally, adoption on the basis of abandonment or desertion required proof that the parent subjectively intended to give up the parent-child relationship, a meaning of abandonment imported from property law. Note, Child Abandonment: The Botched Beginning of the Adoption Process, 60 Yale L.J. 1240 (1951). Strictly applied, this meant that a parent who expressed the desire to maintain parental status could not be found to have abandoned a child, regardless of how he or she had behaved. Many modern statutes, including the Uniform

Adoption Act, like the statute applied in *Rodgers*, ask whether the parent has failed without adequate cause to communicate with or support the child for some statutory period. Uniform Adoption Act §6(a)(2) (1969); Uniform Adoption Act §3-504 (1994). What is the practical significance of this change? Do the older statutes sacrifice children's interests to parental rights, or do the newer statutes give inadequate protection to parental rights?

2. How and why do the three opinions in *Rodgers* reach different conclusions about whether the mother had an adequate reason for not contacting her children after the father was awarded sole custody?

3. The concurring judge argues that the mother could not be expected to understand that she could still communicate with her children in light of the trial court's order but concludes that she should be held responsible for not providing for their support, even though the trial court explicitly declined to enter a child support order. Why does the judge treat these two aspects of the trial court order so differently?

4. Traditionally, parents facing involuntary termination of their parental status through an adoption proceeding had no right to publicly provided legal assistance if they were indigent, but courts in several states have held that due process requires provision of counsel in such cases. See Patricia C. Kussmann, Right of Indigent Parent to Appointed Counsel in Proceeding for Involuntary Termination of Parental Rights, 92 A.L.R.5th 379 (2009) (with weekly updates). A case reaching this conclusion and discussing cases from other states is In re Adoption of J.E.V., 141 A.3d 254 (N.J. 2016). Other cases have held that failure to provide counsel to an indigent parent in a contested adoption, when the state provides counsel to parents in termination of parental rights cases in juvenile court, violates equal protection rights. *See, e.g.*, Matter of Adoption of Y.E.F., 171 N.E.3d 302 (Ohio 2020).

PROBLEMS

1. Mary was 17 years old, unmarried, and unemployed when her baby was born. She gave the baby to her 26-year-old stepbrother and his spouse shortly after birth. Mary visited the child about twice a year and gave her stepbrother small amounts of money irregularly. She is now 23, married, and settled down. She has asked her stepbrother to return custody of her child, but he has refused, and he and his spouse have filed an adoption petition alleging that Mary's consent is unnecessary because she has abandoned the child. Mary insists that she wants and has always wanted to raise her child. What arguments should each side make?

2. Timmy was born to Margaret and Dave, a married couple. Margaret and Dave were divorced when Timmy was one year old. Margaret was awarded custody, and Dave was granted visitation and ordered to pay child support. For the last two years Dave has irregularly and reluctantly paid child support, and he has rarely visited Timmy. Recently, though, he told Margaret that if he had to pay, he wanted to see Timmy more often and that he might even seek custody. Margaret, who is 23, and her father, who is 50, suggested instead that Dave relinquish his parental rights and consent to Timmy's adoption by Margaret's father. Margaret and Timmy often see Margaret's parents, who live in the same town, although they do not live with them. If Margaret and her father file the adoption petition, along with Dave's written consent, is a court likely to grant the adoption? Why or why not?

3. Don lived with Tara for about five years. During that period, Tara gave birth to a son, Eric. Tara ended the relationship with Don when Eric was two and a half, and married Sam a few months later. Don continued to visit Eric but did not contribute financially. About a year after Tara's marriage to Sam, Tara asked Don about allowing Sam to adopt Eric in part so that Sam would be able to add Eric to his medical insurance. Don agreed pursuant to an agreement with Sam and Tara that he could continue to visit Eric. When they went to court to obtain the forms for the adoption, they asked the clerk whether they could modify the consent form to recognize Don's right to visit. The clerk indicated that "there wasn't any way to change the wording." Don signed the unaltered form.

Following the adoption, Don continued to visit Eric, although over time Tara became increasingly reluctant to permit the visits. About a year after the adoption, Tara and Sam ceased permitting Don to visit the child and obtained a permanent injunction forbidding Don from contacting Eric. Don filed a "Verified Motion to Set Aside Adoption Decree," but the trial court denied the motion to set aside the adoption decree, finding that the father's consent to the adoption was "knowingly and intelligently and voluntarily executed." Don appealed. What arguments would you make on Don's behalf? What arguments would you make on behalf of Tara and Sam?

2. Establishing the New Parent-Child Relationship — Independent Versus Agency Adoption and Adoption of Special-Needs Children

Five states — Colorado, Delaware, Indiana, Ohio, and West Virginia — require that all adoptive placements be made by a state child welfare agency or a private child placement agency licensed by the state. Four additional states — Kentucky, Louisiana, Missouri, and Rhode Island — require agency approval unless the adoption is with a stepparent or other relative. Nine states — Florida, Kentucky, Maryland, Massachusetts, Minnesota, Missouri, New Mexico, Rhode Island, and Wisconsin — require parents to obtain permission from the state child welfare agency or a court before they make a private placement. Child Welfare Information Gateway, Who May Adopt, Be Adopted, or Place a Child for Adoption? (2020), available at http://www.childwelfare.gov/systemwide/laws_policies/statutes/parties.cfm (last visited Aug. 27, 2022). Even in some of these states, agencies still have a role to play in private adoptions, since statutes require that a licensed agency evaluate the adoptive parents' home and make a report to the court recommending for or against adoption. These "home studies" are typically waived in stepparent and relative adoptions. *See, e.g.*, Uniform Adoption Act part 2.

In the remaining states private adoptions — that is, ones not arranged by an agency — are permitted. Private adoptions may be arranged directly between the biological parents and adoptive parents or through an intermediary such as a doctor or lawyer. In most states it is a crime to offer or receive money or any valuable consideration for relinquishing or accepting a baby for adoption. However, it is not illegal to pay expenses to the biological parents, including pre-birth and birth medical expenses and professional fees of adoption agencies, lawyers, and doctors. Where offering or receiving money for an adoption is not illegal, payment to a mother may render her consent involuntary. Some states recognize an exception where the agreement promotes the child's welfare and the parent is not in a position to furnish proper care for the child.

As the number of newborn adoptions has declined, adoptions involving agency placement of older, hard to place children have increased? The movement to find adoptive homes for hard to place children — which include older children; children with physical, mental, or emotional disabilities; children of color; and sibling groups — began in the 1970s. Judith K. McKenzie, Adoption of Children with Special Needs, 3 The Future of Children 62 (1993). In practice, placing special-needs children largely means finding adoptive placements for foster children whose parents' rights have been terminated. In addition to increased agency emphasis on placing these children, a number of programs facilitate such adoptions. Some state child welfare agencies encourage people to become foster parents with the promise that they will be able to adopt their foster child if she or he becomes free for adoption. With the support of federal funds, parents who adopt children who have been in the child welfare system may receive subsidies for medical and educational expenses up to the amount of foster care payments until the child is 18, under some circumstances. Almost all the people who adopt older foster children—80 to 90 percent—have been the child's foster parents first. *Id.* at 71.

Because adoptive parents ordinarily must pay an adoption agency or intermediary and often pay expenses of the biological mother, adoption can be expensive. Agency adoptions typically cost from $30,000 to $60,000, and independent adoptions cost from $25,000 to $45,000. Adoptions of children from foster care technically are free of cost, but there are court costs that range from $500 to $2,000, attorney's fees that can cost up to $4,500, and various other expenses incurred in the adoption process. International adoptions are $20,000 to $50,000. Planning for Adoption: Knowing the Costs and Resources (2022), Child Welfare Information Gateway, U.S. Department of Health and Human Services, Children's Bureau, available at https://www.childwelfare.gov/pubPDFs/s_costs.pdf (last visited Sept. 7, 2022).

As a practical matter, the Internet has changed the nature of adoption practice. The Internet has made it easier to facilitate private placements with or without agency involvement. In addition, the information on the Internet makes it easier to track birth families. The Evan B. Donaldson Adoption Institute found the following:

- A growing "commodification" of adoption and a shift away from the perspective that its primary purpose is to find families for children. This is particularly the case in domestic infant adoption, where a scarcity of babies available to be adopted heightens competition. Unregulated websites compete with traditional practitioners, sometimes by making claims and utilizing practices that raise serious ethical and legal concerns.
- Finding birth relatives is becoming increasingly easy and commonplace, with significant institutional and personal implications, including the likely end of the era of "closed" adoption and a growth in relationships between adoptive families and families of origin.
- An indeterminable but growing number of minor adopted children are contacting and forming relationships with biological siblings, parents, and other relatives, sometimes without their adoptive parents' knowledge and usually without guidance or preparation about the complex emotional and interpersonal repercussions for everyone involved.
- A rising number of useful, positive sites, such as ones that expedite the adoption of children and youth who need families, notably including those with special needs; and more places to get information and education, networking opportunities, support services, and other resources that are a clear contribution to professionals, policy makers, researchers, journalists, and the millions of personally affected individuals.

Jeanne A. Howard, Untangling the Web: The Internet's Transformative Impact on Adoption (2012), available at https://www.anniec.org/untangling-the-web-the-internets-transformative-impact-on-adoption/. *See also* Michelle M. Hughes, Internet Promises, Scares, and Surprises: New Realities of Adoption, 41 Cap. U. L. Rev. 279 (2013); Mary Kate Kearney & Arrielle Millstein, Meeting the Challenges of Adoption in an Internet Age, 41 Cap. U. L. Rev. 237 (2013); Heather A. Bartel, From Orphan Trains to Underground Networks: The Need to Get on Board with Adoption Reform, 48 Suffolk U. L. Rev. 823, 843 (2015).

3. Child Placement, Native American Heritage, Race, and Religion

Racial and religious matching of adoptive parents and children was customary and even legally required through the first two-thirds of the twentieth century. Historically, most of the agencies that arranged foster and adoptive placements were religiously affiliated, and they strongly tended to serve only or primarily adults and children who belonged to their denomination. In addition, as we have seen, until fairly recently the dominant approach to adoption has been the "complete substitution" theory, in which adoptions are made to mimic biological parent-child relationships as much as possible. Consistent with this approach, a 1954 survey of more than 250 adoption agencies about their placement practices found that the following factors were ranked as the most important matching factors for adoption: intelligence and intellectual potential, religious background, racial background, temperament needs, educational background, and the adoptive parents' physical resemblance to the child. Laura J. Schwartz, Religious Matching for Adoption: Unraveling the Interests Behind the "Best Interests" Standard, 25 Fam. L.Q. 171, 173 (1991).

During the late 1950s and into the 1960s, adoption practice moved away from this approach and toward greater acceptance of transracial adoption, in part because of the general social changes wrought by the civil rights movement. The emergence of international adoption following the Korean War accelerated the practice, since most international adoptions are transracial. Arnold R. Silverman, Outcomes of Transracial Adoption, 3 The Future of Children 104, 107 (1993). However, transracial adoption became the subject of strong criticism in the 1970s. Objections were particularly vehement to the high incidence of foster care and adoptive placement with white parents of African-American children.

Sharp criticism was also leveled at placing Native American children with non-Native families. In 1978 Congress enacted the Indian Child Welfare Act (ICWA), 25 U.S.C. §§1901-1963, which explicitly requires placing Native American children with Native American foster and adoptive parents. Following enactment of ICWA, adoption of Native American children by non-Native parents dropped dramatically. Silverman, above, at 107.

Mississippi Band of Choctaw Indians v. Holyfield
490 U.S. 30 (1989)

BRENNAN, J. . . . The Indian Child Welfare Act of 1978 (ICWA), 92 Stat. 3069, 25 U.S.C. §§1901-1963, was the product of rising concern in the mid-1970's over the consequences to Indian children, Indian families, and Indian tribes of abusive child welfare practices that resulted in the separation of large numbers of Indian children from their families and tribes through adoption or foster care placement, usually in non-Indian homes. Senate oversight hearings in 1974 yielded numerous examples, statistical data, and expert testimony documenting what one witness called "the wholesale removal of Indian children from their homes, . . . the most tragic aspect of Indian life today." Studies undertaken by the Association on American Indian Affairs in 1969 and 1974, and presented in the Senate hearings, showed that 25 to 35 percent of all Indian children had been separated from their families and placed in adoptive families, foster care, or institutions. Adoptive placements counted significantly in this total: in the State of Minnesota, for example, one in eight Indian children under the age of 18 was in an adoptive home, and during the year 1971-1972 nearly one in every four infants under one year of age was placed for adoption. The adoption rate of Indian children was eight times that of non-Indian children. Approximately 90% of the Indian placements were in non-Indian homes. A number of witnesses also testified to the serious adjustment problems encountered by such children during adolescence, as well as the impact of the adoptions on Indian parents and the tribes themselves.

Further hearings, covering much the same ground, were held during 1977 and 1978 on the bill that became the ICWA. While much of the testimony again focused on the harm to Indian parents and their children who were involuntarily separated by decisions of local welfare authorities, there was also considerable emphasis on the impact on the tribes themselves of the massive removal of their children. For example, Mr. Calvin Isaac, Tribal Chief of the Mississippi Band of Choctaw Indians and representative of the National Tribal Chairmen's Association, testified as follows:

Culturally, the chances of Indian survival are significantly reduced if our children, the only real means for the transmission of the tribal heritage, are to be raised in non-Indian homes and denied exposure to the ways of their People. Furthermore, these practices seriously undercut the tribes' ability to continue as self-governing communities. Probably in no area is it more important that tribal sovereignty be respected than in an area as socially and culturally determinative as family relationships.

1978 Hearings, at 193. *See also* id., at 62. Chief Isaac also summarized succinctly what numerous witnesses saw as the principal reason for the high rates of removal of Indian children:

One of the most serious failings of the present system is that Indian children are removed from the custody of their natural parents by nontribal government authorities who have no basis for intelligently evaluating the cultural and social premises underlying Indian home life and childrearing. Many of the individuals who decide the fate of our children are at best ignorant of our cultural values, and at worst contemptful of the Indian way and convinced that removal, usually to a non-Indian household or institution, can only benefit an Indian child.

Id., at 191-192.[7]

The congressional findings that were incorporated into the ICWA reflect these sentiments. The Congress found:

(3) that there is no resource that is more vital to the continued existence and integrity of Indian tribes than their children . . . ;

(4) that an alarmingly high percentage of Indian families are broken up by the removal, often unwarranted, of their children from them by nontribal public and private agencies and that an alarmingly high percentage of such children are placed in non-Indian foster and adoptive homes and institutions; and

(5) that the States, exercising their recognized jurisdiction over Indian child custody proceedings through administrative and judicial bodies, have often failed to recognize the essential tribal relations of Indian people and the cultural and social standards prevailing in Indian communities and families.

25 U.S.C. §1901.

At the heart of ICWA are its provisions concerning jurisdiction over Indian child custody proceedings.

NOTES AND QUESTIONS

1. In 2022, the Supreme Court granted certiorari in a series of cases challenging ICWA's constitutionality. Decisions in these cases is pending at the time this book is going to press. Brackeen v. Haaland, 994 F.3d 249 (5th Cir. 2021), *cert. granted sub nom.* Nation v. Brackeen,

---

7. One of the particular points of concern was the failure of non-Indian child welfare workers to understand the role of the extended family in Indian society. The House Report on the ICWA noted: "An Indian child may have scores of, perhaps more than a hundred, relatives who are counted as close, responsible members of the family. Many social workers, untutored in the ways of Indian family life or assuming them to be socially irresponsible, consider leaving the child with persons outside the nuclear family as neglect and thus as grounds for terminating parental rights." House Report, at 10, U.S. Code Cong. & Admin. News 1978, at 7532. At the conclusion of the 1974 Senate hearings, Senator Abourezk noted the role that such extended families played in the care of children: "We've had testimony here that in Indian communities throughout the Nation there is no such thing as an abandoned child because when a child does have a need for parents for one reason or another, a relative or a friend will take that child in. It's the extended family concept." 1974 Hearings 473.

142 S. Ct. 1204, and *cert. granted*, 142 S. Ct. 1205, 212 L. Ed. 2d 215 (2022), and *cert. granted sub nom.* Texas v. Haaland, 142 S. Ct. 1205, 212 L. Ed. 2d 215 (2022), and *cert. granted*, 142 S. Ct. 1205, 212 L. Ed. 2d 215 (2022).

2. In *Holyfield* the Supreme Court concluded, years after the children had been placed with the would-be adoptive parents, that the court that granted the adoption had wrongfully asserted jurisdiction. In the meantime, of course, the children and the adoptive parents had been living as a family. When an error of this kind is made, what should be the remedy? Does it make sense to ignore all the expectations and relationships that have developed over time? On the other hand, is any other remedy effective?

If a Native child is being placed for adoption, ICWA provides that without good cause to the contrary, a state court must give preference to a member of the child's extended family, to other members of the Indian child's tribe, or to other Indian families. 25 U.S.C. §1915 (2022). A regulation issued in 2016 elaborates: "A placement may not depart from the preferences based solely on ordinary bonding or attachment that flowed from time spent in a non-preferred placement that was made in violation of ICWA." 25 C.F.R. §23.132(e) (2022). The regulation is discussed in In re Alexandria P., 204 Cal. Rptr. 3d 617 (Cal. App. 2016).

In *Holyfield* the Court held that the case had to be returned to tribal court:

> On February 9, 1990, four years after the Holyfields first brought the twins home from the hospital, Choctaw Tribal Court Judge Roy Jim granted Joan Holyfield's petition to adopt them. Given the Tribe's interest in raising Choctaw children, not to mention the Tribe's significant legal efforts in asserting jurisdiction, one might have expected the Tribal Court to return the twins to the Tribe. However, the Tribal Court balanced the Tribes' interest in keeping tribal children in tribal communities against the children's interests in continuity and stability. . . . Even though she was an "older parent," a number of factors favored Joan. First, the twins had lived with her all their lives and "it would have been cruel to take them from the only mother they knew." Second, by all accounts, she was a loving parent who provided a stable home environment. Third, the twins had not been raised in a Choctaw home and did not speak or understand the Choctaw language, which, according to a 1974 survey, was the predominant language spoken in eighty percent of Choctaw homes. . . . Still, Judge Jim was not willing to sever the children's ties to the Tribe completely; he ordered that they maintain contact with their extended family and other tribal members.

Solangel Maldonado, Race, Culture, and Adoption: Lessons from Mississippi Band of Choctaw Indians v. Holyfield, 17 Colum. J. Gender & L. 1, 17-18 (2008). Maldonado further observes that Mr. Holyfield, the adoptive father, was one-quarter Choctaw, but that the tribe only granted tribal membership to those who were at least one-half Mississippi Choctaw. *Id.* at 23-24.

3. Whose interests is ICWA designed to protect? In *Holyfield*, the lower court found that the twins' mother "went to some efforts to see that they were born outside the confines of the Choctaw Indian Reservation" and that the parents had "promptly arranged for the adoption by the Holyfields." The Supreme Court, however, responded, "Tribal jurisdiction under §1911 (a) was not meant to be defeated by the actions of individual members of the tribe, for Congress was concerned not solely about the interests of Indian children and families, but also about the impact on the tribes themselves of the large numbers of Indian children adopted by non-Indians. . . ." Does that mean that ICWA subordinates the child's interests to those of the tribe? What theory of the best interests of the child supports the ICWA approach to custody?

4. A critical question for purposes of determining the applicability of ICWA is whether the child whose custody is at stake is an "Indian child." The statute defines this term to include any unmarried person less than 18 years old who is an enrolled member of an Indian tribe, the biological child of a member of an Indian tribe, or the biological child of a member of an Indian tribe who is also eligible for membership. 25 U.S.C. §1903(4) (2022). The tribe of which the child may be a member has the exclusive authority to determine whether the child is in fact an Indian child. 25 C.F.R. §23.108 (2022). Tribes vary in how they determine tribal membership.

5. ICWA applies to foster care and preadoptive placements, adoption, and termination of parental rights of Indian children, but not to custody disputes following divorce. 25 U.S.C. §1903(1) (2022).

NOTE: ADOPTIVE COUPLE v. BABY GIRL

Twenty-four years after *Holyfield*, the Supreme Court revisited ICWA in another private adoption case involving an "Indian child," Adoptive Couple v. Baby Girl, 133 S. Ct. 2552 (2013). The case involved the newborn adoption of a baby born to unmarried parents whose relationship fell apart before the birth. The mother decided to place the child for adoption, informing the adoption agency that the child's father was Native American. Because of errors in the request for information, the father's tribe inaccurately reported that he was not an enrolled member. The would-be adoptive parents filed in South Carolina without giving the father notice, but he learned of the adoption, and the tribe intervened in the proceedings. The trial court held that the father was entitled to ICWA protections that he had not received and that, therefore, the child should be placed with the father. The Supreme Court reversed, interpreting ICWA as not granting a biological father whose legal paternity had not been established and who had never had physical or legal custody of a child the procedural safeguards that would otherwise be mandated by ICWA.

On remand, the South Carolina Supreme Court ordered the transfer of Baby Veronica to the adoptive parents. It held that the father's consent was not required for an adoption under South Carolina law and that once a final adoption decree had been entered, "the relationship of parent and child and all the rights, duties, and other legal consequences of the natural relationship of parent and child" existed between the adoptive couple and the child. The court emphasized the need for an expeditious resolution of the case and concluded that "Adoptive Couple is the only party who has a petition pending for the adoption of Baby Girl, and thus, theirs is the only application that should be considered at this stage." It rejected consideration of a best-interest standard on the basis of the ties that had developed during the father's custody of the child for the preceding year and a half. Adoptive Couple v. Baby Girl, 746 S.E.2d 51, *order vacated on reh'g*, 746 S.E.2d 346 (S.C. 2013).

While *Adoptive Couple* quoted verbatim from *Holyfield*'s description of the legislative history of ICWA condemning the involuntary removal of Indian children from their families, *Holyfield* had also emphasized that "Congress was concerned not solely about the interests of Indian children and families, but also about the impact on the tribes themselves of the large numbers of Indian children adopted by non-Indians. . . ." *Adoptive Couple*, in contrast, gave little weight to tribal interests. Professor Rolnick commented:

> The blow struck by [*Adoptive Couple*] . . . is significant. As the Court recognized in *Holyfield*, ICWA is about preserving the relationship between an Indian child and her tribe. The tribe has an interest in its children that may be separate from the interests of the Indian parents. The child's interests are likewise served by maintaining a connection to her tribe and her extended family, even if she no longer has a relationship with her parents. In this case, the Cherokee Nation supported [the father's] effort to regain custody, but tribal intervention does not always (or even usually) mean returning the child to her Indian parent. By focusing so much on the father's actions in the case, the Court has allowed tribal rights to be subsumed by an individual

parent's lack of responsibility. This is precisely the opposite of its holding in *Holyfield*, and it significantly undermines the spirit of the law.

Addie Rolnick, Adoptive Couple v. Baby Girl (1 of 4): Why the Court's ICWA Ruling Matters (June 29, 2013) available at http://prawfsblawg.blogs .com/prawfsblawg/2013/06/adoptive-couple-v-baby-girl-1-of-4-why-the-courts-icwa-ruling-matters-.html.

On the other hand, the child's mother, who decided to place the child for adoption after receiving a text from the father that she interpreted as meaning he did not want to be involved, wrote:

> For 27 months, I watched Veronica grow and thrive with Matt and Melanie [the adoptive couple]. I got regular updates, talked to her on the phone and watched her open presents at Christmas. They are wonderful parents, and I felt proud of the decision I had made for my child. But after more than two years in her happy home, a court ruled that my choice meant nothing.

Christy Maldonado, Baby Veronica's Birth Mother: Girl Belongs with Adoptive Parents, Wash. Post, July 12, 2013, available https://www.washingtonpost.com/opinions/baby-veronicas-birth-mother-girl-belongs-with-adoptive-parents/2013/07/12/40d38a12-e995-11e2-a301-ea5a8116d211_story.html. For an argument that ICWA, rather than constitute a unique response to Native American history, is in fact very similar to modern child welfare policies that promote family reunification, kinship care preferences, cultural competency considerations and community involvement, *see* Marcia Zug, ICWA's Irony, 45 Am. Indian L. Rev. 1 (2021).

NOTE: TRANSRACIAL PLACEMENT

In 1972 the National Association of Black Social Workers (NABSW) adopted a resolution, to which it still adheres, that provides in part:

> [W]e have taken the position that Black children should be placed only with Black families whether in foster care or adoption. Black children belong physically, psychologically and culturally in Black families in order that they receive the total sense of themselves and develop a sound projection of their future. Human beings are products of their environments and develop their sense of values, attitudes and self-concept within their family structures. Black children in White homes are cut off from the healthy development of themselves as Black people.
>
> Our position is based on:
>
> 1. the necessity of self-determination from birth to death of all Black people.
> 2. the need of our young ones to begin at birth to identify with all Black people in a Black community.
> 3. the philosophy that we need our own to build a strong nation.
>
> The socialization process for every child begins at birth. Included in the socialization process is the child's cultural heritage, which is an important segment of the total process. This must begin at the earliest moment; otherwise our children will not have the background and knowledge which is necessary to survive in a racist society. This is impossible if the child is placed with White parents in a White environment. . . .
>
> We the participants of the workshop have committed ourselves to go back to our communities and work to end this particular form of genocide.

Quoted in Rita J. Simon & Howard Altstein, Transracial Adoption 50, 52 (1977). After the NABSW issued its statement, transracial adoption declined sharply. From a peak of 2574 transracial adoptions in 1971, the number fell to 831 in 1975. Elizabeth Bartholet, Where Do Black Children Belong? The Politics of Race Matching in Adoption, 139 U. Pa. L. Rev. 1163, 1180 (1991).

The 1994 Multi-ethnic Placement Act (MEPA-IEP), as amended in 1996, prohibits discrimination in a child's placement on the basis of the race, national origin, or ethnicity of the child or the prospective foster or adoptive parents. The 1996 amendments deleted language that permitted an agency to "consider" the child's cultural, ethnic, or racial background as a factor in assessing the parents' ability to meet the needs of the child. The Act imposes obligations on agencies to seek out potential adoptive families of the races and ethnicities of the children needing placement. 42 U.S.C. § 1996b (2022).

Two trends have produced renewed interest in transracial adoption. The first is emphasis on placing foster children. More than half of all children waiting in foster care to be adopted are children of color. In 2020, 20 percent of the children entering foster care, and 22 percent of those waiting to be adopted—but only 17 percent of those actually adopted—were African-American; 21 percent of those entering foster care, 23 percent of those waiting to be adopted, and 20 percent of those actually adopted were Hispanic (of any race); and 44 percent of those waiting to be adopted, and 51 percent of those actually adopted were non-Hispanic white children. Children's Bureau, The AFCARS Report #28—Preliminary FY 2020 Estimates as of October 2021, available at https://www.acf.hhs.gov/sites/default/files/documents/cb/afcarsreport28.pdf (last visited Sept. 7, 2022). Scholars have sought to address the reasons African-American children are more likely to be placed in foster care and less likely to be adopted. For an assessment, *see* Elizabeth Bartholet, The Racial Disproportionality Movement in Child Welfare: False Facts and Dangerous Directions, 51 Ariz. L. Rev. 871 (2009); Solangel Maldonado, Discouraging Racial Preferences in Adoptions, 39 U.C. Davis L. Rev. 1415, 1431 (2006).

The second trend, as we noted in the begininning of this chapter, is continued interest in international adoption as a way of finding available infants. As a result of these trends, the number of interracial adoptions has increased significantly. In 2001, "14 percent of all adoptions were transracial" while by 2011, 44 percent of all children adopted in the United States were adopted across racial lines. Sara Miller Llana, "We're Not Projects": Transracial Adoptees Insist on Being Seen, Christian Sci. Monitor (Dec. 1, 2020), https://www.csmonitor.com/The-Culture/Family/2020/1201/We-re-not-projects-Transracial-adoptees-insist-on-being-seen.

Twila L. Perry

Transracial and International Adoption: Mothers, Hierarchy, Race and Feminist Legal Theory
10 Yale J.L. & Feminism 102, 115-116, 121-122 (1998)

One troubling aspect of both transracial and international adoption is that each often results in the transfer of children from the least advantaged women to the most advantaged. At the same time, such adoptions, per se, do nothing to alleviate the conditions in the societies or communities from which the children come and thus do nothing to change the conditions that place some women in the position of being unable to care for their children themselves. Perhaps for these reasons, at least in part, recent scholarship by women of color on transracial adoption suggests that many of them are less than enthusiastic about the practice. . . .

There are probably many reasons why Black women often appear to be ambivalent or even hostile toward transracial adoption. Some of the reasons certainly involve perceptions about the needs of individual Black children—there is skepticism about whether white women can provide Black children with the skills they need to survive in a racist society. Some Black women may also feel that white women often raise white children with a sense of superiority over Blacks and that they will naturally raise Black transracially adopted children to feel the same way. Some Black women may simply believe that white people cannot love a Black child the same way they would love a white one. They understand that however precious Black children may be to Black people, for many whites seeking to adopt, a Black child is a second, third or last choice, behind children that are white, Asian or Hispanic. Some Black women are quite critical of the mothering skills displayed by white mothers with respect to their own children, and thus view arguments of some advocates of transracial adoption that white families may be able to parent Black children better than Black families with amused contempt. . . .

I offer two additional explanations for the feelings some Black women may have toward transracial adoption—feelings unrelated to concerns about the competence of white women to raise Black children. I argue that many Black women feel that arguments in favor of transracial adoption that minimize the role of race in parenting devalue an important part of what motherhood means to them—a historical and contemporary struggle to raise Black children successfully in a racist world. In addition, many Black women may also resent transracial adoption because they see it as part of a larger system of racial hierarchy and privilege that advantages white women while it devalues and subordinates women of color. . . .

There are important links to be drawn between the transracial adoption of Black children in the United States and the adoption of children of color from Asia and Latin America. The factors of racism and economic discrimination that result in large numbers of Black children being separated from their biological parents in this country have counterparts in the international context, where a history of colonialism, neocolonialism, cultural imperialism, and economic exploitation often results in mothers being unable to keep the children to whom they have given birth. Thus, both domestically and internationally, transracial and international adoption often result in a pattern in which there is the transfer of children from the least advantaged women to the most advantaged women. Despite the differences between the specific circumstances of Black women in America and some other third world women, there is a connection in terms of a struggle by both to function as mothers under political and economic conditions which severely challenge their ability to adequately parent their own children. Moreover, many transracial adoptions, international adoptions, and adoptions in which racial and ethnic differences are not a factor, also share another connection—a link to the institution of patriarchy.

Elizabeth Bartholet

International Adoption: The Child's Story
24 Ga. St. U. L. Rev. 333, 338-348 (2007)

The issues at the heart of international adoption have to do with children too young to make decisions by themselves, and often too young even to voice feelings, desires, and views. Millions upon millions of infants and young children are growing up in orphanages or on the streets having been orphaned, abandoned, or placed in institutions by parents unable to care for them, or removed from such parents. . . .

International adoption is heavily regulated by the state, with applicable law typically describing itself as guided by the best interest of the child. Such law includes the domestic law of what are called "sending" and "receiving" countries, and international law like the Convention on the Rights of the Child, and the Hague Convention on Intercountry Adoption. All this law has tended to function generally to restrict rather than to facilitate international adoption. The law focuses on the bad things that might happen when a child is transferred from a birth parent to an international adoptive parent and then purports to try to protect against those things happening. . . . There are very typically so many restrictions that even when international adoption is officially allowed, it is in effect not allowed, except for a tiny percentage of children in need, leaving the rest to grow up in institutions or on the streets.

. . . [C]ritics of international adoption have been both active and significantly successful. For example, Romania was forced to eliminate international adoption in 2004 as a condition of being admitted to the European Union by those in control of the European Parliament's process at the time, who relied on the U.N. Convention on the Rights of the Child and the European Convention for the Protection of Human Rights and Fundamental Freedoms to argue that international adoption was inherently a violation of children's rights. . . . New governmental restrictions on private intermediaries involved in international adoption has resulted in significantly closing down such adoption in many countries in South and Central America, including Paraguay, Chile, Bolivia, Peru, Ecuador, Honduras, and El Salvador. The result has generally been to limit the numbers of children released so that only a relative few get out, and these only after having spent two or three years or more in the kind of institutional care that puts children at high risk for permanent disabilities.

II. CONFLICTING VERSIONS OF THE CHILD'S STORY

. . . [L]et's imagine one child whose situation is typical of many others. Let's imagine the infant in a large institution. . . .

If we could have a rational conversation with this infant about her needs and wants, and about the choices she would make among the real-world options she has, how would this conversation go? First the infant would presumably want on an immediate basis to be held, fed, comforted, and played with, and kept clean, dry and warm. She would want attention when awake, and someone to respond when she cries. As months of infancy went by, she would want to see a familiar face, to connect with someone emotionally. If we could explain to her about childhood development, about the social life that normal non-institutionalized adolescents and adults live, about education and the world of work, she would want to make sure that she got the nurturing and education as a child that would enable her to grow up as the kind of emotionally and physically healthy person who could have good relationships with friends and family, and who could survive and thrive in the world of work.

. . . To help the infant make a rational choice among possible future options we should give her some more information. She knows from her daily experience that the orphanage is a horrible place. . . . When she screams for attention because she is hungry or cold or wet or just alone, nobody comes—attendants arrive only every four or six hours and then leave immediately after hurried diaper-changing and bottle-propping events. . . .

We should also give the infant other information. We should tell her that many adults in the world place significant value on birth and national heritage. We should tell her that if she were to grow up adopted abroad, many people would ask about her "real parents," referring to her birth parents. . . . We should [also] tell her that the research shows adopted children do very well on all measures that social scientists use to assess human happiness, and that it reveals no evidence that children are in any way harmed by being placed internationally. Finally, we should tell her that the research shows that children raised for significant periods of time in institutions do terribly badly on all of those social science measures. . . .

NOTES AND QUESTIONS

1. Both proponents of domestic racial matching and critics of international adoption suggest that children's interests lie with connection with home countries, families of origin, and the culture associated with them. They support devoting greater resources to children's needs before they are separated from their birth families or, failing that, more extensive efforts to support children in the communities of their birth. Advocates of cross-racial adoptions like Elizabeth Bartholet address children's needs in the context in which the children exist at the time the children become available for adoption. This debate raises the question of what could be done to reduce the number of children who are separated from their birth parents.

In 2021, Nancy D. Polikoff & Jane M. Spinak observed that:

> State removal of children from their parents is an act of violence and cruelty. That is why the Trump administration faced near universal condemnation for its 2018 policy of separating parents and children at the US-Mexico border. With this symposium, *Strengthened Bonds: Abolishing the Child Welfare System and Re-Imagining Child Well-Being*, we call attention to the enduring, devastating, American practice of separating parents and children through state agency and court procedures cloaked under the misleading name of the *child welfare* system. Those family separations are no less traumatic and consequential than the ones that were denounced at the US-Mexico border, and they will be harder to end. The Articles and Comments in this and the subsequent symposium issue seek to contribute to abolishing the system that allows those separations to continue, and to reimagining and replacing it with policies and practices that facilitate the flourishing of all children within their families, tribes, and communities.
>
> Twenty years ago, in *Shattered Bonds: The Color of Child Welfare*, law professor Dorothy Roberts systematically dismantled any pretense that the child welfare system functions to serve the interests of children. Through data, documentation, history, analysis, and family narratives, Professor Roberts called out the racism at the heart of a system that has destroyed hundreds of thousands of families. "If you came with no preconceptions about the purpose of the child welfare system," she wrote, "you would have to conclude that it is an institution designed to monitor, regulate, and punish poor Black families." Professor Roberts built on earlier analyses of child protection intervention that identified poverty as the leading reason for the state removing children from their families, and on the long legacy of early Progressive activists' efforts to assimilate immigrant families who were a threat to "American" norms by conditioning assistance on intrusive and punitive interventions in their lives. Even before this late 19th century Progressive effort began, the legally sanctioned destruction of Native American families was already operating--a systemic genocide that has yet to abate fully. All of these practices are rooted in the idea of saving children from their families and communities.

Nancy D. Polikoff & Jane M. Spinak, Foreword: Strengthened Bonds: Abolishing the Child Welfare System and Re-Envisioning Child Well-Being, 11 Colum. J. Race & L. 427, 430-433 (2021). These scholars criticize the regulation of families who seek public assistance, the often coercive removal of children from their birth parents described in Section I.A, and the failure to prioritize kinship care and the maintenance of community ties. *See also* Dorothy E. Roberts, Torn Apart: How The Child Welfare System Destroys Black Families—And How Abolition Can Build a Safer World (2022).

A similar critique exists in the context of international adoption. Some critics argue that "international adoptions based on poverty [are] cruel and unethical, compounding the vulnerability and suffering of the poor with the loss of their children, and absurdly spending tens of thousands of dollars for an intercountry adoption when perhaps one hundred dollars or less would have been sufficient to maintain the child with her family." David M. Smolin, The Corrupting Influence of the United States on a Vulnerable Intercountry Adoption System: A Guide for Stakeholders, Hague and Non-Hague Nations, NGOs, and Concerned Parties, 15 Utah L. Rev. 1065, 1072 (2013). Barbara Stark similarly suggests that international adoption should be addressed as part of a global system of governance that examines the root causes of poverty and violence and that the best way to address children's needs is to focus on the forces that separate them from their birth families in the first place. Barbara Stark, Toward a Theory of Intercountry Human Rights: Global Capitalism and the Rise and Fall of Intercountry Adoption, 95 Ind. L.J. 1365 (2020).

Would abolition of the child welfare system that removes children from their birth families and the international adoption system that facilitates transracial and transcultural adoptions improve the well-being of children? If you agree that the ideal solution involves devoting greater resources to struggling families starting at birth, what role would you see for adoption in such a system? If you believe that abolishing these systems is impractical, what reforms would you implement?

2. Does some form of open adoption, with ongoing contact between an adopted child and his or her family of origin, allow the child to form an identity that includes both families and cultures? *See* Solangel Maldonado, Permanency v. Biology: Making the Case for Post-Adoption Contact, 37 Cap. U. L. Rev. 321 (2008); Ashley Albert & Amy Mulzer, Adoption Cannot Be Reformed, 12 Colum. J. Race & L. 1, 3 (2022) (arguing for the abolition of "the practice of permanently severing the legal bonds between a parent and child and 'replacing' them with new ones via formalized adoption").

3. How should a public adoption agency proceed in the following case, which occurred in Cincinnati, Ohio, the seat of Hamilton County?

> Leah, who is two, is Black and was born with Fetal Alcohol Syndrome and a form of dwarfism. After she had been in the permanent custody of the county for about six months, a married couple, the Atkinsons, inquired about the possibility of adopting her. The Atkinsons had three biological children, each of whom had significant special health needs, and they were longtime foster parents to a fourth child, an Alaskan Native who, like Leah, had a form of dwarfism as well as other special needs. The Atkinsons learned about Leah from Little People of America, a national advocacy group in which the Atkinsons were active. The Atkinsons are white and live in North Pole, Alaska, a suburb of Fairbanks.

Is it legally permissible for the agency to inquire about the racial composition of the Atkinsons' neighborhood or church, or about the Atkinsons' attitudes or plans for raising an African-American child in Alaska? Is it permissible for the agency to delay in responding to the Atkinsons for several months while it determines whether other (perhaps more racially suitable) placements are available? Is it legally permissible for the agency to consider the presence of another child with dwarfism in the household and to make that a basis for selecting the Atkinsons over another couple? *See* Julia Steggerda-Corey, Altering the Legal Adoption Framework to Serve Historically-Underserved Transracial Adoptees, 54 Tex. Tech L. Rev. 537, 540 (2022) (suggesting reforms to address the mental and emotional health and development of transracial adoptees through the home study, placement, and adoption processes).

4. Professor Barbara Fedders reports that many private adoption agencies, which are less regulated than public agencies, charge higher fees for the adoption of white infants than Black infants. Barbara Fedders, Race and Market Values in Domestic Infant Adoption, 88 N.C. L. Rev. 1687 (2010). *See also* Marcia Zug, ICWA's Irony, 45 Am. Indian L. Rev. 1, 78 (2021) (describing how in private adoptions, which are not subject to the MEPA-IEP, "race-matching is open and notorious.") Should the agencies be required to charge race-neutral fees even if that means that fewer African-American children will be adopted? Does the response to this issue replicate many of the same issues Professors Perry and Bartholet discuss?

5. Two international treaties address adoption. The first, the Convention on the Rights of the Child, was approved by the United Nations in 1989. The United States is the only UN Member Nation that has not ratified it. Article 20 sets forth governmental obligations in protecting a child's identity and continuity of cultural background, providing that "due regard shall be paid to the desirability of continuity in a child's upbringing and to the child's ethnic, religious, cultural and linguistic background."

The second treaty, the Hague Convention on Protection of Children and Cooperation in Respect of Intercountry Adoption, was adopted in 1993. Article 16 states that a child's country of origin must "give due consideration to the child's upbringing and to his or her ethnic, religious and cultural background" and "determine, on the basis in particular of the reports relating to the child and the prospective adoptive parents, whether the envisaged placement is in the best interests of the child."

Congress enacted the Intercountry Adoption Act of 2000, which brings this country into compliance with Hague Convention requirements. Finding Families for African-American Children: The Role of Race and Law in Adoption from Foster Care 23 (2008), above, at 16-17. In complying with the Hague Convention, the United States requires counseling for adoptive parents about how to meet a child's racial and ethnic needs.

A little-known development is that the United States has also become a source of children adopted abroad, often African-American children from foster care. Twenty states sent children abroad, with Florida sending the most children. The two most popular destination countries for American children are Canada and the Netherlands. An American child adopted abroad retains his or her American citizenship. Cynthia R. Mabry-King, Outgoing Adoptions: What Should Happen When Things Go Wrong?, 44 Cap. U. L. Rev. 1, 3, 5, 7 (2016). The Hague Convention provisions also apply to these children.

The Convention itself is available at the home page of the Hague Conference on Private International Law, http://hcch.e-vision.nl/index_en.php (last visited Sept. 7, 2022).

For a comparison of race matching in the adoption process with race matching in the selection of gametes for assisted reproduction, see Dov Fox, Race Sorting in Family Formation, 49 Fam. L.Q. 55, 56 (2015).

RELIGIOUS MATCHING

Legally, religious matching in adoption and foster care, like racial matching, has been transformed from a mandatory rule to a discretionary policy. In the late 1980s one-third of the states had some form of religious matching provision regarding adoption. Note, Gregory A. Horowitz, Accommodations and Neutrality Under the Establishment Clause: The Foster Care Challenge, 98 Yale L.J. 617, 624 (1989). Professor Clark has argued that religious matching rules were created to impose a truce on proselytizing and to avoid conflict among religious groups. Homer H. Clark, Jr., Domestic Relations in the United States §20.7, at 917 (2d ed. 1988).

Religious matching, which varies from state-to-state, was most deeply entrenched in New York, where it has been the subject of substantial litigation. See Martin Guggenheim, State-Supported Foster Care: The Interplay Between the Prohibition of Establishing Religion and the Free Exercise Rights of Parents and Children: Wilder v. Bernstein, 56 Brook. L. Rev. 603, 605 (1990). Most of the litigation in New York and other states has involved parents' claims that their own free exercise rights require that their children be placed with foster parents of the same religion. These requests are typically honored if possible, and, at least in New York, if a child is placed with foster parents of a different religion, the agency is supposed to provide support and supervision to the foster parent to ensure that the child's religious practices are protected. See, e.g., Bruker v. City of New York, 337 F. Supp. 2d 539 (S.D.N.Y. 2004); Whalen v. Allers, 302 F. Supp. 2d 194 (S.D.N.Y. 2003).

In Fulton v. City of Philadelphia, Pennsylvania, 141 S. Ct. 1868 (2021), the Supreme Court considered whether the City of Philadelphia could terminate its contract with Catholic Social Services (CSS) because of the agency's refusal to certify married same-sex couples as foster parents in violation of the city's anti-discrimination laws. The Supreme Court concluded that Philadelphia's actions violated the Free Exercise Clause of the First Amendment. At least ten states now have laws that permit foster care and adoption agencies to discriminate on the basis of their religious or moral beliefs, and a number of others, including Iowa and Massachusetts, are considering such legislation. Lawrence G. Sager & Nelson Tebbe, Discriminatory Permissions and Structural Injustice, 106 Minn. L. Rev. 803, 807 (2021). Among the factors that the Supreme Court considered in *Fulton* were the facts that "no same-sex couple has ever approached CSS, but if that were to occur, CSS would simply refer the couple to another agency that is happy to provide that service — and there are at least 27 such agencies in Philadelphia." *Fulton*, 141 S. Ct. at 1886. How might the ruling in *Fulton* affect agencies' ability to honor birth parents' requests for placement with heterosexual parents? For a discussion of the likely legal treatment of these issues, *see* Leslie C. Griffin, A Word of Warning from a Woman: Arbitrary, Categorical, and Hidden Religious Exemptions Threaten LGBT Rights, 7 Ala. C.R.-C.L. L. Rev. 97, 104-105 (2015); Matthew A. Issa, Guaranteeing Marriage Rights: Examining the Clash Between Same-Sex Adoption and Religious Freedom, 18 Geo. J. Gender & L. 207, 228 (2017).

PROBLEM

The juvenile court ordered that 14-year-old Liz be placed in foster care after finding that her mother had physically and emotionally abused her. Liz was placed in the foster home of Susan, a single mother living with two children. Liz thrived in Susan's home. Her grades improved, her depression lifted, and she described herself as happier than she had ever been in her life. After Liz had been in Susan's home for three months, Liz's mother learned that Susan is a Catholic. Liz has been raised to be an observant Jew. Statutes in this jurisdiction provide that:

> Whenever a child is committed to an agency, such commitment shall be made, when practicable, to an authorized agency under the control of persons of the same religious faith as that of the child. The placement of any child thus committed must, when practicable, be with or in the custody of a person or persons of the same religious faith or persuasion as that of the child.

Liz was not placed in a Jewish foster home originally because none was available when she was removed from her mother's home. Citing this statute, Liz's mother has asked that Liz be moved from Susan's home to the home of practicing Jewish foster parents. While Liz has resided at Susan's home, she has attended synagogue and observed Jewish holidays. However, prior case law in this jurisdiction provides that the religious matching requirement is not satisfied by placing a child with a person of another faith, even if that person tries to protect the child's faith. Liz vehemently objects to being removed from Susan's home. She believes that her mother's request has nothing to do with religion but is part of her continuing effort to control her.

Based on all the materials we have read so far and assuming that the religious-matching statute does not violate the First Amendment, how should the lawyers for Liz's mother argue that Liz must be moved to the first available Jewish foster home? Assuming that Liz is granted party status and that her guardian ad litem agrees with her position, how should Liz's lawyers argue that she should be allowed to remain at Susan's home?

B. ALTERNATIVE REPRODUCTIVE TECHNOLOGIES

1. Artificial Insemination and In Vitro Fertilization

The most common, most basic, and simplest "alternative reproductive technology" is artificial insemination, a relatively old, relatively simple process. The first recorded application occurred in London in 1785 when Dr. John Hunter impregnated the wife of a linen merchant with her husband's sperm. The use of donor sperm was much more controversial, however, and when the first acknowledged instance occurred in 1884, the doctor did not tell the mother that the sperm came from someone other than her husband. By the end of the 1940s, married couples had quietly begun to use artificial insemination by donor (AID) in substantial numbers in cases where the husband was infertile. So long as the couple stayed together, the child's origins usually remained secret; if the couple divorced, however, questions often arose about the child's legal status and the husband's liability for child support and right to visitation. The answers to these questions in the initial cases were divided. Leading cases imposing a parent-child relationship between the husband and child on the theory that he had voluntarily taken on responsibility for the child by assenting to AID include Levin v. Levin, 626 N.E.2d 527 (Ind. 1993); People v. Sorensen, 437 P.2d 495 (Cal. 1968) (en banc); and Strnad v. Strnad, 78 N.Y.S.2d 390 (N.Y. Sup. 1948). *But see* Gursky v. Gursky, 242 N.Y.S.2d 406 (N.Y. Sup. 1963) (discussing child support for a child considered illegitimate because the husband and wife acknowledged that a donor had supplied the sperm for the child's conception but nonetheless held the husband liable for his support because of his consent to the insemination).

To clarify parental status, these techniques have been the subject of a number of uniform acts, most notably the Uniform Parentage Act of 1973, which was adopted by 18 states. The Uniform Parentage Act of 2002 substantially changed the 1973 Act. By 2017, Alabama, Delaware, Illinois, Maine, New Mexico, North Dakota, Oklahoma, Texas, Utah, Washington, and Wyoming had adopted the 2002 Act. In light of the *Obergefell* decision, the new version of the Act approved in 2017 incorporates gender neutral language. As of 2022, five states have enacted the 2017 version of the Uniform Parentage Act (described as applied to parentage rights in Chapter 13), two more enacted something substantially similar, and three states have introduced the bill. *See* Uniform Parentage Act (2017), Uniform Law Commission, available at https://www.uniformlaws.org/committees/community-home?CommunityKey=c4f37d2d-4d20-4be0-8256-22dd73af068f (last visited Sept. 7, 2022).

UNIFORM PARENTAGE ACT (2017)

§702. A donor is not a parent of a child conceived by means of assisted reproduction.

§704. (a) Consent by a woman, and the individual who intends to be a parent of a child born through assisted reproduction must be in a record.

(b) Failure to consent in a record as required by subsection (a), before or after birth of the child, does not preclude a finding of parentage if the woman giving birth and the individual, during the first two years of the child's life resided together in the same household with the child and openly held out the child as their own. A period of temporary absence is part of the period.

§705. (a) Except as otherwise provided in subsection (b), an individual who, at the time of the child's birth, is the spouse of the woman who gives birth to a child by means of assisted reproduction may not challenge his paternity of the child unless:

(1) within two years after learning of the birth of the child the spouse commences a proceeding to adjudicate his paternity; and

(2) the court finds that the spouse did not consent to the assisted reproduction, before or after birth of the child.

(b) A proceeding to adjudicate paternity may be maintained at any time if the court determines that:

(1) the spouse neither provided a gamete for, nor consented to, assisted reproduction by his or her spouse;

(2) the spouse and the woman who gave birth to the child have not cohabited since the probable time of assisted reproduction; and

(3) the spouse never openly held out the child as his own.

(c) The limitation provided in this section applies to a marriage declared invalid after assisted reproduction.

§706. (a) If a marriage is dissolved before placement of eggs, sperm, or embryos, the former spouse is not a parent of the resulting child unless the former spouse consented in a record that if assisted reproduction were to occur after a divorce, the former spouse would be a parent of the child.

(b) The consent of an individual to assisted reproduction under Section 704 may be withdrawn by that individual in a record with notice to the woman giving birth at any time before placement of eggs, sperm, or embryos. An individual who withdraws consent under this section is not a parent of the resulting child.

§707. If an individual who consented in a record to be a parent by assisted reproduction dies before placement of eggs, sperm, or embryos, the deceased individual is not a parent of the resulting child unless the deceased spouse consented in a record that if assisted reproduction were to occur after death, the deceased individual would be a parent of the child.

Gatsby v. Gatsby
495 P.3d 996 (Idaho 2021)

MOELLER, Justice. We have before us an appeal in a custody case brought by a woman whose same-sex former spouse conceived a child through artificial insemination during their marriage. . . .

The district court affirmed the magistrate court's ruling that Appellant Linsay Gatsby ("Linsay") had no parental rights to the child under Idaho's common law marital presumption of paternity because she conceded that she lacked a biological relationship with the child. The district court also affirmed that Linsay had no parental rights under the Artificial Insemination Act because she did not comply with the statute's provisions. The district court further ruled that Linsay would have had parental rights if she had filed a voluntary acknowledgment of paternity or adopted the child, but she did not do so. Finally, the district court affirmed that Linsay did not have third party standing to seek custody and, in the alternative, that custody or visitation would not be in the child's best interest if Linsay did have third party standing. For the reasons set forth below, we affirm the decision of the district court.

I. FACTUAL AND PROCEDURAL BACKGROUND

Linsay and Kylee Gatsby married in June 2015. They later decided Kylee would attempt to conceive a child through artificial insemination, using semen donated by a mutual friend. They elected to attempt this procedure on their own, without using the services of a physician. Additionally, without consulting an attorney, Linsay, Kylee, and the semen donor signed an artificial insemination agreement Linsay found online, listing the friend as "donor" and both Linsay and Kylee as the "recipient." The agreement included acknowledgements that the recipient intended to become pregnant and to have rights to the child, and that the donor would not have parental rights or obligations to the child. Linsay performed the insemination procedure on Kylee in their home. After several attempts, Kylee became pregnant. On October 29, 2016, Kylee gave birth to the child. It is undisputed that Kylee is the child's biological mother. Linsay was present at the birth. The birth certificate worksheet, which Kylee signed, designates Kylee as "mother," and the word "father" on the form is crossed out and "mother" written by hand in its place to also identify Linsay as the child's mother. The Idaho Department of Health and Welfare issued a Certificate of Live Birth identifying both Kylee and Linsay as the child's mothers. The child resided with Linsay and Kylee, who held themselves out as the child's parents. Both Kylee and Linsay shared in caregiving, but Kylee was the child's primary caregiver.

The following summer the couple had an argument. Both Linsay and Kylee had been drinking, and Kylee became drunk. Kylee shoved Linsay off a bed. Then Linsay punched Kylee, breaking her nose. The child was in the bedroom during the fight, and Linsay's two children from a prior relationship were also in the home. Kylee was arrested and subsequently pleaded guilty to domestic battery, a misdemeanor. Kylee had also committed an act of domestic violence years earlier. On July 5, 2017, a No Contact Order ("NCO") was issued, which prohibited Kylee from seeing the child except at daycare. On August 29, 2017, Linsay filed for divorce. Kylee filed an Answer and Counterclaim, asserting that Linsay had "no legal claim or standing to any custody or visitation" to the minor child.

Due to the NCO, Linsay had sole custody of the child from Kylee's arrest on July 3, 2017, until December 27, 2017, when the magistrate court issued a Temporary Order giving Kylee and Linsay equal custody. In the meantime, Kylee had successfully participated in a Domestic Violence Offender Intervention/Treatment class. After sharing custody for nearly one year, on November 15, 2018, the magistrate court granted sole custody of the child to Kylee. The magistrate court found that Linsay was not the child's legal parent, Linsay had established no third-party rights, and, in the alternative, it was not in the child's best interest for the court to award Linsay custody or visitation rights as a third party based on the evidence in the record. . . .

III. Analysis

This case deals with the sensitive issue of artificial insemination and the rights of spouses who are non-biological parents to children conceived through artificial insemination using a third-party semen donor. Although the issue in this case comes to us in the context of a same-sex marriage, it would be an issue of first impression regardless of the genders of the spouses.

A. The District Court Did Not Err in Concluding That Linsay Does Not Have Parental Rights to the Child.

1. The Artificial Insemination Act Is the Controlling Statute in This Case.

As a threshold matter, we must first hold that the Artificial Insemination Act (I.C. §§ 39-5401 – 39-5407) ("AIA") is the controlling statute in this case. We acknowledge that there has long been a common law marital presumption of paternity in Idaho. . . . Nevertheless, the legislature adopted the AIA in 1982 to specifically address issues that are unique to artificial insemination — including "[t]he relationship, rights and obligation between a child born as a result of artificial insemination and the mother's husband . . . "). I.C. § 39-5405(3). . . .

This Court has long held that "the legislature clearly has the power to abolish or modify common law rights and remedies." . . . Therefore, because the AIA . . . is the more specific statute and has provisions that address how parental rights are established, we conclude that the AIA is controlling with respect to the case at bar. Therefore, neither the common law marital presumption of paternity nor the Paternity Act should be applied to resolve this case. In fact, the application of either would undermine the consent and recording requirements of the AIA. . . .

The AIA expressly states: "Artificial insemination shall not be performed upon a woman without her prior written request and consent and the prior written request and consent of her husband." I.C. § 39-5403(1). Further, the AIA provides that a child and husband will have the same legal relationship as a child naturally conceived if the husband consented to the performance of the artificial insemination . . .

The AIA goes on to require the filing of the request and consent with the state registrar of vital statistics:

> (2) Whenever a child is born who may have been conceived by artificial insemination, a copy of the request and consent required under subsection (1) of this section shall be filed by the physician who performs the artificial insemination with the state registrar of vital statistics. . . .

I.C. § 39-5403(2). The remaining sections of the AIA address regulations that promote health and safety. For example, Section 39-5402 provides that "[o]nly physicians licensed under chapter 18, title 54, Idaho Code, and persons under their supervision may select artificial insemination donors and perform artificial insemination." . . .

Under *Obergefell v. Hodges*, 576 U.S. 644, 135 S.Ct. 2584, 192 L.Ed.2d 609 (2015), the AIA must be read in a gender-neutral manner. When read in that manner, there is no equal protection concern because the AIA would apply to opposite-sex couples and same-sex couples in the exact same manner. . . .

2. The Parties Did Not Comply with the Artificial Insemination Act.

At the time the child in this case was conceived, . . . the Department of Health and Welfare required the use and filing of a specific "Request and Consent for Artificial Insemination" form, which can also be read in a gender-neutral manner:

> **900. Requests and Consent for Artificial Insemination**
>
> **01. Form Content.** The form for reporting the birth of a child who may have been conceived by artificial insemination shall be known as "Request and Consent for Artificial Insemination." The form shall be signed and dated by the wife, husband, and the physician who participates in the procedure of artificial insemination. The form shall include the statement:
> "The undersigned husband and wife do hereby consent of their own free will and choice to said artificial insemination.
> The undersigned have been advised of, and understand the provisions of Title 39, Chapter 54, Idaho Code, including, but not limited to, the provision that if the physician who performs the artificial insemination does not deliver the child conceived as a result of the artificial insemination, it is the duty of the mother and her husband to give that physician notice of the child's birth. We do hereby agree to be bound by such provision. . . ."

IDAPA 16.02.08.900 (repealed 2019)

The magistrate found that Linsay did not "register[ ] a written consent agreement as contemplated by the Artificial Insemination Act," which prevented her from benefiting from the law. The district court observed further that, contrary to the statute, Linsay and Kylee did not use a licensed physician to perform the insemination, nor did they file the required consent with the state registrar of vital statistics, as is required in section 39-5403(2). . . .

Additionally, the agreement itself suffers from severe inadequacies. . . . Critically, the on-line agreement does not contain any language indicating that Linsay, in her capacity as Kylee's spouse, consented to Kylee being inseminated. The agreement does not purport to grant Linsay any parental rights relative to the contemplated child as a nonbiological parent, which is precisely what she is attempting to accomplish by enforcing the agreement. In fact, the agreement contains language appearing to do just the opposite. Section 10 of the agreement contains this problematic provision: "*Each party* relinquishes and releases any and all rights *he or she may have* to bring a suit *to establish paternity*." (Emphasis added). Later, in Section 13 of the agreement, it states that "[e]ach party acknowledges and agrees that the relinquishment of rights, as stated above, is final and irrevocable."

Although it is far from clear in the text of the online form used, even if it is inferred from the circumstances that Linsay consented to Kylee being inseminated, compliance with the AIA requires more. For example, the AIA required both Kylee and Linsay to use a licensed physician to perform the insemination. Additionally, the agency rule applicable at the time required Kylee, Linsay, *and the physician* to sign the consent form. IDAPA 16.02.08.900.01 (repealed 2019). Further, the consent form had to be "filed by the physician who performs the artificial insemination with the state registrar of vital statistics." I.C. § 39-5403(2). We cannot assume that such requirements merely reflect a bureaucratic penchant for paperwork and forms. They are an important part of the myriad legal documents which define and protect Idaho families — like marriage licenses, birth certificates, and even decrees of divorce — and they should not be treated cavalierly. Thus, they cannot be easily tossed aside as mere pieces of paperwork.

. . . Notably, Linsay does not argue that the registration requirement and the mandate that the insemination be performed by a physician place an unfair burden or unreasonable restriction on the use of artificial insemination by same-sex couples. Rather, Linsay asserts that she complied with all the code sections *that applied to her*, meaning that she could satisfy Idaho Code section 39-5405(3), which states that the "mother's husband" will have parental rights "if the husband consented to the performance of artificial insemination." According to Linsay, the only thing that matters is her consent to the artificial insemination, and she claims her consent is clear because: (1) Linsay, Kylee, and the donor filled out a form together that Linsay found online; (2) Linsay performed the insemination on Kylee; and (3) Linsay's name was on the birth certificate. In sum, Linsay asks this Court to read Idaho Code section 39-5405 in isolation from the rest of the AIA. We cannot do this. . . .

Without stating so explicitly, by faulting the majority for its "rigid" adherence to the AIA, the dissent is essentially arguing that we should not strictly enforce a statute when a party has substantially complied with it, or we disagree with it. . . . Additionally, it would be illogical to conclude that the legislature did not intend to require strict compliance with these provisions inasmuch as it made failure to comply with the requirements a misdemeanor. I.C. § 39-5407. . . .

Additionally, the dissent faults the majority for focusing too heavily on the inadequacies in the parties' agreement. However, the majority has merely taken the agreement as it found it and applied it as written. It is neither hyper technical nor "clever" for us to note the many inadequacies of the online form used by the parties in this case. The dissent correctly observes that we should exercise care in our decisions to protect the family unit because of its "essential role in the welfare of our society." *Pedigo v. Rowley*, 101 Idaho 201, 205, 610 P.2d 560, 564 (1980). However, this cuts both ways. It is not unreasonable or improper for the state to promote a policy requiring a married couple to act carefully and responsibly when making the important and life-altering decision to bring a child into their home through artificial insemination from a third-party semen donor. Such an agreement should not be entered into lightly. Ensuring that such choices are made with due consideration to the legal and medical consequences to the parties and the child is a legitimate public policy concern. . . .

The dissent further notes that while this matter was under advisement before this Court, a key provision in the AIA, Idaho Code section 39-5403, was amended by the Idaho legislature. . . . The amended version of section 39-5403 no longer places a duty on the physician who performed the procedure to file the consent form with the state registrar and removes the requirement for the State Board of Health and Welfare to promulgate rules concerning record keeping.

We note that there is no language in the amended statute suggesting that the change should be applied retroactively. However, even if the amended statute were retroactively applied to this case, it does not materially change the Court's analysis. The fact remains that the parties did not comply with the other material provisions of the AIA. . . .

C. The District Court Did Not Err in Affirming the Magistrate Court's Conclusion That It Was in the Child's Best Interest for Kylee to Be Awarded Sole Custody of the Child.

. . . The magistrate's best interest determination was within the boundaries of that court's discretion and in accord with the U.S. Supreme Court's decision in *Troxel*, in which the Court determined "(1) there is a presumption that a fit parent acts in the best interests of his or her child; (2) a judge must accord "special weight" to a fit parent's decision; and (3) a court may not "infringe on the fundamental right of parents to make child rearing decisions simply because [it] believes a 'better' decision could be made." *Leavitt*, 142 Idaho at 671, 132 P.3d at 428 (citing *Troxel*, 530 U.S. at 68, 71–73, 120 S.Ct. 2054).

The magistrate court made the following findings and conclusions:

> Kylee is a fit parent. This Court has minimal concerns about Kylee's ability to properly care for [the child]. While it is recognized that Kylee drank alcohol excessively and she committed acts of domestic violence on her partners, this is not a case in which the Court believes at this time her fundamental and constitutional rights to raise her child should be restricted. Kylee has a good healthy relationship with [the child]. Kylee has a constitutional right to make decisions regarding the care, custody, and control of her child. Kylee wishes to restrict Linsay's access to the child.

Important factors cited by the magistrate court in finding Linsay should have no custody or visitation were: (1) the severe "toxicity" and animosity in Linsay and Kylee's relationship, which the magistrate court found would continue if they interacted with one another through the child; (2) that Linsay had not spent much time as the primary caregiver and failed to act in the child's best interests during the period when she temporarily had sole custody by leaving the child with others for thirty-one overnights during a six month span; (3) that Kylee has a healthier relationship with the child than Linsay does; (4) that Linsay creates conflict in the child's community by excluding a beloved daycare provider and grandmother figure—with whom the child has been close since birth—from the child's life; (5) that the existing joint custody schedule has not created stability for the child; (6) that Linsay lied to the court and has a reputation for dishonesty; and (7) that Kylee's history of domestic violence does not indicate that the child is in danger. We note that substantial and competent evidence in the record supports these findings. . .

Linsay maintains the magistrate court abused its discretion because it failed to consider Idaho Code section 32-717B(5), which provides there will be a presumption that joint custody is not in the best interest of the child if one of the parents is "found by the court to be a habitual perpetrator of domestic violence as defined in section 39-6303." However, section 32-717B is inapplicable to this situation because Linsay seeks custody as a third party. We have noted previously that Idaho Code section 32-717, which codifies the best interest of the child factors, applies almost exclusively to custody disputes between parties with equivalent legal interests in the child. . . .

. . . While the magistrate admittedly did not apply a presumption against Kylee, the magistrate clearly considered the nature of the domestic violence matters and still concluded that it was in the child's best interest for Kylee to be awarded full custody. . . .

STEGNER, J., dissenting. In this case, a married couple (albeit of the same sex) undertook to have a child together through artificial insemination. Now, during the process of divorce, the biological mother of the resulting child seeks to deprive her acknowledged spouse of any recognized legal relationship to the child, the effect of which will render the marriage a nullity and deprive the child of parental and financial support. Today, the majority agrees with the biological mother and issues a decision which effectively says that a parent who has consented to (and participated in) her spouse being artificially inseminated is not entitled to be a parent of the resulting offspring because neither she nor a physician filed a never-used and now-obsolete form with the State Registrar of Vital Statistics. In so holding, the majority has delegitimized the non-biological mother's efforts to establish her parental rights and responsibilities. However, the most lasting error in this decision is not the majority's disregard of Linsay's (and also Kylee's) efforts to establish and recognize a parental relationship; it is the refusal to grapple with the consequences of this decision. I think the effect of the majority's opinion is contrary to the public policy of Idaho and jeopardizes the legal protections of a parent whose child was conceived by artificial insemination. For these reasons, I respectfully dissent.

1. The Majority's Rigid Interpretation of the AIA Is Not Only Incorrect as a Matter of Law, but Also Turns a Blind Eye to Idaho's Public Policy Favoring Legitimacy. . . .

The majority's requirement of strict compliance with every section of the AIA undermines this bedrock policy of Idaho's support for the family. The majority states that it refuses to read Idaho Code section 39-5405 in isolation, and that the Legislature mandated strict compliance with *all* sections of the AIA in order for the protections of section 39-5405(3) to apply. . . . As a result, the majority ignores the parties' express intent and undertaking to establish a parent-child relationship within their legally recognized family unit. *This intent matters.* How can the majority jettison all relevant evidence of consent and intent — evidence that a married couple definitively and consciously undertook the awesome responsibility of parenthood — because a single form was not filed? Linsay assisted in the insemination of her wife Kylee. If that does not evidence her consent, what would? The result of the majority's holding is that the core legal protections of a child conceived by artificial insemination during the course of a marriage would be determined strictly by the filling out and filing of a particular piece of paperwork, rather than by the documented actions and intentions of the spouses.

The majority contends that the consent and notice section sets a requirement for more than a "mere piece of paperwork," equating such a form with those involved in applications for marriage licenses, birth certificates, and divorce decrees. However, this reasoning does not withstand scrutiny. In February 2021, the Idaho State Registrar of Vital Statistics James Aydelotte testified before the Senate Health and Welfare Committee that there has "*never been such a filing [of a couple's written consent to artificial insemination] with the Bureau of Vital Records (BVR) and no purpose exists for either the BVR or the DHW to receive the consent forms.*" *Relating to the State Registrar of Vital Statistics: Hearing before the Senate Health & Welfare Committee*, 66th Leg., 1st Reg. Sess. (Idaho, Feb. 8, 2021) (italics added) (testimony of State Registrar James Aydelotte). Notwithstanding the State Registrar's recognition that there has "never been such a filing . . . and no purpose exists for either the BVR or the DHW to receive the consent forms . . ." the majority concludes otherwise. The effect of which is to dispossess Linsay of her parental rights and responsibilities.

In addition, the majority's erroneous interpretation has significant implications. If the most recent amendment to Idaho Code section 39-5403 is not retroactive, as the majority incorrectly concludes, then all children born by artificial insemination in Idaho until July 1, 2021, are now presumptively illegitimate. The majority invites challenge to the status of these children's recognized relationships in contexts including immigration, citizenship, inheritance, intestate succession, and the rights and benefits of survivors, as well as to child custody, support, and visitation. There will be profound ramifications, many untoward, from today's majority decision. The majority's narrow view of what will satisfy the AIA creates a legal morass and undermines Idaho's public policy of favoring family units.

Whatever the future may bring for those Idaho children created by artificial insemination, the deepest wound wrought *today* by the majority's interpretation is how it renders Linsay's marriage to Kylee a nullity, and eviscerates the legal protections for their child that would otherwise inhere to the family unit. . . .

2. Kylee and Linsay Complied with the Consent Requirement of the AIA and Their Child Is Entitled to the Protection of Idaho Code Section 39-5405(3)

. . . Linsay and Kylee complied with the "written request and consent" requirement of Idaho Code sections 39-5405 and 39-5403(1). Although "consent" is not defined in the AIA, *see* I.C. § 39-5401, Black's Law Dictionary defines "consent," in relevant part, as "[a] voluntary yielding to what another proposes or desires; agreement, approval, or permission regarding some act or purpose, esp. given voluntarily by a competent person; legally effective assent." *Consent*, BLACK'S LAW DICTIONARY (11th ed. 2019). Linsay and Kylee both signed the artificial insemination agreement, which contemplated their use of donated semen, and delineated that the donor would have no rights to any child(ren). The parties memorialized in writing their intent to undergo artificial insemination and to "sever any and all parental rights and responsibilities" of the donor. This is an "agreement" and "approval" regarding the "act or purpose" of artificial insemination. . . .

Instead of acknowledging what the agreement *says*, the majority emphasizes what the agreement *does not* say: the agreement does not specify "the intended recipient of the semen[,]" nor does it "purport to grant Linsay any parental rights relative to the contemplated child as a nonbiological parent." But these are not required by the statute. These omissions do not change the intent or the written consent of the parties in agreeing that artificial insemination will occur. There is simply no other interpretation of this agreement. . . .

3. The Legislature's Recent Amendment to Idaho Code Section 39-5403 Renders the Majority's Analysis of Linsay's Compliance with the AIA Incorrect

. . . It is not difficult to divine why the Legislature made the act retroactive. The Legislature clearly did not want to leave children conceived by artificial insemination in legal limbo. Yet, that is the effect of today's decision. . . .

Under the recently amended version, Linsay also complied with the consent requirements of the AIA. . . . In other words, the Legislature has recognized that the previous statute was much too stringent in its requirements and the amended statute is much more permissive in what is required to comply with the statute. As set out above, Kylee and Linsay entered into an artificial insemination agreement with the donor — in writing which was signed by the parties including Kylee and Linsay. The majority's opinion is too clever by half in its analysis of this agreement. Nothing more than written consent is now required by Idaho Code section 39-5403, and written consent was clearly given. . . .

Curiously, the majority says it does not have to consider Linsay as being different than a man because it would hold similarly if Linsay *were* a man. Think about that result for a moment. Assume Kylee's spouse is a man named Leonard rather than a woman named Linsay.

Leonard is incapable of fathering a child. As a result, Kylee and Leonard download a form from the internet identical to the one signed by Kylee and Linsay. They importune a friend to contribute his semen which will then be used to impregnate Kylee. All three sign the same document, just as Kylee, Linsay, and the semen donor did in this case. Leonard assists Kylee in her artificial insemination, and she delivers a healthy baby girl. Kylee fills out a worksheet which results in Leonard being identified as the father on the birth certificate even though his DNA did not contribute to the baby girl's birth. The marriage disintegrates and divorce proceedings result. Do we tell Leonard that he is not the father of that baby girl and he has no further obligation to her? Do we tell him he needed to adopt that baby girl because he did not do enough under the law to be her father? I think the simple answer to both questions is no; we should not. Such a result flies in the face of Idaho's frequently espoused public policy and exalts form over substance. . . .

Let us also examine this decision with the shoe on the other foot: Assume Kylee now wishes to hold Leonard responsible for the financial support which would otherwise be due. This decision will be used by lawyers going forward and putative — but not biological — parents in the future to resist child support payments that would otherwise be lawfully owed. The unintended consequences of this decision are hard to quantify, but it is safe to say they will be myriad.

NOTES AND QUESTIONS

1. *Compare* the Uniform Parentage Act of 2017 *with* the statute in *Gatsby*. Under what circumstances do each terminate the parental status of the donor? Under what circumstances do the acts recognize the parental status of an intimate partner without a biological tie to the child?

The Uniform Parentage Act of 1973 terminated a donor's parental obligations only if the donor provided the semen to a licensed physician for insemination. Twenty-one states adopted either the 1973 Uniform Parentage Act or other statutes referring to the execution of the procedure by a physician. Although the Uniform Parentage Act of 2002 dropped the requirement (as does the 2017 Uniform Parentage Act), at least 18 states continue to require physician involvement to terminate the parental status of a donor. Many states also continue to limit the termination of the donor's parental status only where the gamete donation is made to a married person although 13 states have codes that do not specifically mention marital status as a requirement. *See* Douglas NeJaime, The Nature of Parenthood, 126 Yale L.J. 2260, 2367 (2017) (summarizing state statutes).

The remaining states have no legislation addressing artificial insemination. These jurisdictions often employ common law principles, such as estoppel or in loco parentis, to recognize a mother's partner as a parent in case-by-case adjudications. *See* Deborah L. Forman, Exploring the Boundaries of Families Created with Known Sperm Providers: Who's In and Who's Out?, 19 U. Pa. J.L. & Soc. Change 41 (2016). *See more generally* Naomi R. Cahn, Test Tube Families: Why the Fertility Market Needs Legal Regulation (2009); Courtney I. Joslin, Protecting Children(?): Marriage, Gender, and Assisted Reproductive Technology, 83 S. Cal. L. Rev. 1177 (2010); Michael J. Yaworsky, Rights and Obligations Resulting from Human Artificial Insemination, 83 A.L.R.4th 295 (1991, with weekly updates).

Given the court's reasoning in *Gatsby*, could Kylee sue the sperm donor for child support? Could the donor establish paternity and seek to share custody of the child?

2. The majority's conclusion that the parties must strictly comply with the statutory provisions for Linsay to acquire parental status is a matter of statutory construction under Idaho law. What arguments do the majority and the dissent make for their respective constructions of the statute?

Both opinions refer to "Idaho's support for the family," but appear to interpret the policies underlying family support quite differently. What did you understand each opinion to have in mind in terms of promoting families?

The dissent emphasizes that "the majority ignores the parties' express intent and undertaking to establish a parent-child relationship within their legally recognized family unit. *This intent matters.* (emphasis in original)." How does the majority respond? What role does intent play in each opinion?

While the litigation was pending, the Idaho legislature amended the statute to eliminate the requirement that the participating doctor file the requisite form establishing parenthood with the state. State officials had testified that there had *"never been such a filing [of a couple's written consent to artificial insemination] with the Bureau of Vital Records (BVR) and no purpose exists for either the BVR or the DHW to receive the consent forms."* If the statute does not apply retroactively, what are the implications for children born through the use of artificial insemination in Idaho before the statutory revisions? Why does the majority conclude that retroactivity does not affect the outcome of this case?

For an alternative interpretation of a state sperm donor statute, *see, e.g.*, Harrison v. Harrison, 643 S.W.3d 376, 383 (Tenn. App. 2021), *appeal denied* (Feb. 10, 2022) (holding that Tenn. Code Ann. §68-3-306 does not require a written agreement between spouses for a child conceived through artificial insemination to be deemed a legitimate child of the marriage; the statute requires that the artificial insemination be performed *"with consent* of the married woman's husband.").

3. The majority opinion in *Gatsby* differs notably from decisions in other states not just in the way that it construes the Idaho artificial insemination statute but also in the way that it applies other doctrines that might establish parenthood. Which bases for parenthood, discussed in Chapter 13, might apply here?

Why does the court conclude that the marital presumption does not apply? Could the marital presumption be an independent basis for establishing parenthood? Is this opinion consistent with the Supreme Court's ruling in Pavan v. Smith, discussed in Chapter 13? For an alternative approach to the marital presumption, *see, e.g.*, Treto v. Treto, 622 S.W.3d 397, 403 (Tex. App. 2020).

The dissent notes further that while Linsay did not specifically plead the issue of equitable estoppel, "Kylee undertook the process to have Linsay listed as the child's 'Mother' on the birth certificate, and—like Linsay—signed the insemination agreement which set out the parties' intentions at length. Kylee's change in position squarely implicates the issue of equitable estoppel." The opinion asks: "should Kylee be permitted to challenge Linsay's assertion of parental rights when she has taken a diametrically opposed position previously? Several states would answer "no, she may not." For an example of a case suggesting that the doctrine of equitable estoppel precludes a legal parent from challenging her same-sex spouse's legal parentage after agreeing with her assumption of a parental role, *see* Strickland v. Day, 239 So. 3d 486, 488 (Miss. 2018).

4. The states vary substantially in the extent to which they allow pre-birth agreements to determine parentage. In Kansas, for example, the state supreme court refused to recognize the parental status of a sperm donor who argued that he intended to play a parental role on the basis of that state's artificial insemination statute. The statute provides that "[t]he donor of semen provided to a licensed physician for use in artificial insemination of a woman other than the donor's wife is treated in law as if he were not the birth father of a child thereby conceived, unless agreed to in writing by the donor and the woman." Kan. Stat. Ann. §23-2208(f) (2022). In In Interest of K.M.H, 169 P.3d 1025 (Kan. 2007), the court held that (1) the plain language of the statute adopts an "opt out" rule in which the donor does not have parental status unless he signs a written agreement to the contrary, and (2) the statute is constitutional even in circumstances in which the donor claims to have relied on an oral agreement that he would have parental rights.

The state of Washington, pursuant to a statute identical to the one in Kansas, concluded that the statute did not apply when the mother and father were in a romantic relationship and used in vitro fertilization rather than artificial insemination with the intention of raising the children together. *See* In re Parentage of J.M.K., 119 P.3d 840 (Wash. 2005).

The Georgia Supreme Court in Patton v. Vanterpool, 806 S.E.2d 494 (Ga. 2017), held that the Georgia artificial insemination statute, which creates an "irrebuttable presumption" of legitimacy with respect to "[a]ll children born within wedlock or within the usual period of gestation thereafter who [were] conceived by means of artificial insemination," did not apply to children conceived by means of in-vitro fertilization ("IVF"). Accordingly, a husband who consented to his wife's use of IVF with donor sperm was not the father of the child pursuant to the statute.

Virginia Code §20-158(A)(3) (2022) provides that "[a] donor is not the parent of a child conceived through assisted conception, unless the donor is the husband of the gestational mother." The Virginia Supreme Court nonetheless found that when a donor provided sperm to an unmarried woman pursuant to an agreement that he would play a parental role and where the parties signed a voluntary acknowledgment of paternity, the statute did not apply and would raise constitutional issues if it did because of the donor's clear intent to retain his parental standing. L.F. v. Breit, 736 S.E.2d 711 (Va. 2013). In a later Virginia case, the parties disagreed about whether they intended the biological father to play a parental role. The court found, however, that the statute did not apply because use of a turkey baster is not "assisted conception" within the meaning of the statute. Bruce v. Boardwine, 770 S.E.2d 774, 775 (Va. App. 2015).

5. The states also differ in the extent to which they allow post-birth contact to determine parental standing. In Jacob v. Shultz-Jacob, 923 A.2d 473 (Pa. 2007), a Pennsylvania appellate court found a known sperm donor liable for child support on equitable estoppel grounds in light of the sperm donor's voluntary provision of some support and involvement in the children's lives. The court awarded the donor partial custody while also finding the child's biological mother and her partner financially liable for the children.

In Jason P. v. Danielle S., 215 Cal. Rptr. 3d 542 (Cal. App. 2017), *rev. denied* (2017), Jason provided sperm to Danielle for use in IVF. His name did not appear on the birth certificate, he did not acknowledge paternity, and the parties did not have an agreement that he would play a parental role. After the birth, however, Jason regularly saw and spent time with the child. The California appellate court concluded that although California's sperm donor statute precluded him from establishing parentage on the basis of his biological connection to the child, it did not prevent him from establishing paternity by welcoming the child into his household and holding him out as his own, under a different part of the statute. As a practical matter, this meant that while Jason may not have been the child's legal father at birth, he became a father through his post-birth actions.

For a review of the known sperm donor cases suggesting that the solution might be third-party visitation or some status short of full parentage, *see* Susan Frelich Appleton, Between the Binaries: Exploring the Legal Boundaries of Nonanonymous Sperm Donation, 49 Fam. L.Q. 93 (2015).

6. Is egg donation the same as sperm donation? Approximately 12 states have statutes that terminate the parental status of egg donors as well as sperm donors. Should donor status be determined differently when a woman donates eggs to her partner with the intention they will raise the resulting children together? In K.M. v. E.G., 117 P.3d 673 (Cal. 2005), the California Supreme Court addressed such a fact pattern. California had adopted the Uniform Parentage Act of 1973, providing that a man is not a father if he provides semen to a physician to inseminate a woman who is not his wife, but the court held that the Act did not apply where a woman donated the egg with the intention that she would participate in raising the child in the home she maintained with her partner. The ruling generated a vigorous dissent objecting that the decision destabilizes preconception agreements about parental status in the context of ovum donation and surrogacy. For a comparison of the egg and sperm markets, *see* Kimberly D. Krawiec, Sunny Samaritans and Egomaniacs: Price-Fixing in the Gamete Market, 72 Law & Contemp. Probs. (Summer 2009). *See also* D.M.T. v. T.M.H., 129 So. 3d 320 (Fla. 2013) (holding that a woman who donated an egg to her same-sex partner with the intention that they would raise the child together was constitutionally entitled to recognition as a parent notwithstanding Florida statute to the contrary).

7. While many of these doctrines rely on consent to be a parent or an agreement between the parties to assume joint responsibility for the child, these agreements should not be understood to be purely private contracts. The courts have routinely held that parents cannot establish parentage solely by contract nor waive their obligations to the child solely on the basis of an agreement between the adults. Instead, these "parentage agreements," when binding, establish the elements such as consent to insemination of a partner necessary to establish parentage under the applicate state law. For an explanation of the difference between private contracts and legally enforceable parentage agreements, *see* Gregg Strauss, Parentage Agreements Are Not Contracts, 90 Fordham L. Rev. 2645, 2650 (2022).

8. Should children have a right to learn identifying information about the donor? *See* Wendy Kramer & Naomi Cahn, Finding Our Families: A First-of-Its-Kind Book for Donor-Conceived People and Their Families (2013); The Donor-Sibling Registry, available at https://www.donorsiblingregistry.com/ (last visited Sept. 7, 2022). In 2022, Colorado passed the Donor-conceived Persons and Families of Donor-conceived Persons Protection Act, Colo. Rev. Stat. Ann. §25-57-102 (2022), becoming the first state to limit anonymous egg and sperm donation.

PROBLEMS

1. Hank and Wendy, a married couple, went to Dr. Donaldson to discuss artificial insemination of Wendy by a donor. Hank did not consent in writing to the insemination then or at any later time, but Dr. Donaldson artificially inseminated Wendy with semen from an unknown donor three times, and Wendy became pregnant and gave birth to a healthy child. Under the Uniform Parentage Act (2017), who is the child's legal father? In a state with no legislation on the subject?

2. Helen decided to conceive a child by artificial insemination and to raise the child jointly with her partner, Victoria. Helen chose Mark as the semen donor. Helen now claims that she made clear to Mark that he was to have no role in the child's life, while Mark says that he and Helen agreed that he would see the child regularly and act as a father. Victoria, who is a nurse, performed the artificial inseminations with Mark's semen. Helen became pregnant and gave birth to a baby girl. Mark was listed as the father on the birth certificate. Mark visited Helen in the hospital several times, purchased gifts for the baby, and visited at least monthly until last month, when Helen cut off the visits. The baby is now 18 months old. Victoria and Helen have remained together, and Victoria actively participates in raising the baby. Mark has filed a paternity suit against Helen, seeking a declaration of paternity and visitation rights.

    a. How should this suit be resolved under the Uniform Parentage Act of 2017? In a state with no sperm donor statutes?

    b. How would Mark's suit be resolved if he had impregnated Helen through intercourse? Why should artificial insemination change the result? Or should it?

    c. What if Helen and Mark had signed a written agreement that provided that Mark would not petition for paternity and waived all claims to legal parenthood? What if they had signed an agreement providing that Mark would waive all claims to legal parenthood, but Helen agreed that he would be able to see the child at least once a month?

    d. Would the result change if Helen and Victoria were married at the time of the child's birth? If Helen and Victoria were married and they agreed that Mark would retain his status as a father, would the state recognize all three of them as parents? If not, how would the state choose between Victoria and Mark if both had a relationship with the child?

3. After having created embryos through in vitro fertilization, a married couple divorced. They could not agree about the disposition of seven frozen embryos stored in a fertility clinic. The mother, Mary Sue, asked for control of the embryos so that she could have them implanted in her uterus and perhaps bear a child. The father, Junior, objected because he was not sure he wanted to become a parent and asked that the embryos remain in cold storage. As the case progressed, both changed their minds: Mary Sue wanted the embryos donated to a childless couple, and Junior wanted them destroyed. Should the embryos be treated like children and the dispute between Mary Sue and Junior handled like a custody fight? Are the embryos property, subject to equitable division between them? If the parties have entered into an agreement with the fertility clinic about the disposition of the embryos in a situation like this, should the agreement be specifically enforced? Is either party entitled as a matter of constitutional right to control the destiny of the embryos?

4. Robert and Denise, a married couple, arranged with a fertility clinic to use in vitro fertilization to attempt a pregnancy with donated ova and Robert's sperm. Denise successfully bore a resulting child. During the same time period, Susan, a single woman, arranged with the same clinic to attempt a pregnancy using donated ova and sperm. She also successfully bore a resulting child, giving birth ten days after Denise. Ten months later, the fertility clinic informed the three parents that the clinic had mistakenly implanted embryos fertilized with Robert's sperm into Susan, and that Robert was the genetic father of the child to whom Susan had given birth. Robert, Denise, and Susan all seek recognition as parents and custody of the child. What is the likely result?

2. Surrogate Motherhood and Gestational Carriers

The idea of "surrogacy" — of a person carrying a child to term to be raised by another — generates enormous legal and ethical disagreement. To some it is "baby selling;" to others it is an acceptable innovation that assists in the creation of families of choice. With the advent of in vitro fertilization and the possibility of separating genetic and gestational motherhood, the use of a "gestational carrier" to give birth to a child to whom she is not genetically related has become more acceptable. The law in this area has shifted dramatically over the last ten years, from prohibition to recognition of intended parents' and surrogates' rights under state statutes governing gestational surrogacy. Rachel Rebouché, Contracting Pregnacy, 105 Iowa L. Rev. 1591, 1592 (2020). In 2022, only two states, Michigan and Louisiana, prohibit paid surrogacy, and three states, Nebraska, Arizona, and Indiana, treat surrogacy agreements as unenforceable.

The first surrogacy case to capture national attention involved "simple" or traditional surrogate motherhood, that is, artificial insemination of a genetically-related surrogate to create a child with sperm from the intended father. William Stern and Mary Beth Whitehead entered into a contract providing that Whitehead would bear Stern's child, who would also be Mary Beth Whitehead's genetic and gestational child. The New Jersey Supreme Court ruled in that case that, absent adoption, Whitehead was Baby M's legal mother. In re Baby M, 537 A.2d 1227 (N.J. 1988).

The *Baby M* decision today seems unremarkable. Most courts would continue to find that Whitehead and other traditional surrogates are the mothers of the children they bear. A notable exception, however, to recognizing the parental rights of traditional surrogates is a Wisconsin case in which the traditional surrogate persuaded an infertile couple she knew not only to allow her to bear a child conceived with the intended father's sperm, but to do so through artificial insemination rather than use of donor eggs. The Wisconsin Supreme Court held that while the surrogacy agreement could not terminate the surrogate mother's parental status, it should be enforced absent a showing that it was contrary to the best interests of the child. In re F.T.R., 833 N.W.2d 634 (Wis. 2013).

The more complicated — and more common — cases involve gestational surrogacy. In these cases, the sperm and an egg are combined in vitro and implanted in the womb of the gestational surrogate who is genetically unrelated to the resulting child or children. The case below involves an intended father who provided sperm, an egg donor, and a gestational surrogate.

P.M. v. T.B.
907 N.W.2d 522 (Iowa 2018)

WATERMAN, Justice. . . . P.M. and C.M. were high school sweethearts but parted ways when P.M. joined the Navy upon graduation. After marrying and divorcing other spouses, they reconnected and married each other in 2013. They now live in Cedar Rapids. . . . The Ms were nearing age fifty and wanted to have a child together. C.M. was no longer able to conceive, so the Ms placed an advertisement on Craigslist in 2015 seeking a woman willing to act as a surrogate mother.

T.B. and D.B. married each other in January 2009 and live in Muscatine. T.B. has four children from a prior marriage; D.B. has no children and had never been married. The Bs want to have children together. In 2010, T.B. had a tubal pregnancy which was life-threatening and incapable of leading to the birth of a viable child, so she surgically terminated the pregnancy. T.B. and D.B. continued to try to conceive without success. The Bs realized they would need the services of a reproductive endocrinologist in order to have a child. T.B. learned that the Bs' insurance would not cover infertility treatment or in vitro fertilization (IVF). They decided they needed to supplement D.B.'s income to pay for assisted reproduction procedures.

T.B. responded to the Ms' Craigslist advertisement. The four met for dinner in Coralville and got along well at first. They agreed that T.B. would gestate two embryos fertilized in vitro with P.M.'s sperm and the eggs of an anonymous donor. The Ms selected Midwest Fertility Clinic (Midwest) in Downers Grove, Illinois, to perform the IVF and embryo transfers. Midwest required a written contract between the parties, so the Ms hired a lawyer to draft the agreement. Its stated purpose was "to enable the Intended Father [P.M.] and the Intended Mother [C.M.] to have a child who is biologically related to one of them." In exchange for the gestational service, the Ms agreed to pay up to $13,000 for an IVF procedure for T.B. to enable her and D.B. to conceive their own child. This payment was conditioned upon T.B. surrendering custody of a live child upon birth. . . .

T.B. and D.B. did not exercise their right to consult a lawyer before the Surrogacy Agreement was signed by all four parties. . . .

On March 27, Midwest implanted two embryos into T.B.'s uterus. The embryos were the ova of an anonymous donor fertilized with P.M.'s sperm. On April 4, blood testing confirmed

T.B.'s pregnancy. The parties' relationship soon began to break down over their disagreement as to payment of medical expenses. All four attended the first ultrasound, which D.B. video-taped. The Ms later objected to his videotaping and to T.B. posting information about the baby on social media.

Their relationship worsened after the women exchanged text messages on April 13. They were discussing whether T.B. could attend a doctor's appointment scheduled by the IVF coor-dinator when C.M. wrote, "Well we have to go next Thursday [because the coordinator] made the [appointment] and this is our journey not anyone else's. She said you have to end with [a doctor's] exam in Chicago and [a] couple more ultrasounds. . . ." T.B. replied, "I'm not going through this with you today. She just called me." C.M. replied, "We are in charge we hired you so just let us be parents and enjoy this ok!"

A second ultrasound confirmed that T.B. was carrying viable twins. T.B. shared that news with the Ms, but the relationship remained rocky. In late April, C.M. texted this to T.B.:

> Every time we question you or try to make a decision (as we should be able to) we are paying you, we hired you, and we are in charge, you get mad and upset and blow up. A carrier shouldn't act like that as the doctors told me they should be saying yes ma'am Whatever you guys want to do. But you can't stand not being in charge and you have some mental disorder for sure but yet you blame everything on us. . . . So if you wanna say u have it bad try feeling how we feel. This is our baby not yours and imagine how U would feel. I know u don't care but just for a moment stop blaming us and look what U have done to us only cuz we have ask[ed] u to do something. Compare the two and u will see we have NEVER did u wrong. This is a nightmare.

When T.B. replied, "You're crazy," C.M. wrote back, "Oh really that's what everyone says about u[.]" T.B. then stated that "everything can be handled through attorneys from here[.]" The Bs retained an attorney to speak for them and cut off direct communication with the Ms, who nevertheless persisted in trying to reach them for updates on the pregnancy.

In a May 20 letter from her attorney, T.B. sought more money from the Ms beyond the $13,000 agreed to in their contract so she could use a costlier clinic for her own IVF. T.B. wanted to replace Midwest because it insisted she use her own medical insurance and because C.M. told her Midwest employees said T.B. was crazy. The clinic T.B. wanted to use charged over twice as much—$30,000—for IVF. T.B. insisted that the Ms pay the higher cost for her to continue to serve as a gestational carrier.

On August 19, P.M. sent Facebook messages to D.B.'s sister, using racial slurs and profan-ity to insult D.B. D.B.'s sister shared the communication with T.B. On August 24, C.M. sent an email to T.B. and T.B.'s attorney, triggering a lengthy exchange, during which C.M. called T.B. the "N" word. That statement, along with the comments P.M. sent to D.B.'s sister, con-vinced T.B. that the Ms were racist. T.B. then called the Ms' attorney. When T.B. expressed concern that the Ms would not pay her, the Ms' attorney assured T.B. that the money for the Bs had already been set aside. The Ms' attorney attempted to make payment arrangements with T.B. and arrange P.M.'s listing on the birth certificate, but those matters remained unre-solved. Later that day, T.B. decided that she would not turn over the babies to the Ms.

Twin babies were born thirteen weeks prematurely on August 31. T.B. did not tell the Ms about the birth. The babies were placed in the neonatal intensive care unit. One died eight days after birth. T.B. did not inform the Ms about the baby's illness or death. The Bs unilater-ally arranged for the deceased baby's cremation.

On October 24, the Ms, still unaware of the birth, filed a petition for declaratory judg-ment and temporary and permanent injunction. . . .

We must decide whether the district court erred by enforcing the gestational surrogacy contract, terminating the presumptive parental rights of the surrogate mother and her hus-band, and placing permanent custody of Baby H with the biological father. . . .

A. Overview of Gestational Surrogacy Arrangements

"In general terms, surrogacy 'is the process by which a woman makes a choice to become pregnant and then carry to full term and deliver a baby who, she intends, will be raised by someone else.'" In re Paternity of F.T.R., 349 Wis.2d 84, 833 N.W.2d 634, 643 (2013). The woman who carries the child is the "surrogate mother." An "intended parent" is "an individual . . . who manifests the intent . . . to be legally bound as the parent of a child resulting from assisted or collaborative reproduction." *Id.* Surrogacies are categorized as "traditional" or "gestational."

> In a traditional surrogacy, the surrogate is the genetic mother of the child and is artificially inseminated with the sperm of the intended father or a sperm donor. In a gestational surrogacy, the surrogate is not genetically related to the child; instead, "sperm is taken from the father (or from a donor) and an egg is taken from the mother (or from a donor), fertilization happens outside the womb (called *in vitro* fertilization), and the fertilized embryos are then implanted into the surrogate mother's uterus."

Id. This case involves a gestational surrogacy because T.B. is not genetically related to the child. T.B. is the surrogate mother, while P.M. and C.M. are the intended parents. . . .

> IVF, egg donation, and gestational surrogacy are decidedly modern phenomena. Indeed, not all that long ago, IVF was still (literally) the stuff of science fiction. *See* Aldous Huxley, *Brave New World* 1 (1932). The first IVF-assisted human birth didn't occur until 1978, and it wasn't until the mid to late 1980s that doctors began to use gestational surrogates in conjunction with IVF procedures.
>
> To be sure, IVF and other assisted reproductive technologies represent revolutionary biomedical advances; they have enabled countless couples to conceive who otherwise couldn't have had children biologically. But these advances are not without their complexities. IVF-assisted reproduction involving (as it does here) third-party egg donors and gestational surrogates "raise moral and ethical issues" that can affect multiple, and often divergent, interests—among them, those of biological fathers, egg donors, surrogate mothers, and the resulting embryos. Not surprisingly, the States have tackled IVF- and surrogacy-related issues in very different ways.

Morrissey v. United States, 871 F.3d 1260, 1269 (11th Cir. 2017) (citations omitted); *see generally* George L. Blum, Annotation, *Validity of Surrogate Parenting Agreement*, 19 A.L.R.7th 179 (2017) (describing how different states have addressed the validity of surrogacy agreements). . . .

A majority of states lack statutes addressing surrogacy. As a result, "cases often involve ad hoc procedures attempting to effectuate the parties' intent by analyzing surrogacy issues under the state's statutes for [termination of parental rights], adoption, custody and placement, and the like." *Id.* . . .

In the minority of states with statutes specifically addressing surrogacy, the enactments generally impose greater restrictions on traditional surrogacies, and most of the statutes can be grouped into three categories:

> First, some states have legislatively prohibited all surrogacy contracts, declaring their terms unenforceable and, in some instances, imposing criminal penalties for those who attempt to enter into or assist in creating such a contract. *See, e.g.,* . . . Mich. Comp. Laws Ann. §§ 722.851–.863 (declaring surrogate parentage contracts, as defined by statute, to be "void and unenforceable" and imposing criminal penalties for participation in a "surrogate parentage contract for compensation" or a surrogacy contract involving a surrogate who is an unemancipated minor or who has "a mental illness or developmental disability"). A second category of states prohibit only certain types of surrogacy contracts—typically those involving a traditional surrogacy. *See, e.g.,* Ky. Rev. Stat. Ann. § 199.590(4) (prohibiting traditional surrogacy contracts, as defined by statute, without addressing gestational surrogacies); N.D. Cent. Code

§§ 14–18–05, –08 (declaring traditional surrogacy agreements void but allowing gestational surrogacies by providing that "[a] child born to a gestational carrier is a child of the intended parents for all purposes and is not a child of the gestational carrier and the gestational carrier's husband, if any"). Finally, states in the third category authorize both traditional and gestational surrogacy contracts, subject to regulation and specified limitations. *See, e.g.*, N.H. Rev. Stat. Ann. §§ 168–B:1 to –B:32 (generally permitting traditional and gestational surrogacy agreements subject to certain conditions, including a traditional surrogate's right to revoke the agreement within seventy-two hours of birth); Va. Code Ann. §§ 20–156 to 20–165 (generally permitting surrogacy contracts, as defined by statute, and providing a multi-step process for judicial pre-approval of such contracts).

In re Baby, 447 S.W.3d 807, 819–20 (Tenn. 2014). The Tennessee Supreme Court held that the public policy of that state "does not prohibit the enforcement of traditional surrogacy contracts" yet concluded many contract terms were unenforceable, including compensation "contingent upon the termination of the surrogate's parental rights." *Id.* at 840 (adjudicating claim of surrogate birth mother who was the biological, genetic mother). . . .

The Ohio Supreme Court held *gestational* surrogacy contracts are enforceable in the absence of enabling legislation. *J.F. v. D.B.*, 116 Ohio St.3d 363, 879 N.E.2d 740, 741–42 (2007) ("[N]o public policy is violated when a gestational-surrogacy contract is entered into, even when one of the provisions requires the gestational surrogate not to assert parental rights regarding children she bears that are of another woman's artificially inseminated egg."). And the California Supreme Court enforced a gestational surrogacy contract in favor of the biological parents and rejected constitutional challenges by the gestational surrogate before that state enacted legislation regulating surrogacy contracts. *Johnson v. Calvert*, 5 Cal.4th 84, 19 Cal.Rptr.2d 494, 851 P.2d 776, 784 (1993) (en banc). . . . The Wisconsin Supreme Court held that a traditional surrogacy contract was enforceable without enabling legislation "unless enforcement is contrary to the best interests of the child." In re Paternity of F.T.R., 833 N.W.2d at 638. But the New Jersey Supreme Court held that a traditional surrogacy contract was unenforceable without legislative authorization. *In re Baby M*, 109 N.J. 396, 537 A.2d 1227, 1264 (1988). . . .

B. Whether the Surrogacy Agreement Is Enforceable Under Iowa Law

T.B. argues the Surrogacy Agreement is unenforceable under Iowa law as inconsistent with statutory provisions and public policy. . . . We find no . . . statutory or judicial prohibition in our state. To the contrary, the Iowa legislature tacitly approved of surrogacy arrangements by exempting them from potential criminal liability for selling children. "Also, we need to consider the public policy implications of an opposite ruling." Banning gestational surrogacy contracts would deprive infertile couples of perhaps the only way to raise their own biological children and would limit the contractual rights of willing surrogates. We join the better-reasoned cases from other jurisdictions rejecting arguments that gestational surrogacy contracts are void against public policy.

1. Whether the Surrogacy Agreement is Inconsistent with Statutory Provisions

Iowa Code section 710.11 expressly exempts surrogacy arrangements from criminal liability for selling children and provides,

> A person commits a class "C" felony when the person purchases or sells or attempts to purchase or sell an individual to another person. This section *does not apply to a surrogate mother arrangement*. For purposes of this section, a "*surrogate mother arrangement*" means an arrangement whereby a female agrees to be artificially inseminated with the semen of a donor, to bear a child, and to relinquish all rights regarding that child to the donor or donor couple.

Iowa Code § 710.11 (first emphasis added). This provision was enacted in 1989, 1989 Iowa Acts ch. 116, § 1, one year after extensive national publicity over the decision of the New Jersey Supreme Court invalidating a surrogacy contract as contrary to that state's adoption statutes, including its "baby selling" prohibition on payment of money to adopt a child. *In re Baby M*, 537 A.2d at 1250 & n.10. Importantly, the *Baby M* court stated, "[O]ur holding today does not preclude the Legislature from altering the current statutory scheme, within constitutional limits, so as to permit surrogacy contracts." *Id.* at 1235. The Iowa legislature did just that for our state in its next session — expressly exempting surrogacy arrangements from the criminal prohibition on selling babies. The Iowa enactment tracked the surrogacy arrangement at issue in *Baby M*.

In *Baby M*, a married couple, William and Elizabeth Stern, wanted to raise a child, but Elizabeth feared her medical condition rendered pregnancy a serious health risk. Mr. Stern's family had perished in the Holocaust, and as the "only survivor, he very much wanted to continue his bloodline." He responded to the advertisements of a fertility clinic. *Id.* at 1236. So did Mary Beth Whitehead, who was motivated by "her sympathy with family members and others who could have no children (she stated that she wanted to give another couple the 'gift of life'); she also wanted . . . $10,000 to help her family." *Id.* Stern and Whitehead entered into a surrogacy contract. *Id.* "The contract provided that through artificial insemination using Mr. Stern's sperm, Mrs. Whitehead would become pregnant, carry the child to term, . . . [and] deliver it to the Sterns" for $10,000 to be paid after the child's birth. *Id.* at 1235. Whitehead agreed in the contract to "do whatever was necessary to terminate her maternal rights so that Mrs. Stern could thereafter adopt the child." *Id.* The artificial insemination was successful, and Whitehead gave birth to Baby M after an uneventful pregnancy. *Id.* at 1236. Whitehead, however, had developed a strong emotional attachment. *Id.* When the Sterns arrived at the hospital to see the baby, Whitehead "broke into tears and . . . talked about how the baby looked like her other daughter." *Id.* She made clear to the Sterns that she was unsure she could give up the child. Three days after the birth, she turned the baby over to the Sterns, who "were thrilled with their new child." *Id.* But their legal battle ensued over custody and contract rights, with the New Jersey Supreme Court ultimately invalidating the surrogacy contract, awarding custody of the child to the Sterns, and allowing Whitehead visitation. *Id.* at 1234, 1263. . . .

We conclude, based on the timing of the enactment of Iowa Code section 710.11, the very next legislative session, that our state's general assembly chose in 1989 to allow surrogacy arrangements, not prohibit them. Section 710.11 specifically mentions artificial insemination of the birth mother (who is the genetic or biological mother, as in *Baby M*), but we decline to infer the legislature intended to allow only traditional surrogacy when the birth mother is the genetic mother and yet criminalize gestational surrogacy arrangements. IVF, allowing implantation in the surrogate mother of embryos from donor eggs, was then in its infancy and had not been the subject of a court decision of national prominence. As other courts have noted, a gestational surrogacy in which the birth mother lacks a genetic connection to the child raises fewer concerns than the traditional surrogacy expressly mentioned in section 710.11. The legislature's decision to allow traditional surrogacy arrangements can be taken as a signal that it would also allow gestational surrogacy arrangements. We conclude that neither traditional nor gestational surrogacy contracts are prohibited under section 710.11. . . .

Another reason the Surrogacy Agreement does not violate Iowa Code section 710.11 is because the Ms' payment was for T.B.'s gestational services rather than for her sale of a baby. The Surrogacy Agreement states,

> The consideration of this agreement is compensation for services and expenses as limited by law and in no way is to be construed as a fee for termination of parental rights or a payment in exchange for consent to surrender the child for adoption.

The California Supreme Court held under equivalent circumstances that the contractual payment is for gestational services, not for the sale of a baby. *See Calvert*, 19 Cal.Rptr.2d 494, 851 P.2d at 784 (explaining that the payments to the surrogate mother "were meant to compensate her for her services in gestating the fetus and undergoing labor"). . . .

T.B. relies on Iowa Code section 600A.4, which requires parents to wait seventy-two hours after a birth before signing a release of custody for an adoption. . . . We agree with other courts that recognize the difference between surrogacy arrangements and giving up one's own genetic child for adoption. . . .

> There is no doubt but that [the statute prohibiting baby selling] is intended to keep baby brokers from overwhelming an expectant mother or the parents of a child with financial inducements to part with the child. But the central fact in the surrogate parenting procedure is that the agreement to bear the child is entered into *before* conception. The essential considerations for the surrogate mother when she agrees to the surrogate parenting procedure are *not* avoiding the consequences of an unwanted pregnancy or fear of the financial burden of child rearing. On the contrary, the essential consideration is to assist a person or couple who desperately want a child but are unable to conceive one in the customary manner to achieve a biologically related offspring.

Surrogate Parenting Assocs., Inc. v. Commonwealth ex rel. Armstrong, 704 S.W.2d 209, 211–12 (Ky. 1986), *superseded by statute*, Ky. Rev. Stat. Ann. § 199.590(4) (West, Westlaw through 2017 Reg. Sess.)

This is not a situation in which T.B. is choosing to give up her own genetically related child in order to avoid the consequences of an unwanted pregnancy or the burdens of childrearing. Instead, T.B. agreed to carry a child for the Ms after responding to their advertisement on Craigslist. But for the acted-on intention of the Ms, Baby H would not exist. The Ms would not have entrusted their embryos fertilized with P.M.'s sperm to T.B. if they thought she would attempt to raise the resulting child herself. . . .

2. Whether the Surrogacy Agreement is Against Public Policy

T.B. also claims enforcement of the Surrogacy Agreement violates Iowa's public policy. We disagree based on the freedom of contract enjoyed by consenting adults. . . .

T.B. argues a surrogacy agreement violates public policy against the exploitation of women, and contends,

> Surrogacy agreements, if enforced embody deviant societal pressures, the object of which is to use the woman, and destroy her interests as a mother to satisfy the desires of third parties. Surrogacy exploits women by treating the mother as if she is not a whole woman. It assumes she can be used much like a breeding animal and act as though she is not, in fact, a mother.

Yet T.B. entered into the Surrogacy Agreement voluntarily. She had given birth to four children of her own before signing the Surrogacy Agreement and was no stranger to the effects of pregnancy. T.B. does not allege she signed the Surrogacy Agreement under economic duress or that its terms are unconscionable.

The California Supreme Court rejected a similar exploitation argument in *Calvert*:

> Although common sense suggests that women of lesser means serve as surrogate mothers more often than do wealthy women, there has been no proof that surrogacy contracts exploit poor women to any greater degree than economic necessity in general exploits them by inducing them to accept lower-paid or otherwise undesirable employment. We are likewise unpersuaded by the claim that surrogacy will foster the attitude that children are mere commodities; no evidence is offered to support it. . . .
>
> The argument that a woman cannot knowingly and intelligently agree to gestate and deliver a baby for intending parents carries overtones of the reasoning that for centuries prevented

women from attaining equal economic rights and professional status under the law. To resurrect this view is both to foreclose a personal and economic choice on the part of the surrogate mother, and to deny intending parents what may be their only means of procreating a child of their own genetic stock. Certainly in the present case it cannot seriously be argued that Anna, a licensed vocational nurse who had done well in school and who had previously borne a child, lacked the intellectual wherewithal or life experience necessary to make an informed decision to enter into the surrogacy contract.

19 Cal.Rptr.2d 494, 851 P.2d at 785. California courts continue to reject the view that surrogacy agreements unfairly exploit women. We reach the same conclusion.

T.B. alternatively argues the Surrogacy Agreement violates the state's public policy favoring families. . . . T.B. characterizes surrogacy agreements as deliberately destroying the surrogate mother–child relationship (a relationship, we note, that would not exist but for the Ms' contribution of their embryos in reliance on T.B.'s willingness to serve as a gestational carrier). We conclude that gestational surrogacy agreements *promote* families by enabling infertile couples to raise their own children and help bring new life into this world through willing surrogate mothers. We agree with the Wisconsin Supreme Court that

> [e]nforcement of surrogacy agreements promotes stability and permanence in family relationships because it allows the intended parents to plan for the arrival of their child, reinforces the expectations of all parties to the agreement, and reduces contentious litigation that could drag on for the first several years of the child's life.

In re Paternity of F.T.R., 833 N.W.2d at 649–50. . . .

For these reasons, we hold the Surrogacy Agreement is enforceable under existing Iowa law. . . . We do not foreclose the possibility that a surrogacy agreement in a particular case could be subject to specific contract defenses, such as fraud, duress, or unconscionability.

C. WHETHER T.B. IS THE "BIOLOGICAL" MOTHER OF BABY H UNDER THE IOWA CODE

T.B. claims that as the birth mother she is the legal and biological mother of Baby H and that she therefore is entitled to custody of Baby H unless and until she is proven unfit by clear and convincing evidence. . . . We must determine T.B.'s parental rights as a gestational surrogate birth mother. This is a question of statutory interpretation. . . .

Iowa Code chapter 232 defines "parent" as

> a *biological or adoptive mother or father* of a child. . . .

Iowa Code § 232.2(39) (emphasis added). . . . "Biological parent" is defined as "a parent who has been a biological party to the procreation of the child." *Id.* § 600A.2(3). . . . Chapter 600A fails to separately define "biological party" or "procreation." It is undisputed that P.M. (not D.B.) is the biological father of Baby H, as confirmed by DNA testing; and it is undisputed that the embryos implanted in T.B. came from the ova of an anonymous woman, not T.B., as confirmed by DNA testing. We agree with the district court's interpretation.

> [I]n using the term biological party, the Iowa Legislature was referencing a party connected by direct genetic relationship. In using the term procreate, the legislature was referencing the act of begetting a child. Thus, a biological parent is a parent whose egg or whose sperm was used to beget a child. Only such a person would have a direct genetic relationship to procreation of the child.

This interpretation fits with the dictionary definitions of "biological" and "procreate." *See Biological, Black's Law Dictionary* (10th ed. 2014) (defining "biological" as "genetically related" in the context of biological parents); . . . *Biological mother, Black's Law Dictionary* (defining "biological mother" as "[t]he woman who provides the egg that develops into an embryo");

Procreate, Merriam-Webster's Collegiate Dictionary (11th ed. 2014) (defining "procreate" as "to beget or bring forth offspring").

We hold the statutory definition of "biological parent" of Baby H does not include a surrogate birth mother who is not the genetic parent. The ordinary meaning of "biological parent" is a person who is the genetic father or mother of the child. That is also the established legal meaning of "biological parent." . . .

D. Whether Enforcement of the Surrogacy Agreement Violates T.B.'s Substantive Due Process and Equal Protection Rights

T.B. claims that she has a fundamental liberty interest in the parent–child relationship. . . . T.B.'s constitutional claims rest on an incorrect premise — that she has parental rights in Baby H without being the child's genetic mother. Any constitutionally protected interest she may have as the surrogate birth mother is overcome by P.M.'s undisputed status as the biological and intended father of Baby H. . . .

NOTES AND QUESTIONS

1. In addressing gestational surrogacy, the Iowa Supreme Court quoted at length from Calvert v. Johnson, one of the earlier gestational surrogacy cases. In *Calvert*, the California Supreme Court applied the Uniform Parentage Act of 1973 and concluded that two women met that statutes' test for parenthood: the genetic (and intended) mother who had supplied an egg with the intention she would raise the child and the birth mother, who under the 1973 Act was treated as a parent by virtue of having given birth. The *Calvert* court concluded that where more than one woman (along with the genetic father) met the statutory definition of a parent, intent was the "tiebreaker," and the two intended (and genetic) parents were the legal parents. How does the Iowa court resolve the issue of maternity? How many legal parents does the opinion recognize? Would the reasoning in this decision apply to a case in which a single woman gave birth to a child using a donor egg? Would the woman in such a case be a "biological mother"? Would she be a legal parent in Iowa? If so, on what grounds?

Scholars continue to debate the respective weight that should be given to gestation versus genetics in determining parenthood. *Compare* Julie Shapiro, For a Feminist Considering Surrogacy, Is Compensation Really the Key Question?, 89 Wash. L. Rev. 1345 (2014), and E. Gary Spitko, The Constitutional Function of Biological Paternity: Evidence of the Biological Mother's Consent to the Biological Father's Co-Parenting of Her Child, 48 Ariz. L. Rev. 97 (2006) *with* Lynda Wray Black, The Birth of a Parent: Defining Parentage for Lenders of Genetic Material, 92 Neb. L. Rev. 799 (2014), and Andrea B. Carroll, Family Law and Female Empowerment, 24 UCLA Women's L.J. 1 (2017).

2. Section 803 of the Uniform Parentage Act of 2017 provides:

> (a) If the requirements of subsection (b) are satisfied, a court may issue an order validating the gestational agreement and declaring that the intended parents will be the parents of a child born during the term of the of the agreement.
>
> (b) The court may issue an order under subsection (a) only on finding that:
>
> (1) the residence requirements of Section 802 have been satisfied and the parties have submitted to the jurisdiction of the court under the jurisdictional standards of this [Act];
>
> (2) unless waived by the court, the [relevant child-welfare agency] has made a home study of the intended parents and the intended parents meet the standards of suitability applicable to adoptive parents;

(3) all parties have voluntarily entered into the agreement and understand its terms;

(4) adequate provision has been made for all reasonable health-care expense associated with the gestational agreement until the birth of the child, including responsibility for those expenses if the agreement is terminated; and

(5) the consideration, if any, paid to the prospective gestational mother is reasonable.

If the parties do not comply with these requirements, the Act recognizes the gestational mother as the mother of the child. If Iowa adopted these provisions, how would they affect a subsequent case similar to P.M. v. T.B.? Would such provisions have helped to avert the conflicts in *P.M.*? Would legal representation for the gestational carrier at the time of the agreement make a difference? Contemporary state statutes governing surrogacy require independent representation for the surrogate, though fees may be paid by intended parents.

3. Though the trend is to permit surrogacy contracts, states continue to vary widely in their regulation of surrogacy. For a summary of existing state laws, *see* Joseph F. Morrissey, Surrogacy: The Process, the Law, and the Contracts, 51 Willamette L. Rev. 459, 468 (2015); Susan Hazeldean, Illegitimate Parents, 55 U.C. Davis L. Rev. 1583, 1703, Table 5 (2022). Forty-seven states currently permit gestational surrogacy contracts, either through statute or case law. Rachel Rebouché, Contracting Pregnancy, 105 Iowa L. Rev. 1591, 1603 (2020). New York became the forty-seventh state to permit surrogacy when it adopted a compensated gestational surrogacy statute that went into effect in 2021. N.Y. Fam. Ct. Act §§581-101 to 581-704 (2022). P.M. v. T.B. identified the differences among the states, but given the large number of states like Iowa with no comprehensive surrogacy statutes, local practices may vary even more than the differences between statutes suggest. Rebouché describes how surrogacy agreements fill in many of the gaps, often including provisions that, while they may not be legally enforceable, attempt to shape the parties' expectations.

In addition, the lower courts have struck down a variety of surrogacy restrictions as unconstitutional, though the precise contours of constitutional protection have yet to be determined. The courts in three cases, for example, have invalidated statutes that refused to recognize a genetic mother as a legal parent where the genetic mother transferred eggs to a surrogate (or a same-sex partner) with the intention that she would be the legal parent of the resulting children. J.R. v. Utah, 261 F. Supp. 2d 1294, 1296-1298 (D. Utah 2002); T.M.H. v. D.M.T, 79 So. 3d 787 (Fla. App. 2011); Soos v. Superior Court in & for Cty. of Maricopa, 897 P.2d 1356 (Ariz. App. 1994). *Cf.* LeFever v. Matthews, 971 N.W.2d 672, 685-686 (Mich. 2021) (finding that where one woman carried her partner's fertilized egg to term with the intention that they would jointly raise the resulting child, the state's surrogacy law did not apply and both partners were mothers under Michigan's parentage and custody law). The Utah Supreme Court also invalidated a statute that required "medical evidence" "show[ing]" that the intended mother is unable to bear a child or is unable to do so without unreasonable risk to her physical or mental health or to the unborn child" because it did not permit male couples to obtain the benefits of the statute. In re Gestational Agreement, 449 P.3d 69, 72 (Utah 2019). For a more general discussion of the importance of surrogacy to gay men, *see* Michael Boucai, Is Assisted Procreation an LGBT Right?, 2016 Wis. L. Rev. 1065 (opposing a biologically based definition of family).

If state law provides that the woman who gives birth and her husband are the legal parents absent adoption, would that law violate the constitutional rights of a biological father who supplied sperm (combined with donor eggs) pursuant to an agreement that he would be the legal father of the resulting child? How would you reconcile the results in surrogacy cases

782 Part III Children, Parents, and the State

with the sperm donor cases discussed above or the application of the marital presumption in *Michael H.* (described in Chapter 13)?.

4. Surrogacy contracts typically provide that the intended parents have the right to decide whether to abort a pregnancy, but such clauses are widely viewed as unenforceable. *See* Rebouché, above. Fertility clinics often implant more than one embryo to increase the odds of pregnancy but caution that higher order pregnancies increase the risk of birth defects. In a recent California case, a gestational carrier became pregnant with triplets. The genetic father, who was a single parent, wished to abort one of the fetuses. The gestational carrier refused to abort a healthy child and offered to take custody of one or all of the triplets. C.M. v. M.C., 213 Cal. Rptr. 3d 351 (Cal. App. 2017). The carrier could not be compelled to have an abortion, but the California courts affirmed the father's status as the sole legal parent of the triplets, and he assumed custody immediately after their birth. How can such conflicts be avoided or resolved once they arise? *See* Deborah L. Forman, Abortion Clauses in Surrogacy Contracts: Insights from a Case Study, 49 Fam. L.Q. 29, 31 (2015); Susan L. Crockin & Gary A. Debele, Ethical Issues in Assisted Reproduction: A Primer for Family Law Attorneys, 27 J. Am. Acad. Matrimonial Law. 289 (2015).

5. One of the objections to the use of gestational surrogates involves fear of the exploitation of the surrogate carrying the child. Agencies, however, screen for reliable surrogates and prefer women of childbearing age who have given birth before. Empirical research in the United States and Britain does not support the stereotype of poor, single, young women whose family, financial difficulties, or other circumstances pressure them into surrogacy arrangements. Nor does it support the view that surrogate mothers are naively taking on a task unaware of the emotional and physical risks it might entail. Rather, the empirical research establishes that surrogates are mature, experienced, stable, self-aware, and extroverted nonconformists who make the initial decision that surrogacy is something that they want to do. *See, e.g.,* Lina Peng, Surrogate Mother: An Exploration of the Empirical and the Normative, 21 Am. U. J. Gender Soc. Pol'y & L. 555 (2013); Pamela Laufer-Ukeles, Mothering for Money: Regulating Commercial Intimacy, 88 Ind. L.J. 1223 (2014). *See also* Rebouché, above on p. 72 at 1636-1637 (observing that "many surrogates, in the United States at least, are middle-class, married, white, with at least one child, and in their late twenties or early thirties".) Nonetheless, the potential for exploitation exists, particularly when the parties arrange surrogacy agreements on their own over Craigslist as the parties did in P.M. v. T.B. Are surrogacy agencies part of the problem or part of the solution for dealing with potential issues of exploitation? *See* June Carbone & Jody Lyneé Madeira, The Role of Agency: Compensated Surrogacy and the Institutionalization of Assisted Reproduction Practices, 90 Wash. L. Rev. (Online) 7 (2015).

6. In the period from 1999-2005, less expensive surrogacy options became available in India, Thailand, Russia, and elsewhere, and Americans began to seek these options abroad. Since 2006, many of these countries have regulated surrogacy more strictly, either limiting the practice or adopting residency requirements. As a result, the number of non-U.S. residents coming to the United States to access surrogacy arrangements has increased and constituted 18.5 percent of all gestational carrier cycles in 2013. Kiran M. Perkins et al., Trends and Outcomes of Gestational Surrogacy in the United States, 106 Fert. & Sterility 435 (2016).

The COVID pandemic and the war in Ukraine have created turmoil for surrogacy arrangements. The New York Times reported "an approximately 60 percent decrease in potential surrogates, according to the 10 agencies The New York Times spoke to, along with doubled wait times and significantly higher fees." Danielle Braff, Desperately Seeking Surrogates, April 2, 2022, available at https://www.nytimes.com/2022/04/02/style/surrogate-shortage-us-pandemic.html (last visited Sept. 2, 2022). The decline in the United States reflected uncertainties related to the COVID pandemic, including vaccination requirements.

Id. After India, Thailand, and other countries restricted international surrogacy, Ukraine became a surrogacy hub, second only to the United States in the number of cross-border surrogate arrangements. A major reason was the lower price in Ukraine, with the process costing $43,000 there, compared with $130,000 in the United States. Isabel Coles, Ukraine Is a World Leader in Surrogacy, but Babies Are Now Stranded in a War Zone, Wall Street Journal, March 12, 2022, available at https://www.wsj.com/articles/ukraine-is-a-world-leader-in-surrogacy-but-babies-are-now-stranded-in-war-zone-11647081997 (last visited Sept. 2, 2022). Both the COVID pandemic and the war in Ukraine restricted the ability of intended parents to travel, often leaving the babies stranded with gestational carriers who were not necessarily prepared to care for them. If you were to add a clause to a surrogacy agreement to deal with such contingencies, what would you propose? *See* Rachel Rebouché, Bargaining about Birth: Surrogacy Contracts in a Pandemic, 100 Wash. U.L. Rev. (forthcoming 2023) (detailing how the COVID-19 pandemic shaped surrogacy agreements).

7. For proposed reforms, *see* Yehezkel Margalit, From Baby M to Baby M(Anji): Regulating International Surrogacy Agreements, 24 J.L. & Pol'y 41, 78 (2015); Seema Mohapatra, Adopting an International Convention on Surrogacy — A Lesson from Intercountry Adoption, 13 Loy. U. Chi. Int'l L. Rev. 25 (2015).

PROBLEMS

1. Under the *P.M.* court's analysis, if a surrogate and a married couple entered into a contract providing that she would be artificially inseminated with one spouse's sperm and that the married couple would have custody of any resulting child, who would be the child's other legal parent?

2. If Mary donated an egg to be fertilized with John's sperm and the fetus was gestated by John's partner Wendy, who would be the child's legal mother under *P.M. v. T.B.*? Would it matter whether Wendy and John were married?

3. Alison gestated a fetus conceived from the egg and sperm of anonymous donors, agreeing that the child would be adopted by Barbara and George. Shortly before the child was born, George filed for divorce, alleging that no children were born of the marriage. Barbara responded that she and George expected to adopt the soon-to-be-born child of Alison and sought custody and a child support order against George. After the baby was born, Alison made clear that she did not want custody. The trial judge ruled that the baby had no legal parents. What arguments should Barbara and George make on appeal?

4. A married couple who lived in a state that bans paid surrogacy and restricts abortion entered into a contract with an agency in Connecticut that recruited a Connecticut woman to act as a gestational carrier. The contract specified that Connecticut law, which treats gestational contracts as enforceable, would apply. The contract further provided that the couple would contribute a donor egg and the husband's sperm, and that the married couple would be recognized as the child's legal parents. The contract also provided that the couple had the right to elect an abortion on terms of their choosing. Early in the pregnancy, the couple learned that the gestational carrier was carrying twins and that one of the twins had serious birth defects. The couple wanted the carrier to have a "selective reduction," aborting the twin with the birth defects. The carrier refused and fled to Michigan, which recognizes the woman giving birth as the legal mother. She gave birth to twins, one of whom had serious birth defects. The carrier placed the twins for adoption in Michigan.

What were the commissioning couples' options when the carrier refused to go through with the abortion? Did they have any recourse after the birth of the children? Does it matter whether abortion is still legal in all of the relevant states?

5. Jill and Jackie had lived together for a number of years. When Jill was diagnosed with cancer, she froze some of her eggs before the doctors removed her uterus. In the meantime, Jackie attempted to become pregnant using donor sperm. She miscarried and discovered that she was a carrier for mitochondrial disease, which is transmitted through the DNA in the cytoplasm of the egg. The nuclear DNA, which determines most of the child's features, does not transmit mitochondrial disease. Jill agreed that Jackie could use her frozen eggs in an effort to have a healthy child. Jackie arranged to have her own eggs fertilized with sperm from her friend, Brian. The doctors also fertilized Jill's eggs with Brian's sperm. They then took one of the fertilized eggs from Jill, removed the nucleus, and added the nucleus from an embryo created using Jackie's eggs. Shortly after Jackie became pregnant, Jill and Jackie broke up. Jackie gave birth to a healthy baby boy, Tony. The baby is genetically related to Jackie (given the use of her nuclear DNA), Jill (given the use of her mitochondrial DNA), and Brian.

If the parties signed no agreements before the birth, who should be recognized as Tony's father?

If the parties signed an agreement indicating that Jackie, Jill, and Brian should all be recognized as parents, would the agreement be enforceable?

If the parties used a gestational carrier pursuant to an agreement that all three intended to be recognized as parents, would the agreement be enforceable? If they did so in a jurisdiction that banned surrogacy and recognized the woman giving birth and her husband as Tony's legal parents, would they have a viable claim that the surrogacy ban violated their constitutional rights to be parents?

TABLE OF CASES

Principal cases are indicated by italics.

A

A.A., In re, 706
A.A. v. B.B., 731
Abate, Estate of, 182
Abbott v. Abbott, 640, 644
Abitz v. Abitz, 384, 385
Abrams v. Massell, 183
A.C. v. D.R., 216
A.C.H., In re, 724
A.D., In re the Parental Responsibilities of, 715
Adams v. Jankouskas, 31–34
Adoption of. *See name of party*
Adoptive Couple v. Baby Girl, 751
Agulnick v. Agulnick, 211
Ahmed v. Ahmed, 641
A.H. v. W.R.L., 736
A.L., State Dep't of Children and Family Servs. ex rel. v. Lowrie, 730
Alejandro v. Alejandro, 211
Alexander, Estate of v. Alexander, 188, 189
Alford v. Alford, 271
Alison D. v. Virginia M., 12
Allen v. Allen, 655
Allen v. Farrow, 462
Alliance for Marriage & Family v. A.A., 731
Allison v. Medlock, 706
Alphin v. Alphin, 473
Altman, In re Marriage of, 265
Altman v. Altman, 533
American Healthcare Ctr. v. Randall, 357–359
A.M.S. ex rel. Farthing v. Stoppleworth, 348
Andersen v. King Cnty., 126
Anderson v. Deas, 604
Andrews v. Andrews, 370
Ankenbrandt v. Richards, 650–652
Ansin v. Craven-Ansin, 516
Arlene's Flowers, Inc.; State v., 127
Arlene's Flowers, Inc. v. Washington, 127
Armstrong v. Mayor, 21–24
Arneault v. Arneault, 241–246
Arnold v. Price, 626
Arnott v. Arnott, 443–446
Aronson v. Aronson, 210, 219

Arroyo; State v., 377
A.S. v. I.S., 698
Asfaw v. Woldberhan, 344
Askins v. Askins, 262
A.T., In re, 635
Attorney Grievance Comm'n of Md. v. O'Leary, 567
Atwood v. Fort Peck Tribal Court Assiniboine, 656, 657

B

Baby, In re, 776
Baby M, In re, 773, 776, 777
Backman v. Backman, 507
Baehr v. Lewin, 114, 125
Baehr v. Miike, 125
Baer v. Town of Brookhaven, 20
Bailey; United States v., 656
Baker v. Baker, Eccles & Co., 620
Baker v. Nelson, 115
Baker; State v., 20
Balfour v. Balfour, 513
B and L v. UK, 141
Barber v. Barber, 610, 651
Bartsch v. Bartsch, 604
Basileh v. Alghusain, 612
Basolo v. Basolo, 445
Bass v. Bass, 183
Bates and Bates, In re Marriage of, 375
Baton Rouge, City of v. Myers, 20
Battersby v. Battersby, 343
Baumann-Chacon v. Baumann, 53
Bautista v. Picone, 433
Baxter v. Baxter, 644
Beasley v. Beasley, 539
Becker v. Johnson, 604
Beckman v. Beckman, 473
Bedrick v. Bedrick, 515–518
Beekman v. Beekman, 459
Begins v. Begins, 459
Belger, In re Marriage of, 371
Bell v. Bell, 281
Belle Terre, Village of v. Boraas, 18, 19

Bender v. Bender, 300
Bennett v. Bennett, 73, 654
Benson ex rel. Patterson v. Patterson, 363
Bentz v. Bentz, 363
Bercume v. Bercume, 542
Bergeron v. Mackler, 554
Berle v. Berle, 268
Bernacki v. Bernacki, 556
Bessette v. W.B. Conkey Co., 395
Beverly v. Beverly, 385
Bingham v. Bingham, 431
Bishop v. Clark, 184, 185
B.J.H., In re Paternity of, 678
Black v. Black, 599
Blaisdell, Matter of, 207
Blige v. Blige, 498
Blumenthal v. Brewer, 15, 183
B.M.H., In re Custody of, 715–721
Boemio v. Boemio, 285
Bogan v. Bogan, 370
Boggs v. Boggs, 41–45
Bonds, In re, 490, 497
Booth v. Booth, 273
Borelli v. Brusseau, 508–513
Borough of. *See name of Borough*
Boston-Edison Protective Ass'n v. Paulist Fathers, 22
Boulds v. Nielsen, 184–186, 196, 304
Bowen v. Bowen, 318
Bowen v. Volz, 318
Bowers v. Hardwick, 114
Bowman v. Bowman, 612
Boyter v. Commissioner, 224
Brackeen v. Haaland, 749
Braddock v. Braddock, 268
Bradley v. Superior Court, 395
Brandt v. Brandt, 628–633
Brantley v. Brantley, 498
Brantner, In re Marriage of, 274
Braschi v. Stahl Assocs. Co., 8–11
Bratton v. Bratton, 518
Brennan-Duffy v. Duffy, 529
Brooke S.B. v. Elizabeth A.C.C., 12, 723
Brooks v. Brooks, 510, 511, 515
Brouillet v. Brouillet, 429
Brown v. Board of Educ., 88
Brown v. Brown (507 A.2d 1223), 34
Brown v. Brown (820 S.E.2d 384), 603
Brown v. Brown (142 So.3d 425), 209
Brown v. Hall, 526
Bruce v. Boardwine, 770
Bruker v. City of New York, 758
Burgess, In re Marriage of, 447
Burnham v. Superior Court, 605
Burns v. Edwards, 349
Burnside v. Burnside, 245
Busche v. Busche, 370
Butler v. Butler, 34

C

Caban v. Mohammed, 686–688
Cabrera v. Mercado, 626
Caldwell-Faso, In re Marriage of, 497
Califano v. Jobst, 112
Califano v. Webster, 66
California v. Superior Court, 657
Callahan, In re Marriage of, 543
Callahan v. Callahan, 655
Callender v. Skiles, 681
Cameron v. Cameron, 240
Campaign for S. Equal. v. Mississippi Dep't of
    Human Servs., 725
Cannon v. Cannon, 463
Caplan v. Donovan, 604
Carabetta v. Carabetta, 132
Carey v. Population Servs. Int'l, 88
Carter, In re Estate of, 172
Carter v. Fairchild-Carter, 506
Cash v. Catholic Diocese, 18
Castleman; United States v., 85
Catalano v. Catalano, 161
Cates v. Swain, 187–189, 190
Catz v. Chalker, 654
C.C. v. A.B., 681
C.C. v. J.A.H., 83
Ceja v. Rudolph & Sietten, Inc., 177
Centazzo v. Centazzo, 262
Center for Inquiry, Inc. v. Marion Cir. Ct. Clerk,
    132
Chamberlain, In re, 406–408
Chapman v. Chapman, 533
Chapman; State v., 395
Chappell, People v., 480
Charter Twp. of Delta v. Dinolfo, 19, 20
Chatterjee v. King, 715
Chaudry v. Chaudry, 519
Cheryl, In re Paternity of, 706
Chevalier v. Barnhart, 655
Chick v. Chick, 625
Child Support Enf't Agency v. Doe, 384
Ching v. Ching, 344
Ciesluk, In re Marriage of, 444
Citizens for Equal Prot. v. Bruning, 115
City of. *See name of city*
C.J.L. v. M.W.B., 431
Clark v. Clark, 158
Clevenger v. Clevenger, 708
C.L.O., In re, 695
C.M. v. M.C., 782
Coleman v. Coleman, 626
Coles v. Granville, 655
Collins, Ex parte, 634
Collins, In re Marriage of, 224
Colonna v. Colonna, 347
Columbia v. Lawton, 703
Comer v. Comer, 395

Commodity Futures Trading Comm'n v. Walsh, 224
Conaway v. Dean, 126
Conde-Vidal v. Rius-Armendariz, 599
Connell v. Francisco, 193–195
Conover v. Conover, 723
Conrad, In re Marriage of, 534
Conzelman v. Conzelman, 221
Cook v. Cole, 84
Cook v. Cook, 378, 599
Cook v. Sullivan, 723
Cooke v. Adams, 60
Copeland, In re Adoption of, 639
Copeland v. Copeland, 356
Costello v. Costello, 107
Cox v. Cox, 344
Craig v. Boren, 56, 64–66
Crain v. Crain, 393
Crawford v. Washington, 75
Crews v. Crews, 375
Cross v. Cross, 265
Currier; State v., 393
Curtis v. Kline, 354
Custody of. *See name of party*
CYFD, State of N.M. ex rel. v. Donna J., 630

D

Daigrepont v. Daigrepont, 346
Dalip Singh Bir's Estate, In re, 162
Damico v. Damico, 395
Danaipour v. McLarey, 644
Darín v. Olivero-Huffman, 645
Davidson, In re, 11
Davis v. Davis, 188
Davis v. Washington, 75
Davis v. Wicomico Cnty. Bureau, 706
D.C. v. D.C., 478
Dean v. Dean, 599
Deboer, In re Marriage of, 363
Debra H. v. Janice R., 12
Deffenbaugh v. Deffenbaugh, 258
Deitz v. Deitz, 262
Denton and Denton, 321
Department of Revenue v. Miller, 697
Department of Revenue Child Support Enf't v. Grullon, 392
DePasse, Estate of, 133
DeSouza, In re Marriage of, 39
Des Plaines, City of v. Trottner, 19
Desrochers v. Desrochers, 215–216
DeTevis v. Aragon, 384
Deyle v. Deyle, 435–439
Dier v. Peters, 698
Division Youth & Family Servs. v. M.Y.J.P., 639
D.M.T. v. T.M.H., 771
Dobbs v. Jackson Women's Health Org., 15, 16, 85, 86–91, 92, 93, 125

Dodson v. Dodson, 498
Doe, In the Interest of, 638
Doe, Matter of Adoption of, 695
Doe v. State, 83
Doe v. *See name of opposing nongovernmental party*
Doty-Perez v. Doty-Perez, 723
Downing v. Downing, 343
Draper v. Burke, 612
Dred Scott v. Sandford, 120
Drewes v. Ilnicki, 654
Dubay v. Wells, 698
Duffey v. Duffey, 384
Duff-Kareores v. Kareores, 291
Dugama v. Ayatew, 430
Duncan, In re Marriage of, 558
Duncan v. Duncan, 128–131
Durham, Town of v. White Enters., Inc., 19
Durr v. Blue, 729
Dyas v. Dyas, 343
Dycus v. Dycus, 217

E

Eagley v. Eagley, 344
Earle v. Earle, 49
E.B., Adoption of, 731
Eder v. Grifka, 55
Edwardson v. Edwardson, 492
Edwin K. v. Bonnie W., 370
Egelhoff v. Egelhoff, 308
Eggemeyer v. Eggemeyer, 240
Eisenstadt v. Baird, 88, 91
Elisa B. v. Superior Court, 711–714
Elk Grove Unified Sch. Dist. v. Newdow, 655, 656
Elkus v. Elkus, 323
EM (Lebanon) v. Secretary of State for the Home Dep't, 462
Employment Div., Dep't of Human Res. v. Smith, 127, 149
E.N. v. T.R., 722
Eori ex rel. Eori v. Eori, 361
Epler, In re Marriage of, 420
Erler v. Erler, 506
Ermold v. Davis, 127
Erpelding, In re Marriage of, 489
Erwin L.D. v. Myla Jean L., 698
Escalante v. Escalante, 208
Estate of. *See name of party*
Estin v. Estin, 601, 602
Evens v. Evens, 208
Everett v. Everett, 600
Evtimov v. Milanova, 281
Ewell v. State, 53

F

Faherty v. Faherty, 572
Fall v. Eastin, 603

Fanelli v. Fanelli, 324
Farrey v. Sanderfoot, 409
Fawzy v. Fawzy, 570–574
Featherston v. Steinhoff, 190
Feely v. Birenbaum, 18
Feltman v. Feltman, 384
Felty v. Felty, 637
Fenn v. Lockwood, 196
Fernando A.; State v., 82
Finan v. Finan, 250
Fink, In re Marriage of, 238
Finnerty v. Boyett, 729
Fisher v. Fisher, 248, 344, 378
530 Second Ave Co., LLC, Matter of
     v. Zenker, 11
Flanagan v. Flanagan, 217–220
Fleckles v. Diamond, 626
Fonken v. Fonken, 744
Fonstein, In re Marriage of, 271
Fore v. Fore, 208
Foretich v. United States, 479
Foster v. Foster, 636
Fox v. Fox, 604
Foy, Estate of, 175
F.R. v. Adoption of Baby Boy Born November 2,
     2010, 740
Francis v. Francis, 324
Frazier v. Goudschaal, 715
Frey v. Frey, 378
Friezo v. Friezo, 497, 506
F.T.R., In re Paternity of, 773, 775, 776, 779
Fulton v. City of Phila., Pa., 127, 759
Fulton v. Vickery, 130
Furr v. James, 706

G

Gabel v. Gabel, 555
Gainey v. Gainey, 534
Galassi v. Galassi, 281
Gallaher v. Elam, 384
Gamino, In re, 551
Gant v. Gant, 490
Garden State Equality v. Dow, 125
Gardner v. Gardner, 209, 221
Gardner v. Perry, 385
Gatsby v. Gatsby, 684, 761–768
GDK v. State, Dep't of Family Servs., 678
Geen v. Geen, 729
Geldmeier v. Geldmeier, 269–270
Gelkop v. Gelkop, 603
Geraghty, Matter of, 158–161
Gershman v. Gershman, 250
Gestational Agreement, In re, 781
Geyer, Estate of, 485, 487
Ghazel and Ghazel, 162
Gil v. Van Nostrand, 172
Gilbert, In re Marriage of, 348

Gimbel Bros., Inc. v. Pinto, 59
Glassboro, Borough of v. Vallorosi, 23
Glona v. American Guarantee & Liab. Ins. Co.,
     671
Godin v. Godin, 700, 703
Golan v. Saada, 646–649
Golipour v. Moghaddam, 506
Gomez v. Perez, 697
Gomprecht, Matter of, 61
Gonzales v. City of Castle Rock, 83
Goodridge v. Department of Pub. Health, 114,
     125
Goodright v. Moss, 670
Gorcyca, Judge, Sixth Circuit Court, In re, 478
Gordon v. Gordon, 378
Grabe v. Hokin, 496
Graby v. Graby, 371
Grant v. Hager, 347
Gray v. Gray, 626
Green; State v., 149, 150
Greenberg, Matter of, 344
Greer ex rel. Farbo v. Greer, 674–679, 726
Griego v. Oliver, 125
Griffin v. Griffin, 610
Grigsby; United States v., 394
Griswold v. Connecticut, 13, 85, 88, 91
Guardianship of. *See name of party*
Gunderson v. Golden, 187
Gursky v. Gursky, 760
Guy, In re, 209

H

Haaland v. Brackeen, 635
Haddock v. Haddock, 593
Hadeen, In re Marriage of, 470
Haefele v. Haefele, 343
Halberstam v. Halberstam, 556
Hall v. Duster, 172
Hall v. Hall, 514
Halvey v. Halvey, 620
Hamilton v. Hamilton, 612
Hansen, In re Marriage of, 281, 427
Hanson v. Denckla, 607
Hanson v. Hanson, 99
Hardesty v. Hardesty, 105, 374
Harman v. Rogers, 183
Harmon, In Matter of, 223
Harris, In re Marriage of (877 N.W.2d 434),
     429
Harris and Harris, Marriage of (244 P.3d 801),
     319–323
Harrison v. Harrison, 769
Harrison v. Tauheed, 441
Harrod v. Harrod, 603
Harrold v. Collier, 669
Harte v. Hand, 381–383
Hatch v. Hatch, 240

Hayes; United States v., 84
Haymes v. Haymes, 210
Health Care & Ret. Corp. of Am. v. Pittas, 361
Heath v. Heath, 160
Hedin v. Hedin, 273
Hein, In re Marriage of, 344
Heller v. Doe, 89
Hemenway v. Hemenway, 604
Henderson v. Henderson, 596
Henry, In re, 209
Henry v. Beacham, 343
Herald and Steadman, In re Marriage of, 310
Hereford, In re, 541
Hermesmann, Kansas ex rel. v. Seyer, 697
Hernandez v. Robles, 126
Herrick v. Herrick, 601
Hewitt v. Hewitt, 183
H.H., In re Paternity of v. Hughes, 706
Hicks v. Feiock, 389, 395, 396
Highfill v. Moody, 632
Hill v. Bert Bell/Pete Rozelle NFL Player Ret.
    Plan, 177
Hines v. Hines, 384
Hirst v. Tiberghien, 644
Hisquierdo v. Hisquierdo, 309
H.K. v. A.K., 592
Hockema v. Hockema, 248
Hodge v. Craig, 698
Hodge v. Hodge, 603
Hoffman v. Germany, 696
Hoffman v. Sender, 644, 645
Hofstad v. Christie, 190
Hogan v. McAndrew, 617
Holder v. Holder, 645
Hollett, In re Estate of, 497
Hollis v. Hollis, 210
Holm v. Holm, 374
Holm; State v., 148–154
Holman v. Holman, 307
Holmes v. Holmes, 460
Hornbeck v. Hornbeck, 265
Howell v. Howell, 309
Hresko v. Hresko, 531–533
Huege v. Huege, 636
Huff v. Director, 176
Hughes v. Hutt, 698
Hunter v. Hunter, 420
Hunter v. Rose, 683
Huss v. Weaver, 521–527
Hutchinson, In re Marriage of, 534
Hutchinson v. Hutchinson, 371
Hyde v. Hyde, 600

I

In re. *See name of party*
International Shoe Co. v. Washington, 596, 605,
    606

Isaacson v. Isaacson, 343
Ivey v. Ivey, 603

J

Jackson v. Sollie, 310
Jacob, Matter of, 12
Jacob v. Shultz-Jacob, 730, 770
Jaggi v. Switzerland, 696
Jago v. Jago, 304
Jason P. v. Danielle S., 770
Jaymot v. Skillings-Donat, 184
J.B. v. W.B., 356
J.C.G., People in Interest of, 715
J.D. v. M.D.F., 75–81
J.D. v. Tuscaloosa Cnty. Dep't of Human Res.,
    639
Jefferson v. Jefferson, 344
Jeffers v. Wibbing, 473
Jenkins v. Jenkins, 211
Jersey Shore Med. Ctr. v. Baum, 60
Jesusa V., In re, 715
J.E.V., In re Adoption of, 745
J.F. v. D.B., 776
J.K.N.A, In re, 172
J.M.K., In re Parentage of, 770
Joel and Roohi, In re Marriage of, 102
Johns v. Cioci, 429
Johnson v. Calvert, 776, 778–779
Johnson v. Johnson, 306
Johnson v. Muelberger, 598
Johnson; United States v., 656
Johnston v. Johnston, 108
Jones v. Brennan, 656
Jones v. Graphia, 190
Jones v. Jones, 101, 310, 474
J.P.D. v. W.E.D., 385
J.R. v. M.S., 422–427, 428, 430, 447
J.R. v. Utah, 781
J.S., In re Adoption of, 695
J.S. v. C.C., 341
J.W.T., In the Interest of, 681

K

Kallas v. Kallas, 473
Kampf v. Kampf, 82, 285
Kansas ex rel. Hermesmann v. Seyer, 697
Kaplan v. Kaplan, 285
Kasner, In re, 534
K.D., In the Interest of, 584
Keeler v. Keeler, 542
Kelcourse v. Kelcourse, 496
Kelm v. Kelm, 574
Kennedy, In re, 556
Kennedy v. Eldridge, 556
Kennedy v. Plan Adm'r, 308
Kerrigan v. Commissioner Pub. Health, 125
Kerry v. Din, 72

Kesler v. Weniger, 524
K.I., In re, 420
Kidane, In re Marriage of, 100
Kiken v. Kiken, 363
Kimbrough v. Kentucky Child Support Div. ex rel. Belmar, 384
Kirchberg v. Feenstra, 36, 66
Kirkpatrick v. District Court, 147
Klemm v. Superior Court, 550
Klotz v. Celentano, Stadtmauer & Walentowicz LLP, 60
Klutchko v. Baron, 324
K.L.W., People In Interest of, 730
K.M. v. E.G., 715, 770
K.M.H, In Interest of, 769
Knappenberger, In re Conduct of, 555
Knorr v. Knorr, 523, 526
Kober v. Kober, 107
Konzelman v. Konzelman, 379
Koon v. Koon, 217
Koontz v. Scott, 356
Kovacs v. Brewer, 620
Koychev v. Bulgaria, 696
Krafick v. Krafick, 299
Kraisinger v. Kraisinger, 524, 527, 528
Krampen v. Krampen, 333
Krause v. Krause, 301
Krejci, In re Marriage of, 255
Kreyling v. Kreyling, 209
Krigel, In re, 695
Kristine H. v. Lisa R., 715
Krone, In re Marriage of, 343
K.T.D. v. K.W.P., 432
Kucera v. Kucera, 205–207
Kugler v. Haitian Tours, Inc., 600
Kulko v. Superior Court, 605–607

L

Labine v. Vincent, 671
Labuz, In re Marriage of, 514
Ladue, City of v. Horn, 16–19
LaFleur v. Pyfer, 172
Lambert v. Lambert, 260
LaMusga, In re Marriage of, 447
Lane v. Lane, 490–494
Lannan v. Maul, 654
LaRocque v. LaRocque, 315
Laurie R., Matter of, 639
Law v. Whittet, 453
Lawrence v. Texas, 88, 91, 114, 121, 149, 153
LC v. MG & Child Support Enf't Agency, 684
L.D. and P.K. v. Bulgaria, 696
Lee, In re, 579–582
LeFever v. Matthews, 781
Lehr v. Robertson, 685–690
Lepis v. Lepis, 375

Leseberg v. Taylor, 405
LeTellier v. LeTellier, 612
Levick v. MacDougall, 132
Levin v. Levin, 760
Levy v. Louisiana, 671
Lewis v. Department of Soc. Serv., 356
Lewis v. Harris, 125
Lewis v. Lewis, 514
L.F. v. Breit, 770
Lien v. Lien, 373
Likine; People v., 394
Lincoln v. Lincoln, 423
Lindberg v. Lindberg, 439
Lindsey, In re Marriage of, 194
Linn Cnty. v. City of Hiawatha, 23
Lister v. Lister, 208
Liu, In re Marriage of, 105
Liu v. Mund, 506
Lochner v. New York, 121
Logan v. Logan, 473
Lombardi v. Lombardi, 285
London v. Handicapped Facilities Bd. of St. Charles Cnty., 18
Lopez, In re, 261
Love v. Love, 444
Loving v. Virginia, 87, 109–111, 115
Lovlace v. Copley, 420
Lowe v. Swanson, 142
Lozano v. Montoya Alvarez, 640, 644
LP v. LF, 723
L. Pamela P. v. Frank S., 698
Lukumi Babalu Aye, Inc. v. City of Hialeah, 149
Lumsden v. Lumsden, 273
Lutwak v. United States, 97–100, 101
L.W.K. v. E.R.C., 363
Lynch; State v., 129, 132
Lyons v. Lederle Labs., 358

M

MacGregor v. Unemployment Ins. Appeals Bd., 12
MacIntyre v. MacIntyre, 654
Mackey v. Lanier Collection Agency & Serv., Inc., 46
MacPhail; United States v., 655
Madelyn B., In re Guardianship of, 715
Madison v. Osburn, 706
Maeker v. Ross, 183
Mallen v. Mallen, 490, 497
Malousek v. Meyer, 137
Malters, In re Marriage of, 260
Mandell v. Mandell, 591
Mansell v. Mansell, 309
Marez and Marshall, In re Marriage of, 478
Marquardt v. Marquardt by Rempfer, 372
Marriage of. *See name of party*
Marshall v. Marshall, 105, 656, 724

Martel, In re, 250
Martin v. Martin, 444, 463
Martini v. Price, 743, 744
Marvin v. Marvin, 181–182, 184, 187, 246
Mary L.O. v. Tommy R.B., 343
Masterpiece Cakeshop, Ltd. v. Colorado Civil
    Rights Comm'n, 126–127
Mathews v. Eldridge, 390
Mathis; United States v., 101
Matter of. *See name of party*
Maturo v. Maturo, 340
Maxwell v. Maxwell, 34
Maxwell Schuman & Co. v. Edwards, 558
May v. Anderson, 620, 626, 639
Mayfield v. Mayfield, 281
Mayland v. Mayland, 208
Maynard v. Hill, 110, 111, 117
May's Estate, In re, 161
M.C. v. T.K., 338
McAlear v. McAlear, 395
McAllister v. McAllister, 731
McCarty v. McCarty, 309, 429
McClure v. Haisha, 348
McCoy v. McCoy, 265
McDermott, Marriage of, 625
McElreath v. McElreath, 603
McFarlane v. McFarlane, 248
McGee v. Gonyo, 699–705
McGowan v. McGowan, 323
McGuire v. McGuire, 46–49
McHugh v. McHugh, 517
McKim v. McKim, 224
McLaren v. Gabel, 190
McLaughlin v. Cotner, 655
McLaughlin v. Jones in and for Cnty. of Pima, 684
McLeod v. Starnes, 350–352, 354
McMaster v. Columbia Bd. of Zoning Appeals,
    20
McNeil v. Hoskyns, 534
McPeek v. McCardle, 162
McQuillen v. Hufford, 706
McReath v. McReath, 312–316
Meagher and Malek, In re Marriage of, 105
Medellín v. Texas, 642
Medlin v. Medlin, 101
M.E.F. v. A.B.F., 61
Meredith, In re Marriage of, 73
Meyer v. State of Neb., 88, 110, 664
Meyers v. Handlon, 557
M.H.B. v. H.T.B., 698
Micaletti, In re, 344
Michael George K.; State ex rel. v., 679
Michael H., Adoption of, 695
Michael H. v. Gerald D., 680, 683, 726, 727, 729
Michelson v. Michelson, 238

Mickey v. Mickey, 297–303
Mick-Skaggs v. Skaggs, 208, 221
Midyett v. Midyett, 618
Millar v. Millar, 105
Miller, In re Marriage of, 356
Miller, In the Matter of, 456–460
Miller v. Deal, 393
Miller v. Miller, 248, 526
Mississippi Band of Choctaw Indians v. Holyfield,
    748–749
Mitchell v. W.T. Grant, 82
M.J.M. v. M.L.G., 441
M.L.K., Matter of Interest of, 639
M.N.M., In re, 691
Modnick, In re Marriage of, 532
Mohen v. Mohen, 467
Moix v. Moix, 473
Monasky v. Taglieri, 639–643
Moncrief's Will, Matter of, 102
Monty S. v. Jason W., 737–738
Mooney v. Mooney, 657
Moore v. City of E. Cleveland, 18, 88
Moore v. Jacobsen, 374
Moore v. McGillis, In re, 724
Moore v. Moore, 317
Moreau v. Sylvester, 701, 722
Morgan v. Foretich, 476–477
Morgan v. Pfau, 617
Morris v. Moller, 435
Morrisey v. Morrisey, 542
Morrissey v. United States, 775
Moss v. Superior Court, 393
Mota v. Castillo, 645
Moynihan v. Lynch, 183
Mpirilis v. Hellenic Lines, Ltd., 101
M.S.B., In the Interest of, 639
Mueller, In re Marriage of, 310
Mullane v. Central Hanover Trust Co., 606
Mumma v. Mumma, 523
Murdoch v. Murdoch, 34
Murphy, Ex parte, 542
Murphy v. Carron, 136
Murphy v. Murphy, 281
Muth v. Frank, 142

N

N.A.H. v. S.L.S., 679
Nail v. Nail, 317
Naim v. Naim, 109
Nancy M. v. John M., 431
Nation v. Brackeen, 749
Neely, In re, 127
Nelson v. Evans, 669
Neyman v. Buckley, 600
Nguyen v. Holder, 138–140

Nicholas H., In re, 713, 715
Nichols v. Nichols, 539
Nicholson v. Pappalaardo, 645
Niemann v. Niemann, 448–451
Nilles, In re Marriage of, 543
Norman v. Thomson, 182
Norman v. Unemployment Ins. Appeals Bd., 12
Nugent v. Nugent, 374
Nurie, In re Marriage of, 632
Nuzman; State v., 392

O

Oakley, In re Marriage of, 133–136
Oakley; State v., 395
Obergefell v. Hodges, 8, *12–14*, 15, 27, 88, 91,
        113–124, 167, 172, 198, 379, 599, 682,
        763
O'Brien v. O'Brien, 255–260, 323, 529
Ocegueda v. Perreira, 625
OCS/Pappas v. O'Brien, 610–616
Ogawa v. Ogawa, 624
Olson v. Mohammadu, 370
Olson v. Olson, 551
Olszewski v. Jordan, 558
Olver v. Fowler, 194
O'Neil v. O'Neil, 618
Open Door Alcoholism Program, Inc. v. Board of
        Adjustment, 24
Orr v. Orr, 65, 232
Ortner, In re the Discipline of, 545–548
Osicka, In re Estate of, 262
Otis v. Otis, 273
Owens v. Auto Machinists Pension Trust, 304

P

Pacelli v. Pacelli, 514, 516
Painter v. Bannister, 413–416
Palmore v. Sidoti, 474, 656
Partanen v. Gallagher, 715
Passemato v. Passemato, 343
Paternity of. *See name of party*
Pathak v. Bhardwaj, 603
Pattee v. Pattee, 366
Patterson, In re, 343
Paul v. Paul, 379
Pavan v. Smith, 125, *682–683*, 769
Pazhoor, In re Marriage of, 278–284
Peacock, In re Estate of, 132
Pearson v. Pearson, 343
Pedigo v. Rowley, 764
Peerenboom v. Peerenboom, 314, 344
Penhallow v. Penhallow, 503
Pennington, In re Marriage of, 196, 197
Pennoyer v. Neff, 606
People v. *See name of opposing party*
Pereira v. Pereira, 261

Perry, In re Marriage of, 555
Personnel Admin. v. Feeney, 67
Peterson v. Peterson, 372–374
Pezas v. Pezas, 53
Philipp v. Stahl, 617
Phillips v. Phillips, 463
Pickard v. Pickard, 131, 132
Pierce v. Pierce, 370
Pierce v. Society of Sisters, 14, 88
Pierron v. Pierron, 428
Pierson v. Pierson, 248
Pilati v. Pilati, 532
Piscopo v. Piscopo, 319
Pitts v. Moore, 722
Planned Parenthood of Cent. Mo. v. Danforth,
        94
Planned Parenthood of Se. Pa. v. Casey, 85, 86
Plessy v. Ferguson, 88
P.M. v. T.B., 773–782
PNC Bank Corp. v. W.C.A.B. (Stamos), 167
Poe v. Seaborn, 401
Pohlmann v. Pohlmann, 384
*Porter v. Department of Health & Human Servs.,
        143–146*
Posner v. Posner, 488
Powell v. Powell, 101
Presbyterian Med. Ctr. v. Budd, 361
Prime v. Prime, 540
Prospect Gardens Convalescent Home, Inc. v.
        City of Norwalk, 19, 24
Puddicombe v. Dreka, 431
Pulkkinen v. Pulkkinen, 618
Pundt, In re Marriage of, 428
Purganan, In re Marriage of, 618
Pusey v. Pusey, 440

Q

Quilloin v. Walcott, 686, 688

R

Racine v. Nelson, 695
Rademan v. City and Cnty. of Denver, 19
Raley v. Raley, 243
Ramirez, In re Marriage of, 103–106
Ramsey's Marriage, In re, 603
Randolph v. Randolph, 490, 497
Raphael P., In re, 683
Ray v. Ray, 533
Raybeck, In the Matter of, 376–378
Reaser v. Reaser, 547
Reed v. Parrish, 186
Reed v. Pieper, 441
Reed v. Reed, 64
Rehak v. Mathis, 183
Renaud v. Renaud, 462
Rennels v. Rennels, 420

Reno v. Flores, 89
Reynolds v. Reynolds, 106
Reynolds v. United States, 149, 154
RHM Estates v. Hampshire, 11
Richardson v. Kohlin, 367
Richardson v. Northwest Christian Univ., 20
Richardson v. Richardson, 543
Ricketts v. Ricketts, 220
Riley v. Riley, 215
Rios v. Ferguson, 604
Risinger v. Risinger, 350
Rivera v. Rivera, 132
R.L.S., In re, 669
Roberts v. Locke, 603
Robertson v. Western Baptist Hosp., 22
Robinson, In re, 566
Robinson v. Robinson, 273
Robinson and Thiel, In re Marriage of, 558
Rockwell v. Rockwell, 539, 542
Rodgers v. Rodgers, 742–744
Rodrigue v. Rodrigue, 45
Roe v. Doe, 356
Roe v. Wade, 85, 86
Roepenack, In re Marriage of, 533
Rogers v. Office of Pers. Mgmt., 177
Romer v. Evans, 114
Romulus v. Romulus, 292
Rose ex rel. Clancy v. Moody, 348
Rosenstiel v. Rosenstiel, 600
Ross, In re Marriage of, 675
Ross, Matter of, 211
Rothman v. Rothman, 240
Rozanski v. Poland, 696
Rubin v. Rubin, 301
Rubin v. Salla, 346
Russell v. Cox, 632
Russo v. Russo, 603
R.W., In re, 639

S

Sahin v. Germany, 696
Sanjari v. Sanjari, 262
San Luis Obispo Cnty. v. Nathaniel J, 697
Santa Barbara, City of v. Adamson, 19, 20
Sarah Ashton McK. v. Samuel Bode M., In re, 626
Sarah D. v. John D., 454
S.B. v. State, 639
S.B. v. W.A., 519
Schaeffer v. Schaeffer, 107
Schaub v. Schaub, 105, 106
Schechter v. Schechter, 576
Schibi v. Schibi, 99, 100
Schultz v. Schultz, 478
Schwartz v. Merchants Mortgage Co., 532
Schwartz v. Philadelphia Zoning Bd. of
    Adjustment, 20

Schwegmann v. Schwegmann, 183
Schweiker v. Gray Panthers, 62
Schweiker v. Hansen, 682
Scoffield, In re Marriage of, 271
S.D.W., In re Adoption of, 691–695
Secretary of Dep't for Children & Families, State
    ex rel. v. Smith, 705
Self v. Self, 363
Selley, In re Marriage of, 344
Sexton v. Sexton, 356
Shaffer v. Heitner, 603, 606
Shah v. Shah, 604
Sharon S. v. Superior Court, 724
Sharp v. Keeler, 463
Sharpe v. Sharpe, 365–369
Sharpe Furniture, Inc. v. Buckstaff, 54–56
Sheetz v. Sheetz, 698
Sherrer v. Sherrer, 597–598
Shih Ping Li v. Tzu Lee, 533
Shippy, In re Estate of, 162
Shofman v. Russia, 696
Short v. Short, 344, 364
Shortt v. Damron, 528
Sickels v. Sickels, 428
Sickler v. Sickler, 395
Sidell v. Sidell, 617
Siderius, Ex parte, 621–625
Siefert v. Siefert, 252–254
Silvan v. Alcina, 281
Silverman v. Silverman, 497
Simcox v. Simcox, 650
Simeone v. Simeone, 484–488
Simmons v. Simmons, 285, 300
Simons v. Miami Beach First Nat'l Bank, 602
Simons v. Simons, 247
Simpson v. Simpson, 209, 374
Simpson Garment Co. v. Schultz, 55
Singletary v. Singletary, 447
Sinnott v. Peck, 723
Sistare v. Sistare, 610
Sistersong v. Kemp, 626
Skinner v. Oklahoma ex rel. Williamson, 88, 93,
    110, 111, 394
S.L.F., In re, 691
Smith, In re Marriage of, 258, 260
Smith v. Cole, 729
Smith v. Jones, 729
Smith v. Lewis, 295
Smith v. Martin, 669
Smith v. Organization of Foster Families for
    Equality & Reform, 687, 689
Smith v. Smith (358 P.3d 171), 310
Smith v. Smith (224 So.3d 740), 137
Smith v. Smith (93 S.W.3d 871), 254
S.N.V., In re, 683
S.O., In re Petition of, 739

Solomon v. Guidry, 600
Sommerfeld v. Germany, 696
Sonder v. Sonder, 526
Sonnicksen, Estate of, 510, 511
Soos v. Superior Court in & for Cnty. of
     Maricopa, 781
Sorensen; People v., 760
Sorensen v. Sorensen, 317
Spearman v. Spearman, 174–176
Spears v. Spears, 176
Spencer v. Spencer, 604, 616
Spheeris v. Spheeris, 313
Srivastava v. Srivastava, 210
Srock v. Srock, 271
Staats v. McKinnon, 631
Stallings v. Stallings, 265
Stanley v. Illinois, 93, 685, 686
Stanton v. Stanton, 65
State v. *See name of opposing party*
Steele v. Neeman, 356
Stephen K. v. Roni L., 698
Stern v. Marshall, 656
Steuart v. McChesney, 525
Stevenson, In re Marriage, 344
Stevenson v. Stevenson, 208
Stewart v. Stewart, 543
Stone v. Stidham, 395
Stone v. Thompson, 166–171
Stoneman v. Drollinger, 636
Stoner v. Stoner, 516
Strack v. Strack, 216
Strickland v. Day, 769
Strnad v. Strnad, 760
Stromsted, Estate of, 55, 60
Suggs, In re Marriage of, 73
Sullivan, In re Marriage of, 344
Sullivan v. Sullivan, 210
Surrogate Parenting Assocs., Inc. v.
     Commonwealth ex rel. Armstrong, 778
Sveen v. Melin, 308
Sweeney v. Sweeney, 601
Swicegood v. Thompson, 172
Swing, In Marriage of, 370
Swoap v. Superior Court, 358, 359–360
Syracuse, City of v. Snow, 22

T

Tacchi v. Tacchi, 107
Tatum v. Tatum, 174
Tavli v. Turkey, 696
Taylor, In re, 409
T.D. v. M.M.M., 726–729
Tedford v. Dempsey, 364
Texas v. Haaland, 750
Theisen v. Theisen, 53
Thetford, In re, 555

Thieme v. Aucoin-Thieme, 265–267
Thomas v. 5 Star Transp., 172
Thomas J.R., In re, 639
Thompson v. Thompson, 657
Thompson, State ex rel. v. Dueker, 556
Thornhill, In re Marriage of, 529, 530
Thornton, In re Estate of, 183
Throckmorton; United States v., 532
Tidwell v. Tidwell, 208
T.L. v. W.L., 604
T.M.H. v. D.M.T., 781
T.N.G., In re, 626
T.N.S.R. v. N.P.W., 432
Toni v. Toni, 535–541
Town of. *See name of town*
Traster, In re Marriage of, 519
Treto v. Treto, 684, 769
Trimble v. Gordon, 671
Tropea v. Tropea, 447
Troxel v. Granville, 413, 419, 663–668
T.S., In re, 562
Tuan Anh Nguyen v. INS, 683
Tuckman v. Tuckman, 339–342
Tuetken v. Tuetken, 574
Turk, In re Marriage of, 345–347
Turner v. Rogers, 388–391
Turner v. Safley, 88, 93, 112, 115
Turner v. Turner, 208, 273, 344
2-4 Realty Assocs. v. Pittman, 11

U

Ulrich v. State, 53
Underwood v. Underwood, 375
United Mine Workers of Am. v. Bagwell, 395
United States v. *See name of opposing party*

V

Vahey v. Vahey, 216
Van Camp v. Van Camp, 261
Vanderbilt v. Vanderbilt, 601–602
Vandervort v. Vandervort, 221–223
Van Dyke v. Thompson, 384
Van Orden v. Van Orden, 530
Van Weelde v. Van Weelde, 706
Varnum v. Brien, 125
Vaughan v. Smithson, 654
Velasquez v. Funes de Velasquez, 645
Ventrice v. Ventrice, 585
Verna v. Verna, 354
Versalle, In re Guardianship of, 669
Vileta v. Vileta, 105
Village of. *See name of village*
Vincent v. State of Cal., 510
Virginia; United States v., 66
V.L. v. E.L., 725
Vlach v. Vlach, 132

Voigt v. Voigt, 539
Voisine v. United States, 85
Voyles v. Voyles, 373

W

W., In re Marriage of, 730
W.A., State ex rel., 639
Wagner v. Wagner, 632
Walker, In re, 625
Wallis v. Smith, 698
Walsh v. Reynolds, 194
Ware v. Ware, 210, 497, 551
Warner and Ryan v. Heiden, 54
Warrender v. Warrender, 600
Warrington v. Warrington, 540
Washington v. Davis, 67
Washington v. Glucksberg, 86
Watt v. Watt, 443
W.C.F. v. M.G., 441
Webb v. Sowell, 350
Weber v. Aetna Cas. & Sur. Co., 671
Weesner v. Weesner, 603
Weinberger v. Wiesenfeld, 56
Weinstein v. Barnett, 559
Weisberger v. Weisberger, 464–469
Weishaus v. Weishaus, 375
Welch, In re Marriage of, 271
Westinghouse Elec. Corp. v. Gulf Oil Corp., 555
Weston v. Weston, 355
Whalen v. Allers, 758
White v. White, 261
White Plains, City of v. Ferraioli, 19
Williams, In re, 639
Williams, In re Marriage of, 250
Williams v. North Carolina, 595–597
Williams v. State, 70–72
Williams v. Williams, 177, 217

Williamson v. Lee Optical of Okla., Inc., 89
Williamson v. Williamson, 347
Windsor; United States v., 114, 124
Winer v. Winer, 265
Winston v. Lee, 88
Wisconsin v. Yoder, 687
Witmayer v. Witmayer, 526
Wood v. Wood, 344
Woronzoff-Daschkoff v. Woronzoff-Daschkoff, 107
Worthley v. Worthley, 610
Woytas v. Greenwood Tree Experts, Inc., 387
Wright v. Dropik, 187
Wright v. Hall, 102
WSC Riverside Drive Owners LLC v. Williams, 11

X

Xiong v. Xiong, 177

Y

Yaghoubinejad v. Haghighi, 133
Yaman, In re, 645
Yang v. Tsui, 645
Yannalfo, In re, 497
Yarbrough v. Celebrezze, 176
Yasmin S., In re Adoption of, 725
Yates v. Yates, 523
Y.E.F., Matter of Adoption of, 745
Yelin v. Yelin, 107

Z

Zablocki v. Redhail, 112, 115, 394
Zaleski v. Zaleski, 281, 286–290
Z.N.H, In re, 555
Zold v. Zold, 342

INDEX

Principal cases are indicated by italics.

A

AAML. *See* American Academy of Matrimonial
 Lawyers
Abandonment
 child, 626, 695, 741–745, 749
 divorce and, 209, 593
Abortion, 85–95
 overturning constitutional protection, 28,
  85–92, 112, 626
 parental notification and consent, 95
 spousal notification and consent, 94
 state laws, 93–95
 substantive due process rights, 93
 surrogacy and, 483, 782
Adoption, 733–759
 abandonment or desertion as basis for, 741–745,
  749
 agencies for, 736–737, 746–747, 757
 best interests of the child, 734, 751, 756
 child's consent to, 740
 commodification of, 747
 complete substitution theory, 747–748
 consent to adopt, 736–741
  lack of consent, 695, 697, 741–746
 costs and payments, 746–747, 757
 demographics, 735–736, 753
 equitable, 736
 of foster children, 734, 735, 739, 746–747, 753,
  758
 full faith and credit, 725
 history of, 733–735, 747–748
 home studies, 746
 infant, 734–735, 746, 751–752, 754–755, 757
 international, 735, 747, 748, 753–758
 Internet, impact of, 747
 interstate placements, 639
 jurisdiction, 637–639, 750
 Native Americans and, 748–752, 756
 new parent-child relationship, 746–747
 non-exclusive, 740
 older children, 740, 746–747
 open, 737–739, 740–741, 757
 out-of-state, recognition of, 725
 overview, 733
 placement in, 747–759
 polyamorous relationships, 731
 post-adoption contact agreements, 730,
  740–741, 757
 private, 735, 739, 746–747, 757
 racial matching, 747–748, 752, 755–758
 religious matching, 747, 758–759
 by same-sex couples, 128, 724–725, 759
 second-parent, 12, 724–725
 secrecy, anonymity, and sealing records of, 734
 special-needs children, 746, 747, 757
 statutes of limitation and, 691
 stepparents, 690, 724–725, 741–744
 stranger, 724
 terminating the first parent-child relationship,
  736–746, 755–757
 transracial, 748, 752–758
 two-stage process of, 736
 UAA, 637–639, 739, 744–745, 746
 unmarried parents' rights, 685–697, 736,
  751–752
 U.S. children adopted abroad, 758
Adultery, 147, 207–208, 210, 211, 249. *See also*
 Infidelity
Affinity, relationship by, 83, 138
Africa, same-sex couple legal recognition in, 128
Age
 of majority, 350
 marriage restrictions, 101, 143–147
Aid for Dependent Children, 550
Alimony. *See* Spousal support
ALI Principles of the Law of Family Dissolution
 child custody, 433–434, 440–441, 452–453,
  528, 530, 569
 child support, 333–335, 338, 363, 383, 528, 724
 cohabitation, 193, 196
 domestic violence, 196, 452–453
 goodwill, treatment of, 317
 parenthood, 723–724, 731
 parenting plan, 433–434, 569
 premarital agreements, 484, 505–506
 property division at divorce, 239, 249, 261, 262,
  317
 separation agreements, 521, 529, 530, 542
 spousal support, 285, 286, 363, 375
Alternative dispute resolution, 568–592
 arbitration, 553, 570–577, 584–585, 586
 collaborative practice, 565, 585, 587–592

costs of, 585–586
defined, 569–570
lawyer's role, 552–553, 564–566, 568–592
mediation, 454, 552–553, 565–566, 577–587
online, 586–587
overview, 568–570
triage (differentiated case management),
    585–586
Alternative reproductive technologies, 760–784
artificial insemination, 125, 715, 760–772, 773
contracts and agreements, 483, 769–771, 772,
    781
egg donation, 770–771, 773, 781
in vitro fertilization, 770, 772–773
legal parenthood and, 682–684, 715, 730–731,
    760–784
overview, 733
racial matching, 758
sperm donors, 682–683, 731, 760, 768–771,
    773, 781–782
surrogacy, 483, 683, 715, 772–784
UPA, 760–761, 768, 770–771, 780–781
American Academy of Matrimonial Lawyers (AAML)
advocacy, bounds of, 560–562, 564–565, 583
joint representation, 551
postnuptial contracts, survey on, 519
spousal support guidelines, 273, 286
standards of conduct, 566–567
Annulment, 101–102, 106–108, 136–137, 203
Antenuptial contracts. See Premarital agreements
Anti-miscegenation laws, 109–113
Arbitration, 553, 570–577, 584–585, 586
Artificial insemination, 125, 715, 760–772, 773
Asia, same-sex couple legal recognition in, 128
Attorneys. See Lawyers
Australia
child support enforcement in, 399
dispute resolution forums in, 565
legal statuses for intimate partners in, 193
property division at divorce in, 248
same-sex couple legal recognition in, 128
Automatic stays, 409
Autonomy
client, 560, 561
family, 51–52, 53, 59, 198
parental, 326
women's, 7, 72, 379, 599

B
Bankruptcy, 231, 271, 375, 405–409, 656
Bastardy action, 672
Belgium, registered partnerships legal status in, 199
Bigamy, 100, 147–158, 162, 172, 177
British Forced Marriage (Civil Protection) Act of
    2007, 107–108
Bulgaria, paternity rights in, 695

C
Canada
family dispute resolution in, 575
legal parenthood definitions in, 731
legal statuses for intimate partners in, 193
same-sex couple legal recognition in, 128
U.S. children adopted in, 758
Capitalization rates, 318
CARES Act (2020), 400
Caretaker-dependent relationship, 5
Catholic Social Services, 759
Central America
international adoptions in, 755
same-sex couple legal recognition in, 128
Child abandonment, 626, 695, 741–745, 749
Child abduction, 83, 478–479, 620, 635–636,
    639–650, 657. See also Parental
    Kidnapping Prevention Act
Child abuse. See also Domestic violence
allegations of, 84, 431, 443, 456–463, 470–471,
    478–479, 626
polygamy and, 156
Child custody, 411–481
abduction to avoid, 478–479, 620, 635–636,
    639–650, 657. See also Parental
    Kidnapping Prevention Act
abuse, allegations of, 84, 431, 443, 456–463,
    470–471, 478–479, 626
alienation issues and, 430–432, 443, 448, 462
ALI principles, 433–434, 440–441, 452–453,
    528, 530, 569
arbitration and, 574–577
attorney-client privilege and duty to disclose,
    480–481
changes of circumstances, 420, 431, 433–434,
    443–448, 451
childcare arrangements, 441
childrearing responsibilities, 277, 293, 435–442
child's objection clause, 645
child's preferences, 430, 434, 470, 478–479,
    645
child support. See Child support
cohabitants, 12, 472–473
demographics and trends, 385–387, 398–399
dependency exemptions, 404–405
disqualifying conduct, 413, 443
domestic violence issues, 84, 431, 443, 448–455,
    579, 583–584, 626, 634, 636–637,
    646–650. See also abuse, this heading
evaluators, 576–577
"friendly parent" provision, 431, 432, 460
gender and, 411–412, 440–441, 462
grandparents and, 413–420, 441, 478–479,
    663–669, 710
habitual residence and, 639–648
history of, 411–412, 421–422

interstate child snatching, 620, 636. *See also*
    Child abduction
joint. *See* Joint custody
jurisdictional issues, 620–650
    home state/extended home state jurisdiction,
        625–626, 627, 633–634
    initial jurisdiction, 621–627
    international enforcement, 635, 639–650
    interstate enforcement and modification,
        627–637
locating parents, 635–636
marital home and, 272
mediation and, 454, 577–585
military and deployed parents, 634
modification of orders, 432, 439–449, 451, 528,
        620–621, 627–637
ne exeat clause, 644
new partners, 472–473
noncustodial fathers, contact with their children,
        326, 395
parentage determination in context of, 413, 662,
        670–708
parental consent to marriage and, 147
parental preference, presumption of, 419–420
parental rights to, 411–412
parenting coordinator, 432–433, 569, 584
parenting plans, 432–435, 448, 462–463, 530,
        569
past caretaking, prioritization of, 440
racial and ethnic issues, 474–475
religious issues, 463, 464–472, 473
relocation of custodial parent, 439–440,
        443–448
same-sex couples, 12, 473, 575, 710
separation agreements, 520–530
split physical custody, 348, 428–429, 471
spousal support and, 277, 293
standards for determination of, 412–476
    best interests doctrine, 412–421, 428,
        429–431, 440–442, 451, 574, 668–669
    expert witnesses, role of, 420, 460–461
    primary caretaker, 435–442
    shared or joint custody, 421–435
    shared parenting, 443–476
    unfitness, 413
tax credits, 404–405
"tender years" doctrine, 412, 440
unborn child, 625–626
unfriendly co-parenting, 448–464
unmarried parents, 441, 521–528, 672,
        685–697, 729–730
visitation, 476–481
    abduction to avoid, 478–479
    abuse allegations, 462–463, 478–479
    child's preferences, 462, 478–479
    contempt sanctions, 478–479

    deliberate interference with, 395, 618
    denial of, 453, 462–463
    enforcement issues, 476–481, 644, 646
    functional parents, 710, 715–723
    grandparents, 419–420, 663–669, 710
    new partners, 472–473
    nonparental statutes, 668
    parenting plans, 462–463
    parenting time, 427–428
    postadoption, 739, 740–741
    romantic cohabitation in presence of
        children, 472–473
    stepparents and, 710, 721–722
    supervised, 453, 463
    therapeutic, 462
    third-party, 668–669, 715–723, 731. *See also*
        grandparents and functional parents, *this
        heading*
    wrongfully removed or retained children, 639,
        644–645. *See also* Child abduction
Childrearing. *See also* Parenting
    cost of, determining for child support, 327–333,
        336–337
    earnings capacity and, 276–277
    politics and social value of, 293–295
    primary caretaker, 435–442
    spousal support, 275, 276–277, 285, 292–295
Children
    abuse of. *See* Child abuse
    adoption of. *See* Adoption
    age-based marriage restrictions, 101, 143–147
    care for/raising. *See* Childrearing
    conflict effects on, 420–421, 451–452
    continuity, need for, 447
    custody of. *See* Child custody
    in divorce, 224, 230, 420–421, 568
    forced marriage of, 108, 147
    lawyer's obligations to, 561–562
    parents of. *See parent-related entries*
    Social Security benefits for, 371
    support for. *See* Child support
    tax benefits associated with, 400, 404–405
    of unmarried parents. *See* Unmarried parents
Children's Rights Council, 336
Child support, 325–357
    ability to pay and, 392–393
    active concealment of child, effect of, 395
    additional dependents, adjustments for, 383
    ALI principles for, 333–335, 338, 363, 383,
        528, 724
    alternative reproduction and liability for, 770
    arbitration, 576
    arrears in, 399, 400
    bankruptcy and, 405–408
    change of circumstances, 363–365
    childcare expenses, 331, 333

children's medical expenses, 331, 333, 387–388
civil vs. criminal contempt proceedings, 388–397
cohabitation and, 172, 381
college expenses, 343, 350–357, 406–408, 528
constitutional challenges to guidelines, 384
continuity of expenditure approach, 333–339
contracts, 344
control of children and, 325–327, 349–350, 356
cost-of-living adjustments, 364
cost-shares approach, 336–337
criminal nonsupport statutes, 394
current model, 327–333
custody and visitation, 326, 327, 348, 385–387,
    395, 404–405, 576, 618
death of obligor, 363, 387
de facto parents, 724
Delaware Melson Formula, 330, 336
demographics, 385–387, 394, 398–399
different families of children, 381–383
disabled children, 355–356, 371
earnings capacity, 364, 370–371
ELS Model, 338
emancipation, 349, 356
enforcement, 326–327, 385–400, 609–620
escalator clauses, 364
exemption, 348
expedited processes, 397
expenditures model, 327–339
family expense statutes, 326–327
federal intent for, 336–337
flat percentage guideline, 329
formulas for, 339–349
guidelines, 327–333, 342–344, 348–349
high-income cases, 343
history of, 325–326
incarcerated parents, 349
income decreases, voluntary vs. involuntary,
    365–372, 394
income of new spouse, 384–385
income of residential vs. nonresidential parent,
    345–348
income shares formula, 329–333, 337, 338, 345
informal and in-kind, 399–400
inheritances, treatment of, 344
interests of child, 334–335
interests of nonresidential parent, 335
interests of residential parent, 335
international enforcement, 619–620
interstate modification and enforcement,
    609–620
involuntary servitude, 393
jailing "deadbeat" parents, 388–397
jurisdictional issues, 605–620, 626
liens, 387, 398
life insurance for, 387
locating parents, 398, 618, 635
long-arm jurisdiction, 605–609

low-income parents, 348–349
marginal expenditures model, 334, 335
misappropriation, 332–333
modification and termination, 363–385,
    535–544, 609–620
necessaries doctrine, 62, 326–327
new families and, 381–385
overview, 325
parenthood determination, 400, 662, 670–708,
    729–730
parenting time adjustment in, 345, 348
percentage of income model, 330–333, 338,
    343, 344
post-majority support, 349–357, 406–408, 528,
    616–617
poverty, 398–400
premarital agreements, 496–497, 502, 504
prior support orders vs. new orders, 610–617
private enforcement mechanisms, 387–388
public assistance payments, 348–349, 355–356,
    400, 550, 673, 706–707
public opinion on, 338–339
remarriage and, 353, 381, 383–385
retirement and, 370
S corporation earnings, treatment of, 343
separation agreements, 355, 520–530, 535–544
standard of living, 330, 334–335, 338, 496–497
state differences, 330–331, 344, 345, 354–355
stepparents, 172, 381, 384–385
taxation, 231, 331, 337, 343–344, 398, 402,
    404–405
unemployment or underemployment, 365–372,
    392
unmarried parents, 325, 327, 339, 671–672,
    697–708, 729–730
wage withholding, 397–398
Wisconsin formula, 332, 344
Child Support Recovery Act, 394
Civil service pensions, 310
Civil unions, 126, 128, 198–199, 600, 730–731. *See
    also* Same-sex couples
Cohabitation, 3, 7–12, 165–199
    ALI principles, 193, 196
    business relationships and, 183, 190
    child custody and, 12, 472–473
    child support and, 172, 381
    choice-of-law problems, 191
    committed intimate relationship, 196–197
    common law marriage, 166–174, 182, 187, 196
    community property and, 197
    contractual and equitable remedies, 181–193,
        483, 507
    defined, 379
    demographic data, 179, 180
    divorce and, 179, 210
    domestic partners, 126, 186–187, 193,
        196–197, 198–199

domestic violence and, 82–83
economic advantages, 165–166, 179–180, 229
family and, 15, 195–198, 661
fiduciary duties, 187
financial management, 179–180, 184
increase in, 3, 165, 178
legal treatment of, 7–8, 15, 166, 196, 197–199
marital status discrimination, 20
meretricious relationships, 180, 197, 379
motivations for, 165–166, 179–180
nonmarital relationships, 3, 195–196, 197, 236–237
parenthood relations and, 661
property rights and, 8, 197, 264–267, 304
public benefits, entitlement to, 8, 12, 172–173
putative spouses, 174–178, 180, 182
reciprocal beneficiary relationships, 198–199
recognition of, 197–199
registered partnerships, 197–199
restitution, 190
same-sex couples, 8–12, 15, 126, 198–199, 264, 379, 473
spousal support and, 53, 372, 376–381
statistics, 178–179
taxation, 401
types of, 178–179
Uniform Cohabitants Economic Remedies Act, 190–191
unjust enrichment, 184, 187–190, 197
unmarried cohabitants, 178–199
zoning ordinances, 16–25
Collaborative lawyering, 565, 585, 587–592
Collusion, 211, 221–224
Common law
adoption, 734
age of consent to marriage, 143
child custody, 411, 412
child support, 697
contract doctrine, 484, 513
fraud, 566
marital property. *See* Common law marital property
marriage, 166–174, 182, 187, 196
necessaries doctrine, 54–57, 59–62, 326–327
parentage, 670, 672, 681, 711, 768
Common law marital property, 29, 30–35, 36
child support and, 384
choice-of-law issues, 268
death of spouse, 30, 35
divorce and property division, 232, 237, 238–240, 252, 255, 261–262, 268
gifts, 34, 252, 255
taxation, 402
traditional, 30
trusts, 31–35
women and, 30–31

Community property, 29, 35–40
business exception, 37–38
child support and, 384
choice-of-law issues, 268
cohabitation and, 197
debt division, 271
divorce and property division, 232, 233, 237–238, 239, 252, 255, 261, 268, 271
employment-related and public benefits, 45–46
fiduciary duty, 39
gifts, 36, 252, 255
inception of title rule, 261
management power, 36–39, 57–59
premarital wealth not, 35–36, 38
quasi-community property statutes, 268
Roman-Dutch law, 35
Spanish law, 35, 36
taxation and, 402
women and, 36–37
Condonation defense to grounds of divorce, 210
Conflicts of interest, 549–559, 562
Connivance as factor in divorce, 210
Consanguinity statutes, 83, 138–142
Conservators, 136–137
Consolidated Appropriations Act of 2022, 605
Constructive trusts, 31–35, 190, 247
Contraceptives, 85, 92, 93, 95, 209, 697, 698
Contracts
alternative reproduction, 483, 769–771, 772, 781
antenuptial. *See* Premarital agreements
capacity to contract, 137
child support, 344
cohabitation contractual and equitable remedies, 181–193, 483, 507
family, 483–544. *See also* Family contracts
fraud, 107
marriage as, 5–6, 107, 203, 217, 226, 483, 574, 595
parent-child, 326
post-adoption contact, 730, 740–741, 757
postnuptial, 508–520
registered contractual relationships, 198
separation. *See* Separation agreements
surrogacy, 483, 771, 772–784
Convention on the Rights of the Child (UN), 430, 754, 755, 757–758
Copyright Act of 1976, 45–46
Cousin marriage, prohibitions on, 138, 141–142
Covenant, marriage as, 203, 217, 226, 483, 574
Coverture, 276–277
COVID-19 pandemic
adult children at home, 355
dating relationships, 83
earnings capacity and work changes, 496
immigration and, 102
international adoption decline, 735

online dispute resolution, 586–587
online legal representation, 553–554
surrogacy effects, 782–783
vaccinations for children, 472
Creditors. *See also* Bankruptcy; Liens
    child support and, 326, 384, 393–394
    marital property and, 28–29, 30, 35, 41, 54–57,
        59–60, 63, 268–271, 384
    parent support suits, 361–362
Cruelty and divorce, 208–209, 210
Custody of children. *See* Child custody

D
Deadbeat Parents Punishment Act, 394
Death benefits, 307–308
Debt. *See* Bankruptcy; Creditors; Liens
Defense of Marriage Act (DOMA), 27, 124–125
Deferred marital property system, 239–240
Desertion. *See* Abandonment
Disabilities, persons with
    adoption of, 746, 747, 757
    adult children's support for parents, 357–362
    child support, 355–356, 371
    disability benefits, 297–304, 307, 349, 371
    mental capacity, 133–138. *See also* Mental capacity
    spousal support, 371
Discounted cash flow method, 296
Discrimination
    children of unmarried parents, 670–671
    familial status, 20
    gender, 64–68, 276. *See also* Women
    marital status, 20
Dispute resolution. *See* Family dispute resolution
Dissolution. *See* Divorce; No-fault divorce
Divisible divorce, 601–604
Divorce, 203–230
    abandonment and desertion, 209, 593
    administrative, 204
    adultery and, 207–208, 210, 211
    age-based factors, 146
    alternative dispute resolution and, 552–553,
        564–566, 568–592
    American system of marriage and, 226–230
    bankruptcy and, 405–406
    bargaining, 521
    certificate of marital termination, 225
    children in, 224, 230, 420–421, 568. *See also*
        Child custody; Child support
    cohabitation and, 179, 210
    collaborative, 585, 587–592
    collusion and, 211, 221–224
    common law marriage and, 171–172, 173
    condonation, 210
    connivance and, 210
    "cooling off" periods, 221
    cruelty and, 208–209, 210

economic awards, history of, 231–232
economic consequences for women and children,
    230, 232–237, 275
economic disparity between men and women
    following, 233–234
education programs, 230–231
equitable estoppel and, 600
exit costs, 228–229, 230
ex parte, and jurisdiction, 595–596, 598, 601,
    602–603
family structure and, 227–228
fault system, 204–212, 217–221, 231–232, 272,
    292
foreign, recognition of, 600
history of, 203–204, 212–213
insanity and, 209–210
irretrievable breakdown/irreconcilable
    differences, 213–217, 221, 224
jurisdiction and, 176, 224, 593–604
lawyers and, 545–592
length of marriage and, 225
Mexican mail-order, 600
new property and, 295–324
no-fault. *See* No-fault divorce
pipeline effect, 227
property division. *See* Property division at divorce
rate of, 226–228, 230
recrimination and, 210–211
reform, 236
religion and, 7, 203, 575–576
remarriage, 236, 594
same-sex couples, 599–600
separation agreements. *See* Separation agreements
separation and, 217–221
spousal support at, 272–295. *See also* Spousal
    support
summary dissolution, 224–226
tax consequences of, 402–405
tort suits and, 251
traditional, 204–212
UMDA. *See* Uniform Marriage and Divorce Act
unilateral, 217, 228, 234, 600
voidable marriage, 101
waiting periods, 221, 230–231
DNA tests. *See* Genetic tests
DOMA (Defense of Marriage Act), 27, 124–125
Domestic partnerships, 126, 186–187, 193,
    196–197, 198–199, 402
Domestic relations, federal court jurisdiction over,
    650–657
Domestic support obligations, 405. *See also* Child
    support; Family support; Spousal support
Domestic violence, 68–85. *See also* Child abuse
    child abduction and, 83, 646–650
    child custody and, 84, 431, 443, 448–455, 579,
        583–584, 626, 634, 636–637, 646–650

children, effects on, 451–452

cohabitation and, 82–83

constitutional limits on state's authority to define conduct as, 73, 74, 84

"cooling-off strategies," 69, 74

criminal justice system and, 50, 68, 69–75, 83–84

defined, 452–453

divorce and, 230, 590–591

emotional distress, intentional infliction of, 251

federal legislation, 84–85

firearms, availability of to offenders, 83, 84–85

Hague Convention and, 646–650

harassment, 81–82

history of reform against, 69–70, 73

immigration rules related to, 72, 102–103

insanity and, 209–210

jurisdiction and, 604–605, 626, 634, 636–637, 646–650

mandatory arrest and no-drop policies, impact of, 70, 74–75

marital rape, 73

mediation and, 454, 583–584, 586–587

polygamy and, 156

premarital agreements and, 502

privacy issues, 28, 69, 73, 74

property division at divorce and, 249

protective (restraining) orders, 75–84, 107–108, 604–605

same-sex couples, 83

stalking, 83

UCCJEA and, 636–637

victim, testimony of, 68, 70, 74–75

Domicile, 595–601, 620

Dower rights, 30, 602–603

Dual paternity, 726–732. *See also* Multiple parenthood

E

Earned income tax credit, 402, 405

Earning capacities. *See also* Income

child support and, 364, 370–371

as divisible property, 319–324

premarital agreements and changes in, 496

speculative estimates, 371

spousal support and, 275–277, 319–324, 364, 370–371

Economic Impact Payments, 400

Education

child custody and, 428, 439

child support for college, 343, 350–357, 406–408, 528

as divisible property, 295, 319–324

on divorce, 230–231

economic value of, 319, 352

marriage and, 3

on mediation, 585–586

premarriage, 569

Elderly adults

adult child support for, 357–362

cohabitation, 179

mental capacity, 137–138

Elizabeth Morgan Act (1996), 479

ELS (Equal Living Standard) Model for Child Support Awards, 338

Employee Retirement Income Security Act of 1974 (ERISA), 41–46

anti-alienation provision of, 41, 46, 304

benefit plans covered by, 46

divorce and beneficiaries of pension plans, 46, 297, 304–305, 307–308, 403, 655

marital property, 41–46, 297, 304–305, 307–308

state laws and, 41–46

Employment benefits plans. *See also* Pensions and retirement plans

children, medical insurance for, 387–388

divisible at divorce, 233, 297–311, 403

domestic partners, 402

group health and life insurance, 305–306, 308

marital property, 40–46, 297–311

taxation, 402, 403

Equal Credit Opportunity Act of 1974, 60

Equal Living Standard (ELS) Model for Child Support Awards, 338

Equal management system, 37–38

Equitable distribution

of debts, 270–271

defined, 31, 240–251

of marital property, 35, 232, 238–252, 262, 603

pure, 238

Equitable estoppel, doctrine of, 600, 769, 770

Equitable parents, 711. *See also* Functional parenthood

Equity, defined, 31

ERISA. *See* Employee Retirement Income Security Act of 1974

Eugenics, 137

Europe. *See also* specific countries

child visitation rights in, 462

international adoptions in, 755

paternity rights in, 696

registered partnerships legal status in, 199

same-sex couple legal recognition in, 128

European Convention for the Protection of Human Rights and Fundamental Freedoms, 141, 462, 696, 755

F

Fair Housing Act of 1968, 20

Family, 3–25, 27–95

autonomy, 51–52, 53, 59, 198

cohabitation and, 3, 7–12, 15, 195–198, 661. *See also* Cohabitation

contracts within. *See* Family contracts
defining, 3–25
division of labor within, 57
divorce and, 227–228, 231. *See also* Divorce
federal court jurisdiction over, 650–657
functional, 19, 25
governance of, courts and, 49, 650–657
grandparents. *See* Grandparents
homemakers for, economic value, 56–57,
    233–236, 246–248
husband as head of, 27–28, 36, 57, 69
importance of being, 27–95
marriage and, 3–16, 27–28, 97, 138–142, 161.
    See also Marital property; Marriage
new families and support orders, 372–385
parental roles. *See parent-related entries*
power and authority in, 51–52, 57
privacy, notion of, 27, 28, 51, 52, 57, 69, 73,
    74, 85–86
same-sex couples, 8–16, 27. *See also* Same-sex
    couples; Same-sex marriage
security and stability, 4–5
single-parent, 293, 441, 661
social history of, 51–52
structure of, 227–228, 661–663
support for, 46–62, 357. *See also* Child support;
    Spousal support
as a unit (entity), 27–28, 51–53, 57, 361, 402
value of caregiving in, 293–295
violence. *See* Domestic violence
zoning ordinances and definition of, 16–25
Family and Medical Leave Act of 1993, 92
Family contracts, 483–544
    defined, 483
    overview, 483–484
    postnuptial agreements, 508–520
    premarital agreements, 100, 484–508, 570,
        575–576
    separation agreements, 520–544
    spousal contracts during marriage, 508–520
Family dispute resolution
    lawyers and, 545–592
    paradigm shift in, 545, 568–569
Family expense statutes, 60, 326–327
Family Law Act of 1970, 551
Family support, 46–62, 357. *See also* Child support;
    Spousal support
Federal Consumer Credit Protection Act, 398
Federal Fugitive Felony Act, 636
Federal Gun Control Act of 1994, 84
FFCCSOA (Full Faith and Credit for Child Support
    Orders Act), 610, 616, 618, 621
Fifth Amendment, 85, 599
Filial support laws, 361–362
Filiation suits, 672. *See also* Parenthood
First Amendment, 73, 85, 126–127, 132, 470–471,
    759

Foster care
    adoption of children in, 734, 735, 739,
        746–747, 753, 758
    interstate placements, 639
    Native American children, 751
    racial matching, 747–748, 752, 758
    religious matching in, 747, 758–759
    same-sex couples, 127, 759
    transracial placement and, 748, 752–753, 758
Fourteenth Amendment, 84, 85–86, 93, 112, 125,
    599
Fourth Amendment, 74, 85
Fragile Families and Child Wellbeing Study,
    399–400, 706–707
France
    non-judicial dissolution of marriage in, 204
    registered partnerships legal status in, 199
Fraud
    adoption, 736
    annulment for, 106–107
    bigamy and polygamy, 154, 155, 156
    divorce collusion as, 221–224
    immigration, 103
    intrinsic vs. extrinsic, 533–534
    lawyer's, 549, 566
    lawyer's withdrawal for client's, 566
    marriage, 101, 102, 106–107, 154–156, 161
    parenthood, 672, 698, 705, 706
    postnuptial agreement as product of,
        514–515
    separation agreements, 531–534, 543
    statute of frauds, 484, 514, 520
Full faith and credit, 594–601, 603, 605–621, 725
Full Faith and Credit for Child Support Orders Act
    (FFCCSOA), 610, 616, 618, 621
Functional parenthood, 661, 708–726
    de facto parenthood, 710, 711, 721–724
    holding out doctrine, 708, 710, 714–715,
        722
    same-sex couples, 710, 711–715, 723,
        724–725
    second-parent adoption, 724–725
    stepparenthood, 708–711, 721–722,
        724–725

G
Genetics, 141–142. *See also* Heredity
Genetic tests, 661–662, 673, 674–680, 696,
    699–705, 707
Germany, parental rights in, 696
Gestational surrogacy. *See* Surrogacy
Goodwill, 295–296, 311–319
Grandparents
    child custody, 413–420, 441
    parental rights of, 663–669, 708, 710
    paternal rights and, 478–479
Guardians, 136–137, 361, 411, 562, 706, 726

H

Hague Convention on the Civil Aspects of International Child Abduction, 479, 639–650

Hague Convention on Protection of Children and Cooperation in Respect of Intercountry Adoption, 754, 758

Hague Convention on Recovery of Child Support and Other Forms of Family Maintenance, 619–620

Heredity, 137, 141–142, 735

Holding out doctrine, 672, 708, 710, 714–715, 722

Housekeeping allowance, 58

Housing discrimination, 20

I

ICWA (Indian Child Welfare Act), 635, 748–752

Immediate relative status, defined, 102

Immigration, 27, 72, 97–101, 102–108, 267, 506–507

Immigration fraud, 103

Incest, 138–142, 161

Income. *See also* Child support; Earning capacities; Spousal support
    gender gap, 63–64, 275, 276, 495
    from marital property, 262
    marriage and, 3, 4
    valuing streams of, 296–297, 305, 318

Indian Child Welfare Act (ICWA), 635, 748–752

Indian tribes. *See* Native Americans

India, surrogacy in, 782

Individual Retirement Accounts (IRAs), 305, 403

Infidelity, 107, 208, 462. *See also* Adultery

Inheritance
    children of unmarried fathers, 671
    child support and, 344
    community property and, 36
    equitable adoption doctrine and, 736
    marriage and, 97, 137–138, 162
    postnuptial agreements and, 514
    probate exception to federal jurisdiction, 656
    separate property and, 252, 255–261

Insanity, 209–210. *See also* Mental capacity

Intercountry Adoption Act of 2000, 758

Interest rates, 296–297

International Marriage Broker Regulation Act, 103

Interstate Compact on the Placement of Children, 639

In vitro fertilization, 770, 772–773

IRAs (Individual Retirement Accounts), 305, 403

Irretrievable breakdown, 213–217, 221, 224

J

Joint custody, 421–435, 443–476
    abuse allegations, 431, 443, 456–463, 470–471
    changed circumstances, 433–434, 443–448, 451
    children's preferences, 430, 434, 470
    child support, 327, 348
    cohabitation, 472–473
    domestic violence, 431, 443, 448–455, 579. *See also* abuse allegations, *this heading*
    growing use of, 413, 422
    history of, 421–422
    legal vs. physical, 427–428, 435, 447, 469
    mediation, 578–579
    parental alienation, 430–432, 443, 448, 462
    parental conflict, 421–422, 429, 430–432. *See also* domestic violence and parental alienation, *this heading*
    parenting coordinator, 432–433, 569, 584
    parenting plans, 432–435, 448, 462–463, 530, 569
    parenting time, 427–428, 429–430, 447
    presumptions, 413, 429–430, 439
    race and, 474–475
    religion and, 463, 464–472, 473
    relocation and, 443–448
    shared parenting, 443–476. *See also* Shared parenting
    split physical custody, 348, 428–429, 471
    unfriendly co-parenting, 448–464

Joint management system, 37

Joint ownership, 29, 30, 103

Joint tenancy vs. tenancy by the entirety, 30

Judicial estoppel, doctrine of, 132

Jurisdiction, 593–657
    adoption, 637–639, 750
    child custody, 620–650. *See also* Child custody
    child support, 605–620, 626
    cooperation among courts, 635
    divisible divorce, 601–604
    divorce, 176, 224, 593–604
    domestic violence and, 604–605, 626, 634, 636–637, 646–650
    emergency, 626
    equitable estoppel and, 600
    ex parte divorce and, 595–596, 598, 601, 602–603
    fairness and out-of-state proceedings, 608
    federal courts and domestic relations, 650–657
    forum non conveniens, 634–635, 636
    full faith and credit, 594–601, 603, 605–621
    in personam, 604, 620
    in rem, 595, 601, 603
    international enforcement
        child custody, 635, 639–650
        child support, 619–620
    interstate enforcement and modification
        child and spousal support, 609–620
        child custody, 627–637
    long-arm, in support cases, 605–609
    marriage and divorce, 97, 176, 224, 593–604, 650–657

ne exeat clause, 644
overview, 593–594
personal liability and, 594
probate exception, 656
property division at divorce, 268, 601–604
protective orders, 604–605
res judicata, 594, 598, 645
spousal support, 601–604, 605, 609–620
"tag," 605
women, federal courts, and, 653–654

K
Kidnapping. *See* Child abduction; Parental
        Kidnapping Prevention Act

L
Lawyers, 545–592
    adoption process, 746, 747
    advocacy, bounds of, 560–562, 564–565, 583
    alternative dispute resolution, 552–553,
        564–566, 568–592
    alternatives to, 553–554, 564
    attorney-client privilege, 480–481, 556
    client emotions, 562
    conflicts of interest, 549–559, 562
    counseling, negotiation, and client relations,
        559–568
    divorce process, 545–592
    dual or joint representation, 550–553
    duties to clients and the court, 545–549
    failure to disclose information, 480–481
    family members, prior representation of other,
        556
    fee arrangements, 557–559
    former clients, duties to, 554–556
    fraud and misconduct by, 549, 566
    ghostwriting legal documents, 554
    limited scope representation, 552–554, 589
    mental capacity, ability to address, 567
    obligations to children, 561–562
    online platforms vs., 553–554, 564
    premarital agreement legal advice, 498–499,
        500, 501, 503–504, 505, 506
    professional conduct rules, 481, 549–550, 553,
        554–556, 558, 559–560, 566–567, 583
    prospective clients, representation adverse to, 555
    right to counsel, 393, 745
    sale of practice, 317–318
    sexual relations with clients, 566–567
    skills necessary for family law, 563–564
    unbundled legal services, 553
    withdrawing from cases, 566
LGBT couples. *See* Same-sex couples
Liens, 387, 398, 409
Lord Mansfield's Rule, 670

M
Mahr agreement, 519
Maintenance. *See* Spousal support
Mann Act, 653
Marital property, 28–68
    asset valuation, timing of, 262
    challenges to classification of, 262–263
    characterization as, 252–264, 318
    common law system. *See* Common law marital
        property
    community property. *See* Community property
    copyrighted works and, 45–46
    debt and creditor liability, 28–29, 30, 35, 41,
        54–57, 59–60, 63, 268–271, 384
    deferred, 239–240
    defined, 239, 262
    degrees and licenses as, 295, 319–324
    disability benefits as, 297–304, 307
    division of, 231–272, 295–324. *See also* Property
        division at divorce
    equitable distribution, 35, 232, 238–252, 262, 603
    equity vs. equitable, 31
    family contracts on. *See* Family contracts
    family support duties, 46–62. *See also* Child
        support; Spousal support
    fraud and misconduct, 102, 250
    gifts, 34, 36, 252, 255, 260
    goodwill as, 295–296, 311–319
    income produced by, 262
    joint tenancy/ownership, 29, 30, 103
    management and authority over, 36–39, 57–59,
        237
    meretricious relationships and, 180, 197
    necessaries, liability for, 54–57, 59–62, 326–327
    overview, 28–29
    ownership and control of wealth, 30–38
    pensions and other employment-related benefits
        as, 40–46, 233, 267, 295–296, 297–311,
        318, 403
    professional practices and other closely held
        businesses, 311–319
    public benefits, 40–46, 61–62
    putative spouse doctrine, 177
    separate property vs. *See* Separate property
    sharing principles, 235–236
    spousal contribution, 233, 247–248, 271
    spousal support issues, 53, 61–68. *See also*
        Spousal support
    summary dissolution, 225
    tenants by the entirety, 30
    tenants in common, 30
    workers' compensation benefits as, 297
Marriage, 97–163
    agreement to marry, 97–108
        capacity to agree, 133–138

American system of divorce and, 226–230
annulment. *See* Annulment
anti-miscegenation laws, 109–113
benefits associated with, 4–5, 12–16
bigamy, 100, 147–158, 162, 172, 177
ceremonies, 128–132, 166
civil, 5–7
cohabitation vs. *See* Cohabitation
common law, 166–174, 182, 187, 196
conflict of laws regarding, 158–163
constitutional protection for right to marry, 109–128
as contract, 5–6, 107, 203, 217, 226, 483, 574, 595
as covenant, 203, 217, 226, 483, 574
date of termination, 262
decision making within, 51, 59, 237
declining importance of, 165–166
defined, 165
demographic trends, 3, 227
divorce. *See* Divorce
under duress, 107–108
economic partnership theory of, 262–263
eligibility for, 97
enforcement of bargains in, 49–51
equality within, 237
exit costs from, 179–180, 228–229, 230
family and, 3–16, 27–28, 97, 138–142, 161
federal court jurisdiction over, 650–657
forced, 107–108, 147
formalities, 128–133, 162
fraud and, 101, 102, 103, 106–107, 154–156, 161
as a fundamental right, 112
gender roles within, 237, 275
government and, 7, 650–657
immigration issues, 27, 72, 97–101, 102–108, 267, 506–507
interracial, 93, 109–113
interstate recognition of, 158–163
jurisdiction, 97, 593–601, 650–657
licenses, 128, 132–133, 162, 177
limited purposes, 100, 101
mail order brides, 103
marital unity, myth of, 27–28, 36, 38, 513
monogamy, 154–155
nonmarriage vs., 3, 165–166, 195–196, 197, 236–237. *See also* Cohabitation; Unmarried parents
parental consent for, 143–147
parental presumption of, 16, 661, 670–684, 705, 708, 715, 726, 769–770
polygamy, 147, 154–157, 384, 653
premarriage education, 569
presumptions about, 174–178

property rights. *See* Marital property
putative spouses, 174–178, 180, 182
registered partnerships vs., 198
religious, 6–7, 69. *See also* Religion
remaking of, 237
remarriage, 236, 353, 372–376, 381, 383–385, 594
requirements for, 97
restrictions on, 128–158
    age, 101, 143–147
    bigamy and polygamy, 147–158, 162, 653
    child support obligors, 112
    constitutional framework for, 109–128
    formalities, 128–133, 162
    mental capacity, 133–138, 141
    prisoners, 112
    racial, 109–113
    relationship, 138–142, 161
"romantic relationship," 53
same-sex. *See* Same-sex marriage
social and legal norms, effect of, 237
spousal contracts during, 508–520
taxation and, 400–402
termination of. *See* Annulment; Divorce; Separation
UMDA. *See* Uniform Marriage and Divorce Act
validity of, 97, 100–102, 132–133, 136, 158–163, 174–178
"void" and "voidable," 100, 101–102, 133
women's vulnerability within, 6–7
Marriage Act of 1753 (England), 166
Marriage Fraud Amendments of 1986, 103
Married Women's Property Acts, 30–31, 36
Maternal mortality rate, 92
Mediation, 454, 552–553, 565–566, 577–587
Medicaid, 61–62, 92, 361–362
Medicare, 61
Mental capacity
    collaborative divorce and, 590–591
    consent to adoption and, 740
    hereditary restrictions, 137, 141
    insanity, 209–210
    lawyer's ability to address, 567
    marriage restrictions, 133–138, 141
    mediation and, 583–584
Meretricious relationships, 180, 197, 379
Mexico, mail-order divorces, 600
Military personnel
    child custody, 634
    retirement benefits, 309–310
Minors. *See* Children
"Mock priest" rule, 132
Model Marriage and Divorce Act, 363
Multiethnic Placement Act of 1994 (amended 1996), 753, 757
Multiple parenthood, 661, 662, 726–732, 740

N

National Association of Black Social Workers (NABSW), 752
National Conference of Commissioners on Uniform State Laws (NCCUSL), 500, 577, 619, 621, 636
National Society of Genetic Counselors (NSGC), 141–142
National Woman Suffrage Association, 156
Native Americans
    adoption issues, 748–752, 756
    child custody issues, 635, 645, 751
    domestic violence jurisdiction, 605
    ICWA, 635, 748–752
    marriage ceremonies, 128, 132
    same-sex marriage laws, 125
    traditional lifestyle and child support, 370
Necessaries of life, spousal liability for, 54–57, 59–62, 326–327
Netherlands
    divorce process in, 225–226
    registered partnerships legal status in, 199
    U.S. children adopted in, 758
New property, 295–324
    defined, 296
    divorce and, 295–324
    pensions and employment-related benefits, 295–296, 297–311, 318
    professional practices and other closely held businesses, 311–319
    valuing payment streams, 296–297, 305, 318
New Zealand
    legal statuses for intimate partners in, 193
    same-sex couple legal recognition in, 128
No-fault divorce, 212–226
    collusion, 221–224
    divorce rates and, 226–228
    economic consequences, 231, 232–237
    as equalizer among women, 278
    fault coexistence with, 217–221
    fault system vs., 207
    history of, 204, 212–213
    irretrievable breakdown and, 213–217, 221, 224
    pipeline effect, 227
    property division under, 232–237
    separation and, 217–221
    spousal support, 221, 272–274, 275, 278
Nonmarital relationships, 3, 165–166, 195–196, 197, 236–237. *See also* Cohabitation; Unmarried parents
NSGC (National Society of Genetic Counselors), 141–142

O

Office of Child Support Enforcement, 332, 397, 399, 619
Online dispute resolution (ODR), 586–587
Open adoption, 737–739, 740–741, 757

P

Parallel parenting, 453
Parens patriae, 521, 574, 575
Parental alienation, 84, 430–432, 443, 448, 462
Parental Kidnapping Prevention Act (PKPA), 621, 627, 628, 635–636, 637, 657
Parenthood, 661–732
    adoptive. *See* Adoption
    alternative reproduction. *See* Alternative reproductive technologies
    best interests of the child, 680, 681, 706, 726
    biological relations, 661–662, 697–708, 729–730
    birth certificate identifying, 673, 682–684
    blood test evidence, 672, 680, 707
    constitutional rights, 663–670
    custodial and support duties, determining in context of, 400, 413, 662, 670–708, 729–730
    de facto, 668, 710, 711, 721–724, 729
    demographics and trends, 661–662
    disestablishing, 698, 706
    by estoppel principle, 711, 723–724, 768
    fraudulent, 672, 698, 705, 706
    functional, 661, 708–726
    genetic tests, 661–662, 673, 674–680, 696, 699–705, 707
    holding out doctrine, 672, 708, 710, 714–715, 722
    in loco parentis, 668, 698, 710, 711, 768
    "lie about contraception" rule, 697, 698
    marital presumption of, 16, 661, 670–684, 705, 708, 715, 726, 769–770
    multiple parents, 661, 662, 726–732, 740
    overview, 661–663
    paternity, voluntary acknowledgments of, 672–673, 683, 691, 699–708, 760
    premarital agreements on, 494
    psychological, 668, 710, 711, 724
    reforming law of, 670–671
    same-sex couples. *See* Same-sex couples
    "statutory rape" rule, 697–698
    stepparents. *See* Stepparenthood
    unmarried parents. *See* Unmarried parents
Parenting. *See also* Childrearing
    co-parenting, 294–295, 453
        unfriendly, 448–464
    parallel, 453
    shared, 275, 345, 443–476. *See also* Joint custody
Parenting coordinators, 432–433, 569, 584
Parenting plans, 432–435, 448, 462–463, 530, 569
Parent Locator Service, 618, 635–636
Parents
    abortion notification and consent, 95
    adoptive. *See* Adoption
    adult children's support of, 357–362
    autonomy of, 326
    consent to minor's marriage, 143–147

constitutional rights of, 663–670
foster. *See* Foster care
legal. *See* Parenthood
low-income, 348–349
mental capacity, 136–137
same-sex. *See* Same-sex couples
single, 293, 441, 661
stepparents. *See* Stepparenthood
unmarried. *See* Unmarried parents
working, empirical data on, 293
Parent support, 357–362
Paternity. *See* Parenthood
Pensions and retirement plans
civil service, 310
contributory vs. noncontributory plans, 304
defined benefit plans, 303–304, 305
defined contribution plans, 303–304, 305
as divisible property at divorce, 45, 233,
       295–296, 297–311, 318, 403
domestic relations exceptions, 655
marital property, 40–46, 233, 267, 295–296,
       297–311, 318, 403
marital vs. nonmarital shares, 306–307
military retirement benefits, 309–310
putative spouses, 177
QDROs, 304–305, 308, 318, 403
Social Security and other federal plans, 297,
       308–310
survivorship rights and death benefits, 307–308
transfer of, taxation issues, 403
valuation of, 304–305
vested and matured, 304
"Pension socialism," 40
PKPA (Parental Kidnapping Prevention Act), 621,
       627, 628, 635–636, 637, 657
Polyamorous relationships, 147, 157, 731
Polygamy, 147, 154–157, 384, 653. *See also* Bigamy
Polygyny, 147
Poor Laws (English), 325
Postnuptial agreements, 508–520
duress or fraud, product of, 514–515
enforceability, 513–520
premarital agreements vs., 518
religion and, 519
separation agreements vs., 519–520
statistics, 519
UPMAA, 518
Poverty, 398–400, 756
Preemption, 41–46, 654
Preexisting duty, doctrine of, 514
Pregnancy
annulment for undisclosed, 107
assisted. *See* Alternative reproductive technologies
termination of. *See* Abortion
Pregnancy Discrimination Act of 1978, 92
Premarital agreements, 484–508
ALI principles, 484, 505–506
amendment or revocation, 502

arbitration clauses, 570, 575–576
bargaining power, 489, 494–495, 497
child support and, 496–497, 502, 504
demographics, 490, 495–496
earnings capacity changes and, 496
enforceability, 484, 496–507
fair and adequate terms, 489–490, 496, 500, 503
full disclosure requirements, 489–490, 496,
       497–498, 501, 502, 503, 506
gender and, 489, 490, 494–495
history of, 484
marriage validity and, 100
optimism for marriage success and, 499–500
parenthood and, 494, 496–497, 502, 504
postnuptial agreements vs., 518
spousal support and, 501, 502–503, 506–507
unconscionability, concept of, 496, 501,
       502–503, 504, 506
UPAA, 484, 500, 502–505, 506
UPMAA, 484, 500–502, 503–505
Prenatal abandonment theory, 695
Preventing Sex Trafficking and Strengthening
       Families Act, 619
Property division at divorce, 231–272, 295–324
appreciation of value, 260–261
asset valuation, timing of, 262
bankruptcy and, 271, 405–406, 409
business partnership and, 247, 311–319
challenges to classification of property, 262–263
characterization of property as separate or
       marital, 252–264, 318
choice-of-law issues, 268
civil service pensions, 310
cohabitation remedy and, 264–267
collusion on, 221–224
commingled property, 252, 260, 261
contempt proceedings for enforcement, 395
death benefits, 307–308
debt division, 268–271
deferred marital property, 239–240
degrees, licenses, jobs, and earning capacity, 295,
       319–324
disability benefits, 297–304, 307
domestic violence and, 249
economic awards, history of, 231–232
economic consequences of no-fault divorce, 231,
       232–237
economic need, consideration of, 248–249, 271
equitable distribution, 35, 232, 238–252, 262,
       270–271, 603
family contracts on. *See* Family contracts
goodwill and, 295–296, 311–319
homemaking, economic value of, 233–236,
       246–248
inception of title rule, 261
income from marital vs. separate property, 262
jurisdiction, 268, 601–604
large marital estates, 247–248

marital and nonmarital shares, 306–307
marital fault and, 249–250
marital homes, 272
marriage termination date and, 262
military retirement benefits, 309–310
misconduct and, 249–250
new property and, 295–324
overview, 231
partnership analogy and, 247, 262–263
pensions and employment benefit plans, 45, 233,
    295–296, 297–311, 318, 403
professional practices and other closely held
    businesses, 311–319
QDROs, 304–305, 308, 318, 403
remarriage and, 236, 375
separate property, 235, 237–238, 247–248,
    252–265, 268, 271, 318
separation agreements on. See Separation
    agreements
sharing principles, 235–236
Social Security benefits, 297, 308–309, 310
"special contributions" principle, 248
spousal contribution, 233, 247–248, 271
spousal support vs., 272, 375. See also Spousal
    support
survivorship rights, 307–308
taxation and, 231, 402, 403
title-based distribution, 237–238
tort suits and, 251
totality-of-the-circumstances test, 375
UMDA on, 238–239, 240, 249, 261, 262, 273
valuing payment streams, 296–297, 305, 318
workers' compensation benefits, 297
Property, marital. See Marital property
Protective orders, 75–84, 107–108, 604–605
Psychological parenthood, 668, 710, 711, 724
Public benefits, 40–46. See also Social Security
    benefits
child support and, 348–349, 355–356, 400,
    550, 673, 706–707
cohabitation and entitlement to, 8, 12, 172–173
marital property, 40–46, 61–62
marriage and, 97, 112–113, 155
necessaries and, 61–62
parenthood establishment and, 706–707
parent support and, 361–362
premarital agreements and eligibility for,
    502–503
separation agreements and reliance on, 529
Putative father registry, 691
Putative spouses, 174–178, 180, 182

Q
Qualified domestic relations order (QDRO),
    304–305, 308, 318, 403
Qualified medical child support order (QMCSO),
    387–388

R
Railroad Retirement Act, 308, 309
Rape. See also Domestic violence
    adoption of child from, 741
    marital, 73
    statutory, 697–698
REACT (Retirement Equity Act) of 1984, 41,
    304–305
Reciprocal beneficiary relationships, 198–199
Registered contractual relationships, 198
Registered partnerships, 197–199
Relative responsibility statutes, 361
Religion
    adoption and foster care matching, 747,
        758–759
    arbitration and, 575–576
    child custody and, 463, 464–472, 473
    divorce and, 7, 203, 575–576
    enforcement of bargains in marriage, 51
    marriage ceremonies, 128, 132, 166
    polygamy and, 154–157, 384
    postnuptial agreements and, 519
    religious marriage, 6–7, 69
    same-sex couples and, 126–127, 759
Reproductive choice, 85–95, 394–395. See also
        Abortion; Contraceptives
Reproductive technologies. See Alternative
        reproductive technologies
Res judicata, 594, 598, 645
Resulting trusts, 31–35, 190
Retirement. See Pensions and retirement plans
Retirement Equity Act (REACT) of 1984, 41,
    304–305
Revised Uniform Arbitration Act, 577
Romania, international adoptions in, 755
Russia, surrogacy in, 782

S
Same-sex couples
    adoption by, 128, 724–725, 759
    alternative reproduction, 125, 682–684, 715,
        730–731, 761–769, 771, 781
    child custody and visitation, 12, 473, 575, 710
    civil unions, 126, 128, 198–199, 600, 730–731
    cohabitation, 8–12, 15, 126, 198–199, 264,
        379, 473
    domestic partnerships. See Domestic partnerships
    domestic violence, 83
    equal access to benefits and protections, 113–128
    functional parent doctrine, 710, 711–715, 723,
        724–725
    marriage of. See Same-sex marriage
    as parents, 12, 125, 128, 662, 672–673,
        682–684, 710, 723, 724–725, 730–731,
        761–769, 771, 781
        foster, 127, 759
    registered partnerships and, 199

religion and, 126–127, 759
Social Security benefits, 310
spousal support, 379
statistics, 126
tax treatment of, 401
Same-sex marriage, 113–128
    civil unions vs., 126, 128. *See also* Civil unions
    common law, 172
    conflict of laws regarding, 27, 124–125
    divorce, 599–600
    domestic partnerships vs., 126, 128. *See also*
        Domestic partnerships
    international recognition of, 128
    interstate recognition of, 27, 125, 162, 599
    jurisdiction, 599–600
    legalization and recognition of, 8, 12–16, 27, 93,
        113–128, 162, 199, 599
    marital property, 267
    Native American tribes, 125
    parental presumption, 682–684
    premarital agreements, 495
    public officials' refusal to participate in, 127
    state vs. federal law, 113–128
    statistics, 126
    tax laws, 401
Second-parent adoption, 12, 724–725
Separate property
    appreciation of, 260–261
    choice-of-law issues, 268
    control of, 58
    debt liability, 271
    divorce and division of, 235, 237–238, 247–248,
        252–265, 268, 271, 318
    enforcement of bargains in marriage, 50
    income produced by, 262
    mixing with marital property, 252, 260, 261
    premarital property as, 35–36, 38, 252, 264–265
    tracing out, 260, 261
    transmutation, 252–255, 260, 262–263
Separation. *See also* Separation agreements
    divorce and, 217–221
    domestic violence as cause for, 68
    history of, 203
    jurisdiction, 593
    spousal support and, 272
Separation agreements, 520–544
    ALI principles, 521, 529, 530, 542
    arbitration clauses, 576
    child custody, visitation, and support provisions,
        355, 520–530, 535–544
    collusion and, 211
    concealment of assets, 533–534
    enforceability of, 520, 541–542
    fraud and, 531–534, 543
    full disclosure, failure to provide, 533–534
    incorporation of into divorce decree, 534,
        541–543

modification of, 529, 535–544
    permissible scope of, 520–530
    post-decree attacks, 531–535
    postnuptial agreements vs., 519–520
    spousal support, 520–521, 528–529, 535–544
    UMDA, 520, 528, 529, 543
    unconscionability standard, 520, 529–530, 533,
        543
Shared parenting, 275, 345, 348, 443–476. *See also*
        Joint custody
Single parents, 293, 441, 661. *See also* Unmarried
        parents
Socialism, defined, 40
Social Security benefits
    child support and, 348, 371
    disability payments, 61, 349, 371
    as divisible property, 297, 308–309, 310
    marital status and, 27, 97, 112–113, 267
    parent support, 361
South Africa, same-sex couple legal recognition in,
        128
South America
    international adoptions in, 755
    same-sex couple legal recognition in, 128
Special needs trusts, 356, 362
Sperm donors, 682–683, 731, 760, 768–771, 773,
        781–782
Spousal abuse. *See* Domestic violence
Spousal contracts during marriage, 508–520. *See also*
        Postnuptial agreements
Spousal immunity, 73
Spousal support, 272–295
    AAML guidelines, 273, 286
    ALI principles, 285, 286, 363, 375
    annulment and, 102
    bankruptcy and, 231, 375, 405
    change of circumstances, 363–365, 376, 379
    childrearing and, 275, 276–277, 285, 292–295
    clean break philosophy, 273
    cohabitation and, 53, 372, 376–381
    compensatory payments, 285, 324
    cost-of-living adjustments, 364
    coverture and, 276–277
    death of the obligor, 363, 387
    divorce grounds affecting, 221, 231–232,
        272–274, 275, 278, 292
    duration of, limitation on, 286–292
    earning capacities, 275–277, 319–324, 364,
        370–371
    economic consequences of no-fault divorce, 231,
        232–237
    economic need, consideration of, 380
    fraud and, 102
    gender-based issues, 62–68, 232, 274–275,
        379–380
    guidelines, emergence of, 286–292
    history of, 231–232, 272

human capital and, 274–275
income decreases, voluntary vs. involuntary, 365–372
indefinite alimony, 291–292
interstate modification and enforcement, 609–620
jurisdiction, 601–604, 605, 610, 618
length of marriage, 290, 291–292
marital fault and misconduct, 292
modification and termination, 363–385, 529, 535–544, 609–620
necessaries doctrine, 61–62
new families, 372–381
overview, 231, 272
postmortem alimony, 387
postnuptial agreements, 513–514
premarital agreements, 501, 502–503, 506–507
professional practice and goodwill as basis, 318
property division at divorce vs., 272, 375. *See also* Property division at divorce
race, privilege, and dependency, 277–278
rehabilitative vs. long-term, 286–292, 324, 363
reimbursement alimony, 290–291, 324, 363
remarriage and, 236, 372–376
retirement and, 370
separation agreements, 520–521, 528–529, 535–544
standard of living, 375
summary dissolution and waiver of, 225
taxation, 231, 402, 403–404, 529
theory of alimony, 275–276
totality-of-the-circumstances test, 375
transitional alimony, 290
Stalking, 83
Statutory rape, 697–698
Stepparenthood
adoption and, 690, 724–725, 741–744
child support and, 172, 381, 384–385
functional parenthood, 708–711, 721–722, 724–725
visitation, 710, 721–722
Substantial relationship test, 554–555
Summary dissolution, 224–226
Supplemental needs trusts, 362
Supplemental Security Income benefits, 172–173, 348, 355–356
Surrogacy, 483, 683, 715, 772–784
Survivorship rights, 307–308

T
Taxation, 400–405
childcare tax credit, 405
child support and, 231, 331, 337, 343–344, 398, 402, 404–405
child tax credit, 400, 404–405
community property states, 402
after divorce, 402–405
divorce collusion and, 224
earned income tax credit, 402, 405
married couples, 400–402
pensions and related assets, 403
progressive, 401, 402
property division and, 231, 402, 403
recapture rules, 404
spousal support and, 231, 402, 403–404, 529
Temporary Assistance for Needy Families (TANF), 349, 356
Tenants by the entirety, 30
Tenants in common, 30
Thailand, surrogacy in, 782
Third Amendment, 85
Thirteenth Amendment, 393
Time value of money, 296
Title-based property distribution, 237–238
Trial marriage, 165, 178
Trusts
child support, 343, 356, 387
constructive and resulting, 31–35, 190, 247
educational, 343
parent support and, 361, 362
special needs, 356, 362
supplemental needs, 362

U
Ukraine, surrogacy in, 782–783
Unbundled legal services, 553
Unconscionable agreements, 496, 501, 502–503, 504, 506, 520, 529–530, 533, 543
Uniform Adoption Act (1994), 637–639, 739, 744–745, 746
Uniform Child Custody Jurisdiction Act (UCCJA), 621, 626, 636, 638, 646
Uniform Child Custody Jurisdiction and Enforcement Act (UCCJEA), 621, 625–637, 645–646
Uniform Cohabitants Economic Remedies Act, 190–191
Uniform Collaborative Law Act, 589
Uniform Collaborative Practice Act, 589–590
Uniform Commercial Code (UCC), 499, 500, 504
Uniform Deployed Parents Custody and Visitation Act (UDPCVA), 634
Uniformed Services Former Spouses' Protection Act (USFSPA), 309
Uniform Family Law Arbitration Act, 577
Uniform Interstate Family Support Act (UIFSA), 608–609, 610, 616–619, 621
Uniform Law Commission. *See* National Conference of Commissioners on Uniform State Laws
Uniform Marital Property Act, 38
Uniform Marriage and Divorce Act (UMDA)
child custody and support, 528
common law marriage, 172

divorce, 204, 214
irretrievable breakdown, 214
property division at divorce, 238–239, 240, 249, 261, 262, 273
putative spouses, 177
separation agreements, 520, 528, 529, 543
spousal support, 272–273, 293
Uniform Parentage Act
1973 version, 760, 768, 770–771, 780
2002 version, 760, 768
2017 version, 671, 672–674, 680, 684, 691, 695, 760–761, 768, 780–781
Uniform Premarital Agreement Act (UPAA), 484, 500, 502–505, 506
Uniform Premarital and Marital Agreements Act (UPMAA), 484, 500–502, 503–505, 518
Uniform Probate Code (UPC), 514
Uniform Reciprocal Enforcement of Support Act (URESA), 610
Unilateral divorce, 217, 228, 234, 600
United Nations Convention on the Rights of the Child, 430, 754, 755, 757–758
Unjust enrichment, 184, 187–190, 197
Unmarried cohabitants, 178–199. *See also* Cohabitation
Unmarried parents
adoption rights, 685–697, 736, 751–752
child support, 325, 327, 339, 671–672, 697–708, 729–730
custodial rights, 441, 521–528, 672, 685–697, 729–730
discrimination against children of, 670–671
inheritance, 671
legal parenthood, 661–662, 670–671, 685–708, 729–730
separation agreements, 521–528

V

Violence. *See* Child abuse; Domestic violence
Violence Against Women Act of 1994 (VAWA), 84, 604–605

Visitation. *See* Child custody
Voluntary separation, 217–221

W

Women
autonomy, 7, 72, 379, 599
black, and transracial adoption, 753–754
child custody, gender issues regarding, 411–412, 440–441, 462
cohabitation issues, 180, 183, 197
constitutional decisions regarding role of, 64–68
earnings, gender gap in, 63–64, 275, 276, 495
economic consequences of divorce for, 230, 232–237, 275
jurisdiction, federal courts, and, 653–654
labor force participation rate, 293
maternal mortality rate, 92
mediation views, 578–579
money control and management, 57–59, 237
polygamy and equal rights for, 155–156
premarital agreements, gender issues and, 489, 490, 494–495
property rights, 30–31, 36–37, 50. *See also* Marital property
race, privilege, and dependency, 277–278
religious marriage and, 6–7
reproductive choice, 85–95. *See also* Abortion; Contraceptives
Roman law, rights under, 69
spousal support, gender issues and, 62–68, 232, 274–275, 379–380
violence against. *See* Domestic violence
work by, economic value of, 56–57, 233–236, 246–248, 276–277
Workers' compensation benefits, 297

Z

Zoning ordinances, 16–25